Lehner's Encyclopedia of
U.S. MARKS
— ON —
Pottery, Porcelain & Clay

LOIS LEHNER

COLLECTOR BOOKS
A Division of Schroeder Publishing Co., Inc.

Letters of inquiry to the author may be sent to the publisher but must be accompanied by a self-addressed, stamped envelope to receive an answer.

Contents

Introduction

What The Book Covers and What It Is Supposed To Accomplish

There are over 1,900 companies, potters, potteries with over 8,000 marks, logos, symbols, etc. divided about equally among the old folk potters, studio potters, dinnerware manufacturers, selling agencies or distributors, decorative or art pottery, decorators, decorating companies and decorative tile.

This book represents about eight years of intensive work on my part and I have researched potteries altogether for books for about 15 years. But if all of the years of research of all of the writers quoted in this book were added together, then this book would represent hundreds of years of very hard work trying to discover facts pertaining to our American ceramic industry. As monumental as the mound of written material is now, we need at least that much more work before we will begin to conquer the subject. In-depth research on local levels is needed. If the overview presented here spurs people to go on with this type of research, the book will have been a success. Also, I hope the readers gain an appreciation of our American potters who have left us such a legacy of beautiful and serviceable products in spite of the trials and tribulations they endured. And last, but most important, I hope the book is a tool to help identify all kinds of American made ceramic ware.

The word American comes so natural to use, but I did not include Canadian made ware. I wanted to try to do so, but the United States was more than one book could hold, and the task of adding marks from another country was more than this author could handle. Once in a while a listing crept into the book that probably did not belong in a strict sense of American affiliations, such as Bernard Leach, an English potter or Lefton, or Fitz and Floyd, who did not sell American-made pottery products. But Leach was so important in the teaching of our American studio potters, and Lefton, and Fitz and Floyd illustrate very well the distributors of today.

There are many lists and indexes in the back of the book to help the reader locate a mark or a potter. The numerous footnotes give the readers further reading on each potter in most cases. In a book this size, it is possible to touch upon only what might be compared to the "tip of the iceberg" of information available to us today. All of us are fortunate that so many people have spent years and years of their lives researching various facets of the American pottery industry, and that publishers and individuals have taken the risk to publish and make the material available to us. You will find their names cited all through this book.

This book was planned to be a simple listing of all of American pottery marks this author could find. No matter how many marks we do find, we may rest assured that this will only be half the number that existed. For every potter listed here, we could find ten more not listed and we will find many more. Ceramic products in many forms have been constantly used by every American who ever lived. It took a huge amount of people working with clay to supply the varied needs of such a great number of people. Many of these potters never were in a listing of any kind. They were not important enough to be included in directories, etc; they may not have even owned a piece of property to be recorded in a court house. Once the people who knew them was gone, there was no one to tell they had existed. Then a piece of pottery with an identification mark of some kind comes to light. The search may go on for years and still no reasonable amount of information may turn up about the maker of a specific item. But we will keep on trying!

Not all entries are covered equally. For the distributors or sales agencies, I did not try to tie down beginning and ending dates, nor did I attempt to show all of their marks. I used mainly those marks that distributors or sales agencies had patented. I tried to use only distributors who sold some American product at one time or another. For all of the other categories I hoped to get location, beginning and ending dates, type of products made and marks used. From potter to potter and factory to factory, this varied greatly for several reasons. If the information was not widely dispersed about a particular business, I tended to want to write and tell more if I could find it. It was hard at times to limit the amount of information I gave. Then some of the businesses received little coverage because I just couldn't manage to find much on them. Those will have to have more work from the researchers yet to come. Some potteries have so much written on them already that it seemed appropriate to give the basic information and to point out the material available and not to elaborate on these potteries.

If a pottery stayed in business for 50 to 100 years, they made it all! They would not have stayed in business if they hadn't changed their products to suit the change in consumer taste. Listing such a pottery for a single item ot two in the back of the books is presumptous, but the lists do give collectors somewhere to start to look for certain types of ware. We haven't really begun yet to determine what all was made by most of the big factories.

In the separate listings in the back of this book, you will find folk potters (stoneware and redware); dinnerware manufacturers; decorators; distributors; decorated tile; electrical porcelain. These lists could be very helpful in searching for a particular mark or manufacturer. I decided not to list "art" potters as opposed to simple decorative pottery, because I did not want to get into the controversy about what is and what isn't art pottery. Let if suffice to say that almost every factory that existed made some pieces that could be called decorative ware at sometime or other, but few reached a level of aesthetic value or had the individual attention that constitutes a real piece of artistic pottery. Anytime Paul Evan's name is cited for information, the reader can rest assured that pottery has now been accepted as a real art pottery.

Not many words in this book have been spent considering the art in the work of the various potters whose lives have spanned the long period of time that this book covers. This author trusts as the reader holds an object in his or her hands, and reads, attempting to identify or verify the piece, that the effort, the art, the talent, the work of the maker will make themselves known to the collector.

Glen Lukens, a brilliant studio potter and teacher of ceramics at the University of California, won awards such as an honorary doctorate from Oregon State University and the Charles Fergus Binns Medal, and in 1951 the government of Haiti awarded him L'Ordre National Honneur et Merite. He was able to see the connection between all potters over the expanse of time including the old stoneware potters, the studio potters, the dinnerware designers, the art tile makers and the art pottery manufacturers when he said: "The new in art is incredibly old and the old is still vastly new."

Talking About "Tools of the Trade" for Researching

Directories as a tool for writing this kind of research are a really big help in many ways. First, they do prove a pottery or business did exist. Many times directories provide the first hint to an author that such a pottery did exist. They provide some indication of the years the company existed and what its name might have been. Sometimes directory listings are all we can find! On the other hand, directories often times list potteries and companies long after they ceased to exist. Terrace Ceramics, Inc., a jobbing concern between factories and distributors ceased to exist as such in 1975. Since 1975, Terrace Ceramics, Inc., is a consulting agency only. John F. Bonistall, the last president of Stangl Pottery, works as a management consultant to pottery and dinnerware industries. He keeps the name Terrace Ceramics, so it is still listed in 1982 under "tableware resources" for "casual dinnerware, cookware, oven to table ware, casseroles, mixing bowl, ceramic canister sets" and on and on. Yet they have not sold any of these things since 1975. Older directories are notorious among research writers for spelling the same name in several ways in just the same number of years.

There are disagreements about the writers of the past. Modern writers all have favorites among the older writers that they feel secure in quoting. The modern day writers do not agree on which of the writers in the olden days were right and which were not quite accurate. By this time I have quoted most of the older writers and been told by some current authors that I have chosen the wrong source. It didn't seem to matter what I used from the wealth of material written, someone did not like that source. So, in this book I often give the conflicting dates of various authors. Edwin Atlee Barber's marks are the most authentic copies of marks I have found by any author. When I do find a very old dish and compare the actual mark to his drawn copy, they are exact or almost exact. Photographs of marks do not necessarily provide a better way to show marks because too many times the photographs do not show the mark clearly. This is because the mark on the dish was not clear to start with. In this case, a person with the piece in hand may produce a better copy than a photograph. Hardly any of the authors of books of marks have drawn their marks themselves for the books. It is possible that Thorn did. But mostly the marks are drawn by some artist who makes them so fancy that they lose their original look. The Ramsay book, *American Potters and Pottery*, is the greatest example of this. Ramsay's marks are very pretty, but they don't look like the original marks often times.

The Ramsay book is an incredible work! It is a work few people would ever attempt-to catalog the redware and stoneware potters up to 1900. Many times it is the only source that can be found with information on some of these potters. Another really fine researcher in American potteries in the Zanesville, Ohio, area, Norris Schneider, had this to say about Ramsay: "There is no question about Ramsay's standing as one of the greatest authorities on American pottery who ever lived. But in addition to his own human falibility, he was dependent upon historical information furnished by others. Sometimes his informants had accepted unverified statements." I wholeheartedly agree with every word. This book is also dependent on the work of others and may sometimes be a compounding of other peoples' errors. One thing that bothers researchers and writers about Ramsay's book is that he only tried to determine if a pottery were still in business up to or in 1900. So all of his listings ended at 1900 even if the pottery were still in business. Some of the potteries lasted another 50 or 60 years, but many writers and researchers took the 1900 as an ending date. Also, I imagine Ramsay was trying to make each listing as brief as possible. So, if he had discovered no mark for a potter, he put just, "no mark," instead of "no discovered mark." Many marks have shown up for potters that Ramsay had listed "no mark," but I am sure he knew this would happen and assumed his readers knew he meant he didn't know of a mark yet.

Many of the old time potters that Ramsay wrote about could not read or write. Long ago it was hard to hire people with enough schooling to make them capable of taking the directory listings. This mostly accounts for the differences in spelling between the written records and what is on the jugs when we do find a marked one. There are a few people who have written books on American pottery that have come to be known as the old masters in the field such as Barber, Ramsay, Thorn, Wilbur Stout, etc. In our modern day we have Paul Evans; the Kovels; Lucile Henzke; Georgeanna Greer; Susan Cox; Pat Johnson; Duke Coleman; Jo Cunningham and so many more whose names appear throughout the book. It is never my intention to be critical of anyone who has spent years of his life researching in this field to provide information for use by many people. I will be pointing out some weaknesses and contradictions only to explain the difficulties encountered in compiling a work of this sort and to help to clarify some facts for the readers. I encourage the readers to go to the original source listed for pictures and additional information whenever I quote a book. My biggest hope is that I quote correctly and with the author's intent.

Where These Marks Came From

The studio potters drew their own marks on the questionnaire they answered. Some of these have been reduced in size, other than that, they are the copies they sent. All through the book you will see Tom Turnquist's name as a researcher of American potteries. He sent many studio potters' marks and information. Another major source of the studio potters' marks was the booklet by Linda Steigleder, published by the Everson Museum of Art to accompany the 1978 exhibition, *A Century of Ceramics in the U.S.*

The stoneware potters' marks were drawn from looking at pictures of crocks, jugs and other pieces in all of the books cited with the potter. There is not enough praise or gratitude to express the appreciation to those writers and publishers who allowed me to draw marks from the pictures in their books. A magnifying glass was an indisposable item in this effort!

Some of the marks on dinnerware came from the factories themselves if they could help me and were still operating-such as Salem China Company, Homer Laughlin China Company, Shenango China Company, Mayer China Company, Taylor, Smith and Taylor, Royal China Company and others. Then for one whole summer, every Friday, I carried a bushel basket of mostly cracked plates and dishes to the copy machine to copy the marks. This process warranted some unusual looks, almost comparable to the puzzled looks I got from the dealers who sold me the old, cracked, damaged pieces. Some of the most important marks were sent by collectors and readers and authors whose names appear throughout the book as having contributed the mark. Articles and books are cited as well. Quality Stamp Company of East Liverpool, Ohio, was a source of hundreds of the marks. Also, Waldorf Stamping Device Company, London, Ohio and Commercial Decal, East Liverpool, Ohio, were other sources. Probably the most important source of the marks were the patent and copyright office registrations researched by Linda Cleveland, which provide us with the most authentic dates we will have for any marks.

We drew the incised marks as closely as we could. The marks we obtained from Quality Stamp Company we got by stamping the little metal die pieces in ink and transferring it to paper. The metal pieces are used to make the rubber stamps for the factories (these stamps are exactly like those used to stamp "paid" or your address, etc.). Great pressure of hundreds of pounds is applied by a machine to imprint the rubber from the metal die pieces. Sometimes the ink smeared as we worked with the small metal pieces trying to stamp off hundreds of marks at Quality Stamp Company. These were then placed on the copy machine to even up the lines and again we darkened in almost all of these marks to get the reader a decent copy. Some still aren't too good, but they are authentic marks. Woodrow Price is the owner of Quality Stamp Company.

Dating Marks and Factories

The marks filed with the patent office have proved one thing-trying to date marks from trade journals, trade catalogues and various advertisements proves only that the pottery made the product the year it was advertised. Potteries could have made the product long before or after the period for which it was advertised. Collectors want specific dates when a mark was used. The writers have attempted every means under the sun to comply with that wish and have made a lot of errors. If the production dates come right from the factory that did the manufacturing, such as the dates they reported on mark registrations, those are mostly reliable dates. Since many of the factories that E.A. Barber wrote about were in business when he wrote the book, I tend to believe his dates. Also since the book was published in 1904, we know the marks were used before that time. Anytime Barber is given as a reference, the reader should know the mark is an old mark before 1904.

There are reasons why the factories do not have records of marks and products made. In the first place, the factories do not need the records. We, the collectors and writers, need the records but the factories do not. They need the room the files would fill. Seldom do factories go into the past to produce an item of years ago. Strangely enough, these reproductions have generally not made money for the factories anyway. After the income tax requirements are fulfilled, many factories throw out the records. Secondly, certain facts the collectors seek, never did exist to begin with. Warwick China and Mt. Clemens Pottery (when owned by Kresge) made hundreds of patterns that were known and ordered by numbers only. These dishes never did have names! Fires have been a terrible threat to potteries. Pottery after pottery has had at least one or more big fires. Many of these fires destroyed records. Floods also have taken their toll of records.

Concerning starting and ending dates for factories, the collectors and researchers want nice "cut and dried" dates for the beginning and ending of factories. In an effort to provide this, all of the writers, both the old time and current, tried to make check lists with specific dates, which sometimes resulted in errors.

A recent publication gave 1900 as a starting date for Canonsburg Pottery. Well, it was, and it wasn't correct! Construction started on the building in 1900 (according to historical information sent to me by the factory) and the first ware was made in 1901. So, I had used 1901 as my starting date. Both writers were **not** wrong. But the readers have a hard time figuring out which was right! Sometimes a potter starts out making pottery as a hobby. Slowly but surely, the pottery making grows into a business over a period of years. Where in this process do we conclude was the starting date? When I talked to some of the individual potters, they had a little trouble deciding on an exact starting time. Sometimes potteries organized, but never did make a piece of ware. Several times the name of the factory was changed soon after it was organized under another name. Also, only a few factories incorporated very near the beginning of their existance.

Potteries don't end any more conclusively than they get started. Many times family members try to continue a business after the death of the main potter or owner until the business finally fades away. This happened even in the days of the old stoneware potter. Factories which are getting ready to go out of business have periods of layoffs and are generally open and closed for awhile before a final bankruptcy sale. Oftentimes, there is a last effort to save the business by completely changing the product made or the name of the business. After a sale of a factory or pottery, the new owner may buy and use the old name even though the product and every aspect of production is different. Rights to names and patents may be purchased, and long after the original manufacturing site is completely dismantled, the name may be used or product may be made.

The factories themselves sometimes pass on incorrect dates to writers. A glass factory owner told me, by letter, he started at a specific date. Later, I had occasion to call him, and again the beginning date was mentioned. I went back to the first letter to see if the dates were the same — they were not! So a third communication tied down the date the glass maker wanted to use. He was simply having trouble making up his mind when his hobby became a business. **The date after the words "at present" is the date the research was done for this book or when this author last communicated with the factory.**

Information About Marks

The word "mark," as used in this book, is anything used by a company to identify their ware. That includes ink stamped marks, impressed or stamped-in marks, incised marks, paper labels, logos, marks in the molds which are sometimes raised or sometimes recessed, advertising trademarks such as the ones used on boxes, and even decals on the front of the piece were included in a very few instances. I tried to tell the reader what kind of a mark it was. Sometimes the marks were sent to me by various people without that information. Directories never say how a mark is applied or whether it is a paper label or not. The registrations with the copyright and patent office did not say how the mark was applied.

On old stoneware, the marks were either scratched into the soft clay with a variety of tools, or they used different kinds of stamps made of metal or wood which were used to stamp or **impress** the mark. The marks written in by hand are called **incised** and were generally one-of-a-kind mark when on old stoneware. Dinnerware makers used an ink stamp mark and later they also used decals on the back as a regular mark. (See Royal China Company for an explanation.) A stamped mark for a stoneware potter would mean **impressed** mark. A stamped mark on dinnerware would mean **ink stamped** mark or **back stamped** as they are called. At the time I wrote the American dinnerware book, I did not know how the marks really got on the backs of dishes. I had envisioned a machine applying these marks, until we went to Quality Stamp Company in East Liverpool, Ohio, and saw that the backstamps were applied with a rubber stamp just like the one I use to put my name on envelopes. Even though one writer had quite a bit to say about my use of the word "backstamp," that word is not even in the *American Dinnerware* book. Anytime a mark shown in this book came from Quality Stamp Company, the reader should know it is an ink stamped mark. Marks copymachined from dishes are almost always inkstamped. This book includes any type of an identifying mark that I think will help the reader to identify a piece of ware.

A **drawn** or **painted** mark is written on the surface of the piece with paint or ink, sometimes underglaze, sometimes not. Studio potters use a zinc oxide that becomes permanent in the firing process. The old stoneware jugs and other pieces sometimes had painted names and marks on them that identified the maker. These old marks were underglaze or fired in. Some advanced collectors can even recognize design or paintings used for decoration as belonging to a certain potter.

What May Be Found In A Mark

The contents of a mark varies from product to product. Probably dinnerware is the hardest to tell what the mark does say. The name in the mark that has come to be known as a pattern name, may be a shape name or a decoration name. There are lists of shape names included for some of the factories in this book.

Many books are available on individual potteries which give us help with this information. **Shape is the key to identifying dinnerware.** If the collector is lucky enough to find two plates from the same company shaped exactly alike with different decorations and the name in the mark is the same on both plates, then you have a shape name. If the plate has Bluebells on the front for decoration and the mark said "Bluebells," it is not hard to tell that the plate had been marked with the name of the decoration.

The complexity of identifying shapes of dinnerware is compounded by the practices of the potteries. For instance, one decoration could be used on several shapes. Sometimes they were given different names if the shape was changed and sometimes they were not. Mostly, as the shape changed, the pattern name changed. But on a big promotion deal where a huge quantity of china was needed to fill orders, shapes could be mixed as long as they had the right decoration. For example, a cream and sugar of a different shape from the rest of the set could be substituted. Also many companies used the same decals. You will find listed as many as three potteries making the same dishes for some big promotions such as for a chain of grocery stores.

I asked Mr. Harrison Keller, president of the Salem China Company at present, for a "guesstimate" of how many pattern names or marks that Salem China might have used. There is no real way to tell, but he guessed 500! I have over 150 marks for Salem in this book, but that leaves a long way to go. On the number of shapes, Mr. Keller said they brought out a new shape every other year, making the number of shapes around 40 to 50.

An example of the above would be "Woodland" and "Woodhue." Woodhue and Woodland had exactly the same decoration. Woodhue was "Flair" shape, which is really the name for a square coup shape. "Coup," by the way is a misunderstood word. Coup refers to shape, but it is not really a shape name. There are many shape names within the coup shape. Complicated? Right! I didn't get this all figured out by myself either. Thanks to Mary Eckstein, a long-time employee at Salem China Company, I understood. She said, "Coup means no rim on surface, it can be round or square as long as it has the smooth no-rim lines." Finally it began to fit together for me. Woodland was also a coup shape, but round, with an Anniversary shaped cream and sugar set. Woodland was a huge promotion deal, sold to many grocery stores to use as premiums in 1954. So, if a collector wanted to put together a set of either of these dishes, there should be plenty around.

Art pottery pieces may have a decorator or artist's mark as well as a factory name. Studio potters sometimes stamp their logo into the damp clay as well as to incise their initials or name. See the listing, "Marks on Dishes, Various Kinds." Also, see the listing of "Decorators and Decorating Factories" in the back.

Why Distributors Are Included

Someone may question why I included distributors or sales agencies in this book. Distributors that used their own marks on pottery, rather than the mark of the manufacturers, are a source of trouble to the collector who is trying to identify the maker of a piece he has acquired. Sometime just knowing the mark is a distributor's mark may help the collector greatly, then he can take the research from there. The distributor played a very important role in our ceramic industry and I hope to bring this fact to light.

Literally hundreds of marks for foreign made ware were filed for registration in the patent and copyright office of this country by the distributors and selling agencies of this country. Generally, these marks were eliminated from the book if I could tell they were definitely foreign-made or were easily identified as foreign ware by the mark on the ceramic piece. I included distributors if I could discover that at some time they did sell American-made goods. There was just no way I could tell whether some of the marks filed for registration in the patent office for distributors were to be used on American-made products. Sears and Roebuck, familiar to us all, sold foreign and American made products. When I could relate the products to one of our factories, I did. In regard to the really big selling agencies and distributors in New York City and Chicago, if I could find no American made product sold by them, they were not included.

Selling agencies that bought foreign blanks and did their own decorating and then sold the products are included in the book. If a seller did some part of making the finished product and I could make the connection, they were listed.

Some huge American distributors will be found listed with only one or two marks out of the dozens they had because these few were the only American products I found for sure that they sold. There were also foreign distributors with offices in America and I couldn't tell whether the mark was on foreign or American ware.

I wanted to include a large variety of types of organizations that owned their own marks, including fraternities, big department stores, museums that also sold pieces, ten-cent stores, tea companies, food companies, antique dealers, souvenir shops, metal cookware, manufacturers, hotel, restaurants, publishers, furniture stores, grocers, fast food chains and appliance manufacturers such as Norge. I think it is important we realize that so many different groups had their own marks, but it is impossible to find out where all of the products were made. But I think they should be included to tell what American companies owned the mark and approximately when it was used.

During World War II and for a very short time afterwards, big distributors sold some American products even if they never did before or after that period. These distributors may be famous for having been an important or sole distributor for a foreign product such as Levy Brothers selling French Haviland; Marks and Rosenfield who sold Colclough English bone china; William S. Pitcairn Corporation sold Irish Belleek; Fondeville and Company sold Embassy Ware, Ambassador Ware, Susie Cooper Ware, Paragon Bone China and Burleigh Ware, all from England in 1945. Fondeville and Company had two lines of American-made ware, "Rochelle Fine China," and "Laurelton" ware.

I did not mean to minimize the importance of our large American distributors by not including the foreign ware sold by them. They were extremely important to our potteries. In this study, it seems to me, that if an American pottery got a large distributor to sell their products then they were a successful pottery. Those that lacked this representation seemed to have a much harder time to survive.

Then there are a few distributors included who, I know, did not sell American products, but whose marks could be taken to be American. Or if over the years I have been asked repeatedly about the marks, I included those distributors and said the ware was foreign made. Hence, some foreign marks will be found in this book under the various distributors. Probably the most difficult part of this book was to decide which distributors to use and those not to be included. I wrote up many I have since taken out of the book. These were American companies with American patents and copyrights on foreign products. It was hard to tell what to do with them.

After around 1960, most of the products would have come from overseas. By the 1980's you can almost count on the fact that practically all of it did! Yet there were more patents filed in the first four years of the 1980's than any other time in history. These then would be American distributors with American patents or copyrights on products they had ordered from overseas.

As of this writing in 1987, very little pottery is made in big factories in this country. It is very sad, but so true, some areas of our American ceramic industry are coming to an end.

The Importance and Understanding of Studio Potters

Studio pottery bears many of the qualities of real art pottery. It undoubtedly is the most artistic ware being made in this country today. But whenever I am faced with tying down a definition in this area, I always turn to Paul Evans' book, *Art Pottery of the United States*, which gives the strictest definition of any of the books on art pottery. Evans, on page five, says, "The distinguishing characteristics of art pottery and studioware can best be delineated by a comparative study of both. In place of the division of labor which became a part of the art pottery industry, one person, the studio potter himself, was responsible for a piece from the beginning to the end: from pugging of the clay to the firing of the kiln and the removal of his personally thrown and decorated piece from it."

The studio potter works in a place of his own rather than a large pottery. The reader will note a great variation in the selection of a workplace for these potters as we tell their histories. Sometimes the studio potter is affiliated with a University or will work in a group with other potters, but still the potter works independently.

Prior to 1920, according to Evans, the person with the same approach to making pottery as that of the studio potter could still find work in our art potteries which gave them the satisfaction they were seeking, but after 1920 the "breakdown between the artistic and technical expression within a commercial framework was obvious, and a definite division between the two approaches was taking place." It was from that time on that the studio pottery movement really started to grow. Between 1894 and 1907, Evans names five Universities that established departments to teach ceramics. Today there are hundreds of colleges and universities offering such courses. In talking to Paul Evans by telephone, he stated he had made a list of over 800 studio potters mentioned in the ceramic magazines in the 1930's. Today these studio potters have to number into the thousands in this country. Their products are completely hand-crafted, one-of-a-kind pieces. The names of these potters included in this book are only a tiny fraction of those that exist today. But maybe in reading about these, an appreciation and recognition of this type of pottery may begin on a wider basis. I truthfully believe that we will never be able to identify one-half of the studio pottery that has been and will be produced in this country. We will have to learn to appreciate a well executed piece and collect the pottery because of the piece in spite of the fact that the maker can't be identified.

A Word On Plaster — Hobby Painting

All over the country now, people are painting on low fired mold cast ceramic ware, making pieces that are about like chalkware or plaster ware. I did not include much of this type in this book. This is in no way a sign of disapproval. I have tried to paint on some of the ware too. Some people are able to turn out beautiful pieces that may make the veteran pottery collector look twice before deciding if the piece is this low fired type of ware or a piece of commercial pottery, especially when some of our commercial factories made ware that was no more vitrified than the hobby type ceramics. There are several shops catering to this hobby trade in every big city and lots of little towns have at least one shop selling these molds. A few of the makers of these items marked their unfired pieces; a very few of these may be found in the book. Mostly the pieces came to the hobbyest unmarked and a variety of names and initials of the person doing the painting or decorating will be found on the pieces. This may cause a great deal of confusion for a beginning pottery collector, but presents no problem whatever to the average pottery collector. Holland Mold, Atlantic Mold, Arners, Sciota Mold are all makers of plaster molds for the hobbyest.

Why So Many Pieces Are Not Marked

Until pottery making of all sorts became a mass production business, adding a mark only added a time consuming chore for the potter. Marks were thought unnecessary in the very early stoneware and redware days because ware was shipped for fairly short distances over a long period of time from one specific area to another for general use. The further the pottery was shipped, the more apt it was to be marked. For instance, the potteries of New Jersey and New York shipped into more populated areas and used more marks than the stoneware potters of Ohio, where there was a potter near many towns who supplied just his own town. The consumer didn't care if a piece wasn't marked and the potter didn't bother to mark it. Then when dinnerware became a factor in the trade, the manufacturer wanted the consumer to think it was foreign made, so marks were deceiving if they were used at all. Redware, stoneware, early glazed earthenware and fine thin porcelain were seldom marked. More marked stoneware can be found than marked redware because redware was generally made earlier.

If a pottery made a special ware and was particularly proud of that production, the effort was put into marking the product. Once in a great while, stoneware potters got an artistic notion and painted a design or marked a variety of things on a single piece of ware. Sometimes they were proud enough of a piece to scribble or paint their name on it and these became the one-of-a-kind pieces so cherished by collectors. But unless there was some reason for the trouble involved in marking the pieces, they weren't marked. One present day studio potter wrote that he never marked his pieces because he thought the ware should be recognized or identified by its own characteristics and merit. I'm sure many stoneware potters felt this same way.

For some reason, very large pieces such as huge jardinieres, etc. were left unmarked by many of the later commercial factories such as Roseville Pottery. Perhaps, it was too hard to get a mark on them. Also, I learned at Ludowici Celedon that just because a mark is in the mold does not mean it will show up on the finished piece. Sometimes it does and sometimes it doesn't. All in all, we can assume there are several times as much unmarked ware in existance as there are pieces with marks.

From the few pieces, we are able to identify by marks and other means, as having come from the old potters and potteries we can learn to recognize the type of ware made by a specific potter, so that when we find unmarked pieces we know who made them. But that is not the only reason we search for marked pieces.

John Ramsay in "Marks of China and Pottery," *Hobbies*, July 1949, pp. 80, 81, said:

"We Americans have become too dependent on labels. But grandma and greatgrandma, unprotected by law and custom, were less fortunate. They had to depend on their own taste and appreciation, their knowledge of quality and workmanship and their own shrewdness and, at that, were too frequently deceived. So, if we want to buy the things grandma and greatgrandma liked and bought, we have to remember that marks did not mean a great deal to them, so that, on their china and pottery, they are often omitted, occasionally impossible to identify from our present data, and not infrequently misleading."

How To Use This Book To Find A Mark Or To Identify A Potter On Your Own

First, try the huge index in the back. The name of the pottery or potter may be listed. Initials are listed, as are pattern names, etc. If this doesn't help, turn to the factories that are listed by place. Sometimes a pottery in the same location will have a mention of the one you are seeking; this is especially true of the way the stoneware potters are written. There are also a list of the various potteries by products. Determine what the piece is and use the product listing. Study the listing of stoneware potters to discover initials. Sometimes the companies used marks that were a composite of their names such as "Ambisco" for American Bisque Company.

If you are seeking a date for a piece and a date is not given, such as for dinnerware pieces, study the pattern lists; some tell when they were discontinued; but either way, you have an idea of time.

Because there are so many marks not yet discovered or identified, many of these suggestions are aimed at helping the reader to find a possible identity on his own with the help of this book even though the mark is not shown. If a company like Salem China, French Saxon or Royal has a large number of identical marks with only a change in pattern name, there are bound to be more just like the ones shown.

If the reader is interested in what kinds of pottery were made in a specific area of the country, he should turn to the place list and read what is written about several potteries in the area. This will give a fairly good idea as to what was produced there.

Credits

Throughout this book the names of dozens of authors, writers, researchers and librarians who have helped me by granting their permission to use their material may be found, then adding new material to what was known at the time. Dozens of people furnished marks for the book. The publishing companies were very kind about granting permission. I will not repeat all of the names here that are mentioned throughout the book. Instead I will use this space to thank the people who worked so diligently behind the scenes. Linda Cleveland searched all of the patent and copyright reports for the book. Ben Cash responded to my request for directory listings by making trip after trip to the library of a University to copy telephone directories. Ben is in his 80's; he had to park his car, walk and climb stairs, etc. but the directories kept coming and he helped so much.

E.S. Carson, Homer Laughlin China Company, Harrison Keller from Salem China Company and Woodrow Price, owner of Quality Stamp Company, have helped me tremendously through all the years I have been researching pottery.

Several writers and editors sent not only the material that is credited to them but they furnished a great deal of source material as well: Susan Cox, editor of *American Clay Exchange*; Pat Johnson, editor of *Pottery Collectors News*; Garth Clark; Dave Newkirk; Thomas G. Turnquist; Jim Martin; Annise Heavilin; Edison Shrum; Henry Heflin; Warren F. Broderick; Grace Allison; Don and Irma Brewer; Doris and Burdell Hall; Jack Tod; Herbert Peck and Jack Chipman.

Individuals who worked in and around the potteries and were always willing to help me include Norris Sowers of Crooksville and S.H. Butler of Bloomingdale, near Roseville, Ohio.

June Kass Jackson (Kass China Company) sent magazines and directories that proved to be invaluable.

Names that do not appear in the credits are Joseph Gregory who researched Virginia potters for the book. Martha Brisker of Brisker's Antiques; Elizabeth Vaughn of Beechwold Antiques; Wilma Hock; Francis Andrews; Connie Rogers and Rena London have all searched out the unidentified marks for me for many years.

A project of this sort involves the whole family of the author. No one escaped numerous tasks involving the book. Every piece of pottery that came near a family member got inspected for a mark "Mom" didn't have. They furnished transportation, moral support and helped in many ways.

Shelly Lehner, my daughter-in-law, typed the book from my rough scribbled sheets. Sometimes we rewrote as many as three times when new material came along, or other authors or publishers wanted changes made. She never complained, she just kept saying "we will get done sometime!"

After eight years spent on this particular book in which I have written hundreds of letters for information and help, I'm sure I may forget to mention someone who should be given credit here. Please know I appreciated all of the help I received, and I hope the book meets the expectations of all of the contributors.

A

A. and A. Pottery. Cotopaxi, Colorado. 1971 to present (1983). Studio potters, Alan and Anita Yarmark make high fired salt glazed stoneware and porcelain into dinnerware, sculptured pieces and various artistic ceramics. Both received B.F.A degrees from Denver University. They participate at various shows around the country. A great deal of hand painting on sculptured pieces was shown in the brochure they sent including various mugs or steins with Alice in Wonderland sculptured faces, pirates, womens faces, etc. A hand painted honey pot with a little bear on top and a sculptured automobile were a couple of the pieces shown. (Mark No. 1 is logo used on brochure. No. 2, 3 & 4, I would assume, are inscribed marks.)

1.

A & A POTTERY

2.

3.

4.

Abbe, Paul O., Inc. Little Falls, New Jersey. Filed for registration of this mark on September 21, 1959, for use on porcelain grinding jars, claiming use since September 1958.

LUMARD

Abbott, Charles. Ogunquit, Maine. 1940 to present (1984). In 1934, Abbott graduated from Syracuse University with a degree in Architectural Engineering. In 1938, Abbott gave up architecture and enrolled in graduate work at University of Michigan to study oriental art. From there he went to Cranbrook Academy to study ceramics under Maija Grotell. In 1951 he studied ceramics at Alfred University. Since 1940, Abbott has been making artistic pieces of ceramics. From 1941 to 1951, he operated a pottery in South Berwick, Maine. In 1948, he became an associate professor at Massachusetts College of Art in Boston, where he started the program that allowed students to earn a degree in ceramics. He later headed the Ceramic Department and finally retired in 1975. While holding the various positions, Abbott always continued as a working potter. After retirement from teaching, he set up a full time studio pottery in Portland, Maine, and then moved

to Ogunquit, Maine, where he still works. Abbott considers himself a functional potter. But like Warren MacKenzie, he has raised the level of ordinary vessels to art pottery. (Information: Thomas Turnquist, ''Charles E. Abbott Vessel Mastery,'' *American Art Pottery*, November 1983, p. 4. Mark: incised, sent in letter by Turnquist.)

C E a

Abcock. Area of New York, Missouri. This potter ceased operations in 1854. His mark is unusual because the name is split by the gallonage numeral. Made stoneware. (Information: Edison Shrum, author for various collector's papers, by letter. Marks: drawn from pictures sent by Edison Shrum.)

Ab 2 cock

Abingdon Potteries Inc. in Abingdon, Illinois. In 1908, Abingdon Sanitary Manufacuring Company started to make plumbing fixtures. In 1933 or 1934 a line of art type pottery including vases, cookie jars and other decorative pieces were started to be made. In November 1950, the art pottery kiln was destroyed by fire, and the emphasis was once more on plumbing fixtures. The company eventually became the Briggs Manufacturing Company, well known for sanitary fixtures. The name was changed from Abingdon Sanitary Manufacturing Company to Abingdon Potteries Inc. in 1945. (Information: London, Rena, ''Out of the Mould,'' *The National Glass, Pottery and Collectable Journal*, February, 1979, p. 10. Also, Hurlburt, Betty, ''Collectors of Abingdon Pottery Organize Group,'' *Tri-State Trader*, April 15, 1978, p. 10). Marks 1, 2 from pieces. Marks 3, 4, 5, 7, Norma Rehl and Connie DeAngelo, ''Abingdon,'' *National Glass, Pottery and Collectables Journal*, December, 1980, pp. 20, 21. Mark 6, *Better Homes and Gardens* advertisement, February, 1949. Mark 8, sent by Don and Irma Brewer, dealers and authors. No. 9 sent by reader. 10, 11, Deb and Gini Johnson, p. 107, 12-14, Rena London, article as cited. 15, Norma Rehl article cited. 16, 17, Lehner *American Kitchen and Dinnerwares*, p. 178.

ABINGDON
USA
P 6

1.

ABINGDON
USA

2.

3.

4.

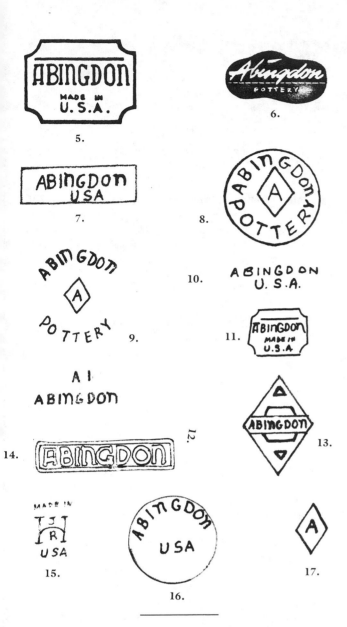

5.

6.

7.

8.

9.

10.

11.

12.

13.

14.

15.

16.

17.

Abraham & Strauss, Inc. Brooklyn, New York. Distributors. Filed December 23, 1936 for rights to this mark to use for china tableware, porcelain table and kitchenware, vases, jars, crocks and jugs, claiming use of this mark since November 1, 1936.

World's Fair

Absecon China and Glass Decorators. Absecon, New Jersey. This company was a decorating company that existed in the 1940's, according to Woodrow Price, owner of Quality Stamp Company. I found no listings at all for this decorator.

Acacia China Company. East Liverpool, Ohio. 1972-1974. Made decorative line of vases, elephants, etc., using mottled glazes and weeping gold decorations. (Information: Jenny B. Derwich and Dr. Mary Latos, *Dictionary Guide to U.S. Pottery and Porcelain*, p. 21. Mark: Quality Stamp Company.)

Ack Potters. Mooresburg, Pennsylvania. 1857-1909. Daniel Ack came to Mooresburg in 1854 from Reading, Pennsylvania. Made stoneware with elaborate cobalt decorations of flowers, birds, etc. Daniel had two sons, John F. and Edward, both potters, who assisted him then carried on the business for a while after he quit. Edward left and John F. worked alone until 1904. John F. Ack reared his nephew, Clyde, and taught him to be a potter, but Clyde left at an early age to be a photographer. A jug as shown had cobalt decoration of flowers and leaves and an impressed or stamped mark in blue. (Information and mark: Jeannette Lasansky, *Made of Mud*, pp. 34, 36.)

J.F. ACK & BRO.
MOORESBURG, PA.

Acme Craftware, Inc. in Wellsville, Ohio, was in business 1946-1970, making a decorative type of pottery, vases, bowls, etc. (Information: Lois Lehner, *Ohio Pottery and Glass, Marks and Manufacturers*, p. 93. Marks: no. 1, stamped mark from Quality Stamp Company, East Liverpool, Ohio; no. 2, incised on piece.)

Acme Pottery (or Porcelain) Company in Crooksville, Ohio, 1903-1905. Makers of semi-porcelain dinnerware. (Information: *Second Annual Crooksville-Roseville Pottery Festival Booklet*, 1967, p. 38.)

Acoma (Indian Pottery). Acoma (Sky City), on top of an isolated mesa in west-central New Mexico, was the site of several revivals of Pueblo pottery making from the 17th century on. Acoma pottery has been popular with the tourist/collector market during the 1900's. Early pieces had simply Acoma painted across the base, but more recently signatures and design marks of individual potters are being added. Lucy M. Lewis was in Indian potter who began making pottery at age seven. By 1950, when she was in her fifties she had become well known. She taught her daughters to make pottery. Dolores Lewis Garcia, Emma Lewis Mitchell, Mary Lewis Garcia, Anne Lews Hansen, are all making pottery. They study the old designs, etc. from books. Dolores was the first of the group to use the old Mimbres designs. Marie Z. Chino, another potter, taught her daughters the art also. Rose Chino Garcia said, ''The forming of the pot is done by pinching if it is small or by coiling on the larger pieces. We use gourds for scraping and a pumice stone for sanding. The drying is done on the stove or in the sun for three or four days. The white slip is applied and polished with a smooth stone, then we paint them with a mixture our mother taught us how to make. We use cow and sheep manure for our firing and cover the pots with shards so they don't get clouded.'' (Quote from Stilwell article as cited.) Guagliumi as cited said, ''Acoma pueblo designs often cover most of a vessel's surface. In the older type the elements have a tight formal arrangement. The later style, while still curvilinear, is much looser. Bird and plant forms have been introduced, as well as hatching. Acoma potters consider hatching to be a color between black and white. Acoma pots, noted for their thin walls, sometimes have a fluted neck. (Information: Arthur Guagliumi, ''Donna Rosa and Black Pottery of Oaxaca,'' *Pottery Collectors' Newsletter*, November, December 1979, p. 7; Kathleen Stilwell, ''Acoma Pottery,'' *American Clay Exchange*, August 15, 1984, pp. 4, 5. Marks: no. 1, Stilwell, as cited; no. 2, staff written, ''Questions,'' *Pottery Collectors' Newsletter*, January, February 1976, p. 10.)

1.

ACOMA
2.

Acorn Pottery. Red Oak, Louisiana. Gordon T. Will, potter, filed for registration of this mark on October 7, 1969, claiming use since October 6, 1966, for wheel thrown pottery of earthenware, stoneware and porcelain in bowls, cups, pitchers, bottles and jugs.

Adams, Allison and Company. Akron, Summit County, Ohio. Around 1860. Stoneware. Mark shown was on cylinder brown glazed molded ink. (Information and mark: Blair, C. Dean, *The Potters and Potteries of Summit County, Ohio*,

1828-1915, published by the Summit County Historical Society, Akron, 1965, p. 25.)

Addington, William R. This potter worked in the 1880's in Jackson County, Georgia, at Jug Hill. By 1880, he was located near Gillsville. He made salt glazed over Albany slip stoneware utilitarian pieces. John A. Burrison, *Brothers in Clay*, pp. 225, 226, said the salt glaze left a mustard tan glaze or green patches where it contacted the Albany or brown slip. (Information and mark: Burrison, as cited.)

WR ADDINGTON
MAYSVILLE GA.

A.F.K. Industries. Addison, Illinois. See Morton Pottery for information. Used mark, ''A.F.K.'' Items with mark are quite scarce.

Aitken, Russell Barnett. Cleveland, Ohio. Aitken was a studio potter who graduated from the Cleveland School of Art in 1931 and studied abroad in 1932-1933. He was one of the artists who worked with Cowan, but it had to be very early in Aitken's career, because the Cowan Pottery closed in 1931. Aitken exhibited in outstanding galleries, such as Sloane Galleries, Ferargill Galleries, Brownell-Lamberton Galleries in New York City and the Neue Gallerie in Vienna. He had one man shows at the Cleveland Museum. You will find his name listed often in the awards presented by the Syracuse Ceramic Nationals as listed in the back of this book. He was still living in 1978. (Information: Gartha Clark, *A Century of Ceramics in the U.S.*, p. 269. Mark: incised; Linda Steigleder, from the booklet published by the Everson Museum of Art to accompany the 1978 exhibition, ''A Century of Ceramics in the U.S.,'' with Curators: Garth Clark and Margie Hughto.)

Akron China Company. Akron, Ohio. 1894-1908. Made ironstone or white granite and hotel ware. This company used a confusing mark because it had nothing to do with the name of the company, ''Revere China/Akron, Ohio'' in a circle with ''A.C. Co.'' monogram in the center. This company was formerly the *Akron Queensware Company* between 1890 and 1894, which used the mark ''A.Q.W. Co. Warranted Iron Stone China, Akron, Ohio'' in a circle stamped underglaze. Barber shows the same mark for Akron China as he did for the American China Company, Toronto, Ohio. There is no

15

way to determine if this is an error or if they both did use the same mark. Sometimes companies in more modern times did use the same mark. (Information and marks: Barber, E.A., *Pottery and Porcelain of the United States*, New York: G.P. Putnam's Sons, 1893, p. 138; Blair, C. Dean, p. 26; Stout, W., *History of Clay Industry in Ohio*, p. 83: Ries and Leighton, around 1921. Also published in full in the *Geological Survey of Ohio*, Columbus, 1923, Fourth Series, Bulletin 26, p. 83.)

Akron Pottery Company. See Johnson, Whitemore, and Co. for history.

Alamo Pottery, Inc. San Antonio, Texas. 1944 to early 1950's. According to Betty Latty, "On the Firing Line," *The Glaze*, March 1978, p. 10, they made vases, patio pieces, pots, jardinieres, pitchers, etc. Later they began to manufacture vitreous china plumbing fixtures. A swan was found by Rena London with the Alamo Pottery mark. The copy of the mark shown was in 1952 *Crockery and Glass Journal*, p. 163. They were not listed in the same reference in 1954. They also made a hand cast tableware with fiesta-like colors. Alamo Pottery had acquired a second plant at Hondo, Texas, and in the early 1950's both plants were purchased by the Universal Rundle Corporation.

Alatoria Pottery. Topeka, Kansas. 1976 to present (1984). Studio potters, Alan and Toria Friedlander, make stoneware into functional ware, one of a kind vessel oriented pots, tile murals and dinnerware. They use an oxidation process fired to cone 6 with crystalline glazes on some pieces. Toria painted pictures before marrying Alan, who was already a potter. Together they started Alatoria Pottery. Pieces of their work has been exhibited at Birdlamp Gallery, Kansas City, MO: Mulvare Art Museum, Topeka KS; also in Wichita and also Albrecht Art Museum, St. Joseph, MO; Harry Hendron Gallery, St. Charles, MO; KACA exchange exhibit in Paraguay. Art pieces are signed "Alatoria" and production work is marked with stamp as shown. Alan did undergraduate work at the School of Visual Arts and received a masters from Pratt Institute, both in New York City. Toria has a B.F.A. degree from City College in New York. Their work is represented in the National Slide Registry of American Craftsmen in Washington D.C.

 Alatoria

Albeco Ceramics. Columbus, Ohio. 1969-1974. Al and Bea Conroy made molded pieces fired to 2,300 degrees into chess sets, Christmas trees, churches, owls, frogs, monkeys, teddy bear lights, etc. which they sold at shows, flea markets and their place of business. Al Conroy died in 1974. They were producing up to the time of his death. Marks are impressed as shown.

ALBECO

Alberhill Pottery in Alberhill, California, was made in connection with the Alberhill Coal and Clay Company for two years only, while Alexander W. Robertson worked for James H. Hill, president of the Alberhill Coal and Clay Company. From 1912 to 1914, he produced artware, hand thrown, some glazed but mostly bisque, in a range of colors from red terra cotta to white and pink. Besides the two marks shown, Paul Evans tells us the company also used the mark "A.C.C. Co. Cal." (Information: Paul Evans, *Art Pottery of the United States*, New York: Charles Scribner's Sons, 1974, pp. 9, 10.)

ALBERHILL

Albery Novelty Pottery. Evanston, Illinois. 1913-1915. Duane F. Albery was a ceramic engineer who worked at the American Terra Cotta and Ceramic Company, but for a couple of years in 1913 to 1915 he and his wife, Frances Huxtable made decorative pottery in the backyard of their home. Some of the glazes resembled Teco ware. (Information and marks: in mold; Sharon S. Darling, *Chicago Ceramics and Glass*, p. 73.)

ALBERY   ALBERY EVANSTON. ILL.

Albright China Company. Carrollton, Ohio. 1910 to the early 1930's. They had a second plant at Scio, Ohio, which later became the home of Scio Pottery. They made dinnerware of semi-porcelain marked "Albright China Company," also "Albright/Carrollton, Ohio." The plant in Scio operated from around 1920 to 1927. A reader writing to *Collector's News* sent a photograph of a plate made by this company, marked "Celebron/Albright/Carrollton, Ohio, U.S.A." It was described as beautiful dinnerware and the picture showed a sailing ship decal. In *Crockery and Glass Journal*, December 18, 1924, p. 153, the Albright China Company advertised three shapes, "Glendere," a fancy shape; "Highland," a plain shape; and "Pilgrim," an octagon shape. They advertised factories at Carrollton, Ohio, and Scio, Ohio, with sales offices in Chicago, Illinois.

Alcas Cutlery Corporation. Olean, New York. Company filed for registration of this mark on September 1982, claiming use since December 1981, for china dinnerware.

KENSINGTON

Alexander, S. and Sons. 38 East 21st, New York, New York. This was a decorating company that existed in the 1940's, according to Woodrow Price, owner of Quality Stamp Company, East Liverpool, Ohio. I found no listing at all for this decorator.

Alexandria, Virginia, Potters and Dealers. Alexandria, Virginia (a suburb of Washington D.C.). **Wilkes Street Pottery** started before 1815 until 1876. On March 2, 1815, the first public announcement of stoneware produced at this pottery appeared in the *Alexandria Gazette*. **John B. Swann** was the first potter in the pottery on Wilkes Street. Before Swann, only earthenware had been made in Alexandria; he was the first to make brown stoneware. Swann had learned the trade making redware apprenticed to a **Lewis Plum** in Alexandria. Later, Swann began to produce gray stoneware with blue decorations, employing 6 men and 2 boys around 1820. In 1822, Hugh Smith and Company loaned Swann a large amount of money to keep him from bankruptcy, but Smith had to foreclose in 1825. Smith operated the pottery until 1841, by hiring men to do the potting. After 1841 until the closing in 1875 the potter **Benedict C. Milburn** and his sons, Stephen and William Lewis, were the owners, making gray utilitarian stoneware with blue leaves, flowers, and so forth painted on, also stove pipe, flower pots and fruit jars. From 1833 until 1841, Milburn had leased the pottery from Smith. He may have worked there even before that time. Benedict Milburn died in 1867, and was followed by his son, Stephen, and by 1873, William Lewis, another son, had taken over from Stephen. In Alexanderia, a dealer named **Robert Hartshorne Miller** established an importing firm selling china, glass and earthenware in 1822. In 1856, his son **Elisha Janney Miller** joined him. Robert retired in 1865 and Elisha continued alone until 1895. In Elmer L. Smith's book, *Pottery, A Utilitarian Folk Craft*, are pictured three gray stoneware crocks with blue sten-

ciled letters. The first initial looks very much like an "r" but it is actually an "e." causing Smith to think the name was R.J. Miller not E.J. Miller. Smith has good pictures of these crocks; it is just that the impressed lettering is poor. According to Myers, p. 77, "no stoneware was ever stenciled in Alexandria. When the Alexandria potters quit, E.J. Miller imported stenciled pieces from James Hamilton and Company of Greensboro, Pennsylvania. See that listing. (Information: Suzita Myers, *The Potters Art, Salt Glazed Stoneware of the 19th Century Alexandria*, published by Alexandria Archaeological Research Center in Alexandria, 1983; Mary G. Powell, *The History of Old Alexandria Virginia - From 1749-1861*, Richmond, Virginia: William Byrd Press, 1928, p. 305. Marks: impressed. No. 1, Smith, p. 16; no. 2, sent by collector and researcher, Joseph F. Gregory who helped to gather the material on these potters. Mark 3, Myers, p. 50, Mark 4, Myers, p. 60. Mark 5, is a water container or water fountain incised on the front, J.W. Smith, who was probably a relative for whom the container was made. On the back is "Smith/Alexa./D.C." Alexandria has not been in the D.C. district since 1846. Nos. 6, 7, 8, Elmer L. Smith, *Pottery, A Utilitarian Folk Craft*, p. 17.)

B.C. MILBURN
1.

B.C. MILBURN
ALEXA.
2.

J. SWANN
ALEX.ᴬ
3.

H.C. SMITH
ALEX
D.C.
4.
4

ON FRONT

J.W. SMITH   5.

E.J. MILLER & CO.
ALEXANDRIA
6.

ON BACK

ALEXA/D.C.

E.J. MILLER & SON
DEALERS IN
7. CHINA AND GLASS
WARE
ALEXANDRIA, VA.

E.J. MILLER & CO.
WHOLESALE
DEALERS IN
QUEENSWARE, CHINA,
GLASSWARE & C.
6 S KING ST.
ALEXANDRIA. VA
8.

Alexis Stoneware Manufactuing Company/Alexis Pottery Company. Alexis, Illinois. 1892-1895. The pottery was organized August 12, 1892, and operated until June 1895. It was sold at auction January 31, 1896. William S. Weir became the owner in 1896 and incorporated the name as the Alexis Pottery Company, which he operated until July 1899, at which time Weir sold his interest. In September 1900, the building was destroyed by fire and never rebuilt. Weir went on to build the Weir Pottery Company. See that listing. (Information and marks: Jim Martin and Bette Cooper, *Monmouth Western Stoneware*, pp. 28, 29.)

Alld, John. Hollis, Maine. Before 1820 until after 1860. John Alld made hand thrown redware and brownware jars, jugs, flower pots, etc. (Information: M. Lelyn Branin, *The Early Potters and Potteries of Maine*, pp. 18-21. Mark: same source, p. 222.)

J Alld

Allegheny China Company. Warren, Pennsylvania. Founded 1952, sold to Buffalo China in 1962 and the factory is still operated by Buffalo China Company. Made hotel and restaurant china. (Information: Lehner, *American Kitchen and Dinner Wares*, p. 21. Also Buffalo China Company information. Marks: The mark shown predates 1959, according to Frank L. Rudesill of Buffalo China, Inc.)

ALLEGHENY
CHINA
VITRIFIED
WARREN, PA.

Alliance China Company. Alliance, Ohio. A distributor associated with Cunningham and Pickett. See Cunningham and Pickett for history. (Marks: on china.)

Alliance Vitreous China Company. Alliance, Ohio. Started 1918 (Stout p. 88.) until the Depression era. Most of the stock was owned by George H. Bowman Company of Cleveland around 1919. They made hotel and restaurant ware and china bathroom accessories. Do not confuse with the Alliance China Company, a distributor. (Information: Lehner, *Ohio Pottery and Glass*, p. 17. Mark: patent office report filed January 2, 1925 which claims the mark had been used from October 1, 1924, for hotel china.)

Allied Stores Corporation. Wilmington, Delaware. This was a giant nation-wide retail syndicate. In April 1951, they added Stern Brothers of New York to the chain. The price was said to exceed $8 million according to the *China, Glass and Decorative Accessories Magazine*, May 1951, p. 35. This was the 75th store to become a part of the Allied Stores Corporation. (Mark no. 1 was filed by Allied Stores Corporation doing business as The Bon Marche, Seattle, Washington, on December 5, 1940 for use on ceramic dinnerware, claiming use of this mark since August 30, 1940. Mark 2 file May 5, 1944 for same use. By the time of the second registration Dey Brothers and Company, Syracuse, New York and the Quackenbush Company of Paterson, New Jersey had been added to the Allied Stores Corporation. No. 3 filed August 19, 1957 claiming use since 1950 for china dinnerware. No. 4 filed February 16, 1982 for glassware beverage sets, and dinnerware made of copper, wood, steel, ceramics and rattan. The company undoubtedly owned many more marks over the years and the products could have been made anywhere. No. 5 by the time this mark was filed October 6, 1964, the name used to file was Bon Marche, Inc. claiming first use June 1954, for earthenware vases, candy dishes, trays, shakers, etc.

1.   2.

WENTWORTH   CHEF WORKS
3.   4.

5.

Alpaugh and McGowan. See Trenton Potteries Company.

B. Altman and Company. New York, New York. Department Store. Filed for registration of this mark on December 8, 1948 to be used on china and earthenware for domestic and household purposes; namely dinner and table ware, vases, ornamental boxes and receptacles for general use, claiming use of this mark since 1915. In the *Crockery and Glass Journal Magazine*, November 1954, p. 36, under "Industry News," is the story of a promotion held by B. Altman and Company, to promote five new dinnerware patterns by Sascha Brastoff, famous California designer. Also, a wall was filled with the designer's one-of-a-kind paintings and a collection of large tile by Brastoff valued at $25,000.00 at that time. See the listing for Brastoff. B. Altman and Company also sold Morgan Belleek China. (See that listing.) In the article "First Showing of Special Castleton China Exhibit at Altman," *Crockery and Glass Journal*, December 1942, pp. 24, 25, is described the special china which Louis E. Hellman, president of

Castleton China commissioned important American painters to design decorations for an expensive and beautiful line of china. Some of the pieces pictured were "Hunters" by Paul Sample which had a full hunting scene and sold for $100.00 per plate. "Wild Flowers" by Ernest Fiene which had a picture of flowers at $800.00 per plaque. "Dance of the Flower Maidens" by Salvador Dali. This ceramic plaque sold for $1,000.00 in 1942. Service plates entitled "Portraits" designed by Elsie Shaver were $1,000.00 per dozen. These had a picture of a little girl with a border of large daisies. In 1986 Altman introduced Homer Laughlin's new line of Fiesta. See Homer Laughlin listing for more.)

Aluminum Cooking Utensil Company, Inc. New Kensington, Pennsylvania. Filed for registration of this mark on November 27, 1956, for table chinaware. There is no connection between this company and Alcoa-Aluminum Company of America. Nancy Prentiss was the Director of the Westmoreland Advisory Service which was a Division of Aluminum Cooking Utensil Company, Inc. She was portrayed as the "perfect hostess," giving advice on table settings, silver, glassware, etc. She was given as author of *The Perfect Hostess* printed in several editions between 1946 and 1954, at Kensington. Dinnerware made by Pope-Gosser China Company, Lenox, Inc., Syracuse China and Castleton China were featured in the booklet.

NANCY PRENTISS

American Art Ceramic Company. Corona, New York. Started 1901 to make artistic terra-cotta and pottery. Evans, p. 11, concluded they were no longer producing art pottery by 1909. (Mark: Barber, *Marks of American Potters*, p. 87.)

Americana Art China Company. Sebring, Ohio. 1949 to present (1983). At first Americana Art China Company decorated pottery pieces only. Then around 1960 they started manufacturing also. The company was started by E.B. Willis and Dean Grindley. These men also started Americana Glass Company which decorated glass. In 1983, Americana Art China Company and the Queens China Company are owned by the families of the two founders. **Queens China Company** was started in 1955 and was purchased by the Grindley and Willis families in the 1960's. Presently, the Queens China Company manufacturers ware for Americana Art China Company to decorate. There is no pottery manufactured at Americana Art China Company at present; they decorate in that building only. In 1981 the Grindley family purchased the **Modern China Company** which had been operating since 1947. Modern

China and Queens China both make a pottery of good quality, a hard body with a fine glaze into cups, pitchers, bowl sets, planters, thimbles, elephants, bells, shoes and all kinds of animals. A great deal of the ware is marked only with "Made in U.S.A." and a lot number. A great deal of pottery is made to customers specifications, decorated and marked only with the distributors names with no manufacturer's name on the piece. At the factory, I saw very attractive large ashtrays marked only with "Indianapolis Motor Speedway Corporation" on the bottom. (I didn't have any real conclusive marks to show in the book even though we went to the factories. Mark 1 is the logo for Modern China Company used on letterheads and boxes etc. which tells us they are still operating under their own name even though owned by Grindleys. Mark 2 is a decal used on the bottom of the ashtray made for Indianapolis Speedway. The stamped mark Ben Silver Creations was dated 2/24/81. Marks 2, 3, 4 were given to me at Americana Art China Company. Further note: In April 1985, Dean Grindley sold the Americana Art China Company. He said as far as he knows they will continue to operate under the same name.)

MODERN CHINA COMPANY 1.
368 EAST VERMONT AVE. P.O. BOX 309
SEBRING, OHIO 44672

2. INDIANAPOLIS MOTOR SPEEDWAY

500 COLLECTOR'S LIMITED SERIES
PLATE NO OF 500

CROWN FAVOR CO.
BOX 310 3.
SEBRING, OHIO 44872

4. **BEN SILVER CREATIONS**
133 PLANDOME RD.
MANHASSET L.I.N.Y. 11030
516-627-8103

American Art China Works. Trenton, New Jersey. Founded 1891 and out of business before 1900, owners were **Rittenhouse and Evans.** Made a thin artware resembling Belleek called "American China" in plain white and decorated ware. (Information and marks: Barber, *Pottery and porcelain of the U.S.*, p. 241.)

American Art Clay Company, Inc. Indianapolis, Indiana. 1919 to present. At present Amaco, the name used by the company, sells all kinds of potters supplies, such as clay, kilns, potter's wheels, glazes, etc. The company now concentrates on school ceramic supplies and ceramic supplies for the hobby field under the "Reward" trade name. According to John F. Gormley who was president of Amaco from 1967 to 1977, the company started to make commercial pottery in 1930. The ceramic designer and manager of the ceramic department was Jaroslov Marek. He and his wife graduated from a ceramic college in Czechoslovakia. The ware included lamp bases, sculptures and vases produced at cone 10 using a white vitreous body. The exclusive distributor was Soovia Janis, still in business in New York City (1983). The retail outlets were very prominent stores such as Peacock's in Chicago, Marshall Fields, Hudsons in Detroit, etc. World War II brought an end to the manufacture of pottery pieces at Amaco. (Information: furnished by John F. Gormley. Mark on beautifully glazed maroon colored vase.)

American Art Clay Works/Edgerton Art Clay Works. Edgerton, Wisconsin. 1892-1903. Made busts, statuettes, ceramic sculpture. The name was changed to **Edgerton Art Clay Works** in 1895. (This is not the same pottery as Edgerton Pottery.) The pottery was idle from 1900 to 1902, then worked a short time, ending in 1903. (Information and marks: Paul Evans, *Art Pottery of the United States*, New York: Charles Scribner's Sons, 1974, pp. 12-14.)

SAMSON BROS. & CO.

American Art Clay Works

Est'd 1892

Edgerton, Wis.

American Art Potteries. 503 West Jefferson Street, Morton, Illinois. 1947-1963. After the Rapp brothers had severed their relationship with Midwest Potteries in 1943, they worked in various potteries in California, Wisconsin and Illinois. After renovating an old garage and equipping it for pottery making, the Rapp brothers opened American Art Potteries in 1947. The products were similar to those made at Cliftwood Pottery and Midwest Pottery when the Rapps were there. None of the products were marked except with a paper label "Norwood Pottery," according to Doris and Burdell Hall in *Morton's Potteries: 99 Years*, p. 46. The pottery made decorative or art ware with unusual colors and mottled appearance. Vases shown in book cited with Matt glaze inside and colored bisque with high gloss spatter outside. Some of these are marked with mark of Planter, Inc., Chicago, Illinois, for which the line was made. The other pottery operating in Morton, Illinois, at this time was the Morton Pottery Company. Both potteries were operated by people whose ancestors had started the first Rapp Brothers Brick and Tile Company. The

American Art Potteries was associated with Andrew Rapp's family; Andrew was also one of the original six brothers who founded the first brick and tile company. The American Art Pottery's shapes and designs are numerous and very attractive, including vases with applied flowers, planters with birds, a swan, frogs, pig figurines, various parts of dolls, bird vases, etc. all beautifully spray glazed. The pottery ended when it was sold for taxes in 1963. (Information: Doris and Burdell Hall, *Morton's Potteries: 99 years*, Morton, Illinois; privately printed, 1981, pp. 46-52. Marks: 1952 *Crockery and Glass Journal Directory*.)

American Beleek Company. Fredericksburg, Ohio. In business for one year only in 1937. See Fredericksburg Art Pottery listing.

American Bisque Company. Williamstown, West Virginia. 1919 to August 1982. Was started in 1919 to supply the shortage of china doll heads which originally came from Germany until World War I. American Bisque turned to making other products - cookie jars, salad bowls, serving dishes of various kinds, ashtrays, etc. - all have been made by this company in huge quantities.

In 1922, B.E. Allen who started Sterling China Company in Wellsville, started to invest in American Bisque, and in order to protect his interests, he finally purchased all of the stock.

American Bisque Company has had its share of hardships so typical of our American Glass factories and potteries. They are in the high water area of the Ohio river and in 1937, ten and one-half feet of water covered the factory floor. On July 28, 1945, the factory burned completely. After rebuilding, all products were made by Ram press only; these use no casting. They had two large kilns operating; one was one-hunded feet long, the other was thirty-five feet in diameter. A sixty-foot decorating kiln was also used. They employed around one hundred people in the peak of the season in 1980. American Bisque used two trademarks. "Sequoia Ware" was sold in gift shops, and "Berkeley" was sold in chain stores, etc. At one time their cookie jars bore a label which looked like a child's blocks with A.B.C. on them. In August 1982, the company was sold to a man from India, named Bipin Mizra, who was operating under the name, **American China Company**, making high fired thin rectangular and square dishes to fit into trays for use on airlines. In 1983 the plant was completely closed and the equipment was sold. (Information: A.N. Allen, last owner of the factory and son of the founds, B.E. Allen. Charles Allen, son of A.N. Allen, works in management at the factory at present for Bipin Mizra. Marks: nos. 1 and 3, sent by company; nos. 2, 3, 5, on pieces. No. 6 was used on paper labels. No. 7 was a roughly incised mark found on several nice pieces of florist or decorative type pottery with dark green mottled glaze. This mark was used for many years around the 1930's according to A.N. Allen. See American Pottery Company for more on the history of American Bisque Company.)

1.

4.

6.

DESIGN
PATENT
APPLIED
ABCO

2.

DESIGN
PATENT
REG 120
A.B.CO.

3.

Patent Applied
Turnabout
The A B Co
USA

5.

AMBISCo
WARE

7.

American Can Company. Greenwich, Connecticut. Filed for registration of this mark on December 18, 1968, claiming use since August 14, 1968, for use on ceramic cups, dishes, plates and bowls.

MIRAWARE

American Ceramic Products Company. See Winfield Pottery.

American Ceramic Society. Columbus, Ohio. The A.C. Society was incorporated in 1899 under the direction of Edward Orton Jr. For the next 19 years the organization was an academic one, publishing *Transactions* and having winter and spring meetings. Then before 1918, the society added in Industrial Division to serve the needs of industrialists and research development as well as the educators. The early organizations was under the direction of such men as Ross Purdy who became General secretary in 1922, and Charles F. Binns of Alfred Unviersity, George H. Brown of Rutgers Univeristy and Homer F. Staley (who was with the National Bureau of Standards.) Purdy became full time editor of *The Journal; Ceramic Abstracts; The Bulletin*, (is often quoted in the book.) Eventually the Ceramic Division of the National Bureau of Standards in Pittsburgh, Pennsylvania was founded due to the influence of the A.C. Society. Purdy was made an honorary member and given recognition for his work in the society in 1942. The Ross Purdy Museum was recently founded in Columbus in connection with the A.C. Society.

American China Company. Toronto, Ohio. Organized in 1894, went into receivership and reorganized in 1897. Closed in 1910. American China Company manufactured a high grade of white granite and semi-porcelain table and toilet ware in white and decorated. They made novelties, jardinieres, souvenir goods and loving cups in artistic shapes. (Information: Lehner, *Ohio Pottery and Glass*, p. 92. Marks: 1, 2, 4, 5, Barber, p. 137, *Marks of American Potters*; No. 3, 6, 7, mark on dishes.)

1.

2.

3.

4.

5.

MADE BY
THE
AMERICAN CHINA CO.
TORONTO. OHIO

6.

7.

American Chinaware Corporation. Had offices in Cleveland, Ohio. Was a combination of several potteries trying to fight the depression: Knowles, Taylor, Knowles; National China Company of East Liverpool, Ohio; Smith Phillips China Company; Carrollton Pottery, Pope-Gosser, E.H. Sebring China Company; The Sebring Manufacturing Company; Morgan Belleek China, Canton, Ohio; lasted only from 1929 to 1931. I had thought previously that American Chinaware Corporation had lasted a year or so longer than 1931, but in *Sebring, Ohio, A Brief History*, 1949, published by the Sebring 50th anniversary committee, p. 17, the unnamed author tells us the corporation was declared bankrupt at that time.

The second mark shown was from a patent office report to be used on plates, dishes, platters, cups etc. made of semi-porcelain. Use was claimed since June 20, 1929. Both marks shown are stamped. The first mark was on a dish.

1.

2.

American China Manufactory. See William E. Tucker.

American China Products Company. Chesterton, Indiana. Pottery was in business as the American China Products Company from 1919 to 1923. In November 1923, the plant was sold to Fraunfelter China Company and operated until December 1925. Fraunfelter China Company sold the plant in May 1931, but it had been inoperable since 1925. Marks shown were used before November 1923. Products made at the Chesterton plant were mainly heavy white hotel china, plain banded or with a logo. Later, a finer decorated china with a bluebird and flower pattern was made. Turtle paperweights, small decorated shoes and salt and pepper shakers were also made by American China Products Company. The Chesterton China (marks shown) was made only for one and one-half years, from April 1922 to December 1923, according to Mrs. Hopkins as cited. (Information and mark no. 2: sent by Eva Hopkins, researcher on Chesterton, Indiana, potteries. Mark 1 was sent by Larry Paul, researcher and writer.)

1.

CHESTERTON
CHINA
A.C.P. CO.

2.

American Crockery Company. Trenton, New Jersey. In business 1876 and out before 1900. Barber showed marks they used in 1890. Made white granite dinnerware. (Information: Lehner, *American Kitchen and Dinner Wares*, p. 24; Barber, *Pottery and Porcelain of the U.S.*, p. 305. Marks: Nos. 1, 2, Barber, *Marks of American Potters*, pp. 59, 60; no. 3, on piece; no. 4, sent by Larry Paul.)

1.

AMERICAN CHINA
A.C.CO.

2.

3.

AMERICAN CHINA
A.C. Co.

4.

American Dinnerware Service. Sioux City, Iowa. Milton J. Soelberg, a distributor filed for rights to this mark on September 19, 1950 to be used for earthenware and porcelain dinnerware; namely cups, saucers and plates, claiming use of this mark since January 1, 1944.

American Encaustic Tiling Company, Ltd. The factory was in Zanesville, Ohio, and the offices and owners were in New York, New York. In 1875 the city directory listed Fischer and Lansing, proprietors of the American Encaustic Tile Company (Benedict Fischer and G.R. Lansing). Fischer and Lansing financed and experimented with making tile for several years, but they were not potters. They lived in New York City. A man named F.H. Hall came to Zanesville around 1874 or 1875 and he was successful in making tile of American clay with American workmen giving the English and Germans the first real competition they had in the field. One of their very first jobs was to make tile for the floor of the Muskingum County Courthouse in 1877. Between 1877 to 1879 George A. Stanberry became general superintendent. He was responsible for divising methods to make floor tile by machinery on a large scale. On March 15, 1879, the name became American Encaustic Tiling Company, Ltd. Other well known ceramists worked at the American Encaustic Tiling Company over the years. Herman C. Mueller went to work there as a modeler in 1886 or 1887 until 1893. Karl Langenbeck came to the plant around 1890. Lawton Gonder worked in the research department from 1915 to 1926. Fred Rhead was another skilled technician who worked there before 1927. In 1875 to 1879 the company operated on Hughes Street in Zanesville, Ohio. In 1879 to 1892 they were on Mareta Road. Then in 1892, they moved to a new plant on Linden Avenue. President McKinley gave an address. A four inch square tile with a woman's head and banner was made to commemorate the opening of the plant on Linden Avenue. Political tile were made over the years such as the Republican State Convention in 1896. For more on these, see Norris F. Schneider, "Souvenir Tile," *Zanesville Times Signal*, October 30, 1966 (no page no.). One of the problems with the business end of the American Encaustic Tiling Company was absentee ownership. Right from the start to finish, the majority of owners and later the stockholders were in New York City. Competition from overseas increased. The stock market fell and the company operated at about fifty percent in 1931 and 1932. By 1933, little tile was made. Refinancing was attempted in December 1934 through the Reconstruction Finance Corporation, but in 1935 the plant was closed permanently. In 1937, the building was opened as the Shawnee Pottery. (Information: Norris Schneider, "Lawton Gonder," *Zanesville Time Signal*, September 22, 1957 (no page no.); Norris Schneider, "H.C. Mueller Contributed to Industrial Life of City," *Zanesville Times Recorder*, March 7, 1971 (no page no.); Norris Schneider, "American Encaustic Tile Company's First Plant Here is Demolished," *Zanesville Times Recorder*, October 27, 1963 (no page no.); Norris "American Encaustic Tile Company," *Zanesville Times Recorder*, in several parts, May 14, 1961, May 21, 1961, May 28, 1961, June 4, 1961. Marks: nos. 1 and 2 were filed April 8, 1905 for ceramic tile and ceramic ware. No prior use was listed. No. 3 was filed April 16, 1921 for ceramic wall, floor and ceiling tile, claiming use since November 1920. No. 4 is a drawn copy of actual mark 5. A recessed mark was found on a vase made of the same vitrified clay with heavy glaze. No. 6 is a recessed mark found on highly vitrified soap dish held in the air by a nude lady figure. No. 7 is from Deb and Gini Johnson, *Beginner's Book of Pottery*, p. 99.)

1. **A.E. TILE CO.**

2. **A.E.T.Co.**

3. **VITKA**

4. **AETCO STUDIO**

5. **AETCO STUDIO**

6. **A.E.T.CO.**

7. **A.E. TILE CO. LIMITED**

American Fine China. Warrington, Pennsylvania. 1977 to present. This is a company I will have to sneak into the book with only a logo to show. The logo was in the letterhead. However, there is a concept represented in this company that I want the readers to know and understand. The following paragraphs are from a letter received from the company in February 1978.

"American Fine China is a company which represents a type that exists in the United States today. We manufacture our dinner ware, kitchen ware and accessory pieces under private label for other people who have sales and marketing organizations. There is a great amount of china and ceramics sold in the United States under the names of people who do not in fact manufacture it, but buy it or import it with their name on the back.

Our company is very young, since we only started in May of last year, and cannot begin to meet the demand that exists at the moment. However, within a year or two we hope to be able to satisfy that demand with the construction of a new factory.

For example, Sears markets many items under their own brand names, such as Kenmore and Tower, etc., which are in fact made by well known American and Foreign companies."

american fine china

American Greeting's Corporation. Cleveland, Ohio. See Taylor, Smith, and Taylor, for some marks.

American Haviland. See Shenango China Company.

American Heritage Publishing Company, Inc. New York, New York. Company filed for registration of this mark on February 19, 1981, claiming use of mark since December 1964, for use on ceramic plates, bowls, dishes and cups; glass vases, bowls, beverage-ware, candlesticks and tankards; ceramic trivets, coffee pots, teapots, creamers, sugar bowls, pitchers, and trays; cheese trays, food serving scoops, salt and pepper shakers, cream pails, storage boxes and glass and ceramic jars.

AMERICAN HERITAGE

American Home Products Corporation. New York, New York. They filed for use of mark one on December 13, 1968, for china dinnerware. Mark 2 filed October 1971 claiming use since July 1970 for earthenware, stoneware and porcelain dishes. The pieces were unidentified as to maker.

PRUDENCE
1.

2.

America House, Ltd. New York, New York. Selling agency. Filed for registration of this mark on March 12, 1956, claiming use since 1943, for pottery, earthenware, and porcelain plates, bowls, cups, saucers, pitchers, mugs, cases, bottles, soup bowls, cereal bowls, sugar bowls, creamers, teapots. This company sold products made by the studio potter, Dorothy Jervis. (See that listing.)

AMERICA HOUSE

American Lava Corporation. Chattanooga, Tennessee. Manufacturers of industrial ceramics who filed for registration of mark no. 1 on June 21, 1961, claiming use since March 1961. Mark 2 was filed June 9, 1949, claiming use since May 1949, for ceramics involving industrial arts.

ALZIRCON
1.

ALSIBASE
2.

American Porcelain Manufacturing Company. Gloucester, New Jersey. Operated 1854 to 1857, became **The Gloucester China Company** 1857-1860. Made white ware and porcelain dinnerware etc. (Information: Barber, *Pottery and Porcelain of the U.S.*, p. 183. Marks: *Marks of American Potters*, p. 69.)

A.P.M.Cº

American Pottery Company. Marietta and Byesville, Ohio. American Pottery Company started as the Stoin-Lee Pottery Company and was incorporated, in Ohio in March 1942, with principal offices in Byesville. In December 1942, the name became American Pottery Company and in 1944 the offices were moved to Marietta. During 1944, J.B. Lenhart acquired the majority of outstanding stock and was treasurer and general manager until 1961. Lenhart was followed by Braden as owner but Braden served on the Board of Directors only. In 1962, John F. Bonistall became president and general manager under Braden's ownership. The pottery went out of business in 1965 and the plant was torn down later. They made cookie jars, some marked "Turnabout," decorative pieces marked "Marietta Modern," kitchenware, etc. The confusing part of the history of this company far as collectors go is as follows: American Pottery Company was owned on a fifty-fifty basis by J.B. Lenhart and A.N. Allen for a period of years. Mr. A.N. Allen was the sole owner of American Bisque Pottery. J.B. Lenhart, besides owning half and later a greater share of American Pottery, also worked at American Bisque for Mr. Allen as his sales manager. With both men having such connections, we get an interchange of products between these two companies. See American Bisque and Terrace Ceramics for more on American Pottery Company. (Information: John F. Bonistall and A.N. Allen by telephone and letters. Marks: no. 1, copyright report filed July 1, 1944, claiming use since 1943 for ceramic cookie and candy jars, also used by American Bisque Company. Mark no. 2, on decorative dish.)

TURNABOUT
"THE FOUR-IN-ONE"   1.

Marietta Modern
  2.
        M-5

American Pottery Company of Peoria, Illinois. See Peoria Pottery for history.

American Pottery Works. East Liverpool, Ohio. Started 1887, by 1902 moved to Sebring, Ohio. American Pottery Works was purchased in East Liverpool, Ohio, in 1887 by the Sebring brothers. There were six brothers, who by working very hard, acquired enough money to purchase a one-kiln pottery which employed ten men in East Liverpool. Their business prospered, and by the 1893 and 1894 *Factory Inspection Reports*, they were employing close to one-hundred people. In these reports, the name was simply **Sebring Pottery** at East Second Street in East Liverpool, making white and decorated ware. By the 1902 *Factory Inspection Report*, the Sebring Pottery had been moved to the town of Sebring which the brothers founded around 1889 or 1890. George, Jr. went to buy land for the town of Sebring as early as 1888, for $1.25 per acre. The sole purpose for founding Sebring was to make a pottery manufacturing town. A pottery was one of the first buildings built, then followed a succession of potteries. By the end of two years, the town of Sebring was pretty well established. See French China, French Saxon China, Limoges China Company, Oliver China, Sebring China, Sebring Manufacturing Company, Saxon China, Royal China, for more on various Sebring, Ohio, potteries. According to Wilbur Stout in *Clay Industry in Ohio*, p. 72, the factory made some bone china, but judging from the texture of these two pieces I have found, this factory didn't seem to have the skill or technique. (Information: Lehner, *American Kitchen and Dinner Wares*, pp. 25 and 26. Mark: copy machined from dish.)

American Terra Cotta and Ceramic Company/Gates Potteries. Terra Cotta, McHenry County, Illinois, near Crystal Lake, forty-five miles northwest of Chicago. In 1885, William D. Gates acquired the property as part of his inheritance from Simon S. Gates, his father. He founded the company to make architectural terra cotta and also created an art pottery called "Teco" ware which was first made public in 1901. Gates created many shapes but also hired company designers to make over 500 shapes. Several writers agree that around early 1920's ended Teco ware production. The last advertisement found was 1923. Barber, *Marks of American Potters*, p. 162, describes Teco ware as being made with plain shapes, usually with modeled or relief designs, covered with a dull or matt glaze of peculiar grayish-green tint. Evans, pp. 278-281, gives a splendid description of the ware and glazes, etc. involved in making it. According to several newspaper accounts from *The Herald*, sent by the McHenry County Historical Society at Union, Illinois, the largest building was built in 1904. In 1930 the American Terra Cotta and Ceramic Company was sold and called the American Terra Cotta Corporation to make architectural products. Shortly after the company started fabricating steel, still operating today as Terra Cotta Industries, Inc. There is some disagreement about when Teco ware was first introduced, but Evans, pp. 278, gives 1901 with evidence to back it up. Perhaps the 1903 or 1904 date grows out of the fact that in 1904 the Gates Potteries were the first to show ware of this kind at the St. Louis Exposition. Also that year, the new big building was constructed. This particular building was torn down in 1972 after the Terra Cotta operation was phased out in the 1960's. (Information: Paul Evans, as cited; Darlene Dommel, "Teco Pottery," *Antique Trader*, June 8, 1977, p. 76. Marks: nos. 1, 2, from *American Clay Exchange*, November 8, 1982, p. 15, in an old advertisement; and staff written "Terra Cotta Teco Pottery Brought Early Fame to C.L.," *Crystal Lake Herald*, July 1, 1974, p. 8.) the mark was filed for registration on May 10, 1905 for ornamental pottery-ware comprising vases, bowls, lamp bases and jars. No prior claim to use was given. Nos. 3-6, Sharon S. Darling, *Chicago Ceramics and Glass*, pp. 57, 169. Nos. 3 and 4 are on art pottery; nos. 5 and 6 were used on architectural pieces.)

Teco   1.   Teco   2.

WM. D. GATES   3.   TECO   4.

AMERICAN
TERRA COTTA   5.   6.   AMERICAN
CHICAGO   TERRA COTTA

American Wholesale Corporation (also known as Baltimore Bargain House). Baltimore and Cumberland, Maryland. A selling agency, which filed May 23, 1910, for mark one, used ten years prior to 1910, for crockery cooking utensils, flower pots, porcelain and earthenware vases, porcelain table and kitchen ware, jardinieres, porcelain toilet sets and crockery dishes. They filed September 25, 1919 for registration of mark two to use on crockery, cooking utensils, flower pots and porcelain and earthenware vases, porcelain table and kitchen ware, jardinieres, porcelain toilet sets and crockery dishes, claiming use since June 27, 1919.

1. Baltimore Bargain House

American Wholesale Corporation
2. **Baltimore Bargain House**

Amish Pottery. See Morton Pottery Company.

Amoges China Company, Inc. Dentzville, Trenton, New Jersey. Filed for registration on this mark on May 11, 1945, for use on decorated chinaware, vases, urns, perfume bottles, jars, candy boxes, apothecary jars and flower pots, claiming use since May 15, 1944. Amoges China Company wasn't listed in the directories until 1948 when the Trenton City Directories listed it that year only. This was apparently a short lived pottery. I don't find another pottery listed later at the address of Amoges which was 213 Bunting Avenue.

Amoges

Amos, F.M. and W.H. (two separate potters). W.H. Amos had a stoneware factory in Baltimore, Maryland, in the early 1830's. See the listing for B.C. Miller, a potter who worked for Amos in Baltimore. Also, in Antioch, Monroe County, Ohio, a potter named F.M. Amos made early stoneware pieces. This imprinted mark was found on a late 19th century stoneware crock at the Ohio Ceramic Center in Zanesville, Ohio.

F. M. AMOS
ANTIOCH
OHIO

Amway Corporation. Ada, Michigan. Distributors of Amway products, such as cleaning products, deodorants, all sorts of chemicals for home use, filed for registration of this mark on April 13, 1966, claiming use since November 1963, for use on chinaware plates, cups, saucers, platters and bowls. No doubt, these were used as a premium in various promotions of Amway products.

AMWAY

Anchor Hocking Corporation. Lancaster, Ohio. This company has a long, well-known history in the field of glassmaking, but their interests in pottery making is less well known. Anchor Cap Corporation was incorporated September 13, 1928, and as of December 31, 1937, was consolidated with Hocking Glass Company which had already merged with General Glass and Standard Glass and the name became Anchor Hocking Glass Corporation. From that time on, company after company was consolidated, controlled, merged or was formed by or with Anchor Hocking. Included were American Metal Cap of Brooklyn; Salem Glass Works, Salem, New Jersey; Gas Transport, Inc., Ohio; Maywood Glass Company, Los Angeles; Carr-Lowrey of Baltimore, Maryland; Glass Crafters, Inc., Baltimore; Tropical Glass and Box Company, Zanesville Mould Company, Zanesville, Ohio; Anchor Hocking Inter America, Ltd. (to purchase distributorship in Puerto Rico); Plastics, Inc., St. Paul; Lindner Industries, Netherlands. Moldcraft, Inc., was acquired and Ravenscroft, Ltd. was a formed company. This is a very sketchy outline of the formation of the present corporation and is mentioned here only to give an indication of the complexity of the corporation that has also become a part of the pottery industry in America. In March, 1973, Anchor Hocking Corporation acquired Taylor, Smith and Taylor, of Chester, West Virginia, a manufacturer of stoneware and ceramic dinnerware. (See Taylor, Smith and Taylor.) Then in 1975, the Taylor, Smith and Taylor Company was dissolved and the plant was operated as a division of Anchor Hocking Corporation. The name Taylor, Smith and Taylor was phased out. In 1982, Taylor, Smith and Taylor was closed permanently. See that listing for the Anchor Hocking marks. Also, see Ravenscroft, Ltd. listing. On June 2, 1979, Shenango China Company became the property of the Anchor Hocking Corporation and has remained so until present (1986). See Shenango China Company listing for marks registered in the Anchor Hocking name.

Anchor Pottery. Trenton, New Jersey. 1893 to 1926. In the *1902 Glass Factory Directory*, they were listed as making dinner sets and toilet sets. They were listed in the *Trenton City Directories* until 1927 as Anchor Pottery, but they were purchased by Fulper Pottery in 1926. In the Stangl Company booklet is the following statement regarding Anchor Pottery: "In 1926 the company (Fulper) had also taken over the Anchor Pottery Company, Trenton, New Jersey, which had been owned by the Grand Union Tea Company and was used to manufacture premiums that Grand Union gave away in its house-to-house sales program." (Information: Barber, *Pottery and Porcelain of the United States*, p. 161, and the *1902 Glass Factory Directory* listing: *Stangl, A Portrait in Progress*, privately printed by Stangl Pottery Company, 1965. Marks: nos. 1-7 and 10, Barber, as cited; nos. 8, 9, 12, on dishes; no. 11, Ramsay, p. 252.)

1.

2.

3.

4.

5.

6.

7.

8.

9.

10.

11.

ANCHOR
JEN

12.

Andersen, Weston and Brenda. East Boothbay, Maine. In business in 1985. Studio potters, Weston and Brenda Andersen, make very attractive ceramic birds, animals, bowls, vases, etc. by making molds from their original designs and then slip casting pieces which then receive a bisque firing, are decorated and refired to 2,200 degrees F. (Mark: incised on piece. Requests for further information were not answered.)

Anderson, Ken D. Mt. Morris, Michigan. Studio potter making stoneware and porcelain into decorative and functional pieces from 1976 to present (1983).

Andrea's, Inc. Kenosha, Wisconsin. Company filed for registration of this mark on November 6, 1978, for use on earthenware mugs.

HOMETOWN MUG

Andreson, Laura. Los Angeles, California. 1933 to present (1984). Laura received a B.A. degree from University of California in Los Angeles in 1932 and a M.A. from Columbia University in 1937. She began teaching in the art department at U.C.L.A. in 1933 until 1970. By 1936 she began making pottery and continued to do so all of the time she was teaching. Until 1948 she made earthenware vases and decorative pieces. Between 1948-1957 she worked with stoneware. After 1957 she used a porcelain base to make artistic pieces. Since 1970, Laura has participated in over 68 invitational and one person shows or exhibitions. (Information: Tom Turnquist, "Studio Pottery" *Antique Trader*, July 4, 1984, 0. 75. Marks: no. 1, Tom Turnquist, by letter. Mark no. 2 is from Linda Steigleder, from the booklet published by the Everson Museum of Art to accompany the 1978 exhibition, "A Century of Ceramics in the U.S.")

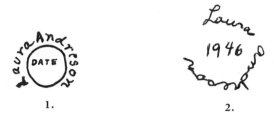

1.

2.

Anna Pottery. Anna, Union County, Illinois. 1859 to 1894. Cornwall and Wallace Kirkpatrick were owners and operators of the Anna Pottery. From 1837 to 1839, Cornwall, at age twenty-three, worked in a pottery started by his father in Urbana, Ohio. His father had moved to northern Illinois. Andrew Kirkpatrick had also worked in Fredericktown, Ohio, as far back as 1820, making earthenware. Cornwall established a second pottery at Covington, Kentucky, where he worked until 1848, then he moved on to Point Pleasant, Ohio. In 1857 he moved to Cincinnati, to work in the Fulton Pottery until 1857. In 1857, Cornwall, Wallace and Andrew had a pottery in Mound City, Illinois, and in 1859 they moved on to Anna, Illinois, where they fired their first kiln in 1859. In 1868 they discovered a fine bed of kaolin clay and sold clay as well as making various utilitarian pieces of pottery. The products were earthenware and later stoneware. Their pig flasks are well known and avidly sought by collectors. Besides basic items such as drain tile, fire brick, they made jugs, dogs, owls, frog mugs, frogs, snake jugs, etc. Wallace made at least two complete farm scenes of stoneware, both described in magazines; one in September 18, 1878, *Farmer and Fruit Grower*, and the other in the November 28, 1883 issue of the same magazine. It was a complete miniature farm scene with snakes, frogs, cabins, wagons, barns, etc. Products made by the Kirkpatrick brothers are in collections at the Smithsonian Institute, the New York Historical Society and many private collections. (Information: Ellen Paul Denker wrote her thesis on the Anna potters, and later an article, "The Kirkpatrick's Anna Pottery," *Antique Trader Weekly*, January 12, 1977, pp. 42, 43. Denker states her material was constructed from W.H. Perrin, *History of Alexander, Union, and Pulaski Counties, Illinois*, 1883, pp. 73, 82; also, E.M. Ayers, Art in Southern Illinois, 1865-1914, *Journal of the Illinois State Museum*, Volume 36, June 1943, pp. 164-189. Marks: inscribed mark no. 1 from Harold Guilland, *Early American Folk Pottery*, p. 227. Various inscriptions may be found on the pig flasks. In the Denker article cited, a pig is pictured with "Centralia has struck coal and is jubilant, November 1874." On p. 145 of *The Art of the Potter*, by Dianna and J. Garrison Stradling, is pictured a pig with "Latest and Most Reliable Railroad and River Guide/Compliments of Anna Pottery/With a little good old rye." Mark no. 2 is inscribed on a pig flask identified by the owner as having been made by the

Kirkpatricks, but it did not say Anna Pottery. It looked very much like the various pigs pictured in books.)

April, Nancy. Rosendale, New York. 1971 to present. Studio potter making art pieces which are Raku fired. She won a banner award at the Winterfair Show in Columbus, Ohio in 1981.

Apple Tree Lane Pottery. Darien, Connecticut. Dorothea Warren O'Hara, a studio potter, writer, illustrator and teacher studied art in Munich, Paris and London. She held her first exhibition of pottery at the Royal College of Art in London. She returned to the U.S. to open a studio in New York, where she taught classes and made pottery. She wrote and illustrated articles for the *Ladies Home Journal* for seven years and was a correspondent for *Keramik Studio* for sixteen years. In 1915 she won a gold medal at the Panama-Pacific International Exposition in San Francisco, for her pottery pieces. Two of her vases were bought by the Japanese for display in the Tokyo Museum. In 1920 she started the Apple Tree Lane Pottery in Darien. She made pieces of red clay and a white tin glaze with high relief modeling on vessel forms. She made some pieces with Egyptian blue glaze. Her work is in collections in th Metropolitan Museum of Art, New York; the Everson Museum of Art, Syracuse, New York; the William Rockhill Nelson Gallery, Kansas City, Missouri; the Henry Ford Museum, Dearborn, Michigan; and the Museum of the Cranbrook Academy of Art, Bloomfield Hills, Michigan. O'Hara was a member of the Society of Designers and Craftsmen of New York and an Honorary Life Member of the Keramik Guild of New York and the Pen and Brush Club. (Information: Garth Clark, *A Century of Ceramics in the U.S.*, p. 315. Incised mark: Linda Steigleder, from the booklet published by the Everson Museum of Art to accompany the 1978 exhibition, "A Century of Ceramics in the U.S.")

Arcadia Export-Import Corporation. New York, New York. Had this mark listed in 1950's directories. Shenango China Company and Jackson China Company both had this mark in their materials, so they both made products for Arcadia Export-Import Corp.

Arc-En-Ciel Pottery. Zanesville, Ohio. 1903-1905. In 1903, John Lessell and several other men purchased the A. Radford Co. and named it Arc-En-Ciel which is a French word for rainbow. In 1904 the pottery exhibited at St. Louis Exposition. A year later it made cooking ware in stippled blue, brown and green in a Rockingham finish. They made gold lustre vases. In 1905 the name was changed to Brighton Pottery. (Information: Norris Schneider, "Many Small Art Potteries Once Operated in Zanesville," *The Times Recorder and The Zanesville Signal*, February 4, 1962, no page numbers in notebook. Marks: No. 1, Lehner, *Ohio Pottery and Glass*, p. 95; No. 2, Evans, *Art Pottery of the U.S.*, p. 16.)

Archie Bray Foundation/Western Clay Manufacturing Company. Helena, Montana. The Western Clay Manufacturing Company in Helena, Montana, began making bricks and press-molded decorations for early neoclassical architecture in 1911. In the early 1940's the plant was owned by Archie Bray. Pete and Henry Meloy were allowed to fire the pots, they had made, at the company kiln. Bray became interested in the work of these studio potters. He had graduated from Ohio State University in 1911 in ceramic engineering and was devoted to arts in general. In 1951, Bray suggested that Peter Voulkos, Rudy Autio, Branson Stevenson and the Meloys build a pottery at the brick yard. This pottery became the basis of the Archie Bray Foundation also established in 1951. After graduation, Voulkos and Bray became resident artists there and the pottery became a center for ceramic art in the Northwest United States. (See the listing for marks and information for the various potters who were associated with the pottery as lecturers and teachers, or were trained themselves at the foundation: Peter Voulkos; Ken Ferguson; David Shaner; Bennett M. Welsh; Rudy Autio; Bernard Leach (an Englishman); Marguerite Wildenhain; Daniel Rhodes; Antonio Prieto; Robert Arneson; Wayne Higby; Warren MacKenzie; Ruth Duckworth; and many others in this book. For a very comprehensive account of the work done at the foundation and history on the various potters see La Mar Harrington, *Ceramics in the Pacific Northwest*, published by the University of Washington Press: Seattle, Washington, 1979.)

Arequipa Pottery. Fairfax, California. Founded in 1911. Incorporated in 1913. Closed during World War I. Pottery started as therapy for tuberculosis patients in a Arequipa sanitorium. The pottery had a selling booth and demonstrations at the Panama-Pacific Exposition in 1915. Pottery was closed around 1918. Ware was hand thrown, some cast and large pieces pressed. The glazes were outstanding. Skilled ceramists such as Frederick H. Rhead and Louis M. Solon were employed at various times. See Paul Evans, *Art Pottery of the United States*, pp. 17-21 and Kovels, *Collector's Guide to American Art Pottery*, pp. 1, 2, for history, techniques and pictures. (Marks: Evans, p. 21; Kovel, p.2)

1.

2.

3.

4.

5.

6.

7.

Ariel of California. See Hillcrest Pottery, Berkeley, California.

Arita Tabletop Company. Anaheim, California. 1976 to present, is a wholly owned subsidary of International Air Services of Burlingame, California. They are a rapidly growing dinnerware concern supplying wares to outstanding stores all across the country. The company's products include a fine porcelain and an excellent grade of stoneware, beautifully decorated. Many shapes and lines were included in Lehner, *American Kitchen and Dinnerwares*, p. 27.

Arlen China Company. See Harlem Crockery Company.

Armstrong, Joe. Roseville, Ohio. Around 1895. Made stoneware. There was a John Armstrong listed in 1850 Census for Clay Township (Roseville, Ohio, area.) Perhaps this Joe Armstrong was his son. (Mark 1, obtained from picture of huge thirty gallon jug owned by local resident in area. Mark 2 on stoneware jug. E.M. Ransbottom was one of the four brothers who owned Ransbottom Brothers Pottery Company in 1906. (See that listing.)

MADE BY
JOE ARMSTRONG
30
APRIL 29ᵗ 1895
ROSEVILLE, O.

1.

MADE FOR
E.M. RANSBOTTOM
ROSEVILLE
BY
JOE ARMSTRONG
OCT 10ᵗ 1895

2.

Armstrong and Wentworth. Norwich, Connecticut. Thorn, p. 116, dates this potter 1814-1828 and Ramsay, p. 199 gives 1812-1834. Mark impressed. Made stoneware. Ramsay describes a mark "A & W" impressed. (Marks: Thorn, p. 116.)

ARMSTRONG & WENTWORTH
NORWICH

E. WENTWORTH
NORWICH

Arneson, Robert. Sculptor, studio potter, teacher, Robert Arneson, studied at College of Marin, Kentfield, California, from 1949 to 1951. He received his B.A. degree from California College of Arts and Crafts in Oakland, California, in 1954, then a M.F.A. degree from Mills College in Oakland, in 1958. He taught in high schools in Oakland, and then at Mills College and in 1962 became head of the ceramics department of University of California, until the present. Arneson has had many one man exhibitions, including shows at the Museum of Contemporary Art in Chicago, and the San Francisco Museum of Modern Art. His work is included in several collections, including San Francisco Museum of Modern Art; The Oakland Museum; University Art Museum, University of California, Berkeley; Whitney Museum of American Art, New York; Guggenheim Museum, New York; Philadelphia Museum of Art, Pennsylvania; Stedelijk Museum, Amsterdam, Holland; and the Hirshhorn Museum and Sculpture Garden, Smithsonian Institution, Washington, D.C. Arneson has been recognized as one of the most outstanding sculptors and teachers of modern times. In the words of Garth Clark in *A Century of Ceramics in the U.S.*, p. 272: "Arneson's work represents one of the most extraordinary contributions to American ceramics – a contribution that can be likened only to that of the Della Robbias of the Renaissance in Italy and Bernard Palissy, the French mannerist. In common with these ceramic masters of the past, Arneson's work exhibits considerable skill, formal accomplishment and a unique and commanding personal vision. He is also a true maverick and his work, while cognizant of mainstream art movements and at times freely satirizing and commenting on these developments, is nonetheless outside any of the identifiable genres or schools of contemporary art today." To describe this man's work without pictures might be compared to teaching a youngster the alphabet without pictures of the letters. His earlier work seemed to be calculated to shock the observer. Sex organs, toilet facilities, an electric toaster with fingers protruding and a typewriter with red painted fingernails for keys, were some of the subject matter Arneson explored with his sculptured pieces. Arneson's subject matter changed as his life expanded. His work represented an ongoing dialogue with himself. One can almost feel the sculptor fighting the battles of environment and conventionalism when looking at the pictures of his pieces. By the 1970's he was doing self-portraits and portraits of friends. Color, texture and force were important elements in the work. To this author, he displays humor, but always with a sense of satire and ridicule. Arneson has been written about in articles in many magazines, including *Craft Horizons; Art in America; Cleveland Press; Art News; Ceramic Review; Arts Magazines; Ceramics Monthly* and others. For a list of the above articles, names of his sculptured pieces, many fine pictures and a fine description of Arneson's work, see Garth Clark, *A Century of Ceramics in the U.S.*, pp. 270-272. (Information: Clark, as cited; also, *Robert Arneson: A Retrospective*, The Des Moines Art Center, 1985. Marks: Linda Steigleder, from the booklet published by the Everson Museum of Art to accompany the 1978 exhibition, "A Century of Ceramics in the U.S.")

ARNESon

ARN=N

ARNESON

ARNESON 1976

Arquette, Cliff. Gettysburg, Pennsylvania. Arquette filed october 3, 1960, for registration of the marks shown to be used on ceramic ware, namely cups, saucer, steins, ashtrays and tumblers, claiming use since March 1959.

Arrowmont School of Crafts. Gatlinburg, Tennessee. Many times this school has been mentioned in this book. As part of the training and education of the various studio potters. The school is a descendent of the Pi Beta Settlement School founded in 1912 which operated to teach mountain children until the 1940's at which time this settlement school was turned over to the crafts people. Now 1,000 people from teenage to their eighties take summer course in crafts at the Arrowmont School of Crafts. Marian Heard was director after 1946. She was also a teacher at the University of Tennessee after 1936.

Art China Company. Sebring, Ohio. Researchers have looked for this company but it did not exist. See E.H. Sebring China Company for mark and history.

Artistic Potteries Company. Pottery had showrooms in Los Angeles, California, and the manufacturing plant in Whittier, California. In business in the 1940's. Makers of art ware, vases, figurines, novelties, lamp bases, etc. I found two listings for this pottery, the 1945 *Crockery and Glass Journal Directory* and the 1948 *China and Glass Red Book Directory*. I did not find them listed in the 1950's. (Marks: no. 1, 3, inscribed on a fancy flower bowl or dish; mark no. 2 was sent by Elizabeth Vaughn, dealer, Columbus, Ohio.)

Artistic California 505

1.

Artistic Potteries California

2.

Artistic Potteries, Inc. Calif, U.S.A.

3.

Arwood, Barbara. Columbus, Ohio. Studio potter who started in 1981 to make functional stoneware and some one of a kind pieces marked with monogram B.J.A.

Asbury, Carolyn. Cambridge, Massachusetts. 1980 to present (1984). Teaches at Mudville School (see that listing). Carolyn attended the University of Massachusetts in Amherst in 1980 and then started teaching at Mudville. She makes wheel thrown, high fired, stoneware, painted with cobalt, iron and porcelain slip designs. Also pieces carved with iron oxide geometric designs are made. Pieces include mugs with feet, shoes, animals in mugs and all sorts of functional pieces. Glazes are high gloss blues, browns, tan and white. She sells her pieces at the school shows and craft stores, fairs, etc.

Associated American Artists. New York, New York. This group originated Stonelain pottery pieces. The A.A.A. was founded by Reeves Lewenthal in 1933 and is still operating. By 1935, they were issuing a mail order catalogue and had a gallery, offices and mail order department. They handled the work of America's best painters and artist of the day, such as Peggy Bacon, Thomas Hart Benton, George Biddle, Grant Wood and several others. By the late 1940's they also offered works of European artists. The group offered prints, books, bronze sculpture, Christmas cards, etc. In the early 1940's until around 1952, the A.A.A. produced pottery. A large facility for pottery was established with three gas fired kilns. Master potters, William Soini and Frances Server were hired to handle the production and technical aspects. Various artist made the designs and sketches for forms and shapes, and then the two men produced them and copyists decorated them, creating a delicate balance between artist and artisan. Dozens of fine American artists became involved in clay and fine art objects of ceramics were created at the A.A.A. while they were making Stonelain pottery. Stonelain was the name of the pottery made. The facility was not called by that name. The marks shown were filed in the name Associated American Artists, Inc. The importance of Stonelain pieces may be seen in the people who participated in the makings such as: Thomas Hart Benton, Aaron Bohrod, John Steuert Curry, Alexander Archipenko, Joseph Hirsch, Adolf Dehn, Gwen Lux, Nancy Dryfoos, Sylvia Shaw Judson, Arivi Tynys, Jason Seley, Edward Chavez, Alphonse Shum, Robert Cronbach, Dorothea Greenbaum, Irma Rothstein, Julio de Diego, Georges Schrieber, Richard Davis, Berta Margoulies, Jo Davidson, Carl Walters, Nathaniel Kaz, Arnold Blanch, Nicolai Cikovsky, Doris Lee, Louis Quintanilla, Ramon Prats and others worked for A.A.A. on Stonelain. (Information and mark 1: Thomas Turnquist, "New York City Ceramics, Part II: Stonelain Pottery," *Journal of the American Art Pottery Association*, May 1985, pp. 8, 9. Marks: no. 1, 1967 *Gift and Tableware Reporter Directory*; marks 2 and 3, filed July 13,

1951, claiming prior use since August 4, 1950, for bowls, pitchers, decorative plates, vases, serving tile, etc., of ceramic material. According to Turnquist, AAA was an early mark.)

1.

STONELAIN

2.   3.

Atcheson and Associates. Annapolis, Indiana. 1841 to after 1904. The pottery was started by D.L. Atcheson in 1841 to make stoneware. Mark impressed. Notice the "e" in Atcheson here. As was the picture in the Baker article telling about the other Atchisons (with an "i"). In 1847 the firm became **Atcheson and Lee.** Lee left the next year, but returned in 1849 to buy out the new partners of Atcheson, namely Laughlin and Welch. In 1900, Howard R. Atcheson, became a partner and the name became **Atcheson and Son.** Howard R. bought out his father's interests in 1904 and started stamping the ware "H.R. Atcheson, Annapolis, Ind." (Information: Peggy A. Loar, *Indiana Stoneware*, (a catalogue of exhibit), Indianapolis: Indianapolis Museum of Art, 1974. Mark: sent by Mel Davies, author of *Clay County Indiana, Traditional Potters and Their Wares*.)

D.L. ATCHESON
ANNAPOLIS, IA.

Atchison, H.K. New Geneva, Pennsylvania. Came to New Geneva in 1855, died in 1893. There was also a Henry P. Atchison working as a potter in New Geneva in 1876. Baker said he might have been Henry K's son. (See Debolt and Atchison for more.) Made stoneware with freehand decoration. (Information and mark: Gordon C. Baker, "Early New Geneva Stoneware Potters," *Spinning Wheel*, May 1979, pp. 17, 18.)

H.K. ATCHISON
NEW GENEVA, PA

Atlan Ceramic Art Club. Chicago, Illinois. 1893 to 1921. The Atlan Ceramic Art Club was organized by a group of ladies who decorated china. They wanted to develop their own style of painting on china which was "Original" and "American." For a list of the members see Sharon S. Darling, *Chicago Ceramics and Glass*, printed by the Chicago Historical Society, Chicago, Illinois, 1979, pp. 18 to 26. (Information and mark: Darling, as cited.)

Atlas China Company. New York, New York. 1918 to present. In the *Crockery and Glass Journal Magazine*, January 1943, p. 80, in the article, "Atlas Celebrates 25th Anniversary," was the following:

"Twenty-five years ago, Samuel Bernthal and Nathan Zank started a small dinnerware decorating business in Brooklyn, producing perhaps twenty-five dozens a day of gold-stamped thirty-two piece dinner sets. Beginning in January, 1943, these same two men, now the Atlas China Company, will celebrate their twenty-five years in business producing an infinitely greater number and quality of china pieces; more than six hundred dozen pieces of vitrified china gold encrusted ware leave their kiln daily. As part of an expansion program, Atlas China Company has taken space at 137 Fifth Avenue, New York, on the ground floor to act as an additional showroom and storage space."

In the 1952 *Crockery and Glass Journal Directory*, p. 133, advertisement for Atlas China, gave the above addresses and advertised themselves as "producers of Grandma Moses plates, Charles Addams cartoons, Currier and Ives wall plates, a Dicken's series, Liberty Bell, gold encrusted ware, children's dishes, cake sets, dinnerware, short set, etc." In a news item and picture in *Crockery and Glass Journal*, August 1950, p. 70, it was stated that the first four pieces of Grandma Moses decorated china out of the kiln were being presented to her by Bernard Bernthal, president of Atlas China, the decorators and by Vincent Lippe, the distributor of the plates. According to Jenny B. Derwich and Dr. Mary Latos in *Dictionary Guide to U.S. Pottery and Porcelain*, p. 29, the present day Atlas China Company which is well known for collector's plates is operated by the son of the founder of Atlas China Company of New York City. The company is presently located in Great Neck, New York. Bernard W. Bernthal, son of the founder has retained the name of Atlas China Company and he works as a designer, consultant and business agent. (Marks: Atlas China applied for mark no. 1 on March 4, 1948 for china tableware, claiming use since June 1930. Mark no. 2 from plate. Marks 3-9, from Quality Stamp Company. Nos. 10 and 11, from 1952 *Crockery and Glass Journal Directory*. Mark 12 was filed by Bernard Bernthal of Long Island City, New York on August 24, 1960 claiming use since January 3, 1958 for ceramic wares, namely cups, saucers, plates, bowls, pitchers, jars, lamp bases, vases, ash trays and figurines. No. 13 is an advertisement from *Crockery and Glass Journal*, March 1949, p. 74 which shows several logos or marks for Atlas China Company. These may have been used only as symbols rather than actual identifying marks. Do not confuse this company with Atlas China of Niles, Ohio.)

ATLAS SATIN GOLD

1.

2.

WARRANTED 22 KARAT GOLD

3.

4.

5.

6.

WARRANTED 22 KARAT GOLD

7.

MADE IN U.S.A.

8.

9.

10.

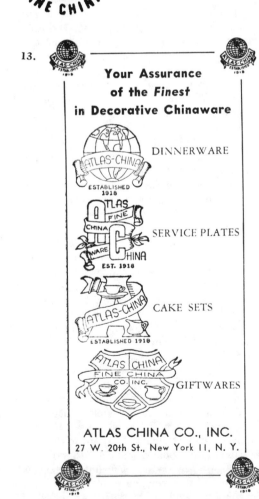

ATLAS

12.

11.

13.

Your Assurance of the *Finest* in Decorative Chinaware

DINNERWARE

SERVICE PLATES

CAKE SETS

GIFTWARES

ATLAS CHINA CO., INC.
27 W. 20th St., New York 11, N. Y.

Atlas China Company. Niles, Ohio. 1922 to 1925. See Bradshaw China Company for history. (Mark from Quality Stamp Company, East Liverpool, Ohio.)

Atlas Globe China Company. Cambridge, Ohio. 1925 to 1934. See Bradshaw China for history. (Marks: no. 1 was filed June 27, 1927, claiming use since November 1926 for use on china, porcelain, pottery and earthenware, and decorated and plain dinnerware. Mark no. 2, filed June 27, 1927, claiming use since June 13, 1927 for use on china dinnerware. Mark nos. 3, 4 on semi-porcelain dinnerware.)

1.

LOVE BIRD

2.

3.

victoria
Dinnerware
WARRANTED
22-K GOLD
TULIP
1-37

4.

Aust, Gottfried. Bethabara and Salem, North Carolina. Aust was a master potter in Bethbara, from 1755 to 1771, and a master potters in Salem, from 1771-1788. This potter contributed more than any other of the six really outstanding potters who were members of the Moravians, a religious society. Also, see the listings for Rudolf Christ, John Holland, Henry Schaffner. Aust was able to make a large quantity of pottery while maintaining quality, and making tests on various clays, etc. and developing new forms. Some of the potters he taught may have been more imaginative or artistic, but he accomplished so much and taught others as well. Aust learned the potter's trade as an apprentice to Brother Andreas Dober in Silesia, Germany. Aust worked at Bethlehem, Pennsylvania, for ten months under the master potter, Michael Odenwald, before going on to Bethabara. Aust made hand thrown earthenware, fired twice, once as biscuit ware and again after glazing. Aust made stove tile, clay pipes, all kinds of utilitarian pieces to be used by the Moravian community. In Salem, Aust made Queensware, which was a fine high fired creamware. William Ellis, an itinerant potter, was in Salem, around 1773, to teach Aust and the other Salem potters how to make the Queensware or fine pottery forms. As most all of the pottery made by the Moravian potters in Salem was unmarked, no specimen in the book showed an inscribed mark for Aust. Pictured is the trade sign used by Aust in 1773 in Salem, decorated with white and green slip over a red body. The scrollwork is filled with white slip. (All of the foregoing information and sign are from John Bivins, Jr. *The Moravian Potters in North Carolina*, published by The University of North Carolina, Press of Chapil Hill for Old Salem, Inc., of Winston-Salem, North Carolina. This is a beautiful book of over 300 pages on the Moravian settlement lifestyle and potters, etc. Sign shown on front cover. Aust was discussed throughout most of the book off and on, but pp. 16-25 and pp. 117-122, used mainly here.)

Autio, Rudy. Rudy, professor of ceramics, potter, metal sculptor, was in the U.S. Navy from 1943 to 1944, and in 1950 he received a B.S. degree from Montana State University at Bozeman, and an M.F.A. degree from Washington State University at Pullman. From 1952 to 1956 he was resident artist at the Archie Bray Foundation. During that time, according to Clark, he produced a number of architectural commissions, including a ten by thirty foot ceramic wall relief depicting, "The Sermon on the Mount." For a time in 1957 he was assistant curator at the Montana Museum in Missoula, and then went on to be a professor of ceramics at the University of Montana, from 1957 to 1971. (Information: Garth Clark, *A Century of Ceramics in the U.S.*, p. 272; also, *Rudy Autio*, University of Montana, 1983. Painted mark: Linda Steigleder, from the booklet published by the Everson Museum of Art to accompany the 1978 exhibition, "A Century of Ceramics in the U.S.")

AUTIO
66

USN

Autio 64

USA
Autio

Automatic Electric Company. Northlake, Illinois. From 1929 to 1951 this company sold "Dry Spot" insulators with white and brown glaze which were made for Automatic Electric Company by the Molded Insulation Division of the Square-D Company in Peru, Indiana. Square-D Company is now a part of General Telephone and Electronics Corporation. For a detailed discussion of the intricate use of this telephone insulator, see Jack H. Tod, *Porcelain Insulators Guide Book for Collectors*, p. 121. Automatic Electric Company never did manufacture any insulators. They were a selling agency only. (Information and embossed mark: Tod, as cited.

A.E. Co. INC.
CHICAGO ILL
Front side

PAT. PEND'G.
Back side

Avera, John C. Crawford County, Georgia. Worked in 1870's. According to John A. Burrison, *Brothers in Clay*, pp. 159, 160, John C. Avera was listed as a carpenter in the 1860 census, but by 1870 he was a "jug turner." He married the daughter of Jesse Long and their son, Jerome, also became a potter at Jesse Long's "jug factory." (See the listing Long Family Potters.) (Mark: The inscribed mark shown is on a highly decorated jug with inscribed X's clear around the jug which is supposed to be a stylized woods and a fox fleeing from a hunter. This is not really a "mark," but an inscription on a one-of-a-kind piece. Mark Burrison as cited.)

J MARSHALL'S JUG
MADE AND WARRANTED BY J.C. AVERA
AUG the 31st 1871

Avery's Ceramic Products, Inc. San Antonio, Texas. Company filed for registration of this mark on September 24, 1982, claiming use of the mark since August 1959, for china dinnerware, porcelain dinnerware, earthenware dinnerware, porcelain casting slip and plaster molds for the making of ceramic goods.

AVERY'S

Avon Faience Pottery Company. Tiltonsville, Ohio. Made artware in very early 1900's. The early history of this pottery is taken from *Twentieth Century History of Steubenville and Jefferson County, Ohio and Representative Citizens* by Joseph B. Doyle. (1910 published by Richmond Arnold Publishing Company, Chicago, Illinois.) 1880 to 1882, James Geisy built and organized a cooperative pottery to manufacture yellow ware and Rockingham in Tiltonsville. In 1882 to 1884, the pottery was taken over by the Tiltonsville Pottery Company composed of Wilbur Medill and some Wheeling gentlemen. They added a line of novelties. From 1884 to 1885, the plant was leased to John Schneider and Company. Then in 1885 to 1893, the plant was sold to Francis J. Torrance of Pittsburgh and Mason of Wheeling, plus others, who reorganized as the Western Sanitary Ware Company and ran until the plant burned in 1893. The plant was rebuilt in 1894, operated six months, went bankrupt and into receivership, was reorganized again under Medill and managed to operate until 1897 when it went under again. From 1897 to 1900, the factory lay idle. In 1900 or 1901, the plant was sold to John Don Passos of New York. He had it for about a year. In 1902, Passos sold the plant to J.N. Vance and Sons of Wheeling, who organized the Faience Pottery Company, to turn out a most artistic line of fine ware. In 1902 or 1903, the plant was disposed of to the Wheeling Potteries Company. For a discussion of the artware made at this plant, see Evans, pp. 303-306. (Marks: 1, 2, 3, W.P. Jervis, "World's Pottery Marks," *Pottery, Glass and Brass Salesman*, October 23, 1913, p. 15, April 22, 1915, p. 15; no. 4, Barber, p. 152; no. 5, Kovel, *Collector's Guide to American Art Pottery*, p. 4; no. 6, 7, Evans, p. 306, no. 8, Lehner, *Ohio Pottery and Glass*, p. 89.)

1.

2.

3.

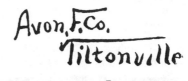
4.

AVON
5.

VANCE
F. CO.
6.

Avon.F.Co.
Tiltonville
7.

8.

Avon Pottery. Cincinnati, Ohio. Established 1886. Only lasted about one and one-half years. Karl Lagenbeck left Rookwood and was instrumental in forming the Avon Pottery for the production of art pottery. After Avon failed, he worked for Weller and Owens, at different times, in Zanesville. One variety of pottery made at Avon was yellow clay decorated in colored slips, etched in part, then treated to a dull finish. They also used white clay decorated with atomized colors and painted designs on biscuit covered by glaze. They were listed only once in a city directory in 1887, as located at the Northeast corner of 8th and Lock. (According to Paul Evans, p. 24, this is the only known mark for Avon Pottery. Thorn, p. 116 had shown a mark that was for Avon Faience Company of Tiltonsville. Several authors, this one included, followed Thorn's error in my *Ohio Pottery and Glass* book, p. 28. Information and mark: Barber, *Marks of American Potters*, p. 126 and 127.)

AVON

Aw Pottery. Berkeley, California. Susan Aw came from Malaysia in October 1980 to Berkeley where she started the Aw Pottery. The tradition behind the Aw Pottery dates back more than a century in China when the first Aw became famous for his pottery. Eng Kwang, Susan's father, is the fourth generation of those potters. He went from China to Southeast Asia to Johore, Malaysia. In 1983 he planned to join Susan in the United States. In Malaysia, Eng Kwang worked with a staff of one-hundred people, including his four sons and one daughter. Eng Kwang Aw has made pottery for fifty-one years and Susan has been a potter for ten years. They have learned from other members of the family. The pieces made at Aw Pottery in Berkeley, are hand thrown, hand decorated with Oriental influence and beautiful clear glazes. They are high fired and many have etched or raised designs. Pieces are animals, kitchenware, vases, pitchers, hanging flower pots, flower pots with oriental faces and forms. Susan's work is very nice but her father's work is breath taking! We can only hope he comes to this country as she says he plans to do at this writing! His pieces are stoneware and porcelain with metallic glazes such as copper when fired correctly giving a deep liver-red color and the hand painted designs are fabulous.

B

Bacerra, Ralph. Los Angeles, California. Bacerra, a studio potter, decorator, teacher, received a B.F.A. degree from Chouinard Art School in Los Angeles, in 1961. He later became the chairman of the ceramics department at the same school. He is a skilled decorator with a number of techniques, including overglaze painting and incising in the clay. He makes porcelain pieces in his studio at present and is a consultant to the ceramics industry. (Information: Garth Clark, *A Century of Ceramics in the U.S.*, p. 273. Incised mark: Linda Steigleder, from the booklet published by the Everson Museum of Art to accompany the 1978 exhibition, ''A Century of Ceramics in the U.S.'')

Bacharach, Inc. 1150 Broadway, New York City. Filed June 20, 1956, for this mark for use on ceramic dinnerware, claiming use since December 15, 1955. This company was listed in the 1952 and 1954 *Crockery and Glass Journal Directory* for decorated and plain colored domestic dinnerware of earthenware and porcelain. In the 1949 *China and Glass Red Book Directory* Bacharach, Inc. was listed for T-Ball teapots. See Hall China Company for the mark used on these teapots that Hall China made for Bacharach.

SKY FLOWER

Bachelder, Carlton. Menasha, Wisconsin. 1850 to 1895. Made gray salt glazed stoneware crocks, jugs, churns, etc. with impressed mark shown. Some are marked just ''Ohio Stone/Menaska, Wis.'' During the 1850's, Calvin B. Bachelder, brother of Carlton was in business with him. See the listing, Omar Khayyam Pottery for the family connections. (Information: Pat H. Johnston, ''Omar Khayyam Pottery,'' *Antiques Journal*, September 1974, pp. 2-7. Mark: on front cover of *Pottery Collectors' Newsletter*, August 1973.)

Bachelder, Oscar Louis. See Omar Khayyam Pottery.

Bachman, Kathy. Logan, Ohio. Mrs. Bachman and her husband, Tim are involved in establishing an artist's collective in Rushville, Ohio, called the Rushcreek Craftworks. Bachman did her first student shows in 1973. She has work-ed in workshops under Paul Soldner, Byron Temple and Bob Nichols, all very well known in the fields of studio pottery. Some pieces are signed with Kathy's signature, and since 1979 she has used a logo which incorporated her initials K.B. and also shows a heart on the wheel head. She makes hand-crafted stoneware.

Baggett, Michael. Thompson, Georgia. Operating at present (1985). Michael is a studio potter who studied under Kenneth Ferguson, Victor Babu and George Timock at the Kansas City Art Institute in Kansas City. He makes wheel thrown and hand cast porcelain decorative pieces fired to cone 10 by reduction method. (Information and inscribed mark: Beverly F. Stoughton, ''Michael Baggett, The Potters Art,'' *American Clay Exchange*, September 15, 1984, p. 8.)

Baggs, Arthur E. Columbus and Cleveland, Ohio. Arthur graduated from the College of Ceramics at Alfred University in Alfred, New York, around 1905 where he was a student of Charles Fergus Binns. He also studied at the Art Students League in New York, and Harvard University. In 1908, he was asked to organize Marblehead Pottery as a handicraft program for the mentally ill. He acted as director there until 1915, when he became owner of the pottery. From 1925 to 1928, he worked as an associate ceramist at Cowan Pottery and also taught at the Cleveland School of Art, where he also obtained an M.A. degree in 1928. Later in 1928, the Ceramic Art School was founded in the Fine Arts Department of Ohio State University in Columbus, Ohio, and Baggs was chosen to head the Ceramic Art School. In the summers, Baggs always returned to work at Marblehead Pottery until it closed in 1936. (See Marblehead Pottery listing.) Baggs was still listed as a professor in the School of Fine and Applied Arts in the *Ohio State University Directory of 1945-1946*. Baggs died in 1947. The ware he designed and helped to make at Marblehead was mostly hand thrown simple straight sided shapes with muted matt glazes of green, blue, brownish yellow. At Ohio State University, Baggs was instrumental in having Edgar Littlefield added to his staff in 1929 and Carlton Atherton in 1930 and Paul Bogatay in 1934. (See individual listings for these potters.) The instructors were there to assist students but were permitted to do work of their own. There were no secrets and no private glazes and all of these talented potters worked together. Baggs explored patterns for reproduction in decalcomania on tableware. He worked with salt glazing of pottery as an art form. One beautiful salt glazed stoneware cookie jar won first prize at the 7th Ceramic

National Exhibition in 1938. (See listings of these winnings in the back of the book. Baggs won several awards at these exhibitions.) One glaze that Baggs and Edgar Littlefield perfected was the copper red glaze. Silicon carbide added to a glaze formula acted as a reducing agent in an oxidation kiln, when the glaze melted the compound broke down to carbon and silica, robbing oxygen elements from copper to produce red. Baggs won many honors: In 1915 the Armour prize for pottery at the Chicago Exhibition of Applied Arts; Boston Society of Arts and Crafts award in 1925; the Charles Fergus Binns Medal in 1928. (Information: Elaine Levin, "Arthur Baggs and Glen Lukens," *Ceramics Monthly*, January 1976, pp. 24-30; Edna Marie Clark, M.A., *Ohio Art and Artists*, Richmond: Garrett and Massie, 1932, pp. 171, 440; Garth Clark, *A Century of Ceramics in the U.S.*, pp. 273, 274. Marks: incised marks found on two pieces shown in Linda Steigleder, from the booklet accompanying the 1978 exhibit, "A Century of Ceramics in the U.S.," with curators, Garth Clark and Margie Hughto, published by the Everson Museum of Art.)

Bahl Potteries, Inc. Carrollton, Ohio. 1940 to 1941. Made dinnerware called Sandela Ware in Nova Rose pattern, from local clay and it resembled the old yellowware of East Liverpool. John Bahl, founder, died in August, 1941. He designed the original Blue Bird Calendar plate while working for Edwin M. Kowles. The plate was given as a premium by the Jewell Tea Company in 1910. The Iris Art Company was operated around 1920 for a short time by John I. Bahl and H.W. Foltz to decorate china. (Information: Mrs. John Bahl by letter; Lehner, *Ohio Pottery and Glass*, p. 27.)

Bailey, Clayton. Hayward, California. Bailey, a studio potter and sculptor, received his M.A. degree at the University of Wisconsin, in 1962. He taught at several universities in the mid-west and became an instructor of ceramics at the University of Wisconsin in Whitewater. He was a guest artist at the University of California, in Davis, for two semesters, then settled to teaching at the California State University at Hayward. By 1970's, Bailey's work had dealt with a series of themes ranging from pornography, the medical establishment, primitive man, to staged events and workshops that

were termed a "neurotic search for new glazes and craft skills to cure imagined creative skills," by Clark in the book cited. Clark also said Bailey's work was the most truly "Funk of the Bay Area Artists." He did gain much recognition in major one man shows, including one at the Museum of Contemporary Crafts in New York in 1964, and one at the Milwaukee Art Center in 1967. Much has been written about Bailey. There is an extensive list of bibliographical material in the Clark book. (Information: Garth Clark, *A Century of Ceramics in the U.S.*, pp. 274, 275. Incised mark: Linda Steigleder, from the booklet published by the Everson Museum of Art to accompany the 1978 exhibition, "A Century of Ceramics in the U.S.")

Bailey-Walker China Company. See Walker China for history and marks.

Baker, Oscar F. Milwaukee, Wisconsin. 1851-1854. Oscar F. Baker was another grocer who turned to pottery making in 1851. He started the **Milwaukee Stoneware Factory** from 1851 to 1853. In 1854, he sold the business to John B. and Amos Maxfield and died of cholera that same year. He made salt glazed stoneware pieces with cobalt blue decorations and the impressed or stamped mark shown. (Information: Kenneth Dearolf, *Wisconsin Folk Pottery*, p. 20. A booklet written in cooperation with the Kenosha Public Museum.)

O.F. BAKER & CO.
MILWAUKEE

Baldauf, Stephen. Sauk Village, Illinois. 1972 to present (1983). This studio potter makes outstanding sculptures hand painted and glazed. Pieces are all types of figures of considerable size; many are more than one foot tall.

Ball, F. Carlton. Northern California. Studio potter, graduated from University of Southern California in 1933. He taught art a couple of years then began his sixth year of college training at University of Southern California, where he studied with Glen Lukens. In 1936, he accepted a position teaching pottery at the California College of Arts and Crafts in Oakland. In 1938, he taught at Sacramento High School and from 1939 to 1949 at Mills College where he started a pottery program. From 1950 to 1957, he worked in collaboration with Aaron Bohrod, a famous painter. Ball was a painter as well as a potter. But for seven years, Ball potted and Bohrod decorated nearly 600 pots which Thomas Turnquist in "Aaron Bohrod and Carlton Ball: Synergism," *American Art Pottery*, August 1983, p. 1, describes as pots which soared to great artistic heights. From 1948 to 1973, Bohrod was Artist in Residence at the University of Wisconsin at Madison. In 1950 and 1951, Ball taught pottery at the Univeristy of Wisconsin, where he became acquainted and associated with Bohrod. They continued to ship pots and travel back and forth to work together after Ball left Wisconsin to teach at University of Southern Illinois at Carbondale. (Information: Thomas Turnquist as cited. Mark: sent by Turnquist by letter.)

F. C. Ball

J.B. Ball and Company. Poughkeepsie, New York. Around 1820. Made stoneware. Mark impressed. (Information and mark: John P. Remensnyder, ''The Potters of Poughkeepsie,'' reprinted from *Antiques Magazine* in *The Art of the Potter*, edited by Diana and J. Garrison Stradling, p. 124.)

J.G. BALL & CO.
POUGHKEEPSIE

Ball and Morris, 1845 to 1855/**McGilvary and Orr,** 1855 to 1857/**Croxall and Associations,** 1857 to 1914/**American Porcelain Company**, 1914 to 1932. Second Street and Cherry Avenue, East Liverpool, Ohio. From 1845 to 1914, under a succession of owners, this plant made Rockingham and yellowware. From 1914 to 1932, electrical porcelain was made there. The various associations with Croxall were Croxall and Cartwright, 1857 to 1888, when Croxall bought Cartwright's shares and became J.W. Croxall and Sons until 1898. From 1898 to 1914 the plant was called just Croxall Pottery. (Information: Jack H. Tod, *Electrical Porcelain Industry in U.S.*, p. 71. Marks: no. 1, Annise Heaivilin, author of *Grandma's Tea Leaf*. Marks 2, 3, Tod, p. 104, on electrical porcelain.)

CROXALL & CARTWRIGHT
EAST
LIVERPOOL
1.   OHIO

AMERICAN
2.

3.

Ballard, Various Potteries. Gardiner, Maine and Burlington, Vermont. **A.K. Ballard** operated alone until 1872 making stoneware. Impressed mark may be seen on crock in picture in Stewart and Consentino, p. 80. The Ballard Brothers followed **Nichols and Boynton,** 1856 to 1859, who had followed **Nichols and Alford** after 1854. In June 1854, three brothers in the Ballard family, Orrin L., Alfred K. and Hiram N. took over a mortgage on a pottery in Gardiner, Maine, which had been owned by Thompson and Company. The Ballards only remained in Gardiner, about a year, but pieces marked ''Ballard and Brothers/Gardiner, Me.,'' are found in reasonable quantity. After 1859 until 1867, O.L. and A.K. were back in Burlington, where they made pottery together until

1867. (Information: M. Lelyn Branin, *The Early Potters and Potteries of Maine*, p. 127, and Ramsay, pp. 189, 190. Marks: nos. 1-2, Stewart and Consentino, *Stoneware, A Guide for Beginning Collectors*, p. 80; no. 3, M. Lelyn Branin, as cited, p. 224.)

O.L. & A.K. BALLARD   1.
BURLINGTON, VT.

2.   A.K. BALLARD
BURLINGTON, VT.

BALLARD & BROTHERS
GARDINER   ME   3.

Baltimore Clayworks. Baltimore, Maryland. Started September 1980 to present (1984). Owner and studio potter, Peter Kaiser, makes functional stoneware. All of his work is signed with what Peter termed a ''chop'' on the bottom or side of pieces as shown. Mark is impressed into clay. Peter produces a line of cookware including colanders, canisters, porcelain teapots, fish-shaped platters. These potters offer a cookbook they composed to go with their cookware! Peter favors clean, basic shapes with heavy glaze and hand painted decorations which complement the form. Special courses and programs are offered at the Clayworks throughout the year.

L. Bamberger & Company. Newark, New Jersey. Distributor. Filed for rights on this mark on September 27, 1929 to be used for chinaware, porcelain ware and earthenware, claiming use of this mark since July 19, 1924.

Super-Saving

Bangor Stone Ware Company. Bangor, Maine. 1880 to around 1917. Bangor Stone Ware Company was established by Anders Persson, native of Sweden, and made stoneware churns, hanging vases, cuspidors, jugs, mugs, soap dishes, milk pans, etc. Anders's son, Peter, changed his name to Pearson, and he worked at his father's factory, until 1893, when he moved to Calais. The pottery at Bangor employed around sixteen or seventeen people in 1888 or 1890, using thirteen wheels for the hand thrown ware. M. Lelyn Branin, in his book, *The Early Potters and Potteries of Maine*, p. 176, said there may have been a very limited amount of manufacturing done after the W.W. I. (Information: Branin as cited. Marks: Branin p. 223.)

BANGOR STONEWARE CO.
BANGOR MAINE

BANGOR STONE WARE CO.

BANGOR MAINE   **BANGOR**

Barker Brothers, Inc. Los Angeles, California. A department store filed for registration on mark one on March 23, 1931, to be used for crockery, earthenware and chinaware such as dinner sets, breakfast sets, coffee sets, tea sets, vases, bowls, jardinieres and lamp vases, claiming use of this mark since February 1, 1931. In *Crockery and Glass Journal*, November 1943, p. 21 is the article "Castleton China Exhibit shown at Barker Bros. "which tells about the pieces of dinnerware with designs taken from original works of various artists such as Salvador Dali, Elsie Shaver and Thomas Hart Benton. Prices for the pieces were $400.00 and up. In 1964, the Barker Brothers were a Division of City Products Corporation of Los Angeles, when they filed for "Bel-Aire" to be used on mattresses and box springs. Mark no. 2, "Barkertone" was a two tone Montecito tableware, made exclusively for Barker Brothers by Gladding, McBean and Company in 1939. These dishes were made to be sold at the Golden Gate International Exposition. They also made a series for them; "California Missions," "Winning of the West," and "California Wild Flowers." No. 3 was a two tone earthenware, coral and white, sold to Barker Brothers by Gladding, McBean and Company, 1940 to 1945.

"CALIFORNIA-COLONIAL"   **FRANCISCAN** MADE IN CALIFORNIA **BARKERTONE**

1.   2.

3.

Barringer, Mary. Hartford, Connecticut. 1973 to present (1984). Mary Barringer, studio potter, graduated from Bennington College in Bennington, Vermont, with B.A. in art in 1972. Prior to that, she had also attended Pratt Institute in Brooklyn, New York, to study sculpture. She also studied at University of Connecticut in 1980-1981, was apprenticed to Michael Frimkess in Venice, California, in 1971 and in 1970 she spent three months on a cross country trip visiting working potters, museums and university ceramics departments. From 1973 to 1976, she managed the **Park Street Potters**, a studio workshop and gallery. While there she managed the workshop, taught and produced pieces of her own. In 1979, Mary Barringer won the Individual Artist's grant for hand built vessels and research on indegenous ceramic materials from the Connecticut Commission on the arts. Mary has taught at the Greater Hartford Community College, the Wesleyan Potters in Middletown, Connecticut, the Farmington Valley Arts Center, the Hartford Public Schools and Park Street Potters. She has given lectures and demonstrations at the Talcott Mountain Science Center and the Hartford Conservatory. A selected few from her long list of exhibitions including one woman, two women and invitational group shows were at the Elements, Greenwich, Connecticut; Currier Gallery, Manchester, New Hampshire; Butterworth Gallery at the Hartford

College for Women in Hartford; the Joseloff Gallery at University of Hartford; Widener Gallery at Trinity College in Hartford; the National Paper and Clay Exhibition at Memphis State University, Memphis, Tennessee; Salmon Kill Gallery, Lime Rock, Connecticut; the New England Crafts Exhibition at the Slater Memorial Museum, Norwich, Connecticut; the Women's Interart Center, New York City, the Northeast Craft Fair, Rhinebeck, New York.

Barth Equipment Company, Inc. New York, New York. Selling agency filed for rights on this mark August 24, 1928, to be used on crockery, earthenware and porcelain, claiming use of the mark since about July 10, 1928. See Warwick China Company and McNicol China Company for Barth Equipment marks on restaurant and hotel china.

Basch, Carol. Golden, Colorado and Anchorage, Alaska. 1968 to present. Carol graduated from Loyola University in Chicago, then studied in various seminars and art schools from 1970-1976 with very well known potters as teachers such as Paul Soldner, Wally Soderquist and many more. From 1976-1979, she was artist in residence at the Colorado Academy in Denver. She is a member of American Crafts Council. Her work is sold through galleries. Carol's pieces are true art pottery. She works with high fired porcelain bodies and crystalline glazes to make the beautiful one of a kind crystalline glazed porcelains into vases, bottles, platters, etc. She makes some functional pieces and architectural pieces such as tiles, murals, etc. These are of high fired stoneware or terra cotta. Marks are incised or written in India ink on the bottom with date added. **Genesee Mountain Pottery** is the name Carol uses for her pottery in Alaska.

Basch 83

Bastian, Jacob. Milton, Pennsylvania. 1823 to 1858. Jacob, a redware potter, followed Adam Gudenkunst, in Milton, Northumberland County, Pennsylvania. According to Jeannette Lasansky, in *Redware Pottery, 1780-1904*, pp. 20, 21, there were twenty-two potters who worked in the northern part of this country before 1882. William Freed, a redware potter also, purchased Jacob's shop when Jacob died in 1858. Products were jugs, bed pans, crocks and other utilitarian pieces. (Information and mark: Lasansky, as cited. The mark shown was slip trailed in a crude fashion on a redware plate.)

Jacob
Bastian
Milton
1858

Bastine Pottery. Noblesville, Indiana. Dan and Sherry Bastine are working in their own pottery in 1984. Dan Bastine worked for three years at the Conner Prairie Historical Museum pottery. The ware is traditional handthrown folk pottery type which Sherry paints with cobalt blue and iron red in the old patterns or designs. The stoneware is oven and food safe. The Bastines also make miniature pieces marked as shown.

1984.
Bastine

Baston, Prescott. Lee, New Hampshire. Baston was born in 1909 in Arlington, Massachusetts. In 1928, he entered Vesper George School of Art in Boston and worked part time in a drug store. His father worked for Olmstead Brothers, an architectural firm in Brookline, where he made miniature replicas of bridges, buildings and whatever the architects needed. Baston went to work part time there, but very quickly the depression came and his father died. He had to provide an income for himself and his mother. He worked on miniature models wherever he could get work. He learned the techniques of miniaturization such as scale, perspective, color and materials to use. In the middle to late 1930's, he received several commissions to paint large murals in the Boston area through the Federal Art Project. In 1938, Baston was asked to design a small set of Amish or Shaker people for a promotion at the Shaker Glen House Restaurant. The owners ordered four dozen and then a thousand. Baston went to Carbone, Inc. in Boston (see that listing) to see if they would be interested in selling a line of ceramic miniatures portraying famous American couples. To create a line, they told him to make a dozen different pairs. They accepted his work and showed it at the Boston Gift Show in 1939. Baston received orders for several thousands of miniature figures at that show. He quit all his various odd jobs and set up a studio in his Arlington basement and "Sebastian Miniatures" were officially born. Carbone, Inc. decided to sell the line nationally. Baston employed twelve people who each worked a half of a day casting, cleaning the pieces for painting and painting some of the larger areas of the figurines. Baston did all the fine detail work. In 1941, Baston designed a set of six birds and "Secrets," a pair of kittens. W.W. II came and Baston volunteered for a job in the Massachusetts Institute of Technology again making miniatures of whatever was needed in studying the war effort. One project involved a system of bomb release which was later used over Germany. Baston's wife, Marjorie, supervised work at the studio, and Armando Carli made the molds for Baston's designs during the wartime. In 1946, following other war effort jobs, Baston moved his family and studio to Marblehead. At this time he signed a contract with Schmid Brothers of Boston to make

"Folks in Little." The years 1946 to 1950 were the most productive years for the company outside of the 1980's when the collector's interest has begun to reach a peak. A famous American series began in 1947 with Washington, Lincoln, Roosevelt, Jefferson and others. Between 1951 and 1968, Baston created 137 figurines for various commercial sales or promotions, including the Shawmut Bank, an S.O.S. lady for the scouring pad company, and Chiquita Banana design for the United Fruit Company's account. Strangely enough, these sales promotion items are the hard ones to find today and command good collector's prices. In 1969, Baston started designing plates, figurines and other pieces for the Lance Corporation in Hudson, Massachusetts. By 1975, Lance Corporation had grown into an important business in the American gift industry and by 1976 Lance Corporation had taken over the production and distribution of Sebastian Miniatures. Large promotions followed. The Sebastian Collectors Society was formed and Baston began to travel for personal appearances. The number of the miniatures created and the complexity of the story involved in the life of Prescott Baston can only be explained in a book. Luckily there is a book depicting the figurines with an explanatory paragraph on each. The forgoing material also came from this book as cited. (Information: from the company; and De. Glenn S. Johnson, *The Sebastian Miniature Collection*, published by Lance Corporation in 1982. Marks: nos. 1, 2, in 1938 before larger productions began, Baston stamped or imprinted "Copr. P.W. Baston U.S.A." on bottom of pieces. In 1939 the imprint was "P.W. Baston U.S.A." After 1940, Carbone, Inc. had him to remove all identification. So these very early imprinted pieces are rare. No. 3 is a silver-green label which Baston attached to the pieces he made at Marblehead. These are also rare pieces. Nos. 4, 5 are inkstamped signatures on Lance Production pieces. These pieces also had labels attached as follows. Nos. 6-10 are the copies of labels shown which were sent by the company. Many Sebastian Miniatures were produced from 1946 to the present. Labels and permanent painter signatures have become a convenient method of determining the years of production and hence, of approximate rarity. The following are helpful tips in determining the age of a Sebastian Miniature: **Arlington** vs. **Marblehead** (1938-1945 vs. 1946-1975); When Baston began production Sebastians, he produced in relatively small quantities. The quantities were so small that he could imprint a "COPR. P.W. BASTON U.S.A." with a stamp in the base while the liquid material was hardening. The stamp had to be applied when the Ceramastone was hard enough to "remember" the imprint, and still wet enough to accept it. This method was obviously impossible with higher production runs. In 1939, Baston changed his imprint to "Sebastian Miniatures P.W. BASTON, U.S.A." Carbone had him remove all identification after 1940, so both imprints are quite rare. Many Arlington pieces appear with no imprint or label. Since many of the Early Pair Series were produced into 1958, there is no way of idenifying Arlington vs. Marblehead production with these pieces.

Marbelhead vs. **Lance**: Baston had designed and produced 368 designs and 192 variations (a total of 560 collectible miniatures) from 1938 through 1975. Since that time, Lance has continued production on 133 of those variations, or less than one-quarter. Therefore, identification of Marblehead vs. Lance is not a problem with 427 designs and variations. All production on them ceased when Lance entered the picture. It is with the 133 continued designs that an identification problem exists. Baston attached a silver-green label to the base of his Marblehead produced pieces. If that label on an old piece is still affixed, that means it is a ''Marblehead Piece,'' or rare.

Lance Production: When Lance began production in January, 1976, it affixed a four-digit blue-on-white label on the base. Lance continued this practice until May 1976, when the company added a white-copy on lime-green paper label that said ''Sebastian Miniatures, Hudson, Mass.'' Then, in November, the company replaced the white-lime green label with a black-copy on dark green paper label. This was used until the end of December, 1978. In 1979, the company used a pastel blue label, 1980 a yellow label and 1981 a red label. In 1982, a purple label was being used. Also, painters were required to sign their initials, the year of painting and the location of painting on the base beginning in 1979. A - 1979; B - 1980; C - 1981; 1 - Lee, New Hamsphire; 2 - Hudson, Massachusetts; 3 - Martha's Vineyard, Massachusetts. Thus, a blue label marked ''JP/A/2'' meant that Joan Priest painted that miniature in 1979 in Hudson. Production in Martha's Vineyard stopped in 1980 and in Hudson in early 1981. Now all miniatures are made in Lee. Here are tips on identifying years of production: SML 163 Phobe was unmarked. It was produced from 1950 to 1975 for the retail line. Since Lance did not continue production, it had to be Marblehead, whether it had a Marblehead label or not.

SML 277 Colonial Glassblower with a Marblehead label: The label certifies the miniature is produced from 1957 to 1975 and is a rare Marblehead piece.

SML 277 Colonial Glassblower has a yellow label and was produced in 1980.

SML 277 Colonial Glassblower with no label, but marked ''DM/B/1'' on base in pencil and was produced in 1980.

SML 277 Colonial Glassblower with no label and no marking. This is the worst condition for classification and the only area where identification is a problem. The piece could be Marblehead and could be 1976 to 1978 with the label off in both cases. It could be 1979 on, since the pencil marking would be obvious. In all cases of this one type, the piece should be brought to a Certified Sebastian Appraiser for final judgment.)

Batchelder, Ernest A. Los Angeles & Pasadena, California. Batchelder graduated from Massachusetts Normal Art Institute in Boston, and received training at Harvard Summer School of Design under Denman Ross, a designer for Dedham Pottery. In 1903, he helped to found the Minneapolis Handcraft School and then taught there for a time. In 1904, he went to California to work at Throop Polytechnic Institute. Around 1910, he started a decorative tile business in Pasadena. In 1916, he moved the business to Los Angeles. The tiles were molded non-vitreous slip decorated or engobe finished and fired with figures, corbels, borders, etc. Lucian H. Wilson and Mr. and Mrs. Engel worked with him as sculptors, etc. In 1932, the bank took the business and the firm was sold to Bauer Pottery. In 1938, he started **Kinneloa Kiln** to make tile. He exhibited at arts and craft shows and shared a permanent show room with Joy Thompson. Some pieces are marked ''Kinneloa Kiln.'' He died in 1957. Batchelder was a writer for the magazine, the *Craftman*. He wrote *Principals of Designs* and *The Inland Printer*. Elva Meline, in article cited, said that a dozen differnet cyphers or marks are known for the tile. The earliest marks are ''Batchelder/Pasadena.'' (Information and marks: Elva Meline, ''Art Tile in California, The Work of E.A. Batchelder,'' *Spinning Wheel*, November 1971, pp. 8, 9, 10; Alice Stone, ''Sincerity of Purpose, The Work of Ernest Batchelder,'' *American Clay Exchange*, November 1982, p. 10, 11, 12, 13.)

B - 25-1
Batchelder

BATCHELDER
LOS ANGELES

Bauer, Fred and **Warashina, Patti.** Fred Bauer and Patti Warashina are studio potters, both of whom received a B.S. and M.F.A. degrees from the University of Washington in Seattle, the latter degree in 1964. These two potters were married in the 1960's and both achieved a great success in the field of ceramics. In 1972, Fred retired from making pottery to become a farmer, but while he had worked in clay he had been a prolific outstanding producer. Patti continued to work in clay. Fred's work won him the Louis Comfort Tiffany Foundation grant in 1966 and he worked at the Archie Bray Foundation in Helena, Montana, in 1964. He taught at the Univerisity of Wisconsin, in Madison, in 1964-1965; the Aztec Mountain School of Craft in Liberty, Maine, in 1967; the University of Michigan, Ann Arbor, from 1965-1968; and the University of Washington, in Seattle, from 1968-1971. Fred's earlier work was functional stoneware pieces, but later he made sculptured pieces of stoneware and porcelain that expressed a certain irreverence, according to Garth Clark. Clark said the pieces were in the Funk/Super-Object vein. Patti's work was functional stoneware in the 1960's with a strong Japanese influence. In 1968, she started painting holloware with bright acrylic paint. In the 1970's, her work took on more of a message, slab built or hand built pieces such as ''After the Catch.'' Clark lists: ''Air Stream Turkey,'' which converted the bird into an American-dream caravan; a motor car series; ''They Thought it was my Last Trip,'' etc. The work in the 1970's dealt with fantasies and personal references. (Information: Garth Clark *A Century of Ceramics in the U.S.*, pp.

275, 276, 339. Marks: Linda Steigleder, from the booklet published by the Everson Museum of Art to accompany the 1978 exhibition, "A Century of Ceramics in the U.S.," Curators: Garth Clark and Margie Hughto. No. 1 is painted and no. 2 is stamped. Mark no. 3 is for Fred, which is a stamped mark.)

Bauer

1.

3.

Patti Warashina

2.

Bauer, Various Potteries. Paducah, Kentucky; Atlanta; Georgia; Los Angeles, California. In 1885, John Bauer organized the **Paducah Pottery** in Paducah, Kentucky, to make stoneware and earthenware jugs and crocks, etc. In 1898, he died; his family continued the business. In 1909, the Bauer Pottery was started on Avenue 33 in Los Angeles, California, and operated until late 1950's or 1960's (see footnote). In Atlanta, Georgia, before 1909 John Andrew Bauer made sanitary whiteware. The pottery was closed and re-opened again from 1938 until sometime before 1948. In 1932, the Bauer Pottery in California started to make a fiesta type dinnerware for which it became well known. According to Evans, p. 26, Bauer sold the plant around 1922-1923 and then reorganized J.A. Bauer Pottery Company, Inc. with W.E. Bockmon as president. The pottery also made a line of art ware in art deco shapes with pastel matt glazes or dark high fired glazes. Herb Brusche joined the firm in the early 1950's. He was married to Bauer's granddaughter. He was responsible for two line of dinnerware, "Al Fresco" and "Contempo." W.E. Bockmon had crockery marked with his name, "Bockmon's Quality Pottery," around 1940. According to Barbara Jean Hayes this ware was actually made at Red Wing Pottery during production difficulties at Bauer Pottery. Crockery was discontinued in1949-1950. (Note on closing date: Paul Evans, p. 26, gives the closing date for the Bauer Pottery around 1958. Jack Chipman said it closed around 1962, after a labor dispute. (Information: Barbara Hayes, *Bauer - The California Pottery Rainbow*, Venice, California; Salem With Antiques, 1975; Evans, *Art Pottery of the United States*, pp. 25, 26; Jack Chipman and Judy J. Stangler, "Bauer: A California Success Story," *The Glaze*, May 1980, pp. 11-14. Also letters from Chipman and Hayes in 1980 and 1982. Marks: no. 1, logo for Bauer from Hayes, p. 32; no. 2, on dish; no. 3, Hayes, p. 7; no. 4, 5, hayes, p. 22. No. 6 from various diectories in the 1950's. See Brusche Ceramics for an explanation of this mark.)

1.

BAUER
MADE IN
USA
LOS ANGELES

2.

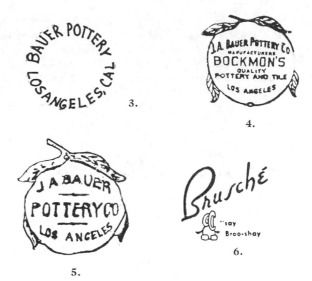

3.

4.

5.

6.

Baum, J.H. Wellsville, Ohio. The older writers agreed that Baum did exist and made white granite and used the mark shown. When he existed seems to be another story. He operated from around 1880 (Ramsay, p. 232, or Thorn, p. 116), or from 1888 (Stout, p. 87) until 1895 (Ramsay, p. 232) or to 1897 (Barber, p. 128). This is typical of many of the conflicting dates left to the researcher who is supposed to come up with "the true facts." (Marks: no. 1, Barber p. 128. No. 2 Ramsay, p. 253.)

1.

Printed

2.

Bayer, Joseph. Washington, Missouri. Around 1885. Made stoneware. Mark found impressed on 2 gallon crock. (Information and mark: Henry W. Hefflin, pottery collector and researcher.)

JOS BAYER
WASHINGTON MO

Baynes, Mary Phelan. Arlington, Virginia. Filed for registration of this mark on September 24, 1954, claiming use since November 1944, for use on ceramic artware and tableware, namely, table china, vases, trays and planters.

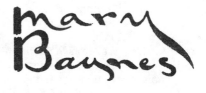

Beamish, Joan. Lewiston, Idaho. Apprentice Potter, who works at the Michael Wendt Pottery. Presently, Joan makes pieces of pottery on her own and someday plans to have her own studio or business. The first mark she used was the J.B. monogram as shown which was inscribed in the wet clay. Second mark used was ''J. Beamish.'' The current mark (1985) is a Hummingbird as shown with ''J. Beamish'' and a date. The last two marks are stamped marks.

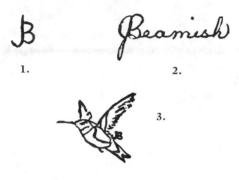

1.

2.

3.

———

Beasley, James. Montrose Baldwin County, Alabama. Around 1880. Made alkaline glazed stoneware. (Information and impressed or stamped mark: E. Henry Willett and Joey Brackner, *The Traditional Pottery of Alabama*, p. 55.)

JAMES BEASLEY MONTROSE

———

Beaumont Pottery. York, Maine. 1970 to present (1986). Jerry Beaumont completed his education at Alfred University's New York State College of Ceramics in 1973. He has taught at Stonybrook University and the Usdan Center for the Peforming Arts in Long Island. In 1970, Beaumont started making pottery in the basement of his father's house in Huntington, Long Island, New York. In 1973, Jerry brought a small farm in the Adirondack Mountains in Andover, New York, where he made pottery. Then in 1975, he moved to Strawbery Banke Historic Preservation in Portsmouth, New Hampshire. By August 1979, he had left Strawbery Banke where he made hand thrown, salt glazed stoneware in the Beaumont Heritage Pottery. The pottery had cobalt tulips and slip trail birds. Before leaving New Hampshire, he produced a special collector's crock marked, ''Beaumont Pottery, York, Maine.'' While in York, Maine, ''The Magnolia Crock'' was advertised and pictured in the *American Colletor*, October 1979, p. 21. It held ½ gallon, was 8″ high with a beautiful cobalt blue Magnolia flower on the front. The Magnolia crock limited to 5,000, carried a cross, the benchmark of the firm and the Beaumont Heritage Stamp with a number and date. This same advertisement said Beaumont had trained workmen and built three kilns in Water Valley, Mississippi, at this same time to make stoneware. The attempt at a partnership in Mississippi, was short lived and the Beaumonts settled down in York, Maine, and built the business until the article by Marty Le Blanc, ''York Pottery is Well-Known Secret,'' *York County Coast Star*, June 19, 1985, Section B, p. 1, called it the second largest pottery in New England at present. Two thousand pieces of hand thrown, decorated salt glazed stoneware are made each week. Crocks, jar, jugs, etc. are patterned after the style of the Brown Bros. of Huntington (see that listing). Handpainted cobalt blue birds, flowers, etc., are on the pieces. Jerry Beaumont sees his work as reviving a lost art; just as redware potter, Lester Brieninger is attempting to revive the art of making the old redware pieces. The work of both men has been well received and both are recognized as true artists. In the staff written article, ''American Salt Glazed Reproductions,'' *Pottery Collectors Newsletter*, March 1978, Jerry Beaumont gave a description of his marks as follows: 1970-1973 - Stamp, ''J. Beaumont,'' Huntington, L.I.; 1973-1975 - ''J. Beaumont,'' Alfred, N.Y.; 1975-present - ''Beaumont Pottery,'' Portsmouth, N.H., ''J. Beaumont,'' Portsmouth, N.H., ''J. Beaumont,'' Strawbery Banke, N.H. Decorators: C.R. - Chris Robinson; D.W. - Dorma West; C.C. - Christian Colby; E.P. - Erica Pyle; B.W. - Bobbie Warthold; P.W. - Pat Wallace. (Information: from article, as cited, and Jerry Beaumont, by letter. Marks: no. 1 is the logo used at Beaumont Heritage Pottery. No. 2 is the logo at present. No. 3 is the cross used with a date on the bottom of each piece.)

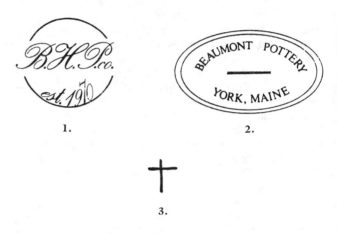

1.

2.

3.

———

Beaver Falls Art Tile Company. Beaver Falls, Pennsylvania. The company was organized December 30, 1886 and incorporated in 1906 by Francis William Walker to make art tile. In 1908, the Beaver Falls Art Tile Company took over the Robert Rossman Company of New York, New York which was a jobbing house of long standing. Rossman Company handled most of the Beaver Falls Art Tile Company sales as well as a complete line of foreign tile. In 1927, the Rossman Corporation was formed from the two companies with Walker as chairman. But in 1931, operations ceased due to inadequate investments and banking directions and support. The Beaver Falls Art Tile Company made many tiles for stove decorations in the early years. Later they made wall tile and finally specialized in white wall tile. (Information: Staff written, ''Francis William Walker,'' *Bulletin of American Ceramic Society*, August 1939, pp. 227, 228. Raised mark: sent by Elizabeth Vaughn, Beechwold Antiques, Columbus, Ohio.)

———

Beck, R.K. R.K. Beck was a wild life painter, whose works were faithfully reproduced on dishes with decals in the early 1900's. In *The Book of Buffalo Pottery*, by Seymour and Violet Altman, pp. 55, 58, are pictures of pieces made by Buffalo Pottery, using these decals. Pieces include a large oval fish platter, which had six little plates and an oval platter with white tailed deer. The deer platter was in the Larkin catalog from 1909 to 1914. Altmans dated the fish platter 1909 or 1910. A piece marked "Florence," as a back stamp with an R.K. Beck scene on the front of three cows was made by the Steubenville Pottery in the very early years. (Mark: furnished by J.F. Vogel.)

Beech, Ralph B. Kensington, Philadelphia, Pennsylvania. 1845-1857. Maker of Japanned and painted earthenware, Rockingham, porcelain vases with full length figures, gilt, scroll work, clusters of fruit, mother-of-pearl inlaid, etc. (Barber, *Marks of American Potters*, p. 25.)

L.B. Beerbower & Company. Elizabeth, New Jersey. Started around 1816 to make stoneware. Later, yellowware and Rockingham were made. By the time the Barber book was written in 1893, they had manufactured ironstone china, semigranite, cream-colored ware and print decorated ware as well. They closed prior to 1902. (Information and marks: Barber, *Marks of American Potters*, p. 69, and W.P. Jervis, "World's Pottery Marks," *Pottery, Glass & Brass Salesman*, December 16, 1917, p. 37. Mark no. 1, Ramsay p. 254.)

1.   2.   3.

Beerbower and Griffin. See Phoenixville Pottery for history. (Mark Barber, *Marks of American Potters*, p. 29.)

Beittel, Kenneth R. Dr. Beittel received a B.F.A. degree from Carnegie Mellon University in Pittsburgh in 1948 and his doctorate in art education from Pennsylvania State University in

1953. Since then he has taught ceramics graduate art seminars at Pennsylvania State. In the 1950's he built a series of kilns and experimented with local clay near the University. In 1967, he apprenticed with Manji Inove in Japan to work at throwing porcelain on a potter's wheel. He has exhibited regionally and nationally in juried, invitational and group shows. He has been the subject of many one-man shows such as the one at the Museum of Art at the Pennsylvania State University in 1977 and Everson Museum of Art in 1978. His colors and textures are quiet and natural. The pieces are hand thrown and slab built porcelain and stoneware with drawing, carving and stamping for decoration and division of space. (Information: Program, "Kenneth Beittel," issued by the Everson Museum of Art to accompany the show August 25 to September 12, 1978. Mark: tooled into bottom of piece, sent by Thomas Turnquist, research writer.)

Belcrest, Inc. Clifton, New Jersey. Around 1963 to present (1986). Belcrest, Inc. is a decorating company owned by Bernard Blum, which decorates imported china. They also decorate plastic, glass and wood. From 1963 to 1970, the company operated a plant in Hackensack, New Jersey. They also operated a plant in Norwood, New Jersey, from 1963 to 1977. In 1977, they moved to Moonachie, New Jersey, and at present they operate a plant in Clifton. (Marks: no. 1, obtained from the Waldorf Stamping Device Company in New London, Ohio. Nos. 2, 3, 4, from Quality Stamp Company, East Liverpool, Ohio. These marks were used on china. See Commerce-Pacific for a different Aladdin mark.)

1.   2.

3.   4.

Bell Buckle Pottery. Bell Buckle, Tennessee. 1960 to present (1985). Anne Hall White is a studio potter, making functional pieces of stoneware, usually with strong textured surface treatment. She called her pottery "traditional with a whimsical flair." Anne also teaches art at Webb School in Bell Buckle. Anne received her basic training at the Archie Bray Foundation in Helena, Montana. She studied with Rod Kendall of Great Falls, Montana. She attended college in Murfreesboro, Tennessee. She has been working, studying and showing pottery in Tennessee, and the middle U.S., for the last twenty years. She has been doing an Educational Art Series on Channel 8 (Nashville), for over nine years. For a few years now, the name of the studio has been **Bell Buckle Crafts** and other products such as baskets, soft goods (quilts, etc.), have been added to the sales line.

Anne White
Bell Buckle Crafts

Bell Buckle Pottery

Anne White

Bell, Various Potters. The first Bell potter was **Peter Bell, Jr.** in partnership as **Leisinger and Bell** 1800 to 1803, in Elizabeth Town (now Hagerstown,) Maryland. From 1804 until 1824, Peter operated alone in Hagerstown then moved to Winchester, Virginia in 1824-1845. His son was **John Bell** who made pottery in Chambersburg, Pennsylvania, from 1833 to 1880. The son of John Bell was **John W. Bell**, a potter from 1881 to 1895. **Upton Bell** was another son of the first John Bell. He made pottery from 1895 to 1898. The other two sons of the very first Bell potter, named Peter, were **Samuel Bell** and **Solomon Bell**, who made pottery in Strasburg, Virginia from 1834 to 1882. Of these two, Samuel had the children who carried on the family tradition of potting. They were **Richard Franklin Bell, Damuel Bell, Jr.** and **Charles Bell**, from 1882-1908. The various Bell potters made a great variety of utilitarian articles in redware, brownware and Rockingham. The marks shown were all impressed. (Information: Ray, Marcia, "A.B.C.'s of Ceramics," *Spinning Wheel*, June, 1968, p. 19. Marks: Christensen, E.O., *Early American Deisgns, Ceramics*, Mark no. 2, p. 21; Smith, E.L., *Pottery, A Utilitarian Folk Craft*, Marks numbered 5, 6, 8 page 25; Wiltshire, W.E., *Folk Pottery of the Shenandoah Valley*, Mark no. 8, p. 58, Mark no. 7 p. 83. Mark no. 3 p. 32. marks 9 through 18 are shown in Thorn, p. 117. Sometimes the Thorn dates given for these potters vary one year from the authors in articles footnoted. (I add this to assure the critics I know it, not to criticize Thorn. He may be correct!)

P. BELL
1.

JOHN BELL
WAYNESBORO
2.

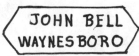
3.

J Bell
4.

JOHN W. BELL
5.

SOLOMON BELL
6.

SOLOMON BELL STRASBURG. VA.
7.

S. BELL & SON STRASBURG
8.

J. BELL
9.

JOHN BELL
10.

SƁ
11.

S. BELL STRASBURG, VA.
12.

P. BELL
13.

UPTON BELL WAYNESBORO
14.

S. BELL
15.

S. BELL & SONS
16.

BELL
17.

JOHN BELL WANESBORO, PA.
18.

Bell, Joseph. Putnam, Ohio. Started around 1827 to make stoneware until 1850. (Information: John Ramsay, p. 228. Mark: Thorn, p. 117.)

JOSEPH BELL

Bell Pottery Company. Findlay, Ohio. Around 1888 they started making vitreous tableware. Around 1903 the company moved to Columbus, Ohio and started to make hotel ware. In 1906 they went bankrupt. They also made semi-porcelain dinner sets and short sets of odd dishes. Part of the time, ware was manufactured in Columbus and decorated in Findlay. The Findlay building later housed U.S. Electrical Co. and the Columbus building was sold to Sanitary Earthenware Company. (Information: Lehner, *American Kitchen and Dinner Wares*, p. 29. Marks: Barber, *Marks of American Potters*, p. 138.)

BELL CHINA
B. P Co.
Findlay, Ohio

THE BELL POTTERY CO
FINDLAY OHIO

B P Co
F O

Belmar of California. Los Angeles, California. Company was listed on Slauson Avenue in the 1965 and 1967 *Gift and Tableware Reporter Directory*. (Mark: found on little aqua colored decorative piece.)

Belmar - Calif
439
USA

Bellmark Pottery Company. Trenton, New Jersey. Started in 1893 (Barber, p. 65) and was listed through 1921 in *Trenton City Directories*. Not listed in 1922. Made plumbers and druggists earthenware. This company had a bell mark very similar to one used much later by the sales agency Ebling Reuss.

Bel Terr China, Inc. East Palestine, Ohio. 1961 to present (1983). Makers of high fired china or stoneware accessories, cups, vases, planters, etc. In the 1960's and 1970's they made a hand thrown art line called "Good Earth Pottery" which was made by potter Belden Ham and his wife Terry Ham, who started the pottery. At the factory, we saw attractively styled brown bean pots and cups of stoneware, drip glaze creamers and sugars more highly vitrified than semi-porcelain, so again it would have to be termed a high fired china. They make commercial type pottery to customer specification, such as ware for decorators, etc. A great part of the ware is marked Bel Terr and sold under the pottery name. Bel Terr China made the "Holly Ross" line. (Marks nos. 1, 2, were early marks used by Mr. Ham. Nos. 3, 4, impressed marks on ware. Nos. 5, 6 stamped marks on ware.)

1. *Bel Terr China*

2. *Good Earth Pottery*

3. *BTC USA 92428*

4. *BEL-TERR CHINA*

5. *Dixon Art Studio USA*

6. *Bel-Terr China U.S.A. 22 KT. GOLD*

Belvedere, Inc. Lake Geneva, Wisconsin. 1947-1950. Herbert and Thomas Dee started in the Chicago area in 1945 to make porcelain, then moved to Lake Geneva in 1947 when their new building was completed. A Mr. Mackelfresh, who has been a consulting engineer for Owens Illinois Glass Company, was vice president. Sculptors and designers were hired. Products were dinnerware and artware of porcelain which was a translucent hand decorated chinaware. In 1949, the plant became idle and in 1952, the plant was purchased by Trostel Packings, Ltd. The pottery kilns were dismantled and removed. It is possible they were moved to California, but I have found no listing to verify this. The Belvedere of California mark is dated about right to allow time for the company to get started in another state. This mark was inscribed underglaze on an aqua colored piece of decorative pottery. The industrial directories I had for this period were no help. (Information: Jenny B. Derwich and Dr. Mary Latos, *Dictionary Guide to U.S. Pottery and Porcelain*, p. 33. Marks: nos. 1-3, Quality Stamp Company, East Liverpool; no. 4, Robert Thayer, dealer and researcher of American pottery.)

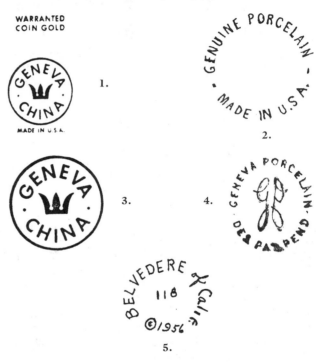

Bengston, Billy Al. Bengston became involved in ceramics when he attended Manual Arts High School in Los Angeles. From 1953 to 1956 he studied at the Los Angeles City College and at the Otis Art Institute in Los Angeles, in 1956 and 1957. He was a part of the group of experimental artists who worked around Peter Voulkos. Then he worked mainly in painting pictures until the 1970's, when he returned to ceramics again. He participated in the "New Works in Clay by Contemporary Painters and Sculptors," exhibition at the Everson Museum of Art in 1975. For a description of this work, see Clark book cited. (Information: Garth Clark, *A Century of Ceramics in the U.S.*, p. 276. Incised mark: Linda Steigleder, from the booklet published by the Everson Museum of Art to accompany the 1978 exhibition, "A Century of Ceramics in the U.S.")

Bengston

Benjamin, James, Stoneware Depot. Cincinnati, Ohio. Latter part of 19th century. Distributor or retailer of stoneware jugs, crocks, etc. In discussing Zanesville stoneware potters, Norris Schneider in "Thirty-one Potteries Operated in City During Late 19th Century," *Zanesville Times Signal*, November 24, 1957, said James Benjamin, J.C. Gillespie, and Hudson C. Ward were the three principal wholesale dealers or outlets in the country for stoneware. Ward was located in Zanesville, Ohio. I didn't find a location for Gillespie. It is entirely possible that stoneware will be found with the names of these two dealers as we did for James Benjamin.

Bennett, Various Potteries. The first Bennett, whose name was James, began in the pottery business in this country by starting the first pottery that was in East Liverpool, Ohio, in 1839. From 1839 to 1841, he operated alone. Then from 1841 to 1844 he was joined by his brothers, Daniel, Edwin and William. In 1844, Edwin, Daniel and James moved to Birmingham, Pennsylvania, where they started a small pottery. In 1846, Edwin went on to Baltimore, Maryland, where he operated the E. Bennett Chinaware Factory until 1848. In 1848, William left Birmingham to join Edwin in Baltimore, and the name became E. & W. Bennett until 1856. Meanwhile, back in Pittsburgh, James had retired and Daniel carried on alone until 1849. From 1856 to 1890 the name of the factory was the Edwin Bennett Pottery and from 1890 to 1936 the title was Edwin Bennett Pottery Company. The Bennett products evolved through the various types familiar to this country. From stoneware, yellowware, Rockingham and majolica in the earliest years, to cream-colored ware, stone china, or granite earthenware in the late 1800's, to Parian, some fine china and artware, before they started back down the scale to plain, semi-porcelain and common china prior to closing their doors in 1936. Bennett's products were beautiful and outstanding in the early years. He even made a Belleek (fine, thin china) and a Rebekah-at-the-Well Rockingham teapot. Thelma Shull's "American Scenes for the China Collector" in *Hobbies*, June, 1942, p. 66, said that Bennett made tableware from transfer prints as the medium for picturing historical scenes. Also see "Bennett Pottery," staff written, in *Spinning Wheel*, November 1958, p. 22. (The following are the dates Barber gave for the marks in his book, *Marks of American Potters*, pp. 143-146. No. 1, around 1850 to 1856. Then according to Barber, no mark was discovered for the firm until around 1875, when no. 2 came into use on white granite ware. No. 3, 1880 on stone china; no. 4 on cream

colored ware, 1884; nos. 5, 6, 7, were used on Parian plaques around 1884-1885; no. 8 in 1886 on Ivory chamber pots; nos. 9 and 10 in 1886 on stone china; nos. 11, 12, 13 were used after 1890 on all semi-porcelain ware; no. 14 in 1892 on semi-granite; no. 15 in 1896; no. 16, paper label, in 1894 on high glazed majolica; no. 17 in 1895 on slip painted ware called Albion. Nos. 18, 19 & 20 with decorator marks: Kate De Witt Berg and Annie Haslam. No. 21 used in 1896 on fine hard china. No. 22 in 1897 on cream colored ware. Nos. 23, 24 & 25 on semi-porcelain ware of a much later date, taken from dishes. Bennett Bakeware was probably made before closing in the 1930's. The mark was on a poor semi-porcelain plate that did not look as if it could stand baking use.)

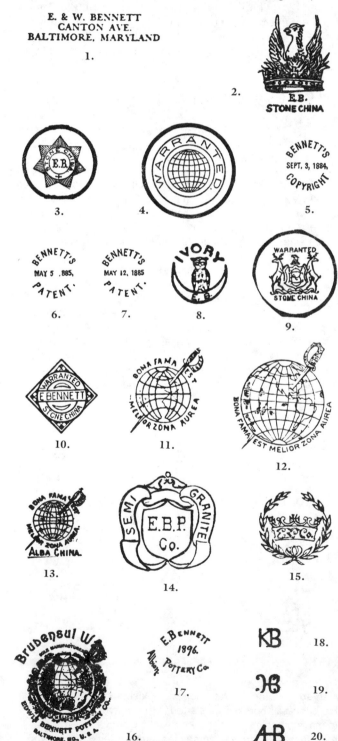

21.

22.

WARRANTED

23.

24.

25.

Bennington Potters. Bennington, Vermont. 1948 to present (1985). David Gil started the Bennington Pottery in 1948. He graduated from Alfred University. By 1969, he employed sixteen. His stoneware and semi-porcelain pieces are marketed all over the country. Another well-known potter who works at the Bennington Pottery is Steve Ballard whose impressed mark is shown. The logo of the pottery is the fork. (Information: Jenny B. Derwich and Dr. Mary Latos, *A Dictionary Guide to U.S. Pottery and Porcelain*, p. 34. Marks: on pieces.)

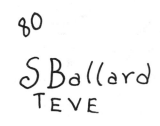

Bennington Potters. Inc.

Bent and Company, Inc. New York, New York. A distributor filed for registration of this mark on January 7, 1927 to be used for porcelain and china, bedroom chambers, cereal sets and chinaware, claiming use of this mark since 1879.

Benton Crock and Pottery Company. Benton, Arkansas. In the *Pottery Collectors' Newsletter*, November 1976, p. 97, is an article by Judy Smith entitled "Niloak Pottery, Benton, Arkansas." In the article she said between 1868 and 1898 there were a dozen pottery plants in operation in the Benton area but by 1898, Hyten, in the Eagle Pottery was the only potter operating. I had no further information on the potteries in Benton, Arkansas, but if what she says is correct, the Benton Crock and Pottery Company should have been gone by 1898.

BENTON CROCK
AND
POTTERY COMPANY
BENTON, ARKANSAS

Berea College. Berea, Kentucky. The college was started in 1855, and has an unusual approach to higher education. Part of their curriculum is a unique labor program which allows students to work in a variety of areas while learning. In crafts, they learn and work with woodcraft, needlecraft, weaving, wrought iron, lapidary, broomcraft and ceramics. Then there are local outlets for the sale of the products the students make such as the Log House Sales Room. Pictured is an inscribed mark no. 1 found on an ashtray, or nut dish of red clay, with brown glaze, made at the college by some student before the Berea College Ceramic Apprenticeship Program; Student Craft Industries was initiated in 1970, under the direction of Walter E. Hyleck, Assistant Professor of Art. All work produced by that program is signed with Berea College's symbol "B", and the individual student maker's stamp. See mark no. 2. See the listings for Deaver Studios and Sarah L. Culbreth for potters who trained at Berea College.

BEREA
COLLEGE   1.
AK

2.   B

Berggren Trayner Corporation. Chicago, and Libertyville, Illinois. 1950 to present (1987). The company was incorporated in Chicago, in December 1950, and moved to Libertyville, in 1953 to present. Berggren Trayner Corporation silk screens designs on ceramic tiles. They also create silk screened ceramic decals for decorating porcelain pieces, such as mugs, cups, saucers, plates, accessories, serving pieces, etc. The blanks are imported from Japan. All of the pieces are fired after decals are applied. The designs are Scandinavian folk art motif. Special orders are made for all types of businesses, associations, museums, churches, etc. Products are also sold from a factory outlet store in Libertyville. Audrey Berggren decided to while away the time her husband, Arthur, was in the Army during W.W. II, by painting Swedish pictures on plates. She had such talent and energy that Marhsal Fields and Company of Chicago, bought all she made during the war. When Arthur came home, they hand painted on wooden plates for several years, and in 1950 they started working with ceramics. They made hand painted tile with old style Swedish designs with inscriptions of old Swedish proverbs. They started silk screening the designs on the tile, and the business was an instant success, so they incorporated and moved as already stated. Other items have been added to decorated lines such as enamelware coffee pots and tea kettles, also wooden cutting boards, metal cannister sets, and trivets. All are beautifully decorated. (Information: from company. Marks: no. 1 is a foil label with red lettering dated 1965. No. 2 is a new label sent by the company. Nos. 3, 4 are a paper label and impressed mark found on the same tile. no. 5 is a paper label.)

FINE PORCELAIN CHINA
Swedish Help Yourself
BERGGREN TRAYNER CORPORATION
○ Berggren Originals
LIBERTYVILLE ILLINOIS

1.

DESIGN No. 193
This original design is
handscreened.
© 1965 BERGGREN TRAYNER CORPORATION
Berggren Originals
LIBERTYVILLE ILLINOIS

2.

Design No 115

. . . .

This original design is hand
screened and fired for perma
nence

THE BERGGREN, SHELTON, TRAYNER CORP.
LIBERTYVILLE, ILLINOIS

Shelton

3.

4.

BERGGREN TRAYNOR CORP
LIBERTYVILLE ILL.

5.   design hand screened

Berndae, Inc. New York, New York. A decorating plant. They filed for registration September 1, 1953, claiming use of this mark since July 30, 1953, for use on earthenware ceramic plates and ornamental serving tile. This company was not listed in the 1952 *Crockery and Glass Journal Directory*, but they were listed in 1954 under decorators.

DEGAS

Berninghaus Company. Cincinnati, Ohio. Eugene Berninghaus was listed in the *R.G. Dunn and Company Mercantile Directory* for 1922 as manufacturers of barber chairs and suppliers of furniture and accessories. Some of those accessories were shaving mugs. Berninghaus decorated some of the mugs. (Marks: found on mug.)

BERNINGHAUS
TRADE
CLIMM
MARK
CINCINNATI. O.

Bethel Pike Pottery. Albany, Indiana. 1967 to present. Alan K. Patrick, studio potter, makes a line of repeated forms of domestic ware in cone 10 stoneware. He also makes one-of-a-kind stoneware pieces and porcelain with overglaze lusters

and enamels. He received a masters degree in ceramics from Ball State University and apprenticed with Byron Temple in 1965.

Beuter, John, Pottery. Waynesburg, Pennsylvania. This pottery made stoneware with stenciled mark and decorations in the 1880's. (Information and mark: Phil Schaltenbrand, *Old Pots*, p. 30.)

J. BEUTER
WAYNESBURG

Big Creek Pottery. Davenport, California. 1967 to present. Bruce McDougal, who operates the Big Creek Pottery with his wife, Marcia, has been making pottery since 1953, but didn't start Big Creek Pottery until 1967. He conducts live-in workshops at the pottery where he and other famous potters teach pottery making, such as John Reeve, Ruth Duckworth and Warren MacKenzie. McDougal makes functional stoneware and small sculpture pieces.

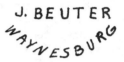

Big Lick Pottery. New Haven, Kentucky. Mike Imes, studio potter, began making pottery in 1972 and in 1980 he started the Big Lick Pottery where he makes stoneware pinch pots and organic vessel forms. An apprentice, Dawn Van Kley, works with him making slab baked pieces and figurative animals and plant motifs. Mike has won many awards at fairs, artists guilds, etc.

BLP

Imes

Van Kley

Big Witch Pottery. Knoxville, Tennessee. 1973 to present (1985). Studio potter, Gina Anderson, makes functional stoneware. She received a Masters Degree from the University of Tennessee. She has worked full time at potting since 1977, before that, part time. She exhibits extensively in galleries and does shows on the east coast. She is a member of the Southern Highlands Guild, the Foothills Craft Guild, Tennessee Artist Craftsmen Association.

Biloxi Art Pottery. See George Ohr.

Binns, Charles Fergus. Binns was a ceramic expert, born in Worcester, England, in 1857. He was the son of the director of the Royal Porcelain Works in Worcester. Binns was in charge of various departments there between 1872 to 1896. In 1896 he came to the United States to be principal of the Technical School of Science and Art in Trenton, New Jersey, from 1897 to 1900. From 1900 to 1931 he was director of the New York State College of Ceramics in Alfred, New York. He published *Ceramic Technology* in 1896; *The Story of a Potter* in 1897; *The Potter's Craft* in 1909, among his several publications and articles. He was an ordained minister in the Protestant Episcopal Church. Levin, in article cited, said Binns was generally acknowledged as the "father of contemporary American ceramics." In 1899, he helped to found the American Ceramic Society. When Adelaide Robineau, a famous decorator, became interested in making pottery as well as decorating it, she worked with Binns several weeks at Alfred University, and then continued to experiment on her own to develop high fired porcelain bodies. This was the connection between Binns and Robineau, made in the article cited. (See the listing for Robineau.). (Information: *Encylcopedia Americana*, Volume 31, 1961, p. 717; Elaine Levin, "Charles binns and Adelaide Robineau," *Ceramics Monthly*, November 1975, pp. 22-26. Incised marks: Linda Steigleder, from the booklet published by the Everson Museum of Art to accompany the 1978 exhibition, "A Century of Ceramics in the U.S.")

Bitterroot Pottery and Glass Company. Victor, Montana. 1969 to present (1983). Peggy Steffes is a studio potter making stoneware and porcelain, functional and sculptural. She had a solo exhibit at the University of Montana in 1982. She graduated from the University of Wisconsin in 1969 and received an M.F.A. in 1971. She has had built and operates in a solid stone pottery shop and has enjoyed a steadily growing business since 1969.

Blackburn, Edward. Blackburn, a studio potter, received a B.A. and an M.F.A. degree from the San Francisco Art Institute in the early 1970's. He taught at the University of Washington, in the 1974-1975 school year, and since 1975 he has been teaching at the California State University. He has done numerous one-man and invitational shows. He uses techniques involving underglazes, lustre glazes and china paints on earthenware pieces. He hand builds or molds pieces, adds successive layers of colors and fires the pieces several times at different temperatures. (Information: Garth

Clark, *A Century of Ceramics in the U.S.*, p. 277. Incised mark: Linda Steigleder, from the booklet published by the Everson Museum of Art to accompany the 1978 exhibition, "A Century of Ceramics in the U.S.")

Black, Harding. San Antonio, Texas. Early 1930's until present (1984). Harding started to study the making of ceramics following an archeological expedition to the Big Bend country of Texas during the depression. There he helped to dig shards of pottery with a group from San Antonio's Witte Memorial Museum. The director brought back a little stock Venus and Harding decided to duplicate the figure which he fired in his mother's own cook stove. He had one year of college before he had to quit because of money. With no equipment and no knowledge, he began to learn by trial and error to make what finally resulted in beautiful art pottery. His first attempt at glazing of a sort was using ashes of Johnson grass or dank leaf mold fired in the open, over charcoal to get a glossy black finish. Fifteen years and over 10,000 tests later he had discovered the ancient Chinese method of making copper-red glazes which he places over fragile porcelain pieces. The oxblood, pigeon blood, Chun, celedon, crackel effects have become his trademark. He is still experimenting with the copper reduction involved in making the glazes. Thin, irridescent glazes are used on stoneware and porcelain pieces, such as pots, plates, bowls and various artistic pieces. Mr. Black has always used native Texas clay. In the last fifty years, Harding figures he has made 200,000 pieces working from 7:00 a.m. to 4:00 p.m., seven days a week. He has been at this present location on Broadway Street since the early 1950's, in his large building, which houses the latest equipment including three gas kilns and many display cases. He has been teaching classes for years. As early as January and February 1953, he was written about in the *Ceramic Monthly* under the staff written profile, "Harding Black." Many other articles in papers followed as his experiments gained success. In 1976, his work was shown at the Star of the Republic Museum in Washington, Texas and his work was pictured in the booklet, *Texas Pottery*, by Sherry B. Humphreys and Johnell L. Schmidt, pp. 36, 37. It shows a porcelain jar with reduction fired Chun glaze and a stoneware bowl with oxidation fired oilspot glaze. (Information: from Harding Black. Mark: from booklet cited.)

Black Knight China. This was the name of a china line made in Bavaria. It is included here because it was distributed by Graham and Zenger, Inc. of New York City in the 1930's. The dishes are porcelain and of such a quality and beauty that many collectors ask for information about them. The china was sold by Ovingtons, New York City and John Wanamaker in Philadelphia. One reader wrote to me about a piece marked "made expressly for the Drake Hotel Company furnished by Albert Pick and Co." Manufactured 1926. In the 1930's a service for eight cost around $500.00 depending on the complexity of the decoration, according to an add in *Art and Decorators*, November 1930.

This hallmark on fine china is a warrant of beauty and an assurance of quality.

This hallmark on fine china is a warrant of beauty and an assurance of quality.

A.C. Blair China Studios. Chester, West Virginia. Around 1945 to 1960 or 1961. Blair was a china decorator not to be confused with William Blair of Blair Ceramics. (Marks: Quality Stamp Company, East Liverpool, Ohio.)

Blair Ceramics, Inc. Ozark, Missouri. Founded 1946, closed in 1950's. William Blair, owner, made hand painted, mold formed, oven proof dinnerware, employing around thirty people producing 3,600 piece weekly. (Information and mark: Jo Cunningham, "The Collector's Encyclopedia of American Dinnerware," Paducah, Kentucky: Schroeder Publishing Company, Inc., 1982, p. 28.)

Blair, Sylvester. Cortland, New York. 1829-1837. Made stoneware. Mark impressed. (Ramsay, p. 191, Thorn, p. 118.)

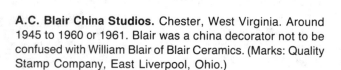

Blank Pottery. Boonville and California, Missouri. August Blank and F.X. Blank operted a pottery in Boonville, Cooper County, Missouri, during 1880's and early 1890's. August went to California, Missouri, in late 1890's and early 1900's. The mark shown is positively identified as coming from that pottery, but no explanation for the initial "W" was given. (Information: Charles Van Ravenswaay, "Missouri Potters and

Their Wares, 1780-1924," *Missouri Historical Society Bulletin*, July 1951, pp. 465, 467. Mark: shown in plate 5 of same source.)

Blazys, Alexander. Cleveland, Ohio. Blazys was an outstanding sculptor, designer, modler. He was born in Lithuania, in 1894. He was associated with the Cleveland School of Art and worked at the Cowan Pottery as a designer. In 1926, 1927 and 1928, he won a first prize for sculpture at the Cleveland Museum of Art's May Show. A group of figures called "Russian Dancers," won first prize in 1927. The mark shown was incised on the top base of the accordian player in the group of figures. (Information: Edna Maria Clark, *Ohio Art and Artists*, p. 443. Mark: Linda Steigleder, from the booklet published by the Everson Museum of Art to accompany the 1978 exhibition, "A Century of Ceramics in the U.S.")

Block China Company/J & I Block Company/Rosenthal Block China Company. New York, New York. These were selling agencies listed in very late 1940's through 1967 in the directories I had. I found no connection to the manufacturing concern, Richard G. Block Pottery of California. My first listing for **J & I Block Company** at 1225 Broadway, was in the 1949 *China and Glass Red Book Directory* for Bavarian china and domestic pottery. They continued to be listed until after 1954. My next directory was 1961 and they were no longer listed. Joseph Block was president of the company. By 1953, Joseph Block was listed as president of **Rosenthal-Block China Corporation** at 21 East 26th Street. This company was not listed for any domestic or American pottery, only Bavarian dinnerware. This company continued to be listed through 1961. In 1963, we have a registered mark for **Block China Company** at 25 East 26th Street, claiming first use since 1962. See mark no. 1. This Block China Company was headed by Jay L. Block and Robert C. Block, and they have continued until the present. In the directories of 1966, 1967, Block China Company was listed as selling American ironstone. At present, they sell a wide selection of foreign made products. In the 1960's, Rosenthal continued alone at 21 East 26th Street, when the name was no longer Rosenthal-Block. Rosenthal China Corporation is still in business, listed for selling German china, crystal, silver and figurines. In all of the directories, these distributors had a wide variety of marks. Shown are only those filed for registration. (Marks: No. 1 filed by Block China Company, January 28, 1963, claiming first use in October 1962, for chinaware and porcelain items, namely plates, platters, cups, saucers, dishes, coffee potes, tea pots, creamers, sugar basins, water pitchers, milk jugs, sauce boats, mustard pots, marmalade and jelly jars, egg cups, salad bowls, cookie jars, soup bowls, tureens, casseroles, chafing dishes, relish dishes and vegetable dishes. No. 2 filed by Block China Company, claiming use since January 1, 1964, for the same articles as no. 1, except in no. 2, the clay was earthenware, ironstone and semi-porcelain, as well as porcelain. No. 3 were shown in various directories. No 4 was filed by the Rosenthal-Block China Corporation on December 29, 1959, claiming use since January 1, 1959, for chinaware and porcelain items, namely plates, platters, cups, saucers, dishes, coffee pots, tea pots, creamers, sugar basins, water pitchers, milk jugs, sauce boats, mustard pots, marmalade an djelly jars, egg cups, salad bowls, cookie jars, soup bowls, tureens, casseroles, chafing dishes, relish dishes and vegetable dishes. Nos. 5, 6, were filed under the name Rosenthal-Block China Company. No. 5 on October 20, 1955 and 6 on October 21, 1952.)

1.

LIBERTY HALL

2.

LORELEI

4.

Script

5.

3.

6.

Block, Richard G., Pottery. Santa Monica Blvd., Los Angeles, California. The pottery was listed as manufacturers in the 1948 and 1949 *China and Glass Red Book Directories*, for figurines, ash trays, animals & birds, vases, bowls, wall pockets, savings banks, & baby novelties. The mark shown sent by a reader shows a 1940 copyright date so the pottery operated throughout the 1940's, but I found no listings in the 1950's. In 1948, Richard G. Block was president. In 1949, the president was Frieda C. Block. I could find no connection to the Blocks in the distributing business in New York City. See that listing.

© 1940
BLOCK
POTTERY
CALIFORNIA

Bloor, William. East Liverpool, Ohio & Trenton, New Jersey. Bloor moved back and forth between these two cities several times between the middle 1850's until after 1875. In the middle 1850's, Bloor was associated in Trenton, with James Taylor and Henry Speeler (Barber, *Pottery and Porcelain of U.S.*, p. 208). By 1859, he was back in East Liverpool, Ohio, according to W.A. Betz, "It All Started in East Liverpool," *Crockery and Glass Journal*, April 1955 from which the following quote is taken.

"William Bloor, in partnership with William Brunt, Jr., purchased the old Woodward, Blakely and Company plant in 1859 and made the first white ware in East Liverpool the following year. It was an exceedingly white Parian Ware, quite translucent and thoroughly vitrified. Much of it was unglazed on the outside and had only

a thin covering of glaze on the inside; and much of it was decorated with artistic designs which were painted by hand. The color scheme most used was a light blue background with the design in relief in clear white. Mr. Bloor made staple goods, hotel ware and such novelties as vases, mugs, fancy dishes, curtain knobs, fancy butter dishes and Parian busts of noted statesmen. Practically everything made in this plant was by the "casting" method; liquid clay (or "slip") was poured into two-part plaster molds. After awhile, when the mold had absorbed some of the water in the slip, causing the slip to adhere to sides of the mold, the excess slip was poured off. What remained was allowed to dry further. Then the mold was opened and the ware removed for further decorating, glazing and firing."

In 1863, Bloor was back in Trenton, New Jersey, and with Thomas Booth (not Brewer, as has been reported in error) and Joseph Ott, where he helped to found the Eturia Pottery. (See that listing for information.) Later, John Hart Brewer purchased Bloor's interest and the firm became Ott and Brewer by 1865. In 1875, Bloor was back in East Liverpool and became part of Brunt, Bloor, Martin and Company. (See that listing for information.) (Mark: raised in mold, Thorn, p. 118. Bloor also used the recessed mark, "W. Bloor," in block letters.)

Blue Arrows Decorating Workshop. New York, New York. Decorating workshop owned by Robert Bloch. Hand decorating done on china, earthenware, pottery and glass, such as figurines, jardinieres, flower bowls, florist ware and lamps. (Mark: from 1945 *Crockery and Glass Journal Directory*. Crossed arrows of one kind and another were used by several foreign countries. This mark won't do much good in identification unless compared to marks in a book showing foreign marks. Also in 1945, Orsay Porcelaine sold by Herman Kupper, and a ware sold by Arnart Imports in 1959 had similar marks shown under American selling agencies that sold foreign products.)

Blue Bird Pottery. Crooksville, Ohio. 1974 to 1977. Owner, Warren Driggs, made caste novelty pieces fired to around 1900 degrees with a good heavy glaze. Employed six to make planters, decorative pieces and some dinnerware. Mostly unmarked, but stamped mark on some pieces.

BLUE BIRD POTTERY CO.

Crooksville, Ohio

Blue Wave. Kennebunk, Maine. Sarah S. Fletcher, doing business as the Blue Wave, filed October 8, 1943, in the names of Norman K. and Anne B. Wiggin for a copyright on this mark to be used on ceramic vases and tableware, claiming use since July 1922.

Boehm, Edward Marshall, Inc. Trenton, New Jersey. Around 1950 to present. Edward Marshall Boehm was one of the world's most renowned sculptors. He was also dedicated to preserving wildlife and to present it in a form that captured the very essence of living nature through his sculptured pieces. Boehm did not work at sculpting until after W.W. II when he was in the Air Force Convalescent Center in Pawling, New York, and became interested in modeling clay. In 1944, Edward and his wife, Helen, settled in Great Neck, New York, and Edward spent all of his spare time modeling and as much time as he could in Trenton, learning about pottery and porcelain manufacture. He worked for a short time as an apprentice with Herbert Haseltine. Around 1950 or 1951, Boehm had succeeded in making hard paste porcelain and doing it well. A studio was opened in Trenton, but as an unknown artist, Boehm found sales difficult at first. His wife, Helen, continued her job, but she started spending her spare hours visiting galleries and promoting his work. Because of the excellence and quality of Boehm's work, the marketing had to start at the top with buyers that few artists ever sell to in a whole lifetime. In 1951, Helen convinced the curator of the American Wing of the Metropolitan Museum of Art to purchase some of Boehm's pieces. A Hereford Bull was presented to the Eisenhowers. Following that, several museums began to purchase the pieces. Helen's marketing efforts began to pay off. Edward Boehm was a self-taught artist, a breeder of champion cattle, dogs and horses, a horticulturalist of note, an entomologist, a breeder of tropical saltwater fish and a world renowned aviculturist who brought back exotic birds from Africa, South America, New Guinea, Borneo, Australia and the Himalayas; one hitherto-unknown species he netted was named for him Flycatcher *boehmii*. He maintained seventeen aviaries to house as many as three hundred and fifty-seven species. Many had never before been seen in captivity, and many of them bred in the well-feathered nests of Boehm. He had an intimate knowledge of birds and most of the other animal species. Boehm died in 1969 at the age of fifty-six. Since Edward's death, Helen has expanded their studios in Trenton, New Jersey, and added two studios in the beautiful Cotswold town of Malvern in England. She has increased business volume to well over ten million dollars a year (the private company publishes no earnings figures). The lifesize Mute Swans, which took two years and five hundred molds to make, were Richard Nixon's gift to Chairman Mao Tse-tung on the President's historic trip to Peking in 1972. Mao Tse-tung thought they were real birds which had been stuffed. Helen Boehm was invited by the Egyptian government to recreate in porcelain some twenty-seven of the Treasures of Tutcankhamun in 1977. Helen Boehm, and no one else, runs the business. One of her decisions each year is to select the pieces that one hundred and eighty artisans will produce in Trenton and Malvern. Many editions

are limited to no more than one thousand pieces each; the more valuable will be limited to two hundred. The most costly will be priced at thirty-five thousand dollars and limited to twenty-five pieces. At the lower end of the scale, the firm sells thousands of "open" (unlimited) porcelains in the one hundred and fifty dollar to three hundred dollar range. There is a backlog of between six months and two years on many pieces; at one point the backlog of orders stretched to four years. Boehm porcelain sculptures are represented in one hundred seventeen museums, royal palaces and cultural centers throughout the world, including: the White House, Washington, D.C.; the Metropolitan Museum of Art, New York, New York; the Smithsonian Institute, Washington, D.C.; Buckingham Palace, London; Royal Palace, Stockholm; Royal Palace, Monaco; Tokyo National Museum, Tokyo; Royal Ontario Museum, Toronto; Los Angeles County Museum, Los Angeles, California; John F. Kennedy Center, Washington, D.C.; The Vatican, Rome; and Elysee Palace, Paris. The pope was presented with a piece for the Vatican Museum called "Cerulean Warblers" with Wild Roses. The Eisenhowers gave Prince Philip of England, the sculpture of the Prince on his Polo pony. (Information: company literature; and Michael Demarest, "The Arts," *Avenue*, May 1979, pp. 44 to 47. Marks: furnished by the company.)

EDWARD MARSHALL
BOEHM
Trenton, NJ, U.S.A.
Nonlimited sculptures
1958–1970 (1950–
present)

1.

EDWARD MARSHALL
BOEHM
Trenton, NJ, U.S.A.
Nonlimited sculptures
1971 (1950–present)

2.

EDWARD MARSHALL
BOEHM
Trenton, NJ, U.S.A.
Nonlimited sculptures
1971 (1950–present)

3.

EDWARD MARSHALL
BOEHM
Trenton, NJ, U.S.A.
Porcelain
1952–1954 (1950–
present)

4.

Boehm

EDWARD MARSHALL
BOEHM
Malvern, England &
Trenton, NJ, U.S.A.
Porcelain. Variations in
wording
1954–present (1950–
present)

5.

EDWARD MARSHALL
BOEHM
Trenton, NJ, U.S.A.
Porcelain, figurines
1951–1952 (1950–
present)

6.

EDWARD MARSHALL
BOEHM
Trenton, NJ, U.S.A.
Limited editions
1958–1970 (1950–
present)

7.

EDWARD MARSHALL
BOEHM
Malvern Link,
Worcestershire, England
Porcelain
1975+ (1950–present)

8.

Bogatay, Paul. Bogatay was a graduate of the Cleveland School of Art and worked at the Cowan Pottery around 1929 into early 1930s' as a designer and decorator. He joined the staff at Ohio State University in 1934, and was named a professor of ceramic art in 1945, where he worked with Arthur Baggs (see that listing). In 1953 he received the Charles Fergus Binns medal for outstanding achievement in ceramic art. The medal is awarded by Alfred University in honor of its first director of ceramics, C.F. Binns. (See the listing for Charles Fergus Binns.) In the Ninth Annual National Ceramic Exhibition at Syracuse (see the various listings of winners for these in the back of the book). Bogatay submitted "Colt," in unglazed red terra cotta which was described as a small figure with great strength and sculptural soundness in "Ninth Annual National Ceramic Exhibition," *Bulletin of American Ceramic Scoiety*, November 1940, p. 453. Mr. Bogatay has had many prize-winning entries in exhibitions throughout the United States. The "Baboon," a ceramic sculpture, which won the purchase award at the Wichita Art Association Exhibition in 1953. He received prizes at the National Ceramic Exhibition at Syracuse in 1949, at the Columbus Art League Exhibition in 1950, and at the Butler Art Institute in 1952. He has also exhibited in Europe and Canada and has served on various show juries. Bogatay died in 1972. (Mark: sent by Ben Hutslar, Ohio State Historical Society Museum, Columbus, Ohio.)

BOGATAY 60

Boggs Pottery. Prattville, Alabama. 1830 to present. In 1830 A.T. Boggs came to Randolf County, Alabama, to make stoneware jugs and churns. The family continued to make pottery in the Randolf location for almost 100 years. In 1929, J.A. Boggs moved to the outskirts of Montgomery and a little later he moved to Prattville where the pottery was still operating in 1983 when the exhibition, "The Traditional Pottery of Alabama," was held at the Montgomery Museum of Fine Arts. In the catalogue to accompany the exhibit written by Henry Willett and Joey Brackner, pictured on p. 62 is a salt glazed jug with the mark inscribed as shown, except I couldn't see all of the date in the picture which was June 19, 1895. (Information: Willett and Brackner as cited, p. 46.)

J a Boggs
June ?

Bohemian Pottery. Zanesville, Ohio. 1900 to 1918. According to Norris Schneider, as cited, the pottery was started by Edwin Munch and John H. Stroop. He said it is believed they made kitchen ware rather than art pottery. There were so many of the little potteries that started up in Zanesville, tried a variety of products to stay in business, but were short lived when in competition with the art pottery giants of the area. See Ohio Porcelain, Brighton Pottery, Nouvelle Pottery and Imperial Porcelain listing for examples. (Information: Norris Schneider, "Many Small Art Potteries Once Operated in Zanesville," *Zanesville Times Recorder*, February 4, 1962 no page number. Mark: found on little salesman's sample crockery bowl.)

"BOHEMIAN"

Bonnema, Garret and Melody. Bethel, Maine. 1973 to present (1984). Studio potters, make lamps, garden furniture, dinnerware, wall and floor tile, umbrella stands, covered casseroles, etc., by handhrown, hand cut and molded methods. (Information: Susan Cox, "Bonnema," *American Clay Exchange*, September, 1983, p. 3. Mark incised.)

BONNEMA

Bonnin (Goussin) and Morris (George Anthony). Philadelphia, Pennsylvania. 1769 to around 1774. This was a short lived pottery that failed due to many difficulties. They made china dinner services, tea sets and small table accessories of porcelain and cream ware. (Information: John Spargo, *Early American Pottery and China*, pp. 76 to 83. He tells us George Anthony Morris furnished most of the capitol and Bonnin was an English potter. The factory was built in the Southwark section in Prime Street. He tells of several interesting advertisements in newspapers for this company. They asked for children between the ages of 12 and 15 for apprenticeship with the men they had brought from England to do the potting. They also advertised for men to do the throwing, turning, modeling, moulding, pressing and painting. They asked for beef and hog bones to buy for their bone china. Zaffera or Zaffer was needed to make the paste porcelain. In 1772, they advertised for 50 wagon loads of white flint stone to make opaque ware. Spargo said the mark "P" from Barber as shown here could have been just a benchmark of the decorator and not really an identifying mark for the pottery. (Information: Spargo, as cited. Marks: E.A. Barber, *Marks of Americna Potters*, p. 11.)

P

Bonzi, William, Company. Pasadena, California. Started around 1945 and was still listed in 1952 *Crockery and Glass Journal Directory*, but was not listed in 1954. William Bonzi graduated from University of California at Berkeley in 1921, according to Derwich and Latos, p. 38. He obtained a plant in Pasadena in 1945. He was listed in the directory as making porcelain figurines. (Marks: 1952 Directory as cited.)

BONZI PORCELAIN

T.G. Boon and Company. Poughkeepsie, New York. Around 1840. Made stoneware. Mark impressed. (Information and mark: John P. Remensnyder, "The Potters of Poughkeepsie," reprinted from *Antiques Magazine in The Art of the Potter*, edited by Diana and J. Garrison Stradling, p. 124.)

T.G BOON & CO.
PO'KEEPIE, N.Y.

Borgfeldt, George, Corporation. New York, New York. In business before 1891. A selling agency, advertised as manufacturers' representatives of American and import lines of glassware, china, earthenware, dinnerware, art pottery, gift and houseware items in 1952 directory. Emerling China Company, East Liverpool, Ohio, decorated ware for them. The company filed for registration on the mark no. 1 on March 17, 1933, to be used on chinaware, crockery and earthenware, such as tableware, dinner sets, fancyware, candy jars, bon bon dishes, vases, jardinieres, flower pots, boxes, marmalade jars, ornamental trays and receptacles, etc., claiming use since 1933. Mark no. 2 was filed July 27, 1945 for the same articles, claiming use since January 8, 1902. Mark no. 3 was filed on December 8, 1929, for the same articles. Mark no. 4 was file July 3, 1937 for the same articles, claiming use since November 1936. Mark no. 5 is from 1952 *Crockery and Glasss Journal Directory*. Marks nos. 6 through 14 are from Quality Stamp Company, East Liverpool, Ohio. Mark 15 filed April 15, 1915, for plates, plaques, mugs, cups, china bric-a-brac, fern dishes, washstand sets, dresser sets, table sets, writing desk sets and vase, claiming use since 1915. Mark 16 filed July 4, 1922, claiming use since 1915 for use on china tableware. Mark 17 filed July 14, 1917, for use on all articles mentioned for mark 15 plus tea, coffee and chocolate sets, mugs, jugs, pitchers, cabarets, olive dishes, bulb bowls, jardinieres, candelabra, trays, etc. Mark 18 filed July 14, 1917, claiming use since July 1, 1917, for same articles as mark 17. Mark 19 filed January 19, 1953, claiming use since November 24, 1952, for use on porcelain and earthenware for domestic purposes, namely, dinner and table use. Borgfeldt sold American and foreign ware under these marks.)

DAMASKINE

1.

2. **CORONET**

DIANA

3.

4.

5.

6.

7. EXQUISITE

8. NANCY

9. BERTHA

10. FOREVER

11. MORESQUE

12. DELLRAY

13. SILVER PUPPY

14. DELLROSE

15. FLOSSIE FISHER'S FUNNIES

16. REX

17. WHITE HOUSE

18. Buckingham Palace

19. *Blossomtime*

Borg-Warner Corporation, Inc. Detroit, Michigan. Filed for registration of this mark on March 11, 1936, to be used for crockery, porcelain and earthen cooking hollow ware, tableware and refrigerator dishes, claiming use since February 2, 1935. In the reports, this company made several requests for registrations of marks to be used on refrigerators, refrigerator units and parts for replacement and repair, claiming use on the refrigerators and parts since 1878.

NORGE

Boss Brothers. Middlebury (Akron), Ohio. There is confusion on date for this company. Thorn, p. 118 and Ramsay, p. 207 give 1874 and Blair, p. 26 gives 1860. The company made utilitarian stoneware ink and beer bottles, marked as shown.

Bosworth, Stanley. Hartford, Connecticut. Around 1873. Made stoneware. (Information and marks: Lura W. Watkins, *Early New England Potters and Their Wares*, p. 250.)

STANLEY BOSWORTH
HARTFORD, CONN.

S.B. BOSWORTH
HARTFORD, CT.

Boughner Pottery and **Vance Pottery.** In 1811, Daniel Boughner started a pottery in Greensboro, Pennsylvania. In 1809, Spargo, p. 215, lists **Alexander Vance** as making pottery in Greensboro. Ramsay, p. 68, states Alexander Vance was there as early as 1800. At any rate, Daniel Boughner married into the Vance Family and became a partner around 1812. Daniel's sons were Alexander V. and William Boughner who carried on the pottery business for over fifty years. The exact ending date is not determined; I found dates from 1870 to 1890 for an end. The Vance family came to Cincinnati, Ohio, to make pottery around the 1830's. How long the Vances and the Boughners worked in a pottery together is another one of the dates not agreed upon. Guappone, p. 10, shows an 1860 advertisement for A. & W. Boughner making stoneware jars, milk pans, butter pots, jugs, pitchers, etc. from one to thirty gallons. Baker tells us the Vance family made unmarked redware usually with a dark brown or black slip glaze. He said they were hard to distinguish from those around the country. (For further information, see Gordon C. Baker, "Pottery of Greensboro and New Geneva," *Spinning Wheel*, November 1973, pp. 14-17. Marks: no. 1, Phil Schaltenbrand, *Old Pots*, Hanover, Pennsylvania; Everybodys Press, 1977, p. 10. No. 2, Spargo, plate 59; and Guappone, p. 15. No. 3, Gordon C. Baker, as cited, p. 15; nos. 4, 5, Thorn, p. 119.)

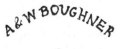

1.

BOUGHNER
GREENSBORO
PA.

2.

A V. Boughner,
Greensboro, Pa.

3.

ALEXANDER BOUGHNER
GREENSBORO
PA.

4.

A. W. BOUGHNER
GREENSBORO
PA.

5.

Bovano Industries, Inc. Cheshire, Connecticut. Filed for registration of this mark on August 6, 1969, claiming use since March 18, 1958, for articles made by fusing glass and porcelain on metal, such as copper, namely, bowls, plates, etc.

BOVANO

J. Bower. Fredericktown, Pennsylvania. Around 1820's. This mark is on a section of stoneware water pipe shown in an article by Philip Schaltenbrand, "Stoneware Potteries of Fredericktown, Pennsylvania," *Spinning Wheel*, November/December 1982, p. 53.

J. BOWER. 1824. PATENT

Bowman, George H. Company. See Cleveland China Company for history and marks.

Boyd, William. Beverly Hills, California. Company filed for registration of this mark on November 9, 1950, for use on dinnerware for children, made of china and porcelain, claiming use since March 26, 1950.

Boyer, John. Schuylkill County, Pennsylvania. Around 1810. Made stoneware. (Information and mark: Thorn, p. 119.)

JOHN BOYER

Boynton, Calvin. West Troy, and Albany, New York. This stoneware potter came from Cavendish, Vermont, and was a brother of Jonah Boynton. He settled first in Albany, then in 1825 he purchased William Lundy's interest in the Hill Street Pottery in Troy. Boynton and Russell Elsworth worked together as **C. Boynton and Company**. In May 1829, the partnership was dissolved and Boynton worked alone until 1837. In January 1837, the Troy, New York, Hill Street Pottery of Boynton was destroyed in a landslide. He died in West Troy, New York, in 1848. (Information and mark: Warren F. Broderick, researcher, writer and collector.)

Bradford Exchange. Chicago, Illinois. Selling agency in 1980's for decorative plates made in association with the Edwin M. Knowles China Company name. (See Edwin M. Knowles for history of that company.) Mark no. 1 shown registered in name, Edwin M. Knowles China Company, September 30, 1982, for use on art objects, namely decorated plates. Mark no. 2 filed September 30, 1982 under the name Edwin M. Knowles China Company, claiming first use on August 5, 1980, for same product as no. 1.

EDWIN M. KNOWLES

1.

2.

Bradley, Mildred. Centerville, Iowa. 1955 to around 1986. In 1953, Mrs. Bradley was introduced to ceramics when she took a course at Community College. By 1955, she had converted the family's four car garage into a studio which she named **Hillcrest Hobby House**. She decided to discover a local clay which she could develop for her own use. A long time of trial and error followed before she found a lovely cinnamon colored clay in Appanoose County where she lived. She was able to finish the clay to a coppertone with the right glaze. She swirled the colored clay to a coppertone with white clay and produced beautiful vases, bowls and all sorts of decorative pieces. She has won many prizes at Midwest Ceramic Shows. Just recently Mrs. Bradley sold the business and is traveling. (Mark: inscribed on bottom of swirled brown and white clay coaster. No doubt this potter used other inscribed marks over the years.)

Iowa Clay Ceramics
Mildred Bradley
Lake Rathbun
Iowa

Bradshaw China Company. Niles, Ohio. Started around 1901, and by 1902 was listed in the *Complete Directory of Glass Factories and Potteries in the U.S. and Canada*, for semi-porcelain and china dinner sets, toilet sets, and short sets of odd dishes and novelties, some decorated. The book, *A History of Niles, Ohio*, by the Niles Centennial History Club of McKinley High School, written 1934, said that William H. Tritt purchased the pottery in 1910 and it was incorporated in 1912 with a capitol of 100,000, employing 25 people to make porcelain and semi-porcelain dinnerware. Floyd W. McKee in *A Century of American Dinnerware Manufactories*, said F.H. Sebring purchased the plant and sent Tritt to manage it. Tritt had gone to work for the Sebring's in their various potteries at age twenty-two. In the *Warren, Niles and Girard, Ohio City Directory for 1916*, W.H. Tritt was listed as president and general manager. The researchers generally agree the plant was sold in 1921, to A.O.C. Ahrendts. Some

say it operated for a short time under the name, Crescent China Company, but was shortly changed to Atlas China Company. The Sebrings were operating a plant named Crescent China in Alliance, Ohio, from 1920 to 1926 and two Crescents would cause confusion. The building had a bad fire in 1925. McKee says it was not rebuilt, but the *History of Niles, Ohio*, said that it was. McKee said a new building was constructed in its place by A.O.C. Ahrendts. At any rate, the *Warren, Niles, Girard City Directory*, 1925 lists Atlas China Company with Ahrendts as president and treasurer. In 1926, the two plants under Ahrendts's ownership, the Atlas China Company of Niles, Ohio, and the Globe Pottery of Cambridge, Ohio, were consolidated under the name **Atlas Globe China Company** with the two plants operating in their respective towns. I had previously thought the whole operation was moved to Cambridge, but the *1929 Directory of Manufacturers*, published by the Division of Labor Statistics lists an Atlas Globe China Company as operating in each town. In the 1930's, another big reorganization took place under O.C. Ahrendts and several partners. By this time the factory in Niles, Ohio, had been closed but Ahrendts was still in possession of Oxford Pottery and the Atlas Globe China Company in Cambridge. The Atlas Globe China Company was forced into some kind of liquidation in the early 1930's. It was settled out of court through the holdings Ahrendts had in Oxford Pottery. Then in 1934 the buildings became the **Universal Potteries, Inc.** According to McKee the main finances were supplied by a family of McClellands who had made money in the wholesale grocery business. Donald Agnew was the manager. See Universal Potteries, Inc. for more history. (Mark shown is for Bradshaw China Company from Barber, *Marks of American Potters*, p. 137.)

Brahm, Johannes. Los Angeles and Reseda, California. Around 1945 to 1956. Pottery started in Los Angeles area around 1945 to make exquisite decorated ware. In the 1952 *Crockery and Glass Journal Directory*, they were listed as making art pottery of earthenware such as candy boxes, console sets, vases, etc. In 1948 the company was moved to Reseda, California, and incorporated in 1953. They stopped production in 1956. (Information: Jenny B. Derwich and Dr. Mary Latos, *Dictionary Guide to United States Pottery and Porcelain*, p. 41. Mark: Ada Read.)

Branum Pottery. Milaca, Minnesota. 1973 to present. Wayne Branum, studio potter, makes wood fired, salt glazed, stoneware and porcelain. He studied under an N.E.A. Craftsmen Fellowship Award.

BRANUM POTTERY
MILACA, MN.

Brastoff, Sascha, of California, Inc. West Los Angeles, California. November 1953 to present. Sascha Brastoff is an internationally known designer, artist, sculptor, ceramist, with works in several permanent collections in the Los Angeles County Museum of Art, the Sculpture Center in New York and other galleries (Derwick and Latos, p. 42.). Mr. Brastoff also worked with metal arts. Listed in 1967 *China, Glass and Tablewares Directory* for decorative accessories, ceramics, enamel on copper and platics. In an advertising brochure which came with a set of beautiful handmade china sold in 1958 was the statement that "In his southern California studios, Brastoff has labored toward a double objective - the offering of unexceled quality in the medium itself and the bringing of fine art into every day living." The brochure mentioned he was a sculptor and a dancer which gave grace and fluidity to his designs. The dinnerware had a soft satin finish or glaze, an off white body. Susan N. Cox, "Sascha Brastoff, Innovator For All Times," *American Clay Exchange*, November 1983, p. 10, gave the dates in business as shown. She tells us the plant covered a full block, even though it was considered a studio plant which operated from 1953 to 1973. Sascha did all of the designs, then he had a staff of twenty artists who worked to his specifications. If he did the piece himself it was signed with his full name, If he supervised the making, the piece was signed "Sascha B." A line of hand painted china with about a dozen designs was produced. Also a full line of dinnerware was made. Pieces cost from $25.00 into the thousands of dollars for other pieces when sold new. At present he is producing very expensive holograms. (Information as cited. Marks: no. 1, a gold label, possibly a backstamp shown in the 1967 directory. Marks 2, 3, the Cox article cited. Mark 4 was filed May 4, 1959, claiming use since January 1948. Mark 5 was filed April 14, 1959, claiming use since January 1952. Both registrations stated that these names stood for Mr. Sascha Brastoff, vice-president of the applicant corporation, consent of record. The name was to be used on earthenware art pottery, namely, ash trays, bowls, dishes, plates, vases, figurines, plaques, china and dinnerware. See B. Altman Company for more.)

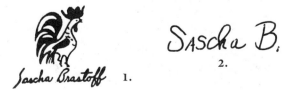

Sascha Brastoff 1.

Sascha B. 2.

Sascha Brastoff 3.

SASCHA B. 4.

5. SASCHA BRASTOFF

Brayton and Associates. Utica, New York. **J.F. Brayton** made stoneware from around 1830 to 1833. From 1833 to around 1837 the listing by Stewart and Consentino, p. 122 was the **J.F. Brayton and Company**. Then in 1827 to around 1832, Barbara Franco in "Stoneware Made by the White Family in Utica, New York," Stradling book, p. 134, also lists a firm of **Brayton, Kellogg and Doolittle** organized shortly after 1825. Ramsay, p. 204 lists this last firm 1827 to around 1840. He listed them for stoneware and possibly redware. (Mark: Stewart and Consentine, *Stoneware*, p. 31.)

J. F. BRAYTON & CO.
UTICA

Brayton Pottery (also referred to as **Brayton Laguna Pottery**). South Laguna Beach, California. 1927-1963. Durlin E. Brayton, graduate of Chicago Art Institute started making pottery in his home in 1927 or 1928 at the 1500 block of South Laguna Beach. The business flourished and grew and is widely collected today. Beautiful hand crafted dinnerware with matte glaze, lamp bases, cookie jars, a "Rascha" Polish peasant type cookie jar decorated with tin glazes, figurines, a pair of standing zebras, Mammy stovetop shakes and salts, and some tile were some of the articles produced in a wide array of colors. He had a limited wholesale business. In 1948, Webb Brayton, Durlin's wife died. Durlin died in 1951, and the employees continued the business. Japanese imports were again plentiful after W.W. II and by 1963 the doors to the pottery were closed. (Information from John Jacob Schram, of Jacob Schram Antiques, South Laguna, California, and former employee at factory, Margaret Blodget, Redding, California. Mark 1, registration applied for February 23, 1935, claiming use since 1930. Mark 2 on piece. No. 3 in *Crockery and Glass Journal Directory* for 1945.)

Brayton Laguna 1.

WEBTON·WARE 2.

Brayton Laguna Pottery 3.

Breininger, Lester and Barbara. Robesonia, Bucks County, Pennsylvania. Around 1965 to present. Lester and his wife, Barbara, are studio potters making red ware pieces in the old tradition, molded from antique molds, or slab built and hand thrown. Decorations are hand painted, slip trailed, sgraffito, etc. in the old Pennsylvania Dutch style. Lester received an M.A. Degree from Pennsylvania State University and Kutztown University. He has received several honors as a teacher of biology. His interest in the old pottery grew out of his Pennsylvania-German ancestry. His family and his wife Barbara's family have lived in the county since the 1700's. He wrote articles for magazines and historical societies on numerous antique artifacts, including *Potters of Tulpehocken*, which led to a study of the old potters tools and a desire to try to make the pieces himself and Lester became a potter. He studied with Thomas Alexander Robesonia; James Seagraves of Trexlertown; Phil Richards, Pequea; and Russel Stahl, Powder Valley; all potters in Pennsylvania. Lester, his wife, his beautiful pottery and his home have been written about in many articles, including a feature article by Carol McCabe, "Pennsylvania Redware: Continuing A Tradition," *Early American Life*, October 1984, pp. 34 to 41. Also, Tony Lucia, "Top Potter, Craftsman Turns Back Time for Clay art," *The Reading Eagle*, August 26, 1984, Section 3, pp. 71, 87. There was also an article in *House Beautiful*, in January 1986, mentioned in the potter's resume: The Breininger's pottery was featured in a two page advertisement by Museum Editions, Ltd., in the *Early American Life* magazine, already cited, whereby a piece was shipped each month for a set price. The Breiningers use quaint little sayings as a part of their marks as did the old Pennsylvania potters. That is what the words "getting colder" represent in the mark shown. One of these old time sayings a potter used on a piece long ago was, "Out of the earth with understanding the potter makes everything." And the latest product from clay in 1986 is automobile parts! The potter who wrote that saying would never dream of that! The "T.M." shown in one of the marks was for Taylor Mansion, Breininger's house.

Robesonia,
19 PA 71
B.L.Breininger

L. Breininger
Robesonia, Pa
Oct. 17, 1985
getting colder

Breininger Pottery
Robesonia, Pa.
1986

Breslauer-Underberg, Inc. New York, New York. A distributor or selling agency. They were listed in the 1945 *Crockery and Glass Journal Directories* as wholesalers of earthenware figures, figurines, miniatures, glass novelties and decorative accessories. On January 2, 1947, mark no. 2 was registered under the name, Elfinware, Inc., of New York, New York, for use on miniature porcelain boxes, trays, dishes, etc., claiming use since May 15, 1945, made in *Germany*. I was able to include them in this book because in the 1951 *Crockery and Glass Journal Directory*, p. 127, Breslauer-Underberg, Inc. had an advertisement showing "California Pottery," by Johannes Brahm, picturing a cigarette set of three pieces, ashtrays and a box.)

1.

Elfinware
2.

Brighton Pottery. Zanesville, Ohio. 1905-1907. Arc-En-Ciel Pottery changed its name to Brighton Pottery in 1905 and then only lasted two more years, closing in 1907. The plant made cooking ware, mixing bowls, tea pots, soup bowls,

cups, cracker jars and honey dishes. Spatterware type of teapot pictured in Lehner, *American Kitchen and Dinner Wares*, p. 31. (Information: Norris Schneider, "Many Small Art Potteries Once Operated in Zanesville," *The Times Recorder and The Zanesville Signal*, February 4, 1962, no page numbers in notebook. Mark: on teapot.)

Bringle, Cynthia. Penland, North Carolina. 1965 to present (1985). Cynthia Bringle is a very well known studio potter who has taught since 1970 at Penland School of Crafts and also at her Pottery Studio. She makes Raku, porcelain and stoneware into functional and decorative pieces which have won many honors for Cynthia. She received a B.F.A. degree from Memphis Academy of Arts in 1962, and an M.A. degree from Alfred University in Alfred, New York, in 1964. Cynthia has also taught at Haystack Mountain School of Crafts in Deer Isle, Maine; the Memphis Academy of Arts; Arrowmont School of Crafts in Gatlinburg, Tennessee; and Naples Mill School in Naples, New York. Her pottery is in collections in the Smithsonian Institution; Brooks Memorial Art Gallery in Memphis, Tennessee; Mint Museum of Art in Charlotte, North Carolina, and the Atlanta Arts Festival in Atlanta, Georgia, to name some of the places. She answered my questionnaire about awards won with "numerous." Following her graduation in 1964, Cynthia had her first studio in Eads, Tennessee, in an old house she rented there. By 1965 she had her pottery shop set up and operating. She moved to Penland in 1970 and has stayed since. She wants the pieces she makes to be used, so they are of a functional type, but the graceful shapes and form of the pieces are beautiful, and she adds to the piece by incising, cutting, carving, stamping and hand painting on designs that make the pieces truly unique. The marks are incised in the clay or written with iron slip before firing. (Information: John Coyne, *The Penland School of Crafts Book of Pottery*, New York: Bobbs-Merrill, 1975, pp. 116-136. Mark: from Cynthia Bringle.)

Bringle

Cynthia Bringle

Brinn's China and Glassware Company. Pittsburgh, Pennsylvania. Company filed for registration of this mark on October 28, 1966, claiming long use since 1934, for ceramic ornamental houseware and ceramic tableware, namely china dishes, plates, cups, saucer, platters, vase, salt and pepper shakers, sugars and creamers, canisters, oven bakingware and florist pottery such as platters, pots and jardinieres.

BRINN'S

Broadmoor Pottery. Denver and Colorado Springs, Colorado. 1934 to 1939. The pottery made a fine quality of color glazed industrial artware. The pottery was established as the Broadmoor Art Pottery and Tile Company in Colorado Springs, in 1934, with P.H. Genter as president. Glazes included metallic bronze, copper, crackle, matt and shiny glazes used on bowls, vase, lamps, novelties, planters, plates, etc. In 1937, Genter moved the pottery to Denver, where starting in October that year the company produced one thousand pieces per day consisting of over two hundred shapes. The plant closed in April 1939. (Information: Tom Turnquist, "Broadmoor Pottery," *American Art Pottery*, July 1979, p. 5. Marks: no. 1, Turnquist article cited. No. 2, Annise Heaivilin, author of *Grandma's Tea Leaf*. No. 3, Ben Cash, researcher.)

1.

```
"SHIP TAVERN"
BROWN PALACE HOTEL
      DENVER
2.
BROADMOOR POTTERY CO.
  DENVER. COLO.
```

```
BROADMOOR POTTERY
Colo SPRINGS, Colo.
   P. H. GENTER        3.
```

Brockville Pottery. Schuyllkill County, Pennsylvania, near Brockton, (which is ten miles north of Pottsville). There were two potteries in the Brockton area in the second half of the 19th century and both were closed by 1907 according to Mildren Veley Hardcastle in "Pottery, Patterson-Brookville-Brockville, near Pottsville, Pennsylvania," *Pottery Collectors' Newsletter*, October 1973, pp. 7, 8. They were the J.B. Patterson Fire Clay and Brockville Pottery. The Brockville Pottery made pieces of yellow clay similar to mocha ware also tan stoneware and Hardcastle described shards ranging from dark to light gray in color as well as brown and tan or Bennington type coloring. (Information: Hardcastle, as cited. Mark stamped into clay. Copy machine of shard sent by James R. Mitchell, curator; State Museum of Pennsylvania, in Harrisburg. Shown is a drawn copy.)

```
BROCKVILLE WORKS
      NEAR
POTTSVILLE, SCH'L CO.
      PENNA.
```

Brockmann Pottery Company. Cincinnati, Ohio. 1888 to 1912. This pottery had it origin in 1854 when **Brewer and Tempest** operated as partners until 1856, then **Tunis Brewer** operated alone until 1859. It became **Tempest, Brockmann and Company** from 1862 until 1881. From 1881 to 1888 the pottery was owned by **Tempest, Brockmann and Sampson**. From 1888 to 1912, the pottery was **C.E. Brockmann Company**. In the 1902 *Glass Factory Directory* the company was listed as making white granite and some porcelain dinner sets, toilet sets and short sets of odd dishes. They also made ironstone china and cream colored ware according to Ramsay. (Information and marks: Barber, *Marks of American Potters*, p. 118 and Ramsay, p. 211.)

E.O. Brody Company. Cleveland, Ohio. Started around 1950 to present. A distributor that used own mark on glass and pottery. (Lehner, Lois, *Ohio Pottery and Glass*, p. 35.)

```
E.O. BRODY
   A 541
```

```
05015
  BY
BRODY
```

Brookcroft Pottery. Plymouth Meeting, Pensylvania. 1939 until after 1974. Mildred Davis Keyser started Brookcroft Pottery in 1939 and it was being run by her daughter, June Adams, yet in 1974. Mildred Keyer's interest in pottery making was born in 1938 when she took a Works Progress Administrtion (W.P.A.) course in Ambler, Pennsylvania, with William Gleaves, a potter from England, who had a pottery on Doylestown Pike. She had always been interested in handicraft work and her husband, C. Naaman Keyser's Pennsylvania Dutch background and the many stories she had heard spurred her to study the work and visit with many of the old potters. What started out as a craft school soon turned into a way to make a supplementary income. Mr. Keyser was in the landscaping business and the Keysers had reared four children and bought a fourteen acre farm on his meager earnings. Mildred had attended Pennsylvania State College as did her husband, where he majored in horticulture. Fame came to this pottery very quickly and by 1939 her pottery was exhibited at the World's Fair. By the end of three years, her work had been exhibited in the Woman's National Exposition of Arts and Industries in New York City. The Pennsylvania Museum in Philadelphia had displays and exhibits of her work. The pieces were a revival of the old Pennsylvania Dutch pottery. She made Sgraffito, slip ware, with tulips, pomegranites, hearts, peacocks, deer, etc. She made slip ware from red clay and Sgraffito from a Pennsylvania black clay. For many years, she taught students at Brookcroft. (Information: no author, "Mildred David Keyser," *Bulletin of American Ceramic Society*, Volume 22, No. 1, January 15,

58

1943, pp. 2-5; also, Grace Ramey, Early German Art Revived, "Historic Materials Used By Mrs. Keyser," *Evening Public Ledger*, Philadelphia, Pennsylvania, November 25, 1939. Mark: on piece at American Ceramic Society Museum in Columbus, Ohio. Many pieces signed with just pine tree and "K." This piece also had signature.)

Brook Pottery. Madison, New Hampshire. 1979 to present (1984). J. Thomas Flavin, studio potter, makes wood fired stoneware porcelain, some decorative, but mostly utilitarian such as tea pots, dinnerware, casseroles, mugs, platters, pitchers, pots and porcelain sinks. He does some sculptural work, grave markers and tiles. He received a B.F.A. degree from the Kansas City Art Institute. He used inscribed and stamped marks as shown.

Brooks, Hervey. Goshen, Connecticut. Around 1802 to around 1873. Brooks was born in 1779. He kept records of his accounts from the year 1802 until he died in 1873. From these records, Lura Woodside Watkins gives us a complete account of this stoneware potter's various activities in the book, *Early New England Potters and Their Wares*, pp. 173-176. His records reads: "one day digging clay, a day glazing and painting, a day setting, a day chopping wood," etc. He left a record of hauling wood, speading manure, grafting trees and splitting nails, even butchering a calf. It's a wonder these old potters left as many pieces of pottery to posterity as they did! He made utilitarian pieces, milk pans, jugs, etc.. (Information: Watkins, as cited. Mark: *Regional Aspects of American Folk Pottery*, printed by Historical Society of York County, Pennsylvania, p. 40.)

H. BROOKS

Broome, Isaac. Potter who worked at Ott and Brewer in Trenton, New Jersey. He also modeled tile for **Trent Tile Company** of Trenton, New Jersey and the **Beaver Falls Art Tile Company**. Broome and Matt Morgan operated the **Dayton Porcelain Works** for a very short time around 1880. In *Ohio Pottery and Glass* the dates were given as 1882 to 1884 as they were sent to me by a librarian and taken from Dayton City Directories in the Dayton Public Library. However, according to Paul Evans, *Art Pottery of the U.S.*, pp. 80-81, Isaac Broome had returned to Trenton by 1882 and Matt Morgan, the other partner had gone to Cincinnati to establish his art pottery. (Information and marks: Barber, *Marks of American Potters*, pp. 53, 54.)

Brouwer Pottery. See Middle Lane Pottery.

Brown Brothers. Huntington, Long Island. See Huntington Pottery.

Brown, Becky. Bloomington, Indiana. 1940 to present (1987). Becky is the wife of Karl Martz (see that listing) and is a fine potter in her own right. She makes handbuilt stoneware animal sculptures and hand thrown functional pots. She also makes animals of earthenware and some clay fired portrait heads. In 1937 and 1938 Becky was artists' representative at the Brown County Art Gallery in Nashville, Indiana. In 1939, she and Karl set up the studio pottery in Nashville and she began to learn slip casting and various ceramic processes. Karl did the designing and Becky served as an apprentice and a sales representative. Around 1943, she decided to have a career of her own in ceramics and studied design with Alma Eikerman at Indiana University. When she and Karl moved into a new home-studio in Brown County, Indiana, she started to throw on a wheel and do her own personal designs in clay while she continued her other jobs of casting, glazing, etc. Becky made buttons designed by Karl in press molds. In 1969, she received an A.B. degree in English from Indiana University. In 1970, she joined The Gallery in Bloomington as a full partner where she worked until 1975. Becky has traveled widely for fairly long periods of time to study and see various collections of ceramics and observe potters at work. She spent five months in New York City, five months in Kyoto and Tokyo, Japan, six weeks in Mexico and six weeks in the Scandanavian Countries. She has exhibited her work since 1951 at various times at the Evansville Museum of Arts, De Pauw University, Indianapolis Museum and others. Becky sent pictures of a rabbit with hat and baseball bat and ball and also a frog on a lily pad. Both were attractive, unique, thoughtful hand built sculptures. Becky displayed "Gazelle with Sackbut" at the Indianapolis Museum of Art exhibit entitled "Works in Clay" in a solo exhibition in 1980. (A sackbut is a medieval trombone.) Becky sent the double B monogram for her mark. She has also made pieces with the inscribed signature shown.

BECKY
BROWN

Brown, Cedric and Christy. Fresno, California. 1972 to present. Studio potters making sculptured pieces and hand thrown dinnerware. Christar pottery has been widely distributed throughout California and as far as Virginia via the San Francisco Gift Show and Merchandise Mart. They often produced forty handthrown 7" planters a day; almost all were thrown by Cedric Brown. They also produced a line of macrame slings utilizing a patented beaded adjustable basket. They now do custom artwork and deal in art and antiques. They produce little pottery at this time (1982).

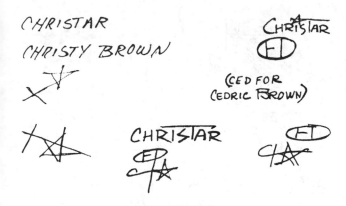

Brown Family, Various Potteries. The history of the various Brown family potteries goes back for eight generations of Browns to John Henry Brown who came from England. There is some disagreement as to who comes next in the family history. "The History of the Brown Family Potters," sent by the Brown Pottery in Arden, North Carolina, states that Bolden (or Bowling) was the son of John Henry Brown. However, John A. Burrison, *Brothers in Clay*, pp. 167 & 311 tells about a will from a William Brown of Pike County, Georgia, to his son, Bowling in 1851. So possibly there was one or two more Browns between John Henry and Bowling. At any rate, Bolden (or Bowling) was born in 1806 and worked with a wheel run by foot power and a horse-drawn clay mill. His mixture for glaze was just sand and ash. Bolden had been the first potter to come to that Jugtown area and he worked there until he moved to Howell's Mills before 1860. Thomas O. Brown had a son, James Osborn Brown, who lived from 1866 to 1929, mainly in the Atlanta area. The son of James Osborn was Davis P. He is the one who left Atlanta and started the Brown Pottery in Arden, North Carolina, around 1924 which still exists today. Louis, the son of Davis, owned and operated the pottery from 1967 to to 1976, when his sons, Charlie and Robert became the owner-operators. These Browns were asked by the Smithsonian Institute to represent the United States in the Festival of American Folklife held at the Exposition in Montreal in 1971. One of their current products in 1978 was French style earthenware. They make flameproof, earthenware cooking ware, dishes and all types of kitchen pottery as well as garden pottery and artware, many pieces made to custom order. Not everything is handmade, but the handmade pieces are so marked. (See mark no. 2.) James O. Brown, born in 1866, learned potting by apprenticing with Charlie Kline (see that listing) for eight years. He was listed as a potter by the Census when he was still a teenager. By 1920, he had six sons who were also working as potters. James could almost be called an itinerant potter as much as he and his family moved from pottery to pottery to work. But he rented farms and maintained homes for his family in various locations. He worked in the Atlanta, Georgia area, also Oakwood, Hall County, Georgia, and at Jugtown, at various times. Various potters for whom he worked were: W.T.B. Gordy; the Meader's family; a man named Covett in Manchester; Milton Puckett at Oakwood and others. This family of Browns has a shop in Alvaton, Georgia, for about six months in the early 1920's. James O. Brown's sons' names were: William O.; Charles Robert; Davis P.; Evan Javan; James Otto, Jr. (called Otto); and Rufus E. James Otto, Jr. moved to Bethune, South Carolina in the early 1930's. In 1953, he set up the first shop of his own. In 1968, in the article by Courtney Carson, "Seven Generations of Pottery

Makers," *Sandlapper*, August 1968, pp. 18-20, it said James (Otto) Brown, Jr., had taken over the management, but James O. Brown was still working. Both men are dead in 1986. The children of Otto, Jr., Kenneth, Carolyn, and Annette, were also learning the trade in 1968. And this doesn't begin to tell the story of the people named Brown, all from one family that made pottery. It only leads up to the two that remain in business today in Arden, North Carolina, and Bethune, South Carolina. there are twenty-two Browns listed on p. 311 of John A. Burrison's book, *Brothers in Clay*, with names, dates, places they worked and a brief description of known marks. Out of all these Brown potters I only have two marks to offer. (Information: as cited. Marks: no. 1 for James Osborn was shown on a two handled churn with lid made of stoneware and glazed with Albany slip in Burrison, p. 70. No. 2 was sent by Brown's Pottery in business now in Arden, North Carolina.)

J O BROWN   1.

2. Brown's Pottery Arden, N. C. Handmade

Brown County Pottery and **Brown County Hills Pottery.** See Claude Graham listing.

J.S. Brown. Carthage, Missouri. Around 1889. Made stoneware. Stamped mark on crock. (Information and mark: Henry W. Heflin, pottery collector and researcher.)

CARTHAGE

The Brown Jug Pottery. Lake Placid, Florida, and Cookeville, Tennessee. 1971 to present (1985). Studio potter, Margaret S. Burnham, makes functional stoneware in pastel colors. Margaret uses underglaze decoration, carved or painted flower designs and a spray on clear glaze. Margaret maintains two studios, one in Lake Placid and one in Cookeville. In the winter months, she does ten or twelve shows in Florida, and then in summer, she shows in Tennessee, Illinois, as far north as Chicago. She taught art for four years in Texas, North Carolina, and also Venezuela, before starting the studios.

Brundin, Ernest W. Montibello, California. A distributor, filed for rights to this mark on May 22, 1939, to be used for receptacles, such as urns, pots, trays of pottery used for growing plants without soil, claiming use since May 9, 1939. Brundin was listed as a florist in 1938 when they patented a new plant culture.

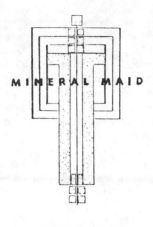

M I N E R A L   M A I D

Brunt, Bloor, Martin and Company; The Dresden Pottery Works; The Potters Co-operative Company; and **The Dresden Pottery Company.** East Liverpool, Ohio. In 1875 (1876 according to Barber, p. 111), William Brunt, Jr., Henry Brunt, William Bloor and a man named Martin started **The Dresden Pottery Works of Brunt, Bloor, Martin and Company**, to make white ware, some decorated, and hotel ware. The company lasted until 1882, (1892 according to Ramsay, p. 218) when they sold the plant to the Potters Co-operative, not becoming a member of the Co-operative as was suggested by the listing in Barber. *Marks of American Potters*, by Barber was published in 1904. Allowing a year or so for publication, we can assure he was writing about the pottery after 1900 sometime when he said under the Potter's Cooperative Company listing that: "The mark of this company, now used on white granite ware is a wreath, enclosing name Dresden." **The Potters Co-operative** was founded in 1882 when eight local potteries banded together, according to William H. Vodrey, Jr., "Record of the Pottery Industry in East Liverpool," *Bulletin of American Ceramic Society*, Volume 24, No. 8 (1923 original listing) 1945, p. 284, and lasted until 1925 when according to the same source, the name was Dresden Pottery Company. In 1927, the business was discontinued. (Vodrey, p. 284). Products of these potteries were white granite and semi-porcelain with stamped or impressed marks. The following marks for the Dresden Pottery were used while the pottery was under the management of the Potters Cooperative. (Marks 1-4 copy machined from dishes. The remainder of the marks from Barber, *Marks of American Potters*, pp. 111, 112.)

1.

2.

3.

4.

5.

POTTERS
CO-OPERATIVE CO.
SEMI
· VITREOUS ·

6.

7.

DRESDEN
HOTEL CHINA   8.
WARRANTED

DRESDEN
HOTEL CHINA
9.

YALE   Dresden   Madrid   California

10.   11.   12.   13.

DRESDEN
WHITE GRANITE   DRESDEN
SEMI PORCELAIN   DRESDEN
CHINA

14.   16.

15.

Brunt Family Associations. 1847 until after 1903, including the **Great Western Pottery, Phoenix Pottery** and **G.F. Brunt Porcelain Company.** East Liverpool, Ohio. Makers of Rockingham ware, yellow ware, Rockingham door knobs, and later white granite and porcelain insulators. The **William Brunt Pottery** was run by William from 1847 to 1856. His son, Henry Brunt, joined him from 1856 to 1895. This firm was listed in Howe's *Historical Collections of Ohio* in 1888 as **H. Brunt, Son and Company**, employing thirty-one. The company was also known as the **Riverside Knob Works**, making door knobs and electric porcelain. William Brunt, Jr. became involved in the **Phoenix Pottery** from 1862 to 1866, at which time the pottery was sold to the West Hardwick Company which continued to operate the Phoenix Pottery until 1868, when it went to George Morley until 1884. One of the Brunt's (probably William, Jr. when he left Phoenix Pottery) started the **Great Western Pottery** with a Mr. Hill as his partner from 1867 to 1874. They were followed by a John Wyllie from 1874 until some time after 1900. Here they made mostly white granite. In what was his third pottery, William Brunt, Jr. was in business with his son from 1879 to 1894 and this plant was called **William Brunt, Son and Company**, with the mark of two lions and a shield and "W.B.P. CO. Warranted Ironstone." Henry's sons became the third generation of Brunts in the pottery business when Henry Brunt retired in 1895. The door knob part of the business was taken over by William H. Brunt and the electrical porcelain part was operated by George F. Brunt. The dates and names given for the electrical porcelain part of the operation by Jack H. Tod, *Electrical Porcelain Industry in the U.S.*, p. 74, were as follows: 1895, Brunt (G.F.) and Thompson; 1897, G.F. Brunt Porcelain Company; 1911, General Porcelain Company; 19??, G.E. Company (by T.F. Anderson); 1930, Riverside Knob Comapny (Miller). The history of the door knob part of the business under William, according to Tod, as cited, was as follows: 1895, Riverside Knob Works (William H. Brunt); 1917, General Porcelain Company, 19?? operations suspended; 19??, G.E. Company (by T.F. Anderson); 1930, Riverside

Knob Company (John C. Miller). According to Jack H. Tod, General Porcelain Company used an embossed ''G.P.Co.'' marking on their dry press insulators, cleats, knobs, etc. But they also had on hand the old press dies from the former and now defunct properties and plant dumpage indicates they were not adverse to using those old dies as is, as opposed to making new dies or reworking old ones to change the marking. The embossed markings on porcelains are repetitive, and made by punching the letters into the die surface. To expunge the marking from the die, it is necessary to braze-in the old, unwanted punchings and regrind the surface smooth, all a laborious and expensive thing. After General Porcelain purchased the plant they continued to use the name ''Brunt.'' See Brunt, Bloor, Martin and Company. (Information: Lehner, *Ohio Pottery and Glass*, p. 42; Jack H. Tod, *Electrical Porcelain Industry in the U.S.*, p. 74. Marks: nos. 1-10, Barber, *Marks of American Potters*, p. 107; no. 11, mark on dish; no. 12, Lehner, ''American Dinnerware and Commercial Pottery,'' *Antique Trader*, May 14, 1980, p. 81; nos. 13, 14, Annise Heaivillin, *Grandma's Tea Leaf*, p. 150, and by letter. Nos. 15, 16; On some split knob insulators the word ''Cinch'' is found with ''Brunt,'' according to Tod, as cited.)

Brusche Ceramics/Brusche Ceramics of California. Whittier, California. There was no listing for Brusche Ceramics

in the 1948 *China and Glass Red Book Directory*. Then for one year, 1949, Brusche Ceramics was at 1456 Workman Mill Road in Whittier. From 1950 the name became Brusche Ceramics of California, and was listed at 415 West Avenue in Los Angeles, which is the same address as the Bauer Pottery. J. Herb Brusche, worked for the the Bauer Pottery. But for a short time around 1949, he had a pottery of his own at 4960 South Workman Mill Road in Whittier, California, where he made tableware. Brusche was the husband of Bauer's granddaughter. After 1950 he made his own line at the Bauer plant. While at Bauer Pottery, he created a line named for him, some marked Brusche; and some marked Brusche Bauer. (See Various Bauer Potteries listing for information on these lines.) Brusche Ceramics of California, continued to be listed at the same time as the Bauer Pottery listings at the same address as Bauer Pottery at 415 West Avenue, Los Angeles. But by now it probably was used as a selling agency for Bauer Pottery. J.W. Brockman was general manager and sales manager at Bauer Pottery, and he was also sales manager of Brusche Ceramics of California. The products in 1952 for Bauer Pottery were stoneware, florists ware, solid-color dinnerware, baking and cooking ware, and garden pottery. Brusche Ceramics of California, listed solid color dinnerware, baking and cooking ware, Al Fresco ware and Brusche ware. When Brusche was alone in Whittier, for one year, 1949, he listed only informal dinnerware as his product. J.H. Brusche was listed as the owner. This was the only listing that showed him in a managerial position. (Marks: no. 1, from the various directories is shown under the Brusche Ceramics of California name with the Bauer Pottery address, so it would really be found on products made by Bauer Pottery. No. 2 and no. 3, sent by Rena London, found on solid color dinnerware which she said looked much like that made by Gladding, McBean and Company, so it must have been of good quality.)

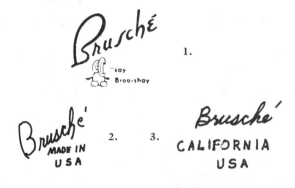

Brush, George S., Pottery. Zanesville, Ohio (the first Brush Pottery.) 1907 to 1908. George S. Brush started making pottery in the site of the Union Pottery in 1907 and the building burned in 1908. From 1909 to 1911 he worked for J.W. McCoy Pottery in Roseville. In 1911, the two men started the Brush McCoy Pottery with one plant operating in Roseville and one in Zanesville. See Brush-McCoy Pottery for more history. Also see the listing for second Brush Pottery, and see the listing for the Nelson McCoy Pottery which was the second McCoy Pottery. According to Norris F. Schneider ''Brush Pottery,'' *Zanesville Times Signal*, September 9, 1962 (no page no.) for its one year of existence the Brush Pottery used the Union Pottery molds for cereal bowls, mixing bowls and kitchen ware. I doubt that we are ever going to find a piece marked with the first Brush Pottery mark because its existence was so short and some old molds were used. However, I thought it important to list the pottery to explain we had two potteries by the name Brush.

Brush Pottery (the second Brush Pottery) Roseville, Ohio. 1925 to the middle of 1982. This pottery was an outgrowth of the Brush-McCoy Pottery and had nothing to do with the first Brush Pottery. Brush Pottery made a variety of well vitrified products, decorative items, kitchen ware, vases, cookie jars, patio ware, garden ware, etc. Brush Pottery made between forty and fifty designs in cookie jars, now highly collected. They also make unglazed redware garden pots. In December 1978, Barnett sold Brush Pottery to C.S.C., Inc. of Chicago. In December 1979, Virgil Cole and John O. Everhart bought the pottery to make garden dishes and specialty items. They made the lamp bases for the Lamplight Farms. **Brush Line, Incorporated** was the last name used for Brush Pottery. In January 1982, the pottery was closed for awhile and then reopened under the same owners but this time without Union labor. The pottery only lasted a few more months, then closed for good in the middle of 1982. A liquidation sale was held leaving an empty building. (Information and marks: E. Lucille Barnett, and company furnished material. Mark no. 9 was taken from broken pottery oil lamps in the factory trash pile in 1980. Seconds were destroyed because they were not perfect. See Lamplight Farms for more. Most of the Brush marks were incised or impressed marks as found on pieces.)

The

Brush

Pottery

Co.,

Zanesville,

Ohio

IN USE
1927-29

REVISED 1958-68

1.

2.

3.

1965-72

W 24
USA

4.

H4
Brush
U.S.A.

5.

Brush H122 U.S.A.

6.

BRUSH USA 692

7.

BRUSH USA 629

8.

LAMPLIGHT U.S.A FARMS

9.

718 BRUSH QUALITY USA

10.

Brush-McCoy Pottery. Roseville, Ohio. 1911 to 1925. Brush-McCoy Pottery followed the first Brush Pottery operated by George S. Brush from 1907 to 1908 and the J.W. McCoy Pottery which operated 1899 to 1911. The first Brush Pottery burned in 1908 and Brush went to work for McCoy. They also had a plant in Zanesville, Ohio, where the artware was made until the factory burned in 1918. Brush-McCoy made all types of kitchenware. The old Brush-McCoy catalog has now been reprinted in book form by Sharon and Bob Huxford. To give an idea of the products made by Brush-McCoy the 1923 catalog included jardinieres in Nuglaz, Higloss and Egyptian; and vases, bulb bowls, candlesticks and jardinieres in Art Vellum (ancient parchment) Onyx (high-glazed;) Jewel (mat body with high gloss jewel design;) Zuniart (high gloss decoration on clay body-Indian designs;) Jet-wood (black tree design on shaded background;) Stonecraft (gray body, fluted sides - decorated at top). There were cuspidors and pitchers. The kitchen lines were in the yellow "dandy-line," brown "nurock" and white "bristol" trimmed in blue. There were bristol combinets and toilet sets. A flier found in the catalog listed the "jug-time" clock. (Company furnished information. Lehner, *Ohio Pottery and Glass*, p. 78.) Brush McCoy Pottery filed for rights to the mark shown on November 28, 1914, claiming use since November 14, 1914, for use on china bowls, platters, plates, cups, saucers, vases, ewers, pots and earthenware bowls (except closet-bowls), cuspidors or spittoons, cullinary utensils, dishes, basins, funnels, hearths, jars, jugs, mugs, plates, platters, pots, vases, combinettes, chambers, jardinieres, pedestals, umbrella stands and towel urns.

Buckeye Pottery. Macomb, Illinois. 1882 to 1941. Around 1853 an Austrian immigrant, Joseph Pech, started a pottery in Madison, Wisconsin, later moved to Atwater, Ohio. Joseph Pech had a son, Washington Pech, born in Akron, Ohio, in 1855 who grew up making pottery with his father. Washington moved to Macomb, Illinois, in 1878, and by 1882 he had established the Buckeye Pottery Company using around 4,000 gallons of clay slip per week. By 1941, the Buckeye Pottery had been working on a lease basis on W. Carroll St. and was purchased by Haeger, Inc. (Information: Bateman and Selby, *Historical Encylcopedia of Illinois and History of McDonough County*, Volume 2, pp. 617-1055. Mark: sent by Janice T. Wass, Curator of Decorative Arts, Illinois State Museum, on piece of stoneware.)

Buckeye Stoneware. Crooksville, Perry County, Ohio. Before 1893. They became plant no. 1 of Star Stoneware. The building was operated by Star Stoneware until around the depression. The company was listed in the *1893 Factory Inspection Report for Ohio*, as employing twelve to make stoneware. In 1902, they employed ten. They made utilitarian stoneware crocks, mugs, jugs, etc., with white interiors and red clay very similar to Weller's products in that category. An incised mark on such a mug was verified by Norris Sowers, who started his career of working in the various potteries when he went to work at age seven or eight in 1913 at Buckeye Stoneware. He became a well known art pottery collector, dealer in the area and has handled all of the now famous lines of Zanesville pottery. He ran (carried) molds at Buckeye for $.60 a week! There was a Buckeye Pottery at Saltillo, near New Lexington or White Cottage, south of Crooksville, which was listed as Buckeye Cottage Stoneware, employing twelve in 1894. This was not the same pottery as Buckeye Stoneware. The Saltillo plant was leased for awhile by the Ransbottom Brothers around 1903 or 1904 to make stoneware and then the plant was abandoned around 1910.

BUCKEYE

Buckley, Newhall Company. New York, New York. A distributing corporation, filed for rights to these marks on March 31, 1931 for use on crockery and dishes of porcelain and china, claiming use since 1910.

BLUE RIBBON

Buffalo Pottery. Buffalo, New York. 1901 to present (1986). The first kiln was fired in 1903. The pottery was organized by William J. Rea to supply the pottery needs of the Larkin Soap Company. (See the listing Larkin Company.) Rea had worked at Mayer China and the Trenton Potteries Company before coming to Buffalo. He was the one responsible for the manufacturing of Old Willow or Blue Willow and Deldare Ware. He was superintendent of the pottery until 1925. Production was completely molded, either by jiggering or casting and was decorated both underglaze or overglaze. According to Evans, the company made its own underglaze colors and used decalcomania as well as hand decorating. Until around 1916 the company made semivitreous ware, and that year they changed to vitrified china. In the *1902-1903 Complete Directory*, Buffalo Pottery was listed as manufacturers of semi-porcelain dinner sets and toilet sets. The Buffalo China mark was first used in 1915 but the name of the pottery was not officially changed to Buffalo China Company until 1956. Buffalo China now makes only hotel and institutional type of ware, very nicely decorated. In the very early 1980's, Buffalo China opened a new addition on the Buffalo, New York site, which doubled their capacity to the 1977 levels. Allegheny China is a wholly owned subsidiary of Buffalo China, and about twenty-five percent of Buffalo China's output comes from the Allegheny facility. (See the listing for Allegheny China.) In the early days, many serving pieces were made including chocolate pots, salad or fruit bowls, cake plates, oatmeal sets, cracker jars, fruit sets, teapots, butter tubs, children's dishes and much more that was used as tableware. According to an article in *China, Glass and Lamps* entitled "American Pottery Trade Marks," September 3, 1923, p. 15, Buffalo Pottery, in 1905, produced the first underglazed blue Willowware ever made in America. The article went on to say that demand for the product increased so steadily that another plant was built in 1914 adjoining the original pottery, with each plant operating independently. In 1923 both plants were producing hotel and dinnerware with no semi-porcelain having been made since 1917. 1n 1923, Buffalo Pottery had fourteen general kilns and eight decorating kilns occupying eight acres of ground. The article mentions "Deldare," an original production with olive green body and hand decorations after old English subjects. The following is a list of dinnerware patterns which includes some as late as 1922. These are from the excellent book, *The Book of Buffalo Pottery*, by Seymour and Violet Altman, published by Crown Publishers, New York, 1969, pp. 157-158. The list is reprinted with the authors' and publisher's permission.

"Given below are the names of the dinnerware patterns, the years in which they were offered in the catalogs, and details about them taken from the catalog descriptions. It is not known whether any of this ware was offered through other distribution outlets of the pottery.

Lamare, 1904 through 1908:
Sprays of poppies, choice of dove, dark blue, green or brown. Embossed work in pure gold.

Modjeska, 1904 through 1909:
Pink roses or blue forget-me-nots. Pure gold trim.

Wild Poppy, 1905 through 1908:
Borders of wild poppies in olive green.

Bonrea (named for Louis Bown and William Rea), 1905 through 1916:
Ornate scroll border in myrtle green with pure gold

Old Blue Willow Ware, 1905 through 1917.

Color Band, 1909 through 1910:
Plain with wide color band and two pure gold li

ing each piece. Comes in apple green, turquoise or maroon.

Miana, 1909 through 1910:
Border pattern of Persian design in Oriental colors, dark and light blue and green predomiating.

Kenmore, 1909 through 1911:
Art Nouveau and floral border in green decor, illuminated in gold and gold trim.

Buffalo, 1909 through 1914:
Sprays of roses and altheas in natural colors. Full gold trim.

Maple Leaf, 1909 through 1914:
Small border of green maple leaves and pink flowers with full gold trim.

Princess, 1909 through 1914:
Green floral border with full gold trim.

Seneca, 1909 through 1914:
Border of flowers. Choice of green or dark blue. Gold handles and embossed work.

Tea Rose, 1909 through 1914:
Small border of pink roses and green leaves with full gold trim.

Gold Band, 1909 through 1915:
Plain white with a wide pure gold band.

Forget-Me-Not, 1909 through 1917:
Forget-me-nots in border pattern with full gold trim.

Florence Rose, 1910:
Double border of pink roses and green leaves with edges and embossed work in gold.

Gold Lace Border, 1911 through 1914:
Gold border in a lace design. Edges and embossed work in gold.

Pluto, 1911 through 1916:
Wide border of pink roses and green leaves, in natural colors. Edges and embossed work in pure gold.

Queen, 1911 through 1917:
Narrow border of pink roses and green leaves in natural colors, edges and embossing in gold.

Minerva. 1913 through 1916:
Sprays of pink roses and spring beauties. Full gold trim.

Vienna, 1915:
Designs in dark blue underglaze. Full gold trim.

Vassar, 1915 through 1916:
Designs in conventional dark green underglaze.

Empress, 1915 through 1917:
Green conventional border. Full gold trim.

Fern Rose, 1915 through 1917:
Border design of small pink roses and green leaves with full gold trim.

Wild Rose, 1915 through 1917:
Wild roses and spring flowers in natural colors with gold trim.

Gold Line, 1916 through 1917:
Plain white, decorated with two narrow gold lines.

Rosebank, 1917:
Wide border of pink roses and green leaves in natural colors. Edges traced in gold.

Spray Decor Tea Set. 1919 through 1920:
Vitreous china. Sprays of pink roses. Very realistic and can hardly be told from hand-painting.

Blue Bird Tea Set. 1919 through 1922:
Vitreous china. Bluebird decor in full natural colors.

Bungalow, 1920 through 1921:
Vitreous china. Fine latticework alternated with a fine floral decoration in red, green or yellow. Blended and dotted beneath with little flowers. Full gold trim.

Dresden, 1920 through 1921:
Vitreous china. Delicate pink roses and blue flowers intertwined and arranged in panels on a dainty ivory background. Edges and handles traced in coin gold.

Glendale, 1920 through 1921:
Vitreous china. Comes in green, golden brown and turquoise blue. An Unusual festoon design surrounding pink roses. Edges and handles traced in coin gold.

Pink Rose, 1930 through 1922:
Vitreous china. Sprays of pink roses almost like hand-painting. Gold border.

Beverly, 1921:
Vitreous china. Conventional border interspersed with pink roses and green leaves. Pure coin gold handles.

Coin Gold Band, 1921:
Vitreous china. Single band of coin gold 3/16th inch wide. Pure gold handles.

Luckily, a lot of the early Buffalo Pottery stamped marks included a date. Another very important factor in dating these marks according to Frank L. Rudesill, Vice-President in Charge of Sales, was that customer's names were not used as part of the mark since in the 1930's. Many of these marks show customers' names and pre-date 1940. Mr. Rudesill, in a letter (December 1977), said that no. 64 was the only trade mark used by them since around 1964. He said it was a matter of manufacturing economics. The company did file one other mark for registration in 1968 (see no. 65). (Marks: nos. 1-9 from Altman's *Book of Buffalo Pottery*, p. 31. Nos. 10-16 taken from a Wanamakers catalogue of 1930's, which was sent to this author by researcher Larry Paul. (See the Wanamaker listing.) Mark no. 17; notice the word, "Lamelle," was not actually filed for registration until April 28, 1945, but use was made of the mark according to the patent since March 15, 1932. Nos. 18, 19, on Railroad China from Richard Lickin, *Dining on Rails*, p. 161 and 242. Nos. 2-24, from Stephen S. Sandknop, pp. 57-64. No. 25, Annise Heaivilin's book, *Grandma's Tea Leaf*, p. 155. Nos. 26-54 from Quality Stamp Company, East Liverpool, Ohio. No. 35 says "Multifleur Lamelle." The marks from Quality Stamo Company are marks of the 1920's and 1930's. Nos. 55-62 were all copy machined from dishes. No. 63 from Dee Albert Gernert, "Buffalo Pottery's Deldare Ware," *Spinning Wheel's Complete Book of Antiques*, p. 120, on the front of a salesman sample and is more of a decoration than a mark. Deldare Ware was made in early 1900's and some in 1920's after W.W. I. No. 64 was used from 1964 to 1980's. Nos. 64-65, see text for discussion of these two marks. No. 66 was a raised mark in the mold on a cup I found and was used as a stamped mark, too. It was filed for registration on July 15, 1985, first being used in commerce October 1956. So this mark would be used over thirty years. No. 67 was filed February 28, 1985, claiming first use in October 1956, also.)

1.

CINDERELLA
B.P.

2.

3.

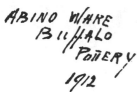

ABINO WARE
BUFFALO
POTTERY
1912

4.

5.

BUFFALO POTTERY
SEMI-VITREOUS
1908

B. P.

RoBin HooD
UNDERGLAZE
1906

6.

SEMI-VITREOUS
BUFFALO POTTERY
1907
No. 1319.

7.

UNDERGLAZE
BUF FALO
WARRANTED
POTTERY
1908

8.

MADE AT
19 BUFFALO 09
POTTERY

9. DELDARE WARE
UNDERGLAZE

Ye Olde Ivory
Buffalo China

10.

PAT. 1,840272
ColoriDo WARE
LAMELLE BuffaloCHINA

11.

BLUE
LUNE WARE
Buffalo China

12.

ColoriDo WARE
Buffalo China

13.

Buffalo CHINA
1930
ROUGE WARE
PATENT
APPLIED FOR

14.

Buffalo CHINA
LUNE LAMELLE
PATENT
1849272

15.

Buffalo CHINA
ROUGE LAMELLE
PATENT
1845272

16.

LAMELLÉ

17.

CHINA
Ye Olde Ivory
SOUTHERN RAILWAY SYSTEM

18.

MADE ESPECIALLY
For
ERIE RAILROAD
DESIGN PATENTED
Buffalo CHINA

19.

Ye Olde Ivory
Buffalo China
MADE EXPRESSLY
FOR
CHESAPEAKE & OHIO-R.R.
DGR

20.

Ye Olde Ivory
Buffalo China
FLORA OF THE SOUTH
MADE ESPECIALLY FOR
ATLANTIC COAST LINE
RAILROAD

21.

BUFFALO CHINA
SOUTHERN RAILWAY
SYSTEM

22.

Buffalo CHINA
MADE FOR
CB&QRR

23.

CHINA
Ye Old Ivory
SOUTHERN RAILWAY
SYSTEM

24.

VASSAR

25.

MADE BY
Buffalo Pottery
JAMES M. SHAW & Co.
Louis Sherry
New York

26.

Buffalo Pottery
1923
ROYCROFT

27.

Cafe Ware
Buffalo China

28.

Olde
Ivory Ware
Buffalo China

29.

Nathan Straus & Son
NEW YORK
BUFFALO CHINA

30.

FURNISHED BY
HOTEL SUPPLY
San Francisco Co
Buffalo China
OAKLAND CALIF

31.

Buffalo China

32.

Buffalo China
1926
MADE FOR
ALBERT PICK & COMPANY
CHICAGO

33.

Buffalo CHINA
Nathan Straus & Sons
AVE NEW YORK CITY

34.

Buffalo China
REGISTERED
PATENT 845272

Q.M.C.
1919

35.

MADE ESPECIALLY
FOR
THE
PALACE HOTEL CO
BUFFALO CHINA
1933

36.

Lune Ware
Buffalo China

37.

CAFE AU LAIT
Buffalo China

38.

Buffalo China
MADE FOR
SPERRY SERVICE
NEW YORK
WESTMINSTER PATTERN

39.

ALBERT PICK-BARTH COMPANY
CHICAGO NEW YORK
Buffalo CHINA

40.

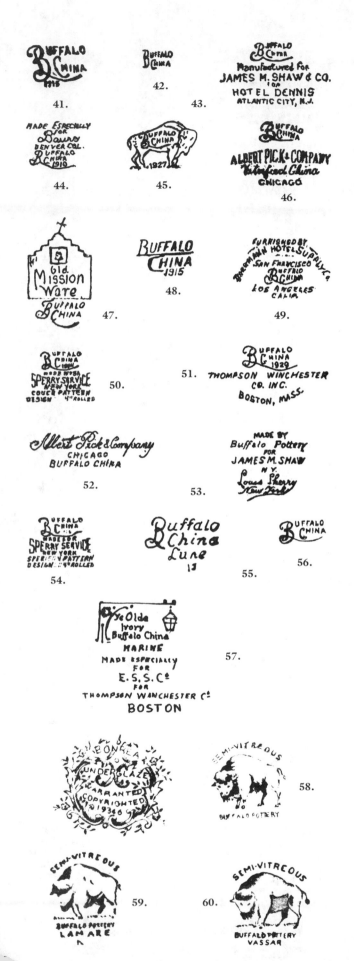

Q. M. C.

62.

BUFFALO
CHINA
U.S.A.
303

64.

MARK
BUFFALO

65.

DELDARE WARE

63.

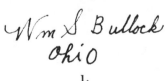

66.

BUFFALO CHINA

67.

Buford, Molly B. Cartersville, Georgia. 1973 to present. She makes handthrown pottery on a wheel working out of her home. She received a degree in apart from Agnes Scott College. No glazes are used as she prefers a natural clay look. (Information: Staff written, ''Molly B. Buford,'' *Pottery Collectors Newsletter*, October, 1976, p. 83.)

Molly

Bullock, William S. Roseville, Ohio. 1870 to 1885. Stoneware. Mark pictured was painted on the front of a large storage crock or jar with handles. Picture was furnished by Lei Cannon of Leica Ceramics, White Cottage, Ohio, a potter and designer near Roseville. (Information: Ramsay. p. 229 lists a W. Bullock with above dates, using an impressed mark ''W. Bullock/Roseville, O.'' The above W.S. could be a son, then the dates would be a little later. Mark no. 2 is shown in Thorn, p. 120 with same dates as Ransay.)

W. BULLOCK
ROSEVILLE, O

2.

Wm S Bullock
Ohio

1.

Bunting W.C. Company. Factory in Wellsville, Ohio. Offices in East Liverpool, Ohio. 1880 to present. Decorators of blanks, such as mugs and similar items for fraternities, universities, churches, etc. Made a seal of Ohio plate in 1968. (Information: company. Marks on products.)

1.

2.

Burden China Company. San Gabriel, California. Pottery started in 1945. In the 1977 *California Manufactures Directory*, they were listed for restaurant coffee mugs, custom decorating and cresting. They employed five people. Mark no. 1 was filed December 9, 1968, claiming use since October 1968, for china dinnerware, including cups, saucers, plates, platters and chinaware oven ware, including side dishes, teapots and coffee mugs. Mark no. 2 was file January 5, 1970, for use on china dishware, claiming use since December 1969.

1. # CALIFORNIA GOLD

2.

Burford Brothers Pottery. East Liverpool, Ohio. 1879-1904. They made a variety of products including semi-vitreous porcelain ware, which was plain white, also decorated. They also made cream-colored ware, hotel ware and granite or ironstone. In 1902, they were listed as making semi-porcelain dinner sets, toilet sets, short sets of odd dishes, hotel ware, plain and decorated. (Information: *Complete Directory of the Glass Factories and Potteries if the United States and Canada for 1902 and 1903*, published by Commoner Publishing Company, Pittsburg, Pennsylvania. Marks: no. 1 and no. 2, on dishes; rest are from Barber, *Marks of American Potters*, p. 116.)

1.

BURFORD
BROS.
E. L. O.

2.

3.

4.

5.

6.

7.

8.

9.

HOTEL

10.

11.

BURFORD BROS

12.

BEAUTY

13.

Burford Bros
CHAMPION

14.

ELECTRIC

15.

Burger, John and Associates. Rochester, New York. From 1852 to 1854 the name was **Harrington and Burger**. Then John Burger operated alone from 1854-1867. John Burger, Jr. joined his father in 1861. They were makers of salt glazed stoneware. He took full control in 1878 and operated until 1890. In 1867 to 1871, a brother must have been in the business; the name was **Burger Brothers and Company**. Then from 1871-1878 it was **Burger and Lang**. The dates given for Burger in *Pottery Collectors' Newsletter*, vary a little from above, dating John Burger around 1855-1866. (Information: Stewart and Consentino, p. 39, 123. Mark: Stewart and Consentino, *Stoneware*, p. 38. Mark no. 2, front cover of *Pottery Collectors' Newsletter*, June 1974, p. 121.)

J. BURGER JR.
ROCHESTER. NY.

1.

JOHN BURGER
ROCHESTER

2.

Burgues Porcelains, Inc. Lakewood, New Jersey. 1964 to present. Dr. Irving Carl Burgues was born the son of a farmer in a small town, not too far from Vienna, Austria. He spent his youth roaming the forest studying the birds, flowers and trees. He earned a doctor's degree in denistry to please his father, but with that accomplished, he went to Vienna to attend the Academy of Fine Arts. Then he studied in Paris with the artist, Mollet. Next, he traveled to Italy where he painted murals in a cathedral. He painted and sculptured, but he wanted another way to make nature endure in art. So he started traveling again, this time to South America, Peru, Cuba, and even spent a year in the Amazon jungles studying the tropical birds and animals. He came to America in 1934 where he studied art at the Brooklyn Museum and the Art Students League in New York. While teaching anatomy at the Newark Fine Arts School he met a chemist who recognized Burgues's desire to create lovely art forms in fine porcelain, so he gave him money for equipment and supplies. Five years passed in intensive study and experimenting. Burgues didn't actually open his own studio until 1964, but years were spent in preparation for that event. He trained a staff of 10 artists, including Carol Werner, who became his wife. She had received a BFA degree in fine arts in Hagen, Germany, and studied in Dusseldorf. She also was a painter who became interested in ceramics as the perfect medium for the combination of color and form. In 1986, Dr. Burgues has been sculpting for 34 years and Carol for 24. The Burgues had a brief venture into the very popular field of souvenir plates in 1978 and 1979 but they returned to their sculpting for fear the plates would rob them of too much time. The Burgues' pieces are delicate, hand painted, high fired porcelain sculptures of birds, animals, flowers, figures and vases, ranging in price from $75.00 to $15,000. They have 96 different pieces in production now, but add only 8 to 10 new pieces each yer. The production of any edition may take several years for them to prepare and sculpt. Examples are: 1981, "Brown Bears," 9 x 14 inches in an edition of 250 at $550.00 each; 1980, "Desert Spring," in an edition of 5 pieces at $15,000.00 each. In the miniature Rose series, 1982, "Love You," and "Cinnamon," in editions of 200 at $75.00 a piece. A line of vases in 1982 were designed and autographed by Carol Werner Burgues. Twelve shapes were completed by 1981 with ten more to come. The prices ranged from $24.00 to $60.00 on these. The Burgues' pieces are represented in all major museums. (Marks: no. 1, used on sculptures; no. 2, used on vases; no. 3, gold foil label; no. 4, card attached to pieces.)

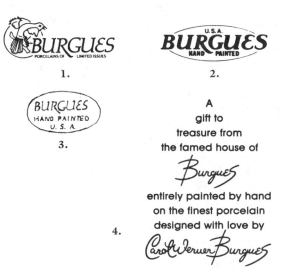

1.

2.

3.

A
gift to
treasure from
the famed house of

Burgues

entirely painted by hand
on the finest porcelain
designed with love by

Carol Werner Burgues

4.

Burke, Bill. San Francisco, California. Operating in 1976 as a studio potter making hand thrown pottery on a wheel. (Information: Murphy, Rose, "The Signing of Pottery," *Ceramics Monthly*, April 1976, pp. 42, 43.)

Burke, Ron. Shapleigh, Maine. 1960 to present. Studio potter making artistic and commercial pieces of slab built and hand thrown on a wheel ware in stoneware body. Also uses some porcelain slip heated to cone 10 to 12. He owned a tile factory for eight years. Ron Burke has an M.F.A. degree from Cranbrook Academy of Art which he received in 1962. He was at the University of Manitoba in Winnepeg, Canada, from 1962-1964. From 1964 to 1965 he was at the Penland School of Crafts in Penland. From 1965 to 1972 he had the Rock Tavern Pottery, Rock Tavern, New York. He also taught and studied at Haystack Mountain School in Liberty, Maine and Deer Isle, Maine.

Burley Potteries. Crooksville, Ohio. **John Burley** purchased a pottery from a man named Castele as early as 1825 which burned down in 1828, according to *The History of Zanesville and Muskingham County, Ohio*, 1927, p. 365, and was rebuilt by John Burley in 1831 and operated until 1885. **Lazalier Burley** was the next Burley from 1846 to 1860's. He was a Bluebird Potter operating at home in yard and sheds. In 1872, William Newton Burley and Wilson WInter started as **Burley and Winter** which was Burley Winter and Brown in 1885. Burley and Winter operated a general store from 1876 to 1901. They were makers of "Heart Brand" stoneware and in later years, the "Bur-win" garden ware. They made both highly glazed stoneware, bisque fired ware and painted wares. Brown left the plant in 1892 and the plant became known as the **Burley and Winter Pottery**. Between 1900 and 1904, Z.W. Burley and S.V. Burley, two brothers started the Keystone Pottery. In December 1909, the John G. Burley Pottery Company was incorporated by John G. Burley and two of Wilson Winter's sons. Around 1912 the Keystone Pottery, the J.G. Burley Pottery and Burley and Winter Pottery all merged. This plant continued until 1932 and a complete liquidation sale was held in 1937. In 1942, the property was sold to Maurice A. Knight and Sons of Akron, Ohio. Shortly after 1912, Z.W. Burley bought the old Globe Stoneware Company and named it the **Burley Pottery Company** and operated it until 1922 when it sold to the Watt Brothers. Z.W. Burley then went to Zanesville and with his brother, Dr. S.V. Burley, started the **Burley Clay Products Company** in 1923, which is still operating today and managed by N.R. Burley and his brother, C.D. Burley. These are the sons of Z.W. Burley and grandsons of W.N. Burley, and great grandsons of Lazalier Burley. Burley Clay Products Company started making one to twenty-five gallon stoneware jars and one to five gallon stoneware jugs. Five years later they changed to red clay flower pots for florists and glazed art ware. Four years later they changed to garden pottery and bird baths and beautiful little garden statues made of a buff high fired stoneware clay. They have successfully continued this line for fifty years now. One more Burley should be mentioned: A John Burley was a very early potter who made stoneware at Mt. Sterling, Muskingham County, Ohio, from 1840 to 1850. (Information: by letter in 1973 from N.R. Burley of Burley Clay Products Company. Impressed marks shown are for the Burley and Winter Pottery. The "C. Winter" mark found on an old piece of stoneware in the area, was probably a relative of Wilson Winter. "The "B. & W.P. Co." mark was on an old stoneware jug.)

B. & W. P. Co.
CROOKSVILLE
O

Burroughs, Edgar Rice, Inc. Tarzana, California. A distributor, filed for rights on this mark on October 19, 1933 to be used for jugs, mugs, childrens' eating bowls, dishes, plates and cups of earthenware and porcelain, claiming use since July 22, 1933.

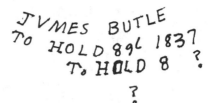

Burroughs and Mountford Company. Trenton, New Jersey. 1879 until 1882 (ending date, Ramsay, p. 183). They produced artware according to Ramsay, but Barber says they also produced a large line of table and toilet ware. They made various grades of white granite and cream-colored wares, some with printed decorations. A variety of marks was shown in Barber. (Information: Barber, p. 60. Marks: no. 1, Ramsay, p. 256; the remainder from Barber, *Marks of American Potters*, p. 60.)

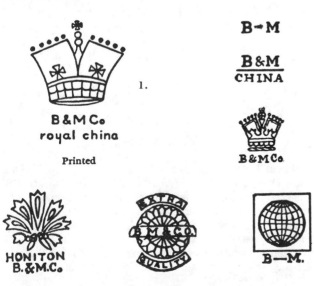

Bustle, James and Bussell, James M. James M. Bussell, a potter in Georgia, was the son of James Bustle according

to John A. Burrison, *Brothers in Clay*, pp. 126, 312. James Bustle was listed as "jug maker" in the 1830 Census in Hancock County and in 1860 he was in eastern Crawford County. Also, according to Burrison, James M. Bussell was listed by George E. Ladd, "A Preliminary Report on a Part of the Clays of Georgia," *Geological Survey of Georgia*, Bulletin No. 6A, 1898, pp. 150, 151, as potting in Northern Washington County in the 1870's. He had come from eastern Crawford County. The mark shown in Burrison as cited, p. 127, is in the earliest piece of documented pottery made in Georgia. It is inscribed on the side of a large double handled jug with what looks like a series of horizontal lines. The spelling of the name is understandable in older times of scarce schooling. (Information and example of a one of a kind, hand inscribed mark, from Burrison, as cited.)

JVMES BUTLE
TO HOLD 89ᴸ 1837
To HOLD 8 ?
?

Butler, Julia Bolin. Worthington, Ohio. 1977 to present (1987). Julia, a studio potter, graduated from Ohio State University in 1981 with a B.F.A. degree in Ceramic Art. Presently, she owns the Colonial Sampler Shop in Powell, Ohio, and makes wheel thrown, hand decorated stoneware. She started making pottery in 1977 in her hometown of Warren, Ohio. Mark is incised.

Butler, A.J. and Company. New Brunswick, New Jersey. Thorn, p. 120, dates this stoneware potter 1879-1882. Ramsay, p. 172, dates him around 1850. (Mark: Thorn, p. 120.)

A.J. BUTLER & CO.
NEW BRUNSWICK
N.J.

Bybee Pottery. See Cornelison Bybee Pottery.

Byrdcliffe Pottery. Woodstock, New York. Around 1903 to after 1928. An art craft colony was founded in 1902 by Ralph Radcliffe Whitehead, at Woodstock. In 1903, pottery was made at a summer school session at the colony. Soon after a pottery was founded at the colony by Edith Penman and Elizabeth Hardenbergh of New York, and called the Byrdcliffe Pottery. Charles Volkmar fired the first pieces (see that listing). Paul Evans, *Art Pottery of the U.S.*, pp. 38, 39, said work continued until 1928 when Zulma Steele Parker made "Zedware," at the pottery that year. Pieces may be seen at the Newark, New Jersey, Museum. The work of the pottery won recognition at the exhibitions held by the New York Society of Keramic Arts. Pieces were made entirely by hand and fied in open air kilns. The colors of the glazes used was the outstanding characteristic of the pieces made. (Information and mark: Evans, as cited.)

C

Cabbages and Kings Pottery. Oak Ridge, Tennessee. 1966 to present. Studio potters, Laurence Knauff and his wife Eileen Knauff make hand thrown, hand painted stoneware, each having their own designs and basic lines, in baking dishes, vases, lamps, bowls, plates, etc. Laurence and Eileen Knauff, both received a B.A. Degree from the University of Illinois in 1967. Both did post-graduate study in the Oxford-Berkeley Summer School in England. Eileen taught at the University of Illinois in 1966, 1967 and at the Old Town Art Center in 1967, 1968. Between 1966-1976 Laurence worked at University of Illinois in Physics Research Equipment Design, also at Bastian-Blessing in R & D Design, and the Univeristy of Illinois as Safety Engineer, while he worked as a part time potter. In 1975, he became a full time potter. There are seventy shops and galleries selling products from the Cabbages and Kings Pottery in many states. (Marks: nos. 1, 2, 3, are marks for Laurence Knauff. Nos. 4, 5, for Eileen Knauff.)

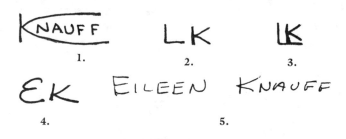

Cahoy Clay Company. Colome, South Dakota. 1974 to present. Emil Cahoy, owner, makes hand thrown and slip caste ware from local clay using twenty tons of clay in six years. The highly vitrified ware is variegated and swirled in color combinations of cream, tan, yellow and deep brown. The clay furnishes the color covered by a clear hard glaze. "Marblestone Products" is the trade name used on paper labels with pieces.

Cahoy

EMIL CAHOY

COLOME, S. DAK.

Caire Pottery. Poughkeepsie, New York. Around 1840 to 1842 the pottery was founded by **John B. Caire** who came to American from Bavaria in 1939. Jacob Caire, son of John, followed in the pottery under the name **Jacob Caire and Company** until 1857 when the pottery was taken over for a few months by Thomas Lehman and Philip Reidinger and operated as **Lehman and Reidinger**. Still in the year 1857, Adam Caire, one of Jacob's brothers came back to Poughkeepsie and the pottery was operated as **Reidinger and Caire** for the next twenty years until Reidinger died in 1878. Adam Caire operated alone until 1896. (Information: John P. Remensnyder, "The Potters of Poughkeepsie," Stradling book, p. 125. Marks: Stewart and Consentino, *Stoneware*, pp. 67, 69; Thorn, p. 146; Christensen, p. 13; and Stradling, p. 126. The mark Lehman and Reidi is for Lehman and Reidinger in Stradling book, p. 126.)

F.J. CAIRE

ADAM CAIRE POKEEPSIE, N.Y.

JACOB CAIRE NY POKEEPSIE

S.B.CAIRE&CO. POKEEPSIE NY

JACOB CAIRE & CO. PO'KEEPSIE

RIEDINGER & CAIRE POKEEPSIE, N.Y.

RIEDINGER & CAIRE POUGHKEEPSIE

LEHMAN AND REIDI... POUGHKEEPSIE, NY

JACOB CAIRE

JACOB CAIRE POKEEPSIE

JACOB CAIRE POTTERY POUGHKEEPSIE N.Y.

Caldwell Potters. Callaway County, Missouri. Family of potters in business from 1827 to around 1891 (Ramsay, p. 209), making sewer tile and utilitarian pottery such as crocks, jugs, mugs, etc. in various locations in the county. Mark found stamped on dark brown stoneware jug was T. and J. Caldwell. Henry W. Heflin, pottery collector and researcher, also listed Newton G. and Thomas H. Caldwell around 1827 in Callaway County. (Information and mark: Henry W. Heflin.)

T.& J. CALDWELL CALLAWAY·CO

California Art Products Company. See Southern California Ceramic Company.

California Belleek Company. Was listed at 527 West Seventh Street, Los Angeles in the 1948 *California Manufacturers Directory*. At Quality Stamp Company in East Liverpool, Ohio, I found the address California Belleek Company, M.H. Strikow, 5064 W. Adams, Blvd., Los Angeles, California, which was the address in the 1952 *Crockery and Glass Journal Directory*. However, in the directory for 1967 the address had changed to 1826 East 43rd Street in Los Angeles. These were the only listings I could find. (Marks 1-7 from Quality Stamp Company, East Liverpool, Ohio. No. 8 from the 1952 directory cited. No. 9 from *Gift and Tableware Reporter*, August 21, 1967, the directory issue.)

California Ceramics/Ceramic Manufacturing Company. Craftsman Center, Calabasas, California. In business before 1948 to around 1955. This pottery must have been short lived or changed names. I found only the three listings in the directories I had. In the 1954 *Crockery and Glass Journal Directory* they were listed as Califronia Ceramics, making dinnerware in various patterns, "Orange Blossom," "Hawaiian Star," "Orchard," "Cherry," "Lava," "Mandalay." In 1957, they were listed as the Ceramic Manufacturing Company at the same address with the mark shown. Also see Rio Hondo Potteries for the use of the trade name "California Ceramics."

California Cleminsons. El Monte, California. 1941 to 1963. George and Betty Cleminson started **Cleminson Clay** in 1941 and in 1943 the name became California Cleminsons. They started in their garage and grew until they employed 165 to 170 people to make artware and novelties. Each piece was hand decorated with colored slip. Lazy susans, bowls, pitchers, pie birds, spoon holders, etc. were made in novelty shapes and decorations. See Betty Newbound, "Along the Flea Market Trail," *Depression Glass Daze*, July 1984, p. 5, for several pictures. She shows wall pockets in the shape of coffee and tea pots. Some complete dinnerware lines were made. (Mark: Jenny Derwich, "Cleminson Mark," *American Clay Exchange*, September 15, 1986, p. 9.)

California Dresden. Glendale, California. In the 1951, 1952 and 1954 *Crockery and Glass Journal Directory*, they were listed for earthenware and china figurines, figures and miniatures. Also, art or decorative pieces with china body such as vases, console sets, etc. These were the only three listings I could find in all my directories for this company. They were not listed at all in the *China and Glass Redbook* or the *California Manufacturers Directories*.

California Exposition and Fair Corporation. Sacramento, California. Filed for registration of this mark on September 29, 1967, claiming first use August 30, 1966, for tableware of china, porcelain, crockery and earthenware.

California Faience Company. Berkeley, California. Art pottery was produced by William Bragdon and Chauncey Thomas under several names between 1916 and 1930. Some tile was made after that time and the facilities were used by local artists according to Evans, p. 41. Dave Rago in "American Art Pottery" column in the *Antique Trader Weekly*, September 9, 1981, p. 91, said California Faience remained in production until the late 1930's. The first company name was **Bragdon and Thomas**, then in 1924 the name was **California Faience**. In the 1924, *Manufacturers Directory of*

California, there are two listings, "California Faience Co., 1335 Hearst Ave. (art)," also, "Tile Shcp, The, 2330 San Pablo Ave. (California Faience)." The pottery was sometimes referred to as the Tile Shop, but that name may have applied only to the separate building listed in the directory as shown. For one year, around the mid 1920's, Bragdon and Thomas made art pottery at the West Coast Porcelain Manufacturers building, but they still worked for California Faience. So we have one firm making a product called California Porcelain in another's building under some arrangement. Also see West Coast Porcelain Manufacturers listing. (Marks: Paul Evans, p. 42. Evans said the "S L T" mark was for designer, S.L. Towne.)

California Faience

STL

California Figurine Company. See Max Weil of California.

California Fruitgrowers Exchange. Los Angeles, California. Distributor. Registered this mark on February 18, 1938, for use on ceramic bowls, claiming use since December 28, 1937, which were made by Gladding, McBean and Company. See that listing.

Sunkist

California Originals. See Heirlooms of Tomorrow.

Camark Pottery. Camden, Arkansas. Founded in 1926 by Samuel Jack Carnes. According to Don Brewer in the article "Camark," *Depression Glass Daze*, June 1982, p. 25, Carnes sold the plant in 1966 after which Brewer stated it was operated mainly as a retail operation by Mary Daniel. In the 1945 *Crockery and Glass Journal Directory*, Camark Pottery was listed as manufacturers and decorators of earthenware-art pottery and decorative accessories. Camark Pottery is important because art pottery was made there. Professional potters and artists like John Lessell (formerly a Weller employee) and his wife were hired to work there. See listing for Lessell.) The Le-Camark line is similar to Weller's La-Sa line. For more on various workers, see the Brewer article already cited. (Marks: no. 1 was filed November 21, 1927, claiming use since March 1, 1927 on pottery, crockery and earthenware. Mark no. 2 was filed December 8, 1947, for use on pottery, crockery and earthenware, namely flower pots, ornamental vases, bowls, dishes, plates, cups and saucers, pitchers, condiment containers and fish bowls. No. 3 was sent by Edward Blas, researcher in American pottery. It is a gold metalic label with blue art and lettering. No. 4 was found in a 1954 directory and is probably a paper label. So the early patented mark was still in use. No. 5 was impressed marks on pieces. No. 6 was a mark in a molded piece. No. 7 shows a paper label copymachined on the bottom of a piece. No. 8 probably a paper label, shown in 1945 *Crockery and Glass Journal Direc-*

tory. No. 9 stamped mark, sent by Don Brewer, researcher on potteries. He also sent a picture which shows no. 1 used as a stamped in gold ink mark.)

1.

2.

3.

4.

CAMARK

5.

2 2 4
Camar k
U.S A

6.

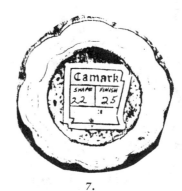

7.

8.

CAMARK
HAND PAINTED
MADE IN USA   9.

Camark Pottery (the second). Camden, Arkansas. Gary and Mark Ashcraft purchased the Camark Pottery building in January 1986. Gary has a B.A. in Graphic Design from Henderson State University at Arkadelphia, Arkansas. Mark has a B.A. in Economics, Business and Accounting from Hendrix College at Conway, Arkansas. This sounds like qualifications for a successful business venture. They plan not to use the old Camark molds and plan a limited production to start with using a mark of their own, not yet designed. (Information: Doris and Burdell Hall, "Camark, A New Beginning," *American Clay Exchange*, September 16, 1986, p. 5.)

Cambridge Art Pottery. Cambridge, Ohio. In 1901, the first ware was made according to Evans, p. 43. Made art ware vases, jardinieres, pedestals, clay specialties. In *1902-1903 Complete Directory* they were listed as making dinner sets; short sets of odd dishes and novelties. From 1909 to around

1924, the plant was called the **Guernsey Earthenware Company**. Around 1924, the building became part of the pottery complex under the ownership of O.C. Ahrendts and his partners C.S. Wardeska, C.R. Ahrendts, Stevens and Gilmer. In 1934, this building became a part of those used by Universal Potteries, Inc. according to William G. Wolfe, *Stories of Guernsey County*, privately printed in Cambridge, Ohio, 1934, p. 770. See Bradshaw China for the history of the holdings of O.C Ahrendts. In a letter from Harold Bennett, owner of Guernsey Glass Company and the Cambridge Glass Museum, both in Cambridge, Ohio, were some facts about marks on Cambridge Art Pottery pieces. Harold has many pieces in the museum. He said "CAP" was used from about 1902 to 1910. He said the mark was generally under the glaze but not always. Bennett said that after 1907, for a short time the pottery used a mark "Otoe" (name of a line). According to Evans, p. 43, the "Otoe" line was very ordinary, made with a matt green glaze and a few pieces had a webbed effect. According to Bennett, 1902, was the only year the pottery made the brown glazed ware. He said red ware and matt green was made from 1907 to 1910. See Evans, pp. 43-45 for a great deal more on various lines and products. See Oxford Pottery Company for the connection between Globe China Company and Guernsey Earthenware Company. (Marks: nos. 1-4, Barber, *Marks of American Potters*, p. 137; nos. 5-7, Evans, p. 45; no. 8, Lehner, *Ohio Pottery and Glass*, p. 24. Impressed or recessed mark no. 9, "Otoe," furnished by Harold Bennett. See further information on an acorn mark under listing Oakwood, various potteries. Impressed mark 10 furnished by Wilma Hock, antique dealer, found on a decorative vase.)

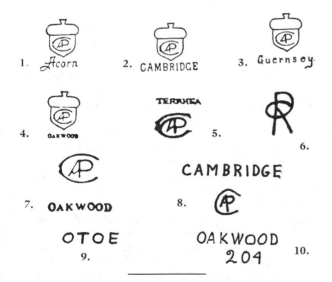

1. Acorn
2. CAMBRIDGE
3. Guernsey
4. OAKWOOD
5. TEROMEA
6.
7. OAKWOOD
8.
9. OTOE
10. OAKWOOD 204
CAMBRIDGE

Cambridge Tile Manufacturing Company. Covington, Kentucky. A brick yard by the name Busse Brothers was at the corner of 16th and Woodburn in Covington. In 1886 the the Busse Brothers started to sell enameled tile and changed the name of the plant to **Mount Casini Art Tile Company**. In 1887, a sales company was formed which the Busse Brothers called the **Cambridge Art Tile Company**. Then in 1889, they incorporated the businesses under the name **Cambridge Tile Manufacturing Company** under Kentucky laws and in June 1906 the company was dissolved and reincorporated under Ohio law. In 1927, the plant in Covington was abandoned and the company bought the Wheatley Pottery Company in Cincinnati, Ohio, and named it the **Wheatley Tile and Pottery**

Company around 1929. (Information: Everett Townsent, "Development of the Tile Industry in the U.S.," *American Ceramic Society Bulletin*, May 1943, p. 131. Mark: raised mark sent by Elizabeth Vaughn, Beechwold, Antiques, Columbus, Ohio.)

Cambridge

Camden Pottery Company. Camden, New Jersey. Around 1906. Manufacturer of sanitary ware basins, sinks, closet bowls, etc. of earthenware. Company filed for registration of mark shown on May 31, 1906. They gave no length of prior use.

Cameron Clay Products Company. Cameron, West Virginia. In the 1958, *Crockery and Glass Journal Directory*, Cameron Clay products was listed as making "Sevilla" earthenware which was sold through J. and I. Block Company of New York City. In 1962, *West Virginia Manufacturing Directory*, they were listed as making semivitreous pottery. There was a very early pottery in Cameron, West Virginia, listed as **Cameron Potteries Company** in the 1902-1903 *Complete Directory*. The Eljer Company started in this building in 1907. (*American Ceramic Society Bulletin*, May, 1946, p. 78.) Cameron Potteries Company also made tableware. However, the mark shown was found in the big record book at Quality Stamp Company of East Liverpool and belonged to the later company.

Camp and Thompson. Akron, Ohio. Around 1870 to 1880. Made stoneware brownware. Mark is impressed. (Information and mark: Thorn, *Handbook of Old Pottery and Porcelain Marks*, p. 121; Ramsay, *American Potters and Pottery*, p. 206.)

CAMP & THOMPSON

Campbell, William, Factory Studio. Cambridge Springs, Pennsylvania. 1969 to present (1983). Mr. Campbell's studio makes 30,000 pieces a year of stoneware and porcelain into beautiful shapes and pieces, both functional and decorative. His display in a show that featured ninety potters created a lasting impression on this author. On the questionnaire, Mr. Campbell replied that he had done many shows and won many awards and I'm sure he has. (All marks prior to 1981 were dated. From 1969 to 1980, marks 1, 2 were used with a date. Important pieces were signed with full name and date such as mark no. 3. Marks no. 4, 5 are current marks. Sometimes a pair of circles is used with mark no. 5.)

1.

2.

3.

4.

5.

Camp Del Mar Pottery. Capitola, California. Late 1940's and early 1950's. Listed in the 1948 *China and Glass Red Book Directory* for "Campo," California porcelain tableware, flower containers, accessories and novelties. They were not listed in 1954. (Mark: 1952 *Crockery and Glass Journal Directory*.)

Canonsburg Pottery. Canonsburg, Pennsylvania. 1901 to 1978. In 1978, a public sale dispersed the property. Just before 1900, when W.S. George was induced to help start a pottery in Canonsburg, Pennsylvania, he was also operating a pottery in East Palestine, Ohio, known as the East Palestine Pottery Company, which had been formed in 1884. As early as 1899, George explored the possibility of locating a plant in Canonsburg. By October, 1899, an organization had been formed and a board of directors elected. In April, 1900, construction began on a $50,000 building, and the pottery was in operation by the beginning of 1901, operating as the **Canonsburg China Company.** (From history sent by the company.) The company was listed in the *1902-1903 Complete Directory* as the Canonsburg China Company making semi-porcelain dinner sets, toilet sets and short sets of odd dishes, some decorated. On March 2, 1909, the assets of the Canonsburg China Company were purchased by a newly formed corporation called the Canonsburg Pottery Company. John George, brother of W.S. George, was elected president. He served in that capacity until his death in 1920, when he was succeeded by Willard C. George, John's son. In 1931, Canonsburg Pottery employed three-hundred six people. In 1938, W.C. George was followed by John George II, who was Williard's son. John II has a brother, William R. George, and in 1976 the last two Georges in the pottery business sold the Canonsburg Pottery to Angelo Falconi. Then on May 18, 1978, a complete dispersal bankruptcy sale of all machinery and equipment was held. The plant had stood idle following a fire around 1975. Prior to 1975, for a period of four or five years, the pottery had been making crock-pot inserts. See W.S. George Pottery listing for his involvement in the plant he owned in Canonsburg. Pope Gosser China Company, Coshocton, Ohio, develped a popular line of ware called Rose Point. (See Pope Gosser listing.) At some point, the Rose Point molds were sold to the Steubenville Pottery Company.

When the Steubenville Pottery Company closed in 1959, the building was sold to Barium and Chemicals, Inc. of Canonsburg, and the Canonsburg Pottery bought the Steubenville Pottery molds and equipment. (Marks: No. 1, "Rose Point by Steubenville" was actually made by Canonsburg Pottery after 1959. Also marks nos. 2-19 were all made at Canonsburg Pottery even though they say Steubenville. We found these marks at Qualty Stamp Company of East Liverpool, Ohio, and some of them were stamped with later dates (see mark no. 2). I had mark no. 3 as a Steubenville Pottery mark in the *American Kitchen and Dinner Wares* book. These marks will cause confusion for years to come, but thanks to Mr. W. Price at Quality Stamp Company, maybe the collectors can avoid some errors in identification between Steubenville Pottery and Canonsburg Pottery pieces. In the 1965, China and Glass Red Book Directory, the name used was Steubenville Pottery with address Canonsburg; John George, president. The name and trademark rights had all been purchased by the Canonsburg Pottery. Mark no. 20 is a very early mark around the opening time of the factory. Nos. 21, 22 and 23 are very early marks, probably around 1920's or before. Some very nice highly vitrified ware is found with marks involving the name Willard George, nos. 24 and 25. Willard George was president of the company between 1920 and 1948, so the dishes were a special effort in that period. The most commonly known Canonsburg marks involve the little cannon. See marks 26-44. Some form of this mark was used for a long period of time. No. 44 was shown in 1952 *Crockery and Glass Journal Directory*. The mark was still being shown in the 1967 *China, Glass and Tableware Directory*. I found dishes that appear to be made in the 1930's with this mark. For a mark very similar to no. 45, see the Keystone Pottery. Nos. 46 and 47 are on a plate of 1930's with raised design borders. The Washington Colonial plate had a large Currier and Ives scene decaled in the center. No. 49 is a Canonsburg Pottery mark found at Quality Stamp Company. No. 48 is an English mark with a very similar name shown here to avoid confusion. Nos. 49-76 are all distributors marks found under Canonsburg Pottery at Quality Stamp Company, East Liverpool, Ohio. Some of these distributors are discussed elsewhere in the book: no. 56, Stanley Home Products,, no. 59, Ebling Reuss, nos. 60, 61, National Silver Company. No. 77 found on green butter dish made in 1960's. The remainder of the marks are all later marks found on dishes or at Quality Stamp Company. No. 58 was a mark used on a series, some of which were "View of Conestoga Wagon, 1800;" "View of Treaty in Greenville, 1795;" "View of Lincoln's Departure, 1861;" "View of Chicago Water Tower, 1870;" "View of Chicago River, 1868." (Information: Lehner, *American Kitchen and Dinner Wares*, p. 38; no author, *A History of the Canonsburg Pottery Company*, Canonsburg, Pennsylvania, June 20, 1972, issued by the company; also, *20th Century History of Washington and Washington County, Pennsylvania and Representative Citizens*, published 1910 (sent to me by company with no author); and Minie Merick, by letter from Jefferson County Historical Association, Inc., Steubenville.)

1.

75

_by_
Steubenville
MADE IN U.S.A.
LADY ESTHER   2.

COLOR FAST-OVEN PROOF-DETERGENT SAFE
BY SKILLED AMERICAN CRAFTSMEN FOR
LASTING BEAUTY.
3.   _Steubenville_
POTTERY CO.
U.S.A.
FAIRLANE

_by_
Steubenville   4.
MADE IN U.S.A.
MAYTIME

hand painted
—color fast —oven proof
COLOR FAST-OVEN PROOF-DETERGENT SAFE
HAND DECORATED IN UNDERGLAZE COLORS
5.   BY SKILLED AMERICAN CRAFTSMEN FOR
LASTING BEAUTY.
Steubenville
POTTERY CO.
U.S.A.

DOMINO   COTILLION
_by_   By
Steubenville _Steubenville_
U.S.A   U.S.A.
6.   7.

DIMENSION   SEQUENCE
By   By
Steubenville _Steubenville_
U.S.A.   U.S.A.
8.   9.

USA
EPICURE
Steubenville
10.

APR 6 - 1967

Steubenville
POTTERY CO.
U.S.A.
11.

OVEN PROOF
STEUBENSTONE
JAMAICA
STEUBENVILLE DIVISION
CANONSBURG POTTERY CO. U.S.A.
12.

OVEN PROOF
STEUBENSTONE
TANGIERS
STEUBENVILLE DIVISION
CANONSBURG POTTERY CO. U.S.A.
13.

OVEN PROOF
STEUBENSTONE
SARDINIA
STEUBENVILLE DIVISION
CANONSBURG POTTERY CO. U.S.A.
14.

OVEN PROOF
STEUBENSTONE
EXPRESSO   15.
STEUBENVILLE DIVISION
CANONSBURG POTTERY CO. U.S.A.

OVEN-PROOF PARTIO-WARE
Designed by Irene Pasinski

16.
The Steubenville Pottery Co.
Fine American Dinnerware Since 1879
"HOMESPUN PATTERN"

OVEN-PROOF PARTIO-WARE
Designed by Irene Pasinski

17.
The Steubenville Pottery Co.
Fine American Dinnerware Since 1879
"BROWNSTONE PATTERN"

OVEN-PROOF PARTIO-WARE
Designed by Irene Pasinski

18.
The Steubenville Pottery Co.
Fine American Dinnerware Since 1879
RONDELAY 4504

OVEN-PROOF PARTIO-WARE
Designed by Irene Pasinski

19.
The Steubenville Pottery Co.
Fine American Dinnerware Since 1879
MAYTIME 4503

20. 21. 22.

MADE IN CANONSBURG POTTERY USA

23.

WILLARD GEORGE
CANONSBURG
CANONSBURG PA.
Pussy Willow
24.

Willard George

Willard George 25.

THE HALLMARK
KEYSTONE
OF QUALITY
"Moonglo"
26.

Citation
OVEN PROOF
THE 27.
HALLMARK OF QUALITY
Canonsburg
U.S.A.

THE HALLMARK
OF QUALITY
"EMPRESS CHANTILLY"
AAA-1 QUALITY
24 KT. GOLD
28.

SIMPLICITY
THE HALLMARK
OF QUALITY
WARRANTED
22 KT. GOLD
MADE IN U.S.A.
BERMUDA ROSE-A-1
29.

THE HALLMARK
OF QUALITY
OVEN PROOF
Temptation - A-1
30.

THE HALLMARK
OF QUALITY
WARRANTED
22 KT. GOLD
American Beauty
31.

FOR SUN GLO STUDIOS
32.
WINTER PASTIME
Currier and Ives Reproductions-Americana Series

Liberty China
WARRANTED
22 CARAT
GOLD
33.

THE HALLMARK
OF QUALITY
OVEN PROOF
Playmates
34.

THE HALLMARK
OF QUALITY
OVEN PROOF
Romance A-1
35.

SIMPLICITY
THE HALLMARK 37.
OF QUALITY
SWEETHEART

SIMPLICITY
THE HALLMARK
OF QUALITY
WARRANTED
22 KT. GOLD
MADE IN U.S.A.
Temptation 39.

MADE IN AMERICA
THE HALLMARK
OF QUALITY
BY UNION LABOR 41.

Liberty China
WARRANTED
22 CARAT
GOLD
43.

KEYSTONE
MADE IN USA
CANONSBURG
POTTERY CO.
45.

American Traditional
Canonsburg Pottery Co.
Canonsburg, Pa.
U.S.A.
47.

SIMPLICITY
THE HALLMARK
OF QUALITY
36. LADY LOCKET

THE HALLMARK
KEYSTONE
OF QUALITY
"YELLOW ROSE BY EMPRESS"
AAA-1 QUALITY
24 KT. GOLD
38.

SIMPLICITY
THE HALLMARK
OF QUALITY
Temptation-A-1
40.

THE HALLMARK
OF QUALITY
OVEN PROOF
42.

44.

WASHINGTON COLONIAL
MADE IN U.S.A.
46.

(ENGLISH MARK)
48.

Royal Wilton

FIRST QUALITY
ORIGINAL
Warranted 22 KT Gold

49.

*"A Housekeeping
Meadow Flower"*

50.

Lojean
WARRANTED
22 KARAT GOLD

51.

CHATEAU FRANCE
By
BETTER LIVING
WARRANTED
22 KT. GOLD
MADE IN USA

52.

53.

Leon's Jewelry
259 E. LINCOLN HIGHWAY
COATESVILLE, PA.

GOURMET

COUNTRY SQUIRE

54.

Jefferson Styled
DINNERWARE
UNION MADE · 22 KT. GOLD

55.

DURA-GLOSS PATTERN UNDERGLAZE
EXCLUSIVE
"STANHOME"
· PATTERN ·
MADE IN
U.S.A.
CANONSBURG POTTERY

56.

*Reliable Home Equip.-Co.
Richmond, Va.
Summer Garden*
22 KT. GOLD

57.

*Mid·America
Heritage*
oven proof
*Canonsburg Pottery
U.S.A.*

58.

E.&R.
INC
AMERICAN
ARTWARE

59.

NASCO
TEABERRY
22 KT. GOLD

60.

61.

NASCO
SURREY
22·KT. GOLD

A KATHY KALE CREATION

62.

63.

Royal Queen

FIRST QUALITY
ORIGINAL
Warranted 22 KT. Gold
ANN LOUISE

64.

Royal Tudor
FIRST QUALITY ORIGINAL
Warranted 22 KT. Gold
MADE IN U. S. A.
PUSSY WILLOW

65.

Royal Tudor
66.
FIRST QUALITY ORIGINAL
Warranted 22 KT. Gold
MADE IN U. S. A.
Pine

Royal Tudor
67. FIRST QUALITY ORIGINAL
Warranted 22 KT. Gold
MADE IN U. S. A.
PINK T ROSE

Royal Tudor
FIRST QUALITY ORIGINAL
Warranted 22 KT. Gold
MADE IN U. S. A.
LINDA

68.

ROYAL
Monarch
FIRST QUALITY CHINA
ORIGINAL
WARRANTED PLAT. AND GOLD
Queen Elizabeth

69.

Royal Monarch
FIRST QUALITY CHINA
ORIGINAL
IMPORTED BAVARIAN DECOR.
Windsor
70.

Royal Monarch
FIRST QUALITY CHINA
ORIGINAL
WARRANTED PLAT. AND GOLD
IMPORTED DECAL HOLLAND
71.

Royal Monarch
FIRST QUALITY CHINA
ORIGINAL
Warranted 22 KT. Gold
Radiant Rose
72.

Royal Monarch
FIRST QUALITY CHINA
ORIGINAL
WARRANTED PLAT. AND GOLD
IMPORTED DECAL HOLLAND
Queen Anne
73.

Royal Monarch
FIRST QUALITY CHINA
ORIGINAL
UNDERGLAZE HAND PAINTED
Lady Jane
74.

Royal Monarch
FIRST QUALITY CHINA
ORIGINAL
Princess Anne
75.

"Indian Rose"
By
Empress Sterling
76.

'ROUND THE CLOCK
Bermuda Rose
77.

GUARANTEED OVEN PROOF DETERGENT PROOF
THE PATTERN IS HERMETICALLY SEALED UNDER GLAZE
A
DURA-GLOSS
DECORATION
MADE IN U.S.A.
BY CANONSBURG POTTERY CANONSBURG, PENNA.
78.

Citation
OVEN PROOF
THE HALLMARK OF QUALITY
Canonsburg
U.S.A.
79.

TERRASTONE
THE CAREFREE
IRONSTONE
by Canonsburg

USA
80.

U.S.A.
YELLOWSTONE
WARE
by Canonsburg

81.

Mid-American Heritage
oven proof
Canonsburg Pottery
U.S.A.

(The four below go with above mark.)
82.

(1) VIEW OF CONESTOGA WAGON 1800
(2) VIEW OF TREATY OF GREENVILLE 1795
(3) VIEW OF LINCOLN'S DEPARTURE 1861
(4) VIEW OF CHICAGO WATER TOWER 1870

GENUINE HAND PAINTED DESIGN
USA
SANDSTONE
405
Canonsburg
POTTERY CO.
OVENPROOF · DISHWASHER · SAFE · DETERGENT · PROOF
83.

GENUINE HAND PAINTED DESIGN
USA
AQUAMARINE
408
Canonsburg
POTTERY CO.
OVENPROOF · DISHWASHER · SAFE · DETERGENT · PROOF
84.

GENUINE HAND PAINTED DESIGN
USA
YELLOWSTONE
403
Canonsburg
POTTERY CO.
OVENPROOF · DISHWASHER · SAFE · DETERGENT · PROOF
85.

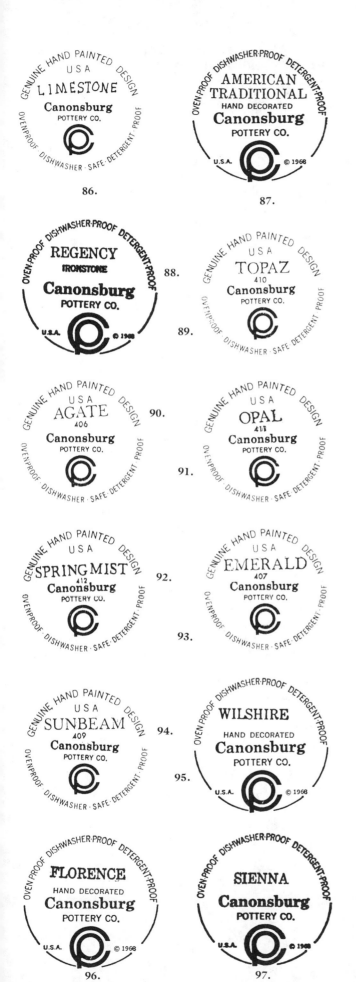

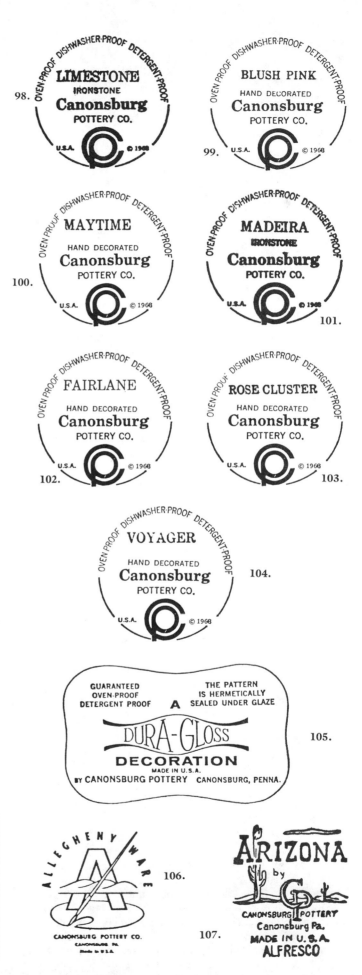

GENUINE HAND PAINTED DESIGN
USA
LIMESTONE
Canonsburg
POTTERY CO.
OVENPROOF · DISHWASHER · SAFE · DETERGENT · PROOF
86.

OVEN-PROOF DISHWASHER-PROOF DETERGENT-PROOF
AMERICAN TRADITIONAL
HAND DECORATED
Canonsburg
POTTERY CO.
U.S.A. © 1968
87.

OVEN-PROOF DISHWASHER-PROOF DETERGENT-PROOF
REGENCY
IRONSTONE
Canonsburg
POTTERY CO.
U.S.A. © 1968
88.

GENUINE HAND PAINTED DESIGN
USA
TOPAZ
410
Canonsburg
POTTERY CO.
OVENPROOF · DISHWASHER · SAFE · DETERGENT · PROOF
89.

GENUINE HAND PAINTED DESIGN
USA
AGATE
406
Canonsburg
POTTERY CO.
OVENPROOF · DISHWASHER · SAFE · DETERGENT · PROOF
90.

GENUINE HAND PAINTED DESIGN
USA
OPAL
411
Canonsburg
POTTERY CO.
OVENPROOF · DISHWASHER · SAFE · DETERGENT · PROOF
91.

GENUINE HAND PAINTED DESIGN
USA
SPRING MIST
412
Canonsburg
POTTERY CO.
OVENPROOF · DISHWASHER · SAFE · DETERGENT · PROOF
92.

GENUINE HAND PAINTED DESIGN
USA
EMERALD
407
Canonsburg
POTTERY CO.
OVENPROOF · DISHWASHER · SAFE · DETERGENT · PROOF
93.

GENUINE HAND PAINTED DESIGN
USA
SUNBEAM
409
Canonsburg
POTTERY CO.
OVENPROOF · DISHWASHER · SAFE · DETERGENT · PROOF
94.

OVEN-PROOF DISHWASHER-PROOF DETERGENT-PROOF
WILSHIRE
HAND DECORATED
Canonsburg
POTTERY CO.
U.S.A. © 1968
95.

OVEN-PROOF DISHWASHER-PROOF DETERGENT-PROOF
FLORENCE
HAND DECORATED
Canonsburg
POTTERY CO.
U.S.A. © 1968
96.

OVEN-PROOF DISHWASHER-PROOF DETERGENT-PROOF
SIENNA
Canonsburg
POTTERY CO.
U.S.A. © 1968
97.

OVEN-PROOF DISHWASHER-PROOF DETERGENT-PROOF
LIMESTONE
IRONSTONE
Canonsburg
POTTERY CO.
U.S.A. © 1968
98.

OVEN-PROOF DISHWASHER-PROOF DETERGENT-PROOF
BLUSH PINK
HAND DECORATED
Canonsburg
POTTERY CO.
U.S.A. © 1968
99.

OVEN-PROOF DISHWASHER-PROOF DETERGENT-PROOF
MAYTIME
HAND DECORATED
Canonsburg
POTTERY CO.
U.S.A. © 1968
100.

OVEN-PROOF DISHWASHER-PROOF DETERGENT-PROOF
MADEIRA
IRONSTONE
Canonsburg
POTTERY CO.
U.S.A. © 1968
101.

OVEN-PROOF DISHWASHER-PROOF DETERGENT-PROOF
FAIRLANE
HAND DECORATED
Canonsburg
POTTERY CO.
U.S.A. © 1968
102.

OVEN-PROOF DISHWASHER-PROOF DETERGENT-PROOF
ROSE CLUSTER
HAND DECORATED
Canonsburg
POTTERY CO.
U.S.A. © 1968
103.

OVEN-PROOF DISHWASHER-PROOF DETERGENT-PROOF
VOYAGER
HAND DECORATED
Canonsburg
POTTERY CO.
U.S.A. © 1968
104.

GUARANTEED OVEN-PROOF DETERGENT PROOF
THE PATTERN IS HERMETICALLY SEALED UNDER GLAZE
A
DURA-GLOSS
DECORATION
MADE IN U.S.A.
BY CANONSBURG POTTERY   CANONSBURG, PENNA.
105.

ALLEGHENY WARE
A
CANONSBURG POTTERY CO.
CANONSBURG, PA.
Made in U.S.A.
106.

ARIZONA
by
CANONSBURG POTTERY
Canonsburg Pa.
MADE IN U.S.A.
ALFRESCO
107.

108.

109.

110.

Capistrano Ceramics/John R. Stewart, Inc. San Juan Capistrano, California. This was listed entirely separate from the Capistrano Mission Potteries in Los Angeles, by two different directories. The company's name was John R. Stewart, Inc., manufacturing "Capistrano Ceramics," which were figurines, ash trays, boxes, animals, vase, bowls and wall pockets. (*China and Glass Red Book Directories* and *Crockery and Glass Journal Directories* for 1948-1949 and 1951 listed the two potteries. Stewart, Inc. was not listed in 1953 either. Mark: *1951 Crockery and Glass Journal Directory*.)

Capistrano Mission Potteries. Los Angeles, California. The 1948 and 1949 *China and Glass Red Book Directories* and the 1951 *Crockery and Glass Journal Directory* listed this pottery for dinnerware, salts and peppers, etc. They were not listed in 1953 in any directory I had. (Mark: from 1951 *Crockery and Glass Journal Directory*. This is not the same company as the Capistrano Ceramics. See that listing.)

Capri Creations. Philadelphia, Pennsylvania. Capri Creations assigned the rights to mark one to Lafair and Sons Company, operating as the Capri Candle Company and Capri Creations on March 3, 1961, claiming prior use of the mark for one month only to be used on salt and pepper shakers, planters and candle holders. Mark no. 2 filed February 7, 1962, claiming use for one year on salt and pepper shakers, planters,

candle holders, smoker sets, banks, candle climbers, pitchers, cups, egg cups and decorative pieces.

1.

2. **CAPRI**

Capsco, Capitol Souvenir, Inc. Washington, D.C. A distributor used a mark found with a W.S. George Pottery mark, saying "a Capsco product." Used 1930's or earlier judging from the little cup plate souvenir.

WARRANTED
22 KARAT GOLD

Carbone, Inc. Boston, Massachussetts. Selling agency for domestic and imported stoneware, china, pottery and glass pieces, including dinnerware, ovenware and all types of dinner service. In the 1945 *Crockery and Glass Journal Directory*, Carbone, Inc. was listed as selling American dinnerware among other products. In 1952, they were listed for art pottery, earthenware vases, console sets, candy boxes, etc. They were also listed for County Fare Hostessware and Taylor Ceramics. Country Fare Hostessware was made by the Zanesville Stoneware Company exclusively for Carbone for several years. Taylor, Smith and Taylor made Taylor Ceramics. In the 1967 *China, Glass and Tableware Directory*, they were listed with the importers. They were listed in the 1977-1978 Directory, but not in the 1981-1982 listing. (Marks: In May 1926, Carbone filed for registration on the mark no. 1 shown, claiming use since 1922 to use on pottery. Mark no. 2 was found at Quality Stamp Company on the page of marks ordered by Hall China. No. 3 was filed for registration January 8, 1960 for use on stoneware, earthenware and ceramics, namely, cups, pitchers, mugs, bowls, plates, saucers, decanters, trays, platters, vases, tea pots, coffee pots, salt and pepper shakers, tureens, casseroles, trivets, water coolers, cruets, bean pots and other dinnerware items, claiming use since October 31, 1946, for the same articles as no. 3. No. 5 was filed September 4, 1951, claiming a long use since November 29, 1940, for the same articles.)

Castelli
1.

Carbone
2. MADE IN U.S.A.

VINTAGE
3.

HARVEST
4.

Country Fare
5.

Carborundum Company. Niagara Falls, New York. Maker of industrial ceramics. Filed for registration of this mark September 1961, claiming use since 1959, for shaped ceramic bodies, having high thermal shock resistance and low thermal expansion.

LITHAFRAX

Carborundum Museum of Ceramics. Niagara Falls, New York. Demonstrations were conducted at the museum featuring various potters. Exhibits of U.S. pottery and porcelain made by early potters were shown there. There was also a gift shop in connection with the museum. Some ware had the "CMC" monogram shown. The museum closed February 2, 1976. (Information: Jenny B. Derwich and Dr. Mary Latos, *Dictionary Guide to United States Pottery and Porcelain*, p. 54. Mark: sent by Jenny B. Derwich.)

Cardinal China Company or Carteret China Company. Carteret, New Jersey. Listed in March 15, 1952 *Crockery and Glass Journal Directory*, with five retail outlets in Texas, California and New York. Cardinal China Company was a distributor that used their own marks on cookie jars and decorative pieces, etc. Their ad to dealers in the 1952 directory cited, said "Cardinal features a complete line of low cost business builders" and "instant turnover and best sellers." They had permanent showrooms in New York city, Chicago and Los Angeles. A 1960, order blank included casseroles, all kinds of dinnerware, cake sets, three tier plates, ashtrays, all types of bowls, cookie jars, tea sets, etc. (Marks: no. 1, Quality Stamp Company; mark no. 2 and 3, incised or stamped into pieces. No. 4 is the way the mark was filed for registration on July 19, 1956, claiming use since May 18, 1948, for ceramic giftware and houseware, such as vase, planters, spoon rests, egg dishes, hors d'oeuvres dishes, lighting receptacle switch plates, gravy ladles, salt and peppers and kitchen utility items.)

Carteret China Co.
Warranted 22 Kt. 1.
MADE IN U. S. A)

© CARDINAL
2. 1579 USA

CARDINAL
CHINA CO.
PAT.
PEND. 3.

CARDINAL
4.

Caribe China Corporation. Vega Baja, Puerto Rico. The mark shown was filed for registration on Janury 18, 1956, claiming use since October 11, 1951, for use on china tableware. See Sterling China Company and Iroquois China Company for history and marks of Caribe China.

CARIBE

Carlock, Elaine D. and Daniel M./Cranberry Hill Studio. Pontiac, Michigan. Elaine D. Carlock is a nationally known sculptor. From around 1940 to 1950, for a period of ten years or so, Elaine sculptured models of little porcelain figures to be made in quantity for Coventry Ware, Inc. of Barberton, Ohio (see that listing). In 1951, she moved to Cranberry Hill, in White Lake Township, near Pontiac, Michigan. She began by making her own models and then molds. In 1970, she designed eight pieces which she planned to produce and sell in a gift shop in Ann Arbor, Michigan. They sold well and Cranberry Hill Studio was born. The studio makes a collection or line of children's figures of high fired vitreous stoneware. They are simplified, stylized, impressions that show the essence, spirit and wonder of childhood. The clay is formed into basic shapes and while still soft, ribbons, bows, ruffles, flowers, grass and leaves are hand applied, giving an individuality to each piece and each is a true work of art. Some hand painting is done and then each is dip glazed and a little more color added. Each piece is signed before the last high firing is done. Elaine's son, Daniel M. Carlock, is the owner and manager of the studio at present. He has worked as a studio potter since the early 1970's, during which time he made mostly raku pieces. Now his interest is in stoneware and porcelain pieces which he marks as is shown in mark no. 2. This work is in addition to running the studio. The newest line of the studio is "Simple Joys," a line of Amish children done in porcelain. (Marks: nos. 1, 2, incised mark of Elaine. No. 3, Daniel's mark, incised.)

Elaine Carlock 1.
Elaine Carlock 2. *DMC* 3.

Carmichael, Michael M. Tyler, Texas. Filed for registration of this mark on December 10, 1954, for use on porcelain objects for the aquarium, claiming use since May 30, 1950.

Carnegie, Hattie, Inc. New York, New York. Company filed for registration of this mark on May 27, 1965, claiming a long use since November 8, 1938, for gift items made of crockery and porcelain, such as urns, vases, picture frames, bowls, jeweled boxes, card boxes, cosmetic trays, perfume jars, cotton jars and powder boxes.

Hattie Carnegie

Carol Ann Pottery, Ltd. Boulder, Colorado. 1973 to present. Several studio potters work with Carol Ann Wilson to create hand thrown dinnerware of stoneware which is oven and microwave proof. The CAW trademark is placed on each pot along with the stamp of the thrower that made the piece. Also shown is a list of the potters and their marks and the dates they worked at the pottery.

	Terry Geosits	10/73 - 5/78
	Maia Sampson	1/74 - 9/75
	Susan Cordova	6/74 - 12/76
	Judy Stone	7/74 - 3/78
	Michael Ryan	10/74 - 6/75
	Bob Osif	10/75
	Joy Eisen	6/75 - 3/76
	KAREN CONDUFF	
	Alice Rubenstein	6/75 - 8/77
	Gini Ingraham	1/76 - 6/77
	Lyle Horn	12/76 -
	Carol Sobieniak	10/77 - 6/78
	Gayle Barnes	2/78 -
	Ted Sowinski	2/78 -
	Jane Maxwell	10/78 -
	KATHY FRANTZ	

Carpenter, Frederick in **Mystic River Works.** Charlestown, Massachusetts. Around 1880 - still operating around 1810, but didn't exist too long. An indepth research has been done on this potter by Lura Woodside Watkins, resulting in the article footnoted. She concluded that just as Edmands and Burroughs used the same "Charlestown" mark as Carpenter, that Carpenter and Jonathan Fenton both used just the mark "Boston." Made stoneware, pickle pots, jugs, etc. with a brown stain or glaze in oval-like and curved shapes. See Emands and also Fenton for a comparison of marks. (Information: Lura Woodside Watkins, "New Light on Boston Stoneware and Frederick Carpenter," *The Art of the Potter*, published by *Antiques Magazine*, 1977, edited by Diana and J. Garrison Stradling, pp. 81-86. Marks: Stradling, pp. 85. 86.)

BOSTON   CHARLESTOWN

BOSTON
1804

Carr China Company. Grafton, West Virginia. 1916 to 1952. The company was chartered on June 7, 1916, the principal office was in Grafton, West Virginia. In 1938, they employed two-hundred thirty people to make hotel ware. The pottery was started by Thomas Carr, son of a potter who learned the trade in England, then moved to this country. Seeing the advantages of the Monongahelia Valley region for operating a pottery, Thomas Carr moved from the New York area where his father had operated, to Grafton. (James Carr operated in the New York City Pottery for years. Thomas may have been his son.) William Frey developed a color application that helped the already successful plant to do even better. The floor space of the plant covered 75,000 square feet, kilns were fired day and night and several shifts of employees maintained. The plant operated until July, 1952. Pieces described by a Carr china collector were a "Blue Willow" pitcher, "Washington" plate, "Blue Onion" ice cream dish, "Rho-Dendra" mug with yellow , blue, green slip color application, a miniature Toby mug of George Washington made for the 1939 World's Fair in New York, a cream and sugar in marblized pink and white. (Information and marks: Nos. 1-4 were furnished by Imelda Dowden, Grafton, West Virginia. No. 5 was sent by Connie Rogers on Blue Willow pattern. The mark stamped so dark I drew a copy which is no. 6. Other marks were found on various pieces of hotel and restaurant china.)

Rho Dendra
Carr China
1.

"ONION"
CARR CHINA
GRAFTON
W. VA.
2.

Rho Dendra
Carr China
Grafton, W. Va.
3.

Grafton
CARR China Co
4.

5.

6.

STANDARD SAMPLE
9017-6-31-6
CARR CHINA
GRAFTON, W.VA.
7.

8.

CARR
CHINA CO.
9.

10.   11.

CARR CHINA CO.
LOUIS . POLSTER
COLUMBUS, O.

12.

Carroll, Carolyn. Palatine, Illinois. 1976 to present. Studio potter making porcelain pieces, slab-built, functional but definitely sculptural in nature. Pieces include lamps, vases, pitcher and tumbler sets, platters, serving pieces, large decorative vases, etc. Ware is white to creamy with a glossy clear glaze, fired to a come 9-10. Ware is fired three times, the third firing adding lusters of pink, blue, brown, grey and some gold for accent. Carolyn received a B.F.A. degree from State University of New York at Brockport, suma cum laude. She won several first place awards in street fairs in New York State in the years 1977 through 1981. She also has done shows in California. Mark used in 1981 on ware produced by Carroll's studio assistant, Martha Hill bears a bean imprint as well as Carroll's signature. Martha made ware to Carroll's designs. The 1982 mark by Martha is marked Carolyn Carroll Studio. All work by Carolyn is signed with her name and dated.

Carolyn Carroll
1/22/82

Carolyn Carroll Studio

Carrollton Pottery Company. Carrollton, Ohio. 1903 to late 1930's. Makers of high grade semivitreous porcelain china or "American China." In June 1914, fire destroyed half of the plant which was rebuilt and enlarged in 1915. They employed 350 people in 1915 with an annual production of one-half million dollars. In 1929, they merged with seven other companies to form American China Corporation. They did not go under with the demise of the corporation as a patent office report shows they were still active as late as 1936. I had thought they were gone sooner. Building was used, after it was no longer a pottery, to refine beryllium, then burned in fall of 1955. No. 4 was filed for registration for copyright on January 2, 1917, claiming use since October 1, 1916 for use on semi-porcelain dinner sets and toilet sets manufactured from domestic and imported kaolin or china clays and producing a semivitreous white body to which a white translucent glaze is applied, producing clear white ware for table service or use. Consisting of regular line of plates, cups, saucers and kindred articles of dinner service. No. 6 from

a patent office registration granted June 23, 1936, claiming use since 1932, for use in semi-porcelain dinnerware. (Information: Lehner, *Ohio Pottery and Glass*, p. 27, Marks: nos. 1, 2, 3 and 5 from dishes.)

1.   2.

3.

4.

5.   6.

Carson Pirie Scott and Company. Chicago, Illinois. A large department store. Filed for rights to mark no. 1 on July 3, 1943, claiming use since February 1, 1943; filed on mark no. 2 on October 26, 1940, claiming use since October 1938; filed on mark no. 3 on April 9, 1937, claiming use since March 1937, for use on table chinaware, breakfast, luncheon and dinner dishes of china and porcelain. Mark no. 1 included bakers, nappies, salad bowls, casseroles, platters, plates, fruit dishes, cereal dishes, soup cups, pickle dishes, sauce boats, sugars, creamers, teapots, coffeepots, cups and saucers. In the *Crockery and Glass Journal*, August, 1944, p. 37 in little newsnotes about various companies, Carson Pirie Scott was selling Paden City Pottery's "Della Robia" and "Morning Glory" dinnerware.

Plantation Rose

1.

2.

MONTICELLO

3.

Carteret China Company. See Cardinal China Company.

Cartwright Brothers. East Liverpool, Ohio. There were Cartwrights in the pottery business in East Liverpool from 1864 until 1924. The early Cartwrights made Rockingham, yellowware and creamware. In 1880, the name became **Cartwright Brothers** and continued under that name until operations were suspended in 1924. Cartwright Brothers made white granite and semi-porcelain. They started making Tea Leaf pattern in 1881. The *1902-1903 Complete Directory* lists the Cartwright Brothers as making white granite, common china dinner sets, short sets of odd dishes and jardinieres, some decorated. They were the makers of the Garfield Drape plates in mottled blue and light green glaze copied from a pressed ware pattern according to Ramsay. (Information: Lehner, *American Kitchen and Dinner Wares*, p. 40; John

Ramsay, "American Majolica," *Hobbies Magazine*, May 1945, p. 45; Jeanette Ray, "Story of Tea Leaf Ironstone," *Antiques Reporter*, November 1973, p. 16. Marks: nos. 1-5, Barber, *Marks of American Potters*, p. 112; no. 6, on ironstone dish.)

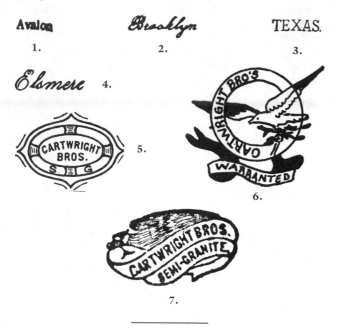

1. Avalon
2. *Brooklyn*
3. TEXAS.
4. *Elsmere*
5. CARTWRIGHT BROS. S.E.G.
6. CARTWRIGHT BRO'S WARRANTED
7. CARTWRIGHT BROS. SEMI-GRANITE

Castle, Nancy Jurs. Scottsville, New York. 1962 to present (1985). Studio potter, making raku and porcelain into unique one of a kind pieces. Nancy's earliest mark was simply her first name as in mark 1. Jurs was added to the inscribed mark in late 1960 and all of the 1970's. 1983 was the first year she has used the complete name as shown in mark 3.

1.

2.

3.

Catalina Marks. Used by two companies, Catalina Pottery and Gladding, McBean and Company. (See the listing for Gladding, McBean and Company.) In 1927, the Catalina Pottery was started on Santa Catalina Island to make clay building products. Around 1930 decorative and functional or utilitarian type pottery was added to the line. Between 1931 and 1937, the company made a full line of color-glazed dishes in whiteware and brownware. In 1937, the plant was sold to Gladding, McBean and Company at which time the pottery was made only on the mainland and the island plant closed. Gladding, McBean and Company continued some of the Catalina lines and used the Catalina trademark until 1947, at which time the ownership of the trademark returned to the Catalina Island Company as was originally agreed. Besides decorative pieces, a large amount of dinnerware was made under the name of Catalina, including plates, cups, coffee servers, saucers, mugs, tumblers, casseroles, pitchers, servers, relish and vegetable dishes, etc., in bright solid colors with fine glazes in bright and dark blue, reddish orange, yellow, green, etc. (Marks: the early marks before 1937 involve the words, Catalina and Catalina Island. Nos. 1-10 are early marks and are incised or stamped or imprinted and are taken from the book by A.W. Fridley, *Catalina Pottery The Early Years*, 1927-1937, Costa Mesa, California: 1977. Nos. 11, 12 and 14 to 24 are marks used after 1937, sent by Interpace Corporation, formerly Gladding, McBean and Company. Nos. 11, 12 are printed with ink and used from 1937 to 1942. No. 13 is a copy of the "Rancho" mark sent by a reader. Nos. 14, 15, 16 are impressions made with a pointed tool by Gladding, McBean and Company. Nos. 17, 18 are backstamps printed with ink 1937 to 1942. Nos. 19, 20, 21 are impressions made in case molds. There was a cactus holder in the form of a cat imprinted with "Lina," on the side. Nos. 22. 23, also impressions, made around 1937. No. 24 was a paper label used by Gladding, McBean and Company. Nos. 14 to 16 are the marks most apt to give the collector's a problem, because "Catalina" and "Catalina Island" are generally associated with the Catalina Island Pottery, but the marks shown were sent to me by Fanciscan Interpace around 1976, and were used by Gladding, McBean and Company.)

Catalina Ware, Made By Gladding, McBean and Company

Line or Pattern	Active Period
Angeleno Art Ware	1942-1942
Aurora Art Ware	1937-1942
Avalon Art Ware	1937-1942
Avalon Table Ware	1937-1938
Catalina Art Ware	1937-1941
Duotone Table Ware	1940-1942
Floral Art Ware	1940-1942
Montebello Art Ware	1940-1942
Nautical Art Wre	1939-1942
Ox Blood Art Wre	1938-1942
Rancho Table Ware	1937-1941
Reseda Art Ware	1940-1942
Saguare Art Ware	1940-1942
Terra Cotta Specials	1937-1940

1. CATALINA ISLAND REG. U.S. PAT OFF.
2. CATALINA ISLAND
3. CATALINA ISLAND (PAPER STICKER)
4. CATALINA

Catalina

5.

CATALINA
REG. US.
PAT. OFf

6.

CATALINA

7.

Catalina

8.

Catalina
Island

9.

CATALINA
ISLAND

10.

CATALINA
MADE IN
U. S. A.
POTTERY

11.

CATALINA
REG. U.S.
PAT. OFF.
RANCHO

12.

CATALINA
REG. U.S.
PAT. OFF
RANCHO

13.

Catalina
Island

14.

CATALINA

15.

Catalina

16.

CATALINA
MADE IN
U. S. A.
POTTERY

17.

CATALINA
MADE IN
U.S.A.
POTTERY

18.

CATALINA
C 60 N

19.

CATALINA

20.

CATALINA
ISLAND
624

21.

CATALINA

22.

RANCHO

CATALINA
RANCHO

CATALINA
C 806
POTTERY

23.

24.

Cauter Porcelain Company. New York, New York. Miss E. Cauter and Miss B. Cauter were listed in the 1946 *Crockery and Glass Journal Directory*, as manufacturers of hand modeled and decorated porcelain figurines. This was the only listing I had for this company, but a full page advertisement in the same directory showed eighteenth century figures of fanciful dressed ladies and men. The ad also stated the factory and showroom were at 245 Grand Street. The West coast representative was a Clarence Bauman in Brack Shops building in Los Angeles.

Cavendish Trading Corporation. New York, New York. A selling agency filed for registration on these marks in November, 1944 to be used on tableware (a full service including sugars and creamers, etc.) baking dishes etc. made from porcelain or chinaware, claiming use of this mark since June 1, 1935.

White Beauty
CAVENCREST

Celestial China Corporation. San Diego, California. Company filed for registration of this mark on February 18, 1960, for use on china dinnerware, claiming use of the mark since June 1, 1959.

CELESTIAL

Cemar Clay Products Company. Los Angeles, California. They were found listed from 1945 through 1957 in the directories I had. They were listed in the 1948 China and Glass Red Book Directory for artware and figures and solid color dinnerware. According to Lucile Henzke, by letter, they produced a line of art deco figurines and animal figurals in quaint form. She said they made a line of dinnerware with strawberries, apples, etc. Jesse Abrams was the distributor in New York City for Cemar Clay Products Company. In the *Crockery and Glass Journal Magazine*, August 1950, p. 52, in an advertisement is pictured a full service line of ware shaped like pineapples, cups, plates, cookie jar, sugar, creamer, etc. in moss green and lime. (Mark: sent by letter by Lucile Hanzke.)

cemar

Century Service Corporation. Alliance, Ohio. A distributor associated with Cunningham and Pickett. See Cunningham and Pickett for history. (Marks: on dishes.)

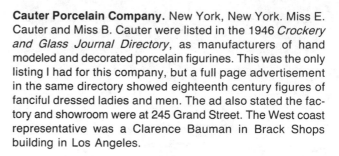

Ceramic Art Association. Los Angeles, California. Filed for registration of this mark on Novebmer 5, 1912, claiming use since March 1912, for vases of earthenware and pottery.

DECA'S CERAMIC

Ceramic Arts Studio. Madison, Wisconsin. Started January 1941. In business until 1955. Lawrence Rabbett and Ruben Sand planned to make wheel thrown products, vases, etc. from Wisconsin clay. However, need created by W.W. II led them into making a fine grade of expensive molded figurines in original designs. These sold for $9.00 in 1944 through jewelry stores, etc. When imports resumed after the war Sand closed the pottery around 1955 and retired. (Information: Chester Davis, "Ceramic Arts Studio of Madison, Wisconsin," *Spinning Wheel*, January-February 1975, p. 59. Marks: all from Quality Stamp Company.)

CERAMIC ARTS
STUDIO

ARABESQUE

Ceramic Manufacturing Company. Calabasas, California. See under Southern California Ceramic Company.

Ceramic Originals. Laguna Beach, California. 1944 to 1955. In a staff written article, "Artware Pottery Gossip from Southern California," *Crockery and Glass Journal* magazine, December 1944, p. 69, is the following account of this company:

"One of the newest pottery companies destined for a bright future in the giftware market, is the recently formed Ceramic Originals of Laguna Beach. The two owners, Russell Leidy, and Cloyd Leland Freeman, are well known to the gift an artware trade. Leidy was formerly associated with Dick Knox, when their concern was kown as the **Knox Leidy Company**. His work in the ceramic field has endowed him with a valuable background for his new business venture. Freeman has gained recognition on two separate counts. His mural decorations grace the walls of many of the finer ballrooms and hotels in the San Joaquin Valley as well as other fine structures in Northern California. He is noted also for creating unique window display ideas which he sold to Barker Brothers over a period of years.

Modern adaptations of beautiful antique candy boxes, jars and objects of art, as well as modern pieces such as Russell Leidi's circus horses and circus wagon, are rapidly creating recognition for Ceramic Originals." (Mark: from Jenny Derwich.)

FReeman - Leidy
Laguna Beach, CaL.

Chadwick China Company. Trenton, New Jersey. This pottery was only listed in the *Trenton City Directories* for one year, 1946, at 1150 Southard Street. In the 1945 and 1946 *Crockery and Glass Journal Directory*, Howard Kiehl was general manager. A selling agency named Jess Abrams with branches in Lose Angeles, San Francisco, Dallas and New York, advertised Chadwick China as a distinguished line of fine American china. The directories listed china earthenware, art pottery, figures and figurines and miniatures for Chadwick China Company. Abrams represented Coventry Ware, West Coast Porcelain and Chadwick China. Jess Abrams was listed through middle 1950's, but not in 1960's. (Mark: 1946 directory as cited.)

Chambers Street Pottery, Ltd. New York City. 1979 to present (1985). Studio potters, Jo Ann Meehan and Jerry Ospa are co-owners of the Chambers Street Pottery. They make high fired stoneware and reduction fired to cone 10, into decorative and one of a kind pieces for wholesale and retail trade. The pieces are wheel thrown and hand built. The work of three other potters is represented at the Chambers Street Pottery. Michael Bayer who signs his work with his full name; Michael Kasdan who signs his work "Kasdan;" and Pat Saab who signs her work "Saab" or with an "S." The last three make stoneware and porcelain pieces. Jo Ann Meehan has had a varied work and educational experience. She was a class and studio manager at the Baldwin Pottery in 1976 and 1977 and had her work on exhibit there in 1976 and 1977. She has taught classes for teachers in New York City and also taught at the Community Center Ceramics Workshop. Her work may be seen at Vitti Artisan's Gallery, Upper Montclair, New Jersey; Salarry in New York City; Crafty Fox, Nyack, New York; Margal Gallery, New York City, etc. Jerry Ospa received a B.A. from the Hunter College of the City University of New York in 1975. He was given a scholarship to attend the Brooklyn Museum School of Art in Brooklyn, in 1967. He has taught at Apple Skills Exchange and the Studio Workshop on 18th Street, both in New York City. He listed many group shows in which he has participated.

M   Meehan

Jo Ann Meehan

A.B. Chance Company. Parkersburg, West Virginia. In 1956, A.B. Chance Company acquired the two plants of the Porcelain Products, Inc., in Carey, Ohio, and Parkersburg, West Virginia. Insulators were made in both plants. For types of insulators and processes used in making, see Jack Tod, *Porcelain Insulators Guide Book for Collectors*, p. 114, and *A History of Electrical Porcelain*, p. 92. Also, see the listing in this book for the Porcelain Products, Inc. Chance continued the "P.P." marking at Parkersburg until late 1958, but used the "Chance" marking thereafter. In 1959, the wet process operation at Parkersburg plant became an operating division of Chance, and the dry process operation at Carey, Ohio, was sold to the Clarken Company, St. Louis, Missouri. The Carey plant operated as "Porcelain Products Company," and they used on porcelain the markings of a rectangle with "P.P" and a rectangle with "P.P./CO." In 1975, Porcelain Products Company bought out Knox Porcelain Company, Knoxville, Tennessee. Thereafter, insulators made at both Carey and Knoxville were marked with both the "P.P." and "Knox" markings. Tod dated the marks as follows: no. 2, 1958; no. 3, 1963; no. 4, 1967; no. 5 1967 and later. (Information and marks: Tod, as cited, and by letter.)

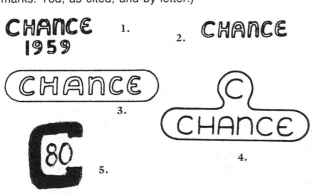

Chandler, Thomas M. Edgefield, South Carolina. Started around 1838. In 1850, he employed eleven workmen and he advertised his jugs marked "Chandler Maker, Warranted." He made stoneware. Thomas died in 1854. (Information and marks: staff written, *Early Decorated Stoneware of the Edgefield District, South Carolina*, p. 8.)

CHANDLER
MAKER

Chapman, Josiah. Troy, New York. He was in Troy as early as 1799. On February 15, 1803, an ad was in the *Troy Gazette* for his "Stone Ware, manufactured in Troy." On December 31, 1979, an article in the *Northern Budget* said the firm of "Chapman and Taylor" is dissolved. (It is possible they were distributors.) Chapman was listed as a "potter" on 1806 Town of Troy Jury List, and also in "Kiln Tile" which appeared in the 1811 Troy Budget. He was a Quaker and active in the

formation of the Troy Monthly Meeting shortly after 1800. The business was sold to Israel Seymour around 1818 to 1819. His second wife, Ann, moved to Wrighstown, Pennsylvania, in 1817, and he followed a year or two later. He died at Frankford, Pennsylvania, in May 1826. In 1828, Ann deeded her right to property in Troy to Israel Seymour. (Information: Warren F. Broderick, writer, researcher and collector. Mark: impressed; Stradling, p. 132.)

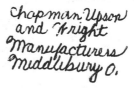

Chapman, Upson and Wright. Middlebury (Akron), Ohio. Stoneware potter who worked around the middle of the nineteenth century. Robert Treichler, who is currently researching the potters of this area has photographed a piece with an eagle in slip decoration from this pottery.

Chapman Upson
and Wright
Manufacturers
Middlebury O.

Charleton Decorating Company. New York, New York. Decorators, filed for a claim on mark 1 on December 9, 1947, for use on chinaware such as dinnerware, tea sets, vases, boxes, flower pots, cake plates, coffee pots, etc., claiming use since December 4, 1941. Mark 2 is a copy of a gold paper label sent by Annise Heaivilin, author of *Grandma's Tea Leaf*, found on a decorated plate. The A.W. Company would be for the distributor Abels, Wasserberg and Company, Inc. for which Charleton decorated the plate. In the 1948 *China and Glass Red Book Directory* was an advertisement by Abels, Wasserberg and Company, Inc., New York, New York, for "Charleton" decorated china and glass, both imported and domestic.

Charleton
1.

2.

Chase, L. and B.G. Somerset, Massachusetts. Around 1850. Impressed mark. Ramsay, p. 187 lists Phineas Chase around 1850 at Amesbury, Massachusetts, making redware. (Information and mark: Thorn, p. 122.)

L. & B.G. CHA.
SOMERSET

Chatham Potters, Inc. Chatham, New Jersey, later, in Oswego, Kansas. 1941 to December 1984. Started in 1941 by Frank and Margie Goss in Chatham, New Jersey. In 1964, they incorporated under the name of Chatham Potters, Inc. and the company continued to grow because of the high quality product it manufactured. In 1965, Costas Kalogirou, who came from Greece, where his family had been potters for four generations, was appointed manager of the plant in New Jersey, at which time new shapes and designs were introduced. In 1967, Kalogirou purchased the company. The search for room to expand and a better supply of gas caused the company to relocate in Oswego, Kansas, in June 1976, with sales offices in Chatham, New Jersey, and in Oswego, at the factory site. Chatham Potters made a very fine grade of stoneware high-fired at a temperature of 2,300 degrees for superior strength. The dinnerware was handcrafted by hand painting and each piece bears the artist's signature. The pottery closed in December 1984. The "C.P." mark shown was filed for registration March 22, 1966, claiming use since May 1, 1966, for use on handcrafted stoneware, mugs, pitchers, casseroles, dinnerware, etc. (See Lehner, *American Kitchen and Dinner Wares*, pp. 41, 42, for pattern information.)

CHATHAM
POTTERS, INC.

Cheesequake, Various Potters. South Amboy, Middlesex County, New Jersey. The Cheesequake Creek was near or in the town of Madison, New Jersey which was a part of South Amboy until 1869. Along this creek, a number of small potteries were built. Joshua Warne lived 1740-1814. His son, Thomas Warne was born 1763 and in 1814 the son of Thomas by the name of James Morgan Warne was appointed administrator of Thomas's estate. In the neighborhood another piece of property was owned by a Joshua Letts prior to 1816 when he deeded it to James Morgan. Joshua Letts married Melody Morgan Warne. The "T.W.J.L." mark probably stands for Thomas Warne and Joshua Letts, and Warne and Letts in the marks would be these two men. Ramsay, p. 180 dates Warne and Letts firm around 1778 to around 1820. All any of the writers have to go on, on these potters are a few marriage records and quite a few marked jugs. (Information: Robert J. Sim and Arthur W. Clement, "The Cheesequake Potteries," Stradling book, pp. 119-122. Marks: nos. 1, 2 and 9, Thorn, pp. 152, 134; nos. 3-8, Stradling, pp. 107, 201, 121.)

J. L.

1.

WARNE & LETTs
S. AMBOY
N. JERSEY

2.

T·W·J·L

3.

WARNE ∨ LETTs 1806
S·AMBOY·N·JERSY

4.

 LIBERTY FORE V
WARNE & LETTs 1807
S·AMBOY·N·JERSY

5.

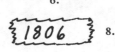 LIBERTY·FOR·EV
6.

 1806
8.

S. AMBOY N. JERSEY
WARNE
7.

9. MADE· BY·J·LETTS

Chelsea China Company. New Cumberland, West Virginia. W.P. Jervis in "A Dictionary of Pottery Terms," *Pottery, Glass and Brass Salesmen*, p. 99, dates this company from 1888-1896. This short lived company made white granite ware, according to Barber, *Marks of American Potters*, p. 153, and he shows these two marks.

CHINA   WHITE GRANITE

Chelsea Keramic Art Works. Chelsea, Massachusetts. James Robertson arrived from Scotland in 1853 and with Nathaniel Plymptom he started the **Plympton and Robertson Pottery** on Condor Street in East Boston, not too long after his arrival in this country. In 1866 his son, Alexander, started a pottery on the corner of Willow and Marginal streets in Chelsea. In 1867, Hugh, brother to Alexander, came to work with him and they operated as A.W. and H.C. Robertson and they began to make glazed artware, copying early Greek, Roman and Egyptian vases in red bisque with black decorations and modeled decorations in relief. They also made Chelsea faience. The father, James, left Plympton in 1872 and came to work with his sons in Chelsea. In 1878, they received first place at the Massachusetts Charitable Mechanics Association under the name **James Robertson and Sons** with the firm name of **Chelsea Keramic Art Works**. Decorative tile were made under the supervision of James and designed by John G. Low, who later started Low Art Tile Works in Chelsea. James died in 1880 and Alexander went to California. Hugh began experiments on an apple green glaze. He went on to discover the process for making crackleware. Hugh was forced to close in 1889 even though his shelves were filled with beautiful example of his efforts because there was no market for them. In 1891, a group from Boston raised the money to reopen the pottery with Hugh as manager and the name was **Chelsea Pottery**. Chelsea was located in too damp a climate to make the beautiful crackleware, so the pottery was moved in 1894 to Dedham, Massachusetts and in 1895 production began again. See the Dedham Pottery listing for more. (Information: J. Milton Robertson (grandson of Hugh), "The Background of Dedham Pottery," *Bulletin of American Ceramic Society*, Volume 20, no. 11, 1941, pp. 411-413. Marks: nos. 1-3, Barber, *Marks of American Potters*, p. 97; nos. 4-5, Evans, p. 51; decorator marks A, B, C, D, E, also Evans, p. 51. Marks impressed; decorator marks incised.)

CHELSEA KERAMIC
ART WORKS
ROBERTSON & SONS.

1.

2.

3.

CHELSEA KERAMIC ART WORKS
ROBERTSON & SONS.

4.

5.

	A.	Hugh C. Robertson
	B.	Josephine Day
	C.	G.W. Fenety
	D.	Franz Dengler
	E.	Alexander W. Robertson

Chelsea Lamp and Shade Company. New York, New York with branch offices in Dallas, Texas and Chicago, Illinois. The name of this company is misleading. In the 1945 and 1946 *Crockery and Glass Journal Directories* they were listed for much more than lamps and lamp shades. In both directories they were listed as manufacturers of art pottery with a china body, earthenware figures, figurines and miniatures. Actually, I believe them to be decorators of their products. In 1945 they had glass novelties listed also. In the material copied at Quality Stamp Company of East Liverpool, Ohio were rubber stamps, used to apply decorations, made there for this company, and the mark shown which may have been used as a paper label. The company was not listed in the 1952 directory.

CHELSEA
Lamp & Shade Co.
NEW YORK, N.Y.

Chemical Gardens, Inc. New York, New York. Filed for registration of this mark on August 26, 1940, claiming use since March 1, 1940, for use on pottery flower pots.

CHEMI-GARDEN

Cherokee China Comany. Jonesboro, Tennessee. This pottery was listed in the *Crockery and Glass Journal Directories* and the *China and Glass Red Book Directories* from 1948 through 1954. The closest directories I had to these dates were 1946 and 1961 and the company was not listed in either. They were listed for florists ware, dinnerware, tea sets and artware of earthenware. (Mark: was ink stamped on a hand-painted little cream pitcher.)

CHEROKEE CHINA CO.
JONESBORO, TENN.
HAND PAINTED

Cherokee Pottery/Cherokee Nation Pottery, Inc. Porum and Tahlequah, Oklahoma. A Cherokee Pottery was still being maintained in Porum in 1983, but a new building was being built at Tahlequah. The pottery is sold at the Tsa-la-gi Inn, which is a part of a tribal business and industrial facility in Tahlequah, Oklahoma. In 1978, $7.5 million dollars was earmarked by the Cherokee Nation for industrial development and $5 million went into this huge complex with all sorts of industry. The pottery has the word, "Cherokee," printed on the bottom. Other Cherokee potter's products are sold at the Tsa-la-gi Inn, such as Grace Thorpe (see that listing), Jess Vana and Mike Daniel. When the new pottery building was built in the industrial complex, the name became Cherokee Nation Pottery, Inc. This operation in Tahlequah, was to operate under a management contract with Haeger Pottery of Dundee, Illinois. The new pottery was sponsored by the Bureau of Indian Affairs, the Creek Nation's Council, the local Industrial Committee and the Frankoma Pottery of Sapula, Oklahoma. In 1971, David Greer, a Cherokee Indian designed "Sequoyah," the first issue of plates with a border of the Cherokee alphabet of eighty-six letters. (Mark: shown on pottery made at Porum.)

Chesapeake Pottery/D.F. Haynes and Son Company. Baltimore, Maryland. Pottery was started at the corner of Nicholson and Decatur streets in Baltimore, Maryland, in 1880 by Henry and Isaac Brougham and John Tunstall. In 1882, D.F. Haynes and Company purchased the Chesapeake Pottery. In 1879, **D.F. Haynes and Company** were jobbers located at 347 West Baltimore Street in Baltimore, Maryland. After enthusiastic expansion, the Chesapeake Pottery experienced some financial difficulties and was put up for sale in 1887 and purchased by Edwin Bennett. Edwin Bennett already owned one pottery at Canton and Central Avenues. (See Bennett Pottery Company.) So just a few years later, Bennett sold the Chesapeake Pottery to his son, E. Huston Bennett and David F. Haynes, then the name became **Haynes, Bennett and Company**. E. Huston Bennett retired in 1895 and his interest was purchased by Frank R. Haynes son of D.F. Haynes, and the firm became **D.F. Haynes and Son** in 1896. When David died in 1908, his son Frank assumed complete control. In 1914, the American Sugar Refining Company purchased the property and the pottery business was discontinued at the Chesapeake Pottery site. The Maryland Queensware Factory also made pottery for D.F. Haynes. (See Maryland Pottery Company.) In a *1902-1903 Complete Directory*, D.F. Haynes was listed as making semi-porcelain toilet sets, odd sets of dishes, jardinieres and novelties. Ramsay listed them as making Majolica between 1881 and 1890 and Parian after 1895, then some white granite and semiporcelain. Barber said a product belonging to the Majolica family was marked "Clifton." He also describes "Avalon" with a fine body, ivory tint, and soft rich glaze ornamented with sprays of flowers in relief. "Calvertine" was similar to Avalon but decorated differently, turned on a lathe with spaces for bands, over which were laid relief ornaments. Other products made at the Chesapeake Pottery were jugs, plates, cups, lamps, vases, clocks, etc., and much that would be considered artware. "Severn" ware made around 1885 had a fine vitreous body of a subtle grayish-olive tint. There are many pieces of this pottery pictured in the Barber book. From about 1887 to 1890, or perhaps a little later according to Barber, three intertwining circles were used to indicate the shapes of dinner services made at Chesapeake Pottery, such as the "Arundel" shape. The letters C.C.P. stood for Chesapeake Pottery and H.B.H. for Haynes and Bennett. These marks were printed on the glaze in the same colors as the overglaze decorations. The "Avalon" mark was used on toilet wares and may have been used on other wares, too, according to Barber. (Nancy Fitzpatrick, "The Chesapeake Pottery Company," *Spinning Wheel*, September, 1957, p. 14; also Barber's *Pottery and Porcelain of the U.S.*, p. 323. Lehner, *American Kitchen and Dinner Wares*, p. 42. Marks: The first eight marks are from Barber, *Marks of American Potters*, p. 148, and were used before 1900. After 1900, the Haynes marks were adopted which are nos. 9, 10, 11. No. 9 is Barber, p. 149. Nos. 10, 11 were sent by Darlene Tates.)

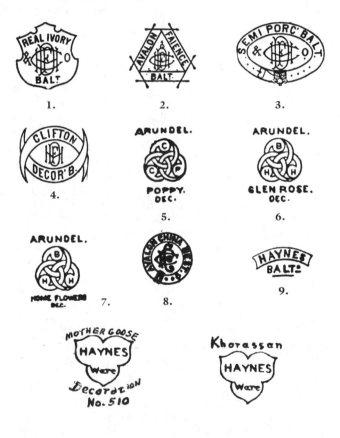

1.
2.
3.
4.
ARUNDEL. POPPY. DEC. 5.
ARUNDEL. GLEN ROSE. DEC. 6.
ARUNDEL. HOME FLOWERS DEC. 7.
8.
HAYNES BALT? 9.
MOTHER GOOSE HAYNES Ware Decoration No. 510
Khorassan HAYNES Ware

Chesnutt, Corinne. Muskogee, Oklahoma. Filed for rights to this mark April 27, 1948, to be used on pottery, namely dishes, cups, powder puff containers, vases, pitchers, claiming use since January 6, 1948.

Chester Pottery. Phoenixville, Pennsylvania. See Phoenixville Pottery for history. Barber, *Marks of American Potters*, p. 31, said these marks were used between 1895 and 1899.

Chicago Crucible Company. Chicago, Illinois. In 1920, the Chicago Crucible Company was acquired by the Northwestern Terra Cotta Company. (See that listing.) In between making architectural terra cotta, some decorative pottery was manufactured. The pieces were bulbous vases, wall plaques, frogs, ashtrays and lamp bases with speckled and blue or yellow-green glazes. The line was phased out after a few years. Information and raised in mold mark: Sharon S. Darling, *Chicago Ceramics and Glass*, pp. 70, 71.)

CHICAGO CRUCIBLE — CO — CHICAGO, ILL

CHICAGO CRUCIBLE CO. CHICAGO, ILL

Chicago Terra Cotta Works (or Company). Chicago, Illinois. 1868 to 1879. Company made terra cotta pieces for architectural purposes such as window caps, cornices, trim and tile, also statues, urn, fountains and vases. For a complete history of this company see Sharon S. Darling, *Chicago Ceramics and Glass*, pp. 162 to 167. (Information and mark: Darling, as cited.)

CHICAGO TERRA COTTA WORKS 1876

Chic Pottery. Wellsville and Zanesville, Ohio. Information on this pottery is very scarce. The pottery started in the late 1930's and operated until the middle 1950's. For several years the pottery was located in Wellsville, Ohio. In January 1943 and January 1944 advertisements in the *Crockery and Glass Journal* magazine, the Chic Pottery Company was said to be in Wellsville, Ohio. Then either a plant or an office was established in Zanesville by December 1947 because the

Crockery and Glass Journal that month gave Zanesville as an address. The first listing I had in the *Zanesville City Directories* for Chic Pottery as a manufacturer was in 1940. But very often it takes the directories a year to pick up on the existance or non-existance of a business. The last listing in the directories was 1954. This gives approximate dates and places for Chic Pottery. There is a variety of small decorative items being found with the marks shown. There was patent granted to Dana K. Harvey doing business as Chic Pottery Company in Wellsville, Ohio. The application was made October 25, 1943, for an ornamental savings bank designed by Hugh Garee. Many of their items had gold trim. Some of the pieces shown in the advertisements cited were spotted hound dogs in all sorts of positions, a spotted giraffe, a cow creamer which came in six assorted colors, etc. Art Wagner worked at Chic Pottery at one time. (See that listing.) (Marks: from pieces, and Quality Stamp Company, East Liverpool, Ohio.)

Children's Television Workshop. New York, New York. Filed for registration of this mark on November 9, 1981, claiming first use since August 1979, for use on dinnerware and kitchenware, such as plates, bowls, tumblers, mugs, cake molds, cake pans, cookie jars, cookie cutters and stampers, lap trays and serving trays.

China Bull. Liberty, Missouri. Paul McNeely graduated from Kansas City Art Institute in 1955. He is a painter, ceramist and sculpter. He first designed stained glass windows and developed a new medium in stained glass, called "Imprisoned Glass." Paul received the Allied Arts Award given by American Institute of Architects for a stained glass window he made. Around 1970, he decided to make a career out of making miniatures which had always been his first love in the art field. His first business name was **Bespoke Miniatures** at which time he started a how to do it magazine for the trade entitled *Miniature Forum*. In April 1979, to present (1983) McNeely switched entirely to ceramic miniatures under the name The China Bull. Since that time he has made 1,000 tiny molds and sold over 8,000 pieces. Paul stated he hadn't "used enough clay in the past four years to throw one big

healthy pot." He has created beautiful artistic highly decorative tiny ceramic pieces that even experts have told him they could never be made. Six months after he started making the ceramic pieces he won several awards in the Kansas City Ceramic Show in professional competition. In 1981, he received three awards for best in the category entered, three firsts, three seconds and one third. Some of the pieces include: toby mugs and pitchers, a forty-two piece set of "Tea Leaf," Victorian pitchers, Blue Willow pattern dishes, a nativity scene with thirteen figures, chocolate set, fish set, game bird set, duck set, berry set, Meissen arbors and figurines, all in miniature. In 1983, he is scaling ½ inch to one foot. And each tiny piece goes through exactly the same step in the making as a large piece of porcelain. (Information and marks: furnished by Paul McNeely. The marks are sometimes embossed in the mold or scratched onto the greenware. Some are painted with gold or a color used on the piece. Dates are not always added. The full name was used with a date on larger pieces. Each year the identification will be treated differently.)

1979

1980

1981

1982

1983

China Craft Inc. Sebring, Ohio. Started during W.W. II and closed around 1978. This pottery employed around twenty to twenty-five people in the 1940's and 1950's making novelties, lamps, vases, etc. I found a good grade of semi-porcelain little vase decorated with decales and gold trim. A very late product was a highly vitrified, heavily glazed stoneware planter dish with mark no. 1 impressed. (No. 1, 2, 5, on vases No. 3, 4 from Quality Stamp Company, East Liverpool.)

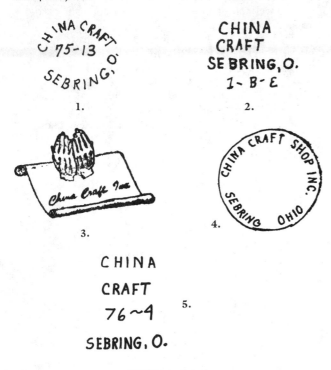

China and Glass Decorators. 158 W. Long Avenue, DuBois, Pennsylvania. Decorators listed in the late 1950's and early 1960's. Marks obtained at Quality Stamp Company, East Liverpool, Ohio.

LIBERTY CHINA
DuBOIS, PA.
MADE IN U S. A.
Alabama Pattern

LAURENTIAN CHINA
DuBOIS. PA.
MADE IN USA

China and Glass Distributors, Inc. New York, New York, distributors who became known by their "Charm House" marks, filed for a claim on mark no. 1 shown in the 1940's, for use on chinaware, pottery, crockery and porcelain pieces such as tea pots, sugar bowls, creamers, pitchers, relish trays, vases, compartment plates and jugs, claiming use of mark since December 30, 1946. Mark no. 2 is the actual mark that was used, obtained at Quality Stamp Company. No. 3 is a mark filed July 17, 1947, for use on chinaware, potter, crockery, porcelains, cookie jars, salt shakers, pepper shakers, sugar bowls, creamers, icebox sets, bean pots, teapots and pitchers, claiming use since February 26, 1947. Marks nos. 4, 5 and 6 from Qualty Stamp Company. No. 7,

1957 *China, Glass and Tableware Directory*. Other brand names were the "Tomatoe Line," "Hospitality," and "Pot of Gold Teaware." Glass brand names included, "Crown Jewell," "Jewell Crystal," and "Parti Aide." All listed in 1948 *China and Glass Red Book Directory*. "Parti Aide" was a mark on glass. Stanford Pottery made "Pantry Parade" in 1949.

Chittenango Pottery Company. Chittenango, New York. 1897 to around 1901. They started in 1897 to make white granite and only lasted a short time due to disastrous fires. They were still in business in 1901 because Barber said they furnished china for the Buffalo Exhibition. Then in the *1902-1903 Complete Directory* the only pottery listed in Chittenango was the Athison Pottery Company making china dinner sets and short sets of odd dishes. W.P. Jervis in "Chittenango Pottery Company," in "A Dictionary of Pottery Terms" in *Pottery, Glass and Brass Salesman*, December 13, 1917, p. 99, said the pottery was established to manufacture porcelain, but was abandoned after the fire and the works were converted to the manufacture of terra-cotta. (Information and marks: Barber, *Marks of American Potters*, p. 86.)

C.P.Co.
CHITTENANGO,N.Y.
CHINA

Chollar and Various Associations. Cortland, New York. **Thomas O. Chollar**, 1832-1842, making redware and stoneware, followed by **Chollar and Bennet**, 1842-1844, then **Chollar and Darby**, 1844-1849. In Thorn, p. 131, the mark no. 1 showed the name Bennet first as is shown. Ramsay, p. 258, describes the same mark with Chollar's name first. Robert D. Grant, "Collecting 19th Century Stoneware," *Mid American Reporter*, June 1972, p. 8, tells about a Thomas D. Chollar, 1844-1849 who produced dark gray crockery by scorching it in the kiln. The Everson Museum of Art in Syracuse has a jug marked "Thomas D. Chollar, Cortland."

BENNET & CHOLLAR   CHOLLAR & DARBY

HOMER   HOMER, N.Y.

Chrisshaun Art. Roseville, Ohio. 1984 to present (1986). Owner and potter, Bud Hoadley, makes art pottery with painted and carved designs in action scenes, such as Custer's last stand, nautical and Indian scenes. Hoadley has been an artist since childhood, but didn't work with pottery until 1984. His sister is the mother of the well known potter-artist, Rick Wisecarver (see that listing). Another sister of Hoadley's, Florence Moore of Sanford, Florida, also makes and sells hand painted pottery pieces. This is an extremely talented family.

Chrisshaun Art Pottery Roseville O.

Bud Hoadley

Christianson Pottery. Lindstrom, Minnesota. 1977 to present. Linda Christianson, studio potter, makes functional stoneware, salt glazed and wood fired. She studied at Hamline University, St. Paul, Minnesota and Banff Centre, School of Art, Alberta, Canada.

Christ, Rudolf. Bethabara and Salem, North Carolina. 1766-1821. Christ was one of several outstanding Moravian potters. The Moravians were a group of people who came from Pennsylvania and central Europe, to settle in North Carolina. They had a community life founded in religion. They constituted one of the first Protestant moves tracing their religion back to John Hus, who was burned at the stake in 1415. (For a better understanding, see the introduction to *The Moravian Potters in North Carolina*, by John Bivins, Jr., published by University of North Carolina Press: Chapel Hill, North Carolina, 1972.) Rudolf Christ worked as an apprentice to Gottfried Aust from around 1766 to 1773. He worked as master potter in Bethabara, from 1786 to 1789, and then as master potter in Salem, from 1789 to 1821. The pottery pieces were either thrown on a wheel or press molded, led glazed with copper green, or shades of light brown to black. White slip was used on the inside of hollow utility pieces, mugs, bowls, etc. The thrown pieces were thin and of fine quality earthenware. Some pieces were slip decorated with beautiful designs. (Information: John Bivins, Jr., in work cited, pp. 30-33, 77, 84, 85. Mark: same source, p. 153. Christ is mentioned off and on throughout the book. This is an outstanding book on a very interesting group of people and the potters who served them. Material is factual, well presented in a scholarly fashion with fine photos.)

R.C.
Bethabara
Jan. 6
1789

Cincinnati Art Pottery. Cincinnati, Ohio. 1879 to 1891. In 1879 a joint-stock company was organized under the title Cincinnati Art Pottery. When the pottery was formerly incorporated in 1880, T.J. Wheatley was one of the incorporators. He was associated with the venture until 1882. In fact the name Cincinnati Art Pottery was not used much until he left. From 1879 to 1882, the T.J. Wheatley name was mostly in use. Evans, p. 54, said this was an attempt to raise more funds for Wheatley's work in the underglaze Cincinnati faience development. This particular product was made only while Wheatley was with the Cincinnati Art Pottery. See the Dayton Street/Coultry Pottery listing for early history of T.J. Wheatley. Also, see the listings T.J. Wheatley Pottery and the Wheatley Pottery Company for more on him. Kezonta Ware was an Ivory colored faience made into vases and bowls, etc., and decorated with gold scroll work and colored flowers. Kezonta was produced until 1891. William Dell was foreman of the Cincinnati Art Pottery, and by 1887 he was superintendent and manager. After the Cincinnati Art Pottery closed, Dell formed his own pottery. (See that listing.) E.A. Barber, *Marks of American Potters*, p. 125, describes a variety of artistic ware such as underglaze faience, barbotine ware, "Hungarian," "Portland Blue," and "Ivory Colored Faience.". (Information: Paul Evans, *Art Pottery of the U.S.*, pp. 54, 55; E.A. Barber, *Pottery and Porcelain of the U.S.*, p. 300. Marks: E.A. Barber, *Marks of American Potters*, p. 125. No. 1 was used in 1886. He said a plain turtle mark was used before that time, but Evans, p. 55, said no examples of the mark have been found. No. 2 is an impressed mark used on plainer ware. No. 3 was used around 1890 to closing and the initials, "CAP Co.," was used according to Barber.)

KEZONTA

City Pottery. Trenton, New Jersey. Began in 1859 and ran under a succession of owners until sometime before 1900. Made white granite and cream-colored ware. They were not listed in the directories that I had, which started with 1900. The first owners were **Rhodes and Yates** in 1859, followed by **Yates and Titus** in 1865, then **Yates, Bennett and Allen** in 1871. (Information and marks: Barber, *Marks of American Potters*, p. 46.)

Clark, Nathan and Associates. Athens, New York. 1805 to 1900. These dates are from Janet R. Macfarlane, "Nathan Clark, Potter," Dianna and J. Garrison Stradling's book, *The Art of the Potter*, which is a reprint of articles from the *Antiques Magazine*, p. 129. She said that papers from the Greene County Court House such as invoices, broadsides, bills of lading and letters extend the dates this pottery had been thought to be in business. Nathan Clark also started potteries in Lyons, Mt. Morris and Rochester, New York, according to Macfarlane. This has caused confusion among the various writers in their attempts to date the various potteries, especially those in Lyons. See Lyons Pottery listing. The dates and various owners given in the Macfarlane article for potters in Athens, are as follows: Howe and Clark, 1805 to 1813; N. Clark, 1813 to 1829; Clark and Fox, 1829 to 1838; E.S. Fox, 1838 to 1843; N. Clark, Jr., 1843 to 1892; Athens Potery (1 "t"), 1892 to 1900. The owners name from 1892 to 1900 was Ryans. (Marks: Staff written, "Pre-Industrial Salt Glazed Ware," *Ceramics Monthly*, February 1980, p. 44; Ramsay, p. 187; Thorn, p. 123; Stradling, pp. 129, 132; Guilland, pp. 105, 138, 234; Stewart and Consentino, *Stoneware*, p. 59; *Old Bottle News*, August 1976, p. 47; also, Bill Grande, "N. Clark and Co., Rochester," *American Collector*, November 1980, p. 24.)

N. CLARK JR. ATHENS

N. CLARK & CO. LYONS

N.CLARK JR. ATHENS, N.Y.

NATHAN CLARK

NATHAN CLARK, LYONS

E.S. FOX ATHENS

N. CLARK ATHENS, N.Y.

N. CLARK ATHENS

CLARK & FOX ATHENS

HOWE & CLARK ATHENS

N. CLARK JR.

Clark Stoneware. Zanesville, Ohio. In 1894, the Clark Stoneware Company was listed as employing forty-three in the *Factory Inspection Reports for Ohio*. William E. Clark started the American Pottery Company in McLuney (near Crooksville) in 1898. This was a steam operated pottery listed as employing ten in 1902, to make stoneware. These were fairly shortlived potteries. Stamped mark on stoneware piece.

CLARK BROS
PAT MAY 1892
ZANESVILLE
O.

Clark, William and Company. Cannelton, Perry County, Indiana. Around 1872-1875. Manufactured stoneware. (Information and mark: staff written, "Indiana Earthenware and Stoneware," *Pottery Collectors' Newsletter*, September, Ocotber, 1979, p. 39).

MANUFACTURED
★ BY ★
Wm. CLARK & Co.
CANNELTON, INDIANA

Clay City Pottery, Inc. Clay City, Indiana. 1885 to present (1987). Beryl Griffith started the pottery in a log house behind the present pottery. Early pieces were handthrown. Pieces are now made by casting and jiggering. Clyde Griffith, son of Beryl, became the operator of the pottery in 1911 and in 1927 Lloyd, the son of Clyde came to work at the pottery. In 1938, Lloyd assumed management. Then in 1979, Lloyd turned the operation over to his daughter, Cheryl Griffith Baughn, the present owner-operator. Clyde rebuilt most of the buildings and added new ones. Lloyd installed electric motors to replace the old steam engine and boiler. He changed the coal fired kilns to gas and remodeled the buildings in the 1970's. Cheryl has improved and expanded the marketing facilities and changed the items made to fit demand. In the early years the pottery made crocks, churns, kraut jars, jugs, etc. Today they still manufacture a large amount of blue crocks using their old molds. Blue pitchers and soap dishes are made by special order. Garden ware is also made. In 1985, to celebrate their 100th birthday, the pottery made a pint jug with the names of five generations of Griffith potters and a quart blue bowl with the 100th anniversary inscription on the bottom. Most of the products are sold wholesale, but an outlet is maintained that sells pieces made at the pottery and pieces from other potteries as well. (Information: sent by company. Mark in the mold as it was sent by Cheryl Baughn.)

Clay City Pottery

CLAY CITY POTTERY
1885-1985
Cheryl Baughn
100TH
ANNIVERSARY

Clay County, Indiana, Various Potters. Before 1900 there were over eighty men who have been identified as potters in Clay County, Indiana. Very often there were several potters from one family. For instance, four named Torbert and four different Kelseys. But in Melvin Davies, *Clay County Indiana Traditioanl Potters and Their Wares*, a catalogue to accompany an exhibition in 1981, is a list of the over 80 potters. Over 30 percent of them had moved to Indiana from Ohio. And by 1900 to 1910 all had stopped operating except the Clay City Pottery (see that listing.) Also, see the listings for Francis Nolen, George Husher, William R. Torbert, Standard Pottery and Kelsey family potters. The mark shown was copied from a piece of stoneware but I couldn't determine which potter in Brazil Township, Clay County, Indiana made the jug because there were several; D.F. Huggins; J. Kelsey; Isaac Cordery; Levi Brackeny and Cyrus Rinehart; and Lawrence Torbert.

```
CLAY COUNTY
  BRAZIL
    IND.
  BRAZIL
```

Claycraft Potteries. Los Angeles, California. 1921 until late 1930's. Incorporated in 1921 to make chemical stoneware, decorative art tiles, garden pottery, etc. The tiles were Faience, claycraft and handmade Faience, according to a catalog. Many tiles were unmarked. Pictures on tile included Spanish scenes, flowers, Woodland scenes, fruit, etc. Shorty after the incorporation in 1921, Fred H. Robertson joined the firm as general superintendent. Then in 1925, George B. Robertson, Fred's son, became assistant superintendent. The two men developed outstanding clay bodies and glazes for the Claycraft Potteries' products including lamp bases. Around 1934, they left Claycraft to start the Robertson Pottery. See that listing. Evans, as cited said few pieces of Claycraft were marked. (Information and mark: Douglass Scott, "Claycraft Potteries of California," *American Clay Exchange*, October 1983, pp. 10, 11. Also, Paul Evans, *Art Pottery in the U.S.*, pp. 239, 240.)

```
CLAYCRAFT
```

Clay Craft Studios. Winchester, Massachusetts. Four women formed a small studio pottery in 1931, called Clay Craft Studios. The women were Mary Hodgdon, Ann Norton, Rowena Hollowell and Carol Nickerson. Hodgdon graduated from Newcomb College in 1922, the others had studied at the Paul Revere Pottery in Brighton, Massachusetts. By 1934, Hodgdon had moved to California to succeed Glen Lukens at Fullerton Jr. College teaching ceramics. Ann Norton had also left by 1934. Hollowell and Nickerson purchased the equipment, moved it to their own homes. Clay Craft Studios had been on Norton property. They worked together until 1954. Nickerson worked alone five more years in Winchester then two more winters in Florida before retiring. Exactly how long the name, Clay Craft Studios, was used is not known to this author, but individual marks are shown for all of these potters except Norton. The pieces were hand thrown, hand decorated, some slip ware and some highly decorated pieces. See the listings for M.Y. Hodgdon. (Information: Thomas Turnquist, "Clay Craft Studios," *American Art Pottery*, July 1983, pp. 1, 3. Marks: sent to author by Thomas Turnquist. No. 1, is Clay Craft Studios mark; no. 2, for Carol Nickerson; no. 3, for Rowena Hollowell; and no. 4, Mary Hodgdon. All marks incised.)

1.

2.

3.

4.

Clay and Fiber Studio. Medina, Ohio. 1974 to present (1985). Kathleen Totter Smith, studio potter, makes hand thrown stoneware, hand decorated pieces, incised Totter. Kathleen received an M.A. Degree in Ceramics from Kent State University in 1969.

Totter

Clayfields Pottery. Larry Schiemann, a studio potter operating in Streetsboro, Ohio, 1972 to present (1983) making pottery that this author could not resist buying. It is "Country Style," which is Larry's terminology, with hand painted slip decoration, into jugs, mugs, etc. which are patterned somewhat after the earlier stoneware pieces but yet they retain the characteristics of today's studio potters. The jugs had delicate painted flowers in three or four colors on the front. This potter had many pieces with a beautiful cobalt blue color of decorations.

Clayhorse Pottery. Stone Mountain, Georgia. Filed for registration of both marks on May 21, 1984, claiming use since February 2, 1982, for clay flower pots and figurines.

NOAH AND HIS ARKERS

ARKERS

Clays in Calico. Cardwell, Montana. Started around 1960 to present (1986). Wesley Van Gorden and Virginia Van Gorden in partnership filed for registration of mark no. 1 on April 14, 1969, for use on flower vases, coffee carafes, pitchers and mugs, bowls, bean pots, plates, teapots, creamers and sugars, salt and pepper shakers, beer steins and condiment serving jars made of china, porcelain or earthenware, claiming use since October 1960. (Mark: no. 2 was incised and found on a small vase with variegated colors of brown, tan, yellow swirls and clear glaze.)

1. **CLAYS IN CALICO**

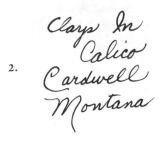

2.

Clay Sketches. 30 S. Chester Avenue in Pasadena, California. This pottery was started in 1943 by Cy Peterson and another man to make figures and figurines with outstanding detail and color. They were listed in the *Manufacturer's Directory of California*, in 1955, but were not listed in 1957 which was my next directory. This potter was not listed in the various trade directories. (Information and marks: Danny Brown, "Those California Figurines," Ace, October 15, 1985, pp. 10-12.)

Clay Sketches
by BALL-Calif.

Claysmiths. San Gabriel, California. Listed in 1948 and 1954 *Crockery and Glass Journal Directory*, under art china of porcelain and earthenware, including vases, console sets, candy boxes, etc. Also listed under figurines of china and earthenware. They were listed under trade names for the name, Will-George. (Mark: on piece at American Ceramic Society Ross Purdy Museum, Columbus, Ohio)

Will-George

Clayworks Production Studios. Hamburg, New York. 1972 to present (1984). Linda Kitchen, studio potter, makes woodfired porcelain pieces into functional ware and vessels. She also makes wall sculptures. She received a B.A. Degree from Empire State College in 1981. Before that she had attended classes at University of Alabama in 1965 and Fredonia State College. She also studied at the Evanston Art Center. She has done many shows including the "Linda Kitchen Woodfired Porcelain," one man show at Point of View Folk Art in Williamsville, New York. She was artist in residence at Artpark in 1979, 1980, 1981. She has pieces on exhibit in New York, Connecticut and Pennsylvania.

Clay Works. Nashville, Tennessee. 1968 to present (1985). Burneta Clore Clayton, studio potter, has operated the Clay Works since 1972, where she makes functional pieces from porcelain, fired in a reduction atmosphere to cone 10. She also works with stoneware and occasionally uses terra cotta. Pieces are mostly wheel thrown, but she builds some from slabs and extrusions. She uses brushwork overglaze decorations. She has one full time apprentice and some part time labor and conducts a self supporting business selling through craft fairs, shops and galleries throughout the country. Burneta received a B.A. degree in Commercial Art from Southern Methodist University, and then worked ten years in advertising art before becoming interested in ceramics. She received her training in ceramics by attending various workshops of two to five days with Paul Soldner, John Glick, Catherine Hierseoux, Byron Temple, Wally Smith, Paula Winokur, Don Rietz and others. In 1983, she was commissioned to make 1,200 small porcelain bowls used as favors for the Tennessee Govenor Alexander's pre-inaugural dinner. In 1981, she was commissioned to make 1,200 candlesticks for his fund raising dinner party. In 1976, she won the Gallery of Honor award at the Tennessee Crafts Fair with Toshiko Takaezu as juror. She listed many craft fairs in Texas, Michigan, Illinois, etc. She gives wheel throwing demonstrations in various places and has had teaching sessions in many high schools. Her work is at present represented in about forty galleries throughout the country. Each piece is stamped "Clay Works," as in mark no. 1, and most are incised with her signature shown in mark no. 2. Mark no. 3 is a logo used in various ways.

Cleveland China Company or the **George H. Bowman Company.** Cleveland, Ohio. A distributing company. Bowman operated a jobbing and import concern in connection with a large retail store in Euclid Avenue in Cleveland. At one time the company had fifty men selling on the road. The Cleveland China or Bowman marks are found on all types of dishes from fine thin vitrified china to hotelware and semi-porcelain. From the 1890's until sometime in the 1930's, the Bowman Company or Cleveland China Company was in operation and an influence in the pottery industry. Iroquois China of Syracuse, New York, Summit China of Akron, Alliance Vitreous China of Alliance, Ohio, all made pottery products for Bowman, and he no doubt used a great many more. Imported china may be found with a Bowman mark and that of a foreign maker. In 1939, Iroquois China was sold at bankruptcy. It has been under the control of George H. Bowman. Mr. Bowman went to work selling for Homer Laughlin China Company & retired around 1950. In 1954, George H. Bowman and Son were listed in business in Salem, Ohio. Illinois China Company must have made products for Bowman, too. (Information: Lehner, *American Kitchen and Dinner Wares*, p. 43. Marks: Nos. 1 to 4 and 6, 7, on dishes; no. 5 from Quality Stamp used by Bowman and Son in Salem, Ohio around 1954.

1.

2.

3.

4.

5.

6.

7.

Clewell Pottery. Canton, Ohio. C. Walter Clewell started around 1906 until his death in 1966 at age 86. He made beautiful shrouded and bronze art pottery with ceramic lining into ornamental and ceremonial utility vessels. He purchased blanks for the coated pieces and made his own molds for the solid clay pieces. (Marks: nos. 1, 2, inscribed in base, from Lehner, *Ohio Pottery and Glass*, p. 27; nos. 3, 4, impressed marks shown in Evans, p. 58.)

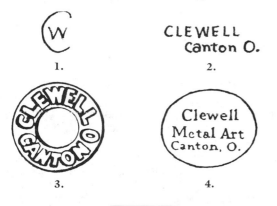

1.

2.

3.

4.

Clews, James, Manufacturers. See Indiana Pottery Company.

Clifton Art Pottery. Newark, New Jersey. Started by Fred Tschirner and William A. Long. From 1905 to 1911 the company made art pottery, then shifted to tile and by 1914 the name became the Clifton Porcelain Tile Company, employing around twelve people. Paul Evans, *Art Pottery of the U.S.*, pp. 59-62, tells us there were two distinct types of art pottery made at this pottery. Crystal Patina and Clifton Indian Ware. For a thorough description of these lines, see the Evans book. In 1909, Long returned to Ohio, to work at Weller Pottery. The production of tile at the factory was under Charles Stegmeyer. (Information: Evans, as already cited. Marks: nos. 1-5, Evans, p. 62; no. 6, Deb and Gini Johnson, p. 91.)

1. **CLIFTON**

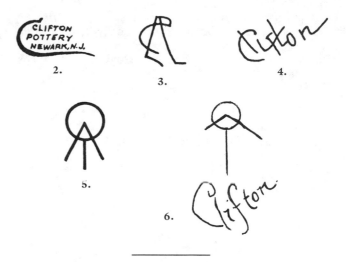

2.

3.

4.

5.

6.

Cliftwood Art Potteries. Morton, Illinois. For history see listing, Rapp Brothers various Illinois potteries. (Marks: no. 1, 2, 3, 6, Doris and Burdell Hall, *Morton's Potteries: 99 Years*, pp. 85, 86; no. 4, Deb and Gini Johnson, *Beginner's Book of American Pottery*, p. 106. Mark no. 1 incised, and the others are paper labels. No. 6 is the actual copy of a paper label. No. 5 is a drawn copy of no. 6. "Pollworth Art" was made in 1930's and early 1940's according to Burdell Hall.)

1.

2.

3.

4.

Paper sticker.

5.

6.

Clinchfield Artware Pottery. Irwin, Tennessee. 1945 to present (1986). Ray and Pauline Cash founded the pottery. They are makers of hand painted semi-porcelain pieces such as bowls and pitcher sets, vases, etc. According to author, Betty Newbound, this pottery purchased molds from liquidation of Southern Potteries, Inc. and since both potteries hand painted ware, there may be some confusion between the products of the two companies, especially by beginning collectors. The pottery is also called the **Cash Family Pottery**. Also, do not confuse the marks of this pottery with the very early marks of Southern Potteries, inc. when that pottery was called the Clinchfield Pottery. See Southern Potteries, Inc. for history. Pitchers and pitcher sets were their specialties. The ware met all standards for safety for eating and drinking. The pieces were distributed all over the United States. In October 1984, the Cash family sold the pottery to Rick Daughtroy. They are now making lamp bases and statuary, some were glazed and some were not, according to Betty Newbound, by letter. She said they also made Indian character jugs in heavily spattered brown. (Information: Betty Newbound,

"Along the Flea Market Trail," *Depression Glass Daze*, May 1979, and August 1980, p. 43. Also, Jenny Derwich, "Clinchfield Artware Pottery," Pottery Collectors Newsletter, October, 1974, p. 9. Marks: nos. 1, 2, Betty Newbound; nos. 3-7, on pieces.)

1.   2.

Clinchfield
Artware Pottery   3.
Erwin, Tenn.

Clinchfield Artware
Hand Painted   4.
Erwin, Tennessee

CLINCHFIELD
ARTWARE POTTERY   *Clinchfield*
Hand Painted   *Artware*
ERWIN, TENNESSEE   6.   HAND PAINTED
5.   ERWIN, TENN.

Made By Cash Hamily
7.   *Hand Painted*
USA

Clinchfield Pottery. See Southern Potteries, Inc.

Clinton Pottery Company. Clinton, Missouri, 1885 to 1898 became **Clinton Stoneware Company** from 1898 to 1906 when it became Plant 6 of Western Stoneware Company and operated until 1910 when plant was completely closed. By 1891, they were manufacturing $50,000 in ware per year, or one-third of the output of the entire state. The Clinton Pottery was a large steam operated pottery. The main output was brownware with an Albany slip glaze, in crocks, jugs, utilitarian ware. By May 1897, the pottery was in financial trouble with the bank, L.E. Culbertson bought the notes held by the bank and purchased the remainder at a forced sale in March 1898. Clinton Stoneware Company was incorporated the same month. The plant was still a productive one as late as 1908 when according to Clarence N. Roberts in *Developments in the Missouri Pottery Industry, 1800-1950*, p. 468, the pottery was still a leader in the state, producing $29,000 in pottery per year. This would be after the organization of the Western Stoneware plants. (Information and mark no. 1:) Jim Martin and Bette Cooper, *Monmouth Western Stoneware*, Des Moines: Wallace Homestead Book Company,

1983, p. 38. Mark no. 2 from Henry W. Heflin, pottery collector and researcher, found on a blue stenciled stoneware 20 gallon crock. Mark 3 found on light beige colored stoneware jug with blue decoration and stamped mark. Starting date from "Statistics of the Stoneware and Earthenware Potteries in Missouri in 1892" *Missouri Geological Survey*, Vol. II pp. 356, 357.

MANUFACTURED
BY   1.
CLINTON POTTERY CO.
CLINTON MO.

CLINTON Pottery Co.
MFGS. OF
2.   STONEWARE
CLINTON, MO.

CLINTON POTTERY 3.

Clough and Calhoun. Portland, Maine. In 1846, Levi Clough and William Calhoun started making stoneware utilitarian pieces in what had been the old Crafts pottery in Portland. In 1847, a third man, John T. Winslow, joined the firm; he had been a grocery store owner and his store had burned. Calhoun died in 1848 and the partnership was Winslow and Clough. Then Winslow purchased Clough's share and moved the pottery to Westbrook Point. Winslow employed the potter, William Fives, and a couple of other potters and continued the business. In M. Leyln Branin's book *The Early Potters and Potteries of Maine*, several land transactions involving John T. Winslow and his brothers, David and James N., took place before 1867. Between 1864 and 1867, James N. Winslow acquired all titles to the properties and mortgages held against them and in 1867 he formed the Portland Stoneware Company. (See that listing.) John T. Winslow in the years he controlled the pottery, made pots, jars, jugs, butter pots, spittoons, etc. in salt glazed stoneware, using three hundred tons of clay and five hundred cords of wood per year. (Information: M. Lelyn Branin, as cited, pp. 61-64. Marks: same book, p. 223.)

J T WINSLOW

CLOUGH CALHOUN
& CO.
PORTLAND MAINE

Clouse Pottery. Erwin, Tennessee. Around 1940, for a short time. Potter made cream colored translucent porcelain decorative pieces. Molds and equipment sold to Clinchfield Art Pottery. (Information: Jenny B. Derwich and Dr. Mary Latos, *Dictionary Guide to United States Pottery and Porcelain*, p. 64. Marks: stamped; sent by Jenny B. Derwich.)

CLOUSE   CLOUSE
HAND PAINTED   HAND PAINTED
ERWIN, TENN

Clow, Bonnie L. Kansas City, Missouri. 1978 to present (1984). An award winning sculptor. Makes stoneware sculptured pieces, which are unique caricatures of the animal world. Bonnie is a graduate of Kansas State University and she attended the Kansas City Art Institute. Her works are displayed in numerous private and corporate collections throughout the Midwest. She exhibits regularly in galleries in Kansas, Missouri, and New Mexico. She listed 23 juried shows and exhibits where she had shown.

Club Aluminum Products Company. Chicago, Illinois. Distributors. Filed for rights on this mark June 21, 1943, to be used for ceramic tableware, refrigerator dishes and ovenware, claiming use since February 1, 1943.

Coffman Potters. Mt. Herman (near Elkton), Virginia. Operated from before 1753 until after 1900. These are very approximate dates. **Andrew Coffman**, whose mark no. 1 is found on a lidded stoneware jar with brushes painted flowers died at age 57 in 1753. **J. Coffman** made Andrew a pottery grave marker so dated. **William Coffman** operated the pottery later. William Coffman's sons **William, Robert, and Edward Coffman** were potters as were some of his grandchildren **Clinton Coffman**, grandchild of the founder, was the last of the Coffman potters born in 1873. Made salt glazed stoneware, and earthenware with a red lead glaze. The only other key we have to dates for this pottery is the August 1860 in the second mark. The wording for mark no. 2 is not complete as shown because it was not shown in the picture in Smith's book. The hand written, incised inscription said, "For Dr. L.L. Painter, made by B.R.L. Coffman, August 18th, 1860." Mark no. 1 is an unevenly impressed mark. (Information and marks: Elmer L. Smith, *Pottery A Utilitarian Folk Craft*, Lebanon, Pa.: 1973, pp. 26, 27.)

1. A. COFFMAN
   ROCKINGHAM VA.

2. By BRL Coffman August 18, 1860

Cofield, T.W. Atlanta area, Georgia. Around 1880 to 1900. Cofield worked as a potter in various potteries in the area including the Rolader Pottery of Howell's Mills. He was in partnership for a while with Edward C. Brown, son of Bowling P. Brown. Pictured in John A. Burrison, *Brothers in Clay*, p. 7 is a stoneware pitcher with Albany slip with the stamped mark shown. (Information: Burrison, as cited, pp. 71, 191, 195, 199.)

TW COFIELD
HOWELL MILL
GA.

Cohen, Michael. Amherst, Massachusetts. 1961 to present. Studio potter making mostly functional stoneware until 1982 when he started also making porcelain. He works with celadon, creamy white and rust on stoneware. The porcelain has pink and white decorations. Michael received a B.F.A. Degree from Massachusetts College of Art and did graduate work at Cranbrook Academy and Haystack School of Crafts 1957, 1960. He has taught ceramics in many places of importance, Penland School, 1964, 1972; Haystack School of Crafts, 1963; Ohio State University (workshop), 1965; Colby Junior College (workshop), 1968; Notre Dame, Artist in Residence, Summer 1976; Creative Arts Center, New Haven (workshop), 1978; Frog Hollow Craft Center, Middlebury, Vermont (workshop), 1979; Association of San Francisco Potters (lecture), 1979; Berkeley Potters Guild (lecture), 1979. His list of exhibitions is very impressive; he listed nine selected group exhibitions, five one person exhibitions and has pieces in six museum collections, the Museum of Modern Art, Design Collection, New York; Museum of Contemporary Crafts, New York; Everson Museum, Syracuse, New York; Walker Art Center, St. Paul, Minnesota; Addison Gallery, Andover, Massachusetts; Johnson Wax Collection of Contemporary Crafts. (Marks: Nos. 1, 2 were used before 1961, nos. 3, 4, 5 used after 1961.)

1. ||||||||||

2. Mike Cohen

3. **MICHAEL COHEN**

4. **COHEN POTTERY**

5.

Coiner, John, Pottery/Earth Works Pottery. Minneapolis, Minnesota. John Coiner, studio potter, is currently working with Peter Deneen as Coiner-Deneen Pottery. See Deneen Pottery listing. Before that time, John Coiner ran a pottery of his own for thirteen years from 1968 to 1981. In 1967, he received a B.A. degree and in 1968 an M.A. from the University of Northern Iowa in Cedar Falls, Iowa. He studied under Marguerite Wildenhain and Warren McKenzie. He taught classes on a graduate level for three years and started a pottery of his own. He makes functional and decorative pieces, sculptured and hand thrown. Both the John Coiner Pottery and Coiner-Deneen Pottery print a brochure for ordering by mail. Both catalogues contain some of the nicest, unique items I have seen made by studio potters. These two men are talented, artistic, original. Both potteries have offered a set of twelve face mugs, a cowboy, Viking man and woman, a king and queen, a pilot, smoker, wizard, unicorn, dog, cat, frog, with faces in sculptured raised designs that are extraordinary. See Deneen Pottery listing for more on products. John has used quite a variety of marks as shown.

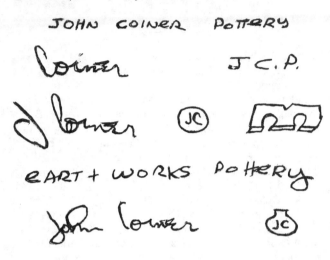

Colchester Pottery. Colchester, Illinois. Little concrete information was found for this pottery. The pottery was founded in 1890. Joe Young, an early worker at the pottery held a record of making 550 one-gallon jugs in nine hours and two minutes. Pottery employed forty men and made stoneware jugs, flower pots, cuspidors, etc. (Information: June Moon, *History of Colchester, Illinois* (no page no.), sent by the Macomb City Public Library. Mark: on old stoneware jar, from Janice T. Wass, curator of Decorative Art, Illinois State Museum.)

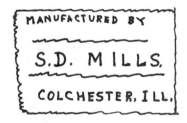

Cole, A.R. Pottery. Sanford, North Carolina. 1934 to present. Arthur Ray Cole, son of Ruffin Cole, brother to C.C. Cole, came from a family of potters. Since the death of A.R. Cole in 1974, the family shop has been operated by his daughters, Neolia Cole Perkinson, and Celia Cole Perkinson. Another member of this family who operates his own pottery in Sanford, is A.R. Cole's son, G.F. Cole. In 1927, A.R. Cole built his first shop in Seagrove, where he made brightly colored earthenware. In 1934, he moved to Sanford, to be accessible to a main highway. A.R. Cole learned potting from his father and he, in turn, taught all of his children the trade. In 1971, they were forced to move their business because a new highway took their property, but they just went a few miles up the road and rebuilt. Pieces are made from a bluish gray clay with streaks of white and red, which is dug in

Smithfield. The ware is hand thrown on a wheel, including candle holders, kitchen and tableware, jardinieres, pitchers, jugs, bowls, tea sets, miniature animals, etc. (Information: Nancy Sweezy, *Raised in Clay, The Southern Pottery Tradition*, pp. 183-186. Impressed mark: on aqua colored small relish tray with a handle.)

Colonial Pottery Company. East Liverpool, Ohio. 1903-1929. So as not to be confusing, there was a building called the Colonial Pottery when occupied by Wallace and Chetwynd. (See that listing.) Later, when the East Liverpool Potteries Company dissolved in 1903, a new Colonial was formed in the Colonial Pottery building. Their products were ironstone and semi-porcelain (W.P. Jervis, ''Dictionary of Pottery Terms,'' *Pottery, Glass and Brass Salesman*, May 20, 1915, p. 13.) This Colonial Company operated until 1929 according to Vodrey (Vodrey, William H., ''Record of the Pottery Industry in East Liverpool District,'' *Bulletin of American Ceramic Society*, XXIV, August 1945, p. 284.) I have found several pieces by this company. The semi-porcelain is heavy and does not have the ring of Crooksville China Company's ''Stinthall.'' I had attributed marks nos. 1, 6, to Crooksville China Company in my book, *American Kitchen and Dinner Wares*. In coloring of clay and glaze, Colonial made a nice white product similar to Crooksville's best china but Colonial China ware is much thicker and does not have the ring of Crooksville China Company's products. The similarity of this mark to other Colonial marks was also a determining factor. All of the several pieces of Colonial Company's dishes that I found have a great deal of gold trim and very pretty old decaled decorations. Marks copy machined from dishes except no. 4 shown in W.P. Jervis, *World's pottery Marks*, Janaury 20, 1919, p. 15.)

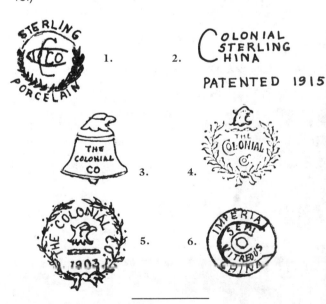

Colonial Silver Company, Inc. Orlando, Florida. Mark no. 1 was filed for registration by this company on Februbary 12,

1957 claiming use since May 10, 1956. Mark 2 was copy machined from a dish. In the dinnerware book I had attributed mark 2 to a Colonial Company in Pittsburgh, Pennsylvania in the 1956 through 1970 directories. That was an error. Both of the companies were distributors. The plate was made by Taylor, Smith and Taylor and the mark was sent to me from the factory just before it closed.

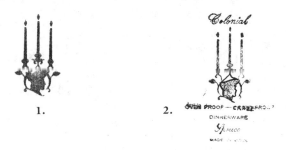

1.   2.

Colorcrete Industries, Inc. Holland, Michigan. Filed for registration of this mark on March 8, 1951, for use on several flower boxes, vase, urns and jars, made of artificial stoneware, claiming use since December 1927.

COLORCRETE

Columbia China. Porter (near Chesterton), Indiana. December 1922 to July 1925. Anton Schmid began the American China Products Company (see that listing), and he left that company in 1920. In 1922, he started a manufacturing company called Columbia China to make a fine thin decorated china. The plant burned in July 1925. The china is marked with "Columbia China, Porter, Indiana," and a man's half silhouette and "C.Ch. Co." is on the cups. Pieces were found decorated by Pickard Studios. (See that listing.) (Information and marks: Mrs. Hugh Hopkins, who is currently compiling a book on Chesterton, Indiana, potteries. Marks nos. 1, 3 are actual copy machine copies; nos. 2, 4 are drawn copies.)

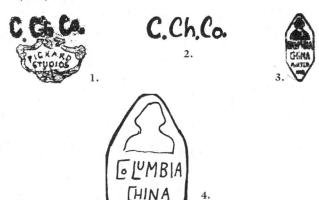

Columbian Art Pottery Company. Trenton, New Jersey. 1893 to around 1902. It was founded in 1893 by W.T. Morris and F.R. Willmore, according to Barber, at Trenton for the manufacture of table and toilet china and artwares in a Belleek body. "Thin Belleek china and ivory ware of a fine

quality are made here in original forms and decorations and include articles of utility and ornamental pieces, such as candlesticks, umbrella holders, tea pots and specialties." (Barber, *Pottery and Porcelain of the U.S.*, p. 242.) This company was listed under general pottery wares in the *Trenton City Directories* for the years 1901 and 1902. I found no further listings. They used a shield mark on Belleek as shown. On opaque china, Barber said they used a miniature copy of the Liberty Bell. (Marks: no. 1, Ramsay, p. 270; nos. 2, 3, Barber, p. 68; no. 4 shows decorator marks from Ramsay, p. 270.)

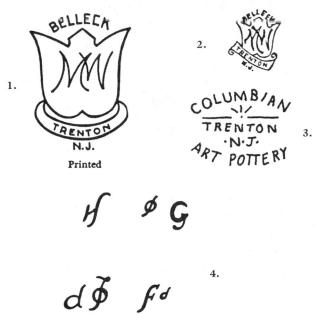

1.   Printed

2.

3.

4.

Comanche Pottery, Inc. Comanche, Texas. 1973 to present (1985). Don Allen and his son have perfected a line of pottery which should be admired and loved for years to come. They use a self-firing process fired by chemical that results in a porous yet highly durable product perfect for plants. The decoration or design is something similar to Niloak with variegated colors from different colors of clay. The name for this particular ware is "All Earthen Pottery." Patents for the manufacture of this ware was applied for in 1973 and 1978 after the Allens had worked on the process since 1971. Pieces of this colorful ware are all sorts of vases and planters of frogs, swans, turkey, cow, shoe, deer, turtle and an assortment of the bowl type flower pots from tiny to huge. The designs result from the colors in the clay and no two are alike. Some have designs incised in the clay as well. Statues of Indian and busts of Indians in the beautiful variegated clay are detailed, authentic and highly desirable. In 1978, the Comanche Pottery opened a second plant in Oxford, Mississippi, and fourteen months later, the third plant was opened in Lumberton, North Carolina. In 1981, a distribution center was opened in Orlando, Florida. The pottery is presently distributing to all of the states and Canada, and showing at all the major shows in New York City, Atlanta, Houston, Dallas, Tampa, etc. They manufacture thousands of pieces in an eight hour period. Most of the pottery is marked with the name "Comanche Pottery" inscribed inside the piece and or a paper label as shown. This is a kind of pottery that will be easily and quickly recognized by collectors because of the variegated colors. (Mark no. 1 is an inscribed mark in very large letters clear around the inside bottom of a pot fifteen inches across and thirteen inches high. No. 2 is a paper label. No. 3 was filed for registration on November 20, 1979 claiming use since January 1, 1977 for pottery flower pots, bird and animal figures. Louisville Pottery also used Comanche marks.)

1.

2.

3.

Combs, Bill. Murfreesboro, Tennessee. 1982 to present (1985). Bill received a B.F.A. degree from Middle Tennessee State University in December 1981. He apprenticed with Lewis Snyder of Murfreesboro, and started his own studio pottery in 1982, making functional stoneware and Raku pieces.

Combs

Commeraw, Thomas (also spelled Commerau in Stewart and Consentino, p. 123). Around 1797 to around 1819 (Stewart and Consentino dates). Other authors mentioned, spelled the name Commeraw. In Coerlears Hook, New York (spelled Corlears in Ramsay, p. 197, and Guilland, p. 106.) In Guilland, p. 106, is shown a very clear picture of a jug with the **Cor**lears spelling. See mark no. 1. In the text Guilland used Corlears. In Webster, p. 62, is a very clear picture with the name spelled **Coer**lears. See mark no. 2. In the text Webster uses Coerlears.) Coerlears Hook was in what is now the Manhatten part of New York City around 1797. The marks were probably applied with woodblock stamps and whoever made one of the two blocks used made an error. Mark no. 3 is the spelling used in Thorn, p. 123. Both stoneware jars pictured had double applied handles, an incised floral decoration and enamel like glaze. The foot of each pot had rims around the bottom. Altogether they were very beautiful pots. (Marks: Guilland, p. 106, 150, 191, 252; no author, *Regional Aspects of American Folk Pottery*, p. 43; Thorn, p. 123. Notice the marks with a backward "s".)

CORLEARS HOOK

COMMERAWƧ
STONEWARE

1.

COERLEARS HOOK   N·YORK

2.

COERLEARS
HOOK
N·YORK

3.

COMMERAW

5.

COMMERAW:Ƨ
STONEWARE
NEW YORK

4.

COMMERAWƧ
STONEWARE
CORLEARS
HOOK
N·YORK

6.

Commerce-Pacific, Inc. Los Angeles, California. A selling agency with a great deal of marks used on foreign ware. To clarify some confusion, china marked "Aladdin," had nothing to do with the Aladdin Lamp Company, as some writers have tried to make a connection. On April 1, 1949, Commerce-Pacific, Inc. filed for registration of the mark shown for use on Japanese made dinnerware. This mark is not to be confused with Aladdin marks used by Belcrest, Inc., a decorating agency. See that listing.

Commerce Pottery. Commerce, Missouri. Operated long before the Civil War and lasted into the 1890's. The Commerce Pottery is thought to have been established in 1834 by William and Samuel Gracey of Philadelphia. During the late 1870's the wares if this pottery bore the name mark "P. Rodenbaugh," and "P. Rodenbaugh & Sons." Other potters marks found on ware at the dump site were "A.A. Austin & Co." and "C.C. Bowen" who was known to be the last potter at the Commerce Pottery. (Information: Edison Shrum, author for various collector's paper, by letter. Mark: drawn from pictures sent by Edison Shrum.)

P. RODENBAUGH & SON
COMMERCE M⁰

Conaway, Mary S. Columbus, Ohio. 1953 to present (1984). Studio potter. Makes high fired functional and decorative stoneware. Studied ceramics at Ohio State University. Mark inscribed. Found vase with several bright colors of green, yellow and brown glazes.

Mary S.
72
Conaway

Confort China Company. Bronx, New York. I found only two listings for this company, in the 1948 and 1949 *China and Glass Red Book Directories*. Charles Confort was president. The company listed ceramic artware, figurines, Madonnas, animals, birds and ashtrays. The drawn copy of the mark was sent to me by a reader some time ago.

Confort
China Co.
Sculptured by
Tamic Lietti
USA

Congress Pottery. South Amboy, New Jersey. Around 1850. A. Cadmus made Rockingham, brownware. Mark impressed. (Information and mark: Ramsay, p. 180; Thorn, p. 121.)

A. CADMUS
CONGRESS POTTERY
SOUTH AMBOY
N. J.

Connell, R.O. Albany, New York. Around 1850. Stoneware potter. Mark impressed on jug owned by New York State Historical Association.

R.O.CONNELL
ALBANY

Conner Prairie Pioneer Settlement. Noblesville, Indiana. 1974 to present (1987.) In 1823, William Conner built a mansion on the present site of the Conner Prairie Settlement. In 1964, the home was restored by Eli Lily and he donated the home and some land to Earlham College. It has since grown into an educational-recreational area where visitors may try weaving on a loom, chopping or carving wood or help make candles, etc. This is a very large commercial venture as well with a huge restaurant, a museum shop, picnic area, etc. Pottery was first made at the settlement in 1974. (Marks: Pieces were marked in several ways over the years. The marks were impressed; except sometimes "C.P." and the dates were inscribed on some pieces. The date was almost always included with the impressed pieces. The only potter that I know for sure that made pieces there was Mel Davies, (see that listing). Most of the potters did not sign their own mark but used the various marks of the settlement as shown. The settlement didn't send a list of the potters who have worked there. No. 1 is the logo also used as an impressed mark.)

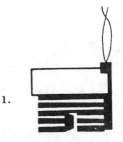

1.

CONNER PRAIRIE
IND

CONNER PRAIRIE
INDIANA

CONNER PRAIRIE (in a half circle)
IND

Conner Prairie

Conner Prairie (a stamp in script)
Indiana

BAKER POTTERY

Conrad Crafters, Inc. Wheeling, West Virginia. Around 1952 to present. Around 1951 when the Warwick plant was in the process of fading from view, two of their big dinnerware customers, the American Hostess Corporation (a party plan company) and the Dean and Kite Company, had many people with half completed sets of dishes. Four of the Warwick employees were offered the job of decorating for a while, to help complete the sets. The whiteware stock of Warwick China Company was purchased and Charles Conrad, Ralph Knight, Albert Lewis and Carolyn Conrad found themselves in the decorating business. Albert Lewis was the kiln-man, the others were the decorators. The white ware blanks purchased from Warwick only lasted about one year, and the group turned to decorating souvenir and giftware, which has been their business ever since. The Conrad Crafters was incorporated in 1957. Many nice items may be found with their mark.

CONRAD CRAFTERS, INC.
"Custom Made Gifts"
WHEELING, W. VA.

A. Conrad and Company. New Geneva, Pennsylvania. Around 1880. In a chart in Schaltenbrand, p. 75, Conrad used 250 tons of clay annually to make stoneware, with an average income of $4,860. By 1890, only one potter named Williams was operating in New Geneva, according to Schaltenbrand, p. 22. See Robert T. Williams. He had come to own the pottery formerly owned by Alexander Conrad. (Marks: Guappone, pp. 33, 34; Schaltenbrand, p. 19; Smith, p. 8.)

A.CONRAD
NEW
GENEVA, PA.

A.CONRAD & CO.
NEW GENEVA, PA

A.CONRAD
NEW GENEVA
FAYETTE CO.

A.CONRAD
NEW
GENEVA
PA
4

A.CONRAD
NEW
GENEVA, PA.

A.CONRAD.NEWGENEVA
FAYETTE CO.

A.CONRAD
NEW GENEVA

A.CONRAD
NEW GENEVA
PA.

NEW GENEVA
POTTERY

Conrad, J.W. The report, "Statistics of the Stoneware and Earthenware Potteries of Missouri in 1892," which is contained in the *Missouri Geological Survey*, by H.A. Wheeler, Vol. II, p. 357, lists this potter as starting in 1887. (Mark: found on five gallon crock with blue stenciled mark sent by Henry W. Heflin, pottery collector and researcher.)

J.W. CONRAD
STOUTSVILLE
→ MO ←

Consolidated Cosmetics. Chicago, Illinois. Distributors of cosmetics filed for a claim on this mark on April 20, 1946 to be used on china dinnerware and tea pots, also china and earthenware chambers, pitchers, cuspidors, bowls, etc., for bedroom use, claiming use since April 17, 1946.

TABU

Contemporary Ceramics. Chatham, New Jersey. Became Chatham Potters. See that listing. (Information: 1967 *China, Glass and Tableware Directory* in listing for Chatham Potters. Mark: found on piece.)

contemporary
ceramics
chatham, n.j.

Continental Ceramics Corporation. New York, New York. Distributor. Listed in the 1945 *Crockery and Glass Journal Directory* as distributors of American dinnerware among other products. They filed July 25, 1928 for registration on mark no. 1 and on February 16, 1935 for mark no. 2, for use on dishes, plates, cups, saucers, casseroles and other similar articles of tableware and porcelain and chinaware of all kinds.

CONTINENTAL.

1.

2.

Continental China Company. See W.S. George Pottery Company, East Palestine, Ohio, for history.

Continental Kilns, Inc. Chester, West Virginia, 1944-1957 was chartered on October 16, 1944, with the principal office on Carolina Avenue in Chester, West Virginia. The company was dissolved on June 28, 1957. (Information furnished by Anna Gayle Harvey of the secretary of state's office in West Virginia.) The company was formed, according to McKee, p. 37, with Vincent Broomhall, former art director of the E.M. Knowles Company as the "leading light," with James Robson, Howard Scweitzer and Alf Duhrssen furnishing part of the capital. Their plan was to manufacture a Belleek-type body and to produce a high art article in a renovated factory which had at one time been the Davidson Porcelain Company on Route 2 between Chester and Newell, West Virginia. In staff written, "Vincent Broomhall Opens China Firm," *Crockery and Glass Journal*, December 1944, p. 71, Broomhall was quoted as saying, "I have been anxious to create a china gift line based on individuality. The "Vincent" line will be made of fine translucent china body, the decorations will be handpainted over embossed flowers and special attention will be given to workmanship." The article said Mr. Broomhall adopted the motif of the Lotus Tree blossom which was embossed and handpainted. Production was to be underway by January 1, 1944, employing fifty people. To my knowledge, so far the dishes that have been found are semi-porcelain, often hand painted with raised designs but nothing at all like Belleek. (Information: Lehner, *American Kitchen and Dinner Wares*, pp. 44, 45. Floyd W. McKee, *A Century of American Dinnerware Manufacture*, p. 37. Marks: on dishes and from Quality Stamp Company, East Liverpool, Ohio.)

Woodleaf
by
CONTINENTAL KILNS
Underglaze
Hand Painted
U. S. A.

Puritan
HAND DECORATED
22 K. GOLD
CONTINENTAL KILNS INC.
U.S.A.

Tahiti
by
CONTINENTAL KILNS
Underglaze
Hand Painted
U. S. A

Woodleaf
by
CONTINENTAL KILNS
Underglaze
Hand Painted
U. S. A.

Tahiti
by
CONTINENTAL KILNS
Underglaze
Hand Painted
U. S. A.

CONTINENTAL
KILNS
Hand Painted

CONTINENTAL.
KILNS
Hand Painted

Stardast
by
CONTINENTAL KILNS
Underglaze
U. S. A.

CONTINENTAL
KILN

Cat Tail
by
CONTINENTAL KILNS
Underglaze
Hand Painted
U. S. A.

Puritan
HAND DECORATED
22 K. GOLD
CONTINENTAL KILNS INC.
U. S. A.

China by *Vincent*

Cookingware - A Discussion of Unidentified Marks. Between approximately 1890 and 1930, a vast quantity of cookingware was manufactured which defies identification by the various authors. This book could have been completed much sooner if this ware did not exist. Two things need to be kept in mind in researching the ware discussed here. "German" was a name for a type of ware used by many potteries and many used the terms "fire clay," "acid prood," and "sanitary." Secondly, there was no Star Stoneware in Akron. Lyndon Viel who was the first to put up a very valiant, honest and sincere attempt at unraveling the cookware "mess" gave us many pictures to work with in his two books, *The Clay Giants I and II*. I have gone practically the same complete route behind him and if it weren't for the patent reports we found, I wouldn't have much more than he did and without his research to guide me, I would never have achieved what he did. He made one error, there was no Star Stoneware in Akron, Ohio. Robert Treichler, Tallmadge, Ohio, is preparing a book on the Akron geographic area which will deal with potters until 1875 and C. Dean Blair wrote *The Potters and Potteries of Summit County 1828 to 1915*, which was published by the Summit County Historical Society. Neither have found a Star Stoneware in Akron. By the time Viel wrote his second book, published in 1980, he had realized there was no such pottery. In the article, "Red Wing Update-Rare," *The Glaze*, August 1978, p. 8. Viel said "There was no Star Stoneware Company of Akron, Ohio." He went on to talk

about Star Stoneware of Crooksville then. Viel searched long and hard for a catalog for the North Star Pottery of Red Wing, Minnesota and Star Stoneware of Crooksville and found none to exist. The products seem to come from two major areas of the country, the Crooksville, Zanesville, Roseville area of Ohio and the various potteries of Red Wing, Minnesota area. The products are somewhere in between the hardness of stoneware and the softness of pottery. Most are glazed inside with a light blue, pure white or dark brown. The color of the clay is a light tan which darkens with use. The various potteries added unusual materials to the clay trying to make it more durable and functional. The Lowry Pottery of Roseville added asbestos to the clay giving the pieces a slightly speckled look. I didn't discover who used radium ore in clay mixture. Mark no. 1, as shown, was on a blue and white spatterware bowl and the mark covered the bottom of the bowl. This particular bowl was glazed inside and out. Then there is a water cooler made with radium ore which according to Dave Huebner in, "Beware of the Revigator," *Red Wing Collectors Newsletter*, Volume 3, no. 4, August 1979, p. 9, tested a little high in the chemistry laboratory. He suggested the maker was the Revigator Radium Ore Company with clay from the Denver area. No. 2 is the mark going down the side of the cooler which is glazed white with spigot. There is other printing on the piece not discernable in the picture and the lid had the mark, "Radium Ore," on it. A letter of inquiry in, "Readers Say," in the *Depression Glass Daze*, May 1984, p. 88 told the instructions for use printed somewhere on the jar such as drinking upon arising and to average six glasses a day.

The next group of marks 3 to 6 are for "German" bake and cookware. I wanted so badly to attribute these to Star Stoneware of Crooksville, Ohio. A few people in that town are certain the Star Pottery made the blue and brown lined cookware with a large star that covers the bottom of the piece and the words "German" and "New German," but months of inquiring and searching brought no conclusive evidence. These look far too late, possibly around 1920 or early 1930's to be attributed to North Star Pottery (see that listing.) See the listings for Lowry Pottery, Tycer Pottery, J.W. McCoy Pottery and the patent dates will tell you these pieces are made 1900 through 1930's. Wilbur Stout in *History of the Clay Industry in Ohio*, published in 1923, p. 61, tells us "At present (around 1922) ware of this class (earthen cooking and serving ware) is produced by most firms in Roseville and Crooksville, among which may be mentioned the Nelson McCoy Sanitary and Stoneware Company, Star Stonewre Company, Ransbottom Brothers Pottery Company, Burley and Winter Pottery Company, Burley Pottery Company, A.E. Hull Pottery Company and the Crooksville Stoneware Company." Prior to the 1922 date, H.R. Bodine and the Lowry Pottery were both full time manufacturers of cookware. Most potteries made some cookware in the area but Bodine and Lowry made a specialty of it. Weller, Zanesville Art Pottery, Roseville Pottery, Ohio Pottery, the Guernseyware Company, Brush McCoy and Fraunfelter, all made cookingware but it is more identifiable and a much better product than the pieces causing the utter confusion. For one thing these companies, last named, issued catalogs to help identify the pieces. The lesser companies did not. And some of the big companies did not advertise their cookware.

For example, in "Many Small Art Potteries Once operated in Zanesville," by Norris Schneider, *Zanesville Times Recorder*, February 4, 1962, (no p. no.) is an account of all the little potteries that started up in Zanesville and disappeared very quickly when they tried to compete with Weller and the other pottery giants. Several of these potteries that were formed to make art pottery ended up making mainly cookingware. Arc-En-Ciel made cookingware in stippled blue, brown and green. Bohemian Pottery Company was formed to make art pottery but Schneider said they made mostly cookingware instead. C.B. Upjohn Pottery, established 1904, was incorporated 1905. Upjohn had been designer for Weller. He created Weller's Dickenware. City directory of 1905 said he made German Sanitary cookingware in mottled decoration. (Springware) Upjohn left in 1905 to teach art at Columbia Univesity. He was followed by John Rice in 1905 who continued to make cookware. In "Weller Pottery," *Zanesville Times Signal*, by Norris Schneider, he said in 1920 Weller bought the Zanesville Art Pottery on Ceramic Avenue from David Schmidt who had owned it for twenty years. Culinary ware has been manufactured at the Art Pottery and this will be continued. This became Weller Plant No. 3. In 1924, the building was remodeled to make art pottery, but for four years Weller made cookware and so had the Zanesville Art Pottery. J.B. Owens made "fire clay" cooking vessels around 1893 and 1894. (See that listing.)

The Roseville Pottery Company acquired the old Mosaic Tile Company in 1902 and had 50 men making "German" cooking ware in four kilns on Muskingum Avenue. There are reasons why we get duplication in product, shape, designs and marks in various Crooksville, Roseville, Zanesville potteries. Many of the same men in the area worked in more than one of the potteries. Also new potteries were organized by the men running the already existing potteries and they became the first shareholders. For example, L.S. Kildow was a partner with Lowry in 1896, but he had been with Williams and McCoy in 1890 and then by himself before 1896. Wilson Winter of Burley-Winter was one of the organizers of the Star Stoneware. The name A.E. Hull, who founded Hull Pottery, shows up with some sort of involvement with several potteries. He helped to organize Star Stoneware and was president of Globe Pottery. According to Norris Schneider, "Hull Pottery," May 2, 1965, A.E. Hull traveled for the Star Stoneware Company before 1900 as a salesman. A.E. Hull's older brother J.J. Hull was president and general manager of the Star Stoneware Company. There will always be a problem identifying exactly which of the factories used which mark and made a certain piece because of the deep involvement of management and employees with several plants. J.W. McCoy Pottery, Lowry Pottery, National Pottery, Star Stoneware, Burley-Winter, Pace Brothers all made pretty much the same cookware starting around 1900. Then shortly after came Tycer Pottery and Watt Pottery to carry on the cookware traditions, all in the Roseville-Crooksville-Zanesville area. See listings for all of these potteries for various marks.

The color of the interior glaze didn't prove to be of any help either. Some of the "German" pieces have a beautiful sky blue glaze. J.W. McCoy, A.E. Hull Pottery, the Logan Pottery Company and several others used this glaze. McCoy used the terms "fire clay" and "Sanitary" in advertisements in the *Collectors Catalogue of Brush-McCoy Pottery*, by Sharon and Bob Huxford, pp. 28, 48. I was very dissapointed we did not find "Sanito," marks 13, 14, in the patent reports, because the mark says it was a registered trademark of the United States patent office. Maybe the next researcher can find it. Mark no. 15 was said to be a mark for Star Stoneware of Crooksville but I am not convinced. I found no real evidence that this is true. Also, there was a Syracuse Stoneware Company in Syracuse, New York, in 1896 as makers of Rock-

ingham and Yellow Ware in the various utilitarian pieces. I have never found a mark for the company nor do I know how long they stayed in business as manufacturers or sellers. (Staff written "Rebekah Teapots," *Spinning Wheel*, July, August 1968, p. 28.) All of the marks shown except no. 2 cover or stretch out across the bottom of the ware. Also, all but no. 2 are recessed-built into the mold. They have almost exactly the same color of clay with white, brown or blue glaze inside and none out. No. 1 is a spatterware decorated piece. Except for design (of which there are few) they look as if they could have come from one company or area – but they did not! I don't honestly think we will ever know exactly which of the potteries mentioned used these marks. Our only hope is to find catalogs or advertisements picturing the pieces and identified with the company. Chances are these will never be found. We will just have to enjoy them knowing they are a good old piece of kitchenware **Made in America**.

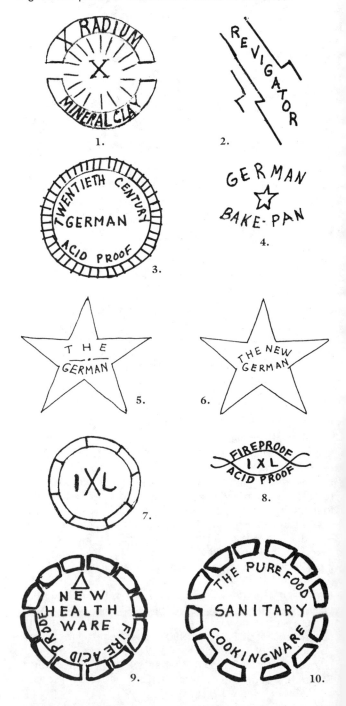

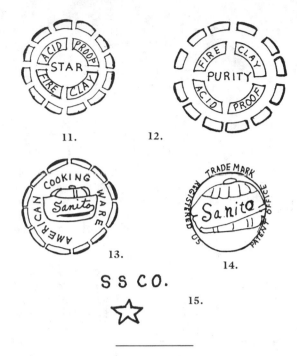

11. 12.

13. 14.

S S CO.

15.

Cook Porcelain Insulator Corporation. About 1920 to 1930's. Had a factory at Byesville and offices at Cambridge, Ohio. Makers of insulators marked "Cook." (Information and marks: Jack H. Tod, *Porcelain Insulators Guide book for Collectors*, privately printed, 1976, p. 122.)

COOK

Cook Pottery. Trenton, New Jersey. Around 1893 to around 1959. Sometime around 1930 the name became Cook-Ceramic Manufacturing Company, after Cook Pottery consolidated with the Ceramic Allied Products, Inc. The Cook Pottery was founded by Charles Howell Cook in Trenton, New Jersey, in 1893 or early 1894, in the building formerly owned by Ott and Brewer called the Etruria Pottery. (See Etruria Pottery.) In the *1902-1903 Complete Directory*, Cook Pottery was listed as making semi-porcelain, hotel ware, white granite dinner sets, toilet sets, short sets of odd dishes and jardinieres, some being decorated. According to Barber, p. 54 Cook made Belleek on which he used a three feather mark and also produced a good grade of Delft ware. Cook also had a plant at Trenton, New Jersey, called the Prospect Hill Works of the Cook Pottery. (See Prospect Hill Pottery). In the 1946 *Crockery and Glass Journal Directory*, the Cook-Ceramic Manufacturing Company was listed as manufacturers of art pottery with a china body, figures, figurines and miniatures. Also they made lamp bases, containers, novelties, etc. P.H. Cranmer was the president. In *A History of the Electrical Porcelain Industry* by Jack H. Tod, p. 77, Tod tells us that in 1932 Cook Ceramic Company purchased the New Brunswick Porcelain Manufacturing Division of Circle-F Manufacturing Company and porcelain insulators were manufactured at the Cook plant on Prospect Street, where the Cook Pottery had first started. Cook Pottery used "C.P." on insulators and also the tradename "WEDGE" on nail knobs. (See the Tod book cited, p. 14, for specific information on these types etc.) Cook was head of the Cook Pottery until illness caused him to quit in 1926. ("Charles Howell Cook," *American Ceramic Society Bulletin*, XIII, February

1925, p. 48.) In the *Trenton City Directories*, Cook China Company was listed by this name through 1929. Cook Ceramics was no longer listed after 1959 in the Trenton directories. Cook Pottery used "Mellor and Company" in its marks because F.G. Mellor was one of the original founders and early owners. (Information: Barber, *Marks of American Potters*, p. 54. Marks: nos. 1, 2 Evans, p. 64, used on art pottery. See Evans book for discussion. Nos. 3, 4 on dishes. No. 5 Spargo, p. 366. Remainder of marks from Barber, p. 54. See Evans, p. 64 for a detailed discussion of art pottery made by Cook Pottery. He pictures a piece marked "Nipur." Cook's markings verified from plant dumpage at plant site on Prospect Street in Trenton, by Tod. Marks 6, 7 on insulators were "C.P." and "WEDGE.")

1. 2. 3.

4. 5. 6.

7.

8. 9. 10.

11. 12. 13. 14.

Cooksburg Pottery. Cooksburgh, Pennsylvania. 1975 to present. Studio potters, Tim Galligan and Kathy Kellagher make salt glazed stoneware with cobalt decorations marked Cooksburg Pottery and initials or name and the year. In printer's type the small pieces are stamped Cooksburg Pottery. Under awards and shows they listed Yankee Peddler 1976 through 1981 and Functional Ceramics 1980 and 1982.

COOKSBURG POTTERY
Jim 1982

COOKSBURG POttERY
KK '82

"COOKSBURG POttERY"

Cookson Pottery Company. Roseville, Ohio. 1945 to present (1987). Started by Gerald Cookson who died in 1966. His son, Ronald, took over the business. They made planters, vases and garden ware. It was sold to a man named Murdoch in May 1982 but still operating in 1985 under the name Cookson and making the same products. (Information: from company. Marks: on pieces.)

COOKSON
603

COOK
SON 325

CP

Cookware Associates. Bucyrus, Ohio. In the 1945 and 1946 *Crockery and Glass Journal Directories*, this company was listed for ceramic cookware using the mark shown, but the directories didn't specify whether the company manufactured or were a selling agency. These were the only listings I found.

OLD HICKORY
Ceramic Cookware
by COOKWARE ASSOCIATES
BUCYRUS · OHIO

H.F. Coors. Inglewood, California. 1925 to present. Was founded by Mr. and Mrs. Herman F. Coors in 1925 at 8729 Aviation Boulevard, Inglewood, California. The owner in 1978 was their son, Robert M. Coors. This company has made many ceramic products since its beginning, including doll heads, wall tile, soap dishes, handles, faucets and shower heads. But they are currently making a fine grade of hotel china called "Alox" and a line of hotel porcelain cooking ware called "Chefsware." This company was in no way connected with the Coors Company in Golden, Colorado. Some collectors are not aware of this company's existence and are confusing their products with those of the Golden, Colorado, company. (Marks: no. 1 was filed for registration May 23, 1934, for us on hard glaze porcelain, claiming use since September 1, 1929. Nos. 2, 3 in company information; nos. 4, 5 on pieces; no. 6, Deb and Gini Johnson, *Beginner's Book of Pottery*, p. 50. The word Alox was filed for registration September 13, 1968 for use on porcelain dinnerware and cooking ware.)

COORSITE 1.

ALOX®

ALOX® 2.

H.F. Coors Company, Inc.
Inglewood, California
52 •••

H.F. Coors Company, Inc
Inglewood, California
52• 3.

Roca®
220 4.

CHEFSWARE

GENUINE
COORSITE
PORCELAIN 5.

Chefsware USA 6.
BLACK VELVET
BY
H.F. COORS

Coors Porcelain. Golden, Colorado. 1910 to present. Was founded as **Herold China and Pottery Company** in 1910 by J.J. Herold and the name was changed to Coors Porcelain in 1920. Still in business making chemical porcelain, electronic ceramics, nose cones for rockets, etc. The pottery made art pottery and dinnerware before 1939, but none since. (Marks: nos. 1 and 2, on dishes; no. 3 filed December 30, 1932, for use on porcelain teapots, drip coffee makers, casseroles, pie plates, service trays, salt and pepper shakers, bowls, sugar and creamers, refrigerator sets and cake spatulas, claiming use since December 1, 1928; no. 4, mark on ashtray for Governor's Conference, 1969; no. 5-9, Deb and Gini Johnson, *Beginner's Book of Pottery*, p. 50. Nos. 10, 11 on dishes. No. 12 filed for registration on March 24, 1966, for use on high temperature resistant translucent industrial ceramics, claiming use since February 1966.)

COORS U.S.A 1.

COORS PORCELAIN GOLDEN COLORADO 2.

THERMO 3.

A.COORS.CO GOLDEN·COLO 4.

A. COORS GOLDEN.COLO. 5.

COORS GOLDEN COLORADO POTTERY 6.

COORS THERMO PORCELAIN Reg. US Pat. off. 7.

COLORADO STATE FAIR COORS BEER 1939 8.

COORS 9.

COORS ROSEBUD U.S.A. 10.

COORS COOK N SERV WARE 11.

VISTAL 12.

Coplin, Alexander. Troy, New York. Around 1829 to around 1832. Alexander Coplin was a stoneware potter who worked for I. Seymour. (See the listing for I. Seymour.) Warren F. Broderick, writer, researcher and collector of stoneware, said the mark shown would be something of a one of a kind piece because it was made by Coplin while he worked for Seymour. Coplin did not have a pottery of his own. (Mark: Dianna and J. Garrison Stradling, *The Art of the Potter*, reprint of articles from *Antiques Magazines* p. 133.),

ALEXANDER COPLIN TROY
NOV, 1829

Copperstate Supply Company/Loma Manufacturing Company. Phoenix, Arizona. W.O. Bodine, filed for registration of this mark on March 14, 1952, for use on kiln-fired glazed earthenware, such as pottery type dinnerware, kitchenware and trays, claiming use since June 1951.

Cordelia China Company. Dalton, Ohio. 1944 to 1952. In 1944, Ed Hazel, who had been a designer for Shawnee Pottery, helped to organize Cordelia China Company which was owned by a man named Jones. Cordelia China was listed in the 1952 *Crockery and Glass Journal Directory*, but not listed in 1954. Products named were decorative china, such as vases, console sets, figures, figurines, miniatures, florist ware, salt and peppers. Various outlets were in Ohio, Virginia, Kansas and Kentucky. Pieces were hand decorated, some dipped in glaze, others spray glazed. The coloring was a part of the clay mixture. (Information: Norris F. Schneider, "Shawnee Pottery," *Zanesville Times Signal*, October 16, 1960.)

Cordey China Company. See Boleslaw Cybis.

Cornelison Pottery/Bybee Pottery. Bybee, Kentucky. According to information from James Andrew Cornelison, the first Cornelison Pottery had its beginnings as early as 1809, giving the pottery now existing, the claim to being the oldest pottery west of the Alleghanies. From 1845, records were kept and some writers use that as a starting date, but it was started in 1809 by Webster Cornelison. Jame Eli Cornelison, the son of Webster, probably began the record keeping and is sometimes credited with the founding of the pottery, but it was his father who founded it. James Eli was followed by his son, the first Walter Cornelison. He was in charge of the pottery until 1939 when Ernest became the owner. The present owner, the second Walter, took over in 1969. The sons of Walter II, are James Andrew and Robert Walter Cornelison, and they are working at the pottery at present (1986) which is still owned by Walter II. In 1954, the name was officially changed to the **Bybee Pottery**. Howard G. Selden was a New York businessman, gift dealer, importer, who created the Bybee Pottery Company of Lexington, Kentucky, to distribute the products of several potteries. He registered the Bybee trademark and for a few years the Bybee Pottery in Bybee, Kentucky, couldn't use "Bybee Pottery" as a mark. In 1930, they regained the right to use that name when the retailer Selden went out of business with the beginning of the Depression. The pottery made at Bybee Pottery over the years varied from salt glazed stoneware in the early years to a more

sophisticated type of glaze after World War I. Ramsay, p. 240, described the old ware as stoneware, some with Albany slip. Today molds are used for items made in large quantites. Some are still hand thrown on a wheel. A variety of colors have been developed in the glazes over the years. The pottery always was and still is made from local clay mined in open pits. (Information: James Andrew Cornelison, by telephone. Duke Coleman, "Letters and Such," *American Art Pottery*, January 1978, pp. 3, 4; Glenn Kerfoot, "Bybee Pottery: The Old Way," *Tri State Trader*, May 19, 1979, p. 23. Marks: no. 1, Coleman, as cited above. No. 2, incised on pottery vase. A glob of glaze covered the date, but Coleman shows it as 1000, probably from a piece he had. No 3 may be found with various wording in the outline of the state of Kentucky. The present marks are "BB" or "Bybee Pottery" and occasionally the stamp is still used. Some pieces are unmarked. Special orders have the customers name and date.)

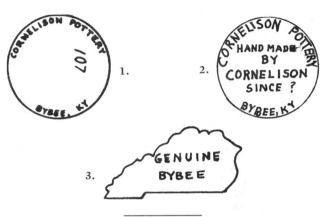

Corona Pottery. Corona, Long Island, New York. See listing W.P. Jervis.

Cosmic Clay Studio. Dowelltown, Tennessee. 1975 to present (1985). Louis and Christine Colombarini are studio potters. The pottery made by the Colombarinis is wheel thrown utilitarian pottery and hand built sculptured pieces, also Raku. Louis received an Associate of Art Degree and then received a B.A. degree from the State University of New York at Geneseo, New York, in 1971 and from 1974-1979, he studied at Florida Atlantic University in Boca Raton, Florida, in a program of professional advancement. Christine received an A.A. degree with honors in 1976 and a B.F.A. degree with honors from Florida Atlantic University in 1978. Louis gave ceramics instructions at the Appalachian Center for Crafts in Smithville, Tennessee, in 1980-1981. He was an Art Appreciation instructor at Broward Community College in 1977. He has given numerous demonstrations on the art of making pottery in Tennessee and Florida. Between 1977 and 1983, Louis and Christine listed twelve joint pottery making demonstrations they have done together, most of which was on handbuilding and the firing of Raku at such places as the Appalachian Center for Crafts; the University of Akron, Ohio; the Ceramic League of Palm Beach and Riveria Beach, Florida; and the Florida Atlantic University. Forty-six exhibitions at Art Fairs, Craft Fairs, Festivals, Galleries, etc. were listed for these two very busy potters between 1977 and 1984, in Tennessee, Florida, Illinois, California, Virginia, Ohio, Texas, Wisconsin, Maryland, Michigan, New York and Pennsylvania, at such places as Festival of the Masters at Disney World in Florida;

the Ninth Biennial Tennessee Artist-Craftsmen Association at Memphis State University in Memphis; The Spotlite 1982 Southeastern Crafts Show at Arrowmont School of Arts and Crafts in Gatlinburg, Tennessee; the Boardwalk Arts and Crafts Show Virginia Beach, Virginia; the Florida Atlantic University Gallery Art Show at Boca Roton, Florida, ec. The Colombarini's won awards at 23 of these shows. At the South Miami Chamber of Commerce Art Festival in Miami, they won four awards. Their work is also sold through galleries in California, New Mexico, New York, Florida, Tennessee, Illinois, Oklahoma, Maryland and Alabama. They belong to American Craft Enterprises, Inc. in New Paltz, New York; The Tennessee Artist-Craftsmen Association; the North Shore Art League in Winnetka, Illinois; and the Southeastern Center for Contemporary Art in Winston-Salem, North Carolina.

Coultry Pottery. See Dayton Street Pottery.

Coventry Ware, Inc. Barberton, Ohio. 1932 to late 1960's. Coventry Ware, Inc., started in Barberton, Ohio, as Dior Studios in 1932. In the 1960's they moved to Barberton, but closed sometime in the late 1960's. Mrs. Carrie Daum, a widow, started the business to make art objects, wall plaques, etc. of plaster products. Around 1940, the firm began to produce a more vitrified ware, ceramic figures, etc. with gold accents. Designer and sculptress, Elaine Carlock, worked at Coventry Ware, Inc. At one time, 30 people were employed and products were shipped all over the country. (Information: Jenny B. Derwich and Dr. Mary Latos, *A Dictionary Guide to U.S. Pottery and Procelain*, p. 69. Marks: nos. 1, 2, Quality Stamp Company; no. 3, 1957 *Crockery and Glass journal Directory*, No. 4 on vase with art deco shape. No. 5 was filed for registration March 15, 1948 for use on flower holders, hanging wall shelves, bells, vases, urns, cream and milk pitchers, candy dishes, decorative mugs, flower and fruit bowls, shakers, jam and mustard jars, etc., claiming prior use for one month only.)

Cowan Pottery. 1912 to December, 1931. Started on Nicholson Avenue, Lakewood, near Cleveland from 1912 to 1917. R. Guy Cowan went to war; when he returned the pottery was reopened. He moved to Rocky River when his gas well ran out in Lakewood. From 1912 to 1917, he used red clay body, but he changed to high fired porcelain at the rocky River location. By 1921, he had twelve hundred outlets for his pottery. Also at that time a commercial line was developed, tiles for floor, counters, walls, etc. In 1925, Cowan made complete table settings, console sets and figurines. Cowan made ceramic desk sets for Wahl Pen Company in 1930. Planters and ivy jars were made in 1930. Most important of Cowan's work was the beautiful art pottery that he produced throughout his years in business, for which he won many outstanding awards. His material was shown at the Cleveland Museum of Art, the Pennsylvania Academy of Art, the Pennsylvania Academy of Art, the Metropolitan Museum of Art, etc. In 1930, the name was changed to Cowan Potters, Inc., and the pottery was reorganized as a center for an artist's colony. The plan did not succeed; the pottery went into receivership December, 1930 and operated only one more year, closing December, 1931. Brodeck says many great works of art came out of the pottery in its last year of operation. The name of the pottery was incised on early pieces, then later a black stamp with just "Cowan" or "Cowan Potteries," his initials "R.G." and "Cowan" in a circle were used. From the book, *Ohio Art and Artists*, pp. 166-170, by Edna Maria Clark, is the following quote. The book was written in 1932.

"It is in ceramic sculpture that we find the most distinctive output of the Cowan Potters. The molds are of plaster of Paris, and made directly from the sculptor's original work, which usually is executed in a patent clay mixed with oil to prevent its drying. The making of the mold is a most delicate and difficult operation, involving cutting the mold into many intricate sectional divisions in order that the cast may not be broken as it is removed. Frequently these molds, which fit together like a puzzle, will contain as many as a dozen sections. A great many examples from the Cowan Studio are made only in limited numbers. After the predetermined lot has been successfully cast and fired, the mold is destroyed, just as an etcher will destroy his plate after a limited output has been produced.

The men who perform the many operations in the Cowan Pottery are truly artists in their particular work. The personal work of Mr. Cowan as a sculptor has brought him as much recognition as his achievement as a craftsman. His figures are distinguished by delightful delicacy and a strong sense of the decorative. His "Adam and Eve," a pair of charming figures, are akin to the sculpture of Paul Manship in positions and archaistic tendencies. He is a modernist in his sympathies and execution, yet a fine restraint keeps his work from degenerating into the grotesque. There is a freshness and refinement of taste in everything he does. The Cowan pottery is attracting such artists as

Alexander Blazys, Waylande Gregory, Margaret Postgate, Thelma Frazier, Paul Bogatay and A.D. Jacobson.''
(Information and marks: Donald Caulkins, ''Cowan Pottery,'' *Antique Trader Weekly*, November 30, 1977, Annual VIII, p. 4; John Brodbeck, ''Cowan Pottery,'' *Spinning Wheel*, March 1973, pp. 24-27. Grace C. Allison, ''Cowan-Ohio Pottery of the Roaring Twenties,'' *American Clay Exchange*, February 1984, pp. 7-9. Marks nos. 1-6, Caulkins, as cited. Nos. 7-13, Linda Steigleder, from the booklet published by the Everson Museum of Art to accompany the 1978 exhibition, ''A Century of Ceramics in the U.S.'' Nos. 7-9 are incised marks. Nos. 10-13 are stamped or impressed marks.)

2. COWAN Pottery

3. LAKEWOOD WARE

4. LAKEWARE

5. COWAN POTTERY

6.

7. Cowan Pottery

G. I. R.

8. Cowan

9. R. G. Cowan

10.

11.

12. COWAN

13.

Cowden Pottery. Harrisburg, Pennsylvania. Some members of the Cowden family in various associations made pottery from 1861 to 1915. Business continued until 1923. **John Wallace Cowden and Company** started in the **William Moyer Pottery** in 1861 until 1870. John W. was joined by his son, Frederick, until Frederick went to the Civil War. They made brushed floral designs on cobalt blue stoneware. From 1870-1881, the pottery became **Cowden and Wilcox** under John W. Cowden and Isaac J. Wilcox. John W. died in 1872 but his sons Frederick and Wilcox continued. During this period the ware was salt glazed, blue decorated with men, birds, flowers, etc. They also made some slip trail decorated pieces. From 1881-1888, Frederick operated alone as **F.H. Cowden**, during which time he introduced straight shapes and stencil designing. From 1888 to 1904, Frederick's son John Wallace Cowden II, was a partner under **F.H. Cowden and Son** name. During this period molds were introduced. The products were no longer all hand thrown on a wheel. Terra cotta building products were added during this itme.

From 1904 to 1915, John W. Cowden II became owner after Frederick's death and called the pottery **Cowden and Company**. The pottery stopped making pottery in 1915 but continued as jobbers until 1923 until the building became a part of R.R. Rhoads Company, a building materials supplier. (Information: Eleanor C. Stipp, ''Cowden Stoneware and The Cowden Pottery,'' *Antique Trader*, June 8, 1976, pp. 52, 53; Mildred Veley Hardcastle, ''The Cowden and Wilcox Pottery Story,'' *Antiques Journal*, January, February, 1968, pp. 38, 39. Marks: Hardcastle, p. 39; Smith, p. 8; Guilland, p. 248; Stewart and Consentino, p. 60. Also, see Jeannette Lasansky, *Made of Mud*, pp. 45, 48, for slight variations of dates from those given by the authors cited. Lasansky's work was very thorough and it is probably a matter of interpretation. For example, Lasansky said Frederick Ack died in 1904 and it took John W. Ack II, a few years to become the sole owner, although he was operator after 1904. So where exactly does the name change come?

F H COWDEN HARRISBURG

COWDEN & WILCOX HARRISBURG

COWDEN & WILCOX

F. H. C.

COWDEN & WILCOX HARRISBURG, PA.

Cox, Paul E. Pottery. New Orleans, Louisiana. Paul E. Cox was a ceramist who made hand thrown pieces and mixed glazes at the Newcomb Pottery from 1910 to 1918. (See the listing for New Orleans, Louisiana potteries.) He taught at Iowa State College Ceramic Department in Ames, Iowa, sometime between 1924 and 1930. (See that listing.) In Garth Clark's *A Century fo Ceramics in the U.S.*, p. 331, in Clark's discussion of the potter, Rudolph Staffel, Clark states that Staffel worked at the Paul Cox Pottery in Louisiana around 1937. Staffel worked part time while he taught at the Arts and Crafts Club there. Clark goes on to say that Cox had established a sophisticated production pottery to make strawberry-canning pots for the Louisiana jam industry. In the page of ''News,'' *Crockery and Glass Journal*, May 1943, p.37, is a paragraph stating that the Paul E. Cox Pottery of New Orleans would be closed for the duration of the war. The article went on to say Cox was working in the Abrasive Company of Philadelphia, making grinding wheels. In *Kovel's Collectors Guide to Art Pottery*, by Ralph and Terry Kovel, p. 345 is described a paper label used by Cox with his name and address, 8 Pine Street, New Orleans, found on a piece of block glazed ware. (Marks: Ross Purdy Museum of American Ceramic Society, Columbus, Ohio.)

THE PAUL E. COX POTTERY NEW ORLEANS, LA.

Coxon and Company. Trenton, New Jersey. This company made cream colored ware and white granite. They merged with the Empire Pottery. See Trenton Potteries Company for history. (Information and marks: Lehner, *American Kitchen and Dinner Wares*, p. 152; Barber, *Marks of American Potters*, p. 56.)

Coxon Pottery. Wooster, Ohio. From around 1926 to around 1930. Failed due to depression. Prior to that time Fred Coxon had operated a pottery for a short time in Fredericksburg, Ohio. When Fred Coxon moved to Wooster, he was joined by his brother, Edward Coxon, Sr., and Edward's son, Edward Coxon, Jr., to make a fine china called "Coxon Belleek," a rich ivory, thin, high-fired porcelain. Also see the Morgan Belleek Company. (Information: Lehner, *American Kitchen and Dinner Wares*, p. 46. Marks: on dishes.)

Craft, Beverly H. Omaha, Nebraska. This mark was filed for registration on October 24, 1965, claiming use since May of that year, on decorative jugs, made of crockery.

JOY JUG

Crafts Potters. Nashua, New Hampshire and Whately, Massachussetts. 1802-1861. Thomas Crafts made earthenware in Whately from 1802 to 1833 at which time he started making stoneware. Three of his sons were also potters, James, Martin and Elbridge. Also one brother of Thomas's named Caleb was a potter. The original pottery belonging to the family was in Whately but a second pottery was operated in Nashua. Lura Woodside Watkins gives these dates for the various family members. In Whately: Thomas, 1802-1861; Caleb, 1845-1854; Martin, after 1856. In Nashua: Martin and James M., 1838-1841; Martin and Caleb, 1841-1845; Martin alone, 1845-1851. Marks included: T. Crafts and Co./Nashua; Martin Crafts/Nashua; Martin Crafts/Nashua, N.H.; C. Crafts and Co./Whately, Mass.; T. Crafts & Co./Whately; M.

Crafts/Whately; Martin Crafts/Whately. These were big operators for the times. In the 1850 Nashua Directory they were listed as employing nine men and doing $16,000 worth of business a year. (Information: articles in *The Art of the Potter*, taken from *Antiques* magazine, edited by Diana and J. Garrison Stradling entitled, "The Crafts Pottery in Nashua, New Hampshire," by F.H. Norton, pp. 97, 98. Also, "A Check List of New England Stoneware Potters," by Lura Woodside Watkins, pp. 77-80. Marks: nos. 1-5, drawn from pictures in the same articles; nos. 6, 7, Thorn, p. 123 and 124. Also see the listing for Martin and Caleb Crafts in Portland, Maine.)

Crafts, Martin and Caleb. Portland, Maine. Martin Crafts from 1833 to 1837; and Caleb Crafts from 1837 to 1841. For the history of the whole Crafts family in New Hampshire and Massachusetts, see the listing the Crafts Potters. However, I thought Martin and Caleb should be considered separately because the pottery organizations were separate. In 1833, Martin Crafts left Whately, Massachusetts, and went to Portland, Maine. He bought a property from John D. Gardner, a merchant, (see the listing for the Gardiner Stoneware Company) and started producing stoneware in Portland, in 1834. Early in 1835, Martin Crafts was joined by Eleazer Orcutt, of Whately, whose father had made pottery in Whately, in 1797. (See the listing, Eleazer Orcutt, and various associations.) Orcutt stayed in Portland, until 1837. In 1835, Martin Crafts purchased a building that had been a distillery and Orcutt and Crafts Pottery was founded in Portland, to make utilitarian stoneware, such as jugs, milk pans, pitchers, fire brick, etc. Another potter from Whately, named David Belding, worked with Orcutt and Crafts in Portland, around 1837 to around 1842. In 1837, Caleb Crafts, an uncle of Martin's, came from Troy, New York, to Portland, very shortly after Caleb's arrival. Martin sold the pottery to Caleb and left Portland. Caleb operated the pottery under the name Caleb Crafts and Company. A man named William Fives worked with Caleb from 1837 until 1841. The property was sold for taxes in 1843. Crafts went to Nashua, in 1841. (Information and marks: M. Lelyn Branin, *The Early Potters and Potteries of Maine*, 1978, pp. 53-58 and 223.)

Craig, B.B. Vale, North Carolina. Burlon Craig learned to make pottery in his childhood by working for pottery Jim Lynn, a potter in the Catawba Valley of North Carolina. He also worked with the Reinhardts, Seth Richie and Propst potteries at various times. He served in the navy in W.W. II. After the war he worked in a furniture store and made pottery at nights and on the weekends for over nineteen years before pottery making became his full time occupation. He makes stoneware from local clay on an old kickwheel, using alkaline glaze, fired in an old groundhog kiln. Pieces include face and snake jars, milk crocks, churns, etc. Craig also makes a clear-glazed swirled pottery and dark Albany slip glazed pottery. He digs and grinds his own clay and grinds glass bottles to use in the ash glaze. (Information: Nancy Sweezy, *Raised in Clay*, pp. 89 to 92. Sweezy gives a fine description of the process Craig uses to make the pottery and a good description of the kiln; also, Karol K. Brookhauser, "Country Potter," *Country Home* magazine, February 1985, pp. 62, 63. Impressed or stamped in mark: shown on a cup made of cream colored clay with dark brown heavy glaze.)

B. B. CRAIG
VALE, N.C.

Crane China Company. See Iroquois China Company.

Craven Art Pottery. East Liverpool, Ohio. Around 1905 and out of business before 1908. W.P. Jervis, author and potter, started the pottery in 1905. W.P. Jervis in "A Dictionary of Pottery Terms," *Pottery, Glass and Brass Salesman*, December 5, 1918, p. 13, had this paragraph about the pottery he made. He was quoting Marcus Benjamin, author of "American Art Pottery," published in *Glass and Pottery World*, just after the turn of the century. Dr. Benjamin in his work on American ceramics says in part: "The product of this pottery is an earthenware body with a matt glaze peculiarity of which is the production of different tones of shades on the same piece, thus avoiding the monotony of the usual matt glazes. This result he has succeeded in obtaining by a radical departure in precedent in the manipulation of the coloring oxides. It is the purpose of this pottery to produce articles of every-day use rather than merely ornamental pieces." See the listing W.P. Jervis, for his involvement with various potteries, also various credits for marks, etc. (The mark shown is the one Jervis said was used at East Liverpool, in 1906 to 1907. Also shown in W.P. Jervis listing, see that listing.)

Craven Family Potters. Steeds, North Carolina. Around 1750 to 1917 (Stewart and Consentino, p. 123). Starting with Peter Craven, around the middle of the 18th century. According to L.G.G. Ramsey in *The Complete Encyclopedia of Antiques*, p. 832, Craven made the plainest of "dirt dishes" in supplying common vessels to Southern distilleries, etc. Peter had a son, Thomas, and Thomas had a son, John, all of whom were very early potters. John's sons were Enoch, Anderson and an H. Craven. Anderson's son, John Dorris Craven is the potter whose mark is shown on a stoneware jar made around 1897 with frogskin glaze, p. 39, of *The Traditional Pottery of North Carolina* by Bob Conway. John D. Craven's sons were I. Frank and Daniel Z. I. Frank had a daughter, Bessie, who married Bryan D. Teague, and today their grandson operates the Teague Pottery (see that listing). Another well-known member of the Craven family of potters was Charles, who was one of the three sons of Daniel Z., who was a son of John D. Craven. Charles, born in 1909, worked at North State Pottery, for two years around age nineteen or twenty. He also worked for Herman Cole at Smithfield for 12 years where he learned to make very large pots. Cole went out of business in 1940 and Charlie went to Royal Crown Pottery, Merry Oak, North Carolina, until the pottery closed in 1942, because of war-time restrictions on glazing material. He also made some pottery for Teague Pottery in Robbins, North Carolina. In 1973, he bought an electric wheel and set up a small shop in his own back yard in Raleigh, North Carolina. In 1982, he arranged to have his stoneware pieces fired at Jugtown Pottery in Seagrove, North Carolina. Pieces include stoneware jugs, jars, pitchers, candlesticks, etc. (Information: Nancy Sweezy, *Raised in Clay*, pp. 93-96. Mark: Zug, p. 39.)

Crawford Ceramics. Carey, Ohio. 1965 to present (1983). Make low-fired ceramic items cast in molds. Decorative pieces.

Creek-Turn Pottery. Haines Port, New Jersey. 1927 to present (1987). Herman Kleiner, Jr. started making pottery in 1927. His father, Herman Kleiner, Sr., was a sculptor who made ornamentation for churches and theaters. He made some ceramic or pottery pieces, but was well known for the larger sculptured pieces. Herman Kleiner, Jr. studied sculpturing, painting and ceramic engineering at the Trenton Industrial School. The school was operated by the big potteries in Trenton to train workers for their factories. Creek-Turn Pottery was closed during World War II, then started operating again. In the 1949 *New Jersey Industrial Directory* the pottery was listed under art pottery. At present the company does custom work such as restoration work, custom made-to-order tiles, etc. Creek-Turn Pottery also sells all sorts of raw materials such as glazes, tools, etc. for the potter. Herman specializes in glazes, bodies and slips. Creek-Turn Pottery made a figurine of St. Francis for Carbone, Inc. to sell. They made lamp bases for Colonial Premier which in turn sold them to Mutual Sunset. (Information: by telephone from Herman Kleiner, Jr. Impressed mark: sent by reader, found on lidded jar with no handles.)

Crescent China Company. Alliance, Ohio. See Leigh Potters, Inc. for history. (Marks: no. 1, 2, 3, dishes; no. 4, 5, Quality Stamp Company.)

 1.

 2.

 3.

 4.

 5.

Crescent Pottery. Trenton, New Jersey. See Trenton Potteries Company for history. The marks shown are from Barber, *Marks of American Potters*, pp. 62, 63 and were used sometime before 1903 on white granite and semi-granite dinnerware, some with underglaze decorations.

Crest China Company/Royal Crest China Company. Santa Ana, California. Started before 1949 until before 1954. They were found listed in the 1949 *China, Glass and Tableware Directory* as Crest China Company at 1335 Santiago Avenue. In the 1952 *Crockery and Glass Journal Directory*, they were listed at the same address as Royal Crest China, using the mark shown. They were not listed in 1954. They manufactured figurines, smoking accessories, flower vases, boxes, table decorations, miniature cups and saucers and miniature vases.

Crest Studios. New York City, New York. Started 1950 to present. Decorators of china.

Cribbs, Daniel. Tuscaloosa, Alabama. A stoneware potter named Daniel Cribbs came from Ohio and may have been in Alabama as early as 1829. His son was a sheriff and potter in Tuscaloosa during the Civil War. Daniel's brother Peter was also a potter, and the son of Peter was Fleming, who was making pottery in Sulligent around 1900. (Information: E. Henry Willett and Joey Brackner, *The Traditional Pottery of Alabama*, p. 38. Mark: some source, p. 42, on gray salt glazed stoneware jar, made around 1850.)

Crisman, W.H. Strasburg, Virginia. Ramsay, p. 242, dated this potter around 1890. He made stoneware. In Smith, p. 22, is a drawn mark for this potter, "W.H. Cristman," which is probably misspelled. According to several sources, the spelling is "Crisman."

Crockett Pottery. Bell Buckle, Tennessee. 1976 to present (1985). Pamela Crockett, studio potter, makes high-fired stoneware and porcelain functional pieces such as dinnerware, etc. She has done shows across the country, from Seattle, Washington, to Washington, D.C. She signs her pots, Crockett, in a circle on the bottom or foot of the pot.

CROCKETT

Crolius Pottery. Manhatten Wells, New York City, New York. John William and Peter Crolius, brothers, were listed on the "roll of freemen" of the city of New York for 1737, both described as stoneware potters (Spargo, p.67). The properties of the Remmey and Crolius families were contiguous on Potter's Hill, but they were not connected in the pottery business. John Remmey and William Crolius married sisters name Cortselius, but were not in business together. Spargo used five full pages, 67-72, to disprove Barber's statement that the families were in business together at any time. John Crolius, son of William Crolius was born in 1733. Son of John Crolius was Clarkson, born October 3, 1773. It is quite possible that he made the jug showing mark no. 1 as was shown in Jervis, "Worlds Pottery Marks," *Bulletin of the American Ceramic Society*, April 1, 1915, p. 13. Spargo said it could have been made by Clarkson Crolius II, son of Clarkson Crolius I. Also bearing on the proper dates for the Crolius potters is one more statement from Spargo, p. 71: "After the death of his father, John Crolius, the business was carried on by Clarkson, and when, in 1812, Potter's Hill was leveled and Collect Pond filled in, he moved the pottery to 65 Bayard Street, where the business was carried on until 1848, Clarkson Crolius II, having in the meantime succeeded his father." I found such discrepancies in the dates listed for these potters. There was just no agreement among authors at all. The Spargo research seemed to be extensive and authentic but incomplete when it came to listing dates when these people worked as potters. The listing that seemed to fit in best with Spargo was from Stewart and Consentino, p. 123: William John Crolius, around 1728; William Crolius, around 1770 to around 1779; John Crolius, around 1785-1808; Clarkson Crolius, around 1794-1838; Clarkson Crolius, Jr., around 1835-1849. Very close to the Stewart and Consentino dates were these from Thorn, p. 124. Thorn also said "Manhatten Wells" was probably not used after 1814. Thorn listed John Crolius for latter half of 18th Century and mark was impressed; Clarkson Crolius, Sr., in New York about 1794-1837; Clarkson Crolius, Jr., in New York, about 1838-1850. (Information: John Spargo, *Early American Pottery and China*, Garden City, New York: Garden City Publishing Co., Inc., 1926, pp. 67-72. Marks: nos. 2-6, all from Guilland, pp. 109, 149, 163, 237, 287; no. 1, W.P. Jervis, as cited p. 13.)

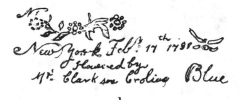

1.

C. CROLIUS
NEW YORK

2.

C. CROLIUS

3.

C. CROLIUS
MANUFACTURER
NEW YORK

4.

C. CROLIUS
MANHATTEN WELLS
NEW YORK

5.

6.

Cronin China Company. Minerva, Ohio. 1934 to 1956. It was founded in 1934 in Minerva, Ohio, and manufactured a very nice grade of semi-porcelain dinnerware until 1956 when the United States Ceramic Tile Company acquired all the stock of Cronin China. The plant still operated under the Cronin name manufacturing wall and floor tile as was listed in the 1960 *Directory of Manufacturers for Ohio*. Marks nos. 1-4, The Pottery Guild, was made for Block China Company (See Block China Company's listing) in late 1930's and early 1940's. These marks were found at Quality Stamp Company, East Liverpool, Ohio, listed under Cronin China. It is possible some other factory made Pottery Guild pieces also, but I don't think so. We searched long and hard for the maker of these handpainted, attractive, well-designed pitchers, platters, large bowls, etc. Other pieces made by Cronin China Company that made the researcher work were marked, "Hamilton Ross." The Hamilton Ross marks shown here, nos. 5, 7, 8, were also found at Quality Stamp Company. No. 8 says "Hamilton Rose," and I never decided if it was an error in spelling or a pattern name that went with the decoration. The mark and design are just as they were found at Quality Stamp Company. No. 6 was sent by Connie Rogers, researcher, writer on Blue Willow. No. 10 was filed for registration February 24, 1938, for use on semi-porcelain ware, namely dishes, claiming use since July 10, 1937. I found this mark on a heavy stoneware serving bowl with a pink color and incised mark. Nos. 11 and 12 are for "Colorama," which was probably Cronin's attempt at Fiesta type dishes. These dishes came in several colors, none of which were very pretty. Most of the Cronin China products were very nice, a good grade of semi-porcelain and well decorated. "Sevilla" was also a trade name listed for Cameron Clay Products Company in the 1954 *Directory*, p. 159. Perhaps my pink bowl belonged to them, but the mark is the same one shown in this patent report. I haven't seen Cameron Clay Product's "Seville," and the bowl looks much older than the 1950's. Bake Oven ware was nicely decaled baking dishes of various kinds being collected now. The rest of the marks came from Quality Stamp Company, or were copy machined from dishes. Hermitage China Company and Floriesta China Company marks are marks of distributors for which Cronin China Company made products. The Hamilton Ross products were made for some distributor, more than likely, but I could not discover which. On a gold covered ceramic spoon and kitchen fork, I found the mark "Lady Hamilton" with the same printing.

HANDPAINTED
Pottery Guild
OF AMERICA
2

1.

HOSTESS WARE
Pottery Guild

2.

HOSTESS WARE
Pottery Guild

BAKE OVEN
3.

HAND PAINTED
By Pottery Guild
4.

HAMILTON ROSS
MING RED
DINNERWARE
UNDERGLAZE
C 53

6.

Hamilton Ross
5.

Hamilton Ross
Lady Godey
7.

Hamilton Rose
WARRANTED
22 KARAT GOLD
8.

Lady Hamilton
WARRANTED 22 K
9.

Sevilla 10.

Cronin Casuals 11.

COLORAMA

COLORAMA
BY
CRONIN
12.

SILVERBROOK(?)
22 KT. GOLD
MADE IN U.S.A.
13.

HERMITAGE CHINA CO.
MADE IN U.S.A.
WARRANTED 22 KARAT GOLD
UNION MADE
14.

CRONIN CHINA
MINERVA,
O.
WARRANTED
22 KARAT GOLD
15.

FLORIESTA CHINA CO
MINERVA, OHIO
16.

CRONIN CHINA
MINERVA,
O.
17.

Románce by CRONIN
18.

Rosemarie by CRONIN
19.

HAND PAINTED
By Pottery Guild

20.

ROYAL IRIS
CRONIN CHINA CO.
MINERVA OHIO
21.

ROYAL EMPEROR MAROON
22 K GOLD
CRONIN CHINA CO
MINERVA, OHIO
22.

ESTHER
BY
CRONIN CHINA CO.
GOLDEN POPPY
23.

CRONIN CHINA
MINERVA,
O.
24.

BAKE OVEN

THE CRONIN CHINA CO.
NATIONAL BROTHERHOOD
OPERATIVE POTTERS
MINERVA, OHIO
25.
66

ROYAL RAJAH MAROON
22 K GOLD
CRONIN CHINA CO.
MINERVA, OHIO
26.

CUMBERLAND WARE
CRONIN CHINA CO.
27.

BAKE OVEN
28.

BAKE OVEN
29.

Crooksville China Company. Crooksville, Ohio. 1902-1959. They started in business employing 125 people and by 1931 were employing 250, and at the time of closing, 300 people. Crooksville Pottery products are of a good grade of semi-porcelain that at times comes close to a fine vitrified ware. They used quaint, old country-type decorations. Crooksville "Pantry-Bak-in" ware had a smooth, hard body with attractive decalcomania. The line started in a small way with a waffle set before 1930 which was greatly extended in 1932. Bowls in five sizes, two different teapots, two sizes of covered jugs, a fruit juice set, coffeepots, three sizes of baking dishes, cookie jars, four spice jars, strands for baking dishes and three different covered baking sets were just some of the items in the line. (*China, Glass and Lamps* advertisement, November, 1923, p. 19.) The finest, thinnest, semi-porcelain of Crooksville's older ware is marked "Stinthal China." There is no mention of Crooksville Pottery in the mark. Stinthal was a special ware made by the pottery which was thin, highly vitrified, almost porcelain and very pretty. Crooksville's "Pantry Bak-in Ware" had many different decals for decoration, one of which was a very attractive type of needlepoint. "Sun Lure" is a mark which refers to the light cream-to-yellow color of the ware. Hardly any pattern names may be found on the Crooksville ware; it is hard to identify as to pattern. (Information: Lehner, *American Kitchen and Dinner Wares*, p. 48. Marks: no. 1, W.P. Jervis, "The World's Pottery Marks," *Pottery, Glass and Brass Salesman*, May 15, 1913, p. 15; no. 2, E.A. Barber *Marks of American Potters*, p. 136. The rest of the marks were found on dishes. Nos. 1-5 older marks.)

1.

2.

3.

4.

5.

6.

7. DELMAR DIANA WARRANTED 22-KT GOLD

8.

9.

10.

11.

12.

13.

14.

15.

16.

17.

18.

19.

Cross, Peter. Hartford, Connecticut. 1805 until around 1818. Stoneware potter who made impressive pieces, but was not very successful in business, according to Lura W. Watkins. He worked in two different buildings in Hartford, in the few years he was there. Watkins describes a urnshaped water color which was in the Deerfield Memorial Museum when she wrote her book in 1950. He made many presentation pieces with incised decorations. (Information: Lura Woodside Watkins, *Early New England Potters and Their Wares*, p. 194. Mark: C. Jordon Thorn, *Handbook of Old Pottery and Porcelain Marks*, p. 124.)

P. CROSS

HARTFORD

Crownford China Company. Broadway, New York. Importers and selling agency, was listed in 1952 and 1954 *Crockery and Glass Journal Directory* for English, German and Italian dinnerware. Company included here because Crown mark is very similar to that used by other factories, particularly Robinson Ransbottom. Also see Tebor Inc. for another "Crownford" mark. I didn't make a connection between the two companies but I believe there may have been one.

TRADE MARK

Crown Pottery and Crown Potteries Company. Evansville, Indiana. 1891 to around 1955. In 1882, A.M. Beck came from England and started a pottery in Evansville, Indiana, to make majolica. In 1884, Beck died and the pottery was sold to **Bennighof, Uhl, and Company**, who began the manufacture of whiteware. (Barber p. 163). By 1891 the pottery was organized as Crown Pottery Company by the Flentke family. (McKee p. 31). In 1902 Crown Pottery Company took over the Peoria Pottery Company in Peoria, Illinois, and the two companies assumed the name of **Crown Potteries Company**. In 1904, Peoria Pottery was closed for good. (See Peoria Pottery.) Barber gives a variety of marks for Crown Pottery and if you will notice, they look very much like English marks, as they were intended to do. Crown Pottery made ironstone china, "Crown Porcelain" dinnerware, toilet ware, semi-porcelain and in the *1902-1903 Complete Directory* they were listed as making semi-porcelain and white granite dinner sets, toilet sets, and short sets of odd dishes, some decorated. According to McKee, Crown had been one of the plants selling a good part of its production to jobbers in plain white when Scio cut in. Being hemmed in by city streets with no room for expansion for proper kilns added to Crown's troubles in the 1950's. Crown Potteries went out of business between 1954 and 1958. The last listing I had for them was 1954. I did not have the directories for the years between 1954 and 1958, but they were no longer listed in 1958. (Information: Lehner, *American Kitchen and Dinner Wares*, p. 49. Also E.A. Barber, *Marks of American Potters*, pp. 163-164. Nos. 1 to 14, E.A. Barber, as cited. No. 15 shown in 1951 and 1954 directories. Nos. 16-17, Quality Stamp Company, East Liverpool, Ohio. No. 18 on plate with Grandma Moses decal. Nos. 19-20, on dishes.)

1. JEWEL / C.P.Co.

2. C P. CO. / REX

3. CROWN HOTEL / WARE

4. C. P. CO. / ROYAL

5. REGINA / C P. CO.

6. HELEN.

7. HOBSON

8. ALMA

9. RENA.

10. IRONSTONE CHINA / WARRANTED

11. CROWN / SEMI-PORCELAIN / C P CO / WARRANTED

12. Crown Porcelain.

13. REX.

14.

15.

16. CROWN POTTERIES CO. / MADE IN U S A

17. CROWN POTTERIES CO. / MADE IN U S A. / 12 43

18. CROWN POTTERIES CO. / MADE IN U S A. / EVANSVILLE. IND. / Ovenproof

19. SEMI PORCELAIN / C. P. CO.

20. COLONIAL DAMES / BY / CROWN

Croydon China Company/Ceramic Decorating Company, Inc. The company listed in *Trenton, New Jersey, City Directory*, from 1943 into the 1960's for general ware, china decorating for the trade. In 1961, they employed four people. In the 1952 *Crockery and Glass Journal Directory*, they were listed for figures, figurines, miniatures, bakeware and cookware. The company decorated products for Tebor Inc. See that listing for the marks found under the Croydon China Company name at Quality Stamp Company in East Liverpool, Ohio.

Crystal Springs Studio. New Albin, Iowa. 1973 to present (1986). Studio potter, Dale A. Raddatz, makes raku fired to 2,000 degrees and other decorative pieces. Dale studied with

Margaurite Wildenheim in the summer of 1967. He graduated from Northern Illinois University in 1973 with a M.A. degree. He signs his pottery as shown.

RADDATZ / CSS.   RADDATZ

Culbreath, Sarah L. Berea, Kentucky. 1972 to present. Since 1980, Sarah has maintained her own studio pottery shop in Berea, where she makes utilitarian ware from highly vitrified red clay with a full signature on the bottom of each piece. She makes bead lamps, butter dishes, bowls, cannister sets, coffee makers, honey pots, juice sets, spoonbread bakers, etc. Beginning in 1972 she was trained and worked in the Berea College program (see that listing for information on the program) under Walter Hyleck and John Eden, an English potter. During the six years from 1972 to 1980, Sarah used the Berea College stamp, mark no. 1, and her stamp as is shown in mark 2. In 1974, she was an instructor at the "Westervelt" workshop at Berea College. In 1978, she studied and worked at the David Leach Workshops. She worked as an instructor in Berea College Workshops, "An Experience in Clay," in 1984 and 1985. Sarash has made special orders of dinnerware to be sold by Neiman-Marcus Company and Marshall Fields Company. (See the listing for these selling agencies.) She has done many shows, exhibitions and crafts fairs.

1. BB   **2.** LEE

3. Sarah Culbreth

Cumbow China Decorating Company. Abingdon, Virginia. 1932 to 1980. Jacob Zacariah Ruskin, from Zurich, Switzerland, had started the business which was continued after his death by Mrs. Ruskin. They were decorators and restored fine china. They decorated quality old fashioned beautifully designed ware with many decorations. Mrs. Mabel Cumbow Ruskin died April 11, 1980 and the business was discontinued. (For a discussion of this company, see Annise Heaivilin, *Grandma's Tea Leaf Ironstone*, pp. 160-161. Marks: no.1, Heaivilin, as cited. No. 2 filed for registration on November 14, 1941, claiming use since January 1936. No. 3 filed for registration on May 2, 1944, claiming use since January 1935. No. 4 filed for registration on October 22, 1941, claiming use since January 1936. No. 6 filed for registration on November 14, 1941, claiming use since January 1933. Nos. 2-6 were all said to be used on table and cooking ware, vases, jars, jugs, jardinieres, crocks, cuspidors and flower pots.)

1. Pat. No. / 187996 / Tea Leaf / from West / CUMBOW CHINA / DECORATING CO. / ABINGDON VA

2. *Louis XV*

3. *Williamsburg*

4. *Old School*

5. *Abingdon*

6. *Cumbow*

Cunningham Industries. A distributor associated with Cunningham & Pickett. See Cunningham & Pickett for history. (Marks: from Quality Stamp Company.)

AVOCADO GREEN

Cunningham and Pickett and Associated Companies. Alliance, Ohio. Alfred Cunningham was the owner of a series of jobber or retail agencies in Alliance, Ohio. The first and last dates for when these names were used to order products were supplied by E.S. Carson of Homer Laughlin Company from copies of order sheets at the factory. A great deal of the dishes distributed under these various names used by Cunningham were made by Homer Laughlin Company so they are a nice quality of semi-porcelain, well decorated and collectible.

Customer (jobber or retailer)	First Purchased	Last Purchased
Cunningham and Pickett, Inc.	1938	1968
Alliance China Company	1958	1968
Century Service Corporation	1953	1968
Laughlin International China Co.	1961	1964
International China Company	1958	1968
International D.S. Co.	1961	1968
Lifetime China Co.	1953	1968
Cunningham Industries, Inc.	1967	1969

(See *American Kitchen and Dinner Wares* for pictures and pattern names.)

Cushing, Val Murat. Alfred, New York. Early 1950's to present (1986). Studio potter and professor of ceramics, Val Murat Cushing, received a B.F.A. degree in 1952 and a M.F.A. in 1956, both from Alfred University in Alfred, New York. In 1956, he taught at the University of Illinois, Urbana, and directed a summer school course at Alfred University from 1957 to 1965. In 1978, he was teaching at Alfred University when Clark and Hughto's book was published. He has done many one-man and major group shows, and in the 1970's, he won the Binns Medal of the American Ceramic Society. (Information: Garth Clark, *A Century of Ceramics in the U.S.*, p. 280. Painted marks: Linda Steigleder, from the booklet published by the Everson Museum of Art to accompany the 1978 exhibition, "Century of Ceramics in the U.S.")

Cushing

Val cushing

Cushman, Paul. Albany, New York. 1809-1832. Some in-depth research on this potter seems to have upset the old established dates for this potter. In a very authorative article by Robert G. Wheeler, "The Potters of Albany," in *The Art of the Potter*, edited by Diana and J. Garrison Stadling (composed of articles from *Antiques*), pp. 131-133, Mr. Wheeler gives 1809-1832 as dates of existance based on letters and various records. (Thorn, p. 125 and Ramsay, p. 186 had dated this potter 1805-1825.) Cushman died in 1832 and his widow sold the stoneware pottery to Jacob Henry and Edward Selby who operated it with Charles Dillon and Nathan Porter under the firm name **Charles Dillon and Company** until 1836. (Marks: Barber, *Marks of American Potters*, p. 74 and Barber, *Pottery and Porcelain of the U.S.*, p. 113, and Stradling, p. 131.)

PAUL CUSHMAN

PAUL · CUSHMAN · STOE · WARE
FACTORY · 1809 · HALF · A · MILE
WEST OF ALBANY GOAL

PAUL CUSHMAN'S STONE WARE FACTORY 1809
HALF A MILE WEST OF THE ALBANY GOAL

Cutting, Heyward Jr. Staunton, Virginia. 1974 to present. Heyward Cutting Jr., a studio potter, makes porcelain functional pieces. He received a M.F.A. Degree from Ohio University in 1979. He has worked as Head Resident in several workshops, a teaching assistant to undergraduates in college, etc. He has a list of sixteen shows and exhibitions where he has participated in eleven different states. His mark is his signature.

Heyward Cutting Jr

Cybis, Boleslaw and Related Companies. Boleslaw Cybis was a Polish born artist, graduate of Fine Arts Academy in Warsaw, a winner of Paris International Exhibitions Grand Prix. He had paintings, sculptures and Al Fresco murals exhibited in many cities. In 1938, he came to this country by invitation to paint murals for the Polish Pavilion at the World's Fair of 1939 in New York. He was headed for home when Poland was invaded by Germans. He came back to the U.S. and stayed. He and his wife founded **Cybis Art Productions** in New York City making plaster of Paris figurines and artware pieces for a few years. They moved to Trenton, New Jersey. In 1942, Boleslaw Cybis, Harry Wilson and Harry Greenberg founded the **Cordey China Company** in Trenton. Cordey China Company and another company named Schiller Brothers were acquired by the Lightron Corporation in 1969 and operated as the Schiller Cordey Company. Between 1942 and 1949, Cordey China made some very fine articles, such as tea and coffee pots with procelain lace and ribbons and tiny flowers. Giftware production made of a cream colored semi-porcelain body, called "Papka" was discontinued after W.W. II because of Japanese imports, and only high fired white translucent porcelain sculptures were made. Until after the Korean War, Cordey made items elaborately decorated with hand shaped roses and other flowers such as coffee sets, lamps, candy dishes, etc. After W.W. II Boleslaw Cybis made a diversified line of religious items also. Then, following the Korean War, Crodey began to make lamps exclusively after the acquisition by Lightron Corporation described. Boleslaw Cybis died in 1957 and his wife, Marja Tym, died in 1958, but his work has been carried on apparently in two locations by two companies. Exactly when Cybis Porcelain came into existence as a company name I could not determine. Around 1960, Cybis Porcelains began to be listed at 65 Norman Avenue. They employed 45 in 1978, to make porcelainware. Cordey China Company at 356 Enterprise Avenue was still listed under the name Cordey in 1978 employing 50 to make porcelain ceramic lamps. From 1960 to 1969 Cybis Inc. was listed at 315 Church Street. Cybis Porcelain Art was listed from 1965 through 1970 at 340 W. State Street. This is all very confusing, I know, but we have three groups of beautiful products to collect that have grown from the Boleslaw Cybis heritage. There are the early delicate porcelain products made by Corday before 1950. And the lamps made by Schiller-Corday are hand crafted and made of porcelain. A third group, the delicate beautiful Cybis Porcelain Company figurines which include carousel horse, owls, skylarks and all sorts of figures from an enchanted world and which according to a December 1977 advertisement of the *Smithsonian*, p. 32, range in price from $25.00 to $5,000.00, would make great collectibles for anyone who can afford them. See the articles cited for numerous pictures of the various figurines. The information I had from the com-

pany centered on the products and history since 1969. There are eleven companies in the Lightron group including Schiller-Cordey, Laurel Lamp and others, making the beautiful decorated lamps. (Information: Rena London, "Cordey," *Antique Trader Weekly*, July 16, 1980, pp. 52-55; Staff written, "What Happened to Yesterdays Artistic Craftsmen?" *Home Lighting and Accessories*, May 1973 (no page numbers in reprint); Chester Davis, "Cordey China," *Spinning Wheel*, January, February, 1973, pp. 10, 11. Marks: no. 1, mark as shown in 1971 *China, Glass and tableware Directory*; no. 2, mark from same directory in 1967 and 1976. The rest of the marks are from "Cybis Porcelain Cats," by Marilyn Dipboye, *Antique Trader Weekley*, January 1, 1986. p. 50.)

1.

2. Porcelain Enchantments.

Porcelains
3. 1940-1957

4. 1942-1950

5. CYBIS 1945

6. 1947-1951

7. 1952-1966

8. 1953

Publications

9. 1950-1960

10. 1953-1957

11. 1960-1965

12. CYBIS 1962-1971

13. 1969

14. CYBIS GRAPHICS 1970

15. 1973

16. 1973-1975

17. 1976

18. 1980

19. CYBIS Porcelains that fire the imagination

D

D and D Pottery. Roseville, Ohio. January 1977 to early 1980's. A small two or three member family business making novelties with a one-fire process from greenware to bisque ware, then just paint added to outside. They were caste pieces, not very vitrified. Clarence Dalrymple was a die maker at the Nelson McCoy Pottery in 1977. He worked for the old Crooksville China years ago. Clarence died in October 1981 and his son, Roger, made some pottery pieces on a limited basis for a while, but was not in production in 1983. Shown are the two paper labels used by Clarence on part of the ware. He had a couple of old Weller molds that he made pieces from with the Weller mark shown. But since they were just painted and not refired and not vitrified, there was no attempt at deception. Clarence just probably liked the shapes. One was a basket; the other was a small vase.

D & D POTTERY
34 East Athens Rd.
Roseville, Ohio 43777
697-7844

Daga Design. Minneapolis, Minnesota. 1969 to present (1985). Maigon Daga has been making pottery since 1954. The first eleven years of pottery making were in Australia. Maigon was born in Latvio and studied economics at the University there until the communists came. In 1945, he escaped to Germany, where he started modeling in clay. In 1948, he emigrated to Australia, where he found odd jobs to pay for continuing his study of sculpture and ceramics at the Adelaide School of Fine Arts. In 1957, he opened his first studio in Adelaide, Australia, and started selling through galleries and shops. In 1964, he came to the U.S., and opened a studio in Chicago. In 1966, he moved to Minneapolis. He sculpted for a couple of Minneapolis firms developing his own unusual style and glazes and in 1969 he opened Daga Design. Maigon still works at his own private studio, but his most recent venture is **MSM Ceramics**, a company formed to produce high-quality studio-crafted pottery, ceramics and sculpture for nationwide sales. Maigon Daga excels at wildlife sculptures, made of stoneware and porcelain. He has done many one man and group exhibitions. His glazes give a stone like appearance to the piece. A brochure showed a seal on a piece of ice, brown bears on a rock, polar bear on ice, buffalo, bull, various fish, birds, a raccoon and many other animals, all beautiful, all lifelike. This potter has gained a reputation as one of the country's finest sculptors.

Daley, William. William Daley, an architectural ceramist and teacher, received a Masters in education in 1951, from Col-

umbia University Teachers College in New York City. He taught in Iowa, New York, New Mexico, before going to teach at the Philadelphia College of Art in 1966. He was still teaching there in 1978 when Clark wrote the book cited. He makes large press molded stoneware vessels and has done many architectural commissions for murals in bronze or ceramics. Some of these were for the Atlantic Richfield Corporation, the South African Airlines Office in New York, and for the IBM Pavilion in Seattle. (Information: Garth Clark, *A Century of Ceramics in the U.S.*, p. 180, 281. Mark: stamped/incised along rib. Linda Steigleder, from the booklet published by the Everson Museum of Art to accompany the 1978 exhibition, "A Century of Ceramics in the U.S.")

WM DALEY
JULY 1977

Dalton Pottery or Houghton Pottery. Dalton, Ohio. Started in 1842 and made pottery until 1951. In 1842, this pottery was established by Curtis Houghton. Curtis was followed by Edward, his oldest son, in 1864, who was followed by Edwin in 1890, and on to Victor, the fourth generation of Houghtons to run the pottery. In 1890, Frank Horbach started the Horbach Pottery to act as a distributor for Houghton's products. The pottery made stoneware jugs, chicken waterers and all sorts of hand thrown, heavily brown glazed utilitarian stoneware in the early years. In the later years, they made several lines of decorative pottery. Mark no. 2 is on the bottom of a vase of variegated colorful circular rings with the color in the clay, similar to Niloak, yet very different. Dr. James D. Houdeshell in "Houghton Pottery Began in 1842," *Tri State Trader*, September 10, 1893, names other lines as Egyptian, Rebecca, Tulip, Sepia and the striped ware just described, he said was called Indian. In 1951, the pottery was sold and only tile was made there for several years. They were still in the 1960 *Directory of Ohio Manufacturers*. The only pottery in the yellow pages for Dalton, Ohio, in 1984 was the Old Church Studio. Even the tile factory was gone by this time.. (Information: Joanne Amstutz, by letter in 1973 and "Pottery Party Line," *Pottery Collectors Newsletter*, August 1977, p. 67. Marks: no. 1, impressed on old brown glazed chicken waterer in the shape of a jug. Notice the one "t" in pottery. No. 2, stamped on Indian line vase; no. 3 was raised on a little brown pitcher which looked like Hull Pottery brown kitchenware; no. 4, incised on bottom of a very small chicken waterer at Brisker's Antiques, Richwood, Ohio; no. 5 in Lehner, *Ohio Pottery and Glass*, p. 41; nos. 6, 7, Amstutz article as cited; nos. 8-12, Houdeshell article as cited. Dr. Houdeshell is writing a book on Dalton Pottery.)

DALTON POTERY 1.

HOUGHTON & CO.
DALTON OHIO
USA
2.

3. DALTON USA

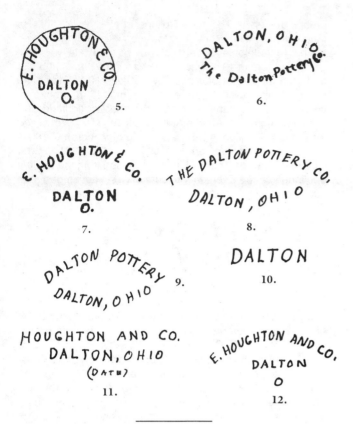

5.

6.

7.

8.

9.

10.

11.

12.

passed it on to customers over the bar or to take away in the customer's containers. By 1870, containers of glass and pottery were starting to be used with the name of the distiller added for advertising purposes. These have provided the collectors with a multitude of collectibles. Shown are a couple of marks as seen on jugs in Donna A. Christian, "Jack Daniel Collectibles," *Antique Trader Weekly*, January 11, 1984, pp. 47-49. (Marks: no. 1 on very old brown and white gallon jug. No. 2 on late modern shaped new looking jug.)

JACK DANIEL'S
OLD No 7
LYNCHBURG.TENN.
1.

2. TENNESSEE WHISKEY

Daubt Glass and Crockery Company. Toledo, Ohio. In business from 1886 to 1929. A distributor. Used this mark around 1909 on fancy and ornamental glass and crockery table pieces. (Information: Lehner, *Ohio Pottery and Glass*, p. 89. Mark: Peterson, Arthur, *400 Trademarks on Glass*, p. 13. Morgan J. Barclay, Toledo - Lucas County Public Library by letter.)

Dauffenbach and Gieseke. New Ulm, Minnesota. Around 1871-1873. Made stoneware jugs, crocks, etc. (Information and marks: sent by Dave Newkirk, co-author of *Red Wing Dinnerware*.)

Dana (sic. Daney, Dany). **Thomas.** Ellsworth, Maine. In *The Art of the Potter*, p. 76, a book composed of articles from *Antiques* magazine, edited by Deanna and J. Garrison Stradling, is a small gray handled jug with the name, "Thos. Daney/Ellsworth," stamped or impressed on the side. The caption under the picture said the potter was unknown and not listed by Lura W. Watkins in her various writings. A possible explanation for the mark is as follows: in *The Early Potters and Potteries* of Maine, by M. Lelyn Branin, pp. 121-124, is discussed a potter, named Edmund Dana, in the area of Hallowell, Maine, who had ten children, one of whom was named Thomas. In 1792, Dana purchased land in Kennebec County, and built a house and pot shop. He made pottery until 1810 when he committed suicide. At the time of his father's death, Thomas was under the age of fourteen and considered a minor at that time. Around 1850, Elisha Jones established a pottery in Ellsworth, Maine, and remained in existance for about ten years. He hired two potters, Samuel F. York and Richard Treat, but Thomas Daney's (or Dana) name was not listed in the population census of 1850, researched by Branin, but Daney could have worked there before 1860. Martha Moore Ballard took care of Mrs. Dana at the birth of most of her children. Martha kept a diary in which she referred to Mrs. Daney spelled with a "y." So the name was subject to variations within the district. This potter was not in any other reference cited in the bibliography. (Information: Branin, as cited. Mark: Stradling, as cited.)

THOS. DANEY
ELLSWORTH

Daniel, Jack, Distillery. Lynchburg, Tennessee. After Civil War to present (1985). After the Civil War, Jack Daniel started distilling whiskey which he sold by the barrel to retailers who

Davidsen, Laura. Los Angeles, California. Filed for registration of this mark on March 24, 1921, for use on hand painted china, claiming use since March 9, 1921.

FLORAMERICANA

Davidson, Taylor and Company. Wheeling, West Virginia. Jobbing concern that sold dishes made by Homer Laughlin China Company to Sears around the turn of the twentieth century. See Sears and Roebuck for marks.

Davies, Melvin L. Flatrock (near Shelbyville), Indiana. Mr. Davies is a studio potter, and noted research writer on the stoneware potters of Indiana. Since 1973 to present he has made wood fired, salt glazed utilitarian pieces of Indiana clay. He dates many of them and most are impressed with his stamp as shown. Some are inscribed with his signature. From 1973 until 1976, he was at Conner Prairie Pioneer Settlement, setting up the pottery at the museum. Conner Prairie Pioneer Settlement is owned by Earlham College which is located near Indianapolis. (See the listing for Conner Prairie.) He has been responsible for or helped to organize several exhibits of Indiana stoneware, such as a large exhibit at Conner Prairie in 1979, followed by a traveling exhibit of thirty-five pieces. In 1981, Clay County, Indiana, had an exhibit in the Riddell National Bank Gallery. Davies prepared the catalogue for that exhibit searching deeds, census reports, business directories, geological reports, etc. He has furnished information for this book. Davies's mark is a stylized "MLD" in a circle impressed in the ware. (Information and mark: Melvin Davies, by visit, letter and *Clay County Indiana Traditional Potters and Their Wares*, p. 4)

Dawson and Sons. Calhoun, Missouri. Around 1874. Made stoneware. (Information: Henry W. Heflin, collector and researcher of Missouri stoneware. Mark: blue stenciled mark on crock.)

DAWSON & SON
CALHOUN, MO.

Day, Evangeline. New York, New York. Filed for rights to this mark on January 31, 1939 to be used on teacups and bowls made of china, porcelain and other earthenware, claiming use since January 20, 1939.

WORLD WISHING BOWL

Dayton Porcelain Works. See Isaac Broome.

Dayton Street Pottery/The Coultry Pottery. Cincinnati, Ohio. The Dayton Street Pottery was started in 1859 by Samuel Pollock, who died in 1870. The Pollock family continued the business until P.L. Coultry took over in 1874. An advertising card for the Dayton Street Pottery listed various products, domestic ware, variegated, Rockingham, and yellowware, tobacco pipe heads, ale and porter bottles, preserve jars, stove linings, furnace bricks, garden vases and flower pots, for the Dayton Street Pottery under Pollock. At first, Coultry continued the manufacturing of yellowware and Rockingham. In 1877, Mary Louise McLaughlin (see separate listing) began experiments at the Coultry Pottery to reproduce the Haviland faience decoration and she succeeded in making the first piece of this ware in Cincinnati. By early 1879, Coultry had hired a young artist, T.J. Wheatley, to decorate

pieces and to teach classes. Also in April 1879, the Cincinnati Pottery Club was formed (see that listing) and their work was fired in Coultry's kilns for a short time until they began to work through the Hamilton Road Pottery of Frederick Dallas (see that listing). In the very early 1880's, a second plant was built in Ironton, Ohio, called the Ironton Pottery (see that listing). Coultry was also still producing yellowware and Rockingham besides the art ware. However, by 1882 the Coultry Pottery in Cincinnati, was closed and the Ironton Pottery in Ironton, was sold at sheriff's sale before the machinery was ever installed. (Information: Wilbur Stout, *Clay Industry of Ohio*, Geological Survey of Ohio Bulletin 26, p. 20; also, Paul Evans, *Art Pottery of the U.S.*, pp. 66-68, and p. 145. Marks. Evans, as cited, p. 68.)

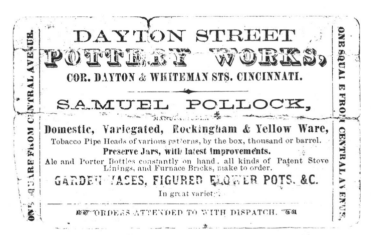

Dean, Jesse, Inc. Trenton, New Jersey, and New York, New York. In W.P. Jervis, *Pottery, Glass and Brass Salesman*, May 20, 1915, p. 13, Jervis stated Jesse Dean, a decorator deserved notice on account of the excellence of his work. Jervis said he introduced new processes for decorating and competed successfully with foreign competition. In the *Pottery, Glass and Brass Salesman*, March 7, 1918, was an advertisement showing mark no. 2 and describing the glass and china decorated with incrusted gold, etched with acid with monograms, crests and designs of the purchaser's choice. Each piece had a style of its own and no two were alike. Jesse Dean, Inc. carried their own lines of decorated glass and china as well. The factory and warehouse were in Trenton, New Jersey, and the show rooms in New York City. The glass and china decorated were foreign and domestic blanks.

Deaver Studios. Berea, Kentucky, and various places. 1970 to present. Teresa and Ron Deaver are studio potters. Both

Teresa and Ron have B.A. degrees from Berea College. At various times, they have maintained studios in Murfreesboro, Tennessee; Ashville, North Carolina; and Cruso, North Carolina. They have had their studio in Berea, since 1980. They make tableware and accent pieces in their studio where they also maintian a residence and showroom. They have been making the wheel thrown tableware since 1978. Some of the decorative or accent pieces are a vitreous redware such as drape molded bowls or slab built pieces. They also make decorative tiles. (Marks: no. 1 is Teresa's stamped mark used from 1974 to 1980. No. 2 is Ron's stamp mark used from 1974 to 1982. Since 1980, they have not used any stamped mark consistently, but they sign the piecs with their written name as shown.)

Debolt and Atchison. In 1849, George Debolt started a pottery in New Geneva, Pennsylvania. In 1855, he took a partner from New Jersey, Henry A. Atchison, who eventually lost an arm in the Civil War and never made any more pottery. In 1876, there was a Henry P. Atchison working as a potter in Greensboro. (Information: Gordon C. Baker, "Pottery of Greensboro and New Geneva, Pa.," *Spinning Wheel*, November 1973, pp. 14-17. Mark: Gordon C. Baker, "Early New Geneva Stoneware Potters," *Spinning Wheel*, May 1979, p. 17. In the November 1973 article, Baker spelled Debolt as "Debelt" but evidently he had found the pot which he pictured in May 1979, and changed the spelling to Debolt or it may have been a typesetter's error.)

Decora Ceramics, Inc. Inglewood, California. This pottery was listed in the 1952 *Crockery and Glass Journal Directory*, but was not listed in 1954. They were not in the 1948 *Directory of California Manufacturers*. They were listed under art pottery made of earthenware, also decorative wall plates. (Mark: found on earthenware cup with hand painted apple.)

Dedham Pottery. East Dedham, Massachusetts. 1895 to 1943 (Evans, p. 83). Was preceded by Chelsea Pottery (1891-1895). The products of this company are considered to be art pottery, but according to Paul Evans in *Art Pottery in the United States*, New York: Scribner's, 1974, p. 84, they did produce over fifty patterns of tableware "spanning the

gamut of any zoo and greenhouse" (in decoration). Rabbits, ducks, grapes, azaleas, magnolias, turkeys, clover, elephants, etc. (See Evans for more.) Stiles, p. 193, said they specialized in crackleware with freehand decorations in cobalt blue. The designs were unusual and the crackle pattern, sometimes in the form of a spider web was most interesting. She also stated that the Rabbit decoration was designed by Joseph Linden Smith and was the best known design of the Dedham Pottery, and was adopted as their trademark. James Robertson, the founder, was the fourth in line of a family of Scottish potters and was followed in this country after 1853 by seven more generations of Robertsons in that business. Frederick W. Allen in "More About Dedham Pottery," *Hobbies*, September, 1952, p. 80, gave us the spelling "Craquleware" for the popular ware made by Robertson. This author had a letter from J. Milton Robertson in which he told how a drawing of a rabbit would vary so much from decorator to decorator, that at first the company put a raised design on the plate so that all the artist had to do was to follow the design and the rabbits would be alike. However, in the drying and shrinking process in the mold, frequently the plate did not release from the mold without cracking. By the time this raised decoration was eliminated from the molds, the decorators were used to the design. The fact that the early plates had a raised design, and the later pieces did not, has great significance for the collector. However, any of this ware today has a great value. (Information: Lehner, *American Kitchen and Dinner Wares*, p. 51 and 52. Paul Evans in *Art Pottery of the U.S.*, pp. 82-86 gives a fine account of the various products of Dedham. Marks: No. 1 Harry Roff "A Rare Dedham," *Glaze*, April 1982, p. 8. No. 2, 3, Barber *Marks of American Potters*, p. 97. No. 4, 5, Evans p. 86.)

D E D H A M
T E R C E N T E N A R Y
1636 - 1936

5.

Deer Foot Pottery. Pueblo, Colorado. 1970 to present (1984). Lyle L. Clift, studio potter, makes functional and decorative stoneware. Lyle participates in shows, art fairs, etc. (Mark no. 1, is recessed stamp of print similar to that made by a deer's foot. Also shown is very attractive logo used on cards, etc. featuring deer feet.)

Deese, Rupert J. Born in Guam in 1924. Rupert received

a B.A. degree from Pomona College in 1950 and an M.F.A. degree from Claremont Graduate School in 1957. He has been a studio potter since 1950 and has worked with Harrison McIntosh. He studied ceramics with Richard Petterson at Claremont and studied sculpture with Albert Stewart at Scripps. He then taught ceramics from 1957 to 1971. Rupert worked mainly as a ceramic designer and model maker for Franciscan Interpace, during the 1964-1983 period. He is presently working again as full-time studio potter at Harrison McIntosh's studio at Padua Hills near Claremont, California. His awards include an Honorable Mention at Syracuse in 1950 and Sweepstakes Prize (IBM) at Syracuse in 1960. (Information and marks: Thomas Turnquist, pottery researcher and writer.)

De Haven, Abraham. Middlebury (Akron), Ohio. Around the middle of the nineteenth century, this potter made stoneware utilitarian pieces. Mark verified by Robert Treichler, who is currently working on a publication about potteries in the Akron area, prior to 1875. Middlebury became a part of Akron in 1872.

A. DEHAVEN
MIDDLEBURY

Delaware Pottery. Trenton, New Jersey. See Trenton Potteries Company for history. (Marks: Barber, *Marks of American Potters*, p. 62.)

Delft Blue Ltd. or **Van Rossum Gallery.** Ellicott City, Maryland. 1963 to present in America, but the heritage dates back to 1821 in the Netherlands, when the Van Rossum family painted tiles and earthenware. Pierre Van Rossum, his artists and craftsman carry on the tradition by making completely hand painted Delftware of the finest quality bisque clay with glazes suitable for hot or cold dinner settings. Mr. Van Rossum holds a Master of Fine Arts Degree from The Sarbonne, Paris, and has displayed his work around the world. (Information and mark from company.)

De Lime Studios. St. Petersburg, Florida. De Lime Studios was listed in 1965 *Gift and Tableware Reporter Directory* for decorator earthenware. This directory didn't distinguish between manufactureres and distributors. The company wasn't in any of the *Crockery and Glass Journal Directories*. (Mark: shown is paper label from small decorative dish.)

De Lite Manufacturing Company, Inc. New York, New York. Filed for registration on this mark December 18, 1942, for use on porcelain vases, claiming use since 1936. This company was listed in the 1945 *Crockery and Glass Journal Directory* as importers and decorators of pottery figures, hand made glassware and novelties.

ETON

Dell, William, Pottery. Cincinnati, Ohio. 1891 and 1892. For only about a year, William Dell made pottery from molds acquired from the Cincinnati Art Pottery. He died in 1892 at age 35. He had been a superintendent and manager at the Cincinnati Art Pottery before it closed. See Evans, p. 87, for more information and pictures of beautiful art ware. (Information and mark: Evans, *Art Pottery of the U.S.*, p. 87.)

Delta-Star Electric Division (H.K. Porter Company). Lisbon, Ohio. In 1957, the R. Thomas and Sons Company of Lisbon, Ohio, (see the listing Thomas China Company) was acquired by the H.K. Porter Company and absorbed into the Delta-Star Electric Division of that company. Suspension type insulators with a sand blasted mark as shown were made there until 1963 when Porter closed the plant. (Information and sand blasted mark: Tod, *Porcelain Insulators Guide Book for Collectors*, p. 122. Tod said by letter, "If they continued making pin types as their cataloging indicated, they probably were unmarked or continued to be marked 'Thomas.' We have never found any pin types with a Delta-Star marking, only suspension insulators.")

Deluxe Decorating Works, Inc. 12 W. 18th St., New York, New York. This address was listed for them in the 1954 *Crockery and Glass Journal Directory*. In the *China, Glass and Tableware Directory* of 1967, there was a Deluxe Designs, Inc., 22 Wyckoff St., Brooklyn, New York, 1967 as decorating contractors for lamp china and giftware trade. In 1982, Deluxe Designs, Inc. were listed as "decorators of ceramic and glass, decal." I assume that means they decorate glass and ceramics with decals. In 1982, they are listed in Trenton, New Jersey. I did not make a positive connection between Deluxe Decorating Works, Inc. and Deluxe Designs, Inc. The mark shown is for Deluxe Decorating Works, Inc.

Deneen Pottery, Inc./Coiner-Deneen. St. Paul, Minnesota. 1970 to present (1984). Studio potter, Peter Deneen, operated alone until 1981, when he was joined by John Coiner. They make hand thrown, hand decorated stoneware artware, dinnerware, gift ware and gourmet pieces which are very beautiful and wholesaled nationally. Pieces shown in brochures sent included candle sconces, hanging baskets, vases with painted and incised ribbed designs, flower pots of various sizes and shapes, complete sets of dinnerware, kerosene lamps, various kitchen accessories. Also pictured were adorable pottery sculptures and there were little animal sculptured figures sitting on the edge of some of the bowls or on the lid of a casserole. (Marks: no. 1, inscribed mark, used 1970-1976; no. 2, impressed mark, used 1976-1981; no. 3, used in 1981; no. 4, used 1982-1984 and at present.)

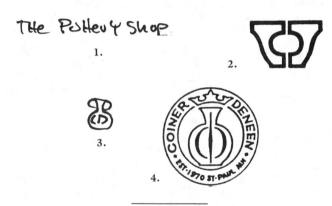

Denlinger, Ding. Columbus, Ohio. 1969 to present. Studio potter making "fantasy" or sculptured and wheel thrown earthenware and porcelain. Mrs. Denlinger's pieces are highly artistic and imaginative. She does shows at cultural art exchanges, fairs, etc. Mark No. 1 is a clay stamp. No. 2 is a small wad of clay added to the pieces marked with no. 1 or 3. No. 3 is the mark for Denlinger's Lotus design ware.

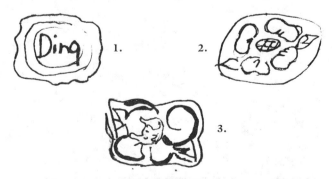

Denver China and Pottery Company. Denver, Colorado. 1901-1905. Organized by William A. Long. They made primarily art pottery but also made a flint blue line which included table pieces such as bowls, mugs, etc. (See Paul

Evans, *Art Pottery of th U.S.*, p. 88 for a complete history and discussion of products. Marks and information: Evans, p. 88.)

Derry China Company. Derry Station, Pennsylvania. Operated for what was apparently a short time around 1900. In the *1902-1903 Complete Directory* they were listed as starting in 1902 with seven kilns to make semi-porcelain and hotel ware, dinner sets, toilet sets and short sets of odd dishes. Barber also listed them as in operation making semi-vitreous china around 1904. My next listing was for 1916 and there was no listing of a pottery in Derry after that, so they had either moved or quit. (Mark: Barber, *Marks of American Potters*, p. 36.)

Desert Sands Pottery. Boulder City, Nevada, and Barstow, California. Started in middle 1940's. For early history of the Evans family potters, see the listing Evans Pottery in Dexter, Missouri. Arthur Evans, son of Hugh Evans started the Desert Sands Pottery in his basement while holding a job with the Bureau of Mines. Arthur's son Ferrell and Arthur's nephew named Terrell, both worked with Arthur. Arthur died in 1966 and Ferrell and Terrell continued to make pottery in Boulder City, until around th 1960's when Ferrell decided to go to Barstow, California, where he opened his own studio and pottery. Ferrell died in 1975, but Terrell was still making pottery in North Las Vegas, according to Jenny B. Derwich and Dr. Mary Latos, *Dictionary Guide to Pottery and Porcelain in the U.S.*, p. 88. Many of the Desert Sands Pottery pieces are handthrown, swirled or striped around with color which is added to the clay. Colors are dull gray, red brown, cobalt blue, green, yellow and black. The glaze is clear over the colored clay. Jo Hamm in "Desert Sands Pottery," *Antiques Journal*, February 1971, pp. 24, 25, said "Desert Sands" became an Evans trade name when Ferrell and Dorothy Evans made and sold their product in Boulder City, Nevada, prior to 1962. (Information: as cited. Marks: 1, 2, Deb and Gini Johnson, *Beginner's Book of Pottery*, p. 98, 99.

Design Technic. New York, New York. Around 1944 to around 1953. Sam and Bee Rosen made lamps, vases, bowls and other small clay objects, most of which was cast in molds with excellent glazes and forms. Some very important potters worked for Design Technic. They were: Vivika Heino,

Sam Haille, David Weinrib, David Gil, Rita Sargen-Simon and Nancy Wickham. Pieces were marked with an in mold mark as shown. (Information and mark: from Tom Turnquist, researcher and writer on potteries.)

DESIGN
TECHNIC

De Staebler, Stephen. Stephen, a studio potter, studied at Black Mountain College in 1951 and received his B.A. Degree in religion from Princeton University in 1954. In 1955, he served in the army in Germany. At Black Mountain College, he studied with Ben Shahn and Robert Motherwell. In 1957, he studied ceramics with Ka-Kwong Hui at the Brooklyn Museum School and in 1958 he worked with Peter Voulkos at the University of California, at Berkeley. After 1967, he became associate professor of sculpture at San Francisco State University. He has exhibited widely, had a major one man show at the Oakland Museum, and has done many important commissions. Some of his pieces are standing sculptures as large as eight or nine feet high. (Information: Garth Clark, *A Centuryf of Ceramics in the U.S.*, p. 282. Mark: Linda Steigleder, from the booklet published by the Everson Museum of Art to accompany the 1978 exhibition, "A Century of Ceramcis in the U.S." Mark is incised.)

DE
STAE
BLER
1977

Deutch, Eugene. Chicago, Illinois. Eugene Deutch was born in Budapest, Hungary, in 1904, where he had two years of business college and also worked as a carpenter. He went to France in 1923 and there he took courses in crafts amd sculpture and had study time with Brancusi. In 1927, he came to Chicago. He and his brother, Alfred, produced pottery, wood inlays and painted fabrics. He taught in Chicago schools under W.P.A. projects and also at Hull House. In 1934, he opened his own pottery in a converted garage on La Salle Street. He made wheel thrown high-fired functional and art pieces from Kentucky and Tennessee clay. He also taught at the Art Institute in Chicago, the Evanston Art Center, New Trier High School in Winnetka and in groups at his studio. Exhibitions were many. Those outstanding were at the Art Institute of Chicago, Chicago Public Library, Museum of Modern Art, the Syracuse Museum of Fine Art, the Chicago Historical Society, etc. Deutch's work is considered to be very fine art pottery. Thomas Turnquist stated "The artists and collectors who purchased Deutch's work realized the very simple truth that his creations were timeless classics that would always be aesthtically correct." (Information: Thomas Turnquist, "Eugene Deutch, Chicago's Potter," *American Art Pottery*, November 1983, pp., 3, 5. Mark: incised, sent by Turnquist.)

E. Deutch

Diamond Brand Stoneware. See Pittsburg Pottery.

Diamond Stoneware Company. Crooksville, Ohio. 1892 to around 1945 when it became the **Diamond Novelty Company**. Diamond Stoneware made utilitarian, crocks, jars, etc. The Diamond Novelty Company made a line of decorative ware, lamp bases and planters from 1945 to 1959 when the plant was sold to the Knight Brothers, and by 1970 it had become the home of the Spring Lumber Company. In the 1954, *Crockery and Glass Journal Directory* for 1954 the pottery was listed as the Diamond Pottery Corporation with a factory in Crooksville and an office in New York City. (Information: Guy E. Crooks, *History of Crooksville*, 1945, p. 31. Marks: no. 1 was on a very old squatty stoneware canning jar; no. 2 inscribed on decorative piece.)

DIAMOND POTTERY
©
CORPORATION
MADE IN USA

1.   2.

Dick, Jacob. Tuscarawas County, Ohio. Thorn dated this potter around 1835; Ramsay dates around 1830 to 1840. Maker of stoneware. Mark impressed. (Information: Thorn, p. 125; Ramsay, p. 134.) I made no connection, but there was a Jake Dickes in Muskingum County, Ohio around 1892 that operated in the Hoover Pottery according to information in the *Crooksville-Roseville Festival Booklet*, 1967. He made fruit jars in quart and gallon sizes. With the errors in spelling and the lack of records in the old days, it is possible this potter could be the same as Jacob Dick.

JACOB DICK
TUSCARAWAS CO.   J. DICK
OHIO

Dickey Clay Manufacturing Company. Corporate Headquarters, Pittsburg, Kansas, has manufacturing facitlities at present in Lehigh, Iowa; Pittsburg, Kansas; Saspamco, Texas; Texarkana, Texas; Port Manatie, Florida. 1885 to present. The W.S. Dickey Clay Manufacturing Company was started in 1885 by Walter S. Dickey to make silo blocks, bricks and all sorts of vitrified clay products, such as field tile, drain tile and all sorts of clay pipe. This is a very large important factory in the manufacturing of industrial ceramics. In a recent book on collectible pottery, the impressed mark, "Dickey Clay," was found on some decorative type piece. The company sent a lot of material on industrial type pottery. In a letter from the company was one sentence I leave for the next pottery researcher to unravel: "No vases or presentation gifts were ever manufactured by Dickey Clay, although there may be items with our name on them that were purchased from other pottery manufacturers." (Marks shown are the impressed, "Dickey Clay," and three paper labels.)

CLAY PIPE

NEVER WEARS OUT

STAYS ROUND

IN THE GROUND

Dickota Pottery and Dickinson Clay Products Company. Dickinson, North Dakota. 1892 until shortly after 1938. Dickota Pottery started as the Dickinson Fire and Pressed Brick Company in 1892, in Dickinson, North Dakota. The company was purchased by the Dickinson Clay Products Company in 1934, and pottery production was started to give the men work when the brickyard could not operate in the cold winter months. While most of the pottery made at the Dickota Pottery was of the decorative type, a line of pottery dishes was introduced in 1938, just before the pottery closed. Their mark was "Dickota" scratched on the article, also sometime paper labels were used. (Information: Darlene Dommel, "Dickota Pottery," *Antique Trader Annual of Articles* for 1974, p. 337. Marks: Deb and Gini Johnson, p. 102. No. 1, incised; no. 2, paper label. Marks 3-7 Susan Cox, "W.P.A. Pottery" *American Clay Exchange*, July 1982, p. 12. This article was one of a series on W.P.A. Pottery (Works Progress Administration/Federal Arts Project).

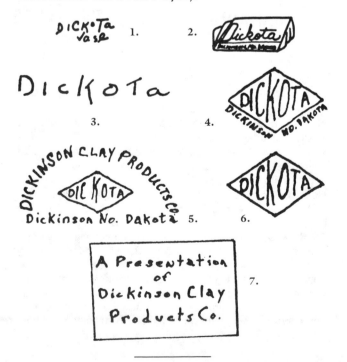

Diederich, Hunt. Hunt was a sculptor, born in Hungary,

studied in Paris, and Rome, also the Pennsylvania Academy of Fine Arts in Philadelphia. He sculptured mainly in bronze, but in the mid 1920's he produced ceramic pieces which he painted, also. He designed pieces for mass production, also. He had work shown at the International Exhibition of Ceramic Art. Diederich died in 1953. (Information: Garth Clark, *A Century of Ceramics in the U.S.*, p. 284. Painted mark: Linda Steigleder, from the booklet published by the Everson Museum of Art to accompany the 1978 exhibition, "A Century of Ceramics in the U.S.")

Dilliner, Leander B. New Geneva, Pennsylvania. 1874-1880. Leander was a son of S.R. Dilliner. He sold his pottery to John P. and Thomas Eberhart in 1880. Made stoneware with impressed mark. There were two more men named Dilliner who were potters in New Geneva, Charles E., and Joseph E. mentioned by Baker. Also Dilliner and Stantz were mentioned as being in Greensboro around 1876. (Information: Gordon C. Baker, "Dilliner Potters," *Spinning Wheel*, July-August, 1979, p. 29. Marks: Guappone, p. 35, and Baker, p.29.)

L.B. DILLINER & CO.

NEW GENEVA, PA

L.B. DILLINER

L.B. Dilliner

NEW GENEVA PA.

L.B. DILLINER KEYSTONE

L.B. DILLINER NEW GENEVA PA.

L.B Dilliner. NEW GENEVA PA.

Dilliner, Samuel R. New Geneva, Pennsylvania. 1854-1866. Samuel R. Dilliner started the pottery business when he was 52 years old. Baker said he may not have been a potter himself but owned the business and employed 15 men to do the potting. In March 1874, he was listed as a general store owner. Most of his stoneware was unmarked; some marked with impressed mark as shown, some was decorated with free hand artwork. (Information and mark: Gordon C. Baker, "Dilliner Potters," *Spinning Wheel*, July-August, 1979, p. 29.)

S.R. DILLINER

NEW GENEVA

Dillon, Charles. Albany, New York. Charles Dillon worked alone from 1824 to 1826. Then from 1827 to 1834 the name became **Tyler and Dillon** when he worked with Moses Tyler. In 1834 to 1836, Jacob Henry and Edward Selby worked with Dillon as **Charles Dillon and Company.** Then the name became **Dillon, Henry, and Porter** when Nathan Porter joined the group. Selby apparently left at that time. These potters made stoneware. See Tyler for a Tyler and Dillon mark. (Information: Warren F. Broderick, New York State Archives and Robert G. Wheeler, "The Potters of Albany," Stradling book, p. 132, and Guilland, p. 188. Marks: No. 1 Wheeler as cited.)

C. DILLON&CO.
ALBANY

DILLON & PORTER
ALBANY

1.   2.

Diona, Sister Mary. Kensington, Maryland. Filed for registration of this mark on July 23, 1979, claiming use for that year only to be used on ceramic pieces. The mark is the word, "Diona," with the second letter "i" in the form of a footed cross.

D✝ONA

Dior Studios. Barberton, Ohio. See Coventry Ware, Inc.

Dipple Pottery. Lewistown, Mifflin County, Pennsylvania. 1850 to 1929. The pottery was in operation by John Dipple until 1872. His widow, Margaret, operated from 1875 to 1890 at various times in partnership with Austin L. Hyssong, her son-in-law, before her son, Andrew Gregg Curtin Dipple, took over in 1894. The pottery was still listed as producing pottery in the *Eleventh Industrial Directory of Pennsylvania*, in 1922 at Lewistown. The pottery made stoneware jugs, milk pan, crocks and other utilitarian pieces which were either salt glazed or with brown and white glazes. In 1929, the company stopped manufacturing and became a selling agency until 1952 when A.G.C. Dipple died. (Information: Mildred Veley Hardcastle, "The Hyssong Potters," *Spinning Wheel's Book of Antiques*, New York: Grosset and Dunlap, 1975, no page numbers in the book. Also, Jeannette Lasansky, *Made of Mud*, pp. 15, 16, 56. Marks: Lasansky, as cited, pp. 14, 15, 16, as seen on pieces of stoneware. No. 1, painted in cobalt blue. No. 2, hand inscribed. No. 3, impressed mark. Other marks given by Lasansky include "A.M. Dipple/Lewistown, Pa.," "J. Dipple/Lewistown, Pa.," "J.H. Dipple/Lewistown, Pa." "J.H. Dipple/Lewistown, Pa." "J.H. Dipple/Pa./Lewistown," and "A.G.C. Dipple/Lewistown, Pa." Thorn, p. 125, and Ramsay, p. 259, had an error for the A.G.C. Dipple mark. The town is Lewistown, Mifflin County, not Lewisburg, Union County. On p. 56 of Lasansky's book are several variations of the marks for J.H. Dipple.)

a. m. Dipple & Son
Lewistown

1.

Mrs. A M Dipple

LEWISTOWN
POTTERY

2.   3.

A.G.C. DIPPLE
LEWISTOWN

4.

J.H. DIPPLE
LEWISTOWN
PA.

5.

Disney, Walt, Productions, Ltd. Los Angeles, California, filed for a copyright on mark 1, November 8, 1930, to be used on dishes, chinaware, porcelain and crockery, claiming use since October 22, 1930. Mark no. 2 was found on an older cookie jar, yellow clay, heavy black glaze and a raised Donald Duck on the front. Many of the potteries made products for the Disney Corporation or with their permission for use and to market. See Ludowici Celadon Company. Also, see Sebring China Company.

Mickey Mouse 1.

DONALD DUCK
©WALT DISNEY PROD. 2.

Dodge Pottery. Portland, Maine. Around 1794 to 1875. The pottery was started by Benjamin Dodge to make earthenware utilitarian pieces. In M. Lelyn Branin's book, *The Early Potters and Potteries of Maine*, pp. 42-45, he lists some of the 27 real estate transactions in the town of Portland, bearing Benjamin Dodge's name, involving various lots and buildings. In 1822, the town of Portland had a disasterous fire, which destroyed 20 buildings. Dodge was named as one of those who sustained the greatest amount of loss, but the pottery on Green Street did not burn in the fire. Dodge built an inn on the side of Green Street near the pottery. From then on Dodge was listed as a potter and innkeeper in the directories. From around 1837, Benjamin Dodge, Jr. worked with his father in the pottery until Benjamin, Sr. died in 1875. (Do not confuse Benjamin Dodge with Samuel Dodge of the Exeter Pottery Works.) (Information and mark: M. Lelyn Branin, as cited. Mark on p. 222.)

B. DODGE
PORTLAND

Dohrmann Hotel Supply Company. San Francisco, California. A selling agency filed for use of this mark August 27, 1945, for use on crockery and chinaware, such as tableware and kitchenware, claiming use since March 1, 1928. Warwick China Company made products for this company. See that listing for mark.

Dollings, John and W.C. Muskingum County, Ohio. Both of the Dollings were bluebird, stoneware potters working in the 1870's. John made a black man head jug in the 1870's in the possession of Museum of the Ohio Historical Society, Inc. in Columbus, Ohio. At the National Road-Zane Grey Museum in Norwich, near Zanesville, Ohio, is a large brown jug with handles in the form of snakes made by W.C. Dollings Norris Schneider in "John Dollings Credited With Making Stoneware in 1870's," *Zanesville Times Signal*, December 8, 1957 (no. p. number), said E. Hall (see that listing) and Dollings were the only Muskingum County potters who displayed any originality in their work. The rest made utilitarian pieces such as jar, jugs, crocks, etc. Other potters listed in the area in the 1870 era were L. Brown and later a G.W. Brown, also C. Green; D. Horn; R.G. Russell; J. James; G.W. Ranken; D. Thomas; A. Wilson; J.B. Wyiel; Joseph Rambo; A. Smith; L. Williams; W.R. Bell; G.D. Burley; C. Hughes; W.A. Morrison; P. Stines; G. Wise; and many others. (Mark: Copied from jug at the National Road-Zane Grey Museum of the Ohio Historical Society, Inc., Norwich, Ohio, where jug may be seen on display.)

W.C. Dollings
Maker
March 17, 1892
Yours Truly

A.P. Donaghho (also spelled Donahoo and Donnaho according to Schaltenbrand, p. 26, Ramsay, p. 226, spelled it Donahue and Donagno.) After 1843, earthenware and later stoneware was made in Fredericktown, Pennsylvania, by Polk Donaghho. In 1855, Donaghho took a partner, Charles Bower for three years. By 1860, a large stoneware factory of Donaghho and Beale was operating until around 1870. Then Ramsay, p. 226, dates Donaghho in Parkersburg, West Virginia, from 1874 until 1900 or after. In Parkersburg, the pottery was called **Excelsior Pottery**. (Marks: no. 1, Schaltenbrand, *Old Pots*, p. 27; mark no. 2, 3, Smith, p. 13 and Raycraft *Decorated Country Stoneware*, p. 55. Information and mark no. 4; Schaltenbrand, "Stoneware Potteries of Fredericktown, Pennsylvania," *Spinning Wheel*, November/December 1982, pp. 50-53.)

AP DONAGHHO
FREDERICKTOWN, PA   1.

EXCELSIOR
POTTERY   2.
PARKERSBURG

A.P. Donaghho   3.
Parkersburg W. Va.

AP DONAGHHO
FREDERICKTOWN,   4.
PA.

Dona Rosa (Indian potter). Oaxaca, Mexico (not New Mexico). Dona Rosa made the now famous black pottery and maintained a small pottery shop in Oaxaca, and was still working in 1979 although she was very old at the time. At least one major publication confused this Mexican Indian potter with potters in New Mexico. For more information on this potter see Arthur Guagliumi, "Dona Rosa and the Black Pottery of Oaxaca," *Pottery Collectors' Newsletter*, November, December 1979, pp. 51-53. (Mark: staff written, "Question Box/On Indian Pottery," *Tri State Trader*, November 10, 1979, p. 9.)

DONA ROSA
S B Coyo Tepec
OAX MEX—

Dorchester Pottery Works. Boston, Massachusetts. 1895 to early 1980's. They were makers of high-fired stoneware for acid proof use in 1,700 items for medical, jewelry and food companies. They used a lead stamp for a mark until 1941. The pottery in Boston, also made wheel thrown, decorated pottery as was pictured in the article by Harry and Stephen Roff, "Dorchester Pottery," *Glaze*, May 1984, p. 9. It was heavy stoneware pieces with hand decorated designs by various decorators in traditional styles and simple forms. Pictured were a pinecone teapot, a cobalt blue basket, a cup and saucer and sugar container. I had a letter initialed only C.A.H. from the factory in 1978. Charles A. Hill was a brother to the wife of the founder. He was a manager and also decorated in the later years of the factory. Nando Ricci was the modeler. The pottery closed in the the early 1980's. (Information: from company. Marks: no. 1, is an early impressed mark found on an old stoneware crock at the Ohio Ceramic Center at Zanesville; no. 2, is a fairly late mark shown in the article already cited. Mark 3 according to Marcia Ray *Collectible Ceramics* p. 72 the Henderson Patented Footwarmer was made as late as 1920 by the Dorchester Pottery Works. Ray, p. 71 has a picture of the footwarmer with mark. This pottery is not to be confused with the Dorchester Pottery of Millville, New Jersey, which was in fact a division of the Stangl Pottery and which was in existence only a few months in 1976 when a fire destroyed the plant before the first dinnerware was made. They did make a few crockpots in the New Jersey plant. (Later information from Edna Mae Hicks, secretary to Frank H. Wheaton, owner of Stangl Pottery.)

DORCHESTER   Dorchester
POTTERY WORKS   Stoneware
BOSTON, MASS.   C.A.H.
                        N. Ricci
   1.   2.   fecit

HENDERSON
FOOT WARMER   3.

Doriot, Helen. Goshen, Indiana. Potter makes porcelain, hand painted, molded, birds, lamps, vases and little people called "the Gossips." Helen started in 1961 at age 61. She was still making the artistic ware in 1976. (Information: Jenny B. Derwich and Dr. Mary Latos, *Dictionary Guide to United States Pottery and Porcelain*, p. 79. Mark: inscribed; sent by Jenny B. Derwich.)

Doubenmier, Cecil. Parkville, Missouri. 1973 to present (1984). Studio potter, makes decorative and functional stoneware, fired to cone 7. (Mark: is bisk stamp pressed into clay.)

Drach, Rudolf. Bedminster, Pennsylvania. 1780-1800. Made slip decorated, sgraffito and plain redware. (Information and mark: Ramsay, p. 164; Thorn, p. 24.)

R. Drach

Dresden Pottery Works. See Brunt, Bloor, Martin and Company and other potteries for history.

Drexel Furniture Company. Drexel, North Carolina. Filed for registration of this mark on March 12, 1952, for use on china and pottery dinnerware and decorative ceramics, such as vases and bowls, claiming use since August 14, 1951.

Dryden Pottery. Dryden Pottery was founded in Ellsworth, Kansas, in 1946 by James Dryden. In 1956, the pottery was moved to Hot Springs, Arkansas. Dryden Pottery specializes in one of a kind signed collector's pieces. James Dryden studied chemistry at the University of Illinois, and art at Kansas University. He served in the army in W.W. II and returned to Kansas University in 1946 to study ceramics. In a sixty foot by sixty foot quonset hut, Dryden started his pottery that same year. He made molded pieces from his own plaster molds and glazes made with volcanic ash from Ellsworth County and other ingredients in a two fire method. In 1947, Dryden exhibited at the Kansas Manufacturers show in Wichita, and was turning out two thousands pieces per week. A fiesta type dinnerware was produced in the late 1940's. By 1948, Dryden was distributing his products to six hundred stores in twenty-two states. In 1955, a Dutch potter, John Van Wunnik, joined the Dryden staff. He made hand thrown pieces on a wheel. In the 1950's, Dryden sold some pottery to the Van Briggle Pottery to offset his loss in over the counter sales. To get more tourist trade, Dryden moved to Hot Springs,

Arkansas, in 1956, where the pottery has been very successful since. Since the late 1960's, most of the pieces have been wheel thrown, but some are still hand cast. The pieces made in Ellsworth County were made with a dark tan clay. The Hot Springs pieces have a pure white clay. This is a good way to tell earlier Dryden pieces. According to Rita C. Mortenson in article cited, all pieces of Dryden were signed. A black panther and some other pieces similar to Dryden's molded pieces were made by several potteries. For pictures of a fine collection of this pottery, see the Mortenson article cited. (Information: Rita C. Mortenson, "Dryden Pottery," *Antique Trader Weekly*, January 19, 1983, pp. 81-85; Martha E. Andrews, *From The Hills of Kansas, The Story of Dryden Pottery*, forty-six page booklet, no date, no publisher. Marks: nos. 1-6, Rena London, "Out of the Mould," *National, Glass, Pottery and Collectables Journal*, August 1980, p. 4 and by letter from that author. Marks 7-10, Deb and Gini Johnson, *Beginners Book of Pottery*, p. 101; nos. 11, 12, from company information.)

Dry, John (Drey, Johan). Dryville, Pennsylvania. Started in the old Melcher Pottery in 1804 to around 1880. John Dry lived from 1785 to 1870. Three sons worked with John Dry, Daniel, Nathaniel and Lewis. Nathaniel did the decorating. Names of individuals were written across plates in large letters in slip. Pottery made earthenware whistles, smoking pipes using brass molds and utilitarian pieces. (Information: Guy F. Reinert, "History of the Pennsylvania German Potteries of Berks County," *Bulletin of America Ceramic Society*, January 1940 p. 19. Marks: Ramsay, p. 166; Thorn, p. 125; no. 3, Barber, p. 14.)

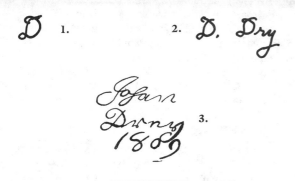

Dubois and Kinsey. Zanesville, Ohio. Samuel Sullivan was the first potter in Zanesville, Muskingum County, Ohio around 1810. Prior to that time he had made redware in St. Clairsville, Ohio, from 1804 to 1809. His pottery was at Third and Market Streets in Zanesville. In 1818, Samuel Frazey bought the Zanesville pottery and made clay marbles. Around 1819, Oliver Dubois and a man named Kinsey became the operators after Frazey. The inscribed mark on the bottom of a five gallon stoneware wine cask with incised bird and fish and blue decorations. (Information: Norris Schneider, "Clay Industry," *Zanesville Time Signal*, November 3, 1957 (no page no.). Mark: Harold F. Guilland, *Early American Folk Pottery*, p. 180.)

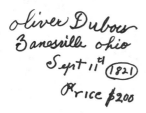

Duché Family Potters. Duché, Anthony was manufacturing a stoneware product in Philadelphia by 1730. Rudolf Hommel in his article, "Colonial Master Potters" in *Hobbies*, May, 1949, p. 80, felt that Duché had been neglected by the historians in telling the whiteware story in this country. Andrew Duché, third son of Anthony, moved from Philadelphia, where he worked with his father in the 1730's, to Charleston, South Carolina around middle 1730's and then on to New Windsor (near North Augusta) Georgia, where he tried to make white porcelain for a year or so. By 1738, he was in Savannah, Georgia, still experimenting with the manufacture of porcelain. While trying to perfect his porcelain ware, Andrew made pots, pans, bowls, jugs, etc. to sell for a living. According to Burrison as cited, p. 105, the pieces were made of lead-glazed earthenware rather than salt glazed stoneware. A lead glazed earthenware jar with the initials A.D. is shown

in Burrison, p. 106, and has been attributed to Andrew Duché although Burrison said this was not verified as yet. (Information: Hommel, as cited, and John A. Burrison, *Brothers in Clay*, pp. 101 to 107. There is a detailed account on Duché in Burrison's book supported by many early newspaper clippings.)

Duckworth, Ruth. Chicago, Illinois. Ruth, a studio potter, was born in Germany, and then studied in England at the Liverpool School of Art from 1936 to 1940. By 1958, she also studied at Hammersmith School of Art and the Central School of Arts and Crafts in London. She worked as a sculptor, carving stone at first then clay. In 1960, she taught at the Central School and came to the U.S. to teach at the University of Chicago in 1964. She established permanent residence and a studio in Chicago. She has a wide range of talents and has made massive stoneware murals, free-outstanding sculptural forms and delicate porcelain pieces. She has had many one-woman shows and done many group exhibitions and various commissions. (Information: Garth Clark, *A Century of Ceramics in the U.S.*, p. 283. Mark: Linda Steigleder, from the booklet published by the Everson Museum of Art to accompany the 1978 exhibition, "A Century of Ceramics in the U.S.")

Duffy, Mary Ellen. Miami, Florida. Filed for registration of this mark on January 25, 1951, for use on ceramic trays and urns, claiming use since August 1, 1950.

CONCHETTE

Dunn, Vera La Fountain. Hollywood, California. Listed in the 1945 *Crockery and Glass Journal Directory Journal* for barnware and figurines. This was the only listing I could find. (Mark: directory as cited.)

Durant Kilns. Bedford Village, New York. For the early history of Leon Volkmar see the listing Volkmar Kilns. In the summer of 1910 a small workshop was organized by Mrs. Jean

Rice with the aid of Leon Volkmar. She furnished the facility and he furnished the technical direction. Production began in 1911. In 1913, a gallery was leased in New York City to show the ware which was maintained until 1918. After that Arden Studios became the sole distributors in New York City for the products of Durant Kilns. Jean Rice died in 1919, leaving Volkmar a life interest in the business and land with the right to buy the remainder. He became sole owner in 1924 and operated as the Durant Kilns until around 1930, the name was dropped and Volkmar operated more as a studio potter from then on. Volkmar died in California in 1959. In addition to Volmar's other involvements described under the two Volkmar potteries listed, he also taught at Columbia University and the University of Cincinnati. Some of his students became well known also. Manuel Jalanovich of San Francisco (see that listing) was one of his students. Durant Kilns products are represented in several museums. They made artware and tableware. Outstanding glazes were developed in cooper blues and reds, etc. See Evans, p. 92 for a good description of products and how they were developed. Volkmar received a Bronze Medal at the Paris Exposition in 1937 for a cream earthenware with Near Eastern influence which he developed. (Marks and information: Paul Evans, *Art Pottery of the U.S.*, pp. 91-93. In 1919, the stylized V was used. It had also been used earlier by the two Volkmar potteries. See those listings.)

Duval, Benjamin B. and Company. Richmond, Virginia. Around 1800, Benjamin B. DuVal II, was an apothecary selling "miracle cures for assorted diseases," who advertised for a potter in 1791 to make containers for his wares. The impressed mark shown was used between 1811 and 1817 on a salt glazed three gallon jug with two handles. In 1808, DuVal formed the **Richmond Tile Manufactory** to make roofing tile. In 1811, DuVal announced the opening of **Richmond Stoneware Manufactory** with the firm name of **Benjamin Duval and Company**. The tile and pottery were manufactured at the same location. The stoneware products were jugs of assorted sizes, pots, bottles, pitchers, milk pans, inks, pocket flasks, etc. The pottery was taken over by Benjamin's son, James in 1817. Benjamin DuVal II died in 1826. The drug business was the only enterprise left in his will. Evidently, the pottery was sold or gone. (Information and mark: Bradford L. Rauschenberg, "B. DuVal and Co./Richmond: A Newly Discovered Pottery," first printed in *Journal of Early Southern Decorative Art*, May 1978, and reprinted in *Pottery Collectors* Newsletter, Volume III, No. IV, no date, pp. 26, 36. Mr. Rauschenberg is a Research Fellow at the Museum of Early Southern Decorative Arts.)

Dynasty Limited. Los Angeles, California. Patrick O'Neill filed for registration of this mark on November 1, 1962, claiming use for one month prior for china and chinaware, dinnerware dishes, cups, saucers, plates, platters, etc.

E

Eagle Porcelain Works (Henry Gast). Lancaster County, Pennsylvania. 1838 to about 1894. Made redware, yellowware and a limited amount of white ware, fancy figures, fountains and statuettes were made in red clay. (Information and mark: M. Luther Heisey, "The Makers of Pottery in Lancaster County," Lancaster, Pa.: Lancaster County Historical Society, Volume I, nos. 4 and 5, 1946, p. 120.)

Eagle
Porcelain Works
Lancaster City, Pa.
Henry Gast, S Q St.

Eagle, Various Potteries and Companies. The Eagle mark shown is from Jack H. Tod, *Electrical Porcelain Industry of the U.S.*, p. 107, and was used by the **Eagle Electric Manufacturing Company**, Long Island, New York, on radio antenna insulators. There was also an **Eagle Pottery** in Trenton, New Jersey, started by Richard Millington, and later owned by Burroughs and Mountford (see that listing). The Eagle Pottery in Trenton, was listed as late as 1900 in the *Trenton City Directories* at North Clinton, and Perrine Avenue, but was not listed after that. There was also an **Eagle Electrical Porcelain Company** on Princeton and Chadwick Avenues, in Trenton, listed in the directories for one year only in 1924. Tod, p. 78, said only that they made electric porcelain prior to 1930 and were probably only a sales agency in later years. There was an Eagle Pottery in East Liverpool, Ohio. See the listing, Goodwin Pottery. There was also and **Eagle Porcelain Works** in Lancaster County, Pennsylvania, and an **Eagle Pottery Company** in Macomb, Illinois. Both are listed separately. James Hamilton and Company of Greenboro, Pennsylvania, also used the mark Eagle Pottery. See that listing. For an **Eagle Pottery** in Benton, Arkansas, see the listing for the Niloak Pottery Company. The eagle in stenciled form shows up even today on stoneware jugs with no real identifying mark made in different places.

EAGLE

Eagle Pottery Company. Macomb, Illinois. 1875-around 1900. J.M. Forest and A.W. Eddy started in 1875. In 1877, the firm name was J.M. Forest and Company. In 1879, it became J.S. Patterson and Company. In 1881, this building was sold to Ragon and Asker Blount and became known as the Eagle Pottery Company, still operating in 1885 to make stoneware utilitarian pieces such as crocks, jugs, etc., with blue stenciled marks and decoration. (Information and mark: Jim Martin, by letter, co-author with Bette Cooper of *Monmouth Western Stoneware*.)

Earl, Jack. Lakeview, Ohio. 1963 to present (1985). Studio potter, making sculptured pieces marked "Jack Earl." I believe due to modesty, some of the most outstanding potters have sent me very little information on the form I sent out. Such was the case with Jack Earl. Fortunately, an article by Jack Klassen, "A Conversation with Jack Earl," *Ceramic Monthly*, October 1981, pp. 68-70, made me realize this potter's importance. Concurrent exhibitions of glazed porcelain sculpture by Jack were presented in 1981 at Exhibit A. Gallery in Chicago, Illinois, and Massillon, Ohio. Jack attended school at Bluffton College, where he became interested in ceramics. He received an M.A. at Ohio State University in Columbus, Ohio. He taught at the Toledo Museum Art School of Design for nine years, from 1963 to 1972, then at Virginia Commonwealth, in Richmond, for six years. He returned to Lakeview, Ohio, and started working full time sculpturing. Theo Portney Gallery in New York City sells most of his work.

JACK EARL

East End Pottery Company. Began in 1894, at the north side of Railroad Street in East Liverpool, Ohio. In 1901, East End Pottery joined the East Liverpool Potteries Company, which was partially dissolved July 7, 1903. (See East Liverpool Potteries Company.) By 1905, East End Pottery was operating on its own and later was called the **East End China Company**. The plant was taken over by Gus Trenle who filed to change the name to Trenle China Company in January 1909 (*Secretary of State Report for 1910*). See Trenle China. The East End China Company or Pottery made a very fine grade of semi-porcelain. According to Annise Heaivilin, this company also made ironstone in a Tea Leaf pattern. (Information: Lehner, *American Kitchen and Dinner Wares*, p. 54; William H. Vodrey, *Record of the Pottery Industry in East Liverpool*, Vol. 24, No. 8, 1923, pp. 282-288. Marks: Barber, *Marks of American Potters*, p. 115.)

Eastern China Company, Inc. New York, New York. A selling and decorating agency. (Mark no. 1, shown in directories of the 1950's and mark no. 2, was found listed for them in Quality Stamp Company of East Liverpool, Ohio, material.

1.

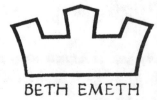

2.

Eastern Outfitting Company. Los Angeles, Pasadena, and Long Beach, California. A selling agency which filed for registration of this mark on May 29, 1939, claiming use since March 1938 for use on ceramic dinnerware and cooking ware.

East Liverpool Pottery Company. East Liverpool, Ohio. Early products were plain and decorated ironstone china. Later, they made a good quality of semi-porcelain ware from around 1884 to 1903. They became one of the six companies to join the East Liverpool Potteries Company from 1901 to 1903. (Marks: nos. 1-4, Barber, *Marks of American Potters*, p. 114; nos. 5, 6, on dishes; no. 7, sent by Elsie Kilmer, *Tri-State Trader*, editor.)

E.L.P.CO.
WACO CHINA

2.

WACO CHINA.

3.

ELPCO
MADE IN USA
CHINA

5.

6. WARRANTED

7.

E.L.P.Co.

East Liverpool Potteries Company. East Liverpool, Ohio. A group of six companies which organized to better compete with Homer Laughlin, Knowles, Taylor and Knowles and others. Established in 1900 to 1903, when the group was dissolved. The following companies were members: The Globe Pottery, Wallace and Chetwynd Pottery, East Liverpool Pottery Company, The George C. Murphy Pottery, East End Pottery, all of East Liverpool, and The United States Pottery of Wellsville, Ohio. During the combination of these companies, a uniform mark was used, but they probably continued to use their own individual factory marks as well. (Information: Barber, *Marks of American Potters*, p. 114; Lehner, *Ohio Pottery and Glass*, p. 44.)

EAST LIVERPOOL
POTTERIES CO.

East Morrisania China Works. New York City, New York. D. Robitzek, owner, was making white granite, cream-colored and decorated ware around 1893. (Barber, *Marks of American Potters*, p. 83.) Jervis in *Pottery, Glass and Brass Salesman*, April 17, 1913, p. 13 said they were not now in business. (Mark: Barber, p. 83.)

East Palestine China Company. Canonsburg, Pennsylvania. See W.S. George Pottery Company for history. (Mark is stamped, used around early 1900's.)

East Palestine Pottery Company. A pottery was started in East Palestine, Ohio, in 1880 to make yellowware and Rockingham. In 1881, the pottery was called **Feustal and Nowling Pottery Company.** In 1884, it became the East Palestine Pottery Company, at which time it was sold to a group of potters from East Liverpool, Ohio, and incorporated in 1889. They enlarged the plant and began making white and decorated ware. For the fifth time the plant was near bankruptcy when George E. Sebring was hired as manager in 1893. He put the pottery on a paying basis. In 1896, Sebring left the East Palestine Pottery to go on the other side of town to start the **Ohio China Company.** By 1904, the controlling interest in the pottery had been purchased by W.S. George. In 1904, W.S. George built a new plant which adjoined on the west to the East Palestine Pottery Company. The new plant was called **Continental China Company.** In January, 1909, the names of the plants were changed to the **W.S. George Pottery Company.** (Secretary of State Report for 1910). By 1912, 750 of the 1,800 people in the town worked in the W.S. George Pottery. The first building built to house the East Palestine Pottery Company burned in 1912 and was not replaced until 1924. In 1955, the W.S. George Pottery went into bankruptcy. In 1960, the plant was reorganized and operated by **Royal China Company** of Sebring, and known as plant No. 4 or Royal China Inc., East Palestine Division. Royal sold all their interest to Jeannette Glass Company of Jeannette, Pennsylvania, on October 1969, and at that time Jeannette idled the East Palestine Company and kept the Sebring branches running. Articles made in the East Palestine Pottery when they started in 1880 were Rockingham and yellowware. Then they went to decorated ware and white ware. Barber, p. 136, listed the East Palestine Pottery Company as makers of semi-porcelain, jardinieres and specialties, plain and decorated. (Information: Martha McCloskey, in an article in the *East Palestine Daily Leader Newspaper*, February 1961. Marks: nos. 1-3, Barber, *Marks of American Potters*, p. 136; nos. 4-6, marks on dishes.)

1.

COLUMBIA

2.

REVERE

3.   4.

5.   6.

East Trenton Pottery. Trenton, New Jersey. Barber in *Pottery and Porcelain of the United States*, p. 47, mentions this company as being in business in 1888. They made plates with portraits of the presidents in the 1888 presidential year. The last listing in the *Trenton City Directories* was in 1905. There were several marks for this company as shown. They made white granite, opaque china.

Ebeling and Reuss Company. Philadelphia, Pennsylvania (1940's) and Devon, Pennsylvania (1983). In 1982 directory, Henry O. Ebeling is listed as president of this selling agency for English bone china, earthenware, bone china, giftware, glass, Italian ware, Austrian giftware, Dutch ware, etc. There have been a variety of marks in the directories for this company over the years, and practically all of their wares were foreign such as "Ridgeway," "Royal Winton," English; "Bluebird," Canadian; "Keramos," Austrian. In the 1940's, Ebeling and Reuss used a mark on American made china of a bell and "E.R." or a bell with "E.R." and "American Artware." This mark was found at Quality Stamp Company, East Liverpool, Ohio, and had been made for the Canonsburg Pottery. There was an egg plate with this mark, made at Canonsburg Pottery for Ebeling and Reuss. In 1945 they were listed for domestic as well as foreign lines of china, glass and pottery. In 1952, an advertisement in the *China and Glass Red Book Directory* included Dee Mar Ceramics from California, as being sold by Ebeling Reuss. These were cigarette sets, candy boxes, ash trays, etc. Of course, that same year, Ebeling Reuss had china and glass from England, Germany, Italy and Norway. In the 1951 *Red Book Directory*, p. 125, was an advertisement for Ebling Reuss, as sellers of Robert Simmons Ceramics, which were well modeled animal figures, made in this country. Also advertised in the ad were the egg

plates already mentioned. In the 1946 *Crockery and Glass Journal Directory*, "St. Regis" was listed as American made porcelain sold by this company. (The "St. Regis" mark is from Quality Stamp Company.)

Eberhart, John R. and Thomas. New Geneva, Pennsylvania. Purchased Dilliner pottery in 1880. Made stoneware. (Information: Gordon C. Baker, "Dilliner Potters," *Spinning Wheel*, July, August, p. 29. Marks: nos. 1-4, Guappone, p. 36; no. 5, Schaltenbrand, p. 19.)

Eberly Pottery. Strasburg, Virginia. 1880-1906. Jacob Jeremiah Eberly established a pottery in 1880 but he was not a potter. He hired local potters and his son, Letcher learned to make earthenware. The first stamped imprint or impressed mark used was "J. Eberly & Co., Strasburg, Va.," then "J. Eberly & Bro., Strasburg, Va." The last stamped imprint was "Eberly & Son, Strasburg, Va." (Information: William E. Wiltshire III, *Folk Pottery of the Shenandoah Valley*, New York: E.O. Dutton & Co., Inc., 1975, pp. 12, 13. Redware sculptured pieces shown in Wiltshire pp. 80, 90. Marks: 1, 2, Smith p. 22. Nos. 3, 4, Thorn, p. 125.)

```
J. S. EBERLEY
STRASBURG    4.
VA.
```

Eckhardt, Edris. Cleveland, Ohio. Edris Eckhardt graduated from the Cleveland Institute of Art in 1932, where she had participated in a collaborative ceramics program of the Cleveland Art School, the Cleveland Museum of Art and the Cowan Pottery. In 1933 to 1934, she was involved for five months in a pilot program for the Public Works of Art Project (see that listing). She also set up her own studio at this time. In 1935, when the WPA-FAP began a local operation, she was made director of the Cleveland department and held this position until 1941 when the program was discontinued. For this program, she had the idea of producing small-scale sculptures for use in children's library programs with figures based on *Alice in Wonderland*, and W.H. Hudson's *Green Meadows*. In 1947, she produced a major work, "Painted Mask," which was exhibited in the May Show in Cleveland, that year. In 1953, she began to work in glass. See the Clark book cited for a discussion of that work. Edris won a Guggenheim fellowship in 1956 and one in 1959. She also received a Louis Comfort Tiffany fellowship for her work in stained glass. She did many one-woman and group shows throughout the country. (Information: Garth Clark, *A Century of Ceramics in the U.S.*, p. 286. Incised mark: Linda Steigleder, from the booklet published by the Everson Museum of Art to accompany the 1978 exhibition, "A Century of Ceramics in the U.S.")

Edris Eckhardt

Eden Roc China Company. Eden Roc China Company was a trade name used by Salem China Company and Paden City Pottery in the 1950's for a very short time. When the Paden City Pottery closed, Salem China purchased some of their molds and lines. The Eden Roc line was one of them. Mr. Harrison Keller said it wasn't so successful and not continued too long. Some pieces have been found by researcher, Gerald Barnett, with the Paden City Pottery mark and Eden Rock mark. The mark shown is a Salem China mark because of the stars and the date 1956. The Eden Roc name was used for a party plan promotion. See Salem China for more information on the use of stars in a mark and some other party plan marks. (Information: Harrison Keller, president and owner of Salem China Company. Mark: Gerald D. Barnett, "Collectable American China," *National Glass, Pottery and Collectibles Journal*, April 1979, pp. 25, 27.)

Edgerton Pottery. Edgerton, Wisconsin. 1894 to 1901. This was a short-lived pottery formed after the Pauline Pottery went into bankruptcy. The Edgerton Pottery made a utilitarian type of pottery such as a water filter for H. Geissel and Company of Chicago. But there was also an art pottery called "Rock Pottery" made there. Edgerton is in Rock County, on the Rock River, hense the name Rock Pottery. Paul Evans in *Art Pottery of the U.S.*, pp. 94, 95, said the pieces found have a marked similarity to Pauline Pottery pieces. Perhaps the molds were sold with the building. However, Evans did not believe Pauline Jacobus was ever associated in any way with this pottery. Information about this pottery is very scarce. There are four marked examples in the Lincoln-Tollman Museum collection. Two are pictured in Evans, one is a yellowware with a blue, green and brown geometric design. The other is a vase with a clover leaf design. Both are very attractive. (Information and marks: Evans, as cited.)

Rock Pottery.
Edgerton, Wis.

Edmands and Various Associates. Charlestown, Massachusetts. 1812-1905. Webster, p. 167, identifies the mark "Charlestown" as a mark for Barnabus Edmands and William Burroughs between 1812-1850, operating as **Edmands and Burroughs**. In a pamplet "Forms From the Earth, 1000 Years of Pottery in America," published by the Museum of Contemporary Art of the American Craftsmen's Council in New York City, is a very good picture with a plain mark of a stoneware jar with blue underglaze deer decoration marked **Edmands and Co.**, also in Charlestown, from 1850-1868. The name was **Powers and Edmands** for a while after 1868 and then **Edmands and Hooper** to 1905. In the article by Lura Woodside Watkins, "New Light on Boston Stoneware," *The Art of the Potter*, published by *Antiques Magazine* and edited by Diana and J. Garrison Stradling, pp. 81-86, she says identical jugs, some with the "Charlestown" marking have been attributed to Frederick Carpenter, a potter in Charlestown, at the same time as Edmands. The Charlestown mark shown here is on p. 86 of the Stradling book. In Thorn, p. 125, is mark no. 3, which has to be a mistake in spelling because mark no. 2 is clear on the picture of the crock as credited above.

```
CHARLESTOWN              EDMANDS & CO.
     1.                        2.

BARNABAS  EDMUNDS
      &   CO.          3.
  CHARLESTOWN
```

Edwards and Minish. Calhoun, Missouri. Around 1892. Made stoneware. Mark on large tan handled crock. (Information and mark: Henry W. Heflin, pottery collector and researcher.)

```
-FROM-
EDWARDS  &  MINISH
   CALHOUN, MO.
```

Eerdmans, Jennifer. Granville, Ohio. 1973 to present (1987). Jennifer, a studio potter, attended Antioch College from 1973 to 1976, where she worked with Karen Shirley, instructor and Michael Jones, visiting artist. She has done numerous craft and arts shows in Michigan and Ohio. She makes an attractive red slipware with the old Pennsylvania Dutch designs. Presently, she signs the pieces, "Jenny," as shown, but plans to have a stamp made of the logo shown.

Efcolite Corporation. Trenton, New Jersey. Distributors. Filed for rights to this mark December 2, 1933 to be used for a china coffee maker, claiming use since September 20, 1933.

CHINA BREW-BEST

Eiler (or Euler) Pottery. East Birmingham (later Pittsburg), Pennsylvania. Name was spelled Euler by Ramsay and as Eyler, Eiler, and Euler in city directories. The mark pictured on a stoneware crock in an article by James M. Harrison, "The Case of the Disappearing Potters," *Antiques Journal*, March 1979, pp. 32, 33, 49, seems to bear out the Eiler spelling. Harrison found these listings in the *Pittsburgh City Directory*: Eiler and Sunshine, 1857-1862; P. Eiler, 1863-1882. (Information and mark: article already cited.)

```
P. EILER
EAST
BIRMINGHAM
POTTERY
```

El Monte, California Various Potteries/Miali Pottery/Hueckel China and Porcelain. I have very little information on these potteries. The only listing I could find in any of the directories listed in the bibliography for Miali Pottery in El Monte, was the 1977 telephone book. The pottery was located on Shirley Avenue. The mark shown was sent by Rena London, researcher and writer, and was found on a yellow stoneware piece, sold by Sears. A letter to the pottery in 1983, was returned by the Postal Department. The other pottery listed in El Monte in 1977 was Hueckel China and Porcelain on Durfee Avenue. This pottery started in 1953 and employed 40 in 1977 to make porcelain and chinaware dinnerware.

```
MIALI PO
SINCE 1906
EL MONTE CALIF
```

Elverson, Sherwood and Barker Pottery. New Brighton, Pennsylvania. Started with Thomas Elverson, 1862, making yellowware, Rockingham and brownware. Elverson and Sherwood were listed around 1870 making stoneware (Ramsay, p. 225). Then Joseph H. Bausman in the *History of Beaver County*, New York: Knickerbocker Press, 1904, p. 710, tells us the Sherwood Brothers (G.W. and W.D.) started their own pottery in 1879, which included the Elverson, Sherwood and Barker Pottery. By 1904, and through miscellaneous directories until 1950, the Elverson Pottery was listed as operating independently again. In the 1931 and 1935 *Industrial Directories for New Jersey*, Elverson Pottery Company was listed as making pottery and chinaware employing 50 people. Through 1950, they were listed the same way, but by 1953 they had become Friedle-Elverson Pottery as they were listed on through 1975, making pottery products not classified under dinnerware. (Mark: no. 1 on cover picture of *Antique Trader Annual*, Volume X, is for Elverson, Sherwood and Barker Company; no. 2 on gray crock written with blue is for Elverson Pottery.)

1.   2.

Empire China Company. Burbank, California. Empire China Company was listed in the *Manufacturer's Directory of California* for 1924 as making hotel and semi-vitreous tableware. (Mark: found on semi-porcelain saucer by Priscella Wegars, researcher in the Laboratory of Anthropology, University of Idaho, Moscow, Idaho.)

Empire Crafts Corporation. Newark, Wayne County, New York. This company sold pottery, dinnerware, crystal, etc., on a salesman, door to door basis. The Princess China mark is also to be found under Jackson China Company as it was furnished by Robert B. Bernstorf of Commercial Decal Company, East Liverpool, Ohio. Empire Crafts Corporation filed for registration of mark no. 1 on August 9, 1956, claiming use since May 29, 1956, for use on semi-vitreous dinnerware. Mark no. 2 filed December 19, 1951, for use on china dishes, claiming use since 1945 on the words "Princess China." Also, see Louis E. Hellman for a Princess China mark. No. 3 was filed March 26, 1957, claiming use since July 16, 1956, for semi-vitreous dinnerware. Mark 4 was filed July 25, 1957, claiming first use July 16, 1956, for semi-vitreous and fine china. No. 5 filed May 28, 1959, claiming use since October 1951, for china dishes. No. 6 filed October 31, 1963, claiming use since July 26, 1963, for china dishes.

LADY EMPIRE

1.

2.

3. **NOBILITY PERMAWARE**

NOBILITY   **PRINCESS**

4.   5.

6. **CAMEO ROSE**

Empire Pottery. Trenton, New Jersey. See Trenton Potteries Company for history.

Empire State Glass Decorating Company. 197 Grand Street, New York City. They were listed in the early 1950's in the various directories as decorators and distributors. They used the mark, "Esco," and "Esco Products," as shown. In 1955, a distributing agency named Esco Products, Inc., Avenue J, Brooklyn, New York, was started by Joseph Malamet, who was an inlaw of the Katz family, who were the founders of Empire State Glass Decorating Company. The companies had no direct connection, but one was the outgrowth of the other through the relatives. Mark no. 1 was found at Quality Stamp Company and attributed to the Empire State Glass Decorating Company, which also decorated or sold some ceramic products; in this case, hotel ware. Mark no. 2 was found in the 1951 *Crockery and Glass Journal Directory*. Esco Products, Inc. under the direction of Allen Malamet, presently is listed for sculpture and art reproductions.

1.   2.

Empire State Glass Dec. Co.
197 Grand St., N. Y.

Enco, Inc. 242 Fourth Avenue, New York City. Company was found listed in 1949-1950 and again in 1965 *Gift and Art Buyers Guide Directory*. These were the only listings I found for them. This company seemed to be listed with only this particular directory and were not found in the *Crockery and Glass Journal Directory*, etc. Many times companies had themselves listed in only one of the many types of directories issued. The marks shown were found on blanks made by Salem China Company. I don't know if Enco, Inc. was the decorator or if Salem decorated the plates and cups and Enco, Inc. only sold them. (Marks: copy machined from pieces.)

Eneix, James E. New Geneva, Pennsylvania. Around 1880 to before 1890. In 1890, only one potter named Williamson was operating in New Geneva, according to Schaltenbrand, p. 22, so we may assume Eneix was gone. Made stoneware. Information on this potter was very scarce. According to Dr. C.A. Guappone in his book, *New Geneva and Greensboro Pottery*, McCellandtown, Pennsylvania, privately printed, 1975, p. 37, a Joseph Eneix was listed as a potter in 1870 census in New Geneva. I also found **Eneix and Frankenbery** and **Eneix and Evans** in New Geneva mentioned by Gorden C. Baker in "Pottery of Greensboro and New Geneva, PA.," *Spinning Wheel*, November 1973, pp. 14-17. He said "About a mile out of New Geneva, James Eneix operated a pottery with various partners under the style of Eneix and Evans and Eneix and Frankenbery." (Marks: Guappone, pp. 37, 38.)

Enterprise Pottery Company. New Brighton, Pennsylvania. 1883 to around 1900. In the *Factory Inspection Reports for State of Pennsylvania*, Enterprise Pottery Company employed 44 people in 1895 and 45 in 1900 to make stoneware. They made jars, ink bottles and a white glazed handthrown stoneware Carter's Ink bottle was found with mark impressed, "Enterprise Pottery Company, New Brighton, Pa." Around 1900, the pottery was purchased by F.G. Barker and in 1904 had become the property of the W.H. Elverson Pottery. (Information: Joseph H. Bausman, *History of Beaver County, Pa.*, 1904, p. 710. Mark stamped in or recessed on Carter's Ink bottle sent by Robert and Beka Mebane, collectors and writers. Also see listing Elverson, Sherwood and Barker Pottery.)

CARTER'S INKS

ENTERPRISE POTTERY CO. NEW BRIGHTON PA.

Enterprise Pottery Company. Trenton, New Jersey. Founded before 1880. In 1892, became one of five companies that founded Trenton Potteries Company. The Enterprise Pottery was listed until 1916 in Trenton City Directories. See the Trenton Potteries Company for history. (Marks: no. 1, Barber, *Marks of American Potters*, p. 64; no. 2, Thorn, p. 126.)

Enterprise Pottery Co

1.

ENTERPRISE POTTERY CO.

2.

Entis, Ann. Marysville, Ohio. 1960 to present. In the last 22 years that Ann has been working in a studio making one of a kind clay sculptured pieces, she has won awards and attended so many professional shows that she said there were too many to mention on the questionaire. She signs all pieces with her full name and uses no other mark.

Ann Entis

Eturia Pottery. Trenton, New Jersey. Was built in 1863 by Bloor, Ott and Booth. In 1865, the firm became **Ott and Brewer** when John Hart Brewer entered the firm. In 1893, the firm was followed by Cook Pottery Company. ("Charles Howell Cook," *American Ceramic Society Bulletin*, August 1925, p. 415.) This company is especially well known for at least two things that they did. One was to hire Isaac Broome who modeled some famous Parian portrait busts and figure vases that were exhibited in the 1876 Centennial Exposition. They were also the first American company to make the famous thin eggshell china with the lustre glazes called Belleek. Opaque china tablewares were made at the Eturia Pottery and marked with a Maltese Cross surrounded by a ribbon, or occasionally a circular rising sun device containing the firm name of Ott and Brewer. The company also made semi-porcelain and ironstone china. (Information and stamped marks: Barber, *Marks of American Potters*, pp. 52, 53; Lehner, *American Kitchen and Dinner Wares*, p. 56. The first three marks are from Ramsay's book. No. 4 is from the Barber, *Marks of American Potters*, was supposed to say "Royal Crown," I am sure. I have included some of Ramsay's marks throughout the book to show how an over zealous

artist can draw the marks so beautifully that they no longer look like the original marks. No. 5, J.G. Stradling, American Ceramics and the Philadelphia Centennial," *Antiques*, July 1976, p. 150. The rest of the marks are from Barber as cited.

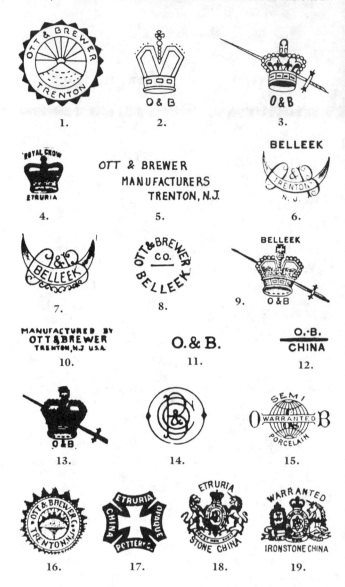

Evans Ceramics, Inc. Healdsburg, California. 1974 to present (1985). Evans Ceramics, Inc. was started by Tony Evans to make functional and decorative high-fired stoneware and low-fired Raku. Mr. Evans has been making pottery since 1960, but started his present business in 1974. Tony stated on his questionnaire that Evans Ceramics, Inc. is the largest commercial producer of Raku in the world. The company sells to the furniture and the gift industry all over the U.S.A. A brochure had pictures of absolutely beautiful pieces made specifically for interior design in a great variety of glazes, a Raku luster, Raku copper, Raku White Crackle, Red Calligraphy, Plum Blossom glaze and a very dark Raku finish called Pit Fire. Each was a one of a kind piece and each is signed and numbered. A certificate of originality comes with each piece. A line called "Landscape" has hand painted scenes. Evans Stoneware is a line of cookware with all sorts of pieces with hand painted designs. Some of these are scenes, delicate little flowers or a drip edging, etc.

Evans, Norris. New York, New York. A distributor, filed for a claim on this mark on February 7, 1933, for use on coffee pots, teapots, chocolate pots, fish platters, vegetable dishes, cereal dishes, baby dishes, deck service dishes, all sorts of cups, etc. made of stoneware, pottery, earthenware, dinnerware, porcelain and stoneware, claiming use since October 15, 1932.

Evan's Pottery. Arden, North Carolina. Evan Javan Brown, Jr. is from the sixth generation of Brown family potters in the U.S. He was raised in the pottery business and began producing traditional handmade pottery in early childhood. He created his first commercially successful glaze (red-brown) at age 17 and gave the formula to his father (famous artist Javan Brown) and Uncle Davis Brown when Evan left the pottery business in World War II to serve as an air traffic controller in the Navy. After the war he opened his first shop in Forest Park, Georgia, operating it part-time while working full-time as an aircraft controller at the Atlanta airport. After moving to Arden, North Carolina, in 1955, he gradually built a house and the current shop on Clayton Road. Through the years he designed many bright, colorful glazes to complement the traditional blacks, browns and whites. His work may be viewed at the Smithsonian Institution, Washignton, D.C.; Mint Museum, Charlotte, North Carolina; other museums in Atlanta and elsewhere. Evan is still in business at the present. (Information: from Evan Javan Brown, Jr. Evan stamps or imprints the pieces with various marks as shown. See the listing Brown Family Potters for more history of family.)

Evan's   *Arden, N.C.*

Handmade

Evans Pottery. Dexter, Stoddard County, Missouri, near Crowley Ridge. Around 1849, Hugh Evans started to make pottery including utilitarian, wheel thrown stoneware jugs, mugs, bowls, crocks, etc. The clay was buff to brown with a clear flecked glaze. He worked at first for a man named Simmermon, married Simmermon's daughter and eventually owned the pottery. Hugh Evans had two sons, Randal and Arthur. Arthur's son was Ferrell Evans and Randal's son was Terrell Evans. Randal continued in his father's pottery at Dexter, until Randal died in 1971 when the pottery closed. Arthur, on the other hand, started a pottery in Boulder City. (See the listing Desert Sands Pottery.) Pieces were made at this pottery with natural and dyed clay or mineral clay to give a variegated colored swirled effect similar to Niloak or Desert Sands. Some are marked "Dexter, Mo." or "Ozark M. Mo." according to Jo Ann Rogers in "The Evans Family Potteries," *Antique Trader*, June 1, 1977, pp. 74 to 76. Also, be sure to see the listing for the Ozark Pottery Company. (Information: Jo Hamm, "Desert Sands Pottery," *Antiques Journal*, February 1971, pp. 24, 25. Also, a very informative article with a very misleading titles is Clair Davidson, "The Ridge Pottery of Evans Crowley," *Antiques Journal*, August 1972, pp. 17, 18. This title and the picture captions were no doubt assigned by a copy editor rather than the author as is generally the case. The title should have read, "Evans Pottery of Crowley Ridge." If the reader gets past the title, the author makes it clear that Crowley Ridge is a place where Evans worked. Also, I think I would never have understood the confusion over Terrell and Ferrell except for Jenny B. Derwich an Dr. Mary Latos's book, *Dictionary Guide to Pottery and Porcelain in the U.S.*, p. 87, 88. Marks: nos. 1, 2, very old impressed marks on stoneware sent by Henry W. Heflin, pottery collector and researcher. Marks 3, 4, from Deb and Gini Johnson, *Beginner's Book of Pottery* pp. 98, 99. Mark no. 3 is stamped and mark no. 4 is inscribed. No. 5, staff written, "Questions," *Pottery Collectors Newsletter*, July 1974, p. 149 has not been verified as a mark belonging to the Evans Pottery, but the mark was found on the variegated type ware made by the pottery and they used Ozark as part of a mark.)

EVANS POTTERY
DEXTER, MO.

1.

EVANS POTTERY
HAND MADE
DEXTER, MO.

2.

EVANS POTTERY
HAND MADE
DEXTOR, MO.

3.

Crowley

4.

OZARK
SKAG
U.S.A.
REG.
15488

5.

Everedy Company. Frederick, Maryland. A distributor filed registration of this mark by May 29, 1939 to be used for crockery and ceramic cooking ware, claiming use since May 15, 1939.

SIZZEROLE

Everlast Company. New York, New York. The Everlast Company was a selling agency for Everlast Metal Products Corporation and the Goldcrest Ceramics Corporation as advertised in a 1948 *China and Glass Red Book Directory*. The ad said "presenting America's preference in forged and hammered aluminum hostess accessories and home items, also presenting a series of figures, animals, smoker's accessories, figurines, etc." (Marks: no. 1 on a decorative piece at the showroom of the American Ceramic Society in Columbus. At the time of our visit, the American Ceramic Society was preparing to open a museum or display room for the miscellaneous pieces they had. Mark 2 was shown in various directories during the 1940's. This particular mark from *China and Glass Red Book Directory*, 1948.)

1.

2.

Excelsior Works. Rices Landing, Pennsylvania. 1870-1880. Mark stenciled in blue. Isaac Hewitt made stoneware. Schaltenbrand, p. 26, tells us that Hewitt with six workers and three wheels made 45,000 gallons of stoneware or about $6,500 worth in 1870's. (Information: Schaltenbrand, *Old Pots*, p. 26; Ramsay, p. 228. Marks: no. 1, Thorn, P. 131; no. 2, Smith, p. 7; no. 3 Schaltenbrand, p. 68.)

ISAAC HEWETT
EXCELSIOR WORKS
PRICES LANDING
PENNA.

1.

2.

3.

Exclusive China Company. Broadway, New York, New York. Sales agency for English bone china giftware, etc., listed in 1967 *China Glass and Tablewares* Directory. Not to be confused with various American Maddock pottery's marks. The mark shown is for English made pottery.

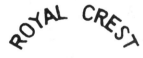

Exclusive China Co. (1)

Exeter Pottery Works. Exeter, New Hampshire. The pottery was an outgrowth of the old Dodge Pottery which operated from 1771 to 1819, when Samuel Dodge built a new pottery building and called it the Exeter Pottery Works. Later from 1838-1884, the owner was Asa B. Lamson, and the pottery began to be known as the **Lamson Pottery**. Frank H. and

Rufus Lamson, both sons of Asa, were known as the **Lamson Brothers,** from 1884 to 1886. From 1886 to 1889, Frank H. Lamson operated alone again. From 1889 to 1905, Frank H. Lamson had a partner, Henry C. Fields, under the name **Lamson and Fields**. At this time the pottery was already selling products not made there. They advertised glassware and graniteware as well as pottery. After 1895, the pottery manufactured no more. They were a selling agency only, until around 1936, when F.H. Lamson died. The pottery made redware with different colored glazes, green, black, brown, etc. in milk pans, cooking dishes, custard cups, washbowls and pitchers, jars, vases, pots, jugs, etc. (Information: Everett C. Lamson, Jr., *The Old Exeter Pottery Works*, Barre, Vermont: privately printed 1978, pp. 19 to 23. Marks: Lamson, pp. 51, 54, 57, 59, 61.)

LAMSON BROS.
EXETER, N. H.

FRANK H. LAMSON
EXETER
N. H.

FRANK H. LAMSON
EXETER, N. H.

FHL
1819

F.H.L.

E-Z-Cook, Inc. Lakeville, Indiana. Selling agency filed for registration of mark 1 in May 1960, claiming use since July 1958. Mark 2 was filed November 1960 and used after October 24, 1960. Both were for porcelain dinnerware. See Crest China Company, Santa Ana, California for another "Royal Crest" mark.

ROYAL CREST
1.

2.

F

F and M Artware Company. See Paden City Artware Company.

Faience Manufacturing Company. Greenpoint, New York. 1880-1892. Edward Lycett joined the company in 1884 and left in 1890 to go to Atlanta, Georgia, to work in a pottery studio with his son. He made beautiful luster glazes. Mark no. 1 used on early ware, majolica and barbotine wares. No. 2 used on finer china bodies and was printed beneath the glaze. No. 3 was used on decorated faience between 1886 and 1892 and was printed in black under glaze. (Marks: E.A. Barber, *Marks of American Potters*, pp. 83, 84. See Edward Lycett for his mark.)

FMG
1.   2.   3.

Fairbanks Ward Industries, Inc., assignee of **Alldec Corporation.** Chicago, Illinois. Filed for registration of this mark on February 11, 1965, claiming use since January 7, 1965, for use on china dinnerware. See French China Company for mark.

EVERSTONE

Fajans, Caroline R. New York, New York. Filed for registration of this mark on April 30, 1947, to be used on chinaware, namely, china dishes, cups, bowls, saucers and pitchers, claiming use since April 21, 1947.

"HAPPI-MAP

Farber Brothers. New York, New York. 1916 to 1965. Farber Brothers sold table accessories in chrome and fine glass for the most part, but they did have pieces with ceramic inserts. Lenox and Fraunfelter China Company are two potteries who made inserts for Farber Brothers. The compotes, candy dishes, butter dishes, mustard, syrups, salt and peppers, etc. were sold through gift shops and leading department stores. *Better Homes and Gardens* and other ladies' magazines had many advertisements for this ware in the 1930's through 1950's. The metal holders were made of chrome, silverplate or mosaic gold. Farber Brother's mark and the mark of the pottery that manufactured the ware may be found on the piece. In most cases, the Farber Brothers pieces will have glass inserts. (Information: Julie Sferrazza, "Farber Brothers Facts," *Daze*, July 1980, p. 1. Marks: two paper labels from *Better Homes and Gardens*; no. 1, 1946; no. 2, 1948.)

 1.   2.

Farber, Samuel P. New York, New York. Mark no. 1 filed August 17, 1951, by Samuel P. Farber, for use on china dinnerware service plates, claiming use since July 1951. In the *Gift and Tableware Reporter Directory*, August 16, 1965, p. 43, there are so many companies listed with Farber as part of the name that I could not assign this mark to one of them. They are: Farber Bros. Company, Crosby Street, New York, New York (see that listing); S.W. Farber, Inc., Bruckner Blvd., New York, New York; Sydney Farber and Son, Inc., Shepard Ave., Brooklyn, New York. These were all selling agencies.

Royal American

Farm Pond Workshop. Guerneville, California. Frans and Marguerite Wildenhain are studio potters, both still living in 1978. Marguerite came to this country around 1938 and Frans joined her in 1947. In 1942, Marguerite started the Pond Farm workshop, studio and school, where she teaches and makes pottery. The background for these two potters while in Europe is outstanding. Marguerite was educated in France, England and Germany. Her early art training was at the School of Fine and Applied Arts in Berlin. She studied with Max Krehan and the sculptor, Gerhard Marcks, at the Bauhaus in Weimar, Germany, where she stayed six years. She headed the ceramics department of the Municipal School for Arts and Crafts in Halle-Saale. In 1933, she and Frans were married and set up a workshop together in Putten, Holland, until she came to the U.S. Frans attended the Bauhaus and studied with the same outstanding men between 1924-1925. He received his M.A. at the Municipal School for Arts and Crafts and later taught there. In 1941, he moved to Amsterdam and then joined his wife in 1947. In reading about the various potters discussed in this book you will find several outstanding potters who studied at the Farm Pond workshop. In the 1978 exhibition, "A Century of Ceramics in the U.S.," sponsored by the Everson Museum of Art in Syracuse (formerly the Syracuse Museum of Fine Art), Frans was represented by a stoneware pot entitled, "Mushroom Pot." In the same exhibit, Marguerite had a tea set of glazed stoneware which had at one time been shown in the Eleventh Ceramic National exhibition at the Syracuse Museum of Fine Arts in 1946. She had won best ceramic design suitable for mass production with the tea set in 1946. (Information: Garth Clark, *A Century of Ceramics in the U.S.*, pp. 340, 341. Mark: Linda Steigleder, from the booklet published by the Everson Museum of Art to accompany the 1978 exhibition, "A Century of Ceramics in the U.S." The mark shown is painted and stamped.)

Farrar, William H. and Company. Syracuse, New York, and Kaolin, South Carolina. 1841 to 1856 or 1857 and Geddes, New York, 1857 to 1868. Made stoneware with blue painted designs in jugs and other utilitarian ware. In Arthur W. Clement's article "Ceramics in the South," pp. 22, 23 of Stradling's book, he states, "a pottery was established in 1856 by W.H. Farrar in Kaolin, South Carolina, who had been a stockholder in Fenton's pottery at Bennington, Vermont." Others associated with the pottery were Decius W. Clark and Alexander H. Stephens. (Information: Regina Stewart and Geraldine Consentino, *Stoneware, A Guide for the Beginning Collector*, p. 123; Bill Grande, "Stoneware Pottery," *American Collector*, April 1980, p. 12, gives the same information and shows this mark; John Spargo, *The Potters and Potteries of Bennington*, pp. 143, 144. See John Spargo's book for more information on this potter. (Mark: Barbara Perry, Everson Museum of Art, from jug at museum.)

W.H.FARRAR&CO.
GEDDES.N.Y.

Farrell Porcelain. East Killingly, Connecticut. Sandra and Richard Farrell, studio potters, make dimensional tiles, dinnerware and decorative accessories of porcelain. Sandra started in 1967 and Richard joined her and they began working as a team in 1972. They make simple graceful forms that are functional and durable. They make their own glazes which are used in multiple overlays. The interaction of these layers of glazes creates new colors in the firing, such as a range of copper reds to steel blues, etc. The Farrells have been written about in the *New York Times, Connecticut Magazine, State of the Arts, Providence Journal, Hartford Currant, Westchester Weekend, American Crafts,* etc. They have work in permanent collections in the Delaware Art Musuem, Wilmington, Delaware; Slater Memorial Museum, Norwich, Connecticut; Parkview Hilton, Hartford, Connecticut; and numerous private and corporate collections. Sandra was director of various art and pottery programs in Boston and Newton, Massachusetts, in 1967 to 1970. In 1968 and in 1972 she worked at the Penland School of Crafts doing graduate work and attending summer programs in ceramics. She received a degree in ceramics from Massachusetts College of Art in Boston. Richard worked as a publishing researcher in the field of electronics from 1967 to 1972. He has an M.A. degree in physics from Brown University in Providence, Rhode Island. On Peep Road Mill Road, they re-adapted a beautiful historic setting into studios, residence and exhibition space where they have organized and presented a series of self sustaining multimedia exhibitions. They have given panel presentations or acted on juries at the following conferences: 1979, "Supermud, NCECA National Conference," Penn State, Pennsylvania; 1979, "Technical Innovations in Clay and Metal," Rhode Island College, Providence, Rhode Island; 1981, "Connecticut Crafts Council," several places in Connecticut; 1981, "Marketing Crafts," Hartford, Connecticut; 1982, "New England Buyers Market," Boston, Maine; 1983, "Society of Connecticut Craftsmen," Farmington, Connecticut; 1984, "Percent For Art," Danielson, Connecticut. Just a partial listing of the many shows and exhibits for the Farrells since 1980 is as follows: 1980, "Seven From Connecticut," Creative Arts Workshops, New Haven, Connecticut; 1980, "Three Centuries of Country Folk Art," The Wadsworth Atheneum, Hartford, Connecticut; 1980, "For the Tabletop," American Craft Museum, New York, New York; 1980, "Architectural Crafts," Creative Arts Workshops, New Haven, Connecticut; 1981, "Jubilee 50," Currier Gallery of Art, Manchester, New Hampshire; 1981, "New England

Ceramics," Fitchburg Art Museum, Fitchburg, Maine; 1981, "Art for the Tabletop," Carol Hooberman Gallery, Birmingham, Michigan; 1983, "Table Art 1983," Benchmarks Gallery, Washington, D.C.; 1983, "Crafts USA in Iceland 1983," Kjarvalsstadir Museum, Reykjvik, Iceland. These few exhibitions listed show the great scope of their work. Some awards won are as follows: 1972, "Best of Show," Craft and Photography Show, Cambridge Art Association, Cambridge, Maine; 1975, "Purchase Award," Delaware Art Museum, Wilmington, Delaware; 1976, "Artists Project Grant," Connecticut Commission on the Arts - to develop vacuum forming technique and new glaze effects; 1978, "Best of Show," West Palm Beach Craft Exhibition, West Palm Beach, Florida; 1979, "Best of Show," Guilford Handcrafts Exhibition, Guilford, Connecticut; 1976-1981, "Court of Honor," Berkshire Craft Show, Great Barrington, Maine - work selected to represent show's highlights, three years; 1984, "Artists Project Grant," Connecticut Commission on the Arts - to produce architectural scale works. Each piece is signed on back or bottom as shown.

Farrell

Farrell, William. Chicago, Illinois. Farrell, a studio potter, born in Pennsylvania in 1936, received a B.S. degree at Indiana State University in 1958 and a M.A. degree from Pennsylvania State University in 1961. He was teaching at The Art Institute of Chicago in 1978, when Clark and Hughto wrote the book cited. Clark describes Farrell's work as showing an involvement with Abstract Expressionism, an affinity to Pop Art and Minimalism. He experimented and developed a technique for covering unfired clay with wet, plastic, forms of latex. Farrell was a founding member of the National Council for Education in the Ceramic Arts and has exhibited his work extensively in the U.S. (Information: Garth Clark, *A Century of Ceramics in the U.S.*, pp. 286, 287. Mark: Linda Steigleder, from the booklet published by the Everson Museum of Art to accompany the 1978 exhibition, "A Century of Ceramics in the U.S." Mark is stamped.)

BILL FARRELL

Farr Pottery. Oskaloosa, Iowa. 1907 to 1915. Charles L. Farr and John M. Farr were twin brothers, listed as makers of art pottery. They had a small business in a shed in the back yard of their home where they did make true art pottery. Their glazes were of beautiful colors, red, orange, blue, green and many hand thrown pieces had a second color dipped for decoration on very nice shapes. They also used a matt glaze. (Information and marks: all furnished by Maxine Gray of Maxine's Hen House, Oskaloosa, Iowa.)

Farr
MDCCCCIX

Farr
1908

Farr
1909

Farr Pottery

Farrar Potters, Various. Fairfax, Vermont. After 1798-1838. Isaac Brown Farrar was born 1771. He was in Enosburgh, Vermont, in 1798 and settled in Fairfax, some time later. He died in 1838. By 1840, George W. and J.H. Farrar, Isaac's sons, were running the pottery making covered butter pots, churns, jugs, sweetmeat jars, straight sided pots with narrow mouths, beer bottles, water fountains, etc. Another mark that may be found is "E.L. Farrar/Fairfax, Vt." and "E.L. Farrar." These were also sons of Isaac Brown Farrar. All members of the family had left Fairfax by 1871. E.L. Farrar went on to build the pottery which became Nichols and Alford in 1854. See that listing in Burlington, but by 1859, he was back in Fairfax. In 1859, there were three stoneware potteries in Fairfax: the E.L. Farrar Pottery; Farrar and Sterns; and Lewis and Cady. (Information: Lura W. Watkins, *Early New England Potters and Their Wares*, p. 148. Mark: Thorn, p. 126 and E.A. Barber, *Pottery and Porcelain of U.S.*, p. 438. Cabeb Farrar was another potter who operated in Middlebury, Vermont, from 1812 to 1850 making earthenware and white tableware. This Farrar sold to James Mitchell and Mitchell sold to Nakum Parker. Before 1900, the building had been converted to a home.

I.B. FARRAR & SONS

Feats of Clay. Austin, Texas. April 1976 to present (1983). Feats of Clay began at 1521 West Anderson Lane as a partnership of three potters, Judy Conroy, Dorothy Cavanaugh and Cindy Stewart Phillips with Jim Phillips as showroom manager, bookkeeper and kiln operator. All of these potters had been working in individual studios for at least seven years prior to forming Feats of Clay in 1976. They made hand thrown dinnerware, kitchen items of all sorts and decorative pieces and whimseys such as elves, castles, frogs, etc. Cindy studied at the University of Texas under Ishmael Soto. In 1979, the first partnership was dissolved and Judy Conroy continued the name Feats of Clay in partnership with James S. Lanham in a new location, 4630 Burnet Road still in Austin with a nice large shop of 2,000 square feet. There she and Lanham make stoneware and porcelain functional wheelthrown and also sculptured pieces. The year of manufacture is added to most of the pieces. Marks 1-6 are marks used by Judy Conroy. Marks 7-10 are marks for James S. Lanham. No. 11 is a paper label in use in 1983. Before 1979, Cindy Stewart Phillips signed her ware "Cindy," "Stewart," "Cindy Stewart" and also "Feats of Clay." Dorothy Cavanaugh signed her work "Cavanaugh," (sometimes with a date) "Dorthalee" and "Dorothy Cavanaugh."

FEATS 1.

Judy Conroy FEATS OF CLAY 2.

JC 3.

Conroy 83 4.   5. Conroy

Conroy FEATS 6.

7. Lanham

Lanham 8.

Lanham 9.   Feats of Clay

JSL 10.

Federal Porcelain Company. Carey, Ohio. Founded in 1917 and became part of Porcelain Products, Inc. in 1927. Made dry press electrical insulators. Letters are embossed on the insulator crown. (Information and mark: Tod, *Porcelain Insulators Guide Book for Collectors*, p. 111.)

Feliciano China and Glass. Puerto Rico. This was either a decorator or distributor whose mark was found at Quality Stamp company in East Liverpool Ohio. Sterling China probably made products for this company to sell. See that listing.

CHINA AND GLASS
FELICIANO
GUARANTEED
22 KT GOLD

Fell & Thropp. See Trenton Pottery Company for history.

IRON STONE CHINA
WARRANTED
F. & T. CO.

F & T Co.

LIBERTY AND PROSPERITY
F. & T. CO.

Fennell, Helen Studio. Davenport, Iowa. 1955 to present (1985). Helen Fennell makes porcelain pieces in molds such as angels, madonnas, birds, animals, a nativity scene, a Christmas tree, etc. The products are sold wholesale to about 300 various stores and gift shops throughout the country. Helen has five full time employees and extra help during the busy season. (Information: Derwich and Latos, *Dictionary Guide to U.S. Pottery and Porcelain*, p. 89. Mark from the potter.)

Helen

Fenton, Jonathan. Jonathan Fenton was born in Mansfield, Connecticut in 1766. He worked as a potter in New Haven, Connecticut, in 1792 until he went to Boston, Massachusetts, from 1793 until 1796. In January 1797, he went to Walpole, New Hampshire and after that he lived in Dorset, Vermont, where he started a pottery in 1801. In Boston, he worked with Frederick Carpenter as a partner (see Carpenter listing). Made stoneware jugs, pitchers, etc. "after the manner of imported Liverpool ware." Jonthan came from New Haven, Connecticut, where he had probably been trained by his brother, Jacob, who had a pottery there. Jonathan Fenton was the father of Christopher Webber Fenton (see the U.S. Pottery listing). Because the Lynn Street Pottery in Boston was closed in 1796, according to Watkins in footnoted article, the jugs marked "Boston 1804" were not made by Fenton, but by Carpenter. However, some marked "Boston" without a date were attributed to him. I recommend that anyone lucky enough to own one of these jugs should read the actual articles to determine the maker. Glaze, shape, how handles are made, etc. all enter into identifying the maker of these pieces as Watkins explains. (Information: Lura Woodside Watkins, "New Light on Boston Stoneware and Frederick Carpenter," *The Art of the Potter*, published by *Antique Magazine*, 1977, edited by Diana and J. Garrison Stradling, pp. 81-86. Marks: no. 1, Thorn, p. 126; nos. 2, 3, Stradling, p. 82.)

JONATHAN FENTON 1.
DORSET, VT.

2.

BOSTON 3.

Fenton, R.L. and Company. Dorset, Vermont. 1801-1834. Jonathan Fenton established a pottery in Dorset, Vermont, in 1801. John Spargo, as cited, p. 173 describes an inkwell made at this pottery as a very dark, almost black, high fired earthenware body and greenish lead glaze. Spargo said only redware and coarse stoneware were ever made at this pottery. The pottery in Dorset was operated until around 1834, by Jonathan Fenton and later by his sons, Richard Lucas Fenton and Christopher Webber Fenton until 1834. (Information: John Spargo, *Early American Pottery and China*, p. 173. Marks: C. Jordan Thorn, *Handbook of Old Pottery and*

Porcelain Marks, p. 126. Also, Spargo Plate 18 on lidded, handled stoneware crocks with painted flower designs.)

R L FENTON & CO.
EAST DORSET

Fenton, Richard Webber/ also **Fenton and Hancock.** St. Johnsbury, Vermont. Richard Webber Fenton was a brother to Jonathan Fenton. In 1808, R.W. Fenton started a pottery in St. Johnsbury and he was succeeded by his son, Leander W. Fenton, who operated the pottery until 1859 making utilitarian ware such as earthen milk pan, plates and stoneware jugs. In 1852, Frederick Hancock was a partner of Leander W. Fenton. By 1859, he had left the company. See F.B. Norton Pottery for more on Hancock. See United States Pottery for more on Fenton. (Information: John Spargo, *Potters and Potteries of Bennington*, p. 2; also Spargo, *Early American Pottery and China*, pp. 173, 174. Marks: C. Jordan Thorn, *Handbook of Old Pottery and Porcelain Marks*, p. 126.)

L W FENTON
ST. JOHNSBURY, VT.

FENTON & HANCOCK
ST. JOHNSBURY
VT.

FENTON & HANCOCK
ST. JOHNSBURY, VT.

Ferguson, Kenneth. Shawnee Mission, Kansas, with summer studio in Centennial, Wyoming. 1954 to present (1985). Kenneth Ferguson, a well-known studio potter, received a B.F.A. degree from Carnegie Institute of Technology in Pittsburg in 1952. After that he studied with Charles Harder at Alfred University, New York, and received his M.A. degree at Alfred in 1954. During the years at Alfred, Kenneth Ferguson's work was termed hard-edged, matte finished stoneware pieces with a Scandinavian influence. He went on to teach at several institutions including the Carnegie Institute, Alfred University and the Archie Bray Foundation in Helena, Montana. While at the latter school, he developed a line of utilitarian stoneware with Early American and Scandinavian techniques and images. Ferguson has at various times made functional and nonfunctional pieces of stoneware and porcelain, salt glazed and raku by wheel throwing, hand forming and also casting. Ferguson has done innumerable demonstrations, one-man shows, etc. In 1797, the Nelson Art Gallery in Kansas City had the exhibit consisting of 201 pieces entitled, "The Three Kilns of Ken Ferguson." A series of "Adam and Eve" plates was in the exhibit. One pictured three apples. All that was left of one of the apples was the core, portraying the message, the deed had been done! Ferguson's pots are aggressive in scale, sometimes very large, slumped or sagging. One pot Ferguson said looked like him; "It sort of sagged on me, it looks like me. It's a man's belly, hanging over his belt." Ferguson can turn the perfect functional pot and does, but he is not afraid to experiment and let the clay lead him to its ultimate conclusion and thus has created works of art. Ferguson was represented in 1978 at the Elverson Museum of Art in "A Century of Ceramics in the U.S.," created by curators, Garth Clark and Margie Hughto. (Information: Donald Hoffman, "The Creative Wheel," *Kansas City*

Star, October 16, 1983, pp. 1E, 7E. Also, Clary Illian, "The Three Kilns of Ken Ferguson," *Ceramic Monthly*, March 1980, pp. 47-50; and Garth Clark and Margie Hughto, *A Century of Ceramics in the U.S.*, p. 287.

Ferguso

Ferrell (or Ferrel), **Frank.** (Norris Schneider and Paul Evans both use one "L" in his name. Mark uses two "L's" and Evans gives both spellings.) Ferrell designed, modeled and decorated artware for various Zanesville, Ohio, potteries. Ferrell studied art with Karl Kappes in Zanesville, Ohio, and with the local Art Club composed of various employees of Weller Pottery, Mosaic Pottery and the American Encaustic Tile Company. From 1897 to 1905, Ferrell worked for the Weller Pottery. After 1905, for a short time, he worked for the J.B. Owens Pottery. In 1912, Ferrell was at the Peters and Reed Pottery where he designed the Moss Aztec. Weller had rejected this line when Ferrell suggested it to him, according to Norris F. Schneider, "D.W. Frank Has 500 Pieces of Weller and Roseville Ware," *Zanesville Times Recorder*, September 30, 1962 (no page no.). In 1918, Ferrell became art director for the Roseville Pottery Company, but he designed products for them earlier than that according to Schneider, as cited. Ferrell designed Dogwood made in 1916 to 1919. He designed the "Pine Cone" line which became one of Roseville Pottery's most profitable lines, now widely collected. "Ferella" also was designed by Ferrell. He refused to allow the line name to be "Ferrell," but settled for "Ferrella." At Roseville Pottery, Ferrell designed two lines a year from 1918 to 1954. (Information: Schneider, as cited, and also by Schneider, "Roseville Pottery," *Zanesville Time Signal*, in a series of articles, March 15, 1959, March 22, 1959, March 29, 1959. Mark: found on a piece with raised flowers and no other mark. At that time several years ago the price seemed so high I did not buy it. So, I can't identify which of the potteries Ferrell signed it for. It was a commercial artware piece. Sometimes the various pieces were signed "Ferrell" or "FF".)

Ferrell

Feustal and Nowling Pottery Company. See East Palestine Pottery Company.

Field, L.F. (and/or T.F.). Utica, New York. T.F. Field is dated 1828 to 1830 by Stewart and Consentino, p. 123, making stoneware jugs, etc. L.F. Field is shown in Thorn's book, p. 126, and dated around 1860 to 1870. (Mark: impressed; Thorn, p. 126.)

L.F. FIELD
UTICA
N.Y.

Figley, Joseph. New Philadelphia, Tuscarawas County, Ohio. Made stoneware. (Information and mark: Thorn, p. 126, and Lehner, *Ohio Pottery and Glass*, p. 73.

J. FIGLEY

Wm. Filene's Sons Company. Boston, Massachusetts. Distributor. Filed for a claim on this mark on September 13, 1929, for use on salt and pepper shakers, dishes, trays, vases and jars, kitchen spice sets, figurines of men, animals, etc. made of porcelain, crockery and earthenware, claiming use since January 1, 1928.

Fina, Angela, Pottery Studio. Amherst, Massachusetts. 1978 to present. Angela taught in colleges for 16 years before starting her own studio pottery in 1978. She makes porcelain, hand thrown, functional ware. She uses an apricot colored "shino" glaze and various transparent glossy glazes. Her list of shows and awards was given as "numerous."

Finch, Kay, Ceramics. Corona Del Mar, California. After study and travel around the world, Kay Finch opened her studio in 1935. Items were designed by Kay or her son, George, also an artist and sculptor. Braden Finch, her husband, was a guiding light on the business end while he lived. Operations ceased in 1963. Pieces include a variety of animals. All Kay Finch's pieces were hand decorated. (The foregoing is from Jenny B. Derwich, "Kay Finch Ceramics," *Pottery Collectors Newsletter*, July-August, 1980, p. 36.) In August 1984, this author received a letter from Dorothy Lombard, a long time friend of Kay Finch. She stated that Dorothy and Kay's son, George, were again making pieces from the original molds which contain the original marks. Kay Finch is still living at age 87 (September 1987).

Findlay Porcelain Company. Founded in 1911 until 1927 making all types of dry press and wet process pin type porcelain insulators. In 1927, they became one of six companies that merged to form Porcelain Products, Inc. In 1928, all operations ceased in Findlay, Ohio, and the factory operations were moved to the Carey, Ohio, and Parkersburg, West Virginia plants. The head office remained in Findlay until

1960. (Information: Tod, *Porcelain Insulators Guide Book for Collectors*, p. 111, and Don E. Smith, author of the book *Findlay Pattern Glass*, by letter. Incised or stamped marks: Tod, as cited, p. 11. Tod shows several sizes of the diamond-F mark.)

FINDLAY

First Thought Pottery/Cottage Craftsman. Sandpoint, Idaho, 1970 to present (1985). Kaaren Stoner, studio potter, makes reduction fired stoneware and some salt glazed ware into functional pieces, such as dinner sets, casseroles, pitchers, kitchenware, planters, etc. She also makes a line of animal banks, jugs, bears, etc. From 1973-1977, Kaaren lived and worked in Port Orchard, Washignton. From 1977-1983, First Thought Pottery was in Orient, Washington. In 1984, they moved to Sandpoint, Idaho, where she and her husband sell the pieces from their shop. Kaaren said she had attended far too many shows to list, mostly in the Pacific Northwest. She did say she attended the Pacific Northwest Arts and Crafts Fair in Bellevue, Washington, every year between 1972 and 1982. Kaaren earned an M.A. in Fine Arts from University of Puget Sound, Tacoma, Washington, in 1973. Prior to 1973 her work was signed "K.S." The "K.S." evolved into the "K" and straight line mark shown. The "F.T.P." mark is a stamped mark used after 1983 on some of Kaaren's pieces, for the name First Thought Pottery.

Fischl, Janet W. Plandome Manor, New York. Filed for registration of this mark April 10, 1956, claiming use since February 27, 1956, on crockery, tea cups and saucers.

Fisher, Bruce and Company. Philadelphia, Pennsylvania. Selling agency, listed in various directories that I had from 1950's into 1980's. In the 1967 *China, Glass and Tableware Directory* they showed the marks and were listed as selling Baronet china from Bavaria, Aynsley from England Luneville from France, etc. But they also showed these two marks for Lamberton China, made by Scammell China Company and Sterling China Company. In the 1945 *Crockery and Glass Journal Directory* this company was listed as distributors of American dinnerware among other products. At that time, they were selling the Stangl Pottery's Della Ware line. See Stangl for marks. Windsor Ware was English earthenware filed for registration in 1961 by Fisher, Bruce and Company, claiming use since 1940.

Fisher, Bruce & Co., 221
Market St., Phila., Pa.

Fisher, Bruce & Co., 221
Market St., Philadelphia, Pa.

Fisher, J.C. Hartford, Connecticut. 1805-1812. Impressed mark on redware and stoneware. This man may have been a relative of the Jacob Fisher who was at the Lyons Pottery. Jacob followed T. Harrington at Lyons and T. Harrington came from Hartford. But I could not positively connect the two Fishers. In another area, there were two Fishers in Berks County, Pennsylvania, a John Fisher Pottery, around 1879, and a Michael B. Fisher Pottery, around 1891. The latter known by the name Fair Pottery. These men seemed to have no connection to each other either. (Information: Guy F. Reinert, "History of Pennsylvania-German Potteries of Berks County," *Bulletin of the American Ceramic Society*, January 1940, p. 26.)

J. FISHER

Fitz and Floyd. Dallas, Texas. Late 1950's to present. Pat Fitzpatrick and Bob Floyd were distributors and a selling agency which started in late 1950's. Fitzpatrick died, and Floyd carried on in the late 1960's. He introduced the idea of mix and match dinnerware in 1972. In 1983, at age 52, Floyd spend four months per year in Japan to work with his seven designers. One-third of his time is spent in Dallas, working with his salesmen and department heads. Palm Springs, California, is the site of his first retail store where he spends the remainder of his time. He has a residence in all three locations. The ideas, designs and specification for the dinnerware and decorative pieces come from Fitz and Floyd, are made in Japan and sold in this country. This American distributor of foreign made ware is included to give an understanding of today's mode of operation in the dinnerware industry. Besides individual distributing or selling companies, many of the companies that were formerly manufacturers of dinnerware, now import the dinnerware and sell only. See Salem China Company, Scio China Company and Gorham China Company for examples. (Information: "Robert Floyd," *The Dallas Morning News*, October 23, 1983, pp. 1, 4. Marks: sent by Rena London. Mark 1 filed January 15, 1981, claiming first use in commerce in 1965.)

1.

FF 2.

FITZ AND FLOYD, INC.
© MCMLXXV
FF

Fletcher Pottery Works. Mason, New Hampshire. 1974 to present (1984). Liz Fletcher, studio potter, makes mostly stoneware sculpture and a small amount of functional ware. (Marks: no. 1, is used on sculptured pieces; no. 2, incised on pottery; no. 3, stamped on pottery.)

LIZ FLETCHER
1984

1.

LIZ

2.

LIZ FLETCHER
MASON, NH

3.

Fleuron, Inc. North Tonowanda, New York. This company was not listed in the 1922 R.G. Dun and Company's huge directory of manufactuers, so they must have started between 1922 and 1927. Mark no. 1 was filed for registration October 19, 1928, claiming use since October 18, 1927 for pottery vases, lamp bases, jardinieres, flowerpots of ceramic products. Mark no. 2 was found on little unglazed vase of heavy red clay which looked like field tile clay. I found no further listings and no telephone was listed at present.

1.

2. FLEURON
N.TONOWANDA, N.Y.

Flintridge China Company. Pasadena, California. 1945 to 1970. Flintridge China Company was started in Pasadena, California, in 1946 by Thomas Hogan and Milton Mason. Both men had developed their expertise in china manufacturing by working at Gladding McBean. Their manufacturing skills helped them to develop a thinner china that used a high Nepheline syenite body at cone 7. A series of outstanding china designs came along that rapidly expanded the plant to a full city block in 1963. One original design which is still highly popular today is Black Contessa. In March 1970, Flintridge China was acquired by the Gorham Division of Textron, Inc. (See that listing.) (Marks: no. 1, from Quality Stamp Company, East Liverpool, Ohio, also known in various directories. Mark no. 1 was also used by Gorham after 1970. They had purchased all rights. No. 2 filed for registration on December 15, 1947, for use on dinnerware manufactured of clay, claiming use since 1946. Mark 3 filed on December 18, 1964, claiming use since July 1964, for use on china dinnerware. No. 4 filed for registration on November 30, 1959, claiming use since June 1958, for table china. No. 5 filed on December 8, 1958, claiming use since June 16, 1952. No. 6 filed on August 12, 1957, claiming use since July 29, 1957.)

1.

2.

ROYAL DEVON

3.

4.

FLINTRIDGE

5.

BON-LITE

6.

Floch, Jenny. Columbus, Ohio. 1952 to present (1985). Studio potter, Jenny Floch, makes functional and decorative stoneware. The list of juried group shows attended by Jenny since 1959 is quite impressive, including shows at the Everson Museum of Fine Art, Syracuse, New York; Cooper Union Museum, New York City; Akron Art Institute, Akron, Ohio; Batelle Memorial Institute, Columbus, Ohio; Butler Art Institute, Youngstown, Ohio; Columbus Museum of Arts; and Schumacher Gallery at Capitol University, Columbus, Ohio. A partial list of one- or two- person shows include many of the same places plus the Philadelphia Art Alliance; the Zanesville Art Institute at Zanesville, Ohio; Pennsylvania State University; the Matrix Gallery, Indiana State University; and several other galleries in various states. The list of invitational shows is also impressive and Jenny has pieces on exhibit at: the Sand Museum, Palm Springs, California; Zanesville Art Institue, Zanesville, Ohio; Wehrle Gallery, Ohio Dominican College, Columbus, Ohio; Massilon Museum, Massilon, Ohio; Ceramic Monthly Collection, Columbus, Ohio; Hebrew Union College, Jewish Institute of Religion at Los Angeles; Muskingum College, Muskingum, Ohio. Awards won by Jenny include: 1961, Court of Honor, York State Crafts Fair, Binghamton, New York; 1963, Award of Merit, Artist-Craftsmen of New York, Cooper Union Museum, New York; 1966, Exhibition '66, Columbus Museum of Fine Art, Columbus, Ohio; 1968, Exhibition '68, Columbus Museum of Fine Art, Columbus, Ohio; 1970, 1974, 1977, Purchase Award, Columbus Art League Show; 1979, Purchase Award, Columbus State House Show; 1979, Purchase Award, Liturgical Arts Show, Columbus, Ohio; 1970; Award of Merit, Ohio Designer Craftsman Show, Columbus, Ohio; 1982, Purchase Award, Ohio Arts Council at Winterfair. Jenny's work has been discussed in articles in *Ceramic Monthly*, September 1970, *Designer Craftsmen*, October 1970, and *Craft Horizons* in various reviews between 1966-1978. This potter also found time to serve in various capacities, plus she now works as a jury member in judging shows. Professional service includes: 1970-1972, State Representative and Treasurer, North Central Assembly, American Crafts Council; 1970-1971, First Vice President, Ohio Designer Craftsman; 1975, member of the Advisory Panel, Artist's File, Columbus Museum of Fine Art; 1976, member of the Task Force for grants to individual artists, Ohio Arts Council; 1981-present, member of the Artists Services Committee, Greater Columbus Arts Council.

Florence Ceramics. Pasadena, California. Florence Ward started making ceramic jewelry in the 1930's. Her business grew into a factory at South Gabriel. She sold the business in 1964. The largest amount of production was made during the 1940's. Pottery listed in 1954 directory with outlets in New York City, Chicago, Washington, Atlanta, Dallas and San Francisco. Florence made molded and hand decorated figurines with marks shown. (Information from Libby Monson, Libby Monson Unique Items, El Macero, California). In 1964, the business was sold to the Scripto Company. They continued under the same name, but made mugs, cups, ashtrays, etc., even mugs for the Rose Bowl Tournament of Roses one year. They were still listed in the *China, Glass, and Tableware Directory* for 1977, but that year the inventory was sold & the building vacated, according to Derwich and Latos, *Dictionary Guide to U.S. Pottery and Porcelain*, p. 92. (Marks: nos. 1, 2, sent by letter, Lucille Henzke, no. 3 from R.R. Rider.)

Florence Pottery. Mount Gilead, Ohio. 1920 to 1941. A man named McGowan started two early stoneware potteries in the town, with one on each end of town at various times. To date no marked specimens from McGowan have been found. Florence Pottery, an outgrowth of the old potteries, became of interest to collectors when it was learned that Rum Rill was made there in the late 1930's until the pottery burned in 1941. See Rum Rill for more on this. Lawton Gonder managed the Florence Pottery from 1938 to 1941 and from there he went to Zanesville, Ohio, and started the Gonder Ceramic Arts Company. See Gonder Ceramic Arts for more information. I have never found a mark that Florence Pottery used except the "Rum Rill" mark. See Red Wing Pottery for dates on these registered marks. Also see listing for Rum Rill.

Florentine Pottery. Started around 1900 in Chillicothe, Ohio, and moved to Cambridge, Ohio, in 1919. (Stout, pp. 88, 97.) According to Barber p. 138, they made faience and artware vases, pedestals, etc. around the early 1900's. Listed in the *Factory Inspection Report for Ohio* in 1902, as employing 31 to make pottery. In 1906, they employed 36. Made a ware called "Effeco." In 1905, the pottery started manufacturing sanitary ware. (Mark: Barber, p. 38.)

Foell and Alt. East Birmingham (later Pittsburg), Pennsylvania. 1857-1885. The mark pictured was on a stoneware crock with a cobalt eagle with flowing banner with nine stars and the words "Foell and Alt/Manufacturers" above the eagle and "East Birmingham" below the eagle. It was shown in the article by James M. Harrison, "The Case of the Disap-

pearing Potters," *Antiques Journal*, March 1979, pp. 32, 33, 39.

Fondeville, Eugene L. New York, New York. Distributor, filed for registration of mark no. 1 on June 20, 1942, for use on ceramic tableware, claiming use since June 8, 1942. In the 1946 *Crockery and Glass Journal*, Fondeville and Company was listed as selling "Rochelle," mark 3, an American made fine china in fancy ware, but it didn't say which pottery made it for them. Mark 3 is in the 1946 *Crockery and Glass Journal Directory*. See the section in the introduction on distributors for a discussion on Fondeville.

Ford China Company. Ford City, Pennsylvania. Was started in 1898 by John Wick, Jr. and John B. Ford. Around 1904, **Cook and Company, Inc.** owned the plant. It was sold to **Pennsylvania China Company** of Kittanning, Pennsylvania in 1912, who manufactured tableware, plain and decorated jardinieres and ornamental vases. In 1918, the plant was purchased by the **Eljer Company** of Cameron, West Virginia which made sanitary ware. They employed around 600. (Lehner, *American Kitchen and Dinner Wares*, pp. 57 and 118; Joseph F. Gregory, researcher, by letter; also, J.H. Beers, *History of Armstrong County, Pa.*, 1914, p. 128.)

Ford, Henry, Pottery Shop. See the listing Greenfield Village Pottery for information.

Forrest Valley Galleries. Nashville, Tennessee. 1975 to present (1984). Owners and studio potters, Ronald and Judi Lederer makes wheel thrown or slab built high fired stoneware, all hand glazed, decorated or carved in a wide variety of colors and scenes. Every piece in the two small brochures sent had pictures painted on them. Pieces made are cannisters, cookie jars, pitchers, bowls, steins, mugs, cups, lamps, vases, pyramids, etc. Ronald graduated from the University of Wisconsin, where he studied artistic design, architecture and sculpture. He came from Wisconsin to Nashville to take the job as city planner. The demand for his pottery forced him into pottery making full time.

Lederer '83

Fort Dodge, Iowa, Various Potteries. Fort Dodge, Iowa. Martin White founded **White's Pottery Works** around 1870 in Fort Dodge. The early pieces are sometimes marked with the pottery name and Fort Dodge, Iowa, on the opposite side. White made stoneware with dark brown glaze or Albany slip into crocks, jugs, churns, etc. Mr. White had a partner named Meggs for three years around 1880. Then Meggs left and started his own pottery which soon failed. That pottery was taken over by Martin White and his two sons, and then they operated in two buildings. An early map shows a third pottery owned by the Whites, called **Union Pottery Works** and some pieces were so marked. Mr. White passed away in 1890 and in 1892 the sons established the firm name of **Hartwell and Bower, Inc.** Mr. Hartwell and Mr. Bower were the two silent backers of the pottery in Fort Dodge. Around this time the name **Fort Dodge Stoneware Company** began to be used. In 1906, the pottery was one of the seven potteries that were merged to form Western Stoneware Company. Fort Dodge Stoneware became Plant 7. (Information and marks: Elva Barglof, "The Four Faces of Fort Dodge Pottery," *Antique Trader*, April 2, 1980, pp. 62-64. Marks as seen on crocks in pictures in article. No. 1-3, marks for Fort Dodge Pottery, heavily impressed on bottom of crock. No. 4 is a printed square mark on side of crock. Mark 5 sent by Barglof by letter.

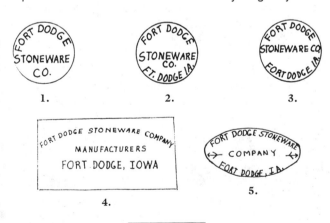

1.   2.   3.

4.   5.

Fort Edward Pottery Company. Fort Edward, New York. 1859-1861 (Stewart and Consentino Stoneware, dates, p. 123). Made stoneware. There was also a Fort Edwards Stoneware Company (see Haxstun and Company listing). (Marks: Guilland, p. 110.)

FORT EDWARD POTTERY CO. 1.

FORT EDWARD POTTERY CO.
FORT EDWARD, N.Y. 2.

Fortescue, Cecily. New York, New York. 1974 to present (1984). Studio potter, makes slab stoneware, dinnerware and large one of a kind pieces. Sells products chiefly to Henri Bendel's and Macy's. Mark incised.

Fort Hays State College Pottery. Fort Hays, Kansas. Produced from 1935 to 1948 at Fort Hays Kansas State College within the Department of Art. The pottery was produced under the direction of John Strange, as a segment of the National Youth Administration. Strange was the ceramic instructor at Fort Hays. The College employed some of its students to work in the process of producing art pottery and other pottery items. Clay for the pottery came from Ellis and Russell counties in Kansas. All the equipment was produced by Strange and the students. Pottery is marked Fort Hays Kansas State College, impressed as shown in Deb and Gini Johnson's book, *Beginners Book of American Pottery*, p. 107. (Information: sent by Thomas Turnquist, researcher and writer on American pottery.)

Fort Hays
Kansas State
College

Fort Ticonderoga Pottery. Fort Ticonderoga, New York. In 1931, a non-profit membrship corporation was formed for the purpose of restoring and preserving the old fort located between Lake Champlain and Lake George, well known to students of the Revolutionary War. Mr. and Mrs. Stephen Pell, descendants of the first Pell who purchased the ground in 1820, were the guiding lights of the organization. During the 1930's and 1940's, a potter named Henry Graack worked as a potter at the Fort making pieces for the tourist trade to buy. See the listing H.A. Graack Art Pottery for more on Graack. (Information and marks: Bob Doherty, "Fort Ticonderoga Pottery," *American Clay Exchange*, February 1984, p. 3. Marks impressed.)

FORT TICONDEROGA

FORT TICONDEROGA

Fosdick, Marion Lawrence. Marion Fosdick studied at the school of the Museum of Fine Arts in Boston from 1900 to 1912 and also studied in Germany in 1912 and 1913. She came back to the United States to do special work at the art museum school and then joined the staff of Alfred University as a professor of design and drawing until 1920 when she taught pottery and sculpture. During the late 1930's and 1940, she won several important awards. See the lists in the back for the Syracuse Ceramic National Prizes. She received the Binns Medal and a medal from the Boston Society of Arts and Crafts. (Information: Garth Clark, *A Century of Ceramics in the U.S.*, pp. 287, 288. Marks: no. 1 is a painted mark; no. 2 is a paper sticker; Linda Steigleder, from the booklet published by the Everson Museum of Art to accompany the

1978 exhibition, ''A Century of Ceramics in the U.S.,'' with Curators: Garth Clark and Margie Hughto.)

FOSDICK

1.

MARION L. FOSDICK

2.

Foxhill Pottery. Parkville, Missouri. Studio potter, Jane Turner, is working at present (1984) to make stoneware, porcelain into special orders. Jane also gives private lessons in pottery making.

Fox Pass Pottery. Hot Springs, Arkansas. January 1972 to present (1984). Owners, James and Barbara Larkin, studio potters, make vitrified stoneware and some porcelain into kitchen and dinnerware and other functional as well as decorative pieces. They have won many awards at arts and craft shows in various locations in Arkansas. No. 1 is Barbara's drawing of a stamped mark used at Fox Pass Pottery. No. 2 is Jim's inscribed mark; no. 3 is Barbara's mark.

1.

Larkin

2.

B. Larkin 3.

Frackelton, Susan. Milwaukee, Wisconsin. 1876 to 1910. Susan Frackelton, a china painter or decorator, was also a writer and lecturer and she illuminated manuscripts. She worked in ceramics from 1876 until 1910. In 1893, she founded the Frackelton China Decorator Works. She also helped to form the National League of Mineral Painters. She used applied, incised and cobalt decorations, also underglaze slip decorating in Delft type designs on stoneware pieces. Frackelton wrote a handbook for china painters, entitled *Trial by Fire*, published in 1885. (Information: Dave Rago, ''American Art Pottery,'' *Antique Trader*, April 7, 1982, p. 97. For a description of several pieces of her ware, see Paul Evans, *Art Pottery of the U.S.*, p. 105-109. Marks: hand incised or inscribed. No. 1, Rago, as cited; no. 2, Linda Steigleder, from the booklet published by the Everson Museum of Art to accompany the 1978 exhibition, ''A Century of Ceramics in the U.S.'')

1.

2.

1893

Framae Art Pottery. Sheffield Lake, Ohio. 1979 to present (1983). Owners Frank and Anna Mae Steel make slip cast, hand decorated art pottery vases, ewers, pitcher and bowl sets, jardinieres, steins, mugs, plates, lamps, etc. in a two fire process fired at 1,900 degrees. The pieces are decorated with birds, Indians, animals, flowers, etc. First marks were ''FraMae hand painted,'' or just ''Hand Made'' with the date from 1979 through 1981. The 1982 mark was ''FraMae'' and a number designating glaze and date made. The last letter being A or F for Anna or Frank, whichever made the piece. The glazes come in a beautiful brown, soft matte blue and a beige to brown color. The pieces are hand painted with portraits and regular hand painted scenes built up with layers of slip and then painted. Mark no. 1 incised on piece. Mark 2 filed for registration Juen 30, 1981 claiming use since July 1980 for art pottery vases and receptacles.)

HAND MADE
FRA MAE
ART POTTERY

1.

FRAMAE ART POTTERY

2.

Frankenthaler, Helen. Helen received her education at Bennington College, Vermont. She is a painter and sculptor, whose work has been widely exhibited. She participated in the Art in America project in 1964 with her paintings. She uses a technique of stain painting in which she washes colors into unprimed canvas. In November 1975, she worked at the Clay Institute in Syracuse, in the Everson Museum's ''New Works in Clay by Contemporary Painters and Sculptors.'' Her works in clay has been sculptured pieces. (Information: Garth Clark, *A Century of Ceramics in the U.S.*, p. 289. Painted mark: Linda Steigleder, from the booklet published by the Everson Museum of Art to accompany the 1978 exhibition, ''A Century of Ceramics in the U.S.'')

frankenthaler

Franklin, Ben, Stores. Chicago, Illinois. A distributing agency with a chain of stores still operating in 1980's. The mark shown was under the French Saxon Pottery Company marks in the material secured from Quality Stamp Company of East Liverpool, Ohio.

BEN FRANKLIN DINNERWARE

U. S. A.

Franklin Factory. Cincinnati, Ohio. In the *Dictionary of Antiques* by L.G.G. Ramsey, p. 870, is described a ten inch brown-glazed jar made for tobacconist H. Thayer which was marked ''Franklin Factory/1834/S. Quigley.'' The finding of this jar gives the mark authenticity. (The mark had been questioned by John Ramsay in *American Potters and Pottey*, p.

210, and C. Jordon Thorn in *Handbook of Old Pottery and Porcelain Marks*, p. 144.)

**S. QUIGLEY
FRANKLIN FACTORY
CINCINNATI**

Franklin Porcelain Company. Norristown, Pennsylvania. Early 1920 to around 1928 or 1929. The company made electrical porcelain, mainly insulators, which were sold by the Electric Service Supplies Company which purchased the controlling interest in the Franklin Porcelain Company. (Information and incuse (stamped) marks: Jack H. Tod, *Porcelain Insulators Guide Book for Collectors*, p. 123.)

FP

Franklin Pottery Company. Franklin, Ohio. 1880-1884. Made semi-porcelain, granite ware. Ramsay called this plant the **Franklin Porcelain Company** with the same dates. (Information: Lehner, *Ohio Pottery and Glass*, p. 59. Mark: Thorn, p. 126.)

$$\frac{F\,PC}{F}$$

Frankoma Pottery. Sapulpa, Oklahoma. 1936 to present. The success of this pottery is the result of the efforts of one truly remarkable family. John Frank, the founder, died in 1973 and the control of the pottery passed into the hands of his daughter, Joniece Frank. John had a B.A. degree from the Chicago Art Institute and Joniece graduated from Hockaday College Preparatory School in Dallas, Texas, then received a degree from the University of Oklahoma and later studied two months in Europe. John Frank served as an instructor of Art and Ceramics at the University of Oklahoma from 1927 until he started Frankoma Pottery in 1936. The pottery was practically wiped out by fire in 1943, and again in September 1983, and was rebuilt both times. Another daughter of John's, Donna Frank, has written an interesting and informative book about John and the factory called *Clay in the Master's Hands*.

One line introduced in the 1940's was Mayan-Aztec. Besides the beautiful lines of dinnerware, Frankoma is well known for a series of Christmas plates, sculptured items designed by John's wife, Grace Lee Frank, flower containers and all sorts of novelty items. The Christmas plates as listed in a brochure sent by the company were: "Jesus, the Carpenter," 1973; "David, the Musician," 1974; "Jonathan, the Archer," 1975; "Dorcas, the Seamstress," 1976; "Peter, the Fisherman," 1977; "Martha, the Homemaker," 1978; "Daniel, the Courageous," 1979; "Ruth, the Devoted," 1980; "Joseph, the Dreamer," 1981. There was also a series of state plates made at the pottery. These were available in desert gold, white sand, prairie green and flame. Colors used on other pieces of Frankoma are a Robin egg blue, autumn yellow, onyx black, terra cotta brown, satin, etc. The color-

ing of the pieces is vivid and outstanding. Grace Lee Frank, wife of John, is an artist in her own right. She designed such plates as, "The Grace Madonna," in 1977 and "The Madonna of Love," in 1978. Also, she has designed a variety of birds and other pieces. (Information: Lehner, *American Kitchen and Dinner Wares*, p. 58; brochures, etc. sent by factory. Marks: nos. 1 through 11, from Susan Cox, *The Collectors Guide to Frankoma Pottery*, Book II, 1983, p. 19. Nos. 1, 2, 3, John Frank's initials or name used around 1927 to 1933, according to Cox as cited. No. 4, rare mark, 1938. Nos. 5, 6 incised or rubber stamped, used around 1933. No. 7, incised, rubber stamped, impressed, used around 1934 to 1936. No. 8, impressed, on small pieces, only Frankoma was sometimes used, 1940 to 1946. No. 9, 1942 to present. No. 10, current initials for Joniece Frank Duane. No. 11, Frankoma Pottery initials used around 1960 to present. No. 12, on a limited edition vase issued 1972: Frankoma and V4 were raised letters; John Frank and the number 2442 was incised; from article, "Frankoma Pottery Vases," *Antique Trader*, July 22, 1981, p. 79. No. 13, raised mark on plate. Nos. 14, 15, marks shown in brochure and various articles for Frankoma.

Fraunfelter China Company. Zanesville, Ohio. 1923 to 1939. Fraunfelter China Company followed the **Ohio Pottery** which had operated from 1900 to 1923. Ohio Pottery made chemical items when they started and added hotel ware and a true hard paste dinnerware to line around 1918-1920. Charles Fraunfelter became director of pottey in 1915. In 1923,

Fraunfelter also purchased **American China Products Company** of Chesterton, Indiana. He made dinnerware in both plants. The Chesterton plant closed in 1925 when Charles Fraunfelter died. Fraunfelter China failed during the depression, reorganized and reopened, then closed for the last time in 1939. Some very interesting marks are found on Fraunfelter china. The Ohio Pottery and Fraunfelter China Company both sold large quantities of blanks for decoration, since they were one of the very few American firms that made porcelain of European quality and still be competitive in price. Norris Schneider in "Fraunfelter China Company," *Zanesville Time Recorder*, January 21, 1962 (no page number in notebooks) said that Fraunfelter never decorated any artware as such. In mark no. 1, the Warwick China mark is overstamped by a Fraunfelter, Albert Pick mark. Mark sent by Larry Paul. No. 2, the Royal Rochester mark is not a label; it is a colored mark under glaze. This would be a distributor's mark. (See the Robeson Rochester Corporation listing). No. 3 shows us that Ohio Pottery as well as Fraunfelter China made products for Robeson Rochester Corporation. No. 4 is a variation of the decaled Royal Rochester mark. No. 5. is the Fraunfelter mark as it was filed for registration January 15, 1925, claiming use since 1924 for use on china tableware, dinner ware, china cooking ware, china chemical laboratory ware and china ornaments. No. 6 found without manufacturer's mark. No. 7 furnished by Brisker's Antiques, Richwood, Ohio. The rest are stamped marks are photostatic copies on dishes.

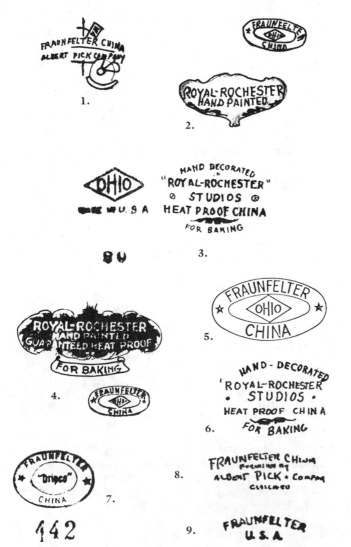

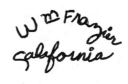

Frazier, Inc. North Hollywood, California. This company was listed at 7333 Coldwater Canyon Ave. in 1960 *Giftware Buyers Guide* as a manufacturer. This was the only listing I found. (Mark: was inscribed on an earthenware dish with a speckled rose and brownish gray glaze, sent by Darlene Reynolds.)

Fredericksburg Art Pottery. Fredericksburg, Ohio. In 1910, a pottery was built in Fredericksburg, Ohio, by Walter and George Spencer, where they made bean jars and other utilitarian type pieces. Then in 1913 or 1914 the pottery was sold to the **Wooster China Company** with Al Harrison, Fred Coxon and Fred Bell as the owners. In 1921, the pottery again changed hands and became a branch of the **National Sanitary Company**, Salem, which made iron and enamel products. I suppose they made basins, pots, etc., among other things. In 1923, that same company acquired a third plant in Clarksburg, West Virginia. In 1927, all three plants were sold to the **Elger Manufacturing Company**, which made bathroom fixtures. The plant was abandoned in 1936 or 1937 with no machinery on the premises. Then, in late 1937, Joe Imler leased the plant for one year to the **American Beleek Company**. In Fredricksburg, this American Beleek Company only lasted six months and then left the town and their debts behind. And so no more was heard from them in Fredericksburg. In 1939, John McClain reorganized the plant, along with George Heisler. At one time, these men employed 210 people making novelties, vases, cookie jars even wooden whatnots. Then, in 1949, after the plant had been closed down for six months, it was sold to the Pilgrim Pottery Company, with George Stanford of Sebring as president, John McClain as vice president and a C.V. Martin as manager. Around 1951, they were employing 112 people, and they were still making a novelty line. On May 26, 1965, the plant burned down completely. (Information: Mrs. V.D. Sterling, *A History* *of Fredericksburg and Community, Salt Creek Township, Wayne County, 1951. Marks: impressed or incised on pieces.)*

FreDericksburg
Art
Pottery
U.S.A.

1.

PATENTED
Puss 'n Boots
USA

2.

F.A.P. co.

3.

F.A.P.co

4.

I. Freeman and Son. Had two addresses in the 1952 *Crockery and Glass Journal Directory*, one in New York City and the other in Los Angeles. The mark shown was registered to New York City address April 14, 1952, claiming use since September 17, 1948, for use on chinaware and crockery, namely, cups, saucers, plates, bowls and platters as decorative ware and collectors' items. There was also a Martin Freeman Company in New York City in 1952. This was a separate company. Mark shown was not found under foreign or domestic trade names. So, I don't know if it was French or American made ware.

PORCELAINE

DE PARIS

Freeman-McFarlin Potteries. El Monte, California. 1951 to 1980. Gerald H. McFarlin and Maynard Anthony Freeman started the pottery in 1951 in El Monte. In 1980, the plant was sold to Hagen Renaker, Inc. in San Marcos (see that listing). In the 1977 *California Manufacturers Directory*, Freeman-McFarlin was listed as a Division of International Multifoods employed 200 people to make art or decorative pottery. There must have been many marks for this company, but I can only show two that I found inscribed on pieces. One was a large decorative bowl. The other piece was a cigarette box with a beautiful glaze that looked almost like marble and part of the box was a dull black matt finish, very attractive. The only reponse I was able to get from letters was from Maxine Renaker of Hagen Renaker, Inc.

Anthony ©
475 U.S.A.

F - McF
©
USA
319

Freimarck, John. Mechanicsville, Virginia. John started in Rochester, New York, 1970-1973, then moved to his present site in Mechanicsville. He is a studio potter making functional stoneware. In 1980 and 1981, he made 7,000 to 8,000 pieces each year of leach type slag marked "Freimarck" usually ac-

companied by a brushed mark "F." John has done many shows including the Virginia Craft Biennial, 1974, 1976, 1978, 1980. He also lists the Virginia Museum in Richmond and the Mint Museum for shows and awards.

FREIMARCK
J

French China Company. Sebring, Ohio. Founded shortly before 1900. In 1916, the pottery became part of the **Sebring Manufacturing Company** when the French China Company, the Saxon China Company and the Strong Manufacturing Company were consolidated under one management. All three plants retained their original name under this ownership. The Saxon China Company was founded in 1911, according to *Sebring, Ohio, A Brief History*, p. 16. The Sebring Manufacturing Corp. joined the American Chinaware Corp. in 1929. The American Chinaware Corp. failed in 1931. The same soource said that both the French China and Saxon China companies passed out of existance in 1932, after the American Chinaware Corp. was dissolved. Around 1934, the Saxon China Company was reopened as the French-Saxon China Company. The first ware was shipped in January 1935. The buildings were greatly expanded and improved. In 1949, French Saxon China Company employed 380 people to make semi-porcelain dinnerware and various accessory pieces. In 1964, French Saxon-China Company was purchased by Royal China Company, also of Sebring, Ohio, and was operated as a wholly owned subsidary. See Royal China listing. See the Stetson China listing for more on French Pottery building. See Saxon China Company listing for marks for that company. (See *American Kitchen and Dinner Wares*, p. 58, for picture of ware made by French China Company, Marks: no. 1 filed March 4, 1916, under the French China Company name for use on ceramic tableware, claiming use for one month. Both plants made semi-porcelain dinnerware with this mark. Marks nos. 1-7, Barber, *Marks of American Potters*, p. 135; nos. 9-16, on dishes.)

MARTHA
WASHINGTON

1.

PLUTO
F.C.CO.

2.

TIGER

3.

CUPID

4.

LYGIA

5.

Greek

6.

La Francaise
Porcelain

7.

Kenneth

8.

F.C. CO.
MARTHA
WASHINGTON
A-22

9.

10.

F.C. CO.
VICTORIA
A-22

French China
Co
FII 27B

11.

12.

F.C. CO.
26-E

13.

14.

LA FRANCAISE PORCELAIN

LA FRANCAISE SEMI VITREOUS

LA FRANCAISE SEMI VITREOUS A B

15.

16.

French Saxon China Company. Sebring, Ohio. See French China, Sebring, for history. (Marks: no. 1 is the mark most commonly known for French China as it was filed for registration October 8, 1945, claiming use since the year 1936. See Promotions, Inc. for marks put on ware made by French Saxon China Company. Nos. 2, 3, are marks, probably paper labels, shown in the 1952 and 1954 *Crockery and Glass Journal Directory*. The directories never tell how the lable or mark is applied. A few of the remainder of the marks came from dishes, but almost all of them were listed under French Saxon at the Quality Stamp Company in East Liverpool, Ohio. I believe "Victory" to be used in marks by several companies during the W.W. II. I have seen several. The only reason I can identify this one is that it was under French Saxon material at Quality Stamp Company. Salem China had a "Victory" mark, also. Nasco is a mark used by National Silver Company, a distributor. See the National Silver Company listing. Marks 4-14 are part of a mark – they would be found in conjunction with the shield and armour mark or the National Silver Company mark. Many backstamps are applied by two stamps. The marks shown are all backstamps.)

FRENCH SAXON CHINA

1.

FRENCH CHINA SAXON

2.

THE F-S CHINA CO.

3.

JONQUIL
UNION MADE
U.S.A.
22 KT GOLD

4.

CELADON
UNION MADE
U.S.A.
22 KT. GOLD

5.

POPPYWHEAT
U.S.A.

6.

Good Housekeeping
DINNERWARE
22 KT. GOLD
U.S.A.
FAIRFAX

7.

Vanity Fair
DINNER WARE
NANCY LEE
22 K. GOLD
U.S.A.

8.

COSMOPOLITAN
DINNERWARE
22 K. GOLD
SPRING FLOWER
U.S.A.

9.

SANDRA
22 Kt. Gold 10.
U.S.A.

SPRINGTIME
22 K GOLD
SPRINGTIME
22 K. GOLD

11.

BLUE MIST
UNION MADE
U.S.A.
22 KT. GOLD

12.

CORAL ROSE
UNION MADE
U.S.A.
22 KT. GOLD

13.

14.

FAIRBANKS-WARD
ARISTOCRAT
22 KT. GOLD
MADE IN U.S.A.

UNION MADE NASCO U.S.A.

BOUQUET
22 KT. GOLD
DECORATED

15.

UNION MADE U.S.A.

22 K. GOLD
U.S.A.

16.

UNION MADE NASCO U.S.A.

ROSE OF PARADISE
22 KT. GOLD
DECORATED

17.

UNION MADE NASCO U.S.A.

22 K. GOLD
U.S.A.

18.

UNION MADE NASCO U.S.A.

19.

JUANITA
22 KT. GOLD
DECORATED

FRENCH SAXON CHINA

20.

CORAL GARDEN
UNION MADE
22 KT. GOLD
U.S.A.

FRENCH SAXON CHINA

21.

UNION MADE
U.S.A.
22 KT. GOLD

Florence

FRENCH SAXON CHINA

22.

UNION MADE
U.S.A.
WARRANTED
22 KT. GOLD
DUSTY ROSE

FRENCH SAXON CHINA

23.

UNION MADE
U.S.A.
22 KT. GOLD

Empire

UNION MADE NASCO U.S.A.

CAROLINE
22 KT. GOLD
DECORATED

24.

UNION MADE NASCO U.S.A.

LORRAINE
22 KT GOLD
DECORATED

25.

UNION MADE NASCO U.S.A.

PRINCESS ELIZABETH
22 KT. GOLD
DECORATED

26.

UNION MADE NASCO U.S.A.

ROSE OF PARADISE
22 KT. GOLD
DECORATED

27.

UNION MADE
U S A
SOUTHERN
ROSE

28.

UNION MADE
U.S.A.
22 KT. GOLD

La Fleur Bran

FIRST QUALITY

2706H

29.

UNION MADE
U.S.A.
SILVER
SYMPHONY

30.

UNION MADE
U.S.A.
Dehaviland

31.

U S A
22 KT. GOLD
GOLDEN HARVEST

32.

UNION MADE
U.S.A.
WARRANTED
22 KT. GOLD
GOLD BORDER

33.

UNION MADE
U.S.A.
ROSE GARDEN

34.

U.S.A.
Star Flower
2885-S-56

35.

UNION MADE
U.S.A
22 KT. GOLD
GOLDEN
POPPY

36.

CORAL BOUQUET
UNION MADE
U.S.A.
22 KT. GOLD

37.

UNION MADE
U.S.A.
Carolyn Rose

38.

39.

UNION MADE
U.S.A.
22KT. GOLD
Wedgebine

UNION MADE
U.S.A.
Pine Cone
2837-S-54

40.

UNION MADE
U S A.
COSMOS

41.

UNION MADE
U.S.A.
African Violet

42.

UNION MADE
U.S.A.
BURGUNDY
LACE

43.

UNION MADE
U.S.A.
GLENNDALE

44.

5

UNION MADE
U.S.A.

"Rose Dogwood"

52/1   45.

U.S.A. - 2
STAR FLOWER
2885-S-56
22 KT. GOLD

46.

3

UNION MADE
U.S.A.
THISTLE

47.

U.S.A.
BREEZE
2926-S-58
22 KT. GOLD   48.

ROMANY
F. S. C. CO.
Sebring. Ohio
U.S.A.
Union Made

49.

Rancho
DINNERWARE
BY
FRENCH SAXON

50.

VICTORY
UNION
MADE
U.S.A.

51.

Aloha
Dinnerware
by
FRENCH SAXON
CHINA

52.

THE FRENCH SAXON CHINA CO.
NATIONAL BROTHERHOOD
OF CO-OPERATIVE POTTERS
SEBRING, OHIO

U.S.A.

53.

The French Saxon China Co.
MADE IN USA
Hand Decorated
FOR
BEN GROSS CO.

54.

Frey, Viola. Oakland, California. Middle 1950's to present (1985). Studio potter and teacher makes ceramic dogs, cats, roosters, birds, etc., using china paintings to change the surface of the forms. She uses overglazes to give them alertness, vividness, etc. Viola received a B.F.A degree at the California College of Arts and Crafts in 1956 and an M.F.A. degree in 1958 from Tulane University in New Orleans, Louisiana. From 1970 to the present, she has taught at the California College of Arts and Crafts. In July of 1984, she had a one-person exhibition at the Whitney Museum of Art. She is now making eleven foot high figures. (Information: Garth Clark, *A Century of Ceramics in the U.S.*, p. 290; also, *It's All Part of Clay: Viola Frey*, Philadelphia, Pennysylvania: Moore College of Art, 1984. Mark: Linda Steigleder, from the booklet published by the Everson Museum of Art to accompany the 1978 exhibition, "A Century of Ceramics in the U.S.")

V·FREY

Friendship Pottery. Roseville, Ohio. February 1973 to present (1986). Owners, Terry Zahn and Frank Rossi, bought the former Melick Pottery. They are makers of crock pots, high vitrified mixing bowl sets, etc. In May 1984, Ungemach Pottery was sold to the owners of Friendship Pottery and became Friendship No. 2. In 1985, they were making decorative ware in one building and functional pieces in the other. (Marks: no. 1 is a raised mark in the mold on the bottom of an excellent mixing bowl. No. 2 is a paper label used in 1984. Some hand decorating is done on some pieces, such as pie bakers with blue birds and little sayings, etc.)

1.

2.

Frimkess, Michael. Very active in 1960's and 1970's. This talented studio potter was admitted to the Otis Art Institute in 1952 at the age of 15, as one of the youngest students ever to attend there. He studied under Peter Voulkos. He learned a special technique to throw a hard clay without water. He studied the Greek ceramics in the New York Metropolitan Museum of Art which had probably been made by this method. Garth Clark describes his work as having bright overglaze decorations with some purely decorative motifs and some with comic illustrations of Frimkess's experiences in Boyle Heights, where he grew up in a Jewish family. Japanese, Chicano and Black children were all in his neighborhood, an ethnic melting pot. (Information: Garth Clark, *A Century of Ceramics in the U.S.*, pp. 290-291. Mark: Linda Steigleder, from the booklet published by the Everson Museum of Art to accompany the 1978 exhibition, "A Century of Ceramics in the U.S." Mark 1, painted; no. 2 incised.)

1.

FRIM.60
2.

Fulkerson, Jude M.J. Topeka, Kansas. Filed for registration of this mark on April 3, 1979, claiming use since January 1, 1970, for use on pottery and earthenware teapots, wine decanters, toothbrush holders, vases, planters, coffee cups, cookie jars.

Fulton, G.N. Jordan Mines, Virginia. Located between the mountains of Virginia and West Virginia, near Potts Creek. 19th Century. Made bluish gray stoneware, according to Elmer L. Smith in his book, *Pottery A Utilitarian Folk Craft*, p. 31. Fulton's name was hand painted on a stoneware jar with a large flower. Fulton had a kiln that could hold 1,000 gallons per firing. I could find no further information on the potter. (Mark: same source.)

L.D. Funkhouser and Company. Strasburg, Virginia. Thorn, p. 126, dates this pottery 1889 until 1905. Made stoneware. Mark impressed. (Marks: no. 1, Smith, p. 23; no. 2, Thorn, p. 126.)

1.

L.D. FUNKHOUSER
STRASBURG
VA.
2.

Furman, Noah. Cheesequake, New Jersey. 1840-1856. Made stoneware, jugs, crocks, etc. mostly cylindrical in shape. A straight sided jug marked "N. Furman, South Amboy" within an oval was found. (Information: Robert J. Sim and Arthur W. Clement, "The Cheesequake Potteries," reprinted from *Antiques Magazine* in *The Art of the Potter*, edited by Diana and J. Garrison Stradling, p. 122. Mark: Thorn, p. 126.)

N. FURMAN NO.39, PECK SLIP N.Y.

G

Galesburg Pottery Company/Galesburg Stoneware Manufacturing Company. Galesburg, Illinois. Pottery built in 1891 by a stock company. They made brown and white stoneware crocks, jugs, churns, water pitchers, tea pots, etc. The plant had a very bad fire in 1897 but was able to go on until after the turn of the century. In 1893, the company was listed as the Galesburg Stoneware Manufacturing Company employing 23 in the *Factory Inspection Reports* for Illinois. (Information and marks: Janice T. Wass, curator of Decorative Arts Illinois State Museum. Marks: no. 1, stenciled on stoneware crock. Nos. 2-3, inscribed mark on bottom of stoneware piece.)

Galesville, Various Potters. Galesville (Washington County), New York. There were several potters in Galesville, New York, between 1850 and the late 1860's, according to Warren F. Broderick, researcher and writer, who sent the following information. Otto V. Lewis and William A. Lewis are listed separately. See that listing. Frederick A. Gale operated in the 1850's and 1860's and used the Galesville mark shown which may be seen pictured on a salt glazed jug with trailed blue slip flowers pictured in Guilland, p. 235. Gale also used the marks, ''Frederick A. Gale/Galesville,'' and ''F.A. Gale/Galesville.'' Moses Farrar and Burtis Soper, around 1853 to 1855, used the mark, ''Farrar and Soper/Galesville.'' John H. Giles, around 1863-1866, used the mark, ''John H. Giles/Galesville.'' All of these men were stoneware potters. (Information and marks: Warren F. Broderick, as cited.)

GALESVILLE NY

Galloway and Graff. Philadelphia, Pennsylvania. Started 1868 (Thorn, p. 126) Barber, *Marks of American Potters*, said they were operating at the time the book was first published in 1893. Evans, p. 52, said Galloway and Graff became the Galloway Terra-Cotta Company of Philadelphia. This company made terra cotta artware, pedestals, fountains, statuary, vases in Greek shapes. Later, they made all garden ware. Advertisements in the 1930's and 1940's referred to the company as the **Galloway Pottery.** In *American Homes*, July 30, it is advertised, ''decorative pottery of high-fired beautiful Terra Cotta for garden, sun room and porch made by Galloway Pottery at 3214 Walnut Street, Philadelphia.'' In *House and Garden*, March 1940, the pieces mentioned are jars, vases, benches, gazing globes, bird baths, etc. of same material, all large pieces suitable for garden and outdoors use. The shapes are outstanding. (The magazine clippings were sent to me without page numbers.) Mark: Barber, *Marks of American Potters*, p. 32)

Gallstyn Company, Inc. New York, New York. Company filed for registration of this mark on January 21, 1972, claiming use since November 16, 1971, for ceramic and stoneware kitchen ware, cook ware and cooking utensils.

Gamtofte Pottery. Ripley, Ohio. 1952-1957. Elizabeth Barrett Jensen and Jens Jensen were decorators at Rookwood Pottery. Jens, born in Fynen, Denmark, studied art in Jutland, came to America in 1927, and worked at Rookwood from 1927 to 1948. Elizabeth Barrett, born in Maysville, Kentucky, studied at Cincinnati Art Academy and University of Cincinnati, decorated at Rookwood Pottery from 1924 until her marriage in 1931. She worked part time after 1931 at Rookwood. In 1952, the Jensens began making pottery in the Gamtofte Pottery that they established near a little stone house they had purchased. In 1957, the Ohio Department of Highways relocated the main road and cut around in back of the pottery. They realized the futility of trying to attract customers from the road on which the house was located and gave up on the commercial venture. They undoubtedly made some pieces for their own pleasure after that time which were fired in a kiln belonging to Mrs. Jensen's sister. Jens has been dead for several years; he died sometime after 1977. Elizabeth is no longer able to be contacted; she suffers from glaucoma and emphasema and should not be bothered by collectors or writers. Elizabeth, while she was still able, made some commercial items to be sold in a Maysville, Kentucky store, such as souvenir mugs with the Kentucky Cardinal on them. Another line of plates, cups, teapots, etc. was called ''Tuckaho Pottery'' marked with a T.P. monogram above Elizabeth's initials. Mark 1 is the mark used by Elizabeth at Rookwood Pottery. Mark 2 was used by Jens at Rookwood Pottery. Marks 3, 4, 5 are the marks found on the Tuckaho Pottery pieces. (Information: Frederick O'Nan by letter, January 29, 1983 and article, ''A Rookwood Romance, Elizabeth Barrett and Jens Jensen,'' *American Art Pottery*, August 1977, p. 1. Marks: furnished by Frederick O'Nan.)

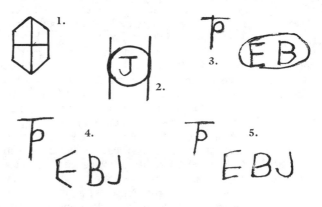

Gamza, Steve. Burnsville, North Carolina. 1970 to present (1984). Steve is a studio potter of great promise; he graduated from Michigan State University in 1976 with a master's degree in fine arts. Before that, he attended Indiana State University and the New York College of Ceramics at Alfred University. He uses a low-firing approach to make vessels of a decorative nature, "their function is to shed a bit of light to their immediate surroundings," said Steve. Since 1970, he has been doing craft fairs and he listed 25 exhibitions he has done since 1977 in 13 different states! Among them was the National Raku Exhibition, Peters Valley, Layton, New Jersey. Others were held at Detroit Institute of Art, Columbus Gallery of Fine Art, Clemson University at Clemson, South Carolina, North Carolina Museum of Art and many more we just can't list here. Steve was associated with the Penland School of Crafts from 1979 to 1983; then in 1984, he established himself as a studio artist in Burnsville. He has worked and studied in Germany and Italy as an independent studio artist. He was a visiting instructor of ceramic art at Alma College in Alma, Michigan. He has conducted workshops at various colleges and studios in several states and Brazil.

So Gamza

Ganse, Henry. Lancaster County, Pennsylvania. Around 1894. The mark shown must have been poorly inscribed on a pot found by Thorn, p. 126, or someone, who gave the mark to him. Probably the "e" was illegible. Other pieces marked by Ganse were redware moulded pieces, according to M. Luther Heisey in "The Makers of Pottery in Lancaster County," published by Lancaster County Historical Society, Volume I, nos. 4 and 5, 1946, p. 120. Heisey said after Henry Gast died, Henry Ganse took over the Gast pottery in 1894. The Ganse family had been potters near Dorwart since 1843.

H. GANS

Gardiner Stoneware Manufactory. Gardiner and Farmingdale, Maine. 1876 until around 1890. For early history, see the listing Plaisted Pottery. In 1876 to 1878, the Gardiner Stoneware Manufactory was owned by Charles Swift and William M. Wood. In 1878, Swift sold his part of the plant to Anders Persson, one of the potters who worked there. Persson resold his share one year later to Elias S. Brown and went to Bangor, Maine, to establish the Bangor Stone Ware Company (see that listing). Many more changes of ownership occurred throughout the history of this pottery, but the name always remained Gardiner Stoneware Manufactory. In the M. Lelyn Branin book, *The Early Potters and Potteries of Maine*, he tells about all of the real estate transactions recorded for all of the various Maine potters. It is the most thoroughly documented book I have found on the old earthenware and stoneware potters. On p. 132, he tells of what were the last two transactions on this property. The owners in 1890 were Lennan and Billings. Billings sold his share in 1890 and Lennan in 1892, and the pottery ceased to operate around that time. Products were stoneware crocks, jugs, jars, churns, etc., some with incised figures of a cow, swan or eagle, etc. (Information: Branin, as cited, p. 223; and

"Regional Aspects of American Folk Pottery," published by Historical Society of York County, Pennsylvania, 1974, p. 50.)

GARDINER

GARDINER ME

Garzio, Angelo C. Garzio came to the United States in 1930 and received a B.A. and B.S. (liberal sciences) from Syracuse University in 1949. He received a Diploma di Proffito, University of Florence, Italy in 1950. Also an M.A. (art history) from University of Iowa, in 1954 and an M.F.A. (ceramics) from the University of Iowa in 1955. He was the winner of three Fulbright Awards. He has won prizes in pottery at: 1958 Brussel's World's Fair; 1959 Ostend International Ceramics Competition; 1959 Miami National Ceramic Competition; 1963, Rocky Mt. National Ceramic Competition, and was the winner of 15 regional and state competitions. He has been represented in collections in the Smithsonian Institute, Syracuse Museum and Alfred University. He is presently professor of art at Kansas State University, since 1957. Pots are marked incised with "Garzio." (Information and mark: Thomas Turnquist, pottery researcher and writer.)

Garzio

Gates Potteries. See American Terra Cotta and Ceramic Company.

Gautier, Josie. Gautier, Mississippi. Filed for registration of this mark on February 5, 1951, for pottery and ceramics, such as vases, tableware and jewel cases, claiming use since April 15, 1950. (The potter's name and the town name were the same on the report.)

Gayet Ceramics. Temple City, California. Ethlyn B. Gaylord filed for registration of this mark on April 14, 1952, for use on ceramic articles, such as dishes, spoon drip holders, salt and pepper shakers, tea bag drainers, egg cups, cruets, planters, salt boxes, cookie jars, decorative wall plates, razor blade banks, toby mugs, pin cushions, candy boxes, picture frames, tea balls, tooth paste and brush holders or dishes, claiming use since April 4, 1945.

Geijsbeek Pottery Company. Denver and Golden, Colorado. Started in 1899 (Barber, p. 165). Also according to Barber, *Marks of American Potters*, p. 165, some marks used said Denver, Colorado. Marcia Ray, p. 248, called the Geijsbeek Pottery "a commercial venture where three kilns turned out whiteware said to be very much like modern Delft without the blue decoration." In "Samuel Geijsbeek," *Bulletin of American Ceramic Society*, Volume 23, no. 2, 1944, p. 66, Sameul Geijsbeek reproduced for J.B. Owens Pottery, without much trial, the brown underglaze decorated artware first made by McLaughlin in Cincinnati. Geijsbeek was superintendent of J.B. Owens Pottery for two years, 1896 to 1898. In 1898, he joined Sherwood Brothers of New Brighton, Pennsylvania, as assistant superintendent and chemist. In 1899, he equipped and operated a vitrified dinnerware plant of his own in Denver, Colorado. In 1900, he became secretary and general manager of the Geijsbeek Pottery in Golden, Colorado, where according to this same article, he made the first whiteware made west of the Mississippi River. He made the ware from Colorado clay. From 1903 to 1906, he was assistant superintendent and chemist for the Winkle Terra Cotta Company of St. Louis, Missouri. In the article, seven more moves and positions changes were made by Geijsbeek before his death in 1943. But none of these mentioned the Geijsbeek Pottery. It may have lasted only until 1903 when Geijsbeek went to St. Louis. I could find nothing more on the pottery. (Marks: no. 1, on piece at American Ceramic Society, Columbus, Ohio; nos. 3, 4, 5, from E.A. Barber, *Marks of American Potters*, p. 165.)

Gem Clay Forming Company. Sebring, Ohio. Incorporated in 1907, the company originated in East Liverpool, Ohio, and moved to Sebring, according to *Sebring, Ohio, A Brief History*, a 50th Anniversary publication, with no author given, Sebring, Ohio: 1949. They started by making gas mantle rings, tips, pins and stilts. The plant burned in 1908. After moving to new quarters, they manufactured parts for space heaters, electrical porcelain, lamp bases and parts for cooking ranges. In the 1930's, they made a line of figurines or comedy figures in form of the "Our Gang" comics. In the 1950's and 1960's, they made lamp bases. Gem Clay was still listed in 1960 under ceramics, floor and wall tile in the directory. At present, only furnace liners are made in the building by Ferro Corporation. Gerald Barnett found the mark shown on a refrigerator dish or pitcher marked "Kelvinator." (Mark: Gerald Barnett, "Spotlight," *National Journal*, March 1979, p. 25.)

General Ceramics Company. New York, New York. Manufactured chemical and industrial stoneware. They also owned **Carillon Ceramics Corporation** prior to 1944 when it became a separate company. Then in 1945, Carillon Ceramics was sold to the Richmond Radiator Company of New York, New York. The first three marks shown below are for acid proof industrial and chemical stoneware, all patented in 1931, by General Ceramics. The fourth "Carillon" mark is the patent mark for china dishes and vases filed for May 15, 1940, claiming use since April 1940. An advertisement in *House and Gardens*, December, 1940, p. 16b, showed a deep glazed porcelain bowl made by Carillon Ceramics Corporation which was owned by General Ceramics Company at this time. In *House and Garden*, October, 1940, is an advertisement for "Carillon China made by American craftsmen with fascinating glazes and simple beauty" with a vase pictured.

PYROTONE   CERAMCO

CERAMIT   **CARILLON**

General Housewares Corp., Holt-Howard Division. Hyannis, Massachusetts. Listed in 1971 and 1977 in *China, Glass and Tableware Directory*, for ceramics, gourmet cookware, kitchen accessories, mugs, salts and peppers, trivets, cutting and serving boards and sugars and creamers.

General Mills. Minneapolis, Minnesota. Distributors of food products, filed for a claim on Mark 1, on February 8, 1937, to be used for earthenware, mugs, baking dishes, sugar bowls, tea cups, salt cellars, etc., claiming use since January 25, 1937. Mark 2 was filed February 2, 1942, for use on ceramic dishes, claiming use since January 22, 1941. Mark 3 was filed October 8, 1959 claiming use since April that year for china and earthen dinnerware. Mark 4 was filed August 8, 1967 for use on the same articles.

ROMANY
1.

2. **BETTY CROCKER**

TWIN STAR
3.

4. **PATIO**

General Porcelain Company. Parkersburg, West Virginia. Company was formed in 1913, by the consolidation of three porcelain companies. One in New Lexington, Ohio, also Sun Porcelain Company and Diamond Porcelain Company, both of Trenton, New Jersey. The company made electrical porcelain insulators with incuse or stamped in marks as shown. (Information and marks: Tod, *Porcelain Insulators Guide Book for Collectors*, p 112. Tod showed various kinds of lettering for the General Porcelain Company's mark.)

Geneva Porcelain. See Belvedere, Inc.

George-Good Corporation. City of Industry, California. Listed in the 1981-1982 *China, Glass and Tableware Directory* for ceramic figurines, mugs and woodenware. A distributor or selling agency owned the marks shown. Nos. 2 and 3 were found on a fine little porcelain figurine, the other on a semi-porcelain plate. To keep collectors from confusing mark no. 1 with a mark for W.S. George, I have included this distributor. The pieces I have seen with these marks are of excellent quality.

George Street Pottery. New Haven, Connecticut. 1974 to present (1984). Maishe Dickman, studio potter, received a B.S. degree in Industrial Design from University of Bridgeport in 1971. She studied later in North Africa, and also studied with Mick Casson and Don Reitz. For three years, she worked as an industrial designer in New York City and then started the George Street Pottery in 1974. In 1983, she conducted two workshops at Cambridge School, Weston, Massachusetts, and at the Creative Art Workshop in New Haven, Connecticut. She listed eight group and six one-man shows she had done in the last two years plus several craft exhibitions and some juried shows in seven different states. At the George Street Pottery, Maishe makes functional and sculptural stoneware, signed with her name.

W.S. George Pottery Company. East Palestine, Ohio; Canonsburg, Pennsylvania; Kittanning, Pennsylvania. For the early history of W.S. George Pottery Company in East Palestine, see the listing for the East Palestine Pottery Company. William Shaw George was also involved in two different locations in Pennsylvania, in Canonsburg and Kittanning. Around 1900, W.S. George was involved in the founding of the Canonsburg Pottery Company, but he also had a pottery of his own which was listed in Canonsburg, but was actually in Strabane, Pennsylvania, which was a mile away from the Canonsburg Pottery in Washington County. See East Palestine China Company for mark. See the Canonsburg Pottery listing for W.S. George's involvement in that operation. From 1913 or 1914 to 1927, W.S. George Company owned a plant in Kittanning, Pennsylvania. See the Wick China Company listing for the history of that plant. W.S. George Pottery was still listed in Kittanning, in Armstrong County, as late as 1935, in the *Pennsylvania Industrial Directory*. I was missing directories between 1935 and 1947, so I don't know exactly when W.S. George Pottery Company closed the plant in Kittanning. Through all of the directories, the Canonsburg Pottery and the W.S. George Pottery Company were both given separate listings in Washington County, Pennsylvania. McKee, p. 27, said W.S. George Pottery Company suspended operations in December 1955. I am afraid this was not the case. The W.S. George Pottery Company in Canonsburg, Washington County was still listed in the *Industrial Directory of Pennsylvania*, in 1959. My next directory was 1962 and they were no longer listed. I believe there was a bankruptcy suit in 1955, and some sort of reorganization by the George Brothers, but the potteries continued for a while longer. W.S. George Pottery was still listed in the 1960 Telephone Directory for the Salem, East Palestine area. W.S. George died in 1925, but the family members continued the potteries.

Some of the very early products for the W.S. George Pottery were semi-porcelain dinnerware, plain and fancy table and toilet ware, hotel ware, which was half an inch thick and had a welded edge, white and decorated goods. (Stout, p. 84.) (Information: Lehner, *American Kitchen and Dinner Wares*, pp. 59-61. Marks: W.S. George Pottery used stamped marks. The Argosy shape (see marks 1, 2, 3) was introduced in the late 1920's. No. 4, Bolero shape. Nos. 5, 6, Lido shape. No. 7, Rainbow were all introduced in the 1930's. No. 8, Del Rio Ochre was introduced in 1934, according to Harvey Duke. Nos. 9, 10, 11, 12, 13, are marks of late 1930's and into the 1940's. Nos. 14, 15, 16, are marks used in 1940's. Nos. 17, 18, 19, are distributor's marks found under W.S. George at Quality Stamp Company. No. 20 is a distributor's mark, stamped over a W.S. George mark and is from 1952 *Crockery and Glass Journal Directory*. Nos. 21, 22, Jo Cunningham *American Dinnerware*, pp. 84. 85. The rest of the marks are the later marks used in very late 1940's or in the 1950's, before the plant closed. Marks were obtained from making photostatic copies from marks on dishes or at Quality Stamp Company in East Liverpool, Ohio. I have not been able to identify what was called the "Cavett Shaw Division," except W.S. George's middle name was Shaw, and it was probably one of the four plants. The mark was used in the late 1930's and possibly 1940's.)

W.S. George
4. *Bolero*

5. LIDO
W.S. GEORGE
WHITE
MADE IN USA

6. L I D O
W.S. GEORGE
CANARYTONE
MADE IN USA
1 0 2 A

7. *W.S. George*
Rainbow
9 8 5 A

8. *W.S. George*
Del Rio
Ochre

9. RADISSON
W. S. GEORGE
MADE IN U.S.A.
0 1 8 B

10. ELMHURST
W. S. GEORGE
MADE IN U.S.A.

11. ASTOR
W. S. GEORGE

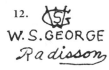
12. W.S. GEORGE
Radisson

13. DERWOOD
W.S. GEORGE
1 6 5 D

14.

15. *W.S. George*
HALF CENTURY/FINE DINNERWARE

CO791

16. *W.S. George*
HALF CENTURY/FINE DINNERWARE
1904-1954

17. *Bralex's*
ROYAL MONARCH
FIRST QUALITY

18. *Jardine*
FIRST QUALITY
ORIGINAL
Guaranteed 22 Kt Gold
MADE IN U.S.A.

19. *Royal Wilton*
FIRST QUALITY
ORIGINAL
WARRANTED 22 KT. GOLD

20. THE
W. S. George
POTTERY CO.
EAST PALESTINE, OHIO

W.S. George
21. *Georgette*
2 8 3 A

22. *W.S. George*
Fleurette
1 8 6 A

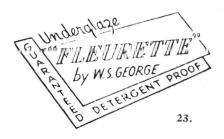
23.

CHINA-CRAFT
by W.S. George
24.

WARRANTED
22 KARAT GOLD

OVEN PROOF DISH WASHER PROOF
UNDERGLAZE
Mulby ☆
Starglow
BY W. S. GEORGE
25.

W. S. George
26.

Mulby Rose
BY W. S. GEORGE
OVEN PROOF DISH WASHER PROOF UNDERGLAZE
27.

Cavitt-Shaw
1950
28.

Cavitt-Shaw
DIVISION
29.

Cavitt-Shaw
DIVISION
W. S. GEORGE
2 9 8 A
31.

Hand Glazed
by
Cavitt-Shaw
DIVISION
30.
W. S. GEORGE

FOREST FLOOR
BOX 626
MONROE MICHIGAN
MADE IN U.S.A.
32.

33. Chip Resistant
W.S.G.
Oven Proof

34.

Underglaze
"MAYFAIR"
by W.S. GEORGE
GUARANTEED DETERGENT PROOF

35.

Underglaze
"Sherwood"
by W.S. GEORGE
GUARANTEED DETERGENT PROOF

36.

Underglaze
"MAYFAIR"
by W.S. GEORGE
GUARANTEED DETERGENT PROOF

37.

Hopalong Cassidy
BY
W.S. GEORGE

38.

COMMUNITY WARE
by
W.S.G.
MADE IN U.S.A.

39.

COMMUNITY WARE
by
W.S.G.

Georgiana Ceramics. Marietta, Georgia. Listed in 1952 *Crockery and Glass Journal*, not listed in 1954. Listed for decorative china, vases, console sets, candy boxes, ash trays, florist ware, etc.

Georgiana china

C. Gerlach. Pennsylvania. Ramsay, p. 186, said exact location and date for this very old potter unknown but redware marked with his name had been found. (Mark: Thorn, p. 127.)

c. gerlach

German-American Stoneware Works. New York, New York. Filed February 26, 1913, for registration of this mark, claiming prior use since September 1912, for use on acid-proof chemical stoneware, pitchers, jugs, evaporation dishes, subliming dishes, stoneware funnels, retorts, carboys, acid pots, acid storage and transportation pots, coils, tourills, stone balls, stone stirrers, acid stone elevator, stone dishes and stone crystallizing dishes. Various companies used the word, "German," as part of their marks on stoneware utilitarian pieces. Do not try to attribute any bowl marked "German," to this company. "German" seems to be used to classify a type or brand of stoneware. I was unable to get more information on this particular company.

Gerson, Samuel L. Wilmington, Delaware. Filed for registration of this mark on April 15, 1952, for use on cooking ware made of semi-vitreous china, such as casseroles, bean pots and tureens, claiming use since January 30, 1952.

Pot Luck

Gerstung, John. Logansville, Sugar Valley, Clinton County, Pennsylvania. Between 1870 to 1880 Gerstung was taxed as a potter in Logansville in Sugar Valley, Pennsylvania (Logansville now Loganton). He made ironstone utilitarian ware marked "Sugar Valley" some of which had blue flowers, animals and landscapes painted on. There are several other potters who worked in the Loganton area listed in Lasansky, p. 26 but definite marks have not been attributed to them. (Information and impressed mark: Jeannette Lasansky, *Made of Mud*, pp. 26, 54. There was a variation of the mark shown spelled with one "l.")

SUGAR VALLEY, PA.

Gift Horse Creations. San Mateo, California. Milton E. Stackpole filed for registration of this mark on May 13, 1952, for use on ceramic tableware, such as glasses and tumblers, claiming use since October 1, 1951.

GIFT HORSE

Gilmer Potteries. Gilmer, Texas. 1951 to present (1985). Started in 1951 by a group of local people who purchased stock in the factory with Carlton Rowe and Dick Potter as managers. The pottery makes cast ware. In the beginning a very decorative type of ware was made before 1960. Then in 1970 the emphasis was on bathroom accessories with some decorative items still being made, but earlier emphasis was on well vitrified cast decorative pieces. (Marks: no. 1, recessed, on green decorative molded vase. No. 2 also recessed and no. 3 inscribed.)

Gimbel Brothers, Inc. New York, New York. A large department store which filed for registration of the two marks shown on August 1, 1984, claiming use for three months prior to that time for porcelain and earthenware dinnerware including serving trays, dishes, bowls and platters; baskets, trays, drinking glasses, bowls, cookware, coffee and tea pots, bottles, salt and pepper shakers, non-electric coffee makers and pasta-making machines and wine coolers.

G and J Decorating Company. Beloit (near Sebring), Ohio. Company existed for a time in the 1940's, according to Woodrow Price, owner of Quality Stamp Company, East Liverpool, Ohio. I found no listings at all for this decorator.

Gladding, McBean and Company. Glendale and Los Angeles, California. 1875 to 1984. Organized to make sewer pipe in 1875 by Charles Gladding, Peter McGill McBean and George Chambers, all of Chicago, who had been attracted to California by the discovery of fire clay deposits at the little foothill town of Lincoln in Placer County. In 1884, terra-cotta for buildings was manufactured for the first time and today Gladding, McBean and Company's products, particularly terra-cotta, are well known worldwide. Other products followed: hollow tile in 1890, face brick in 1891, roof tile in 1893, enamel brick in 1899, vitrified brick in 1902 and coated brick in 1915.

Tropico Pottery which started in 1904 to make faience and floor tile on Los Angeles Boulevard, Los Angeles County, later made a line of garden ware. Gladding, McBean and Company acquired Tropico Pottery in 1923 and combined the garden line with one made at the Lincoln plant; which

is now the Glendale plant, where the facilities were greatly expanded by Gladding, McBean and Company. From April 15,1935, to December 31, 1937, Tropico Pottery also produced a line of artware and mixing bowls which became part of the Franciscan products.

Catalina Ware and Catalina Art Ware were originally made by Santa Catalina Island Company, Pottery Division, Avalon, California. The product is identified by numbers with the prefix ''C.'' Catalina glazes are identified by numbers with the prefix ''CA.'' In 1937, Gladding, McBean and Company purchased the Catalina Island Company. Early Catalina Pottery is also identified by the name ''Catalina'' inscribed in the ware. After 1937, the impressions were replaced with a stamped inscription. In 1947, the use of the Catalina trademark was relinquished as was previously agreed. Catalina products were sold under various names identifying lines patterns. (See the listing Catalina marks.)

In 1933, Gladding, McBean and Company acquired the West Coast properties of the American Encaustic Tiling Company, which for many years has been the largest manufacturer fo floor and wall tile in the world. In December, 1943, Gladding, McBean and Company acquired the plants of the Stockton Fire Brick Company at Pittsburg, California. This was followed in September, 1944, by the addition of the two plants of the Emsco Refractories Company to make silica brick.

In 1934, the company began the manufacture of dinnerware and art pottery which was marketed under the name of Franciscan Ware. The first dinnerware was made in plain shapes and bright colors, reminiscent of the old Spanish days. Later on, other graceful shapes and subdued or pastel colors were added. This style of dinnerware, together with the beautifully modeled underglaze patterns that were developed, have won national acclaim. In 1942, fine thin china was manufactured at the Glendale plant and also marketed under the Franciscan name. This transulucent vitrified china is inspiring. Typically American in body and decoration, it was accepted with great response in the field of fine china. Franciscan has three distinct lines: masterpiece china, quality translucent fine china; earthenware, cream-colored ware in a variety of decal and hand decorated patterns; and whitestone ware, white earthenware. Franciscan earthenware was first made in 1934 and is unquestionably the largest selling, best known of its type. The famous Desert Rose pattern is the most popular dinnerware ever made in the country. Gladding, McBean and Company made decorative tile. In 1942, they furnished the tile for a huge and colorful mural for the National Broadcasting Company Building in San Francisco. G.J. Fitzgerald designed the mural which was 40″ high by 16′ wide, telling about the radio station's service to the world. There were 114 different colors of glazes used on 6″ x 6″ tile. (''Radio's Greatest Mural Unveiled,'' *Bullentin of American Ceramic Society*, February 1942, p. 33.) In 1962, Gladding, McBean and Company merged with Lock Joint Pipe Company to form International Pipe and Ceramics Corporation. In 1963, the name was changed to Interpace Corporation. (See the listing for Interpace Corporation.) In April 1979, Josiah Wedgwood and Sons were negotiating to buy the Gladding, McBean and Company plant from Interpace. The transaction was completed and Wedgwood operated the plant until around the middle of 1984 when the plant was closed. As of January 1986, the plant has not been dismantled or sold, according to an employee who was taking care of the plant, but no product was being made there.

The following list of shape or pattern names was furnished by Franciscan Interpace Corporation.

Year	Shape or Pattern	Product
1934	Cielito Art Ware	Franciscan
	Cocinero	Franciscan
	El Patio Table Ware	Franciscan
	Garden Ware	Tropico
	Miscellaneous Ware	Special
	Special Ware	Special
1935	Coronado Art Ware	Franciscan
	El Patio Nuevo	Franciscan
	Franciscan Ruby Art	Franciscan
	Tropico Ware	Tropico
1936	Capistrano Art Ware	Franciscan
	Coronado Table Ware	Franciscan
	Florist Special	Franciscan
	Flower Pots & Saucers	Tropico
1937	Aurora Art Ware	Catalina
	Avalon Table Ware	Catalina
	Catalina Art Ware	Catalina
	Del Mar Table Ware	Franciscan
	Del Oro Table Ware	Franciscan
	Encanto Art Ware	Franciscan
	Lamp Bases	Special
	Mango Table Ware	Franciscan
	Montecito Table Ware	Franciscan
	Padua Table Ware	Franciscan
	Pueblo Table Ware	Franciscan
	Rancho Table Ware	Catalina
	Terra Cotta Specials	Catalina
	Tiger Flower Table Ware	Franciscan
	Willow Table Ware	Franciscan
1938	Fruit Table Ware	Franciscan
	Hawthorne Table Ware	Franciscan
	Hotel Ware (1000)	Franciscan
	Kitchen Ware	Franciscan
	Ox Blood Art Ware	Catalina
1939	Geranium Table Ware	Franciscan
	Hotel Ware (1000)	Franciscan
	Max Shonfeld Art Ware	Franciscan
	Nautical Art Ware	Catalina
	Silver City Special	Special
1940	Apple	Franciscan
	Duotone Table Ware	Catalina
	Floral Art Ware	Catalina
	Merced Shape	Masterpiece
	Metropolitan Service	Franciscan
	Montebello Art Ware	Catalina
	Reseda Art Ware	Catalina
	Saguaro Art Ware	Catalina
	Victoria Service	Franciscan
1941	Arden	Masterpiece
	Arcadia Blue	Masterpiece
	Arcadia Gold	Masterpiece
	Arcadia Green	Masterpiece
	Arcadia Maroon	Masterpiece
	Beverly	Masterpiece
	Cherokee Rose Green	Masterpiece
	Cherokee Rose Palomino	Masterpiece
	Dainty Bess	Masterpiece
	Del Monte	Masterpiece
	Desert Rose	Franciscan
	Gold Band 302	Masterpiece
	Laguna	Masterpiece
	Mountain Laurel	Masterpiece
	Wishmaker Table Ware	Franciscan
	Woodside	Masterpiece
1942	Angeleno Art Ware	Catalina
	Arcadia Cobalt	Masterpiece
	Balboa	Masterpiece
	Beverly Cobalt	Masterpiece
	Carmel (turquoise)	Masterpiece
	Cherokee Rose Gold	Masterpiece
	Crinoline	Masterpiece
	Desert Blossom	Masterpiece
	Fremont	Masterpiece
	Gold Band 101	Masterpiece
	Gold Band 201	Masterpiece
	Gold Band 202	Masterpiece
	Gold Band 302	Masterpiece
	Larchmont	Masterpiece
	Monterey Cobalt	Masterpiece
	Northridge	Masterpiece
	Ovide or Redondo Shape	Masterpiece
	Polynesian Art Ware	Franciscan
	Shasta	Masterpiece
	Westwood	Masterpiece
	Wild Flower Table Ware	Franciscan
	Wilshire	Masterpiece
1943	Blue Jessamine	Masterpiece
1944		
1945	Rossmore	Masterpiece
1946	Blossom Time	Masterpiece
	Chinese Yellow	Masterpiece
	Cobalt	Masterpiece
	Del Rey Shape	Masterpiece
	Elsinore	Masterpiece
	Emerald Green	Masterpiece
	Fuchia	Masterpiece
	Lorraine Green	Masterpiece
	Lorraine Maroon	Masterpiece
	Maroon	Masterpiece
	Peacock Green	Masterpiece
1947	California Manor	Masterpiece
	California Wheat	Masterpiece
	Lorraine Grey	Masterpiece
1948	Cameo Pink	Masterpiece
	Domino Black	Masterpiece
	Dove Grey Gold	Masterpiece
	Encanto Shape	Masterpiece
	Huntington 401	Masterpiece
	Ivy	Franciscan
	Jade Green	Masterpiece
	Jasper Green	Masterpiece
	Platinum Band 606	Masterpiece
	Primrose Yellow	Masterpiece
	Robin Egg Blue	Masterpiece
1949	Breakfast Sets	Masterpiece
	California Rose	Masterpiece
	Cimarron	Masterpiece

	Dove Grey Platinum	
	Encino Shape	Masterpiece
	Fruit (1400 line)	Franciscan
	Gold Band 101 (E)	Masterpiece
	Gold Band 301 (B)	Masterpiece
	Mariposa	Masterpiece
	Monterey	Masterpiece
	Platinum Band (E)	Masterpiece
	Renaissance Grey	Masterpiece
	Ridgewood	Masterpiece
	Sonora	Masterpiece
	Tiempo	Franciscan
1950	California Poppy	Franciscan
	Canton	Masterpiece
	Chelan	Masterpiece
	Granada	Masterpiece
	Mesa	Masterpiece
	Olympic	Masterpiece
	Palo Alto	Masterpiece
	Tahoe	Masterpiece
	Sierra	Masterpiece
1951	Franciscan Wheat	Franciscan
1952	Appleton	Masterpiece
	Aragon	Masterpiece
	Birchbark	Masterpiece
	Carmel	Masterpiece
	Celadon (Flambeau)	Masterpiece
	Claremont	Masterpiece
	Concord	Masterpiece
	Magnolia	Masterpiece
	Maroon (Flambeau)	Masterpiece
	Renaissance Crown	Masterpiece
	Sandalwood	Masterpiece
	Spruce	Masterpiece
	Starry Night	Masterpiece
	Teak	Masterpiece
	Willow	Masterpiece
1953	Franciscan Wheat	Franciscan
	Regency	Masterpiece
1954	Echo	Franciscan
	Eclipse Shape	Franciscan
	Eclipse White	Franciscan
	Flair Shape	Franciscan
	Flair White	Franciscan
	Dawn	Masterpiece
	Encanto Rose	Masterpiece
	Pomegranate	Franciscan
	Starburst	Franciscan
	Willow Bouquet	Masterpiece
	Winter Bouquet	Masterpiece
	Woodlore	Franciscan
	Trio	Franciscan
1954	Autumn	Franciscan
	Contours Art Ware	Masterpiece
	Huntington Rose	Masterpiece
	Oasis	Franciscan
	Silver Pine	Masterpiece
1956	Ballet	Masterpiece
	Brentwood	Masterpiece
	California Wheat	Masterpiece
	Del Rio	Masterpiece

	Encore	Masterpiece
	Duet	Franciscan
1957	Ferndel	Franciscan
	Gold Leaves	Masterpiece
	Montecito	Masterpiece
	Sunset	Masterpiece
1958	Acacia	Masterpiece
	Debut	Masterpiece
	Family China	(3000 line)
	Indian Summer	Family China
	Larkspur	Franciscan
	Radiance	Family China
	Spring Song	Family China
	Sycamore	Family China
	Winsome	Family China
1959	Arabesque	Masterpiece
	Cameo	Masterpiece
	Capri	Cosmopolitan
	Cosmopolitan China	(NTK Japan)
	Crown Jewel	Masterpiece
	Happy Talk	Whitestone
	It's a Breeze	Whitestone
	Lucerne	Cosmopolitan
	Malaya	Cosmopolitan
	Nassau	Cosmopolitan
	Merry go Round	Whitestone
	Newport	Cosmopolitan
	Pink a Dilly	Whitestone
	Sommerset	Masterpiece
	Swingtime	Whitestone
	Tapestry	Masterpiece
	Tara	Cosmopolitan
	Trianon	Cosmopolitan
	Twice Nice	Whitestone
	Valencia	Cosmopolitan
	Whitestone Ware	(TTK) Japan
1960	Daisy	Franciscan
	Cloud Nine	Whitestone
	Cortina	Cosmopolitan
	Interlude	Masterpiece
	St. Moritz	Cosmopolitan
	Whitel a Gig	Whitestone
1961	Corinthian	Masterpiece
	Glenfield	Porcelain
	Fan Tan	Whitestone
	Melrose	Procelain
	Patrician	Masterpiece
	Platina	Porcelain
	Porcelain	(NTK Japan)
	Simplicity	Porcelain
	Snow Pine	Porcelain
	Spice	Franciscan
	Swirl Shape	Masterpiece
	Talisman	Porcelain
1962	Cypress	Franciscan
	Dusty Rose	Regal China
	Medallion	Family China
	Platinum Swirl	Regal China
	Renaissance Gold	Masterpiece
	Renaissance Platinum	Masterpiece
	Rondelay	Masterpiece
	Silver Mist	Masterpiece

	Silver Wheat	Regal China
	Simplicity	Regal China
	Wedding Band	Regal China
1963	Blue Fancy	Whitestone
	Fruit (2200 line)	Franciscan
	Sierra Sand	Franciscan
	Snow Crest	Franciscan
	Tulip Time	Franciscan
	2200 Shape	Franciscan
1964	Classic	Regal China
	Hacienda	Franciscan
	Malibu	Franciscan
	Merry Mint	Whitestone
	Ring A Ling	Whitestone
1965	Cantata	Whitestone
	Emerald Isle	Discovery
	Hacienda (green)	Franciscan
	Pickwick	Whitestone
	Tahiti	Discovery
	Terra Cotta	Discovery
	Topaz	Discovery
	Walden	Whitestone
	Discovery (new name)	Family China
1966	Antique Green	Masterpiece
	Antigua	Whitestone
	Brown Eyes	Whitestone
	El Dorado	Earthenware
	Martinque	Masterpiece
	Midnight Mist	Masterpiece
	Moon Glow	Masterpiece
	Nightingale	Masterpiece
	7000 Shape	Masterpiece
1967	Constantine	Masterpiece
	Chalice	Masterpiece
	Garland	Earthenware
	Hawaii	Whitestone
	Madeira	Earthenware
	Montago	Earthenware
	Zinnia	Earthenware
1968	Applique	Masterpiece
	Bird 'N Hand	Whitestone
	Monaco	Masterpiece
	Regalia	Masterpiece
	Royal Renaissance	Masterpiece
1969	Gabrielle	Masterpiece
	Kasmir	Masterpiece
	Pebble Beach	Earthenware
1970	Indigo	Masterpiece
	Medallion Plate	Masterpiece
	Millbrook	Ironstone
	Nut Tree	Earthenware
	Peacock Plate	Masterpiece
	Yellow Bouquet	Ironstone
1971	Ariel	Masterpiece
	Castile	Masterpiece
	Golden Gate	Whitestone
	Happenstance	Whitestone
	Larami	Stoneware
	Petals & Pods	Whitestone
	Quadrille	Masterpiece
	Sequoia	Stoneware

	Silver Lining	Masterpiece
	Taos	Stoneware
	Yuma	Stoneware
	Zanzibar	Earthenware
	Cimmaron	Stoneware
	Floral	Earthenware
1972	Abstract	Gourmet
	Apache	Ind. Stoneware
	Brush	Gourmet
	Cane	Ind. Ironstone
	Circles	Gourmet
	Crinoline	Masterpiece
	Dotted Stripe	Ind. Porcelain
	Yellow Zebra	Ind. Porcelain
	Flame	Ind. Porcelain
	Gold Plate	Ind. Porcelain
	Gourmet	Gourmet
	Gray Wave	Ind. Porcelain
	Kachina	Ind. Stoneware
	Lariat	Ind. Stoneware
	Moondance	Earthenware
	Nouelle Ebony	Masterpiece
	Nouelle Ivory	Masterpiece
	Nuts and Bolts	Ind. Porcelain
	Petalpoint	Masterpiece
	Plain White	Ind. Porcelain
	Pueblo	Earthenware
	Rimrock	Earthenware
	Rodeo	Ind. Stoneware
	Silver Plate	Ind. Porcelain
	Sonora	Ind. Stoneware
	Stripes	Gourmet
	Sundance	Earthenware
1973	Amapola	Earthenware
	Creole	Earthenware
	Jamoca	Earthenware
	Madrigal	Masterpiece
	Mandalay (Neptune)	Masterpiece
	Mary Jane	Ironstone
	Minaret	Masterpiece
	Natchez	Masterpiece
	Ondine	Masterpiece
	Picnic	Earthenware
	7700 Line	Masterpiece
	2600 Line	Earthenware
	2700 Line	Earthenware
	Shalimar	Masterpiece
	Yankee Doodle	Ironstone
1974	Garden Party	Earthenware
	Ginger Snap	Earthenware
	Limerick	Ironstone
	Madrigal	Masterpiece
	Mandalay	Masterpiece
	Minaret	Masterpiece
	Maypole	Earthenware
	Ondine	Masterpiece
	Picnic	Earthenware
	Shalimar	Masterpiece

1975	Crown Daisy	Earthenware
	Dogwood	Earthenware
	Fallbrook	Ironstone
	Greenhouse Series	Earthenware
	Mirasol	Earthenware
	Pillowtalk	Ironstone
	Swirl	Masterpiece
	Wrightwood	Masterpiece

(Marks: No. 1 was filed for registration with patent office under the name, Gladding, McBean and Company in Los Angeles, California. Dates of filing: no. 1, February 25, 1938; no. 2, December 31, 1934; no. 3, January 5, 1953, claiming use since October 1, 1934; no. 4, October 13, 1955; no. 5, July 21, 1955; No. 6, June 25, 1956; no. 7, November 7, 1957, claiming use since April 1954; no. 8, June 16, 1958. All were filed shortly after they started being used except no. 3 and no. 7. All were for fine china dinnerware, except no. 1, "Rancho," which was earthenware flower pots, garden pottery, jardinieres, art pottery, glazed and unglazed bowls. No. 2, "Franciscan," included tableware and art pottery. No. 9 was filed under the name, International Pipe and Ceramics Corporation, March 23, 1964, claiming first use July 17, 1963. In 1934, the company started making dinnerware and art ware, which they marketed under the name, Franciscan. But the very early dishes made between 1934 and 1938 had the "G.M.B." mark similar to no. 10. No. 11 was filed January 26, 1935, claiming use since January 1, 1920. When the company decided to have a mark to go with the name, Franciscan, in September 1938, they used nos. 12, 13, until February 1939. For a short time, around 1938, no. 14, Franciscan Pottery, replaced the big "F," but was soon changed to Franciscan Ware, no. 15. Over the years, after 1938, the name Franciscan Ware was used almost entirely, but the Gladding, McBean and Company's name also showed up in some of the marks. No. 16 was a decal on an ash tray for office use, made between 1941 and 1947. No. 17 was dated 1954. No. 18 was used from 1941 to 1947. No. 19 was started in use in 1953 and in January 1955, the C and R were added. Nos. 20-21 were made in ¾" and 1" stamps used from February 1939 to August 1940. After July 1940, the "Hand Decorated" was used on some of the pieces. From 1947 to 1949 numbers were added to this mark. See nos. 22-23. No. 24 was used February 1953 to July 1958. No. 25 was used on Coronado ware only from 1954 to 1956. No. 26 was used February 1954 until July 1958. No. 27 was used from 1949 to Feburary 1953. "Masterpiece China," a fine thin china was first made in 1940, and by 1941 there was a large production of it. See the chronological list of products. No. 29, the name had to be omitted in February 1963, after Gladding, McBean merged with Lock Joint Pipe Company in 1962, no. 30. Then in April 1963, the name Interpace, was added. No. 31 shows the initials, R.K. below the stamp which stands for kiln run or seconds, which were sold at the Franciscan shop outlet. Nos. 32-43, all put into first use between 1958 and 1971 for Franciscan Earthenware, seem to be very much alike at first glance, but they all have small changes to accomodate changes in name, etc. No. 32 was first used in 1958, stamped in brown rather than black. No. 33 was to remove the name, Gladding, McBean, at the merger of G.McB. and Lock Joint Company. No. 34 added the name, Interpace, in 1963. No. 35; This stamp was made in September 1966 to use with dark glazes. The lettering and frame were heavier and still a lighter colored glaze than the ware had to be used to cover the mark. No. 36, first used January 25, 1971. Nos. 37-43; other variations of the Franciscan Earthenware marks first put into use as stated. No. 44: This mark used on Franciscan Earthenware , made in England. In 1974, Interpace acquired the Alfred Meakin plant in Tunstall, England. (See the listing, Interpace Corporation.) Nos. 45-52, for Franciscan Family China, went through the same name changes as the Masterpiece China and Earthenware China. Nos. 45-47, with the name, Gladding, McBean and Company, before the merger in 1962. Then for a short time before April 1963, no name is shown in nos. 47, 48. After April 1963, Interpace was added in nos. 49, 50. The first Franciscan Family China mark was used in 1958. Nos. 51-53 are for Franciscan Porcelain which can be dated the same as 45-52, by the name changes. Notice this ware was made in Japan. No. 54, Cosmopolitan China was also made in Japan from 1959 to 1961, when the line was discontinued. Nos. 55-57, another Japanese made ware of the 1960's. Nos. 58, 59, Discovery replaced Family China in December 1964. Nos. 60, 61 were adopted in 1974 to further the idea that the dinnerware was handcrafted. Epoxy type stamping agents had started to be used to make a more legible backstamp. Nos. 62, 63: These are copies of paper labels shown in the various trade directories. Nos. 64, 65; marks found in the company material used on products for railroads. The Southern Pacific ware was made in 1939 for "Daylite" trains between San Francisco and Los Angeles. No. 66, used on china art ware named, "Contours," between July 1955 to December 1956. This mark was a decal. No. 67 was a backstamp on an ashtray given away in 1950 at an open house for employees and their families at the 75th anniversary celebration. No. 68, Pueblo Pottery, stamped on a premium ware, but the company material didn't say what company used it as a premium. No. 69, stamped on child's cup and plate in Apple or Desert Rose. Nos. 70-73, El Camino China and Wilshire China were the names used on china sold in the Franciscan shop only. The marks were generally stamped in gold on seconds in the 1950's. No. 74, backstamp used on an ashtray made in 1938. No. 75 was a decal used on the front of an ashtray as a decoration for a company gift when the Glendale Research Center opened. Nos. 76, 77, 78, only the artwork for these backstamps was found in the company files. It is possible they were never used. No. 76 would date around 1952, if such a mark is ever found on a piece. The company thought the Coronado mark in no. 78, could have been used with "Made in California, U.S.A. and Gladding, McBean and Co.," as a center insert. See the Tropico Pottery listing for that mark. See Catalina Pottery for marks and information on that part of the Gladding, McBean operation. No. 79, "California Manor" was a mark used on a special pattern for Faye Eggleston, a California designer. No. 80 was a decal backstamp used on china made for Abbey Rents, Los Angeles in 1947. See the following companies for more on Gladding, McBean products and marks: Regal Corporation, National Silver; Carole Stupell, Ltd.; Max Schonfield; the Barker Brothers, for marks used on ware made by Gladding, McBean and Company. Information and marks were furnished by the Franciscan Interpace Corporation in 1979 for the *American Kitchen and Dinner Wares* book by this author.)

1. RANCHO
2. FRANCISCAN
3. Franciscan
4. CONTOURS

5. *Color-Seal*

6. **ENCORE**

7. STARBURST

8.

9.

10.

11.

12. F
MADE IN
U. S. A.

13. F
MADE IN
U. S. A.

14. FRANCISCAN POTTERY

15. FRANCISCAN WARE
MADE IN U. S. A.

16.

GLADDING, McBEAN & CO.

17. MADE IN
CALIFORNIA
USA
✦
GLADDING
McBEAN
& CO.

18.
FRANCISCAN CHINA
MADE IN CALIFORNIA

19.
Franciscan fine China
made in California USA
GLADDING McBEAN & CO.
CLAREMONT

20.

21.

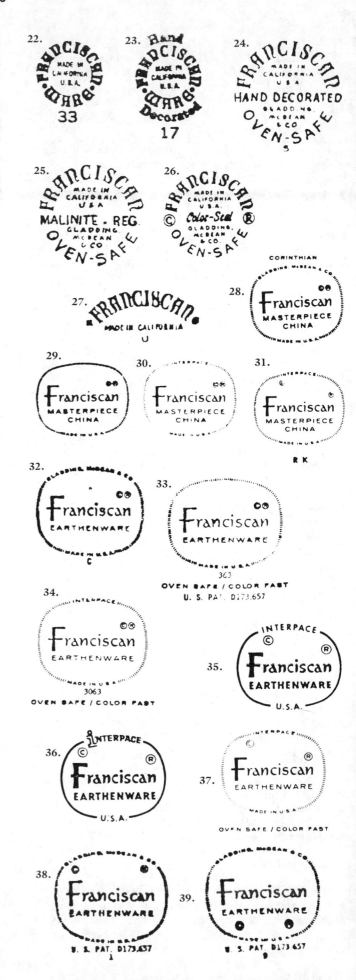

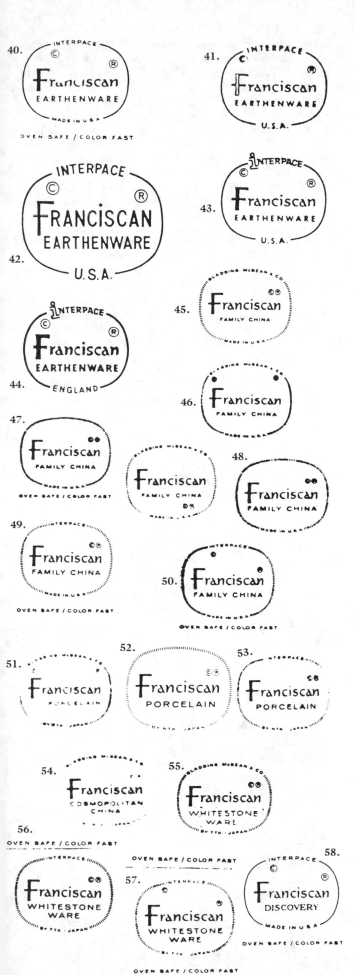

40. INTERPACE © ® Franciscan EARTHENWARE MADE IN U S A OVEN SAFE / COLOR FAST

41. INTERPACE © ® Franciscan EARTHENWARE U.S.A.

42. INTERPACE © ® Franciscan EARTHENWARE U.S.A.

43. INTERPACE © ® Franciscan EARTHENWARE U.S.A.

44. INTERPACE © ® Franciscan EARTHENWARE ENGLAND

45. GLADDING McBEAN & CO. Franciscan FAMILY CHINA MADE IN U S A

46. GLADDING McBEAN & CO. Franciscan FAMILY CHINA MADE IN U S A

47. Franciscan FAMILY CHINA MADE IN U S A OVEN SAFE / COLOR FAST

48. GLADDING McBEAN & CO. Franciscan FAMILY CHINA MADE IN U S A

49. INTERPACE Franciscan FAMILY CHINA MADE IN U S A OVEN SAFE / COLOR FAST

50. INTERPACE Franciscan FAMILY CHINA MADE IN U S A OVEN SAFE / COLOR FAST

51. GLADDING McBEAN & CO. Franciscan PORCELAIN OVEN SAFE / COLOR FAST

52. Franciscan PORCELAIN BY NTK JAPAN

53. INTERPACE Franciscan PORCELAIN BY NTK JAPAN

54. GLADDING McBEAN & CO. Franciscan COSMOPOLITAN CHINA OVEN SAFE / COLOR FAST

55. GLADDING McBEAN & CO. Franciscan WHITESTONE WARE BY TTK JAPAN OVEN SAFE / COLOR FAST

56. INTERPACE Franciscan WHITESTONE WARE BY TTK JAPAN

57. INTERPACE Franciscan WHITESTONE WARE BY TTK JAPAN OVEN SAFE / COLOR FAST

58. INTERPACE © ® Franciscan DISCOVERY MADE IN U S A OVEN SAFE / COLOR FAST

59. INTERPACE © ® Franciscan Discovery MADE IN U.S.A. OVEN SAFE / COLOR FAST

60. The California Craftsmen since 1875. FRANCISCAN © EARTHENWARE OVEN·SAFE · COLOR·FAST · X10·74 © INTERPACE · MADE IN U S A

61. The California Craftsmen since 1875. FRANCISCAN Interpace Corporation 2901 Los Feliz Blvd Los Angeles 90039

62. Franciscan FINE DINNERWARE

63. FRANCISCAN WARE CALIFORNIA REG. U.S. PAT. OFFICE

64. PULLMAN CO.

65. S P Co FRANCISCAN WARE SOUTHERN PACIFIC LINES

66. Franciscan fine China MADE IN U.S.A. © ®

67. COMPLIMENTS GLADDING McBEAN & CO. OPEN HOUSE 1950

this is my first piece of Franciscan Ware MADE IN U.S.A.

68. PUEBLO MADE IN U.S.A. POTTERY

69. EL CAMINO PROD. CA. 235 0 USA

70. EL CAMINO CHINA MADE IN U S A

71. EL CA. 235 D

72. EL CAMINO CHINA MADE IN U. S. A. California "Wheat"

73. EL CAMINO CHINA MADE IN U. S. A.

WILSHIRE

74. SAN FRANCISCO 1938

75.

INTERPACE

GLENDALE RESEARCH CENTER

76. FRANCISCAN WARE OVEN·SAFE

77. FRANCISCAN HAND DECORATED

78. FRANCISCAN CORONADO

79. "California Manor"

80. TIFFANY
Arcadia Gold

Gladding Ceramic Insulator Company, Inc. San Jose, California. This company was formed by the Gladding family of Gladding, McBean & Company around 1924 to make tile, and they began to manufacture porcelain insulators in 1964. The insulators have been marked with the incuse or recessed mark shown. (Information and mark: Jack H. Tod, *Porcelain Insulators*, p. 140.)

GLADCO
U.S.A.

Glaser, Louis J. Rochester, New York. Filed for registration of this mark September 19, 1929, for use on ceramic cups, saucers, plates and pitchers, claiming use since August 22, 1929.

GLACO
SOUVENIRS

Glasgow Pottery. Trenton, New Jersey. Started in 1863 by John Moses. (There was a typesetter's error in my dinnerware book giving this date as 1893.) (His brother, James Moses started Mercer Pottery, Trenton, in 1858, and John and James were both associated with James Carr and Edward Clark for a few months in 1879 in the International Pottery.) This firm made a great variety of articles and used several marks. They started with Rockingham and yellowware

in the early years and then later made cream-colored ware, white granite or ironstone, thin hotel ware, a completely vitrified china and steamboat china. They made ware for the armed forces stamped "Q.M.D." and "U.S.M.C." At the Centennial Exhibition, they exhibited stone china, decorated ware and majolica. A plate, decorated with "Philadelphia" in a circle around "1873," then in a larger circle "Centennial Commemorative of the Boston Tea Party, Dec. 1773" all of this on the front, was pictured in "Memo from Marcia," *Spinning Wheel*, January-February, 1973, p. 72. The plate was impressed "Glasgow Pottery Company, Trenton, New Jersey." The Glasgow Pottery was listed only until 1900 in the *Trenton City Directories*. Between 1901 and 1905 the company was listed as **John Moses and Sons** making general pottery. The *1902-1903 Complete Directory* listed the company as making semi-porcelain, white granite, in common china dinner sets, toilet sets and short sets of odd dishes, some decorated. A mark used in 1876 was the American eagle and shield, on white granite. A similar mark was used on semi-porcelain in 1878. In 1880, a wreath enclosing the date was the mark for the same ware. In 1882, white granite was marked "Glasgow China," in a circle. In 1884, the monogram of John Moses, surrounded by the name of the ware, was printed on white granite in black. On the same grade of ware, in 1893, a diamond-shaped mark was printed. (Information and marks: E.A. Barber, *Marks of American Potters*, pp. 50-52.)

SAPPHO
J. M. & S. CO.

GLASGOW CHINA
VITRIFIED
TRENTON. N J

BERKELEY
J. M. & S. CO.
TRENTON. N. J.

GLASGOW POTTERY CO.
TRENTON. N. J.

SAPPHO
J. M. & S. CO.

Glazier, Henry. Huntingdon, Pennsylvania. Henry and his son, John, made earthenware and stoneware pottery. Henry had worked alone making earthenware pieces for 15 or 20 years before he was joined by his son in 1831, and they started making stoneware. Henry retired in 1847. Around 1854, John quit making pottery and held some various public offices instead. (Information and impressed mark: Jeannette Lasansky, *Made in Mud*, pp. 17-19.)

HENRY GLAZIER
HUNTINGDON, PA.

Glenmoor Pottery. See University City Pottery.

Glen View Pottery. See Pennsbury Pottery.

Glidden Pottery. Alfred, New York. 1940-1957. Pottery was founded by Glidden Parker, graduate of Bates College. He attended University of Vienna, and in 1938 he did graduate work in ceramics at Alfred University. He was assisted by the help of Marion L. Fosdick, an associate professor of ceramic design. At the peak of production, 55 were employed. Parker left ceramics to work in stained glass. A complete line of dinnerware and various art objects were made at Glidden Pottery, including unusual shapes and colors in bowls, ash trays, teapots, relish dishes, vases, platters, etc.

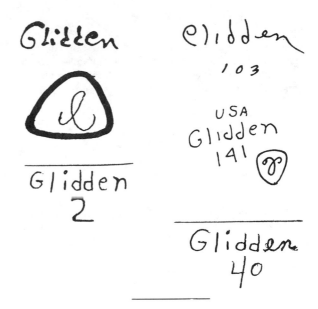

Globe China Company. Cambridge, Ohio. See Oxford Pottery.

Globe Pottery Company. Succeeded Frederick, Schenkle, Allen and Company (1881-1888) in 1888 in East Liverpool, Ohio. Around 1900, Globe Pottery joined the East Liverpool Potteries Company. That company dissolved in 1903. The Globe Pottery was listed last in 1912. They had continued for a while after the East Liverpool Potteries Company was dissolved in 1903. Early products were Rockingham, cream-colored ware, later semi-porcelain dinnerware and various utilitarian pieces. (Information: Lehner, *American Kitchen and Dinner Wares*, p. 67. Marks: nos. 1-7, Barber, *Marks of American Potters*; nos. 8, 9, on dishes.)

Goldcrest Ceramics Corporation. Trenton, New Jersey. Around late 1940's and early 1950's, for a very few years. Listed for china figurines and lamps sold by the Everlast Company, New York, New York. See that listing for a mark.

Goldenberg's. Washington, D.C. Selling agency. Filed for registration of this mark July 8, 1916, under a 10-year proviso to be used on crockery, earthenware and porcelain, consisting of teapots, pitchers, vases, salad sets, tea sets, bureau sets, jardinieres, sugar and cream sets, dinner sets, dinnerware, bowls, umbrella-racks, hair-receivers, puff boxes, comb and brush sets, comb trays, plaques, toilet sets, chambers, cuspidors and mugs, claiming use since January 1895.

Golden Rule, Inc. Columbus, Ohio. Distributors. Filed for registration of this mark on March 29, 1926, for use on china dishes, claiming use since January 22, 1926.

Goldman Costume Company. New York, New York. A distributor. Filed for registration of this mark January 24, 1917, for use on crockery, earthenware, porcelain and china dishes and kitchen receptacles, claiming use since January 5, 1917.

Goldscheider Pottery. Trenton, New Jersey. Listed as Goldscheider Everlast Corporation. Trenton City Directories listed this pottery from 1943 through 1950. They were also listed in the *1952 Crockery and Glass Journal Directory* as the Goldscheider Ceramics at 1441 Heath Avenue. They were not listed in 1954. From the *American Ceramic Society Bulletin*, "Goldscheiders Produce New Porcelain Base," Volume 25, No. 12, 1946, p. 494, we get this quote:

> The Goldscheider family, famous for three hundred years as Viennese craftsmen, has discovered a new porcelain base.
>
> The Goldscheiders, refugees from their native Vienna from the day Hitler invaded it, are producing their products in Trenton, NJ, and Goldscheiderware has obtained a higher production level here than in the non-profitable days of old Vienna.
>
> Erwin F. Goldscheider, vice-president of the company in charge of production, is responsible for the ceramic discovery. The direct result will be an immediate change from the present china body to an additional and stronger porcelain body. The porcelain base is a combination of American air-floated and magnetically purified kaolin feldspathic rock, and silica.
>
> The Goldscheider's new fine-china body apparently assumes extra hardness when fired to vitrification, retaining the highest possible degree of pure whiteness. This permits the most delicate underglaze decoration to be applied on its surface, as well as unlimited nuances of color shading. Since it is leadless, it will retain its original sheen, a goal of ceramists for hundreds of years.

These new translucent porcelains will be decorated exclusively, in gold, platinum and overglaze colors for extreme delicacy of ornament, and in unlimited colors and shades for general production. Production has begun at once for early shipment to American stores first, then global exportations to follow.

In 1952, they were listed for art or decorative china, figures, figurines and miniatures only. So they made mainly art or decorative china. (Marks: no. 1, on piece at American Ceramic Society in Columbus, Ohio; No. 2, *1952 Crockery and Glass Journal Directory*, p. 166.)

Gonder Ceramic Arts. Zanesville, Ohio. 1941 to 1957. On December 8, 1941, Gonder purchased the former Zane Pottery Company which had just closed. Gonder made a higher priced grade of commercial art pottery. Jamie Matchet and Chester Kirk both were outstanding designers with many exhibits and awards. Also Helen Conover and F.F. Greene were designers for Gonder. Flambe was developed which looks like a red flame with streaks of yellow. Gold crackle, and Chinese crackle glazes were used. Gonder duplicated old Chinese museum pieces. For more on Lawton Gonder, see Elgee Pottery and Florence Pottery. In 1955, Gonder Ceramic Arts was converted to the manufacture of tile due to the injury to our potteries by foreign imports that put so many out of business in the 1950's. In 1957, Gonder was about finished. Norris Schneider in "Lawton Gonder," *The Zanesville Time Signal*, September 22, 1957, said Gonder converted his entire production to other types of ceramic products. (Marks found on pieces are all incised or impressed except one paper label is shown.)

Goodale, Daniel. Hartford, Connecticut. 1818-1830. Marks used were D. Goodale; D. Goodale/Hartford; Goodale & Stedham/Hartford/1822. (Information: Lura W. Watkins, ''A Check List of New England Stoneware Potters,'' *Antiques*, August 1942, reprinted in Stradling, p.80. Marks: Stradling, p. 80. Same mark in Guilland, p. 254.)

D. GOODALE
HARTFORD

GOODALE & STEDMAN
HARTFORD
1822

Good Earth Studio. Williamston, Michigan. 1968 to present (1985). Terry Emrich, studio potter, started making functional and non-functional stoneware and porcelain pieces, both thrown and hand formed in 1968. In 1971, he started potting full time in the Good Earth Studio. He also makes architectural tile. Terry received a B.S. degree in art education from Manchester College in 1970 and an M.F.A. degree from Michigan State University in 1978. Terry has been an instructor in ceramics at Lansing Community College on a part time basis since 1972 to present. At some time or other, Terry has participated in most of the art fairs in the Midwest and won many awards. The most recent award was a purchase prize from *Ceramics Monthly* magazine. Most of the best galleries in the Eastern part of the U.S., carry Terry's work. (Mark 1 is a brush application of initials on pot. Mark 2 is scratched into the clay.)

1.   2. OV

Goodwin Pottery. East Liverpool, Ohio. The Goodwin family was involved in the pottery business in East Liverpool, Ohio, and Trenton, New Jersey, starting as early as 1844. John Goodwin made the old yellowware and Rockingham in East Liverpool from 1844 to 1853. He sold the pottery to the Baggott Brothers and moved to Trenton until 1863. He then came back to East Liverpool to work at various potteries. In 1872, John Goodwin purchased the old Broadway Pottery of T. Rigby and Company. It was here that he began preparations to make whiteware. He died in 1875. James, son of John, began whiteware production in 1876. The firm became the Goodwin Brothers until 1893 when it became the Goodwin Pottery until 1912. The building was purchased by Hall China Company in 1919, but between 1912 and 1919 it may have been vacant for quite time. Goodwin Pottery Company made a pear-white, a cream-colored ware, and some decorated ware. In 1902, they were listed in the *1902-1903 Complete Directory* as making semi-porcelain and common china dinner sets, toilet sets and short sets of odd dishes. (Information: ''James H. Goodwin,'' *Ceramic Society Bulletin*, February 1925, p. 34; Lehner, *America Kitchen and Dinner Wares*, p. 68; W.P. Jervis, ''Worlds Pottery Marks,'' *Pottery, Glass and Brass Salesman*, April 17, 1913, p. 18. Marks: nos. 1-5, Barber, *Marks of American Potters*, pp. 105, 106; no. 6, Hazel Hartman, *Porcelain and Pottery Marks*, p. 112; no. 7, on dish; no. 8, J.B. Stradling, ''East Liverpool, Ohio, an

American Pottery Town,'' June 1982, p. 1368. This mark on experimental custard cup made by John Goodwin. The building had burned in 1857, and the cup was excavated from the rubble.)

Goodwin, Various Potteries. Hartford, Connecticut. **Seth Goodwin** was the first Goodwin in Hartford to make redware from 1795 to 1828 (Thorn, p. 192 and Ramsay, p. 193). **Thomas O'Hara Goodwin** was a son of Seth who made redware and later stoneware. Thorn dates Thomas 1820-1870, but Ramsay said Thomas lived around 1828 to 1880. **Horace Goodwin**, a brother of Seth, also had a pottery and operated around 1800 to 1810 making redware. According to Stewart and Consentino, p. 33, Horace had a partner named M.C. Webster, from 1810 to 1840. In Donald Blake Webster's book, *Decorated Stoneware of North America*, p. 97, is a fine picture of a jug marked ''Goodwin and Webster'' and this author said that Goodwin and Webster operated two potteries in Hartford around 1830-1840. Webster also had a pottery with his son, Charles T. Webster, called **M.C. Webster and Son**, from before 1840 until 1857. Charles T. Webster operated with O.H. Seymour from 1857-1873 as **Webster and Seymour**. (See various Seymour Potters for more.) ''A Checklist of New England Potters,'' by F.H. Norton, in the *Bulletin of the American Ceramic Society*, Volume 18, May 1939, pp. 181, 182, lists a Goodwin around 1870 in Elmwood, Connecticut, and Thomas O. Goodwin Pottery in Hartford, from 1820-1870, and a Harvey Goodwin from 1820-1870. In 1856, Norton gives us the names Harvey Goodwin and Thomas Goodwin as owners. (Information: Lura W. Watkins, ''A Checklist of New England Stoneware Potters,'' *Antiques*, August 1942, reprinted in Stradling, p. 80. Marks: Stewart and Consentino, p. 32; no. 2, Stradling, p. 69, nos. 3, 4, Thorn, p. 128.)

GOODWIN
&
WEBSTER
1.

GOODWIN & WEBSTER
2.

T.O. GOODWIN
HARTFORD
3.

SETH GOODWIN
4.

Gordy Family Potters/Georgia Art Pottery. Several locations in Georgia. In 1907, W.T.B. Gordy and a potter named Edwards L. Stork obtained a shop from potter Frank Gibson in Alvaton, Georgia. A year later, Gordy and Stork moved below Atlanta, Georgia, for six months or so making a shop in an old log house. They moved on to Aberdeen, and the partnership dissolved in 1909. Stork settled at Orange, seven miles east of Canton, and Gordy stayed in Aberdeen until 1918. Gordy then returned to Alvaton until 1935 when he moved to Primrose, eight miles north of Greenville on Highway 27. Gordy made stoneware jugs, mugs, homebrew crocks, etc. with Albany slip or salt glazed. For a full description see Burrison as cited. His jugs were sometimes human figure forms or had applied decorative motifs such as grape clusters and vines, ear of corn, lizards and butterflies. W.T.B. Gordy had two sons, William J. and Dorris Xerxes. They learned to throw pottery on a wheel as teenagers. As a young adult, William J. Gordy traveled around to various potteries learning to make different shapes and products. In 1935, he established the Georgia Art Pottery on Highway U.S. 41, five miles north of Cartersville, Georgia. D.X. Gordy took over his father's shop at Primrose in 1955. He made some clay sculptured pieces, including some religious groupings for his own satisfaction and not for sale. In 1969, he left Primrose to develop the pottery section of the museum of Westville in Lumpkin, Georgia, where he constructed a replica of folk-pottery based on his memory of his father's shop. The shop is an old double log pen with a mule-powered clay mill in front, and a hand made kick wheel, etc. For a full description see Burrison as cited, p. 177. D.X. Gordy was competent as both a folk and studio potter. He trained men to carry on with the making of folk pottery at Westville and returned to his Primrose shop to create a line of ware with delicately painted rural scenes such as farm buildings, spinning sheels, etc. He demonstrated pottery making at the Second Georgia Folklife Festival in Atlanta in 1981. For much more on all of the Gordy potters, see Burrison as cited. (Information: John A. Burrison, *Brothers in Clay*, pp. 172 to 178; also, William J. Gordy, "A Part of My Experience in the Pottery Business and My Father's Experience," *American Ceramic Bulletin*, Volume 17, no. 10, October 1938, p. 374. Marks: no. 1, Burrison as cited, p. 71; no. 2 from Melvin L. Davies, research potter; no. 3, Charles Counts, also a potter and research writer; nos. 4-5, from the Ross C. Purdy Museum at the American Ceramic Society building in Columbus.)

Gorham Company. Providence, Rhode Island. They made fine china dinnerware from 1970 to 1984. Company was started in 1831 by Jabez Gorham. Jabez's son, John, was primarily responsible for developing the manufacturing techniques that enabled the company to become the world's leading silversmiths, famous for sterling flatware as well as silver hollow-ware. In 1967, Gorham became a division of Textron, Inc. of Providence, and then began developing the total tabletop marketing approach by acquiring the Reizart Crystal Company. On March 23, 1970, Gorham acquired the Flintridge China Company of Pasadena, California. Flintridge had begun operations in 1945 as a partnership of Thomas Hogan and Milton Mason. See the Flintridge China listing. Their manufacturing skills helped to build Flintridge into a small, but highly respected china company. Beginning with a top quality product, Gorham added its design and marketing strengths and within eight years expanded from 30,000 square feet of manufacturing space and four kilns to over 80,000 square feet and eight large quality-designed kilns. According to Virginia Lirio, sales promotion manager at Gorham Fine China, the company stopped manufacturing their own china December 31, 1984, and started importing it. She wasn't sure what had been done with the building that Gorham had bought from Flintridge China Company.

(Information: company furnished information by the Gorham Division of Textron of Providence, Rhode Island. Marks: no. 1 was originally a Flintridge China Company mark which was also used by Gorham after the purchase of Flintridge China Company in 1970. No. 2 was filed in the name of Gorham Manufacturing Company on December 27, 1951, claiming use since August 29, 1951, for tableware bowls, vases, made of high fired ceramic material. It was to be expected that Gorham would sell dinnerware along with their silver, even before they owned their own factory in 1970. I don't know which pottery made "Vitrion" for Gorham, but it was probably Flintridge China Company. NOTE: all of the rest of the patent office registrations shown for Gorham were filed in the name of Textron, Inc., and all for china dinnerware. No. 3 filed October 21, 1970. No. 4 filed for registration on September 9, 1970. No. 5, "Black Contessa," was also made for Gorham before they acquired a factory and continued until after they stopped manufacturing and started importing ware again. In fact, most of the patterns named in these marks should still be available in imported china made for Gorham. Many housewives would hope that they would be. "Black Contessa" is a very popular pattern. Mark was filed for registration on December 18, 1981, claiming use since June 30, 1969. Nos. 6, 7 were both filed for registration on December 18, 1981, claiming use since June 30, 1971. Nos. 8-11 were filed for registration on December 18, 1981, claiming use since January 30, 1977. Nos. 15, 16, 17 were filed for registration on December 18, 1981, claiming use since June 30, 1978. Nos. 18-22 filed for registration on December 18, 1981, claiming use since June 30, 1979. Nos. 22, 23 filed for registration on December 18, 1981, claiming use since June 30, 1980. No. 24 filed for registration on August 22, 1983, claiming use since May 23, 1983. Nos. 25, 26, 27 filed for registration on February 10, 1983, claiming use since November 17, 1982.)

1.
W.T.B. GORDY

HAND MADE
BY
W.J. GORDY
2.

3. GA. Art Pottery

GA. ART
POTTERY

GA. ART
POTTERY
5.

4. W W.G.

1.

2. **VITRION**

GORHAM

3.

FLINTRIDGE

4. HISPANA

5. BLACK CONTESSA	17. ROYALSTON
6. MEDICI GREEN	18. PRINTEMPS
7. BRIDAL BOUQUET	19. FLEURS DE FRANCE
8. ROYAL BUTTERCUP	20. RONDELLE
9. FAIRMEADOWS	21. GRANDE MOTIF
10. KINGSBURY	22. BEAU JARDIN
11. CHANTILLY LACE	23. SPRING LAUREL
12. PASTELLE	24. CHERRYWOOD
13. LONG MEADOW	25. ARIANA
14. WINTER BLOSSOM	26. CHATHAM
15. LADY MADISON	27. JULIANA
16. APRIL SHOWERS	28. CAMELLIA

Gort China Company. Metuchen, New Jersey. 1944 to after 1954. Potters, Eric and Walter Gort, produced fine bone china figurines. Eric was an artist and sculptor. Walter was a ceramic engineer. The figurines were molded in many parts with intricate detailed sculpturing down to stitches in buttons and eye lashes. They were still listed in the 1954 *Crockery and Glass Journal Directory*, but closed sometime in the 1950's, according to Derwich, as cited. (Information: Jenny B. Derwich and Dr. Mary Latos, *Dictionary Guide to United States Pottery and Porcelain*, p. 104. Mark no. 1, stamped mark from 1954 directory cited. Mark no. 2 filed for registration on March 19, 1945, for use on bone china, ornamental and utilitarian, namely, candy boxes, vases, bowls, powder boxes, perfume bottles, trays, sugar bowls, creamers, egg cups, cups and saucers, plates, terrines, salt shakers, mustard jars and jam jars, claiming use since February 10, 1945.)

Graack, H.A. Bradentown (became Bradenton in 1920's) and Silver Springs, Florida. A pottery was founded by a Mrs. Ward in 1915, and she threw the pieces alone at first. Decorators were neighborhood women, Carrie Philips, Francis Wiggins, a Mr. Ireland and a Mr. Thompson doing typical Florida scenes of pine trees, peacocks, etc. on decorative items such as vases, ash trays, candlesticks and lamp bases, all unglazed and only varnished on interior. In 1920, H.A. Grack bought the pottery and made pieces with the stamped mark shown.

Production ceased in the 1920's in Bradenton. In the 1930's, Henry Graack had a concession to sell pottery at Silver Springs, Florida, where he made a hand swirled ware which Deb and Gini Johnson described as not being the natural earth tones of Niloak, but pleasing to the eye. The texture was smooth, but not velvety. Interiors were glazed. Graack died in 1965, and Stell Phillips continued in his place. She made hand thrown terra cotta flower containers, candle holders, etc. signed "S.P." or "S" and "Hand Made at Silver Springs, Florida." The Silver Springs mark shown was used by Graack and was found on the piece described by the Johnsons. (Information and mark 1: Allen Wunsch, "West Coast Florida Art Pottery," *American Art Pottery*, December 1980, pp. 1, 3. (Information and mark 2: Deb and Gini Johnson, *Beginners Book of American Pottery*, p. 99, and Jenny B. Derwich and Dr. Mary Latos, *Dictionary Guide to U.S. Pottery and Porcelain*, pp. 210, 211.)

Grab, Elaine. Dublin, Ohio. 1973 to present (1983). Studio potter making wheelthrown stoneware which won two second places and one third place prize at the New York State Fair. She learned to make pottery from her father George Rosenthal (see that listing) and a couple of formal classes in pottery making. Elaine operated in Fayetteville, New York, from 1973 until 1982.

Gracetone Pottery. Muskogee, Oklahoma. In September 1958, John Frank, owner of the Frankoma Pottery, purchased the Synar Ceramics Company of Muskogee, Oklahoma, and operated it until May 31, 1962. He changed the name to Gracetone Pottery in 1959. In 1962, part of the business was purchased by John Taylor, a long time employee of Frankoma Pottery, and he remained in business for a time after 1962. A line of dinnerware called "Gracetone" was made during Frank's ownership of the facatory. (Information: Susan Cox, editor of *American Clay Exchange*. Marks: sent by Elizabeth Vaughn, Beechworld, Antiques.)

Graham, Charles Pottery. Brooklyn, New York. Started in 1880. Until shortly after 1900 the pottery made artware. After that time Graham made chemical pottery such as acid receivers, vats, jars, etc. (Information: Evans, p. 114 and p. 115. Marks: no. 1, Barber, *Marks of American Potters*, p. 85; no. 1, 2, Evans, p. 115.)

1.   2.

Graham, Claude/Brown County Hills Pottery/Brown County Pottery. Nashville, Tennessee. A family named Griffith, from Fort Wayne, opened a pottery called the Brown County Pottery Works in the early 1930's. They hired a potter named Claude Graham to work for them, doing odd jobs. The pottery made a molded dinnerware, highly decorated with pine forests, dogwood flowers, deer, etc. Some were pictured in *House and Gardens* magazine, August 1942, p. 58. The really prized pottery that came from this venture was made by Claude Graham. While working around the shop, he decided to learn to make pottery on a wheel. In one week, he was able to turn out saleable products, and in two years time, his pieces were being shipped to Macy's, Marshall Fields, and L.S. Ayers. The hand thrown pieces made by Graham at this pottery should not be confused with the molded ware. Some of the same decorations were used. Pieces included dinnerware, tiny animals, people, vases, flower pots, chocolate pots, lamps, tile, etc. Some pieces had raised designs of fruit or flowers; some of the pieces were very simple. In 1942, Graham left to go to war. He was a maintainance man at Camp Atterbury and served six years and six months. When he came home, he didn't return to potting immediately. He worked at carpentry and electrical work until 1957 when he returned to potting in a shop of his own until 1970, called the Brown County Hills Pottery. Graham died in 1982. Graham's early work was signed "Brown County Pottery," or with the initials, "B.C.P." Mark no. 2 was found roughly incised on a hand thrown piece. In the 1950's and until 1970, the pieces were marked as shown, "Brown County Hills Pottery."

On Graham's Dogwood pieces, he often used a raised pattern of Dogwood and each petal was formed separately and attached or else the Dogwood was painted freehand. He applied apples, grapes and bittersweet decorations the same way. The only pieces Graham made in molds were oversized pieces such as huge clam shells and large flower pots. There has been and will be confusion over which was Graham's work and which should be credited to the Griffith's Brown County Pottery. Either would be very nice collectables. I didn't have a conclusive ending date for the Brown County Pottery, but the last listing I had for them in *Indiana Industrial Directory* was 1954-1955. They were not listed in 1958-1959. (Information and marks: Jerry Kay Cannon, niece to Claude Graham, who has been researching and collecting his pottery. Also, "The Mould of A Man's Fortune is in His Own Hands," *Nashville Tribune*, July 31, 1967.)

Brown County Hills
1.   Pottery   2.

BrowN
CouNTY

Grand Feu Art Pottery. Los Angeles, California. Started around 1912, remaining in production through 1918. Founder and owner was Cornelius Brauckman. Some of the pottery is marked with the name **Brauckman Art Pottery.** See Paul Evans, *Art Pottery of the U.S.*, p. 116, for a description of beautiful art pottery made there. (Information: Dave Rago, "American Art Pottery," *Antique Trader Weekly*, September 9, 1981, p. 91. Marks: Paul Evans, *Art Pottery of the U.S.*, p. 117.)

BRAUCKMAN
ART   T T
POTTERY

GRAND FEU
POTTERY   T T
L. A., CAL.

Grand Ledge, Michigan, Various Potteries. Grand Ledge in Michigan, is west of Lansing, located near a section of land in Grand River Valley which has a superior grade of sandstone, coal and clay. **Grand Ledge Sewer Pipe Company** was formed in the 1880's. They were purchased by Universal American Sewer Pipe Company of Cleveland in 1898, which later became plant no. 32 of American Vitrified Products Company until late 1960's when it closed. **Grand Ledge Clay Products Company** was formed in 1906 to make conduit pipe for underground wiring. The plant had a disasterous fire in 1937. It was reopened and made only sewer pipe. It is still operating in the 1980's. The workers at the potteries listed made whimseys or folk art pottery pieces at the factory. Several reclining lions made at Grand Ledge Clay Products Company were pictured in the book, *Cast in Clay*. The lions were made in a mold. Harry Poole, a worker in the potteries, said just before noon, when time was available, a worker would pack the mold with clay and leave it to dry until the next day. When the lion was taken out of the mold the next day, the workers smoothed it by licking their thumb. Some made mouths and tongues in the lions and "fixed" or sculptured on them with pen knives, pencils or whatever was available. The piece was then fired in the big tile kilns. Pieces were sometimes stamped with a mark (mark no. 2) or incised (marks, nos. 3 and 4) with a date and the worker's initials. The date, not visable in the picture, on the piece with mark no. 4, was November 7, 1936, when Tom Carter, worker, made his lion whimsey. "RCP," the initials of a worker (mark no. 5) were found on an ashtray. Other pieces shown were cats, alligators, a vase with a flag etched on it with "Grand Ledge" on one side and "My Flag" on the other (mark no. 6). Also frogs, a head of Lincoln, dogs, religious statues, turtles, tree stump flower urns, book ends and even a tombstone were made by the workers in the various Grand Ledge, Michigan, potteries. Some of the pieces shown were very artistic, some very crude as the talents of the workers varied. Mark no. 7 was used on sewer pipe. The mark "R.C.P." is for Roy C. Poole, a brother to Harry Poole mentioned. (Information and marks: Marsha MacDowell and C. Kurt Dewhurst, *Cast in Clay: The Folk Pottery of Grand Ledge, Michigan.* East Lansing, Michigan: The Museum, Michigan State University, 1980. Marsha McDowell is the Curator of Folk Art at Michigan State University.)

1. **GRAND   LEDGE**

GRAND   LEDGE,   MICH.
2.

3. *NOV 12 1903 EME*

4. *MADE BY TOM CARTER*

5. *RCP*

6. *AVP CO GRAND LEDGE*

7. *MY FLAG GRAND LEDGE*

W.T. Grant Company. McKeesport, Pennsylvania. A chain of variety stores. In late 1985, the W.T. Grant Company stores were sold to Ames Department Stores. (Mark no. 1 filed on July 6, 1954, for use on china and earthenware tableware. The other marks were on plates made by Salem China Company for the Grant Ten Cent stores. The pink ''Crocus'' pattern was made at Salem China Company. W.T. Grant sold foreign and domestic ware.)

GRANT·CREST

GRANT CREST COUNTRY CHARM

Gray, Verdelle. Asheville, North Carolina. 1962 to present. Mrs. Gray is a studio potter. She makes handthrown pottery on a wheel and hand built sculptures. She is a graduate of the School of American Craftsmen, Alfred University, Alfred, New York. (Information: Staff written, ''Verdelle Gray,'' *Pottery Collectors Newsletter*, October, 1976, p. 85.)

Verdelle

Greber Pottery. Upper Hanover, Montgomery County, Pennsylvania. 1848-1855. Made earthenware and redware. (Information: Spargo, p. 168; Ramsay, p. 184. Mark: Thorn, p. 129.)

C. Greber

Greenfield Village Pottery. In Greenfield Village, Dearborn, Michigan. 1933 to present (1985). This pottery is part of the Edison Institute founded by Henry Ford around 1922, with craft shops, a blacksmith shop, a tin type studio, etc. Adjoining the Greenfield Village is the Henry Ford Museum. Dr. Mary Latos and Jenny B. Derwich in their book, *Dictionary Guide to U.S. Pottery and Porcelain*, 1984, p 106, gives us this list of potters who have worked at the Greenfield Village Pottery: John A. Foster, early 1930's; Frank Greenwald, 1937; Peter Sultarski, 1954; Dale Huffman, 1954; Gordon Orear, 1960-1965; Norman Yanke, 1965-1969; Vey Valentine, 1965 to present; Bryan R. Van Benschoten, 1976 to the present; Ellen Bailey 1980 to the present; William Fluharty, 1980 to the present; David Hopwood, 1980 to the present. Pictured logo probably used a paper label. Some pieces sold at the shop were made in England by Simpsons, Ltd. an affiliate of Phaltzgraph Company and these were decorated by Cumbow China Decorating Company. See that listing. (Mark 1 shown in various directories. Mark 2 Annise Heavilin, *Grandma's Tea Leaf*, p. 161.)

1. 2.

Green Hills Pottery. Madison, Indiana. 1971 to present (1985). Dixie and James McDonough are studio potters, making earthenware custom designed mugs, with personal names, etc.

Green Hills Pottery *GHP*

Greenleaf Pottery, Inc. East Hartford, Connecticut. 1975 to present (1984). Studio potter, John Macomber, makes functional stoneware fired to cone 10, in a reduction atmosphere. He worked two years as a potter before starting the Greenleaf Pottery. He has done many craft shows. Pieces are signed with name and year. Pieces in pictures sent were large distinctive shapes with beautifully hand painted designs in ginger jars, fancy jugs, plates, vases, bowls, etc. John makes some limited editions and custom designed pieces. His pieces are richly colored, delicately designed and extremely durable.

John Macomber 1984

Green Thumb Products. Toledo, Ohio. Filed for registration of this mark on October 3, 1952, claiming use since April 30, 1952, for use on clay flower pots.

GREEN THUMB

Greenwood China Company/Greenwood Pottery. Trenton, New Jersey. Greenwood China was organized in 1868 out of a pottery which had been started in 1861 by Stephens, Tams and Company. In 1886, the name "Greenwood China" was first impressed on ironstone or white granite, according to Barber. Before that time, the company used a mark showing the coat of arms of the state of New Jersey (mark no. 1). Sometimes the initials of the company were used. The *1902-1903 Complete Directory* listed Greenwood Pottery as making hotel ware, sanitary ware, dinner sets, toilet sets and short sets of odd dishes, some decorated. In searching for an ending date for the Greenwood Pottery, I had the *Trenton City Directory* listings from 1900 to 1975; I didn't have the ones before 1900. The two names, Greenwood China Company and Greenwood Pottery were listed entirely separate, with separate names, addresses, etc., but they were under the same management and were the same business which caused confusion among writers. Greenwood China was at North Clinton Avenue opposite Oak, 1900 until 1905.

They operated 20 kilns with around 300 workers. Then in 1905, Greenwood China had two addresses, North Clinton opposite Oak, and at Muirhead opposite Ott. In 1908, the two addresses were no longer listed. Only the one at North Clinton was listed until 1918 when the Muirhead address showed up again and was the only address given until 1924, for the name Greenwood China. Greenwood Pottery was listed at North Canal and Grand (sometimes Grant) Streets until 1917, when the address for Greenwood Pottery became Canal Street and Clinton, until 1933, which was probably about the time the whole business ceased to exist. Proof of their inter-relationship was an advertisement in a 1913 *Keller's Pottery and Glass Annual Directory*. Marks nos. 2 and 3 were shown in the ad. At the top it said Greenwood China and across the bottom, Greenwood Pottery Company. The company made a variety of products including stone china, a fine translucent dinnerware, restaurant china, door knobs, porcelain insulators, etc. They made art pottery vases, plaques, with ivory finishes or white enamel with gold, silver and bronze effects. (Marks: nos. 2 and 3 were shown in the advertisement and were labeled "old trademark" for no. 2 which was first used around 1886, and "new trademark" which came into use around 1910. See mark no. 11. Nos. 1, 4 to 7, E.A. Barber, *Marks of American Potters*, pp. 46, 47. No. 7 is Barber's version of no. 2 from ad. No. 8 was impressed on a vitrified hotel plate. No. 9 sent by Linda Cleveland is a stamped mark found on hotel plate in addition to impressed mark no. 8. Both marks on the same plate. No. 10, Hazel Hartman, *Porcelain and Pottery Marks*, p. 112. No. 11: Just this portion of mark no. 3 was filed for registration on September 20, 1910 for chinaware, no prior use was claimed.)

1.

2. GREENWOOD CHINA
TRENTON, N. J.

3.

4.

5.

6. **G.P. Co.**

7. GREENWOOD CHINA
TRENTON, N.J.

8. GREENWOOD
CHINA
P

9. PATENT...

10.

11.

GREENWOOD CHINA

Celebrated for its strength and durability and especially adapted for Hotel, Restaurant, and Steamship Use. Please read our Trade Mark

New Trade Mark

1862 GREENWOOD CHINA TRENTON, N.J. 1876 REG. U.S. PAT. OFF.

Old Trade Mark
GREENWOOD CHINA
TRENTON, N. J.

and do not be deceived by similar Trade Marks. Address all communications to

The Greenwood Pottery Co.
TRENTON, N. J.

Greer, Georgeanna H. San Antonio, Texas. 1956 to 1966. Greer, a studio type potter, worked mainly in a classroom situation and did not go on to establish a studio. Rather, she is known for the knowledge she has acquired and dispensed about pottery. Her most recent publication is *American Stonewares, The Art and Craft of Utilitarian Potters*, Exton, Pennsylvania: Schiffer Publishing Company, 1981, dealing with methods of production. Other writings are: "Alkaline Glazes and Groundhog Kilns: Southern Pottery Traditions," *Antiques* 61, no. 4, 1977, pp. 42-54; "Basic Forms of Historic Pottery Kilns Which May Be Encountered in the United States," *The Conference on Historic Site Archaeology Papers 1978,* pp. 133-147, Columbia, South Carolina: Institute of Archaeology and Anthropology, University of South Carolina, 1979; "The Folk Pottery of Mississippi," *Made by Hand: Mississippi Folk Art*, pp. 45-54, catalog of an exhibition held at Mississippi State Historical Museum, Jackson, January 22-May 25, 1980; "Groundhog Kilns: Rectangular American Kilns of the Nineteenth and Early Twentieth Centuries," *Northeast Historical Archaeology 6*, no. 1-2, 1977, pp. 42-54; "Meyer Family Pottery: A Ceramics Monthly Portfolio," *Ceramics Monthly*, June 22, 1974; "Preliminary Information on the Use of Alkaline Glaze for Stoneware in the South, 1800-1970," pp. 159, 161-162, *The Conference on Historic Site Archaeology Papers 1970*, vol. 5, Columbia: Institute of Archaeology and Anthropology, University of South Carolina, 1971; "The Wilson Potteries," *Ceramics Monthly 29*, no. 6, 1981; "Harding Black," *The Meyer Family: Master Potters* of Texas, San Antonio, Texas: Trinity University Press for San Antonio Museum Association, 1971. Georgeanna made utilitarian stoneware vessels with a hand inscribed mark as shown.

g. greer

_____

Gregory, Waylande. Sculptor Waylande Gregory studied at Kansas State Teacher's College in Emporia, Kansas, then at the Art Institute in Kansas City. He then went to Chicago, to study at the Art Institute, under Lorado Taft. After that, he studied for a time in Florence, Italy. He worked in bronze and ceramics. From 1928-1932, he worked at Cowan Art Pottery. In 1932 and 1933, he was an artist in residence at the Cranbrook Academy of Art in Bloomfield Hills, Michigan, for a short time before moving to Bound Brook, New Jersey, to set up his own studio. Waylande died in 1971. In 1933, at the Second National Ceramic Exhibition at Syracuse Museum of Fine Arts, Waylande Gregory won first prize for ceramics sculpture for "Girl with Olive." In 1934, he won first honorable mention for "Head of a Child." In 1935, he won first honorable mention for "Kansas Madonna." In 1939, he received special recognition for work on an outdoor ceramic sculpture which comprised of 12 ceramic figures, each of which weighed one ton. He called the work, "The Fountain of Atoms," and it was exhibited at the 1939 Worlds' Fair. The mark shown was on the piece, "Europa," of unglazed earthenware, exhibited at the Golden Gate International Exposition in San Francisco, and the Seventh Ceramic National in 1938. (Information: Ross Anderson and Barbara Perry, *Diversions of Keramos*, Syracuse, New York: Everson Museum of Art, 1983, pp. 3-23; also, Garth Clark, *A Century of Ceramics in the U.S.*, pp. 293-194; and Helen Stiles, *Pottery of the U.S.*, pp. 307-315. Mark: Linda Steigleder, from the booklet published by the Everson Museum of Art to accompany the 1978 exhibition. "A Century of Ceramics in the U.S." A very similar mark to the one shown was in the book by Clark, which was found on a piece made by Gregory, when he worked at Cowan Pottery.)

WAYLANDE GREGORY

_____

Grindley Artware Manufacturing Company. Sebring, Ohio. 1933 to 1952. Started in 1933, during the depression. They stopped working in 1947 to rebuild after a disasterous fire. They operated again but were completely out of business by 1952, according to Dean L. Grindley, son of the founder, Arthur Grindley, Sr. Both of Arthur Grindley's sons, Arthur, Jr. and Dean, worked at Grindley Artware before its closing. The pottery made cow creamer and syrups and other novelty items. In the 1952, *Crockery and Glass Journal*, they were listed under teapots, art china, such as vases, console sets, candy boxes, etc. They were also listed under cooking ware, but not dinnerware. See Americana Art China Company for more on Dean Grindley and his involvement in Sebring, Ohio, potteries. (Marks: from Quality Stamp Company, East Liverpool, Ohio.)

_____

Grossman, Edward, doing business as **The Spitler**. Chicago, Illinois. Filed for a claim on this mark on September 28, 1942, for use on earthen and porcelain cuspidors, claiming use since April 1, 1942.

The Spitler

_____

Grotell, Maija. Grotell, studio potter, instructor, sculptress, was born in Helsinki, Finland, where she studied at the School of Industrial Art and learned painting, design and sculpture. She studied and worked in Europe, with Alfred Finch, then came to the United States in 1927. She taught at the Henry Street Settlement House. Then from 1936 to 1938, she instructed potters at Rutgers University. In 1938, she joined the staff of the Cranbrook Academy of Art in Bloomfield Hills, Michigan, where she was head of the ceramic department until 1966. She won 25 major awards and is listed several times in the Syracuse Nationals Ceramic Awards in the back of this book. (Information: Garth Clark, *A Century of Ceramics in the U.S.*, p. 294. Marks: incised; Linda Steigleder, from the booklet published by the Everson Museum of Art to accompany the 1978 exhibition, "A Century of Ceramics in the U.S.," with Curators: Garth Clark and Margie Hughto.)

MG MG MG

_____

Grueby-Faience Company, 1894-1909; **Grueby Pottery Company**, 1907-1911; **Grueby Faience and Tile Company**, 1909-? Boston, Massachusetts. The actual dates of the beginning of Grueby Faience and Tile Company are a little difficult to ascertain. On the copyright report no. 8, the Grueby Faience and Tile Company claimed use of this mark from 1888. Evans, p. 118, says William Henry Grueby started a plant in Revere, Massachusetts, in September 1890, to make architectural faience, and in 1891, the plant became Atwood (Eugene R.) and Grueby. In 1894, the Grueby-Faience Company began operations at the same address and was incorporated in 1897. Then in 1907, the Grueby Pottery Company was incorporated in Boston, Massachusetts, although the Grueby Pottery mark was used as early as 1899, with both plants operating. The name of Grueby Faience Company was changed to Grueby Faience and Tile Company following a bankruptcy and a receivership in 1909. Grueby Faience and Tile Company suffered a fire in 1912, (Kovel, p. 50) or in 1913, (Evans, p. 121). They rebuilt the plant, which was sold to C. Pardee Works of Perth Amboy, New Jersey. In 1921, Pardee moved the Grueby operaion to New Jersey. But all of the copyrights were filed by Grueby Faience and Tile Company of Boston, Massachusetts, and Philadelphia, Pennsylvania, in 1926, and 1928. Writing the history of this pottery is doubly confusing because the dates of the use of the marks in no way coincides with the name or product changes or factory loction. Seldom do three authorities such as Barber, Evans and the Kovels have conflicting information for the same pottery. Barber, *Marks of American Potters*, p. 99, said Grueby Faience Company was organized in June 1896. It was incorporated then but organized much earlier. Experimenting with the making of art pottery was done on a limited basis between 1894 and 1897, according to Evans. Whatever the name and whatever the location, art pottery was made by Grueby until 1910. The 1910 date is Evan's, p. 49. Barber, p. 99, described the early ware as hand thrown in a hard semi-porcelain body, highly decorated in an opaque lustreless enamel of great smoothness and satin finish. The products were vases and decorative pieces that ended up in many museums. For a great deal of information on the products, decorators and modlers, see Evans, *Art Pottery of the U,S,*, pp. 118 to 123 and Kovel's *Collector's Guide to American Art Pottery*, pp. 47 to 56. The first five marks are from Barber, *Marks of American Potters*, p. 99. No. 6 was filed for copyright on February 5, 1920, claiming use since 1913, on Faience. No. 7 was filed February 5, 1926, claiming use since 1921, on Faience. No. 8 was filed June 15, 1928, for pottery and Faience, claiming use since 1888, on pottery and tile. No. 3 was filed for registration April 8, 1905, but no date was given for first use. The company filed for registration of just the Lotus flower as seen in the center of the various marks in November 1899, under the name Grueby Faience Company, claiming it was used after October 26, 1898.

GRUEBY 1.

GRUEBY
BOSTON.MASS
2.

3.

4.

GRUEBY POTTERY
BOSTON.U.S.A.
5.

HAUTEVILLE 6.

7.

GRUEBY 8.

Marks used by Grueby decorators
(Barber, p. 100)

 Miss Ruth Erickson
Mr. Kiichi Yamada

 Miss Gertrude Stanwood
Miss Ellen R. Farrington

 Miss Florence S. Liley
Miss Annie V. Lingley

 Miss Wilhelmina Post (2)

 Miss Lillian Newman
Miss Gertrude Priest

S M.S Miss Marie A. Seaman (2)
Miss Norma Pierce

G.T. Chemical Products, Inc. San Diego, California. Filed for registration on this mark on July 27, 1981, for use on drinking mugs, planters, bath accessories, such as drinking glasses, soap dishes, toothbrush holders and covered containers, animal figurines and gourmet cookware, made of clay and ceramics, claiming use of this mark since January 1977.

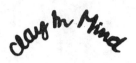

Guernsey Earthenware, formerly the **Cambride Art Pottery**, became Guernsey Earthenware 1909 to around 1924. Makers of cooking ware, hotel ware and chemical porcelain (Stout, p. 62, 89). Some of the cookingware had an earthenware body, some of it was porcelain after 1914. All had a fine white lining. During 1918 the hotel ware line was added to supply government needs and shortages due to the war. For more on history of Guernsey Earthenware Company, see Cambridge Art Pottery. (Marks: on pieces of highly vitrified hotel ware and a teapot.)

GUERNSEY WARE
HOTEL
VITRIFIED
USA   GUERNSEY WARE
HOTEL
U.S.A.   GUERNSEY
CA
COOKING WARE

Gump, S. and G. Company. San Francisco, California. A very large store. In May 1951, *China, Glass and Decorative Accessories Magazine*, p. 28, in "Current on the Coast," by Edna M. Craig, was a news item that the Gump Store in Honolulu had to be sold to settle the estate of A.L. Gump. The Honolulu branch had operated for 22 years. (Mark: They filed for use of this mark on figurines in November 1947, claiming use since July 5, 1928. Then they filed on the same mark again on November 15, 1947, to be used for earthenware and porcelain, such as bowls, vases, plates and dinner sets, claiming use since June 1930. This was the only time we found that a company filed on exactly the same mark twice, besides Homer Laughlin. Gump sold pottery made by Jalanivich and Olsen of San Francisco, California. See that listing.)

GUMP'S

Gunther and Berns. Sheboygan, Wisconsin. 1862-1886. Peter Berns operated a pottery to made redware, and in 1862, he became partners with Theodore Gunther to make stoneware crocks, jugs, churns, etc. A very few of the pieces had some cobalt decorations. Some were marked with the impressed mark shown. Many pieces were undecorated and unmarked. In 1866, Gunther became the sole owner and worked until 1886. (Information: Kenneth Dearolf, *Wisconsin Folk Pottery*, pp. 22 and 24. A booklet written in cooperation with the Kenosha Public Museum.)

H

M.A. Hadley Pottery, Inc. Louisville, Kentucky. 1939 to present. The pottery got its initial start in 1939 when Mary Alice Hadley brought home pieces of pottery to hand decorate. After she decorated them, she took them to the Louisville Pottery Company for glazing and firing. The demand for her pottery increased, so she hired help to decorate, then rented a room at the Louisville pottery in which to work. The business grew, and in 1944, the Hadleys were looking for a small pottery to buy. They bought the building at 1570 Story Avenue in Louisville, Kentucky in October of that year. By December, they had the first kiln ready to fire. In 1948, they added a second kiln and new processing equipment. Until 1969, the ware was either cast (in molds) or jiggered (thrown on a wheel).

In 1969, a Ram Press was put into operation for making plates and similar items. The Hadley Pottery Company was always operated by George and Mary Alice Hadley as a cooperative effort. In the early years, the business had grown so rapidly that George had to quit his job to devote full time to the pottery. In 1960, the name was changed from the Hadley Pottery to Hadley Pottery, Inc. Mrs. Hadley died in 1965. The same attractive, hand-decorated pieces of kitchenware and pottery are still available at the pottery, using the patterns that were originated by Mary Alice Hadley.

She painted in water colors and oils long before she became involved in pottery decorating. She had received awards and recognition and had exhibited paintings in New York, Boston, Los Angeles and other cities. The Hadley designs used on the pottery were unique. Hadley pottery is made from native clays with a modified stoneware body similar to ironstone. The decoration is applied on the unfired pieces, which are then sprayed or dip-glazed and fired in a single-fire process at 2,300 degrees. This produces maximum bond between the body and decoration which is under the lead-free glaze, making a very durable product. The Hadley Pottery produced a complete line of dinnerware and numerous ornamental and incidental pieces. Open stock was maintained in eight patterns and marketed as ''M.A. Hadley Designs'' in all 50 states and Canada. The Hadleys also made attractive pottery lamps. By 1950, the list of dinnerware patterns had grown to eight designs. ''Pear and Grape,'' ''Green Bird,'' ''Fisherman'' and ''Country Scene'' which came in eight scenes (a farmer and wife, son, daughter, horse, cow, pig, etc.) were all introduced before 1943. Others were ''Blue Horse'' in deep blue and white and ''Ship and Whale'' (also called ''Three Masted Schooner and Whale''). By 1950, a ''Scalloped Edge'' was listed in solid white or green glaze. ''Three Leaf Clover'' was another, but wasn't listed for very many years. In 1952, ''Brown Fleck'' with a straight-edge design was chosen by the Selection Committee of the Museum of Modern Art of New York for the museum's ''Good Design'' Exhibition. The list of kitchenware items made by Hadley is extensive: saltbox, matchbox, coffee urns, canister-type jars for tea, coffee, sugar, etc., a little dipper to use in canisters, a syrup pitcher, cinnamon shaker, mustard jar, even a dish for the dog and one for the cat. There were also many figure pieces made at Hadley Pottery. In 1979, Kenneth Moore became the owner of the Hadley Pottery with Virgil Kendall as the general manager in 1986. (Mark: was filed for registration on January 7, 1985, claiming use since 1940 for pottery pieces.)

M. A. Hadley

Haeger Potteries, Inc. Two plants in Macomb and one in Dundee, Illinois. 1871 to present. In 1871, David H. Haeger purchased an interest in the Dundee Brick Yard in Dundee, Illinois. Before passing away in 1900, Mr. Haeger added two other brick and tile factories to his holdings, which earned him a comfortable fortune. After 1900, the management fell to his sons who added flower pots to the products in 1912. In 1914, they began to glaze pottery and Haeger Potteries, Inc. was given birth. A few days before World War I, the pottery launched its artware efforts, sending the first shipment to Marshall Field and Company of Chicago. The ware was widely accepted, and in July 1919, Edmund H. Haeger purchased the pottery at Dundee from the family corporation and doubled the factory output by constructing another kiln. Output and sales kept gradually increasing as the years went by until, in 1939, Haeger Potteries, Inc. took over the Macomb Pottery at Macomb, Illinois, to convert the plant exclusively to artware. A second tunnel kiln was built at Dundee in 1941. In 1934, the Haeger Potteries exhibited at the Century of Progress in Chicago in a separate building which housed a complete pottery plant. Marshall Field and Company catalogs show Haeger luncheon and tea sets made in 1938 in four colors, blue, rose, yellow and green with attractive shapes and a fine glaze. Also pictured in an ad for 1976 was the ''Country Classics,'' a hand-decorated tabletop collection in early American tradition which were made of ironstone in Leather Brown and Orange Peel. According to the article, staff written, ''Newsletter,'' *China, Glass and Tableware*, August 1979, p. 17, Haeger Potteries, Inc. introduced a dinnerware line in the fall of 1980, named ''Cherokee Stoneware'' which was designed by Ben Seibel. In 1969, a second plant to make lamps was purchased in Macomb, Illinois. The plant is under the direction of Nicolas Edmund Haeger (fourth generation).

In 1979, the Creek Indians built a pottery which was to be operated under the direction of Haeger Potteries, Inc. See the listing Cherokee Pottery/Cherokee Nation Pottery, Inc. Many famous designers designed pieces for Haeger Potteries at one time or other: Ben Seibel; Sascha Brastoff; Eric Olsen and Lee Secrist. Mr. Secrist came to Haeger Potteries, Inc. in 1946. He was hired to supervise and create designs for both Haeger Potteries, Inc. in Dundee, and Haeger Lamp Company in Macomb. Secrist had studied at the Chicago Academy of Fine Arts; the Chicago Art Institute; the Yale School of Fine Arts and also studied in Florence, Italy.

February 1947, was their 75th anniversary celebration; they sponsored an art competition supervised by Mr. Secrist. A total of $2,000 in prizes was awarded for pottery designs best suited to large scale production. Vases, figurines and console sets were the pieces the artists designed. Eric Olsen was also outstanding in the ceramic field. Mr. Olsen, a Norwegian, is best known in the United States for his work on Wedgwood and Spode china. In 1930, he was engaged by Josiah Wedgwood as a designer and modeler. He joined Spode in 1932 where he remained as designer and modeler until 1942, when he joined the Norwegian Quartermaster General. He was selected in 1936 as National Register Designer under the auspices of the English Board of Trade, and in 1937, he gave a private exhibiton in London which was opened by the Queen of Norway. In 1971, a line of about 50 pieces named ''Esplanade'' was designed for Haeger Potteries, Inc. by Sacha Brastoff (see the listing for Brastoff). The pieces had a silver or bronze metallic finish and were decorated with Spanish or Florentine designs. Lamps, vases, covered boxes, ashtrays, planters, plates and serving platters were produced. A few pieces of handmade wheel thrown pottery was still being made in the late 1970's at Haeger Potteries, Inc. in Dundee, Illinois. Sebastiano Maglio produced miscellaneous pieces. Maglio came from Sicily, where he was a professor of art. He is the seventh generation in his family of potters. In 1976, he had worked at Haeger Potteries for 13 years making unique items which were displayed at the various Haeger plants and other places. One vase Maglio made was 8' tall and used 650 pounds of clay which will remain on display in Haeger's public showroom in Dundee.

Around a quarter of a million visitors come there each year. The beautiful large vase was completed in December 1977 and had scenes depicting potters at work. The designs painted on the vase were executed by Glenn Richardson, chief staff designer. Today, artware is made in the old Buckeye Pottery building in Macomb (see that listing), and lamps are made in a building used at one time by Western Stoneware. Both plants have been modernized. Art and florists ware are made in the building in Dundee. (Information: staff written, "History of Haeger Potteries, Inc.," *American Ceramic Society Bulletin*, XXIV, October 1945, p. 356; Lois Lehner, *American Kitchen and Dinner Wares*, pp. 72-73; Rena London, "Haeger Pottery - Royal, Doubly Royal and Plain," *National Glass and Pottery and Collectables Journal*, May 1979, pp. 20, 21; some material sent by company.)

Marks: no. 1 was filed for registration May 15, 1941, claiming use since 1914 for use on vases, bowls, flower pots, console sets and novelty plant or flower holders, made of earthenware and porcelain. No. 2 was filed June 28, 1951, claiming use since 1914 for various ceramic articles, namely, vases, bowls, pots, flower pots, console sets, novelty plant holders and novelty flower holders. No. 3 was filed May 15, 1941, claiming use since August 1939 for the same articles as listed in no. 1. No. 4 was filed June 28, 1951, claiming use since August 1939 for various ceramic products, namely, vases, bowls, fish bowls, pots, flower pots, console sets, novelty plant holders, novelty flower holders and mugs. No. 5 was on a vase at the Ross Purdy Museum of the American Ceramic Society in Columbus, Ohio. Nos. 6, 7, 8 are a variety of marks found on pieces of Royal Haeger. The name Royal Haeger has been used and discontinued several times throughout the years on various pieces. In 1966, just "Haeger" was being used, but by 1979 the Royal Haeger crown label was in use again. No. 9 was sent by Edward Blas, researcher; mark is a paper label used around 1933-1934. Nos. 10-11 are labels shown in advertisement in *House and Gardens*, February 1949 as sent to this author by Edward Blas. Nos. 12-14 would probably be used as paper labels. These are logos shown in various directories. No. 12 was 1945 and no. 13 is from 1967 Directory. No. 15 is a gold foil label, and the rest of the marks were copied from pieces.)

1.

Haeger

2.

3.

4.

ROYAL HAEGER
BY
ROYAL HICKMAN
MADE IN U.S.A.
223

5.

Royal **Haeger** USA○

ROYAL HAEGER
R1903 USA

7.

6.

HAEGER POTTERY DUNDEE ILL.

9.

Royal **Haeger** USA

8.

Royal **Haeger** Lamp

10.

Haeger POTTERY

11.

Haeger

12.

HAEGER

13.

ROYAL **Haeger** POTTERY 75th Anniversary

14.

COPYRIGHTED **Haeger** ®

15.

Haeger 3758 U.S.A

16.

TF3
TELEFLORA
BY
Haeger ©
USA 1977

17.

Craftsmen for a century

18.

HAEGER

19.

HAEGER © 231- U.S.A.

20.

MADE FOR ®
FTD
© F.T.D.A. 1979
BY HAEGER USA

21.

Hagen-Renaker, Inc. San Dimas, California. 1945 to present (1983). In 1945, Maxine Hagen Renaker and her husband John Renaker started a pottery business in their garage in Culver City, California. In 1946, they moved to a factory building in Monrovia, California, which had been built by Maxine's father, Ole Hagen, who became a partner. The first pieces made were wall plaques and decorative plates and bowls. These had handpainted underglaze flowers, fruits and birds and were signed on the back in engobe signatures with "Hagen-Renaker, Calif." and the initials of the particular painter. A few figurines were added to the original line, and it soon became apparent that the little animals were the most popular. Helen Perrin and Maxine Renaker were the designers of the Hagen-Renaker Miniatures, a line that has grown steadily since 1948. In the 1950's and 1960's, the company produced a line of larger animals. Hagen-Renaker produces some animals for Disneyland and Disneyworld. In the late 1960's, Hagen-Renaker became a California Corporation; in 1966 they moved the factory to San Dimas.

Three of the four Renaker children are working in pottery, two in businesses of their own, the third as treasurer-controller of the corporation. According to Mrs. Renaker, the miniatures are too small to mark, but come with card attached with the name and address of the factory. Hagen-Renaker, Inc. also has a wholesale nursery business in Encinitas. These labels are reprinted from the *Hagen-Renaker Collector's Catalog* by Cheryl Abelson, p. 6, with her permission (privately printed, 75 pp., 1982.). Labels were printed on foil-type paper in various colors. There were four "Famous Thoroughbreds" designed by Maureen Love (Swaps, Silky Sulivan, Man O' War, Terrang and Kelso). Four of these had race ticket labels as shown. Kelso did not have the ticket attached. "Kelso" was made in 1961-1962, 1963-1968 and again in 1973-1974. The early issue had black and gold labels. Later Kelso labels were green and gold. (Information furnished by Maxine Renaker. Marks as already cited.)

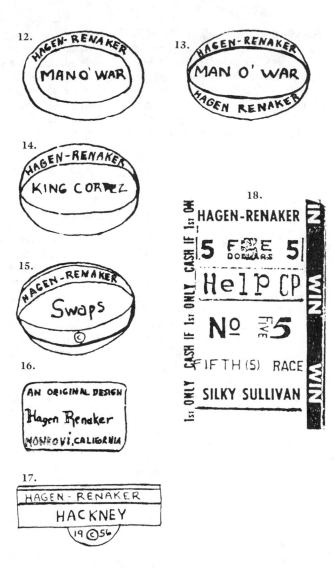

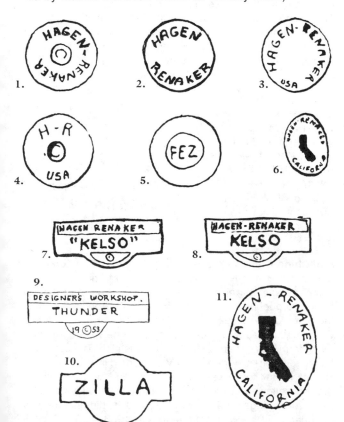

Hagy Ceramic Studio. San Antonio, Texas. 1939 to 1953. Tom Hagy first became interested in making pottery through a ceramic course offered at the Witte Museum in San Antonio, Texas. He then enrolled in Alfred University in Alfred, New York, before W.W. II sometime. In 1939, he started his studio in San Antonio, hiring Mexican students to trim the greenware and do the hand painting making approximately 2,000 pieces per month. The ware was caste, art tiles with nursery rhyme characters, etc.; figurines of ducks, dogs, chickens, birds, etc.; a line of planters with a swan, fish, dogs, cats, etc. Sears and Roebuck and Company was a big customer for Hagy ceramics, although he had at least a dozen outlets across the country. (Information: Jenny B. Derwich and Dr. Mary Latos, *Dictionary Guide to United States Pottery and Porcelain*, p. 111. Marks: stamped; sent by Jenny B. Derwich.)

Haig Pottery. Philadelphia, Pennsylvania. Pottery was started by Thomas Haig in 1812 and operated by him until 1833 when his sons, James and Thomas II, took over until around 1890. The pottery made Rockingham, brownware, cow creamer, log cabin bank, Washington-Masonic pitchers of stoneware using local clay. In 1826, Thomas II won a bronze medal from Franklin Institute for pottery. (Information: Ramsay, p. 45; Spargo, p. 221. Mark: Thorn, p. 129.)

T. HAIG

1852

Halcyon Art Pottery. Halcyon (near Pismo Beach), California. 1910 to 1913, also 1931 to 1932. Halcyon began as a settlement of a communal group called the Temple Home Association in 1903. In 1910, as part of their program to regenerate man, they started the pottery. Under the direction of Alexander W. Robertson, they were firing their first pieces made of unglazed red clay with modeled decorations by 1911. The pottery closed in 1913, but was opened for a short time in 1931, under the guidance of Gertrude Wall (see Walrich Pottery). Then in 1932, the pottery operated a short time under the direction of the University of California, Extention Department. In the 1930's, white clay was used and glazes applied. The pottery was idled again in 1931, and in 1940 it was completely dismantled. The Temple Home Association was dissolved in 1949. Many of the later pieces were unmarked, but sometimes no. 4, the "H.P." symbol was used. (Information and impressed marks: Paul Evans, *Art Pottery of the U.S.*, pp. 124-126.)

1. *AwR*   2. HALCYON CALIF.   3. HALCYON CAL   4. HP

Haldeman Potteries. Burbank and Calabasas, California. From 1933 to 1951, Virgil K. Haldeman had a pottery in Burbank. From 1951 to 1953, they relocated in Calabasas. The pottery made art or decorative ware in beautiful pastel colors with soft glazes. Before having his own pottery, Haldeman had developed glazes for Santa Catalina Clay Products Company for the Catalina art pottery pieces. (Marks: no.1, filed for registration on December 2, 1947, claiming use since 1935 for pottery vases, bowls, baskets, planters, cups, saucers, sugar bowls, creamers, plates, dishes and platters; no. 2, yellow and gold foil label on aqua colored fancy bowl; no. 3, roughly inscribed name, Haldeman, California, on artistic bowl. For a discussion of the life of Haldeman and various positions he held, see Jenny B. Derwich and Dr. Mary Latos, *Dictionary Guide to U.S. Pottery and Porcelain*, p. 112.)

Caliente

1.

2.

3. *r85*

Haldeman California

Hall, Charles, Inc. New York, New York. Charles Hall, Inc. was a sales agency or distributor listed in *1952 Crockery and Glass Journal Directory* for porcelain and earthenware dinnerware, art or decorative china and earthenware candelabra, cups and saucers, figurines. Also glass tableware, etc. In the 1945 *Crockery and Glass Journal Directory*, they also listed various lines of domestic decorative ware as well as imported products.

HALL HOUSE NEW YORK

E. Hall. Newton Township, Muskingum County, Ohio. (Both Ramsay and Thorn said Hall was in Tuscarawas County, and I picked up on this error in my Ohio book) 1828-1856. Made earthenware and stoneware, some highly decorated. In the words of Norris Schnieder, "Blue Bird Potteries," *Zanesville Times Signal*, December 1, 1959, "Occasionally a potter with an innate and untutored sense of the beautiful would decorate his ware." Pictured in the same article is a cookie jar with modeled clasped hands that are characteristic of Hall's work. It is decorated with stars, diamonds and bunches of grapes. The handles appear to be held in place by imitation screw heads made of clay. Hall's most ambitious work is an elaborate stoneware water cooler. (Marks: picture no. 59 in Ramsay following p. 204; Lehner, *Ohio Pottery and Glass*, p. 92.)

MADE BY E. HALL OF NEWTON TOWNSHIP MUSKINGUM CO. OHIO AT W.P. HARRISES FACTORY. A HOLE-SALE AND RETAIL DEALER IN STONE WARE. BUCK AND BRECK TO JOSHUA CITES. JANUARY 13, 1856

E. HALL OHIO

E. HALL NEWTON TOWNSHIP TUSCARAWAS CO. O

Hall China Company. East Liverpool, Ohio. The company was founded August 14, 1903 and is still in business. The company was started at East Fourth and Walnut Streets in East Liverpool by Robert Hall and his son, Robert T. Hall in the plant formerly operated by the East Liverpool Potteries Company. It was a hard beginning for a new company suffering from lack of capital and stiff competition. The company had hardly gotten started when Mr. Hall died in 1904. His son, Robert T. Hall took over the company and kept it going by making whiteware from 1905 to 1911 such as toilet sets, bed pans, mugs, jugs, etc. From 1908 to 1911, dinnerware was manufactured, then discontinued until 1936. Robert T. Hall was a man with a dream, which was to develop a new glaze that was single fire, non-lead, hard, non-porous and craze proof. In 1911, Robert Hall was successful, and he produced a ware that is hard, non-porous, craze proof and beautiful. The company labeled this line of one-fire ware, "Secret Process," and it is still a most important part of their production. From then on, the Hall story is one of growth, constant need for new facilities, etc. In 1914, Hall China made casseroles, teapots, coffee urn liners for institutional trade. Hall China cookingware became so popular that in 1919 they bought the old Goodwin Pottery Plant at East 6th and Broadway to make gold decorated teapots, and soon became a leader in decorated teapots. In 1920, soon after the death of Robert T. Hall, Malcolm W. Thompson joined the company. In 1927, the third plant was opened to make soda fountain jars. The year 1928 saw the advent of decorated cookingware. In 1930, the three old pottery plants were abandoned, and a new building was built which was added to eight times.

The principal products of the company today are Hall Fireproof China casseroles and other baking dishes, teapots, coffee pots, serving dishes and storage dishes; many were used in restaurants, hotels, hospitals, airlines, railroads and other institutions. Hall Gold Label teapots and cooking china were sold in leading department stores. Hall's superior quality dinnerware and fine china was available through stamp stores and large merchandising centers. Super-Ceram is a type of coffee and tea service which has a tough, white ceramic body. In *China, Glass and Lamps*, June 18, 1923, p. 21, Hall China Company's ad read, "48 different teapots, no two alike. Every pot is craze proof, non-absorbent fire-proof china from the largest manufacturer of fireproof cooking china in the world."

(Information: from company; also, "History of Hall China Company," *6th Annual for Tri State Pottery Festival*, June 1973, p. 9. Marks: A few of the marks have hand written or stamped dates beside or above them. These are the dates the hand stamps were made by Quality Stamp Company, East Liverpool, Ohio. Almost all of these marks came from that source. A few are copied from dishes. No. 1, "Hall" in a circle was filed for registration February 10, 1930, claiming use since October 1903 for fireproof china teapots, coffeepots, sugar bowls, cream pitchers, beanpots, shirred-egg dishes, pudding pans, bakers, casseroles, spittoons, ice bowls, stock jars, steam-table insets and soda-fountain jars. The Hall in a circle in various forms was shown right on into the 1970's in the directories you may find listed in the bibliography; so it was used over a long period of time. No. 2 was filed September 20, 1933, claiming use since August 8, 1903, for vitrified chinaware, china kitchenware, china bakingware, china cookingware, china tableware and plain and decorated chinaware comprising apple baking dishes, bake or salad pans, baking dishes, casserolettes, chili bowls, chocolate tumblers, cocottes, comb and brush trays, creamers, cream bottles, custards, drawn butter servers, egg cups, fruit cocktail cups, hospital sets, ice cream jars, ice tubs, insets for cold tables, insets for steam tables, jelly moulds, jugs, kitchen bowls, little brown jugs, marmalade jars, mugs, mustards, napples, pans for steam tables, petite marmites, pin trays, pot pie or pudding dishes, punch bowls or salad bowls, ramekins, relish dishes, refrigerator pans, salad dishes, sauce boats, sole dishes, souffles, sugars and creamers, sugars, stew pots, teapots, teapot tiles, twin-tea sets, urn liners, vases, water servers and Welsh Rarebit dishes. Nos. 3, 4, 5, are also very early marks, according to Harvey Duke, Hall China, Book I, p. 12. You will find several more marks shown with the word "Hall" in a circle. No. 6 was filed June 1, 1939, claiming use for one month before

that time. No. 7 and 8 were filed April 12, 1961, claiming use for one month prior. No. 9, "Hall" in a rounded rectangle gives us a key to the date of several marks shown, and it was filed for registration February 20, 1969, claiming use since Janury 6, 1969. No. 10 was filed May 11, 1984, and first used July 14, 1981. No. 11 and all of the marks very similar to this one, were used over a long period of time, also. Harvey Duke gave a beginning date around 1932, and it was still shown in the *Gift and Tableware Reporter Directory* in August 1967, used on kitchenware. Nos. 12, 13: notice the last line in nos. 12 and 13 - "Dec. 80" does not mean December 1980 - Dec. could be for decoration. These were on dishes made in 1930's or 1940's. Nos. 14, 15, 16, "Harmony house" were on products made for Sears. No. 17, "Hallcraft," was designed by Eva Zeisel (see that listing).

Nos. 18 to 21 were on products made by Hall for the Red Cliff Company (see that listing). Nos. 22, 23, 24, "Owens-Illinois:" This glass company had ceramic plates made to give to druggists who ordered pharmacy bottles. No. 24 is the design used on the front of the plate which was registered by Owens-Illinois Glass Company on August 5, 1963, claiming use since 1958 for use on china dinnerware and coffee pots. Notice the wide variety of customers that Hall China Company made products for such as railroads, airlines, restaurants and various selling agencies such as Montgomery Wards, Sears and Roebuck and the Jewell Tea Company. But please remember, these customers ordered from many different potteries besides Hall China Company. See the listing Tea, Various Companies for a McCormick Tea mark.)

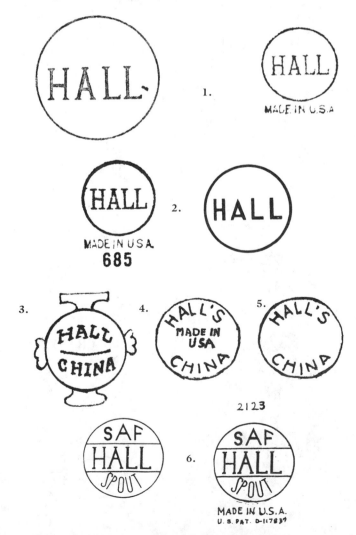

1.

2.

685

3.

4.

5.

2123

6.

7.

Super-Ceram

8.

9.

Hall

10.

Hi-TECH

GOLDEN OAK
PATTERN

HALL'S
SUPERIOR
QUALITY
Kitchenware

MADE IN
U. S. A.

11.

HALL'S
SUPERIOR
QUALITY
Kitchenware

MADE IN
U. S. A.

12. HALL CHINA.
SET. NO. 2
BLUE BELL
DEC. 80 BLUE

13.
HALL CHINA
SET NO. 2
BUTTERCUP
DEC. 80 BLUE

14.

15.

16.

HARMONY HOUSE
QUALITY · DESIGN · COLOR
4538-MARCIA.
H.H. PACIFIC BLUE
and
H.H CHERRY PINK

17.

HALLCRAFT

18.

Red-Cliff Ware

19.

RED·CLIFF
IRONSTONE
Fine China
"Wheat"

20.

RED·CLIFF
IRONSTONE
Grafio

21.

RED-CLIFF
IRONSTONE
Tea Leaf
TRADEMARK

OWENS
22. ILLINOIS

23. OWENS-ILLINOIS

24.

HALL

MADE IN
U. S. A.

25.

SPRINGTIME
PATTERN

HALL'S
SUPERIOR
QUALITY
Kitchenware

MADE IN
U. S. A.

26.

© Hall ®

27.

Hall

© ®

MADE IN U.S.A.

2975

28.

AUG 3 - 1979

Hall

© ®

MADE IN U.S.A.

29.

HALL

MADE IN U.S.A

355

30.

HALL

31.

Hall

MADE IN U.S.A.

291

32. A.I.S

HALL
MADE IN U.S.A.

33.

HALL'S
SUPERIOR
QUALITY
KITCHENWARE

MADE IN
U. S. A.

34. ROSE Parade
1259

1623

HALL

35.

MADE IN U.S.A.

PANAGRA

MFG. BY
THE HALL CHINA CO.

36.

HALL
MADE IN U.S.A.
38. **479**

HALL CHINA
37. UNDERGLAZE

39.

TRICOLATOR
PRODUCT

40.
MADE IN U.S.A.

SUPERIOR HALL QUALITY
DINNERWARE

PEACH BLOSSOM
MADE IN
41. U.S.A.

nov. 15 1962

MADE EXCLUSIVELY FOR
WESTINGHOUSE
42. BY
The Hall China Co.
MADE IN U.S.A.

PATTERN BY
HALL CHINA
ANOTHER
43. ANNIVERSARY
EXCLUSIVE

PRIMROSE
PATTERN BY
HALL CHINA
ANOTHER
GRAND UNION
EXCLUSIVE
44.

MARDI-GRAS
PATTERN BY
HALL CHINA
ANOTHER
ANNIVERSARY
EXCLUSIVE
45.

MARDI-GRAS
PATTERN BY
HALL CHINA
ANOTHER
ANNIVERSARY
EXCLUSIVE
46.

"TIP-POT"
PAT.
PEND.
The ultimate in serving hot tea or coffee
10 CUP · FIREPROOF · HALL CHINA
ANOTHER
FORMAN FAMILY
USA PRODUCT
47.

GOLDEN GLO

WARRANTED
22 CARAT GOLD
48.

Pam Pam
MADE BY
HALL CHINA
49.

HALL
2210
50.

SUPERIOR HALL QUALITY
DINNERWARE
GOLDEN OAK
PATTERN
51.

SUPERIOR HALL QUALITY
DINNERWARE
SPRINGTIME
PATTERN
52.

MADE EXPRESSLY
FOR
MINNERS & CO.
NEW YORK, N.Y.
BY
THE HALL CHINA CO.
53.

Made Exclusively For
MONTGOMERY WARD & CO.
CHICAGO
BY
The Hall China Co.
54.
5121

THE HALL CHINA CO. OHIO
EAST LIVERPOOL
55.

STANDARD AIRWAYS
BY
HALL CHINA
56.

APR 1 - 1977

Adjusto®
Tea Pot

ADJUST STRENGTH OF TEA TO YOUR TASTE

EXCLUSIVE PRODUCT

FORMAN (4) FAMILY

HALL PORCELAIN

57.

JUN 13 1968

MADE EXPRESSLY FOR

WESTERN
AIRLINES

BY

HALL CHINA CO.

SUPPLIED BY

MINNERS & CO.

U. S. A.

58.

THE ENTERPRISE ALUMINUM CO.
MASSILLON, OHIO
SUPERIOR QUALITY
KITCHEN WARE
Drip-O-lator
TRADE MARK REG. U.S. PAT. OFF.
PATENT NOS. 1370782-1743925

59.

MADE EXPRESSLY FOR

EASTERN AIRLINES

BY

HALL CHINA CO.

FURNISHED BY

MINNERS & CO.

CA-0034

60.

PAL

MADE IN USA

61.

JUN 6 - 1978

HALL CHINA
OVEN-PROOF GOLDEN GLO

Heat gradually to desired temperature. Wash by hand only with
mild soap. Do not use abrasives
or detergents.

62.

HALL CHINA CO.

FOR

GUMP'S - SAN FRANCISCO

T. W. A.
PART #44-1136
HALL CHINA
FROM
MINNERS & CO. INC.

63.

STEPHEN LEEMAN
PRODUCTS COMPANY
WEST NYACK, N. Y.
EPICURIO No. 971
MADE IN U. S. A.

64.

MAY 2 3 1978

ORIGINAL DESIGN
FROM THE
OHIO A A A
COLLECTION GALLERY
1909 WHITE
HALL MADE IN U.S.A.
1978

65.

AMERICANA
OF
NEW YORK
BY
H. FRIEDMAN & SONS
NEW YORK

HALL

66.

MADE IN
U. S. A.
1973

SEP 27 1972

innkare

mfg for IMART Memphis Tenn 38118
U.S.A.

67.

JUL 1 2 1974

innkare®

MADE IN U.S.A.

69.

Hall
ARTISTONE

HANDCRAFTED BY 68.

DENBY

ENGLAND

ERNEST
S t
John
CREATIONS
MADE IN
U S A

70.

duPont

H O T E L

duPont

WILMINGTON, DELAWARE

71.

MADE
EXPRESSLY FOR
INTERNATIONAL
HOTEL SUPPLY CO.
BOSTON, MASS.

1554-IHS 31

HALL 72.

MADE IN
U. S. A.

THE
CUBE
REG. TRADE MARK
REG. No. 693783
Brit Pats 110952 & 258456
AND ABROAD
U.S.A. PAT. 1380668-21
1599957-6
73.
CUBE TEAPOTS Ltd
LEICESTER

MADE IN U.S.A.

PAL
74.
MADE IN USA

Size   Medium
Brunswick Corporation
Mfg. by Hall China Co.
East Liverpool, OH U.S.A.
Date   75.

85.
MADE IN U.S.A.
-2923

86.
MADE IN U.S.A.
-2923

COLD   SPOT
REFRIGERATOR DISH
BY
THE HALL CHINA CO.
76.

T-BALL TEAPOT
MADE FOR
BACHARACH
BY
HALL CHINA
COMPANY
PATENT APPLIED FOR

77.
3272

87.

Kraft
INC

MADE EXPRESSLY FOR
KRAFT INC
BY
THE HALL CHINA CO.
MADE IN U S A

Made Exclusively for
WESTINGHOUSE By
The Hall China Co.
MADE IN U.S.A.
88.

MADE IN U.S.A.
1320

H. FRIEDMAN & SONS
N.Y.C

78.

MADE IN U.S.A.
2649

79.

Hall
©   ®

MADE IN U.S.A.
2953

80.

HALL
MADE IN U.S.A.
5074
MADE EXCLUSIVELY
FOR
WESTINGHOUSE

89.

American Airlines
73-PO-15

Hall   90.

MADE IN U.S.A.

HALL'S
SUPERIOR

TESTED
AND APPROVED
BY
Mary Dunbar
JEWEL
HOMEMAKERS
INSTITUTE

QUALITY
KITCHENWARE

81.

SUPERIOR HALL QUALITY
TESTED
AND APPROVED
BY
Mary Dunbar
JEWEL
HOMEMAKERS
INSTITUTE
DINNERWARE

82.

AUG 2 4 1978

AMERICAN AIRLINES

HALL
MADE IN U.S.A

91.

SUPERIOR HALL QUALITY
TESTED
AND APPROVED
BY
Mary Dunbar
JEWEL
1978
DINNERWARE

83.

HALL'S
SUPERIOR

TESTED
AND APPROVED
BY
Mary Dunbar
JEWEL
1978

84.

QUALITY
KITCHENWARE

Don
STAKUPS ©
by Hall ®

92.

73-DI-36

APR 1 6 1973

HALL CHINA
OVEN-PROOF SILVER GLO

Start with cold oven. Heat
gradually to desired temperature. Wash by hand with mild
soap. Do not use abrasives or
detergents.

94.

MADE EXPRESSLY FOR
ALLEGHENY
AIRLINES
CR-15
BY
HALL CHINA
SUPPLIED BY   93.
MINNERS & CO.
U.S.A.

MADE EXPRESSLY FOR
NATIONAL AIR LINES
BY
HALL CHINA CO.   95.
FURNISHED BY
MINNERS & CO.

DEC 15 1956

EXPRESSLY MADE FOR
BRANIFF
INTERNATIONAL

HALL
CHINA
1269

96.

HALL
1620
MADE IN U.S.A.
FOR
TRANS-CANADA
AIR LINES
97. SUPPLIED BY
CASSIDY'S LTD.

HALL 98.

421

U A L

D-C-7

5-54

JAN 11 1972

T-10-CP
Aladdin Synergetics, Inc.
NASHVILLE, TENNESSEE
99.

Hall

temp·rite ®
by *Aladdin*
NASHVILLE, TENNESSEE
100.

SuperCeram
HALL
U.S.A.
101.

AUG 3 0 1974

MADE EXPRESSLY FOR
DELTA
AIR LINES
102. BY
HALL CHINA CO.

AUG 1 4 1970

TWA   103.

PART # 44-1370

TWA

HALL
MADE IN
U.S.A.
1616
105.

HALL
MADE IN U.S.A.
O-1660
104. 44-DI-0008
EASTERN

THE
TEXAS T&P PACIFIC
RAILWAY
106.

CANADIAN PACIFIC
B.C. COAST
STEAMSHIPS
107.

(SMALL PRINT;
"WORLD'S GREATEST
TRAIN SYSTEM")

MADE EXPRESSLY FO
108. *DELTA*
AIRLINES
BY
HALL CHINA CO.
THROUGH
WHITLOCK-DOBBS INC

73-DI-32
MADE EXPRESSLY FOR
AMERICAN 109.
AIRLINES
BY
HALL CHINA
SUPPLIED BY
MINNERS & CO.
U.S.A.
1672

NASSAU CHINA CO.
TRENTON, N.J.
110.

CANADIAN
NATIONAL
SYSTEM
112.

HALL
MADE IN U.S.A.
111.

SOUTHERN PACIFIC
113.

*Burlington
Route*
114.

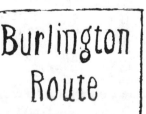
SEABOARD
THROUGH
THE HEART
OF THE
SOUTH
RAILWAY
115.

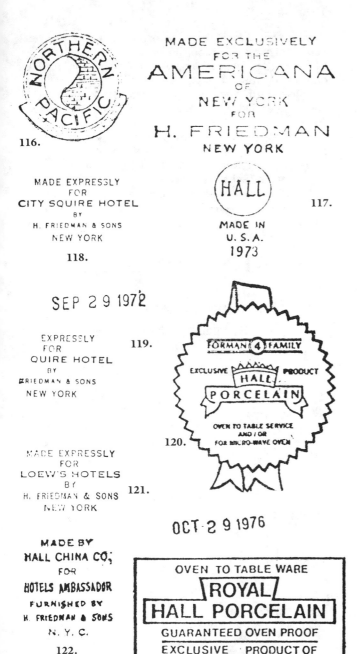

116.

117.

118.

119.

120.

121.

122.

123.

Hallelujah Pottery. Sewanne, Tennessee. Peter Goubeaud, a studio potter, would be better described as a handsome, burly, bearded, six feet tall, well educated, mountain craftsman. Very much the family man who has built his own home as he was able to spare time from potting. Goubeaud received his schooling on the G.I. Bill and football scholarships. He spent one year at Wake Forest University before serving in Vietnam. When he came home, he worked as a brakeman on the railroad. He married in 1968, and in 1971, he started his schooling again at the School of Art in Laguna Beach, California. He received a B.A. degree from Long Island University in New York. For a while, he worked at the Big Star Pottery in Texas until it closed. He then worked for a pottery firm in Florida, in production pottery. Four children were born to the Goubeauds, and when Peter decided to start his own pottery, he had just enough money to buy clay. He made the pots, sold the pots to buy more clay, and from this

humble beginning, Hallelujah Pottery was born out of pure faith. Peter makes stoneware functional pieces fired to cone eleven which he sells at craft fairs, etc. In 1984, he built a wood-fired kiln to make salt glazed stoneware besides his regular stoneware. He incises the mark, "Hallelujah," and the date on the bottom of the pieces when they are leather hard with a little bamboo stick.

Halm Art Pottery Company. Sandy Hills (later Hudson Falls), New York. 1844 to June 1880. The pottery was founded by George R. Halm in 1877, and by 1878 was making 1,000 pieces of terra cotta artware per week. The pottery was not successful and was sold in June 1880, and art pottery probably was not made after that time. The whole operation was closed down by 1887. Evans describes a piece in George S. McKearin's collection which was a "lathe turned vase of classic shape in red earthenware." In the *Pottery Collectors Newsletter*, September 1977, p. 75, a rare and beautiful piece for sale was described as a "bulbous vase, eight inches high, lathe turned redware, with a silver gray color with burnt orange, number and dark red decoration." (Information and mark: Paul Evans, *Art Pottery of the U.S.*, p. 127.)

HALM·ART·POTTERY·CO.
SANDY
HILL
N.Y.

Ham Brothers. Tuscaloosa County, Albama. Around 1880. Made salt glazed stoneware. (Information and impressed mark: E. Henry Willett and Joey Brackner, *The Traditional Pottery of Alabama*, pp. 56 & 57.)

HAM·BROS.

Hamilton, Clem. Tuscarawas County, Ohio. Around 1870. Thorn lists earthenware as product. Ramsay lists brownware. (Ramsay, p. 235,; Thorn, p. 129.)

CLEM HAMILTON

Hamilton, James and Company. Greensboro, Pennsylvania. According to Joseph H. Bausman, A.M. in the *History of Beaver County, Pennsylvania*, New York: Knickerbacher Press, 1904, p. 775, the Hamilton brothers, James and Lute, operated as James Hamilton and Company. They made common stoneware, jugs, crocks, etc. 50 or 60 years ago - making the starting date for the Hamiltons between 1844 and 1854. They got their clay on a hill near the house of John Dickey on the west side of Brady's Run and made the pottery in Bridgewater, Pennsylvania. According to Gordon C. Baker, "Pottery of Greensboro and New Geneva, Pennsylvania," *Spinning Wheel*, pp. 14-17, this partnership continued until 1857, after moving to Greensboro, Pennsylvania, when Leet (Baker's name) or Lute (Bausman's name) left the partnership to form **Hamilton and Company**. Then in 1866, Leet Hamilton formed a partnership with John Jones to become Hamilton and Jones. James continued on his own until 1880 when he sold to T.F. Reppert. (See Hamilton and Jones for more.) (Marks: Guappone, pp. 15-20; Schaltenbrand, pp. 2, 51; Stewart and Consentino, *Stoneware*, pp. 83, 124. The Eagle Pottery mark is attributed to James Hamilton by Gordon C. Baker, p. 15.)

Hamilton and Jones. Greensboro, Pennsylvania. 1866-1898. Formed of partnership John Jones and William Leet or (Lute) Hamilton. (See James Hamilton and Company for previous history.) In 1897, the pottery building burned, and the business was moved into the then vacant Williams and Reppert pottery building, but after one more year, Hamilton and Jones closed, nearly bankrupt. They made stoneware with blue lettering and designs, stenciled and freehand. (Information: Gordon C. Baker, "Pottery of Greensboro and New Geneva, Pennsylvania," *Spinning Wheel*, November 1973, p. 15. Marks: Schaltenbrand, pp. 12, 57; Guappone, pp. 21-27, and the Baker article already mentioned. The Star Pottery mark and a Union Pottery mark are attributed to Hamilton and Jones by Baker, p. 15.)

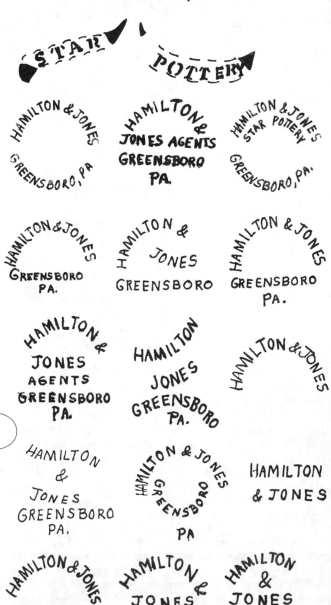

HAMILTON & JONES

Hamilton, Nan. Cambridge, Massachusetts. 1971 to present (1984). Studio potter, makes funtional stoneware and porcelain with cobalt iron sgraffito designs and animals and scenes, all one of a kind. Nan also makes painted tiles with scenes inlaid in handmade tables, cabinets and boxes. Nan is a teacher at Mudville school (see that listing). (Marks: no. 1, incised on tile.)

1. NH (date)   2. (date)

Hamilton Road Pottery. From 1856 to 1865, the pottery was owned by Michael and Nimrod Tempest who made Rockingham, yellowware and brownware fruit jars. In 1865, the pottery was purchased by Federick Dallas which he eventually refitted to manufacturing cream-colored (c.c.ware) and stone china (ironstone) ware. In 1879, two kilns were built to fire decorated ware. (See the listing for Mary Louise McLaughlin for the financing and use of these kilns.) At one time, the Dallas Pottery was firing pottery for over 200 women in Cincinnati when the pottery craze was at its heighth. It was undoubtedly the work of these women of the Cincinnati Pottery Club that made the Dallas Pottery well known, Mary Louise McLaughlin and Maria Longworth Nichols Storer. Their work was first exhibited in 1879 at the seventh Cincinnati Industrial Exposition along with more common household pottery of good quality. Dallas Pottery made the Cincinnati faience pottery, but Evans, p. 77, said most of it must have been unmarked. Few examples have been found. Dallas died in 1881. In 1882, all Cincinnati underglaze faience work stopped, and in July 1882, the announcement of the plant closing was made. (Information and marks: Lois Lehner, *Ohio Pottery and Glass*, p. 30. Paul Evans, *Art Pottery of the U.S.*, p. 78.)

DALLAS

FRED. DALLAS.
Pure Red Clay.
HAMILTON ROAD POTTERY
CIN. O
AUG. 1880

Hamilton Tile Works Company/Ohio Tile Company. Hamilton, Ohio. Before 1884 to 1901. Adolf Metzner, a druggist in Indianapolis, was a talented artist and amateur potter and tile maker. He had relatives in Hamilton, Ohio, and they told him the Royal Pottery was for sale. A Mr. Hatt from Indianapolis and Metzner operated as **Metzner, Hatt and Com-**

pany in the old Royal Pottery. At first they met only with failure. Hatt retired and was succeeded by J.L. Bieler, also of Indianapolis. Now the firm was **Metzner and Bieler**. Finally, they hired a man who knew how to make tile, Robert Minton Taylor, and incorporated the company as the **Robert Minton Taylor Ceramic Company**, but Taylor didn't own any of the business. Taylor didn't stay long, but Metzner never gave up. Finally, he and his sons, Otto and Max, made tile with a splendid clay body, handsome designs and magnificent glazes, according to the article cited. In 1884, Juilius Bunsen (nephew of the inventor of the Bunsen burner) and a Mr. Wild joined the Metzners and the name became the **Hamilton Tile Works**. They failed in 1899, and local people bought the plant and named it the **Ohio Tile Company**. It was not very successful either and lasted only until 1909, and that was the end of tile making in Hamilton. (Information: D.W. McClung, editor, "The Hamilton Tile Works Company, Artistic Hearth and Facing Tiles," *The Centennial Anniversary of Hamilton, Ohio*, 1891, pp. 302, 303.; and Everett Townsend, "Development of the Tile Industry in the U.S.," *American Ceramic Society Bulletin,* May 1943, p. 138. Marks: sent by Helen Miller and Eudell Baker, Butler County Historical Society, Hamilton, Ohio. Notice backward N on mark 2.)

1. THE
HAMILTON
TILE WORKS-CO
HAMILTON
OHIO

2. HAMILTON

3. HAMILTON. O.

Hammond Research Corportion. Gloucester, Massachusetts. Filed for registration of this mark no. 1 on February 8, 1949, for use on cups, saucers, dishes made of china, claiming use since December 21, 1948. Mark 2 was filed December 6, 1950, claiming use since October 2, 1950, for the same products.

1. **STICWARE**

2. **MAGNEWARE**

Hampshire Pottery. Keene, New Hampshire. 1871 to 1923. Started by James Scolly Taft. At first they made very ordinary redware and later stoneware jugs, crocks, flowerpots, milk pans and pitchers. In 1878 or 1879, the firm started making Majolica in green, brown, yellow and blue colors with raised decorations. The early pieces were not marked. In 1883, Wallace L. King was hired to run a department which was to produce decorative pottery. A line of art specialties requiring as many as five firings was developed called Royal Worcester. Several artists were hired, and the emphasis was on art pottery right up to the World War I when the plant was closed temporarily. In 1916, Taft sold the factory to George Morton of Boston. When the factory opened again after the war, white hotel china and mosaic floor tile were added to the line. The factory closed in 1923. A mark used by this pottery was an M inside an O designating Emoretta, wife of Cadmon Robertson who entered the business in 1904. In the *Complete Directory of Glass Factories and Potteries of the United States and Canada*, 1902 and 1903, J.S. Taft and Company were listed as making dinner sets, toilet sets, short sets of odd dishes, some decorated. Evans mentions another pottery that was purchased by Hampshire Pottery by 1874 in Keene. The second pottery was begun in 1871 by Starkey and Howard, later purchased by W.P. Chamberlain and E.C. Baker before being purchased by Hampshire Pottery. (Information: "First Hampshire Pottery Was Made One Hundred Years Ago," staff written, *Tri State Trader*, December 21, 1971, p. 2; and Paul Evans, "Hampshire Pottery," *Spinning Wheel*, September 1970, p. 22; also, Lehner, *American Kitchen and Dinner Wares*, p. 74. Marks: no. 1 on pitcher with handpainted scene of church, trees and flowers and raised design around the upper ⅓ of pitcher. Handpainted, but not artist signed. Nos. 2, 3, Evans, p. 132; no. 4, 5, from pictures of jugs in Joan Pappas and Harold Kendall, *Hampshire Pottery Manufactured By J.S. Taft and Company, Keene, New Hampshire*, p. 7. This is an excellent book full of colored pictures of the beautiful ware. Nos. 6, 7, Deb and Gini Johnson, p. 89; no. 8, Ramsay, p. 281; nos. 9, 10, 11, are very early marks from Barber, *Marks of American Potters*, p. 98.)

1. J.S.T. & CO. KEENE.N.H.

2. HAMPSHIRE

3. Hampshire Pottery

4. J.S. TAFT & CO. KEENE, N.H.

5. J.S.TAFT & COMPANY KEENE, N. H.

6.

7.  Hampshire Pottery

8.

9. 10.

11.

Handicraft Guild of Minneapolis. Minneapolis, Minnesota. 1904 to 1919. The guild provided instruction in various handcrafts including pottery making at 2nd and 10th Streets. The clay used came from Red Wing Pottery. In April 1905, James T. Webb was managing the Guild's pottery production with seven potter's wheels and two kilns. Students, teachers and some artists worked at various times to fill their individual needs. The first pieces were terra cotta with glazing, and later a decoration was added. The Guild incorporated in 1905 and relocated to 10th Street in 1907. Both thrown and molded pieces were made. (Information: Thomas Turnquist, "The Handicraft Guild of Minneapolis, 1904-1919," *American Art Pottery*, April 1983, p. 8. Mark: from Turnquist, sent by letter.)

Handicraft Guild of Minneapolis

Hand, Russ. Columbus, Ohio. 1976 to present. A studio potter making functional stoneware and some sculptured pieces.

Hankscraft Company. Madison, Wisconsin. Hankscraft Company was a manufacturer of electrical appliances sold through catalogs such as the Butler Brothers in the 1920's through the 1940's. Various companies made products for Hankscraft such as inserts for baby dishes, bottle warmers, egg cookers, etc. The inserts were marked as shown. In material dated 1941 sent by Larry Paul, research writer, was a picture of what Hankscraft called a "Hospitality Set" which they sold. Centered on a tray was the electrical toaster made by Hankscraft and ceramic cups, saucers, butter dishes and bread trays, etc. to make a complete set. They made electrically heated children's serving or baby food dishes and an egg cooker. The company began to market the egg cooker in 1920. The recessed mark no. 1 shown was on an egg cup or server.

1. HANKSCRAFT 008

2. HANKSCRAFT 600

Hansen, Gail. Cambridge, Massachusetts. 1978 to present (1984). Studio potter, working at Mudville School (see Mudville listing), makes highly decorative high fired functional ware with decorations carved into cobalt slip of flowers and animals, etc. Results are blue designs on white glossy glazed background.

gail hansen '84

Happy Clay. Emeryville, California. Filed for registration of this mark on October 22, 1981, claiming use since December 28, 1980, for use on ceramic products, such as plates and platters, with painted designs.

HAPPY CLAY

Harder, Charles M. Harder was a professor of ceramic art, a professional and industrial designer of ceramics. In 1919 he attended Texas A and M University. In 1925, he graduated from the Art Institute of Chicago. In 1927, he was teaching ceramics in the College of Ceramics, Alfred, New York. He became an assistant professor at the college in 1931 and received a B.S. degree there in 1935. He did post graduate studies at the Art Institute of Chicago in 1935, and then returned to Alfred to teach again as a full professor. He became head of the design department in 1944 after helping to direct it since 1938. He won many honors and awards, including a Gold Medal at the Paris International Exposition in 1937, the Binns Medal and others. He was made a fellow in the American Ceramic Society in 1947, and he was also a member of the Ceramic Educational Council. (Information: Garth Clark, *A Century of Ceramics in the U.S.*, pp. 295, 296. Incised mark: Linda Steigleder, from the booklet published by the Everson Museum of Art to accompany the 1978 exhibition, ''A Century of Ceramics in the U.S.'')

Hardesty China Company. New Brighton, Pennsylvania. From late 1930's into the 1940's. Eugene Hardesty received a degree in ceramic engineering from Pennsylvania State College in 1929. Then he worked for Mayer China a number of years before starting his own pottery to make a fine thin translucent vitrified dinnerware. He was killed in an auto accident in 1947. But the pottery was not listed in *1947 - 11th Industrial Directory of Pennsylvania*, so it must have been closed before his death. (Information: ''Eugene Hardesty,'' *Bulletin of American Ceramic Society*, March 1948, p. 147. Marks: Quality Stamp Company, East Liverpool, Ohio.)

Brighton China

Harding China Company. See Kingwood Ceramics.

Hare, William. Wilmington, Delaware. This mark was found pictured in Smith, p. 3, who says he made stoneware crocks, jars, jugs, etc. It is not in the Watkins books or any other standard reference book.

WM. HARE
WILMINGTON, DEL.

Harker, George S., Pottery. East Liverpool, Ohio. 1853 or 1854 to 1890, became Harker Pottery in 1890, which became Harker China Company in 1931. There were several owners and combinations of owners after 1840 until the pottery became the George S. Harker Pottery. Benjamin Harker was the first owner in 1840. His sons, Benjamin Jr. and George

S., had various partners such as James Taylor, William G. Smith, and Mathew Thompson. Various books give different dates for the combination of partners between 1844 and 1854. But around that time, the history of the pottery became stable because of George S. Harker who became sole owner. He did take in various partners before his death in 1864, but the name of the pottery remained the same as various people and family members ran the operation. He made yellowware and Rockingham ware. (See listing for Harker Pottery. Mark: J. Agnes Spring.)

Harker Pottery. In 1839, an Englishman, Benjamin Harker, Sr., sold whatever he owned in England, came to Ohio, bought a patch of ground, erected a log cabin, built a beehive kiln, moved his clay down off a big hill by mule, ground it by hand and in 1840, started a pottery business which lasted until 1972 and culminated in the Harker Pottery. The pottery researchers do not agree at all on the dates of the early meanderings and partnerships of the Harkers, and I can't imagine Benjamin and his successors worrying very much about record-keeping as they fought the weather, primitive methods, and bone weary tiredness, just trying to get that clay off the big hill and made into usable products. They probably never dreamed that in the 1980's somebody would be trying to figure out what they were doing back then. There were no good roads and no railroads, but the timber was uncut and served as a source of fuel, even though that meant a lot more work to cut it. A few weeks after Harker arrived, James Bennett came to town and started his pottery in East Liverpool, Ohio, which is considered the first operable pottery in the district. Harker furnished clay to Bennett which gave Harker a little capital. It was after seeing Bennett take the first pottery out of his kiln that Harker got the idea to make pottery too. Up until then he had intended just to farm his ground.

Benjamin Harker didn't live too long. From 1844-1847 his two sons, Benjamin, Jr., and George, operated the pottery now called the **Etruria Pottery**. Some sources say George died as early as 1851, but it seems, perhaps, he lived until around 1864. But it was during this period Benjamin, Jr. had to go to the Civil War. Partners and operators came and went, and confusion reigns in the history books. From 1846 or 1847 to 1851, the name was **Harker** (George), **Taylor** (James) **and Company**. See that listing. From 1851 to 1854, it was **Harker** (George), **Thompson** (Mathew) **and Company**. The companies just listed operated on the River Road east of what became the Homer Laughlin Pottery. When Benjamin and George separated, Benjamin took a partner, William G. Smith, and operated as **Harker and Smith** at the Northeast corner of Second and Washington streets from 1853 to around 1857 when the pottery became **Foster and Garner**. At the time of separation, George operated the **George S. Harker Pottery** which became the Harker Pottery we know. (See the George S. Harker Company listing.) When Benjamin came back from the Civil War, he worked in the Wedgwood Pottery which was sold to Wallace and Chetwynd in 1881. When George died, his sons William W. Harker and Harry N. Harker were very young. A brother-in-law, David Boyce, filled in until the boys were old enough to take over. In 1877, Benjamin, Jr. sold any interest he still retained in the original Harker pottery, and it was George's boys who became responsible for the founding of the pottery that concerns the collectors of dinnerware. In July 1899, the firm incorporated, and from 1890 on it was known as the Harker Pottery with George's son, W.W. Harker as the first president.

The name Boyce runs through the Harker Pottery history. We have mentioned the first Boyce named David who came to the pottery when Benjamin, Jr. went to the Civil War, and who then stayed on until George's sons grew up enough to take over the business. David had a son, Charles R. Boyce, and the sons of Charles Boyce were executives in the pottery around 1940. Their names were David and Robert. Finally, in 1959, David G. Boyce became president. No doubt part of Harker's huge success for so very many years was the fact that not only did the family stay with the business, but a line of faithful employees also stayed, giving the company a certain pride in their products. By 1965 Harker was employing 300 people to turn out 25 million pieces annually, with tunnel kilns and the latest equipment. Harker developed a special engraving process which gave us "Cameoware." They featured a Russel Wright designed dinner service from 1953 to 1958.

According to Harvey Duke in the *Depression Glass Daze*. January 1978, **Columbia China** was a separate sales agency set up by Harker Pottery. He said they used different names and marks so that more than one outlet in a given town might think they were handling Harker Pottery's wares on an exclusive basis. He cited "Hotoven," "Columbia China Company," "Oven Ware," and "Sun Glow Bakerite" as example. "Cameoware" came in many different designs. The design was recessed in a white color. "Quaker Maid" by Harker had a dark brown glaze with drips and blotches of lighter colored glaze around the edges. This was a full line with plates, cups, accessory pieces, etc. "Bakerite" was a line of kitchen accessories including bowls, water bottles, rolling pins, spoons and forks for serving, cake plates, casseroles, etc. (Information: Lehner, *American Kitchen and Dinner Wares*, pp. 74, 75 & 76.; Ramsay, Jervis and Barber's books, as well as the "Oldest Pottery in America Marks Its 125th Anniversary" reprinted from *China, Glass and Tablewares*, January 1965, no page given. Also "Centenary Anniversary of Harker Pottery Company" from the *American Ceramic Society Bulletin*, XX, June 1941, p. 25. For more on patterns and products, see Lehner, *American Kitchen and Dinner Wares*, pp. 75, 76. Marks: The marks shown are photostatic copies from dishes or from Quality Stamp Company, East Liverpool, Ohio, unless otherwise indicted. Nos. 1-6 are copies of the same mark as shown by six different authoratative authors. The mark was used in the 1880-1890 era. This mark has been contested as having been an actual mark by a modern writer, but I don't believe we can ignore the fact that this many writers on marks said that it was used as a stamped mark on dishes. And I believe it should be presented to the readers: Mark no. 1, John Ramsay, *American Potters and Pottery*, p. 262; no. 2, Hazel Hartman, *Porcelain and Pottery Marks*, p. 112; no. 3, H.P. Jervis, "Worlds Pottery Marks," *Pottery, Glass and Brass Salesman*, February 19, 1913, p. 17; no. 4, Ralph and Terry Kovel, *Dictionary of Marks, Pottery and Porcelain*, p. 160; no. 5, John Spargo, *Early American Pottery and China*, p. 366; no. 6, C. Jordan Thorn, *Handbook of Old Pottery and Porcelain Marks*, p. 130. The works quoted were written at all different times from as early as 1913 to 1977. See bibliography for dates for books. The difference between this mark and other Harker

marks is the direction of the arrow. The copies vary a little due to the artists' interpretation. This is a good example of various artists' interpretations. Nos. 7, 8, 9, are very early marks used before 1900 from E.A. Barber, as cited, p. 105. No. 10 is not an early mark. This impressed mark was put on hound handled mugs, etc. of a Rockingham type of ware in the 1960's. These hound handled mugs were even made with an aqua-green glaze. They are collectible, but not old Rockingham. Nos. 11-13, "Cameoware," made in 1940's, was glazed with color, a template placed over it, and then sandblasted to give a recessed design of a different color and then glazed again. The process of manufacturing was expensive. No. 11, from 1945 directory, nos. 12 & 13, are photostatic copies from dishes. No. 14, "The Harker Hot Oven" mark was a colored decaled mark used on ovenware bowls, etc. made in 1930's and 1940's. No. 15, "Royal Dresden" used on semi-vitreous dinnerware in 1930 to 1940 era. There was also a mark written like this that said, "Early American," where this mark says "Royal Dresden." Nos. 16, 17, 18 on products first made in 1930's. See text on Columbia mark. Nos. 19 to 38 were marks used on products in the 1950's, some extending into the 1960's. No. 22, Rena London, "Collecting Harker China," *National Glass, Pottery and Collectable Journal*, September 1980, p. 21. No. 39 was an impressed mark on stoneware dinnerware being made when factory closed, but has been produced for quite a while. Nos. 40 to 42 were found on a translucent vitrified china dinnerware. No. 43 "Quaker Maid," used in 1960's until closing; had a dark brown glaze and was a heavy pottery or ironstone type of ware with a tan drip glaze around the edges. This was a full line of dinnerware and accessory pieces. Nos. 44, 45, used in 1960's until closing. Nos. 46 to 49, Jo Cunningham, *Collector's Encyclopedia of American Dinnerware*, pp. 136, 148, 152, 154.)

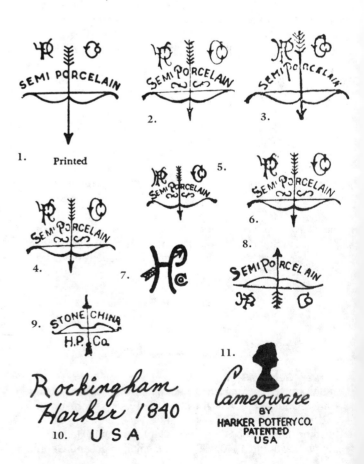

1. Printed

2.

3.

4.

5.

6.

7.

8.

9. STONE CHINA H.P. Co.

10. *Rockingham Harker 1840* USA

11. *Cameoware* BY HARKER POTTERY CO. PATENTED USA

12.  Cameo Ware by HARKER USA

13. *Cameoware* BY HARKER POTTERY CO PATENTED USA

14.  HOTOVEN HARKER THE OLDEST POTTERY IN AMERICA COOKINGWARE

15. *Royal Dresden by Harker Est 1840*

16.  ESTABLISHED 1873 COLUMBIA CHINAWARE

17.  COLUMBIA CHINAWARE

18. BAKERITE OVEN TESTED MADE IN USA WARRANTED 22 K GOLD 391

19.  COLONIAL USA 1840 HARKER STONEWARE OVENPROOF

20.  HARKER Pate sur Pate WARE POTTERY EST. 1840 RESISTS ACID·DETERGENTS·CRAZE

21.  The Harker Pottery Co. QUALITY Made In U.S.A. Since 1840

22. HARKER POTTERY MODERN AGE *The Ware of Tomorrow Made in U.S.A. Established 1840 Oldest in America*

23. *Barbecue* OUTDOOR-WARE by HARKER POTTERY CO. U.S.A.

24. STONE CHINA

25.  *Royal Gadroon* HARKER STONE POTTERY

26. HARKER 1840

27. *Royal Jackson* HARKER OLDEST POTTERY

28. *Harkerware* SINCE 1840

29. HARKERWARE *Russel Wright*

30. HARKER *Chesterton Ware* POTTERY EST 1840

31.  *Laurel* HARKER POTTERY EST 1840 RESISTS ACID·DETERGENTS·CRAZE

32. *Wild Rice* INTAGLIO by HARKER POTTERY CO. U.S.A.

33.  HARKER ENGOBE WARE *Bermuda Blue* U.S.A.

34.  OVEN-PROOF Harkerware SINCE 1840 DISH WASHER PROOF U.S.A.

35.  Harkerware SINCE 1840 U.S.A.

36.  HARKER POTTERY *Harkerware* SINCE 1840 EAST LIVERPOOL OHIO

37. WHITE ROSE *carv-kraft* ❖❖❖ BY HARKER

38. *Corinthian* HARKER U.S.A.

39. *Harkerware* STONE CHINA OVEN PROOF USA

40. *Harker* CHINA COMPANY U.S.A.

41.  Harker CHINA COMPANY U.S.A. TRANSLUCENT THERMOWARE

42. *Whitechapel* TRANSLUCENT THERMOWARE U.S.A.

43.  genuine *Quaker Maid* COOK WARE HARKER CHINA CO. East Liverpool, Ohio, USA

44. COUNTRY STYLE USA HARKER STONEWARE OVENPROOF

45.  COUNTRY STYLE USA 1840 HARKER STONEWARE OVENPROOF DISHWASHER SAFE

46.  ☆*Heritance*☆ BONE WHITE IRONSTONE OVENPROOF U.S.A.

47. *CCC* TRANSLUCENT CHINA U.S.A. *Enchantment*

48.  *Laurelton* HARKER CHINA CO. EST. 1840 U.S.A.

49. *American Engobe* MADE BY HARKER U.S.A.

Harker, Taylor and Company. East Liverpool, Ohio. 1846 to 1851. This was one of the Harker combinations of potters who laid the early foundation for the Harker China Company. See Harker Pottery listing. The mark or embossed inscription is on a yellowware water cooler with this inscription on an applied ornament on the side. (Information and mark no. 1: J.G. Stradling, "East Liverpool, Ohio: An American Pottery Town," *Antiques Magazine*, p. 1367. Marks: no. 2, John Ramsay, *American Pottery and Porcelain*, p. 263; no. 3, E.A. Barber, *Marks of American Potters*, p. 105.)

Harker, Thompson and Company. East Liverpool, Ohio. 1851 to 1854. A ceramic business card had the relief lettering shown in the book, *American Potters and Pottery*, by John Ramsay, figure no. 55, following p. 204. Ramsay dates Harker, Thompson and Company from 1851 to 1854. See the listing, Harker Pottery, for a discussion on the various combinations preceeding Harker China Company. Company made yellowware and Rockingham.

Harlem Crockery Company. 5th Avenue, New York, New York. Distributor or sales agency. Started 1910 and was still listed in the 1954 *Crockery and Glass Journal Directory* for dinnerware. In the 1945 *Crockery and Glass Journal Directory*, the company was listed as selling American earthenware and dinnerware with mark no. 1. By the 1954 listing, they were selling French, German and Italian dinnerware. (Mark 2 was from 1952 *Crockery and Glass Journal Directory*. Mark 3 was filed for registration April 17, 1957, under the name Harlem Crockery Company, claiming use since October 18, 1955, for use on china and earthen dinnerware. Very soon after that time, the company name became Arlen China Company until present.)

Harris, Charles W. Painesville, Ohio. Filed for registration of this mark in June 9, 1949, for use on flower pots of clay and ceramic materials having exterior coating finishes of different colors, claiming use since April 1, 1949.

SUEDE-POT

Harris, Thomas. Cuyahoga Falls (Akron), Ohio. 1863 to 1880. Made stoneware. (Information: C. Dean Blair, *The Potters and Potteries of Summit County, 1828-1915*, p. 27. Impressed mark: Thorn, p. 130.)

THOMAS HARRIS

Hartford Faience Company. Hartford, Connecticut. In the 1860's this was the Atwood Company which became Atwood Faience Company, and in 1900 was known as Hartford Faience Company. In 1905, the company started making electrical porcelain and commenced making high voltage insulators about 1925. Direct sales to utility companies ceased in 1947, and the company started making specialty porcelain products. (Information and incuse mark: Jack H. Tod, *Porcelain Insulators*, pp. 123, 124 and by letter.) Mark no. 1 is on pin type insulators; no. 2 is on dry press insulators; no. 3 is on specialty porcelain.)

H 1. 2. **H. F.** 3. **H. F. Co.**
A106

Hartman's Furniture and Carpet Company. Chicago, Illinois. Retailers filed for a claim to these marks September 22, 1924 and September 30, 1925, claiming use for approximately one year prior to that time. Marks to be used on chinaware and china dinner sets.

Hart, Various Family Potters. Ogdensburg, Sherburne and Fulton, New York (name changed from Oswego Falls to Fulton in 1830's). James and Samuel Hart made utilitarian type stoneware pottery, jugs, etc., in Oswego Falls from 1832 to 1840. James Hart moved to Sherburne in 1841 to open his own pottery, leaving Samuel Hart the sole owner in Oswego Falls or Fulton from 1840 to 1876. From around 1876 to 1895 the pottery was **Hart Brothers** in Fulton. In Sherburne, James was joined by his son, Charles, until 1858. Then Charles operated alone from 1858 to 1866 in Sherburne. In 1866, Charles took his son, Nahum, as a partner. They operated as **C. Hart and Son** until 1885. To complicate the picture, Charles Hart had a son, Charles Hart, Jr., who had a pottery in Ogdensburg from 1850-1858 which became **W. Hart** from 1858 to 1869 and **J.J. Hart** from 1869 to 1872. The following is a list of the potteries in Oswego Falls (Fulton):

James and Samuel from 1832 to 1840; Samuel, alone from 1840 to 1876; Hart Bros. from around 1876 to 1895. In Ogdensburg: J.J. Hart from 1869 to 1872; W. Hart from 1858 to 1869; C. Hart and Company from 1850 to 1858. In Sherburne: James and Charles Hart from 1841 to 1858; Charles, alone from 1858 to 1866; Charles and son, Nahum from 1866 to 1885. (Information: Regina Stewart and Geraldine Consentino, *Stoneware, A Guide for Beginning Collectors*, pp. 29, 71, 124; Marks: Stewart and Consentino, pp. 29, 61; Guilland, p. 238; "W. Hart," in Bill Grande, "Stoneware Pottery," *American Collector*, April 1980, p. 12; also Auction catalogue, "Early American Antiques," Garth's Auction Barn, Stratford, Ohio, August 8, 1970. "Harts-Fulton" mark, Dorothy Hammond, *Price Guide to Country Antiques and American Primitives*, 1975, p. 217.)

HARTS FULTON

C. HART & SON SHERBURNE

C. HART SHERBURNE

C. HART & CO. OGDENSBURGH

W. HART OGDENSBURG

S. HART FULTON

J. HART & SON SHERBURNE

J & S HART OSWEGO FALLS N.Y.

Hartsoe, John L. Near Lincolnton, North Carolina. Used the mark shown around 1923. John L. Hartsoe was one of the sons of Poley Hartsoe. Several generations of the Hartsoe family made pottery from around 1850 until Poley Hartsoe made his last kiln full in 1956. John L. Hartsoe did not make his living from making pottery, but coming from such a family he did learn to make pieces. Some are found marked "J.L.H." For the history of the whole family of Hartsoe potters, see Daisy Wade Bridges, *Potters of the Catawba Valley*, Charlotte, North Carolina: Mint Museum, 1980, pp. 17 to 20. (Information: Bridges, p. 17. Mark: Bridges, p. 56.)

J L H

Hartstone, Inc. Zanesville, Ohio. 1976 to present (1985). Patrick Hart, owner and founder, started in June 1975 in the building formerly occupied by Chatham Potters in Chatham, New Jersey. In October 1979, they started making products in the old J.B. Owen Pottery plant in Zanesville, Ohio. They phased out the plant in New Jersey after a while. They make beautiful cookie molds in the shape of various historical buildings, such as the Metropolitan Museum of Art and the Thomas Jefferson Memorial Foundation building. They make dinnerware and kitchen accessories with underglaze cobalt decorations, some with hand painted slip trail that make the pieces look enameled. The attractive ware is highly vitrified and durable and designed by well-known designers such as Francis Maida, Helena Uglow, Yale and Frances Foreman. (Marks shown are incised in clay on bottom of cups. Also shown is the company logo.)

Hartstone USA

HARTSTONE U.S.A. ©

Hartstone USA ©

© 1980 HARTSTONE

Hartzog, David. Vale, Lincoln County, North Carolina. 1808-1883. Stoneware and earthenware. (Information: Daisy Wade Bridges, *Potters of the Catawba Valley*, Charlotte, North Carolina: Mint Museum, 1980, pp. 15, 55. Mark: same book, pp. 18, 55.)

DAVIDHARTZOGHI2MAKE   D. H.

Haruta, Yosuke. Hanover, Michigan. 1972 to present (1985). Yosuke Haruta, studio potter, makes stoneware into functional and sculptured and slab built pieces, highly glazed and some hand painted. Sprayed oxides are heavily reduced in firing with combustible materials. Some of the pieces Yosuke showed at the December Fair in Columbus, Ohio, 1984 were beautiful wallhangings and all sorts of decorative pieces. Yosuke came from Japan in 1966 and attended Jackson Community College in Jackson, Michigan in 1967. In 1974, he received a B.F.A. Degree from Eastern Michigan University at Ipsilanti, Michigan. He has been working full time at making pottery since 1972. He is an artist as well as craftsman in clay.

Hasting (Wellington) and Belding (David). Ashfield, Massachusetts. (Pottery owned ⅓ share by John Guilford. See Orcutt, Eleazer and Various Associations for more on this.) It was started 1850, and in 1854 went into receivership.

Belding came from Whately, Massachusetts, and a small gray stoneware churn was found marked "D. Belding/Whately." Belding had gone into insolvency in Whately in 1847. Van Loon and Boyden took over the Ashfield Pottery in 1854 with John Guilford still retaining his ⅓ share. (Information and marks: no. 1, Lura Woodside Watkins, "The Stoneware of South Ashfield, Mass.," Stradling book, pp. 102, 103; marks nos. 2-3, Thorn, p. 130.)

HASTINGS & BELDING

1. ASHFIELD, MASS.

HASTINGS & BELDING
ASHFIELD.   **2. ASHFIELD**
3. MASS.

Hawthorn Pottery Company. Hawthorn, Pennsylvania. 1899 until after 1922, and was still listed in *Industrial Directory of Pennsylvania* 1922. From 1892-1894, George W. Arblaster had a pottery at the site of the Hawthorn Pottery. In 1894, W.T. Putney and E.A. Hamilton, operating as **Putney and Hamilton**, updated and expanded the pottery and finally incorporated in 1899 as the Hawthorne Pottery Company. In 1928, the land, buildings and machinery were sold and the pottery was dismantled. (Information and marks: Dr. James Measell, "The Hawthorne Pottery Company," *Pottery Collectors Newsletter*, March 1976, p. 15. Also same title in *Glaze*, January 1980, p. 4)

H.P.Co.
HAWTHORN, PA

H.P.CO.
Hawthorn, Pa

Haxstun, Ottman, and Company. Fort Edward, New York. Raycraft, p. 15 gave dates 1867-1872. Thorn, p. 130, had estimated 1875. Ramsay, p. 192 gave around 1875-1900. Stewart and Consentino, p. 124, gave 1857 to around 1882. In Thorn, p. 130 and Ramsay, p. 192, the spelling was Haxtun, which is an error. On p. 15 of Raycraft's book is a very clear picture showing correct spelling, Haxstun. Made stoneware with mark impressed. (See the listing for Ottman Brothers.) (Marks: Stradling, p. 132 and Don and Carol Raycraft, *Decorated Country Stoneware*, Paducah, Kentucky: Collector Books, pp. 12-15.)

HAXSTUN. OTTMAN & CO.
FORT EDWARD, N.Y.

HAXSTUN & CO.
FORT EDWARD
N.Y.

HAXSTUN & CO.
FORT EDWARD, N.Y.

Headman Pottery. Andrew Headman was in Rock Hill, Bucks County, Pennsylvania. 1806 or 1808 to 1840. Andrew's brother John Headman, 1800 to 1830, had a son Peter Head-

man, 1830 to 1870, and Peter's son, also named John, to after 1904. Andrew Headman also had a son Charles who made pottery from around 1840-1890. The Headmans all made slip decorated, sgraffito and redware with coarse body. Charles used an occassional mark of his name or initials inscribed. (Information: Spargo, p. 161, furnished son's names and dates. Marks: Barber, *Mark of American Potters*, p. 14; Thorn, p. 130.)

A H   **Chas. Headman**   **C H**

Healy, Susan G. Cincinnati, Ohio. 1976 to present. Susan, a studio potter, who makes humorous sculptured pieces has won several awards for her work and participated in the Liturgical Art Exhibit of Ohio, the Cincinnti Art Museum Invitational in 1981, etc. From 1976 to 1980 Susan marked pieces "Healy." From 1980 on the mark has been "S.G. Healy."

HEALY   **S.G.HEALY**

Heath Ceramics, Inc. Sausalito, California. 1945 to present (1986). The story of this company is closely tied to the history of Edith Kiertener Heath, who studied at the Chicago Art Institute for six years, was a supervisor in a federal art project, and who began working in ceramics in 1941 and 1942 by making dinnerware on a potter's wheel. Then in 1947, she designed and began production of Heath dinnerware with 10 employees and Brian Heath as manager. From that almost humble beginning, the Heath Ceramics business grew until in 1960 they moved into a beautiful new building built and designed for their individual company's needs. In 1961, a "Gourmet Line" was developed, and in 1963, the company also started making architectural tile as well as the other products. One great accomplishment was a tile mural 220' long by 10' high in the Occidental Center in Los Angeles. N.S. Gustin Company, Los Angeles, California, distributed the Heath Ceramic products. (Information: from company. Marks: no. 1 filed for registration June 9, 1959, claiming use since May 16, 1950, as shown; claiming also the use of the name, "Heath," since 1945.)

HEATH

HEATH
N. S. Gustin Co.

HEATH
©
MADE IN USA

Heighshoe, S.E. Somerset, Perry County, Ohio. Around 1850. Made stoneware and brownware. (Information and mark: Thorn, p. 131; Ramsay, p. 230.)

S.E. HEIGHSHOE
SOMERSET
O.

Heino, Vivika and Otto. Ojai, California. Vivika Timeriasieff was a native of Caledonia, New York, and studied at Rochester City Normal School, then at the Colorado College of Education with the emphasis on crafts. During the depression era, she studied painting and design at the California School of Fine Arts while she worked to pay her way. In 1937 or 1938, she started making pottery in Manuel Jalanivich's pottery classes, and that determined the course of her life. In 1942, Vivika had a teaching fellowship at Alfred University, where she studied with Charles Harder. She received a master's degree in 1944. For a while, she had a studio in New York City, until she became involved with the League of New Hampshire Craftsmen in their teaching programs, etc.

Otto Heino was a native of New England. He visited English potteries while stationed in England during W.W. II. Otto saw Bernard Leach at work on the wheel. After the war, he began to study with Vivika at the Sharon Art Center in New Hampshire. In 1950, they married and set up their first studio at Hopkinton, New Hampshire. In 1952, the couple moved to California, where Vivika took a job teaching at the University of Southern California, at the invitation of Glen Lukens. Otto also started teaching there in 1953, but in 1955, Otto changed his teaching position to the Chouinard Art Institute until 1963, when they moved back to the east coast. Vivika then taught at the Rhode Island School of Design from 1963 to 1965 and Otto worked in their studio. The Heino's maintained their own studios while teaching all through the years and continued a production that has lasted over 30 years now.

In 1973, they moved to Ojai, California, where they are still making pots (1985) in a beautiful studio, rebuilt and fashioned by Otto's carpentry. Some pieces pictured in various articles included an earthenware, chartreuse crackle lead glazed bowl by Vivika; a plate of stoneware with wax resistant nichel slip design (Bray, p. 55); a bottle of stoneware with ash and iron glaze (Clark and Hughto, p. 254). The couple has produced a wide range of architectural, functional and decorative pieces. The Heinos have received numerous awards for their work. In 1978, Otto received a Gold Medal from the Sixth Biennale Internationale de Ceramique D'Art in Vallauris, France. In 1959, they received a Silver Medal at the 1959 International Ceramic Exhibition at Ostend. Over the years, Vivika's work was included in San Francisco Women Artists' shows and National Ceramic Exhibitions and in displays at the Golden Gate International Exposition. They are among the very most outstanding potters in the country today and have been written about in many books and articles. (Information: Tom Turnquist, "Studio Pottery," *Antique Trader*, July 4, 1984, p. 75; Garth Clark, *A Century of Ceramics in U.S.*, p. 254; Hazel V. Bray, *The Potters Art in California*, pp. 54, 55. Marks: sent by Thomas Turnquist.)

Heirlooms of Tomorrow/California Originals. Manhattan Beach and Torrance, California. 1947 to present (1985). Employs 300 people. In the 1948 to 1953 *China and Glass Red Book Directories*, Heirlooms of Tomorrow was listed for porcelain figurines, cigarette boxes and sets, vases, shoes, slippers, miniature figurines, candy dishes, wall pockets, etc.

The porcelain pieces were decorated with applied lace and fancy roses, etc. By 1953, California Originals, an artware pottery, was listed under the trade name for the company, Heirlooms of Tomorrow. The 1961 listing included pottery artware; bowls, birds, lazy susans and casseroles. By 1965 in the *China, Glass and Tableware Directory*, under company names, Heirlooms of Tomorrow was listed and also California Originals. So the name change for the company was under way, and the name Heirlooms of Tomorrow was dropped in preference to the name, California Originals. William D. Bailey was president and sales manager. According to Derwich and Latos, p. 51, Sears, Penneys, Montgomery Wards and other large department stores have sold the products. This pottery also made liquor bottles for collections, antique and racing cars, etc. The plant covers 147,000 square feet in Torrance, California, at present. Just as Onondago Pottery finally took the tradename, Syracuse, for its proper name, Heirlooms of Tomorrow, seems to have taken the tradename, California Originals, to be the company name. (Marks: nos. 1, 2, from 1952 *Crockery and Glass Journal Directory*. No. 3 is a paper label. The rest are inscribed on various pieces.)

Hellman, Louis E. New York, New York. Selling agency, filed for registration of the name, "Princess China," November 30, 1936, for use on ceramic tableware, claiming use since November 9, 1936. Also, see Empire Crafts Corporation for a "Princess China" mark. Also, see Jackson China Company and Salem China Company.

Helzberg's Diamond Shops, Inc. Kansas City, Missouri. Filed for registration of this mark on July 3, 1968, for porcelain dinnerware.

Henderson, Alison. Dayton, Ohio. 1975 to present (1985). Studio potter, makes wheel thrown stoneware functional ware. Alison apprenticed to a Rhode Island potter. She moved to Chapel Hill, North Carolina, in 1978, then came on to Ohio. She has attended graduate classes at Rhode Island College and the University of North Carolina at Chapel Hill. She operates under the name, "Pottery by Alison."

Henderson, Texas, Various Potters. Henderson, Texas. The only book which listed potteries in Henderson, Texas, was the L.D. Byrd book, *100 Years of Texas Pottery*, pp. 128-133, and he listed five. The potteries Byrd lists were **Rushton Pottery**, 1869-1900, see that listing; **Cogburn and Protho** in Rusk County, 1850-1860; **J.F. Hunt**, 1890-1932; the **Russel Pottery**, 1900-1909; and **John Leopard and Son**, 1850-1879. According to Georgeanna Greer, by letter, the Henderson Pottery operated between 1890 and 1893 making salt glazed and slip glazed stoneware and brick. (Mark: on stoneware piece sent by Sherry B. Humphreys, Star of the Republic Museum, Washington, Texas.)

Henne, T.S. Shartlesville, Pennsylvania. Around 1800. Mark impressed. Made redware. (Thorn, p. 131.) Ramsay, p. 179, lists Daniel P. Henne around 1860-1870 and Joseph K. Henne (Daniel's son) around 1870-1880. (Mark: Thorn, p. 131.)

T. S. HENNE

Hercher, Joseph. Near village of New York, Scott County, Missouri. Sometime between 1830 and 1850. Made stoneware jugs and bottles. According to Edison Shrum, "Industrial Reformers Life Traced to S.E. Missouri Tract," *Tri*

State Trader, October 9, 1982, p. 40, there were seven potteries in this area in the same period. Other names mentioned by Shrum were S.D. Smith, Balsir Oartar and Burkhart Juengling. Bottles and jugs were found marked with their names. (Mark pictured in same article by Edison Shrum. Lettering was very irregularly impressed and the O was left out of county. Shrum said this was corrected in later marks.) Burkhart Juengling, who owned a pottery went out of the business of making stoneware around 1857 but later acquired Eisele's pottery through marriage to Eisele's widow. The Eisele-Juengling Pottery went out of business at the onset of the Civil War. Documents discovered by Shrum indicate that Joseph Hercher worked at both of the Juengling potteries under a lease agreement. (Information: Edison Shrum by letter. Mark: drawn from pictures sent by Shrum.)

JOSEPH HERCHER

JOSEPH HERCHER
SCOT CUNTY

Heritage Company. Uniontown, Pennsylvania. A group of local potters under the direction of P.G. Panky, started around 1975 to make stoneware pots in the old traditional style with Pennsylvania Dutch designs of flowers, hearts, birds, etc. The pieces are hand thrown, hand decorated and hand lettered. All designs are cobalt blue in very attractive blue-gray crocks. One crock was pictured with an Indian bust, a maple leaf and an oil derrick; one had an eagle, a buffalo and a riverboat; another had an anchor, horse's head and 1880's train engine. The brochure sent to me stated that each crock is stamped with the unique potter's mark at the base of the piece or the base of the handle, which serves as the official signature of the maker. But a second query for the marks brought the reply that the company didn't have anything showing the individual potters marks. Many potters have come and gone, and several of the potters are working at the New Geneva Stoneware Company in Masontown, Pennsylvania. Around 1979, Tom Smith became owner of the Heritage Pottery. He had Tom Smith Sales Company in Pittsburgh. No. 1 is the company's logo used while it was the Heritage Company. The remaining are not to be considered marks, they are simply a few of the various decorations used in the front of the pieces. They are decorations because they have no relationship to the maker or place of origin. Linn Newman worked as a logo carver at Heritage Company from 1976 to 1978. He is currently (1986) an owner of the New Geneva Stoneware Company (see that listing). Linn explained how the artwork was done at Heritage. He said, "All of their artwork was stamped from plexiglass carved molds and rubber letters from lettering sets. The cobalt was then trailed over the designs." Linn carved as many as 60 different designs for the Heritage Company.

1.

Hermann Family Potters. Milwaukee, Wisconsin. 1856-1935. Charles Hermann was a potter and grocer who started around 1856. In 1882 Louis Pierron, his stepson, joined Hermann at the factory, and in 1892 Pierron became the sole owner until 1935. The factory became the largest of eight that were operating in Milwaukee. The factory made stoneware crocks, jugs, churns, jars, etc. made from Ohio and Illinois clay. Many had gray and tan salt glaze and cobalt blue decoration. Hermann also made containers for various retail outlets, druggists, whiskey manufacturers and others with their names stenciled on the various pieces. A brother, Frederick Herrmann, (spelled differently) made pottery in Milwaukee from 1848 to 1884 and was followed by his son Albert. No marked examples of their ware has been found. Charles had two other brothers who made pottery, Christian Hermann, who worked for Frederick and then opened his own shop from 1850 to 1856 until he became a grocer. Samuel Hermann, the fourth brother, worked for Frederick from 1850 to 1857, then opened his own pottery in 1857 until 1860 when he died. His wife continued the pottery for a number of years. (Information and marks: Kenneth Dearolf, *Wisconsin Folk Pottery*, pp. 7 to 12. A booklet written in cooperation with the Kenosha Public Museum. Mark no. 1 impressed or hand stamped. The rest of marks shown are stenciled in blue.

C. HERMANN & CO.
MILWAUKEE, WIS.

MANUFACTURED
BY
CHAS. HERMANN & CO.
MILWAUKEE, WIS.

MANUFACTURED AT THE
CHAS. HERMANN
STONEWARE
FACTORY

L.M. PIERRON, PROP.
MILWAUKEE, WIS.

MANUFACTURED
BY
CHAS. HERMANN & CO.
MILWAUKEE, WIS.

Manufactured
BY
C. HERRmann & CO.
Milwaukee

Herold, John J. John J. Herold came to the U.S. from Austria in 1891. He worked four and one-half years in New York, spent a year in a glass factory in Pittsburgh and arrived in Zanesville, in 1898. He worked a year as a decorator for S.A. Weller and another year for J.B. Owens, before going to Roseville Pottery in 1900 (date from Schneider, as cited), where he became superintendent of the art department, and in 1905 he became superintendent of the whole plant. His copper red or oxblood glazes won first prize at the St. Louis Exposition in 1904. In 1908, he left Roseville to go to Golden, Colorado, where he founded Herold China Company to make chemical porcelain. Herold China Company became Coors Porcelain (see that listing). Herold returned to Ohio in the 1920's and became superintendent of the Ohio Pottery. He died on April 18, 1923. (Information: Schneider, ''Roseville Pottery,'' *Zanesville Times Signal*, in a series of articles, March 15, 1959, March 22, 1959, and March 29, 1959. Marks: Foster Hall, *Collector's Guide to American Pottery Artists, Potters and Designers and Their Marks*, p. 7.)

J. H.   J·H·

Herold, Paul G. (not to be confused with John J. Herold). Dr. Herold became instructor in the ceramic department of the School of Mines and Metalurgy, University of Missouri in Rolla, Missouri, in September 1936. He had a B.S., M.S. and a Ph.d in ceramic engineering from Ohio State University. His work was in the field of commercial-type ceramics. He worked at Columbus Tile and Brick; the Ohio Sanitary Company, Salem, Ohio; Old Hickory Clay Company, Paducah, Kentucky; the A.C. Spark Plug Company, Flint, Michigan, etc. He did a great deal of research on high-temperature chemistry of ceramics.

Herring Run Pottery. East Weymouth, Massachusetts. 1953 to present (1985). William Wyman, studio potter, has operated the Herring Run Pottery since 1953, where he makes functional and non-functional stoneware pieces which are hand thrown or slab built. Some of his pots have sgraffito type surfaces with cartoons, poems, little sayings, etc. Wyman has taught at Drake University in Des Moines, Iowa; the University of Maryland in College Park; the Massachusetts College of Art in Boston; and De Cordova and Dana Museum and Park in Lincoln, Massachusetts. (Information: Garth Clark, *A Century of Ceramics in U.S.*, p. 343. Marks: Linda Steigleder, from the booklet published by the Everson Museum of Art to accompany the 1978 exhibition, ''A Century of Ceramics in the U.S.'' Mark no. 1 is stamped and mark no. 2 is incised.)

1.   2. *Wyman 62*

Hickerson, James N. Strasburg, Virginia. 1884 to 1898. Hickerson was a stoneware potter whose daughter married Ernest Keister (see the listing, Keister Pottery), a son of Adam Keister. Both Amos and Ernest Keister worked with Hickerson at various times. (Information: A.H. Rice and John B. Stoudt, *The Shenandoa Pottery*, pp. 85, 107. Mark: Elmer Smith, *Pottery, A Utilitarian Folk Craft*, p. 22.)

J.M. HICKERSON
STRASBURG, VA.

Hickman, Royal Arden. Although Royal Hickman had no formal training, he is considered to have been a genius of design. From 1938 to 1944 he designed most of the pieces in the line Royal Haeger by Royal Hickman for Haeger Potteries, Inc. of Dundee, Illinois (see that listing). During the war years, Hickman operated a small pottery of his own in Tampa, Florida. The pottery was destroyed by fire and Hickman went to Guadalajara, Mexico, where he built a home to retire. However, even after retirement he continued to design some pieces for Haeger up until Hickman died in 1969 or 1970. (Information: Don Brewer, "Haeger Potteries," *Antique Trader*, November 6, 1985, pp. 74 to 76. Marks raised or recessed in molds sent by researcher Edward Blas. See the Haeger Potteries Inc. listing for the Royal Haeger by Royal Hickman marks.)

ROYAL
HICKMAN
USA 474

ROYAL
HICKMAN
FLORIDA
515

HICKMAN
USA
501

Hicks. Crooksville, Ohio. There were two potters in the Crooksville area by the name of Hicks, using the marks shown. E.A. Hicks was a stoneware potter. That mark was on a salt glazed crock made in 1882 with an incised decoration and inscribed mark. Fred Hicks remains pretty much a mystery also. Some of the old timers still remember him as working in some of the local potteries, but none can explain the mark shown found on a grotesque head with brown glaze. I called many people by the name Hicks in the area, but never found the right family. This was apparently some little pottery Hicks had in his home or a bluebird type of operation around 1930.

Higby, Wayne. Wayne, a studio potter, was educated at the University of Colorado in Boulder and received his M.F.A. degree at the University of Michigan, in Ann Arbor, in 1968. Between 1968 and 1973, he taught in Omaha, also Scripps College in Claremont, California, and the Rhode Island School of Design in Providence. In 1973, he became professor of ceramics at the New York College of Ceramics in Alfred. He made raku pieces with landscape imagery. He was given a one-man show at the Museum of Contemporary Crafts in New York City, and he has exhibited widely in many places. (Information: Garth Clark, *A Century of Ceramics in the U.S.*,

p. 298. Stamped mark: Linda Steigleder, from the booklet published by the Everson Museum of Art to accompany the 1978 exhibition, "A Century of Ceramics in the U..S.")

Higgins, A.D. Cleveland, Ohio. Around 1837 to 1850. Made stoneware. Mark impressed. (Information and mark: Lehner, *Ohio Pottery and Glass*, p. 36. Mark 2 on stoneware piece at Ohio Ceramic Center, Zanesville, Ohio.)

A D HIGGINS
CLEVELAND
OHIO

1.

HIGGINS & CO.
2. CLEVELAND, O

C.E. Hill and Company. Kansas City, Missouri. 1870-1880. Made stoneware. Mark on 2 gallon salt glazed stoneware jug. Made whiskey jugs. (Information and mark: Henry W. Heflin, pottery collector and researcher.)

C.E HILL & CO.
MAKERS
KANSAS CITY, – MO.

Hillcrest Pottery. Beldenville, Wisconsin. 1977 to present (1982). Willem G. Gebbon, a studio potter born in the Netherlands, started the Fillmore Street Pottery in Jenison, Michigan, in 1975 and moved to Hillcrest Pottery in 1977. He produces wood fired to 2,300 degrees F. stoneware and porcelain thrown on an oriental kick wheel into a wide range of utilitarian pots for the kitchen and table as well as decorative vases and jars. He received a B.A. degree from Grand Valley State College in Allendale, Michigan, in 1975. He then worked as an apprentice to David Eeles, Mosteaton, Dorset, V.K. A few of the places Mr. Gebbon's work was shown are listed. In 1981, he did a one-man show at Smits International, Delft, the Netherlands. In 1979, 1980 and 1981 he showed his work at Minnesota Craft Council Show in St. Paul.

Personal Stamp

Pottery Stamp

Hillcrest Pottery. Berkeley, California. Lois Walden, a studio potter, started in 1973. In 1976, she acquired the studio in Berkeley, and in 1982 Lois and Jesse Walden added a second studio in Medocino, California. They are makers of high fired functional stoneware, some porcelain studio pieces. Since 1978 they have made an extensive line of "burning" items including six or seven different kerosene lamps, 8 or 10 "bead" candles. Kitchen items include mugs, bowls, goblets, casseroles, etc. A line of jewelry marked "Ariel of California" made of high fired porcelain is made and sometimes marked "AOC" as shown in mark 1. After 1981, no date was added to marks on Hillcrest Pottery ware. Pottery is currently almost 100 percent sold wholesale nationally. (Mark 2 used by Lois Walden until around 1980. Mark 3 used by Jesse Walden until 1981. Mark 4 with some variations was used from 1978 until present (1983). Mark 5 from 1981 to present with some variations. Marks inscribed.)

1. AoC 83   2. ☼   3. ✶   4. W

5. Walden

Hill/Fulper/Stangl/Potteries. Flemington, Hunterdon County, New Jersey (1814 to 1935); Trenton, New Jersey (1928 to 1978). Authorities disagree on beginning date. Numerous sources, including the factory, used 1805 as a starting date. (See mark 5) but Evans, p. 109, said 1814 was the first documented date. Even the copyright registration and marks' dates seem to be exaggerated. Evans based this statement on the research done by M. Lelyn Branin, author of *The Early Potters and Potteries of Maine*, a book often quoted in this book in the discussion of the Maine potteries. Branin did the most thorough job of researching the very old court house records and documents, etc., of any of the authors whose material I have used. Oftentimes when a pottery has made a variety of ware such as was made in Flemington and Trenton, the study and discussion of art pottery or later products may overshadow the fact that for many years the pottery produced other products. Samuel Hill started the pottery at the site and operated for 46 years. He made redware and later stoneware. Abraham Fulper didn't acquire the pottery until 1860, according to Evans, p. 109. Fulper had worked for Hill and may have been renting the pottery from him before 1860, but the purchase took place in 1860. Abraham (also called Abram) Fulper lived until 1881, when his sons operated as G.W. Fulper and Bros. and also as Fulper Bros.

The pottery was incorporated in 1899 as the Fulper Pottery Co. (marks 1 and 2). For the first 100 years, the product of this pottery had been utilitarian stoneware. The piece pictured in Guilland, p. 236, was a gray salt glazed stoneware jug with a stamped or impressed mark and blue slip trailed flower decoration. One of the most unusual products created by the Fulper Pottery Company was a set of stoneware jars to provide clean, cool water. From the upper section the water passed through a specially made filter stone into the lower container, inside of which was a smaller jar to hold ice. The surrounding water, cooled by this "ice-chamber," was drawn off through a spigot. This was the forerunner of today's watercooler. So great was the demand for the "Fulper Germ-Proof Filter," as it was called, that other potteries were often contracted to help make enough to fill the orders. These "watercoolers" were to be found in every railroad station from coast to coast and in office buildings and stores throughout the nation. They were also exported in large quantities to various South American and West Indian countries. When a large American doll manufacturer requested that Mr. Stangl make doll heads to replace the supply cut off from Europe during World War I, Mr. Stangl created the now famous "Fulper" doll heads which are prized by antique collectors throughout the country. Early Fulper products were red earthenware jars and shaving cups, stoneware pipkins, crocks, flowerpots and brown glazed ware, gray pottery jugs with spongework decoration, candlesticks, etc. Other rough cast articles such as bowls and drinking foundations for poultry were added to the line. From 1860 to 1910, production was expanded to include water and vinegar jugs, pickling jars, butter churns, ginger beer bottles and beer mugs. By 1911, J. Martin Stangl was working for Fulper. Between 1915 and 1920, Stangl left Fulper to work for Haeger Potteries. When he came back in 1920 it was to head the pottery, according to company history.

In 1926, Fulper acquired Anchor Pottery Company of Trenton, New Jersey, and by 1929 Fulper had two plants operating in Flemington. In 1930, Stangl acquired the Fulper firm, following a disastrous fire in the Flemington plants in 1929. Vasekraft, an artware, first introduced in 1909, had hundreds of glazes, according to Evans, p. 110, including lustre, crystalline, matt and high gloss finishes. All sorts of decorative and functional pieces were made in this line, a few of which are listed in the copyright registration (see mark 5). Fulper art pottery was mostly made from molds with pottery or stoneware. Much was hand decorated. Every conceivable type of piece was made including vases, lamps, candleholders, etc. Fulper Pottery won some awards in the 1915 Panama Pacific International Exposition in San Francisco. In 1920, Fulper Pottery introduced solid color glazed dinnerware. For many years they used only green, but in 1930 other colors were added to the dinnerware line. On September 19, 1929, disaster struck. The original Fulper Pottery series of buildings caught fire at 5:30 a.m. and burned to the ground.

In 1930, J. Martin Stangl acquired the Fulper firm. The manufacture of art pottery, begun around 1909, was continued until 1935 when the emphasis was changed to dinnerware. Not until late 1955 was the corporate title changed to Stangl Pottery, according to Evans; however, he adds that the Stangl name had been in use for ten years then. So this is one of the cases where it is difficult to tell where one pottery ends and another starts. The same people, the same products to a great extent and then one day a name change! After 1935, all manufacturing operations were transferred to the Trenton plant. In the 1940's, Stangl began to manufacture a finer grade of dinnerware. Stangl initiated hand decorated dinnerware during World War II. From the beginning a distinctive red clay body was used with white clay applied in the front of the red clay body. Sometimes the body was carved to let the red clay show through on the surface. Cheerful and bright underglaze colored decorations were also applied by hand. In 1973, Frank H. Wheaton, Jr. acquired the operation. According to John F. Bonistall, recent vice-president and general manager of Stangl Pottery, the Stangl Pottery was purchased by Pfaltzgraff Pottery on July 31, 1978. Stangl made an Audubon series of birds in the 1940's when imports were curtailed. In addition to the ceramic bird line, Stangl created 12 birds with intricate designs in a porcelain body. Less than 50 of each of the 12 porcelain birds were made. A line of artware Mr. Stangl created had a unique process of applying 22-karat gold brushed on over a mat green glaze. This line was aptly named "Antique Gold." Stangl Kiddieware sets depicted gay, colorful nursery characters. At the time of selling, Stangl was still producing a fine line of dinnerware, including the "Town and Country" line which resembled the old enameled speckled granite ware in decoration and was very nice for today's early American decors. They were also making what they called "an authentic early American stoneware" called "Maize-ware" which was a corn pattern in a medium dark brown glaze. Sometime in the early to middle 1970's, Stangl had stopped making the red bodied dinnerware line mentioned earlier.

The following is a list of pattern names furnished by Stangl Pottery showing the dates of introductions and discontinuation of the various patterns.

Introduced	Pattern	Discontinued
1942	Fruit	
1942	Blue-Yellow Tulip	1955
1947	Garden Flower	1955
1947	Mountain Laurel	1955
1947	Flora	1955
1949	Prelude	1955
1949	Water Lily	1955
1950	Blueberry	1965
1950	Kumquat	
1950	Lime	
1951	Thistle	1965
1952	Star Flower	1955
1952	Magnolia	1956
1953	Pink Lily	1955
1953	Golden Harvest	1964
1954	Lyric	1957
1954	Carnival	1957
1954	Amber Glo	1960
1955	Wild Rose	1963
1955	Windfall	1957
1956	Country Garden	
1956	Country Life	1959
1957	Tiger Lily	1959
1957	Provincial	1962
1957	Frosted Fruit	
1957	Concord	
1958	Fruit & Flowers	1975
1958	Florentine	
1959	Garland	1963
1959	Fairlawn	1961
1960	Bella Rose	1961
1960	Chicory	1963
1961	Florette	1963
1961	Festival	1964
1962	Bittersweet	1969
1962	Orchard Song	1975
1963	Golden Grape	1968
1963	Paisley	1965
1963	Blue Daisy	
1964	Golden Blossom	1975
1965	Maple Whirl	1971
1965	Spun Gold	1971
1965	Rustic	1971
1965	Dogwood	
1965	Apple Delight	1975
1965	Mediterranean	1975
1965	Bachelor's Button	1968
1966	Pink Cosmos	
1966	Sculptured Fruit	
1967	White Grape	
1967	Holly	
1968	Star Dust	
1968	First Love	1970
1968	Treasured	
1965	Inspiration	

(Marks: 1, 2, Guilland, p. 236, Stewart and Consentino, p. 72, and Bottle News, August 1976, p. 48. No. 3 shown in W.P. Jervis, "World's Pottery Marks," Pottery, Glass and Brass Salesman, January 18, 1914, p. 13. No. 4, paper label, Deb and Gini Johnson, Beginner's Book of Pottery, p. 39. No. 5 is the mark as it was registered by the Fulper Pottery Company, September 13, 1911, claiming use since July 12, 1911, for pottery vases, pottery tobacco jars, pottery jardinieres, pottery coffee sets, pottery beer sets, pottery ash trays and pottery fountains. No. 6 was filed for registration on May 7, 1917, claiming use since the year 1840! No. 6 was used on bowls, shapes, vases, flower holders, trays, twig-sticks, book blocks, tobacco jars, door stops, pitchers, pots, jars, urns, plates, money banks, casseroles, coasters, tankards, sconces, of pottery. Nos. 7, 8, 9, impressed marks from Paul Evans, Art Pottery of the U.S., p. 112. No. 9 is impressed mark on cipher of Martin Stangl. No. 10, "Terra Rose" was filed for registration under the name Fulper Pottery Company, Trenton, New Jersey, August 3, 1940, claiming use since July 20, 1940, for glazed pottery tableware and vases. No. 11, photostatic copy of stamped Terra Rose mark. No. 12, drawn copy. No. 13, shown in 1945 Crockery and Glass Journal Directory.

As is always the case with directories, it didn't say how this trademark was used, as just a logo or an actual mark. Nos. 14-19 were used on Stangl dinnerware in 1940's, 1950's, 1960's. See list of discontinued patterns for dates. No. 20 was filed for copyright by Fisher, Bruce and Company, Philadelphia, Pennsylvania, on May 21, 1943, for use on ceramic dishes, flower pots and flower bowls, claiming use since 1940. These articles were made for Fisher, Bruce and Company by Stangl Pottery. Nos. 21 and 22 were the actual marks as they appeared on the very attractive dinnerware. No. 21 was sent by Linda Cleveland. No. 22, Norma Rehl, "Tabletop Fashions of Bygone Days," National Journal, August 1981, p. 3. No. 23, paper label. No. 24 filed April 22, 1964 and no. 25 filed April 26, 1962, both for ceramic tableware with little prior use of mark. No. 26 was part of an advertisement in American Home, July 1945, sent by Rena London, and was verified by John F. Bonistall as being used as a paper label before his tenure. Marks 27-31, sent by Bonistall, are found on Stangl pottery birds and are shown in the book by Joan Dworkin and Martha Horman entitled A Guide to Stangl Pottery Birds, Willow Pond Books, 1977, only plate numbers in book. These authors give explanations for some of the letters and decorator's marks found on the birds. No. 27, impressed mark. No. 28, painted mark. Nos. 29-31 are stamped under glaze. No. 32 is a paper label. Verna M. Fulgham, "Stangl Birds Collect," Pottery Collectors' Newsletter, December 1975, p. 171, said Stangl Birds are marked with name of company, artist and model number. Most are marked on the bottom, a few on the side. The birds are hollow with a hole in the bottom of them. Some have a paper sticker plus the mark. No. 33, Lucile Henzke, "Stangl Audubon Birds," Spinning Wheel, March 1971, pp. 9-11.) NOTE: To clear up a bad misconception that is evidently a typesetter's error in Thorn's book of marks - Lenneth, Pluto, Cupid, Tiger, Greek and Lygia are not Fulper marks. They belong to French China, Sebring, Ohio. The tragedy is that by mislocating one little number the error occurred, and some modern authors have perpetrated the mistake. (See French China.)

1. 4007
    FULPER

2. FULPER BROS.
    FLEMINGTON, N.J.

211

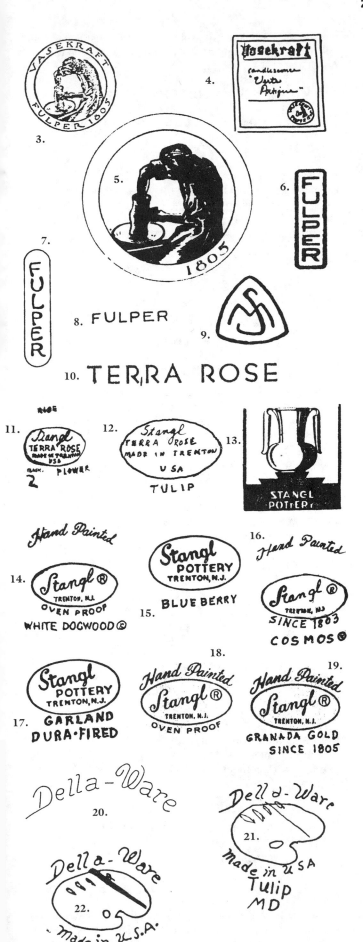

3.

4.

5.

6.

7.

8. FULPER

9.

10. TERRA ROSE

11. Stangl TERRA ROSE MADE IN TRENTON USA — ROSE — PLOWER 2

12. Stangl TERRA ROSE MADE IN TRENTON USA — TULIP

13. STANGL POTTERY

14. Stangl® TRENTON, N.J. OVEN PROOF — Hand Painted — WHITE DOGWOOD®

15. Stangl POTTERY TRENTON, N.J. — BLUE BERRY

16. Hand Painted — Stangl® TRENTON, N.J. SINCE 1805 — COSMOS®

17. Stangl POTTERY TRENTON, N.J. — GARLAND DURA·FIRED

18. Hand Painted Stangl® TRENTON, N.J. OVEN PROOF

19. Hand Painted Stangl® TRENTON, N.J. GRANADA GOLD SINCE 1805

20. Della-Ware

21. Della-Ware Made in USA Tulip MD

22. Della-Ware Made in U.S.A.

23.

24. **GOLDEN BLOSSOM**

DURA-FIRED 25.

26. Stangl Birds

STANGL USA 27.

28. STANGL

29. Stangl

30. STANGL POTTERY BIRDS

31. STANGL

32. Stangl Birds

33. STANGL POTTERY

Hilton Potteries. There were several potters all members of a single family name Hilton (also spelled Helton) in the Catawba Valley area of North Carolina. John Wesley of Propst Crossroads was a farmer, soldier and potter after he returned from the Civil War. He taught his son, Ernest Auburn Hilton to make pottery at a very early age. Ernest worked with his father in McDowell County until 1900. From 1900-1906 he worked at the Oak Grove Pottery. From 1906-1908 he worked with his brother-in-law, Seth Ritchey and George Hilton, a cousin, in Iredell County at Harmony and Houstonville. In 1908, Ernest leased his own pottery near Hickory, where he worked until 1922. There is some uncertainty as to how he spent his years from 1922 to 1934. One version is that he worked in a pottery with his brothers at Oyama, east of Hickory. In 1935, he moved four miles west of Marion to start the **E.A. Hilton Pottery.** During the years Ernest had been in partnership with his brothers, Ernest started to make the fancy "jugtown" pottery rather than the strictly utilitarian pottery he had made before. The ware was glass-like in glaze, high-fired, hand-thrown. Ernest died in September 1948.

Clara Maude Hilton continued making and decorating pottery figurines, doll heads, special Dogwood decorated pieces, etc., for which she became famous. Her work was exhibited in the Metropolitan Museum of Art and other places. E.A. Hilton Pottery closed in 1953. Clara Maude Hilton died in July, 1969. The mark shown is a stamped mark used after World War II. Most of the Hilton pottery was unmarked but pieces have been found with initials and signatures of various family members and workers, such as "Bill H.," "Mrs. F.W. Hilton," also "E & W Hilton/Hickory, N.C." (Information and marks: Bridges, Daisy Wade, *Potters of the Catawba Valley*, Vol. 4 of Journal of Studies Ceramic Circle of Charlotte, N.C., Mint Museum, 1980, pp. 22-32; Fossett, Milded Beedle, "The Hilton Craftsman, *Pottery Collectors Newsletter*, March 1978, pp. 19-21; No author given, "The Craft Potters of North Carolina," *Bulletin of American Ceramic Society*, Vol. 21, No. 6, June 15, 1942, pp. 83, 84.

Hilton

Hindes, Charles Austin. Charles, a studio potter, received B.F.A. and M.F.A. degrees from the Rhode Island School of Design in Providence, in 1968. He has been a strong influence as a teacher and artist, having taught at several schools in Illinois and New York. He was an adjunct professor of ceramics at the Rhode Island School of Design in 1972 to 1973. He then became an associate professor of ceramics at the University of Iowa in Iowa City. He has exhibited widely and participated in numerous workshops. (Information: Garth Clark, *A Century of Ceramics in the U.S.*, p. 298. Incised mark: Linda Steigleder, from the booklet published by the Everson Museum of Art to accompany the 1978 exhibition, "A Century of Ceramics in the U.S.")

Hintze Pottery. Bishop Hill, Illinois. 1982 to 1986. Rick and Gail Hintze, studio potters, working in the Colony Blacksmith Shop, are part of a crafts program sponsored by the Bishop Hill Heritage Association and a percentage of their profit goes to restore the colony buildings at Bishop Hill. Both attended college and studied art. (Information: Dianne L. Beetler, "Hintze Pottery," *American Clay Exchange*, March 30, 1986, p. 12. Marks: nos. 1-3 are used by Rick and nos. 4, 5 are used by Gail. At first, the Hintzes did not mark their pottery. The "H" within a rectangle and the ginkgo leaf within a circle were two of their earlier marks. Usually Rick uses the mark which is a rectangle enclosing two dots and the letters, "B H" to show that the piece was made in Bishop Hill. Gail usually uses the mark with a ginkkgo leaf in a rectangle dividing her initial "G" from the letters "B H" signifying that the pot was made in Bishop Hill.)

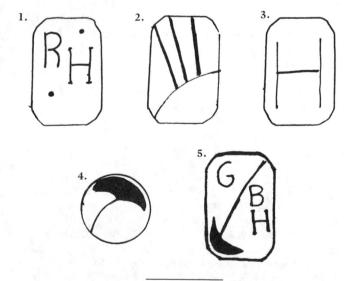

Hirsch Manufacturing Company. The William H. Hirsch Manufacturing Company was listed in only one of the directories I had. In the 1946 *Crockery and Glass Journal Directory*, the company was listed in Hollywood. The mark found stamped on a piece clearly states Los Angeles. In the directory cited, the company made art pottery, figures, figurines,

miniatures, jardinieres, flower bowls and florist ware, also special mold china and earthenware. (Mark: Martha Brisker Antiques.)

Historic Charleston Foundation. Charleston, South Carolina. As a part of their fund raising efforts issue a yearly catalogue advertising paintings, porcelain, silver, furniture and other heirloom reproductions are issued by the foundation. Also, see the listing, "Historic Places."

Historic Places. Various historic places have pottery making demonstrated or they sell pottery made elsewhere with their name or mark, as part of their fund raising activities. Sometimes these are in connection with a specific festival or event. See the separate listings for Monticello, Mt. Vernon, Historic Charleston Foundation, Williamsburg Pottery Factory, Inc., Greenfield Village Pottery and Hintze Pottery. Shown is a mark found on a pair of hand thrown candleholders made in connection with a pottery festival at Jamestown, Virginia. Also see the listing for Old Sturbridge, Inc. The Sturbridge Yankee Workshop issues a yearly catalog from the Colonial restoration village featuring all kinds of basic items for the early American type home.

HMH Publishing Company. Chicago, Illinois. Company filed for registration of both marks on June 13, 1962, claiming use since December 15, 1961, to be used on china dinnerware.

FEMLIN

Hobart, D.P. Williamsport, Pennsylvania. D.P. Hobart was associated with the Moore, Nichols and Company Pottery in Williamsport, Pennsylvania, from 1877 to 1879. But pieces are found with marks with the word agent or manufacturer as shown, suggesting he was also a selling agent or had some business on his own besides. Hobart was a coal dealer. He became a part of the pottery venture with Nichols and Moore to sell them coal. (Information: Jeannette Lasansky, *Made of Mud*, p. 31. Impressed mark: Jeannette Lasansky as cited, p. 56.)

D.P. HOBART, AGENT
WILLIAMS PORT, PA.

Hodgdon, Mary Yancey. Studio potter who was a pioneer in the use of art deco surface decoration to make some of the finest pots made in the 1920's, according to Tom Turnquist in "Mary Yancey Hodgdon Revisited," in *American Art Pottery*, July 1984, p. 5. Hodgdon worked at Iowa State College in Ames, Iowa, from 1924 to 1930 (see that listing). She was one of the founders of Clay Craft Studios in Winchester, Massachusetts, in 1931 to around 1934 (see that listing). She then taught at Fullerton Junior College in Fullerton, California, from 1934 for the next 30 years. Hodgdon pieces are found marked with a "Y" and "ISC, Ames," as shown under Iowa State College listing. At Fullerton Junior College, she incised her name. (Marks: sent by Tom Turnquist by letter.)

MARY YANCEY HODGDON
FULLERTON
JUNIOR COLLEGE

Hoffman China. Columbus, Ohio. March, 1946 to present. Makers of personalized pottery, hand tooled, hand decorated with names, dates and inscriptions, in a variety of Pennsylvania Dutch designs. They also make fine ceramic dinnerware and related items in the Pennsylvania Dutch style. (Information and marks: Lehner, *American Kitchen and Dinner Wares*, p. 77.)

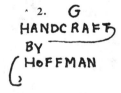

Holcomb, Jan C. Pascoag, Rhode Island. Jan is a professional sculptress. She recieved a B.F.A. degree from the University of Michigan in Ann Arbor in 1975 and her M.A. degree from California State University at Sacramento in 1977. She has worked at the Rhode Island School of Design in Providence as an instructor in the ceramics department from 1977 to 1985 and was acting program head of ceramics in 1983. She has lectured at several universities, and her work may be found in many collections. Her work has been pictured in *Crafts Horizon, New York Magazine, American Craft, Ceramic Monthly* and *American Ceramics*. She listed over 30 major exhibitions from 1974 to 1986. A selective group of these exhibitions is: "Beaux Arts Designer/Craftsman '75," Columbus Gallery of Fine Arts; "Ce-ra-mic," group show, American River College, Sacramento, California, 1977; "Fourth Annual Ceramics and Glass Exhibition," Palo Alto

Cultural Center, 1977; "Massachusetts Regional Artists' Invitational," Southeastern Massachusetts University, South Dartmouth, Massachusetts, 1979; "Clay Metal Fiber," National Invitational, Southeastern Massachusetts University, 1979; One-Man Show, Art Latitude Gallery, New York, New York, November, 1980; "New Fauves," Hadler Rodrigeuz Gallery, Houston, Texas, December 1980; "Imagined Icons," Clark Gallery, Lincoln, Massachusetts, April 1984; Inaugural Show, Dorothy Weiss Gallery, San Francisco, July 1984; Contemporary American Ceramics: Twenty Artist-Newport Harbor Museum, Newport Harbor, California, May-July 1985; and One Man Show, Garth Clark Gallery, New York, May 1986.

Holder, Lily Frona. Temple City, California. Filed for registration of this mark on November 7, 1955, claiming use since September 13, 1955, for use on wedding cups and saucers.

Holiday Designs, Inc. Sebring, Ohio. 1964 to present. Recently changed ownership (1983), but still operating under the same name. Makers of attractive cookie jars, ceramic canister sets, etc. They are located in what was once the Spaulding China building. Products marked occasionally with mark in mold somewhere around the bottom of article, also used paper labels and logo shown. Mostly unmarked.

holiDAY desIgNs
USA

Holland, John Frederic. Salem, North Carolina. 1796 to 1843. John Holland was apprenticed to Rudolf Christ from 1796 to around 1803 in Salem, North Carolina. He worked as a journeyman from 1803 to 1821 and as a master potter from 1821-1843. John was one of the group called Moravians. See the listing for Rudolf Christ for an explanation of the Moravians and the type of ware made by the potters who served them. (Information: John Bivins, Jr., *The Moravian Potters in North Carolina*, published by University of North Carolina Press: Chapel Hill, North Carolina, 1972, pp. 38, 39. Mark: same source, p. 259.)

Holland
5V/A

Holly, Daniel. Vale, Lincoln County, North Carolina. 1811-1899. Made stoneware. (Information and mark: Daisy

Wade Bridges, *Potters of the Catawba Valley*, pp. 15, 51.)

D. HOLLY
2

Hollywood Ceramics. Los Angeles, California. Were manufacturers for Maddux of California. (See Maddux). Hollywood Ceramics was listed at 3061 Riverside Drive in 1948. A change of ownership for Hollywood Ceramics in 1976 is explained in the Maddux of California history. See Maddux of California for mark. Also see Southern California Ceramic Company for "Hollywood Ware."

Home Decorators, Inc. Newark, New York. Filed a registration for no. 1 in August 1959, claiming use since May 1956. Mark 2 was filed August 1968, claiming use since June 1968. Both marks were for china dinnerware. Robert B. Bernstorf at Commercial Decal in East Liverpool, Ohio, said that Jackson China Company made products for Home Decorators, Inc. Also, mark 3 was found at Quality Stamp Company in East Liverpool, Ohio, which made stamps for Jackson China Company. Mark 4 was also found in Jackson China Company's marks and was filed by Home Decorators, Inc., December 28, 1950, claiming use since October that same year for plates, cups and saucers.

1. **PRESTIGE** 2. **PETITE ROSE**

Honey Bear Farm. Genoa City, Wisconsin. Julia Steven Krafft filed for registration of this mark on October 31, 1952, for use on cups and mugs, made of china or ceramic ware, claiming use since June 1952.

Hood, Sylvia Designs. Pasadena, California. The 1960 and 1965 *Gift and Tableware Reporter Directories* listed the Sylvia Hood Designs at 1572 E. Walnut St. These were the only listings I found in any directory. The company was not listed in the same directory in 1967. Products were birds, animals and other figurines. (Mark: impressed between the feet on top of the pedestal of a figurine, sent and identified by Lucile Henzke, by letter.)

Hoover, Joseph C. Villanova, Pennsylvania. Filed for registration of this mark December 28, 1961, for use on ceramic mugs with caricatures, claiming since March 1960.

CELEBRITY MUGS

Hope Chest Company, Inc. Minneapolis, Minnesota. Filed for registration of mark 1 on August 19, 1955, claiming use since August 1, 1955, for use on china dishes. Mark 2 filed April 14, 1958, claiming use since March 5, 1958, for china dishes. Mark 3 filed December 18, 1957, claiming use since August 1954, for dinnerware made of china. Mark 4 filed July 21, 1958, claiming use since November 15, 1955, for use on same products.

1. **Hope Chest** 2. **TREASURE CHEST** 4. **CATALINA**

Hopewell China Company (Ostrow China). Hopewell, Virginia. Started between 1920-1922. The pottery was still listed as Hopewell China in 1929 but a little later became the **James River Potteries** around 1938 to 1940. The mark "Ostrow China" came from the owner's name, Sol Ostrow, which was used on a finer grade of semi-porcelain made at Hopewell China Company. They were makers of semi-porcelain dinnerware. For pattern names, see Lehner, *American Kitchen and Dinner Wares*, p. 78, and the article cited by Marlene Jinkins. (Marks: No. 1 is artist's enlargement of mark 2 found on a cream pitcher of semi-porcelain. Mark 3 was found in an article by Marlene Jinkins, "Hopewell China Company," *Depression Glass Daze*, May 1980, p. 42. Mark 4 sent by author Veryl Marie Worth, author of *Willow Pattern China*.)

Hopewell Township, Muskingum County, Ohio Potters. Hopewell Township, Muskingum County, Ohio. Norris F. Schneider in "John Dollings Credited With Making Stoneware in 1870's," *Zanesville Times Signal*, December 8, 1957, named a list of potters who made pottery in Hopewell Township, in the late nineteenth century. James Peterson was listed among them. The mark shown was stenciled lettering in blue on a gray clay salt glazed crock. The other potters Schneider listed in the township were: Noah Allen; William Bell; George Burley; William Burley; Burgess; John Chappelear; Fawell Dolings; Martin Fountain; Jesse German; Joyce German; Charles Hood; Kreager; Ace Lake; George Maholland; Ora Morrison; James Peterson; Austin Rambo; Lewis Richards; Ashwell Search; Thomas Sears; Jesse Smith; John Stine; and Bogus Van Allen.

Jns Peterson
Hopewell

Hopkins, John. Senaca County, Ohio. Around 1835 (Thorn, p. 131). Ramsay, p. 234, dates this stoneware potter around 1834-1840. (Mark: Thorn, p. 131.)

JOHN HOPKINS

Horn, Martin. Martin Horn was a potter who worked for the Gardiner Stoneware Company with factories in Gardiner and Farmingdale, Maine. Horn worked at the Farmingdale branch. In M. Lelyn Branin's book, *Early Potters and Potteries of Maine*, pp. 132, 133, he suggests a two gallon salt glazed jug with figures of eagles incised on it and "2/M. Horn/1883" incised could have been made for presentation to Horn; but since he was a potter, the jug was probably made by Horn. Martin Horn also had some financial interest in the Bangor Stone Ware Company around 1880. (Information: Branin, as cited, pp. 132, 133, 171, 172. Mark: Branin, plate following p. 147.)

2
M. HORN
1883

Horton Ceramics. Eastland, Texas. 1208 S. Bassett Street. I had listings of this pottery only for the years 1952 and 1954 in the *Crockery and Glass Journal Directory*. I don't know actual dates of existance. In 1952, they were listed as making vases, console sets, candy boxes, etc., of what the directory called art china. (Mark: sent by Frances Andrews.)

horton ceramics
EASTLAND, TEXAS

Hot Springs Pottery. Hot Springs, Arkansas. 1964 to present (1983). Owner Jack Buck served his apprenticeship at the Dryden Potteries for five years to qualify as a master potter. He develops his own glazes, some in solid colors, some mingled tones of brown and yellow or turquoise and green on dinnerware and other utility pieces. Some solid red items were made, but red was discontinued because a separate firing at lower temperature was necessary. Also, the oxides to make red are very expensive. Mr. Buck uses some commercial molds but also makes some of his own. A great deal of wheel thrown pottery is also made. All pottery made to sell at the factory or gift shops is marked "Hot Springs, Ark." Handthrown items have the word "Original" and the initials "J.B." (Information: Rena London, "Hot Springs Pottery," *National Journal*, January 1981, p. 8. Mark sent by Jack Buck. Mark 2 found on piece. Both marks incised.

1.   2.

House of Webster Ceramics. Manufacture in Eastland, Texas. Shipping center is Rogers, Arkansas. Roy and Evelyn Webster have manufactured ceramic products since 1965 to present (1984). But he started in business in 1934 selling wild rare fruit products from Great White River Country of Arkansas, many packed in old Mason fruit jars (replicas still used). In 1957, their "Country Charm" line of early American Electric Appliances were introduced. For instance, at the House of Webster one might buy homemade peach preserves in a pot made in Eastland, Texas, which looks like a shock of wheat gathered in and tied at the center. A ceramic cream can, a 5" brown jug, a 4¾" replica of a bushel basket, a 2 lb. stoneware churn, a 6" red raspberry, 4¾" red apple, a 2 lb. "sack o' something," a 3 lb. red coffee mill, a black pot bellied stove, a red fire hydrant, a ceramic thimble that holds 1¼ lbs. are all some of the ceramic pieces that may be purchased holding a variety of jams, jelly, honey, etc. Roy wrote that they make 200,000 pieces of pottery per year. Their son, Dale, works with Roy and Evelyn. (Marks: no. 1, found stamped on piece. No. 2 may be just a logo and not the one actually on pieces. However, in the letter, Mr. Webster said, "The House of Webster Ceramics logo is on the bottom of the pottery.")

1.   2.

Howell Porcelain. Mt. Pleasant, Pennsylvania. 1977 to present. Karen Howell, is a studio potter making porcelain dinnerware using a mark which is a bird foot print, her last name and copyright symbol with the year.

Ψ Howell © year

Hubener, George. (Barber's spelling, p. 12). Montgomery County, Pennsylvania. Started around 1773 to 1775 until 1798. George Hubener made redware and sgraffito with figures of peacocks, tulips, etc. Occasionally his full name is the mark. (Every one of the older references said how many marked examples there were for this potter, yet they did not agree on the spelling of his name. Ramsay, p. 184, spelled it Huebener as did Spargo, p. 159. Albert Hasting Pitkin in *Early American Folk Pottery*, Hartford, Connecticut, 1918, p. 105, spelled the name Huebener. W.P. Jervis in "The World's Pottery Marks," *The Pottery, Glass and Brass Salesman*, June 21, 1915, p. 15, showed this mark for George Hubener (Jervis spelling) at the **Groffits Pottery** 1785-1798. (Mark: Barber, *Marks of American Potters*, p. 12.)

G H

Hueckel China and Porcelain. El Monte, California. See listing for Various El Monte, California Potteries.

D.F. Huggins and Son. Lakenan, Missouri. Around 1870. Made stoneware. Mark on blue stenciled stoneware crock. (Information and mark: Henry W. Heflin, pottery collector and researcher.)

Hui, Ka-Kwong. Ka-Kwong Hui attended Kong Jung Art School in Canton, China, and the Shanghai School of Fine Arts in Shanghai. Ka-Kwong apprenticed to Cheng Ho, a sculptor, then came to the U.S. in 1948 to work at the Pond Farm in California with the Wildenhains (see that listing). Later, he received his B.F.A. and an M.F.A. degree from New College of Ceramics at Alfred University. He taught at the Brooklyn Art School and Douglass College, which is part of Rutgers University in New Brunswick, New Jersey. In 1964 to 1965, Ka-Kwong collaborated with Roy Lichtenstein to make a series of cup sculptures and ceramic mannequin heads which were later exhibited at the Leo Castelli Gallery in New York City. (Information: Gartha Clark, *A Century of Ceramics in the U.S.*, p. 299. Painted mark: Linda Steigleder, from the booklet published by the Everson Museum of Art to accompany the 1978 exhibition, "A Century of Ceramics in the U.S.")

Hull House Kilns. Chicago, Illinois. 1927 to around 1940. A social settlement formed by Jane Adams an Ellen Gates sponsored three pottery operations including the **Labor Museum**, the **Hull House Kilns** and the **Hull-House Shops**. The Hull House Kilns were an outgrowth of the Labor Museum organized in 1927. The kilns made all sorts of tableware pieces, animal and children figures of dense heavy clays glazed with very bright colors. Some had decorated or hand incised designs. The Labor Museum gave immigrants a place to practice the old country crafts, and then they were exhibited and sold there. The Hull-House Shops conducted evening classes by social workers who belonged to the Chicago Arts and Crafts Society. (Information and marks: no. 1, stamped with ink; no. 2, incised from Sharon S. Darling, *Chicago Ceramics and Glass*, p. 79. For a great deal of information on these groups, see Darling, as cited, pp. 79, 80.)

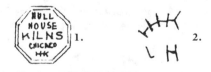

Hull Pottery Company. Crooksville, Ohio. 1905 to 1986. **A.E. Hull Pottery Company** started in 1905 to 1952 when it became the Hull Pottery Company. The plant was inactive following a fire in 1950 until 1952, at which time the name was changed and the initials left off. In 1917, art pottery was added to the line and continued to be made until in the early 1950's. The fact that the company no longer made art pottery makes it a very highly collectible commodity which is still priced within reason. From 1927 to 1929, they made tile in one of their two plants. Many other items were produced: Blue Band Kitchenware, Zane Grey Kitchenware, candlesticks, stoneware jugs, jugs, bowls, vases (art type and for florists), pitchers, a swan vase, poodle dog, duck planters, slippers, baskets, caster sets, ash trays, plates and dinnerware accessories. In 1937, the pottery reached its highest employment of 400 people in fulfilling a nine year contract (1937 to 1946) with the Shulton Company of New York. Hull Pottery ran three shifts and delivered over 11 million pieces of pottery during that time. The flood and fire that destroyed the plant in 1950 didn't stop the company. They rebuilt and operated successfully through the 1960's. But the labor problems which included several strikes and the high cost of fuel and foreign competition that put down so many of our factories in the 1970's and 1980's, finally got to Hull Pottery too. In July 1985, the company was already operating with just a few employees such as watchmen and a small office force. The official closing came in March 1986. (Information: Lois Lehner, *Ohio Pottery and Glass*, p. 40. Marks: no. 1 filed for registration August 16, 1944, claiming use since October 1943. Nos. 2, 3 are the paper labels or impressed mark as it was used; nos. 4-7 are marks shown in directories in 1950's and 1960's. Probably used in form of paper labels. The directories never say in what form the mark appears. No. 8 is a copy of a paper label; nos. 9, 10 are backstamps obtained at Quality Stamp Company, East Liverpool, Ohio. Hull used mostly incised marks or marks built into the mold, and that is what almost all of the marks shown here are. No. 11 was drawn from mark on a fancy footed bowl. The mark was identified by Brenda Roberts in the book, *Hull Pottery*, p. 19. Hull Pottery made ware for many distributors, using their own mark such as Marcrest for Marshall Burns, Leeds China, etc. Nos. 12, 13 are from Brenda Roberts, *Hull Pottery*, p. 16, which she said were used between 1927-1933. The "H" in the circle is a very old Hull mark. Hull Pottery did not use "H" in a diamond; that mark was registered by Carrollton Pottery, Carrollton, Ohio. See that listing. No. 14 was on bottom of heavy mug. The rest of the marks are incised or in the molds from various pieces. According to Brenda Roberts, by letter, also by letter from Bill Callihan of Hull Pottery Company, "Regal" was manufactured and marketed by Hull Pottery to the chain stores. Hull Pottery has had no connection with Regal China Company. The line of very pretty vases and decorative pieces marked "Regal" are definitely a Hull Pottery product. See the Roberts book for various pieces. After 1966 "hull" with a small letter "h" was used. Sometimes just a paper label was used.)

215

6.

7. **HULL** *Modern Art Pottery*

9. *Hull* U̱SA

8.  OVEN PROOF

10. URN-VASE 419 HULL-USA

11. *Imperial* F78-USA

12. HULL TILE

HULL FAIENCE

13. CUSHION

14. *Crooksville* hull *Ohio*

15. hull U.S.A.

16. *Hull*

18. *Hull Art*

17. PAT PEND *Corky Pig* ©USA 1957 HP Co

19. A.E. HULL USA B-15 OVEN PROOF

20. hull *Oven Proof* U.S.A.

21. *Oven Proof U.S.A.*

22. A.E. HULL USA B-15 OVEN-PROOF

23. H.P. © CO. *Oven Proof U.S.A.*

24. 967 *Hull-Ware Little Red Riding Hood Patent Applied For USA*

25. Ⓗ

26. *Hull* USA 29 Ⓖ

27. HULL OVEN-SERV '4 32 OZ USA

28. REGAL USA

REGAL 313 USA

29. REGAL 312-USA

30. hull *Oven Proof* USA

31. *Oven Proof Bake & Serve In This Dish* hull © USa

32. hull © *Gingerbread Man* U.S.a.

33. OVEN-PROOF *Hull* USA No 42-7½"

34. hull © *Crooksville, Ohio Oven Proof*

35. SALAD-BOWL *Hull* USA No 49-10

36. OVEN PROOF *Hull* NO. 83

Humble Mill Pottery. Seagrove and Asheboro, North Carolina. 1964 to present (1985). Jerry and Charlotte Fenberg, studio potters, are making porcelainous stoneware pieces which are hand thrown or press molded into tiles and figurines of birds, fish, etc. and other decorative pieces. They also make press molded dinnerware. They make a sgraffito ware with white slip. Some designs are carved in relief and some are hand painted with a brush. Each piece is stamped, signed and dated as shown. The Fenbergs spent two years, 1967 and 1968, in Japan, studying ceramics under Shoji Hamada and his son. In 1970, they settled in the North Carolina Piedmont where they were joined by Hiroshi Sueyoshi of Tokyo who is now working in Wilmington, North Carolina. From 1970 to 1973 he worked with the Fenbergs to develop a workshop and to do intensive research on using North Carolina clay. The Fenbergs started making pottery in 1964, and said they had several shops since then.

HUMBLE MILL POTTERY 1985

Fenberg

Hummel, John M. Florence, Missouri. Started before 1860 to after 1897. Made stoneware. Mark stamped on salt glazed stoneware crocks, vases, stoves of tile, jars up to ten gallons, sugar bowls, creamers, doorstops, tombstones. John M. Hummel came from Saxony, Germany, and is thought to be a relative of the famous Hummels from that country. By 1860, at age 30, he had several employees working in his pottery. The pottery was a three story building with a kiln in the basement and one out of doors. The stoves made of tile were the most outstanding articles made there. The stoves were 7′ tall and 3′ wide, made of individual pottery tile similar to those made by the Moravian potters. (Information: Ralph O. Lewis, researcher on the Hummel Pottery. Also, Hazel Lang, ''Florence Was Pioneer Morgan County Settlement,'' *Sedalia Democrat*, April 1969, pp. 4, 5. Marks: nos. 1-2, Henry W. Heflin, pottery collector and researcher; no. 3, Ralph O. Lewis.)

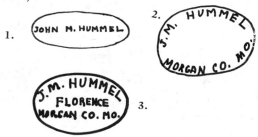

Hunter Street Pottery. Columbus, Ohio. 1978 to present (1982). Thomas Radca, a studio potter, makes functional handthrown stoneware, which he shows at many of the major Ohio craft shows. He adds the year to his mark on larger pieces.

Radca   (circle mark: RAdcA COLS OHIO '82)

Huntington Pottery. Huntington, Long Island, New York. Middle of 18th century to 1904. This pottery started about the middle of the 18th century by a man named Scudder, according to Barber, *Pottery and Porcelain of United States*, p. 543. In the Stradling's book, *Art of the Potter*, is an article, ''The Pottery of Huntington, L.I.'' by Mrs. Irving S. Sammis. She said Sarah and Jonathon Titus sold the land to Willliams, Scudder, Sammis, Fleet and Wetmore, and at times these men used the name Samuel J. Wetmore and Company. Scudder, who had bought out all the other owners around 1824, then deeded the property to Lewis and Gardiner (see that listing). Before 1854 we get marks, Gardiner and Lewis, Lewis and Lewis and just Lewis. In 1854, the owners were Henry Lewis, I. Scudder, Ketcham and Francis Hoyt with Frederick J. Caire as manager until 1863. At that time, the three Brown brothers became the owners, George, Thomas and Stephen Brown. George and his son, George W., continued when Stephen and Thomas left. Work ceased in 1904, and the buildings were torn down in 1918. (Marks: no. 1, Stradling, p. 111, found on a bulbous old jug that the author says was one to be taken to be filled with rum, etc. Dread was not a potter but the person for which the jug was made. No. 2, pictured in L.G.G. Ramsey's (spelled with ''e''), *Dictionary of Antiques*, New York: Hawthorne Books, 1968, plate 305, p. 849. Nos. 3, 4, Thorn, p. 134. No. 5, Stradling, p. 109.)

1. DREAD OF HUNTINGTON

3. HENRY LEWIS

4. LEWIS& LEWIS

5. LEWIS & GARDINER HUNTINGTON, L.I.

Hunt, William Company. Columbus, Ohio. 1966 to present (1983). William Hunt, a studio potter, is currently the editor of *Ceramics Monthly*. He also maintains an active studio career. He has judged or juried many regional and national exhibitions, written widely in the field of ceramics, conducted workshops in various colleges and univerisities in the U.S. and Canada. He has been elected to the International Academy of Ceramics. He makes stoneware, earthenware, Jasperware and porcelain pieces. (Marks no. 1 and 2 were used from 1966 through 1972. Marks 2 and 3 were used from 1972 until the present.)

Husher, George. Brazil, Indiana. Around 1860 to 1877. Husher made salt glazed stoneware utilitarian ware, jugs, crocks, etc. Prior to 1860, Husher had worked with or for Isaac Cordery, who was also a stoneware potter. (Information and impressed marks: Melvin Davies, *Clay County Indiana Traditional Potters and Their Wares*, pp. 15, 16.)

GEO. HUZHER BRAZIL, IND.   GEORGE HUSHER

Hyalyn Porcelain. Hickory, North Carolina. 1947 to present (1986). Company was started in 1947 by two potters from Zanesville, Ohio, one by the name of Leslie Moody. In 1975, Hamilton Cosco of Columbus, Indiana, bought Hyalyn Porcelain. The company operated until 1977 as Hyalyn Cosco in Hickory, North Carolina, manufacturing decorative accessory pieces, canisters, kitchen accessories, planters, etc. In 1977 or 1978, Robert Warmuth became sole owner of the Hyalyn Pottery. This was the name given in the telephone directory. In the 1981 *China, Glass and Tableware Directory*, they were listed for decorative accessories, canisters, ashtrays, kitchen accessories, tiles, cache pots and planters. In the early years, Edgar Littlefield left Ohio State University to work at Hyalyn Porcelain for a short time. See the listing on Littlefield. (Marks: nos. 1-4, on pieces; no. 5, in 1952 *Crockery and Glass Journal Directory*. The word, Hyalyn, as pictured in no. 6, was filed for registration on February 10, 1959, claiming use of the mark since April 1947 for a porcelain line of products; namely vases, bowls, ashtrays, cigarette lighters, plaques, and table service items.)

1.

AMERICA'S FINEST PORCELAIN

2.   635

hyalyn
3.   635

hyalyn
605
4.

hyalyn
PORCELAIN
style   quality
5.

HYALYN
6.

Hyssong/Hissong/Various Potteries. A name change within the family caused a great deal of confusion in the history of these potters. Elijah B. Hissong came to Cassville, Huntingdon County, Pennsylvania, around 1850. (Different dates around 1850 and different first names are given for this potter.) An impressed mark, no. 1, is shown on a pitcher for this potter in Jeannette Lasansky, *Made of Mud*, p. 22, which shows the name clearly spelled with an "i." This potter had 12 children, four of whom became potters, Austin, George, Charles and Russell. Apparently, Austin is the one who made the name change. Mildred V. Hardcastle, in "The Hyssong Potters," *Spinning Wheels Complete Book of Antiques*, p. 72, said a direct descendent, Glenn Hyssong, thought it could have been Elijah or E.B. Hissong, who changed the "i" to

"y." Reasons were unknown. In Huntingdon, which is in the same county as Cassville, Austin used "A.L. Hissong/Huntingdon," for a mark while he worked with his father, E.B. Hissong, and later he used "Hyssong," when he became of age and was in partnership with the Dipples in Lewistown, Pennsylvania, between 1872 and 1876. In 1877, he was in Petersburg, Pennsylvania, for one year and then back to Lewistown, from 1878 to 1880. From 1881 to 1885 he was in Huntingdon, Pennsylvania. In 1891, he purchased a pottery in Bloomsburg, which he operated until he died in 1914. Somewhere along the line he started stamping or impressing his pieces "Hyssong," spelled with the "y." See marks nos. 2, 3. Bruce Hissong, another son of E.B., operated the pottery in Cassville, after his father's death in 1893, until 1912. Russell, brother to Bruce, also had continued to work at this pottery but left earlier than 1912. Charles Hyssong, son of Austin, apparently used his father's name change and operated the pottery in Bloomsburg, Pennsylvania, from 1914 to 1945. The pottery building was then sold to the Long Supply Company and never operated as a pottery again. Two other sons of Austin became potters, Irving and Walter. Products for the various Hissong/Hyssong potteries were crocks, bowls, milkpans, dye pots, pitchers, batter jugs, etc. of stoneware, some with cobalt painted designs, some painted and some impressed marks. (Information: from Hardcastle, as cited previously. She quoted the *Columbia County History of 1915*, and direct descendents of the Hyssongs that she had spoken with. Marks: nos. 1 and 3, Jeannette Lasansky, *Made in Mud*, pp. 22-55; no. 2, *Regional Aspects of American Folk Pottery*, York, Pennsylvania; published by Historical Society of York County, p. 50, is a very plain mark impressed on a stoneware jug.)

CASSVILLE 1.
EB HISSONG

2.   AL HYSSONG
BLOOMSBURG. PA.

A.L. HISSONG
3.   HUNTINGDON

I

Ideal Pottery Company. Trenton, New Jersey. I found this pottery first listed in directories in 1902. In 1892, five potteries went together to form the Trenton Potteries Company. Ideal Pottery Company was built later by Trenton Potteries Company for the sole purpose of making sanitary ware. I found the building listed under the name, Ideal Pottery, but as part of Trenton Potteries Company until 1918. See Trenton Potteries Company for history. (Mark: shown from Barber, *Marks of American Potters*, p. 65.)

Ideas Unlimited. Los Angeles, California. Mark shown registered on September 4, 1945, for use on ceramic containers for fresh and cut flowers.

FLORA-ROCK

Ilka Ceramics. Beloit (near Sebring), Ohio. 1969 to present. Pottery makes customized mugs and steins employing 25 people and selling to 32 states. Started by Robert Taylor, Paul and Charlie Rosse. Plant sold to Sig Kramer in 1975. Much of the ware is marked just "Made in U.S.A."; a lot not marked at all; some marked with distributors and decorators names, such as Star Crest in Philadelphia, and W.C. Bunting Company of Wellsville, Ohio. The company uses no marks of its own now. See W.C. Bunting for marks on ware. Pictured is a logo used on boxes, cards, stationary, etc. (Information: company furnished. Mark: no. 2, was dated May 8, 1975, and made at Quality Stamp Company of East Liverpool, Ohio.)

Illinois China Company. Lincoln, Illinois. Started in Roodhouse, Illinois, then in 1919 the factory was moved to Lincoln, Illinois, under the direction of James H. Smith. A disastrous fire in 1922 burned the entire plant. With $50,000 insurance money and $50,000 raised by selling stock, the factory was rebuilt and started again with four upright bisque kilns, two decorating kilns and six upright glost kilns, all coal-fired (changed to gas in 1935). James Shaw came from the W.S. George Pottery of Canonsburg, Pennsylvania, to the Illinois China Company in 1929, bringing his knowledge of dinnerware manufacture and decorating to the company. On February 1, 1946, the Illinois China Company was sold to Stetson China Company which spent two and one-half million dollars on the plant by 1953, making it one of the most modern plants in America. In the early years Illinois China Company employed between 90 and 185 people according to the season. After Joseph Stetson took over the plant, the number of employees increased to 500. (Information: staff written, "Stetson China Was Moved Here From Roodhouse," *Lincoln Courier*, August 26, 1953, sec. 8, p. 11. Mark stamped on dish.

Illinois Electric Porcelain Company. Macomb, Illinois. Company was incorporated in December 1910, and many plant additions were made over the years. In 1953, the McGraw Electric Company purchased the controlling interest. See that listing. Over the years, the company made wet and dry process insulators including pin types. For complete details of products manufactured and examples of more marks, see Jack H. Tod, *Porcelain Insulators Guide Book for Collectors*, pp. 117, 118. (Information and marks: Tod, as cited.)

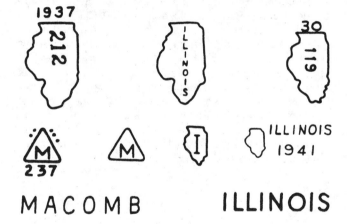

Imperial Porcelain Corporation. Zanesville, Ohio. 1946 until 1960. The company made a series of American folk sculptures of mountain folk, animals, etc. that has caught the eye of the collectors. P.H. Genter was the chief designer, and he secured the help of Paul Webb, the cartoonist who created "Daisy Mae" and "Lil Abner" in a comic strip. The various molded pieces were hand painted and expensive to produce because of royalties due on the copyrights involved. Imperial Porcelain started out making utilitarian ware such as butter dishes, pitchers and trays and ended their career with garden pottery. Of the 14 years of the pottery's existance, not more than 10 years were devoted to the cartoon figures. Ungemach Pottery (see that listing) also made the hill folk figures. In the author's collection, there is a boy on a stump with a fishing pole, straw hat, etc. made by Ungemach. Also, Twin Winton pottery (see that listing) made mugs with hillbilly handles and a pitcher and other miscellaneous pieces in this style. The few Imperial pieces I have had or seen seem to be more detailed, and the features sharper than those by Twin Winton. The Ungemach Pottery boy is nicely detailed and hand painted. (Incised marks: on pieces.)

COPYRIGHT 1947
Imperial Porcelain Corp.
ZANESVILLE, OHIO
Hand Crafted
U.S.A.
No. 99

Paul Webb
MT. Boys
USA ©
no. 29

(on bottom)
COPYRIGHT 1948
Imperial Porcelain Corp.
ZANESVILLE, OHIO
Hand Painted
USA
NO.94

Paul Webb — (on side)
© MT BOYS

Imperial Porcelain Works. Trenton, New Jersey. 1891 to around 1920's. Pottery started in 1891 by F.A. Duggan (who had been with the Trenton China Company) and was listed in the *Trenton City Directories* through 1944. Early in its history this company made some insulators for Fred M. Lock (see that listing) which Jack Tod, *Porcelain Insulators Guide Book for Collectors*, p. 124, says are prized specimens when marked with Imperial name on one side and Fred M. Locke on the other. Imperial then made high voltage pin type insulators until around 1904 marked with the Imperial Crown trademark. See Tod, as cited, for detailed descriptions of various marks, also of marks with errors such as no. 2. (Information and marks: Tod, as cited, pp. 124, 125.)

TRADE MARK. 1.

IMPERIAL PORCELAIN

MANUFACTURED BY
Imperial Porcelain Works.
TRENTON, N.J.
2.

MANUFACTURED BY
IMPERIAL PORCELAIN WORKS
TRENTON, N.J.
3.

Independent Grocers' Alliance Distributing Company. Chicago, Illinois. Commonly known as the I.G.A. stores. Filed for registration of this mark on November 9, 1928, for use on chinaware and crockery, claiming use since September 1, 1927.

Independent Manufacturing Association, Inc. Cincinnati, Ohio. Distributors. Filed for rights to this mark on May 25, 1929, for use on chinaware, claiming use since July 1, 1927.

LIFETIME

Indiana Pottery Company. Troy, Indiana. The company was incorporated January 7, 1837, by James Clews, who came from England. It was thought that whiteware similar to that made in England could be made from the Troy, Indiana, clay, but that soon proved to be false. After about a year, the property was leased to a Samuel Casseday of Louisville, who in turn, leased it occasionally to be used by workmen who came from England. One of the potters who came to Troy was Jabez Vodrey. He worked from 1839 to around 1947 in the Indiana Pottery building making Rockingham, brownware and cream-colored earthenware. See Vodrey and various associates. (Information: Barber, *Pottery and Porcelain of the United States*, p. 159; Ramsay, *American Potters and Pottery*, p. 231. Mark: shown on bottom of blue printed creamware jar for snuff, made around 1837 in L.G.G. Ramsey, *Dictionary of Antiques*, p. 315.)

CLEWS MANUFACTURER'S

Indiana Redware Potters. According to Melvin L. Davies, it has not been realized that Indiana had a few redware potters. Only the stoneware potters have been researched so far. Mr. Davies furnished marks for two of these redware potters as shown. Even though I have no additional information on these potters, I am showing the marks. Mr. Davies has come to be recognized as the outstanding authority in Indiana stoneware potters. (Marks: No. 1 is an impressed mark, No. 2, 3 are inscribed on five pieces of old redware.)

W. W. C.
1.

Wm W Cline
Hartford City
Ind
Aug 16th 1901
282X
2.

Joel Kaufman 3.

International Artware Corporation. Cleveland, Ohio. Listed in 1967 *Red Book Directory* as sellers of ceramic planters, giftware, floral arrangements and glass floral containers. The "Inarco, Cleve., Ohio," part of the mark is permanent stamped mark under glaze. The paper label shows a globe with "Inarco" and "Japan." (Marks: nos. 1 and 2 were on pieces; mark 3 filed for registration September 1, 1965, claiming first use in May 1961 for pottery, ceramics, crockery and earthenware, namely, planters, compotes, vases, cups and saucers, flower holders and other similar decorative items for use in conjunction with floral arrangements. Mark 4 filed August 30, 1965, for the same products.)

1. 2. 3. 4.

International Brotherhood of Pottery and Allied Workers, AFL-CIO. Began in East liverpool in 1890. The International Brotherhood was chartered by the AFL in 1899. Then in 1904, they merged with the Potters National Union which now includes 30 separate trades in the industry. The present name was adopted in 1970. The union works for protection, elevation, and relief of all workers and their families in matters concerning the potters' work. (Information: *12th Annual, Tri-State Pottery Festival Booklet*, 1979, p. 18.) The following is a list of the membership around 1935 of the International Brotherhood of Operative Potters as it was called then, which was found in Salem China records: American Limoges China Company, Inc.; Buffalo Pottery, Inc.; Canonsburg Pottery Company; Cronin China Company; Crooksville China Company; Crown Potteries Company; French Saxon China Company; W.S. George Pottery Company; Hall China Company; Harker Pottery Company; Edwin M. Knowles China Company; Homer Laughlin China Company; Mayer China Company; D.E. McNicol Pottery Company; Paden City Pottery Company; Pope-Gosser China Company; Salem China Company; Southern Potteries, Inc.; Sterling China Company; Steubenville Pottery Company; Taylor, Smith and Taylor Company; Universal Potteries, Inc.; Walker China Company; Wellsville China Company. Brush Pottery organized as Local #135 in 1936. See Universal Potteries, Inc. for more marks.

International China Company. Alliance, Ohio. A distributor associated with Cunningham and Pickett. See Cunningham and Pickett for history. (Marks: on dishes.)

International CHINA CO. ALLIANCE, OHIO GOLD AND TURQUOISE

International CHINA CO. ALLIANCE, OHIO EMPIRE GREEN

International CHINA CO. ALLIANCE, OHIO

International D.S. Company. Alliance, Ohio. A distributor associated with Cunningham and Pickett. See Cunningham and Pickett for history. (Marks: from dishes).

INTERNATIONAL D. S. CO. ALLIANCE, OHIO *Glenwood*

INTERNATIONAL D. S. CO. ALLIANCE, OHIO

International Pottery Company. Trenton, New Jersey. Was formed in 1860 by Henry Speeler (Barber, *Marks of American Potters*, p. 58). In 1868, he admitted his two sons, and the business became Henry Speeler and Sons. Carr and Clark, assisted by John and James Moses, purchased the Speeler works and named it the **Lincoln Pottery**. The name was the International Pottery at the time of the reorganization of the Lincoln Pottery by Edward Clark and James Carr. (See Lincoln Pottery, Trenton.) Later in 1879, Burgess and Campbell became the owners of this pottery. The last listing I found for this company in the *Trenton City Directory* was in 1936 making general and sanitary ware. In *China, Glass and Lamps*, June 4, 1923, p. 76, they advertised hotel ware, semi-porcelain and toilet ware. They made "Royal Blue" and "Rugby Flint" ware. Some of their semi-porcelain ware had blue decorations beneath the glaze, and these had marks printed in the same blue (Barber, p. 59.) In the *1902-1903 Complete Directory*, International Pottery Company was listed as making semi-porcelain, white granite dinner sets, toilet sets and short sets of odd dishes, some decorated. The double shield was adopted as being an appropriate design for the name for the company. (Barber, pp. 57, 58.)

Burgess and Campbell used the same mark as Carr and Clark by just substituting their name under the double shield. One more point on this confusing mark: John Moses was at least a part owner with Carr and Clark in the International Pottery Company, and James Moses was the head of the Mercer Pottery company of Trenton, which was organized in 1868. (See Mercer Pottery.) Mercer and International made the same products and used the same mark. According to Barber, we have three Trenton potteries using the double shield mark. Also, Mr. Campbell must have sold his interest to Burgess in 1903, because the name became **Burgess and Company** at that time, but Mr. Campbell stayed on as treasurer until 1906. (See Glasgow Pottery for more on John Moses as owner of Glasgow Pottery.) The following is a small excerpt on the life of Campbell which tells about his becoming involved with the International Pottery (taken from *Bulletin of the American Ceramic Society*, XXIII, April 15, 1940, p. 128).

"After leaving Princeton in 1876, Mr. Campbell went to New York City to engage in the pottery importing business. He remained there until 1879, when he went to Trenton to become associated with the International Pottery. On October 30, of the same year, he married Fannie Cleveland of Shushan, New York.

"In the Internationl Pottery, he was associated with his former classmate at Princeton, the late William Burgess, with whom he had engaged in pottery jobbing in New York. The pair turned their attention to Trenton as a prospective business field when they found it difficult to obtain regular shipment of goods from England. Trenton at that time was known as "the Staffordshire of America".

"During a conversation with John Moses, owner of the International Pottery, the latter offered to sell a half interest in the plant to the two young men. The offer was accepted and later the youthful partners purchased the remainder of the business from English holders.

"Mr. Campbell became treasurer of International, retaining that position until 1906, when he was made general manager of the Trenton Potteries Company." (Information and marks: E.A. Barber, *Marks of American Potters*, pp. 57-59. All marks shown were used before 1904. The Crown in a circle was first used around 1903. "Albany," "Japonica," "Lotus," "Diamond," found on dinnerware.)

International Silver Company. Meriden, Connecticut. This company has always been listed in the directories for flatware and hollowware of sterling and plated silver. But at some time they evidently had a pottery to make some kitchen piece or pieces to use in a promotion as this mark shows.

MADE EXCLUSIVELY FOR
INTERNATIONAL
SILVER CO.
OVEN TO TABLE
TO DISHWASHER
U.S.A.

Interpace Corporation. Similar to Jeannette Corporation and Anchor Hocking Corporation in that they diversified interests but have been a real factor in the dinnerware field. They are defined as a building and construction products company serving the building, construction, specialty mineral and ceramic markets. A parent company was incorporated in 1914 as Electro-Chemical Engineering and Manufacturing Corporation. In 1962, that company was merged with Lock Joint Pipe Company and Gladding, McBean and Company to form International Pipe and Ceramics Corporation (see Gladding, McBean and Company for history). In April 1963, the name was changed to Interpace Corporation at the time of incorporation. On March 25, 1968, Interpace acquired its second big pottery, Shenango China, which was the owner and maker of "Castleton China." Shenango China had purchased Mayer China in 1964, so Interpace acquired both plants. In February 1974, Interpace acquired Alfred Meakin, Tunstall, England. There is a considerable list of companies owned by Interpace that are not related to the field of pottery. In April 1979, an agreement was reached whereby Josiah Wedgwood and Son, Ltd. acquired the Franciscan Division of the Interpace Corporation. On June 2, 1979, the Interpace Corporation sold Shenango China Company to the Anchor Hocking Corporation. Also in 1979, Interpace Corporation sold Mayer China to a group of private investors. (See Shenango China and Mayer China listings.)

Inwood Pottery Studios. New York, New York. Started 1923 until late 1940's or early 1950's. Studios built by Aimee Le Prince Voorhees and Harry Voorhees, on the site of an old Indian Village called Shorakop-kik. New York City decided the land was to be purchased for a park, and in 1936 the studio had to be moved to 168th Street. The studio was used by various potters, classes were offered and firing was done for people working outside the studio. Harry died in 1936, but Aimee continued to provide a home base for many of New York City's best ceramists. A variety of objects were made there and marked, "Inwood Pottery, N.Y.C." (Information and marks: Thomas Turnquist, "New York City Ceramics, Part I, The Inwood Pottery Studios," *Journal of the American Art Pottery Association*, March 1985, p. 15.

Iowa State College of Agriculture and Mechanical Arts. Ames, Iowa. As early as 1899, research and some instruction had been given in the field of ceramics. The department of ceramics was established and housed in a new building in 1910-1911. Some modelled pottery was made in 1915. In 1923, an electric kiln was set up at the Iowa State Fair, and thousands of souvenirs in the form of miniature drain tiles were given to visitors. In 1924, Mary L. Yancy came to the college to give instruction in the making of art pottery. She stayed until 1930. Paul Cox also taught and made pottery at the college during this period. The vases Mary Yancy made during that period are marked with the "Y" in a circle as shown. The emphasis was strictly on engineering ceramics after 1939, so the art pottery era of the college was from 1924 to 1939 only. Some ware was modelled, some hand thrown, some cast in gang molds, etc. Some had raised and/or painted designs and glazed with a variety of colors or bisque fired at times. Souvenir items such as tiles, trivets, etc. were always mass produced and distributed in connection with the school's spring celebration called Veishea, and after 1939, the souvenirs were sold. Today the focus is on engineering, and in 1975 the ceramics and metallurgy departments merged and presently offer a degree in ceramic engineering. (Information and marks: Elva Barglof, "The Prairie-Style Art Pottery of Iowa State College," *Antique Trader*, December 1, 1982, pp. 70, 71. Marks: are hand applied except on production pieces. Lilian Hall Crowley, "American Art Pottery," *Better Homes and Gardens*, March 1928, pp. 29, and 102 to 104.)

Irish-Hosler Pottery. North East, Pennsylvania. 1960 to present (1985). Doug Irish-Hosler graduated from the University of Cincinnati with a B.F.A. degree and B.S.A.E. degree. He studied at Temple University in England, also the Pennsylvania Academy of Fine Arts, the University of Alaska, and Edinboro State University. At present, he makes porcelain and stoneware, wheel thrown pots which are bisque fired, then sandblasted to produce relief designs or texture, then glazed and fired again to 2,380 degrees F. Many are fired and sandblasted for the third time. The final result is a beautiful, polished, well executed piece of porcelain. Doug also builds slab pieces. He is a potter, sculptor and painter, and his work shows his great talent. He listed many one-man shows and two dozen or so invitational and juried shows and dozens of craft fairs that he has attended in many states. He was written about in *Showcase Magazine* in October and November 1981. The major awards he has won at the many shows are as follows: 1960, Best in State, Tri Kappa; 1961, Best in Show, University of Cincinnati; 1972, Selected for Judging, ACC Northeast Crafts Fair, Bennington, Vermont; 1974, Best in Show, Gallery 1 Sculpture Show, Petosky, Michigan; 1975, Purchase Award, Arts and Flowers Show, Erie, Pennsylvania; 1976, Artist's Selection Award, NEA Show, Erie, Pennsylvania; 1977, Judge's Choice, Boston Mills, Ohio; 1978-1983, Selected for Judging, Boston Mills, Ohio; 1980-1981, Selected for Judging, Artisans' Fair, Boston Mills, Ohio; 1982, Selected for Judging, Ceramics Fair, Boston Mills, Ohio; 1983, Best of Show, Snowtrails Craft Fair, Mansfield, Ohio; 1983, Honorable Mention, Crosby Gardens, Toledo, Ohio; 1984, Best in Show, Three Rivers, Pittsburgh, Pennsylvania; 1984, Honorable Mention, Caine Park, Cleveland Heights, Ohio; 1984, 4th Place, Shadyside Arts Festival, Pittsburgh, Pennsylvania; 1984, Craftsman Special Recognition, Berkshire Crafts Fair, Great Barrington, Maine; 1984, First Place, Counselor Award, Mitchell Museum, Mt. Vernon, Illinois. Doug's one-man shows include: Wolf and Dessaurs, Fort Wayne, Indiana; Gallery 1, Perosky, Michigan;

Townhouse Gallery, Reading, Pennsylvania; Upstairs Gallery, Reading, Pennsylvania; Albright College, Reading, Pennsylvania; Glass Growers, Erie, Pennsylvania; Clay Place, Pittsburgh, Pennsylvania, 1984; Canton Art Institute, Canton, Ohio, 1984. His recent commissions are: Envirogas, Corporate Headquarters, Buffalo, New York; Paul Reifler, Inc., Buffalo, New York.

Iron Mountain Stoneware. Laurel Bloomery, Tennessee. 1965 to present (1984). This might be called the modern version of Southern Potteries, Inc. of Erwin, Tennessee. They make a beautiful line of stoneware dinnerware with the most enticing names. Many of the pieces have hand-painted designs on them. Located at the foot of the Iron Mountains, the pottery has served as an economic development model for the whole area. Sixty workers are employed to hand and machine-make the dinnerware. Machinery is relied upon to process the clay and to fire it. Fitting the clay into the molds, trimming the dried, unfired pieces and decorating are all done by hand. Nancy Pearson, a Los Angeles ceramics designer, and Albert Mock, an architect-businessman, started the pottery in 1965. Their production approach is summed up in the statement by Nancy, "Studio pottery is too small an operation to manufacture items and still keep the unit cost down. A highly mechanized approach is just too expensive. The hand and machine approach is more interesting." Many one-of-a-kind pieces are turned out there, and the decorating varies a little from piece to piece within a given set, as is true of most hand-painted china. (Marks: no. 1, is impressed on all stoneware before it is fired. No. 2, is a copy machine copy of signature incised by Sally Patterson. No. 3, is Jim Kanako's signature added to all of his painted pieces along with mark no. 1. No. 4, is the impressed mark and incised signature on pieces painted by Sally Patterson. These marks were obtained when a secretary at the office darkened in marks on the bottom of pots and made photostatic copies of them. No. 5, is the logo. It shows what part of the impressed mark is supposed to look like.)

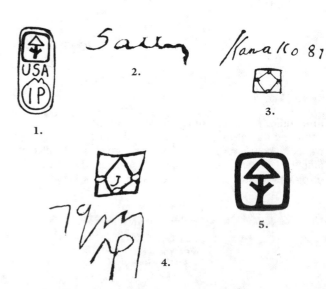

Iroquois China Company. Syracuse, New York. Started in 1905-1969. (McKee date). Between 1905 and 1939, part of that time, the plant was controlled by George H. Bowman who owned Cleveland China, a sales agency (McKee, p. 39). (See Cleveland China Company.) Bowman's mark may be found on some very nice semi-porcelain, and how much of that was made by Iroquois would be very hard to determine. In 1939, the company was owned by a local bank (probably following a bankruptcy), and at that time the plant was sold to Earl Crane, who manufactured only hotel ware until 1946. In 1946, the Iroquois China Company began production of a line of "Casual China" which had been designed by Russel Wright. There were actually three lines made by Iroquois China that became outstanding and will be quite collectible, "Iroquois Casual China," already mentioned and two lines designed by Ben Seibel, "Impromptu" and "Informal." According to Frank L. Rudesill of Buffalo China, Inc. Iroquois stopped their commercial or hotel type ware in the late 1950's or early 1960's, continuing only the lines mentioned. Financial difficulties forced them in and out of production in the late 1960's, and in 1969 they ceased operations permanently. A liquidation sale was held August 12, 1971, and the plant sold to a woodworking company.

In 1947, Iroquois began the building of a plant in Vega Baja, Puerto Rico, to manufacture under the name **Crane China Company**. This project was in conjunction with the Puerto Rico Industrial Development Corporation. In the early 1950's the plant in Puerto Rico was acquired by Sterling China Company of Wellsville, Ohio (with offices in East Liverpool). From that time on the factory in Puerto Rico was known as **Caribe China**, and the products were so marked. The Puerto Rico factory was closed by 1977. (Much of the foregoing information was furnished by letter by Stanley Campion of the Syracuse China Corporation, as well as Frank L. Rudesill of Buffalo China, Inc. See Sterling China and Caribe China for more on "Caribe" mark. Marks: no. 1 filed for registration March 29, 1956, claiming use since March 2, 1956, for tableware. From mark 2, we can see the registered word in mark 1 incorporated in an actual mark. No. 3 was filed June 14, 1917, having been in use since May of that year for use on chinaware. No. 4 was registered September 20, 1954, having been in use since August 1954, for china tableware. No. 5 is a very early mark. No. 6 is an actual mark used as shown in 1967 *China, Glass and Tableware Directory*, and found on dish. No. 7 is an enlarged version of no. 6 shown in *Gift and Decorative Accessories*, June 1960, p. 11. Nos. 8, 9, 10, 11 from 1966 *China, Glass and Tableware Directory*. The rest were photostatic copies made from dishes.)

7. THE MUSEUM COLLECTION © BY IROQUOIS U.S.A.

8. Informal GENUINE CHINA BY Iroquois — A Ben Seibel DESIGN

9. Iroquois CASUAL CHINA Russel Wright

10. FAMOUS Iroquois Impromptu GENUINE CHINA A BEN SEIBEL DESIGN

11. Intaglio A BEN SEIBEL DESIGN GENUINE CHINA BY Iroquois

12. Russel Wright CHINA by Iroquois

13. IROQUOIS CHINA USA PAT

14. IROQUOIS CASUAL CHINA by Russel Wright

15. IROQUOIS China SYRACUSE N Y D-4

16. china by Iroquois USA C6

17. china by Iroquois USA D-2

Impromptu
1.

2. Impromptu IROQUOIS Ben Seibel

IROQUOIS 3.

4. carrara MODERN BY IROQUOIS

IROQUOIS USA CHINA COPYRIGHTED 5.

P 2

THE HENRY FORD MUSEUM DEARBORN MICHIGAN THE GREENFIELD VILLAGE THE MUSEUM COLLECTION © BY Iroquois U.S.A. 6.

Ironton, Ohio, Various Potters. Ironton, Ohio. The Coultry Pottery of Cincinnati, Ohio, needed room to expand, and in 1880 they built a new plant at Ironton, Ohio, called the Ironton Pottery. (See the listing Dayton Street Pottery/Coultry Pottery Company.) By the middle of 1882, three different companies were making the same type of faience as the Coultry Pottery, and in 1882 "the decorated-ware crush was reported as practically played out," according to Paul Evans, *Art Pottery of the U.S.*, p. 67. The Ironton plant which covered almost an acre was sold at sheriff's sale in October 1881 before any machinery could ever be installed in the building. From there on I had to rely on directories for whatever history I could get for this big plant. I found a **Young and Harris** listed from 1882 to 1884. And in the 1888-1889 city directories, a **G.W. Silliman** was listed as proprietor of the Ironton Pottery at Seventh and Railroad Streets. By 1888, the directories listed **E. Manring and Company**. These potteries made stoneware, sewer pipe and terra cotta. (Mark: on a stoneware jug and furnished to the author by Clifford L. Ford. There was one other potter listed in Ironton, Ohio, who did not seem to figure into the progression of this factory. In 1878, before the Ironton Pottery was built, there was a **W.P. Harris** listed at Seventh and Lawrence Streets.)

IRONTON 2 POttery

Irvine, Samuel. Newville, Cumberland City, Pennsylvania. Around 1865 to 1875. Samuel Irvine was a selling agent who had products made for him by the Hayes Pottery. The mark as shown was found on a decorated harvest stoneware jug produced by John S. and Edwin R. Hayes. The body of the jug was gray with blue brushwork of leaves and flowers. (Information and impressed mark: Jeannette Lasansky, *Made of Mud*, pp. 40, 54.)

Irwin, Robert W., Company. Grand Rapids, Michigan. Distributor, filed October 3, 1941, for a claim to this mark to be used on ceramic breakfast, luncheon and dinner dishes, claiming use since January 1, 1940.

Ispanky Porcelains, Ltd. Pennington, New Jersey. Lazlo Ispanky received a degree in 1943 from the Fine Arts Academy in Budapest, where he was born. He came to this country in 1956 where he received a fellowship at Cranbrook Academy of Art in Bloomfield Hills, Michigan. In 1960, he worked for Cybis Porcelains. In 1966, he opened his own studio where he has made detailed porcelain art pieces, each numbered and mold destroyed, etc. In the 1977-1978 *China, Glass and Tableware Directory*, the company was listed for porcelain figurines, bronzes and graphics. In the May 1977 *Smithsonian* magazine was advertised "Washington at Prayer," sculpted by Ispanky, hand cast by Royal Doulton and sponsored by The Freedom Foundation at Valley Forge at $875.00 each. (Information: Jenny B. Derwich and Dr. Mary

Latos, *Dictionary Guide to U.S. Pottery and Porcelain*, p. 124. Mark: 1971 directory as cited.)

I-T-E Imperial Corporation. Victor, New Jersey. I-T-E bought the Victor, New York plant belonging to the Victor Insulators Company, Inc. in 1953 and operated it as the Victor Insulators Division of the I-T-E Imperial Corporation. They are now a major producer of pin type insulators marked with I-T-E trademark and occasionally other letters for the style of the insulator. I-T-E Imperial merged with Gould, Inc. May 1, 1976. The name was changed to Gould, Inc. officially December 1, 1976. The I-T-E marking on insulators at the Victor plant was phased out in 1977, and the pin types were then marked (incuse) with the Gould logo (see mark no. 2). In 1980, Gould entered into a joint venture with Brown, Boveri and Company of Baden, Switzerland, and the Victor, New York plant operated as Gould-Brown Boveri, with continued use of the Gould logo marking. In late 1981, Gould sold its interest to Brown, Boveri and Company, and the former I-T-E divisions became Brown Boveri Electric, Inc., a subsidiary of Brown, Boveri and Company. The insulator marking was then changed to "BBC." See mark no. 3. (Information and mark: Jack H. Tod, *Porcelain Insulators Guide Book for Collectors*, p. 106, and by letter. Mark is incuse (stamped in).

WL 1.

2.

BBC

3.

J

Jabeson China Company, Inc. New York, New York. Filed for registration of mark 1 on September 29, 1943, to be used on ceramic table, cooking ware, bar ware, vases, jardinieres, candy boxes, jars, jugs, flower pots, cuspitors, combinettes, chambers and churns, claiming use since August 15, 1942. Mark 2 is from the 1945 *Crockery and Glass Journal Directory* under the distributor, Bernard Lipman, for figurines. Lipman listed four factories the company represented; Princeton China Corporation, Nancy China, Jabeson China Company, Inc., and the Bristol Ceramic Corporation. This leads me to believe Jabeson was a manufacturer. These were the only listings I found for Jabeson.

 1.

2.

Jackson China, Inc. Falls Creek, Pennsylvania. 1917 to present (1985). **Jackson Vitrified China Company** was founded in 1917 on the site of the old **Bohemian Art Pottery** which had gone bankrupt during World War I. Jackson Vitrified China was not incorporated until 1920. Then in the mid-1920's the company withstood a severe blow when two of the principals of the corporation were killed by a disgruntled debtor of the old Bohemian Art Pottery. Local support and the bank in DuBois kept the pottery going. In 1946, Philip R. Distillator purchased all shares of stock from local stockholders, doubled the floor space, provided modern equipment, and doubled the work force. A decorating plant was operated in New York until it was destroyed by fire in 1967. Jackson Featherweight China, designed by M.A. Van Nostrand, was made after 1939 until the 1960's and was marketed under the name "Royal Jackson," according to company information. At the present time (1985) production is 100% institutional china. In September 1976, Andrew Greystoke purchased the company and the name changed to **Jackson China, Incorporated**. In January 1985, Jackson China encountered some financial difficulties and was reorganized. The new owners became Tim Carr and Robert Hoover.

(Marks: Jackson China seems to have filed few marks for registration. All of their records are destroyed every seven years, so the company couldn't help much. Mark 12, filed December 21, 1953, for decorated and undecorated china dinnerware and hotel-ware, claiming use since 1947. Nos. 1-10 from Quality Stamp Company, East Liverpool, Ohio. Nos. 13-17 from Commercial Decal Company, East Liverpool, Ohio. Robert B. Bernstorf verified these as marks used by Jackson China. Nos. 19-21 are shown in various directories of the 1950's, 1960's. Nos. 22-24 were recent marks sent by the company. The dating code shown was verified by Lee Berry from Jackson Vitrified China Company in November 1981. He said Jackson China used mainly stamped marks. No. 25 on dish.

Jackson China Date Code From 1951

A - 1951	H - 1958	O - 1965	V - 1972	
B - 1951	I - 1959	P - 1966	W - 1973	C - 1979
C - 1953	J - 1960	Q - 1967	X - 1974	D - 1980
D - 1954	K - 1961	R - 1968	Y - 1975	E - 1981
E - 1955	L - 1962	S - 1969	Z - 1976	F - 1982
F - 1956	M - 1963	T - 1970	A - 1977	etc.
G - 1957	N - 1964	U - 1971	B - 1978	

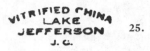

25.

Jackson Internationale. Pelham Manor, New York. 1960's. Listed under importers and American pottery in the 1966 and 1967 *China, Glass and Tablewares Directory.* They were listed as fine china dinnerware sellers, so they evidently handled both American and foreign dishes. The Pelham Manor business burned in the late 1960's and was no longer listed in the 1970's. In the 1967 directory, Philip R. Distillator was the president of Jackson Internationale. He was also president of Jackson China until around 1980 and Vogue Ceramic Industries, which was listed through the 1950's. See the listings for Jackson China Company and Vogue Ceramics Industries.

Jackson, Sharon. Worthington, Ohio. Sharon, a studio potter, started in February 1982 to make functional stoneware on a commercial basis.

Jalanivich (Manuele) and Olsen (Ingvardt). San Francisco, California. Around 1920 to middle 1940's. These potters are what Paul Evan terms transitional potters which had the characteristics of both art and studio potters. Evans said this group of transitional potters existed from 1910 to 1930, but there are studio potters today who make only beautiful art pieces and defy such exact classification as to studio or art potters. Jalanivich, born 1897, was a designer, sculptor, who made hand thrown and molded pieces. He became interested in pottery through George Ohr of Biloxi Art Pottery and Joseph Meyer of Newcomb Pottery. He studied under Leon Volkmar of the Durant Kilns. (See various listings for these men.) Olsen was the technical authority on clay and glazing. He was born in Copenhagen, Denmark in 1888, studied at the Royal Danish Copenhagen Chinese Kilns, and came to the United States at age 20. Around 1935, some molded pieces were made by these potters, but Evans said they lacked the quality of their earlier work. The studio was closed in 1938, and the pair moved to Belmont, California, where they made molded pieces for a few years. Jalanivich died in 1944. From 1937 to 1939, for two years, Jalanivich taught at the San Francisco Art Institute. The two men opened a school of ceramics for women in the Bay Area in 1938. The pieces had a low fired earthenware body, but the glazes were exceptional. They had a crackle glaze and sometimes two glazes were mixed by running one glaze over the top of the other. Designs included Persian, Egyptian and Chinese influences. Gumps of San Francisco sold Jalan pieces. (See the listing for S. and G. Gump Company.) Gumps loaned a bowl and several pieces to the 1939 San Francisco Golden Gate International Exposition for display. The Jalan pieces have received many awards and honors around the world. (Information: Paul Evans,

"Jalan: Transitional Pottery of San Francisco," *Spinning Wheel*, April 1973, pp. 28, 48, 49. Marks: According to Evans as cited, the only marks used by the studio aside from the incised Jalan marks, were "I.O." or "Olie," designating Olsen's work. In Belmont, some pieces were marked with a "B" and a date. Mark is shown from Evan's article as cited, p. 49. The name, Jalan, is also found with San Francisco, below.)

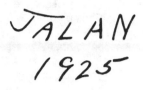

Jam Ceramic Design. Sacramento, California. 1975 to present (1983). At first, Jo Anne Marquardt used the name Jam Creative Pottery. In 1978, she moved to larger facilities, and the name was changed to Jam Ceramic Design. She makes low fired whiteware, highly decorated in a variety of colorful hand decorated functional and decorative pieces. Jo Anne designs all of the pieces, including all kinds of fruit which would be fine for filling artificial fruit bowls; decorative, fruits, chefs, etc. to attach with magnets to kitchen appliances; also what she calls "plant stix," "garden stakes," "plant pols," which are decorative flowers, birds, frogs, etc. for sticking in flower pots with flowers, spoon holders, trivets, ceramic pumpkin faces, salt and peppers in fruits and vegetables and even a complete hamburger sandwich; wind chimes are made in shapes of leaves, fruits, birds, animals, letters, keys, chickens, cows, etc. are just a few of the original designs created by this unusual artist. Pictured are a signed mark and a paper label.

sacramento california

James, Bill Y. Miami, Oklahoma. Filed for registration of these marks in 1969, 1970 and 1971, for use on decorative plates made of earthenware. "First American" and "Keep Forever" were used on dinnerware. This was probably a decorating agency.

GRANDMOTHER'S   MOTHER'S

BRIDAL PLATE

FAMILY

KEEPFOREVER

THE FIRST AMERICANS

James River Potteries. Hopewell, Virginia. See Hopewell China Company for history. (Mark: Connie Roger.)

JAMES RIVER POTTERIES
VIRGINIA   H/P

22 KT. GOLD

Jamestown China. Mt. Clemens, Michigan. See Mt. Clemens Pottery for history.

James Towne Collony Pottery. Williamsburg, Virginia. Started in 1929. Filed for registration of this mark on November 29, 1946, for use on vases, dinnerware, casseroles, baking dishes and water pitchers, claiming use since October 30, 1929. P.M. Griesenauer made pieces similar to the old ware found at Jamestown according to Derwich and Latos, *Dictionary Guide to U.S. Pottery and Porcelain*, p. 127.

James Towne Collony

Janas, Stephanie. Toledo, Ohio. 1950 to present (1983). Stephanie is a studio potter making utilitarian and decorative pieces of stoneware, porcelain and earthenware, which are thrown, cast and handbuilt. During the last three years this potter has been making a Greek Attic type of earthenware with terrasigillata, burnished and unburnished. Stephanie studied at the Toledo Museum of Art, Bowling Green University, and Southern Illinois University. She has pieces in permanent collections in several churches. She has won numerous awards in juried shows in the Toledo area especially.

janas

Jansen, Jenny. Savannah, Missouri. 1981 to present (1984). Studio potter making wheel thrown stoneware into dinnerware, lamps, etc.

Jansen

Jaska of California. Los Angeles, California. Started after 1946 and was listed in the 1948 *China and Glass Red Book Directory* for semi-porcelain as making handmade and hand-painted baby bowls, baby mugs, baby plates, decorated in nursery rhyme characters and animated animals and infor-

mal and patio dinnerware. Pottery was not listed in the 1960's. (Mark: from 1954 *Crockery and Glass Journal Directory*.)

Jeannette Corporation. Had its beginning in 1898 and is another corporation like Anchor Hocking Corporation which is known in the field of glass but which entered into the pottery industry as well. Jeannette Glass Company was incorporated in Pennsylvania on April 8, 1936, to acquire assets and business of its predecessor company of the same name which had been started in June, 1898. The Jeannette Corporation name was adopted in 1971. In 1961, Jeannette acquired McKee Glass and in 1968, Blefeld and Company, an importing company. Then in 1969 they became involved in pottery as a part of their "Tabletop" concept by acquiring Harker Pottery which stopped producing in 1972. (See Harker Pottery.) Also in 1969, they purchased Royal China Company of Sebring, Ohio, which had already purchased French Saxon China of Sebring in 1964 (see French Saxon). Hence, Jeannette acquired both plants. In 1976, the entire Jeannette Corporation was sold to Coca-Cola Bottling Company of New York. See the Royal China Company listing for the intervening events that led to the complete closing of the Royal China factory in 1986. On November 15, 1976, the Jeannette Corporation had purchased Walker China Company of Bedford, Ohio. (See the listing Walker China Company for the events that led to the final closing of that factory on June 16, 1980. See the listings for the potteries for marks used during the Jeannette Corporation ownership.)

Jeffery-Dewitt Insulator Company. Kenova, West Virginia. In 1915, the company built a plant in Kenova to manufacture suspension insulators. In 1921, the company sold to the Champion Sparkplug Company. Then in 1940 the owner became W.L. Stinson. In 1951, the Line Material Company, a division of McGraw Electric Company, bought the plant. Jack Tod's *Porcelain Insulators Guide Book for Collectors*, p. 116, said the mark shown was continued during this period. In 1952, the plant burned and was not rebuilt. For technical information as to types of insulators made there and processes used, see the Tod book. He gives many details. (Information and mark: Tod, as cited.)

J and E Decorators. Zanesville, Ohio. 1956 to 1962. This pottery made birds and lawn ornaments and decorated some decorative pieces. (Information: Jenny B. Derwich and Dr. Mary Latos, *Dictionary Guide to U.S. Pottery and Porcelain*, p. 116. Mark: backstamped on piece.)

J. & E.

Jeffords, J.E. See Port Richmond Pottery Company.

Jegglin Family Potters. Boonville and Calhoun, Missouri, from around 1850 to around 1890's. G.A. Jegglin, around 1881 in Calhoun; E.A. Jegglin, around 1894 in Boonville, Cooper City; J.M. Jegglin, around 1867 in Boonville, Cooper City. Made stoneware. J.M. mark on 6 gallon stoneware crock. Other two marks on brown heavy glazed jugs. (Information and marks: Henry W. Heflin, pottery collector and researcher.)

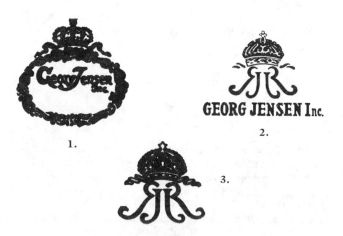

J.M. JEGGLIN
BOONVILLE, MO.

FROM
G.A. JEGGLIN
CALHOUN, MO.

E.A. JEGGLIN
BOONVILLE, MO.

Jensen, Georg, Inc. New York, New York. A selling agency with a Madison Avenue shop that sold many products including a diamond brooch, advertised in *Venture*, June 1964, Vol. 1, no. 1, p. 23. In "Pottery-Making: A Jensen Attraction," *Gifts and Decorative Accessories Magazine*, December 1973, p. 170, is the story of Nancy Patterson, one of the designers of Iron Mountain Stoneware coming to Jensens to set up a potter's wheel to demonstrate pottery making as a promotion for pottery from that company sold by Jensen. In "American Pottery Comes of Age," *House Beautiful*, August 1943, pp. 6, 66, it tells Georg Jensen was selling the "Della Robbia" pattern made by Paden City Pottery. The marks shown were filed by Jensen, but may not have been used on American made ware because the company also sold the finest of imported foreign ware. (Marks: Company filed for rights to mark 1 on January 13, 1948, to be used on crockery and chinaware such as plates, platters and all various dinnerware pieces, coffee pots, teapots, creamers, etc., also basins, mild jugs, mustard pots, marmalade jars, egg cups, salad bowls, cookie jars, etc., claiming use since June 5, 1942. Mark 2 was filed on January 7, 1948, for the same articles, claiming use since January 20, 1940. Mark 3 was filed June 21, 1946, for the same articles, claiming use since 1932.)

Georg Jensen Inc.
1.

GEORG JENSEN Inc.
2.

3.

Jersey City Pottery. Jersey City, New Jersey. 1827 to around 1829. In 1825, it was incorporated as the **Jersey Porcelain**

and Earthenware Company. Jersey Porcelain and Earthenware Company won a silver medal at the Franklin Insitute in Philadelphia in 1826, and their products were good enough that the company should have lasted more than the two years it did. In 1833, the factory was reopened by David and J. Henderson as the **American Pottery Manufacturing Company** until 1840 when the name became **American Pottery Company**. From 1845 to 1854, William Rhodes was the owner and made white granite and cream-colored ware. Jersey City Pottery made eight-sided pitchers decorated with the bust of William Henry Harrison in 1840. (Thelma Shull, "American Scenes for the China Collector, *Hobbies*, June 1942, p. 66.) In 1855, the owners were Rouse, Turner, Duncan and Henry, and later the name was just Rouse and Turner, who made white pottery exclusively. The American Pottery Company imported Staffordshire potters from England in 1840 to make dinnerware in the "Canova" pattern. Canova pictures an urn set in a Venetian background and has a border pattern with flowers, leaves and ships. (Katherine B. Ripley, "Canova Pottery," *Hobbies*, January 1942, p. 58.) Daniel Greatback molded his first hound handled pitcher while working at the American Pottery Company. (Peter Cook , "Bennington's Hound Handled Pitchers," *Antique Trader*, May 25, 1976, p. 332.) Barber states in *Marks of American Potters*, p. 44, the old buildings were torn down in 1892 to make room for modern improvements. Then in *Pottery and Porcelain of the U.S.*, p. 440, Barber states that the last proprietor of the Jersey City Pottery had died. The marks shown with the name Henderson or American Pottery Manufacturing Company may be dated before 1840. Mark no. 13 with initials R. and T. for Rouse and Turner may be dated around 1850 when they became owners. The I.V.W. mark was used around 1880. (Information: Barber, *Marks of American Potters*, p. 41, 44. Marks: nos. 1, 4, 6, 7, 10, 11, 12, 13, Barber, *Marks of American Potters*, p. 41, 44. Marks 8, 9, 14, 15, Ramsay, p. 252. Marks, 2, 3, 5, Spargo, p. 358.)

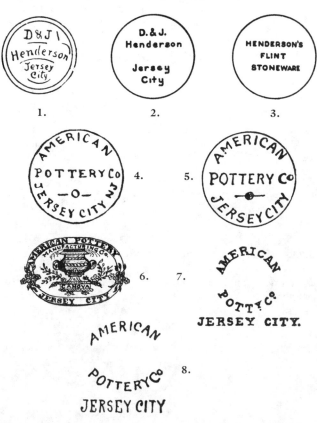

1.   2.   3.

4.   5.

6.   7.

8.

AM. POTTERY MANUF. CO. JERSEY CITY

9.

AM. POTTERY MANUF? Co. JERSEY CITY.

10.

AMERICAN POTT? CO JERSEY CITY

11.

I.V.W.

12.

R. & T.

13.

CANOVA AMERICAN POT MANUF. CO JERSEY CITY

14.

AMERICAN POTTERY CO JERSEY CITY

15. Impressed

Jervis, Dorothy. New York, New York. This studio potter made pottery for a period of 50 years. Born in 1909, died in 1980. She attended Ethical Culture School and considered herself to be a self-taught potter. She sold at craft fairs through the distributor American House (see that listing), G. Fox and Company, and Rena Rosenthal selling agency, among others. She received several awards from various craft groups during her career. (Above information given to Thomas G. Turnquist on October 3, 1984, by letter from Herman Jervis. Incised mark: sent by Turnquist.)

JERVIS

J. and H. International/Jepcor International, Inc. Wilmette, Illinois. J. and H. International was a selling agency out of Chicago, Illinois, based in Wilmette, Illinois. They became Jepcor International, Inc. sometime before the middle of the 1970's. In the 1975 to 1976 *China, Glass and Tableware Redbook Directory*, Jepcor was listed under domestic and imported ironstone and stoneware dinnerware and fine porcelain china and cookware. The Sheffield trademark was used by both companies, according to E.S. Carson at Homer Laughlin China Company. Homer Laughlin made some products with this mark for these distributors. (See the H.L.C. listing.) The marks shown were also on dishes made in America, but I have not identified the maker of the dishes, only the owners of the trademark. There were undoubtedly many more of these Sheffield marks. (Marks: Quality Stamp Company, East Liverpool, Ohio.)

Golden Meadow IRONSTONE
Sheffield ™
● DETERGENT·PROOF
● OVEN·PROOF
● DISHWASHER·SAFE
MADE IN U.S.A.

Sheffield ™
SUPREME
Demur
MADE IN U.S.A.

Sheffield ™
GRANADA
MADE IN USA

Blue Dresden by Sheffield ™ TM
MADE IN U.S.A

Jervis, William Percival. This potter is best known for his writing about pottery. Many times in this book I have shown marks from "The World's Pottery Marks," printed in the *Pottery, Glass and Brass Salesman* magazine in many installments, 1913 through 1916. "A Dictionary of Pottery Terms" in the same magazine, 1917 through 1918, is also very good. He also wrote *Rough Notes on Pottery* and *A Pottery Primer*. Jervis worked in several potteries before starting his own business in 1908. In 1902, he was manager of Vance/Avon Faience and around that time he had a pottery of his own in Corona, New York, which was very short lived because it burned. Norris E. Schneider in "Owens Made Pottery Ware" *Zanesville Times Signal*, April 7, 1963 (no p. no.) said J.B. Owens bought the molds and equipment and moved them to Zanesville, Ohio. Schneider said the Corona pieces resembled a type of bronze ware. In 1904, he had a pottery shop or studio in the Guild Hall, side room of the Rose Valley Pottery, Rose Valley, Pennsylvania. The Rose Valley Association had been formed in 1901 as an arts and crafts colony. In 1905, pottery work at Rose Valley ceased, and Jervis moved again, this time to the Craven Art Pottery in East Liverpool, Ohio, organized in 1904. Jervis stayed in East Liverpool until the Craven Art Pottery was dissolved in 1908.

At this time, he went to Oyster Bay, New York, and started his own pottery, the Jervis Pottery, which operated until 1912. Jervis made art pottery in the different potteries in which he worked. For a full discussion of the pieces, see Paul Evan's book as cited. Jervis used sgraffito as one method of decorating. He preferred matt glazes and subdued colors. Jervis wanted his pieces to be useful or utilitarian ware, vessels, flowerpots, pitchers, vases, etc. (Information: Paul Evans, *Art Pottery of the U.S.*, pp. 65, 74, 75, 133-135, 261-263. Marks: The first four marks are from Jervis's work, "The World's Pottery Works," *Pottery, Glass and Brass Salesman*, April 2, 1914, p. 12, and November 6, 1913, p. 13. Nos. 1, 2, 3 were used at Rose Valley, accoridng to Jervis, as cited. No. 4 was used at East Liverpool, in 1906 to 1907. Jervis said the same mark was used with the word "Briarcliff," in 1913. No. 5 is from Evans, p. 135 and was used at Oyster Bay.)

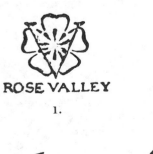

ROSE VALLEY
1.

C C C C C C
2.

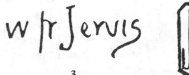

W P Jervis
3.

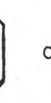

4.   5.

Johns-Manville. New York, New York. 1858 to present. H.W. Johns Manufacturing Company founded in 1858 merged with Manville Covering Company in 1901 to become the H.W. Johns-Manville Company, and later the initials H.W. were dropped from the name. This company is well known for items made of asbestos and other fibrous materials. Johns-Manville, over the years, cataloged and sold porcelain pin type insulators sold by many American manufacturers including Pittsburg High Voltage, Thomas Porcelain, New Lexington High Voltage Porcelain Company, Brooklyn and Ohio Brass. (Information and incuse (stamped) mark: Jack H. Tod, *Porcelain Insulators Guide Book for Collectors*, p. 125.)

JOHNS-MANVILLE

Johnson, Shirley. Stillwater, Minnesota. 1973 to present. Studio potter who works in the same studio with the renowned Warren MacKenzie making utilitarian porcelain and stoneware.

Johnson, Whitmore and Company. Akron, Ohio. 1856 to 1862, became **Whitmore, Robinson and Company** from 1862-1900. They were makers of stoneware, yellowware, Rockingham, and after 1870 they made a white granite with a buff body and an opaque glaze. They employed 129 in 1888. The **Robinson-Merrill Company** was formed from a combination of Whitmore, Robinson and Company and the **E.H. Merrill Company** in 1900, and in 1902 the company was called the **Robinson Clay Products Company**. To go back now to pick up the history of E.H. Merrill; that potter started in Mogodore between 1833 and 1835 to make clay bottles, tobacco pipes, stoneware, etc. (Mogodore became part of Akron). In 1847, he moved to Springfield Township, which also became a part of Akron. There **Edwin and Calvin Merrill** operated from 1847 to 1861. Then from 1861 to 1888 Edwin H. Merrill and Henry E. Merrill called their business the **Akron Pottery Company**. From 1888 to around 1900 the plant was the E.H. Merrill and Company. (There was a second Akron Pottery Company from 1896 to around 1900 according to Blair, p. 10, which was an association of seven firms trying to stay in business in hard times.) In 1920, according to company information from **Robinson-Ransbottom** of Roseville, Ohio, the **Ransbottom Brothers Pottery** of Roseville, Ohio, combined with the Robinson Clay Products of Akron, Ohio, to form Robinson-Ransbottom still active.

The four Ransbottom brothers founded their pottery in Ironspot, one mile north of Roseville, around 1900. Between 1900 and 1910, they also operated a plant in Saltillo, Ohio, for the manufacture of stoneware jars. This plant was incorporated into the Roseville plant around 1910. Sometime before 1920, Robinson Clay Products had shifted its emphasis from utilitarian stoneware to mostly bricks. A cylindar ink and a handled jug in gray and white were found marked, ''R.C.P. Co. No. 2, Akron, O.'' on the base. Also, two cone inks were found marked ''Merrill'' and ''Merrill Pottery.'' Around 1916, Ransbottom Brothers Pottery was the country's largest producer of stoneware jars. They also made preserve jars, churns, milk pans or bowls, poultry fountains, etc. Robinson-Ransbottom Pottery Company in business

now makes a quality product characteristic of the fine products made by the long line of predecessors. Because the products are so good and Robinson Ransbottom uses marks very similar at times to those used by the Roseville Pottery Company, the products of the two companies are confused by some sellers. Both companies marked products just Roseville, Ohio. Study the marks for both companies. Also, look for marks under the names of the various companies underlined. (Information: Lois Lehner, *Ohio Pottery and Glass*, pp. 13, 15; Wilbur Stout, *Clay Industry of Ohio*, Geological Survey of Ohio, Bulletin 26, Columbus, 1923, p. 54. The mark shown is a four leaf clover, which was used very early by the Ransbottom Brothers. The mark is in blue on a brown and white jug.)

Jones, Cecil. Studio potter from England came to this country in 1913 after having been headmaster at the Coalbrookdale School of Art and designed tiles and architectural faience and modeled for different English firms. In 1913, he went to work at the American Encaustic Tiling Company at Zanesville, Ohio, as a modeler. He became head of the department and was transferred to their New Jersey plant. Around 1919, Jones went to California, where he headed the A.E.T. Company's Los Angeles plant until 1930. After that, he worked at Claycraft for two years for the Robertsons. In 1933, he worked at the Van Briggle Pottery in Colorado and helped to organize the Broadmoor Art Pottery. Jones died in 1949. While living in New Jersey, he was a member of the New York Society of Craftsmen. His work represented the American Encaustic Tiling Company at the Metropolitan Museum of Art in 1921, 1922 and 1924. In 1931, his modeled plaques were in special showings at the Los Angeles County Museum. A piece he made was described as cast earthenware with floral design and a brilliantly lustered surface in several reds, orange rose and green colors, dated 1947. (Information: Hazel V. Bray, *The Potter's Art in California*, pp. 50.52. Mark: incised; sent by Thomas Turnquist by letter.)

Jones, Cindy Butler. Tipp City, Ohio. 1973 to present. In 1973, Bill and Cindy Jones started the **Jones Family Pottery** in New Carlisle, Ohio, making functional ware and whimsical pieces such as bells, banks, sculptures, etc. After they moved to Tipp City in 1979, Bill only made pottery for a few more months, but Cindy continued under just her own name Cindy Butler Jones, or M. Lucinda Butler Jones which she signs on pieces with the date or a bisque stamp as shown. They no longer maintain a retail shop, but she sells and shows her work at exhibitions. She had a one-person show at Indianapolis Museum of Art and has had pieces pictured in

Ceramics Monthly and miscellaneous exhibitions she has already done in her short career. She did one private commission in Washington, D.C. for a 6' decorative panel in porcelain.

C. Butler Jones

M. Lucinda Butler Jones

Jones, J.A. Young Cane, Union County, Georgia. Around 1870's. This was one of Georgia's few mountain potteries, according to John A. Burrison, *Brothers in Clay*, p. 117. The jug pictured in Burrison is stoneware with olive brown ash glaze and five pour spouts. (Information and one-of-a-kind inscription: Burrison, as cited. The jug was inscribed to a Miss L.A. Wilborn/a present by J.A. Jones/Young, Ga.)

g J A Jones young ga

Jones, McDuffee and Straton. Boston, Massachusetts. Early 1800's to around 1953. Mark 1 was found in the 1952 *Crockery and Glass Journal Directory*. Sometimes starting dates are a little exaggerated by companies in marks and advertisements, but according to mark 1, the company started in 1810. The company did register the mark "Tournay" in 1877. (No picture of mark available.) In the *Pottery, Glass and Brass Salesman* magazine, October 8, 1914, p. 10, Jones, McDuffee and Stratton advertised Lenox, Onondago China, Greenwood Pottery Company and Knowles, Taylor, Knowles products along with their foreign made ware. They were listed under decorative wall plates in 1952. They were not listed in 1954. See Sterling China Company for mark for Jones, McDuffee and Stratton. (Marks 2 and 3 were both filed for registration on September 4, 1893, claiming use since November 1891 for no. 2, and since April 1, 1893 for no. 1, for use on table and toilet ware. Nos. 4, 5, 6, 7, 8 were all filed for registration on January 11, 1895. All were said to be used only in the year 1894 for prior use. "Bonaventure" was for pottery for household use; the other four were for tableware.)

1.

2.

CAMPANIA

3.

SAINT LAZARE

4.

5. BONAVENTURE

ENGADINE   KREMLIN

6.   7.

CATHERINE MERMET   8.

Jones Pottery. Pittston, Pennsylvania. Around 1800-1880. In Harold F. Guilland, *Early American Folk Pottey*, p. 102, is a picture of a crock that shows the mark of an Evan R. Jones in Pittston, which Guilland dates around 1800. Ramsay, p. 177, lists Evan B. Jones in Pittston around 1880. Both men made stoneware and were probably father and son, but I did not verify any connection between them other than name, place and product. (Mark 2, Thorn p. 131.)

EVAN R. JONES   EVAN B. JONES

PITTSTON PA.   PITTSTON

1.   2.   PENNA.

Jugtown Pottery. Seagrove, Moore County, North Carolina. A Jugtown did mean any little town that had several potters making hand thrown utilitarian jugs, mugs, etc. in older times. Around 1921, Julianna and Jacques Busbee started a pottery which they called Jugtown Pottery. They searched in the area for the old experienced potters who had made these wares to come to work in their pottery. The Busbees had a tea room in Greenwich Village, New York City, and later a shop in Jugtown to sell the pottery. In 1923, they hired Ben Owen as a potter and new shapes and glazes were developed. Jacques Busbee died in 1947. In 1958, Mrs. Busbee became ill, and the pottery was closed in 1959, reorganized and opened again in April 1960 under the direction of John Mare. From 1968 until 1982, Nancy Sweezy was a potter who operated the Jugtown Pottery for Country Roads, Inc. (See the listing for Nancy Sweezy.) In 1982, the Jugtown Pottery was sold by Country Roads, Inc. to Vernon Owens, who had been working there as chief potter since 1960. Country Roads, Inc. had owned the pottery since 1968.

The log home of the Busbees which was later that of Nancy Sweezy was purchased by Owens. (See the listing Various Owen family potters.) A brown glaze called "Tobacco Spit" brown and Jugtown orange were made at the pottery. The shapes were simple yet beautiful. Stoneware was salt glazed and sometimes glazed in white and frogskin glazes. During the Busbee period, Chinese style pieces were also made. Tobacco Spit and orange glazes were used on earthenware during Busbee's period. Since these were lead glazes they were replaced by higher temperature glazes under Nancy Sweezy's direction to avoid using lead. The colors are blue ridge blue, cinnamon, mustard green, white, wood smoke and a new tobacco spit brown and also occasionally the old orange is used on non-food ware. The same Jugtown mark has been impressed in the clay over the years. The ware has not changed a great deal either. (Information: Nancy Sweezy, *Raised in Clay*, pp. 211-217, and by letter. Mark: stamped on piece.)

K

Kahiki Restaurant. Columbus, Ohio. In business at present (1986). Well vitrified, brown glazed pottery, tall drinking containers with totem pole-type face found incised on bottom with restaurant name.

Kahla China Company. New York, New York. I had no way to determine if this was a manufacturer or selling agency. The company filed for rights to the mark shown on January 11, 1926, claiming use since 1925 for use on goods made of china, such as cups and saucers, salad dishes, bowls, sugar bowls, creamers, jugs, mugs, teapots, covered dishes, casseroles, coffeepots, chocolate pots, vegetable dishes, meat platters, covered butter dishes, spoon trays, celery trays, olive trays, bonbon trays, spoon holders, gravy boats, chop plates, hair receivers, puff boxes, comb and brush trays, salt and pepper shakers, toothpick holders, mustard pots, mayonnaise dishes, marmalade jars, condensed milk jars, hatpin holders, sauce tureens, soup tureens, pickle dishes, fruit saucers, cereal saucers, individual plates, bone plates, egg cups, syrup pitchers, ramekins, stands, cracker jars, salt dips, teapot dishes, cuspidors, vases.

UNITY

Kaneko, Jun. Kaneko was a painter in Japan before coming to the U.S. in 1963. In 1964, he studied at the Chouinard Art School in Los Angeles under Ralph Bacerra. He also studied at the studio of Jerry Rothman in Los Angeles and at the University of California in Berkeley with Peter Voulkos and finally at the Claremont Graduate School, Claremont, California, where he received an M.F.A. degree in 1971. Before returning to Japan in 1973, he taught at the Rhode Island School of Design. During his stay in the U.S., Kaneko did many group and one-man exhibitions. (Information: Garth Clark, *A Century of Ceramics in the U.S.*, p. 300. Painted marks: Linda Steigleder, from the booklet published by the Everson Museum of Art to accompany the 1978 exhibition, "A Century of Ceramics in the U.S.")

Karen's Kustom Kreations. Crooksville, Ohio. 1973 - in business 1983. Terry Thompson makes decorative pottery in molds very similar to that by Twin Winton Pottery. Pieces include attractively glazed watering can planters, owls, bowls, pitchers, figurines, etc. A few pieces will be found with the "K.K.K." mark. Most pieces are unmarked.

Karlinsey Pottery, Inc. Tacoma, Washington. 1974 to present (1985). Robert Karlinsey, studio potter, makes stoneware cartoon pottery. From 1974 until 1977, Mr. Karlinsey made pottery somewhere in California. In 1977, he moved to Tacoma. He sculptures cartoon faces on cups, cookie jars, toothbrush holders, money socks, etc. Shown is Karlinsey's logo and a "K" he uses on pieces.

Kass China. East Liverpool, Ohio. Around 1929-1972. John B. Kass was working in pottery in his home in the late 1920's and early 1930's. In my dinnerware book, I gave starting date as 1929 and closing date of 1973 which I still believe to be authentic. William Gates in his book *East Liverpool Pottery District: Identification of Manufacturers and Marks*, California, Pennsylvania: published by Society for Historical Archaeology, p. 97, gave 1935 as a starting date because he states that Kass purchased some equipment and started a back yard pottery operation. June Jackson, daughter of John B. Kass, by letter and telephone assured me he was working with pottery prior to that time. For an ending date Gates had 1978. In my book, I had used 1972 as an ending date which Mrs. Jackson reaffirms as correct. In 1971, the son of John B. Kass, who was operating the business, had a stroke. His wife continued to go to the plant to pack and process a few orders for another year but then her health failed too. A sale of stock, etc. was held in 1978, but the pottery was gone long before that time. Kass China made novelty specialties and did a lot of decorating to order. In the 1950's, they decorated a lot of china for Homer Laughlin. George H. Bowman of the Cleveland China Company had products decorated by Kass. (Information and marks: June Jackson, daughter of the founder John B. Kass.)

Kaufman's Department Stores, Inc. Pittsburgh, Pennsylvania. Distributor. Filed for rights to this mark on August 8, 1924, to be used on brown earthenware bowls for egg beater, porcelain bowls for mayonnaise mixer, earthen dinner ware (English and American made), and earthenware teapots. In crockery, they had jars, jugs, mixing bowls, teapots, cuspidors and combinets. They also listed imported earthenware table and kitchen wares, claiming use since July 1, 1913.

Kaul, Leo. Chicago, Illinois. Filed for registration of mark 1 on December 4, 1937 for use on pottery flower and bud vases, pitchers, powder boxes, perfume bottles, jewelry boxes, tea and coffee sets, urns and baskets, claiming use since November 4, 1937. Mark 2 is from Quality Stamp Company, East Liverpool, Ohio. Mark 2 tells us that Kaul did sell some American made or American decorated products because the mark came from Quality Stamp Company.

 1.   2.

Keeler, Brad. Los Angeles, California. Brad Keeler was the son of Rufus Keeler who was prominent in the tile business in Malibu, California. Brad worked in several potteries in the Los Angeles area in the 1930's. Brad started a pottery in his garage and made 12 Flamingo figurines which he sold to Bullock's Department Store. By World War II, Brad Keeler employed 50 to 60 people. He modeled or sculpted the figures. Then they were made from molds and glazed. Birds of all kinds, lobsters, etc. were made into figurines and also were used to decorate bowls, planters, candlesticks and other decorative pieces. Brad made figurines of Jose Carioca, Donald Duck and other Disney characters. Keeler died in 1952 at age 39. I can find no mention of the American Pottery Company shown in this mark. Betty Newbound, "Along the Flea Market Trail," *Depression Glass Daze*, August 1984, p. 42, is the source of this information on Keeler. She mentions there may have been some connection between Evan K. Shaw and the American Pottery Company. Shaw purchased the Metlox Pottery in 1947, but I have found nothing on the American Pottery Company. (Information and mark: Betty Newbound, as cited, and by letter. No. 2, copy of paper label in metallic gold with black background, sent by Edward Blas, researcher in American pottery. No. 3, incised on leaf type ashtray with two birds on one side, sent by Rena London, writer on American pottery.)

1.   2.

3.

Keepsake House and Madow's. New York, New York. Filed for registration on this mark on October 12, 1964, for use on china dinnerware under the name, Louis Madow, claiming use since March 15, 1955.

KEEPSAKE HOUSE

Keister Pottery. Main and Depot Streets, Strasburg, Virginia. Adam Keister, Sr. came from Pennsylvania to Virginia in the late 18th century to establish a pottery. He was the father of eight children. Adam's son, Isaac, also became a potter and moved to Columbiana, Ohio. Adam Keister, Jr. and Henry Keister, both sons of the first Adam, were merchants and had a pottery in Strasburg. They were not potters, only the owners. Henry lived from 1814 to 1875, giving us some idea of the time they operated. Three more of Adam Sr.'s sons came into the pottery to work in the last quarter of the 19th century. They were Jeremiah, Amos and William. Amos became the owner and manufactured stoneware marked, "A. Keister and Co., Strasburg, Va." He made some slip decorated ware. Around 1885, he took Samuel H. Sonner as a partner. A stoneware crock was found with the mark shown in the Smith book cited. Jeremiah Keister made stoneware in a shop on Washington Street, near Holliday Street, marked "J. Keister and Co., Strasburg, Va.," around 1880. He then moved to Pleasant Dale, West Virginia, to establish a pottery. William Keister moved to Aiken, South Carolina. (Information: A.H. Rice and John B. Stoudt, *The Shenandoah Pottery*, pp. 83-85. Mark: impressed on stoneware jar from Elmer Smith, *Pottery, A Utilitarian Folk Craft*, p. 22.)

```
KEISTER & SONNER
STRASBURG, VA.
```

Keller, William. New Albany, Indiana. Lived 1824 to 1876. Pictured on front cover of *Pottery Collectors Newsletter* for September/October 1979, was a stoneware crock with painted cobalt blue decoration and a large K attributed to Keller.

Kelley, Frank Reuss. Norwalk, Connecticut. A studio potter who was in production by 1925 and continued until 1942. He was considered one of America's finest potters by historian and writer Warren Cox. He made hand thrown or hand built pieces from clays from the Orient, Europe and the United States. He used an open fire method with flames touching pieces. He made crystalline, opalescent, crackle and aventurine glazes. He used slip decoration and sgraffito decorations at times. His mother's maiden name was Reuss, which he incised as a mark or sometimes incised his initials. In 1928, he exhibited at the Metropolitan Museum of Art, New York City; Pennsylvania Museum in Philadelphia; Minneapolis Institute of Art, Minneapolis; Baltimore Museum of Art, Baltimore; Detroit Institute of Art, Detroit; Newark Museum Association, Newark; Carnegie Institute, Pittsburgh, Montclair Art Museum, Montclair, New Jersey; Denks Galleries, New

York City, and at the Exposition of Modern American Decorative and Industrial Art in Chicago. (Information: Thomas Turnquist, "Frank Reuss Kelley: A Potter Remembered," *American Art Pottery*, January 1984, p. 3. Mark: sent by Turnquist in letter.)

FRK   REUSS

Kellogg Studio. Petoskey, Michigan. 1948-1976. Stanley Kellogg studied art at the University of Michigan and two years with the master sculptor, Lorado Taft, of Chicago. He also studied at Cranbrook Academy with Carl Milles, another American sculptor. Together they worked on panel reliefs in Rockefeller Center, the Aloe Fountain in St. Louis and Swedish Monument in Wilmington, Delaware. Following an injury to his spine, Stanley could no longer sculpt with marble, and in 1948 he opened the Kellogg Studio where he designed and made various decorative pieces. In 1972, he died, but his wife continued the business until 1976. Sculptured heads or busts of famous people made by Stanley are in several museums. (Information: Jenny B. Derwich and Dr. Mary Latos, *Dictionary Guide to U.S. Pottery and Porcelain*, p. 130. Mark: on piece.)

Kelloggs Petoskey Mich

Kelly, Peter. Philadelphia, Pennsylvania. Around 1840. Made redware. Mark impressed. (Information and marks: Thorn, p. 131; Ramsay, p. 176.)

PETER KELLY

Kelsey Family Potters. Posey Township, Clay County, Indiana. Jonathon Kelsey came from Ashtabula County, Ohio, to Posey Township, Cloverland area of Clay County, Indiana, around 1840. His sons, Smith A., Orville, and Carlos, were also listed as potters in 1850. The Kelseys sold their acreage and pottery to Lawrence R. Torbert in 1855. (Information and mark: Melvin Davies, *Clay County Indiana Traditional Potters and Their Wares*, pp. 16, 34.)

S.A. KELSEY

Kemp's Pottery. St. Joseph, Missouri. Around 1867. Made stoneware. Mark on five-gallon stoneware crock. Made utilitarian pottery for 18 months. (Information and mark: Henry W. Heflin, pottery collector and researcher.)

KEMP'S POTTERY ST. JO. MO. 5

Kendall, Uriah. Cincinnati, Ohio. 1839 to around 1850. From 1840 to 1850 the factory was owned by Uriah and his son. They made Rockingham, yellowware and stoneware. This impressed mark was found on a gallon crock. (Information: John Spargo, *Early American Pottery and China*, p. 222.)

U KENDALL'S FACTORY CIN. O.

Kenton Hills Porcelains, Inc./Harold F. Bopp Manufacturing Company. Erlanger, Kentucky. Harold F. Bopp, who had worked as superintendent of the Rookwood Pottery from 1929 to around 1939, started the Kenton Hills Porcelains with David Seyler, a talented sculptor and artist, as art director of the firm. Bopp acted as manager and chemist. Decorations and glazes were similar to Rookwood. William Hentschel, another Rookwood employee, modeled some pieces for Kenton Hills Porcelains. Bopp left in 1942, and Seyler continued awhile alone, but W.W. II forced the plant to close, and it was never reopened. David Seyler moved on in 1948 to become the head of the Department of Sculpture at University of Nebraska, and was still there in the early 1970's. Kenton Hills Porcelains' pieces were sold by Nieman-Marcus, Dallas; Marshall Fields, Chicago; Lord and Taylor, George Jensen and Tiffany Company in New York City. For a detailed description of the art pottery pieces, see Evans and Cummins.

(Information: Virginia R. Cummins, "Kenton Hills Pottery," *Pottery Collectors Newsletter*, October 1972, pp. 1-5; Paul Evans, *Art Pottery of the U.S.*, pp. 136-138. Marks: no. 1 was filed under the name, Harold F. Bopp, doing business as the H.F. Bopp Manufacturing Company in Erlanger, Kentucky, January 22, 1940, for pottery tableware and ornamental pottery vases, claiming use since January 18, 1940. No. 2 was filed under the name, Kenton Hills Porcelains, Inc. on February 4, 1942, for use on porcelain products, namely vases, bowls, cups, plates and pitchers, claiming use since October 1, 1940. Marks 3-10 were decorators' marks shown in Cummins and Evans, as cited. No. 11 was shown in both the 1945 and 1946 *Crockery and Glass Journal Directories*, but the plant was nearly inoperative if not gone.)

1.

2.

3. HB	Harold Bopp	7. Hb	William Hentschel
4. B	Julian Bechtold	8. AS	Alza Stratton
5. C	Arthur Conant	9. DS	David Seyler
6. H	Charlotte Haupt	10. RD	Rosemary Dickman

11.

Kettlesprings Kilns. Alliance, Ohio. 1950-present. E.S. "Gene" Cunin, founder of the business, died in June 1982. Dick Faye became the new owner and is still operating under the Kettlesprings Kilns name. This company is well known for commemorative plates designed and decorated by them.

Keystone China. East Liverpool, Ohio. Started in middle to late 1940's. In the *East Liverpool City Directory* they were listed in 1951 through 1954 and were not listed in 1955-1956. In 1951, Keystone advertised artware and china specialties. (Mark shown from 1952 *Crockery and Glass Journal Directory*, p. 167.)

Keystone Pottery Company. Trenton, New Jersey. Started 1892 and was listed in *Trenton City Directory* until 1935. Made mostly sanitary ware. (Marks: no. 1, Barber, p. 66; no. 2 is the mark as it was filed for registration on September 29, 1894, for vitreous china.)

1.   2.

Keystone Pottery Company. Rochester, Beaver County, Pennsylvania, 1890 until after 1904. The Pottery was incorporated in 1890 by William Miller and Sons and John Gripp of Pittsburgh. On June 26, 1895 the plant was destroyed by fire, and the Miller Brick Company was formed at that site. However, Joseph H. Bausman in *History of Beaver County, Pennsylvania*, p. 710, said that in 1904, the Keystone Pottery Company was operating in the old Brewer Pottery building. My next directory was 1916, and the company was no longer listed. They made stoneware jars, ink bottles and other utilitarian pieces, some with white glaze. (Information: Joseph H. Bausman, *History of Beaver County, Pennsylvania*, 1904, pp. 710, 743. Mark: Robert and Beka Mebane, bottle collectors, as found on a Carter's Ink bottle.)

Kingwood Ceramics. East Palestine, Ohio. 1939 to present. Makers of artware marked with a "K" inside a crown. They make pig banks, mugs, tankards, ashtrays, etc. Their fine line was Weeping Gold which had 22 karat gold finish on teapots, creamers, sugars, serving trays, coffee sets, vases, ashtrays, powder boxes, candy dishes with fitted covers, cow creamers, bull sugars, etc. This line is no longer made due to the very high price of gold. Since December 1981, Kingwood Ceramics have decorated only in their original building. In 1981, Kingwood Ceramics purchased **Klare China Company** (or Harding China) which still (1983) operates under the name Klare China. Pressed items are made at Klare China then are decorated at Kingwood Ceramics. These two companies made the Govenor Rhodes decanter, a limited edition liquor bottle for Paramount Distillers, Incorporated, Cleveland, Ohio. Harding or Klare China was started by Robert Harding in 1945 and sold to Kingwood Ceramics in 1981. Articles made by Harding were hand caste until 1974, such as figurines, vases and ceramic pictures. After 1974 the ware was pressed, candy dishes, bicentennial plates, coasters, etc. The articles that were designed by Harding were marked with an "H" and a number. (Mark was "K" in a crown was an earlier mark. No. 2 is a paper label in use in 1983. No. 3 was found on dish. Nos. 4, 5, 6 from Quality Stamp Company. No. 7 impressed mark on liquor bottle; other marks are stamped marks with exception of no. 2, the paper label. No. 8 on very nice cookie jar with raised grape design.)

1.

2.

Hand Decorated
WEEPING BRIGHT GOLD
22k GOLD U.S.A.

3.

Hand Decorated
WARRANTED 22 K. GOLD U.S.A.
Fascination

4.

Hand Decorated
22 K. GOLD U.S.A.
WEEPING-BRIGHT GOLD

5.

Hand Decorated
WARRANTED 22 K. GOLD U.S.A.
Percal

6.

KINGWOOD CERAMICS
OHIO 44413

7.

KINGWOOD CERAMICS
MADE IN AMERICA

8.

Kirby, Orville. 1941 to present (1986). This ceramic potter and sculptor stated by letter that he started his first commercial venture in Los Angeles, California, in 1941, using the name, Orville Kirby Pottery. Next he called his business the **California Pottery**. In 1947, he purchased the **Sleepy Hollow Pottery** at Laguna Beach, California. In November 1954, Kirby moved the operation to Monroe, Utah, where he is still located in 1986. He attended the St. Paul School of Fine Arts in Minnesota and studied for a year at the University of Southern California. He learned modeling working with S. Paul Ward and Ada Mae Sharples. His products include many pieces with Western themes, a series of seven birds made in two part molds, a bull dog, calico cats, many planters, including a horse drawn wagon, a cradle, a washing machine, etc. Some of the pieces are air brush decorated; all are fired twice. Kirby stated that he had never used a particular mark, only paper labels or stamps of the type to suit the name of the business at the time.

```
Sleepy Hollow Pottery
95 W. Center Street
Monroe, Utah 84754
```

Kirchmann, Dennis G. Martinsville, Indiana. 1975 to present (1984). Studio potter Dennis Kirchmann received a B.A. degree in 1969 from Hastings College, Hastings, Nebraska, an M.A. in ceramics in 1970 from Fort Hays Kansas State College and a M.F.A. in 1972 from University of Iowa at Iowa City. From 1972 to 1975 he taught art at Indiana Central University in Indianapolis. From 1975 to 1981 he was an instructor for the Indianapolis Art League. From 1975 to present, he has worked full time as artist and craftsman in ceramics. Dennis makes wheel thrown and slab built stoneware and Raku, primarily decorative or sculptural, but some is functional. He listed only his most recent shows. His recent one-man shows are: Craft Alliance, St. Louis, MO; November 1978; Artworks Gallery, South Bend, Indiana, March-April 1981; The Gallery, Bloomington, Indiana, November 1981; Middletown, Ohio, Fine Arts Center, March-April 1983. Dennis's recent invitational shows from 1978 to 1984 are: Clay, Designer/Craftsman Guild, Ft. Wayne, Indiana; Four-Man Raku Show, Alliance Shop, Indianapolis Museum of Art, Indianapolis, Indiana; "Making It In Crafts: An Indiana Sampler;" 1982 Indiana Clay Invitational, Indiana University S.E.; "Hands of Man," Regional Crafts Invitational, Indianapolis Art League; "Tea-Bowl" National Invitational, Craft Alliance, St. Louis. He also listed eight other recent shows. Art pieces signed Kirchmann as in mark no. 1. Nos. 2, 3, are the stamps on some small pieces.

1.   2.   3.

Kirk China Company. New Brighton, Pennsylvania. 1950's. This company must have existed for a very short time. They were listed in the *Industrial Directory of Pennsylvania* for 1953 under pottery and china ware. They were also mentioned in a 1954 *Crockery and Glass Journal Directory,* for the "Brighton China" dinnerware. They were not listed in the 1949 *China and Glass Red Book Directory* but they were listed in the same directory in 1951, 1952 and 1953 for dinnerware, teapots, teaware and tea sets. They were not listed in the 1960's. (Mark: on dishes purchased by some dinnerware plan from a door to door salesman.)

Hand Painted

Kittler, Joseph R. Chicago, Illinois. Filed for registration of this mark November 19, 1925, to be used on chinaware, ashtrays, bonbon dishes, berry sets, butter cups, cake plates, candy jars, celery trays, chocolate sets, chop dishes, coffeepots, dinnerware, dresser sets, fruit bowls, jardinieres, lemonade sets, mayonnaise sets, mustard jars, nut sets, olive dishes, salt and pepper shakers, sandwich trays, sugar and cream sets, tea sets, vases and whip-cream bowls. Claiming use since September 1, 1922.

Klare China Company. See under Kingwood Ceramics.

Kline, Charles S. Atlanta, Georgia. Around 1883 Kline was making salt glazed cobalt blue decorated churns and crocks at Howell's Mills. John A. Burrison, *Brothers in Clay*, p. 193, said Kline was the only Georgia potter to decorate this way. The looping line used by Kline reminds me of the same type of design used by Adam Welker (see that listing). Burrison said Kline came from Ohio, but I couldn't make a connection to Massillon, Ohio potters. Kline married Emma Brown, daughter of William S. Brown, and Kline worked with James Osborn Brown at Jugtown around 1880. He also worked for W.T.B. Gordy around 1915. (Information and mark: Burrison, pp. 192, 193.)

KLINE & BROWN
MANUFACTURERS
ATLANTA, Ga.

Kline, Phillip. Carversville, Pennsylvania. Established 1808, according to Spargo, p. 162, but he said it was not known how long the potter operated. Spargo said at the time he wrote his book, *Early American Pottery and China* in 1926, there was a jug in the Pennsylvania museum which was signed and dated by Kline. Made slip decorated, sgraffito, plain redware and brick, according to Ramsay, p. 165. (Mark: inscribed, from Thorn, p. 132.)

Phillip Kline

Klinker, Christian. Bucks County, Pennsylvania. There seems to be disagreement on dates for this potter, but an earthenware jar with floral design in slip decoration had the initials C.K. and the date 1773. Klinker died in 1793. Made sgraffito, slip decorated and redware. (Information: Barber, *Tulip Ware of the Pennsylvania-German Potters,* p. 111. Mark: on gray stoneware jug with blue lettering from Melvin L. Davies, research potter.)

C. K.

Klugh, Jesse. Maytowne, Lancaster County, Pennsylvania. This potter was listed in a directory from 1869 to 1870, according to an article by Luther Heisey, "The Makers of Pottery in Lancaster County," in *Lancaster County Historical Society*, Vol. I, No. 5, 1946, p. 126. (Mark: C. Jordan Thorn, *Handbook of Old Pottery and Porcelain Marks*, p. 122.)

Jesse Klugh

Knight, Maurice A., Company. Akron, Ohio, since 1910, and Crooksville, Ohio, after 1942. In 1981, the Maurice A. Knight Company became the Knight Division of Kock Engineering, whose headquarters are in Wichita, Kansas. See Weeks, Cook and Weeks for early history. (Marks: no. 1, filed for registration on June 13, 1922, for use on acid proof chemical stoneware; no. 2, filed for same use October 12, 1924. Both marks claimed use since 1917. No. 3, found on large red clay funnel.)

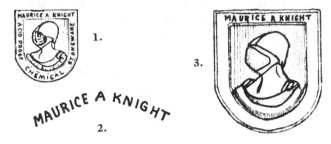

Knowles, Edwin M., China Company. Newell and Chester, West Virginia. 1900 to 1963. There are two companies by the Knowles name that made very fine dinnerware. Knowles, Taylor, Knowles was the first, but Edwin M. Knowles was also an old company which made good quality ware from 1900 to 1963. In 1900, Edwin M. Knowles, son of Isaac W. Knowles, founded the Edwin M. Knowles China Company. Their first plant was located in Chester, West Virginia, later occupied by the Harker Pottery Company. In 1913, they put into operation the building now in existence, but no pottery has been made there since 1963. Under the guidance of Mr. Knowles and his successors, this developed into one of the most modern and best equipped plants in the industry. Edwin M. Knowles Company kept their offices in East Liverpool until 1931. They manufactured in Chester, West Virginia, and from 1913 to 1963 they had their factory in Newell, West Virginia. The only confusing mark used by Edwin Knowles was the big K with the word Knowles. This might be taken for a mark for Knowles, Taylor, Knowles by a beginning collector. Several of the Edwin M. Knowles marks have the name completely taken out. (For a discussion of patterns, etc., see Lehner, *American Kitchen and Dinner Wares*, pp. 85, 86. For several pages of pictures of ware, see Jo Cunningham, *Collector's Encyclopedia of American Dinnerware*, pp. 162-170. (Marks: Knowles filed for copyright on mark 1 on February 21, 1939, claiming prior use for 11 days only. No. 2 was filed for copyright on May 20, 1920. Various forms of this mark as in nos. 3 to 7, were used for many years. On the copy of the patent, I couldn't read how long use was claimed on this mark. No. 3 was in the 1945 *Crockery and Glass Journal Directory*. No. 6 and 7 were on dishes made in the early 1920's or before with the old streaky yellow glaze which represented the various potteries first attempt to add colored glaze for solid colored dishes. The marks are stamped and Goldina for the color is written in gold leaf. Mark 8, "Marion," was for an octagon shape with fluted edges. This is an older mark, around 1920's or 1930's. No. 9, mark on "Mayflower" shape which was pictured in a 1925 *Butler Brothers Catalogue*. No. 10, 1946 *Crockery and Glass Journal Directory*. No. 11, very old mark shown in Barber, *Marks of American Potters*, first used before 1904. No. 12 was filed February 12, 1958, for semi-vitreous dinnerware. "Knowles Utility Ware," no. 13, was a mark of the 1930's and early 1940's, found on kitchenware. No. 14 was filed January 3, 1949, claiming use since December 7, 1948 on the large K. A claim was made since January 1901 as to the use of the word Knowles.)

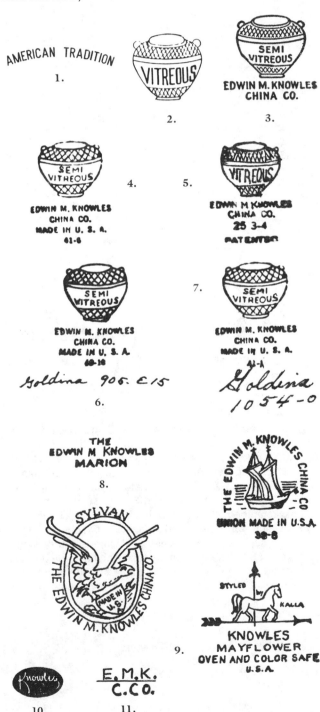

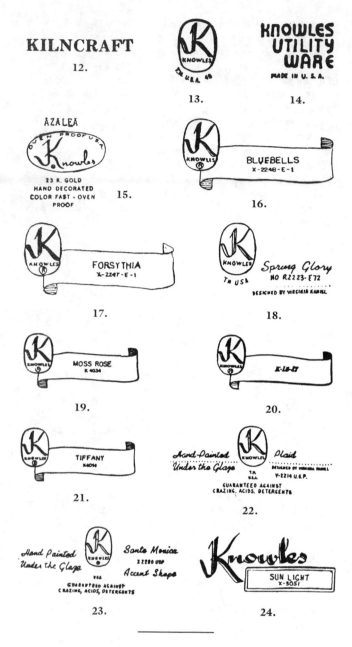

KILNCRAFT

12.

13.

KNOWLES
UTILITY
WARE
MADE IN U.S.A.

14.

AZALEA
Knowles
23 K. GOLD
HAND DECORATED
COLOR FAST - OVEN
PROOF

15.

BLUEBELLS
X-2248-E-1

16.

FORSYTHIA
X-2247-E-1

17.

Spring Glory
NO R2223-E72
DESIGNED BY VIRGINIA HAMILL

18.

MOSS ROSE
K 4034

19.

K-18-D

20.

TIFFANY
X4014

21.

Hand Painted
Under the Glaze

Plaid
DESIGNED BY VIRGINIA HAMILL
V-2214 U.G.P.

T.M.
U.S.A.
GUARANTEED AGAINST
CRAZING, ACIDS, DETERGENTS

22.

Hand Painted
Under the Glaze

Santa Monica
22290 UGP
Accent Shape

USA
GUARANTEED AGAINST
CRAZING, ACIDS, DETERGENTS

Knowles

SUN LIGHT
X-5051

23.

24.

Knowles, Homer, Pottery Company. Santa Clara, California. Started in 1923. In 1923, Homer Knowles of Knowles, Taylor, Knowles, completed a small plant with five kilns in Santa Clara and went bankrupt the same year, according to Jenny B. Derwich and Dr. Mary Latos, *Dictionary Guide to U.S. Pottery and Porcelain,* pp. 133, 134. Some of the ware was backstamped, "K.T.K. of Calif.," or "K.T.K., Hand Made Calif." which was incised underglazed. In October 1924 the plant was sold to Platt's Premier Porcelain (sanitary ware). Finally, in 1937 after being empty for a long time, the building was used as Myers Ceramic Tile Manufacturing Company, or the Santa Clara Tile Company. (Mark: stamped on plate.)

ORCHARD
WARE
By KNOWLES

MADE IN CALIFORNIA

Knowles, Taylor, Knowles. East Liverpool, Ohio. 1854 to 1931. In 1853, Isaac Knowles and Isaac Harvey operated a store boat selling pottery, glass and staples along the Ohio and Mississippi Rivers. In 1854, they started a factory, making yellowware in a single kiln; then added bisque and glostware; still later they added Rockingham. From 1856 to 1870 Isaac Knowles operated alone after buying out Harvey's share of the pottery. In 1870, John W. Taylor, Isaac Knowles' son-in-law, and Isaac's son, Homer Knowles, joined Isaac to form Knowles, Taylor, Kowles. The company was not incorporated until 1891. In 1872, white granite ware or ironstone was added to their line. By 1901, the plant included 35 kilns and covered 10 acres of ground, employing 700 people. In 1888, a new plant had been built called **Art China Works** but it burned right after it was built, and then was rebuilt. In 1888, Joseph G. Lee and Willis A. Knowles were admitted to the firm, and in 1891 a stock company was formed and incorporated for one million dollars. In 1887, the company brought over a manager from an Irish factory, and before 1889 they had made a finely moulded fragile ware called "Lotus Ware." (Another source gives 1893 as the date of perfecting Lotus Ware; another says a considerable amount was made before 1889, when the China Works was built. But this does give an approximate starting date for Lotus Ware.) Homer Taylor, son of John Taylor, gave 1889 to 1896 as the dates for the production of Lotus Ware. A great certainty is that it was a beautiful, superior grade of art china, translucent in character, having a soft transparent glaze, made in artistic shapes and made for just a few short years. High cost of production and fragility which caused high breakage was the cause of discontinuation. In 1929, Knowles, Taylor, Knowles, was one of eight companies that merged to form the American China Corporation. The corporation failed due to the depression. (Information: Lehner, *Ohio Pottery and Glass,* p. 47. Marks: Nos. 1 through 34 were marks shown in E.A. Barber, *Marks of American Potters,* pp. 108, 109, all before 1904. Barber didn't try to date these marks as specifically as he did others. He just said they were used after 1872. The eagle trademark was on ironstone china around 1879 and a variation in 1881. The crescent and star were on Lotus Ware. No. 35 was filed for registration August 9, 1919, for table pottery, claiming use since 1905. No. 36 didn't have a filing date, but the patent was granted September 28, 1926, and was used since January 2, 1926 on dinnerware. Nos. 37 to 39 were on dishes.)

IRON STONE CHINA
KNOWLES, TAYLOR
AND
KNOWLES

1.

STONE CHINA
K.T & K
HOTEL

2.

STONE CHINA
K.T & K.

3.

IRON STONE CHINA
K.T.& K.

4.

NITREOUS PORCEL
K.T.& K. CO.

5.

SEMI-VITREOUS
PORCELAIN
K T & K

6.

KNOWLES VITREOUS PORCELAIN
TAYLOR
EAST LIVERPOOL
OHIO, U.S.A.

7.

8.

LOTUS WARE

9.

LOTUS WARE

10. 11. 12. 13.

14. 15. 16.

17. 18. 19. 20.

21. 22. 23. 24.

25. 26. 27.

28. 29. 30.

31. 32. 33.

34. 35. 36.

37. 38. 39.

Knox Porcelain Corporation. Knoxville, Tennessee. 1936 to 1975. The company made porcelain electrical items by dry and wet processes over the years, including pin type insulators. In 1975, the company was purchased by the Porcelain Products Company. (Information and ink stamped and incuse marks: Jack H. Tod, *Porcelain Insulators Guide Book for Collectors*, p. 126.)

  KNOX

Koch, Charles, Pottery. Commerce, Missouri. Operated before 1870 until Charles Koch died in 1879. A raised mark in a circle read "C. Koch, Com., Mo." I couldn't see it well enough in the picture to have it reproduced here, but there is a small jug in the center of the mark with the initials "C.K." Koch also marked some of his pottery with a blue hand lettered "C." He also dated some of the pieces of stoneware and added a similar design as shown. (Information: Edison Shrum by letter. Marks 1-3, drawn from pictures of stoneware pieces sent by Shrum. No. 4, 5, from pictures of stoneware crock and jug sent by Henry W. Hefflin, pottery collector and researcher.)

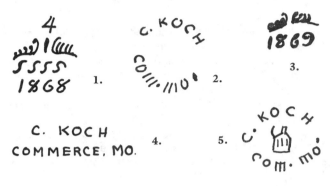

1. 2. 3.

4. 5.

Koch, George and Sons. Evansville, Indiana. Probably were florists. Filed for rights to this mark October 13, 1939 to use on flower pots made of ceramic, claiming use since September 1938.

"EASY-GRO"

Koenig, Diane. Hudson, Ohio. 1976 to present (1987). Diane, a studio potter, makes wheel thrown sgraffito and slipware pieces in attractive blue and white, and black and white color combinations. She graduated with a B.A. degree from Bowling Green State University in 1976 and has attended numerous craft shows. She signs pieces as shown.

KOENIG

Kohler, J.W. Pensacola, Florida. Around 1870's until shortly after 1909. According to Don Fredgant, this potter used three names in various directory listings for his pottery, the **Kohler Pottery**, the **Pensacola Pottery** and the **Southern Pottery Works**. History for this potter was very vague. Pictured was impressed mark on a wheel thrown churn with light brown glaze and darker brown drip glaze and apparently made of stoneware. (Information and mark: Don Fredgant, "T.B. Odom and J.W. Kohler: Two 19th Century West Florida Potters," *Antiques Journal*, June 1981, pp. 26-29.)

JW KOHLER
PENSACOLA
FLA.

Korte Pottery. Cincinnati, Ohio. Pam Korte, a studio potter made pottery marked or impressed with a metal stamp (mark 3) from 1975 to 1977. Then in 1979 she started the Korte Pottery and used the inscribed mark shown. Pam makes porcelain fired to 2,300 degrees into teapots, pitchers and what she terms "altered forms" in fancy bowls, etc. In 1979, she received a M.A. degree from the University of Louisville.

1.　　　　　2.　　　　　3.

Kottler, Howard. Howard is a studio type potter and sculptor, who has developed his own form of expression which displays a comic aspect and a certain sarcasm. He takes already modeled pieces, prepared glazes and junked ceramic objects and builds them into something that expresses his thoughts or feelings and becomes a work of art. One work pictured in the Clark book cited on p. 237, is a molded commercial type house. Next to it is a sack or bag (like a grocery bag) that Kottler built of clay. Where a roof should be, Kottler has walnut shells of clay and on the front of the bag is a little porch that matches the porch of the commercially made house next door. Kottler called this work, "The Old Bag Next Door is Nuts." I loved the work. It made me smile with its sarcastic humor, and I wondered about the creator who could see any part of life in such a fashion. Generally, we do not think beyond the merits of the piece he exhibits. For a better description and understanding of Kottler's work, see Clark's book cited. Kottler received three degrees from Ohio State University in Columbus, Ohio; his B.A. degree in 1952, an M.A. degree in 1956 and a Ph.D. in 1964. He received a M.F.A. degree from Cranbrook Academy of Art in Bloomfield Hills, Michigan, in 1957. He then taught at Ohio State University from 1961 to 1964 and at the University of Washington in Seattle after 1964, and he was still teaching there in 1978 when Clark wrote the book cited. At first he made traditional utilitarian stoneware then went on to develop the style I have tried to describe. (Information: Garth Clark, *A Century of Ceramics in the U.S.*, p. 301. Incised mark: Linda Steigleder, from the booklet published by the Everson Museum of Art to accompany the 1978 exhibition, "A Century of Ceramics in the U.S.")

KOTTLER

Kraus, Anne. Short Hills, New Jersey. Around 1984 to present. Anne received a B.A. degree from the University of Pennsylvania in painting in 1978. She also graduated from the Alfred University in Alfred, New York, with a B.F.A. degree in ceramics in 1984. She calls her pottery pieces "Shining Leaf Slip Ware." Sometimes the words "Shining Leaf" are inscribed with the mark shown. Anne's work is always signed. She makes slip-cast whiteware, oxidation fired. She paints the pieces in bright colors with beautiful full pictures of trees, hills, houses, etc., which are underglaze. Her products may be purchased and seen at Garth Clark Galleries in New York and Los Angeles. She already has an impressive list of exhibitions for such a short career. Her pieces are in many collections including: March/McClennan, New York; Victoria and Albert Museum, London, England; Newark Museum, Newark,

New Jersey; Everson Museum, Syracuse, New York. The exhibitions she has done are as follows: Rituals of Tea, Garth Clark Gallery, New York/Los Angeles; Teapots, Nancy Yaw Gallery, Birmingham, Michigan; Art of the Teapot, San Francisco International Airport; NCECA Group Exhibition, Greenberg Gallery, St. Louis, Missouri; One Person Exhibition, Garth Clark Gallery, New York; Rituals of Tea: International Invitational, Garth Clark Gallery, Los Angeles; One Person Exhibition, Garth Clark Gallery, Los Angeles; Painted Volumes, Chrysler Museum, Norfolk, Virginia; One Person Exhibition, Newark Museum, Newark, New Jersey; and One Person Exhibition, Everson Museum, Syracuse, New York.

S.S. Kresge Company, also called **K Mart Corporation**. Detroit, Michigan until 1972, then in Troy, Michigan until present. 1899 to present (1984). In 1899, the company was founded by Sebastian Spering Kresge, and was incorporated in state of Delaware in 1912. By 1929, Kresge had a total of 597 stores in the U.S. and Canada. In 1962, the first K Mart discount department store was opened in Detroit. Seventeen other K Marts opened the same year, and by 1980 there were 1,885 K Marts and 367 Kresge stores in operation. In 1968, S.S. Kresge Company and G.J. Coles and Coy, Ltd., of Australia, organized the K Mart Limited in Australia with Kresge holding 51 percent of the common stock. In 1977, the name Kresge Company was changed to the K Mart Corporation. In 1980, K Mart signed a license agreement with The Daiei, Inc., the largest retailer in Japan to develop a mass merchandising operation in Japan. Kresges owned the Mount Clemens Pottery of Mount Clemens, Michigan, from around 1920 to 1965 which they operated as a subsidiary to furnish products for their stores. The marks shown would be found on ware made at Mount Clemens Pottery for the most part. (No. 1, was filed on January 31, 1933, for use on tableware of china, kitchenware, crockery and earthenware and porcelain utensils, claiming use since February 1, 1927. Mark no. 2 or "Krest" was used on ceramic cooking and table ware and the patent was granted to Sebastian S. Kresge of Kresge Department Stores in September, 1939. The mark had been used since June 20, 1929.)

   **KREST**

1.   2.

Kromex Corp. Cleveland, Ohio. This company manufactured chromium plated ware. Some of it was combined with glassware and pottery such as holders for casseroles, etc. The company was listed in the 1945 *Crockery and Glass Journal Directory* and as late as 1965 in the *Gift and Tableware Reporter Directory*. These are not the actual beginning and ending dates, only directory listings. (Incised mark: found on lidded, heavily brown glazed casserole with tan to yellow clay.)

KROMEX
Oven Ware
MADE IN USA

Krumeich, B.J. Newark, New Jersey. Around 1845 to 1860. Made stoneware. (Information and mark: John Ramsay, p. 172; and Thorn, p. 133.)

B.J. KRUMEICH

NEWARK

N.J.

Kupper, Herman C. New York, New York. Distributor, who imported and also sold domestic ware. Kupper had the exclusive distributorship for "Monticello," made by Steubenville Pottery in the 1940's and 1950's. Also, they sold "Fine Concorde China," some of which was made by Taylor, Smith and Taylor, and decorated by Zapun Ceramics, Inc. In the October 1944 *Crockery and Glass Journal Magazine's* advertisement, they sold these products all made in America: Monticello dinnerware, Regal Bellum dinnerware, Vontury Art Porcelain and Orsay fine china. Kupper also sold products from Switzerland, France, Bavaria, etc. (Marks: no. 1, from 1945 *Crockery and Glass Journal Directory*. Mark 2 filed February 21, 1951, for pottery vessels for flowers and plants, claiming use since April 6, 1950.)

Kurlbaum and Schwartz. Philadelphia, Pennsylvania. 1851-1855. Started experiments in making hard-paste porcelain in 1851 in Philadelphia, Pennsylvania. They were listed for the last time in business in 1855 at Front and Oxford Streets as manufacturers of porcelain. Barber showed a tea set and bowls made by them. (Information and mark: Barber, *Marks of American Potters*, pp. 26, 27.)

K & S

L

La Luz Clay Products Company. La Luz, New Mexico. Filed for registration of this mark on May 9, 1931, for use on terra cotta pottery, claiming use since November 1930.

Lambert, J.C. Denton County, Texas. Around 1860. Impressed mark pictured on crock on ash glazed stoneware crock. (Information and mark: Sherry B. Humphreys and Johnell L. Schmidt, *Texas Pottery*, Washington, Texas: Star of Republic Museum, 1976, p. 25.)

J.C. LAMBERT

Lamberton Works. Trenton, New Jersey. Dates its foundation from 1869 when three Quakers, George Comfort, Thomas Bell and Jonathan Stewart, started a pottery of two kilns in the part of Trenton called Port of Lamberton where the canal joins the Delaware River. They named the pottery the Lamberton Works.

In 1892, there was a fire in one of the Maddock potteries. At that time the newly formed Maddock Pottery Company purchased the old Lamberton Works. At first, the old plant was used to make sanitary ware until a new building could be built by the Maddocks for that purpose. (There were three Maddock potteries. See Maddock Pottery history.) When the new building was ready to manufacture the sanitary ware, the old Lamberton Works began producing hotel ware called "Trenton China." Barber said that fine grades of semi-porcelain were made at the Lamberton Works under the Maddocks. In 1901, D. William Scammell joined the Maddocks and little by little bought out the Maddocks' interest in the Lamberton Works. (Last listing for Maddock Pottery was 1923.) Around 1923, Scammel and his five brothers purchased the remaining stock and formed the Scammell China Company. Pictured is an impressed mark used before 1890 at the Lamberton Works, according to Larry Paul, researcher and writer on the various Maddock potteries.)

TRENTON CHINA CO.
TRENTON. N.J.

Lamplight Farms. Offices in Brookfield, Wisconsin. 1964 to present (1983). Distributors of all kinds of oil lamps, with wood, brass, pottery bases. Three American potteries have made bases for the pottery lamps for this company; Brush Pottery Company, Regal China Company and Homer Laughlin China Company. See Brush Pottery marks for an impressed mark used on bottom of the lamp bases made by Brush around 1980. Mark shown here is a paper label used on lamps. (Information and mark: from company.)

Lamson and Swasey. Portland, Maine. 1875 to 1884. They operated in the **Portland Earthenware Manufactory**, later called **Portland Pottery Works**. The Portland Pottery Works continued to be operated by owners other than Lamson and Swasey. See Swasey, Jones and Company. Do not confuse the Portland Pottery Works with the Portland Pottery Company. Rufus Lamson and Eben Swasey were probably invited by Benjamin Dodge, Sr. to come to Portland from Exeter, New Hampshire, around 1873 or 1874 to work in the Dodge Pottery. (See that listing.) In February 1978, Lamson and Swasey purchased one-half of the interest in the pottery from John Dodge of Boston, and a couple years later they owned it all. They made redware or earthenware until the late 1870's or early 1880's when they started making stoneware utilitarian pieces, and they imported Rockingham and whiteware to sell. Before coming to Portland, Rufus, who was born in 1844, had owned the Paige Pottery in Peabody, New York, around 1860 to 1870. (For more on Lamson, see the Exeter Pottery Works listing.) The Lamson and Swasey operation must have been ended before 1884, because at that time Rufus Lamson was back in Exeter, working with his brother. For more information, see the listing Portland Pottery Works. (Information: Everett C. Lamson, Jr., *The Old Exeter Pottery Works*, p.22; and M. Lelyn Branin, *The Early Potters and Potteries of Maine*, pp. 30, 31, 67. Mark: no. 1, Stewart and Consentino, *Stoneware*, p. 65.)

LAMSON & SWASEY
PORTLAND, ME.

Lane and Company/Sunkist Creations of California. Van Nuys, California. Before 1956 until after 1967. This company has been of interest to researchers for some time because of the beautiful lamps they found marked with the incised mark and green and silver paper label as shown. The particular lamp which these marks were on was a colorful duck lamp and flower container combination. The company was not listed in any of the *California Manufacturers Directories* that I had, nor was it in *Crockery and Glass Journal Directory*. However, it was listed in the 1960-1961 and the 1965 *Gift and Tableware Reporter Directory* as being located at 14460 Arminta Street, and products were earthenware vases, serving bowls and television and tablelamps. In 1961, the Lane and Company listing said to see Sunkist Creations of California, and that name was used under the individual products listing. In 1965, the name was simply Lane and Company. This directory doesn't specify whether the companies are manufacturers or distributors, but since Lane and Company was not in the state manufacturers' directory, I would believe them to be a jobbing or distributing agency. They sold through Bernard Lipman, Inc., New York City and Bernard Krauss and Associates in San Francisco.

LANE & CO.
VAN NUYS, CAL.
© 1957
P 443

© 1956 LANE & CO.
1958 VAN NUYS. CALIF. USA

Lang, Anton. Oberammergau, Bavaria, Germany. Art potter, born in 1876, came to America in 1922 for an exhibition held in the Grand Central Palace, New York City, December 15, 1922 to January 1, 1923. In the small German town of Oberammergau, which had less than 5,000 people, an eight-hour Passion Play was held every 10 years from the 1600's for which there was no charge for admission. The expense of the play drained all the resources from the little town. A committee of Americans helped to support the craftspeople in the town for a year and then promoted an exhibition of their handicrafts at the Grand Palace, New York City. Anton Lang was an art potter and acted in the Passion Play in Oberammergau, playing Christ in 1900, 1910 and 1922. He made pottery for one year before the exhibition to bring to America to show and sell. A few pieces are showing up in hands of collectors now. While in America, he visited Rookwood and made a few pieces. See the picture, p. 106, Herbert Peck, *The Book of Rookwood Pottery.* (Information: Program booklet, *Oberammergau Grand Central Palace, December 15 to January 1 Exhibition,* New York City: printed by Oberammergau Committee, 1922.)

Anton Lang

Lang and Osgood. New York. Selling agency which followed Lang and Schafer as agents for Wannopee Pottery. According to Paul Evans, *Art Pottery of the U.S.,* p. 321, it seems that E.A. Barber in *Marks of American Potters,* p. 98, started some confusion when he showed this mark under Wannopee Pottery and designated the mark as a monogram for the name "Park Lane Pottery," when it really stood for Lang and Osgood. Barber speaks of Park Lane Pottery under the same management as Wannopee Pottery Company. Evans doubts that evidence can ever be found that the name Park Lane was used in connection with the Wannopee Pottery. In "The Worlds Pottery Marks," by W.P. Jervis, *Bulletin of American Ceramic Society,* October 20, 1914, p. 25, listed this mark with the Park Lane Pottery, 1886, used on bronzed ware. He probably got this from Barber also.

Lapp Insulator Company. Le Roy, New York. Company was incorporated in December 1916 and was producing within

a year. The company made all types of wet process porcelain insulators. For a discussion of the various types, see Jack H. Tod, *Porcelain Insulators Guide Book for Collectors,* pp. 126, 127. In the late 1960's, Lapp built another plant in Sandersville, Georgia. In June 1969, the company became the Lapp Insulator Division of the Interpace Corporation (see the Interpace listing). (Information and marks: Tod, as cited, pp. 126, 127. According to Tod, the early insulators had incuse markings. After 1927 all of the marks were underglaze, but not all insulators were marked. The marks used by Lapp came in a variety of sizes and with a variety of dates and catalog numbers. See Tod, p. 127, for many examples and variations of the mark shown.)

Larkin Company. Buffalo, New York. 1878 to WW II. Elbert Hubbard, founder of the Roycrofters, became a partner with John D. Larkin in 1878 in the business J.D. Larkin and Company. Larkin had started to manufacture soap around 1875. In 1892, the company was reorganized as the Larkin Soap Manufacturing Company with Hubbard as part owner until 1893 when he retired and later founded the Roycrofters. (See that listing). Hubbard was responsible for the merchandising and conceived the idea of premiums. He introduced the idea of a club plan to sell soap with premiums. It was not the company's soap that made them famous. They issued a vast amount of promotional publication, trade cards, catalogues, brochures and flyers. They had their own branch within the post office; their mail was so large, both incoming and outgoing. Premiums included silverware, dishes, toys, furniture, lamps, etc., which came from various companies. In 1901, the Larkin Company founded the Buffalo Pottery Company to produce their ceramic items (see the listing Buffalo China Company for marks). I was really surprised that no marks were registered in the name of Larkin. But since they had their own pottery, they probably felt this was unnecessary. (Suggested reading on the Larkin Company: Seymour and Violet Altman, *The Book of Buffalo Pottery*; Bruce Garret, "Buffalo Pottery and the Larkin Company, *Spinning Wheel,* January, February 1963, pp. 18-20; and Darlene Fox, "Early 20th Century Premiums and Premium Catalogs," *Antique Trader Weekly,* April 8, 1981, pp. 94-100.)

La Rowe, John and Glen. The Mark of the Potter (name for salesroom, home and workshop). Near Clarksburg, Georgia on S.R. 197. Glen, wife of John La Rowe, started making hand thrown pottery on a wheel on a full time basis in 1966. The Mark of the Potter studio was purchased in 1968. John, an architect, worked at making pottery three days a week. They make a stoneware body of red Georgia clay, ball clay, and fireclay into a variety of pieces including jugs and hanging baskets, vases and various decorative pieces. The Mark of the Potter sells the work of many other potters from Georgia and four other states. (Information: Bonham, Roger D., "The Mark of the Potter," *Ceramics Monthly,* November 1973, pp. 28-30. The mark shown was stamped into the ware and the article quoted said it was the only mark they both used.)

Larson, Tyrone and Julie. Royal Oak, Michigan, and later, Bakersville, North Carolina. 1966 to present (1985). The Larsons are studio potters making three distinct types of pottery at present. Both of these very talented potters have been written up in many publications. Both are featured in *The Penland School of Crafts*, a book by John Coyne, *Design Through Discovery* by Marjorie Elliott Bevlin, *American Crafts* by Katherine Pearson and *The Complete Book of Ceramic Art* by Polly Rothenberg. Magazine articles reviews which included the Larsons have appeared in *Craft Horizons, Ceramic Monthly, The Studio Potter*, etc. The types of pottery they make are as follows: decorative stoneware, including limited editions and one-of-a-kind pieces, utilizing gold and platinum luster. The pieces are reduction fired to cone 10 and then the lusters are added and fired to cone 018 to fuse the metallic luster colors. Their most recent work is being done as a team.

They make one-of-a-kind pieces, platters, large vase forms, using stencils of animals, birds and fish forms applied in patterns. The stencils are covered with colored engobes, and after the stencil is removed, they do a great deal of sgraffito drawing on the figures. The pieces are bisqued and glazed with transparent glazes and fired to cone 10 in a heavy reduction atmosphere. The pieces are then lustered with banding and highlighting of gold or platinum luster and fired to cone 018. These pieces are signed in one of the three ways shown in marks 1, 2 and 3. They make functional stoneware. They make limited edition pieces, but they never made large quantities of any ware. They place emphasis on quality construction in their slab building and throwing, spending a great deal of time on each piece. The functional stoneware consists of complex slab constructed canister sets, sets of five and seven mixing bowls, plates and occasionally a dinnerware set. These pieces are all reduction fired to cone 10. They make ovenware which is constructed of a special high-lithium clay body formulated to withstand the stresses of thermal shock. Most of their pieces are thermal open baking dishes, hand-constructed of slabs and extrusions. Glaze techniques have varied on these pieces from pouring and dipping methods to glaze trailing and stencils. The forms are elaborate and time consuming to construct. Most of their ovenwear is octagonal, free-form or rectangular. Many have handles which attach to the basic extrusion by interlocking designs similar to pieces of a jigsaw puzzle. In addition, they have made wheel thrown baking pieces and casseroles with matching trivets. The ovenware is fired to cone 10 reduction.

Tyrone was a self taught potter. He was employed by the U.S. Corps of Engineers as a navigational cartographer from 1955 to 1966. From 1961 to 1963 he served in the U.S. Military Police Corp. In 1966, he and Julie set up their first pottery in Royal Oak, Michigan. In 1971, they moved to the Penland area of North Carolina. Tyrone and Julie, both have taught classes at the Penland School Crafts and the Arrowmont School of Crafts in Gatlinburg, Tennessee. Julie also taught in the art department of Wayne State University in Detroit, Michigan, where she received an M.A. degree (cum laude) in 1966. Both are represented in collections at the Smithsonian Institution, the Utah Museum of Art at Salt Lake City, the Lannan Foundation in Palm Beach, the North Carolina National Bank at Charlotte, North Carolina, the

Kalamazoo Institute of Arts in Kalamazoo, Michigan, the Arts and Science Musuem in Statesville, North Carolina. Tyrone also has pieces in the Hans Behtler Collection in Zurich, Switzerland, at Henry Ford Community College in Dearborn, Michigan, and several more universities and museums. Julie has work in the Columbus Gallery of Fine Art, Columbus, Ohio, the R.J. Reynolds Collection at Winston-Salem, North Carolina, the Melven Maxwell Smith Collection in Bloomfield Hills, Michigan, plus several more universities and museums. The list is just too long to give all of it here. Tyrone received the Master Craftsmen's Grant sponsored by the North Carolina Arts Council for two successive years, 1979 and 1980. As one can imagine, these two potters have done an extensive list of outstanding exhibitions and won numerous awards at these shows. We will list only shows at which awards were won. Julie has won awards at: 20th Exhibition for Michigan Artist Craftsmen, Detroit Institute of Arts, Detroit, Michigan; Michigan Craftsmen's Exhibit, Bloomfield Art Association, Michigan; Michigan State Fair Pottery Prize; Flint Art Fair Pottery Prize; Fourth Bienneal Michigan Craftsmen's Exhibit, Grand Rapids, Michigan; "Exhibition '70" Regional Exhibit, Columbus Gallery of Fine Arts, Columbus, Ohio (Beaux Arts Award); Mint Museum Purchase Award, Piedmont Crafts Exhibit, Charlotte, North Carolina; Winter Park Arts Festival Award In Pottery, Winter Park, Florida; Wiggins Memorial Ceramic Award, Coconut Grove, Florida; Lakefront Festival of Arts, Milwaukee, Wisconsin; North Carolina National Bank Purchase Award, to name only a few.

Tyrone has won awards at: 20th Exhibition for Michigan Artist Craftsmen, Detroit Institute of Arts, "Mt. Clemens Pottery Prize" for a canister set design; Henry Ford Community College Purchase Award, Michigan Craftsmen's Exhibit, Bloomfield Art Association; 21st Exhibition for Michigan Artist Craftsmen, Detroit Institute of Arts, "Mt. Clemens Pottery Prize" for a canister set design; Eastern Michigan University, purchase prize; Pottery Merit Award, North Carolina Craftsmen Exhibit, Raleigh Museum; North Carolina National Bank Purchase Prize, Mint Museum Craftsmen's Exhibit, Charlotte, North Carolina; Pottery Award, Appalachian Corridors Exhibition, Charleston, West Virginia; "Best-In-Crafts" Award, Coconut Grove Arts Festival, Coconut Grove, Florida; Museum Purchase Award, Southeastern Invitational Crafts Exhibition, Greenville County Museum of Art, Greenville, South Carolina; "Ceramics Monthly Magazine Purchase Award," Winterfair, Columbus, Ohio. (Marks: nos. 1, 2, 3, one of these marks is used on the pieces they make together. At present, their new one-of-a-kind "creature" pieces are also signed in this manner. No. 4 is the logo they have used since 1966. No. 5 is Tyrone's mark used on his artistic pieces. No. 6 is Julie's mark on her stoneware decorative pieces. No. 7 is used on ovenware and all baking pieces.)

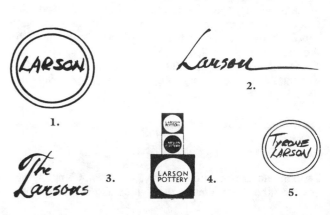

1.

2.

3.

4.

5.

LARSON POTTERY
OVENWARE
3 Quarts

Julie Larson

6.

Julie Larson

7.

La Solana Potteries, Inc./Bergstrom and French. 1946 to present (1985). The factory was located in Mesa, Arizona. The pottery had its early beginning in Glendale, California, in 1946 until 1953 as Bergstrom and French, makers of ovenware. By January 1954, the business was relocated in Scottsdale, Arizona, where the offices are still located with the factory in Mesa. At present, La Salona Potteries, Inc. is listed making earthenware dinnerware, pitchers, tumblers, mugs, cups and saucers, microwave oven-to-table casseroles, serving pieces, bean pots, salad bowls, etc. In 1953, they were listed for ovenware and casual living earthenware. Mark 1 was filed for registration May 14, 1951 for use on flower pots, jardinieres, hanging baskets, birdbaths, ornamental jars, oven ware, casseroles, bean pots, salad bowls, pitchers, relish dishes, shakers, etc. claiming first use of the mark September 15, 1947. No. 2, 3 shown in directories for La Salona Potteries after 1954.)

1.

2.

3.

Lauer's Pottery. Olathe, Kansas. 1970 to present (1984).

James Lauer, studio potter, makes stoneware, dinnerware and elegant lamps. Jim Lauer has a B.F.A. degree from the Kansas City Art Institute and has won awards at various shows, such as first place in ceramics at the Prairie Village Art Fair in Prairie Village, Kansas. He also won second place in Third Dimension category as the Crown Center Art Festival in Kansas City.

LAUER

Laughlin, Homer, China Company and Predecessors. Newell, West Virginia. The pottery had its origin in 1869 when Homer Laughlin came to East Liverpool, Ohio, and began a partnership with Nathaniel Simms until 1872 to make yellowware and stoneware (Ramsay, p. 218.) Then Simms left Laughlin to join Ferguson from 1872 to 1875. In 1873, Homer Laughlin and his brother Shakespeare made stoneware in a plant on Market Street. Also, in 1873 the town of East Liverpool furnished $5,000.00 to build a white ware plant which was still to be known as the Laughlin Brothers. In 1877, Homer bought Shakespeare's interest in the company, making white granite and porcelain. In 1887, they employed 137 people. Homer Laughlin China Company was the name from 1897 to the present. Homer Laughlin manufactured hotelware back around the turn of the century identified as double thick, and again for the government during both WWI and WWII. Then finally in 1949, the hotel china was manufactured on a full time basis. Best China, their vitrified hotel line, has been so successful that even in this short period, they have achieved a position of one of the three leaders in this field. The method of dating their hotel china, sent by the company, is as follows, and while sometimes it may vary, this is the basic outline that has been used. The first shipment of hotelware was shipped June 1959, none dated until May 1960. See marks 50 to 55.

Best China Backstamp Code

Year	Jan	Feb	Mar	Apr	May	June	July	Aug	Sept	Oct	Nov	Dec
1960					AE	AF	AG	AH	AI	AJ	AK	AL
1961	BA	BB	BC	BD	BE	BF	BG	BH	BI	BJ	BK	BL
1962	CA	CB	CC	CD	CE	CF	CG	CH	CI	CJ	CK	CL
1963	DA	DB	DC	DD	DE	DF	DG	DH	DI	DJ	DK	DL
1964	EA	EB	EC	ED	EE	EF	EG	EH	EI	EJ	EK	EL
1965	FA	FB	FC	FD	FE	FF	FG	FH	FI	FJ	FK	FL
1966	GA	GB	GC	GD	GE	GF	GG	GH	GI	GJ	GK	GL
1967	HA	HB	HC	HD	HE	HF	HG	HH	HI	HJ	HK	HL
1968	IA	IB	IC	ID	IE	IF	IG	IH	II	IJ	IK	IL
1969	JA	JB	JC	JD	JE	JF	JG	JH	JI	JJ	JK	JL
1970	KA	KB	KC	KD	KE	KF	KG	KH	KI	KJ	KK	KL
1971	LA	LB	LC	LD	LE	LF	LG	LH	LI	LJ	LK	LL
1972	MA	MB	MC	MD	ME	MF	MG	MH	MI	MJ	MK	ML
1973	NA	NB	NC	ND	NE	NF	NG	NH	NI	NJ	NK	NL
1974	OA	OB	OC	OD	OE	OF	OG	OH	OI	OJ	OK	OL
1975	PA	PB	PC	PD	PE	PF	PG	PH	PI	PJ	PK	PL
1976	QA	QB	QC	QD	QE	QF	QG	QH	QI	QJ	QK	QL
1977	RA	RB	RC	RD	RE	RF	RG	RH	RI	RJ	RK	RL
1978	SA	SB	SC	SD	SE	SF	SG	SH	SI	SJ	SK	SL
1979	TA	TB	TC	TD	TE	TF	TG	TH	TI	TJ	TK	TL
1980	UA	UB	UC	UD	UE	UF	UG	UH	UI	UJ	UK	UL
1981	VA	VB	VC	VD	VE	VF	VG	VH	VI	VJ	VK	VL
1982	WA	WB	WC	WD	WE	WF	WG	WH	WI	WJ	WK	WL
1983	XA	XB	XC	XD	XE	XF	XG	XH	XI	XJ	XK	XL
1984	YA	YB	YC	YD	YE	YF	YG	YH	YI	YJ	YK	YL
1985	ZA	ZB	ZC	ZD	ZE	ZF	ZG	ZH	ZI	ZJ	ZK	ZL

Three plants were operated in East Liverpool until 1932. In 1905, Newell, West Virginia, became the site where Laughlin China built the largest single pottery in the world at that time. Plant no. 4 began operation in 1907. A second plant in Newell, plant no. 5 was built in 1914. Plants 6, 7 and 8 followed by 1931. In the 1970's, Homer Laughlin Company was still employing around 1,500 people to work in five plants. The total capacity of their work force is 2,500. In 1980's, when potteries are facing the hardest times ever, Homer Laughlin China Company is still employing 800, which is a testament to the popularity of their products because of its quality. According to the company, the first trademark used was just "Laughlin China," in a horse shoe. Secondly, after 1890, came the American eagle carrying the lion until around 1900. From then on, the "HLC" monogram with variations was used. In 1900, Homer Laughlin started using a series of numbers which meant the month, a second single numeral identified the year, and a third number identified the plant. Hence 74L would mean July, 1904, factory on the east end of town. In the years 1910 to 1920, the first figure was the month, the next two numbers were the year and the third figure designated the plant. (East end plant was L; number 4 plant was N; and plant 5 was N5.) From 1921 to 1930, a letter was used first to indicate the month such as an A for January, etc. The next single number was the year, and the last figure or letter was the plant. From 1931 to 1969 the month was expressed as a letter, but the year was indicated with two digits. Plant no. 4 was "N," no. 5 was "R," no. 6 and 7 were "C," and no. 8 was listed as "P." During this period, E44R5 would indicate May 1944 and manufactured in plant no. 5. The current trademark has been in use for approximately 70 years, and the numbers are the only indication of the years that items were produced. Beginning in 1970, only the Homer Laughlin name and year of manufacture appears. In 1981, holloware items were marked with a raised logo of the Homer Laughlin trademark. For F.W. Woolworth's 100 year anniversary in 1979, Homer Laughlin China Company produced "Harlequin" in four colors, three of which matched the original colors. Only the salmon was a little deeper in color. The turquoise, yellow and green matched the original colors. The only difference in design was a solid handle on the new sugar as opposed to an open handle on the original. The following information furnished by the company is reprinted almost in its entirety as it was included in *American Kitchen and Dinner Wares*, p. 89:

The Story of Genuine Fiesta Dinnerware (1936-1973)

Fiesta comes in four lovely colors: green, blue, yellow and red, all brilliant, all cheerful, all endowed with a pleasant feeling of good fellowship, informality and gracious living. Whether used for serving breakfast, luncheon, informal supper or buffet, Fiesta makes the meal a truly gay occasion. It's fun to set a table with Fiesta!

Designed by Fredrick Rhead an English Stoke on Trent potter, working under the direction of M.L. Aaron, president and J.M. Wells, secretary and general manager. Design modeled by Arthur Kraft and Bill Berrsford, the distinctive glazes developed by Dr. A.V. Bleininger in association with H.W. Thiemecke. A tale body was introduced for the first time making Fiesta entirely different in body materials and glazes.

Initially 54 items (69 individual pieces) were produced in green, blue, yellow and red. Soon it was apparent that Fiesta was to be all time leader in the colored dinnerware field. Ivory was added in 1936, turquoise in 1938, blue, rose, grey, chartreuse and olive green colors in 1943 to be followed by several other distinct colors over the years.

The original design, colors and name are registered property of Homer Laughlin. The Fiesta trademark was imprinted from the mould or by a rubber stamp hand operations depending upon the method of producing the individual item. Those without trademarks are merely the result of human error and since many imitations appeared over the years, it would be safe to assume that only those items bearing the trademark are genuine Fiesta.

In an effort to serve all markets, especially the syndicate stores, competitive lines identified as Harlequin and Riviera were produced in a slightly different design in the true Fiesta colors and sold without trademark in tremendous quantities for a number of years. In 1941, the continued success of the Fiesta colors was applied to a "Bake & Serve" line identified as "Fiesta Kitchen Kraft."

A juice set consisting of 30 oz. disc water jug with six 5-oz. juice tumblers was produced merely as a special sales stimulator between 1940 and 1943 and was part of a promotional program involving six special items that included the juice set, covered refrigerator jars, casserole and pie plate, handled chop plate, French casserole and individual sugar, cream and tray. These were initially offered for sale at 98¢ detail.

Records list those colors manufactured as royal blue, yellow, old ivory, red, turquoise, forest green, chartreuse, grey, rose, antique gold, turf green and two additional green colors that were never singularly named.

Fiesta Red was discontinued in 1943 because this color was manufactured from depleted uranium oxide, and our government assumed control of uranium oxide at that time. "Fiesta Red went to war."

The color assortment during this period was forest green, chartreuse, grey and rose.

The Atomic Energy Commission licensed The Homer Laughlin China Company to again buy this material and Fiesta Red, the most popular of all colors, returned to the market in May of 1959.

With the return of red, new colors consisting of yellow, turquoise and medium green, replaced the war year colors to more clearly match the original four colors.

Finally, in November 1972, all production of Fiesta Red was discontinued because many of the original technicians who developed this color and maintained control over the complicated manufacturing and firing had retired and modern mass production methods were unsuited to this process.

Silverware and glassware sold in Fiesta ensembles were manufactured by other companies and merely shipped here to our plant and reshipped with the Fiesta and other items included in the ensemble. Records fail to identify the company that may have manufactured these complementary accessories.

The famous old line of Fiesta Ironstone dinnerware was discontinued January 1, 1973.

In 1986, the Homer Laughlin China Company decided to produce a new line of Fiesta Ware. In the 1930's, the line sold millions of pieces annually during its 40 years of production and has become a widely collected dinnerware. The return of Fiesta was marked by a ceremony at The Cultural Center in Charleston, West Virginia, in which Governor Arch A. Moore, along with Homer Laughlin Company and Department of Culture and History officials, unveiled the new line at the State Museum of the Cultural Center prior to its introduction at several major department stores in the United States. Bloomingdale's and B. Altman in New York started selling the Fiesta line in February 1986. It is also being carried by the Main Street stores in Chicago and other retailers nationally. Colors are: black; a slightly different cobalt blue; and slightly different rose than in past years; apricot and stark sugar white. Items being reproduced are the cup and saucer; original sauce boat; two sizes of disk jugs - 2½ quart and 30 ounce; 10¼″ dinner plate; salad plate; cereal/soup bowl; both candleholders (pyramid and round); bud vase; 8″ vase; salt and pepper; individual sugar and creamer; standard sugar and creamer; 8 cup teapot; round platter; 8″ vegetable bowl and the covered casserole. The plates and soup/salad bowls are slightly larger. But the design is the same art deco style as the original. The new accessory pieces are slightly smaller than the originals. Markings will be very similar to the old markings and will be difficult for the novice to tell which is old or new, according to Ed Carson. He feels the advanced Fiesta collector won't have trouble distinguishing old from new markings. See mark 154 for the stamped mark used on the new Fiesta. The caste items in Fiesta are made from the original molds and, of course, those marks are the same as the original because the mark is in the mold.

(Marks: no. 1 is a copy of the very first Homer Laughlin China Company's mark, 1871 to 1890. No. 2 is a photostatic copy of mark used around 1900. Nos. 3-4 are the second trademark with the prostrate lion signifying the end of British domination in the dinnerware field used before 1900. Nos. 5-11, from E.A. Barber, *Marks of American Potters*, pp. 110-111, so they were used before 1904 in order to be in the book. Nos. 12-13, also very early marks around 1905-1910 era. No. 14 was filed for registration on February 27, 1912 and again on April 3, 1956, claiming use on or before December 31, 1879, for use on earthenware table service. Nos. 15-20, all early marks on dinnerware around 1900, just before or after; see patent report on no. 14; also see mark 124 for a later mark of this type. Nos. 26, 27 are on products made by Homer Laughlin for the Alcoa-Aluminum Corp. H.L.C. made three or four patterns for them according to Mr. Carson. Nos. 21, 22, 23 are the marks shown in directories in later years for Homer Laughlin. They are logos or symbols. Nos. 24-32 are marks sent from company. Some are as they were sent with dates. Nos. 33, 34, 35 are marks used on material made for Pearl China Company (see that listing). Nos. 36, 37. The satin textured Wells glazes were developed in the early 1930's. Mr. W.E. Wells died September 18, 1931, and these were probably named in his memory. Joseph Wells and M.L. Aaron developed them. No. 39; "Oven Serve" mark was filed for registration on July 31, 1933, claiming use since July 1, 1933, for earthenware for oven and refrigerator use and table service. This was a very modest description of a ware that was to become so highly collectible. Nos. 38 to 49 show a variety of "Oven Serve" marks and the "Household Institute" marks found on Priscilla pattern oven serve. This was made from 1933 as stated under no. 39, and through the 1940's and 1950's. Marks 50-55, previously explained under hotel and restaurant ware. No. 55 in the 1974 *Tri State Pottery Festival* booklet was the picture of the gladiator shown with the statement under it that it was the "symbol of strength and durability used on all hotel ware." This was not actually used as a mark, but only as a logo in spite of what the booklet said. No. 56-65, "Eggshell" was a fine thin semi-porcelain dinnerware with outstanding decorations. These were first made during W.W. II, but were discontinued after the ware when the imports started flooding the markets again in the early 1950's. The word "eggshell," was for thinness and composition. We can also see the various shapes used on this ware, "Cavalier," "Nautilus," "Georgian," "Theme," and "Swing." No. 66, "Tea Rose" was also made by Taylor, Smith and Taylor for a retail promotion of some sort. Nos. 67-71, verified by company. No. 71, "Sky Tone" was an at-

tractive blue dinnerware and accessory pieces of 1950's. No. 73, from around 1910 for a few years. Homer Laughlin made Art China. Most of it was semi-porcelain. Nos. 74-75, "Historical America" was a line manufactured exclusively for the F.W. Woolworth Company, which was first introduced in 1942 and was made until around 1952, then discontinued. Mr. E.S. Carson, from the Homer Laughlin China Company provided the following list of pieces made in this pattern;

10″ dinner plate of "George Washington Takes Command;" 9″ plate with "Purchase of Manhattan Island;" rim soup with "Ponce De Leon Discovers Florida;" 7″ salad with "Liberty Bell;" bread and butter with "Paul Revere;" dessert fruit with "Lincoln Rail Splitter;" 13″ platter with "First Thanksgiving;" 11″ platter wtih "Clemont;" vegetable with "Pony Express;" oval vegetable with "Lincoln's Gettysburg Address;" cups with "Franklin's Experiment;" saucers with "Mayflower;" cereal soup with "Stage Coach;" sugars and covers with "Barbara Fritchie;" creams with "Star Spangled Banner." In that period, all exclusive F.W. Woolworth patterns were identified by year, as well as the numerical series of those patterns purchased. Thus the "W" indicating Woolworth, and the number "3" indicating the third pattern purchased in 1942. This is true of all exclusive Woolworth patterns manufactured during that period, and as an example W-336 identifies Harlequin and the third pattern purchased by them in 1936 on an exclusive basis. Nos. 76-87; In the 1940's, Homer Laughlin China Company made "Currier and Ives" dinnerware called Americana. In a 1942-1943 *Montgomery Ward's* catalogue, the dinnerware was advertised as an exclusive Ward's pattern. There were 31 different scenes applied under glaze in a soft rose-pink color. Some of the other names included in marks not shown here include: "Landing of the Pilgrims," "Washington Family," "Maple Sugaring," "Signing of the Declaration of Independence," "Western Farmer's Home," "Winter in the Country," "Husking," "Partridge Shooting," "View of Harpers Ferry, Va." Nos. 88-90; Epicure was a shape name filed for use on earthenware table service on March 31, 1955, claiming use since March 22, 1955. No. 90 is mark as it was registered. Nos. 91-103, "Sheffield" was a trade name used by J. and H. International which became Jebcor International. These are marks of the 1960's. (See the listing for J. and H. International.) Mr. Ed Carson, who has worked at Homer Laughlin China Company since 1937 picked out the marks for J. and H. International and Jebcor International that were used on products made by Homer Laughlin. These distributors also used the Sheffield marks on products made by other American and foreign companies. Nos. 104-105, "Shakespeare Country" was made for Laughlin International to sell (see the listing Laughlin International). Nos. 106-114, "Modern Star," "Chateau Buffet," "Fortune," "Pastoral," "Harvest," and "Wild Rose," were marks used on Mother's Oats dishes in the 1940's and 1950's. "Pastoral," and "Fortune" were both made by Taylor, Smith and Taylor as well as Homer Laughlin China Company. Nos. 115-115, "Town House" was a Sears' product. Nos. 117-119, "Triumph" was filed for registration September 4, 1959, claiming use since June 1959 for china dinnerware. No. 120, "Golden Wheat" was made by French Saxon China, Scio Pottery as well as Homer Laughlin, for a grocery store promotion in the 1960's. No. 121 was filed for registration by the H.L.C. Co. on May 31, 1956, claiming use since April 1956, for earthenware table service. No. 122 was filed for registration on March 18, 1948, claiming use since January 1948, for earthenware table service. No. 123 filed May 18, 1940, claiming use since April 30, 1940, for earthenware table service. No. 124 was an earlier mark dated 1920, notice the upper part of mark is the same as no. 14. Nos. 125-126, dates on these marks sent from company were April 26, 1940 on no. 125, and July 11, 1939 on no. 126. Nos. 127-128 were dated by company material. No. 127 on April 14, 1937, and no. 128 on April 9, 1937. Nos. 129-130, "Craftsman Dinnerware" filed for registration on December 20, 1933, claiming use since November 1933. No. 129 is mark as filed. No. 130 is on dish. No. 131, in *Sears and Roebuck Catalogue* for Fall and Winter, 1928, also 1929-1930, the "Sunrise" dinnerware is shown with mark 131. The dated Homer Laughlin mark shown with the "Sunrise" mark would be June 1929, factory N. Nos. 132 and 133 would be later marks than no. 131, but still a Sears' product. Nos. 135-140, see text on Fiesta Ware. No. 134 was filed for registration on March 20, 1937, claiming use since November 11, 1935, for use on earthenware table service. Nos. 137-140, from S. Dan Anderson, "Fiesta Fever," *National Journal*, January 1981, p. 18. Marks similar to 137 and 140 were used as late as 1970's. On the Harlequin reproduction in 1979, the backstamp was the name Homer Laughlin and the year and that appeared only on the dinner plates. No. 141, in the *Montgomery Wards Catalogue*, 1942-1943, was pictured Homer Laughlin's Blue Willow dishes. In the *Sears* catalogue of 1949, was the Willow in pink as well as blue. No. 142, "Virginia Rose" shape was introduced in 1932 and made for several years with an assortment of different decorations. Mark seen dated 1947.

No. 143, "Kennelworth" was a complete line of buffet ware introduced in the middle 1950s. The ware was made for a New York firm on an exclusive basis. No. 144, "Dura Print" was a printing process giving a textural underglazed pattern in color combinations advertised in *Crockery and Glass Journal* for March 15, 1952, p. 40. No. 145, "Ravenna" was an early pattern around late 1920's or very early 1930's. "Ravenna" referred to shape because there are different quaint decaled decorations in center. Plates have raised design on border. The glaze is the old streaky yellow of the early years. Nos. 146-153, according to E. S. Carson, these Kingsway marks were made for the Cunningham and Pickett group of distributors from Alliance, Ohio. See that listing. There were undoubtedly double the number of marks shown here that existed for Homer Laughlin China Company. But this should provide a good start. Many of these marks and much of the information was furnished by E. S. Carson, an employee of the Homer Laughlin China Company. Of all the gentlemen I have talked with in the various potteries, he has been the most informative and willing to help. Woodrow Price of Quality Stamp Company of East Liverpool, Ohio, furnished about one-third of the marks, and the rest were photostatic copies from dishes. The "Currier and Ives" marks were sent to me by Robert LaBelle and Joe Alexander. "Laughlin's Dreamland" sent by Joanne Smith is an older mark, possibly around 1915 to 1920. A vase with this mark and children's figures was found. The vase had exactly the same shape and thin semi-procelain body as a vase with the "Laughlin Art China" mark. A delicate jug with the dreamland mark and children's figures was also found.

1.

KING CHARLES
COPYRIGHTED

2.

Majestic

20.

21. 22.

HOMER LAUGHLIN

23.

American China
MADE IN U.S.A.
by
Homer Laughlin

24.

Preference
BY
HOMER LAUGHLIN CHINA
22 KT GOLD
W.Va.

25.

Kenmark
CHINA
MADE IN U.S.A.

26.

Kenmark
CHINA
MADE IN U.S.A.

27.

Royal Crown
A-A-1
Dinnerware

MAR 8 – 1940
FEB 3 – 1940

28.

ROSE
MEDALLION

29.

The PEARL CHINA CO.
EAST LIVERPOOL, OHIO.
HAND PAINTED

30.

ZYLCO
FINE DINNERWARE
Meadow
MADE IN U.S.A.
OVEN-PROOF
DISHWASHER-PROOF

31.

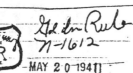
Golden Rule
N-1612
MAY 20 1940

32.

The PEARL CHINA CO.
EAST LIVERPOOL, OHIO
THE VELVARAY

33.

The PEARL CHINA CO.
EAST LIVERPOOL, OHIO
ROYAL GOLD

34.

PEARL CHINA

35.

The
Yelvaray

FIRST QUALITY
WARRANTED
20 KARAT GOLD

Wells
WARRANTED
18 CARAT GOLD

36.

ART
WELLS
GLAZES

MADE IN U.S.A.

37.

GUARANTEED
OVEN SERVE
MADE IN
U.S.A

38.

39.

OVEN SERVE
MADE IN
U.S.A

"Royal"
OVEN SERVE
Guaranteed
100% oven proof

40.

*Kitchen
Kraft*
OVEN SERVE
U.S.A

41.

GUARANTEED
OVEN SERVE
MADE IN
U.S.A.

42.

GENUINE
OVEN SERVE
WARE
U.S.A

43.

HOUSEHOLD
Priscilla
PATTERN
INSTITUTE

Eggshell
NAUTILUS
U.S.
H 42 N 5

44.

HOUSEHOLD
Priscilla
OVENWARE
INSTITUTE
U.S.A.

45.

Guaranteed
KITCHEN KRAFT
OVEN SERV
USA

46.

HOUSEHOLD
Priscilla
OVENWARE
INSTITUTE

47.

Guaranteed
To Withstand Changes of
Oven and Refrigerator Temperatures
OVEN SERVE
"The Oven Ware for Table Service"
The Homer Laughlin China Co.
Newell, W. Va.

48.

49.

HOUSEHOLD
Priscilla
OVENWARE
INSTITUTE

Best China
HOMER LAUGHLIN CHINA
MADE IN U.S.A
B L

50.

HOMER LAUGHLIN
SINCE 1871
SEMI-VITREOUS DINNERWARE
CHINA DINNERWARE
Best China
VITRIFIED HOTEL AND
RESTAURANT WARE

51.

BEST CHINA
HOMER LAUGHLIN
USA

52.

HOMER LAUGHLIN
Best China
U.S.A.
SA

53.

HOMER LAUGHLIN
Best China
U.S.A.
IC

54.

55.

THE GLADIATOR

56.

THEME
EGGSHELL
MADE IN USA
M 39 N 5

57.

Eggshell
NAUTILUS
U·S·A
K 48 N 5

58.

HOMER LAUGHLIN
EGGSHELL
MADE IN U.S.A.
C 44 N 5

78.

79.

59.

HLC
SWING
Eggshell
U.S.A.

60.

HLC
SWING
Eggshell

61.

Theme
HOMER LAUGHLIN
MADE IN U.S.A.
K 52 N 6

80.

81.

62.

EGGSHELL
GEORGIAN
HOMER LAUGHLIN
MADE IN U.S.A.
O 47 N 5

63.

Cavalier
EGGSHELL
HOMER LAUGHLIN
U.S.A.
H 56 N 4

64.

Eggshell
NAUTILUS
U.S.A.

82.

83.

65.

FAMOUS
OLD
SHIPS
HOMER LAUGHLIN
MADE IN U.S.A.
SAN MARTIN

66.

Tea Rose
U.S.A

67.

Trellis
J

84.

85.

Eggshell
NAUTILUS
U.S.A
E 41 N 5

68.

Trellis
L

69.

Moss
Rose
MADE IN U.S.A.

86.

87.

70.

Ivory Color
C

71.

Skytone
by
HOMER LAUGHLIN
USA
K 50 N B

72.

GEORGIAN
DINNERWARE
U. S. A.

88.

Epicure
OVENPROOF
HOMER LAUGHLIN
U.S.A.

89.

Epicure
by
HOMER LAUGHLIN
U.S.A.

73.

Laughlin
ART CHINA.

74.

HISTORICAL AMERICA
BETSY ROSS SHOWING
THE FIRST FLAG >>
HOMER LAUGHLIN CHINA CO.
MADE IN U.S.A.

PICTURE REPRODUCED FROM
ORIGINAL PAINTING BY
JOSEPH BOGGS BEALE
COPYRIGHT - MODERN ENTERPRISES
PHILADELPHIA, PA.

90.

Epicure

Sheffield ™
SEVILLE
MADE IN U.S.A.

92.

Sheffield ™
DINNERWARE
"BRAVADO"
PATTERN
BY J&H INTERNATIONAL
• DISHWASHER-SAFE
• DETERGENT PROOF
• OVEN PROOF
• USPA APPROVED GLAZE
MADE IN U.S.A.

91.

75.

HISTORICAL AMERICA
PAUL REVERE CROSSING BRIDGE
INTO MEDFORD TOWN... 1775
HOMER LAUGHLIN CHINA CO.
MADE IN U.S.A.

76.

HUDSON RIVER-CROW NEST
AN AMERICAN SUBJECT
- FROM -
CURRIER & IVES
PRINTS
MADE IN U.S.A. BY
HOMER LAUGHLIN

77.

SURRENDER OF BURGOYNE 1777
AN AMERICAN SUBJECT
- FROM -
CURRIER & IVES
PRINTS
MADE IN U.S.A. BY
HOMER LAUGHLIN
DECLARATION OF INDEPENDENCE

93.

Sheffield ™
Sierra
Ironstone Dinnerware
• DISHWASHER-SAFE
• DETERGENT-PROOF
• OVEN-PROOF
• USPA APPROVED GLAZE
MADE IN U.S.A.

94.

HERITAGE QUALITY
IMPERIAL
BLUE
1875
Dresden
DINNERWARE
MADE IN U.S.A.
HOMER LAUGHLIN CHINA CO.

HERITAGE QUALITY
IMPERIAL BLUE
Dresden
DINNERWARE
Sheffield
MADE IN U.S.A.
AUG. 10, 1967

95.

Scandia
by
Sheffield
MADE IN U.S.A.

96.

Sheffield
PROVINCIAL
MADE IN U.S.A.

97.

98.

Sheffield
Bone White
China
U.S.A.

Serenade
HAND DECORATED
OVEN PROOF
DETERGENT PROOF
HOMER LAUGHLIN
MADE IN U.S.A.

99.

Serenade
HOMER LAUGHLIN
Made in U.S.A.

100.

Sheffield
SERENADE
MADE IN U.S.A.

101.

Sheffield
SUNGOLD
• DISHWASHER-SAFE
• DETERGENT PROOF
• OVEN-PROOF
• USPA APPROVED
MADE IN U.S.A.

102.

Sheffield
AMBERSTONE
MADE IN U.S.A.

103.

Strathwood Collection
Shakespeare
Country
MADE IN U.S.A.

104.

Shakespeare Country
Scenes Permanently Engraved
by Ceramic Printing
Laughlin International
Newell, W. Va.   U.S.A.

105.

CHATEAU BUFFET
USA

106.

107.

PASTORAL
by
HOMER LAUGHLIN
USA
M 55 N 6

PASTORAL
HOMER LAUGHLIN
USA
M 57 N 5

108.

HARVEST
USA
B 47 N 5

109.

PASTORAL
by
HOMER LAUGHLIN
USA
J 56 N 6

110.

HARVEST
GOLD

111.

Modern Star
MADE IN U.S.A.
HLC

112.

Fortune
MADE IN USA
H.L.C.

113.

Wild Rose
U.S.A.

114.

town house
semi-vitreous
china
DETERGENT-SAFE
OVEN PROOF
U.S.A.

115.

town house
IMPERIAL WHITE
IRONSTONE
MADE IN U.S.A.
DETERGENT-SAFE
OVEN PROOF

116.

117.

Triumph
HOMER LAUGHLIN

Triumph
HOMER LAUGHLIN CHINA CO.
FINE CHINA

118.

Triumph
HOMER LAUGHLIN CHINA CO
FINE CHINA
MADE IN USA
Cynthia

119.

Golden
Wheat
MADE IN U.S.A.
- 22 K GOLD -
OVEN-PROOF

120.

BIG
PAY-OFF
Dinnerware
Designed
by
BESS
MYERSON
THE HOMER LAUGHLIN CHINA CO

121.

Jubilee

122.

ADD·A·PLACE

123.

HOMER LAUGHLIN
EMPRESS
4 20 N

124.

MADE IN AMERICA FOR
FINE
DINNERWARE
★ NOSEGAY ★
★
SEARS, ROEBUCK AND CO.

125.

MADE IN AMERICA FOR
FINE
DINNERWARE
★ ELAINE ★
★
SEARS, ROEBUCK AND CO.

126.

"Buttercup"

127.

"Pasadena"

128.

CRAFTSMAN
DINNERWARE

129.

SUNRISE
BRAND
DINNERWARE

CRAFTSMAN
DINNERWARE
USA
WARRANTED
18 CARAT GOLD

130.

HOMER LAUGHLIN
MADE IN USA
F 9 N

131.

SUNRISE
NATIONAL BROTHERHOOD
OPERATIVE POTTERS
DINNERWARE
MADE IN U.S.A.

132.

Interstate Sunrise Ware

133.

Durastone by Homer Laughlin
OVEN PROOF
DISHWASHER-PROOF
MADE IN U.S.A.

134.

KING QUALITY
HAND PAINTED
War. 22 Kt. Gold
MADE IN U.S.A

151.

152.

153.

GENUINE
fiesta
H·L·C   USA

135.

136.

fiesta
H·L·C   USA

GENUINE
Fiesta
H·L·Co
U·S·A·

154.

155.

Laughlin's Dreamland

fiesta
MADE IN
U.S.A.

137.

GENUINE
fiesta
H. L. Co   USA

138.

fiesta
H L C USA

139.

HOMER LAUGHLIN
UNDERGLAZE
MADE IN
ROYAL MAYTIME

156.

ROYAL CHINA
WARRANTED
22 KT. GOLD

157.

KRAFT PINK
HOMER LAUGHLIN
MADE IN U.S.A.

158.

H L C
fiesta
MADE IN
U.S.A.

140.

WILLOW
U.S.A.
HOMER LAUGHLIN

141.

KRAFT BLUE
HOMER LAUGHLIN
MADE IN U S A

159.

N442

160.

Coronation Rose
MADE EXCLUSIVELY
FOR
HL
WARRANTED
22 KT.
GOLD
FIRST QUALITY
WARE
by
HOMER LAUGHLIN

HOMER LAUGHLIN
VIRGINIA ROSE
MADE IN U S A.
K 47 N 8

142.

HOMER LAUGHLIN

Kenilworth
U·S·A·

143.

ZYLCO
FINE DINNERWARE
Meadow
MADE IN U.S.A
OVEN PROOF
DISHWASHER PROOF

161.

Z
ZYLCO
MADE IN U.S.A

162.

*Designs For Diving
Supreme Quality
Peoria, Ill*

163.

Dura-Print
HOMER LAUGHLIN
MADE IN USA

A 56 N 6

144.

Ravenna

145.

CARNIVAL
HOMER-LAUGHLIN

164.

*Rhythm
by
HOMER LAUGHLIN
J59 N 5*

165.

ROYAL
HARVEST
U.S.A.

166.

Old Classic Prints
"Home Sweet Home"
KINGSWAY
ALLIANCE, OHIO
USA

146.

147.
Old Classic Prints
"A Visit to Grandmothers"
KINGSWAY
ALLIANCE, OHIO
USA

HOMER LAUGHLIN
MADE IN U.S.A.
F 52 N 6

167.

HOMER LAUGHLIN
WARRANTED 22 KT GOLD

168.

Alvarado
IRONSTONE
BY
Homer Laughlin

169.

Old Classic Prints
"Traveler's Welcome"
KINGSWAY
ALLIANCE, OHIO
USA

148.

149.
Old Classic Prints
"New Comers"
KINGSWAY
ALLIANCE, OHIO
USA

Old Classic Prints
"Spring Time on the Farm"
KINGSWAY
ALLIANCE, OHIO
USA

150.

HOMER LAUGHLIN CHINA CO
Color Harmony Dinnerware
MADE BY FAMOUS AMERICAN CRAFTSMEN

170.

IRONSTONE DINNERWARE
GHC
General
Housewares
Corp.
USA
by HOMER LAUGHLIN

171.

COLORAMA
MADE IN U.S.A
BY HOMER LAUGHLIN

172.

MARIO Designer Collection
Wilkne House
AMERICAN MADE IRONSTONE

173.   OVEN-TO-TABLE-
TO-DISHWASHER

EARLY AMERICA
HOMER LAUGHLIN CHINA CO.

174.

SINCE 1871
K
KRISTINA COLLECTION

175.

PREMIUM STONE CHINA
HOMER LAUGHLIN

176.

Debutante
BY
HOMER LAUGHLIN 177.
USA
F 51 N 8

MARRIOT HOTEL
WASHINGTON D.C
BY
HOMER LAUGHLIN

178.

Suntone
BY
HOMER LAUGHLIN

179.

HC
NAUTILUS
MADE IN U.S.A

180.

CORONET
HC
`U·S·A·`

181.

HC
HOMER LAUGHLIN
Golden Harvest 182.
• DISHWASHER-SAFE
• DETERGENT-PROOF
• OVEN-PROOF
USPA APPROVED GLAZE
MADE IN USA

HOMER LAUGHLIN
Montota Meadow 183.
• DISHWASHER-SAFE
• DETERGENT-PROOF
• OVEN-PROOF
• USPA APPROVED GLAZE
MADE IN USA

HC
MADE IN
U.S.A.

184.

Piandilly
HOMER LAUGHLIN
MADE IN U.S.A.
A 40 N G

185.

ROSE
MEDALLION

186.

Royal Crown
A-A-1
Dinnerware

187.

American China
MADE IN U.S.A.
Homer Laughlin

188.

Hand Painted
HOMER LAUGHLIN
MADE IN U.S.A.

189.

190.

HAND PAINTED
HOMER LAUGHLIN
MADE IN U.S.A.

Palette Ware
MADE IN U.S.A.
by
Homer Laughlin

191.

Colorama
MADE IN U.S.A.
BY
HOMER LAUGHLIN

192.

WHITE DOVER
IRONSTONE
MADE IN U.S.A.

193.

Designer Group

WHITE DOVER IRONSTONE 194.

Debutante
BY
HOMER LAUGHLIN
USA
®

195.

HC
VELLUM

196.

HC
Mardi Gras
U·S·A

197.

Spring Garden
by
Homer Laughlin
OVEN PROOF
DISHWASHER-PROOF
MADE IN U.S.A

198.

Wheat
AMERICANA
HOMER LAUGHLIN
USA

199.

WARRANTED
ORIGINAL
MANSFIELD
DINNERWARE
22 KARAT GOLD

200.

FEB ?? 1941
MAR-3--19411

WARRANTED
ORIGINAL
MANSFIELD
DINNERWARE
22 KARAT GOLD

201.

Laughlin International. See Cunningham and Pickett for history.

Laughlin International Newell, W. Va.

Laurel Potteries. Stockton, California. Before 1941 until the early 1960's. They had several addresses for offices in the few California directories I had. In 1941 and 1958, they had offices at 354 Pine Street, San Francisco, a plant on McKinley Road in Stockton, California. By 1954 they were at 322 Hayes Street, San Francisco. In 1957 they were at 1355 Market Street in the same city. In the *Crockery and Glass Journal*, March 15, 1952, p. 143, they had an advertisement for ''California Life'' dinnerware which looked a lot like Steubenville Pottery's "American Modern." This ad showed outlets in several major cities for the ware. They also made "Holiday" pattern. The pottery was listed as manufacturers of earthenware dinnerware and vitrified. (No. 1 was filed June 10, 1946, claiming use since May 1946, for colored pottery dinnerware (rest of the marks were copied from dishes).

1.

Ceramic Studio
Laurel
OF CALIFORNIA

2.

Laurel
of California
★ U S A ★

3.

Laurel
OF CALIFORNIA
U S A

4.

HARMONY HOUSE
BIKINI
AQUAMARINE
MADE IN CALIFORNIA

5.

Lavender, Jane. Atlanta, Georgia. Around 1972 to present (1986). Jane is a studio potter making contemporary art pottery, hand painted with faces, birds, Indian head, etc. in the style of Wisecarver, Fra Mae Art Pottery and others. Each of whom has his or her own style, but for lack of a better description, their work is reminiscent of Weller or Rookwood portrait and floral pieces. In the April 1974 and November 1978 *Pottery Collector's Newsletter* were advertisements by Lavender, showing her work. Repeated letters to this potter have brought no answers. (Marks: Ellen Jennings, "Sleuths," *American Clay Exchange*, September 1984, p. 13.)

Lavender
'71

JL/73

Lawton, James. Penland, California. 1973 to present (1985). James Lawton, studio potter, is presently working at the Penland School of Crafts making sculptural vessel forms. The pieces are Raku fired and glazed with Lawton's personal glaze imagery. Lawton's work appears at the Garth Clark Gallery in New York City and Los Angeles. From October 17 to November 7, 1984, he had an exhibition, "Three Attitudes in Clay," at the Art Gallery of the Georgia State University. Each piece is made with both slab building and wheel throwing. Some parts of each piece are made by these two means. Objects seem to float upon the surface of the pieces. For instance, a teapot pictured had a vase and a grand piano for decoration which stood out in some three dimensional form. The effect was quite stunning and is achieved somehow in the glazing which Lawton calls his "glaze imagery." Lawton actually started making pottery in 1973, but didn't start as a business until 1980. He did his first show in 1976. The Penland School of Crafts and Haystack Mountain School of Crafts have been the major factors in his development as an artist and teacher. Lawton was recently granted a National Endowment Visual Art Fellowship Grant for 1985.

Lawton
85

Leach, Bernard. St. Ives, England. English potter who apprenticed several of our American potters in his studio pottery in St. Ives. Among those who studied with him were Alix and Warren Mackenzie and Byron Temple. As late as 1979, Temple was still working at the pottery with Leach who was then blind and 92 years old! Recently, a piece of Leach pottery went at auction for such a tremendous price that I decided his marks should be included here in order that they not be confused with American potters by that name. (Marks: furnished by Byron Temple.)

Leach, Janet H.B. Columbus, Ohio. 1972 to present (1984). Studio potter. Made high fired functional and decorative stoneware and Raku. Studied ceramics at Ohio State University. Mark inscribed. Not to be confused with Bernard Leach, English potter.

LEACH
W-15
⊕

Leach, Sara Ann. Columbus, Ohio. 1971-1975. Died in 1975. Studio potter. Made high fired decorative and functional pieces. Studied ceramics at O.S.U. Mark incised. Not to be confused with Bernard Leach, English potter.

S.LEACH

Leathers Pottery. Howard and Mount Eagle, Pennsylvania. Around 1862 until before 1887. John B. Leathers built a pottery to make stoneware jugs, pitchers, spittoons, batter jugs, etc. on Bald Eagle Road in Mount Eagle next to his home. In 1870 his nephew, Warren, worked at the pottery with John. From 1878 to 1884 John Leathers and his brother Ira C. Howard were also part of a pottery business which was near to Mount Eagle. By 1887 John B. Leathers was manufacturing wooden ax handles. He died in 1894 at age 61. Some of the pieces were decorated with flowers, stems and leaves. Lasansky said his pitchers were some of the best thrown in central Pennsylvania. (Information and impressed marks: Jeannette Lasansky, *Made of Mud*, pp. 24, 25, 54.)

JB LEATHERS
MT. EAGLE PA.

Leeds China Company. Chicago, Illinois. This selling agency or distributor, held a license to use the Disney characters from 1944 until 1954 in products such as cookie jars, banks, plates, planters, pitchers, figurines, salt and pepper shakers, etc. Some of the Disney characters used by Leeds included Mickey Mouse, Minnie Mouse, Donald Duck, Joe Carioca, Pluto, Dumbo, Bambi, Thumper, Snow White, Dopey, etc. Many of these were made by Ludowici Celedon and other potteries. (See that listing for connection to American Bisque.) Hull Pottery made some liquor bottles for Leeds. (Mark: incised on piece. See Ludowici Celedon for marks found in mold on pieces sold by Leeds.)

PaT. Appl'd For
LEEDS
U.S.A

Leeman, Stephen, Products. Nyack, and New York City, New York. Filed for a patent on this mark on July 23, 1932, for use on pottery bowls, jars and vases, claiming use of this mark since May 20, 1932. In the 1945 *Crockery and Glass Journal Directory*, this company was listed for earthenware fancy ware, decorated novelties, art pottery and containers. (Mark no. 2 was a backstamp from Quality Stamp Company, East Liverpool, Ohio, so I know an American pottery in that area made products for Leeman, although much of the ware the company sold probably was foreign.)

Epi-CURIO
1.

STEPHEN LEEMAN
PRODUCTS COMPANY
WEST NYACK, N. Y.
2.   EPICURIO No. 971
MADE IN U. S. A.

Lefcourte Cosmetics Company. New York, New York. Albert Lefcourte filed for registration on this mark May 30, 1944, for use on empty porcelain cosmetics boxes, claiming use since July 3, 1943.

"COVER GIRL"

Lefevres, Isaac. Vale, Lincoln County, North Carolina. 1831-1864. Stoneware. (Information and mark: Daisy Wade Bridges, *Potters of the Catawaba Valley*, Charlotte N.C. Mint Museum, 1980.)

I.L.

Lefton, George Zolton, China Company. Chicago, Illinois. 1940 to present. A distributor of ceramic giftware made overseas, but they do distribute some American made products such as woodenware, wooden bases for figurines, metal cup and saucer. Showrooms are located in more than 17 cities in the United States, Puerto Rico and Honolulu. Shown are some of the more prevalent forms used in the company's beginning. Items made between 1945 and 1953 were also labeled, "Made in Occupied Japan," as was required by law during General MacArthur's administration of post-war Japan. Some pieces made in the 1950's had the year of copyright placed below the trademark, but usually any number found there is the item identification number. If the number is preceded by letters, these will be the abbreviated factory identification. Trademarks are found in both single color and multi-color styles. Today's trademarks are of similar styles. (Information and trademarks: were furnished by the company, all but no. 9 which was filed for registration on March 7, 1967, for use on chinaware, earthenware and porcelain, namely, dinnerware, mugs, teapots, coffee pots, pitchers, bowls, trays, salt and pepper shakers and planters claiming use since 1953.)

MADE IN OCCUPIED JAPAN	Lefton China Hand painted MADE IN JAPAN	Lefton China Hand painted Reg. U.S. Pat. Off.
1948-1953	1948-1953	1949-1955
1.	2.	3.
Lefton China Hand painted	© geo. Z. Lefton	L
1950-1955	1950-1955	1948-1953
4.	5.	6.

Lefton 7.   8. G.Z. Lefton CREATION

Lefton 9.

W.H. Lehew and Company. Strasburg, Virginia. Ramsay, p. 242, dates this pottery 1885 until after 1900. Also Smith, p. 22 mentions **Lehew, Sonner, and Hickerson** marked pieces. He said these pieces reflect ownership of the pottery; that the stoneware pieces were made by journeymen. Mark impressed. (Information and marks: Smith, p. 22, 23.)

W.H. Lehew & CO.

W.H. LEHEW & CO.
STRASBURG

L. Lehman and Company. Poughkeepsie and New York City, New York. This potter was dated from 1852 to 1856 in Poughkeepsie, New York, in C. Jordan Thorn's book, *Handbook of Old Pottery and Porcelain Marks*. Then from 1858 to 1863 he was in Manhatten, New York City, according to Regina Stewart and Geraldine Consentino in *Stoneware*, pp. 78, 124. William Ketchem, in *Early Potters and Potteries of New York State*, p. 229, also dates the pottery in Manhatten from 1858 to 1863. At that time, in 1863, William MacQuoid bought the pottery works of Lewis Lehman on West Twelveth Street, according to Stewart and Consentino, p. 78. There is a problem about the spelling of the name, Lewis or Louis. Thorn has "Lewis," in the index and "Louis," in the text and mark he shows which is simply the name, "Louis Lehman," impressed. The other authors cited, all use the spelling, "Lewis." (Mark: impressed on crock in picture in Harold F. Guilland's book, *Early American Folk Pottery*, p. 114.)

L.LEHMAN & CO.
WEST 12 ST. N.Y.

Lehner, Ann Berquist. Delaware County, Ohio. 1974 to 1983. Ann made handmade utilitarian pottery on a wheel, some decorative, some functional including full dinnerware sets. She used various colorful and artistically applied glazes. She made a few sculptured pieces. Ann sold from place of business called **The Ivy Tree Greenhouse and Pottery**. She resumed her teaching career in 1983. Ann makes an occasional piece of decorative pottery at present.

Berquist   *Ivy Tree A. Lehner*

Leica Ceramics. White Cottage, Ohio. (near Roseville, Ohio). 1961 to present. Lei Cannon, owner, is an experienced potter and designer. At present, he makes items for custom orders and decorates with silk screening. He does some manufacturing of pottery for his custom work. He also uses the name **Zane Trace Pottery**. He designs and makes all sort of novelty items, souvenir items, etc.

23 K. GOLD
GUARANTEED
Leica Ceramics
WHITE COTTAGE
OHIO

Zane's Trace
POTTERY
ZANESVILLE, OHIO
43701

Leigh Potters, Inc. Alliance, Ohio. 1926-1931. The pottery was first called **Crescent China Company** from 1920-1926. Then it became Leigh Potters, Inc. This pottery was built and owned by some of the Sebring brothers, so the products made here were very similar to those of other Sebring, Ohio potteries. Made dinnerware, kitchenware, a line of decorative pottery called Leigh Art Ware, etc. of semi-porcelain in good shapes, nicely decorated by decals. My source of informa-

tion on the Crescent and Leigh potteries was taken from Edward T. Heald who wrote a four or five volume book on Stark County where he lived. He not only wrote the history of the potteries in Stark County, he wrote the history of every industry that existed there before 1958. I stand by my original source. When Heald says the building was vacant from 1931 to 1940, I believe it was vacant. Here is his paragraph on the potteries as well as the paragraph that preceeded it on the Alliance Manufacturing Company which followed the Leigh Potters, Inc. in the pottery building:

"In 1940 a vacated pottery building on the northeast corner of Lake Park Avenue and South Mahoning Avenue was purchased by the Alliance Manufacturing Company and the two assembling plants on Union Avenue and Riverside were disposed of and all assembling operations combined in the new building. The production plant at 1255 South Mahoning Avenue was continued in operation, however.

The pottery building had been built in 1920 by F.A. Sebring and operated until 1926 as the Crescent China Company with Samuel I. Marley as manager. From 1926 to 1931 it was operated as the Leigh Pottery Company with Charles Sebring, son of F.A., as manager. Another son, Frank Sebring, Jr., operated a pottery plant at Salem, Ohio. James Erdley, now with Spaulding China at Sebring, was an employee. The depression hit the pottery business hard, and the Park Avenue plant was closed in 1931. It remained idle nine years until purchased by the Alliance Manufacturing Company."

(Information: Edward T. Heald, *The Stark County Story*, Volume IV, Part II, "The Suburban Era," 1917-1958. Canton: The Stark County Historical Society, p. 743. Marks: 1, 2, 3, 4, 5, photocopied from dishes; no. 6, Quality Stamp Company; no.7, Gerald, Barnett, "Collectible American China," *National Journal*, March 1979, p. 22)

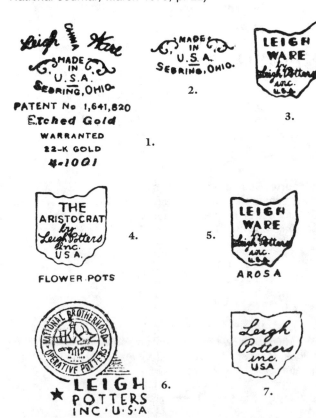

Leman, Johannes (spelled "Lehman," by Ramsay, p. 186). Tylersport, Pennsylvania. Around 1830. Ramsay said this potter made sgraffito pieces, some marked with name at Frederick Hildebrand's pottery. Thorn, p. 134, spelled the name, "Leman," and gave the mark shown.

Johannes Leman

Leneige China, Inc. Burbank California. Before 1934 and out of business before 1955. In the directories, I had Leneige was first listed in 1934 and not listed in 1954. They were listed in the 1952 *Crockery and Glass Journal Directory* for art china of porcelain and earthenware, including vases, console sets, etc. Also cups and saucers, figurines, service plates, tea sets and wall plates. (Mark: 1952 directory cited.)

Leneige

Lenox, Inc./Ceramic Art Company. Trenton, New Jersey. 1894 to present. The following is a reduced version of the material sent by the company for use in *American Kitchen and Dinnerwares*. The long discussion about how chinaware is manufactured at Lenox, Inc. had to be omitted here, also some decoration and shape information. The information that follows tells about the fierce struggle required for success, and in this day and age when almost all of our potteries are gone, Lenox, Inc. is still operating; that requires great admiration for the company.

Walter Scott Lenox was born in Trenton in 1859. As a boy he completed an apprenticeship in how to make pottery. When he was in his 20's he became art director of the Ott and Brewer factory. He saved his money and in 1889, got together $4,000 and became a partner with Jonathan Coxon, Sr., in the Ceramic Art Company. At that time, all fine chinaware was imported from Europe, but the idea of making ware comparable to any in the world was in Lenox's mind from the beginning. It was an idea that was far more daring and far more hazardous as a business proposition than might have seemed on the surface. In the first place, the technique of making fine china was difficult to master; secondly, Americans were strongly prejudiced in favor of the famous European china names; and thirdly, it seemed highly probable that a company would go broke trying to produce high-quality ware while paying American scale wages. About 70 percent of the cost of fine chinaware is labor, much of it highly skilled.

In 1894, when he acquired sole ownership of the company, about all he had was debts and a three-story pottery that had been built, on the insistence of financial backers, so that it could easily be converted into a tenement house if the business failed. If didn't fail, but it would have except for Lenox's ability to make friends. There were many times when he dashed from friend to friend to borrow $500 to meet the payroll; or to borrow from one friend to pay back, often without interest, what he had previously borrowed from another. And there were many times when Harry A. Brown, secretary of the company, stood by as china was taken from the kilns and then, if it had turned out well, hurried to New York to collect in advance enough money to buy more materials for the potter.

At first, Lenox concentrated on production of a rich, ivory-tinted ware referred to as Belleek similar in appearance to the china which originated in Belleek, Ireland. He was forced to import two skilled potters in order to learn the methods but even then the next few years brought more disappointments than successes. The ware lacked the durability of the finest foreign product but Lenox slowly developed his own formula and soon after the turn of the century was making dinnerware comparable to the best. But even then the American buying public wouldn't believe this and the majority kept right on buying foreign-made ware.

Furthermore, personal disaster was descending on Lenox. He was a bachelor whose manner of living was graceful, but soon after the turn of the century, his health began to fail. He was becoming both blind and paralyzed. For a man who enjoyed life as Lenox did, such an illness might have been a shattering blow. Actually, it had the opposite effect on him. He continued to go to the pottery daily and his interest in details of manufacture became more instense as his physical condition deteriorated. Even when he could "see" the chinaware only with his sensitive fingers and when his chauffeur had to carry him piggyback to his desk, he supervised each step in production and ran the business with Harry Brown as his assistant and alter ego.

He formed Lenox, Inc., in 1906 and redoubled his efforts to overcome the prejudice against American-made fine china. Almost at once he got a spectacular break. In 1905, the company had received a large order from Shreve and Company of San Francisco with a request to get the ware there for the opening of their new store. The order was rushed through and shipped to the West Coast just in time to become a casualty of the San Francisco earthquake and fire. Except that it wasn't exactly a casualty; it became proof of Lenox quality. Out of the wreckage was dug a Lenox plate that had been decorated in green and gold. The gold had melted, the green had become streaked with smoke and the design was almost obliterated but the glazed plate was basically as perfect as on the day it was made. With the blackened plate as Exhibit A in his campaign, Lenox concentrated in the next few years on the most expensive market. Tiffany's became the new company's first account.

The encouragement of Tiffany's played an important part in the progress of Lenox and caused other New York and Philadelphia stores to take an interest, but it was not until 1917 that the company received outstanding recognition. Since 1826, Congress had been on record as requiring that, so far as possible, all equipment for the White House should be bought in the United States. No President, however, had been able to find American-made china fit for the White House table and even Theodore Roosevelt, who had scoured the country's potteries, had to admit that "we are dependent upon foreign factories for the very dishes from which the Chief Executive of the United States must eat." Woodrow Wilson, who had served in Trenton as governor of New Jersey, finally broke the precedent with the encouragement of his friend, the late James Kerney, Sr., editor of the *Trenton Times*. Wilson ordered a 1,700 piece dinner set costing $16,000 from Lenox in 1917. Franklin D. Roosevelt and Harry S. Truman followed Wilson's example when they returned to Lenox years later to supplement the White House dinner service. The company has made many dinner sets for state governors, presidents of Latin American countries and dignitaries around the world.

It was introduction of his ware into the White House in Wilson's home, however, that climaxed Lenox's career. He remained in command only two more years.

The real struggle for position in the American market, however, was only begun. Although Lenox had demonstrated that fine china could be made in the United States, foreign firms still dominated the domestic market and produced perhaps eight of every 10 pieces sold in this country. European ideas of shape and design were paramount and were followed here just as American dressmakers followed Paris fashions. It took another 15 years, under the presidency of Harry Brown, to break down this tradition. In the 1930's when the company was still doing considerably less than $1,000,000 worth of business annually, designer Frank Homes began introducing a new style in china that was generally called modern, and represented the first real effort to break away from European traditions. It was clean and simple of line in contrast to the elaborate and often rococo style that had been popular for years in Europe. This modern style, particularly Holmes' unencumbered decorative motifs against ivory backgrounds, soon attracted attention. By the late 1930's the Lenox trademark was on perhaps one of every four pieces of chinaware purchased by Americans.

World War II completed the transition, by cutting off practically all imports of fine china. A dozen American firms, some new and some established companies which had not previously made fine chinaware, got into the field. Starting about 1943, the American market went domestic with a bang. For the first time, it attracted big and aggressive capital, put emphasis on modern business methods as well as high artistic standards and flourished because of American manufacaturing ingenuity, merchandising and sales methods.

With competition mounting among American firms, the old system of having a few salesmen who packed their trunks and toured around to see important customers perhaps once a year was abandoned. A number of sales regions were set up to keep in regular touch with dealers. Merchandising methods such as exhibits, attractive display ideas and publicity programs were introduced. A long-range program of educating women and girls in the use of American-made china was inaugurated and copies of a full-color motion picture demonstrating the making of Lenox China were put into circulation in schools and clubs all over the country. Special training courses were arranged for the sales forces in large stores and recommended coordinations of china design and style with crystal, silver and other table appointments were created in order to increase the harmony of table settings.

But perhaps the most important change broke away from the old European system of selling china services principally by the set, which in practice had required the purchaser to invest perhaps $600 in a lump sum. This tended to limit the market because the average housewife couldn't afford such an investment. The company, instead, began putting emphasis on buying 5-piece place settings or individual pieces.

Today, Lenox, Inc., is a multi-million dollar enterprise. The company has been expanding rapidly into other product lines over the past two decades. In 1962 Oxford bone China, now widely known for its pure white color, translucency, delicate appearance and remarkable strength, was introduced to the American market.

The year 1972 was marked by the much heralded introduction of a versatile new line of super-ceramic, casual dinnerware, Temper-ware by Lenox.

In 1965, Lenox acquired the oldest crystal glass blowing company in the United States and thus Lenox Crystal was born.

Between 1968 and 1972, the Lenox family added Lenox Candles, Paragon Products Corporation, a refiner of custom waxes; Kaumagraph Company, a specialty printer; Carolina Soap and Candle Makers Company, a producer of scented candles, soaps and toiletries; Art Carved, Incorporated, a designer and manufacturer of wedding and engagement rings; H. Rosenthal Jewelry Corporation, a distributor of high fashion jewelry. In late 1972 Lenox acquired the Imperial Glass Corporation, a manufacturer of quality cut glassware. In 1973 Lenox added Taunton Silversmiths, Ltd., makers of silver-plated gifts, serving pieces and accessories. In 1975 Lenox acquired ownership of the John Roberts Company, now known as Art-Carved Class Rings, Incorporated; Eisenstadt Manufacturing Company, a wholesale distributor of jewelry and awards, now named Lenox Awards, Inc. In addition Lenox, Inc. operates two latin American subsidiaries producing melamine dinnerware, stainless steel flatware, sterling silver and silver-plated flatware.

Shown first are the marks Nos. 1A to 7A as they were sent from the company. They were pretty much in agreement with the information filed by the company in the patent reports. We should all recognize the difficult work it is for some office employee to find time to search files and furnish material on inquiry. Many companies just won't do it.

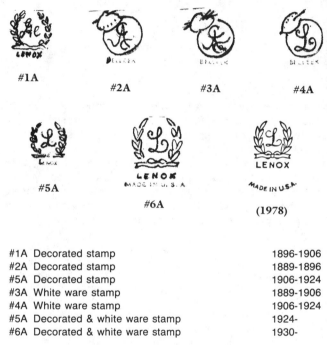

#1A
#2A
#3A
#4A
#5A
#6A
(1978)

#1A	Decorated stamp	1896-1906
#2A	Decorated stamp	1889-1896
#5A	Decorated stamp	1906-1924
#3A	White ware stamp	1889-1906
#4A	White ware stamp	1906-1924
#5A	Decorated & white ware stamp	1924-
#6A	Decorated & white ware stamp	1930-

Nos. 1-5 the Ceramic Art Company from Barber, *Marks of American Potters*, used before 1904. Barber dated the Indian head 1895 and said it was used on undecorated ware. Nos. 6, 7 were said to be Lenox marks by W.P. Jervis, "Worlds' Pottery Marks," *Pottery, Glass, and Brass Salesman*, April 8, 1915, p. 11, to be used on a series of portrait jugs made for a private firm. No. 8 was filed for registration August 18, 1916, claiming use since February 1, 1906 for Belleek. Belleek was an exceptionally fine thin china, but the patent or copyright report said "undecorated table ware of porcelain and earthenware." No. 9 was filed August 18, 1916, claiming use since February 1906, for same products as no. 8. No. 10 filed December 11, 1917 - no prior use claimed for tableware. No. 11 filed July 28, 1925, claiming use for one month prior to registration for pottery plates, cups, platters, bowls and other tableware pottery and vases. No. 12 filed April 20, 1927, claiming use since December 6, 1926 for plates, platters, cover dishes, boats, cups and saucers, coffee pots, teapots, sugars and creamers, pitchers of all sizes, vases of all sizes, mayonnaise bowls, jam jars, flower bowls and flower holders made of china, porcelain or earthenware, china dresser sets. No. 13 filed June 12, 1962, claiming use since February 2, 1962 for dinnerware formed of ceramic material. No. 14 filed August 18, 1963, claiming first use since 1894, for ceramic ware for the preparation and service of food and beverages and for other utilitarian used in homes, hotels, offices and similar places. No. 15 filed April 18, 1963, claiming first use since 1906, about 1894 as to "Lenox" in another display (meaning mark). No. 16 and No. 22 were filed April 18, 1963, with first use in 1949, for ceramic ware for the preparation and service of food and beverages and for other utilitarian uses in homes, hotels, offices and similar places. No. 17, "Lenox," was filed again on October 20, 1965, claiming first use since 1900, for different articles than no. 14 - namely, ceramic vases, pitchers, urns, pin trays, nut bowls, nut dishes, jars, coaster, teapots, candy bowls, candy dishes, serving bowls, relish dishes, ornamental trays, bowls and dishes for use as centerpieces and the like, playing card boxes and boxes and containers for small miscellaneous items. Nos. 18-20 were all filed in May 1983, claiming use for a few months prior to that time for dinnerware. No. 21 filed November 29, 1984, with mark in use one month for dinnerware. The remainder are miscellaneous marks from dishes and directories.)

1.

2.

3.

4.

5.

6.

7.

8.

9. BELLEEK

10.

11. SILVER-LENOX

12.

13. OXFORD

14. LENOX

15.

LENOX

16. LENOX CHINA

17. LENOX

18. LANTANA

19.

20. LENOX CHINASTONE

BOUQUET COLLECTION 21.

22.

23. MARSHALL FIELD & COMPANY CHICAGO

24. LENOX TIFFANY & CO

25. LENOX MADE IN U.

26.

27. OXFORD® BONE CHINA MADE IN U.S.A

28. LENOX MADE IN U.S.A.

29. LENOX © ® MADE IN U.S.A

30. temper-ware BY LENOX

Lent, George. Troy, and Lansingburgh, New York. Seems to have made pottery from around 1800 to early 1840's. This potter was born in 1774 and died 1850. In his very early years, he lived in Cornwall, Orange County, New York, near Nathan Clark. In 1806 he lived in Greenbush, New York. By 1810 he was listed in the census of Troy, New York, and in 1813 he advertised a new stoneware factory at the south part of the village. Warren F. Broderick, researcher and writer, listed several properties or lots purchased by George Lent in Troy, including lots with a home, a warehouse, etc. One of these properties had a store and his partner was a man named Peterson. In 1824, Lent purchased Peterson's share and sold properties to William Lundy for $2,100.00 and then moved to Lansingburgh. In 1825, Lent constructed a pottery in Lansingburgh. William Lent, son of George, worked with his father from 1813 to 1836. By the middle 1840's, Broderick found advertisements where Lent was trying to sell his pottery. Broderick thinks Orcutt may have used Lent's pottery facilities in the early 1840's. (Information and marks: Warren F. Broderick, as cited.)

G. LENT

LANSINGBURGH

G. LENT

TROY

Leonard, S.E. Wallingford, Vermont. Born in 1875. Seth E. Leonard was a blacksmith and hotelkeeper, who had his name put on a jug as did many firms in Bradford, Brandon and Wallingford, Vermont, according to Lura Woodside Watkins in *Early New England Potters and Their Wares*, p. 152. She believed the jug was made in Hartford. (Mark: impressed on jug - illustration no. 100 following p. 290 of Watkins's book.)

S E LEONARD

WALLINGFORD VT.

Le Pere Pottery. Listed at 1470 Greenwood Avenue, Zanesville, Ohio. Started 1936 by Otto and Paul Herold with the help and advice of Albert Lepper, and was last listed in directories in 1961. In 1945 they employed 250 to make hand decorated ware, some gold decorated, a line of copper luster which was a reproduction of Colonial Ware, that sold as fast as it could be made. The ware was fairly vitrified, but still semi-porcelain. Harry P. Moyer's mark seen here was on a decaled, gold trimmed violin planter. He was a modeler and designer at the plant from 1945 until sometime after 1956. Lepper perfected the glazes and named the pottery. (Information: Norris F. Schneider, "Le Pere Plant," *The Zanesville Times Signal*, November 11, 1956, no page no. Marks: on pieces of china.)

Le Pere

Le Pere
POTTERY
U.S.A.

© MOYER

Le Pot Marie. Bastrop, Texas. 1971 to present (1985). Marie Blazek, a studio potter, makes functional porcelain into one of a kind pieces. She graduated from University of Texas in 1969. In 1970 and 1971 she lived and studied in Mexico City. In 1971, Marie studied under Lisalot Schmidt and in 1972 with Gary Huntoon, both of whom studied under Marguerite Wildenheim. In 1973, she was potter in residence at the Peaceable Kingdom School of Crafts. In 1975, she apprenticed with Ishmael Soto and Finn Alban. In 1978, she received the National Endowment grant for residency at the Star of the Republic Museum in Washington, to research early Texas pottery. Marie said that after 10 years of experimen-

ting with clay that she had settled for a pure white porcelain clay imported from England which is translucent when thrown thinly. Marie does extensive slip decoration in bright colors that contrast with the white clay. Marie has done many, many shows over the years and listed many galleries and shops that sell her work. A few recent shows include: 1983, Fayette Heritage Society Show, juried; 1983, M.E.'s Gallery, one-man-show, Houston, Texas; 1983, Texas Designer Craftsmen, juried show, Denton, Texas; 1983, Texas State Arts and Crafts Festival in Kerrville, Texas, juried; 1984, San Angelo Ceramic Competition, winner.

Blazek

Lerner, Claire, Studio. Los Angeles, California. Operated in 1940's until around 1955. The studio was listed in 1954 but not in 1955. Listed as makers of art pottery of earthenware, vases, candy boxes, console sets, trays, cigarette boxes, etc. (Mark: furnished by Martha Brisker, Brisker's Antiques.)

Claire Lerner
Calif
19 © 50

CL 228

Claire LERNER

Lessell Art Ware. Parkersburg, West Virginia. John Lessell was associated with several of the potteries during his career as a designer including Ford City China Company before 1899, the Bohemian Pottery in 1903, and he was one of the incorporators of Arc-En-Ciel Pottery. In 1905, he worked at the J.B. Owens Pottery and produced a line of lustre ware, similar to La Sa line which he later designed for Weller Pottery Company where he worked in the early 1920's. In March 1911, only until the middle of 1912, Lessell had a pottery of his own in Parkersburg where he made art pottery. Until now no marked examples had been known. In 1924, he was head pottery expert for Art China Company of Zanesville, Ohio, another short lived company. Lessell died in the late 1920's. He worked for a short while at Camark Pottery before he died and his wife, Jenny, carried on his designing at Camark. The rare pieces he worked on at Camark are marked "Le Camark." According to Norris F. Schneider, "Veteran Mosaic Tile Employee Compiles Outstanding Display," *Zanesville Times Recorder*, October 30, 1960 (no page no.), Lessell purchased some unfinished ware from Fraunfelter and added his own decoration. Schneider said Lessell owned work studios for short periods of time in Zanesville and Newark, Ohio; Parkersburg, West Virginia. (Information: Paul Evans, Art Pottery in the U.S., p. 140. Joseph D. Alsbrook, "Camark, A Legendary Name in American Pottery," *American Clay Exchange*, June 15, 1985, pp. 8, 9. Very rare stamped mark: from Doris Reddy.)

f 10ª

Lettell and Company. Greensboro, Pennsylvania. (Spelled "Littel," by Baker, and "Lettell," on crock pictured in Guappone, p. 27.) Made stoneware. Ended 1870. (Information: Gordon C. Baker, "Pottery of Greensboro and New Geneva, Pa.," *Spinning Wheel*, November 1973, p. 15. Mark: Guappone, p. 27.)

Leveritt, Joseph. Conway, Arkansas. 1979 to present (1987). Leveritt is a self taught studio type potter, making functional, decorative and personalized pieces in a swirled high temperature stoneware similar to Niloak's swirled ware. The pieces are hand thrown or slab build into vases, bowls, mugs, etc. Several years ago, Leveritt worked in a shop at Pickles Gap Creek Crafts Village, just north of Conway. In the past, he has shipped the beautiful swirled pieces all over the country. Leveritt retired from his regular work as a physical education teacher in 1979 and started making pottery pieces on a full time basis. Leveritt said in a letter, February 1986: "Pottery and art in general have been my hobby for over 60 years. I saw my first potter in action in 1930. Before I was really involved in pottery, I had three or four ideas about kilns, which I learned later were the old Chinese bee-hive kilns. I tell people that I am a reincarnated Chinese potter. I have always been fascinated with what the Chinese called agate ware, which is like the old Niloak pottery from Benton, Arkansas, back in the 1930's. We actually duplicate nature in making the rock which is called agate." (Information: Doris and Burdell Hall, "New Swirl Pottery from Arkansas," *American Clay Exchange*, September 30, 1985, pp. 8-10; and letter from Leveritt. Marks are incised.)

LEVERITT

LEVERITT
AR
CONWAY

Levy Brothers China Company, Inc. New York, New York. Decorators and importers, filed for registration on this mark on January 3, 1940, for use on chinaware vases and dishes, claiming use since 1939. In the 1945 *Crockery and Glass Journal Directory*, they were listed as selling American art pottery and garden pottery. They were also listed as decorators. They also sold foreign ware and were the sole distributors for Robert Haviland Le Tanneur, Limoges, Hampton ware which was artware in vitrified china.

Lewis and Gardiner/Lewis and Lewis/Henry Lewis. See the Huntington Pottery listing.

Lewis, Otto V. This stoneware potter was in several places in New York State. In the years before 1852, he was at Greenwich. From around 1852 to around 1860, he was at Galesville. Then in the 1860's he was at Mechanicville. Bill Grande in "Stoneware Pottery," *American Collector*, April 1980, p. 12, said O.V. Lewis incised two fish on a large water cooler. In 1858, O.V. Lewis helped to open a pottery at Fort Edward. William A. Lewis was in Galesville around 1858 to around 1864 using the mark, "W.A. Lewis/Galesville." Other marks used by Otto were "Otto V. Lewis," and "O.V. Lewis," probably used in 1849's and early 1850's. He also used "O.V. Lewis/Galesville," around 1852 to 1860, in addition to the full name, Otto, as shown. (Information and marks: Warren F. Broderick, writer, researcher and collector.)

OTTO V. LEWIS
MECHANICVILLE
1.

OTTO V. LEWIS
GALESVILLE
2.

O.V. LEWIS
GREENWICH
3.

Liberty China. See Virginia Pottery, New Lexington, Ohio.

Lietzke Porcelains. Mogadore (Akron), Ohio. 1949 to present. Makers of hand crafted items in fine porcelain for use and show including salad sets, tableware, vases, tumblers, porcelain cabinet pulls and door knobs. Their porcelain is marked "Lietzke" with year and date on outside surface. (Information and mark: Lehner, *Ohio Pottery and Glass*, p. 69.)

Lietzke

Lietzke '73

Lietzke
Porcelains
(1949)

Lifetime China Company. Alliance, Ohio. A distributor associated with Cunningham and Pickett. See Cunningham and Pickett for history. (Marks: on dishes.)

Lima Insulator Company. Lima, New York. 1904 to 1908. In 1908, the plant was almost destroyed by fire and purchased by the Locke family in 1909 and became a part of Locke Insulator Manufacturing Company in 1910. (Information and incuse (stamped in) mark: Tod, *Porcelain Insulators Guide Book for Collectors*, p. 107.)

LIMA, N.Y.

Limoges China Company. Sebring, Ohio. 1900 until shortly after 1955 when the pottery went into bankruptcy. Limoges had a daily output of 45,000 pieces of semi-porcelain dinnerware. What I am finding of their ware is very pretty, and it is destined to become a great collectible because there is enough of it around to complete sets. The plant was first called **Sterling China**, then the name was quickly changed to **Sebring China Company**, but that didn't work because the E.H. Sebring China Company was also called the Sebring China Company; so the name was very shortly made Limoges China Company. Several Sterling marks have been attributed to the Limoges Company for the short time the company was called by that name. To tell the truth, we will probably never know which of the Sterling marks they used or even if they used one. See the discussion under the listing Sterling China Marks for more on this. I saw a tall pitcher and mugs with portraits that was almost in the realm of artistic pottery very much like that made by Warwick China Company (only the shading was in orange to tan rather than a brown color) which was made at Limoges China Company in the early years. As late as 1945 and 1946 the *Crockery and Glass Journal Directories* listed dinnerware of china for Limoges. I am sure it was not china at that time, and I have sincere doubts that Limoges ever made what was a true porcelain product. That is not to say they are not attractive or collectible, just not real china. In the late 1940's, Limoges China Company was threatened with a lawsuit by the Limoges Company in France over the name "Limoges," and started calling their product American Limoges. Also, the company name became American Limoges China Company in advertisements, etc. One other name used by Limoges China Company probably for purposes of marketing was the Lincoln China Company. By using more than one name, a pottery could give an exclusive dealership to more than one customer in the same town. Victor Schreckengost worked at times for the Limoges China Company. Six scenes called "Old Virginia Fashionware," in blue, brown, mauve, with a celedon rim and copper line were designed by him in 1942. Helen Stiles in *Pottery in the United States*, p. 78 had a great deal to say about dinnerware made by Limoges in the 1940 era:

"The Manhattan shape as designed by Mr. Schreckengost for the American Limoges China Company has been decorated in a number of interesting patterns. The "Meerschaum" pattern is the color of a mellowed meerschaum pipe with deeper brown flecks. There is a streaked band of darker sepia brown which gives strength and beauty to this pattern. A design called "Red Sails" is printed in brilliant red and black with red band and handle treatment on a soft ivory-toned body. The "Animal Kingdom" consist of eight different characters which are gay and humorous designs in bright red. This design is used for children's sets, and has been very successful for bridge sets. The bridge plate, with well for cup, is one of the new pieces which has been added to the Manhattan shape. Another gay little design is "Ship Ahoy" with nautical flags spelling good luck. Mr. Schreckengost's "Jiffy Ware" is also made by the American Limoges China Company."

The company existed through the 1940's when the emphasis on design became so important to our American potteries. Consequently this company produced some really beautiful ware. In the 1940's, Salem China Company, Sebring Pottery Company, and Limoges China Company were all under the same management. Schreckengost designed for all of them and we get duplication in pattern and designs made during this time as would be expected. (Information: Thelma Shull, "Scenes for the China Collector," *Hobbies*, June 1942, p. 66. See Lois Lehner, *American Kitchen and Dinner Wares*, pp. 98, 99, for a discussion of patterns by Limoges China Company. Marks: no. 1 was an early mark filed November 4, 1918, claiming use June 19, 1917, for china cups, saucers, plates and food dishes. No. 2 was filed for registration of chinaware August 1, 1925, claiming use since July 1925. No. 3 shows the wording as it was used on a deep dark blue plate with a great deal of gold trim. The plate was a good grade of semi-porcelain but not china. No. 4, "Peach Blo," was filed October 2, 1930, claiming use since December 1, 1929, for porcelain and semi-porcelain dishes and tableware. "Peach-blo," "Golden Glo," and "Glo Peach" were used in a wide variety of marks referring to a yellow type glaze that came into use at this time. No. 5, "American Limoges," was filed December 29, 1941, claiming use since June 1941, for china tableware. No. 6, "Made in U.S.A. Limoges," was filed June 3, 1949, claiming use since April 1942, for dinnerware made of earthenware. No. 7 in the 1945 *Crockery and Glass Journal Directory*. No. 8, "Casino," sent by reader, Alice Jamieson. Nos. 9, 10, from Jo Cunningham, p. 214. "Jiffy Ware" was a kitchen ware, shakers, etc. "Regency," "Triumph," and "Diana" were shape names used in 1940's and early 1950's. "Triumph" was found dated in 1940's on a plate. The rest of the marks came from Quality Stamp Company, East Liverpool, Ohio, or were copied from dishes.).

1.

2.

4.

5.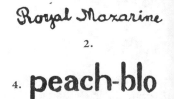

6.

MADE IN U.S.A. LIMOGES

7.

ROSE MARIE

S M Toy

26.

27.

MADE IN U.S.A. LIMOGES

28.

8.

peach-blo by Limoges

9.

L'Exquisite

AMERICAN LIMOGES MADE IN U.S.A.

TRILLIUM 1-15530
WARRANTED 22K GOLD

29.

TRIUMPH
AMERICAN LIMOGES
SEBRING·OHIO

WARRANTED 22·K GOLD
VERMILLION ROSE

30.

PEACH-BLO by Limoges SEBRING OHIO

Silver Moon
4M155

10.

TRIUMPH

MADE IN U.S.A. LIMOGES

UC FOREST GREEN
CHATEAU FRANCE T.S.52
WARRANTED 22K GOLD

11.

TRIUMPH
AMERICAN LIMOGES
SEBRING·OHIO
WARRANTED
22·K·GOLD

31.

32.

TRIUMPH
AMERICAN LIMOGES
MADE IN U.S.A.

PROMENADE
BURGUNDY T-S284 C.D.
WARRANTED 22 K GOLD

AMERICAN LIMOGES

WARRANTED 22K GOLD
TOLEDO DELIGHT-ITC-X

12.

DESIGNED BY ANNE ORR
MADE IN U.S.A. LIMOGES

13.

PEASANTWARE
MADE IN USA
Limoges

14.

TRIUMPH
AMERICAN LIMOGES
SEBRING·OHIO

WARRANTED 22·K GOLD
CORONATION ORANGE
VENETIAN BLIND 1T-S278

33.

TRIUMPH
AMERICAN LIMOGES
MADE IN U.S.A.

CHINA D'OR
1T-S 284
WARRANTED 22K GOLD

34.

Jiffy ware
SEBRING, OHIO U.S.A.

15.

PEARL IVORY by Limoges SEBRING.O

16.

GLO PECHE WARE by Limoges SEBRING, OHIO

BEL CLARE

17.

PEACH-BLO MADE by Limoges SEBRING, OHIO

18.

GLO PECHE WARE by Limoges SEBRING, OHIO

19.

GLO PECHE WARE by Limoges SEBRING, OHIO

20.

CANDLE·LIGHT

MADE IN U.S.A. LIMOGES

WARRANTED 22K GOLD
VIENNA-LC-S360-1
PRESENTED TO
S. T. Pollock
IN APPRECIATION
OF HIS TWENTY YEARS' OF SERVICE TO THE
SEBRING SCHOOL SYSTEM
BY THE
BOARD OF EDUCATION
SEBRING, OHIO
JUNE 1946

35.

AMERICAN LIMOGES

ROSALIE 1 K-NL

36.

MANHATTAN
AMERICAN LIMOGES
SEBRING·OHIO

WARRANTED
22-K-GOLD

21.

CANDLE·LIGHT
MADE IN U.S.A. LIMOGES
WARRANTED
22·K·GOLD

22.

CANDLE·LIGHT
by AMERICAN LIMOGES
CHINA CO. SEBRING·OHIO

NEW PRINCESS -LC

NO LINE

23.

MADE IN U.S.A. LIMOGES

WHEATFIELD
1K-NL

37.

BLUE WILLOW
MADE IN U.S.A. LIMOGES

24.

CANDLE·LIGHT
LIMOGES

25.

AMERICAN LIMOGES MADE IN U.S.A.

OLD DUTCH 44

38.

AMERICAN LIMOGES MADE IN U.S.A.

11

CHATEAU-FRANCE
1K-S518
WARRANTED 22K GOLD

39.

AMERICAN LIMOGES MADE IN U.S.A.
55
WHEATFIELD TC G. F. 2
WARRANTED 22 K GOLD
40.

WESTWOOD *Limoges China*
W
B-48   *1*
SYLVIA
41.

LINCOLN CHINA CO. BY AMERICAN LIMOGES SEBRING-OHIO
42.
WHITE GOLD
WARRANTED 22-K

LIMOGES ·U·S·A· CHINA·CO. 1 27
43.

MADE IN U.S.A. LIMOGES *4*
44.
CHINA ROSE 3 TC-6W
WARRANTED 22 K GOLD

45.   THE LINCOLN CHINA CO
SEBRING, OHIO
U. S. A.
22 K. GOLD

LIMOGES CHINA CO. U.S.A. SEBRING-OHIO
GOLDEN GLOW
PAT. APPLIED FOR
46.

Guild Edge *4*
AMERICAN ROSE DINNER WARE
22 K. GOLD
47.

Glamour BY THE AMERICAN LIMOGES CHINA CO. MADE IN U S A
WARRANTED 22 K GOLD
48.

CAMEO BY AMERICAN LIMOGES SEBRING-OHIO
49.

EMBASSY AMERICAN LIMOGES SEBRING-OHIO
50.

51. SNOWFLAKE AMERICAN LIMOGES SEBRING-OHIO

Lincoln Pottery. Trenton, New Jersey. The pottery was started by James Carr and Edward Clark in 1879 at which time they purchased the old Speeler Pottery of Trenton and organized it as the Lincoln Pottery. Mr. Carr only stayed with the Lincoln Pottery for a very few months. The same mark he used at the Lincoln Pottery may be found on his wares in the New York Pottery which he helped to operate and owned with various partners. (See New York City Pottery for marks and more on Carr.) Barber didn't say if the International Pottery owned by Burgess and Campbell bought the Lincoln Pottery from Carr, but he did say they were the next ones to reorganize the Lincoln Pottery, so we assume they bought it. Then they used some marks similar to the ones Carr had used changing only the initials or adding the names, Burgess and Campbell. See International Pottery listing for marks.

Lincoln, Richard M. Fort Worth, Texas. 1955 to present (1985). Studio potter, Richard M. Lincoln, studied at the Potter's Guild, Ann Arbor, Michigan, under the tutelage of Rhoda Lopez and J.T. Abernathy, potters of national repute, from 1955 to 1957 when he moved to Fort Worth. He received a degree from the University of Michigan. He was assistant professor of French at Texas Christian University until retirement in 1984. His work is mostly functional, traditional stoneware and porcelain pieces, but in recent years, he has moved more toward sculpture. He attains a great originality within a traditional framework of age old techniques and classic forms. In the book by Sherry B. Humphreys and Johnell L. Schmidt, *Texas Pottery*, pp. 38, 39, is pictured a stoneware vase which encompasses slab building, some wheel throwing and press molding, all in one beautiful piece with an opaque white glaze that lets the gray color of the clay show through. Also shown is "Yankee Doodle Stele," a stoneware sculpture built with the same three techniques. This piece has red and blue glazes and gold luster added in the third firing. Pieces are inscribed "RML." Richard listed a few of his national and regional shows as follows: 19th Ceramic National, 1956, Syracuse, New York; 20th Ceramic International, 1958, Syracuse, New York (invitational); Miami National Ceramic Exhibition, 1957 and 1958, Miami, Florida; Young Americans, 1956, Museum of Contemporary Crafts, New York, third Ceramic Prize; Decorative Arts and Ceramics Exhibition, 1957, Wichita, Kansas; Fiber, Clay and Metal, 1958, St. Paul, Minnesota; Michigan State Crafts Exhibition, 1956 and 1957, Detroit, Michigan (work included in museum collection); Michigan Regional Ceramics Exhibition, 1956 and 1957, several prizes including a purchase prize; Ninth Annual Texas Crafts Exhibition, 1957, Dallas, Texas, purchase prize and pottery award; Tenth Annual Texas Crafts Exhibition, 1958, pottery award; First Annual Regional Exhibition, San Antonio, Texas, purchase prize; Twenty-Second Annual Exhibition, Tarrant County Artists, Fort Worth. The principal gallery selling his work at present is the Carlin Gallery, Fort Worth, Texas.

Line Material Company/McGraw Electric Company/McGraw-Edison Company. See the listing Jeffery-Dewitt Insulator Company for previous history. Line Material Company was a subsidiary of the McGraw Electric Company which purchased the Jeffery-Dewitt Insulator Company in 1951, and Line Material Company operated the plant. This plant in Kenova burned completely in 1952. In 1953, McGraw Electric Company purchased Illinois Electric Porcelain plant in Macomb, Illinois, and used the name Illinois McGraw Electric Company after June 1954, which in turn became McGraw-Edison Company in 1957 when the company merged with the Thomas A. Edison Industries. The "IEP" mark (no. 1) shown, stood for Illinois Electric Porcelain, and later Illinois Edison Porcelain, and was used from around 1954 to 1958. The various L.M. marks, nos. 2, 3, 4, stood for Line Material Company and were used until 1967 when the mark became ME, as shown for McGraw-Edison, in nos. 5, 6. (Information and incuse, and stamped blasted, some underglaze marks: Jack H. Tod, *Porcelain Insulators Guide Book for Collectors*, p. 119.)

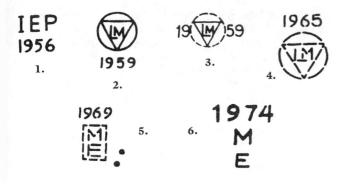

1. IEP 1956
2. 1959
3. 19 59
4. 1965
5. 1969
6. 1974 M E

Lingon, Deborah. Charlottsville, Virginia. 1975 to present (1985). Deborah received a B.S. degree from Longwood College in Farmville, Virginia, in 1967. She attended classes from 1977-1980 at Washington and Lee University, where she studied Chinese art with I-Hsuing Ju. She makes beautiful porcelain pieces fired to 2,300 degrees including a full range of functional and decorative ware.

Link Pottery. Stonetown, Berks County, Pennsylvania. 1865 to 1910. Christian Link who learned pottery trade in Black Forest, Germany, started in Exeter Township to make utilitarian type stoneware, some salt glazed, some dark brown glazed and also redware from local clay. Sometimes the ware was marked just C. Link. He decorated some of his stoneware with branches and leaves in blue. Guy F. Reinert, "A History of the Pennsylvania German Potteries of Berks County," *Bulletin of American Ceramic Society*, Volume 19, no. 1, 1940, p. 28, describes a stoneware jar with a stamped spread Eagle decoration with "Christian Link" above and "Stonetown, Pa." below the Eagle. Ferdinand Winterhalter, who worked for the Troxel Pottery also worked for Christian Link. Christian's sons, James, John, and Christian, Jr., also worked at the pottery. Mark and information: Mildred Hardcastle, "Potteries of Exeter Township, Berks County, Pennsylvania." *Spinning Wheel*, January, February, 1970, pp. 14, 15, 63.)

CHRISTIAN LINK
STONETOWN
BERKS Co. PA.

C. LINK
EXETER

Lion's Head Pottery. Galena, Ohio. 1968 to present. Sara King, owner and a studio potter, makes a variety of artistic, sculptural and functional pieces in stoneware with a rainbow of different glazes. Three other potters work with Mrs. King at Lion's Head Pottery, and they operate a selling establishment, the Pottery Place, in Westerville, Ohio. Sally exhibits every year in Ohio Designer Craftsman shows in Cincinnati, Cleveland and Columbus and has won several awards.

LH   King   K

Lipman, Bernard, Company/Princeton China Corporation. New York, New York. In the 1940's and early 1950's there were various listings in the *Crockery and Glass Journal Directories* for these companies associated or under the direction of Bernard Lipman. The Bernard Lipman Company and Princeton China Corporation had the same address and phone number and were associated, but they were listed entirely separately in the directories with Lipman as president. In the article, "Making American China Artware," staff written, January 1943, *Crockery and Glass Journal*, p. 6, is a full page of pictures and captions showing pottery being caste in molds and decorated at Princeton China Corporation. The line of artware was started in 1942. In the *Crockery and Glass Journal Directory*, January 1943, p. 84, is an article, "New Artware Decoration," telling that the company was announcing a new style of artware decoration, with embossed designs in relief. Lipman said this was the first time this specific type of decoration had been used in this country. The style was French with multicolored florals with gold treatment on satin-like antique finish backgrounds.

In the 1952 and 1954 *Crockery and Glass Journal Directories*, Bernard Lipman Company was advertised as distributors of "Bas Susans," a lazy susan server made by the Bass Products Company, California. The server was made with four chartreuse or green side dishes, a coffee server in center and a mahogany tray. In the 1946 *Crockery and Glass Journal Directory*, Bernard Lipman Company was the selling agency for Nancy China (see separate listing), Princeton China, Jabeson China (see separate listing), and the Bristol Ceramic Corp. I found no information on the Bristol Ceramic Corp. and believe they were probably English. (Marks: no. 1, registration was filed on this mark, May 25, 1944, for use on ceramic ware such as vases, urns, chache pots, apothecary jars, candy boxes, bonbon dishes, coffee pots, pitchers, dinnerware, china console sets, bowls and candleholders, flower pots, china vanity sets, trays, powder boxes and perfume holders. Claiming use since December 22, 1941. Nos. 2, 3, 4, were marks shown between 1945 and 1953 in the *Crockery and Glass Journal Directories* under either Bernard Lipman Company or the Princeton China Corp. names.)

1.

2.

3.

4.

Littlefield, Edgar. Littlefield was a graduate of the Ceramic Engineering Department at Ohio State University, and in 1929 he joined Arthur Baggs to help with the newly established art division in the ceramics department at Ohio State University. (See the listing for Arthur Baggs and also Ohio State University.) Baggs and Littlefield did extensive research in controlling one particular type of glaze, a copper red. They published a paper describing the results in the *Journal of American Ceramic Society.* See the Arthur Baggs listing for a discussion of this ware. These early pieces are made of a very heavy vitrified red clay with the copper-red to orange glaze. A vase was found with roughly incised initials as shown and date 1930. Around the top was an incised decoration. The reddish-orange and shape of the vase gave an oriental impression. (Marks: Linda Steigleder, from the booklet published by the Everson Museum of Art to accompany the 1978 exhibition, "A Century of Ceramics in the U.S." Pieces have also been found with the name Littlefield written out.)

Little-Jones Company, Inc. New York, New York. Selling agency, filed for a patent on this mark on January 1, 1944, for use on ceramic table and cooking ware, claiming use since February 1, 1943. It is very possible this is a mark used on American products. In the 1952 *Crockery and Glass Journal Directory,* Little-Jones Company was listed as selling Italian dinnerware and figurines, but they also carried a line of domestic art china and earthenware. During the war, companies sold American products even if they never sold them before or again.

Little Mountain Studio. Claude and Elaine Graves have a studio located six miles from Columbus, North Carolina, on Peniel Road with mailing address in Tyron, North Carolina. The couple started making pottery in 1968 and established the studio in 1973 to present (1986). The Graves produce a variety of work in six kilns. Domestic ware is fired to cone four in a gas reduction kiln. Sculpture and decorative pottery is fired to cone six in a gas fired salt kiln. Raku fired earthenware is fired in a small electric kiln. Electric kilns are also used for bisque and lustre firings. A wood fired updraft kiln is used to fire glazed and unglazed earthenware. All ware is stamped with impressed mark as shown. The pamphlet sent described some of the work as "contemporary earthenware in the folk art tradition." The Graves sell their pieces at the retail shop near the studio, and hold an open house yearly which attracts up to 1,000 people. Claude built their home and the rough hewn open studio. The couple were students at the University of North Carolina when they met. After graduation, Claude worked as a social worker for two years to save money for them to travel for the next year to Spain, Canary Islands, Mexico and North Africa. They came home and bought the 80 acres and started building the home

and studio. They have done some teaching at schools in the surrounding area. Elaine's work shows her fascination for the figurines of the Aztecs and Incas that she saw in their travels. Claude's dinnerware has endless patterns and shapes, such as Oak Leaf, Dancing Bunnies, Iris, Blue Winter Tree and one called Little Mountain. The couple refuse to hire help, insisting on hand crafting each piece themselves. They have work in public collections in North Carolina State Capitol Building, Raleigh, North Carolina; North Carolina Welcome Center, Columbus, North Carolina; Spartanburg County Art Association, Spartanburg, South Carolina. A list of selected exhibitions they have done are: University of South Carolina at Spartanburg in 1983; Wilson Art Center, Wilson, North Carolina, in 1983; Rutherford County Museum, Rutherfordton, North Carolina, in 1982; Kinston Art Center, Kinston, North Carolina, in 1982; Folk Art Center, Asheville, North Carolina, in 1982; Upstairs Gallery, Tyron, North Carolina, in 1981, 1982; Spartanburg Art Center, Spartanburg, South Carolina, in 1975, 1976, 1977, 1978, 1979, 1980, 1981, 1982; Greenville County Museum of Art, Greenville, South Carolina, in 1980; North Carolina Museum of Art, Raleigh, North Carolina, in 1980; Mint Museum of Art, Charlotte, North Carolina, in 1977, 1978. Also, they have had articles about them in *Ceramics Monthly, Crafts Report* and the *Arts Journal.*

LITTLE
MOUNTAIN
POTTERY

Locke Insulator Company/General Electric Company. Victor, New York, and Baltimore, Maryland. Fred M. Locke, while working as a telegraph operator in the 1880's, started selling electrical supplies and insulators. In 1894 he established a small plant in Fishers, New York, a town near to Victor. He realized the needs in the field of electricity. For a description of the various technical aspects of these needs, see Jack H. Tod, *Porcelain Insulators,* pp. 97 to 104. One would either have to be an insulator collector or electrician to understand the detailed information given by Tod. These books are easily available from Mr. Tod, and they are wonderful for the collector. In September 1902, the Locke Insulator Manufacturing Company was incorporated in Victor, New York, and in 1903, Fred Locke left the business, and John S. Lapp was hired as general manager. In January 1910, Locke Insulator Manufacturing Company bought the Lima Insulator Company of Lima, New York (see that listing). In 1917 the Locke operation was purchased by the Symington family and General Electric became a minority owner in 1918. In 1921, the name was changed to Locke Insulator Corporation. A new plant was started in Baltimore in 1922 by General Electric. At that time, the trade name was changed from "Victor" to "Locke" because Victor, New York, was not the only site of manufacturing. In 1934, General Electric became the sole owner of the Locke Insulator Company. In 1948 the name became Locke, Inc., and in 1951 it became the Locke Department of General Electric Company, and still later it was called Insulator Products Department of General Electric Company. Tod gives a description of shapes, markings, the number of parts in the insulators, etc. He discusses numbers of certain types made and glazes and clays used. (Information: Tod, as previously cited. Markings variously may show "Fred M.

Locke," "F.M. Locke." Sometimes the "Victor, N.Y." address is shown, sometimes the "Victor" tradename, actual dates of manufacture, etc. The very first units may have references to "Imperial." Some of the markings are very wordy, taking several lines of fine print to record all the patent dates involved. Any specimens marked with Fred Locke's name were made before about 1904. The tradename for insulators made by Locke was "Victor" until 1922, and this marking was used on units made up until about 1908. These early Locke insulator markings should not be confused with insulators made from 1935 to 1953 by Victor Insulators, Inc. (trademark of "V" inside a rectangle). Starting about 1908, Lock insulators were marked with a trademark consisting of the outline of a transmission insulator in which were included the tradename "Victor" and the legend "R = oo" (resistance equals infinity). When General Electric started production at their new Baltimore plant in 1922, the word "Victor" was replaced with the word "Locke." This marking was carried in Locke literature until 1932, but it was not used after the Victor, New York, plant was closed by General Electric in 1928. These markings exist in several different sizes and it is difficult to locate specimens which have a nice readable impression. There were a number of Locke markings used at the Baltimore plant after the Victor plant was closed in 1928, and we are fortunate that General Electric was able to furnish a record of their usage. Insulator Catalog No. 8881 is used as an illustration in the following tabulation:

1928 -	1936	LOCKE
1936 - Nov	1938	LOCKE/8881
Nov 1938 - Dec	1939	
Dec 1939 - Sep	1943	LOCKE/8881
Sep 1943 - Aug	1945	LOCKE/8881/USA
Aug 1945 - Mar	1950	LOCKE/USA
Mar 1950 - Nov	1962	LOCKE/8881/USA
Nov 1962 - Dec	1968	LOCKE
May 1963 - Dec	1968	LOCKE R (noise proof units)
Dec 1968 - Jan	1969	GE/8881/69 (year)
Jan 1969 -	1971	GE/8881/70/USA (year)

Some of these markings are illustrated below, along with others which included the "Hi-top" tradename. The G.E. markings are shown in the "General Electric" section. Most of the marks shown are incuse or stamped in, and they are from the Tod book cited, pp. 103-104. Nos. 1 and 2, "Locke" and "Victor" were shown in Tod, p. 103 with "R = oo." Several variations of the mark, "Locke" are shown in Tod's book. Mark 9 is a newer "Locke" mark used from 1962-1968. There were a very few under-glaze early "Fred M. Locke" marks. No. 10, 11 are what Tod terms "error handstamps reported.")

LOCKE 1.

2. VICTOR

FRED M. LOCKE 3.
Victor, N.Y.

4. PAT'D MAY 22 1894
FRED M. LOCKE

LOCKE
44C 6.
USA

F.M.LOCKE VICTOR.N.Y.
PAT. MAY '89 MAY 22,'94

5.

7. LOCKE
H1 TOP
33

LOCKE
HI-TOP
77V
USA
8.

LOCKE
9.

LOCRE
10.

LOCKE
HI-TOP
77V
ASU
11.

Lock Haven, Pennsylvania, Various Potters. William Shroat, age 26, came from Germany in 1840. He lived in Reading and Gettysburg, Pennsylvania, before moving to Lock Haven around 1855. He located his pottery in the rear of Marshall's warehouse which held goods for a grocery and ice cream parlor. Shroat's stoneware utilitarian pieces were marked "Lock Haven." From 1864 to 1866 he paid taxes as William Shroat and Company. He died in 1866, and the pottery ceased. The second potter in Lock Haven, **Bernard Hoffard** (also spelled Bernhardt Hoffart, Hoffert, Huffard, Hufferd) was 49 when he came to Lock Haven from Lewistown shortly after Shroat died. In 1867 Hoffard had a partner William Gopel. Hoffard made pottery in two or three locations in Lock Haven until 1884. Lasansky said he might have also used the mark "Lock Haven." **George Strayer** worked with tin and owned quite a lot of property in Lock Haven (for details see Lasansky, p. 28). In 1877 he bought Hoffard's shop, and by 1883 it was listed under the ownership of the Van Christs with a man named Bernhard making stoneware pots. The pieces were either unmarked or marked "Lock Haven." By 1884 utilitarian pottery was no longer made in Lock Haven. A large sewer pipe and terra cotta industry operated there in 1890. (Information and impressed mark: Jeannette Lasansky, *Made of Mud*, pp. 26, 28, 54.)

LOCK HAVEN, PA.

Logan Pottery Company. Logan, Ohio. Pottery was organized May 29, 1902, and operated until the end of 1964. Makers of stoneware, jugs, milk pans, water kegs, handled jars, flue thimbles, butter pots, mixing bowls, bean pots, etc. The same items were advertised in the 1908 catalogue as were advertised in 1961! Since the same products were made all those years, think how many round salt boxes in blue and white, or jugs with brown and white outside colors etc., would be distributed in that time. The problem is that the only known marked piece was the pottery footwarmer. (Information and mark: Mrs. Helen Mowrey, Hocking County Historical Society.)

LOGAN
POTTERY CO.
LOGAN, O.

Long, Doyle. Delaware, Ohio. 1975 to present (1983) Studio potter making utilitarian stoneware characterized by bold, large, masculine, looking shapes and outstanding glazes.

Long Family Potters. In Eastern Crawford County, Georgia, there were around 65 potters beginning in the late 1820's. They made jugs and jars etc. with lime or ash glaze and Albany slip, marked on the handles with the various maker's marks. Some flowerpot-shaped pitchers, beanpots, coffee pots, etc. were discovered in February 1973 when the site of the Jesse Long pottery was explored by the Georgia State University archaeology students under the supervision of Catherine Lee. A great variety of initials were found in various handles of the shards, including J.B.L. for Jessee Bradford Long, H.D. for Henry D. Marshall, J.H.L. for John H. Long in 1890's, H.N.L., H.N., L., W.M., C.M., L.A. and G.R. John L. Burrison, *Brothers in Clay*, p. 141, said these were possibly initials or marks of the various workers applied in order to keep count of each man's output so he could be fairly paid. It is doubtful that all of these initials will ever be identified with the potters. Jesse Bradford Long was the son of James Long who set up a pottery shop in 1829 in the eastern part of Crawford County, Georgia, to make earthenware and probably stoneware pieces. In Burrison, p. 136, is pictured a tan alkaline 12 gallon jar attributed to James Long in the 1830's or 1840's, marked J.L. in the looped handle with decorations of sprig molding with the head of Andrew Jackson on one side and the face of Thomas Jefferson on the other. Sprig molding is identified by Burrison as "small molds of baked clay containing an intaglio design filled with moist clay to produce the design in relief which adheres to the wall of the formed pot." Joseph Long was another of James's sons who died in 1851. Jesse seems to have been the most prolific and made pottery for around 50 years until he died around 1888. For a detailed account of the various members of the Long family and how the products were made see Burrison as cited. (Information and mark: John A. Burrison, *Brothers in Clay*, pp. 133 to 144.)

J B L   J H L

Lonhuda Pottery. Steubenville, Ohio. Pottery was organized by William A. Long, W.H. Hunter and Alfred Day. Mr. Day also helped to organize the Steubenville Pottery Company. According to Paul Evans, *Art Pottery of the U.S.*, p. 141, this was the first pottery to turn out on a large scale what Evans calls Cincinnati-faience, which was hand decorated with hand painted slipware underglaze. Laura Fry was an outstanding decorator at Lonhuda Pottery. She left the Rookwood Pottery in 1887 and became a professor of Industrial Art at Purdue University in 1891 among other accomplishments. After coming to Lonhuda in 1892, she patented a method of decoration and became involved in a court case with Rookwood. For particulars on this, see Evans, p. 142. In 1894 she went back to Cincinnati, Ohio, and organized the Porcelain League of Cincinnati in her studio. In 1894, Weller acquired an interest in Lonhuda Pottery. The plans were to enlarge the operation in Steubenville, instead the Lonhuda Faience was produced on a large scale in Zanesville, Ohio. Weller renamed the Lonhuda line, "Louwelsa." Long went to work for J.B. Owens in 1899 until he left for Denver to establish the Denver

China and Pottery Company in 1901. Pieces of Lonhuda pottery are in various museums; the Philadelphia Museum of Art, and the National Museum of History and Technology of the Smithsonian Institution. (Information: Paul Evans, *Art Pottery of the U.S.*, pp. 141-143; E.A. Barber, *Marks of American Potters*, pp. 130, 131; and E.A. Barber, *Pottery and Porcelain of the U.S.*, pp. 336, 337. Marks: E.A. Barber, *Marks of American Potters*, pp. 130, 131. Barber said no. 1 was the first mark used and was replaced by no. 2, the solid Indian head in 1893. Next in use was no. 3. No. 4 was used in 1895 to 1896 when Long became partners with Weller.)

1.   2.   3.

4.

268

Other marks which occur on Lonhuda pottery are the initials and monograms of the decorators, as follows:

Miss Laura A. Fry	℟
Miss Sarah R. McLaughlin	S℟
Miss Helen M. Harper	HᴹH
Mr. W.A. Long	℟
Miss Jessie R. Spaulding	℟

The numbers impressed on Lonhuda pieces relate to the forms.

Lon Valley/Lion's Valley. Lon Valley was a mark registered to the Little-Jones Company, New York, New York, in 1944. See that listing for mark. Lion's Valley was a pottery in Lemon Grove, California, from 1974 to 1977 with Sam Aaron as president and general manager. They made fine stoneware dinnerware and accessory pieces. I wrote for a mark, none was sent.

Lord, Various Potters. Before 1725, a Nathaniel Lord was making redware in Charlestown, Massachusetts, according to Lura W. Watkins, *Early New England Potters and Their Wares*, p. 26. A bottle with the impressed mark shown for E.A. Lord was pictured in *Regional Aspects of American Folk Pottery*, p. 51 (staff written). The bottle was dated in the first half of the 19th century, and the potter was from Litchfield, Connecticut.

E·A· LORD

LITCHFIELD

Los Angeles Potteries. Lynwood, California. Before 1941 until after 1967. This pottery was listed in various directories as makers of artware and dinnerware at 11700 Alameda in Lynwood, California. They were not listed in 1971. In 1941, a bowl marked ''Los Angeles Potteries,'' was patented and assigned to Allan Rosenfeld, New York, New York, distributor. Several pattern names for dinnerware were listed for this pottery in the 1954 *Crockery and Glass Directory*, and the pieces these marks were drawn from were nicely vitrified hand molded decorative bowls with a high gloss glaze in pink, gray and yellow. (Marks: no. 1, shown in various directories; the rest of the marks were found on colorful well shaped pieces, flower bowls, etc.)

Santa Rosa
L. A. POTTERIES
CALIFORNIA
1.

Los Angeles
Potteries
PAT. Nº
2.
129517

L.A. POTTERIES
310
3.

Los Angeles Potteries
600
4.

California © 51
LOS ANGELES POTTERIES
297
5.

Lotus and Acanthus Studios/Spence and King. Los Angeles, California. 1932 to 1966. Albert H. King and Harold Spence were studio potters in 1932 in East Los Angeles. They operated as Spence and King. King had acquaintances or associations with Cecil Jones, La Mirada Potteries; Max Compton of Gladding McBean; and George Robertson of the Robertson Pottery (see various listings), and he had been taught to make pottery by Fred Meyers of Meyers Pottery in Los Angeles (see that listing). In 1936, Spence left the pottery, and Albert King and his wife continued under the name Lotus and Acanthus Studios. Louisa Anne Etchevery King was the daughter of a retired potter. She made numerous models for vessels and figurines, and Albert King's glazes continued to be used. The pieces were sold through art galleries and won several awards and honors. Louisa Anne died in 1956, and Albert King continued alone until 1966. (Information and incised marks: Jack Chipman, ''Lotus and Acanthus Studios,'' *American Clay Exchange*, August 30, 1986, p. 9.)

The Kings
PORCELAIN
AK

Louisville Pottery. Louisville, Kentucky. Incorporated in 1906 and went out of business around 1970. (These dates furnished by George Hadley of Hadley Pottery Company, Inc.) In 1971, Louisville Stoneware Company was started in the same building. See Louisville Stoneware Company. Mr. Hadley had the 1940-1944 catalogues for the Louisville Pottery showing stoneware jars, covers, pots, pans, jugs, churns, kegs, pitchers, boxes, bowls, mugs, feeders, casseroles, etc. They also made garden pottery and what they listed as art ware in vases, bowls, jars, pots, etc. Miniatures and novelties were made in a wide range. Before the Louisville Pottery, a similar business had existed in the building from 1896 until 1906. In the 1946 *Crockery and Glass Journal*, the Lousiville Pottery Company was listed for ''Cherokee'' art and garden pottery. They also made ''Indian Head'' pottery. (Marks 1, 2, are from pieces made in the 1930's or a little later.)

JBt
MADE IN USA

John B Taylor
MADE IN
USA

Louisville Stoneware Company. Louisville, Kentucky. 1971 to present (1984). In 1971, John and Vivian Robertson purchased the Louisville Pottery Company from John B. Taylor. The purchase included the building, molds, designs and right to the makers, etc. The old buildings were torn down, and the operation moved to Brent Street in Louisville. Robertson is a ceramic engineer with a degree from the University of Wisconsin. He designed one piece made for the Reagan administration to give as gifts which was a replica of the Executive Office building in form of a box. He won the Best of Show at the Chicago Gift Show in 1979. In the 1930's, Mary Alice Hadley had worked for the Louisville Pottery Company as a designer and painter. Some of Hadley Pottery pieces and the Louisville Pottery and Louisville Stoneware will show a similarity due to her influence. (See Hadley Pottery listing.) The pieces have decorations of birds, flowers, ducks, pears, etc., handpainted on. (Information: Robertson, by telephone. Marks: stamped; Susan Cox, ''Louisville Kentucky Potteries,'' *American Clay Exchange*, January 1982, p. 10.)

LOUISVILLE
STONEWARE
MADE IN KENTUCKY

B Taylor
B
LOUISVILLE, KY.
MADE IN U.S.A.
VINTAGE
Ceramic

made in Kentucky U.S.A.
Bny
Louisville
Stoneware Co.
1981
year of the
107th Kentucky Derby

Louthan Manufacturing Company. East Liverpool, Ohio. 1901 to 1947. They formed as Louthan Supply Company in 1901 to make potter's supplies such as pins and stilts, and around 1911 they made mantle rings for gas lights. In 1913, they purchased **Anderson Porcelain Company** of East Liverpool, Ohio, and began to make refractory back walls and radiants for newly invented gas heaters. In 1916 the company incorporated under the name Louthan Manufacturing Company. In 1924 the entire operation was centered in the building that had been Anderson Porcelain Company, and the pottery began to make parts for electrical appliances. During W.W. II they made vast quantities of electronic parts for the Army and Navy. In 1947, Harbeson-Walker Refractories Company of Pittsburgh, Pennsylvania, purchased the Louthan Manufacturing Company. (Information: "Ceramic Plant Purchased by Harbeson-Walker," *Bulletin of American Ceramic Society*, Volume 26, no. 9, 1947, pp. 361, 362. Mark: was registered April 25, 1956, claiming use since January 1, 1935, for use on foundry cores and articles for industrial use made from porcelain and porous and special refractories.)

Love Field Potteries. Dallas, Texas. The Love Field Pottery Company was built at Love Field in Dallas in 1925 and operated until 1948. There was another mark which is almost the same as the one shown, except that a biplane rather than a monoplane is used, but the monoplane is the most common. (Information: Georgeanna Greer, by letter. Mark: Humphries and Schmidt, *Texas Pottery*, p. 32, stamped in cobalt.)

Loveland Art Pottery. Loveland, Colorado. Mid 1930's until late 1960's. The pottery was owned and operated by Helmer J. Roslund. Made a well vitrified decorative ware. Employed three or four people. (Information: Louise Green of the Rocky Mountain Pottery. Marks: incised, found on two nice decorative pieces purchased at the factory in the 1960's.)

Lovett, Robert E. Los Angeles, California. Company filed for registration of this mark on June 29, 1966, claiming use since April 19, 1965, for use on china dinnerware.

DIPSY DISH

Low Art Tile Company. Chelsea, Massachusetts. 1879 to 1890 (dates from Townsend, as cited). John G. Low, founder of the pottery, worked at the Chelsea Keramic Art Works for Robertson (see that listing). George W. Robertson worked at the Low Art Tile Company where he perfected glazes for the designs of Arthur Osborne. Jugs and vases, some with hand modeled relief, were also made there. Evans p. 153 said there were no marked examples of the art pottery. Marks 1 and 2 were used on art tile. (Information: Everett Townsend, "Development of the Tile Industry in the U.S." *American Ceramic Society Bulletin*, May 1943, p. 129; Paul Evans, *Art Pottery of the United States*, pp. 151 - 153. Marks: No. 1, E.A. Barber, *Marks of American Potters*, p. 101; no. 2, C. Jordon, *Handbook of Old Pottery and Porcelain Marks*; no. 3, Paul Evans, as cited, p. 153, is the firm's trademark or logo probably used as a paper label.)

(A)

1.

J & J G LOW
PATENT
ART TILE WORKS
CHELSEA
MASS. USA

2.   COPYRIGHT 1881 BY J&J.G. LOW

3.

Lowell Stoneware Company. Lowell, Illinois (a few miles from Tonica). 1884 to depression era. Pottery built in 1884 by Stoeffer and Leach to make stoneware, crocks, jugs, etc. Mark stamped using name of nearest larger town. In the late 1920's some pitchers, vases, candlesticks, etc. were produced when stoneware utilitarian ware was no longer needed to such a great extent. After 1930 very little pottery was made at all. In the 1930's, a new road and bridge covered the clay pit, and the pottery never did resume function. (Information and mark: Betty Warner, "Illinois Pottery was in Production Nearly 50 Years," *Tri State Trader*, March 21, 1981, p. 3.)

Lowry, Various Potteries. Roseville, Ohio. From 1886 to middle 1940's. The various potteries made stoneware jugs, drain tile, flower pots, jardinieres and cooking crocks. **W.B. Lowry** was the first in a series of ownerships, starting in 1866 to make stoneware crocks, jugs, etc. with the impressed mark no. 1. Between 1870 and 1880 the demand grew for ceramic vessels for cooking. Prior to that time, metal and yellowware were used. H.R. Bodine in Zanesville patented cooking utensils around 1878, and he operated until around 1900. In 1882, Lyman Lowry established a second Lowry pottery to make cookingware only. In 1923, the company was still making 3,000 pieces per day in two plants. The product was known as "fire clay" cooking ware because it was made off refined clay and crushed asbestos which made it "fire proof." They made everything needed for roasting, baking and broiling.

By 1896 the firm name was **Kildow and Lowry**, under which name mark no. 2 was filed for the purpose of making cookingware. In the Columbian Exposition of 1893, Lyman Lowry won a gold medal and later became known as the "Father of Cooking Ware." In July 1906 he was succeeded by his four sons, and the pottery became **Lowry Brothers Pottery Company**. Curtis Lowry, the oldest of the four sons, was the manager. The pottery employed six people in 1888 and seven in 1902, but a little booklet entitled, "Roseville," written in 1906, no author or publisher given, claimed the pottery shipped 300,000 pieces per year. In 1901, Frederick S. Lowry, son of W.B. Lowry, purchased the pottery, re-equipped it and made fine cookingware also. In the 1944 *Directory of Manufacturers for Ohio*, the W.B. Lowry Pottery was listed as owned by Daisy Culp and employing three. In the middle 1940's the Lowry Brothers' plant closed and was later destroyed by fire. (Information: Norris Schneider, "Roseville," Part IV, *Zanesville Times Signal*, August 2, 1959, (no page number); *Factory Inspection Report for State of Ohio*, 1902; also, the Roseville booklet, as cited, sent to this author by Tom Brown, teacher and researcher in Zanesville, Ohio. Mark: no. 1 on crock at Ohio Ceramic Society Museum in Zanesville, Ohio. Mark 2 was a series of concentric segments or panels spaced circularly around the whole bottom of a cookingware piece. The mark was first used in 1896 when filed. This mark, a large raised design, is found on a variety of kitchen pieces which are well vitrified but probably not as hard as stoneware. No. 3 was filed March 9, 1903, claiming use since 1896 for cookware. The design or mark consisted of a honeycombed or cellular band containing several heart-shaped panels in relief. No. 4 was found on the bottom of a piece that had hearts on the side, possibly as filed in no. 2. The registrations with the patent office do not say where or how the design or mark will be used. See the listing Cookingware, a Discussion of Unidentified Marks.)

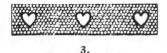

1.

2.

3.

4.

Loy Soloman. Alamance County, North Carolina. Earthenware and stoneware potter around 1805. On the front cover of *The Traditional Pottery of North Carolina*, by Charles G. Zug III, which was a catalog for an exhibition at the Ackland Art Museum in 1981, is pictured an earthenware plate with trailed white and rust bands and triangles on the rim surrounding the potter's signature (mark 1) in the center of the plate as shown. Albert F. Loy, born 1874, was a son of Soloman Loy. He made stoneware slip decorated pieces stamped or impressed "A.F. Loy." (Information: Zug, as cited, pp. 22, 23, 52.)

Luce, Nora. Royal Oak, Michigan. Nora Luce died in 1973. She was a china painter and teacher of china painting as well as a fine artist. (Information: Jenny B. Derwich and Dr. Mary Latos, *A Dictionary Guide to U.S. Pottery and Porcelain*, p. 144.

N. LUCE

Ludowici Celadon Company. New Lexington, Ohio. 1902 to present. In 1902, Celadon Terra Cotta bought the old Imperial Brick Company with the intentions of making clay roofing tile. In 1906 Ludowici bought the plant and named it Ludowici Celadon. They are manufacturers of beautiful roofing tile; the kind found on expensive buildings, and the average home owner just dreams about. For four years during World War II, approximately 1941-1945, this pottery made cookie jars. They were just one of the companies that made the Walt Disney and Turnabout cookie jars. They made the bear, wolf and pig, a Dutch girl and boy. Later some of the molds were sold to American Bisque, and the cookie jars were made again. For pictures of patents on these and considerable further discussion of the cookie jars, see Lehner, "A Cookie Jar Update," *Antique Trader*, February 29, 1984, pp. 72-75. See American Bisque and American Pottery at Marietta for more on cookie jars. (Marks: drawn from molds at the factory. No. 1, 2, are marks found on the tile. The one mark without the ending "i" after the "c" even led some of the residents of the area to pronounce the name of the pottery this way.)

LUDOWIC DI ✕

1.

LUDOWICI CELADON CO. CHICAGO

2.

Belmont

USA

3.

fluffys

USA

4.

USA
Model C
Design No 3   5.

Ltd. Ed. 30 PCS
L C Co. -   1979
6.

WALT DISNEY
DUMBO
2 QT JUG
7.

Patented
TURNABOUT
DUMBO
Walt Disney
8.

©
WALT DISNEY
USA

DUMBO (on side)
9.

DONALD DUCK
and
JOE CARIOCA
from
The
THREE CABALLEROS
10.
©
WALT DISNEY
USA

Lukens, Glen. Los Angeles, California. In 1921, Lukens received a B.A. degree from Oregon State Agricultural College. A year later he was attending an art institute in Chicago. He then worked several years in veteran's hospitals following W.W. I to teach pottery, etc. to help rehabilitate soldiers. In mid 1920's he joined the staff of Fullerton Union High School to teach pottery making. In the early 1930's he moved to the University of Southern California and began training not only potters, but teachers of potters as well. He remained there for 30 years. During the depression, Lukens was hired by the National Youth Administration to set up night classes in ceramics. Over weekends, he and his classes scoured the California deserts all the way to Death Valley, looking for clays, feldspars and talcs. By trial and error, Lukens discovered, as did a number of the other Southern California potters, that liberal use of the soft mineral called talc, which is found in quantities in the desert east of Los Angeles, made for better dishes. They were better because the talc served as a catalyst and stabilizer in the clay, binding the other materials together. Another advantage was that the talc-filled clays could be cooked into earthenware of great strength at relatively low firing heats. His most productive period as an artist came from late 1930's until around 1945, according to Garth Clark. He won awards at the Ceramic Nationals and represented the West Coast at the 1937 Paris Exposition and the 1939 World's Fair in New York. In the article, "Oregon State College Honors Glen Lukens," *Bulletin of American Ceramic Society*, Vol. 18, No. 7, 1939, pp. 258, 259, we learn much of Lukens in his own words. He was given the Honorary Degree of Doctor of Science from Oregon State College in 1939. The rest of the article is the response given by Lukens when he received the degree. He talked about the thousands of people working in the Federal Art Program, and how arrangements were being made to show that work at the 1939 World's Fair in San Francisco. Lukens said his first award came from the National Robineau Society in 1936. He received a citation from Society of Designer Craftsmen in 1938 "for having reached a new high in Ceramic Art in American today." For two years, Lukens worked with Reginald Poland, Director of San Diego Museum of Fine Arts and they exhibited each year at the All-California Exhibition of Ceramics. This had to take place before the article was printed in 1939. Lukens spoke of cooperation from large clay working industries around Los Angeles, such as Gladding, McBean and Company, Pacific Clay Products Company and Vernon Kilns. He said he hoped to see the day that design would catch up with technique. The *Christian Science Monitor* of May 23, 1939, said Luken's work had an authentic, downright beauty in which color, texture, form and function were completely integrated. (Information: *Bulletin of American Ceramic Society*, already cited: Elaine Levin, "Pioneers of Contemporary American Ceramics, Arthur Baggs, Glen Lukens," *Ceramics Monthly*, January 1976, pp. 24-30; Frank J. Taylor, "Dining Off the Rainbow," *Saturday Evening Post*, November 19, 1949, pp. 40, 41, 123, 124, 127; Garth Clark, *A Century of Ceramics in the U.S.*, p. 303; Hazel V. Bray, *The Potter's Art in California 1885 to 1955*, pp. 44, 45. Marks: no. 1, from Tom Turnquist, by letter. Mark is incised or in ink. Incised mark 2 and painted mark 3 are from Linda Steigleder, from the booklet published by the Everson Museum of Art to accompany the 1978 exhibition, "A Century of Ceramics in the U.S.")

Lukens
1.

GLEN
LUKENS
2.

GLEN
LUKENS
3.

Lunning, Frederick. New York, New York. Listed in 1950 and 1960's. Company was a division of George Jensen, Inc. in 1965 (see that listing). In 1952 *Crockery and Glass Journal Directory*, Lunning was listed for domestic and foreign china, glass and earthenware. Lunning was listed in the *Crockery and Glass Journal* as a decorator of ceramics. In the 1961 *China and Glass and Tableware Red Book Directory*, they were listed for all foreign products; Swedish, German and Danish, dinnerware, figurines, glassware, etc. Some of the distributors that never sold American products before or after W.W. II, sold some of them during the war, and right after the war. Both marks shown were probably on foreign made ware of fine quality. (Marks: no. 1 in 1952 directory as cited. Mark 2, *Gift and Tableware Reporter Directory*, August 16, 1965.)

Frederik Lunning Inc.
667 Fifth Avenue
TELEPHONE ELDORADO 5-6630
New York 22, N.Y.
1.

2.   LUNNING

Lutz and Schramm Company. Sales agency. Mark found on gray white wax sealer. The fruit jar also had Sherwood Brothers mark on opposite side. In the book *Fruit Jars*, by Alice M. Creswick, 1970, is listed a similar pottery jar marked "Patented July 19, 1909, by Jos. H. Schramm." There was a Schram Glass Mfg. Company in St. Louis, Missouri, from 1906 to 1925 which made the Schram, Drey and some

Mason jars. This company was spelled with one "m." In 1925 the company consolidated with Ball. See listing Elverson Sherwood, and Barker Pottery for manufacturer of this jar.

PATENT APPLIED FOR
BY
LUTZ & SCHRAMM C⁰

Lycett, Edward and William. Atlanta, Georgia. Edward Lycett, an outstanding china decorator, worked at the Faience Manufacturing Company from 1884 to 1890 (see that listing). As early as 1879 he decorated china for the Homer Laughlin China Company. He then went to Atlanta to work with his son, William, who also painted on china from 1890 to 1909, when Edward Lucett died. He perfected metallic luster glazes. He sometimes signed his work. (For a discusion of his work see E.A. Barber, *Marks of American Potters*, pp. 153, 154 and Evans, pp. 100, 101. Francis Thompson, "Lycett Respected Name in China," *Tri State Trader*, November 8, 1980, p. 12. Marks: Barber as cited. W.P. Jervis, "World's Pottery Marks," *Bulletin of the American Ceramic Society*, April 25, 1914, p. 15.)

E Lycett   1.   2.   E Lycett
  1902   1904

Lyman and Clark. Gardiner, Maine. Around 1837 to 1839. Alanson Potter Lyman and Decius W. Clark both connected with the Bennington potteries at various times, started a stoneware factory in Gardiner, Maine, around 1837. They purchased the land from Robert H. Gardiner and built a building. In 1839 the factory was sold to Robert Thompson and Charles Tarbell (see that listing). The company made a good grade of stoneware pots, crocks, etc. The jugs were ovoidal or pot-bellied in shape and attractively decorated with blue slip on a buff colored body. (Information: M. Lelyn Branin, *The Early Potters and Potteries of Maine*, pp. 425-426. Mark: Branin, same source, p. 233.)

LYMAN ɟ CLARK
GARDINER

Lyons Pottery. Lyons, New York. Around the middle 1800's this pottery as owned by Nathan Clark, Jr. followed by Thompson Harrington in 1867, followed by Jacob Fisher in 1872 until 1902 (also, see listing Nathan Clark, Sr. in Athens). In 1902 until 1904, the name was the Lyons Cooperative Pottery. One mark used by the Lyons Cooperative Pottery Company that might be deceiving is "Lyons Stoneware Co./Established 1825." That mark was used after 1902. Their other marks were the company's name and Lyons. Jacob Fisher was the last of the individual potters to operate in the building before it became a company. (Marks: no. 1, on jug with dog's head design in catalogue for Garth's Auction Barn, Inc., November 28, 1968, no page numbers. No. 2, Guilland, p. 103; no. 3, Spargo, plate 57; no. 4, Christensen, p. 15.)

L Y O N S   2   T. HARRINGTON
                                  LYONS
  1.   2.

MADE
BY   3.   4.   J. FISHER. CO
T. HARRINGTON   ← · →
HARTFORD   LYONS, NY
CONN.

M

Mabbett and Anthone. Poughkeepsie, New York. Late 1830's. Made stoneware. (Information and mark: John P. Remensnyder, "The Potters of Poughkeepsie," reprinted from *Antiques Magazine* in *The Art of the Potter*, edited by Diana and J. Garrison Stradling, p. 126.)

MABBETT & ANTHONE
PO'KEEPSIE, NY

MacDougal, Alice Foote, Coffee Shops, Inc. New York, New York. Filed for a claim on this mark on February 5, 1929, for use on dinner sets, tea sets, cocoa sets, liquor sets, bowls, pitchers, coffee pots and trays, plaques, cornucopias, perfume bottles, etc. made of earthenware, chinaware or porcelain, claiming use since January 1925.

MacKenzie Pottery. Stillwater, Minnesota. Warren MacKenzie, studio potter, has been making pottery since 1947 to present. He graduated from the Art Institute in Chicago in 1947. He worked with Bernard Leach at St. Ives, England, for two years in the 1950's. He teaches at the University of Minnesota in the Twin Cities. He has won many awards and has gained wide recognition, having taught and lectured throughout the country. On my questionnaire, MacKenzie listed his products as utilitarian, stoneware and porcelain. Warren's wife, Alix, also makes pottery, and she studied with him under Bernard Leach in England. Warren MacKenzie had products on display or one-man shows in the following places: Museum of Contemporary Crafts in New York; Chicago Art Institute; Walker Art Center; Renwick Gallery; University of Iowa; University of Minnesota; University of New Mexico in Flagstaff; and Bennington College Gallery. He is a fellow of the ACC and also a fellow of the NCELA. (Marks: no. 1 is MacKenzie's inscribed mark. No. 2 is MacKenzie' stamped mark. No. 3 is a stamped mark used when Alix worked on the pieces with him as a joint production.)

Macomb Pottery. Macomb, Illinois. Incorporated 1880 (Martin and Cooper p. 35). In 1906 became plant no. 3 of Western Stoneware Company until 1956 when the building was sold to Kayson's Inc. Haeger Potteries owns and operates the building at present. Cardinal Brand florists pots, some lawn and garden lines were made here after the pottery became part of Western Stoneware. Impressed mark was found on bottom of gray-white half gallon pottery canning jar with threaded neck, "Macomb Pottery Co., Macomb, Illinois, Pat. Jan. 24, 1899 or 1890." (Information: Jim Martin, "The Pot-

teries of Monmouth, Illinois," *Antique Trader*, December 19, 1979, pp. 62, 63. Marks: Jim Martin and Bette Cooper, *Monmouth Western Stoneware*, p. 36. Western Stoneware Pottery bought the rights to the horseshoe mark.)

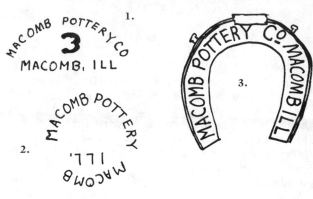

Macomb Stoneware Company. Macomb, Illinois. Started in 1889; became part of Western Stoneware Pottery in 1906. They manufactured all types of utilitarian stoneware pieces, such as jugs, crocks, mugs, etc. They supplied stoneware to the P.F. Pfeiffer Crockery Company of Peoria, Illinois, and jugs to the Lilybeck Drug Company of Memphis, Tennessee. This pottery became plant 3 of Western Stoneware Company and burned down in 1913 and was not rebuilt. (Information and mark: Jim Martin and Bette Cooper, *Monmouth Western Stoneware*, p. 34.)

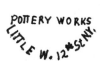

MacQuoid, William A., and Company. New York, New York. 1863 to 1879. Made stoneware. (Information: Stewart and Consentino, p. 80. Marks: pictured on pieces in Christensen, p. 37, Guillland, pp. 98, 99, 102, Stewart and Consentino, p. 79.)

R.H. Macy and Company, Inc. New York, New York. Department store which filed claim for mark no. 1 on September 1, 1925, claiming use since June 1925, for china and porcelain dishes. No. 2 was filed July 28, 1928, claiming use since March 1928, for chinaware. No. 3 was filed October 20, 1983, claiming use since June 1977, for fine china dinnerware.

1.

"ALL-OCCASION

2.

ROYAL GALLERY 3.

Madden, J.M. Roundout, New York (now part of the City of Kingston, New York). Around 1870. Impressed mark found in Thorn, p. 135. This was a seller not a potter according to Warren F. Broderick, researcher and writer.

J.M. MADDEN
ROUNDOUT
N.Y.

Maddock and Miller, Inc. New York, New York. A distributor, filed for rights to this mark June 27, 1936, for use on china and earthenware tableware and vases, claiming use since January 19, 1926. According to Larry Paul, who has authored a book on the Trenton Potteries, Maddock and Miller started as Thomas Maddock and Brother changed to Maddock and Steel then in 1897 became Maddock and Miller at 53 Barclay Street in New York City. According to Larry Paul they imported English ware and also distributed the Trenton product of the Coalport Works, either those made by John Maddocks and Sons or Thomas Maddock and Sons. We will never know for sure until a piece shows up with a mark that can be identified as to maker and is also pictured in a Maddock and Miller advertisement similar to the one we found which dated between 1904 and 1910.

SNOW GLAZE

Maddock, Various Potteries. Trenton, New Jersey. There were three separate potteries operating in Trenton at the same time operated by members of the same family. The Maddock Pottery operated from 1893 to about 1923 in the old Lamberton Works that was eventually to become the home of Scammell China Company. "Lamberton China" was the name given to the hotel china made by Maddock Pottery Company. The name Lamberton came from the location of the pottery at the port of Lamberton on the old Delaware and Raritan Canal, which became part of the city of Trenton.

Thomas Maddock and Sons followed a long line of owners of a pottery on Carroll Street in Trenton, New Jersey. The pottery was first established by **Millington and Astbury** in 1853 to 1859. The owners were **Millington, Astbury and Poulson,** 1859 to 1870, who used the mark "M.A.P. Trenton" in an oval. They were making whiteware goods in 1861 (Barber). In that same year, Mr. Poulson died, and a Mr. Coughley bought his interests, but he died in 1869. Then

Thomas Maddock entered the company by buying Coughley's share and also that of Millington. (Milligton left to start the Eagle Pottery.) From 1875 to 1882 (Ramsay) the firm was Astbury and Maddock. In 1882, Mr. Maddock became sole owner and took his sons as partners. The last listing for Thomas Maddock and Sons in the *Trenton City Directory* was in 1929. The products of the firm went from Rockingham, brownware and yellowware, under Millington and Astbury, to white granite between 1859 and 1875. Then 1875 to 1882, only sanitary ware was listed by Ramsay. Thomas Maddock and Sons made white earthenware in addition to sanitary ware, some decorated ware, souvenir and fraternal pieces. (Marcia Ray in *Collectible Ceramics*, p. 95, gives "Indian Tree" as a pattern made by Maddock and Sons.) Ramsay gives their mark as "T.M. & S" with an anchor. In the *1902-1903 Complete Directory* **Maddock Pottery Company**, which was owned by Thomas Maddock and Sons and operated in the old Lamberton Works, was listed as making white granite dinner sets, toilet sets and short sets of odd dishes, some decorated. (See Lamberton Works for the history of Maddock Pottery Company 1892 to 1922 in the old Lamberton Works.) John Maddock was a son of Thomas Maddock who started a business of his own and took his own sons as partners from 1895 to 1929. As far as I can determine **John Maddock and Sons** made only sanitary ware, sanitary specialties, and plumbers' ware. The Maddocks had three factories operating at once in Trenton. (Used Cloverleaf backstamp.)

Larry Paul, who is currently working on a book on the various Maddock potteries changed a couple of the dates given by Barber to one year earlier and added these notes to the forgoing material. In 1882 for only part of the year the company name was just **Thomas Maddock** and then became Thomas Maddock and Sons. The corporate name for the separate company formed by Thomas Maddock and Sons was **Maddock Pottery Company, Lamberton Works.** (See information under Scammell china.) In 1902, Thomas Maddock and Sons reincorporated as **Thomas Maddock's Son's Company.** This company purchased Glasgow Pottery in 1900. Then later became part of American Standard. Maddock Pottery made both "American China" and "Lamberton China" which were two different formulas. Scammell China made "Trenton China" and "Lamberton China," also different formulas. Lamberton China was the finest grade of ware. The 1938 Lamberton China made for the Fisher, Bruce Company was a dinnerware line for home use. Maddock Pottery had the "in-house" ability to produce their own decals and transfer engravings which continued under Scammell ownership. (Information: Barber, *Marks of American Potters*, pp. 48-49; Larry Paul, researcher and writer on the various Maddocks' potteries; Lehner, *American Kitchen and Dinner Wares*, pp. 100, 101. Marks: nos. 1-7, sent by Larry Paul are Maddock Pottery marks; nos. 8, 9, for Maddock Pottery are from Barber, *Marks of American Potters*, p. 49; nos. 10, 11, are for John Maddock and Sons, from Barber, *Marks of American Potters*, p. 49; no. 12, was filed for use by Maddock Pottery Company on September 30, 1916, claiming use since the year 1893; no. 13 and 14, are marks for Maddock Pottery from Stephen S. Sandknop, *Nothing Could Be Finer*, a compendium on Railroad China, privately printed, 1977; no. 15, for Thomas Maddock's Sons Company was filed April 27, 1915, claiming use since 1877 for use on vitreous china bathroom trimmings and fittings such as comb and brush holders, soap holders, towel bars, etc.; nos. 16 and 17, are Thomas Maddocks and Sons marks from Barber, *Marks of American Potters*, p. 49.)

1. MADDOCK & CHINA AMERICAN BOUTELL BROS MINNEAPOLIS MINN

2. LAMBERTON CHINA L BARTH & SON NEW YORK

3. *Lamberton China*

4. *Lamberton China* M L

5. CHINA L

6. LAMBERTON M CHINA

7. MADDOCK'S AMERICAN CHINA

8. MADDOCK LAMBERTON ROYAL PORCELAIN WORKS

9. M CHINA L

10. JOHN MADDOCK & SONS COAL PORT TRENTON. N.J.

11. WARRANTED VITREOUS GLAZE JOHN MADDOCK & SONS COAL PORT TRENTON. N.J.

12. *Lamberton China*

13. VITRIFIED MADDOCKS AMERICAN CHINA

14. 1827 1927 THE BALTIMORE & OHIO RAILROAD COMPANY Charter granted Feb 28 1827. First stone laid July 4 1828 Reached Elliotts Mills May 22 1830 Steam first used Aug. 30. 1830 Reached Washington Aug. 25. 1835 Reached Wheeling Dec. 25. 1852 First train to St Louis in 1857 First train to Chicago in 1874 First train to Philadelphia in 1886 And Railroad using electric locomotive 1894 Lamberton DESIGN PAT

15. (anchor mark)

16. TM&S (anchor mark)

17. 1859 TM&S (crown mark)

Maddux of California. Los Angeles, California. Started in 1938. Makers and distributors of novelty and figurines, planters, lamps, console sets, decorative bowls and all sorts of ceramic giftware, which were marketed on a very large scale. The year 1974 was their last full year of manufacturing. **Hollywood Ceramics** was a manufacturing corporation for Maddux which was sold in 1976, along with Maddux of California to Norman Bogdanow to form the **Rinor Marketing Corporation**. In August 1977, Carol Lee Tirre became the owner of Maddux of California which became strictly a selling organization. The following detailed history is included here to help the reader to understand the complexity, problems, marketing, etc. of the potteries. This is exactly the way many of them turned to distributing alone.

Maddux of California was founded in 1938 by Bill Maddux. In 1948 it was incorporated and purchased shortly thereafter by Lou and Dave Warsaw. During those early years and proceeding through the mid 50's, the bulk of their volume was sold through the variety chains. Their line consisted mainly of novelty and figurine planters.

In 1956 Dave Warsaw sold his 50% interest to Morris D. Bogdanow and went into the import business. At about the same time, the variety chains began to import low-priced ceramic products from the Orient. During the next five or six years, however, Maddux showed satisfactory increases in volume so that they purchased houses around their location at 303 Fletcher Drive and expanded their production facilities. This culminated in 1959 when they completed their 25,000 sq. ft. factory, employing approximately 75 people. With no tariffs to protect them, the import of foreign ceramics continued unabated. This was and is a labor intensive industry unable to compete, at that time, with low-priced foreign labor. Hence, volume began to fall off during the early 1960's. Lou Warsaw sold out his share and retired. Maddux began floundering around searching out a new market. For a few years they found solace in the department stores aided by their introduction of the Shell Line of Pearltone Serving Accessories. This hot new line gained them entry into almost every major department store nationwide. However, they were never successfully able to follow up this line. They also started doing business with the stamp companies, which were entering their prime during this period. By the mid 1960's they had items listed in every major stamp catalog. This fact, has continued to date.

During the late 1960's, Maddux changed its emphasis to the mass market. This included discount stores, drug chains, hardware-houseware jobbers, etc. They put their emphasis in basic stock programs. They were able to list such chains as Zody's, Caldor, Rinks Bargain City and Community Discount among the accounts they serviced. Community Discount is still being serviced today, some 10 years later. The nation's two largest hardware distributors, Cotter (True Value) and Ace, have also been steady customers for well over 15 years.

In the fall of 1968 Norman Bogdanow joined his father. Utilizing his degree in marketing from U.C.L.A., he began to revitalize the marketing department. While Maddux had always sold through manufacturers representatives, in 1968 they had only five reps doing over $10,000 in annual volume, with two doing over $20,000. Over half of their volume was from stamp companies. By the end of 1974, (their last full year as a manufacturer) they had nine reps over $10,000, eight over $20,000, five over $50,000 and two over $100,000. Only 20% of their volume was from stamp companies.

During the mid 1970's Maddux led the way into the planter boom, having its most profitable year even in 1974. However, the boom was not without its dark side: imports from Brazil, Italy and the Orient began to increase and an economic recession of unknown size and duration was getting into full swing. With all of this in sight, Mr. Bogdanow received and accepted a substantial offer for his factory facilities from Grandinetti Products, Inc.

So, in early 1975, Maddux suddenly found itself with molds, designs and accounts, but no factory. All of this in a year that, while ceramic pots were still in high demand, prices were rapidly falling, as more and more people entered the field. As Maddux shifted from factory to factory seeking out satisfying quality and delivery, its own deliveries to its customers went from bad to worse. To remain competitive, with all of the new entries to the market place, margins were cut. The result was a small loss in dollar volume and a large loss in profit.

In March of 1976, after three months of difficult negotiations, Norman Bogdanow bought the assets of Maddux of California and *Hollywood Ceramics*, Los Angeles, (the former manufacturing corp. for Maddux) from his father. His aims for the first year of operation were to rid himself of unprofitable accounts; to seek out more profitable lines of merchandise; to break-even or show a small profit. Toward these ends, he took on the national representation of Valley Wholesale Supply, a medium-sized manufacturer and distributor of quality picture frames. He also began distributing the *Y.D. Designs* line of stoneware. The end result of these moves was a turn-around. Even after writing off the majority of the high organization expenses, his new corporation, *Rinor Marketing Corporation* showed a small profit.

Marks: no. I is a logo. Nos. 2-4, incised or inscribed marks.

Maddux 1.
OF CALIFORNIA

3. C A L
U S A
7 1 7

Maddux of Calif
3211 2.

M Add u x
U.S.A. 4. 797

Magdich, Jean Pottery. Logan, Ohio. 1974 to present. Jean Magdich, studio potter, makes low fired porcelain into wheel thrown and slab built and hand pulled, decorative pieces with hand painted decorations. Jean received a B.F.A. Degree at Miami University in Oxford, Ohio, in 1974 and started making pottery full time which she sells at invitational shows and fairs, etc.

Mallek, Kay Studios. Tucson, Arizona. 1947 to present (1984). Kay Mallek, who loves working with clay, colors and artistic endeavors, manufactures a line of tiles and commemorative plates along with antique collecting and magazine publishing. For many years, until sometime in the 1970's, Kay Mallek Studios made their own stoneware and porcelain blanks to decorate. Now the blanks are imported, but a silk screen shop for decorating and art work is maintained. Several hundred items are decorated there. A series of Navajo Christmas plates was made between 1970 and 1983, all designed by well known Indian artists. For example, the 1975 was the fifth in the series, designed by Robert Chee, a Navajo, who created his version of Christmas on the reservation. This particular plate was hand jiggered in Arizona of Arizona clay. Each year a different Navajo artist designed the plate. Other very attractive plates included "The Shootout at the O.K. Corral," 1981 designed by Santos Blas Barbosa, a prominent western artist; the "Amish Harvest Plate," designed by Charles A.L. Stephens, who has designed interiors for cathedrals, theaters, theatrical sets, etc.: "Morman Harvest," also was designed by Stephens. Kay Mallek also presented plates with very old designs of the Mimbres Indians of the Southwest. (Information and marks: sent by company. No. 1, is backstamp on plate. The original manufacturers mark is under the mark causing it to appear a little smeared here. The other marks feature the road runner logo used by the company.)

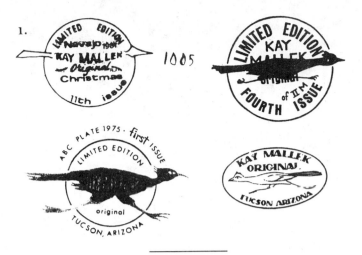

1.

Mallory Randall Corporation. Lake Success, New York. Filed for registration of this mark on August 14, 1970, claiming use since May 1970 for china dinnerware. Joshua Crabtree is the name of a deceased American potter of the 18th century.

JOSHUA CRABTREE, ESQ.

Maloney, Harold J. Kalamazoo, Michigan. Filed for registration of this mark on May 17, 1961, claiming use since February 1961 for ceramics and art objects, such as bowls, plates, cups, saucers, covered jars, pitchers and vases.

HAL

Manker, William. Claremont, California. 1937 to late 1950's. In 1932, Manker opened a pottery studio in Pasadena, California. In 1933, he moved to Padua Hills, north of Claremont, California, where he taught at Scripps College and founded the ceramics department. Soon his ware was being sold in leading stores throughout the United States. Made slip cast ware into cigarette boxes, vases, ashtrays, candleholders, lamp bases, a line of dinnerware in shape of stylized leaf. The dinnerware was produced around 1947 for only a year or so. In 1954, Manker turned the ceramic business over to his son, Courtney, and in the late 1950's the business closed due to foreign competition. The outstanding qualities of Manker's work were his shapes and colors of glazes. In reaching for words to describe Manker's shapes, majestic, modernistic, clean clear cut lines came to this author's mind. About shape Manker said: "I've always maintained that if the shape is beautiful there's no occasion for using decoration on it, and if it isn't, then all the decoration in the world isn't going to make it any more beautiful." (Information: All the foregoing information from an article by Jack Chipman, "William Manker Ceramics Objects of Timeless Beauty," *Antique Trader*, September 28, 1983, p. 72-75. Mark furnished by Chipman. Chipman said about the marks: "During World War II a new ink mark, "William Manker Ceramics/California/U.S.A.," was adopted to stress the fact that it was a California product. After 1954, when son Courtney took over, the mark was changed to "Manker Ceramics/California/U.S.A." The mark shown was inkstamped and used during 1930's.)

Mann, John. Rahway, New Jersey. Around 1830 until after 1900. Potter made redware and black glazed teapots. (Information: John Ramsay, *American Potters and Pottery*, p. 178. Mark: C. Jordan Thorn, *Handbook of Old Pottery and Porcelain Marks*, p. 135)

JOHN MANN
RAHWAY
N. J.

Mapp, E.T. Bacon Level, Randolf County, Alabama. Made alkaline glazed stoneware. (Stamped or impressed mark and information: E. Henry Willett and Joey Brackner, *The Traditional Pottery of Alabama*, p. 65.)

E. T MAPP

Marblehead Pottery. Marblehead, Massachusetts. 1904 to 1936. Marblehead Pottery was a small pottery producing around 200 pieces per week. It was founded by Herbert Hall as a handicraft program for the mentally ill. Arthur E. Baggs organized the pottery and was in charge of various technical aspects of the production for many years. See the listing for Arthur E. Baggs for a more detailed account of his involvement at Marblehead. Most of the ware was done in simple matt glazes of blue, gray, yellow, rose, etc. with classical shapes. Some pieces had hand-carved designs. In 1912, a 10-enameled faience line was introduced. Various ware included teapots, children's cereal sets, mugs, luncheon sets, decorative pieces, bookends, tiles, etc. The decorative pieces are beautiful. (Information: Paul Evans, as cited, pp. 157-160; also, Gail Pike Hercher, "Marblehead Pottery," *American Art Pottery*, March 1982, pp. 1, 6, 7. Marks: no. 1 is the stamp used at Marblehead Pottery as shown in Linda Steigleder, from the booklet published by the Everson Museum of Art to accompany the 1978 exhibition, "A Century of Ceramics in the U.S." No. 2 is the incised initials of Arthur E. Baggs as shown in Paul Evans, *Art Pottery of the U.S.*, p. 160, used on pieces made by Baggs himself with special decorations or glazes. Nos. 3, 4, Dave Rago, "American Art Pottery," *Antique Trader Weekly*, April 30, 1980, p. 77.)

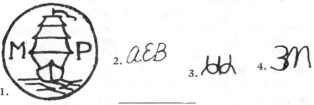

Marco Pottery. Zanesville, Ohio. Found listed in 1939-1940 Zanesville Directory. In 1948 they were listed at 620 Moxhala Avenue, Zanesville, and in 1950 they were at 725 Pine. Not listed in 1952. Mark was stamped in gold on a teapot, sugar and creamer which was highly vitrified cream colored body with violet decals and gold trim. Sam Marsh was the owner and Art Wagner was one of the decorators at Marco Pottery. (See the Art Wagner listing). (Mark: Elizabeth Vaughn, Beechwold Antiques, Columbus, Ohio.)

Marek, J.J. Brownsburg, Indiana. Marek, a studio potter, came from Czechoslavakia, and he had studied in France and Germany. He worked in the United States in the 1940's making deco figurals which were fired under high heat. He used unusual two color mixed glazes. (Information and impressed mark, "JJM": sent by Lucile Henzke, by letter.)

Markell, Immon and Company. Akron, Ohio. (Spelled Markle, Inman and Company in Blair, p. 28.) Were in business around 1869, became **Viall and Markell**, 1869 to around 1890. Made stoneware. Employed 25 in 1888. (Information: Spargo, p. 343, and Ramsay, p. 206. Mark: Thorn, p. 135. This mark shown as Thorn spelled it. Incidentally, Spargo spelled Markell with one L as Markel, Immon and Co. which is also Ramsay's spelling. But I assume Thorn saw the mark somewhere to draw it for the book and chose to use that spelling.)

MARKELL, IMMON & CO.
AKRON
O.

Markham Pottery. Ann Arbor, Michigan, and National City, California. Before 1905 to 1921. Herman C. Markham started making pots to grow and hold his roses, from clay in his own back yard in the late 1800's. By 1905 the hobby had developed into a business, and Markham was joined by his son, Kenneth S. According to W.P. Jervis in "World's Pottery Marks," *American Ceramic Society Bulletin*, April 8, 1915, the early pieces had the "V.P." cipher, and he claimed that mark was abandoned in 1905 in preference to the incised Markham mark. In 1913 the pottery moved to National City, California, and after locating in a couple of different places in the city, the operation ceased in 1921. In 1915, the Markhams worked in a portion of the California China Products Company which produced ceramic tile. In 1915, Markham won a gold medal at the 1915 San Diego Panama-California Exposition for a low fire glazed piece which had the appearance of being buried because of the web of veins or maze of lines rough to touch. (Information: Paul Evans,

Art Pottery in the U.S., pp. 161-163; and Douglas Scott, "Markham Pottery," *American Clay Exchange*, November 1983, p. 13. Marks: no. 1, Jervis, as cited. Nos. 1, 2, Scott, as cited.)

1. ꟿ *Markham* 2.

Marks On Dishes, Various Kinds. Miscellaneous marks found on dishes and other ceramic pieces cause the collectors concern. All sorts of marks may be found that are for factory use or information and were not put there with a collector in mind. On stock numbers, identification numbers, etc., each factory had their own system, and it changed for year to year. Almost all major companies used just U.S.A. on ceramics at various times. There is no way to identify a piece of china from just U.S.A. Many collectors have tried, some even claim to be able to tell their favorite collectible that way, but they are only fooling themselves. Marks 1-4 shown are four "Made in U.S.A." marks used by Gladding, McBean and Company. I can identify these only because they came out of company files, but any number of companies marks could look exactly the same. Nos. 5-6, "C" in circle, and "R" in a circle are for copyrighted and registered. No. 7, "2nd,RK," means the piece is a second or run of the kiln with a minor defect. Sometimes these are sold from store or shop at the factory site. Sometimes they are shipped out of state to be sold. No. 8: This particular set of numbers were used by Gladding, McBean and Company on earthenware pieces only. The letter identified the day of the month beginning with A for the 1st. The next two numbers were for the decorator and last two numbers gives the year. This system of dating was used in 1944 or 1945 and probably would not be found often at all. Sometimes a patent number is added to the mark such as in no. 9, which shows a stock number "C-809" and "patent no. 114,748," used around 1939. No. 10: This particular number is a decorator's number used at the Gladding, McBean and Company factory in 1963. There are long lists of decorators' marks or initials for the major art potteries. No. 11: At the Homer Laughlin China Company outlet shop, I purchased dishes with mark no. 11 from an experimental run or trial. The dishes never were acutally produced so they did not have a regular mark, only an identification number. Nos. 12, 13, 14: The Good Housekeeping Seal of Approval sometimes appears, as does the American Retailers Guild mark, and the Household Institute mark to tell the customer that the dishes were sanctioned by some group. No. 15: On china used by the army, we find "U.S." and "Q.M.C.," the latter standing for the Quartermaster Corp. No. 16: Various brotherhood organizations have their own symbols that can be found such as number 16, Benevolent Paternal Order of Elks. All of the above marks are backstamps except no. 11, written in oxide ink.

1. MADE IN U.S.A.

2. MADE IN U.S.A.

3. MADE IN U.S.A

4. MADE IN U.S.A. 1

5. Ⓒ   6. Ⓡ

7. 2nd RK

8. T 27 62

9. C-809   U.S. Pat No 114,748

10. 44   11. 4915-50   12. Guaranteed by Good Housekeeping

13. AMERICAN RETAILERS GUILD WARRANTED 24 KT. GOLD

14. HOUSEHOLD INSTITUTE Pink Rose DINNERWARE

15. U.S. Q.M.C.

16. B.P.O.E.

Marks and Rosenfeld. San Francisco, California. This selling agency advertised in the 1940's and 1950's in various trade magazines. They sold "Cali Crown" of California, and "Marose" of California, both trade names for ceramic products used by Marks and Rosenfeld, Inc. Marose is a combination of the two names in the company. Pieces advertised were cigarette boxes with sculptured hand made flowers on top and lazy susans in various two tone combinations of glaze. Marks and Rosenfeld also sold glass products. In the 1945 *Crockery and Glass Journal Directory*, they were listed as importers and wholesalers of china, pottery, earthenware, fancy ware, novelties, decorative accessories, etc. They also listed exclusive promotional items in domestic china and glass. (Marks: no. 1, from 1945 directory cited. No. 2, sent by Rena London, researcher and writer.)

MADE IN M&R AMERICA 1.

HAND MADE POTTERY M&R CALIFORNIA 2.

Marshall Burns Company. Chicago, Illinois. A division of Technicolor, a sales agency out of business quite a while. Well known among collectors for heavy brown dinnerware marked "Mar Crest" which was manufactured for Marshall Burns by Western Stoneware Company. (This fact verified by Betty Cooper at Western Stoneware.) Products were made for Marshall Burns with the Mar-Crest mark by potteries other than Western Stoneware Company. (Mark 1 was filed for registration July 7, 1959, for ceramic dinnerware, stoneware mixing bowls and ceramic beverage mugs, claiming first use on August 31, 1954. The other two marks found on the dark brown ware mentioned, a blue well vitrified ashtray and a yellow bulbous pitcher.)

MAR-CREST 1.

MARCREST Ⓡ 75 U.S.A. 2.

MARCREST OVENPROOF QUALITY MADE IN USA 3.

Marshall Field and Company. Chicago, Illinois. A large department store in business at present. This company has sold many American made products over the years. The name appears often as you read about the various potteries. Filed for copyright on use of mark 1 on May 9, 1921, for use on pottery ware, claiming use since 1917. Mark 2, found at Quality Stamp Company, East Liverpool, Ohio. The company sold products for Haeger Potteries, Inc. around 1938.

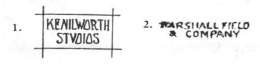

1. KENILWORTH STUDIOS

2. MARSHALL FIELD & COMPANY

Marshall Pottery. Marshall, Texas. 1896 to present. The single kiln pottery was started by a man named Rocker until 1905 when Sam H. Ellis became owner. In spite of a 1912 fire and competition from other small potteries in the area, the pottey grew, and they now supply distributors in 37 states. Today they use over 100 tons of clay a day in two plants making 155 items in stoneware or red clay. Much of the stoneware is hand turned such as butter churns while red clay flower pots are made with modern machinery. Pottery now in hands of third generation of Ellis's. (Information: Company furnished, no author, "The History of Marshall Pottery," six typed pages.)

1. MARSHALL POTTERY 3 MARSHALL, TEXAS

2. HAND TURNED IN THE ANCIENT TRADITION BY SKILLED CRAFTSMAN AT MARSHALL POTTERY

Marshall Studios, Inc. Veedersburg, Indiana. 1951 to present (1984). Gordon Martz, studio potter, makes stoneware pieces fired to 2,350 degrees F. into lamps, dinnerware, trays, clocks, tile, various accessories, etc. From 1926 to 1951, Mr. Martz was in the lamp shade business in Indianapolis, Indiana. Then in 1951 he started the ceramic business at 104 N. Mill Street in Veedersburg. He has pieces in the Museum of Modern Art and the John Herron Museum in Indianapolis.

Martz

Marsh Industries. Los Angeles, California. 1950 to present (1986). This company was started by Arthur Marpet and Mike Shein in 1950 in Glendale, California. In 1959, the company moved from Glendale to Los Angeles, where they are still in business at present making California giftware and "French Chef" cookware. In 1969, Mike Shein retired, and the business was owned by Arthur Marpet and his son, Richard A. Marpet, in 1978. In 1969 the line of "Gourmet Cookware" was introduced. Some of the products are handpainted. (Marks inscribed on various pieces identified from catalogues. Nos. 1-3 logos or used as paper labels.)

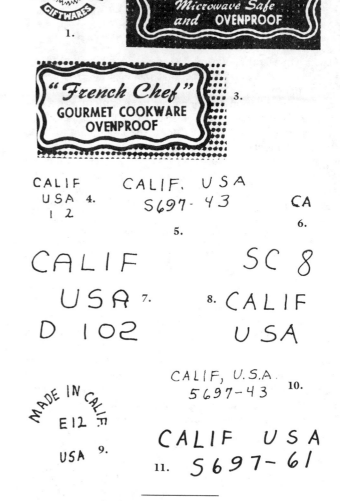

1. MARSH · INDUSTRIES GIFTWARES

2. "French Chef" GOURMET COOKWARE Microwave Safe and OVENPROOF

3. "French Chef" GOURMET COOKWARE OVENPROOF

4. CALIF USA 1 2

5. CALIF. USA S697-43

6. CA

7. CALIF USA D 102

8. SC 8 CALIF USA

9. MADE IN CALIF. E 12 USA

10. CALIF, U.S.A. 5697-43

11. CALIF USA S697-61

Martin, E.G. Camp Point, Illinois. Stoneware potter who operated around 1851 making stoneware crocks, jugs, etc. (Information and mark: Janice T. Wass, curator of Decorative Arts Illinois State Museum.)

E G MARTIN
4
Camp Point. Ill.

Martinez, Maria Montoya and Julian. San Ildefonso Pueblo, approximately 24 miles from Santa Fe, New Mexico. In 1904, Maria and her husband, Julian, demonstrated Indian Crafts at the St. Louis Exposition where she made red bowls. Maria grew up making pottery with her sisters for use and sale. Around 1907 Maria was asked to reproduce a replica of an old Indian pot found by archeologists. She became more involved in making pottery and continued to create her celebrated pieces for the rest of her very long life. Maria died July 20, 1980, at age 96. As late as 1978 she made a trip to the Pennsylvania State University to demonstrate her skills. In 1979, she went to Washington, D.C. to participate in the opening of an exhibit of her ware at the Smithsonian Institution. The process for making the pottery was a very simplified one. Julian dug the clay from a hillside. Some blue clay was brought from the Jemez Mountains. Maria, sitting on the ground, worked and patted the clay with water to form large balls. The balls were worked into rolls and the pots were hand built layer by layer, sun dried, decorated, then fired in an open fire. A grate or some means was used to keep the pieces up out of the actual fire. The pots were covered with pottery shards or tin, and then sheep manure was heaped over all the pile to give the beautiful black color from the smoke. Julian discovered a glaze that left a matt decoration after firing, creating what came to be known as "Black on black." The shiny black which Maria created by rubbing made a beautiful contrast with the dull matt decorative patterns. Maria's form and shape of her pots were controlled and beautiful. She made polychrome and redware, but black pots were what made Maria famous. Making the pottery was a family process. One person would create the form, another would hand paint with yucca leaf paint brushes and another polish. Julian died in 1943 and Santana, who was the wife of Maria's son Adam, worked with Maria until around 1956 when Tony Martinez, another son of Maria began to help her. Tony's Indian name was Popovi Da, and he died in 1968, but his widow Anita, and their three children, Tony, Joyce and Janice, all are interested in Indian art. Julian and Popovi Da both did art work on pieces for Maria.

Over the years, Maria received many awards and honors and her pieces are in outstanding displays and collections in many places. In 1954, she received the Palmes Academique from the French Ministry of Education. In 1974 she received the first annual New Mexico Governor's Award because "she brought honor to her people and the state of New Mexico." She received an honorary doctorate degree from the College of Santa Fe in 1980. Other awards include the Craftsmanship Medal from the American Institute of Architects; Symbol of Man Award from the Minnesota Museum of Art; Presidential Citation from the American Ceramic Society; University Recognition Medal from the University of Colorado; Catholic Art Association Medal; and the Jane Adams Award from Rockford College. She is listed in *Who's Who in America* and is the subject of a book published by the University of Oklahoma Press. The Cleveland Museum of Art has a coil-process set of six pieces and 10 bowls made especially for the museum around 1930. Maria, herself, could not relate accurate dates, as she did not keep records, and being quite elderly when the matter of "dating" pieces became important to collectors and historians, she simply could not put exact dates with her stages of pottery production. Her work was under very primitive conditions and time had little meaning for her. (Information: staff written paragraphs accompanying book review of Alice Marriott's book, *Maria, The Potter of San Ildefonso*, in *Pottery Collectors' Newsletter*, March 1973, pp. 65-66; staff written, "Legend Dies," *Pottery Collectors' Newsletter*, September, October 1980, p. 50; staff written, "Maria Martinez," *American Art Pottery Newsletter*, August 1980, p. 4; Jo Ann Rogers, "The Pottery of San Ildefonso," *Antique Trader*, April 24, 1972, p. 47; Hazel Hyde, *Maria Making Pottery*, 27 page booklet, pp. 3-20; staff written, "On Indian Pottery," *Tri-State Trader*, November 10, 1979, p. 9. Marks: The black pots were first made around 1919. Pots signed "Marie and Julian," were made from around 1923 to 1943. Maria used the name, "Marie," inscribed in script on early pots until around 1948 when she started using Maria. Her Indian name was Poveka which was also usd on some pieces in late 1940's and early 1950's. Santana and Maria

was inscribed after 1943 until Popovi Da worked with Maria. Marks are from Linda Steigleder, from the booklet published by the Everson Museum of Art to accompany the 1978 exhibition, "A Century of Ceramics in the U.S.")

Marie & Julian

Marie

Maria Poveka

Maria & Popovi Da

Marie & Santana .

Martz, Karl. Bloomington, Indiana. 1935 to present (1985). Karl worked as a self-employed potter from 1935 to 1942 and from 1945 until 1977 he was a professor of fine arts-ceramics at Indiana University during which time he produced pieces of his own work as time permitted. Karl made mostly art pottery and some functional container forms. He has worked with earthenware, stoneware and porcelain at various times in his life. His work is sold through The Gallery in Bloomington and sometimes from exhibitions. His schooling consisted of: B.A. in chemistry, 1933, Indiana University. Four quarters of ceramic art, Ohio State University, 1934 and 1939. Two weeks workshop with Shoji Hamada, Bernard Leach, Marguerite Wildenhain, Soetsu Yanagi at Black Mountain College, 1952. Three sabbaticals: New York City in 1952-1953; Kyoto, Japan in 1963-1964; Mashiko, Japan in 1971-1972. A few of the important exhibitions Karl has done are: 1959 - "XXth International Ceramic Exhibit," Syracuse Museum, N.Y. and Metropolitan Museum, NYC; 1963 - "Ninth International Exhibition of Ceramic Art," Smithsonian Institution; 1967 - "Acquisitions," Museum of Contemporary Crafts, NYC; 1975 - "Masters in Ceramic Art," Fairtree Gallery, NYC, Everson Museum, Syracus, NY, and Alfred University, Alfred, NY; and many others. He was appointed "Bingham Professor of Humanities," University of Louisville, 1975. Past President and Fellow of National Council for Education in the Ceramic Arts. Listed in *Who's Who in American Art*. (Marks: Since 1935, Martz has usd the initials in a circle incised or stamped into the clay in 99% of his work. Up until about 1955 the various pieces were dated also. In the 1970's a few pieces were incised "K.M." without the circle.)

KM

Maryland Pottery Company. See Maryland Queensware Company.

Maryland Queensware Company. Built in Baltimore in 1879 by **Hamill and Bullock**. In 1880 they were followed by **Hamill, Brown and Company**. In 1888 the **Maryland Pottery Company** was incorporated. The Maryland Pottery made a variety of dinnerware in white granite, opaque porcelain and stone china. Barber says that Maryland Pottery also used the word "Etruscan" on a black and white granite toilet set. They may have used it on other products they made not knowing that the Griffen, Smith and Hill Company of Phoenixville, Pennsylvania, were using the mark in Majolica. There would be no similarity in the ware, so this should not cause trouble for collectors. The D.F. Haynes and Company shown in the marks was a selling agency. The Maryland Pottery Company made white granite for them to sell around 1879. D.F. Haynes and Son Company later purchased the Chesapeake Pottery Company in 1896 (see that listing). W.P. Jervis in a "Dictionary of Pottery Terms," *Pottery, Glass and Brass Salesman*, May 16, 1918, p. 11, said the Maryland Pottery made decorated earthenware and later, semi-porcelain. Barber said this company was the first to make vitreous plumber's ware around 1891. In *Pottery, Glass and Brass Salesman*, July 2, 1914, p. 15, Jervis stated that tne Maryland Pottery Company was closed at that time, 1914, after a checkered existence. (Information: Lehner, *American Kitchen and Dinner Wares*, p. 102. Marks: nos. 1-10, Barber, *Marks of American Potters*, pp. 147, 148; nos. 11, 12, 13, 14, were all filed for registration on April 27, 1894, claiming use since March 24, 1894, for vitreous china, including plumbers and toilet ware.)

Mason, John. According to Garth Clark and Margie Hughto in *A Century of Ceramics in the U.S.*, pp. 305 and 306, Mason's major contribution to the field of ceramics came between 1958 and 1969 when he produced some of the finest abstract sculptural pieces made in ceramics. Many were permanently installed in public buildings and homes. The sculptures were large free standing forms up to six feet tall and bright monochrome glazes. He had an exceptional piece in the 1972 Ceramic Nationals at Syracuse. Pictured in the book cited is a ceramic wall by Mason, constructed in Los Angeles. In the 1970's, Mason began to make the sculptures and floor pieces with fire brick such as "Installations from the Hudson River" series funded by the National Endowment

for the Arts. Mason received his schooling at the Chouinard Art Institute in Los Angeles. He also taught at Pomona College in Claremont, California; the Otis Art Institute and the University of California, and by 1978 he was teaching at Hunter College in New York. (Information: Garth Clark as already cited. See Clark for a more complete discussion of this man's work. Marks: painted; Linda Steigleder, from the booklet published by the Everson Museum of Art to accompany the 1978 exhibition, "A Century fo Ceramics in the U.S.," with Curators: Garth Clark and Margie Hughto.)

Mason and Russell. (Ramsay, p. 191 uses one "l," and Thorn, p. 146, shows two "l's" for Russell.) Cortland, New York. They both agree this potter made stoneware around 1870.

MASON & RUSSELL

CORTLAND

N.Y.

Massillon, Ohio, Various Potteries. From 1860 to 1891 a potter named Adam Welker made stoneware unmarked except by design. The Daisy and curved lines as shown, is on two pieces made by him in the Massillon Museum. William W. Welker was superintendent of **Massillon Pottery** from 1866 to 1888. Besides the Massillon Pottery there was also a **Massillon Stoneware Company** which was also referred to as the **Boerner Pottery** because Andrew Boerner was president from 1890 to 1902. After 1890 until its closing in 1902 W.W. Welker was superintendent of that pottery also. Another stoneware pottery operated around 1890 to 1905 in the area called the **Navarre Pottery** in Navarre, Ohio (five miles south of Massillon) made stoneware, brown ware, blue spongeware, etc. Also **George Binkley**, was in Massillon from 1822 to 1826 and moved to Canton, Ohio, from 1826 to 1840. He made redware and later brown stoneware with Albany slip glaze. No. 1 is a design used by Adam Welker. No. 2 and 3 are the marks reported to be for George Binkley.

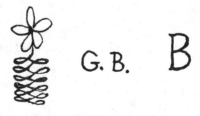

Mather, Tim, Stoneware and Porcelain. Athens, Ohio. 1976 to present (1984). Tim Mather, a studio potter, received a M.F.A. degree from Ohio University in 1967. In 1967 to 1974 he was affiliated with Illinois State University. He also taught the summer of 1971 at Moore College of Art and summer of 1974 and 1978 he was at Penland School of Crafts. Between 1967 and 1984, Tim listed over 125 exhibitions that he has done in colleges, galleries, museums, etc. Colleges sponsoring various exhibitions included: College of Wooster, Wooster, Ohio; West Virginia Weslyan College, Buckhannon, West Virginia; Idaho State University, Pocatello, Idaho; Marietta College, Marietta, Ohio; Ohio University, Athens, Ohio; Murray State Univeristy, Murray, Kentucky; University of West Virginia, Morgantown, West Virginia; University of Rochester, Rochester, New York; Southern Illinois University, Edwardsville, Illinois; University of Akron, Akron, Ohio; Thiel University, Greenville, Pennsylvania; Chadron State College, Chadron, Nebraska; State University, Brockport, New York; Ohio Northern Univeristy, Ada, Ohio; Illinois State University, Lakeview Center, Peoria, Illinois, Eureka College, Eureka, Illinois; Bradley University, Peoria, Illinois; Illinois State University, Normal, Illinois; University of Massachusetts, Amherst, Massachusetts; Western Illinois University, Macomb, Illinois. His pieces were shown at the galleries, art centers and museums included: Columbus Cultural Arts Center and Helen Winnemore Gallery, both in Columbus, Ohio; Contemporary Crafts Gallery, Louisville, Kentucky; Parkersburg Art Center, Parkersburg, West Virginia; Netsky Gallery, South Miami, Florida; Clay and Fiber Gallery, Taos, New Mexico; Renwick Gallery, Smithsonian Institution, Washington, D.C.; Indianapolis Museum of Art, Indianapolis, Indiana; Butler Institute of American Art, Youngstown, Ohio; Kalamazoo Institute of Art, Kalamazoo, Michigan; Memphis Academy of Art, Memphis, Tennessee; Museum of Contemporary Crafts, New York City, New York; Rochester Art Center, Rochester, Minnesota; Everson Museum, Syracuse, New York. This does not begin to tell the impressive resume sent by Tim Mather. A long list of workshops was included and several shows where Tim was a juror to judge the winners. At his studio, Tim makes functional and non-functional porcelain with mark incised on bottom, usually in a circle.

Maurice Ceramics of California. Los Angeles, California. The earliest listing I found for this pottery in the 1967, *China, Glass and Tableware Directory*. They were still in business manufacturing pottery in 1985. The products given in various directories included lazy susans, serving trays, ashtrays, casseroles, tier trays, cannister sets, cookie jars, candleholders, figurines, salad bowl sets, console sets, etc. (Inscribed mark: no. 1, found on a nice big rooster cookie jar. Mark 2 sent by Francis Andrews.)

1. Maurice Ceramics Co. of Cal

2. MAURICE of CALIF

May Department Stores. New York, New York; Akron, Ohio; Cleveland, Ohio; Baltimore, Maryland; Los Angeles, California; Denver, Colorado; and St. Louis, Missouri, filed for registration of this mark March 1, 1939, for use on pottery namely, dinner sets composed of plates, bowls, cups, saucers, platters, serving dishes, sugar bowls, cream pitchers and four piece bowl sets, jugs, water pitchers, salt and pepper shakers, teapots, service, chop and square salad plates. Claiming use since September 2, 1938.

MISSION BELL

Mayer China Company. Beaver Falls, Pennsylvania. 1881 to present. (1985). In 1880, Joseph Mayer came to New York from England to engage in a pottery importing business with his brother, Arthur Mayer. He moved on to Beaver County, Pennsylvania, in 1881 with another brother, Ernest, to organize the **Mayer Potteries Company, Ltd.** on the banks of the Beaver Falls. The pottery was later incorporated as the Mayer China Company. ("Necrology-Joseph Mayer," *Bulletin of the American Ceramic Society*, December 1930, p. 336.) The present product of Mayer China is a fine grade of very attractive hotel ware. But in their long history, Mayer made a great variety of products. Mayer Brothers of Beaver Falls, Pennsylvania, advertised white ironstone underglaze "Lustre Band and Sprig" (Tea Leaf) in 1881. Also an 1893 advertisement of Mayer's said "Lustre Band and Sprig already over 10 years on the market will not wear off." (Jeanette Ray Hutchinson, "Story of Tea Leaf Ironstone," *Antique Reporter*, November 1973, p. 16) Marcia Ray called Mayer China a leading producer of the Tea Leaf pattern. ("A.B.C.'s of Ceramics," *Spinning Wheel*, June 1968, p. 21.) In 1896 the old buildings were destroyed by fire and a new building erected. Listed in the *1902-1903 Complete Directory*, Mayer China was manufacturing white granite, semi-porcelain dinner sets, toilet sets, and odd sets of dishes. In the *1900 Factory Inspection Report*, Mayer was listed as employing 145 to make white granite.

From *The Heritage of a Century*, published around 1915 and copyrighted by Mayer China, is a list of the various kinds of clay used by Mayer. Ball clay from Tennessee, feldspar from Canada, Connecticut, and New York, kaolin from England and Florida, and flint from Illinois. These materials mixed in proper proportions achieved the quality of the Mayer's products. Around 1915, 75% of Mayer's China's output was whiteware and 25% was decorated before it was dipped and glazed. Company information said that about this time (1914 to 1915) the Mayer China Company entered the hotel ware field almost exclusively and gradually discontinued tableware for home use. Shenango China Company of New Castle, Pennsylvania, purchased Mayer China in 1964. (See Shenango.) Then in 1968 both companies were purchased by Interpace. (See Interpace.) Shenango China was sold to the Anchor Hocking Corporation on June 2, 1979, this serving connection with Mayer China. On June 16, 1980, Mayer China took over the Walker China Company which had been owned by the Jeannette Corporation. (See Jeannette Corporation.) On April 3, 1981, Walker China was closed down by Mayer China Company, and the equipment was moved out of the plant. Interpace sold Mayer China also in 1979 to a private group. This group of investors sold Mayer China to the Syracuse China Company on December 14, 1984. The dating code for Mayer China is as follows: the numbers stamped on the china are manufacturing dates; the last two digits are the last two numbers of the year the china was produced. (Information: company information; and Lehner, *American Kitchen and Dinner Wares*, p. 103. Marks: nos. 1-21, Barber, *Marks of American Potters*, p. 33; nos. 22-41,

Quality Stamp Company, East Liverpool, Ohio; no. 41 filed for registration on March 2, 1931, claiming use since January 2, 1931, for use on chinaware; nos. 42, 43, Ramsay, p. 268; no. 44, Father Sandknopp, p. 63; nos. 45-46, on dishes; nos. 47-67, sent by Mayer China in 1978; nos. 81-82, sent by Mayer China in 1981; nos. 74-80, Waldorf Stamping Device, New London, Ohio. No. 83 was filed for registration November 9, 1965, claiming use since July 1965. No. 84 is a version of the same mark from 1967 *China, Glass and Tableware Directory*. No. 85, Larry Paul, research writer on pottery.

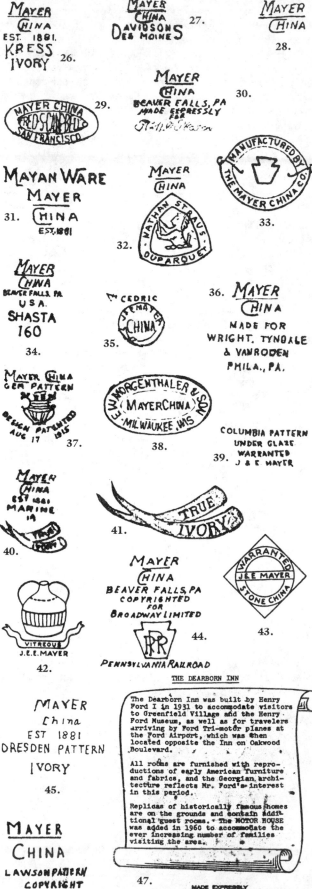

MADE EXPRESSLY FOR
The Gran Crystal Palace
Mayer China
INTERPACE ®
48.

MADE EXPRESSLY FOR
BRIARWOOD RACQUET CLUB
MAYER CHINA
BY INTERPACE U.S.A ®
DISTRIBUTED BY
EZEKIEL &
WEILMAN Co.
RICHMOND, VA.
49.

DESIGNED EXPRESSLY FOR
HOTEL HERSHEY
Mayer China ®
© BY INTERPACE
FURNISHED BY
JOHN WANAMAKER PHILA.
50.

DESIGNED EXPRESSLY FOR
THE STANFORD COURT
Mayer China ®
© BY INTERPACE
51.

MADE EXCLUSIVELY FOR
LOEWS
L'enfant PLAZA
Mayer China
INTERPACE ®
52.

DESIGNED EXPRESSLY FOR
The Mélange
Mayer China
INTERPACE ®
53.
FURNISHED BY
GERBER'S

MADE EXPRESSLY FOR
Holiday Inn
BARBADOS
54.
MAYER CHINA ©
BEAVER FALLS PA
BY INTERPACE U.S.A ®

DESIGNED EXCLUSIVELY FOR
Swedish Club
of Chicago
55.
BY
MAYER CHINA ©
BEAVER FALLS, PA.
U.S.A

Made Expressly For
SKY CLUB
MAYER CHINA
BY INTERPACE ®
U.S.A
SUPPLIED BY
MINNERS & CO.
56.

MADE EXPRESSLY FOR
Minnesota Twins
MAYER CHINA
BY INTERPACE ®
U.S.A
57.
FURNISHED BY
OKen's Inc.

DESIGNED EXCLUSIVELY FOR
ST. THOMAS' CHURCH
ON THE OCCASION OF ITS 150th ANNIVERSARY
Mayer China
INTERPACE ®
58.

Made Expressly For
DUBLIN HOUSE
COLORADO SPRINGS
59.

MADE EXPRESSLY FOR
THE NATIONAL PRESBYTERIAN
CHURCH AND CENTER
MAYER CHINA
BY INTERPACE U.S.A ®
FURNISHED BY
L.N. HILL CO.
WASHINGTON, D.C.
60.

MADE EXPRESSLY FOR
BEL AIR
MAYER CHINA
BY INTERPACE ®
U.S.A.
61.

DESIGNED EXPRESSLY FOR
HOTEL THAYER
THE DESIGN IS BASED UPON
A PATTERN USED IN THE
WEST POINT CADET MESS,
CIRCA 1875.
BY
MINNERS ASSOCIATES
N.Y.C.
Mayer China
INTERPACE ®
62.

MADE EXPRESSLY FOR
Holiday Inn
ST. LUCIA. WEST INDIES
Mayer China
INTERPACE ®
63.

HOTEL DEL LAGO
MARACAIBO
VENEZUELA
64.

MAYER
CHINA
BEAVER FALLS PA
65.

DELTA
AIR LINES
MAYER
CHINA ©
BEAVER FALLS. PA
BY INTERPACE U.S.A ®
67.

DESIGNED EXCLUSIVELY FOR
MEDICENTER
OF AMERICA
MEMPHIS, TENN.
MAYER CHINA
BY INTERPACE ®
U.S.A
370
66.

HANDCRAFTED
BY
MAYER CHINA
BEAVER FALLS. PA
FOR
68. Armstrong World Industries, Inc.
BOARD OF DIRECTORS VISIT
MARCH 29, 1982
BEAVER FALLS PLANT
'IN ITS EIGHTIETH YEAR'

DESIGNED EXCLUSIVELY FOR
THE
PEZZINO FAMILY
AT
CHEZ SAMUEL
SUPPLIED BY
Buffalo Hotel Supply
69.
Mayer ©
CHINA
BEAVER FALLS, PA.

DESIGNED AS A
LIMITED EDITION FOR THE
Claridge
Mayer CHINA CO
© BEAVER FALLS PA
70.

MADE EXPRESSLY FOR
RIDGEWELLS
CATERERS
Mayer CHINA CO
© BEAVER FALLS PA
71.

Produced Expressly For
THE
HOMESTEAD
Hand Paint No.
814
72.
Mayer CHINA CO
© BEAVER FALLS PA

MADE EXCLUSIVELY FOR THE
SECRETARY OF DEFENSE
MEXICO
1981
73.
Mayer CHINA CO.
© BEAVER FALLS PA

Walker China
BY Mayer ®
74.

Mayer CHINA CO.
© BEAVER FALLS PA
K.G.
75.

Bayberry
DESIGNED BY
Mayer CHINA
BEAVER FALLS PA
USA
EXPRESSLY FOR
CHALFONTE-HADDON HALL
FURNISHED BY
JOHN WANAMAKER
PHILADELPHIA
76.

77.

MAYER
CHINA
BEAVER FALLS, PA.
U.S.A.
Furnished By
MINNERS & CO. INC.
NEW YORK CITY

79.

STYLED & DESIGNED BY
Dorothy Draper Inc
FOR
INTERNATIONAL HOTEL
PORT OF NEW YORK AUTHORITY
FURNISHED BY
MAYER
CHINA
BEAVER FALLS, PA.

78.

MAYER
CHINA

81.

MADE EXPRESSLY
FOR
THE HARLEY OF NEW YORK
Mayer CHINA CO
© BEAVER FALLS PA.
U.S.A.

80.

MAYER
CHINA
LAWSON-PATTERN
COPYRIGHT

82.

83.

84.

•BALTIC•
MAYER CHINA
MANUFACTURED FOR
THE F.F. DE BOLT Co

85.

Mayeron Tile Works. St. Paul, Minnesota. 1971 to present. Constance Mayeron started making pottery in 1971 and started the Tile Works in 1980. She is a studio potter who makes tile cut from slabs of clay. She also has gained wide recognition from her wheel thrown and altered stoneware and porcelain functional type of ware. She worked as an apprentice with Curtis Hoard, an instructor at the University of Minnesota. Her work has been shown in articles in *Ceramic Monthly, Craft Connection*, an arts newspaper. In 1982 she showed her work at galleries in Minneapolis, New York City and Bayfield, Wisconsin.

Mayeron

Mayers, W.S. Roseville, Ohio. Around 1870 to 1880. Made stoneware. (Information: Lois Lehner, *Ohio Pottery and Glass*, p. 77.)

W.S. MAYERS
ROSEVILLE
OHIO

McAdam, John. Montrose, Baldwin County, Alabama. This mark was scratched or incised into the hat of a figure head or face vessel with Albany slip glaze made around 1890. The head was 12¼″ x 7¼″. I couldn't see the top line of the mark very well in the picture, but it would be a one of a kind rough

inscribed mark. (Information: E. Henry Willett and Joey Brackner, *The Traditional Pottery of Alabama*, pp. 31 and 61.)

Mc A ?
Montrose
Potter

McCarthy Brothers. Somerville, Massachusetts. Around 1870. Potter made stoneware with name impressed. (Information and mark: John Ramsay, p. 202 and C. Jordan Thorn, p. 137.)

McCARTHY BROS.
SOMERVILLE
MASS.

McCarty Brothers. Sierra Madre, California. 1941 to 1952. Lee and Michael McCarty both had graduated from Pasadena City College and they started their pottery in Sierra Madre, which is Northeast of Pasadena, in 1941. Lee sculpted models of figurines and flower holders such as a Chinese boy and girl called Ching Li and Mei Mei. Others were Mexican children, Lupe and Carlos; a Tibetan boy, Tibi Tan and an Indian girl. From around 1943 to 1947 the McCarty Brothers figurines and flower holders were sold by Walter Wilson (see that listing). From 1949 to late 1950's Stewart B. McCulloch, a distributor, handled their ware. The business closed in 1952 due to the return of foreign competition following World War II. (Information and marks: Jack Chipman, *American Clay Exchange*, November 15, 1986, pp. 8 and 9. After 1952, McCulloch manufactured the line.)

McCarty Bros
California ©47
8-11-47

McCARTY BROS.
SIERRA MADRE, CALIF.

J.L. McClusky. Lakenan, Missouri. Around 1882. Mark on blue stenciled four gallon crock. (Information and mark: Henry W. Heflin, pottery collector and researcher; also *Report of Manufacturers of U.S., 10th Census*, Washington: 1880, p. 357.)

J.L. McCluskey
Lakenan. Mo.

McCormick, Annette. Mansfield, Ohio. 1976 to present. Annette is a studio potter making decorative and functional salt glazed porcelain thrown on a wheel and fired at cone eleven. Some of her pieces have additional hand building on them. In 1971 she received a B.F.A. degree from Florida Atlantic University in Boca Raton, Florida. She has done several major shows in Ohio and won first place in ceramics at the Toledo Festival of Arts.

McCormick

J.W. McCoy Pottery. Roseville, Ohio. 1899-1911. James W. McCoy organized the first McCoy Pottery in 1899. There were two McCoy potteries; see the listing for Nelson McCoy Pottery also. There had been McCoys in the potting business before 1899, but James W. McCoy was the first to make a big contribution. In 1848 the very first McCoy operated a pottery in a small log building. From 1886 to 1890 the Midland Pottery of Kildow, Williams and McCoy made stoneware in Roseville. Later, the plant was called L.S. Kildow. James W. McCoy started a general merchandise store in Roseville, in 1876, which according to *Roseville*, a booklet written in 1906, p. 6, was the first established business in Roseville. In 1901, the active management of the store was turned over to McCoy's son Arthur, but up to that time, J.W. McCoy was a store keeper, not a potter. By 1902, McCoy had the production of pottery up to 5,000 pieces a day, employing 100 workers. He made several lines of art pottery that are highly prized today. Mont Pelee ware, Olympia, Loy-Nel-Art (named for his sons, Nelson and Lloyd) and Navarre were some of the lines. In 1911 the name of the J.W. McCoy Pottery became the Brush-McCoy Pottery when George S. Brush became a partner in the business. George S. Brush had worked for McCoy since 1909 after his own pottery had burned in 1908. See the Brush Pottery listings.

J.W. McCoy Pottery also made jardineres, umbrella stands, a corn line, butter jars and other functional pieces. In the study of the pottery in Roseville, Crooksville, and Zanesville, Ohio, researchers have become involved with the beautiful art pottery made there and largely ignored the fine old cookingware pieces these potteries made in huge quantities just before and after 1900. In 1908 J.W. McCoy filed for registration of mark no. 6 to be used on cooking and culinary articles. The designs on these old cookingware pieces covered the whole bottom of the article. (Mark no. 1 shown was taken from a piece of the "Olympia" line. On this particular mark the Mc is covered by the O in Olympia. The Olympia marks are incised or scratched by hand into the bottom of each piece, therefore they will vary from mark to mark. The Loy-Nel-Art mark is impressed. For a picture of mark no. 5, see Kovel's *Guide to American Art Pottery*, p. 92. See Bob and Sharon Huxford, *Collectors Catalogue of Brush-McCoy Pottery*, pp. 4-8, for much more history. Mark no. 2: "Olympia," as shown in Deb and Gini Johnson, *Beginner's Book of American Pottery*, p. 15; marks 3-4, Lehner, *Ohio Pottery and Glass*, p. 78. Mt. Pelee mark furnished by Betty Blair.)

3. **ROSEWOOD**   4. **LOY-NEL ART**

LOY-NEL-ART
5. **McCOY**

       MT.
7. **PELEE**

McCoy Limited. Zanesville, Ohio. Nelson McCoy, Jr. left the McCoy plant in September 1981. Later he started a sales agency of his own, having pieces made to his specifications using the mark, "McCoy Limited." Two very attractive pieces were an ebony black candleholder in the form of a duck and also a cat candleholder. Mark inscribed.

McCoy Limited
USA
©

_____

McCoy, Nelson Pottery. Roseville, Ohio. In 1910 the company started as **Nelson McCoy Sanitary and Stoneware Company** by Nelson McCoy who was in charge of company for 35 years. He died in 1945. Nelson Melick McCoy took over the management until 1954, and Nelson McCoy, Jr. became president at age 29. He resigned September 30, 1981. In 1967, the plant covered 150,000 square feet of floor space and employed 300 people. The products became so well known that the name McCoy is known universally. Originality, attractiveness and ingenuity have made McCoy Pottery products widely saleable. Cookie jars, kitchen and tableware, garden and florists' ware, heavy dinnerware and cooking utensils, vases and all sorts of ornamental pieces or industrial artware have come from this factory at the rate of five million pieces per year (1967 statistic). McCoy Pottery was purchased by David T. Chase and Chase Enterprises. This management group also owned Mt. Clemens Pottery after 1963 and Sabin Industries as well. After March 4, 1974, McCoy Pottery was owned by the Lancaster Colony group, who also owned Indiana Glass Company. "Floraline" is the name of the line of florists' pieces. "Hostess" was used for serving pieces. Norris F. Schneider, "McCoy Ceramic Collection Features Rare Pieces," *Zanesville Time Recorder*, July 15, 1973 (no page no.), had this to say about McCoy marks:

"McCoy's first mark, a large M superimposed upon a small n, was used from 1934 to the late 1930's (mark no. 16). His second, N and M overlapping side by side with U.S.A., is found on pieces made in the late 1930's and early 1940's (mark no. 3). "McCoy" impressed, later with U.S.A. below it, was adopted in the early 1940's. The same mark embossed is found on ware from the middle 1940's to the 1960's. In the late 1940's "McCoy U.S.A." in a circle was adopted (see marks 9, 10). These marks overlap in time. The molds of a popular line with one mark were utilized for casting after other marks had been introduced."

By 1985 the Pottery Shop outlet was closed. McCoy was employing only 25-30 people in the factory. In 1986 the pottery was sold to people from New Jersey. The plant is supposed to operate again. (Marks: nos. 1-4 are older marks for McCoy; no. 4 was found on old stoneware crock; nos. 5-6 were used by Mt. Clemens Pottery and McCoy pottery while under joint ownership sometime during the period 1967 to 1974; nos. 7-8 were marks used on little brown glazed mustard containers made for the Heinz Company; nos. 9-12 are paper labels; no. 13 is the most recent McCoy logo and used as part of their marks now (1985); nos. 14, 15, from Deb and Gini Johnson's *Beginners Book of Pottery*, p. 15; no. 16, from Betty Latty, "On the Firing Line," *Glaze*, April 1981, p. 17. No. 17 was found on a very nice mixing bowl. This mark is very similar to one used by Watt Pottery. No. 18 on same type bowl as 17. No. 19 used on a stein. McCoy marks are in the mold, not stamped. Some are inscribed. No. 20 was filed on March 2, 1979 for use on dinnerware claiming use since July 26, 1977. No. 20 was filed February 25, 1980 for use on vases, jars, bowls, planters, candle holders, teapots, cups, bells, etc. claiming use since November 1979. No. 21 was filed March 2, 1979 for dinnerware.)

Canyon

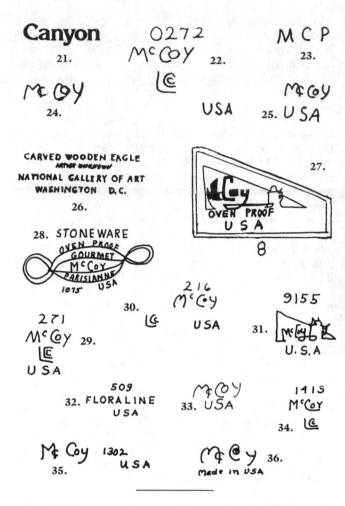

McCoy, Wilbur F. Zanesville, Ohio. Large wholesale dealer in stoneware on Putnum Avenue in 1880's. (Information and mark: Norris Schneider, ''31 Potteries Operated in City During the 19th Century,'' *Zanesville Times-Signal*, Zanesville, Ohio, November 24, 1957.)

W F Mc COY.
WHOLESALE
DEALER IN
STONEWARE
ZANESVILLE, O

McCrory Stores Corporation. New York, New York. Filed for registration of mark no. 1 on May 25, 1937, claiming use since April 1, 1937. On mark no. 2 the claim was filed May 29, 1937 and claimed use since January 1, 1937, on crockery domestic holloware and dinnerware.

McCurdy, I. Newcastle, Ohio. Late 19th century piece of stoneware found with this mark stenciled in blue. I found no further information on this potter. There were two Newcastles in Ohio as late as 1922; one in Coshocton County still had only 150 people; the one in Belmont County had a population of 15.

McCutcheon, James & Company. New York, New York. Filed for registration of this mark January 22, 1935. Claiming use since May 1, 1866 for tea and coffee sets of china and pottery. (1866 was the correct date given on the patent.)

McDade Pottery. McDade, Texas. Around 1890-1920. The pottery in McDade was not yet listed in the 1890-1891 *Texas State Gazetteer Business Directory*, but it was listed in the other directories I was able to obtain, 1892, 1896, and 1914-1915, under the name of R.L. Williams. There was one other pottery listed in McDade in 1892, under the names Dixen and Strollins. They were not listed in my next directory. Mark stamped in blue on white stoneware spittoon. (Information and mark: Sherry B. Humphreys and Johnell L. Schmidt, *Texas Pottery*, Washington, Texas: Star of Republic Museum, 1976, p. 25.)

McGraw Electric Company. Chicago, Illinois, Filed for registration of mark no. 1 on October 21, 1938, claiming use since July 24, 1936, and they filed on no. 2 on October 21, 1938, claiming use since July 24, 1936 on receptacles for household use, namely dishes of pottery. (Also see Line Material Company.)

HOSPITALITY TOASTMASTER
1.   2.

McGray H. Crooksville, Ohio. 1977 to present (1986). This person worked at Nelson McCoy's Pottery before 1977 and since has been decorating pieces marked as shown.

H. Mc GRAY
1977

McIlvain, William Gibbon. Philadelphia, Pennsylvania. Filed for rights to this mark on September 21, 1925, for salt and pepper shakers, talcum powder shakers made of china and vitreous china, claiming use since March 16, 1925.

McIntosh, Harrison. Claremont, California. Started making pottery 1939 until present (1984). McIntosh studied at the Art Center School in Los Angeles in 1938 where he learned drawing. In 1939-1940, he studied pottery making with Glen Lukens in University of Southern California. Following W.W. II, he studied with Albert and Louisa King. In 1949, he attended graduate school at Claremont. By 1952 he had a studio of his own set up. In 1954, he taught at the Otis Art Institute with Peter Voulkos, but since that time he has concentrated mostly on his studio work. His vessels and sculptural pieces are stoneware made with a single fire process resulting in striking work because of his feel for colors and attention to texture and shape. He did several large commissions including an urn with lid for the Scottish Rite Lounge in Los Angeles in 1962, a seven foot stoneware cross from Kingham Chapel for Claremont Community Church, and wind chimes for the thirty foot tower at Claremont Bank of California. (Information: Thomas Turnquist, "Harrison McIntosh, A Concerto in Clay," *American Art Pottery*, April, 1983, pp. 1, 4. Marks: sent by Turnquist in letter.)

   McINTOSH

McIntosh, Martha Lenore. Columbus, Ohio. Studio potter, started 1972 to make earthenware and stoneware into wind chimes, teapots, cups, bowls, decorative vases, birdhouses and some sculptured pieces. She has participated in many craft and juried shows in Ohio and New Jersey. She has pieces distributed over much of U.S., Scotland and England. Mark no. 1 is hand drawn on the bottom of some pieces. Marks 2 and 3 are small stamps found on the bottom or sides of pots.

1.   2.   3.

McKeachie-Johnston Pottery. (Randy J. Johnston and Jan McKeachie-Johnston.) River Falls, Wisconsin. 1972 to present (1983). Randy, a studio potter received a B.F.A. degree from the University of Minnesota in 1972 and apprenticed in Japan before setting up studio. He has taught in several places; Rochester Art Center, Quadna Summer Art Study Center and at the University of Minnesota Studio Arts as a Sabbatical replacement for Warren MacKenzie, also the Bergen School of Art in Bergen, Norway, all in the last 10 years. Randy listed 22 places where he has been invited as a guest artist including the Minnesota Museum of Art, Cleveland Art Institute, the Penland School of Crafts, etc. He has had 24 exhibits in various colleges, galleries and museums between 1972 and 1981. Randy makes utilitarian stoneware and porcelain woodfired to 2,350 degrees. Randy's wife Jan McKeachie-Johnston is also a potter. Her pottery stamp shown below is "M.J." A star in a circle is one of Randy's stamps.

McLaughlin, Mary Louise/Cincinnati Pottery Club/Losanti Ware. Cincinnati, Ohio. 1898 to 1906. Mary Louise McLaughlin became interested in ceramics through china painting. In 1877 she began experimenting at the Coultry Pottery. (See the listing Dayton Street Pottery/Coultry Pottery for early history.) Miss McLaughlin formed the Cincinnati Pottery Club in April 1879. This group worked in a room rented from the Cincinnati Woman's Art Association and fired the products at Coultry Pottery and later at the Hamilton Road Pottery of Frederick Dallas. Miss McLaughlin and Maria Longworth Nichols advanced the cost of building two kilns for firing decorated ware at the Dallas Pottery. One was for underglaze and one for overglaze decorated pieces. According to the May 1881 issue of *Harper's New Monthly Magazine* reprinted in *Hobbies*, February 1947, pp. 100, 101, under the title, "Decorative Pottery of Cincinnati," the club had 12 active and 3 honorary members. Each one of the ladies worked upon some specialty, or at least brought to her work so marked an individuality as to characterize it with distinctive features. All have painted and overglazed; each worked in incised design, in relief decoration and in underglaze color. The members of the Pottery Club were as follows: Miss M. Louis McLaughlin, president; Miss Clara C. Newton, secretary; Miss Alice B. Holabird, treasurer; Mrs. E.G. Leonard; Mrs. Charles Kebler; Mrs. George Dominick; Mrs. Walter Field; Miss Florence Carlisle; Miss Agnes Pitman; Miss Fannie M. Banks; Mrs. Andrew B. Merriam. Honorary members were: Mrs. M.V. Keenan; Miss Laura Fry; and Miss Elizabouth Nourse. (The Cincinnati Pottery Club is not to be confused with the Cincinnati Art Pottery or the Cincinnati Pottery Company.) In 1881, the Club group began working through the Rookwood Pottery where their blanks were made and the pieces fired after the ladies decorated them. In 1882, Rookwood Pottery would no longer accommodate the group and they had to go back to overglaze painting rather than to make the Cincinnati faience underglazed product. For a time, McLaughlin did china painting only. Then in 1894 she worked on what she called "American faience," a type of decoration with inlaid clay. This was fired at the Brockmann Pottery Company. The process involved a colored slip applied to a different colored clay body. (See Paul Evans, *Art Pottery of the U.S.*, p. 147, for more details on this method of inlaying a design.) In 1894, McLaughlin started the Porcelain League of Cincinnati to make hard-paste decorative porcelain. Many different bodies were produced before she achieved a real success in 1900. (Again, see Evans, p. 147, for details.) A creamy white, translucent ware, named "Losanti" was developed and exhibited at the 1901 Pan American Exposition in Buffalo, where it won a Bronze Medal. Miss McLaughlin cut out the design in the clay and filled the opening with glaze to provide even more translucency. Miss

McLaughlin stopped her work with ceramics in 1906 and lived to be 91 in 1939. McLaughlin had many major accomplishments. In the winter of 1879 to 1880, she made a 42" "Ali Baba" vase at the Frederick Dallas Pottery. In 1876 she published a book on china painting entitled *Pottery Decoration Under the Glaze*. She painted the first successful piece of blue underglaze on white ware. (See Coultry Pottery listing.) (Information: Paul Evans, *Art Pottery of the U.S.*, pp. 145-150; and *Hobbies* magazine, as cited. Marks: nos. 1, 2, E.A. Barber, *Marks of American Potters*, p. 127; no. 3, Paul Evans, as cited, p. 149. Evans said all of McLaughlin's work is carefully marked with incised marks. He thought the incised butterfly no. 3 was an early mark. Nos. 4, 5, 6, Dave Rago, "American Art Pottery," *Antique Trader Weekly*, April 7, 1982, p. 97. No. 7 on piece at Ross Purdy Museum of American Ceramics Society, Columbus, Ohio.)

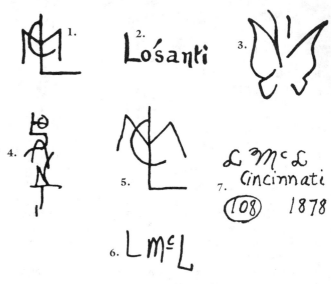

McNicol, Burton and Company. See Novelty Pottery Company.

D.E. McNicol Pottery. East Liverpool, Ohio and Clarksburg, West Virginia. Operated from 1892 to 1920's in Ohio, then this pottery went to Clarksburg, West Virginia, where they were still operating in the 1960's under the ownership of New York interests. Before 1920, D.E. McNicol made whiteware and yellowware and after moving to West Virginia they made mostly hotel ware but they did make some other products. In the *1902-1903 Complete Directory*, D.E. McNicol was listed as making common china and semi-porcelain dinner sets, toilet sets and short sets of odd dishes, some decorated. (Mark no. 1 and no. 4 are Ramsay's and Barber's version of the same mark. Barber, p. 110 would be the most correct. Ramsay p. 268 is mark 1. Nos. 2, 3, 5, 6, on dishes. No. 7 was filed for registration August 24, 1959. The company claimed on the registration that they had used the mark since October 31, 1931. No. 8 was filed April 26, 1960, claiming use since July 11, 1957. No. 9 was filed July 29, 1959, claiming first use was June 29, 1956. Marks were said to be used on china dinnerware, ovenware and food receptacles. In June 26, 1959, when numbers 10 and 11 were filed for registration, the registration stated a change of name from D.E. McNicol Pottery Company of West Virginia, to the McNicol China Company. Nos. 10, 11 were used since July 11, 1957

No. 12 found on rather thin porcelain plate with delicate green-gold trim. The rest of the marks came from Quality Stamp Company, East Liverpool, Ohio.)

1. SEMI-GRANITE / THE DE McN.P.CO

2. D.G. McNicol POTTERY CO. EAST LIVERPOOL, OHIO.

3. D.E. McNICOL EAST LIVERPOOL, O. X O C

4.  SEMI-GRANITE THE D.E.McN.P.CO. LIVERPOOL

5.  BARTH EQUID McNICOL CHINA BARTH EQUIPMENT CO NEW YORK

6. HOLDFAST BABYPLATE MADE BY D.E. McNICOL POTTERY CO. EAST LIVERPOOL OHIO PATENT APPLIED FOR

7.  McNICOL CHINA

8. REVELE

9. 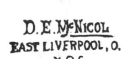 Therm - Oven China PORTION CONTROLLED McNICOL CHINA

10. GRECIAN

11. SENYU

12. IDEAL PORCELAIN ELO

13. Lexington China MADE IN U.S.A. Florella

14. OLD McNicols WEST VIRGINIA STONEWARE CHINA

15. GENUINE CHINA. McNICOL CHINA CLARKSBURG, W.VA. U.S.A

16. GENUINE CHINA McNICOL-MARTIN CLARKSBURG, W.VA. U.S.A.

17. VITRIFIED McNICOL CHINA Distributed by JAMES M. SHAW & CO. NEW YORK

18.  TOULAINE VITRIFIED CHINA SOLD ONLY BY H.L. HOECHSTETTER CO. MADE BY THE D E McNICOL POTTERY CO. CLARKSBURG, W.VA

19.  McNICOL CHINA MANGRUM HOLBROOK SAN FRANCISCO

20.  LIBERTY VITRIFIED CHINA TRADE MARK MANUFACTURED BY D.E. McNICOL POTTERY CLARKSBURG, W.VA. JOHN R. THOMPSON CO.

21.  NATHAN STRAUS DUPARQUET McNICOL CHINA

22.  MORRIS GORDON & SON, INC BOSTON MASS. McNICOL M S CHINA

23. McNICOL CHINA GENUINE CHINA

24.  LIBERTY VITRIFIED CHINA ALBERT PICK CO INC. CHICAGO ILLINOIS McNICOL CHINA CLARKSBURG, W. VA. U.S.A.

25.  MORRIS GORDON & SON INC BOSTON MASS. McNICOL M S CHINA

26. McNICOL CHINA MADE EXPRESSLY FOR SOUTHERN PACIFIC S.S. LINES Jas H SHAW & Co

27. LIBERTY VITRIFIED CHINA TRADE MARK ALBERT PICK & CO L BARTH & CO INC CHICAGO NEW YORK D E McNICOL POTTERY CLARKSBURG, W.VA.

28. McNICOL CHINA BARBIZON - PLAZA HOTEL

29.  MADE FOR INDUSTRIAL SALES CORP. McNICOL CHINA STONEWOOD, W. VA. U.S.A.

30. McNICOL BRENTANO CHINA

31.  LIBERTY VITRIFIED CHINA ALBERT PICK CO INC CHICAGO ILLINOIS D E McNICOL CLARKSBURG W VA

32. McNICOL DELATONE CHINA

33. McNICOL ROSLITE CHINA

34.  BEVERLY McNICOL CHINA Distributed by JAMES M. SHAW & CO. NEW YORK

35. McNICOL PARAGON CHINA

36.  McNICOL PALLADIAN CHINA

37.  McNICOL APOLLO C CHINA

38.

39.

40.

41.

42.

43.

D.E. McNicol and Smith, also McNicol and Corns, and various associates. East Liverpool, Ohio. D.E. McNicol and William Smith started in 1899 until 1907. Smith left and A.W. Corns joined McNicol until 1928 when McNicol left. Corns continued to operate until 1932. Plant made semi-porcelain dinnerware, attractively decorated, also hotel ware. (Mark: stamped on dish.)

McNicol, Patrick. East Liverpool, Ohio. 1886-1927. The Standard Pottery was organized in 1886. Patrick McNicol assumed control around 1894. In 1919 or 1920 the pottery lacked room to expand (McKee, p. 25). The pottery was inoperable for awhile around 1920 and soon after the Cronin family assumed control of the plants with Daniel Cronin as president until late 1920's. (Mark stamped on dish.)

T.A. McNicol Pottery Company. East Liverpool, Ohio. 1913 to late 1920's. Operated in what had been the Old Globe Pottery Company building. Making semi-porcelain dinnerware. (Information and mark: Annise Heaivilin, author of *Grandma's Tea Leaf*, by letter.)

Meader's Pottery. White County, Georgia. 1893 to present (1984). A. Meaders started the pottery in 1893 when he built a log building and hired a potter to throw pots and to teach his six sons to be potters. All but one became potters and worked in four separate shops. One of the sons was named Cheever, and he is the father of the present potter, Lanier. Cheever took over the original pottery in 1920. Eventually Casey built his own pottery, and Cheever replaced the old building with a new one of pine logs. Cheever's wife, Arie, was a potter in her own right. She worked with Cheever and applied designs such as leaves and bunches of grapes to the pieces. She handbuilt chickens, geese, owls, etc. Arie signed the pots. For Cheever, she signed C.M. Her own pieces she signed "A.M." Finally in 1965 when Arie was 60 years old, she started using the wheel. In 1966, Lanier Meaders took over his father's shop and Cheever died in 1967. Lanier, Edwin and Cleater are the only Meaders making pottery today. Lanier's brother, Edwin, is a potter with a shop across the road from Lanier. The amount Lanier makes is very limited, but it sells as fast as he makes it. In 1976, an exhibition, "The Meaders Family of Mossy Creek," was held at the Georgia State University Art Gallery in Atlanta, to exemplify ash glazed stoneware as it was made throughout the 19th century. In 1966, the Smithsonian Institution made a film of the Meaders pottery and family. Ash glaze in a green or very deep dark brown in color with a drip textured surface which the old timers called "tobacco spit," "burnt sugar," and other such names makes a beautiful piece of pottery. For detailed account on how the glaze was made see Joan Falconer Byrd, "Lanier Meaders - Georgia Folk Potter," *Ceramics Monthly*, October 1976, pp. 24, 26, 28; and Nancy Sweezy, Raised in Clay, pp. 108. 109. (Marks: no. 1, "A.M." for Arie, "Meader's Pottery, White County, Georgia," *Pottery Collectors Newsletter*, March 1974, p. 77. No. 2, inscribed on piece.)

1.   𝄢   2. *Lanier Meaders*

Mead, I.M. and Company. Summit County, Ohio. Around 1840 to around 1850. Made stoneware. There is also a piece made by this potter at the Ohio Ceramic Center, Zanesville, Ohio, with mark no. 3. The piece is a stoneware jug with a gray colored clay and blue lettering, "I.M. Mead and Co." (Marks: Robert Treichler, researcher of potters in Akron area.)

I.M. MEAD
PORTAGE CO.   2. I.M. MEAD
1. OHIO

Mear, Frederick/Boston Earthenware Factory. Boston, Massachusetts. Dated 1852 to 1858, by Ramsay, p. 188; and around 1840, by Thorn, p. 137, also in Boston. Mark is sometimes impressed. Made Rockingham, brownware, which was light in color. (Mark: Thorn, p. 137.)

FREDERICK MEAR

Medinger, Jacob. Montgomery County, Pennsylvania (near Neiffer). William Medinger, around 1850-1880, was followed by his son, Jacob Medinger, around 1880 to 1930. A picture of a bill dated March 10, 1926, for redware made by Jacob Medinger had his name as heading and **Limerick Pottery**. Made a lot of ware with mottled olive and satin black glazes. (Information: Ramsay, p. 172. Thorn, p. 137, shows a much different single signature for Jacob than the one I copied from the picture of a pie dish in Stradling, P. 32, as shown.)

I made this dish without a pie now try and make a pie without a dish
Jacob Medinger

Melick, H.H. Roseville, Ohio. Made stoneware around 1875, according to Thorn, p. 79. Thorn spells the name with two l's. At the Ohio Ceramic Center, near Zanesville, Ohio, is a gray piece of stoneware marked with Melick, spelled with one l.

**H H MELICK
ROSEVILLE, O.**

Menchhofer Pottery. Oak Ridge, Tennessee. 1972 to present (1985). Paul Menchhofer, studio potter, makes a complete variety of functional stoneware and porcelain as well as many one of a kind pieces. He is a member of the Southern Highlands Handicraft Guild and the Foothills Craftsmans Guild, and the Tennessee Artists and Craftsmans Association. He has won numerous awards. Paul signs some pieces with his signature as shown, but states he believes that the work should be the signature.

Paul Menchhofer

Mercer Pottery. Trenton, New Jersey. 1868 into 1930's. It was organized in 1868 with James Moses as head of the company. Barber lists this company as making ironstone or white granite, semi-vitreous and semi-porcelain products. The *1902-1903 Complete Directory* listed them as making porcelain and white granite, in dinner sets, toilet sets, short sets of odd dishes, druggists' supplies (such as mortars and pestles, etc.) and sanitary ware. Mercer Pottery was listed in the *Trenton City Directory* until 1937. I found no listing for them in 1937 or after that. But in the listings there were two Mercer factories after 1924. Mercer Porcelain, the second factory, lasted until 1938; there was no listing that year. In the *1931 Industrial Directory for the State of New Jersey*, Mercer Porcelain was listed as making electrical supplies and hardware and bathroom fixtures, located at Penn Avenue and Mulberry. Mercer Pottery was still listed as making general pottery in 1931 at 39 Muirheid Avenue. A Mercer Pottery advertisement in the *Crockery and Glass Journal*, September

9, 1875, showed white granite ware typical of the 1870's. The advertisement mentioned above was reprinted in *Antiques Monthly*, July 1976, p. 156. The double shield mark, formerly used by this company, was the same as that employed by the firms of Carr and Clark and Burgess and Campbell. It was also used at the New York City Pottery by Mr. Carr. When the International Pottery Company was organzied in 1879 by Carr and Clark, assisted by John and James Moses, they adopted the double shield. The same shapes were being made at the Mercer and International Potteries and the goods were interchangeable. Hence the same mark was used by each, the only difference being in the name printed beneath. In September of the same year, Messrs, Burgess and Campbell bought the interest of Carr and Clark and substituted their names beneath the trade-mark. Other marks were a globe impressed on white granite ware. The name of the pottery was impressed. (Information: directories as cited; and Barber, *Marks of American Potters*, p. 57. Marks: no. 1 filed for registration on August 20, 1928, claiming use since July 1, 1928, for use on semi-porcelain dinnerware and semi-porcelain hotel ware, decorated white semi-porcelain dinnerware and cream colored semi-porcelain dinnerware. The remainder of marks are from Barber, as cited.)

Meric Art Studios. East Liverpool, Ohio. In a 1931 *China, Glass and Lamps* magazine was an advertisement showing the logo pictured. The ad showed Meric Art Ware, all flower holders, one with a nude lady with raised design, on with hand painted flowers, etc. If they used a paper lable or a backstamp of any kind, it would probably be very similar to the logo pictured. In the *East Liverpool City Directories*, they were still listed in 1939 at 209 West Fourth Street. The pottery was not listed in 1941.

Merrimac Pottery Company. Newburyport, Massachusetts. 1897 to before 1908. Pottery was incorporated in 1897 as **Merrimac Ceramic Company** to make florists' ware and enameled tile. In 1902, name changed to Merrimac Pottery Company with the emphasis on decorative and glazed artware. Pieces were mostly hand thrown with superior glazes including enamels. For descriptions of the many complex types of fine art ware produced by Merrimac Pottery Company, see Evans, *Art Pottery in the United States*, pp. 168, 171. (Marks shown are a paper label and an impressed or incised marks as shown in Barber, *Marks of American Potters*, pp. 100, 101.)

E.H. Merrill. Springfield (Akron), Ohio. See Johnson, Whitmore and Co. for history. Early products were jugs, stone bottles, tobacco pipes, etc. (Mark: 1, Thorn, p. 138. Mark 2, Richard Stillinger, collector.)

1. E. H. MERRILL
    SPRINGFIELD
    O.

2. E. H. MERRILL & CO.
    AKRON, O.

Merritt Island Pottery. Merritt Island, Florida. 1936 to present (1985). Melvin Casper, assisted by Peggy Jamieson, owns and operates a pottery to make bas reliefs, fountains, tiles, garden statuary. Melvin studied at the Art Institute in Chicago, Illinois, under Eugene Deuch. His glazes are outstanding; some have a metallic finish. He uses a backstamp of his name in Chinese or Merritt Island in script as shown. (Information: Jenny B. Derwich and Dr. Mary Latos, p. 151. Mark: *Pottery Collector's Newsletter*, January, February, 1976, Vol. 5, No. 1, p. 10.)

Metcalf, Thomas D. Sunbury, Northumberland County, Pennsylvania. 1870 to 1889. This potter returned from the Civil War to Northumberland County in 1863. He was taxed or assessed as a potter from 1870 to 1889. He died in 1890. He made utilitarian stoneware with a stamped or impressed mark. (Information and impressed mark: Jeannette Lasansky, *Made of Mud*, pp. 37, 56.)

T.D. METCALF
SUNBURY, PA.

Metlox Potteries. Manhattan Beach, California. 1927 to present (1985). Founded by T.C. Prouty to make the ceramic part of neon signs. The name Metlox (Manufacturing Company) was derived from the metal oxide used in the signs. In 1934, Prouty bought out the Malinite Corp. to produce some solid-colored ware for the May Company. In 1938 the first tunnel kiln was built at Metlox. But the pottery hadn't really gotten heavily into dinnerware yet because World War II came along, and Metlox produced machine parts for the duration. In the article by Jack Chipman, "Discovering Metlox," *American Clay Exchange*, March 1983, pp. 12, 13, he tells us that Metlox hired a designer, Carl Romanelli, to design artware from the late 1930's until around World War II. The facsimile signature, "C. Romanelli," was impressed in the bases of figurines, Zodiac vases, Metlox miniatures. During the war, Metlox made parts for B-25 bombers and the production of the artware was cut. After the war, dinnerware became the main product. During 1946 and 1947, Prouty made some ware for National Silver. The list of discontinued patterns sent by the company started with the year 1941 and listed both Vernonware and Poppy Trail lines.

The real beginning of the Metlox Potteries dinnerware manufacture began when the plant was purchased by Evan K. Shaw in 1947; from the reorganization the success was determined. In 1958, Metlox bought the patterns and equipment from Vernon Kilns. (See Vernon Kilns.) In 1978, Evan Shaw was still the owner of Metlox, and working with Evan was his son and daughter, Ken and Melinda, also Melinda's husband, Kenneth Avery. At present (1985), Kenneth Avery is manager. Both Evan and his son are deceased. For such a large factory to remain in the hands of the family and to be so successful is unbelievable in this country. The "Poppytrail" line is made from original designs reproduced by American craftsman from the finest raw materials, then either cast or molded and fired at 2,100 degrees for 40 hours to make a clean, high-fired bisque. The decorations are then applied by hand and a signature number of the artist is added. A spray glaze is added and the piece refired at 1,875 degrees to seal the pattern under glaze which preserves the decoration for the life of the article. The glaze is hard and beautiful. The designs are timeless and will fit with any style of living. The colors used are gorgeous. The ingenuity and imagination that goes into the Metlox Potteries products have only been rivaled in a very few instances by any other American pottery. "Vernon Ware" is made by much the same careful process as "Poppy Trail." The glaze is porcelain strong, the styles cover a wide spectrum, including modern coupe shapes, luxuriously carved borders, and fluted edges with scalloped rims for the traditional, provincial, or Mediterranean-style home. Metlox Potteries will be recognized as one of our most outstanding potteries.

Metlox Potteries
Discontinued Patterns, 1941-1976

Vernonware

Accents	V611-614
Anytime	V830
Blue Fascination	V981
Blue Zinnia	V640
Butterscotch	V710
Caprice	V982
Castile	V910
Classic Antique	V680
Classic Flower	V670
Fancy Free	V860
Golden Amber	V621
Heavenly Days	V820
La Jolla	V622
Patrician White	V960
Petalburst	V620
Pink Lady	V940
Rose-A-Day	V870
Sherwood	V850
Sierra Flower	V620
Springtime	V760
Sun and Sand	V630
Tickled Pink	V810
Tisket-A-Tasket	V840
Town & Country	V720-750
Vernon Calypso	V626
Vernon Pacific Blue	V628
Vernon Pueblo	V631
Year Round	V880

Poppytrail

Apple	P160
Aztec	P330
Blueberry Provincial	P350
Blue Dahlia	P562
Blue Provincial	P120
California Fruit	P180
California Geranium	P450
California Palm	P540
California Rose	P570
California Tempo	P441-447
Cape Cod	P370
Capistrano	P360
Central Park	P270
Colonial Heritage	P380
Confetti	P430
Contempora	P340
Country Side	P280
Del Rey	P420
Flamenco Red Sc.	P577
Fleur De Lis	P150
Free Form	P310
Golden Fruit	P510
Golden Scroll	P430
Happy Time	P290
Impressions	P320-323
Indian Summer	P260
Indigo	P570
Jamestown	P480
La Casa Brown	P573
Luau	P460
Mardi Gras	P370
Mayan Necklace	P130
Mission Verde	P580
Mobile	P320
Monte Carlo	P210
Navajo	P470
Painted Desert	P530
Palm Springs	P410
Peach Blossom	P220

Peppertree	P520
Provincial Flower	P360
Provincial Rose	P550
Rooster Bleu	P380
Rooster Premium	P410
Shoreline	P230
Solid Colors	P360
Street Scene	P350
Tradition White	P164
Tropicana	P580
Yorkshire	P500

(Information: company furnished. Marks: Due to the importance of the factory I was very disappointed with the marks I have to show in this book. Repeated letters and telephone calls brought no more added information than I had been sent in the 1970's for Lehner, *American Kitchen and Dinner Wares*. I was assured however, that the single words taken from advertising brochures were at least a part of the mark as it was used. Also, Metlox didn't file registrations on nearly as many marks as some of the other big factories. The important thing to notice on the marks filed is the date from which the company claimed the marks were used. Mark no. 1, ''Metlox'' was filed August 28, 1931, claiming use since February 1928, for ceramic letters. So this would be the first mark used but not on dinnerware at this time. No. 2, ''Malinite'' wasn't filed until June 7, 1952, but was used since June 13, 1932, for molded ceramic bodies, namely dinnerware. It was filed in the name, Malinite Corporation, Los Angeles. No. 3, ''Yorkshire'' was filed November 1, 1937, claiming use only one month from October 1, 1937. No. 4, ''Poppy trail,'' (two words) was filed the first time on February 7, 1936, claiming use since March 24, 1934, for ceramic ware, namely tableware, kitchenware, vases, jardinieres, pots, bowls, flower holders, coasters and pet dishes. No. 5, ''Poppytrail,'' (one word) was filed again on November 13, 1959, claiming ''first used at least as early as 1934'' for ceramicware, such as dinnerware, kitchenware and miscellaneous serving dishes. No. 6, ''Vernon Ware,'' (two words) was filed December 7, 1959, claiming use since 1938 for dinnerware. No. 7, ''Camellia'' was filed September 4, 1946, claiming use since July 24, 1946, for earthenware dinnerware. No. 8, ''Colorstax'' was filed November 3, 1978, with first use June 25, 1978, for ceramic dinnerware. No. 9, Maxine Nelson, *Versatile Vernon Kilns*, p. 58. Nos. 10 through 22, from dishes. No. 23 was identified by Jack Chipman, ''The California Firing line,'' *American Clay Exchange*, January 1986, p. 3, as an exclusive line of kitchenware made by Metlox Potteries between 1935 and 1938. Padre Potteries (see that listing) also made a line of dinnerware named ''Mission,'' as listed in 1945 and 1946 *Crockery and Glass Journal Directory*. No. 24 is a recessed mark from Jo Cunningham, *American Dinnerware*, p. 38. The rest of the marks shown are from advertising brochures as discussed earlier in this section. May Department stores filed rights to ''Mission Bell.'' See that listing.)

1. METLOX

2. MALINITE

3. YORKSHIRE

4. Poppytrail

5. POPPYTRAIL

6. VERNON WARE

8. COLORSTAX

7.
Camellia

9. HEAVENLY DAYS
Vernon ware
U.S.A.

10.
VERNON WARE
BY
METLOX
MADE IN CALIFORNIA

11. MEDALLION RED
Poppytrail —METLOX
SAFE TO OVEN and
DISH WASHER • DURABLE
HAND • DECORATED
MADE IN CALIF. • USA.

12. HAND PAINTED
VINEYARD

Vernon ware
U.S.A.
safe in oven and dish washer
BY METLOX

13. PROVINCIAL
BLUE
HAND PAINTED

Poppytrail
PAT.
PEND.
CALIFORNIA MADE • METLOX

14.
Vernon ware
U.S.A.
use in oven and dishwasher

15. WOODLAND
GOLD
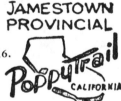
Poppytrail —METLOX
Safe in oven and
dishwasher durable
Hand decorated
Made in Calif • U.S.A

16. JAMESTOWN
PROVINCIAL
Poppytrail
CALIFORNIA
OVEN SAFE

17. PROVINCIAL
BLUE
Poppytrail
METLOX
Safe in oven and
dishwasher • Durable
Hand. Decorated
Made in Calif. • U.S.A.

18.
HAND-PAINTED VERNONWARE
Gigi
FREEZER • DISHWASHER • OVEN
MICROWAVE SAFE
METLOX POTTERIES • CALIF. USA
7-81

19. HAND-DECORATED
8-81
Poppytrail
QUAIL RIDGE
FREEZER DISHWASHER
OVEN • MICROWAVE
SAFE
MADE IN CALIFORNIA • USA • METLOX POTTERIES

20.
HAND CRAFTED
Poppytrail
ANTIQUE
GRAPE
DISHWASHER
OVEN • MICROWAVE
SAFE
MADE IN CALIFORNIA • USA • METLOX POTTERIES
8-81

21. GRAPE ARBOR
Poppytrail
—METLOX
Safe in oven and
dishwasher • Durable
Hand • Decorated
Made in Calif. • U.S.A.
870

22.
HAND-DECORATED
Poppytrail
SCULPTURED
DAISY
DISHWASHER
OVEN • MICROWAVE
SAFE
MADE IN CALIFORNIA • USA • METLOX POTTERIES
9-81

23.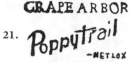
Mission
708
USA
Bell

24. *Mission Bell
California*

25. POPPY TRAIL
BY
METLOX
MADE IN CALIFORNIA
1175

26.
Vernon ware
FINE DINNERWARE

27.
Vernon ware

28. *Poppytrail* ARTWARE

29. *Poppytrail*
POTTERY

30. *Vernon* Monterey

31. *Poppytrail*
MADE IN CALIFORNIA

32. *Vernon* ware

33. *Vernon* OLD CATHAY
HAND-PAINTED

34. OVEN & DISHWASHER-SAFE

Vernon ware BOUQUET
HAND • PAINTED
MANUFACTURED in U.S.A. by

Vernon ware
DIVISION OF
METLOX POTTERIES

35. *Vernon* Antique Blue
HAND CRAFTED

36. *Vernon* Della Robbia

37.
Vernon ware
FINE DINNERWARE

38. *Vernon* ANTIQUA

 39.

40.

  41.

42.

  43.

44. **Poppytrail** ARTWARE

 Wildflower 45.

ARTWARE
46.

LOTUS
47.

48.

MACRAMÉ

49.  **TIFFANY**

 Geranium 50.

51. **Poppytrail** DINNERWARE

 52.

53. *Vernon Rose*®

Flower Basket 54.
HAND-PAINTED

55. BOUQUET
HAND PAINTED

Mesa 56.
HAND-PAINTED

57. *True Blue*

Nasturtium 58.

59. San Fernando

Vineyard 60.

Matilija

Fruit Basket
61.
(White Poppy)
62.

La Mancha
gold
63.

California
Brownstone 64.

Metropolis Bending Company. Metropolis, Illinois. Assigned this mark to Babee-Tenda License Corporation on July 11, 1958, claiming one year's used of the mark on feeding dishes.

BABEE-TENDA

Meyers Pottery. 52nd Street, Huntington Park, California. In business before 1933 to after 1948. Mearl C. Meyers made pottery dinnerware baking and cooking ware with colored glazes, art or decorative ware and garden pottery. They were listed as late as 1948 in the *China and Glass Red Book Directory*. They were not listed in the directories I had for the 1950's. (Marks: no. 1 shown was filed for registration on June 7, 1937, for use on dinnerware, vases, flower pots, urns and mixing bowls, claiming use since 1933. Mark no. 2 was found on a bright orange-red pottery mixing bowl, sent by reader.)

CALIFORNIA RAINBOW
1.

2.

Miali Pottery. El Monte, California. See listing for Various El Monte, California, Potteries.

Michaels and Company, Inc. Brooklyn, New York. Filed for registration of this mark on November 23, 1945, for use on crockery, earthenware and porcelain, namely, dinnerware, cups, saucers, plates, platters, dishes, pitchers, bowls and jugs, claiming use since October 16, 1945.

DINNER CLUB

Middle Earth Studio/Primus Studio. Princeton, Wisconsin. 1971 to present (1986). From 1971 to 1980 the name was Middle Earth Studio, when it was changed to Primus Studio to present. Potter, Robert Carlson, makes hand thrown, hand built, salt glazed, stoneware and porcelain pieces. He also makes Raku. For the past three and one-half years, he has worked with his wife and partner, Marilee Hall, using mark no. 4.

1.

2.

3.

4.

Middle Lane Pottery. East Hampton and Westhampton, New York. T.A. Brouwer, Jr. began experimenting with glazes in 1893 and opened pottery in 1894 in East Hampton. In 1903 he started in a new plant in Westhampton. It is very hard to date the ending of this pottery because Brouwer became involved in so many other things, such as lecturing, making concrete figures, etc. after 1911. In 1925 he did incorporate in state of New York, the **Ceramic Flame Company** for purpose of maintaining a factory, pottery, studio, store, office, etc. to manufacture and sell pottery. Brouwer died in 1932. His corporation wasn't dissolved until 1946. Evans, p. 176, said marked ware of the Ceramic Flame Company was unknown. Marks incised. (Information: Evans, pp. 173-176; Kovel, pp. 6-8. Marks: nos. 1, 2, 3, Evans, p. 176; no. 2, Jervis, *Pottery, Glass and Brass Salesman*, June 25, 1914, p. 17; nos. 1, 2, Kovel, p. 7.)

1.

2.

3.

Midhurst China Company. New York, New York. Company was listed in the 1952 *Crockery and Glass Journal Directory* as distributors of Hallcraft by Eva Zeisel, a dinnerware manufactured by Hall China Company. Also, at the same address, 129 5th Avenue in New York City, was a Midhurst Importing Corporation.

Midland Terra Cotta Company. Chicago, Illinois. 1910 to around 1939. The company made architectural ceramics such as terra cotta columns, pilasters, medallions and various ornamental pieces for buildings. (Information and mark: Sharon S. Darling, *Chicago Ceramics and Glass*, p. 187.)

MIDLAND
TERRA COTTA CO.
CHICAGO, ILL.
SAMPLE No

Midwest Pottery. Morton, Illinois. 1940-1944. See listing, Rapp Brothers various Illinois potteries for history on Midwest Pottery. Also Cliftwood Potteries for label similar to this one. The label shown reads, ''A Cliftwood Creation by Midwest of Morton, Illinois.'' Midwest Pottery followed the Cliftwood Potteries and were still trading on their name with this label. See the listing already mentioned for history on Cliftwood Potteries also. Mark is a paper label shown in Doris and Burdell Hall, *Morton's Potteries: 99 Years*, p. 85.)

Midwest Potteries, Inc.

Midwest Pottery Company. South Milwaukee, Wisconsin. Around 1945 to around middle 1950's. In 1940, the Rapp Brothers had sold the Cliftwood Art Pottery which was purchased by three Peoria businesmen who renamed the plant the Midwest Pottery Company. (See the listing, the Rapp Brothers various Illinois potteries.) In 1941 the plant was sold again to Sherman Deutch of Canton, Illinois. The Rapps continued to manage and operate the plant for a while until 1941, the manager was R.G. Dunn. Deutch went to the army in W.W. II. In 1944 the Midwest Pottery of Morton, Illinois, burned to the ground. Apparently, Sherman Deutch operated another pottery by the name Midwest Pottery Co. in South Milwaukee, Wisconsin, because in the 1945 and 1946 *Crockery and Glass Journal Directories*, we find such a listing with Sherman Deutch as owner and R.G. Dunn as manager. This plant made china art pottery, specialties and florist's ware. One line listed in the 1946 directory was the "Kron" line. By 1952 in the *China and Glass Red Book Directory*, Midwest Potteries Company in South Milwaukee, was listed as selling a "Cliftwood" line, and the "Kron" line of American originals. They were still listed in 1953, but not in 1954. (Mark: sent by Rena London, pottery researcher and writer.)

Kron

Miles, Lewis J. Pottery. Edgefield District, South Carolina. Dave, a slave, was trained by Abner Landrum and worked in the pottery of Lewis J. Miles, which was located on Mile's plantation, Stoney Bluff, in the Edgefield District. Dave threw some of the largest hand thrown production pieces made in that period; some were over 40 gallons in volume. The pottery made alkaline glazed utilitarian stoneware jugs, crocks and storage jars. The "LM" in the mark is for Lewis Miles. Baddler was another man who worked at the pottery. Two jars were marked, "Dave and Baddler." Dave put little verses on a few of his containers. Dave died around 1863 and worked to that date. (Information: *Early Decorated Stoneware of Edgefield District of South Carolina*, published by Greenville County Museum of Art, p. 17. Pictures of Dave's jugs may be seen in staff written, "Neat Piece, Plain Style Furniture of the 19th Century Georgia," *Early American Life*, p. 58, and John A. Burrison, *Brothers in Clay*, p. 21.)

Jan 29 Lm 1859
Dave

Milk Farm. Dixon, California. Company filed for registration of this mark on January 24, 1951, for use on gift shop items, such as earthenware and porcelain dishes, cups, saucers, trays, platters, salt and pepper shakers, bowls, vases, jars and pots, claiming use since September 1, 1942.

Miller, Benjamin C. Baltimore, Maryland. Miller was a stoneware potter who worked at the factory of William H. Amos in Baltimore, in the early 1830's. The factory of William H. Amos operated around 1814 to 1840. (Information and mark: Henry Franced du Pont Winterthur Museum. Mark found on a spool-shaped sander with incurving sides and flaring rim at base. Made of gray clay with cobalt blue splotches over a gray color.)

B C Miller
Maker
Sept 1st 1830
W H Amos

Miller, John Brough. Argyle, Texas. 1964 to present (1985). On the line for a beginning date, J. Brough Miller put 1964. That was also the year that he gave for starting to teach at the Texas Woman's University in Denton, Texas, where he still is a professor of art. The only educational information included was that he was a student of Maija Grotell for two years after 1962. I became aware of this potter from a picture in the book, *Texas Pottery*, by Sherry B. Humphreys and Johnell L. Schmidt, p. 41, showing a beautiful stoneware vase by Mr. Miller, with mark no. 1 as shown. (Mark no. 2 was sent by Miller.) I am sure this is a very important potter, and I'm sorry I was not able to obtain more information. Mr. Miller makes wheel thrown art pottery pieces, some with hand carved decorations. His philosophy as given in the potter's own words for the book cited and is as follows: "Ceramics to me is the synthesis of aesthetics and function. Studio pottery is an art form having the same nonverbal elements as painting and sculpture–line, form, color and texture. In addition, ceramics is a general expression of man's achievement over earth, fire, and water."

1. *Brough TWU*   2. *Brough*

Miller and Rhoads, Inc. Richmond, Virginia. Filed December 10, 1951, for use on this mark on dinnerware of china, earthenware and pottery, claiming use since April 1917.

THE SHOPPING CENTER

Miller, George W. Strasburg, Virginia. Very late 1800's. George Miller purchased the pottery from William H. Lehew and Company (see that listing), and employed George R. Davidson and Theophilus Grim to operate it. The pottery made utilitarian stoneware. When Grim retired, Alexander Fleet became the potter. Fleet had learned potting with the Bell Pottery (see that listing). The partnership became Miller and Fleet. There was also a Miller and Woodard listed in Strasburg. Rice and Stoudt, as cited, gave no particular dates for these potters. Also, in Smith, p. 23, as cited, was a stoneware piece marked "Kenner, Davidson and Miller." It seems Miller, the owner, worked in partnership with whatever potter was doing the throwing. W.B. Kenner was listed in Strasburg just before 1900. (Information: A.H. Rice and John B. Stoudt, *The Shenandoah Pottery*, p. 81. Marks: Elmer Smith, *Pottery, A Utilitarian Folk Craft*, p. 23.)

GEO W. MILLER STRASBURG   KENNER, DAVIDSON & MILLER ST RASBURG, VA.

Miller, George, Family Pottery. Newport, Pennsylvania. George Miller came to the Newport, Pennsylvania, area in 1838 and purchased property on which he started a pottery to make utilitarian stoneware. In 1860 his two sons, George and Michael, 22 and 16 years of age were listed as working with George. Several other potters worked with Miller during that period according to Lasansky, p. 38. Five of George's 10 children also worked in the pottery eventually but Michael and Theophilus were the ones who continued in the pottery after their father died in 1864. In 1877, Henry Markel became the owner and the two brothers continued to work with him, and the name of the pottery stayed the same. In 1890 the pottery was still listed in the state business directory, and in 1893 a newspaper article said the plant was working to full capacity. But by 1908 the pottery was closed and the kiln torn down. For a long and detailed account of the various workers and members of the family associated with the pottery see Lasansky, as cited. (Information and marks: Jeannette Lasansky, *Made of Mud*, pp. 38, 39, 56. No. 1 stamped mark. No. 2 stenciled mark.)

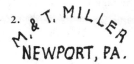

Miller, Marcellus S. Norfolk, Virginia. Filed for registration of this mark on April 14, 1950, for use on plates made of china, claiming use since February 20, 1950.

Millheim Pottery/William S. Maize/H.H. Weiser. New Berlin, Centre County, Pennsylvania. William was the son of redware potter, John Maize. John's father, Adam, was also a potter. These men worked in Centre County, Pennsylvania, between the years 1829 until after 1853 making redware. William worked at the Millheim Pottery after 1847 which operated from 1806 until 1874. The mark shown is not complete. The full mark was "W.S. Maize and H.H. Weiser," on an unglazed stovepipe lid. Only the Maize name showed in the picture. There was a double line around the stovepipe. Weiser worked at the Millheim Pottery in the early 1870's before the pottery closed in mid 1870's. (Information and mark: Jeannette Lasansky, *Redware Pottery, 1780-1904*, pp. 26, 27.)

Millington (Richard), and Astbury (John). Trenton, New Jersey. Started in 1853 on Carroll Street in Trenton, New Jersey. By 1859 the firm was **Millington, Astbury and Poulson.** By 1861 they were making whiteware goods. Barber shows a pitcher with a Civil War scene modeled by Josiah Jones and made at this factory, then decorated by Edward Lycett who had a decorating shop on Greene Street. See various Maddock Potteries listing for history. (Information and impressed marks: Barber, *Pottery and Porcelain of the U.S.*, p. 452.)

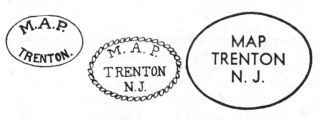

Miltonvale Potteries. Miltonvale, Kansas. Started making pottery April 1949 until around 1956. Miltonvale was offered in nine colors and carried by 150 dealers in 15 states. They made decorative pieces, dogs, flower holders, candleholders, vases, etc. at the rate of 1,000 pieces per day. (Information: Cox, Susan, "Miltonvale Potteries," *American Clay Exchange*, January 1982, p. 6. Mark: on pottery piece.)

SS

MILTONVALE

Miner, William. Symmes Creek, Ohio. Around 1869. Made stoneware. Mark impressed. (Ramsay, p. 231, dated this potter from 1869-1883. Information and mark: Thorn, p. 139.)

MINER

Minich, Lorna. Ada, Ohio. 1963 to present. Studio potter, makes functional stoneware and Raku. Lorna received an associate B.S. degree in applied sciences from Fenn College, she studied with Cleo Ferguson at Ohio Northern University and has attended numerous workshops and conferences. She is a member of Ohio Designer Craftsmen, the Ohio Arts and Crafts Guild and the Black Swamp Potters Guild. She listed seven juried shows and 12 juried fairs she has exhibited at in Lima, Columbus at Ohio State University, Athens, Mansfield, Akron, and Cleveland, at the Museum of Art. She also listed seven invitational shows in as many cities in Ohio. She has won several awards, first places and honorable mentions at many of the shows. Her work may be seen at the Mansfield Art Center, Mansfield, Ohio; the Findlay Art League in Findlay; and the Gallery in Bucyrus.

Lorna   *LM*

Minnesota Pottery Company. Near Red Wing, Minnesota. Around 1870 to around 1875. Pottery started by David Hallem to make salt glazed stoneware crocks, jugs, etc. of gray white clay with inside covered by Albany slip. Pieces had stenciled name in cobalt blue. Hallem worked for the Red Wing Union Stoneware Company after his pottery went bankrupt. (Information: Lyndon C. Viel, *The Clay Giants Book I*, p. 9. Mark: Viel, *Clay Giants Book II*, p. 26.)

Minnesota Stoneware Company. Red Wing, Minnesota. 1883 to 1906. Minnesota Stoneware Company, North Star Stoneware and Red Wing Stoneware formed a selling agency called **Union Stoneware Company** in 1894. The three potteries remained legally independent and separately incorporated until 1906. In the Lyndon Viel book cited, is a reprint of an article from *The Advance Sun* newspaper, September 12, 1894, explaining the organization. (Also, see the listing Union Stoneware Company.) Minnesota Stoneware Company made stoneware, some with Albany slip and some salt glazed. In 1906, the Minnesota Stoneware Company merged with the Redwing Stoneware Company to form the Red Wing Union Stoneware Company (see that listing). (Information: Lyndon Viel, *The Clay Giants Book II*, p. 92. Marks: A variety of marks for this company are shown on the bottoms and sides of various pieces in Lyndon Viel's book cited, pp. 45 to 65, and also David A. Newkirk, *A Guide to Red Wing Markings*, pp. 12 to 18.)

MINNESOTA STONEWARE CO.
RED WING MINN.

MINN. STONEWARE CO.

Miramar of California. Los Angeles, California. This company was established in 1952, and in 1978 they answered my request for information saying they did not manufacture pottery and gave no further information. In the 1977 *California Manufacturers Register*, they were listed as employing 72 people to make plastic holders. Apparently, Miramar did manufacturer pottery when they started in business, and they were still listed in the pottery section of various directories through the 1960's as making planters, casseroles, servers, warmers, lazy susans, lamps and ashtrays. (Marks: inscribed or incised on pieces.)

Mitteldorfer Straus. New York, New York. Started 1907. Distributors. Filed for a claim on mark no. 1 on March 12, 1928, claiming use since January 1913. On mark no. 2 they

filed March 12, 1928, claiming use since January 1928, on mark no. 3 they filed February 2, 1929, claiming use since February 15, 1928. These marks were to be used for pottery, china candy dishes, porcelain plates and dishes. The P.V. trademark shown was put on a set of plates with scenes from operas on them. These were supposed to be made for a time in the U.S. around World War II. The ''P.V.'' mark was filed for registration on September 14, 1950, claiming use since February 15, 1928. Marks 1 and 2 were probably used on foreign ware.

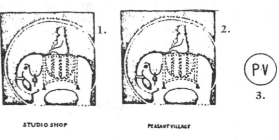

STUDIO SHOP   PEASANT VILLAGE

Modern China Company. See Americana Art China Company, Sebring, Ohio.

Moma Ceramics. See Tierra Royal Potteries, Inc.

Monarch Dinnerware Company. East Liverpool, Ohio. This company was listed as wholesalers of dinnerware in 1939 *Ohio Directory of Manufacturers*. They were also a decorating company. (See that listing for marks.) E.S. Carson at Homer Laughlin China Company, said the Monarch Dinnerware Company bought blanks from them to decorate. (Mark from Quality Stamp Company.)

Monefeldt, Jens. Hayward, California. Company filed for registration of this mark on October 28, 1958, for cotton dispenser in the form of a porcelain bunny with the cotton serving as its tail.

The Cotton Bunny

Monmouth Pottery Company. Monmouth, Illinois. Organized 1893 to 1906. Became plant no. 1 of Western Stoneware Company in 1906. See Western Stoneware. Production ceased in this building in 1930, but the office, garden and salesroom were used until 1954 by Western Stoneware Company, according to Jim Martin, co-author of *Monmouth Western Stoneware*. Early products were spongeware and salt glazed, blue stenciled crocks, jugs, etc. with Albany slip inside. Maple Leaf brand of stoneware was made at plant no. 1, as shown in a 1926 catalog. Ramsay lists a Western

Stoneware Company operating in Monmouth, Illinois, from 1870 to 1890. Jim Martin said by letter that Ramsay is in error, and no doubt Ramsay is. In 1926, Western Stoneware Company introduced a line of artware with the Maple Leaf Monmouth Pottery mark similar to those shown. The line was called Monmouth Pottery Artware. If the maple leaf does not have "Co." on it, it is the Western Stoneware mark. See Western Stoneware Company marks. (Marks: nos. 1, 2, 3, 4, Deb and Gini Johnson, p. 107; no. 5, Barber, *Marks of American Potters*, p. 162; no. 6, sent by letter from Dave Newkirk, co-author of *Red Wing Dinnerware*. The rest of the marks were either sent by letter from Jim Martin or are pictured in the book by Jim Martin and Bette Cooper, *Monmouth Western Stoneware*, pp. 12-27.)

1.
Paper sticker, blue and white.

2.
Raised letters.

3.
Paper sticker, blue and silver.

4.

5.

6.

7.

8.

9.

10.

11.

12.

13.

14.

15.

16.

17.

18.

Monon Center, Inc. Greensboro, Pennsylvania. Filed for registration of this mark on April 17, 1980, for use on hand thrown earthenware pottery, claiming use since April 1, 1976.

Monsarrat Pottery. Friendsville, Tennessee. 1978 to present. Studio potter, Allen Monsarrat makes beautiful functional stoneware. He graduated from the Memphis Academy of Arts in 1977. The mark with Monsarrat in a circle is done in ironoxide of all flat bottomed pieces. "MP" is stamped on tumblers, mugs and bowls.

Monterey Art Pottery. Monterey, California. Around 1948. This pottery made a product called Monterey Jade which looks almost like glass until one looks at the clay on the bottom. Shades of blues and greens create a ware that looks like it should be made into jewelry. In Derwich and Latos, *Dictionary Guide to U.S. Pottery and Porcelain*, p. 153, there are no dates, but there is a discussion about how the ware is made. They say it is molded pottery, bisque fired for 8 hours to 2,000 degrees; several applications of glaze is added and fired again. I didn't have very many California directories, but I found the Monterey Art Pottery listed in 1948 with only a post office box number in the *Manufactures Directory of California* but they were not listed in 1951 or 1955. (Marks: no. 1, on a baby shoe decorative piece sent by Frances Andrews. Mark 2, incised on two beautiful, rather tall cups.)

MONTEREY 1.
Art Pottery
Monterey, Calif

2. Montery Jade

Monticello. Albermarle County, Virginia. Since 1954, a gift shop has been maintained for tourists at the site of Monticello, the home of Thomas Jefferson, third president of the United States. The impressed mark shown has been used on some pieces made there. English pieces at present are marked in ink, "Thomas Jefferson Memorial Foundation." Some hand thrown studio pottery pieces are marked, "Monticello."

Moore, John Hudson Company. Morris Plains, New Jersey. According to Dorothy Lawless in "Those Jolly Sportsman Mugs," *Spinning Wheel*, December 1968, p. 28, the John Hudson Moore Company and their successors, The Lambert Company, sold shaivng mugs with marks very similar to those shown in the 1950's. They were made by a New Jersey pottery. the mugs came with 22 different designs representing all sorts of occupations, including farmer, peddler, doctor, barber, engineer, etc.

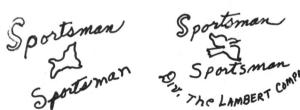

Moore, Nichols and Company. Williamsport, Pennsylvania. 1877-1879. Joseph Nichols (formerly of the Sipe Pottery, see that listing), Logan Moore and David P. Hobart formed a partnership to make stoneware for a couple of years 1877 to 1879. Moore and Young left town and the venture ended. Pieces were pictured in Lasansky, p. 31, with a long bodied lion and another with a man's head with a huge nose. She said there was another with a primitive eagle facing frontward with a shield as it's body. (Information and impressed mark: Jeannette Lasansky, *Made of Mud*, pp. 29, 31, 54.)

MOORE NICHOLS& CO.
WILLIAMSPORT, PA.

Moore, Walter B., Inc. West Lafayette, Ohio. Filed for registration on this mark January 24, 1939, claiming use since November 8, 1938, to be used on hollowware of porcelain. The mark is found on well vitrified coffee pots.

Moore, W.T. Middlebury (Akron), Summit County, Ohio. 1850-1870. The picture of a beautiful jug with floral slip decoration in Guilland, pp. 242, 243, does not show the "e"

on the name Moore, but Guilland has Moor(e) in the text. Also, Ramsay, p. 231, lists an Alvin S. Moore in 1850-1870, in Tallmadge, which is also a part of Akron now. There is probably a connection between the two I couldn't establish.

W.T. MOOR
MIDDLEBURY SUMMIT CO.
OHIO

Moravian Pottery and Tile Works. Doylestown, Pennsylvania. 1912 to 1956, and as a museum from 1969 to present. Henry Chapman Mercer was born in 1856 in Buck County, Pennsylvania. He studied law at the University of Pennsylvania. He became curator of American and prehistoric archaeology at the museum of the University of Pennsylvania. He was also editor of *American Naturalist* in 1893. While searching for tools used by the old potters, Mercer became interested in the potter's art. He built a workshop on the family estate in 1898. In 1912 he built the Moravian Pottery and Tile Works in Doylestown when his little workshop at his home burned. According to E.A. Barber, *Marks of American Potters*, p. 35, he used common red clay from the vicinity, covered with heavy glaze. He decorated the tile in the fashion of the old iron stove plates and earthenware made by Pennsylvania Germans such as the conventionalized tulip, etc. He made sgraffito designs and used some of the old Pennsylvania-German inscriptions. By 1904 he had made sinear glazed, modeled, sgraffito and slip decorated tiles, according to Barber. In 1967 the Buck's County Commissioners purchased the old Moravian Pottery and Tile Works, renovated it and opened the bulding as a museum in 1969. By 1974 the old Mercer molds and equipment were in use in making tile again. They produce tiles as close to those of Mercer as they can in many designs, but their actual output is small. (Information: Duke Coleman, "Henry Chapman Mercer," *American Art Pottery*, January 1979, p. 1; also Ann S. Bland, "Mercer Museum Pennyslvania Wonder," *Collector's News*, August 1977, pp. 14, 15. Marks: nos. 1, 2, stamped or impressed marks in Barber, as cited, p. 35. No. 3, Ramsay; no. 4, a stylized "MOR" and the year of manufacture is stamped on the souvenir tile of recent manufacture or "Mercer" and the date is also used.)

MORAVIAN 1.  3. 4.

Morgan (Matt) Art Pottery. Cincinnati, Ohio. Organized in 1882; incorporated in Jaunary 1883 to the end of 1884. Matt Morgan had worked in the pottery business in Spain before coming to America. His partner in Cincinnati was George Ligowsky, inventor of clay pigeons used for shooting purposes. In 1883 they made Moresque-type pottery with a Spanish accent. Later ware resembled early Rookwood, because some of the Rookwood artists produced art work for the Matt Morgan Pottery. Matt Morgan was a cartoonist in England. He did a series of cartoons for *London Fun*, and *London Punch* magazines. Frank Leslie urged him to come to this country. Morgan was an accomplished artist and designer. When the company was incorporated and placed on a commercial basis, it didn't last long. It failed by the end of 1884. But in its short existance the company made some beautiful pottery. (Information: Lois Lehner, *Ohio Pottery and Glass*, pp. 30-31; also, Duke Coleman, "Matt Morgan, More than a Potter," *American Art Pottery*, November 1977, p. 18. Marks: E.A. Barber, *Marks of American Potters*, p. 126.)

N.J.H.

(FOR N.J. HIRSCHFIELD)

Morgan Belleek China Company. Canton, Ohio. Started in 1923 as the **Rea China Company.** Changed name to Morgan Belleek Company in 1924. In 1929 the company merged with The American China Corporation which closed because of the depression. This company made Morgan Belleek, a thin eggshell like china with a high fired body and beautiful iridescence obtained by means of metallic washes. Morgan Belleek Company employed about 30. The name Morgan was added to the Belleek for William Morgan, first production man at the company. Morgan Belleek Company also made semivitreous porcelain and other pottery products, plain and decorated. A set of cobalt blue trimmed Morgan Belleek cost $1,200 new in 1930. (Information: Heald, Edward T., "The American Way of Life," *The Stark County Story*, vol. 4, pt. 3, Columbus, Ohio: State of Ohio publisher, 1902, p. 114. Marks: taken from patent reports sent by Linda Cleveland. No. 1 patented, December 15, 1924, for crockery, earthenware and porcelain. No. 2 patented September 20, 1927, for chinaware pottery, semivitreous porcelain. Claimed use of mark since September 1, 1926. No. 3 used since December 19, 1927; patent granted January 6, 1928. No. 4 used since December 19, 1927 and patent granted January 6, 1928, for products already mentioned.)

D. Morgan. New York, New York. Around 1794-1804 (Thorn, p. 139). Ramsay, p. 197 dated this very early potter around 1806. Made stoneware. (Mark: Thorn, p. 139.)

D. MORGAN

N YORK

Morgan, Thomas. Baltimore, Maryland. Very early 1800's to 1837. Made stoneware. (Information: John Ramsay, *American Potters and Pottery*, p. 163.)

ON SIDE OF JUG

ON BOTTOM

Morgan maker

Pitt Street Balt

1823

Morgantown Pottery. Morgantown, West Virginia. Started before 1785 until sometime after 1890. James Thompson took over the pottery around 1800 from a man named Foulke. Later his son, Greenland Thompson, ran the pottery. Barber states slip ware and lead glazed pottery were made there in very early years. Later, stoneware was decorated with applied ornaments made in moulds. The glazes range from lustrous yellow to manganese black. Mark impressed. (Information and mark: Barber, *Mark of American Potters*, p. 149 and *Pottery and Porcelain of U.S.*, p. 544. See Webster, p. 46, for tools used by this pottery which are now at the Smithsonian Institution.)

MORGANTOWN

Morley and Company. See Wellsville China Company for information. (Marks: Barber, *Marks of American Potters*, p. 127.)

Morris, Dwight, China. East Palestine, Ohio. 1939 to 1982. The plant operated from 1941 to early 1982 in the same location. Dwight Morris was a nationally known porcelain designer and modeler. He died in December 1982, and the operation ceased shortly thereafter. Dwight sculptured items to be mass produced for S. and H. Stamps, White Owl Cigars, Black Velvet Whiskey, Seagrams and other businesses in need of ceramic items in the commercial field. For many years, Dwight Morris China and Kingwood Ceramics worked together to produce the items. (See the Kingwood Ceramics listing.) At Mt. Vernon, Fairfax County, Virginia, George Washington's home is a gift shop. For years, Dwight Morris shipped them 4,000 pieces of ware annually between 1950 and 1970. (See the Mt. Vernon listing for marks.) Dwight also designed for other china companies such as Mayer China Company. For his own trade he produced: porcelain artware, birds, animals, figurines, vases, pitchers, etc. Trademark was an eagle with raised wings and a large "M" between the wings and "Dwight Morris Porcelain," under the eagle. Earlier pieces had the name engraved on the bottom of ware. (Information: Grace C. Allison, "The Dwight Morris Porcelain Company, East Palestine, Ohio," *American Clay Exchange*, May 1985, pp. 4, 5; and letters from the company in 1977.)

M

Dwight Morris Porcelains

Dwight Morris

Morrison, Inc. Mobile, Alabama. Filed for registration of mark 1 on July 12, 1982, claiming use since July 1980, for china for the table. Mark 2 was found on a hotel ware sauce dish.

MORCO

1.

2.

282

Morton Ceramic Tile Company. See Morton Pottery Company. (Mark shown from picture of a mark in Doris and Burdell Hall, *Morton's Potteries: 99 Years*, p. 86.)

MOR·TILE
48   USA

Morton Earthenware Company. Morton, Illinois. 1915-1917. See listing, Rapp Brothers various Illinois potteries.

Morton Pottery Company. Bloomington Street (now Jefferson Street), Morton, Illinois. 1922-1976, first kiln fired July 7, 1923. The Morton Pottery Company was founded by the sons of Andrew Rapp, one of the original founders of the Rapp Brothers Brick and Tile Company. The Morton Pottery Company purchased a part of the Morton Corporation on Bloomington Street and added a new plant to that building. Also, this was not the same pottery as the Morton Pottery Works. (See the listing Rapp Brothers Various Morton Potteries for Morton Pottery Works.) Before the pottery could really get going, a fire broke out in the Morton Corporation in October which completely destroyed the office building, but the plant part of pottery was saved. Morton Pottery Company sold products made at Cliftwood Art Potteries during the period that Morton Pottery Company was being organized. In 1926 the Morton Pottery brought out the Pilgrim line and produced it for one year only. A second major fire halted the Pilgrim production when the main building and warehouses were destroyed. The next line was the Amish Pottery line brought out in 1929. Morton Pottery Company made utilitarian type of ware. Not until the late 1930's did they bring out a novelty line. They worked very closely through the years with Cliftwood Art Pottery which made the decorative ware and Morton Pottery Company made the utilitarian ware. Some political items were made at Morton Pottery Company. See Doris and Burdell Hall, *Morton's Potteries: 99 Years*, Morton, Illinois: privately printed, 1981, pp. 53-83, for pictures and discussions of products made. In 1956, Morton Pottery added ceramic tile in 12 colors and bathroom fixtures to their line, operating the Morton Ceramic Tile Company, a subsidiary of the Morton Pottery Company. Tiles were marked "Mor-Tile." In 1967, Morton Pottery Company produced a line for Sears and Roebuck, called "The Sears Vincent Price National Treasures Collection," consisting of early American designs in food mold, pitchers, bowls, canister sets, potato mashers, etc. in a brown Rockingham type glaze or blue spatter on white. The line was advertised by Sears in 1967 and 1968 catalogues. In 1969, the pottery was sold to Ronald Cowan and William York who continued to use the name Morton Pottery. These owners filed for voluntary bankruptcy in 1971 and after a great deal of legal maneuvering, the pottery was sold to AFK Industries that same year. AFK Industries sold the pottery to Rival Mfg. Company of Kansas City, Missouri, in

1972. Inserts for crock pots and crock plates for Rival's fast cooker were made there until 1976. The building was torn down in 1979. (Information: Doris and Burdell Hall, *Morton's Potteries: 99 Years*, Morton, Illinois: privately printed, 1981, pp. 53-83. Marks: No. 1-4 from Hall's book as cited, p. 86. No. 5 was filed by Morton Pottery Company in June 1938 for use on pottery ware namely teapots, bowls, casseroles and plates, claiming use since April 15, 1928. No. 6, drawn copy of paper label taken from picture sent by the Halls. No. 7, *China, Glass and Tableware Directory* for 1967. No. 8 was identified by the Halls as a Morton Pottery mark used in the late 1960's, as was no. 9. The Halls said after the National Treasure's Collection failed for Sears, the pottery couldn't use the Vincent Price mark so they used these two marks so items could be identified on the line by the workers. Few pieces will be found with these marks. No. 8 is incised and was found on a planter. No. 9 is a stamped mark. Cookie jars and other pieces had these marks. However, few pieces will be found with these marks. The M.P. mark could very easily be taken or a McCoy mark. "Lincoln Beauty Ware" was another Morton Pottery mark used on cookie jars. Marks and information for marks, 10, 11, were also sent by Halls. No. 10 was unusual because it had the town name as part of the mark. No. 11 was used between 1928 and 1932, according to the Halls. Helmco, Inc. was owned by Grover C. Helm, and based in Bloomington, Illinois. No. 10 found on an ashtray and no. 11 on bottom of one quart stoneware jar.

Morton Pottery Works. Morton, Illinois. 1878-1915. See listing, Rapp Brothers Various Illinois Potteries. (Marks: No. 1, 2, Doris and Burdell Hall, *Morton's Potteries: 99 Years*, p. 86. Mark 3, Don and Carol Raycraft, *Decorated Country Stoneware*, p. 71. Notice backwards S. No. 4, impressed mark sent by Hall's by letter.

1. MORTON POTTERY WORKS

2. MORTON POTTERY WORKS

3. MORTON POTTERY WORKZ

4. M P W

Mosaic Tile Company. Zanesville, Ohio. 1894 to 1967. This company was incorporated in September 1894 and employed 30 people. Among the incorporators were Karl Langenback and H.C. Mueller of the American Encaustic Tiling Company, Ltd. (see that listing). Four new brick buildings were built. The work "Mosaic" means inlaid. The company started by making floor tile, but Mueller and Lagenback hoped to specialize in the manufacture of inlaid mural tile. An example of the Mosaic panels made by this company was the entrance to the St. Nicholas church in Zanesville, Ohio, which depicts the landing of Columbus. By 1925 the plant was employing 1,250 people. A warehouse and branch office were established in New York City as early as 1901. Later, warehouses and sales agencies in Los Angeles, San Francisco, Chicago, Detroit and Boston were added. In 1907 and during World War I, William Shinnick directed important expansion at Mosaic until he died in 1923. By 1920 tile made in Zanesville covered the floors of many large buildings and hotels across the United States. In 1922, Mosaic began making pastel shades of wall tile with a matt finish. In 1920 Mosaic Tile Company acquired the Atlantic Tile Manufacturing Company of Matawan, New Jersey. In 1935 the Carlyle Tile Company of Ironton, Ohio, was purchased by Mosaic. In 1937, Mosaic acquired controlling interest of the General Tile Corporation in El Segundo, California. One of the most outstanding jobs done by Mosaic Tile in early 1940's was the manufacture of two large Faience decorated panels for the Will Rogers Memorial at Fort Worth, Texas, depicting the development of Texas in panels 120' long by 7½' high. The plant closed in 1967. They had stopped making faience tile in the 1950's, and couldn't compete with foreign competition on the miscellaneous pottery products they had tried to produce. (Information: Norris Schneider, "Mosaic Largest U.S. Tile Plant." *Zanesville Times Signal*, September 10, 1944 (no page no.). Marks: no. 1, E.A. Barber, *Marks of American Potters*, p. 134; nos. 2-3, Danny Brown, "Constructing a Collection Tile by Tile," *American Clay Exchange*, April 1983, p. 4; nos. 4-5, marks on tile; no. 6 from sale catalogue for Garth's Auction Barn, Delaware, Ohio.)

1.

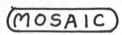
2.

3.

TRADE MARK

THE MOSAIC TILE COMPANY
ZANESVILLE, OHIO
4. NEW YORK
N.Y.

5.
MOSAIC MADE IN USA

6.
MOSAIC

Moses, Grandma, Properties, Inc. New York, New York. Filed for registration of mark one on October 4, 1950, claiming use since June 1, 1950, for china dishes. The consent of Mrs. Anna Mary Robertson Moses, the well-known primitive painter, often referred to as "Grandma Moses," had been obtained by applicant and was made of record in the application. Mark 2 was also filed with the famous artist's consent on March 18, 1952, claiming use since June 1, 1950, for the same article. In the August 1950 *Crockery and Glass Journal Magazine*, p. 70, an advertisement told that Atlas China Company in New York City, decorated Grandma Moses plates and Vincent Lippe distributed them. In the 1970's Syracuse China Company and Ridgewood China Company made some of the plates. In 1980, the Calhoun Collector's Society issued a four plate set.

1. *Anna mary Robertson moses*

2. A GRANDMA MOSES PRODUCT

Moss, David L. and Company. New York, New York. In the 1965 *China and Glass Tableware Red Book Directory*, this company advertised to various decorators of china and glass that David L. Moss and Company sold quality products with the finest English genuine ceramic tile. The mark shown was in the 1967 *Gift and Tableware Reporter Directory*. These tiles are included here because they could have been decorated by many United States decorators.

Mount Clemens Pottery. Mount Clemens, Michigan. 1915 to late 1987. Ground breaking for the building of Mount Clemens Pottery of Mount Clemens, Michigan, took place in May 1914, and by January 1915, the pottery was making its first shipments. Charles Doll served as general manager of the company from the time it started until 1962, when he retired. He was succeeded by one of his sons, Charles E. Doll, Jr., with another of his sons, J. Randolph Doll as assistant manager. By 1964, the company was turning out 240,000 pieces of dinnerware per day. Although the plant was doing well, by 1920 they were needing capital to expand. Doll succeeded in selling all of the outstanding shares of stock to the S.S. Kresge Company, and Mount Clemens Pottery became a wholly owned subsidiary of that company. They always continued to operate completely independently of Kresge, except to furnish them with dishes. Mount Clemens made semiporcelain dinnerware and a solid color ware which came in a dark green, blue and pink was probably Mount Clemens' answer to Fiesta ware. The shape and pattern names for Mt. Clemens are very confusing because in the green room, the sets or shapes went by one name. Then when they were decorated they were given a second name. At this point a few basic shape names might be assigned a lot of new pattern names before leaving the factory. No employee, from the factory that I have corresponded with, can remember the names because they say there were always so very many of them. In 1965, David T. Chase and Chase Enterprise purchased the Mount Clemens Pottery, and later they also purchased Sabin Industries of McKeesport, Pennsylvania. Sabin Industries is a primary decorator of ceramics and glass. In 1967, McCoy pottery had come under the same ownership as Mt. Clemens. See McCoy Pottery listing. In the 1970's the companies underwent another reorganization. By 1974, McCoy Pottery had been purchased by the Lancaster Colony group. Mount Clemens has been formed into a new company called Jamestown China and was being operated by new company owners which were David Chase, C. Ikuta, and the Neachimen Corporation. Sabin Industries was being run as a separate company too, owned by Mr. Chase and Sam Sabin. Then in 1979, Sabin Industries burned to the ground. Whatever was left in the way of equipment and the whole operation was moved to Mt. Clemens Pottery. The manufacturing and decorating were all done in one huge building with David Chase as owner. (Early history of Mount Clemens Pottery is from the article, "Old Timer Gazes Back at 1914," *The Daily Leader*, Mount Clemens, Michigan, May 22, 1939, 25th anniversary issue, pp. 1, 4, 8.) The trade names used in the names used in the late 1970's and 1980 at Mt. Clemens were Jamestown China, Whitehall, Dalton, and Sabina Line. But the name of the factory was changed from Jamestown China back to Mt. Clemens Pottery again around 1980. (Marks: nos. 1-5, on dishes are marks of 1930's and 1940's; no. 6 was mark used by Mt. Clemens and McCoy Pottery when they were under same ownership. The remainder of the marks are for 1970's and 1980's, obtained from company. In early years, Mt. Clemens Pottery did not use a variety of marks. They were all pretty much the same.)

1.

2.

MADE IN USA
12·6R

3.

1124A

4.

632H

TOULON

5.

MONTEL

6.

MOUNT CLEMENS
POTTERY

7.

IRONSTONE
MADE IN USA

MOUNT CLEMENS
POTTERY

8.

UNDERGLAZE
IRONSTONE
MADE IN USA
DISHWASHER-SAFE
DETERGENT-PROOF
OVEN-PROOF

MOUNT CLEMENS CHINA

9.

UNDERGLAZE
IRONSTONE
MADE IN USA
DISHWASHER-SAFE
DETERGENT-PROOF
OVEN-PROOF

MCC-BS-U

DISHWASHER-SAFE
DETERGENT-PROOF
UNDERGLAZE

10.

OVEN-PROOF

JAMESTOWN CHINA

11.

IRONSTONE
DISHWASHER-SAFE
DETERGENT-PROOF
OVEN-PROOF
U.S.A.

12.

DISHWASHER-SAFE
DETERGENT-PROOF
UNDERGLAZE

OVEN-PROOF

13.

Roycroft
stoneware

14.

15.

●DISHWASHER-SAFE ●DETERGENT-PROOF ●OVEN-PROOF
MADE IN USA

Whitehall
Fine China

16.

IRONSTONE
MADE IN USA

17. U.S.A.

18.

Yours...
From the good Earth

DISHWASHER-SAFE   OVEN-PROOF
DETERGENT-PROOF
MADE IN USA

19.

DALTON
STONEWARE

Mountaindale Pottery. Mountaindale, New York. This was a small manufacturer of stoneware dinnerware, mugs and accessories which went out of business around 1984 according to a telephone conversation from a new tenant in the building. The only listing I found was in the 1981-1982 *China, Glass and Tableware Directory*, where Jeff Pullman was president and the mark shown was given. It was probably a paper label.

mountaindale
POTTERY

usa

Mountainside Art Pottery. Mountainside, New Jersey. Around 1929 to around 1941. John Kovacs, an immigrant from Hungary who was associated with the Rutgers University Ceramics Club, started the pottery around 1929 to make hand thrown and modeled art ware such as vases, bowls and figurals. White and red clay earthenware pieces with hand incised marks are found. (Information: Tom Turnquist, "The Broadmoor and Mountainside Potteries," *Antique Trader Weekly*, February 13, 1980, p. 53. Incised marks: Ralph and Terry Kovel, *The Kovel's Collectors Guide to American Art Pottery*, p. 362.)

1. MP   2. MP

Mova Products. San Francisco, California. Sylvester A. Baker from this company filed for a claim on this mark on June 28, 1943, for use on china tableware, vases and jars, claiming use since January 15, 1943.

MOVA WARE

Mt. Vernon Gift Shop. Fairfax County, Virginia. This stamp in varous sizes was found at the Quality Stamp Company in East Liverpool, Ohio, and was used on American made china for souvenir pieces sold at the gift shop at George Washington's home site. One manufacturer for the shop was Dwight Morris China Company in East Palestine, Ohio. See that listing. Dwight Morris made vases, candleholders, toby jugs, and pitchers with decals of George and Martha as decorations, also busts of Martha and George in toby mugs, and other decorative pieces for the gift shop according to Grace C. Allison, "The Dwight Morris Porcelain Company, East Palestine, Ohio," *American Clay Exchange*, May 15, 1985, pp. 4, 5.

Mr. Mugs, Inc. Hallandale, Florida. Company filed for registration of this mark on June 28, 1978, claiming use since December 22, 1974, for use on mugs made of ceramic, porcelain, stoneware and earthenware.

MR. MUGS

Mud Daubers. Kernersville, North Carolina. Filed for registration of this mark on May 17, 1982, claiming use since April 23, 1977, for earthenware, stoneware and porcelain pottery.

Muddy Wheel Gallery. Albuquerque, New Mexico. 1968 to present. Fred R. Wilson, studio potter, started the Muddy Wheel Gallery in 1968 in Van Nuys, California. In April 1971, he moved to Studio City, California. In 1977, he moved to Albuquerque, New Mexico. He has worked as an artist since 1950. Fred makes one of a kind limited forms, slab thrown sculptures such as heads and figures, functional pottery forms in stoneware and earthenware. A graduate with B.A. Degree from La Verne College, Fred did graduate work at Fresno State College and Los Angeles State College from 1959 to 1964. He has won 27 first place prizes in sculpture and painting in various major fairs in California. In 1970 he won top artist out of 400 at the Century City Artist Invitational. He won the Silver Bunyol award in Valencia, Spain. He had a silk screen print, "Whipping Boy," that was on tour of Russia in a cultural exchange program. His awards, shows, etc. are practically a book in themselves and cannot be adequately recounted here. He had a sculpture called "Detroit Pieta"

in the Los Angeles County Museum as of February 1972. His work has been exhibited at New York Museum (a sculpture named "Protection") and in 50 different locations in California from 1960 to 1972, such as the Cultural Fair in Panorama City and the Summer Festival at Westlake. By 1971 he had already taught 3,100 students! He has worked on educational films with Stephen Productions of Hollywood on the complete art of making pottery. Fred is truly an extraordinary man! In 1975 following a auto accident that disabled Fred for eight months, he went on tour in June 1976 and traveled 21,000 miles, exhibiting his work, demonstrating pottery techniques and giving lectures and conducting seminars in Minnesota, Iowa, Colorado, Texas, New Mexico, etc. In 1977 his list of places of exhibits included New Mexico and Colorado. Fred has been on 35 television shows, including Dinah Shore and Steve Allen's shows to demonstrate the art of pottery.

1950-68

One of kind limited forms are signed like prints ⅙ or ⅖ etc.

1968 to present time, year included.

Muddy Wheel Pottery. Lee's Summit, Missouri. 1975 to present (1984). William W. Gardner, studio potter makes hand-thrown functional stoneware with a mark which is either incised or painted on with oxide ink. Each piece is dated with month and year.

Mudville. Cambridge, Massachusetts. 1974 to present (1984). Mudville is a non-profit pottery school which has two shows yearly with students as well as teachers showing their pottery. The school teaches approximately 40 to 60 students at a time. See Nan Hamilton, Gail Hansen and Carolyn Asbury for information and marks for some Mudville potters.

Mueller, Herman/Mueller Mosaic Tile Company. Herman Miller left public school at age 14 to attend the School of Industrial Arts in Nuernberg, Germany. Later he worked as a sculptor in Bremen, Kiel and Hamburg, Germany, before coming to the United States in 1875. He eventually became a modeler in a terra cotta factory in Indianapolis, where he sculpted four faces for the Indiana State House. From 1886 to 1893 he was associated with the American Encaustic Tiling Company, Zanesville, Ohio. In 1893 he and Karl Langenbeck started the Mosaic Tile Company, Zanesville, (see that listing). In 1903 he left Mosaic Tile to work for Robertson Art Tile Company in Morrisville, Pennsylvania. (See that listing). In 1908 or early 1909 he started his own business the Mueller Mosaic Tile Company in Trenton, New Jersey. He remained as president of the company until the late 1930's or early 1940's. There is some conflict about exactly when Mueller died and the plant closed. In the *Bulletin of the American Ceramic Society* as cited here was this statement, "Mueller remained as president of the Company until he died at the age of 87 on September 21, 1941. But Paul Evans cites the same publication for October, 1938, pp. 429, 430 as giving Mueller's death date as 1938. Evans and the Kovels both give the closing date for the factory as 1938. So we are safe in saying Mueller died and the factory closed in the late 1930's or early 1940's. (Information: Staff written "Ceramic History, Herman, Mueller," *Bulletin of American Ceramic Society*, January, 1942, pp. 1-3. Marks: Ralph and Terry Kovel, *The Collector's Guide to American Art Pottery*, p. 107.)

Mullis, Charles, Manufacturing Company. Greenburg, Indiana. Company filed April 28, 1920, for this mark, claiming use since November 1910, for ornamental and ornamented pottery.

Muncie Clay Products Company/Muncie Potteries, Inc. Muncie, Indiana. 1919 to 1939. The Gill Clay Pot Company started in 1880's in Bellaire, Ohio, and moved to Muncie, Indiana, around 1900 when the gas supply ran out in that area of Ohio. In 1908 the company was incorporated as Gill Clay Pot Company. The clay pots this company made were the huge pots made for melting glass and all kinds of furnace materials and fixtures used by the many glass factories that were in the Findlay and Bellaire, Ohio, area. During W.W. I, they made pots to melt metals. Muncie Clay Products Company, a Division of Gill Clay Pot Company was formed in 1919. In the early 1920's, Charles Benham joined Charles Grafton and the Gill family, and a line of decorative pottery was introduced in a new building built for that purpose, including planters, bookends, jugs, wall pockets, pitchers and various art novelties. In 1931 the name became Muncie Potteries, Inc., making the same products. The company ceased operations January 1939. In 1951 the building where the pottery pieces were made was destroyed by fire. Gill Pottery was liquidated in 1967, and that building burned in 1969. The pieces were described by Henzke as having soft flowing glazes with lovely color effects. The colors were blended from pink to green and lavender to blue, etc. She described the shapes as intricate and stunning. (Information: Don Brewer, "What About Muncie," *American Clay Exchange*, January 1984, pp. 10, 11. The beginning dates for Muncie Clay Products Company were from Brewer, who named dates, officers of the company, incorporators, etc. in the article cited. These dates vary somewhat from those reported earlier by other writers, but seem to be founded on considerable research by Brewer. (Information: Don Brewer, as cited; also, Lucile Henzke in "Muncie Pottery," *Pottery Collector's Newsletter*, February 1973, p. 51. Marks: Brewer, as cited. The letters A 1 and A 2, etc. would appear one at a time with the word Muncie.)

MUNCIE
A1 - A2 - A3

Murchison, Loren and Company, Inc. Newark, New Jersey. Filed for registration of this mark on August 14, 1961, for beer mugs.

HERALDO-MUG

Murphy Pottery Company. East Liverpool, Ohio. Shortly before 1900 to 1903. The pottery became a member of East Liverpool Potteries Company which was dissolved in 1903. The pottery made semi-porcelain and porcelain dinnerware. G.C. Murphy plant burned in 1904, and Murphy went into business in Barberton, Ohio. Actually, this was a very short lived pottery, no more than six years of production, if that many. (Marks: Barber, Marks of American Potters, p. 114.)

Museum Pieces, Inc. New York, New York. An advertisement in *Gift and Tableware Reporter*, August 16, 1965, p. 152, showed four reproductions of sculptured pieces by Betti Richard, which had originally been sculptured in stone or terra cotta. The ad said the company, Museum Pieces, Inc., had over 200 pieces for sale, reproduced from pieces in 25 museums by 30 top artists. They were authentic, hand finished, exactly like the original, according to the ad. The "MPI" trademark shown was said to stand for absolute authenticity. (Mark: directory as cited.)

Musick, Irene Kolodziej. Studio potter who received a degree from Western Reserve University in Cleveland, Ohio, in 1938. She taught and continued her studies receiving a master degree in 1942. She then attended Cranbrook Art Academy and worked with Carl Mills, a well known sculptor and studied ceramics under Maija Grotell. In 1947 she headed the ceramics department of the University of Missouri in Columbia, until 1951 when she married Musick, a painting instructor at the University. The couple moved to Colorado Springs, Colorado. He painted and was an active W.P.A. artist; she made pots on commissions and for exhibitions. The pieces were wheel thrown, some hand painted, exquisite shapes and designs and glazed with glazes Musick made herself. Between 1947 and 1957 she won seven major prizes at exhibitions. Irene continued to make pottery until she died in 1969. (Information: Thomas Turnquist, "Musick In Clay," *American Art Pottery*, March, 1984, p. 9. Marks: sent by Turnquist by letter.)

I. KOLODZIEJ

IK   IKM

Mutual China Company. Indianapolis, Indiana. 1861-1972. Was a retail institution that was started in May 1861, by Louis Hollweg. In 1915, the business was incorporated as Mutual China Company. On Janury 29, 1972, the doors were closed following a public auction (JoAnn Rogers, "Mutual China Closes," *Collectors Weekly*, February, 1972, p. 4). The mark they used was for china made in this country and abroad. Sometimes the mark is found alone; sometimes it is accompanied by the maker's mark. This mark found stamped on a piece of hotel ware.

MUTUAL CHINA CO.
INDIANAPOLIS
HAND PAINTED

Myers and Hall. Mogadore, Portage County, Ohio. Around 1872, E.W. Myers worked alone and in 1873 the name became Myers and Hall. From 1874 to 1880 the pottery was **Myers, Baird, and Hall**. (Ramsay, p. 224.) Blair, p. 28, gives 1866 to 1896 for Myers and Hall.

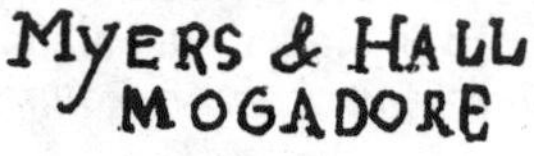

MYERS & HALL
MOGADORE

Myhr, David W. Sevierville, Tennessee. 1969 to present (1985). David Myhr, studio potter, makes stoneware dinnerware and architectural tile with a Smoky Mountain landscape scene in the glaze, featuring a mountain and several trees. He inscribes the bottom of pieces as shown.

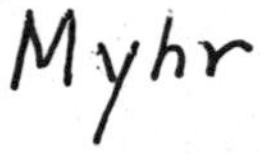

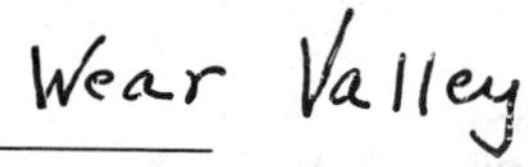

Myhr   Wear Valley

N

Nancy China. Woodbridge, New Jersey. In 1942 the Gerber Plumbing Fixtures Corp. purchased a pottery building in Woodbridge. For a short time during W.W. II, a line of artware was made at the pottery. (Derwich and Latos, p. 162.) The Nancy China, Inc. logo (probably a paper label) was shown in the 1952 *Crockery and Glass Journal Directory*. However, the art line was probably discontinued before that time. In this directory, Nancy China, Inc. was listed at 1133 Broadway, New York, also in Chicago, Illinois. These outlets may have continued to have the china made for them after the Woodbridge plant quit. The patent no. 416457 is part of the mark shown. See the listing Bernard Lipman/Princeton China Corporation.

Nash, Various Potters. In 1784, Jonathon Nash occupied a pot house and works on a road to Springfield, Massachusetts, according to a sale bill discussed in Lura W. Watkins, *Early New England Potters and Their Wares*, p. 94. Watkins said she did not know what became of this Nash. In Jordon C. Thorn, *Handbook of Old Pottery and Porcelain Marks*, p. 139, is an impressed mark for E. and G. Nash in Utica, New York, around 1820. John Ramsay, p. 59 said this second Nash Pottery was built in 1819 and was taken over by Noah White. (Marks: no. 2, the single word, "Nash," found on a gray pottery beer bottle that was certainly not old enough to be either of the above Nash potters. F.M. Nash made stoneware in Scott County, Illinois, around 1850, according to the check list in Betty I. Madden, *Art Crafts and Architecture of Early Illinois*, p. 193. The pottery employed four. Perhaps this is the Nash that made the bottle, but this is not verified.)

Nashville Art Pottey. Nashville, Tennessee. 1884-1889. Pottery started by Bettie J. Scovel, in connection with the Nashville School of Art. Pottery made in molds made from forms modeled by Miss Scovel. Barber, Pottery and Porcelain of United States, pp. 470 and 471, and Evans, p. 178, describe a ware with dark brown glaze over a red body and a ware with white body and red veined effect. Scovel left, and the pottery closed in 1889, according to Barber. (Information: as cited. Mark: Evans, p. 178.)

Nashville Art Pottery

Nassau China Company. Trenton, New Jersey. This company was listed as manufacturers, in the *New Jersey City*

Directory from 1948 through 1956 under pottery products. But I found no listing to tell what those products were. This mark was found under Hall China Company's marks at Quality Stamp Company. It is possible this was a pottery that turned from making pottery to selling to distributing it for a time before closing. Many companies did that.

NASSAU CHINA CO. TRENTON. N.J.

National China Company. East Liverpool, Ohio and Salineville, Ohio. 1899-1931. Was incorporated June 15, 1899, in East Liverpool, Ohio, and moved to Salineville, Ohio, quite awhile before 1923, then operated there until the American China Corporation, which the company had joined in 1929, went under due to the Depression. In East Liverpool, the National China Company made tableware and hotel ware and a fancy shaped dinner service, vase, jugs, etc. In Salineville, efforts were concentrated more on an exclusive line of dinnerware. Around 1923 the company was making only one dinner service called "La Rosa" which had become very popular in the trade. ("American Pottery Trade Marks," *China, Glass, and Lamps*, September 10, 1923, p. 15.) There are several marks shown that were used by this company. They were still in East Liverpool in 1908, because they made a 1908 calender plate marked "N.C. Co. E.L.P." (Information: Lehner, *American Kitchen and Dinner Wares*, p. 111. Marks: no. 1, Jervis, *Pottery, Glass and Brass Salesman*, August 28, 1913, p. 14. No. 2 sent by reader, Grace Blake, Bedford, Pa. No. 2 is monogram N.C.Co. The rest of the marks were on dishes of author.

National Potteries Corporation. Bedford, Ohio (near Cleveland). 1938 to present. They are distributors of pottery and glass. They partially manufacture. They used the trademark "Napco." In the 1981-1982 *China, Glass and Tableware Directory*, they are listed as importers of ceramic, glass, bone china miniatures, holiday decorations, brassware, porcelainware, limited editions, housewares, novelty figurines and silk-like flowers. (Marks: nos. 1-2, copies of paper labels; nos. 3-4, printed marks on pieces. No. 5 was filed for registration September 16, 1965, claiming use since June 1965, for ceramic jars, bottles and tumblers. No. 6 was filed July 27, 1966 for Christmas decorated products, such as centerpiece bowls, Christmas sleigh-planters, candle stands, holly ring planters, dinner bell ornaments, bell shaped salt and pepper shakers, tree shaped three tier serving dishes, etc. all made of earthenware.)

1. ITS Napco ITS NEW!

2. Napco Creation

3. NAPCO USA CLEVELAND,O.

4. C3342C © NAPCO 1958

5. Lady Fair

6. HOLLY DAY

7. NAPCOWARE

National Pottery. On Potters Alley, Roseville, Ohio. Existed in first quarter of 20th century. Found listed in 1922 *R.G. Dun and Company Reference Book*, that tells credit ratings. J. Burgess Lenhart had the National Pottery and then went on to start the American Pottery Company in Marietta, Ohio, in early 1940's. By 1937 the building had been empty for awhile and most of it had burned. In 1937, Fred Ungemach started making pottery in what was left of a 12′ x 12′ office, still standing. (Marks: stamped mark found on 4″ vase with yellow clay and poor streaky aqua glaze; no. 1 is a photostatic copy of stamped mark; no. 2 is a drawing of the mark. No. 3 is found on utilitarian pie bakers, crocks, etc., and will cover the whole bottom of the piece. The mark was apparently in the molds and is a recessed mark. Jack Woodward, president of Robinson Ransbottom and a 50-year employee of that plant, verified the mark. Many pottery collectors, dealers, etc. in the Roseville area have had these pieces. Norris Sowers, whose name is mentioned in connection with several of the potteries in this area also verified the mark. Mr. Sowers, is a lifetime resident, worked in the various potteries and became an art pottery dealer.

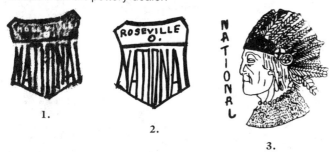

1. ROSEVILLE O. NATIONAL

2. ROSEVILLE O. NATIONAL

3. NATIONAL

National Silver Company. New York, New York. A selling agency of glass, pottery, etc. They used the mark "Nasco" on their ware. Southern Potteries, Gladding, McBean and Company, Santa Anita Pottery and many other potteries made products with National Silver's mark. (Marks: nos. 1-16, obtained at Quality Stamp Company, East Liverpool, Ohio; 1-8, on dishes made by French Saxon China Company; 9-10, on dishes made by W.S. George Pottery; 11-14, on dishes made by Cannonsburg Pottery Company. The round Nasco mark did not have lines, the copy of the mark at Quality Stamp was on lined paper. No. 15 was an incised mark on a cookie jar sent by Edna Myers, writer for *The Glaze*; no. 16, mark on

a highly vitrified Indian tree pattern platter; no. 17, sent by Linda Cleveland who researched the patents; no. 18, filed for registration by National Silver Company, January 3, 1941, claiming use since March 1, 1939, for use on pottery, cooking and tableware; no. 19 filed by National Silver Company on March 24, 1942, claiming use since September 1, 1941, for use on ceramic dinnerware, cookingware, vases, jars, jugs, jardiniers, crocks and flower pots; no. 20, filed April 6, 1949, claiming use for one month for use on pottery cups, saucers, plates, bowls, dishes, tea and coffee pots, casseroles, salad sets, all of which is made of clay and talcs; no. 21, found on nicely vitrified yellow plate. No. 22 filed October 19, 1954, for use on ceramic dinnerware.) Nos. 22-26 were all fired for china or ceramic dinnerware and were only used a month or two before filing. No. 22 filed October 19, 1954; No. 23 filed June 27, 1952; No. 24 filed August 11, 1950; No. 25 filed September 13, 1952; No. 26 filed June 21, 1950; No. 27 filed March 30, 1951, claiming use since May 1949. No. 28 was used on ware made by Gladding McBean and Company for National Silver, from 1934 to 1940. In addition to this mark, the company records showed casseroles were made and stamped, "California Pottery Nasco," and pie plate had an imprint in the mold reading "California Pottery Nasco.")

1. UNION MADE NASCO U.S.A. BOUQUET 22 KT. GOLD DECORATED

2. UNION MADE NASCO U.S.A. ROSE OF PARADISE 22 KT. GOLD DECORATED

3. UNION MADE NASCO U.S.A. JUANITA 22 KT. GOLD DECORATED

4. UNION MADE NASCO U.S.A. LORRAINE 22 KT GOLD DECORATED

5. NASCO U.S.A. 22 K. GOLD U.S.A.

6. UNION MADE NASCO U.S.A. ROSE OF PARADISE 22 KT. GOLD DECORATED

7. UNION MADE NASCO U.S.A. JUANITA 22 KT. GOLD DECORATED

8. UNION MADE NASCO U.S.A. LORRAINE 22 KT GOLD DECORATED

9. NASCO Golden Floral FIRST QUALITY ORIGINAL Warranted 22 KT. Gold MADE IN U.S.A.

10. NASCO Golden Colonial FIRST QUALITY ORIGINAL Warranted 22 KT. Gold MADE IN U.S.A.

11. NASCO SURREY 22·KT. GOLD

12. NASCO TEABERRY 22 KT. GOLD

13.

14. **NASCO**
22 KT. GOLD
'QUEEN'S ROSE'
MADE IN U.S.A.

15.
U.S.A.
N.S.Co.

16. *Nasco*
Indian Tree

18. *DEL CORONADO*

NASCO
THELMA
MADE IN
U.S.A

17.

19.

20.
ROYAL HAWAIIAN
MADE IN
CALIFORNIA

21.

22.

23.

DUNSMUIR
24.

25.

SERVETTE 26.   27. **SCARLET**

OVEN
28. **NASCO**
PROOF

National Specials Company. New York, New York. Frank C. Baxter, doing business as a selling agency under above name filed for use of this mark March 1922, for use on household dishes of crockery, earthenware or porcelain, claiming use since November 1921.

National Unit Distributors, Inc. Boston, Massachusetts. Filed for a claim on this mark on December 28, 1942, for use on semi-vitreous china tableware, claiming use since October 26, 1942.

"UNI-SET"

Natzler, Gertrud and Otto. The couple began working together in ceramics in 1933 with Gertrude hand throwing the pieces, and Otto making and applying the glazes. In 1937 they won a Silver Medal at the Paris International Exposition. In 1938, they came to the U.S. and settled in Los Angeles. They quickly became the leading figures in ceramic art. Their glazes drew a great deal of attention, particularly their volcanic or crater glazes. They won many awards. See the lists for National Ceramic Exhibitions at Syracuse in the back of this book. Their work is represented in more than 35 museums, including The Metropolitan Museum of Art, New York; The Museum of Modern Art, New York; The Art Institute of Chicago; the Philedelphia Museum of Art; and the Los Angeles County Museum of Art. Otto has now begun to work with the forms as well as the glazes, following the death of Gertrud, and in 1977 he held a one-man exhibition of slab-built vessels at the Craft and Folk Art Museum in Los Angeles. (Information: Garth Clark, *A Century of Ceramics in the U.S.*, p. 311. Incised marks: Linda Steigleder, from the booklet published by the Everson Museum of Art to accompany the 1978 exhibition, "A Century of Ceramics in the U.S.")

MΣLER   G   +   O
                NΛΣLCR

MTZLCR   MΣLR

Neff Brothers. Taylorsville, Highland County, Ohio. Had a population of 50 in 1922 with one business, and a general store. Mark was found painted in blue on late 19th century gray stoneware jug.

NEFF BRO'S
MANUFACTURERS
TAYLORSVILLE, O

Neff, Grace V. Chicago, Illinois. Filed for registration of this mark on May 18, 1948, for use on china dinner service, plates, cups, bowls, coffee pot, sugar and creamer, and picture plates, claiming use since January 1942.

KATE GREENAWAY

Neiman-Marcus Company. Dallas, Texas. A large department store. Filed for registration of mark 1 in December 1958, claiming use since October 1958, for use on crockery, earthenware, porcelain and china, namely, casseroles, salt and pepper cellars, bric-a-brac, trays, bowls, vases, cups, saucers, plates, pitchers, coffee pots, teapots, sugar bowls and creamers. Mark 2 was filed July 15, 1965, for the same articles. Sarach L. Culbreath, studio potter, made special order dinnerware for this store. See Culbreath listing.)

1. STACK-PAC

2. TREASURE STACK

Nemadji Earth Pottery Company. Kettle River, Minnesota. 1922 to present (1986). The pottery makes slip cast, hand decorated earthenware into attractive decorative pieces and tile. The tile are heat resistant, scratch resistant and framed in hand finished oak. Wildlife scenes of bears, jackalope, a longhorn bull, deer, elk, etc. are real art designs on the tile, also on coffee mugs. A type of Indian like pottery made of natural earthen clay and hand painted with various color that swirl, drip or bend together make beautiful decorative pieces. The general manager of the pottery is E. Gregory Koivisto, and he holds a masters degree in ceramic engineering and art. (Information and stamped marks from the company. The mark "Garden of the Gods" was on pieces of decorative pottery made by Nemadji Pottery for a company by that name in Manitou Springs, Colorado, in the 1960's for a custom order, according to E.G. Koivisto.)

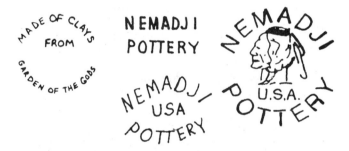

NEMADJI POTTERY U.S.A.

New Castle Pottery (or China Company). New Castle, Pennsylvania. 1901-1905. Was organized in 1901 and they built a six kiln plant on the present site of Shenango China in New Castle, Pennsylvania. The company only operated around four years until around 1905 when it was closed. In 1912 the Shenango Pottery purchased the New Castle Pottery buildings and moved the machinery and equipment to the Shenango plant on Emery Street which had also been started in 1901. (See Shenango.) New Castle Pottery was organized to make vitreous hotel and dinnerware. In 1903 they were listed as making semi-porcelain dinner sets, toilet sets, and short sets of odd dishes. The only piece I have found from this company was a little oval, hotel ware vitreous dish which had an impressed mark, "New Castle China, New Castle, Pennsylvania." (Information: from Shenango China Company, also Barber, *Marks of American Potters*, p. 36. Mark no. 1, Barber; Mark no. 2 impressed on dish.)

NEW CASTLE CHINA
NEW CASTLE, PA.

Newcomb, Inc. Roselle Park, New Jersey, 1950 to 1954. Operated a small plant on Filbert Street. Larry Lafray researched the family in regard to the pottery operation. (Information: Lafray, Larry, information in letter, "*Glaze*," February, 1979, p. 4.)

NEWCOMB
INC
©
ROSELLE NJ

Newcomb Pottery. New Orleans, Louisiana. Tulane University, a women's college, was organized in 1886. In 1895 a pottery was established by the college to train students in conjunction with art and design classes. Ellsworth Woodward was the supervisor, and many well known ceramists worked at Newcomb Pottery. The ware was wheel thrown, and they made their own glazes. The students were really artists who decorated the ware. Paul E. Cox and Mary G. Sheerer were two of the most outstanding. (See separate listings for these.)

Prior to formation of the pottery at the school, women had painted ware thrown by George Ohr and Joseph F. Meyer at the Biloxi Art Pottery. Evans, p. 183, described some of the ware as underglaze painted on a low fired biscuit. Very early pieces were slip decorated. They incised designs on the wet clay, fired it once and then painted and refired. Matt glazes were developed, also. In 1918, Cox left and the pottery was moved to the basement of one of the college buildings. At that time the pottery was no longer a partly commercial, as well as educational, venture. It became a laboratory where students could make a piece of pottery from start to finish rather than just to decorate what some professional potter had made. But Paul Evans, *Art Pottery of the U.S.*, still classified the ware made during the 1918 to 1930 period as art pottery; the students did exceptional work.

After 1930, only a plainware was made and a limited amount was produced into the 1940's under the name the Newcomb Guild. The pottery won medals at many major fairs and expositions and are part of permanent collections in major museums across the U.S. The pottery won medals at the Paris Exposition of 1900 and the St. Louis Exposition of 1904 and is presently included in the permanent collections of the Metropolitan Museum of Art, the Newark Museum, the Museum of Fine Arts, Boston and the Louisiana State Museum. An exhibition organized by the Smithsonian Institution's Travel Exhibition Services and Newcomb College of Tulane University with the Louisiana State Museum, and a tour opened in late 1984 at the Smithsonian's Renwick Gallery and will close at Newcomb College in Spring, 1987. The catalogue for the exhibition, the result of intensive research, is a major publication entitled, "Newcomb Pottery: An Enterprise for Southern Women, 1890-1940," by Professor Jessie Jean Poesch, professor of art history at Newcomb College and Curator of the show. (Information: Paul Evans, *Art Pottery of the U.S.*, pp. 182 to 187. Marks: no. 1 is the official mark of the pottery, generally painted in color underglaze in the early period, later it was not in color. The H. and B. on either side of the Newcomb cipher means hand built. The "M" in no. 3 meant a mold had also been made. See Evans, p. 185, for explanation. Marks nos. 1, 2 were from Linda Steigleder, from the booklet published by the Everson Museum of Art to accompany the 1978 exhibition, "A Century of Ceramics in the U.S." No. 3 was from Paul Evans, p. 186. No. 4, Barber, *Marks of American Potters*, p. 156 and 157. Nos. 5 through 9 are decorators' marks from the booklet by Linda Steigleder, as cited: No. 6, Sabina E. Wells; no. 7, Sadie Irvine; no. 8, Marie Hall Le Blanc; no. 9, Anna Francis Simpson. No. 10 is a paper label from Deb and Gini Johnson, *Beginning Book of Pottery*. No. 11 is Joseph Meyers, one of the main potters. No. 12 through 37 are decorators' marks shown in Barber, p. 127, identified as follows: no. 12, Leoni Nicholson; no. 13, Bessie A. Ficklen; no. 14, Sarah Henderson; no. 15, Hattie Joor; no. 16, Gertrude R. Smith; no. 17, Katherine Kopman; no. 18, Frances H. Cocke; no. 19, Roberta Kennon; no. 20, Mary Sheerer; no. 21, Mary W. Butler; no. 22, Emily Huger; no. 23, Amalie' Roman; no. 24, Mazie T. Ryan; no. 25, Elizabeth G. Rogers; no. 26, Frances Jones; no. 27, Desiree' Roman; no. 28, Mary F. Baker; no. 29, Marie-Hoe-LeBlanc; no. 30, Irene B. Keep; no. 31, Selina E.B. Gregory; no. 32, Raymond A. Scudder; no. 33, Beverly Randolph; no. 34, Esther Huger Elliott; no. 35 Francis E. Lines; no. 36, Mary W. Richardson; no. 37, Olive W. Dodd. There are more Newcomb Pottery decorators' marks shown in the *Kovels Collectors Guide to American Art Pottery*.)

New Distributor System. Fitchburg, Massachusetts. Frank Mastrangelo from this business filed for registration of this mark on December 22, 1945, for use on earthenware and china articles, namely bowls, glasses, cups, dishes, platters and saucers, claiming use since January 1940.

New England Pottery Company. Boston, Massachusetts. E.A. Barber tells us on p. 245 of *Pottery and Porcelain of the U.S.*, that this pottery was founded in 1854 by Frederick Meagher, who made Rockingham and yellowware. But on p. 96 of *Marks of American Potters*, Barber said the pottery was founded for the manufacturing of common white ware. At any rate, by 1875 the plant was owned by Thomas Gray and W.L. Clark and the name became the New England Pottery Company and they made ironstone china and white granite ware. Around 1886 they made "Rieti" ware, a semi-porcelain decorated ware, and they also made porcelain with old ivory and mazarine blue finish. The beautiful old designs used to decorate the pieces were engraved and printed by J.W. Phillips. Thomas H. Copeland modeled most of the pieces. Chocolate jugs, vases, jardinieres, cracker jars, rose jars, etc. were made. (Information and marks: Barber, as cited. Barber dated no. 1 from 1878 to 1883; no. 2 from 1883 to 1886; no. 3 from 1887 until after 1904; no. 4 as "Rieti" ware from 1886 to 1888; and no. 5 was used after 1888 until 1889 when no more "Rieti" was made. The rest of the marks were used before 1904 when Barber's book was published.)

New Geneva Stoneware Company. Masontown, Pennsylvania. 1978 to present (1987). Linn Newman, potter, worked at the Heritage Company in Uniontown, Pennsylvania, as a logo carver in the years 1976 to 1978. (See that listing for his work there.) In 1978, John Whoolery and Linn Newman formed the New Geneva Stoneware Company to produce a combination of freehand painted and free thrown pieces. The pieces are hand thrown on a potter's wheel, from an off-white or tan clay which is then hand-decorated in traditional cobalt-blue floral or bird patterns and fired to 2,360 degrees F. producing a durable stoneware. They use no stenciled or stamped designs; the designs are all hand painted. They dug 30 tons of clay from a site near New Geneva and are still using that clay today to make the tan colored pots. Linn said "we prefer dealing one on one with our customers, keeping prices reasonable and with one or two exceptions, we do not sell to stores or shops." The company has refused many requests to handle their ware (even from a Japanese department store chain.) Currently only the Henry Ford Museum and Walt Disney World sell the products besides the company itself. The majority of their business is mail order. Ads appear regularly in *Country Living, Country Home* and *Colonial Homes*. At present, Wilma Nopwasky and John Whoolery do the potting. Linn Newman does the art work and puts his signature only on the very significant pieces. Other pieces are marked with the stamps shown. The month and date are stamped on most pieces just to keep track of drying time.

NEW GENEVA 1986 STONEWARE CO.

Whoolery

Nopwasky

N. G. S. Co 1986

New Hope Studios. Alexandria, Tennessee. 1977 to present. Maryann Fariello, a studio potter, makes tiles, sculptural and architectural installations, dinnerware, etc. of porcelain. This is a young artist destined to go right to the top of her profession. She received a M.F.A. degree in ceramics in 1977 from the School of Art, East Carolina University, Greenville, North Carolina. She was a ceramics instructor at Vanderbuilt University in Nashville, Tennessee. She has had extensive news coverage of her work; mentioned several times in *Ceramic Monthly*, etc. Showing the beautiful wall hangings in porcelain she has made, such as "Winged Tiles" and "Wall Sconce II." She listed five juried competitions, seven invitational exhibitions, several one and two person shows and several miscellaneous exhibitions. She has worked as ceramic instructor or taught art history in four colleges, East Carolina University, Greenville, North Carolina; Motlow State College in Tullahoma, Tennessee; the School of Arts, Stillwater, New Jersey; and Douglas College Art Dept., New Brunswick, New Jersey. (Marks: no. 1, incised; no. 2, impressed; no. 3, paper label.)

Fariello + date

* BLACK ♥ series, done in collaboration with blacksmith porcelain plates + steel utensils since 1981

impressed griffin

New Hope Studios
Route 1, Box 192
Alexandria
Tennessee 37012

New Jersey Pottery Company. Trenton, New Jersey. Was organized in 1869 and in 1883 became the Union Pottery Company according to Barber in *Marks of American Potters*, p. 58. They made cream-colored and white graniteware. During the presidential campaign of 1880 they issued a series of plates with overglaze printed portraits of the candidates. I found no mention of a Union Pottery listed in the *Trenton City Directory* in 1900 or after, except a Union Electrical Porcelain Works which stayed in business until 1946. (Mark, Barber p. 58.)

Newland, Schneeloch and Piek, Inc. New York, New York. Filed for a registration on this mark September 17, 1937, for use on dishes of china and earthenware, claiming use since September 1936. They were listed in the 1945 *Crockery and Glass Journal* as manufacturers and importers of various pottery and glass products. In the *Crockery and Glass Journal Magazine*, August 1950, on the inside cover, and in several other of these magazines in the 1950's, Newland, Schneeloch and Piek were the distributors for Southern California Ceramics Company's orchard dinnerware. See Southern California Ceramics for that mark.

ROYAL EMBASSY CHINA

New Milford Pottery Company (Wannopee Pottery). New Milford, Connecticut. According to Barber, the New Milford Pottery Company of New Milford, Connecticut, was founded in 1886 as a stock company. According to Evans, the pottery had a kiln in operation by September 1887. The products of the New Milford Pottery Company were the ordinary grades of whiteware and cream-colored ware which was marked with a square and the initials of the company. They also made semi-opaque china marked with an eagle mark. In 1892 the pottery was sold to E.D. Black, L.F. Curtis, C.M. and Merritt Beach (Evans, p. 320). In the *1902-1903 Complete Directory*, the company was listed as **Black and Beach Pottery Company**, making common china dinner sets, toilet sets and short sets of odd dishes. The name was changed in 1890 (W.P. Jervis's date in "Dictionary of Pottery Terms," *Pottery, Glass, and Brass Salesman*, September 26, 1918, p. 11) to the Wannopee Pottery, and the ware was of a fancy decorative type or art pottery type. (For a description of the artware, see Evans' book, pp. 320-322.) In 1903, the pottery stopped operating and was liquidated in 1904. Jervis said they made a lettuce ware of good quality in addition to a general line of colored glazes that entitled them to a longer life-span than they achieved. In the book, *Majolica*, by Wildey C. Rickerson, Chester, Connecticut: Pequot Press, 1972, p. 37, he tells us that in 1904 when Wannopee Pottery Company was liquidated the molds and trademarks were sold to Mr. Charles

Reynolds who had worked at the company as a designer. He moved to Trenton and in conjunction with George H. Bowman Company of Cleveland (The Cleveland China Company, a distributor), he manufactured lettuce leaf ware for several years with mark no. 8, "Trade/lettuce leaf/mark." (Marks: nos. 1-6, Barber, p. 98; nos. 7, 8, Rickerson, p. 37; no. 9 Evans, p. 322 - Evans also showed all of marks shown here. Also see Lang and Osgood for more on marks.)

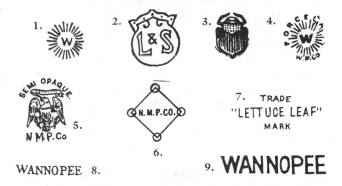

1. 2. 3. 4.

5. SEMI OPAQUE. N M.P.Co

6. N.M.P.CO.

7. TRADE "LETTUCE LEAF" MARK

WANNOPEE 8. 9. **WANNOPEE**

New Orleans, Louisiana, Various Potteries. In late 1880 the New Orleans Porcelain Factory was started by Surgi and d'Estampes and operated until 1883. By March 1881 they had made 6,000 pieces of porcelain. In 1883 d'Estampes left and formed the **French Porcelain Company**, but it didn't last long enough to even get into the directories. In 1883, L.M. Gex operated the plant for a very short time. In the *New Orleans City Directories* from 1884-1889, for over six years, Lucian M. Gex was listed as having a factory of his own at 248 and 250 Carondelet Walk, with offices on North Basin Street. Hernandez and Saloy operated as the **Louisiana Porcelain Manufacturing Company** which Barber, *Pottery and Porcelain of the U.S.*, p. 313, said closed around 1890. In the New Orleans City Directories, the firm was listed as the **Louisiana Porcelain Works of Hernandez and Company**, in 1887, 1888, 1889, at 326 Carondelet Walk. In the same directory, the **New Orleans Art Pottery** was listed one year only in 1889 at 249 Baronne Street. Paul Evans, *Art Pottery of the U.S.*, p. 179, tells us George Ohr (see Beloxi Pottery), and Joseph Meyer (later at Newcomb Pottery) came there to work. Meyer was listed as operating his own pottery in 1881, 1882, 1883, at Bernard Avenue between Prieur and Johnson. The local ladies art league came to the New Orleans Art Pottery failed, the ladies organized the Art League Pottery Club or Art League for Women and called it the Baronne Street Pottery. They continued to fire their pieces and work there. This arrangement went on for about five years until the pottery was established at Newcomb College, Tulane University (see Newcomb Pottery) and Mary G. Sheerer was brought in to supervise the ladies. The mark shown is for the New Orleans Art Pottery firm. Also, see Paul E. Cox Pottery listing. (Information: *New Orleans City Directories, 1880-1900*, sent to author by the Louisiana State Library at Baton Rouge; Paul Evans, *Art Pottery of the U.S.*, pp. 179-182; Ralph and Terry Kovel, *The Kovel's Collector's Guide to American Art Pottery*, pp. 114-117. See both of these books for a much more detailed account and discussion of individual worker and products. Mark: Evans, p. 181.)

N. o. art Pottery

Newton, Dewey. White Cottage, Muskingum County, Ohio. Late 19th century. Made stoneware. (Mark was found on blue spongeware crock of gray clay. Mark hand written in blue.)

DEWEY NEWTON WHITE COTTAGE

New York City Pottery. New York City, New York. 1853-1888. The pottery was started by James Carr in October 1853 (Barber, p. 77) under the firm name **Carr and Morrison**. In 1852, for one year, Carr had operated a little pottery of his own in South Amboy, New Jersey. (J. Stradling, "American Ceramics at the Philadelphia Centennial," *Antiques Magazine*, July 1976, p. 146.) The firm name stayed Morrison and Carr until 1871. Carr continued to operate the New York Pottery until 1888 when the pottery closed. Carr died January 31, 1904, at the age of 84. Carr, an English potter, had worked for Ridgeway and James Clews in England. Carr was a remarkable person who managed in a lifetime to have affiliations with several potteries. (See Carr and Clark in Lincoln Pottery and Carr and Clark at the International Pottery.) According to Ramsay, Carr made a cauliflower majolica teapot, and according to Jervis he made a wide variety of articles in majolica. Carr, in his long career also manufactured Parian, cream-colored ware, and white granite; and his very early products included Rockingham and yellowware. From *The Ceramic Art, the History and Manufacture of Pottery and Porcelain*, by Jennie J. Young, New York, 1878, Harper & Brothers, p. 458, it is found that Carr made six or seven different bodies all composed of American materials. Young also stated that the dinner services were decorated with the same care usually reserved for porcelain. Carr's "semi-china" was nearly as translucent as porcelain, made of American kaolin clay with a large admixture of feldspar and decorated in styles similar to those found on ironstone china, according to Ms. Young. (Marks: nos. 1-9, Barber, *Marks of American Potters*, pp. 77-79; no. 10, from Jervis, "Pottery Marks of the World," *American Ceramic Society Bulletin*, January 1, 1914, p. 15; nos. 11-14, Ramsay, p. 257.)

1. SEMI CHINA J. C.
2. STONE PORCELAIN J.C.
3. MORRISON & CARR
4. JAMES L. RICHARD & CO. HARTFORD PAT. SEPT. 19 -1871-
5.
6. STONE CHINA JAMES CARR N.Y.C. POTTERY
7. TRADE MARK
8. TRADE MARK STONE CHINA
9. J. C. N.Y.C.P.
10.
11. JC STONE CHINA

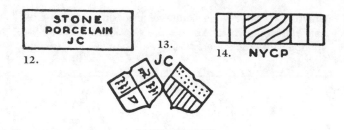

12. STONE PORCELAIN JC

13. JC

14. NYCP

New York, Missouri Area Potters. Balsir Oartar owned the New York pottery for a time in the 1850's. Marks of other potters found on shards at the dump site were "S.D. Smith," "W. Lindsay," "Smith & Fothingham," "G. Ro---?" Made stoneware. A complete shard has not been found for the name starting "G Ro---." All of the marks shown were from the period after the Civil War. (Information: Edison Shrum by letter. Mark: drawn from pictures.)

S.D. SMITH   W. LINDSAY

G. RO — ?   SMITH & FOTHINGHAM

BALSIR OARTAR NEW YORK, MO.

New York State College. Alfred, New York. The New York State College of Ceramics has played a big role in the story of ceramics in the United States. The school was started at Alfred University in 1900. Charles Fergus Binns, well-known studio potter, was the first director. The school was the New York State School of clayworking. The emphasis was on craft pottery, and the graduates went into teaching. The ceramic industry needed technically trained people, scientists, engineers, designers, etc. Hostetter, president of the American Ceramic Society and Ross Purdy, secretary, influenced a change in the Alfred program. The name was changed to The New York State College of Ceramics, a professional faculty hired, and a new ciriculum started in 1932. R. Guy Cowan, a graduate of Alfred and president of the Cowan Pottery Company of Rocky River, Ohio, was responsible for the school's hiring Don Schreckengost, a professional experienced designer who became the college's first professor of Industrial Ceramic Design in 1935. Today the school has the reputation of being the world's leading ceramic college. Many of today's designers are from this school.

New York Stoneware Company. Fort Edwards, New York. 1861-1885 (*Stewart and Consentino Stoneware*, dates, p. 125.) Made utilitarian stoneware. (Marks: Elmer L. Smith, *Pottery a Utilitarian Folk Craft*, p. 6.)

NEW YORK STONE WARE CO.

NEW YORK STONEWARE CO. FORT EDWARDS, N.Y.

Nicholas, Donna L. Edinboro, Pennsylvania. Donna, a studio potter was born in 1938. She received a B.A. degree at Pomona College in Claremont, California, in 1959, and a M.F.A. in 1966. From 1962 to 1964 she studied with Hiroki Morino and maintained a studio of her own in Japan. In 1978, she was teaching art at Edinboro State College in Edinboro, Pennsylvania, where she started in 1969. She has won many grants and awards and exhibited her work in many one-woman and group shows. At present, she sculptures her pieces. (Information: Garth Clark, *A Century of Ceramics in the U.S.*, p. 313. Mark: Linda Steigleder, from the booklet published by the Everson Museum of Art to accompany the 1978 exhibition, "A Century of Ceramics in the U.S." Mark is incised.)

Nicholas 77

Nichols and Alford/Nichols and Boynton. Burlington, Vermont. Pottery was built by E.L. Farrar, but operated by Nichols and Alford from 1854 to 1856. They made hound handled pitchers and other useful and ornamental Rockingham pieces such as pitchers, mugs, book flasks, vases, etc. In 1856 until before 1860 the firm was Nichols and Boynton, and in 1860 it was taken over by H.N. Ballard. (Information: Lura W. Watkins, *Early New England Potters and Their Wares*, p. 150. Marks: no. 1, E.A. Barber, *Marks of American Potters*, p. 96. Mark no. 2, from Stewart and Consentino, *Stoneware*.)

Nichols & Alford Manufacturers 1854 Burlington, Vt

NICHOLS & BOYNTON BURLINGTON, V.T.

Nichols, Elmer L. San Antonio, Texas. Filed for registration of this mark on December 8, 1954, for use on chinaware creamers, although they may be made of other materials, claiming use since April 2, 1954.

HITCHIKER

Nichols Pottery. Avondale, Missouri. Owner Deanna Nichols is a studio potter operating 1965 to present to make functional and decorative stoneware and porcelain salt glazed ware fired to cone 10. She has an M.A. degree from Claremont Graduate School and B.F.A. degree from Kansas City Art Institute. (Mark no. 1 was used from 1965 to 1971 in Castle Rock, Colorado, and Norfolk, Virginia. No. 2 was used 1972 to 1979 in Norfolk, Virginia and Yarnell, Arizona. Nos. 3 and 4 used 1980 to present (1982) in Yarnell, Arizona and Kansas City, Missouri.)

Nichols

NICHOLS FERENBACH

NICHOLS

Nichols

Nichols

W. Nichols. Poughkeepsie, New York. Around 1823. Made stoneware. Mark impressed in a painted circle. (Information and mark: John P. Remensnyder, "The Potters of Poughkeepsie," reprinted from *Antiques Magazine* in *The Art of the Potter*, edited by Diana and J. Stradling, p. 124.)

W. NICHOLS

PO'KEEPSIE

Nicodemus, Chester. Columbus, Ohio. 1935 to present (1985). Produces a vitrified ware from local Bedford shale in vases, pitchers, urns, bowls, dogs, cats, and various other animals, figurines, and birds. Discontinued selling to stores as of Janury 1, 1971; sold privately only in 1973 to present (1985). Nicodemus graduated in 1925 from the Cleveland School of Art. He taught sculpture in the Dayton Art Institute for five years from 1925 to 1930, then came to the Columbus Art School to teach. He taught at the Columbus Art School for 13 years for three days a week and made pottery on the other days. He studied with Arthur Baggs at Ohio State University in the early 1930's. In 1943 he started working a gift ceramic business, although he had been taking some orders before that time. At age 83 in 1985, Nicodemus works at making pottery and is at his shop daily.

NICODEMUS   cN²   (PAPER LABEL 1971)

NICODEMUS
FERRO-STONE

Nielson, Christian/Nielson Pottery. Zanesville, Ohio. Potter born in Denmark in 1870. He studied sculpture at the Royal Academy of Art in Copenhagen and worked in a pottery there for a year. He came to the United States in 1891 and worked in New Jersey and Connecticut before coming to Ohio. In 1893, he designed work which won a gold medal at the Chicago World's Fair while working at Homer Laughlin China Company in East Liverpool, Ohio. In 1894 he went to the American Encaustic Tiling Company for eight years. In 1902 to around 1905 he worked at the Roseville Pottery. Then for just one year Nielson had a pottery of his own. In 1905 the Nielson Pottery was incorporated by Christian Nielson, Henry Roekel, W. Miller and their wives. It was located in Muskingum Ave. at the foot of Pierce Street in Zanesville, Ohio. The pottery only lasted one year because it made too many sales at too low a price according to Schneider as cited. (Information: Norris Schneider, "Roseville Pottery," *Zanesville Times Signal*, March 22, 1959 (no page no.), also, "Many Small Potteries Once Operated in Zanesville," *Zanesville Times Recorder*, February 4, 1962, (no p. no.) Mark: Foster E. and Gladys C. Hall, *Collector's Guide to American Pottery Artists, Potters and Designers and Their Marks*, p. 13.)

C N

Niloak Pottery Company/Hyten-Eagle Pottery Company. Benton, Arkansas. The Hyten Pottery, later called Eagle Pottery, was started before 1900 by J.H. Hyten. By 1909, his son, Charles Dean "Bullet" Hyten was the sole owner. Around 1911 the original pottery burned, and in 1912 a new two story building was built which housed both the Hyten/Eagle Pottery and the newly formed Niloak Pottery Company. The Hyten/Eagle Pottery made stoneware jugs, crocks, churns, flower pots, etc. until around 1938. Some writers refer to "Eagle" as a line name only, rather than a name of the pottery because for a time, both the Eagle Pottery and Niloak Pottery Company operated in the same building on separate floors. Charles Hyten owned the Eagle Pottery and managed the Niloak Pottery Company, and this seems to be the only real connection between the two other than sharing a building.

In 1909 or 1910, Hyten developed a swirled hand thrown artware which has come to be known as "Mission Ware." Hyten did not give the product this name. It was probably assigned by some distributor. Mission Ware was marketed all over the country by such names as Wanamakers, Marshall Fields, the May Company, etc. (See these individual listings.) The Niloak Pottery Company was formed as a stock company around 1911 with Charles D. Hyten as the operator. At one time, six potters worked to hand throw the pieces of "Mission Ware," which was no longer made after late 1930's. In 1929, a showroom was built to try to sell the product in hard times and the plant was heavily mortgaged. The depression came, and by 1934 the mortgage was bought by a group of Little Rock insurance men, and it was at this point that Hyten lost some of his authority over production even though he still owned considerable stock and was more of a figurehead and salesman. In 1941, he sold the rest of his stock. Charles Hyten was a brilliant artist, although it seems doubtful he considered himself as such. He did not exhibit his ware as an artist, but he did receive recognition for "Mission Ware" at the Chicago World's Fair in the Arkansas section. He was born in 1887 and died in 1944. For a time, after he no longer managed Niloak Pottery Company, he worked as a salesman at Camark Pottery from the late 1930's until 1944. "Mission Ware" has become well known among collectors because of its unusual appearance of different swirled colors of clay. To make a piece, colors were carefully planned in relationship to each other for harmony and appearance. No two pieces were ever exactly alike.

In the late 1920's, a less expensive line of solid colored ware called "Hywood" was introduced. The very early pieces were hand thrown, but later after a change of ownership around 1934, the ware was all cast in molds. The Hywood mark was eventually dropped and a great deal was marked Niloak. Collectors are saying a great deal was unmarked. Niloak Pottery made clocks, jardinieres, tumblers, smoking sets, pitchers, steins, umbrella stands, vases, rose jars, tobacco humidors, hand cast animal figures, even gear shift knobs and tile. Several potters have made a swirled clay ware in the United States, with varying degrees of success when compared to Niloak. See the listings for Desert Sands Pottery, Commanche Pottery, Ouachita Pottery and J. Leveritt. The problem with mixing the clays for a swirled combination is to keep the clay from shrinking and separating after it is fired. For a technical discussion of this, see Paul Evans, "The Niloak Pottery," *Spinning Wheel*, October 1970, pp. 18, 19, and also Virginia Coleman Johnson, "Niloak Pottery," *Antiques Journal*, July 1973, pp. 28-30, 45. (Information: Jeannette H. Dixon, "Niloak Pottery," *Hobbies*, March 1973, pp. 109, 113; Evans, as cited; and Johnson, as cited. Marks: Niloak marks are impressed or ink stamped. Molded pieces may have raised lettering for a mark. Besides the name of the pottery, two types of stickers were used. There was blue and white one in the form of a circle with Niloak written on the inside circle, and there was a sticker in the shape of a gold vase with brown lettering, "From-Niloak-Since 1868-In Arkansas." A person may be fortunate even today to pick up a piece of Niloak with an original sticker on it. Niloak was registered as a trademark in 1924, claiming use since 1910. Mark no. 1 was on five gallon stoneware crock pictured in Deb and Gini Johnson, *Beginners Book of Pottery*, p. 31. No. 2 was a photostatic copy from a paper label which was only mark on the piece unless it is marked under the label. All the rest of the marks may be seen in Johnsons' book as cited, p. 30.)

Niloak Pottery and Tile Company. Little Rock, Arkansas. This company filed May 6, 1947 for use of this mark on vitrified dinnerware, claiming use since March 1, 1947. I could make no connection between this company and the well known Niloak Pottery Company of Benton, Arkansas, except that men from Little Rock had purchased the Niloak Pottery mortgage in 1934. There may very well be a connection if only in the persons involved. Someone will have to pursue this at a local level.

BOUQUET

Noguchi, Isamu. Isamu, a sculpturer and studio type potter, spent most of his childhood in Japan. He came back to the U.S. in 1918 to attend the International School in Indiana. He studied with Gutzon Borglum in 1922 before moving back to New York City. He studied scultpure at the Leonardo da Vinci Art School under Onorio Ruotolo. In 1927 to 1928 he studied in Paris, on a Guggenheim scholarship. He became a studio assistant to Constantin Brancusi. From 1930 to 1932, he made a series of ceramic sculptures in Japan. He returned to Japan for a time in the 1950's, also, and did the same type of work. His first large exhibition in the U.S. came in 1954 at the Stable Gallery in New York. (Information: Garth Clark, *A Century of Ceramics in the U.S.*, p. 314. Mark: Linda Steigleder, from the booklet published by the Everson Museum of Art to accompany the 1978 exhibition, ''A Century of Ceramics in the U.S.'' Mark is incised.)

Nolen, Francis. Cloverland, Clay County, Indiana. Around 1849 to 1854. Made stoneware. In the booklet by Melvin Davies for the exhibit *Clay County Indiana Traditional Potters and Their Wares* held in 1981, a salt glazed stoneware jar with an incised floral design in cobalt blue made by Francis Nolen was shown. (Information and impressed marks: no. 1, Staff written, ''Indiana Earthenware and Stoneware,'' *Pottery Collectors Newsletter*, September, October, 1979, p. 41; impressed mark no. 2: staff written, ''Indiana Earthenware, Stoneware Exhibit Opens June 23 at Bank in Fort Wayne,'' *Tri State Trader*, June 21, 1980, p. 7.)

FRANCIS
1. NOLEN   2. FRANCIS NOLEN
            CLAY COUNTY. IND.

Nonconnah Pottery. See Walter B. Stephen.

Norse Pottery. Edgerton, Wisconsin, and Rockford, Illinois. 1903 to 1913. Norse Pottery in Edgerton, Wisconsin, begun in 1903. In 1904 it was moved to Rockford, Illinois, and named the Norse Pottery Company. Production stopped in 1913. Art pottery, consisting of vases, candlesticks, fern pots, cigar jars, bowls, ashtrays, etc. were the products. They made replicas of ancient bronze pieces. Also, a selection of work was shown in the 1904 St. Louis expedition which had a red body painted with oil colors in an ancient Greek style. Examples are at the Smithsonian Institution. (Information: Danny Brown, ''Pitcher Potpourri,'' *American Clay Exchange*, January 1982, p. 10; and Paul Evans, *Art Pottery of the U.S.*, pp. 193, 194. Impressed mark: copy sent by Dave Rago, by letter; also shown in Danny Brown, and Evans, as cited.)

North Dakota School of Mines. University of North Dakota, Grand Forks, North Dakota. Earliest known were dated 1904, made by Marcia Bisbee. The school was first equipped to make pottery in 1910 and continued making ware until 1963. Ceramic courses continued to be taught until 1972. Almost all pieces were made from molds. A few pieces were handthrown by Margaret Cable. Margaret was hired in 1910 and taught at the University until 1949. Piece was marked, ''M. Cable, 1946.'' The wares were sometimes decorated with designs carved in low relief or handpainted with colored glazes. A few pieces were marked, ''U.N.D., Grand Forks, N.D.'' After 1963, the pieces were marked just with the students' names who made them. Only a limited amount of the pottery made at the University was ever sold to the public. Pieces included vases, figurines, cookie jars, lamp bases, ashtrays, tea sets, plaques, etc. Other artist's names found in addition to the stamped mark shown were ''Huck,'' for Flora Huckfield, who taught between 1923 and 1949. Also, ''Agnes Dollahan,'' with date, ''Dec. 1946.'' ''J.M.'' signified Julia E. Mattson, which was found on a brown high gloss vase with raised figures of a cowboy lassoing a horse. (Information: staff written, ''American Art Pottery Gains Attentions of Wide Range of Readers,'' *American Art Pottery*, July 1980, p. 4; Darlene Dommel, ''University of North Dakota Pottery,'' *Spinning Wheel*, June 1973, pp. 30, 31. Mark: no. 1 stamped on piece with very heavy ink. The incised initials ''U.N.D.'' and artists' initials or lot numbers may be found as a mark such as those shown from "University of North Dakota," May 30, 1985, p. 11, and "Pottery Puzzlers," July, 1983, p. 11, in the *American Clay Exchange*.)

UND

North Star Stoneware Company. Red Wing, Minnesota. 1892 to May 20, 1896. The pottery made stoneware crocks, jugs, bowls, etc., sewer pipe and brick. They were short lived, even though they had a good capitol and buildings to start. Lyndon Viel in *Clay Giants Book II*, pp. 69 to 71, gives us great insight into the quick failure of North Star. He said they were quickly running out of clay. They started with 37 acres and were down to six when the factory closed. The Union Stoneware Company, a selling agency (see that listing), had its three member potteries on a quota basis and North Star had the smallest quota. The Red Wing Stoneware Company and the Minnesota Stoneware Company were allowed to sell more to Union Stoneware Company for resale. Also, he states North Star had used up a lot of their capitol trying to perfect a white glaze. (Marks: nos. 1, 2, 3, David Newkirk, *A Guide to Redwing Markings*, p. 19. Mark 1 is a raised star mark with the word, "North," going counter clockwise. No. 2 is a recessed star mark with the letters going clockwise. Shards of lid covers found in the North Star Pottery dump have a plain raised star on the knob or handle of the lids. No. 4 was a stenciled mark on the front of an Albany glazed jug in Lyndon C. Viel, *Clay Giants Book II*, p. 83. No. 5 is from same source and is a recessed mark on the bottom of a butter tub. Viel shows another piece with this mark that has a carmel colored glaze. No. 6 was sent by Dave Newkirk.)

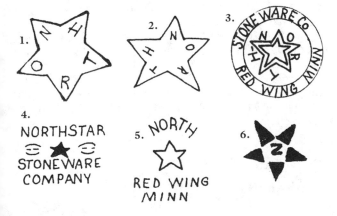

North State Pottery Company. Sanford, North Carolina. 1924 to 1959. Became **Pine State Pottery** from 1959 to 1977. North State Pottery Company produced the old type of stoneware for four years only, then went on to a variety of clay bodies and excellent glazes which eventually included a marbleized or swirl ware, a spider-webbing or crackle-glaze, and an easily identifiable double-dip glaze in a variety of colors, and a great number of shapes, all handmade. See Stuart C. Schwartz, *North State Pottery Company*, Charlotte, North

Carolina: Mint Museum of History, 1977, a booklet of 16 pages containing more on marks, history and products. Publication also included two facsimile catalogs, one for wholesale buyers, the other for the retail trade (out of print), also see the listing various Owen family potters. (Marks: as they appeared in Schwartz book cited, except the first mark which is a 1925 patent office mark, filed for use on crockery, earthenware and porcelain. North State Pottery claimed the use of this mark after November 9, 1925; no. 2, is artist's version of no. 1, as shown on the front of the Schwartz book. The following are Stuart Schwartz's dates for use: no. 3, used 1925 until November 1925; no. 4, December 1925, until 1938 or 1939; no. 5, 1939 to 1959; no. 6, 1959 until 1965; no. 7, after 1965; no. 8, after 1970.)

Northwestern Terra Cotta/Gustav Hottinger. Chicago, Illinois. Gustav Hottinger was born in Vienna, Austria, where he received degrees as an artist and sculptor. At age 19 he came to the United States to work for the Chicago Terra Cotta Works. In 1873, he and several other men formed the Northwestern Terra Cotta Works. The partnership was known as True, Brunkhorst and Company. John R. True was bookkeeper and accountant. John Brunkhorst and Henry Rohkam were the potters. Gustav was in charge of the art work. At first they made flower pots, garden vases and ceramic furniture and small statuary. Later, structural terra cotta became the product and finally became the largest plant in the country making terra cotta by the 1920's. Sometime before 1907 for a short while, possibly 10 years, the pottery made art pottery with a crystalline glaze with an impressed mark, "Norweta." Not all of it was marked. They also made a line of Terra Cotta vases. Gustav Hottinger contributed $50,000 toward the funding of an Industrial Arts School. In the 1930's he also gave his $4 million share in the Northwestern Terra Cotta Company to the 36 men who helped him build his great business. (Information: staff written, "Gustav Hottinger," *Bulletin of the American Ceramic Society*, December 1936, p. 476. Marks: Nos. 1, 2, marks in mold on art pottery; Sharon S. Darling, *Chicago Ceramics and Glass*, p. 70. No. 3 on terra cotta pieces, p. 168.)

1. NORWETA

2. NORWETA

3. NORTHWESTERN TERRA COTTA CHICAGO

Norton, F.B. Pottery. Worcester, Massachusetts. 1858-1894. Franklin (Frank) B. Norton was the grandson of Captain John Norton. Franklin probably apprenticed with his uncle, Luman Norton. In 1858 Franklin and Frederick Hancock began to manufacture stoneware in Worcester, Massachusetts, and operated for 36 years making jugs, jars, pots and other stoneware pieces. From 1858 to 1876 Norton and Hancock operated under the firm name F.B. Norton and Company. In 1876, Hancock sold his share, and the name became Frank B. Norton. When Franklin (or Frank) died, his sons, Myron E. and John E. operated as F.B. Norton's Sons until 1894. See also Richard W. Fenton for more on Hancock. (Information and marks: David J. Corrigan and Norma Feingold, *The F.B. Norton Pottery*, booklet written to accompany an exhibition held October 1980 to January 1981 by the Worcester Historical Museum in Worcester, pp. 2, 3.)

FRANK B NORTON

WORCESTER, MASS.

FB NORTON & CO.

WORCESTER, MASS.

Norton Pottery. Bennington, Vermont. The pottery was established in 1793 by Captain John Norton, who retired in 1823. The first stoneware was made in 1800, prior to that only redware was made. Captain Norton took his two sons into partnership with him. When Luman, Captain John's first son, was taken in, the firm became **L. Norton and Company**, sometimes found with or without the town name of Bennington. This mark was used from around 1823 to the end of 1827 or beginning of 1828 while the pottery was owned by Luman and his brother John. At the beginning of 1828, Luman became the sole owner, and the name and mark became just **L. Norton** until 1833. Then in 1833, Luman took his son, Julius, into partnership and the mark became **L. Norton and Son**, until 1840. (Spargo, p. 20) At the beginning of 1841, Julius Norton began to advertise the business in his own name, and this date is the one when historians assume Judge Luman Norton had left the business; the marks became **Julius Norton** and **J. Norton**. Sometime just before 1845, Christopher W. Fenton, who was married to Julius Norton's sister, became a partner in the Norton Pottery after he had worked there for several years prior to that time. The pottery had been cursed by a bankruptcy in 1842 and a fire in 1845. The pottery was rebuilt and functioning fine, but the partnership did not last long; it was dissolved June 25, 1847, accor-

ding to a newspaper announcement. (Spargo, p. 82). The mark used during the partnership was **Norton and Fenton**, East Bennington, then a little later the East was dropped and just Bennington was used. All pottery marked Norton and Fenton comes from the period 1844-1847, according to Spargo, p. 83. From 1847 to 1850, Julius Norton once more operated alone and marked his pottery in the same way that he had done from 1841 to 1844. Then in 1850, Edward Norton, a cousin of Julius, became a partner in the pottery, and the mark became **J. and E. Norton** until 1859. Julius had only one son, Luman Preston Norton, who was taken into the business in 1859 and until 1861 the firm was **J. & E. Norton and Co.** Between 1859 and 1861, Spargo, p. 98 tells us that two marks were used: "J. Norton and Co., Bennington, Vt.," and "J. and E. Norton and Co., Bennington, Vt." In 1861, Julius Norton died. Edward and Luman Preston Norton continued to operate the firm under the name **E. & L.P. Norton**, and with Bennington, Vermont, this became the mark until 1881. In 1881 Luman P. Norton retired, and Edward Norton became the sole proprietor until 1883 when the name was **E. Norton**, Bennington, Vermont. In 1883, C.W. Thatcher bought half interest in the pottery, and the name became **Edward Norton and Company**. The marks used during this partnership which lasted until 1894, were "Edward Norton and Company" or "E. Norton and Co." and "Bennington, Vermont." In 1885, two years after Thatcher had come into the firm, Edward Norton had died and his son, Edward Lincoln Norton, had taken his father's place. But at the age of 29, Edward Lincoln Norton died in 1894. The Norton Pottery at Bennington, Vermont, made Rockingham, stoneware jugs, crocks, etc. and brown glazed pottery pieces. They also made whiteware for table use, yellowware for domestic utensils such as milkpans, pitchers, mixing bowls, baking dishes, etc. (Information: John Spargo, *Early American Pottery and China*, pp. 172, 173, 256 to 300; also by Spargo, *The Potters and Potteries of Bennington*, pp. 14 to 20, 61 to 69. The chronological list shown on p. 98 of last book named and on p. 371 of first book. The marks shown are repeated in several books. One or more of these marks may be found in the following references: Guilland, pp. 133; Stradling, pp. 78, 88, 89; Revi, *Antiques Book*, p. 79; Spargo, plates following p. 14 and 240; Garth's Auction catalogue of Early Antiques, August 8, 1970; Stewart and Consentino, pp. 63, 65, 70, 81; Thorn, p. 140; Barbara Chiolino, "Folk Art on Utilitarian Stoneware," *Spinning Wheel*, April 1968, pp. 16-19; *Pottery Collectors Newsletter*, May, June 1980, front cover picture and p. 19; and Doris M. Green, "Butter Making," *Antiques Journal*, July 1964, p. 27, which shows E. and L.P. Norton butter churn.)

E. & L.P. NORTON
BENNINGTON VT.

E. NORTON & CO.
BENNINGTON VT.

E. NORTON
BENNINGTON
VT.

EDWARD NORTON & CO.
BENNINGTON, VT.

NORTON & FENTON
EAST BENNINGTON, VT.

NORTON & FENTON
BENNINGTON VT.

NORTON & FENTON
DENNINGTON

EDWARD NORTON CO.
BENNINGTON
V T.

THE EDWARD NORTON CO.
BENNINGTON, VT.

J & E NORTON
BENNINGTON
VT.

J & E NORTON & CO.
BENNINGTON, VT.

J. NORTON & CO.
BENNINGTON VT

J. NORTON & CO.
BENNINGTON VT.

JULIUS NORTON
EAST BENNINGTON
VT.

J. NORTON & CO.
BENNINGTON
V T.

J. NORTON
EAST BENNINGTON

JULIUS NORTON
BENNINGTON
VT.

J & E NORTON
BENNINGTON, VT.

JULIUS NORTON
BENNINGTON, VT.

L. NORTON & SON
BENNINGTON
VT.

J. NORTON
BENNINGTON
V T.

L. NORTON & CO.
BENNINGTON

L. NORTON & CO.

L. NORTON & CO.
BENNINGTON
VT.

L. NORTON
BENNINGTON
VT.

Marks Used by the Norton Potteries

L. Norton & Co., Bennington, Vt.	1823–28
L. Norton, Bennington, Vt.	1828–33
L. Norton & Son, East Bennington, Vt. L. Norton & Son, Bennington, Vt.	1833–40
Julius Norton, East Bennington, Vt. J. Norton, East Bennington, Vt. Julius Norton, Bennington, Vt. J. Norton, Bennington, Vt.	1841–44 (45)
Norton & Fenton, East Bennington, Vt. Norton & Fenton, Bennington, Vt.	1844 (45)–47
Julius Norton, Bennington, Vt. J. Norton, Bennington, Vt.	1847–50
J. & E. Norton, Bennington, Vt.	1850–59
J. Norton & Co., Bennington, Vt. J. & E. Norton & Co., Bennington, Vt.	1859–61
E. & L. P. Norton, Bennington, Vt.	1861–81
E. Norton, Bennington, Vt.	1881–83
Edward Norton, Bennington, Vt. Edward Norton & Co., Bennington, Vt. E. Norton & Co., Bennington, Vt. Edward Norton & Company, Bennington, Vt.	1883–94

(Sometimes the word "Company" is spelled in full)
Edward Norton Company, Bennington, Vt.   1886–94
(This last mark is uncommon.)
Bennington Factory

No-Ten-O-Quah Pottery (Indian name for wind woman). Yale, Oklahoma. 1978 to present (1985). Grace F. Thorpe, studio potter from the Sac Fox Tribe, makes stoneware into animal effegy pots and pieces with old American Indian designs in a high fired process. She studied at Arrowmont School of Crafts in Gatlinburg, Tennessee, and at the Oklahoma State University in Stillwater, Oklahoma. For a mark, Grace draws a duck or animal with her signature in the bottom or side of the pot.

grace thorpe   *Grace thorpe*

Notkin, Richard T. Myrtle Point, Oregon. 1969 to present. Richard is a studio potter using a variety of clays such as stoneware, porcelain, earthenware, some terra cotta and raku to make pieces. He uses a great variety of techniques such as sculpturing, hand throwing, slip casting, etc. Each piece is unique and occassionally a small edition of up to six of something is made, but even though similar they would not be exactly alike. Richard graduated with a B.F.A. degree from the Kansas City Art Institute in Kansas City, Missouri, in 1970, and got a M.F.A. degree from the University of California in Davis, California, in 1973. Between 1971 and 1984, Richard has taught ceramics at several schools: Kansas City Art Institute; Ohio State University; Montana State University; Maryland Institute College of Art; University of Utah; and University of California. Also, he listed 32 workshops and lectures he has conducted between 1977 and 1985 and a sampling of these locations are: School of the Art Institute of Chicago; Purdue University, West Lafayette, Indiana; Northern Illinois University, DeKalb; University of Wisconsin, Madison; Virginia Commonwealth University, Richmond; New York State College of Ceramics, Alfred; Mills College, Oakland, California; California State University, Hayward; University of Washington, Seattle; University of Oregon, Eugene; Pennsylvania State University; Rhode Island School of Design, Providence; University of Montana, Missoula; and Georgia State University, Atlanta. He has received the following grants and fellowships: Fellowship, Western States Arts Foundation, 1976; Emerging Artist Fellowship, National Endowment for the Arts, 1979; Visual Arts Fellowship, National Endowment for the Arts, 1981; and Individual Artist Fellowship, Oregon Arts Commission, 1985. The list of 88 selected group exhibitions that he has participated in since 1971 covers many of the states and reads like a "Who's Who" in important shows. We are listing only the exhibitions since 1983 to give an idea of the scope and importance of his work.

"Clay: A Medium for Personal Iconography," Elements Gallery, New York; "Ronna Neuenschwander and Richard T. Notkin," Hoffman Gallery, Oregon School of Arts and Crafts, Portland; "Tea - A Pot Pourri," Netsky Gallery, Miami, Florida; "Winners" (Oregon NEA Fellowship Recipients), Contemporary Crafts Gallery, Portland, Oregon; "Echoes - Historical References in Contemporary Ceramics," Nelson-Atkins Museum of Art, Kansas City, Missouri; "Ceramic Artists: Distinguished Alumni," Kemper Gallery, Kansas City Art Institute, Missouri; "A Personal View: Seletions from the Joan Mannheimer Ceramic Collection, University of Missouri-Kansas City; "Teapots: Poetry in Mass and Line," Garth Clark Gallery, Los Angeles; "International Tea Party," Contemporary Crafts Gallery, Portland, Oregon; "Clay: 1984, A National Survey," Traver Sutton Gallery, Seattle, Washington; "Image-Vessel-Image," Garth Clark Gallery, New York; "Design in the Service of Tea," Cooper-Hewitt Museum, New York; "Design in the Service of Tea," Cooper-Hewitt Museum, New York; "Oregon Invitational Exhibition," Hult Center for the Performing Arts, Eugene, "Rituals of Tea," Garth Clark Galleries, New York and Los Angeles; "Ceramics and Social Commentary," Laumeier Sculpture Park, St. Louis, Missouri; "Ceramic Invitational," The Canton Art Institute, Canton, Ohio; "The Oregon Biennial 1985," Portland Art Museum; "A Centennial Celebration: Highlights from Kansas City Art Institute Alumni," Nelson-Atkins Museum of Art, Kansas City, Missouri; "Clay: Everyday Plus Sunday," John Michael Kohler Arts Center, Sheboygan, Wisconsin; "Cast Clay," Pinch Pottery, Northhampton, Massachusetts; "Chronicles: Historical References in Contemprary Clay," Nora Eccles Harrison Museum of Art, Utah State University, Logan; "Cups," The Hand and the Spirit Crafts Gallery, Scottsdale, Arizona: "Possibly Functional," Esther Saks Gallery, Chicago, Illinois; "Oregon Invitational Small Sculpture Exhibition," Lane Community College, Eugene; "Our Cup of Tea - Contemporary Crafted Teapots, Cups and Spoons," Renwick Gallery, Smithsonian Institution, Washington, D.C.; "Recent Ceramic Sculpture," University Art Museum, University of New Mexico, Albuquerque; "Northwest Invitational Ceramics Exhibition," Eastern Washington University.

Richard has pieces in several public and private collections. The public collections listed were: National Collection of Fine Arts, Smithsonian Institution, Washing, D.C.; Cooper-Hewitt Museum, New York; Everson Museum of Art, Syracuse, New York; Nelson-Atkisn Museum of Art, Kansas City, Missouri; Victoria and Albery Museum, London, England; Stedelijk Museum, Amsterdam, The Netherlands; Hokkaido Television Broadcasting Company, Sapporo, Hokkaido, Japan; John Michael Kohler Arts Center, Sheboygan, Wisconsin; Nora Eccles Harrison Museum of Art, Utah State Unviersity, Logan City of Seattle, Washington.

Many articles have discussed this artist's work, a few include: *Painting and Sculpture Today: 1976*, Indianapolis Museum of Art, Indiana, 1976; *Eight Artists in Industry*, John Michael Kohler Arts Center, Sheboygan, Wisconsin, 1977; *Ceramics in the Pacific Northwest*, LaMar Harrington, University of Washington Press, Seattle, 1979; *West Coast Ceramics*, Stedilijk Museum Editions, Amsterdam, The Netherlands, 1979; *Porcelain: Traditions and New Visions*, Jan Axel and Karen McCready, Watson-Guptil, 1981; Jan Axel and Karen McCready, Watson-Guptil, 1981; *Forgotten Dimension: A Survey of Small Sculpture in California Now*, Fresno Art Center, California, 1982; "Richard Notkin," Lynn Eder, *Ceramics Monthly Magazine*, November 1982, pp. 59-63; *Art and/or Craft: USA and Japan*, Hokuriku Broadcasting Company, Ltd., Kanazawa, Japan, 1982; *Echoes: Historical References in Contemporary Ceramics*, Garth Clark, The Contemporary Arts Society, Nelson-Atkins Museum of Art, Kansas City, Missouri, 1983; *Ceramics Artists - Distinguished Alumni of the Kansas City Art Institute*, Charlotte Crosby Kemper Gallery, Kansas City Art Institute, Missouri, 1983; *Chronicles: Historical References in Contemporary Clay*, Nora Eccles Harrison Museum of Art, Utah State University, Logan, 1985. (Information: from the potter, Richard Notkin. Marks: hand inscribed. No. 1 was used from 1969 to 1973. No. 2 was used from 1969 to present. Usually the year is hand inscribed under the signature. A very few pieces are stamped "Notkin" in letters, but the stamp is seldom used.)

NOTKIN   *Notkin*

Nouvelle Pottery. Zanesville, Ohio. 1946 to middle 1970's - I had a letter in 1973, they closed shortly after. Makers of all types of glazed, bisque, and decorated pottery such as mugs, novelties, etc. made to customer specification. The only identification of its own that the pottery used was an occasional paper label. Marks of their customers were applied. The mark shown is for a large order of Elmer and Elsie salt and peppers for Borden's Milk Company. Nouvelle Pottery made a bust in two sizes of Alfred E. Neuman of Mad Magazine Fame. They made lamp bases for the Columbian Lamp Company. A.L. Hirsch and Company of New York had them to make a "Watch Dog" holder for the contents of men's pockets. (Information: Lehner, *Ohio Pottery and Glass*, p. 97; Norris Schneider, "Nouvelle Pottery," *Zanesville Times Recorder*, October 28, 1962.)

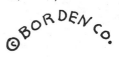

Novelty Pottery Company. East Liverpool, Ohio. This pottery building had a succession of owners between 1863 and 1928. John Goodwin built the plant in 1863; Manly and Riley owned it from 1865 to 1869; A.H. Marks from 1869 to 1870; McNicol, Burton and Company from 1870 to 1892 when it became the D.E. McNicol Pottery Company until 1928. (See separate listing for D.E. McNicol.) Yellowware and Rockingham and semi-porcelain were made. Mark shown was for McNicol, Burton and Company. As shown in *American Kitchen and Dinnerware* on an old discolored yellowware bowl.

O

Oak Creek Kilns. Sedona, Arizona. The mark shown was filed for registration by James M. Relph on April 22, 1966, claiming use since January 15, 1966, for earthenware, tableware, vases and urns. According to Derwich and Latos, *Dictionary Guide to U.S. Pottery and Porcelain*, p. 165, the pottery started in 1966 as a husband-wife team operation, making hand made pottery, hand decorated with Indians, cactus, an owl, the Roadrunner, geese, etc. Articles were windbells, coinbanks, animals, etc.

LEGENDWARE

Oakland (Name) Various Businesses. Oakland, California. On November 3, 1928, the **Oakland China Studio, Inc.** filed for registration of the mark, ''Silverite'' for use on ''dishes made of china and dishes made of porcelain.'' The company claimed use of the mark since August 15, 1926. The patent reports do not give street addresses, and I found no further listings with this name. In the *California Manufacturers Directory* for 1977, the **Oakland China and Glass Studio, Inc.** in Oakland, California, established 1929, was listed for china decorating, glass cutting and decorating giftware, etc. They employed seven in 1977. In 1948, which was the only other listing I had for this second factory, they were listed as china decorators only. In Paul Evans, *Art Pottery of the U.S.*, is an account of the **Oakland Art Pottery**, which existed from around 1887. The Oakland Art Pottery evolved from the original operation, the California Pottery and Terra Cotta Works found by James Miller and Serril Windsor. Around 1887, Miller's name was associated with the Oakland Art Pottery and Terra Cotta Works when it was first listed in directories. The pottery made art pottery, vases, flowerpots, but they also made sewer pipe and chimney tops. Evans doubted the company made any more art pottery after 1906 when the earthquake and fires hit California. He also said little was marked as no marked examples have been found. I have found no connection between these three companies.

SILVERITE

Oakley, Annie, Enteprises, Inc. Los Angeles, California. Filed for registration on this mark on July 19, 1954, for use on cups, saucers, cookie jars of earthenware, claiming use since October 1953.

ANNIE OAKLEY

Oak Tree Studio or Bennett Welsh Studio. Gresham, Oregon. Bennett Welsh has made pottery from 1947 to present (1983). The name used by this master potter and his associates from 1947 to 1960 was the **B. Welsh Studio.** From 1960 to 1973 the name was **Pacific Stoneware, Inc.** and from 1973 to present the name has been the **Bennett Welsh**

Studio. Bennett Welsh guides a group of young professional artists and craftsmen in the production of an outstanding line of functional stoneware, garden ware, dinnerware, bud vases, bonbon dishes, and all sorts of beautiful kitchenware. The patterns are melted into the glaze at 2,300 degrees and can't possibly wear off. The dishes are individually thrown, no molds are used so each is unique yet the sets are beautifully matched. Abigail Welsh-Fuller, Bennett's daughter, is a decorator and designer at the pottery. Individual potters have their own symbols incorporated into a company mark. (Marks: 1-7 are shown below a picture of the individual potters' symbol and the names of the potters as they were sent to me: nos. 8-11 are symbols shown in the material that may be found in use sometime. At present no names were assigned to these symbols.)

Oakwood China Company. Sebring, Ohio. Decorators that existed as early as 1915 until after 1967, and mark no.1 was shown in James Lafferty's book, *1940's Revisited*, p. 120. Lafferty got these marks from a *Crockery and Glass Journal Directory* of the 1940's, but did not state which one. In 1952 and 1954 in the same directories, the Oakwood China Company was listed on East Ohio Avenue. In the 1952 directory, they were listed for decorative wall plates, figures, figurines and miniatures, dinnerware of earthenware and porcelain, cups and saucers, so they must have decorated a variety of ware. (Mark no. 2 is from *Gift and Tableware Reporter Directory*, August 2, 1967. No. 3 is from Quality Stamp Company, East Liverpool, Ohio.)

Oakwood (various potteries). Oakwood was the name used by several potteries in Ohio: Cambridge, Wellsville, Dayton and Sebring. John Patterson and Sons, Wellsville, Ohio, called their pottery, Oakwood Art Pottery, but apparently they used their own name as a mark (see that listing). Oakwood China Company of Sebring, Ohio, were decorators with a variety of marks. Most marks found saying Oakwood, will belong to that company. (See the listing for Oakwood China Company, Sebring, Ohio.) The Cambridge Art Pottery, Cambridge, Ohio, used an impressed, "Oakwood" mark on their Oakwood artware. (See that listing for mark.) Then there was an Oakwood Pottery in Dayton, Ohio, from 1877 to around 1926 making earthenware and stoneware utilitarian pieces such as flower pots, hanging baskets, vases and crocks. Their "Oakwood" mark was incised. It is not as confusing as it sounds if we remember how the mark is applied and what type of ware we are considering. Sebring's Oakwood would be later machine made ware with a stamped mark. Cambridge Art Pottery would be attractive decorative ware as would be that of the Dayton Oakwood Pottery, but Cambridge Art Pottery used an impressed mark and Dayton's Oakwood Pottery used an inscribed mark, according to Paul Evans, *Art Pottery in the U.S.*, p. 198. The acorn mark shown is still unidentified. It has been said to be a Cambridge Art Pottery mark for a line called "Otoe," but according to Harold Bennett, owner of the Cambridge Glass Museum (which also has a lot of Cambridge Art Pottery on display) said this is not a mark for the Cambridge Company. It was found on a matt green little dish, round with straight sides coming up (not like a saucer), probably a bottom to a flower pot. The piece looked very old - but the mark is still unidentified. Also see Gordon T. Will, and Cambridge Art Pottery for other acorn marks.

Oatmeal Companies. Quaker Oats Company, Chicago, Illinois, filed for registration on the mark "Carnival," July 14, 1954, for use on tableware made of china, claiming use since April 1954. **Mother's Oats Company,** Chicago, Illinois, marked dishes "Tudor Rose," in the 1930's. "Harvest," "Pastoral," and "Wild Rose," also came in Mother's Oats during the 1940's and 1950's. See Homer Laughlin China Company and Taylor, Smith and Taylor for copies of these marks.

CARNIVAL

T.B. Odom. Knox Hill, Walton County, Florida. Around 1860. T.B. Odom was found in tax records for the year 1866, but was reported to have been making pottery before 1860. There seems to be a business association with a man named Turnley (or Turnlee). Piece pictured by Fredgant had an impressed mark "T.B. Odom." Red clay body and brownish tan or olive green glazes were found on several pieces in museums in Florida, but history is still very vague. (Information and mark: Don Fredgant, "T.B. Odom and J.W. Kohler: Two 19th Century West Florida Potters," *Antiques Journal*, June 1981, pp. 26-29. Mark 2, Harold F. Guilland, *Early American Folk Pottery*, p. 174 shown on a stoneware jug with olive green spots which Guilland said was typical of the pottery.)

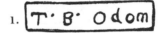

Oestreich Pottery. Taylor Falls, Minnesota. 1971 to present. Jeff Oestreich, studio potter, a maker of functional wood fired stoneware and porcelain. Studied at Bemidji State University, University of Minnesota. Did his apprenticeship in Leach Pottery, St. Ives, England.

Ohio Brass Company. Akron, Ohio. 1888 to present. The company was started in 1888 as a small foundry to make metal fittings for harness. Around 1903 to 1910, Ohio Brass distributed porcelain insulators made by Locke Insulator Manufacturing Company and the Akron High-Potential Insulator Company, Barberton, Ohio. In 1910, Ohio Brass bought the Barberton plant. For just a few years from around 1895 to 1915, the Ohio Brass Company also distributed glass insulators, but they only manufactured ceramic ones after 1910. Jack H. Tod, *Porcelain Insulators Guide Book for Collectors*, p. 130, said the glazes on the Ohio Brass insulators were beautiful, mottled combinations of tan-brown, gray and black. (Information: Tod, as cited, pp. 129-131. A fine detailed history and description of products is given in Tod's book. Marks: nos. 1-3, sent by company with approximate dates. Tod said no. 1 was a logo used on packing cartons and letterheads, never on insulators. No. 2 and its variations is the only mark that appeared on insulators. No. 3 is the newer logo used since 1960. It does not appear on insulators, but is found on some metal parts of insulator assemblies. Nos. 4-7 are a few of the embossed or recessed-embossed marks shown by Tod, p. 131. Tod said in recent years the monogram marking carries a manufacturing date beneath the marking.

The first number (s) is the month, and the last two numbers are the last two digits of the year.)

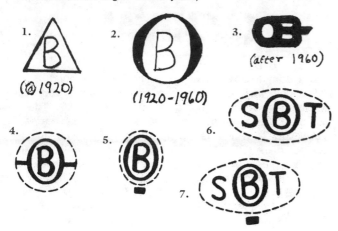

1. B (@ 1920)
2. B (1920-1960)
3. OB (after 1960)
4. B
5. B
6. SBT
7. SBT

Ohio China Company. East Palestine, Ohio. 1896 to around 1912. Started 1896 as the Ohio China Works by the Sebring Brothers. In 1902, this pottery was sold to the Ohio China Company, a company composed of East Palestine Capital headed by O.C. Walker. Made whiteware. (Information: McCord, *History of Columbian County*, p. 173; Ending date of around 1911 or 1912 from "Four Generations of Sebrings," *Bulletin no. 9 of Sebring Historical Society*, July 1971, no page numbers. Marks: No. 1, E.A. Barber, *Marks of American Potters*, p. 136; no. 2, on dish - semi-vitreous with cobalt blue edging, close to flow blue.)

1. OCCO Limoges PORCELAIN
2. OC CO. IMPERIAL CHINA

Ohio China Company. Monroe, Michigan. 1931 to present (1987). (Not to be confused with Ohio China Company of East Palestine.) Marks for this sales agency were found under the Canonsburg Pottery material at Quality Stamp Company in East Liverpool, Ohio. So evidently Canonsburg was one of the potteries that made products for Ohio China Company of Monroe, to sell. In a news note in the May 1951 *China, Glass and Decorative Accessories* magazine, Ohio China was named to represent Canonsburg Pottery in the state of Ohio, as of May 1, 1951. In 1952, Ohio China sold products made by W.S. George Pottery Company, as well as those made by Canonsburg Pottery Company.

MINUET
22 KT. GOLD
Ohio China Co.
MONROE, MICH.

LINDA
22 KT. GOLD
Ohio China Co.
MONROE, MICH.

Ohio Porcelain Company. Zanesville, Ohio. Started around 1940 until after 1956. The directories I had skipped some years. They were not listed in 1937 or 1958. Mark 1, was

found inscribed on attractive vitreous semi-porcelain ashtray with a modeled bird perched on one end and tulips hand painted on the piece. They made an array of decorative pieces nicely vitrified. Mark 2 sent by Elizabeth Vaughn, Beechwold Antiques.

1. CERAMIC FASHIONS BY O.P. CO.
2. CERAMIC FASHIONS @ O.P. CO.
3. PAT-PENDING O.P.CO ZANESVILLE,O USA

Ohio Pottery. Zanesville, Ohio. Around 1900 to 1923. See Fraunfelter China Company for history. (Marks: impressed or incised marks on pieces of pottery, vases, etc. Petroscan stamped mark was on vitrified heavy baking dish with brown lustre glaze.)

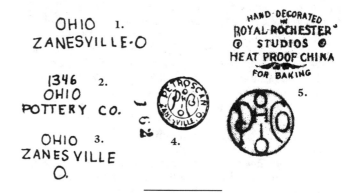

1. OHIO ZANESVILLE-O
2. 1346 OHIO POTTERY CO.
3. OHIO ZANESVILLE O.
4. PETROSCAN (mark)
5. HAND-DECORATED ROYAL ROCHESTER STUDIOS HEAT PROOF CHINA FOR BAKING

Ohio State University. Columbus, Ohio. By 1896 Ohio State University was the first to offer a full four year course in ceramics. In 1927, the University offered a separate ceramics program which included fine arts and art history rather than making that training a part of the ceramic engineering department. Arthur Baggs was chosen to lead the ceramic division of the arts department. By 1930 ceramics engineer, Edgar Littlefield and designer Carlton Atherton had joined the staff. Ceramic sculptor Paul Bogatay and glaze expert Margaret Fetzer were added to the staff in the early 1930's. (See the various listings for these potters.) In 1981, the permanent faculty in the ceramic department was Michael Chipperfield, Stan Fistick, Gene Friley and Bob Shay. Each quarter a ceramic artist visits the University and works with the staff to teach and help in the studio area. The Student League of Independent Potters at the University holds a pottery and ceramic art sale twice a year. Money from part of the sale buys books and sponsors ceramic artists. The inscribed mark shown was in an ashtray or dish probably made by a student to commemorate the 75th anniversary of the University.

The Ohio State University 75th Anniversary 1873-1948 N.J.

Ohio Valley China Company. Wheeling, West Virginia. The **West Virginia China Company** was chartered in Wheeling on August 12, 1887, and a charter was granted on May 8, 1891, to the Ohio Valley China Company. The plant was operative until after 1893, then idle and became known as their Riverside Plant. ("Charles W. Franzheim," *Bulletin of American Ceramic Society*, XX, May 1941, p. 185.) At the Riverside Plant only sanitary goods were made. The Ohio Valley China Company manufactured porcelain in striking shapes and decoration, some of which were exhibited at the Columbian Exposition in 1893. This company produced a fine grade of true hard porcelain in tableware with overglaze colors. They also made a heavy hotel ware and artistic wares already mentioned. (Barber, *Pottery and Porcelain of the United States*, pp. 335, 497.) See Wheeling Potteries Company. (Marks: Barber, *Marks of American Potters*, p. 151.)

Ohr, George E./Biloxi Art Pottery. Biloxi, Mississippi. 1883 to sometime before Ohr's death in 1918. Why George E. Ohr was not classed as a studio potter, according to Evans' definition, I do not know. His work is included in all of the art pottery books, but he worked exactly as a studio potter would. He did all of the work from digging the clay to applying his beautiful glazes. He used local clay fired at a low temperature. His shapes are often more ridiculous than beautiful to me, but they are original and artistic. Some pieces were very thin, some twisted, crushed, folded, dented, sometimes even broken. Writers said he tortured the clay into the unusual shapes - no two alike. George Ohr was an eccentric who has caught the imagination of the pottery collectors. He did such things as to name his children, Leo, Lio, Zio, Oto, Cio, Ojo and George, so their initials could be their first name. He had a mustache so long he wrapped it around his ears or tucked it in his shirt when he made pots. His hair was long and worn in a knot. He traveled to fairs, carnivals and expositions and loved to work before an audience. While he lived, he didn't make more money than he needed to raise his large family.

Because he was so sure his pottery would someday be recognized for the art pottery it was, he packed a great amount of it away before he died. After he died, his family opened a salesroom and again tried to sell it; much of it was packed away a second time. In 1972, it was sold as a lot, and according to Jerard Jordan, "Will Ohr Pottery Find Niche Among Collectors," *Tri State Trader*, Volume 8, No. 7, p. 1, museums purchased 75% of the pieces. The pottery collectors have been scrambling to get it ever since. Ohr was called the "Mad Potter of Biloxi," as was supposed to be in evidence in his pieces with snakes, crabs, seashells, head of a wildcat, lizards, dragons, a puzzle cup for which the puzzle was how to drink from it without spilling the contents all over the drinker! He also made a coffee pot that filled from the bottom with a lid not removable. All of this was a determined part of Ohr's showmanship that he used in an effort to promote pottery sales. He called himself "the world's greatest potter." He won a medal at the St. Louis Exposition in 1904. His pieces are in museums such as the Smithsonian and the State Historical Society of Wisconsin. (Information: Paul Evans, *Art Pottery of the U.S.*, pp. 27-31; no author, "Landmark Exhibition to Be Shown at Cooper-Hewitt Museum," *National Journal*, April 1980, p. 1; Bob and June

Secrist, "A Rare Pottery Find," *Antique Trader Weekly*, March 30, 1977, p. 94; Ralph and Terry Kovel, "The Mad Potter of Biloxi," *Western Collector*, May 1972, p. 1. Marks W.P. Jervis, "Worlds' Pottery Marks," *Pottery, Glass and Brass Salesman*, August 6, 1914, p. 13; nos. 2, 3, Barber, *Marks of American Potters*, p. 155, also shown in Thorn, p. 141; no. 4, Kovels, *Kovel's Collectors Guide to American Art Pottery*, p. 139; no. 5, J.W. Carpenter, "Geo. Ohr's Pot-Ohr-E," *Antique Trader Weekly*, September 19, 1972, p. 42; no. 6, Orva Heissenbuttal, "The Biloxi Art Pottery of George E. Ohr," *American Art Pottery*, October 1976, pp. 1-3. No. 7 is from Linda Steigleder, from the booklet published by the Everson Museum of Art to accompany the 1978 exhibition, "A Century of Ceramics in the U.S.")

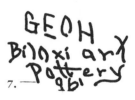

Old Sleepy Eye Collectors Club of America, Inc. Box 12, Monmouth, Illinois, 61462. 1976 to present. Had products made which they distributed at their annual conventions. Western Stoneware made the mugs for the club. The mugs were purchased plain, and the logo, date and place of convention were silk-screened on by another company. The colors were 1976, gray; 1977, caramel; 1978, cobalt blue; 1979, brown; 1980, light blue; and 1981, tan. These were made in limited numbers, and the ones auctioned at the convention's annual sale have been selling high. In 1979, 1980, 1981 and 1982, Western Stoneware produced a numbered and dated, limited edition (not over 500 pieces) Old Sleepy Eye stein, which sold for $100. The 1979 stein was made in the old stoneware body and glazed in blue on gray, the 1980 was brown on yellow, and the 1981, blue on white. The 1980 and 1981 steins were produced in the white ware body. The first year (1979), it had been decided to produce a thousand of these, and since collectors were allowed to choose their numbers on a first-come-first-served basis, some numbers are in the range 500 to 1,000. However, it was later decided to limit the quantity produced to not over 500, so in reality, only 500 or fewer were made, but some numbers on the 1979 steins will be between 500 and 1,000. (Information: Jim Martin and Bette Cooper, *Monmouth Western Stoneware*, p. 113. Jim Martin was instrumental in the founding of the club and has served as president since its inception.)

Old Sturbridge, Inc./Old Sturbridge Village. Sturbridge, Massachusetts. A restored colonial village depicting all aspects of life in the 1700's in America. Pottery, blacksmithing, jewelry, leather work, candle-making and all crafts of the early period are made here for the public to see and buy. Only exceptional crafts people serve here. They filed for registration of mark no. 1 on February 14, 1963, claiming first use since July 25, 1962, for use on bowls, plates, pitchers, flower holders and tiles, made of Delftware. Mark no. 2 filed February 14, 1963, claiming first use since December 14, 1956, for use on pottery tableware and decorative and miscellaneous pottery articles.

1.

2. OLD STURBRIDGE VILLAGE

Oletha Pottery. Limestone County, Texas. Around 1890. Made salt glazed stoneware. Jug shown in Sherry B. Humphreys and Johnell L. Schmidt, *Texas Pottery*, Washington, Texas: Star of the Republic Museum, p. 30, with the name of the Wooten Well Company which was made by the Oletha Pottery.

WOOTEN WELL CO.
WOOTEN WELLS
TEX.

Oliver China Company. Sebring, Ohio. 1899 to 1909. This is another of the companies founded by the Sebring Brothers. This company was supposed to have made porcelain according to their marks, but again I believe it is a loose usage of the term. All the other Sebring wares I have seen are definitely semi-porcelain. In the *1902-1903 Complete Directory*, Oliver China is listed as making semi-porcelain dinner sets, toilet sets and short sets of odd dishes, some decorated. (Marks: Barber, *Marks of American Potters*, p. 136.)

VERUS
PORCELAIN

THE OLIVER
CHINA CO.
SEBRING, OHIO

Omar Khayyam Pottery. Luther, Buncombe County, North Carolina. 1916 to 1935. Oscar Louis Bachelder was producing pottery in Luther from 1911 on, but he didn't open the Omar Khayyam Pottery until 1916. Before 1911, he was an itinerant potter working in many places making utilitarian pottery. Bachelder's stoneware and earthenware was high fired, non-porous, heavily glazed beautiful pieces including vases, pitchers, etc. He used black Albany slip, some with yellow overflow. He said, "There was one thought always before me: art goods. I longed to shape vases in all the lovely forms that flitted through my brain." And this he did at the Omar Khayyam Pottery after working years where he had had to make whatever utilitarian pieces he was told to make. Ross Purdy of the American Ceramic Society wrote that Oscar

Bachelder profoundly influenced the upswing from "jugtown utility" to "jugtown artcraft." In 1919, Oscar received a medal for pottery at the 18th Annual Exhibition of Applied Arts in Chicago. In 1927, he exhibited at the Tricentennial Exhibition of the Society of Arts and Crafts at the Museum of Fine Arts in Boston. He was a member of the Boston Society of Arts and Crafts and the Philadelphia Arts and Crafts Guild. His work is now being shown in museums such as North Carolina State Museum in Raleigh, the North Carolina Potter's Museum in Seagrove. Several of the Bachelders engaged in pottery making, so included here is a short version of the family tree in case someone is lucky enough to find a marked piece by a family member. Jacob Bachelder had a son, Luther, in 1804 in Concord, New Hampshire. Three sons were born to Luther. They were Cleveland, Calvin B. and Carlton. (See the listing for Carlton.) In 1830 the family moved to Exeter, Maine and made pottery. Luther continued the business until 1845 when he moved to Wisconsin. Cleveland, the oldest son, moved to California. In 1852, Calvin B. became the father of Oscar Louis, listed above. Calvin B. and Carlton made pottery in Menaska, Wisconsin, until 1860. Calvin left Wisconsin to go to Ohio and then to Erie, Pennsylvania, on to Fulton, Illinois, and finally to Beaver City, Nebraska. He died in 1906 at age 80. Carlton continued alone until 1895 in Menaska. (Information and mark: All of the foregoing is from an article by Pat H. Johnston, "Omar Khayyam Pottery," *The Antiques Journal*, September 1974, pp. 2-7. Pat was the editor of the very fine paper, *Pottery Collectors Newsletter* for over 10 years.)

Oneida Community, Ltd. Oneida, New York. Filed for use of this mark September 1915, for use on plates, cups, saucers, bowls, pitchers, jars, vases, platters, of crockery, earthenware and porcelain, claiming use since or before October 1914. Filed for registration of mark no. 2, on April 4, 1936, claiming use since October 1914; on mark no. 3, on November 5, 1936, claiming use since October 16, 1936; on mark no. 4, they filed October 26, 1938, claiming use since October 4, 1938, always for use on the same items.

1. **COMMUNITY**

2. COMMUNITY

3. CORONATION

4.

COMMUNITY CHINA

Open Sky Studio. Chesterhill, Ohio. 1978 to present (1984). Bradley and Lynnell Pekoc, studio potters, make functional porcelain and stoneware. (Marks: are incised "pekoc" within a circle or stamped "Open Sky.")

OPEN
SKY

Orchard Kilns Pottery. Cornish, New York. Paul Gaudens was the son of Louis St. Gaudens. Louis was a brother to the famous American sculptor, Augustus St. Gaudens. Louis met Annette Johnson, a young sculptress, when she was working for Augustine. Louis and Annette lived with her parents at the time Paul was born in Flint, Ohio, in 1900. Annette had been a pupil of the Columbus Art School, Columbus, Ohio. She had studied with Twachtman and Saint-Gaudens. She won a silver medal at the Panama California Exposition in San Diego in 1915. It was natural that Paul should follow in her footsteps. He studied drawing, ceramics and sculpture in the United States at the Museum of Fine Art in Boston and also in Europe. In 1921, he built a ground hog kiln behind his mother's studio in Cornish, New Hampshire, and opened the Orchard Kilns Pottery. His mother worked with him. Paul wanted to learn more, and he went to Chandler, North Carolina, to study with Oscar Louis Bachelder (see that listing). He also studied with Frank Applegate, who taught at the Industrial Arts School in Trenton, New Jersey, and Charles Binns, at Alfred, New York. In 1925, he returned to Cornish to work, and soon after an article about him appeared in *Country Life Magazine*, by Alice Van Lee Carrick, entitled, ''The Orchard Potteries,'' January 1926, pp. 48-50, which helped his business to grow. He had a one-man show at the Newark Museum in 1924. With New Jersey clay, an old kick wheel, a wood burning or bee hive kiln, Paul made beautiful ornamental pieces, decorative tile and panels in the Mayan design.

In 1938, he married and moved to Miami, Florida, where he worked and spent his winters until around 1946. He worked in Cornish in the summer and Miami in the winter. Paul's output was small, a few firings a year in each place. Paul died in 1954. Pictured in *Spinning Wheel's* article cited, is a beautiful terra cotta vase with dancing figures in relief made by Annette. Another of her vases had babies in relief. Paul's pieces shown include a vase with relief decoration, and a couple high gloss glazed vases, a plate with hand or slip painted designs, and mugs with modeled figures for handles. All of the work was beautiful. (Information: John H. Dryfhout, ''Paul St. Gaudens and the Orchard Kiln Pottery,'' *Pottery Collectors Newsletter*, September 1974, pp. 171 to 173. Also Chester Davis, ''The Orchard Kilns of Paul St. Gaudens,'' *Spinning Wheel*, March 1974, pp. 54 to 56; and Edna Maria Clark, *Ohio Art and Artists*, p. 493. Marks: Dryfhout, as cited, p. 171, shows the monograms of Annette and Paul.)

SAG   P ST G

Orcutt, Eleazer and Various Associations. Troy, Albany, and Lansingburgh, New York, and Ashfield, Massachusetts. Eleazer was born in 1796 in Whately, Massachusetts, where he was trained by his father to be a potter. In 1823, he and his nephew, Walter, joined with Horace Humiston in Troy to form the firm of **Orcutt and Humiston**. From 1824 to 1826, Eleazer was partners with Orlando Montague as **Orcutt and Montague**. From 1826 to 1828 he worked with William Lundy and Patrick Irwin as **W. Lundy and Company**. In 1828 and 1829, Eleazer Orcutt, Orlando Montague and Horace Humiston made pottery as **Orcutt, Humiston and Company**. In 1831, **Orcutt and Thompson** were listed in Poughkeepsie tax assessments. They also made Rockingham pitchers. For the period of Eleazer Orcutt's life from early 1835 to May 31, 1937, see the listing for Martin and Caleb Crafts in

Portland, Maine. In 1838 to 1840, Eleazer was living in Albany, and was in business with John H. Giles, his brother-in-law. In 1841 to 1842 he worked with Augustus Smith as **Orcutt and Smith**, still in Albany. From 1843 to 1847, Eleazer was in Lansingburgh, New York and used the name **E. Orcutt and Company**. At that time, Eleazer went to Bennington, Vermont; by 1853 he was back in Troy, New York. From 1854 until he died, Eleazer was in Albany, New York, where the pottery was known as **C.F. Orcutt and Company** (Charles Frary), or **E.B. Orcutt** (Edwin B.). Eleazer died in 1864 or 1865. Eleazer had two more sons who were potters, Rodolphus and Walter G. In 1848, Eleazer helped his uncle to build a pottery in Ashfield, Massachusetts, and the name was **W. and E. Orcutt and Company**. One-third interest was held by John L. Guilford because the pottery was on his family land. Around 1848 the company was called **Orcutt, Guilford and Company**, but John Guilford was not a potter. Some pieces are reported to be marked ''W. and E. Orcutt and Co.,'' standing for Walter and Eleazer. Other marks used were ''Orcutt, Belding and Co.'' and also, ''Walter Orcutt and Co.'' A brother of Guilford, William Frank Guilford, sold the goods from a peddler's cart. In 1850, Walter Orcutt sold his share of the stoneware factory to Wellington Hastings and David Belding, while John L. Guilford retained his one-third share. (Information: Warren F. Broderick, researcher and writer. Also, F.H. Norton, ''A Check List of Early New England Potteries,'' *Bulletin of American Ceramic Society*, May 1939, pp. 181-185; Robert G. Wheeler, ''The Potters of Albany,'' reprinted from *Antiques* in book edited by Diana and J. Garrison Stradling, The Art of the Potter, p. 131; Lura Woodside Watkins, ''The Stoneware of South Ashfield, Massachusetts,'' Stradling book, pp. 102, 103. Marks: sent by Warren F. Broderick. Various examples of these marks shown in Ramsay, pp. 187 and 203; Stradling, pp. 102, 103, and 126; Thorn, p. 141. For more information on Ashfield Pottery, see Hastings and Belding. Also, for more on Eleazer Orcutt, see the Martin and Caleb Crafts listing.)

ORCUTT, HUMISTON & CO.
TROY, N.Y.

ORCUTT & THOMPSON

PICTURE
OF
EAGLE

POKEEPSIE

E. ORCUTT & CO.
LANSINGBURGH

ORCUTT, GUILDFORD & CO.
ASHFIELD, MASS.

WALTER, ORCUTT & CO.
ASHFIELD, MASS.

ORCUTT, BELDING & CO.   E. ORCUTT
ASHFIELD   LANSINGBURGH
MASS.

ORCUTT GUILFORD & CO.   WALTER ORCUTT & CO.
ASHFIELD, MASS.   ASHFIELD, MASS.

LANSINGBURGH

Osborne, Beverly. Oklahoma City, Oklahoma. Filed for registration of this mark to be used on ceramic dishes, plates, platters, bowls, cups and saucers, claiming use since September 1936. '

CHICKEN IN THE ROUGH

Ostrowe, Caryn. Albuquerque, New Mexico. 1971 to present (1984). Studio potter. Makes porcelain lamps, dinnerware, bakeware, serving pieces. Also makes sculptures, jewelry and dolls. After 1982, Caryn said she paints a brushstroke of colored slip on the bottom of pieces with signature and year. Dolls are always signed on left side of their necks and as of 1982, they are signed on their feet as well as the soles of their shoes. The earlier mark was applied with a blunt wooden tool. Earrings are signed ''Ció'' or ''Cio.''

Ostrow China. See Hopewell China Company.

Ottman Bros. Fort Edward, New York. 1872 to around 1892. Made gray stoneware crocks, etc. with blue decorations painted on and an impressed mark. (Information and marks: Stewart and Consentino, *Stoneware*, p. 65; also Smith, *Pottery, A Utilitarian Folk Craft*, p. 6.)

OTTMAN BRO'S   OTTMAN BRO'S
& CO.
FORT EDWARD, N.Y.   FORT EDWARD N.Y.

Ouachita Pottery. Hot Springs, Arkansas. Organized early 1900's. The mark shown would indicate the pottery was in business at the time of the Louisiana Purchase Exposition in St. Louis, in 1904 which would explain the St. Louis in the mark. This pottery made a swirled ware similar to Niloak. In fact, according to Paul Evans, ''Ouachita Pottery,'' *Spinning Wheel*, July, August 1977, pp. 33-35, Arthur Dovey, who developed the swirled ware at Ouachita Pottery, was one of the incorporators of Niloak Pottery in 1909. In 1908, the

Ouachita Pottery's name was changed or **Hot Springs Clay Products Company**. (Mark: ''Questions,'' *Pottery Collector's Newsletter*, Vol. VII, No. 3, April 1978, p. 30.)

Overbeck Pottery. Cambridge City, Indiana. Around 1911 to 1955. Was established in a cottage around 1911 and operated in Cambridge City, Indiana, until 1955. Art pottery is the term used to distinguish creative work from the less commercial type of pottery. All of the work of the four Overbeck sisters would have to be considered art pottery, but they did make a kind of dinnerware including plates, tea sets, cups, saucers, tumblers, etc. For lengthy discussions on this pottery see the various fine books now available on American art pottery. The Overbecks made beautiful vases, bowls and a great assortment of figurines. By the time the 1944 article was written (see below) they were doing mostly, or almost completely, art-type pieces. The more functional pieces were early wares. (Information: ''The Overbeck Pottery,'' *American Ceramic Society Bulletin*, XXVIII, May 1944, p. 156. Marks: all Evans, p. 205.)

Overcast Clay Sculptureworks and Crocks. Nashville, Tennessee. 1970 to present (1985). Studio potter, Roy Overcast, makes sculptured pieces, functional ware, and traditional spongeware. He received a B.S. Degree in art education from Tennessee State University, and a Master of Fine Arts from University of Georgia. He had an assistantship at the Arrowmont School of Crafts in Gatlinburg, Tennessee. Many of his pieces are in permanent collections including ones at five universities in Tennessee and Indiana, the Evansville Museum of Art, etc. He has been written about in many publications including *Ceramic Monthly, Crafts Horizons*, and several others. Mr. Overcast has an impressive list of exhibitions and one man shows, such as those at the Hunter Museum of Art in Chattanooga, the Taca Biennial Craft Exhibit for 1970, 1972, 1974 and 1976, the 11th Annual Piedmont Crafts Show at the Mint Museum, the Centennial At Center in Nashville, at Wafford College in Spartinburg, South Carolina, and many others. Roy was in *Who's Who in American Art* from 1977-1978, and in *Who's Who in The South and Southeast* from 1977-1978. He was chosen as one of 250 U.S. craftspeople to attend the ''World Crafts Council Conference,'' held in Kyoto, Japan, in September 1978. Roy was coordinator/participant of panel discussions, for the National Crafts Administrator's Conference, Brandon Springs, Kentucky, November 8-11, 1977; National Endowment for the Arts Crafts Task Force Member, 1980-1981; and Tennessee representative to the American Crafts Council, 1978-1982.

From 1970-1974, he used "Overcast," with the "O" making a circle as a mark. From 1975 to present, he signs "Overcast" without the circle.

Ovington Brothers Company. New York, New York. A selling agency. Filed June 1921, for use of this mark on earthenware, chinaware and porcelain, claiming use since 1895.

OVINGTON'S

Owen, Edward J., China Company. Minerva, Ohio. Operated from 1902 to 1932 and was another one of our potteries that succumbed to the Depression. As early as 1904 the company won a gold medal for the best domestic semi-porcelain at the Louisiana Purchase Exposition in St. Louis. In 1923, the company operated 11 kilns and planned to add 11 more to double their capacity. ("American Pottery Trade Marks," *China, Glass and Lamps*, August 6, 1923, p. 15). The company made dinnerware, calendar plates and some nice hand-decorated pottery under the direction of John I. Bahl who worked at Minerva from 1907 to 1912. (Information and marks 1 and 2, Lehner, *American Kitchen and Dinner Wares*, p. 115. Mark 3, W.P. Jervis, June 26, 1934, p. 13, found on art pottery described as matt metallic luster of copper, gray green, magenta and gold with scenic decorations with trees on white clay body.

Owen and Owens Family Potters. Seagrove, North Carolina. Benjamin Franklin Owen, born in 1848 and died in 1917, was the father of two sons, Rufus (born 1872; died 1948) and James H. (born 1866; died 1923). James H. changed his last name to Owens. So two lines of potters descended from the same family, one by the name Owen, and the other Owens, causing a great deal of confusion over the spelling of the name. Rufus had three sons, Joseph T. (born 1910), Charlie (born 1901), and Benjamin Wade Owen (born 1905; died 1983). Joseph T. operated the pottery in Seagrove, until he died in 1986. At age 18 in 1923, Ben W. Owen started working with Jacques Busbee and his wife Juliana, at Jugtown Pottery in Steeds, North Carolina, where he worked until 1959, when it closed. After 1959 he operated his own Plank Road Pottery until 1972. (See the listing for Jugtown Pottery.) He died October 1983. He stamped his pottery, "Master/Ben Owen/Potter." He was given the title of Master Potter at the Dogwood Festival in Chapel Hill in 1928. Ben W. Owen's work is known internationally and is exhibited at the Smithsonian Institution, the Metropolitan Museum of Art in New York, etc. He used a Chinese blue glaze on some pieces that won great acclaim. James H. Owens, as he prefer-

red his name, was the first to become a potter in this family. When he was 17, he worked at Pascal Marable's pottery in Steeds, North Carolina, in 1883. James had a son, Melvin L. Owens (born 1917), who continued his father's pottery in Seagrove. Melvin L. had a son, Boyd, who is operating the M.L. Owens pottery on the site of his father's pottery in Seagrove, North Carolina, with his sister, Nancy, at present. He makes a beautiful ware fired to cone seven and salt glazed stoneware fired to cone 10. Pieces include vases, decorative pieces, functional, kitchen ware, sculptured pieces and folk art. Billy Ray Hussey is now associated with the pottery and has been making sculptured pieces since 1977 and working on a wheel since around 1975. Nancy has been working at the wheel since 1965, and M.L. Owens has made pottery for over 50 years. Some of the other children of James H., besides Melvin L., who became potters were Walter N., Elvin, James and Jonie. To complicate matters, Walter N. Owen chose not to put the "s" on the name Owen, but used the original version of the name. One other member of the family of James that did not use the "s" was Elvin Owen, a brother to Melvin and Walter. This fact was verified by Boyd Owens, by telephone, after I ended up in utter confusion over the name. Walter N. Owen was the chief potter at North State Pottery after 1927. North State Pottery was started and owned by Rebecca Cooper in 1924. In 1926, Henry Cooper quit his salesmen's job to work with her. Success of the pottery was assured after Walter N. Owen joined the group in 1927. Rebecca died in 1954 and Henry in 1959. The pottery was given to Walter, who had worked there for 32 years. He changed the name to Pine State. By 1977 he was making a very limited number of pieces. Vernon Owens, another son of M.L. Owens, has been the principal potter at the Jugtown Pottery since 1960. In 1983, he purchased the pottery. (Information: Boyd Owens, by mail and telephone. Nancy Sweezy, *Raised in Clay*, pp. 223 to 234. See the book by Stuart C. Schwartz, *North State Pottery Company*, a booklet printed by Mint Museum of History, Charlotte, North Carolina, 1977, for a fine discussion of the products made and methods used by these potters. Marks: See North State Pottery Company for marks for Walter N. Owen. The marks shown here are for the M.L. Owens Pottery in Seagrove, sent by Boyd Owens.)

M.L. OWENS
Seagrove, N.C.

BH

OWENS

Owens

J.B. Owens Pottery. Roseville, and Zanesville, Ohio. J.B. Owens started in Roseville, Ohio, in 1885 at age 25, employing one other potter. He moved to Zanesville, Ohio, in 1891 and built a new pottery, subsidized with a small cash payment from the city plus a building site. Owens began manufacturing art pottery in 1896. First line of ware was "Utopian," similar to "Louwelsea," and "Lonhuda." He developed 12 new lines in just a few years. The mark was the line name and "Owens." Much of his pottery is unmarked. He employed 23 people in Roseville, and 68 after moving to Zanesville. His factory burned in 1902 and was rebuilt, but was in receivership by 1907. After that time, he manufactured architectural tile. By 1912 he had built another plant on Dearborn Street and was employing 400 to make tile. On March 1, 1928, Owens had a second disastrous fire. By 1929 he had another building completed, his "Empire" tile plant, but it never got into operation because the depression came. Barber, *Marks of American Potters*, p. 132, said the company made art vases, lamps, jardinieres, pedestals and specialties with underglaze decorations, which were painted by competent artists. Lines named and described in Evans, pp. 206-211, were a lustre line similar to Weller's "La Sa," developed by John Lessell before he introduced the idea to Weller later. There was Alpine ware in soft mellow tints in blue, green and brown colors with an overglaze free hand decoration. The Henri Deux line introduced in 1900 had Art Nouveau designs cut in the clay. Corona had an earthenware body with mineral colors to look like bronze ware. See Evans, for detailed descriptions of these lines and others. (Information: Norris F. Schneider, "J.B. Owens," *The Times-Signal*, Zanesville, Ohio, July 15, 1951. Marks: The decorator marks shown here are from Barber's book, p. 132. Mark no. 1, Jervis "World's Pottery Marks," *Bulletin of American Ceramic Society*, August 6, 1914; nos. 2-4, Barber, p. 134; no. 5, on vase of collector, Wilma Hock; nos. 6-8, Evans, p. 211.)

J.B. Owens Pottery Decorator Marks
(from E.A. Barber, *Marks of American Potters*, p. 32.)

Estelle Beardsley		H. Hoskins	*HH*
Edith Bell	*EB*	Harry Larzelere	
Fanny Bell	*FB*	A.V. Lewis	*AL*
A.F. Best		Cora McCandless	
Cecilia Bloomer		Carrie McDonald	
Lillian Bloomer		Miss Oshe	*O*
Cora Davis	*C.D.*	Mary L. Peirce	
W. Denny	*WD*	Harry Robinson	
Harrie Eberlein	*HE*	Hatti M. Ross	
Hattie Eberlein	*HE*	R. Lillian Shoemaker	
Cecil Excel		Ida Steele	
Charles Gray		Will H. Stemm	
Martha E. Gray	*M.G.*	Mary Fauntleroy Stevens	
Delores Harvey	*D.H.*	Mae Timberlake	*M.T.*
Albert Haubrich		Sarah Timberlake	*S.T.*
Roy Hook		Arthur Williams	

1. OWENS UTOPIAN 2. HENRI DEUX 3.

OWENS FEROZA 4. 5. 820

6. OWENSART 7. 8. *Owens Utopian*

Oxford Pottery Company. Cambridge, Ohio. Was started in 1913. A.O.C. Ahrendts acquired the majority of the stock in Oxford Pottery in the 1920's (Wolfe, p. 770). McKee suggests this was about the time of the fire at Atlas China, Niles, Ohio, around 1925. Wolfe, p. 770, speaks of the group of men (meaning Ahrendts and partners from Niles) acquiring the ownership of Guernsey Earthenware, also in Cambridge. In 1925, a reorganization took place, and Globe China Company was formed by Ahrendts in Cambridge. I had previously thought that Oxford China was in this reorganization since it was owned by Ahrendts also. But the *Directory of Manufacturers of Ohio for 1929* published by the Division of Labor statistics, lists Atlas Globe China Company on Woodlawn Avenue and Oxford Pottery on Marquand and Burgess Avenue. So it looks as if Guernsey Earthenware, rather than the Oxford Pottery, became Globe China for one year in 1925, and later Atlas-Globe China from 1926 to 1934. However, by the time Universal Potteries, Inc. was formed, the Oxford Pottery building was included. The Oxford Pottery made earthenware similar to that made by Guernsey Earthenware's products; utilitarian ware such as pitchers, bowls, etc. According to Stout, p. 63, the Oxford Pottery products had a white interior similar to Guernsey Earthenware. While most had brown interiors, some came in blue. There is a problem with the Oxford Pottery works. Universal Potteries, Inc. marked products with Oxford marks also. Norris Sowers, who worked in the potteries in the area much of his life and who became a dealer well known to art pottery collectors, identified mark 1 by identifying a square jug-like pitcher as being made by Oxford Pottery, Universal Potteries did make a pitcher in this same shape patented in 1937, but the Universal pitcher had bulging rings around the bottom. The pitcher identified by Sowers was a very old looking piece.

OXFORD-WARE
MADE IN USA

Oxford Tile Company. See Universal Potteries, Inc.

Ozark Pottery Company. St. Louis, Missouri. We have little information on this company beside the patent office registration of the mark, but I feel there is a definite connection between this company, probably a distributor, and the Evans Pottery, Dexter, Missouri. The registration was filed January 25, 1907 with no prior used given for ornamental tiles, jars, pitchers, salad bowls, bowls, steins, table vases, plates, cups, saucers, jardinieres, fancy pottery, vases, umbrella stands, pedestals and shades for lamps, and all of them of earthenware.

ZARK

Ozark Mountain Store, Inc. Windsor, Missouri. Filed for registration of this mark on July 11, 1955, for porcelain, earthenware, and crockery cookie jars, jugs, trays, salt and pepper shakers, cream and sugar bowls, catsup and mustard dispensers, serving trays and butter and hot sauce servers, claiming use since February 28, 1955.

P

Pace, Various Family Potters. Roseville, Ohio. **O.W. Pace** had a dry goods and grocery store and manufactured stoneware crocks, jugs, etc. He was listed in the 1866 Muskingum County, Ohio, Atlas. (Norris Schneider, "Roseville," Part IV, *Zanesville Times Signal*, August 2, 1959, no page no.) In the booklet, *Roseville*, printed 1906, probably printed by the town, no author given, furnished to this author by Tom Brown, Zanesville, and there was a **George W. Pace** who had worked at making pottery for 60 years by 1906. His son was **O.F. Pace**, whom George had trained. The mark shown on a large jar, placed O.F. Pace as making pottery in the 1880's. By 1885 the name was **Pace Brothers Pottery**, and in the 1902 **Factory Inspection Report** they were listed as making stoneware and employing nine people. In the *Factory Inspection Reports for Ohio* for 1902 and 1904, **Pace Brothers and Montgomery** were listed as making ceramic artware, employing eight. Hanging baskets, cuspidors, flower pots, jardinieres, fernpots and cooking utensils were the products listed in the *Roseville* booklet cited. I don't know how long after 1906 the pottery operated. They were in full production and financially sound in 1906. The **Baldoser and Pace Pottery** was organized in 1904. E.A. Baldoser married George W. Pace's daughter and acted as business manager. (Mark 1 furnished by Stratford Auction Barn, Delaware, Ohio. Mark 2 on gray stoneware piece with blue lettering.)

O. PACE
1889
ROSEVILLE
OHIO

*Olla Pace
Roseville
Sept.*
1888

Pacific Clay Products Company. Los Angeles, California. 1881 until after W.W. II. The pottery was established in 1981 according to McKee (p. 49). There was a Pacific Porcelain Ware Company listed in 1924 in Richmond and San Francisco, making sanitary-type products. Around 1930, for a short time, Pacific Clay Products made dinnerware, but went back to technical or commercial products. In the very early years they made stoneware, tile and crocks. Barbara Jean Hayes said by the late 1800's Pacific Clay Manufacturing Company had several plants in Southern California. Elsinore, Alberhill and Riverside were all locations for the very early plants that made yellowware and red clay products. Hayes states that 1931 was the year Pacific Clay began to experiment with bowls, etc., and by 1937 they were in full swing making pottery products such as dinnerware and vases as opposed to the early products of brick and tile. At the beginning of World War II the pottery went to the production of Steatite high frequency insulators for radio equipment and that was the end of the dinnerware production. The dinnerware they made, as described by Hayes, was a pastel-colored ware with low-fired glazes. *American Home*, 1937, had an ad for "Coralitos," a thin dinnerware in chartreuse, ivory, yellow and turquoise. (Information: Barbara Jean Hayes, author of *Bauer, The California Pottery Rainbow* and the *Pacific Pottery Notebook*. Marks: no. 1 sent by Bob Thayer, pottery researcher. No. 2 filed for registration June 19, 1922, for glazed stoneware, milk

pans, water jars, butter jars, churns, preserve jars, pigeon fountains, rabbit jars, chicken feeders, sanitary poultry fountains, casseroles, Boston bean pots, shoulder jugs, mixing bowls, steam table insets, coffee urn jars, fumigating pitchers, combinets, cuspidors, water coolers, buttermilk coolers, cider coolers, claiming use since April 1, 1921. No. 3, the mark "Hostessware," was filed for registration by Pacific Clay Products on February 27, 1935, claiming use since August 31, 1932, for use on earthenware, table ware, art pottery, flower jars, vases and boxes, sand jars, jardinieres, decorative pots, kitchenware, oven ware, stoneware jars, jugs, decanters, spiritous liquor containers, wine containers. No. 4, is a photostatic copy of a stamped mark from a small decal decorated plate. Nos. 5-8 were sent by Barbara Jean Hayes. She said they were used around the 1932 to 1940 period. Nos. 5-7 are incised. No. 8 is stamped in blue. No. 9 is hand lettered on an old stoneware piece.)

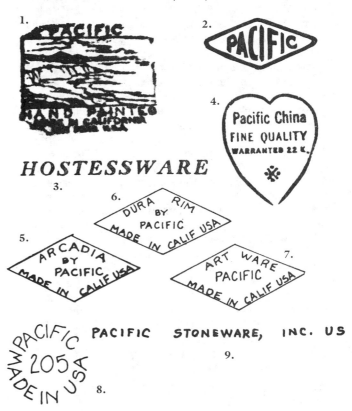

Packing Products Company. New York, New York. Filed for rights to this mark on June 24, 1944, to be used on china tableware, claiming use since January 28, 1941.

Paden City Artware Company. Paden City, West Virginia. 1940 to around 1985. From 1940 to 1956 the name was **F and M Artware**. In 1956 the name was changed to Paden City Artware company. Not to be confused with Paden City Pottery. Company established by Lyle Mitchell and William Ford in 1940. They were a handcraft shop employing around 15 people to make assorted decorative items including jugs, ashtrays, vases, bells, etc. (Marks: 1-2, sent by company.)

F & M
ARTWARE
Hand Made

PADEN CITY
ARTWARE
W. VA.

P. C. A.
HAND CRAFTED
MADE IN USA

Paden City Pottery. Near Sisterville, West Virginia. Was chartered September 15, 1914, with principal offices in Paden City, West Virginia, with a capital stock of $75,000 which was increased to $225,000 in 1921. The company was dissolved on November 12, 1963. The foregoing information was furnished by the Secretary of State's office of West Virginia. The Paden City Pottery was a large manufacturer of a good grade of semi-porcelain dinnerware. The one thing a collector will notice right away about the Paden City ware is that some of their decals looked as if they were handpainted china. Sears sold the "Nasturtium" pattern made by Paden City Pottery around 1940. McKee tells us that Paden City Pottery devised a method for applying the decal underglaze, but went back to decals overglaze because the colors that could be used underglaze with their method were too limited. In single colors of glazed ware, Paden City made some very dark green, dark maroon, etc. as well as the light pastel sets. Paden City made a "Bakserv" line. Gerald Barnett in an article, "Paden City Pottery Company's Shenandoah Ware," in the *National Glass, Pottery and Collectables Journal*, April 6, 1979, p. 38, tells us that there were six different decorations used on the Shenandoah line made by the Paden City Pottery. There was also a line of plain colored "Shenandoah Ware" in pastel colors. (See Lehner, *American Kitchen and Dinner Wares*, pp. 116 and 117, for more on pattern information. Marks: No. 1 was filed for registration July 12, 1943, claiming use since June 17, 1943, for dinnerware made of pottery clay. Caliente was a dinnerware in various solid colors. No. 2 was shown in "Readers Say," *Depression Glass Daze*, June 1984, p. 44. Nos. 3-7 are from Quality Stamp Company, East Liverpool, Ohio. Shell Krest is a mark found on dinnerware in the late 1930's and 1940's. See Jo Cunningham, *American Dinnerware*, p. 223. Shell China Company in Sebring could have been an outlet for Paden City Pottery. This was a common practice - name changes to give an exclusive dealership in one area and then sell the same product under another name in another area. The rest of marks were photostatic copies made from dishes.)

Padre Potteries. Los Angeles, California. This company was listed in the 1945 and 1946 *Crockery and Glass Journal Directories*, also in the 1952 *China and Glass Red Book Directory*, but were not listed in 1953. They manufactured dinnerware, kitchen and ovenware, art pottery and novelties. (Mark: sent by Mrs. A.R.L. Booher, found on pieces of decorative pottery with matte finish.)

PADRE

Paducah Pottery. See Various Bauer Potteries for information.

Paige Pottery. St. Louis, Missouri. Studio potter, Scott Paige, started June 1983 to make wheel thrown stoneware into soap sets, cookware and oil lamps, etc. fired to cone 10. While he earned a B.S. degree in art, he learned metal smithing and studied ceramics.

Palm Springs Ceramics. Banning, California. B.H. Karmen filed for registration of this mark on January 9, 1950, for use on chinaware and earthenware, such as mugs, plates and planters, claiming use since December 5, 1949.

Pan's Dell Pottery. Joplin, Missouri. Filed for registration of this mark on February 24, 1964, claiming use since July 14, 1963, for pottery of the hollowware type.

PAN'S DELL

C. Pardee Works. Perth Amboy, New Jersey and Philadelphia, Pennsylvania. From the registrations of marks filed by the C. Pardee Works we know they were in existance before or around February 1895 because that is when they claimed first use of mark 1. This company made decorative tiles, pottery and faience. In E.A. Barber, *Pottery and Porcelain of the U.S.*, is a description of a few tiles made by Pardee. The tiles had intaglio modeled heads of Emperor Wilhelm, Benjamin Harrison, Grover Cleveland and James G. Blaine. They also made souvenir tiles of Niagara Falls, Plymouth Rock, etc. The pottery made printed underglaze and overglaze tiles. According to Paul Evans, *Art Pottery of the U.S.*, p. 121, Pardee purchased the Grueby Pottery (see that listing) in 1921 and moved the Grueby operation to New Jersey. The two marks shown were both filed in April 1926 and Philadelphia, Pennsylvania is given as the address. I couldn't find C. Pardee Works listed in any of the Pennsylvania directories I had. The registrations were filed for pottery and faience. If this pottery really made faience, it should be the subject of further research in the future.

Paris Decorators Corporation. New York, New York, filed August 28, 1948 for rights to this mark to be used on china and ceramic vases and bud vases, claiming use since November 13, 1936.

Park Lane Pottery. See the discussion under Lang and Osgood.

Parkville Pottery. Parkville, Missouri. 1973 to present (1984). Cecil Doubenmier, studio potter, makes decorative and functional stoneware, marked with a stamp as shown through 1983, and his first name has been his mark after 1983.

Pasmantier, John L. New York, New York. In the 1952 *Red Book Directory* is a half page advertisement for Pasmantier, saying they were exclusive distributors in the East, for Crooksville China Company and Purinton Pottery Company. They filed for registration of this mark on January 25, 1933 to be used on porcelain and earthenware coffee pots, claiming use since January 1, 1932. A second mark for Pasmantier is shown in the 1952 *Crockery and Glass Journal Directory*. It may or may not have been used on American products. See Sterling China Company for marks for Pasmantier.

Patch, Inc. Atlanta, Georgia. Filed for registration of mark on May 15, 1985, for use on decorative tile, earthenware hot pads, coasters for supporting hot and cold containers. Mark in use since December 1980.

Patrick, Vernon. Chico, California. Studio potter had an earthenware glazed, sculptured piece entitled, "Middle American, Post and Lintel," exhibited at the Everson Museum of Art in Syracuse in the 1978 exhibition. The piece was made in 1975. (Information: Garth Clark, *A Century of Ceramics in the U.S.*, p. 235. Incised mark: Linda Steigleder, from the booklet published by the Everson Museum of Art to accompany the 1978 exhibition, "A Century of Ceramics in the U.S.")

PATRICK
1975

Patterson, John, and Sons Pottery Company/Oakwood Pottery. Wellsville, Ohio. Started in 1882, and was reorganized as **Patterson Brothers** in 1900 and in 1917 sold the plant to Sterling China Company. (Information: Wilbur Stout, *History of the Clay Industry in Ohio*, p. 73. Mark: on side of fancy old tea or coffee pot in gold, seen at the East Liverpool, Ohio Historical Society's museum. Also at the museum is a piece impressed, ''J. Pattersons/Wellsville/Ohio.'')

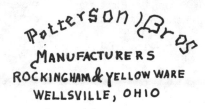

Patterson Bros
MANUFACTURERS
ROCKINGHAM & YELLOW WARE
WELLSVILLE, OHIO

Patterson, Mignon II. Washington, D.C., filed for rights to this mark January 29, 1947 to be used on china cups and saucers and other tableware, claiming use since November 1946.

HANGOVER

Paul, Edward P., and Company. New York, New York. A selling agency. In the 1930's this distributor filed for marks on English made china such as Royal Fenton, which was English Staffordshire China. But in the 1952 *China and Glass Red Book Directory*, the company was listed as selling domestic china along with products made in many other countries. (This mark was shown in a 1950's directory and was probably a paper label used on many products sold by Paul.)

PAUL'S
E.P.P. & CO.
NEW YORK
GIFTS

Pauline Pottery. Chicago, Illinois, and Edgerton, Wisconsin. 1888 to 1909. Pauline Jacobus of Chicago did china painting as a hobby in the 1870's. In 1881 she started modeling her own pieces from clay shipped to her from Ohio. The pieces were then returned to Cincinnati for baking and glazing. Finally, she went to Rookwood to study and to learn to better mix the clay and apply colors, etc. She came back to Chicago in 1883 and started a pottery of her own with two student decorators. They called the new ware, ''Pauline Pottery.'' The business grew; a regular staff of artists were employed and in 1888, Pauline and her husband, Oscar, moved the pottery business to Edgerton, Wisconsin, 125 miles northwest of Chicago, near a fine bed of clay. Around 37 people were employed, 13 of them were women decorators, who painted the artware, such as vases, bowls, ewers, tiles, flower pots, etc. In Chicago, Mrs. Jacobus made several dozen rose

jars for Marshall Fields' retail stores (see that listing). Also, Willard A. Pickard distributed her ware. The pottery was started by selling stock. When Oscar Jacobus died around 1891, the pottery soon closed. In 1894, following bankruptcy proceedings, a new company, the **Edgerton Pottery** was formed. Do not confuse with the American/Edgerton Art Clay Works in the same city. Evans, p. 218, said he found no connection at all between the two, other than the fact that some of the workers may have worked at both plants at different times. (See the listing, American/Edgerton Art Clay Works.) The Edgerton Pottery was formed after the Pauline Pottery failed. It didn't last very long either. It failed in 1901. In 1902, Mrs. Jacobus bought one of the six kilns and had it set up in her back yard and she continued to make some pieces for a short time until around 1909. See the listing for the Edgerton Pottery for that mark. (Information: Thelma Shull, ''The Pauline Pottery,'' *Hobbies*, October 1943, pp. 56 to 58. Marks: no. 1, E.A. Barber, *Pottery and Porcelain of the U.S.*, p. 413. Barber said this mark was impressed at first and later printed. This would be a very early mark. Nos. 2, Paul Evans, *Art Pottery of the U.S.*, p. 221. Nos. 3, 4, Sharon S. Darling, *Chicago Ceramics and Glass*, p. 52. No. 3 is a raised mark and no. 4 is inscribed.)

1.

Trade Mark
2.

PAULINE POTTERY
3. CHICAGO

Pauline Pottery
4. 1883

P. and E. Decorators. Roseville, Ohio. Arthur H. Pemberton and a Mr. Earle decorated accessory and decorative pieces in the late 1940's and early 1950's, stamped with the mark shown.

P & E

Pearl China Company. Now known as a selling operation, but they did have a direct connection with the Pioneer Pottery Company in the middle 1930's to 1958 in East Liverpool, Ohio. In a plant formerly owned by Hall China Company, Mr. George Singer, wanting products to expand his jobbing business, made art and novelty ware until 1958 when he sold to Craft Master of Toldeo. Pearl China Company still exists in East Liverpool today as a huge outlet for pottery. Many pieces of pottery ware may be found with Pearl China marks, ranging from decorative to very functional kitchenware and heavy brown dinnerware. They have used no mark at all for a long time due to the cost of backstamping, according to L.W. Howell, owner and operator. There seems to be some confusion as to the exact role of Pearl China Company in regards to the making of pottery. Mr. George Singer has always maintained a selling operation known as Pearl China, but he did have an influence in making pottery. It was not an uncommon practice for a selling agency to have control over or to own its own pottery where the complete output of that pottery would be channelled through a specific sales agency. Kresge had Mt. Clemens Pottery, G.H. Bowman of Cleveland China had the Iroquois China for a period of time. Bowman even had his own glass cutting plant for a time. But all of these sellers also purchased products from additional sources. The following is from a letter by L.W. Howell in August 1973 to this author: "In the middle 1930's the plant was unused and in very poor physical shape. It had facilities to jigger ware and three periodic upright kilns to fire. The roof was almost completely gone from the building, and Mr. George Singer of the Pearl China Company in East Liverpool wanted to expand his business, and he leased it from Hall China. He began to make art and novelty ware by the casting process. He kept expanding the business and his sales until by the end of World War II, he employed 165 people. Due to various circumstances, by 1958 he sold the business to Craft Master Corporation of Toldeo, Ohio. At this time we went heavily into the business of mugs to be decorated for the college trade, and we're still in that business. In 1968 Craft Master Corp. was purchased by General Mills. They thereby acquired ownership of Pioneer Pottery Company. They were not interested in retaining the ownership so in the beginning of 1973 they sold to the present owner, Pioneer Pottery, Inc." Homer Laughlin China Company and other potteries manufactured a great deal of ware to be sold by Pearl China Company. See the Pearl China marks under the Homer Laughlin listing. Harker made the Quaker Maid Cook Ware for Pearl China. See a similar mark under Harker Pottery. (Marks: no. 1, from Quality Stamp Company; no. 2, stamped on dishes; no. 3, incised mark on piece.) See Pioneer Pottery.

Pear Tree, Inc. Bryn Mawr, Pennsylvania. Filed for registration of this mark on April 3, 1963, claiming use since October 1960, for porcelain dinnerware.

the pear tree

Peeler Pottery. Reelsville, Indiana. Richard and Marj Peeler have been making pottery since 1948, but they started potting full time in 1972 and are working at present. To their credit they have 21 years of teaching ceramics; the last 14 were at De Pauw University. They have written many articles for the *Ceramic Monthly* and have made eight motion pictures for McGraw Hill which are used nationwide in the teaching of ceramics. They make a high fired (2,380 degrees) stoneware on a potters wheel, mostly utilitarian but some

sculptured. These are highly professional experienced potters who turn out 10,000 pieces annually not counting small beads or bird sculptures. All pieces are completely hand crafted. The marks they use are: "RP" on most utilitarian objects. "R. Peeler" on one-of-a-kind or sculptures and sometimes with the date. "Marj Peeler" and "R & M Peeler" are the marks used by Mrs. Peeler.

RP   R & M PEELER

Marj PEELER   R. PEELER
                    1982

Peiser, Jane. Penland, North Carolina. Started early 1960's to present (1984). Studio potter, makes highly artistic pottery pieces decorated with millefiore and hand painted and glazed in a very intricate process requiring several hours per piece. Jane received a B.A. degree from George Peabody College for Teachers in Nashville, Tennessee, and M.A. from Institute of Design in Chicago. She taught at the Institute of Design in Chicago and the Penland School of Crafts. From 1963 to 1974 her work was exhibited at the School of the Art Institute of Chicago; University of Chicago; George Peabody College; Mundelein College; Springfield Art Museum; Hanes Commuity Center; Mint Museum of Art; San Antonio Art Museum; Asheville Art Museum; and American Crafts Council. Jane's work is now in several private collections, also the University of Florida in Gainesville; Mint Museum of Art in Charlotte, North Carolina; Smithsonian Institution in Washington, D.C. (Information: Jane Peiser, "Night Garden With Ladies," *The Penland School of Crafts Book of Pottery*, edited by John Coyne, Indianapolis: Bobbs-Merrill, 1975, pp. 56-75. Mark: was roughly inscribed in circular fashion on a beautiful vase.)

Pelton's Pottery. San Antonio, Texas. 1976 to present (1984). Grace Pelton and her daughter, Mary Pelton, make hand thrown stoneware into many kinds of articles. They indicate the month an article is made by the astrological sign for that month which is signed with their initials. Round mark is a paper label.

MARY J. PELTON   GRACE J. PELTON

Penland School of Crafts. Penland, North Carolina. 1923 to present (1985). A private, nonprofit organizaton, which offers instruction in the major craft areas to a little less than 1,000 students per year. The school has only the very finest resident and visiting instructors available. The school has up to 70 instructors at one time who work for room and board, plus travel expenses, just to be a part of Penland. They are the key to the huge success of the school. It is an honor for a potter to have worked or studied at the school. For marks of individual potters who have worked here, see listings for: Jane Peiser; Tyrone and Julie Larson; Tom Suomalainen; Cynthia Bringle. (Mark: stamped on piece at American Ceramic Society Museum.)

PENLAND'S POTTERY
CHANDLER, N.C.

Pennsbury Pottery. Tyburn Road, near Morrisville, Pennsylvania. 1950-1971. Started by Henry Below to make decorative pottery pieces, such as birds, lamps, tile, teapots, plaques, vases, pitchers, etc., all hand decorated on hand cast pieces, some carved in low relief. In 1967, the son of Henry was in charge after the deaths of Henry and his wife. In 1971, the pottery burned to the ground. (Mark: found on pieces.)

Pennsbury
Pottery.
Morrisville Pa.

Pennsbury
Pottery

Pennsylvania China Company. Kittanning, Pennsylvania. There was no Pennsylvania China Company listed in 1900 or before. They may have come into being at the time they purchased Wick and Ford China Companies in 1912. It was a short lived company as far as I can determine. Pennsylvania China Company manufactured tableware and insulators, plain and decorated jardinieres and ornamental vases. In 1912 the Pennsylvania China Company purchased both Wick China Company and the Ford China Company. (See these listings.) Wick China Company was in turn sold to W.S. George of East Palestine, in 1913 and the Ford China Company was sold to Eljer Company of Cameron, West Virginia, in 1918. An advertisement in the *Pottery, Glass and Brass Salesman*, December 26, 1912, Pennsylvania China Company advertised 17 kilns in Ford City and 7 kilns in Kittanning, with pictures of two large plants in those cities. See Wick China and Ford China Company for marks.

Pennsylvania Dutch Potteries/China Artwares Company, Division of Fitzpatrick Industries. East Palestine, Ohio. 1947 to 1955. The Pennsylvania Dutch Potteries was started in 1947 by Ray Fitzpatrick. In the 1948 and 1949 *China and Glass Red Book Directories*, the pottery was listed for china art ware, figures and figurines, butter mold designs and general specialties. Mr. Fitzpatrick died in 1948 and by 1952, the listing was China Artwares Company, Division of Fitzpatrick Industries, making the same products under the direction of Allan T. White. According to Jenny B. Derwich, in *Dictionary Guide to U.S. Pottery and Porcelain*, p. 175, the Pennsylvania Dutch Ware was discontinued in 1950. In *Crockery and Glass Journal Magazine* for February 1952, p. 63, is an advertisement for the Lady Godey head vases by this company. The impressed mark shown with inscribed numbers was on a beauftiul vase, with green streaked background and a hand painted decoration around upper one-third of vase. Design in dark blue, brown and black. Vase was wheel thrown of very vitrified ware. In 1955, the pottery burned.

DUTCH
POTTERY

8112

Pennsylvania Museum and School of Industrial Art. Philadelphia, Pennsylvania. Started 1903 and Leon Volkmar became head of the new department while he continued his work at the Volkmar Kilns in Metuchen, New Jersey, where he also taught classes (Evans, p. 307). See Volkmar Kilns listing. Barber describes the art ware made at the school as having decorations modeled or carved in relief with shades of yellow, green and blue enamels. Barber was quite impressed with the work of the school. (Information and mark: Barber, *Marks of American Potters*, pp. 36-39.)

J.C. Penney Company, Inc. New York, New York. A company with a chain of stores and mail order businesses, operating at present. They filed for registration of this mark on March 24, 1971, for dinnerware made of china porcelain, probably not American made.

SPRING 'N SUMMER

Pen Yan Pottery. Pen Yan, Yates County, New York. There are two listings for this pottery in Stewart and Consentino, p. 124. **J. Mantell**, from around 1855 to around 1876. A second listing is **Mantell and Thomas** around 1855 to 1876. Thorn's dates, p. 142, vary. He lists the pottery 1830 to 1850. I found no further information. (Marks: Thorn, p. 142.)

PENN YAN

PEN YAN

MANTELL & THOMAS

PEN YAN

Peoria Pottery. Peoria, Illinois. The pottery organized as the **American Pottery Company** in 1859 and started making pottery in 1860. When Christopher Webber Fenton's United States Pottery in Vermont failed because of the high cost of production, he came to Peoria to start the American Pottery Company. The American Pottery made glazed yellowware and whiteware of excellent quality. The pottery closed because of the Civil War. In 1873 when it was opened again it was known as the Peoria Pottery Company which operated until 1904. In 1881 the Peoria Pottery had five kilns to make heavy buff stoneware in all kinds of utilitarian pottery trimmed with blotches, bands, stains and dribbles in red, green, cream, smokey or brown slipware. In 1893, they were making cream-colored and decorated wares, white granite or ironstone. They exhibited fine dinnerware in delicate pastel colors at the Columbian Exposition in 1893. The colors included a pale green and a salmon. In 1902, the Peoria Pottery was taken over by Crown Pottery of Evansville, Indiana, to form the Crown Potteries Company. In 1904, the doors were closed completely. (Information: Jane Rosenow, "Peoria Pottery and How It Grew," *Antiques Journal*, December 1969, p. 30; Barber, *Pottery and Porcelain of the U.S.*, p. 244. Marks: Barber, *Marks of American Potters*, p. 30, all except "Peoria Pottery" found on brown stoneware glazed pitcher with a silvery caste to the glaze. Julian Toulouse in *Fruit Jars*, Camden, New Jersey: Thomas Nelson and Sons, 1969, p. 339, tells about a wax sealer jar circulated around 1885 and later made of slip cast pottery with 16 panels, brown glaze, wide at the shoulder and narrow at the top and bottom which was die stamped "Peoria Pottery.")

Pereny Pottery Company. Columbus, Ohio. Started on Pearl Street in Columbus and was also called the **Pearl Street Pottery**. The pottery existed from 1933 to 1938 when it was purchased by W.I. Tycer Pottery of Roseville. Andrew Pereny made hand molded and hand thrown art pottery with beautiful glazes. Pieces seen were a tall pitcher or ewer shading from yellow to orange and a little greenish blue vase, both with outstanding glaze. (Information: from Pereny. Marks: on pieces. When I first wrote to Mr. Pereny in July, 1973 he told me the mark on his pottery was very much like the logo on his letterhead shown in mark no. 1. Since then I have acquired one piece of the pottery with raised mark no. 3 and seen the stamped mark no. 2, which is very similar to the logo or no. 1, Marks through courtesy of Elizabeth Vaughn, Beechwold Antiques, Columbus, Ohio.)

Perlee, Inc. Trenton, New Jersey. Found listed in directories 1926-1930. According to *Encylcopedia of Collectibles*, vol. B, p. 36, they made Belleek.

Perry, J.S. Putnamville, Putnam County, Indiana. According to Peggy A. Loar as cited, p. 15, J.S. Perry started his pottery around 1831. Melvin L. Davies in the booklet *Clay County Indiana Traditional Potters & Their Wares*, p. 20, lists a Neal Vestal whom Davies thinks worked with J.S. Perry around the late 1830's and early 1840's. Hezekiah Perry, the son of John S. Perry, was born in 1829 and learned the trade from his father. The younger Perry purchased the Vestal Pottery in 1851 and operated until 1871. (Information: Peggy A. Loar, *Indiana Stoneware*, 13 page booklet to accompany 1974 exhibit at Indianapolis Museum of Art, pp. 14, 43; and Melvin L. Davies as cited. Mark: impressed in clay from Melvin L. Davies.)

Perry, Sanford S. West Troy, New York. This stoneware potter came to Whately, Massachusetts, from Troy, New York, just before 1821 where he introduced the manufacturing of black teapots. Very shortly Crafts Pottery was making the same product and Perry and Company left town in 1823. (Information: Lura W. Watkins, *Early New England Potters and Their Wares*, p. 102. Mark: Guilland, p. 256.

Peters, Charles Adolph. Bayside, Long Island, New York, filed for rights to this mark May 25, 1946, to be used on china, porcelain and earthenware articles, namely, vases, flower containers, fruit bowls, urns, tea sets, dinnerware, salt and pepper shakers and dishes. Claiming use since February 15, 1946.

THE THREE MUSKETEERS

Peters and Reed/Zane Pottery. Zanesville, Ohio. John Peters and Adam Reed worked for the Weller Pottery. In 1897 they decided to make pottery on their own. They worked at first in a small workshop they built on Linden Avenue. Then they rented the old Clark Stoneware Company until Young at Roseville Pottery bought it. The Peters and Reed Pottery was incorporated in 1901 in the old South Zanesville Stoneware Company's building. At first they made mostly flower pots and flower containers, but in 1905 Frank Ferrell, who had worked eight years at Weller Pottery, came to design for them. He introduced the Moss Aztec line and Peters and Reed became an art pottery. Ferrell went to the Roseville Pottery in 1919. In 1920, Harry S. McClelland and Reed bought the plant, and in 1921 the name became Zane Pottery Company. Adam Reed died, and McClelland became the sole owner of the Zane Pottery for almost 20 years. C.W. Chilcote was in charge of advertising and design. The first half of every year was devoted to making flower pots or containers. One Cincinnati customer bought 55 car loads a year. The garden line consisted of 60 different pieces and was called "Greystone" until Weller adopted the name and copyrighted it. Then Zane Pottery called their line "Stonetex." McClelland died in 1931, and his wife operated the plant until 1941 when it was sold to Lawton Gonder. (See the listing Gonder Ceramic Arts, Inc.) Brownware was made in the early years with sprigged on decorations of grapes, garlands, flowers, a lion's head, a ladies head, etc. Most of the ware from this pottery was made of red clay. The clay was mined by Peters and Reed near their plant. Schneider, as cited, said they changed to a white body in 1926, so "Moss Aztec" was made of red clay before 1926 and white clay after that time. W. Stout, said in *History of Clay Industry*, in Ohio, p. 61, that the Peters and Reed Pottery started making brownware cookware with a white lining around 1903. He said the body was composed of weathered shale and the white lining was largely of clay. This ware was discontinued around 1906. Peters and Reed made a line marked "Pereco" with a semi-matte finish in plain green, orange and blue. The pieces were mostly artistic such as vases, etc., but they did make bowls in this line. Bowls, covered jars, and trays were made in the "Landsun" line as well as artistic pieces. Some have referred to this line as a "drip" or "sheenware effect." (Information: Norris F. Schneider, "Peters and Reed Pottery," *Zanesville Times Signal*, September 15, 1957; Stout, as cited. Impressed marks: Lois Lehner, *Ohio Pottery and Glass*, p. 101.)

Petterson, Richard B. Studio potter who lived in China until he reached age 18 where he had a youthful interest in Chinese ceramics. He attended Pei Yang University, where his father taught engineering. When he came to this country he attended University of California to study art. He graduated in 1938 and spent a year at University of California at Los Angeles and the University of Chicago. He began to teach at Pasadena City College, and from 1941-1946 he headed a summer art and craft program at University of Chicago. In 1947 he joined faculty of Scrupps College and Claremont Graduate School, teaching design and ceramics. He helped to promote a transition from low fired cast ware to wheel thrown porcelain. He worked with the art section of Los Angeles County Fairs. He acted as a consultant in many areas of industrial ceramics. Described in the catalog by Hazel V. Bray, *Potter's Art in California 1995-1955*, p. 65, was a tall stoneware wine bottle with brown and white engobe designs over incised vertical designs with a cobalt blue glaze. Petterson was a member of the Design Division of the American Ceramic Society, and his work appeared in several National Ceramic Exhibitions. (Information: Hazel V. Bray, as cited. Incised mark: sent by Thomas Turnquist, by letter.)

R.
PETTERSON
B.

Pewabic Pottery. Detroit, Michigan. In the 1880's, Mary Chase Perry Stratton became interested in china painting. She had been born in 1867. Her father, Dr. W.W. Perry, was a physician in Northern Michigan. She was able to travel and study at art schools in Cincinnati, Ohio, and New York. Around 1903 she and Horace Caulkins, a manufacturer of dental kilns, set up a workshop in an old coach house in Detroit. Early names were simply Miss Perry's Workshop, the Stable Workshop or **Revelation Kilns**. Then in 1906 a new pottery was built on Jefferson Avenue, and the name became Pewabic Pottery. By 1904 the work was shown at the St. Louis Exhibition. The glazes made by Mary Chase Perry seem to be the most outstanding characteristic of her work, at least they merit the most discussion in various references.

"Pewabic Pottery on Exhibit in Michigan," *Collectors News*, April 1980, p. 67 (staff written), states that it took Mary C. Perry nine years to develop her first iridescent glaze. Eventually there were six: a green, blue, gold, violet, ruby and yellow. In 1918, Mary married William Buck Stratton when she was 51 years of age. His firm had designed the pottery which had been built in 1906. Mary lived to the age of 94 and seems to have been associated with the pottery right up to that time, around 1961. She taught ceramics at the Wayne State University and the University of Michigan. She wrote *Ceramic Processes*. Around 1966, Henry Caulkins, son of the kiln maker who first worked with Mary, purchased the pottery and put it under the care of the Michigan State University. By 1968 it was operating again. In "Pewabic Pottery Sold," *American Art Pottery*, November 1981, p. 4, is the news item telling the pottery was sold to the Pewabic Society, Inc. because of budget cutbacks at the Michigan State University. The Society was to cooperate with the University to continue to provide ceramic education for academic credit.

Over the years, decorative ceramic tile was a very important product of the pottery. Artware, vases, etc. in a variety of glazes and colors have been widely exhibited. Barber, *Marks of American Potters*, p. 167, decided the early ware as having a hard white body, covered with heavy opaque enamels with simple and graceful forms. The glazes were matte finish. Some pieces had relief decorations. Some had crystalline spots of a lighter shade. Drip glazing was also described. In 1977, the Freer Gallery of Art of the Smithsonian Institution had a large exhibit. In 1981, the Detroit Historical Museum had the pottery on display. In 1969, Jim Powell became an instructor at Michigan State University and his salt glazed pottery was displayed March 7 to May 1, 1976 in the University Ceramics' gallery. In 1974, 20 area potters including Robert Diebboll, participated in an invitational Christmas Show at the Pewabic Pottery. According to Paul Evans, *Art Pottery of the U.S.*, p. 229, the art pottery pieces were carefully marked. He said heavy glaze often obscured the impressed mark. Paper labels were used at times. Also, "MCP," the initials of Mary Chase Perry, and "WBS" for William Buck Stratton may be found on early pieces. Evans said the impressed "Revelation Pottery" mark was used only for a year before 1906. An impressed maple leaf mark was used for a short time, and then the circular impressed "Pewabic Pottery" mark was used. (Marks: nos. 1, 2, Barber, *Marks of American Potters*, p. 167. No. 3, shown in various directories of the 1950's. Nos. 4, 5, 6, Evans, as cited, p. 229. No. 7, stamped mark from Linda Steigleder, from the booklet published by the Everson Museum of Art to accompany the 1978 exhibition, "A Century of Ceramics in the U.S.")

1. **M C P** 🍁🍁🍁🍁 **PEWABIC** 2.

3. 4. 5.

6. 7. PEWABIC DETROIT

REVELATION POTTERY M.C.P. DETROIT.

Pewtress (two potters). S.L. Pewtress and Company, New Haven, Connecticut, started around 1868 to 1887, and made stoneware. Mark shown was on piece in Stewart and Consentino, *Stoneware*, p. 80. There was also a John B. Pewtress in Perth Amboy, New Jersey, around 1849, who made stoneware. His impressed mark was "John B. Pewtress."

S.L. PEWTRESS
NEW HAVEN CONN.

Pfaltzgraff Pottery. York, Pennsylvania. 1811 to present (1987). George Pfaltzgraff, a German immigrant, started in 1811 making redware and stoneware. In the *1900 Factory Inspection Report for Pennsylvania*, they employed 28 to make stoneware under the name J.K. Pfaltzgraff. In the 1931 and 1935 *Industrial Directories for Pennsylvania*, published by the Department of Internal Affairs, they were listed as employing 113 and 104 to make pottery and chinaware. In a 1974 exhibition of regional folk pottery held in York County, Pennsylvania, a plate with brushed slip decoration was shown marked "H.B. Pfaltzgraff." The same mark was found on a 19th century crock. In the lengthy history of the pottery they have expanded their production from that originally made to a wide variety of products. From 1811 to 1913, Pfaltzgraff Pottery produced stoneware; crocks, jugs, pots, etc. In 1913 they started making red clay flower pots which was the major line until 1942 when they started making stoneware again.

In 1947, "Brownie" beanpots were displayed at the Museum of Modern Art, New York City, and chosen as one of the hundred useful objects of fine design for 1947. ("Company News," *Bulletin of the American Ceramic Society*, December 1947, p. 415.) The Gourmet Brown Drip pattern of Pfaltzgraff following W.W. II was the pottery's first success in dinnerware and is much copied according to the article "Pfaltzgraff Not a Dirty Word," *American Art Pottery News*, July, 1976, p. 4. The trademark of Pfaltzgraff shows the outline of a castle still standing in the German Rhineland which bears the Pfaltzgraff name. A variety of marks involving the Pfaltzgraff name have been used over the years; Pfaltzgraff Stoneware Company, Ltd.; B. Pfaltzgraff; H.B. and G.B. Pfaltzgraff; Pfaltzgraff Company; the P.S. Company; and J.K. Pfaltzgraff and currently, Pfaltzgraff Company, a division of the Susquehanna Broadcasting Company. The company has now expanded to include handcrafted pewter, glass, copper, tin and Buenilum products as well as pottery pieces. Pfaltzgraff Pottery purchased Stangl Pottery in Trenton, New Jersey, on July 31, 1978.

A group of character mugs and tumblers, made in the 1940's have become very popular with collectors. These include Derby Dan, Cockeyed Charlie, Handsome Herman, Flirty Girty, Myrtle, Sleepy Sam, Pickled Pete, Burnie and others. See marks 5 and 6. The H.B. was for Henry Pfaltzgraff and G.B. for George Pfaltzgraff. (Information: Mildred Veley Hardcastle, "The Pfaltzgraff Pottery," *Spinning Wheel*, 1972, (no p. no.) and Lehner, *American Kitchen and Dinner Wares*, pp. 118, 119. Marks: no. 1, 2, 3, found on stoneware from Hardcastle article; no. 4 was filed for a patent report on December 19, 1941, for use on ceramic ovenware, claiming use since March 1, 1941; nos. 5 and 6, found stamped on novelty type mugs. Many of Pfaltzgraff marks are impressed as is no. 7. No. 8 was filed for a patent report on November 12, 1931, for stone jars and jugs claiming use since November 4, 1931. No. 9 was filed for a patent on May 5, 1936 for use on jars, jugs, bowls, flower pots made of coarse stoneware, claiming use since September 15, 1934. The H.B. was for Henry Pfaltzgraff and G.B. for George Pfaltzgraff. No. 10, 11 in 1945 *Crockery and Glass Jounal Directory*. No. 12 "Ceramex" in the 1951 *China and Glass Red Book Directory*. No. 13 is a recent raised mark on flower pot. No. 14, 15, Deb and Gini Johnson, p. 107. No. 16 for old stoneware from Thorn, p. 143. Nos. 17 through 32 are marks filed for registration with the patent office, under the name Susquehanna Broadcasting System, for cookware and serving dishes made from ceramics, stoneware or glass or ceramic material and glass. They were filed on the following dates: No. 17, September 4, 1979; no. 18, March 15, 1979; no. 19, November 7, 1979; no. 20, February 1, 1979; no. 21, September 4, 1979; no. 22, February 1, 1979; no. 23, June 30, 1980; no. 24, August 3, 1981; no. 25, August 3, 1981; no. 26, April 30, 1981; no. 27, August 3, 1981; no. 28, October 21, 1982; no. 29, July 6, 1982; no. 30, February 7, 1983; no. 31, April 16, 1984; no. 32, February 2, 1984; no. 33, November 10, 1983; no. 34, May 25, 1984; no. 35, August 1, 1984; no. 36, April 4, 1984; no. 37, November 1, 1984; no. 38, January 9, 1984; no. 39, November 1, 1984; no. 40, September 21, 1984; no. 41, November 1, 1984; no. 42, January 31, 1985; no. 43, March 25, 1985; no. 44, March 25, 1985.) *The Hardcastle article cited was reprinted in *Pottery Collectors' Newsletter*, December 1972, pp. 31, 32 without a page number.

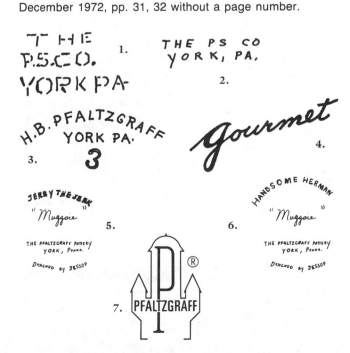

THE P.S.CO. YORK PA 1.

THE PS CO YORK, PA. 2.

H.B. PFALTZGRAFF YORK PA. 3. 3

Gourmet 4.

JERRY THE JERK "Muggsie" 5.

HANDSOME HERMAN "Muggsie" 6.

THE PFALTZGRAFF POTTERY YORK, Penna. Denched by JESSOP

THE PFALTZGRAFF POTTERY YORK, Penna. Denched by JESSOP

7. PFALTZGRAFF ®

8.

9.

10.

11. PFALTZGRAFF *gourmet* YORK PENNSYLVANIA U S A

12.

13. FTD® PFALTZGRAFF USA © FTDA. 1982

14.

15. DESIGNED BY *Georges Briard* THE PFALTZGRAFF POTTERY USA

16. PFALTZGRAFF POTTERY

17. GLASS PFACTORY

18. STONEWARE STEMS BY PFALTZGRAFF

19. GLASS CROCKS BY PFALTZGRAFF

20. A LA CARTE

21. FOLK ART BY PFALTZGRAFF

22. TABLESIDE

23. FARMHOUSE

24.  COUNTRY PFALTZGRAFF COLLECTIBLES

25. WOODCUTS BY PFALTZGRAFF

26. CREATIVE by PFALTZGRAFF COLLECTIBLES

27. FARMHOUSE BY PFALTZGRAFF

28. COUNTRY VICTORIAN

29. THANKSGIVING

30. DESIGNERS PORTFOLIO

31. YANKEE TRADER BY PFALTZGRAFF

32. GAZEBO

33. HEIRLOOM

34. THE VICKIE HANSON COLLECTION

35.  PFALTZGRAFF

36. CHRISTMAS COLLECTIBLES BY PFALTZGRAFF

37. IMAGES

38. FRESH TRADITIONS BY PFALTZGRAFF

39. MEMORIES BY PFALTZGRAFF

40. REMEMBRANCE

41. ELEMENTS

42.

PFALTZGRAFF IDEAL FOR MICROWAVE AND CONVENTIONAL OVENS BAKE AND SERVE IN ONE DISH Not For Stove Top Or Broiler Use STONEWARE

43. SECRETS

44. POETRY

Philadelphia City Directory. See Port Richmond Pottery Company.

Philco Corporation. Philadelphia, Pennsylvania. Filed registration of this mark several times, on February 11, 1942 and March 7, 1944 for ceramic ware such as jars for containing various solids and liquids, plants, and like articles for decorative purposes; and once on May 15, 1945 for porcelain pans used as containers for food, particularly for holding food to be placed in refrigerators. The company claimed use of the mark since 1921.

PHILCO

Phillips, Lz. Omaha, Nebraska. A distributor. Filed for registration of this mark on November 6, 1916, claiming use on crockery and earthenware since January 1912.

THE DUTCH MILL

Phillips Pottery. Catawba County, North Carolina. Thomas H. Phillips was a stoneware potter around 1897. In *Traditional*

Pottery of North Carolina, published by Ackland Art Museum, University of North Carolina, at Chapel Hill, p. 33, has a picture of an alkaline glazed stoneware pitcher with a roughly incised mark as shown.

? Phillips
to Mrs Ba
June 14, 1891

Phinney, Tom. Oberlin, Ohio. 1974 to present (1985). Tom Phinney, studio potter, uses a 50-50 mixture of earthenware and stoneware clay to make pieces. He adds a white deflocculated slip over a red clay and clear glaze over all. He fires by oxidation process. Tom received a B.F.A. Degree from Nova Scotia College of Art and Design in Halifax, Nova Scotia, Canada. He has been operating his present studio since 1979 and has sold to galleries, wholesale only. He particularly focuses on color, pattern, white background and solid functional forms. He applies underglaze pencils and colors. Some of the galleries currently carrying Tom Phiney's pottery are: The Craftsman's Gallery, Scarsdale, New York; American House Gallery, Tenafly, New Jersey; Jackie Chalkley Gallery, Washington, D.C.; Gillette-Frutchey Gallery (formerly Great American Gallery), Atlanta, Georgia; Sylvia Ullman American Crafts, Cleveland, Ohio; Columbus Museum of Fine Art, Columbus, Ohio; Ilona and Gallery, Farmington, Hills, Michigan; Beyond Horizons, Scottsdale, Arizona; and Craft and Folk Art Museum, Los Angeles, California.

Phinney

Phoenix Pottery. Goffstown, New Hampshire. 1951 to present. Gerry Williams, a studio potter, making wheel thrown and slab built stoneware and porcelain into a limited production of utilitarian pottery and some special sculptured pieces. His pottery is sold at his shop and selected stores throughout the country. His special orders range from large coil built pieces to commissioned wall plaque. He has published articles on his techniques called wetfire and photoresist. He listed six of his one man exhibitions. In addition, he has exhibited abroad at the Brussel's Fair, the Ostend International, the New Dehli World Agricultural Fair, the Victoria and Albert Museum, the Art in the Embasssies Program, Objects USA, Ceramics International 1972, and State Department Traveling Shows in Africa. He has taught at Dartmouth College, Sharon Art Center, Willimantic State College, Haystack School of Crafts, Brookfield Center, N.Y. State College at Cortland, the Worcester Craft Center and the Tasmanian College of Advanced Education, Hobart, Australia. He has conducted many workshops in U.S. and Canada. In 1959 he helped to organize an exhibit of American Crafts for the U.S. Government in Delhi, India. He was a part of an exhibition that toured the country, sponsored by Currier Gallery of Art

and Dartmouth College, that featured Indian textiles that Gerry brough back from Mexico. Gerry was born in India and spent his early years there. In 1977 he visited the People's Republic of China with a delegation of artists and craftsmen.

He is a founder and co-editor of *Studio Potter*, a magazine for professional potters, published by the Daniel Clark Foundation, of which he is the executive director. He was the subject of a 36 minute, 16mm color film called *An American Potter*, directed and produced by Charles Musser, a film which has won many awards and has been shown on national educational television. And this is only a small part of the outstanding accomplishments of Gerry Williams, (Marks: No. 1 from 1951-1953 the stamp was impressed with G.W.; No. 2 from 1953-1955 the stamp was used without Gerry's intials; No. 3 from 1955 to present only written signature was used on stoneware and porcelain; No. 4 is a Phoenix stamp used on some production or shopware.

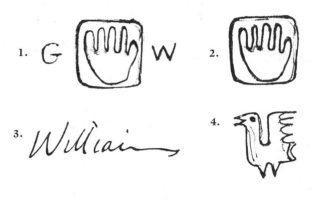

Phoenixville Pottery, Kaolin and Fire Brick Company. Phoenixville, Pennsylvania. Operated from 1867 to 1872 making yellowware, Rockingham and fire brick in Phoenixville, Pennsylvania. In 1872 when the works were leased to **Schreiber and Betz**, animal heads in terra-cotta and Parian were added to the production. Lithophanes and transparencies for windows and lampshades were made and some of these were marked ''Phoenix Pottery.'' In 1877, the pottery was leased by **L.B. Beerbower and Henry B. Griffen** at which time manufacture of white granite was started at Phoenixville. (See L.B. Beerbower and Company.) During 1878 the name was **Griffen, Smith and Company** for a short time. In 1879, the name was changed to **Griffen, Smith and Hill**. In 1880, they began to manufacture their ''Etruscan Majolica.'' They also made a good grade of white and decorated tableware. The company name was changed when Hill resigned. Then around 1882, **Griffen, Smith and Company** started making porcelain. In 1890, a fire destroyed a large portion of the works and majolica was discontinued. In 1889, Smith withdrew and the firm became **Griffen, Love and Company**. In 1891, it was called the **Griffen China Company**, which for just one year manufactured a translucent French-type of china in plain white table service. In 1892, the works closed. Apparently the buildings were not used until 1894 when several different owners used the buildings after that time. From 1894 to 1897 it was called **Chester Pottery** making cream-colored and semi-granite dinnerware. From 1899 to 1902 it became **Penn China Company** making blue mottled dinnerware. Then for less than one year after January, 1902, they were the **Tuxedo Pottery Company**. (Information and marks: Barber, *Marks of American Potters*, pp. 28, and *Pottery and Porcelain of the United States*, p. 267; Lehner, *American Kitchen and Dinner Wares*, p. 119.)

Phoenix Pottery ETRUSCAN

ETRUSCAN MAJOLICA

Other marks found on Phoenix Pottery, sometimes alone or with the other marks shown.

A1   B13   C4   D15   E14

F11   G2   H9   I3   J10

K8   L6   M5   N7   O12

A1, A2, etc., occur on individual butter plates, round, leaf or flower shape.

B1, B2, etc., on pickle dishes, usually of irregular leaf shape.

C1, C2, etc., on cake trays or dishes, of leaf or flower shape, irregular or round.

D1, D2, etc., on plates of various patterns, round, conventionalized leaf or shell shape.

E1, E2, etc., on hollow vessels, such as pitchers, coffee and tea pots, syrup jugs, sugar and slop bowls.

F1, F2, etc., on cuspidors and jardinieres.

G1, G2, etc., on cake baskets.

H1, H2, etc., on bonbon dishes, deep and oval.

I1, I2, etc., on covered boxes.

J1, J2, etc., on comports with pedestals or stands.

K1, K2, etc., on paper weights, pin trays or small flower jars, and occasionally cheese dishes and trays of special form.

L1, L2, etc., on celery vases, mugs, pepper and salt shakers, jewel trays and comports with dolphin-shaped feet. (Barber, p. 29.)

Pick, Albert and Company. Sales organization that operated out of Chicago, Illinois, for a number of years. The marks, with or without the mark of the manufacturer, may be found on a great variety of ware. He was mentioned as operating in 1904 when the *Marks of American Potters* was written by Barber. Albert Pick marks may be found on dishes made by companies in business through the 1930's. They may be seen under several potteries in this book. (Marks: no. 1 is the registered mark filed on May 4, 1927 to be used on china, dishes and crockery, claiming use of the mark since June 1926. No. 2 found on dishes made by D.E. McNicol and no. 3, the mark, "M.L." china was used by the Maddock Pottery. Also, see Fraunfelter China Company, Warwick China Company and others. These marks are photostatic copies from dishes and some obtained at Quality Stamp Company, East Liverpool, Ohio.)

Pickard China. Antioch, Illinois. 1894 to present. Founded by Wilder Pickard in Chicago in 1894 as a decorating establishment, existed for a period of more than 40 years, and achieved a high reputation for painted and gold decorations on fine table china obtained in white form from other china factories. At the turn of the century, Wilder's china decorating studio in Chicago specialized in hand-painted art pieces and dessert and tea sets. Most of the original artists were from Chicago's famous Art Institute. Business mounted swiftly and soon the staff was swelled by renowned ceramic artists from all the countries of Europe. Since most china was manufactured abroad at that time, the Pickard studios imported blank ware to be decorated. These early hand-painted pieces are now sought by collectors. When Wilder's son, Austin, entered the business, he longed for the day that Pickard no longer would be dependent upon outside sources. In 1930, they decided to make china as well as to decorate.

An addition was added to their plant in Chicago and five years of experimentation in manufacture followed. After two more years of test production, a new plant was built in Antioch. Finally in 1938, chinaware made by Pickard appeared on the market. (Eberlein and Ramsdell, *The Practical Book of Chinaware*, Philadelphia: J.B. Lippincott Company, 1948, p. 302.) Pickard China makes wares that are completely vitrified, translucent, with an excellent glaze. In the period of time when Pickard merely decorated and did not manufacture, two marks may be found, one for Pickard and one for the company that made the china. For instance, the Pickard mark and a Haviland mark may be found on the same plate. Before Pickard started making their own china, they used mostly French china to decorate. While the output of the company was virtually confined to tableware, Pickard's early china has become a valuable and desirable collector's item because of the artists and their signatures on the china. Pickard still manufactures a line of decorative accessories introduced by Wilder A. Pickard in 1915, with 23-karat gold hand painted over an intricate rose and daisy design in etched relief.

Pickard began manufacturing an annual series of limited edition Christmas pieces in 1976. Pickard, Inc. was selected in 1977 by the U.S. Department of State to manufacture the official service of china used by our embassies and other diplomatic missions around the world. The special decoration had an embossed gold border of stars and stripes and an embossed gold reproduction of the Great Seal of the United States. (Information: from the company in 1978 used in Lois Lehner, *American Kitchen and Dinner Wares*, pp. 120, 121. Marks: nos. 1, 2, were used around 1895 to 1910. No. 3 is a very old Pickard mark, filed for copyright January 25, 1926, claiming use since September 1, 1925, on pottery and porcelain. No. 4 filed March 18, 1932, for chinaware and pottery, claiming use since December 15, 1931. No. 5 filed July 24, 1947 for use on pottery, earthenware, china and porcelain, namely, large cups, saucers, soup dishes, vegetable dishes, platters, gravy boats, teapots, sugars and creamers, candy dishes, coffee pots, mayonnaise sets, divided relish dishes, cake plates and vases, claiming use since the fall of 1928. Nos. 6 and 7 were both filed July 24, 1947, claiming use since June 1938. No. 6 was for the same articles as no. 5 and no. 7 was for pottery and china articles, namely, cups and salt and pepper shakers. No. 6 was filed again December 22, 1955, claiming first use in 1938, for same products as before. The rest of the marks shown are variations from directories, advertisements using pieces of the marks as they were filed for registration.)

1. 2. 3. 4. 5.

6. 7. PICKARD

Pierce, Howard, Ceramics. Claremont, and Joshua Tree, California. 1941 to present (1984). Ellen and Howard Pierce, studio potters, lived in Claremont, 1941 to around 1961 and then moved to Joshua Tree where they operate today. Howard attended Chicago Art Institute, Pomana College in California and University of Illinois. They are creators of ceramic animals and birds at present. They have made all sorts of decorative pieces and a very small amount of dinnerware to order or for gifts of porcelain fired to 2,150 degrees. Products distributed by N.S. Gustin Company. All pieces spray glazed and use brush to make accents. (Most pieces marked like no. 1, with a "Howard Pierce" rubber stamp. Some earlier pieces marked "Howard Pierce Porcelains." No. 2, incised when they lived in Claremont before 1961. Also used mark "H.P." on some pieces. No. 3, incised. A few pieces made with ash from St. Helens volcanic ash are marked St. Helens and the regular Howard Pierce rubber stamp. Information: Susan Cox, "Howard Pierce Porcelains," *Antique Trader*, August 3, 1983, pp. 60-63. Marks: sent by Susan Cox by letter.)

1. HOWARD PIERCE   2. Pierce

3. Howard Pierce Claremont, Calif

Pierron, Louis M. Pottery. See the listing Hermann Family Potters.

Pigeon Forge Pottery. Pigeon Forge, Tennessee. 1946 to present (1983). Douglas J. Ferguson started the pottery with the help of his father-in-law, Ernest Wilson, to make high fired stoneware with no absorbency, in an old tobacco barn. In 1957, a new building was built. Red or gray clay found in the area is used. The glazes specially formulated often have subdued and delicate tones and the variety of shapes and items are both functional and decorative; many are sculptured. The awards and recognition given to Mr. Ferguson is endless. He has done several architectural works and after 15 months of work in 1979 he completed a mural depicting Appalachia which he called "Heritage," for his Alma Mater, Mars Hill College at Mars Hill, North Carolina. Also for the college in 1982, he built a 12″ thick wall fountain made of blocks, depicting 84 quilt patterns such as "Wedding Ring," "Rose of Sharon," and "Tennessee Star." Mr. Ferguson studied ceramics in 14 foreign countries and is a member of the American Craftsmen's Council and The World Crafts Council.

Ernest Wilson who helped to start the Pigeon Forge Pottery was a potter in his own right. He came from East Liverpool, Ohio, and was a well known ceramist from the T.V.A. Ceramic Research Laboratory. He signed his pieces "E.W." according to his daughter, Mrs. D.J. Ferguson.

Jane Ferguson, daughter of Douglas is a 5th generation potter in a family tradition that goes back to Stoke-on-Trent, England. She makes one of a kind hand thrown forms, utilitarian and architectural of high fired stoneware and porcelain. Jane's pottery is on display and for sale at the Pigeon Forge Pottery sales room. Some pieces that are hand turned on the wheel by two seasonal employees marked "E. Ownby" or "A. Huskey." Jane graduated in August 1983 from California School of Arts and Crafts in Oakland, California.

(Marks and information: furnished by company except no. 6 incised in small bowl. No. 1, inscribed mark of Douglas Ferguson. Nos. 2, 3, 4, Jane Ferguson marks. No. 5 stamped mark. No. 7, inscribed mark.)

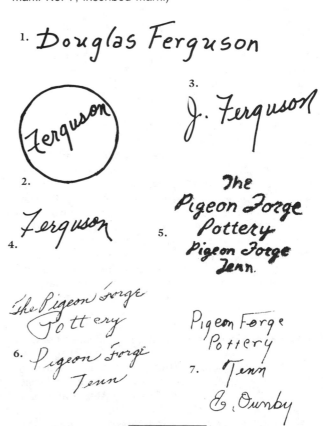

1. Douglas Ferguson

2. Ferguson

3. J. Ferguson

4. Ferguson

5. The Pigeon Forge Pottery Pigeon Forge Tenn.

6. The Pigeon Forge Pottery Pigeon Forge Tenn

7. Pigeon Forge Pottery Tenn E. Ownby

Pilcher, Don. Champaign-Urbana, Illinois. Studio potter, who had a wheelthrown, stoneware bowl and a porcelain salt glazed bottle in the collection of the Everson Museum of Art in Syracuse. The bowl was made around 1969 and the bottle in 1978. (Information: Garth Clark, *A Century of Ceramics in the U.S.*, pp. 193, 256. Incised mark: Linda Steigleder, from the booklet published by the Everson Museum of Art to accompany the 1978 exhibition, ''A Century of Ceramics in the U.S.'')

Pilgrim Pottery. See Morton Pottery Company. Pilgrim Pottery was the name of a line with paper labels as shown made by Morton Pottery Company. (Label shown from Doris and Burdell Hall, *Morton's Potteries: 99 Years*, p. 85. Also see Fredericksburg Art Pottery for another Pilgrim Pottery.)

Morton Pottery Company

Pillin, Polia. Los Angeles, California. Polia was a studio potter, born in Poland in 1909. She came to the U.S. in 1924 at age 15. While working in the garment industry in Chicago, she studied painting and sculpture at the Jewish People's Institute, where she worked under Todros Geller and several other artists. At age 20, she married William Pillin and moved to a small farm in Espaniola Valley, New Mexico. Polia continued to paint in water colors and oil. When a child arrived, they moved back to Chicago. A visit to the Chicago Art Institute was the start of Polia's fascination with pottery. She enrolled in classes at Hull House, Chicago's settlement house, and there she learned to throw on a wheel and slab build pots. Other than this, she was completely self taught in the making of pottery. In 1948, they moved to Los Angeles, where they established a studio in a backyard garage. William began to work full time with the preparation of clay and glazes, casting, firing, etc. Polia continued to paint in oils and water colors and considered painting on pottery an extension of that work. She fits the surface decoration to the form of the clay. She brings a unique quality to pottery making. Her work soon becomes recognizable even without an inscribed mark or signature. She uses colored slip and colors the clay itself with various pigments. Then adds more color with the glaze. She uses sponging, graffito and banding. A ''Byzantine'' quality to her painting carries over to the pictures on her pottery. Her husband, born in Russia, died in June 1985. He had become a well known poet published in more than 100 literary reviews, and he published nine collections of his poems. Her son is pursuing a doctorate in music. Polia has exhibited her work widely and done many one-woman shows. Many of her pieces are in permanent collections, such as: Long Beach Museum; Dallas Art Museum; Syracuse Museum; University of Maine; The A.A. D'Amico Collection; Otis Art Institute and many public and private collections. She has been written about in magazines including: *Arts and Architecture; The American*

Artist; The Arts (Los Angeles); *Los Angeles Times Home Section; Trace* (Los Angeles); *Craftsmen of the Southwest Annual*; and other periodicals. (Information and marks: Thomas G. Turnquist, ''Polia Pillin: Clay Eye Treats,'' *Journal of the American Art Pottery Association*, September, October 1985, pp. 8, 9. Mark 2 is Polia's husband's mark.)

Pinch Pottery. Northampton, Massachusetts. 1973 to present (1982). Studio potter, Barbara Walch, owner of Pinch Pottery also called **East Street Clay Studios**, makes handbuilt and dinnerware of stoneware.

Walch

Pincherry Pottery. Worthington, Ohio. Owners and studio potters are Joseph and Jane Cooper, who have been operating 1970 to present to make functional and architectural stoneware. (Marks 1, 2, 3, 4, are for Joseph Cooper. Marks 5, 6, are for Jane Cooper.)

1. Joseph Cooper

2.   3.   4.

5. Jane Cooper

6.

Pine's End Pottery. Washington, Michigan. 1947 to present (1985). Robert H. Diebboll, accomplished painter and studio potter, made high fired porcelain pieces into functional and decorative ware before 1979. He studied at Society of Arts and Crafts in Detroit, Michigan, (now called Center for Creative Studies), where he taught Life Drawing for 10 years. Since 1979 he has been making salt glazed early American type stoneware pieces with beautiful blue hand painted motifs of his own such as birds, flowers, etc. Mr. Diebboll has been a stoneware collector for 30 years and appreciates the art of the old potter. He has won the Lillian Haas Award, the Richard Weber prize, and the Michigan Potter's Association Award. This is a very modest list of awards he has given this author judging by the picture of beautiful ware he sent with the information. In 1966 he started his present business, but before that time he worked as a sculptor-designer for General Motors for 27 years. Diebboll worked in the early years to perfect his painting, but while teaching at the Society of Arts and Crafts, he became interested in pottery making in the 1940's and worked in that medium from then on. Both talents have reached their heights of perfection in his present work. He makes very large urns, jugs, crocks, covered jars and plates of stoneware with the Early American designs, both sculptured and hand painted. Most of the pieces are thrown on a wheel, but some are slab built with his own special technique of etching a design in styrofoam and rolling the clay into the design. He signs his name as a series of lines as shown. Also pictured is a bird stamp he uses.

Pines Pottery. Chester, West Virginia. 1939 to 1953. Edward Carson and his father, Clyde, went into the distributing business in 1939. Around 1940, Clyde died and Edward went to the army for W.W. II. The business was closed from 1940 to sometime in 1945 when Edward and his wife reopened. In 1948 they sold the distributorship to Ira Sayers, and in 1953 the business closed. There was no manufacturing done at Pines Pottery. They purchased products from Homer Laughlin China Company and Haeger Pottery and Fostoria Glass Company to distribute to the various retail outlets. Many times in this book, you will see the name, Ed Carson. Mr. Carson went to work for Homer Laughlin in 1948 and has been a tremendous help to this author. (Information: Ed Carson. Mark: from Quality Stamp Company, East Liverpool, Ohio. Note: Information on this company in Gates and Ormerod, *The East Liverpool Pottery District Identification of Manufacturers and Marks*, p. 331, is in error.)

Pinewood Pottery. Charlotte, North Carolina, and Fairhope, Alabama. Before 1936 to 1964. Edith Harwell was an accomplished potter who was aided by her husband, Converse, in the manufacture of the pottery in the Pinewood Pottery. Converse became interested in making pottery first, but it turned out that Edith was the talented one in throwing on a wheel. Converse mixed and invented glazes and did the firing, etc. The time of the very early learning process and exactly when the couple set up their first pottery has not been fully established. But by 1936, Edith was good enough to be invited to the Mint Museum in Charlotte to demonstrate and sell her pieces. These pieces made at the museum were marked, "Mint Museum/Pinewood," and dated. Also, they were initialed, "E.H." In the early 1930's, the Harwells had a pottery of their own in Charlotte. Then in 1938 or 1939 they moved to Fairhope, Alabama, and established a pottery there. At Fairhope, Edith taught pottery making at the School of Organic Education until 1971, even though the Pinewood Pot-

tery was maintained only until 1964. The pieces were high fired stoneware with glossy rich colored glazes in decorative and functional ware. Other marks were, "E.H., Charlotte, N.C." and "E.H., Fairhope, Alabama." (Information: Don Brewer, "Pinewood Pottery," and "Pinewood Pottery Update," *American Clay Exchange*, January 15, 1984, pp. 12, 13, and June 30, 1985, pp. 8, 9; also, Thomas Polley, "Pinewood Pottery," *American Clay Exchange*, December 1982, p. 22. Mark: American Ceramic Society, Ross Purdy Museum.)

Pioneer Pottery. Wellsville, Ohio. 1885 to 1896. Pioneer Pottery or Pioneer Pottery Works made white ironstone, graniteware, some with fanciful decorations as is shown on the two handled vase with naturalistic flowers and leaves and the wording shown in mark no. 8, pictured in J.G. Stradling, "East Liverpool, Ohio, an American Pottery Town," *Antiques*, June 1982, pp. 1,366 to 1,373. See Wellsville China Company for imformation. (Marks: nos. 2-6, Barber, *Marks of American Potters*, p. 128; nos. 1, 7, Ramsay, p. 276.)

Pioneer Pottery Company. East Liverpool, Ohio. See Pearl China Company for history. (Mark: found on newer mug.)

PIONEER
USA

Piper, Lucile Seymour, Company. Cincinnati, Ohio. Robert G. Piper, doing business under the above listed name, a selling agency. Filed April 1948, for use of the mark 1, on porcelain dinner and service plates having pictorial designs or pictures on them. Claiming use of the mark since 1936. Mark 2 found on a plate manufactured by Homer Laughlin China Company and distributed by Piper in 1952.

1. **MEMORY PLATES**

2.

Pisgah Forest Pottery. Near Mount Pisgah, Arden, North Carolina. 1926 to present. Walter B. Stephen, formerly of the Nonconnah Pottery started the Pisgah Forest Pottery. (See Nonconnah Pottery listing for early history of Stephen.) Products included Cameo ware, Jasper ware, a crackled glaze ware. The Cameo ware was in blue, green and light brown. After 1926, pieces were dated and marked as shown until 1961 when Stephen died. After that dates were omitted. The marks of the Pisgah Forest period are generally pressed on the base and appear in relief. Some few pieces are incised ''Pisgah Forest'' or ''Stephen.'' One mark was simply impressed and is illustrated as no. 7. The pieces in the third period almost always bear the date of the year and most have variations of a potter at the wheel. For a short period of time in the late 1940's, the pottery name was changed to ''Stephen Pottery.'' (See mark 3.) One vase in the exhibit has an incised logo. (See mark 8.) After 1961, the company continued under the leadership of G.G. Ledbetter, Mr. Stephen's assistant, and T.J. Case, his step-grandson, and dating was omitted. (See mark 9.) (Information and marks: marks as shown are copies from *The Pottery of Walter Stephen*, published by the Ceramic Circle of Charlotte in conjunction with the Mint Museum, pp. 11, 12. Permission granted by Stuart C. Schwartz, Director of Mint Museum.)

1.   2.   3.

4.   5.   6.

7.   8.   9.

Pitman-Dreitzer and Company, Inc. New York, New York. Selling agency which was listed in the 1952 and 1954 *Crockery and Glass Journal Directories* under cookie jars and earthenware decorative pottery, candelabra, carafes, all of earthenware. They also were listed for coasters of metal and glass. This company was listed as a Division of Lancaster Colony Corporation in the 1966 *China, Glass and Tableware*, with a big ad for glass on the back cover. Mark no. 3 was listed as Colony Division of Pitman-Dreitzer. (Marks: no. 1, on cookie jar; nos. 2, 3, from 1971-1972 *China, Glass and Tableware Directory*.)

© F K R 1942 PD & Co. Inc.

1. ALBERT APPLE

   3.

2.

Pitney, William. See the listing The Pot Shop.

Pittsburg High Voltage Insulator Company. Derry, Pennsylvania. The company was established in 1908, and by 1922 they were solely owned by the Westinghouse Corporation. Around 1910, Westinghouse had started selling the company's products, by 1914 they had controlling interest and by 1922 they owned it all. Until 1953, Westinghouse made pin type insulators at this factory. (Information and stamped marks: Tod, *Porcelain Insulators Guide Book for Collectors*, pp. 134, 135.)

1. *"Pittsburg"*   2. Pittsburg

Pittsburg Pottery/Seville Industries. Pittsburg, Kansas. In November 1984, the Pittsburg Pottery was acquired by Seville Industries. The previous owner set the starting date at 1898, but the pottery moved to the present site in 1913. Seville Industries is continuing the same product line that has been manufactured there for some time. This company is one of three or four potteries left in this country making functional stoneware in a factory. The pottery uses a diamond symbol and ''Diamond Brand'' name shown. Over the years, various wording has been used inside the diamond symbol, such as name, location, capacity, etc. The diamond remains constant, however. Products included sets of nested bowls, butter churn, cannister sets, a bowl and pitcher set, strawberry jar (to grow plants in), cheese and butter jars, stone jars and pitchers, vases, urns, etc. Products are made on a jiggering machine - a plaster of paris mold on a potter's wheel. The greenware is trimmed and glazed, then the stoneware is heated for 36 hours, slowly reaching 2,100 degrees Farenheit.

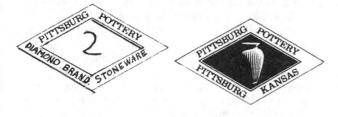

Pixie Potters. Los Angeles and Long Beach, California. Mildred H. Andrews filed for registration on mark 1 on April 12, 1946, claiming use since September 1939 on ceramic figurines, listing her address as Los Angeles. Then on September 1, 1945, mark 2 was filed by John T. Hughes, claiming prior use for the year 1945 for dinnerware, salt and pepper shakers and ornamental flower containers. Both people said they were doing business as the Pixie Potters. This would make a very interesting story, but I don't know it. I found nothing under these names in the 1948 *Directory of California Manufacturers* and nothing in the *Crockery and Glass Journal Directory*. Mark 3 was filed April 3, 1950, for bud vases, bowls, relish dishes, nut dishes and candy boxes.

Plaisted Pottery. Gardiner, Maine. 1855 to 1876. Francis A. Plaisted and William H. Wiles were owners and operators of F.A. Plaisted and Company from 1855 to 1863. From 1863 to 1873 the name was just F.A. Plaisted, after Wiles sold his share to Plaisted. From 1873 to 1876, Francis's son, Frank C., worked with him and the firm was F.A. Plaisted and Son. The pottery employed 10 to 12 people in various census reports to make utilitarian stoneware with an impressed mark. In 1876, the property was sold to Charles Swift and William M. Wood and became the Gardiner Stone Ware Manufactory (see that listing). (Information: M. Lelyn Branin, *The Early Potters and Potteries of Maine*, pp. 128-131. Mark: same source, p. 224.)

F.A. PLAISTED & CO, GARDINER. ME.

MANUFACTURED BY F.A. PLAISTED & SON GARDINER ME

Planned Products, Inc. Eugene, Oregon. Filed for registration of this mark on October 26, 1981, claiming use since June 1981 for cookware, such as baking and warming plates, pan, pots, dishes and tiles made of unglazed stoneware.

Plaster Mold, Various Companies. In business at present. Various plaster mold companies are makers of plaster of Paris molds for the hobbiest, industrial and commercial use at present. They are mentioned here because of the great quantity of pieces found with these mold marks. Some of this ware is more sturdy than some of the ware made in potteries which confuses the beginning collector. Holland Mold, Inc. in Trenton, New Jersey, employed 33 in 1978. Atlantic Mold, also in Trenton, New Jersey, employed 45 in 1978 to make molds for the hobbiest. Kimple Mold Corp., the Kleine Company, and Byron Molds are all names and marks given to me by hobbiests who decorate the molds. Some of these decorators do beautiful work, start shops and make a living from them. These pieces are almost always glazed across the bottom where pieces made by potteries are not generally glazed on the bottom so completely. Placarte Designs Corporation, also in Trenton, New Jersey, were listed in 1978, as employing 10 to make plastercrafts.

HOLLAND © MOLD

KLEINE CO.

ATLANTIC © MOLD

KIMPLE MOLD CORP. 1984

Platecraft of America, Inc. Buffalo, New York. Filed for registration of this mark on January 3, 1956, for use on metal plated ceramic coffee pots, teapots and pitchers, claiming use since December 7, 1955.

PLATECRAFT

Play-Bear, Ltd. Skokie, Illinois. Filed for registration of this mark on May 19, 1971, claiming use since March 12, 1971, for use on pottery, namely, plates, cups, bowls, serving pieces, vases, flower arrangers, made of crockery, earthenware or china materials.

PLAY-BEAR

Plum Tree Pottery. Farmington, Michigan. 1964 to present. John Glick, owner, is a studio potter, making one of a kind pieces of handthrown pottery on a wheel, both decorative and utilitarian. He received a B.F.A. degree from Wayne State University in 1960 and a M.F.A. degree from Cranbrook Academy of Art in 1962. He also received the Louis Comfort Tiffany Grant in 1961. (Information: Staff written, "John Parker Glick, Plum Tree Pottery," *Pottery Collectors Newsletter*, November, 1972, p. 23.)

Plymouth Products. Philadelphia, Pennsylvania. This pottery must have been short lived. I found no connection between this Plymouth Products of Philadelphia and the Plymouth Pottery in Plymouth, Massachusetts. Plymouth Products was listed for one year in the 1959 *Pennsylvania Industrial Directory* at 1501 N. 59th Street. They were not listed 1956 or 1962 which were my directories closest to the 1959 date. Inscribed mark found on 9" x 4" hand made ashtray or decorative dish of white clay, heavy pink glaze, well vitrified.

PLYMOUTH
PRODUCTS
PHILA, PA.

Plymouth Pottery. Plymouth, Massachusetts. 1936 to present (1985). Katherine Alden was the first resident potter in the restored Richard Sparrow house, built around 1640. The Plymouth Pottery Guild was formed in the 1930's and Katherine taught classes. Until 1961 the state of Massachusetts gave aid to the Plymouth Pottery. When aid was withdrawn it became a private business with workshops. In the 1980's the potters in residence were Robert and Laurie DeRosa and Jean Walker. In 1978 the Plymouth Pottery Guild moved to the Antiquarian Museum Carriage House located in downtown Plymouth where they also maintain a shop. Both potteries use a stamp or incised marks, sometimes with the artists name. Products are reminiscent of early pieces with red clay in figures, garden items, miscellaneous decorative pieces. (Information: Jenny B. Derwich and Dr. Mary Latos, *Dictionary Guide to U.S. Pottery and Porcelain*, p. 183. Mark: Deb and Gini Johnson, p. 106.)

Plymouth
Pottery

Plymouth Stoneware Company. Fort Dodge, Iowa. See the listing, Various Potteries of Fort Dodge for information and marks.

Plymouth Wholesale Dry Goods Corporation. New York, New York. Filed for rights to this mark January 28, 1947, for use on china, semi-porcelain and pottery articles, namely, dinner and breakfast sets, bowls, pots and baking dishes, claiming use since February 13, 1945.

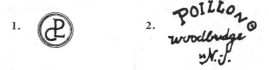

Poillon Pottery. Woodbridge, New Jersey. Clara Louise Poillon and Mrs. Howard A. Poillon did china painting and became interested in making pottery. Around 1901 they started a pottery on Fleet Street with broken machinery and worn out kilns. By 1903 they had a new kiln and incorporated the pottery to manufacture glazes, colors and pottery ware. They had relocated to the old Salamander Works in Woodbridge, New Jersey. (See that listing.) The Poillons lived in

New York City which is close to Woodbridge and this gave them excellent opportunities to exhibit their art pottery. In December 1901 their work was shown at the New York Society of Keramic Arts. According to Paul Evans, *Art Pottery of the U.S.*, p. 230, Poillon earthenware was decorated with gold and orange lusters; they also used matte or high gloss glazes, all of which were developed by Clara L. Poillon. By 1904 they made garden and kitchen pieces such as coffee and teapots. In 1928 Clara L. Poillon retired, and she died in 1936. Evans said the output was rather limited and not particularly noteworthy but a single piece was in the National Museum of History and Technology of the Smithsonian Institution. (Information: Paul Evans, as cited, pp. 230, 231. Mark: No. 1, E.A. Barber, *Marks of American Potters*, p. 70. No. 2, Evans, p. 231.)

Poinciana Chinaware, Inc. Miami, Florida. Operated throughout the 1950's and 1960's. They were not listed in 1949 or 1971 directories. Listed in the 1965 *China, Glass and Tableware Directory* for artware, cups and saucers, china dinnerware, semi-porcelain dinnerware, vitrified hotel ware, service plates, premium assortments (for chain stores and promotions, etc.), teapots, etc. I found nothing in any listing to determine if this company was a distributor or manufacturer.

Poor and Company. Chicago, Illinois, filed for a claim on this mark December 10, 1946, to be used on ceramic and china dinnerware having photographically printed images thereon, claiming use since November 26, 1946.

Promart

Poor, Henry Varnum. 1923 to 1971. Henry Poor studied at Stanford University, Stanford, California, and the Slade School of Art in London. He later moved to Paris to study at Academie Julian. In 1912 he returned to United States to teach at Stanford and at the Mark Hopkins Art Institute, San Francisco. In 1923, Poor turned from painting to ceramics. During the next 10 years he gained a national reputation and won many awards. After that time, he made ceramics but was involved in writing, etc. In 1954, Poor published his book, *From Mud to Immortality*. He died in 1971. In *A Century of Ceramics*, p. 141, by Garth Clark, is pictured a footed, stoneware bowl with underglaze decoration. In Helen Stiles book, *Pottery in the U.S.*, p. 305, she lists Henry Varnum Poor as one of the very outstanding American ceramist whose work was exhibited in Denmark, Sweden, Finland, and England, beginning January 8, 1937. (Information: Garth Clark, *A Century of Ceramics in the U.S.*, pp. 318, 319; also, *Henry Varnum Poor 1887-1970: A Retrospective Exhibition*, The Pennsylvania State University Museum of Art, 1983. Marks: no. 1, sent by Thomas Turnquist, writer and member of American Art Pottery Association. Nos. 2, 3, 4, Linda Steigleder, from the booklet published by the Everson Museum of Art to accompany the 1978 exhibition, "A Century of Ceramics in the U.S." Nos. 2 and 3 are incised and no. 4 is a painted mark.)

1. HP 2. $HP52$ 3. $HP31$ 4. $HP26$

Pope-Gosser China Company. Coshocton, Ohio. Was organized in 1902 by Charles F. Gosser and Bentley Pope. Pope was born in England in 1847 and died in 1911. He was a skillful decorator who came to America in 1870 and worked at Trenton until 1891. He then became manager for Knowles, Taylor and Knowles, East Liverpool, remaining with them until 1903, in which year he formed a partnership with Charles F. Gosser and founded the Pope-Gosser China Company at Coshocton, Ohio, which the combined abilities of the partners soon raised to importance. The ware was excellently potted and the shapes were a departure from existing models. In 1903, the company started to produce a high-grade translucent china body for vases, etc. These very early pieces must have been of excellent quality, highly vitrified and attractive. Finding this type of ware unprofitable, the company changed to dinnerware which was described by Stout, p. 83, as "Not truly vitrified but much harder than semi-porcelain." He said the product was light in weight, decidedly translucent and quite hard, comparing well with any foreign ware. In 1929, Pope-Gosser joined the American China Corporation, a merger of eight companies. (See American China Corp.)

After the A.M.C. was dissolved, Pope-Gosser was reorganized in 1932 by Frank Judge. They still made beautiful semi-porcelain ware until 1958, but it was not as thin or translucent or the quality of the earlier ware. However, Pope-Gosser's late ware was as good or better than most semi-porcelain ware; it was of that good a quality. In 1904, Pope-Gosser China won the silver medal for superior semi-porcelain at the St. Louis Louisiana Purchase Exposition. In 1907, Pope-Gosser received the gold medal for plain and decorated china and semi-porcelain at the Jamestown Tercentennial Exposition. One very popular pattern made from 1935 until closing was "Rosepoint." The Steubenville Pottery bought the molds and Canonsburg Pottery bought the Steubenville Pottery and the molds, so "Rosepoint" marked made by Steubenville was made at Canonsburg Pottery after 1959. (See the listings for Steubenville Pottery and Canonsburg Pottery.) (Information: W.P. Jervis, "Dictionary Pottery Terms," *Pottery, Glass and Brass Salesman*, July 4, 1918, p. 12; also Wilbur Stout, *Clay Industry of Ohio*, p. 83. Marks: nos. 1 and 2 were old marks which W.P. Jervis, "Worlds Pottery Marks," *Pottery, Glass, and Brass Salesman*, February 13, 1913, pp. 13, 17, said no. 1 was used from 1903 to 1913, and no. 2 was used in 1913. No. 3, "Rosepoint," was filed for registration January 3, 1935, claiming use since July 10, 1934, for chinaware, porcelainware, earthenware and potteryware, for table and culinary purposes. This pattern was semi-porcelain with a raised design of roses and different flowered decals in the center. See discussion above. No. 4, "Candlewick," was filed for registration June 22, 1936, claiming use since March 1936 for chinaware, porcelainware, semi-porcelainware, earthenware, potteryware and crockeryware,

for table, culinary and household purposes. No. 5, "Briar Rose," from Jo Cunningham. No. 6, the wreath mark was shown in 1952 *Crockery and Glass Journal Directory*, p. 24. The rest of the marks were used in the 1940 and 1950's. They were from Quality Stamp Company, East Liverpool, Ohio, or copied from dishes.)

Porcelain Design. Ann Arbor, Michigan. 1977 to present (1985). Sharon Hubbard is a studio potter, who describes herself as a ceramic designer, has been making handbuilt porcelain, decorative and sculptural, destinctively designed in asymetrically balanced delicate shapes, glazed with beautiful pastel colors which have pencil lines. The pastel glazes are sprayed on, giving an unusual effect. Each piece is hand signed and dated with blue-green or black oxide stain on the unglazed bottom. She has been at her present location since 1977. She received a B.F.A. Summa Cum Laude from the University of Michigan. Sharon's exhibitions include: Everson Museum of Art, one person show, 1985, Syracuse, New York; "National Clay and Fiber," 1984, Cuyahoga Valley Art Center, Cuyahoga Falls, Ohio; "New Thoughts in Ceramics," 1984, Venture/Habatat Gallery, Lathrup Village, Michigan; "Created by Hand," 1984, AAO Gallery, Buffalo, New York; ACC Craft Fair, 1984, Eastern States Exposition Center, West Springfield, Maine; "Clayworks," 1984, Ann Arbor Art Association, Ann Arbor, Michigan; "Michigan Artists Invitational," 1984, Troy Art Gallery, Troy, Michigan; Ceramic Exhibit 1984, by Foundation Artists, Detroit, Michigan; "Michigan Ceramics 1983," Michigan Potters Assoc., Selo/Shevel Gallery, Ann Arbor, Michigan; "Spring Exhibition," Artisans Gallery, 1983, Great Neck, New York; DeMatt Gallery, 1983, a three person exhibition, Holt, Michigan; "Annual Juried Membership Show 1981," Ann Arbor Association, Ann Arbor, Michigan; "Michigan Ceramics 1981," Detroit Artists Market, Detroit, Michigan; "Focus on Clay," a four person exhibition, 1981, Rackham Galleries, U of M, Ann Arbor, Michigan; "Porcelain and Photography," a two person exhibition by Sharon Hubbard and Joel Hakken, 1980, Northwestern Michigan College, Traverse City, Michigan.

Awards include: Juror's Award, Created by Hands, AAO Gallery, Buffalo, New York, 1984; Best of Show, Art in the Park, Birmingham, Michigan, 1984; Best of Show, East Lansing Art Festival, 1983; Best of Show and Purchase Award, ToledoFest, Toledo, Ohio, 1983 and 1984; Second Place - Ceramics, Crosby Gardens, Toledo, Ohio, 1983; Third Place in Crafts, and Purchase Awards, Miami Beach, Florida, 1983 and 1984; Judge's Recognition Award, Las Olas Art Festival, Ft. Lauderdale, Florida, 1983; Award Winner, 16th Flint Art Fair, Flint, Michigan, 1983; Merit Award, and Honorable Mention, "Images 1983" Show, New Smyrna Beach, Florida.

Sharon's pottery has been displayed in the following galleries: Artisans Gallery, Great Neck, New York; Best of Everything Gallery, Potomac, Maryland; and Washington, D.C.; Kornbluth Gallery, Fairlawn, New Jersey; Masterworks Gallery, Highland Park, Illinois; Canyon Gallery, Ft. Lauderdale, Florida; Detroit Gallery of Contemporary Crafts, Detroit, Michigan; DeGraaf-Forsythe Gallery, Ann Arbor, Michigan and Chicago, Illinois; Venture/Habatat Galleries, Lathrup Village, Michigan; Troy Art Gallery, Troy, Michigan; Ann Arbor Art Association Exhibit Gallery, Ann Arbor, Michigan. Her permanent collections consist of: Penzoil Corp., Johnson Bldg., Houston, Texas; and Greater Toledo Arts Commission, Toledo, Ohio. Sharon was featured in *Ceramics Monthly*, September issue, 1983, pp. 77-79 and also in the April issue, 1984, p. 44.

S. Hubbard '84

Porcelain Insulator Corporation/Pinco Division of Joslyn Manufacturing and Supply Company. Lima, New York. 1920 to present. Company was started at the site of the old Lima Insulator Company which had burned in 1919. Pinco insulators were sold through Joslyn Manufacturing and Supply Company. In 1976 the company was known as the Pinco Division of the Joslyn Manufacturing and Supply Company. Several types of insulators were made there over the years with incuse (stamped in) or hand stamped with ink underglaze marks. (Information: For a long discussion and description of the products, see Jack H. Tod, *Porcelain Insulators Guide Book for Collectors*, pp. 107-109. Shown in Tod, p. 109, is a variety of marks for this company. Only a few of the variations are shown here. The marks vary in size and numbers. There was also a mark, "Patent Applied For" in a circle, which Tod said was used on style U-174. He also includes a date coding for markings 1946 and later. The dot as placed in mark no. 1 designated 1949, and the dot in mark no. 2 meant 1953, according to Tod, by letter. The number 63 in mark no. 2 was a catalog number.)

PINCO 1.

PINCO 63 2.

PINCO-U 3.

PINCO 4.

Porcelain Products, Inc. Organized in 1927 by the merger or purchase of five porcelain companies: Federal Porcelain Company, Carey, Ohio; National Electric Porcelain Company, Carey, Ohio; Findlay Electrical Porcelain Company, Findlay, Ohio; Ravenswood Porcelain Company, Ravenswood, West Virginia; General Porcelain Company, Parkersburg, West Virginia. After several years of organizational and equipment shuffling, the wet process manufacture was conducted at the Parkersburg plant, dry process manufacture was combined and conducted at the original Federal Porcelain plant in Carey, and general offices were located in the old plant building at Findlay. All the other properties of the combined companies were shut down or sold, and even the general offices at Findlay were moved to Parkersburg in 1955. The specific offices for the dry press manufacture at Carey were moved from Findlay to Carey in 1957. The company manufactured only insulators, generally marked with forms of rectangle-PP or rectangle-PP/INC., the latter being an approximation of their registered (1927) trademark. The trademark registration covered crockery, because Ravenswood was a manufacturer of all forms of heavy hotel chinaware. However, there is evidence that Porcelain Products, Inc. never operated the Ravenswood plant, and the latter was shut down almost immediately and sold in 1929. Porcelain Products, Inc. became a wholly owned subsidiary of A.B. Chance Company in May 1956. The subsidiary became an operating division of A.B. Chance in 1958, and insulator markings were then changed from "P.P." to "Chance." (Information: Jack H. Tod, by letter. Marks: no. 1 filed for registration December 1, 1927, claiming use since October 1, 1927, for use on crockery, namely dishes, plates, cups, saucers, bowls, jugs, pitchers, mugs, jars, crocks and vases. Other marks found impressed on insulators. In Jack H. Tod, *A History of Electrical Porcelain*, p. 92, he tells us they used the trademark "Alligator" on assembled split knobs. Also the name "Findlay" was used on earlier made insulators.)

PP
TRADE INC MARK

```
PAT
4-16-29
```

CHANCE

P P

```
P P
1000
```

Porcelier Manufacturing Company. South Greenberg, Pennsylvania and East Liverpool, Ohio. 1927-1954. Started 1927 in East Liverpool and was listed at Dresden and Smith Streets in 1929. In 1930 the company was moved to South Greenberg, Pennsylvania. By 1931 they were employing 302 people to make vitrified china teapots, electric coffee pots, sugars, creamers, cups, bowls, etc. (For more information and pictures, see Lehner, *American Kitchen and Dinner Wares*, p. 123. Marks: from dishes.)

Porcelier
HAND DEC
VITREOUS CHINA
U.S. PATENT APPLIED FOR
DO NOT PLACE OVER
OPEN FLAME
USE A HEAT PAD

Porcelier
TRADE MARK MFG. Co.
GREENSBURG, PA.
2007

Porcelier
TRADE MARK
VITREOUS HAND DEC
CHINA
MADE IN U.S.A.

Porcelier
TRADE MARK
VITREOUS CHINA
MADE IN U.S.A.

Porcelier
TRADE MARK
VITRIFIED
HEAT-PROOF
COOKING CHINA

Portland Pottery Works, 1884 to 1890/ **E. Swasey and Company**, 1892 until the Depression. Portland, Maine. For early history, see Lamson and Swasey listing. In 1884, Rufus Lamson left the partnership of Lamson and Swasey in the Portland Pottery Works and L. Frank Jones, a Portland businessman bought his interests, and the pottery operated as **Swasey, Jones and Company**. Lamson had left following a triple tragedy, the death of his wife and son and a fire in the factory. After a couple of years, he came back to the business and the name was **Swasey, Lamson and Company** until around 1890. In 1890, Lamson established a wholesale and retail crockery business, and Swasey started selling crockery and glass in a business of his own called E. Swasey and Company. Although the pottery may have operated for a very short time after 1890, by 1891 the plant had become part of the **Portland Pottery Company** under Joseph S. Gilliatt. Then in 1892, Swasey again operated the plant as E. Swasey and Company. In 1897, Eben Swasey's son, Perley Ambrose Swasey became the operators of E. Swasey and Company and continued to operate until the depression. Crocks, jars and other salt glazed stoneware pieces in buff and brown, with stamped on or printed marks were made at this pottery. (Information: M. Lelyn Branin, *The Early Potters and Potteries of Maine*, pp. 67-70. Marks: Branin, same source, p. 224.)

```
E. SWASEY & CO.
PORTLAND ME
```

```
E. SWASEY & CO.
PORTLAND ME
USA
```

SWASEY JONES & CO
PORTLAND ME

Portland Stoneware Company/Winslow and Company. Portland, Maine. 1867 to 1969. For previous history, see the listing, Clough and Calhoun. As soon as the corporation for the Portland Stoneware Company was formed, expansion programs and new products were initiated. By 1875 the factory was using steam power and employing 70 men and owned their own vessels for transporting raw and finished materials. The company made garden vases and statuary, chimney tops and flues, and fire proof brick tile. In 1882, the name was changed from the Portland Stoneware Company to Winslow and Company with Edward B. Winslow as superintendent. In November 1886, the company suffered a major fire and destroyed $75,000.00 to $100,000.00 worth of machinery. A new three story building was built. On the first floor, brick and tile were made. Terra cotta pieces, some of which were very expensive were made on the second floor and on the third floor the product was drain and sewer pipe. The number of employees was 250 by 1893. The company survived the Depression, but after W.W. II, they were acting as a distributing agency and in 1969 the Winslow family disposed of what remained of the business. (Information: M. Lelyn Branin, *The Early Potters and Potteries of Maine*, pp. 64-67. Marks: Branin, as cited, p. 224.)

Port Richmond Pottery Company/J.E. Jeffords Company/Philadelphia City Pottery. The pottery started in Philadelphia in 1868 by J.E. Jeffords and Company as the **Port Richmond Pottery Company** and was out of business by 1915. Somehow this company displeased some of the old master writers on pottery. W.P. Jervis in "A Dictionary of Pottery Terms," the *Pottery, Glass, and Brass Salesman*, March 28, 1913, p. 15, said they made a "cheap grade" of earthenware around 1904, and were out of business at the time the article was written. E.A. Barber in *Marks of American Potters*, p. 32, written in 1904, said "they manufacture cow creamers in brown glaze after the old shapes, and while not intended to deceive, these are such excellent reproductions of early patterns that examples frequently find their way into the shops of secondhand dealers and are sold as genuine antiques at high prices." According to Jennie Young, *The Ceramic Art* written in 1878, p. 455, this company made an excellent grade of fine stoneware for household purposes and tableware. She said the pieces usually had mouldings in relief and that they were colored brown and yellow outside and white inside. Probably we will never know which of the writers were correct about the company's products because Barber said much of it was unmarked. In the 1913 *Keller's Pottery and Glass Annual*, p. 50. The Philadelphia City Pottery Company advertised themselves as successors to the J.E. Jeffords and Company, making the "original" Jeffords yellowware, Rockingham, and yellow white lined ware in kitchenware pieces, cups, etc. Other products made by Jeffords were teapots, table and toilet whitewares, jardinieres, Rockingham, yellowware and blue glazed ware. They also exhibited majolica at the Philadelphia Exhibition in 1876. In the 1893 *Industrial Directory of Pennsylvania*, the company was still called the Port Richmond Pottery, employing 150. (Marks: were printed or stamped. No. 1 John Ramsay, *American Potters and Pottery*, p. 265; no. 2, Barber, p. 32; no. 3, Jervis, p. 15.)

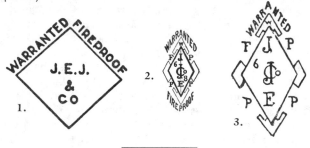

Pots & Stuff. Columbus, Ohio. 1973 to present. Bill Barnett, a studio potter makes wind chimes of stoneware and pottery pieces. He won a Governor's Award in 1975.

Pot Shop. Sharon, Connecticut. Willim E. Pitney, studio potter, received a B.F.A. degree from Pratt Institute Art Education Department, Brooklyn, New York, in 1942, and a M.F.A. degree from New York State College of Ceramics at Alfred University, Alfred, New York, in 1950. He started teaching in 1945 in the Amityville Public Schools; then on to Mohawk College where he was administrative assistant to the Dean; from 1950-1972 he had a full professorship as head of the ceramic division of the department of art of Wayne State University at Detroit, Michigan. In 1972 at age 58, Pitney became a full time studio potter. He set up a studio in Vermont, for a year then went to Sharon, Connecticut, where he converted a two car, two story garage into a ceramic studio to make stoneware and porcelain pieces. He has exhibited at various shows in the Syracuse Museum of Fine Arts; the Brooklyn Museum; the Detroit Institute of Arts; Ball State Teachers College Art Gallery, Muncie, Indiana; the Museum of Contemporary Crafts, New York City; the John Herron Art Gallery, Indianapolis; Habatat Galleries; the Society of Connecticut Craftsmen at Wesleyan University at Middletown, Connecticut; the University of Hartford, West Hartford, Connecticut; the Farmington Valley Arts Center, Avon, Connecticut; Guilford Handcrafts Center, Guilford, Connecticut; and at the Pewabic Pottery in Detroit, a special exhibition of "Bill Pitney and Former Students," was held in 1982. A great number of the shows held at the places listed were one man shows. He is a member of the Michigan Potter's Association, the Connecticut Guild of Craftsmen, the National Association of Handcraftsmen, Inc., American Association of University Professors, the Society of Connecticut Craftsmen, American Craftsmen's Council and has held many offices in these organizations. (Information: Resume by Pitney, sent to author by Thomas Turnquist, who also sent the marks.)

THE POT SHOP

Pot Shop. Anoka, Minnesota. 1974 to present (1984). Studio potter, Barbara A. Hern, makes stoneware and porcelain functional pottery pieces. She maintains a salesroom, also does orders to specifications, as well as teaching pottery making classes to children and adults. Mark is inscribed signature or paper label as shown.

```
The Pot Shop
2527 N. Ferry
Anoka, MN 55303
612-427-7160
```

Potter's Co-operative. See listing for Brunt, Bloor, Martin and Company and other potteries for history.

Potter's Habitat. Columbus, Ohio. Studio potter, Alan B. Jones, started in Brownsville, Nebraska, in January 1975. At present (1982) he is making handthrown functional stoneware in Columbus.

Potter's House. Indianapolis, Indiana. 1972 to present (1983). Trudy Thorn, a studio potter, started in business in New Jersey in 1972 and moved to Indianapolis in 1976. The Potter's House is a school for potters maintaining around 24 students all of the time. Trudy Thorn also makes stoneware, porcelain and some raku for sale in her own show room. Most of the ware is functional such as dinnerware (by special order), mugs, pitchers, bowls, lamps, clocks, etc. Some pieces are decorative, such as vases, etc.

Potter's Mark Studio. Banner Elk, North Carolina. 1970 to present. Bill Dicks, owner, is a studio potter making handthrown pottery on a wheel, specializing in sitting and hanging lanterns. They are indoor/outdoor ceramic lanterns. Each lantern is a one-of-a-kind original, and he glazes them in various colors. (Information: Staff written, "Bill Dicks, The Potter's Mark Studio," *Pottery Collectors Newsletter*, October, 1976, p. 86.)

Potters of Wall Street/Harris Strong, Inc. New York, New York, and Ellsworth, Maine. From 1947 to 1951, Harris Strong and Robert Krassner were co-owners of Potters of Wall Street. Harris Strong attended the North Carolina State College of Engineering, then studied ceramic art under Ruth Canfield at the New York University. In 1952, Strong started a business of his own called Harris Strong, Inc. in the Bronx, and later in Ellsworth, Maine. He made wall pieces, lamps, tile tables and individual tiles. The pieces were signed with paper labels or signed in the clay. The wall pieces usually had a one-letter and one or two-number code hand written on the back. The wall pieces sometimes had mounting brackets on the back that were hinged metal loops. In 1970, Strong moved to Ellsworth, Maine, where the emphasis shifted to prints and graphics. Strong still operates Harris Strong, Inc. in Maine, with almost total emphasis on graphics. (Information: Thomas Turnquist, researcher and writer on American pottery. Marks: also sent by Turnquist, represent photostatic copies from pictures of the actual marks. Also pictured is a drawn copy of each mark.)

> hand crafted by
> harris g. strong
> bronx 55, N.Y.

> hand crafted by
> harris g. strong
> bronx 55, N.Y.

Harris G. Strong
 # 30 of 100

Harris G. Strong
 # 30 of 100

Potter's Supply Company. East Liverpool, Ohio. Company filed for registration of this mark on March 13, 1958, claiming use since July 1950, for pottery kiln room supplies, namely, potter's pins, potter's stilts, potter's spurs and potter's thimbles, made of ceramic material.

PIN-RITE

Pottersville. Near Edgefield District, South Carolina. From around 1810 until after the Civil War there was a village named Pottersville about a mile north of the Edgefield District, South Carolina. Potters in Pottersville in the first half of the 19th Century included Abner Landrum, W.F. Hahn, Harris, Miles, Rhodes, Lofton, Ramey, Gibbs, Drake, Corley, Hill, Mitchell and Wardlaw. Trenton, South Carolina was in the Edgefield District, and W.F. Hahn was one of the early potters. The only other information I found on a potter named Hahn was in John A. Burrison, *Brothers in Clay*, pp. 292 and 315. He lists Hahn Pottery Works in Augusta, Georgia, around 1900 and suggests the potter may have worked in Aiken County, South Carolina. He said the Hahn family is known to have made pottery at Trenton and North Augusta, South Carolina. (Information and mark: Thomas G. Smith, "Potter's

Museum of McClendon," *Sandlapper*, April 1970, pp. 9-11; and Burrison, as cited.)

> W. F HAHN
> TRENTON
> S.C.

The Potter's Wheel. Columbus, Ohio. 1972 to present (1983). Lynda Schaefer Fromm is a studio potter making handmade wheel thrown functional stoneware, averaging 300 to 500 pieces a month in standard and miniature sizes.

Schaefer

Pottery Barn. New York, New York. Paul Secon, representing The Pottery Barn, filed for registration of this mark on August 2, 1956, for dinnerware, ovenware, kitchenware, art and decorative ware, such as dishes, dish services, beverage services, mugs, tiles, trays, bowls, salt and pepper shakers, casseroles, covered pots and pans, vases, flower pots, all made of crockery, earthenware and porcelain.

Pottery Queen. Zanesville, Ohio. Mark Heatwole, owner of the pottery outlet or sales agency called Pottery Queen, used the mark, "Queen Pottery," on pieces decorated at the Pottery Queen. I had quite a problem finding this particular information because the name of the store was Pottery Queen and the mark is Queen Pottery. Heatwole became owner of the stores in January 1954. But he did not start the decorating department until the middle 1960's. In 1973 Heatwole sold the stores. Exceptional glazes were perfected at the Pottery Queen. A pearl-like glaze, more attractive than most, was made. A heavy coating of gold and silver was used on these pieces for trim, and the result is striking. Decorators were Alma Heatwole, Edna Kettlewell and Art Wagner (see the listing for Art Wagner). The Pottery Queen owned many of their own molds and had pottery pieces made to their specifications. Blanks were also purchased from Nouvelle Pottery, Scio Pottery and various plants. The Pottery Queen was located in what had been the old Weller showroom. According to Heatwole, he had a glaze very similar to Weller's, Sicardo, but he didn't make many pieces when he found out the Queen Pottery mark was being erased and the pieces sold as Weller. Some of the pieces are hand painted with landscape scenes that are beautiful. (Marks: no. 1 is the Queen Pottery mark with the decorator mark of Alma Heatwole. No. 2; the initials of Edna Kettlewell may be found with the same mark.)

1.   2.   *E K*

Pottery By Barbara Williams. Kansas City, Missouri. 1982 to present (1984). Studio potter, Barbara Williams, made Raku Ware, white and dark stoneware specialties and functional, both handbuilt and wheel thrown. Barbara has a B.A. degree from Avila College in Kansas City. She studied with some outstanding potters including Joel Souza from Brazil, Donna Polsen and several others.

Pottery By Ward. Victor, Montana. 1973 to present (1983). Studio potter, John E. Ward makes functional and decorative stoneware and porcelain.

Pottery Works. Fitzwilliam Depot, New Hampshire. 1973 to present (1984). Studio potters, Karen Gregory and Terry Silverman make stoneware and porcelain into flameware cooking pots, porcelain mirrors, dinnerware and other functional pieces.

Potting Shed. Concord, Massachusetts. In 1973, Charlotte Star started experimenting to reproduce Dedham Pottery pieces, which she marks with her own marks as shown. In 1977, the Potting Shed was started in West Concord by Charlotte and her two sons, Chris and Rob. The traditional rabbit pattern in cobalt blue remains the outstanding favorite but grape clusters, flowers, dolphins, whales, bees, birds and beasts are also used. An advantage to the new "Dedham" is that it is dishwasher-safe and oven proof. The original Dedham patterns used are azaleas, clover, crabs, ducks, elephants, horse chestnuts and the rabbits. The Potting Shed has added many patterns of its own to their output. They utilize the distinctive crackled glaze finish as well as non-crackled gloss finish. All patterns are available in three colors, blue, moss green and raw sienna, with an off-white background. From 1944 to 1983 the number of outlets for this pottery has grown from 2 to 200. Each piece is completely hand made. First it is handmolded, dried, sanded smooth. A small staff of artists hand paints the designs before the bisque firing at 2,000 degrees, then comes a dip glazing and refiring. The pieces are rubbed with a carbon-water solution to bring out crackles in glaze. The whole process takes a week to complete. Because none of the original Dedham molds were available, no piece is identical in shape to Robertson's Dedhamware. No. 1 is the logo or design used on stationary etc. No. 2, 3, shows the explanations just as they were sent by Rob Star to this author.

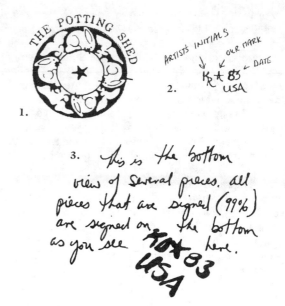

Pound, W.D. Randolf County, Alabama. Around 1920 made salt glazed stoneware. (Information and stamped or impressed mark with backward N. E. Henry Willett and Joey Brackner, *The Traditional Pottery of Alabama*, pp. 66 and 68.)

W D POUND

Prairie House. Springfield, Illinois. This mark filed for registration on September 23, 1971, claiming first use November 1, 1970, for use on pottery jars, bottles, platters, dishes, bowls, casseroles, pots, cups, vases, gobblets, samovars, ladles, shakers, planters, pitchers and tumblers.

PRAIRIE HOUSE

Price, Kenneth. To condense and to describe the work of a studio potter and sculptor such as Price to a small paragraph for such a book as this is almost impossible. I strongly urge the serious student to see the source cited for further information. Price studied at the Chouinard Art Institute in Los Angeles in 1953, 1954, and received a B.F.A. degree from the University of Southern California, in 1956. In 1957, 1958, he worked with Peter Voulkas at the Otis Art Institute. Then he went on to Alfred University to receive an M.F.A. degree in 1956. He had his first one man show at the Ferus Gallery in Los Angeles in 1960. His sculptured pieces had wit, imagination, bright and contrasting colors, and made a strong statement that the common place could be artistic and imaginative. He did a series on cups which was witty and complex and artistic. He took a functional object out of the realm of the ordinary with form and color. (Information: Garth Clark, *A Century of Ceramics in the U.S.*, pp. 319, 320. Mark: incised; Linda Steigleder, from the booklet published by the Everson Museum of Art to accompany the 1978 exhibition, "A Century of Ceramics in the U.S.," with curators: Garth Clark and Margie Hughto.)

PRICE '56

Price, Xerxes. Sayreville, New Jersey. Around 1802. Made stoneware. Impressed mark. (Information and marks: Thorn, p. 143.)

MADE BY XERXES
PRICE S. AMBOY

Prieto, Antonio. Oakland, California. Antonio Prieto is the head of Mills College ceramic department. He is an important professor who influenced many potters, one of whom was Robert Arneson, who worked as an assistant to Prieto, from 1960 to 1962. Prieto had a stoneware vase in the collection at the Everson Museum of Art in Syracuse, which he made around 1950. Clark mentions Prieto several times throughout the book cited, but there is no biographical listing for him to give more complete information. (Information: Garth Clark, *A Century of Ceramics in the U.S.*, pp. 124, 132, 140, 270, 271. Incised marks: Linda Steigleder, from the booklet published by the Everson Museum of Art to accompany the 1978 exhibition, "A Century of Ceramics in the U.S.")

Promotions, Inc. Youngstown, Ohio. Sales agency in business during the 1940's. All of the marks shown are filed by Promotions, Inc. However in *House and Gardens*, July 1945, p. 94, was an advertisement for "Cosmopolitan" dinnerware in Mayfair pattern from **Cosmopolitan Wares**, Youngstown (see mark 1). In *House and Gardens*, September 1945, p. 151, was another ad for "Vanity Fair" dinnerware in Rose Marie pattern by **Vanity Fair Housewares, Inc.** (see mark 3). We didn't find ads for the other two marks shown namely Good Housekeeping and American Homes, but all of this was evidently this distributors way of using several names for his business in different advertisements. This is not an uncommon practice even today. See Cunningham and Pickett for an example. Marks 5, 6, 7, are found on dishes made by French Saxon China Company of East Liverpool, Ohio. There was no listing for any of these names in the 1944 *Ohio Directory of Manufacturers*. (Information: advertisements sent by Linda Cleveland. Marks: nos. 5, 6, 7, from Quality Stamp Company. The company filed for registration on mark 1, on December 18, 1942, claiming use since October 4, 1941; mark 2 filed on May 24, 1943, claiming use since November 14, 1941; mark 3 filed November 10, 1941, claiming use since October 10, 1941; mark 4 filed May 20, 1941, claiming use since May 12, 1941, to be used on dinnerware made of crockery, earthenware or porcelain in sets or separate pieces.)

1. COSMOPOLITAN

2. AMERICAN HOMES

3. **Vanity Fair**

4. GOOD HOUSEKEEPING

5. Good Housekeeping DINNERWARE MADE EXPRESSLY FOR PROMOTIONS INC 22 KT. GOLD U.S.A. ROSALIE

6. Good Housekeeping DINNERWARE MADE EXPRESSLY FOR PROMOTIONS INC 22 KT. GOLD U.S.A. LILLY BELL

7. Good Housekeeping DINNERWARE MADE EXPRESSLY FOR PROMOTIONS INC 22 KT. GOLD U.S.A. GOLDEN LACE

Prospect Hill Pottery. Trenton, New Jersey. Was operated by Dale and Davis in Trenton, New Jersey, from 1880 until 1894 or 1895 making decorated semi-porcelain and white granite dinnerware according to Barber. After that time the pottery was sold to Charles H. Cook of Cook Pottery. There were no listings for the Prospect Hill Pottery in Trenton in 1901, 1902, 1903 or 1904. Then from 1905 until 1920, the pottery was listed every year, so I assume this was the period it was operated by Cook. It was not listed in the *Industrial Directory*, only the city directory so I couldn't tell what products it made that year. After 1920 the Prospect Hill Pottery was not listed until it was listed again in 1925 and 1926. That was the final mention of the pottery. The early marks in Barber for the Prospect Hill Pottery involve the names Dale and Davis. Davis, working alone, had exhibited white granite and decorated crockery in Philadelphia in 1876. (Information and marks: Barber, *Marks of American Potters*, p. 305; Lehner, *American Kitchen and Dinner Wares*, p. 124.)

IRON-STONE CHINA
DALE & DAVIS.

PATENTED AUG. 26th .78.
I. DAVIS.

D—D

I. DAVIS

IRONSTONE CHINA
I. DAVIS

Providential Tile Company. Trenton, New Jersey. Around 1885 to 1913. This company was organized by Joseph L. Kirkham, James H. Robinson, and C. Lewis Whitehead around 1885. Mr. Kirkham sold his share to his partners and started the **Kirkham Art Tile Company** in 1893 in Barberton, Ohio. This last company was listed only a couple of years before Kirkham moved on to Tropico, California, to start the Kirkham Tile and Pottery Company in Tropico, about nine miles from Los Angeles. Mr. Robinson didn't stay in the Providential Tile Company long either, leaving around 1900, but Whitehead continued alone until 1913. The factory was closed and never opened as a tile factory again. Scott Callowhill was the artist and modeler and two of his sons worked as decorators. Some tile and relief designs in highly decorated caps and borders with white glaze and gold. They also made tiles in two colors with part of the design raised. (Information: Townsend, "Development of the Tile Industry in the

U.S.," *American Ceramic Society Bulletin*, May 1943, pp. 133, 134, 148. Mark: raised in mold, sent by Elizabeth Vaughn, Beechwold Antiques, Columbus, Ohio.)

THE PROVIDENTIAL

TILE WORKS

TRENTON, N.J.

Pruden, John. Elizabeth, New Jersey. 1816 to 1879. Potter made slip decorated, sgraffito, plain redware, stoneware, Rockingham, brownware, including a large heavy pitcher with eagle and flag relief. (Information: John Ramsay, *American Potters and Pottery*, p. 166. Marks: Regina Stewart and Geraldine Consentino, *Stoneware*, p. 41; and C. Jordan Thorn, *Handbook of Old Pottery and Porcelain Marks*, p. 144.)

J.M. PRUDEN
ELIZABETH, N.J.

JOHN PRUDEN
ELIZABETH
N.J.

Purdy, George A. Pierce City, Missouri. Around 1883. Made stoneware. Mark found on six gallon stoneware handled crock or churn. (Information: Henry W. Heflin, pottery collector and researcher.)

GEO. A. PURDY
MFR.
PIERCE CITY
MO.

Purdy Potters. Atwater, Summit County, Ohio. Soloman Purdy was in Putnam, Ohio, around 1820 where he made slip decorated ware, plain redware, and earthenware into roofing tile and utilitarian pieces. Purdy lived for a time in the Zoar Community between 1820 and 1850 according to L.G.G. Ramsey, *The Complete Encyclopedia of Antiques*, New York: Hawthorne Books, 1962, p. 832. He was listed in Atwater in 1850, by Ramsay, p. 234. Gordon B. Purdy, Soloman's son was in Atwater as early as 1850 according to Spargo, p. 226. However, Ramsay, p. 207 lists Gordon B. Purdy from 1860 to 1870. He made stoneware with his name impressed for a mark. Fritzhugh Purdy and his partner Loomis operated in Atwater around 1871 according to Spargo, p. 343, making stoneware. (Marks: 1, 2, 7, Lehner, Ohio Pottery and Glass, pp. 18, 102. No. 3 Guilliland, p. 225. Nos. 4, 5, 6, Thorn, p. 144.

1. S. PURDY
ZOAR

2. ZOAR

3. Z•O•A•R•

4. S. PURDY
ATWATER

5. S. PURDY

6. S. PURDY
PORTAGE CO.

7.

Purinton Pottery Company. Shippenville, Pennsylvania. 1941 to 1959. They closed for a while in 1958 but were open again part of 1959. The concept and processes were developed by Bernard S. Purinton in a pilot operation in Wellsville, Ohio, beginning in 1936. Purinton Pottery Company was formed and production begun in 1941 in a plant designed and built for the purpose in Shippenville. Originally all the slipware was cast. (Later on, some was pressed, with the introduction of the Ram Press process.) The strictly free-brush decoration was made of the same slip as the body, with colored minerals added. The decorations were painted on the leather-hard body of the greenware. The decorators were local people trained at the factory. Glaze was applied by dipping the decorated ware, and the ware was fired only once. The body was formulated to stand the handling necessary for this process. Manufacture was ended and the company completely liquidated for economic reasons in 1959. The building was sold for other use. Competition from foreign imports was one of the underlying factors. (Information from Purinton by letter. Mark 1, 1945 *China and Glass Red Book Directory*. The rest of the marks came from pieces.)

Putnam Pottery. Athens, Ohio. 1983 to present (1985). Marcia Madonik, studio potter, makes wheel thrown and slab built functional pieces of stoneware. She specializes in dinnerware which is hand stamped with a sponge. She also makes kitchenware and giftware. Although in business a short time, this potter makes beautiful pottery. She showed at the Decemberfair in Columbus, Ohio, in 1984. Hundreds apply for admission and only a few are selected to show. Marcia received a B.F.A. degree from Ohio University at Athens, Ohio, in 1982.

PUTNAM *Madonik*

Pyramid Alloy Manufacturing Company. El Cerrito, California. Filed for rights to this mark November 28, 1947 for use on household, hotel and restaurant table chinaware including bath vessels and dishes, claiming use since August 21, 1947.

Q

Quality Enterprises, Inc. Shawnee Mission, Kansas. Filed for registration of this mark on February 5, 1962, for use on china dinnerware, claiming use since June 2, 1958.

Celebrity

Queen City Pottery Company. Cincinnati, Ohio. A wholesale outlet which was purchased by Robinson Ransbottom and used as a warehouse and wholesale outlet for the Cincinnati and Kentucky areas. See listing for Robinson Ransbottom.

Queens China Company. See American Art China Company, Sebring, Ohio.

R

Rabb and Rehm. Bloomsburg, Pennsylvania. 1874 to 1891. Charles Rabb and John Rehm started a pottery in Bloomsburg, Pennsylvania, in 1874, making stoneware jugs, batter jugs, crocks and other utilitarian pieces, some decorated in cobalt blue. In 1891, Rabb and Rehm sold the pottery to Austin Hyssong, one of the sons of E.B. Hissong of Cassville (see the Hyssong/Hissong listing). (Information and mark: Jeannette Lasansky, *Made in Mud*, pp. 12, 13.)

RABB & REHM
BLOOMBURG, PA.

Radford, Albert. Albert Radford was born in England in 1862. Several generations of his family had worked for Josiah Wedgwood Pottery. Albert worked there too, until coming to the United States in 1885 to work at the Eagle Pottery in Trenton, New Jersey. In 1889, he won a bronze medal at the Philadelphia Exposition while working at the Eagle Pottery. He constructed his first pottery at Broadway, Virginia, in 1891 and then moved to Tiffin in 1893, where he had a one kiln pottery on the back of his property. Around 1900 he moved to Zanesville to work as a modeler for Weller Pottery and left there in 1903. He was superintendent at the J.B. Owens Pottery and general manager at the Zanesville Art Pottery around 1901. He was largely responsible for a ware called, "La Moro," made at the Zanesville Art Pottery. Radford moved from pottery to pottery very quickly; like Lessell and other ceramists, he saw the big factories making so much money from his designs and formulas while he received little pay. From February to August of 1903, Radford had a one kiln pottery of his own on Coppermill Road, near Zanesville, which he called the **A. Radford Pottery Company**. From Zanesville, he went to Clarksburg, West Virginia, in 1903 and established a pottery there, also called the A. Radford Pottery Company. Radford had a heart attack and died in 1904 at age 41, but the pottery continued until 1912 when all molds and equipment, etc. were sold to the Brush-McCoy Pottery. According to Paul Evans, *Art Pottery of the U.S.*, p. 234, in 1970 to at least 1973, A. Radford's grandson, Fred W. Radford reproduced the Jasper-type decorated ware of the Zanesville variety, using the original molds with the mark, "An A. Radford/Reproduction/by F. Radford." The highest quality of ware produced by A. Radford was made at Tiffin, Ohio. Some of it was marked, "Radford Jasper." In the article by Evan Purviance, "American Art Pottery," *Mid-America Reporter*, November 1972, p. 7, Mr. Purviance said:

> "Radford used the original mold from Wedgwood from designs by Flaxman. Supposedly every piece of Radford Jasper made at Tiffin was created by his grandfather personally. No one in this country at that time possessed the knowledge and skill to produce this type of ware. His molds depict Greek figures, vines and conventional designs. The background colors of the ware made at Tiffin were royal blue, light blue, dove gray and olive green with relief work in white. It is said Radford created his finest art pottery at Tiffin. His ware made there is known and some is marked "Radford Jasper." However, we have in our collection a bowl with fluted top, pictured here, which we purchased in Zanesville. Radford lived next door to its owners and he made the bowl while in Zanesville, and gave it to them. It is marked Radford Jasper. The ware made in Zanesville, often had an overlay of contrasting colored clay,

background pebbly like orange peel or tree bark in matte finish. The colors were usually black, tan, brown, gray or green with backgrounds in lighter shades of blue, pink, dove gray, tan or green decorated with relief in white. Small pieces did not have the pebbly background applied, neither did the tankards, mugs or pitchers. Most of the ware made in Zanesville, was of the bisque type and is so hard it will hold water without glazing."

Ware made in Zanesville, most often bears only a shape number on the base. Pottery made in Clarksburg has the line name impressed and not the Radford name, such as Ruko, Radura and Thera, all made in Clarksburg. (Information: Evans, as cited, pp. 232-234; and also Purviance, as cited. Marks: nos. 1-4, Evans, as cited, p. 234; no. 5, Purviance, as cited.)

1. RADFORD JASPER
2. [THERA.]
3. RADURA.
4. RUKO
5. A. RADFORD POTTERY CO.

Raines, Elsie H. Cincinnati, Ohio. 1971 to present (1983). This studio potter makes porcelain dolls, birds, Christmas ornaments, figurines, etc. These are beautiful bisque looking collectibles marked with the date in most cases.

ER

Ralston Purina Company. St. Louis, Missouri. Filed for rights to this mark on March 23, 1925, for use on chinaware bowls, claiming use since October 13, 1924.

find the bottom

Ramblewood/Anna Mae Burke. Newtown, Pennsylvania. Filed for registration of this mark on February 10, 1965, claiming first use on December 29, 1964, for hand painted and glazed molded earthenware, such as dinnerware and tableware reproduced in quantity from an original drawing in colors applied to the outer or face side of such ware.

Randall, Ruth H. Syracuse, New York. 1923 to 1981. Ruth H. Randall, a sculptress, was born in 1896. She studied at the Cleveland Art Institute, Cleveland, Ohio, from 1915 to 1921, receiving degrees in design and art education. In 1930

she received a B.F.A. degree from the College of Fine Arts at Syracuse University. She taught at this university from 1930 to 1962, as a professor of ceramics and later as professor of design and crafts. In 1932, she went to study in Vienna. Her work became internationally known when it was included by invitation in 1937 for the Exhibition of Contemporary American Ceramics assembled by the Everson Museum for Denmark, Sweden, Finland and England; the Decorative Arts Exhibit in Paris; in the Golden Gate International Exposition at San Francisco and the 1939 World's Fair. Her piece "Madame Queen" appeared in *Fortune Magazine* and is in the permanent collection of the Everson Museum of Art. By 1939 she had also exhibited at the Cleveland Museum of Art, the Whitney Museum of Art, the Philadelphia Art Alliance and in exhibitions of the National League of American Pen Women.

In 1940, she visited Hawaii, Tahiti and Samoa. There were three visits to Peru in 1945, 1953 and 1958, when she had a pottery class in the summer session of the Miraflores Art Center. She obtained several contemporary Peruvian pots for the Syracuse University collection. While on leave from the university in 1947 she wrote the first book on ceramic sculpture published in the United States. It was entitled, "Ceramic Sculpture" and published by Watson-Guptill. That same year she taught part-time at Rhode Island School of Design. On sabbatical leave in 1956, she spent four months in Japan, followed by a trip around the world. She found many examples of Japanese folk art to bring back to Syracuse University. In 1962, Randall retired from Syracuse University and a retrospective exhibition was held at Lowe Art Gallery.

A list of her exhibitions, honors, awards and accomplishments include: Syracuse National Ceramic exhibitions 1932-1962; group shows at the Butler Institute of American Art (Youngstown, Ohio); the Cleveland Museum of Art; the regional shows of the Syracuse, Rochester and Utica museums; the Wichita Associated Artists; the Syracuse Ceramic Guild; the annual faculty shows of the School of Art at Syracuse University; the Philadelphia Art Alliance; the New York and San Francisco World Fairs, the 1936 Exhibition of Decorative Arts in Paris; and the various European travelling shows of the National Ceramic Exhibitions. She has had one-man shows at the Argent Gallery (New York); the Oneonta Art Museum; the New York State College of Education in Cortland; the 1958 State Fair; the Everson Museum of Syracuse (1960) and Hanover Gallery (1980). She was awarded second prize (1940) and honorable mention (1935) in the national ceramic shows, first prizes for sculpture in the Associated Artists Annual (1936, 1938) and the 1954 Syracuse Museum regional show, and the 1953 purchase prize by the Butler Museum of American Art. Her publications include numerous articles on ceramics in *Design Magazine*, the *Everson Museum Bulletin*, *Craft Horizons* and the *Journal of the American Ceramic Society* and her book *Ceramic Sculpture*. Her work appears in the permanent collections of the Everson Museum of Art in Syracuse; in the Butler Museum of American Art in Youngstown, Ohio; the I.B.M. Museum in Endicott, New York; the El Paso Museum, Texas; and Syracuse University. Ruth Randall died in 1983. (Information: Margie Hughto, "Ruthie Hunie Randall Ceramics, 1923-1981," four pages published to go with exhibit at Everson Museum of Art, May 1 to June 7, 1981. Marks: no. 1, Linda Steigleder, from the booklet published by the Everson Museum of Art to accompany the 1978 exhibition, "A Century of Ceramics in the U.S.," mark incised; no. 2, from Tom Turnquist, researcher on ceramics.)

Ruth H. Randall

Ransbottom Brothers Pottery Company. Roseville, Ohio. 1900 to 1920. Alfred Ransbottom operated a small pottery in Roseville, Ohio, before the 1900's. In 1902, his four sons started the Ransbottom Brothers Pottery with F.M. Ransbottom as the active manager. The brothers purchased a small plant, the Oval Ware and Brick Company, and by 1906 the building covered 3½ acres, employing 100 men. See Johnson, Whitmore and Company for more history. (Information: *Roseville*, a 20 page booklet printed in 1906, probably by the town council. No author given. Mark shown was filed for copyright on November 7, 1919, by Ransbottom Brothers claiming use on stoneware and pottery since 1910.)

Ransburg, Harper J. Company. From 1908 to 1912 in Toledo, Ohio. They moved to Indianapolis, Indiana, in 1912. They were still in business in the 1960's. This company did all sorts of decorating, starting with glass cutting, later hand decorated metal kitchenware, even decorated candles. They also patented marks for jars, bowls, trays, cracker boxes, cakes, etc. in 1936, made of crockery, earthenware, etc. (Information: Albert Christian Revi, "Glass of Class," *Spinning Wheel*, July-August, 1966, p. 18. Marks: nos. 1, 2, metallic or foil labels found on pieces. Nos. 3, 4, both filed in 1936, claiming use for that year prior to filing. No. 5 was the copy filed with the patent office December 1, 1950, claiming use since April 25, 1936, for cookie jars, grease jars, pitchers, salt and pepper shakers, salad bowls, mixing bowls, teapots and flower pots, all made of earthenware.)

3. **MUNCH**
4. **SNACK JAR**

Rapp Brothers Various Morton, Illinois, Potteries: Rapp Brothers Brick and Tile Company on 220 Pennsylvania Avenue, in Morton, Illinois. 1877-1936. Six brothers from Germany founded the business to make just brick, but by the mid 1890's the pottery was making mixing bowls, wine jugs, chambers, milk crocks, churns, pitchers, etc. to meet the local demand in the **Morton Pottery Works** which was started in 1878. The second generation of Rapps renamed the pottery

The Morton Earthenware Company in 1915. According to Doris and Burdell Hall in Morton's Potteries, 99 Years, Morton, Illinois: privately printed, 1981, p. 7, the ware made at the pottery didn't change that much, only the name was changed. Rockingham and yellowware were among the early products. A Rebecca at the Well teapot was made at the Morton Pottery Works. The pottery was closed during W.W.I. and opened again under the guidance of one of the original founders, named Mathew, and his four sons in 1920 as the **Cliftwood Art Potteries, Inc.** They made miniature toys and animals and various decorative items. A beautiful brown flow or drip glaze was developed. Art lines were developed and ready for market about five years after Cliftwood Art Potteries, Inc. got started. A jade green color with an irridescent appearance, and a cobalt blue with high gloss glaze were developed and used. The Hall's mentioned 13 different colors were used on ware. Lamps were added to the line in 1932, and were decorated in a separate building called the **Cliftwood Studio**. A little over 100,000 lamps were sold in the first year. During the early 1930's the pottery had a show room in Chicago, and Mathew and his sons built the Cliftwood Inn, where they showed pottery as well as maintained a lunch room, etc. In January 1933, the Inn was sold. The pottery operated at peak production right on through the depression, but after Mathew Rapp died in 1938, the sons only maintained their interest and enthusiasm for two more years. In 1940 the pottery was sold and renamed **Midwest Pottery** which operated until 1944 when the pottery building on Pennsylvania Avenue was leveled by fire. (Information: Doris and Burdell Hall, *Morton's Potteries: 99 Years*, Morton, Illinois: privately printed, 1981 from various pages and pictures throughout the whole book. The marks for the various potteries are to be found under the name of the potteries. See the various listing for marks. See American Art Potteries, Morton, Illinois, for more on the Rapp brothers.

Ratner, Harry, Pottery, Inc. Maspeth, New York. The Harry Ratner Pottery, Inc. filed for registration of mark 1 on July 22, 1940, for use on flower pots.

Rauschenberg, Robert. Robert, a studio potter, attended the Kansas City Art Institute in 1956 on the G.I. Bill. In 1957 he studied at the Academie Julian in Paris. He became very involved with ceramics in 1972 when he stayed for three months at the Graphicstudio at the art department of the University of Southern Florida, in Tampa. See Garth Clark as cited for a description of the work Robert did there. (Information: Garth Clark, *A Century of Ceramics in the U.S.*, p. 321. Mark: Linda Steigleder, from the booklet published by the Everson Museum of Art to accompany the 1978 exhibition, "A Century of Ceramics in the U.S." The mark shown is painted.)

Ravenscroft, Ltd. Sales agency in Lancaster, Ohio, belonging to Anchor Hocking which marketed American-made glass and dinnerware. They did market Taylor, Smith and Taylor dinnerware while the plant was owned by Anchor Hocking. (See Taylor, Smith, and Taylor for more information.)

Raymond's, Inc. Boston, Massachusetts. Filed for registration on this mark on February 16, 1956, for use on china tableware, claiming use since 1954.

INCOGNITO

Read, Thomas. Newport, Ohio (near New Philadelphia). About 1850 to 1865. Made stoneware. (Information: Ramsay, *American Potters and Pottery*, p. 225. Marks: Thorn, p. 144.)

T. READ   T. READ
TUSCARAWAS CO.

Red Bull Inns of America, Inc. Carnegie, Pennsylvania. Company filed for registration of this mark on November 19, 1969, claiming first use March 1, 1968 for use on dishes, such as dinner and bread plates, platters, cups, saucers and bowls of ceramic material.

Red Cliff Company. Chicago, Illinois. 1950 to 1980. This was a decorating and distributing company which decorated beautiful ironstone pieces patterned after old patterns and shapes. According to Annise Heaivilin's book, *Grandma's Tea Leaf*, pp. 178, 179, Hall China Company made ware in the 1950's and 1960's for Fred Clifford, owner of Red Cliff Company. Clifford purchased original English Tea Leaf to use as an example. All Red Cliff ware was clearly marked. There was no attempt at deception. Only a desire to create more of a beautiful saleable product. Heaivilin called the ware beautiful and becoming scarce already. Red Cliff Company had many patterns of old ironstone china. (Marks: nos. 1-3, Heaivilin, p. 179. Mark 4 was filed June 6, 1951, for use on china table and oven ware, claiming use since February 1950.

The rest of the marks are from Quality Stamp Company, East Liverpool, Ohio.)

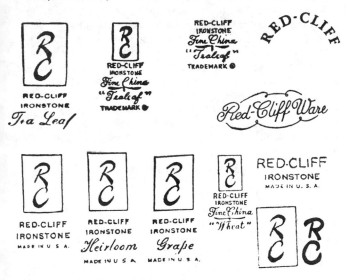

Red Horse Hill Pottery. Portsmouth, New Hampshire. The owners started commercially in 1975, although studio potter, George Sanders Nile, Jr. had been making pottery since 1972 and Cheryl Bucklin Niles since 1972. They make both artistic and commercial stoneware and porcelain fired to cone 10. Both have a B.A. degree from the University of New Hampshire. (Mark 1 is George's mark and mark 2 is Cheryl's mark.)

Niles
date

CBN
date

Redlands Pottery. Redlands, California. Before 1902 and after 1908. Wesley H. Trippett was a designer and modeler of clay in the making of architectural and decorative metalwork. He decided to make the actual pottery pieces when he found a good surface clay deposit. He made his own wheel and started making vases, bowls, plaques, etc. Some of the pieces are glazed, but many are the natural unglazed clay surface to which he added sculptured effects. In 1978, the Oakland Museum showed two covered bonbon dishes with a modeled frog and lizard on the lids. Trippett worked alone for several years. (Information: Dave Rago, "American Art Pottery," *Antique Trader Weekly*, September 9, 1981, p. 91. Mark: shown in advertisement by Antiques Unlimited in the *American Art Pottery* newsletter by Duke Coleman, in various issues.)

REDLANDS POTTERY

Red Wing Stoneware Company, 1878 to 1906 /**Red Wing Union Stoneware Company,** 1906 to 1936 /**Red Wing Potteries, Inc.,** 1936 to 1967. Red Wing, Minnesota. The Red Wing Stoneware Company was founded in 1877, and in 1894 they joined with Minnesota Stoneware Company and North Star Stoneware Company to organize a selling agency called Union Stoneware Company. All three of the potteries re-

tained their own names and legal independencies. They just sold their products through Union Stoneware Company (see that listing). Then in 1906, Red Wing Stoneware Company and the Minnesota Stoneware Company really did have a merger, and the company became the Red Wing Union Stoneware Company which in turn became Red Wing Potteries, Inc. in 1936 to August 1967. Western Stoneware Company of Monmouth, Illinois, was founded just a short time before these Red Wing, Minnesota, potteries joined forces to stay in the competition. The beginning date, 1877 was established by David Newkirk who researched the papers recorded on file at the Goodhue County Courthouse. The actual incorporation took place March 10, 1877. The organization may have started sooner with the purchase of the assets of the small Hallem pottery called the Minnesota Pottery Company (not to be confused with Minnesota Stoneware Company). Hallem continued to work for the Red Wing Stoneware Company (see the listing Minnesota Pottery Company).

According to Dommel in article cited, a partial merger for selling purposes, took place as early as 1892, and the Red Wing Union Stoneware Company's name began to be used. However, Dave Newkirk found the Articles of Incorporation as they were published in the *Red Wing Daily Republican*, March 17, 1906, for the Red Wing Union Stoneware Company formed solely for the purpose of manufacturing. In 1900, the Minnesota Stoneware Company burned to the ground.

Around 1901, Red Wing Stoneware burned, too. In the *Tri State Trader*, October 16, 1982, p. 9, is a story, "Dormant Red Wing Factory Due to Become Office Complex," which states a new building was built in early 1900's, consisting of 100,000 square feet in four stories. That building housed the Red Wing Union Stoneware Company and Red Wing Pottery, Inc., until the plant was closed and 100 workers idled. Later in 1982, after being idle for 15 years, the building was to house retail outlets, restaurants, etc. As with most potteries that operate over a long period of years, the products of the Red Wing potteries changed as time went by. In the early years, the company produced stoneware jugs, crocks, jars, Mason fruit jars, etc. Stoneware was made until 1947. Many pieces are pictured in Viel's book as cited. Around 1920 the company began making vases, cookie jars, jardinieres, bowls, etc. in a more decorative line of pottery. On February 20, 1935, the Rum Rill mark was filed by the Red Wing Union Stoneware Company for use on earthenware vase, jugs, bowls, jardinieres, teasets, console sets, shell luncheon services, water jugs and occasionally china, claiming use since July 1, 1932, which is about the time they started making products for George Rum Rill, a selling agency (see that listing). Then starting in the 1930's, came the hundreds of dinnerware patterns made by Red Wing Potteries and shown so well in Dave Newkirk's book *Red Wing Dinnerware*. Solid color dinnerware became a popular selling item. Later, the hand painting of dinnerware and artware was added, which was to grow until the process required 90 workers.

The following quote from Ms. Dommel's article tells us about the ending struggle of Red Wing and is reprinted with permission of Spinning Wheel's former editor, Albert Christian Revi in 1981.

The 1920's and 1940's were prosperous years and Red Wing became an established leader in the dinnerware field. Red Wing pottery was sold in department stores, gift shops, floral shops, small-town hardware stores, even roadside stands. Then, around 1950, department stores, the major market for dinnerware, began importing increasing quantities. In 1950, about 10 percent of all dinnerware sold by department stores was imported and by 1967, imports had increased to 90 percent. It was difficult to compete with imports since foreign potteries were as modern and efficient but paid wages only a fraction of the United States scale.

Red Wing Potteries showed its first year of loss in 1955 and continued with greater losses until 1958. R.A. Gilmer became president and general manager in that year, and the company started making marginal profits again. As foreign import dinnerware sales continued to wreck havoc, the company sought new markets. Dinnerware was made specifically for trading stamp companies. Supermarkets were also large volume customers but carried lines only a limited time and were not a consistent sales source. As well as facing marketing problems, the antiquated physical plant prevented fluid production flow.

Further diversification was needed. Red Wing Potteries began producing a line of casual dinnerware in 1959 and started making restaurant and hotel china in 1964. Both casual and restaurant dinnerware showed promise of success as well as dinnerware manufactured for Sears, Roebuck and Company . . . .

Nationally recognized as a tourist attraction, the retail store was located across the street from the factory. Annually, thousands of tourists from throughout the country came to purchase second-quality Red Wing wares and tour the plant. In 1966, a gift shop and candy store were added and the retail store accounted for nearly one-fourth of total company sales.

The fatal blow to Red Wing Potteries came on June 1, 1967, when factory workers went on strike for higher wages. Unable to meet the workers' demands, Red Wing Potteries, which gained world-wide fame and stature during 90 years of pottery production, closed on August 24, 1967.

(Information: Lyndon Viel, *The Clay Giants*, Books I and II, see for many pictures; David Newkirk, *A Guide to Red Wing Markings*; Darlene Dommel, "Red Wing and Rum Rill Pottery," *Spinning Wheel*, December 1972, pp. 22 to 24. Marks: nos. 1-10 are for the Red Wing Stoneware Company, taken from Lyndon Viel's book, *Clay Giants, Book II*, pp. 27 through 44, and from David A. Newkirk's, *A Guide to Red Wing Markings*, pp. 5 to 11. These marks are duplicated several times in the two books. Both are excellent source material. No. 1, from bottom of figure of a pig, made around 1893. No. 11, ink stamped mark from Lyndon Viel, Book II, p. 114. No. 12, mark in mold on bottom from Lyndon Viel, Book II, p. 118. No. 13, stenciled mark on front, from Lyndon Viel, Book II, p. 165. Nos. 14, 15, 16, a great variation in stamped marks similar to these is shown in Newkirk's book, pp. 23 to 27.

The remainder of the marks from no. 17 on, are for Red Wing Potteries, Inc. The Rum Rill marks, no. 17, was filed February 20, 1935, by Red Wing Union Stoneware Company, as already explained. No. 18 was filed July 12, 1935, by the Rum Rill Pottery Company of Little Rock, Arkansas, at almost the exact same time. (See the listing for Rum Rill Pottery Company for history). Both claimed use since July 1932. Red Wing Potteries, Inc. made Rum Rill pieces until 1938. No. 19 was the only other mark we found registered by Red Wing Potteries, Inc. It was filed December 29, 1947, claiming use since July 1, 1946, for use on semi-porcelain vases, flower pots, vegetable dishes, mixing bowls, batter jugs, bread and butter plates, cake covers, casseroles, celery trays, compote plates, dinner plates, sugar and creamers, coffee cups and saucers, bouillon cups, egg cups, tea cups, grape fruit plates, ice tubs, mustard cups, oatmeal bowls, relish plates, dessert plates, soup plates, compartment plates, platters, pudding dishes, salad plates and sauce boats. Nos. 20, 21 Saffron Ware, a yellow domestic ware with salt boxes, pitchers, bowls, etc. was introduced in the late 1930's. Red Wing Pottery also made a line of gray kitchenware, called Sponge Band. Saffron was sold plain or with sponge decorations. See Viel's

Book II, pp. 112, 113, for several pictures of this ware, also for Saffron marks shown. Nos. 22, 23, were the marks shown in various directories of the 1950's and 1960's for Red Wing Potteries. No. 24 is the actual mark as it appeared on a dish. Nos. 25, 26, 27, were also photostatic copies from dinnerware. Nos. 28 to 31 were incised or in the mold, on serving pieces and bowls. The remainder of the Red Wing Potteries's marks are from David Newkirks, *A Guide to Red Wing Markings*, pp. 28 to 31. He shows us the mark, "Red Wing, U.S.A." in various forms. The mark came inscribed or recessed in a mold, also raised in the mold. Each time the mark appears a little different. No. 28 was used in the 1950's and 1960's. No. 29 was used in the 1930's and 1940's, according to Newkirk. No. 30, Newkirk pictured a one pint bean pot with a five point star and Red Wing Potteries, in a circle.

Some of the Red Wing Potteries pieces are marked with a pattern name. David Newkirk and Stanley J. Bougie, *Red Wing Dinnerware*, has pictures, dates, pattern names, etc., all taken from actual brochures put out by the company. It is a wonderful help to the Red Wing collector. In an effort to help the reader to date the pattern names, I have included the following list of pattern names from the Newkirk-Bougie book cited, p. 3. From the material in the book, I was able to tell the year that each was introduced. Sometimes the name on the plate will be a pattern name which refers to the decoration. Sometimes the name could be a shape name. A line name is given to a certain kind of dish. For instance, Newkirk tells us that the "True China" line really was made of china clay instead of the coarser pottery clay used up to that time (1964). The "Like China" line was not china, but had the same shape as the "True China" line with a few exceptions he outlines. So line names represent a kind of china, rather than shape or decoration.

From *Red Wing Dinnerware*, by David A. Newkirk and Stanley J. Bougie:

Pattern Name	Shape or Line Name	Date
Adobestone	Ceramastone	1967
Ardennes		1941
Bake & Serve		1963
Blossom Time	Concord	1947
Blue Shadows	Like China	1964
Bob White	Casual	1956
Brittany		1941
Brocade	Like China	1964
Bud	Concord	1947
Buffet Royale		1960
Capistrano	Anniversary	1953
Caprice	Fancy Free	1952
Charstone Bleu	Ceramastone	1967
Chevron	Gypsy Trail	1935
Chrysanthemum	Concord	1947
Colonnes	Futura	1955
Continental Buffet		1956
Country Garden	Anniverary	1953
Crazy Rhythm	Futura	1955
Crocus	True China	1960
Daisy Chain	True China	1960
Damask	Like China	1964
Delta Blue		1954
Desert	Fancy Free	1952
Desert Sun	Cylindar	1962
Diamond Jim's China		
Driftwood	Anniversary	1953
Ebb Tide		1965
Fantasy	Concord	1947
Flight	Cylindar	1962
Fondoso	Gypsy Trail	1938
Frontenac	Futura	1955

Pattern Name	Shape or Line Name	Date
Fruit	Concord	1947
Granada	True China	1960
Greenwichstone	Ceramastone	1967
Golden Viking	Futura	1955
Hamm's Beer Set		1961
Harvest	Concord	1947
Hearthside	Casual	1961
Hearthstone Beige	Ceramastone	1967
Hearthstone Orange	Ceramastone	1967
Heatherstone	Ceramastone	1967
Hotel & Restaurant		
China		1964
Iris	Concord	1947
Kashmir	Like China	1964
Kermis		1957
Labriego		1930's
Lanterns	Concord	1947
Leaf Magic	Concord	1947
Lexington	Concord	1947
Lotus	Concord	1947
Lupine	Futura	1955
Lute Song	True China	1960
Magnolia	Concord	1947
Majestic	True China	1960
Mediterrania	True China	1960
Merrileaf	True China	1960
Midnight Rose	Anniversary	1953
Montmartre	Futura	1955
Morning Glory	Concord	1947
Nassau	Concord	1947
Normandy		1941
Northern Lights	Futura	1955
Orleans		1941
Pepe	Cylindar	1962
Picardy		1960
Pink Spice	Anniversary	1953
Plain	Gypsey Trail	1935
Plum Blossom	Dynasty	1949
Pompeii	Cylindar	1962
Provincial		1941
	(and again in 1963)	
Provincial Oomph		1943
Quartette	Concord	1947
Random Harvest	Futura	1955
Red Wing Rose	Futura	1955
Reed	Gypsey Trail	1935
Round Up	Casual	1958
Smart Set	Casual	1955
Spring Song	Concord	1947
Spruce		1956
Sweden House China		
Tahitian Gold	Cylindar	1962
Tampico	Futura	1955
Tip Toe	Casual	1958
Town & Country		1946
Turtle Dove	Cylindar	1962
Tweed Tex	Anniversary	1953
Two Step		1960
Village Brown		1955
Village Green		1953
Vintage	True China	1960
White & Turquoise	Contemporary	1956
Willow Wind	Concord	1947
Zinnia	Concord	1947

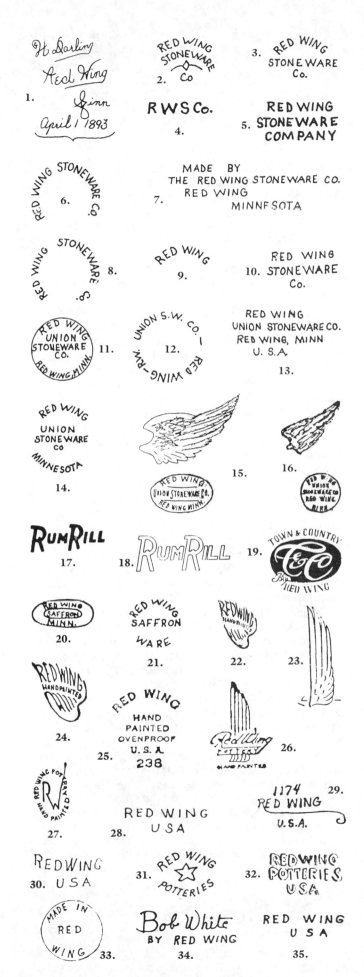

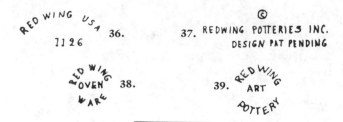

36. RED WING USA 7126

37. REDWING POTTERIES INC.
DESIGN PAT PENDING

38. RED WING OVEN WARE

39. RED WING ART POTTERY

Regal China Corporation. Antioch, Illinois. Started around 1938 to present (1985). Jim Beam Distilleries owns the Regal China Corporation as a wholly owned subsidiary. Royal China and Novelty Company of Chicago is the distributing or sales organization for the corporation. Regal China Company makes the products and Royal China and Novelty Company sells contracts to various industries. Sometime in the 1940's, Regal China Company was purchased by Royal China and Novelty Company. Regal China Corporation is completely separate from Regal Ware, Inc. of Kewaskum, Wisconsin. They have not manufactured any products for Regal Ware, Inc. The Regal Corporation manufactures decorative or art type ware on a contract basis only. J.S. Greenberg, president in 1985 said that no items which carry just the Regal name have been sold to retail trade since he has been there in 1968. Regal China Company, the pottery manufacturing part of the corporation makes bottles for James B. Beam Distilling Company. They made a cookie jar for Quaker Oats around 1976. A milk pitcher was made for Ovaltine. In 1983 they made a ship decanter and coffee mug for Old Spice (see Shulton Corporation listing). They were one of three potteries that made bases for oil lamps for Lamplight farms. (See Lamplight Farms listing.) Regal China Company was one of the potteries that made products for Marshall Burns marked "Marcrest." (See Marshall Burns, Hull Pottery, Western Stoneware listings.) In 1985 they are making a line of vases for Soovia Janis. One of the outstanding lines made by Regal China Company was the Van Telligen pieces. The name Van Telligen comes from the designer, Ruth Van Tellingen, who designed the pieces for the Royal China and Novelty Company of Chicago to distribute. In 1947, Royal China and Novelty Company had Regal China Company make the Van Telligen Dutch Boy and Girl, Mary and Lamb, Boy and Dog, Mermaid and Sailor, Peek-A-Boo cookie jar, Love Bugs, pigs, ducks, animals. Sometime in the 1940's, Royal China and Novelty Company purchased Regal China Company. A Mr. Kravitz was president of both companies. The production of the Peek-A-Boo Cookie Jar was less than a thousand. The animal shakers seem to be more easily found. For vases marked, "Regal," see Hull Pottery. (Information: J.S. Greenberg, president of Regal China Company, by letter and telephone; also, Don Brewer, writer for the *Daze* was the first researcher to discover the maker of the Van Tellingen pieces which he released in two articles, "Van Teelingen Uncovered," *Daze*, July 1983, p. 6, and "More On Van Tellingen," *Daze*, August 1983, p. 8. Marks: no. 1, on piece; mark no. 2 from article by Paul Jeromack, "Who Was Van Tellingen?" *Glaze*, June 1983, p. 6. No. 3 on rabbit piece. No. 4 on giant bear cookie jar made for Kraft, Inc. promotion. No. 5 on Jim Beam whiskey bottle.)

VAN TELLINGEN
1.

PEEK-A-BOO
2. Van Tellingen ©

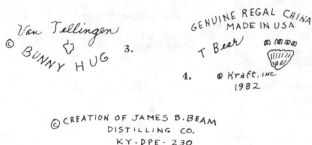

3. © Van Tellingen
© BUNNY HUG

4. GENUINE REGAL CHINA MADE IN USA
T Bear
© Kraft, INC. 1982

5. © CREATION OF JAMES B. BEAM DISTILLING CO.
KY-DPE-230
GENUINE REGAL CHINA 1975
C. MILLER
REGAL CHINA CORPORATION
145
LIQUOR BOTTLE

Regal Ware, Inc. Kewaskum, Wisconsin. Following World War II, in August 1945, J.O. Reigle, a cookware executive from Ohio, was faced with converting the Kewaskum Aluminum Company, from war time to peace time production. The company started making stainless steel sauce pans. Today the company produces dozens of complete lines of cast and drawn aluminum and stainless steel cookware, and a line of polyester-glass microwave accessories. Regal Ware Inc. does not produce any pottery, but they have pottery produced for them which is sold under their trademark. They pack a carafe and mug set made by Kingwood Ceramics, East Palestine, Ohio, with one of Regal Ware's coffee makers. In the marks sent by Franciscan China, formerly Gladding, McBean and Company, was a trademark shown with a notation, "Special dinnerware made for Eternal Stainless Company, late 1962. Distribution in the eastern part of U.S." In a letter from Regal Ware Inc. November 16, 1981, was this line, "The china carrying the Regal trademark was produced by Franciscan China for Regal Ware many years ago and has since been discontinued."

Regal
FINE CHINA
Made in U.S.A.

MADE IN CALIF. U.S.A.

Regan, Peter. New Berlin, New York. 1978 to present, studio potter making stoneware pottery fired at cone 10, vitreous tableware and other funtional items. Some products had incised P or metal stamped P on small items. He attended MFA Rochester Institute of Technology in 1978.

"P"

Registered California, Inc. Offices in Los Angeles, California. A label saying, "Registered California," was used by a group of leading California manufacturers to identify their products as actually, "Made-in-California," according to an advertisement in the *Crockery and Glass Journal Magazine*, for June 1946, p. 59. They held their first annual meeting in 1946 and named Virgil K. Haldeman as president and chairman of the board.

Reiley, James. Troy and Lansingburgh, New York. This potter was born in 1832. He was listed in the 1850 *Census of Troy, New York*, and at that time he worked with his father, Bernard Reiley, at the Troy Pottery. In 1854 he moved to Lansingburgh, and worked for Pliny Thayer. On May 14, 1855, he purchased the pottery and property of Pliny Thayer (see that listing). The firm became J. Reiley and Company. Bernard Reiley had moved his family to join James in Lansingburgh, in 1854 so he became a part of the firm. In 1856, Thayer assigned the remaining mortgage of $305.50 due to Samuel Brooks, and in 1958, Brooks foreclosed on the mortgage and bought the property at auction for $250. In November 1958 the pottery closed and James moved back to Troy. In the *Troy Directory* for 1861, James was listed as a potter. He lived until sometime after 1871. (Information and marks: Warren F. Broderick, writer and researcher.)

T REILEY & CO.
LANSINGBURGH

J. REILEY
LANSINGBURG

JAMES REILEY
LANSINGBURGH

Reinhardt, Various Potteries. Vale, North Carolina. Ambrose Reinhardt immigrated to the Catawaba Valley from Pennsylvania sometime after 1850. His sons, Jim and Pinkney, were also potters. Pinkney had two sons, Enoch W. (lived 1903-1978), and Harvey F. (lived 1912-1960). Both worked in the pottery with their father and pieces with their marks have been found. Enoch stopped making pottery after 1920 until in the 1930's. Harvey continued to work with his father; later he worked for a potter named Lynn. In the early 1930's, Harvey and Enoch Reinhardt built a pottery building and operated it as the **Reinhardt Brothers Pottery** producing utilitarian and a swirled ware or multicolored clay ware. In 1936 or 1937, Harvey Reinhardt set up a shop of his own, but continued to work with his brother. They made the fire brick for their new kiln. Mark 3 was used by Harvey in his own shop. Mark 2 was used by Enoch around the same time. After 1942, Harvey didn't make anymore pottery. He worked in the shipyards and later as a barber. He died at age 48 in Hollywood, Florida, where he was living at the time. Enoch fired his last kiln in 1946. (Information and mark: Daisy Wade Bridges, *Potters of the Catawba Valley*, Charlotte, North Carolina: Mint Museum, 1980, pp. 33-38.)

Reinhardt Bros.
Vale, N. C.
1.

E. W. REINHARDT
2. POTTERY
VALE, NO. CAR.

3. H. F. REINHARDT
VALE, N. C.

Reitz, Donald L. Studio potter and teacher, Donald Reitz, makes hand thrown salt glazed pieces showing great mastery and technique. He received a B.S. degree and an M.F.A. degree from Alfred University at Alfred, New York, in the late 1950's and early 1960's. Since that time, he has taught at the University of Wisconsin at Madison. He does various workshops. In the article by Jerry L. Caplan, ''Don Reitz: New Directions,'' *Ceramics Monthly*, June 1980, p. 64, is a discussion of a workshop he set up at Chatham College in Pittsburgh. He built seven newly constructed works from clay, glass, steel, rope, plastic, rubber, wood and paper in two days before the workshop opened. An example was ''Hanging Clay,'' featuring suspended clay slabs, which had special treatment, hung with bolts and chains, etc. The mark shown was a painted mark on a soup tureen with ladle of salt glazed stoneware, entered in the 1978 Exhibition at the Everson Museum of Art, entitled, ''A Century of Ceramics in the U.S.'' (Information: *Ceramics Monthly*, as cited; and Garth Clark, *A Century of Ceramics in the U.S.*, p. 321. Mark: Linda Steigleder, from the booklet published by the Everson Museum of Art to accompany the 1978 exhibition, ''A Century of Ceramics in the U.S.'')

Reliable Glassware and Pottery Company. Chicago, Illinois. Importers, listed in various directories through 1950 to present, as selling woodenware, brassware, pottery products. The pieces come new with a sticker as shown, but a black stamped mark, ''Relpo'' is left on many pieces after the sticker is gone. (Marks: nos. 1, 2, shown from directories. No. 3, the stamped mark on a piece.)

 1.   2.   3. **RELPO** c 783

Remmey Family, Various Potters. New York City, Philadelphia and Baltimore. Made stoneware. Decorations were hand painted blue, incised and relief or raised designs with a fine glaze. **John Remmey** came to New York in 1735 from Germany and started making pottery on land just north of the present New York City Hall. In 1762, John Remmey died, leaving the pottery business to his son, **John Remmey, II.** He operated the pottery for about 30 years, dying at age 55 in 1793, leaving the pottery in the hands of **John Remmey, III.** This third Remmey was an accomplished writer, soldier in the War of 1812 and even dabbled in astronomy, but he was a fine potter, too. In 1820, he lost his business because he had signed a note for a friend. John Remmey, II, already mentioned, had another son, Henry, who was also a potter. His only child, a son, was **Henry Harrison Remmey**, born in 1794. This branch of the family left New York and migrated to Philadelphia, where they established a pottery on Marshall Street around 1810. Henry Harrison Remmey died in 1878 and his son, **Richard Clinton Remmey**, succeeded him in Philadelphia. It seems Henry Harrison Remmey had established another son, **Henry Harrison Remmey**, in a branch of the pottery in Baltimore around 1818. In 1828, the Philadelphia Remmey pottery was called **Burnett and Remmey** in an advertisement in *The Philadelphian*, May 23, 1828, according to W. Oakley Raymond's article cited later. Richard Clinton Remmey was talented as well as a good business man, assuming full management in 1859 making chemical ware, bricks, as well as Bristol glazed stoneware.

"R.C.R." was stamped on many pieces of the stoneware. He decorated with a feathery blue design. Between 1865 to 1870 he stopped making stoneware and made only brick and commercial stoneware. Richard Clinton's Remmey's son was Robert Henry Remmey. He worked on his father's pottery. In 1904 following his father's death, **Robert Henry Remmey** took his brother, **John Bolgiano Remmey** into partnership. The Cumberland Street factory burned for the second time in its history. This time it was not rebuilt. Instead the Remmeys relocated close to the Delaware River at Hedley Street and from that time on the products were fire brick, refractories, high temperature cement, etc. for commercial use. (Information: W. Oakley Raymond, "Parts I and II of Remmey Family; American Potters," *The Art of the Potter*, published by *Antiques Monthly*, edited by Diana and J. Garrison Stradling, pp. 114-117. Marks: no. 1, no author, *Regional Aspects of American Folk Pottery*, published by Historical Society of York County, York, Pennsylvania, p. 48; no. 2. Guilland, p. 114; nos. 3-4, Stradling, pp. 116, 117. Nos. 5, 6, Thorn, p. 144.)

1. R.C.R. PHILA.

2. J. REMMEY. MANHATTAN-WELLS. NEW YORK

3. R Made by Henry Remmey 1789

4. H. REMMEY BALTIMORE

5. R & Remmey 1872

6. R C R

T.F. Reppert Pottery. Greensboro, Pennsylvania. In 1880, Reppert purchased the James Hamilton Pottery. In 1886, Reppert became partners with W.T. Williams. (They were out of business by 1897 because when the Hamilton and Jones Pottery burned, Hamilton and Jones moved into the vacant Reppert and Williams Pottery.) Made stoneware crocks, jugs, etc. marked and decorated in blue stenciled and freehand. (Information: Gordon C. Baker, "Pottery of Greensboro and New Geneva, Pennsylvania," *Spinning Wheel*, November 1973, p. 15. Marks: Guappone, p. 28, 30, 31; Schaltenbrand, p. 16; Smith, p. 11.)

T F REPPERT SUCCESSOR JAMES HAMILTON & CO. GREENSBORO. PA.

T.F. REPPERT SUCCESSOR TO AND COMPANY JAS HAMILTON GREENSBORO, PA.

T.F. REPPERT SUCCESSOR TO MR. HAMILTON & CO. GREENSBORO, P.A.

T.F. REPPERT GREENSBORO PA.

T.F. REPPERT GREENSBORO PA.

WILLIAMS & REPPERT GREENSBORO, PA.

T.F. Reppert and W.T. Williams. See T.F. Reppert.

Revelation Pottery. See Pewabic Pottery.

Revere, Paul, Pottery/Saturday Evening Girls. Boston and Brighton, Massachusetts. 1906 until 1940's. The Paul Revere Pottery was an outgrowth of the Saturday Evening Girls, a group of immigrant ladies who met on Saturday evening to do craft projects. Around 1906 they included ceramics in their crafts, bought a kiln, and hired a potter to teach glazes and firing. The project grew until in 1908 a regular production was begun, and the business was located in the basement and rear half of the first floor of the Library Club House, near Old North Church in Boston, made famous by Paul Revere, hense the name for the pottery. The pottery was known as the **Bowl Shop**, and paper labels have been found showing that name. In 1915, the pottery was moved again to a new building in Brighton, Massachusetts, which operated into the 1940's.

Despite the fact that the pottery seemed to grow and by 1915 employed around 13 workers, it always needed subsidizing from people such as Edith Brown and others. Products were plain and decorated vases, electric lamps, dinner service, paperweights, ink wells, bookends, tiles, teasets and children's breakfast sets. An exhibit of the pottery was shown at the University of Massachusetts Bicentennial Exhibition in Boston, and for the first time a group of the beautiful pottery was assembled. The pieces were usually surface painted in mineral colors against a light background. About one-fourth of the pieces had incised designs as well. Glazes were semi or high gloss with only an occasional matte glaze used.

Shapes and colors were vast and varied. A covered marmalade jar, attributed to the Saturday Evening Girls, with violet honeybees against a blue, green and cream background, dated Janury 11, 1911, decorated by S. Gainer, was pictured in *American Clay Exchange* under "Arts and Crafts Auction," May 15, 1986, p. 4. There is a little disagreement about what to call the closing date because some people seemed to have worked there individually for a time after the pottery closed as a business. But the pottery faded away by the end of the 1940's. (Information: Paul Evans, *Art Pottery in the U.S.*, pp. 213-216; also Dave Rago, "American Art Pottery," *Antique Trader Weekly*, February 6, 1980, p. 67; and Arthur Guagliumi, "The Saturday Evening Girls: Opening a Door to America," *Pottery Collectors Newsletter*, October, November 1975, pp. 149, 151, 152. Marks: nos. 1, 2, Evans, as cited, p. 216; nos. 3, 4, Guagliumi, as cited, p. 149; no. 5, paper label shown by Ralph and Terry Kovel in *The Kovel's Collectors Guide to American Art Pottery*, p. 189. The identifying marks of this pottery are varied: incised impression of Paul Revere on horse; or initialed "P.R.P.," in dark letters; or "S.E.G." with a date, initial or pottery; or any of the above combinations.)

P.R.P.   **S.E.G.**

Reynolds, J. Proctorville, Ohio. Not a potter. Reynolds was still listed as having a general store in 1922 in Proctorville which had a population of 629. Mark on a 19th century gray stoneware jug with cobalt blue decorations.

J. REYNOLDS
DEALER IN GENERAL
MERCHANDISE

PROCTORVILLE, OHIO

W. Reynolds. Poughkeepsie, New York. 1824-1837. Reynolds acquired the Nichols Pottery after 1824 and held it until 1837. He may not have been active all of this time. Made stoneware. (Information: John P. Remensnyder, "The Potters of Poughkeepsie," Stradling book, p. 123.)

PO'KE' PSIE
W. REYNOLDS

Rhead, Frederick Hurten/Rhead Pottery. The Rhead Pottery was organized by Frederick Hurten Rhead in Santa Barbara, California, and operated from 1913 to 1917. The impressed marks and labels shown were marks for that pottery where Rhead made art pottery pieces. Some showed an Oriental influence, with oxblood black and crackle glazes. He used a technique for decorating which was an inlaid process explained by Evans, p. 236. Rhead was a really great artist and deeply involved in ceramics in several of the potteries.

A brief history of Rhead from staff written, "Frederick Hurten Rhead," *Bulletin of American Ceramic Society*, December 15, 1942, p. 306, is as follows. Frederick Hurten Rhead was born in Hanley, Stafforshire, England, in 1880, the son of Frederick Alfred Rhead. His ancestors had been artists and potters for many generations. He attended Wedgwood Institute in Burslem and the Stoke-on-Trent Government Art School. For three years he was instructor in design in the Government Art School at Longton. No degrees are given in English art schools, but he received diplomas in design, modeling, geometry, perspective and painting. For five years Frederick was apprenticed at Brownfields, Burslem, Staffordshire, and for three years he was art director of the Wardle Pottery, Hanley, Staffordshire. He aided his father in building and organizing the art pottery for Wileman and Company, Longton. Rhead came to the United States in 1902 and became associated with W.P. Jervis at Vance/Avon Faience Company for a while, around 1902 and also served as art director at the Roseville Pottery, Zanesville, Ohio, for four to six years around 1904. For three years he was associated with Taxile Doat as instructor in pottery at Peoples University, University City, St. Louis, Missouri, in 1909. From 1911 to 1913 he joined the Arequipa Pottery.

During the period 1913-1917 he operated a studio pottery in Santa Barbara, California, and for ten years he served as director of the Research Department of the American Encaustic Tiling Company, Zanesville, Ohio. In 1927 he was engaged as art director of the Homer Laughlin China Company, Newell, West Virginia, in which position he continued for 15 years. He died in 1942. Rhead organized the art division of The American Ceramic Society and served as chairman for five years (1920-1925). He also was chairman of the

White Wares Division (1926); vice-president of The Society (1926); and trustee (1926-1027). He was a charter member of the Fellows of The American Ceramic Society. Fred was a member of the Architectural League of New York, the United States Potters Association (chairman, Art and Design Committee), the Masonic Lodge, the East Liverpool Country Club, and the Chemists' Club (London). While in Santa Barbara, Fred edited and published three issues of *the Potter*, a magazine for ceramists. This was under his own sponsorship and was financed entirely by him. For many years, he published weekly in the East Liverpool *Potters Herald*, a series of historical articles on ceramics. At the San Diego Exposition in 1915, Frederick was awarded a gold medal for an exhibit of artware. In 1934, he received from the New York State College of Ceramics the Charles Fergus Binns Medal for his many unselfish activities in the interest of ceramic art. He was chairman of the art and design committee of the U.S. Potters Association. The Evening Pottery School of Newell, under the financial sponsorship of the West Virginia University Extension Department, was one of the enterprises to which he devoted many hours each week, all in the interest of the men and women employees of the potteries in the East Liverpool district." (Marks 1-5: Paul Evans, *Art Pottery of the U.S.*, p. 238.

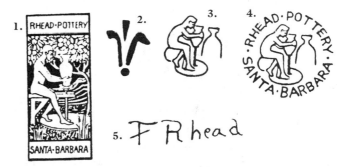

5. F Rhead

RHEAD
6. **SANTA BARBARA**

Rhead, Harry. Zanesville, Ohio. Harry was the art director at the Roseville Pottery from around 1902 to 1908. He was a brother to Frederich H. Rhead. They both came from England. He developed several of the pottery's outstanding lines, including Mostique, Carnelian, Donatello and others. In the article by Norris Schneider, "Roseville Pottery," *Zanesville Times Signal*, March 29, 1959, (no page no.) he said, "Harry Rhead originated Pauleo. He measured Chinese vases in New York museums and copied them for the new Roseville line which was red and brown lustre ware made first in plain blends with dark top and reddish bottom. Later Rhead changed the decoration to different colors at top and bottom with a breaker between. An artistic four-page pamphlet entitled "Pauleo Pottery" was signed by Harry W. Rhead in 1916. He said that the line was started two and one-half years earlier. (Information: Schneider, as cited. Mark: Ralph and Terry Kovel, *The Kovel's Collectors Guide to American Art Pottery Artists, Potters and Designers and Their Marks*, p. 14.)

H Rhead

Rhodes, Collin. Edgefield District, South Carolina. From April 1840 to the fall of 1840, Collin Rhodes was a partner in the establishment of the **Phoenix Factory**. R.W. Mathis, Amos Landrum, T.M. Chandler and others were involved. Collin sold his interest to his brother in 1840. The factory seems to have been shortlived, lasting only until around 1842. Both iron and kaolin slips were used to decorate at this factory and pieces were sometimes stamped "Phoenix Factory, ED., S.C." The next information on this man was that Collin Rhodes sold his Piney Woods Plantation of 2,700 acres in 1853 on which he had a sawmill, a gristmill, and a pottery which all used slave labor from before 1850 to 1853. The pottery was decorated with kaolin slip with folk subjects, such as flowers, birds, snakes, etc., into pitchers, bowls, jugs, storage jars, etc. (Information: *Early Decorated Stoneware of Edgefield District, South Carolina*, published by Greenville County Museum of Art: Greenville, South Carolina, 1976, pp. 13, 14. Slip trailed mark: same source, p.4.)

Rice, Prosper. Putnam, Ohio. About 1827 to 1850. Made stoneware, brownware, Rockingham. (Information: Ramsay, p. 228. Mark: Thorn, p. 144.)

P. RICE

Rice, Tim. Clarksville, Tennessee. 1978 to present (1985). Tim Rice, a studio potter, makes stoneware and porcelain into anagama-mostly sculptured birds. He has won Merit awards in 1979, 1983 and 1984 at the Tennessee Crafts Fair. He signs pieces with his name and the year.

Tom Rice 84

TRice

Ridge Pottery. Franklin, Tennessee. 1970 to present (1985). Charles Akin, studio potter, makes functional pieces, such as lamps, dinnerware, flower containers, etc., of white stoneware and some miniature pieces. He does about 12 craft fairs and shows a year in Gatlinburg, Cincinnati, Nashville, etc. He uses a plaster stamp with his name at present. Before 1980, he signed pieces with his name.

Akin   Akn

Ridgewood China Company/Ridgewood Industries, Inc. Southampton, Pennsylvania, and Burbank, California. Ridgewood China Company started in the late 1940's or early 1950's in Southampton, Pennsylvania, and in 1971 they became Ridgewood Industries, Inc. with plants in Southamp-

ton and Burbank, California. In the 1977 *California Manufacturers Register* the starting date was given as 1952, but it has been suggested by another source that the date could have been in the late 1940's. Seventy-six people were employed in the California plant in 1977. Prior to 1977 they manufactured just one line of translucent fine china with exclusive shapes and hand-decorating. They made a complete dinnerware set with a hard glaze and durable pattern which was sold through franchised dealers. After 1977, Ridgewood discontinued the manufacturing of all fine china and became exclusively a decorating facility. In 1978, they were decorating commemorative pieces only, such as the "Game Bird" series which includes "Ring-necked Pheasant," "Bobwhite," "Woodchuck," etc. Sets of Ridgewood China have now entered the realm of collectors' items. Ridgewood Industries went out of business in 1978, according to a former employee.

Riegger, Harold. Harold Riegger was born in 1913 and in 1938 he received his B.S. degree at Alfred University, and in 1940 he got an M.A. degree from Ohio State University in Columbus, Ohio. After graduating, he moved to Mill Valley in San Francisco, and set up a studio. He made Raku and was interest in primative firing techniques, according to Garth Clark. He wrote several manuals on how to make pottery. He taught at Haystack Mountain School of Crafts in Liberty, Maine; California College of Arts and Crafts, Oakland; California School of Fine Arts, San Francisco; University of Oregon, Eugene; Museum of Industrial Art, Philadelphia; Ohio State University, Columbus. (Information: Garth Clark, *A Century of Ceramics in the U.S.*, p. 322. Incised marks: Linda Steigleder, from the booklet published by the Everson Museum of Art to accompany the 1978 exhibition, "A Century of Ceramics in the U.S.")

Hal 1948   *Riegger '44*

Rio Hondo Potteries. El Monte, California. Before 1945 until before 1955. The first directory listing I had for this pottery was 1945 with Gerald H. McFarlin as general manager making art pottery. This McFarlin became the partner in the Freeman-McFarlin Potteries in 1951. By 1951, P.L., H.N., and B.L. Waters with D.H. Hiffner were the owners making artware and figurines. The company was listed in this manner through 1952. My next listing was 1955, and they were not listed. (Information: *Crockery and Glass Journal Directories*, as cited. Mark: silver paper label sent by Jenny Derwich. In 1946 Rio Hondo Potteries was listed under tradenames as using "California Ceramics" for art pottery. I was not able to make a connection to the pottery named California Ceramics. See that listing.)

MADE IN
CALIFORNIA
RIO HONDO POTTERIES
EL MONTE, CALIF

Ripley, Illinois, Various Potteries. Between 1836 and 1913, Ripley was an important jugtown with many potters making utilitarian type pieces of stoneware. John Ramsay, *American Potters and Pottery*, p. 229, said there were 12 potteries in Ripley in 1880 making brownware and stoneware. He lists only John N. Stout around 1866 to 1880 making brownware. Marjorie Taylor, "Stoneware of Ripley, Illinois," in *The Art of the Potter*, edited by Dianna and J. Garrison Stradling, pp. 143 to 145, lists several: L.D. Stofer around 1847, Adam Stofer and William Shields around 1891, W.H. Hardin in 1836, F.M. Stout and Son around 1878, Charles W. Keith approximately 1849 to 1869, Adam E. Martin around 1852. In 1882, F.M. Stout employed 20 potters, Harvey Irwin employed seven, Stofer and Leach had seven, W.A. Canada employed six, and Crawford and Sons hired three. Jugs, mugs, snuff jars, fruit jars, decorated cookie jars, salt jars, etc. were made in these potteries. Although the potteries were still very active in 1891, they were almost all gone by 1913. In addition to the potters named by Taylor, as cited, Betty Madden, *Art, Crafts, and Architecture of Early Illinois*, pp. 189-194, names John Neff Ebey, around 1836 to 1843, Walter Croxton around 1850, Augustus Pierce around 1850, W.W. Hubbs around 1850, Adam E. Martin from 1852 to 1864, William Glenn and W.W. Haukins after 1860 sometime (no date given). (Marks: The two marks are shown on crocks pictured in the Madden book cited, p. 187, but no dates were given for these businesses. This is an area that needs a book of researching on the local level from court house records, etc.)

J.T. ROBERTS
RIPLEY, ILL

W.H. CLARK
MANY
RIPLEY, ILL.

Rising Fawn Pottery. Rising Fawn, Georgia. 1959 to present (1986). Charles Counts, studio potter, started making pottery of stoneware, both decorative and functional, in 1959 at Beaver Ridge. Then in 1961 he established the Rising Fawn Pottery on Lookout Mountain, nine miles from the town of Rising Fawn. In 1984 he moved to Atlanta to share a workshop with Craig Smith of Atlanta in an artist's building named Tula just completed in Atlanta. He felt the need for a change from the rural scene and a year around market. The Tula building contains 25 or more workshops, studios and galleries for painters, weavers, sculptors, potters, architects, etc. Counts has made pots and clay sculptures and found time to teach over 500 potters in the more than 26 years he has worked in pottery. Counts received a M.A. degree in fine arts at Southern Illinois University. He then interned at Pond Farm Pottery in Guerneville, California, under Wildenhain. This was where Counts learned the Bauhaus concept that all arts should work together, each stimulating the other. This was the idea behind the Tula building. Counts wrote the book, *Common Clay*, in 1972. He did a study for the Smithsonian Institution called, "Encouraging American Craftsmen," in 1970 and 1972, which helped to form the basis of the federal government's policy toward the awarding of grants. He also wrote a how-to-book called, *Pottery Workshop*. It was published by Macmillan Company and has sold 15,000 copies to date. He was elected by 1,500 Southeastern craftsmen in the American Crafts Council to travel and lecture from 1968 to 1971. Counts said we are living in a time when the fine line between arts and crafts has been erased and American are now educated to search out

the value in a given piece of work. Counts is a potter, artist, teacher, philosopher, author, lecturer and altogether one of the South's best known craftsmen. (Information and inscribed marks: from Counts. Beaver Ridge was used from 1959 to 1961. Charles Count or Rising Fawn was used from 1961 to 1984.)

Charles Counts

RISING FAWN

Beaver Ridge

beaver ridge

beaver ridge

Rising Sun Pottery. Victor, Montana. 1976 to present (1985). Studio potters, Randy McClain and Kerry Loveridge, make stoneware functional pieces such as dinnerware, etc. They also make sculptural and decorative pieces such as vases, etc. and raku, which they sign with their names and or the name of the pottery.

Randy

Kerry

The Rising Sun Pottery

Risley Stoneware Pottery. Norwich, Connecticut. Established 1836 by Sidney Risley. Son of Sidney named George Riley, died in 1881, and the pottery was closed and sold. In 1882, the pottery was reopened by B.C. Chace as the **Norwich Pottery Works**. In 1885-1887, George B. Chamberlain was the owner. The owner from 1888 to 1895 was Otto N. Suderberg, who closed the business permanently in 1895. (Information and mark: Henry R. Armstrong, "The Norwich Pottery Works," *The Art of the Potter*, published by *Antiques Magazine*, edited by Diana and J. Garrison Stradling, pp. 99-101. No. 2, Thorn, p. 144.)

NORWICH POTTERY
NORWICH
CONN.

S. RISLEY
NORWICH

Ritchie, Luther Seth. Blackburn, North Carolina. 1867-1940. Stoneware jug shown with dark brownish green cinder streaked glaze. (Information and mark: Daisy Wade Bridges, *Potters of the Catawba Valley*, Charlotte, North Carolina: Mint Museum, 1980, pp. 58.)

L.S.R.
BLACKBURN
N.C.

Ritchie, Thomas. Lincoln and Catawba Counties, North Carolina. 1825-1909. Stoneware. (Information and mark: Daisy Wade Bridges, *Potters of the Catawba Valley*, Charlotte, North Carolina: Mint Museum, 1980, pp. 15, 57.)

T R 1

TR 2

R and N China Company, Inc. Carrollton, Ohio. Started January 1973 to present. Decorate personalized items such as decorated cups, plates, etc. for weddings, or with old fashioned photos, pictures of homes, buildings, etc., all to customer specifications. They decorate a wide variety of message mugs with birds, owls, dogs, kittens, clowns, etc. and cute sayings such as ''Love Me I'm A Golfer,'' etc. They also have a line of handcrafted, hand painted ironstone miniatures.

R and N China Co.
CARROLLTON, OHIO

1988 Loramer Prod
Another Gray Original
from R & N China Carrollton Ohio

R and N CHINA CO.©
CARROLLTON, OHIO

R and N CHINA CO
CARROLLTON, OHIO

Personalized Collector's Plate
Limited Edition Decorative Use Only
R & N China Co. Carrollton, Ohio
This plate is not for food service. Clean
with a quality liquid or paste polish only.
Do not use abrasives or ammonia cleaners

limited edition
R & N China Co.
Carrollton, Ohio

Roark Pottery. Denton, Texas. Around 1880. Made light salt glazed stoneware. (Information and mark: Sherry B. Humphreys and Johnell L. Schmidt, *Texas Pottery*, Washington, Texas: Star of the Republic Museum, p. 30.)

ROARK

Robbins, Carolyn. Fowler, Illinois. 1979 to present (1985). Working with ceramics is not a full time occupation for Carolyn Robbins, but she has been making Autumn Leaf pattern miniature dishes since 1979 and selling at the APEC Show in Springfield, Illinois, and by other means. She started making the miniature dishes because she wanted a set in Autumn Leaf, and making them herself seemed to be the only way to get them. All pieces are molded pieces, hand painted and signed. They are food safe. Carolyn has shipped some as far as Alaska.

Robbins
1985

HAND PAINTED
by
Robbins
1985
Fowler, Il

Roberts, David. Utica, New York. Established a pottery in 1827. By 1832 the White family pottery was the only one left in Utica, so Roberts was gone. Made utilitarian stoneware. (Information and mark: Barbara Franco, ''Stoneware Made by the White Family in Utica, New York,'' reprinted from *An-* tiques Magazine in *The Art of the Potter*, edited by Diana and J. Garrison Stradling, p. 134.)

D.ROBERTS
UTICA
H.S.

Roberts, William. Binghampton, New York. 1848 to 1888. Operated with various members of the White family who came from Utica, New York. Made stoneware. (Information: Stewart and Consentino, p. 108; Guilland, p. 116. Mark: In Guilland, p. 116, was pictured a gray saltglazed stoneware crock with a bird decoration done in a redish-brown and blue slip.)

W. ROBERTS BINGHAMTON, N.Y.

Robertson, Alexander H./Roblin Art Pottery. San Francisco, California. Before 1898 to 1906. For very early history of Alexander H. Robertson see the Chelsea Keramic Art Works listing. Alexander H. Robertson and Linna Irelan made a couple attempts to establish a small studio type pottery before 1898 and both times abandoned the project. But in 1898 they started and worked steadily for eight years making hand thrown art pottery pieces of red, buff and white clay bodies with underglaze slip painting, carving in the clay, incised designs, etc. Mrs. Irelan did the modeling and Robertson developed beautiful glazes. In 1903, Alexander's son, Fred, joined him. A pottery school was established in connection with the pottery and in 1906 the San Francisco earthquake and fire destroyed the school, the pottery and remaining stock of ware. The Robertsons went to Los Angeles. (See the listing for Fred H. Robertson for more history.) A few pieces of the beautiful pottery are in the Oakland, California, Museum, The Smithsonian Institution and Museum of Fine Arts in Boston. They are marked with an impressed bear or firm name. Sometimes Robertson or Mrs. Irelan's initials or full name may be found. An incised spider and web mark or hallmark may also be found. (Information: Paul Evans, *Art Pottery of the U.S.*, pp. 250 to 254. Marks: Evans, as cited. Also, W.P. Jervis, ''Worlds' Pottery Marks,'' *Pottery, Glass and Brass Salesman*, March 1912, p. 15.)

A R C P   Aw.R   ROBLIN   ROBLIN

Robertson, Alexander W. See the Chelsea Keramic Art Works and Halcyon Art Pottery for his mark. Robertson was a potter at both of these potteries at various times.

Robertson, David T. and Shearer, B. Appomattox, Virginia. In the 1952 and 1954 *Crockery and Glass Journal Directories*, David T. Robertson was listed for photography on chinaware. In 1972-1973 *China, Glass and Tablewares Directories*, the listing was Shearer B. Robertson. (Marks: from 1952 directory as cited.)

Fotoware
TRADE MARK REG   PAT APPL'D FOR
NATIONAL PHOTO SERVICE & SUPPLY CO.
APPOMATTOX VA

Robertson, Fred H./Robertson Pottery. Los Angeles, North Hollywood, California. 1934 to 1950. For the early history of Fred H. Robertson, see the listing for Alexander W. Robertson, Fred's father. In 1906, Fred H. started working at the Los Angeles Pressed Brick Company, and at that time he started making art pottery which he fired in their kilns. The first dated pieces found were 1913. By 1915 he was producing luster and crystalline glazed pieces for which he won awards at the San Diego and San Francisco Expositions. In 1921, Fred went to work as general superintendent at Claycraft Potteries (see the listing for Alexander H. Robertson) until 1934, when George B. and Fred H. Robertson started the Robertson Pottery in Los Angeles and in 1935 to 1940 they were located in North Hollywood. Then from 1940 to 1943 they were back in Los Angeles and from 1943 to 1950 in Hollywood again. At least the pottery showroom stayed in one place in Hollywood across from the Hollywood Bowl. Paul Evans, as cited, didn't say why the men moved their workrooms so often. Most of the pieces were wheel thrown, but some molds were used. It was their glazes that made the Robertsons outstanding potters. Besides the luster and crystalline mentioned, they developed a crackle, and Persian blue, green and chartreuse to oxblood and other colors. For a discussion of these glazes, see Evans, as cited. (Information: Paul Evans, *Art Pottery in the U.S.*, pp. 239 to 242. Marks: Evans, p. 242. Evans said some work had an impressed mark, but most was incised or imprinted as shown.)

F. H. R.
Los Angeles

R
Los Angeles

ROBERTSON
HOLLYWOOD

Robertson
Hollywood

Robertson
Hollywood

Robertson, George B. See Claycraft Potteries and the listing Fred H. Robertson.

Robertson, Hugh C. See listing Chelsea Keramic Art Works.

Robeson Rochester Corporation. Rochester and Perry, New York. M.F. Robeson was a manufacturer of cutlery. He started in Elmira, New York, in 1879, moved to Rochester in 1894, and added a plant in Perry in 1900. In 1922, Robeson Cutlery Company was merged with the Rochester Stamping Works started in 1888. A 1931 staff written article reprinted in the *Glaze* entitled "Robeson Rochester Wares," December 1983, p. 7, tells us this company made metal casserole holders, coffee urns, trays, waffle irons, etc. Fraunfelter China Company is one of the potteries that made inserts for these kitchen pieces of Robeson. The marks shown were on a beautifully decorated bowl with a pearl like finish inside and a purple lustre outside. The piece that had the mark, "Royal Rochester Studios," also had an Ohio Pottery mark which was the predecessor company of Fraunfelter. This was a compote with lid with stenciled decorations. It had a metal holder. No. 1, 2, stamped marks also shown under Fraunfelter China Company listing. No. 3 was filed March 13, 1928 for rights to this mark to be used on teapots, sugar bowls, cream pitchers, pie servers, casseroles, sandwich plates, bonbon dishes, syrup pitchers, tea tiles, baking pudding dishes and coffee cups made of china, claiming use since March 31, 1927.

1. HAND-DECORATED
ROYAL-ROCHESTER
• STUDIOS •
HEAT PROOF CHINA
FOR BAKING

2. FRAUNFELTER CHINA

ROYAL-ROCHESTER
HAND PAINTED

3. "*Royalite*"

Robineau, Adelaide Alsop. As a young woman, Adelaide Alsop was a china painter and watercolor artist. In 1899, she married Samuel E. Robineau, a Frenchman who collected Chinese ceramics. Together they founded *Keramic Studio* (later called *Design*), a magazine for china decorators. She became more and more interested in ceramics and worked several weeks with Charles Binns at Alfred University. Adelaide began to experiment with porcelain and had two pieces exhibited in 1901. She learned to throw pieces on a wheel and influenced by Taxile Doat, a French artist's treatise on ceramics, she developed her own glazes and body.

In 1904, her thrown and carved pieces were exhibited at the St. Louis Exposition. She learned to carve clear through the clay making reticulated and excised decorations. Probably her most famous work, the "Scarab" vase, took 1,000 hours to carve. It was exhibited in 1911 in Turin, Italy, where it won the grand prize in ceramics at the International Exposition. The vase is now part of the collection of the Everson Museum of Syracuse, New York. In 1909, Taxile Doat and the Robineaus joined the staff at the beginning of the University City Pottery (see that listing) for a short time.

A. Robineau won many honors. University of Syracuse gave her an honorary doctorate degree in 1917, and she taught there from 1920 to 1929. As a memorial to Adelaide Robineau the Syracuse Museum of Fine Arts (now the Everson Museum of Art) founded the Ceramic Nationals in 1932. (See the lists of winners in the back of the book.) This is a very sketchy account of such a tremendously famous potter's work. The pieces have to be so scarce, according to Paul Evans, as cited, p. 246. In 25 years only 600 pieces of her work was sold. A great many of these are in museums now, the Detroit Institute of Art, Cranbrook Academy of Art, the Metropolitan Museum of Art and the Everson Museum of Art already mentioned. For a detailed account of her work, see the sources cited. Both explain processes and give much more history. (Information: Paul Evans, *Art Pottery of the U.S.*, pp. 243-248; and Elaine Levin, "Charles Binns and Adelaide Robineau," *Ceramics Monthly*, November 1975, pp. 22-27. Incised marks: Linda Steigleder, from the booklet published by the Everson Museum of Art to accompany the 1978 exhibition, "A Century of Ceramics in the U.S.")

6.

7.

8.

9.

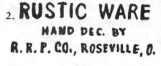

"Old Colony"
HAND DECORATED
R. R. P. CO.
ROSEVILLE O.

1.

2. RUSTIC WARE
HAND DEC. BY
R.R. P. CO., ROSEVILLE, O.

3.

4.

R. R. P. Co.
Roseville, O.
U. S. A.

Robinson Clay Prodcuts Company. Akron, Ohio. See Johnson, Whitemore and Company for history. Early products were stoneware, Rockingham, yellowware, fire brick, paving brick, flue liners and other clay products. This company became a selling agency. After the consolidation with Ransbottom Brothers as discussed in the early history, Robinson-Ransbottom used the facilities of the Robinson Clay Products Company for selling. In the *1951 Crockery and Glass Journal Directory*, Robinson Clay Products Company was listed as wholesalers of dinnerware, pottery, kitchenware and glassware, with outlets in Albany, Syracuse, Rochester, Buffalo, all in New York. Also in East Hartford, Connecticut; Chicago, Illinois, Indianapolis, Indiana; Boston, Massachusetts; Canada and Jamaica. (Marks: Blair, p. 50 and on pieces.)

5.

6. TIONESTA
Art Ware
ROBINSON-RANSBOTTOM POTTERY CO.
ROSEVILLE OHIO

CLAY PRODUCTS
1903 PAPER LABEL

The Robinson Clay Product Co.
Akron, Ohio.

7.

8. Early
STONEWARE
American
ROSEVILLE, OHIO

AKRON SEWER PIPE

THE ROBINSON CLAY PRODUCTS CO.
AKRON OHIO

R.C.P. CO. No.2
AKRON, O

Robinson-Merrill Company. See Johnson, Whitemore and Company for history.

Robinson Ransbottom Pottery Company. Roseville, Ohio. See Johnson, Whitemore & Company for history. (Marks 1 and 2 were used on decorative and functional pieces which were hand decorated under glaze with individual decorations and color combinations. The lines were started in the mid 1930's, and Old Colony was produced until 1940 and Rustic Ware into the 1960's, both under the Crown Pottery brand name. Mark 3 was filed for registration February 17, 1926, for use on pottery, crockery, earthenware and porcelain, claiming use since May 1924. Most of the marks are inscribed on the bottom of the ware. No. 4 and no. 20 are stamped marks, and no. 5 is impressed. Nos. 6-8 are labels sent by the company. A variety of impressed crowns were used such as no. 9, sent by the company, and no. 10 found in Stewart and Consentino's book, p. 56. No. 10, found on an old jug. Nos. 11-19, are inscribed marks found on various pieces. No. 21 was another simple paper label sent by company as such. Nos. 22, 23 were the pictures shown in various directories of the 1950's. No. 12 was a mark on a 1977 piece. An interesting fact about no. 23, Robinson Ransbottom didn't register this mark with the patent office until November 1962 claiming use since June 28, 1921 on stoneware jars. No. 24 was a decorative paper label used in 1986.)

9.

10.

R.R.P. CO
ROSEVILLE, OHIO
308

ROSEVILLE, OHIO
311

11.

RANSBOTTOM
1420
USA
5"
ROSEVILLE, O.

12.

R. R. P. Co.
Roseville OHIO
1500 —
U. S. A.

13.

ROSEVILLE, OHIO
3" 8"

14. U. S. A.
R. R. P. CO.

R. R. P. Co.
ROSEVILLE, OHIO
321 —

15.

R. R. P. CO.
ROSEVILLE, O

16.

17. JPN U.S.A. Roseville, O. R R P Co

18. ROSEVILLE, OHIO 311 8" U.S.A. R. R. P. Co.

19. R.R.P Co. ROSEVILLE, OHIO 312

20. R.R.P. Co. Roseville, O. U.S.A.

21. Our Own FLAME Handcrafted Roseville, Ohio ROBINSON-RANSBOTTOM Exclusive

22. CROWN BRAND

23.

24.

Robinson Studios. Weare, New Hampshire. 1967 to present. Dave and Cathy Robinson and Joanne Watanabe are studio potters making stoneware which is 99% vitreous into functional and artistic pieces. They incise the name Robinson into the bottom of the pieces when they are dried to leather hard consistancy.

Robinson

Rockdale Union Stoneware, Inc. Cambridge, Wisconsin. July 1984 to present. Owner and potter, Peter W. Jackson, started making pots while attending the Philbrook Art Center, Tulsa, Oklahoma, in 1971, when he was in seventh and eighth grades. The following summer he bought a kick wheel kit and built it in his parents basement and started producing. The next summer he bought an electric kiln with his paper route savings and started making pots to sell at local art fairs. The first art fair Peter did was Festival '74 in Tulsa. His father was a fiber artist and opened a small retail store and studio, Cords and Clay, featuring Peter's pottery and his fiber art. Peter received a B.A. in studio art from Knox College in 1980. At present he is engaged in the production of reproductions of 19th century salt-glazed stoneware jugs, crocks, churns, etc. The stoneware is fired to cone 8. He apprenticed with Wayne Branum in Milaca, Minnesota, from 1980 to 1982, firing a two chambered, Japanese style wood-fired kiln. He worked as a production potter for Rowe Pottery Works, Cambridge, Wisconsin, from June 1982 to April 1984. The designs used by Rockdale Union Stoneware are designed by Cynthia Rattmann. On his questionnaire, Peter had this to say about his pottery making. It is included here because it shows one approach to making studio pottery, the artistic versus functional. Also it gives insight into MacKenzie, who seems to talk little about himself.

"I got away from doing "artistic" pieces while pursuing a degree at Knox College, Galesburg, Illinois. I decided that my roots were in the craftsmanship of making functional pieces, and that the validity of such was easier for me to understand. One very special influence on my work was the friendship and guidance of Warren MacKenzie, Stillwater, Minnesota, and the head of the Art Department at the University of Minnesota. I did a workshop with him at Big Creek Pottery, Davenport, California, in August 1979, and he encouraged me not to pursue graduate studies, but to find an apprenticeship, and make pots! He helped set up my apprenticeship with Branum, which we tried to fund through a NEA apprenticeship grant. The grant was not approved, as the program was cut severely by the Reagan Congress. So, I did the apprenticeship with my own money, and tried to support myself by selling the work I produced."

(Marks: nos. 1, 2 are the stamps used on pieces. No. 2 is the current mark. No. 3 shows individual potters' marks with their names. The rest of the very attractive designs shown are decorations on the front of various vessels. *They are not marks* and are not meant to be.)

Decorations by: Cynthia Rattmann

1.

2.

3. Potter's Marks: Peter Jackson

Aaron Netsell

Scott Keith

Cary Hulin

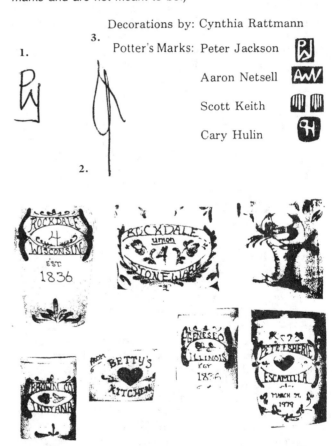

Rockwell Silver Company. Meriden, Connecticut. Filed for rights to this mark on October 11, 1946, for use on china plates and bowls, claiming use since August 10, 1914.

ROCKWELL

Rocky Mountain Pottery. Loveland, Colorado. 1952 to present (1985). In 1953, the pottery was started in Denver, Colorado. Lee Huston was the founder. In 1957, the firm moved to Loveland, Colorado. In 1980, Mr. Huston sold part ownership to the Greens, according to Louise Green, who answered by letters, and then Huston moved to the West Coast. Slip cast ware is made. At one time, presses were used but were unsuccessful, so now and for a long time, hand casting has been used. The pottery made pine scented pottery, bisque fired to white then stained to resemble wood grain and soaked with a pine oil on the bottom to carry the scent. The pieces are heavily glazed on the inside and fired at 1,820 degrees F., to be water tight but the clay had to be soft and porous to absorb the pine oil. The greenware is hand painted in pinecone and wheat patterns. Products are candle holders, mugs, dinnerware, vases, flower holders, etc. Pieces receive a second firing at 1,960 degrees F. with a clear glaze. The finished products are very attractive and durable. The pottery today makes just about the same products as has been made over the years with only a few items discontinued. (Marks: no. 1, is a paper label used now. No. 2 is an older label. No. 3 was filed for registration on February 8, 1960, for use on earthenware articles, namely vases, planters, steins, mugs, wine containers, candy containers, figurines, dinnerware, birdbaths, outdoor urns and outdoor planters, claiming use of mark since November, 1958.)

1.
HANDMADE
BY
**Rocky Mountain
Pottery**
LOVELAND, COLO

2.
THIS IS AN
Original
BY THE
Artists of
**Rocky Mtn.
Pottery Co.**
Estes Park
AND
Loveland,
Colorado

3.

Rogers, John. New York, New York. Around 1859 to 1890. Creator of plaster statuary. In all, he created more than 80 groups which sold more than 100,000 copies, according to Marcia Ray, *Collectible Ceramics*, p. 187. For many years, John Rogers pursued his statue making only as a hobby while he worked as a machinest. As early as 1859 he had a man peddling his ware on the streets in New York. He modeled the statues in clay and then produced them in quantity in plaster. Marcia Ray said Rogers's Groups are always signed. Some of the groups were "Playing Doctor," "Weighing the Baby," "Chickens on the Farm," "The Favored Scholar," etc. On November 14, 1878, John Rogers filed a patent on a "group of statuary," but unfortunately no picture of patent was found. At the time he was in Connecticut. (Mark: Thorn, p. 144.)

**ROGERS
JOHN**

Rogers Jewelers. Columbus, Ohio. 1920 to present (1984). A jewelry store which had their name on dishes sold. (Mark: found on semi-porcelain plate.)

YOURS FROM
ROGERS
Jewelers
:.. a name you can trust in diamonds
COLUMBUS · FOUNDED IN 1920
COLUMBUS · FAMILY · OWNED

Roman Art Company, Inc. St. Louis, Missouri. Around 1907. In the 1949 to 1950 Gift and *Art Buyers Directory*, was an advertisement for "Robia Ware," made by Roman Art Company, Inc. with 42 years of manufacturing experience. Pictured were figurines or statues of religious figures; "Our Lady of Fatima;" "St. Therese;" "Our Mother of Grace;" etc. Also pictured were "Mongolian Man," "Mongolian Woman," a 10" Marquis and a 10" Marchioness. The pictures testify to the fact they were beautiful pieces. The ad said the finishes were superlative. I found them in the directories I had as late as 1965, always listed for figures, figurines and miniatures. (Mark: from 1952 *Crockery and Glass Journal Directory*.)

Roman Ceramics. Mayfield, Kentucky. Before World War II to 1982. About 90 percent of the plant's production in 1979 was figural whiskey bottles with the largest amount sold to Austin-Nichols Distillery of Lawrenceburg (Wild Turkey bottles). Before the 1970's the production was mainly lamp bases. The pottery also has made cookie jars, canister sets, etc. The ware was cast by hand and was hand decorated. Two clay sculptors were responsible for the designs, Shirley Nance and Ronald Hughes. Hughes trained at St. John's University of Minnesota, where he received a B.A. degree. He also studied in Dusseldorf, Germany. Joyce Herdon Roerig, in the article cited, had a W.C. Field's cookie jar in the original box, idenifying the ware as Handcrafted "Cumberland Ware," by the Roman Ceramic Corporation with the "C.W." mark shown. She said they also made a sailor mouse, a monk, Smokey the Bear, all of which were a light tan color. Roman Ceramics also produced Star Wars jars in 1977. (Information: Dona Rains, "Decanter Business Continues to Boom at Roman Ceramics," *Paducah Sun*, Paducah, Kentucky, reprinted in the *Glaze*, November 1981, p. 12; Joyce Herndon Roerig, "Collecting Cookie Jars," *The New Glaze*, January, February, 1985, p. 14. Mark: no. 1, Roerig article.)

U S A

Rookwood Pottery Company. Cincinnati, Ohio, and Starkville, Mississippi. 1880 to 1967. The pottery was started by Maria Longsworth Nichols Storer. The plant was located at 207 Eastern Avenue until 1893. In 1883, she was joined by W.W. Taylor, who became president of the company in 1888. The company first made pitchers, toilet sets, gray stoneware. (Gray stoneware had not been made in Cincinnati before.) The pottery didn't pay its own way for the first nine years of existence, according to Thelma Shull, "Rookwood Pottery," *Hobbies Magazine*, October, 1942, p. 66. In 1884, the development of Tiger Eye or Crystalline glaze was perfected. Around 1904, Vellum, a transparent matte, developed in fire was used first at Rookwood. After 1915, Rookwood developed porcelainized body and added the letter "P," impressed in paste. ("L" was used for standard glaze.) Rookwood became famous for its beautiful art pottery which was the most consistently marked of any pottery, which adds greatly to the charm of collecting Rookwood. In 1941, Rookwood filed bankruptcy and closed in April; a bankrupty sale followed in September. The plant was reopened by a group of new owners in November; Harold and Walter Schott and Lawrence Kyte. In 1942, the pottery was sold again to Sperti, Inc. In 1956, James M. Smith was the owner; in 1959, Herschede Hall Clock Company was owner; and in 1960 the plant was moved to Starkville, Mississippi. In 1967, the controlling interest in Herschede Hall Clock Company was sold and the operation at Rookwood was suspended.

Some pieces were plain but most were incised, or decorated in relief, and cast from a mold in quantity before painting. By being hand decorated, Rookwood was one-of-a-kind merchandise. They made beautiful art vases, garden ware, decorative tile, jugs for packaging toilet water, candlesticks, mugs, ashtrays, book ends, paperweights, chocolate pots, teapots, cigarette and candy boxes, plaques, pitchers, compotes, cups, saucers, clock holders, lamps, dinnerware, statuettes and religious figures using carved, incised and molded techniques. Between 1912 and the late 1930's the Rookwood Pottery made more than 75 different styles and designs of paperweights. For a list of these see Herbert Peck, "Rookwood Pottery Paperweights," *Pottery Collectors' Newsletter*, November 1972, p. 17. In the *Pottery Collectors' Newsletter*, May 1976, p. 43, is a staff written article that tells about "Blue Ship" dinnerware that seems to have been a complete set. Very early in its history, Rookwood Pottery made some dinnerware with commercial transfer printed designs underglaze to try to help meet expenses. The venture was not succesful and the pieces are extremely rare today. If you see a plate with fish, butterflies, birds, frogs, etc. in the old style transfer print, be sure to take a second look; it could be Rookwood Pottery made in early 1880's. In a book this size it is impossible to deal properly with a subject as complex as the Rookwood Pottery. We are very fortunate that so much has been written about the pottery. Each of the artists who worked at the pottery would deserve his or her own listing and discussion if room permitted.

All that can be done here is to give a suggestion of the type of outstanding talented people who made the fabulous Rookwood Pottery pieces. **Louise Abel** worked at the pottery from 1920 to 1932. She decorated and also designed 64 new shapes, including human and animal figures. She had trained with Clement Barnhorn at the Cincinnati Art Academy for five years before 1920. In 1928, she took a leave of absence to go to study in Stuttgart, Germany. Another brilliant young artist was **Grace Young** who studied at the Cincinnati Art Academy and worked at Rookwood Pottery until she got enough money to go to Munich, Germany, in 1891 to study under Frederick Fehr and later Carl Marr. When she ran out of money, she came back to the pottery to work. Even though the pottery was only her stepping stone on her way to becoming a great teacher, the pottery benefitted from her talent in the years she was there. By 1903, she was teaching at the Cincinnati Art Academy. She studied in Paris in 1905 and then returned again to Cincinnati to teach. She left paintings and pottery for us to cherish. **Kataro Shirayamandi** worked at the pottery for 54 years, starting around 1883 or 1884 until he died in 1948. He turned to his native country of Japan just once in 1894, hoping to gain information that would solve some of the early problems Rookwood had with crazing and cracking of the glaze. He was ranked as one of the most outstanding of the Rookwood artists. **Matt A. Daly**, born in 1860, was a pupil of Thomas S. Noble at the Cincin-nati Art School. He studied with Frank Duveneck, a great painter who had studied in Germany and won many honors. Daly's work is represented in the Cincinnati Art Museum and the University of Cincinnati. At Rookwood Pottery he painted a bust length portrait of an Indian warrior, "Weesaw Shoshone," on a vase dated 1899 which was shown in the 1900 Paris Exposition Universelle. This is just a sampling of what Rookwood Pottery so outstanding. (Information: Herbert Peck, *Book of Rookwood Pottery*, and by letter; Edwin J. Kircher, *Rookwood Pottery, An Explanation of its Marks and Symbols*, 19 page booklet, privately printed, 1962; E.A. Barber, *Marks of American Potters*, pp. 118-124; Chester Davis, "The Later Years of Rookwood Pottery, 1920-1967," *Spinning Wheel*, October 1969, pp. 10 to 12; Thelma Shull, as cited; Kenneth R. Trapp, "Rookwood's Printed-Ware," *Spinning Wheel*, January, February 1973, pp. 26-28; Gail Kolakowski, "Louise Abel," *Pottery Collectors' Newsletter*, July 1974, p. 139; Frederick O'Nan, "Grace Young," *American Art Pottery*, April, 1977, p. 1.

Factory Marks

Nos. 1-11 are dates and copies of marks from Barber, *Marks of American Potters*, pp. 119, 120. No. 1, printed underglaze represents pottery kiln and two rooks used from 1880 to 1882; no. 2 was used before 1882; no. 3 is a mark on a trade piece - letters impressed on raised ribbon; no. 4 is a mark adopted as regular trade mark in 1882, according to Barber, but the pottery said 1880 in their copyright registration and the date changed each year - see mark no. 15 when copyright was finally filed on this mark in 1921. No. 5 is stamped mark used around 1883 for a short time; no. 6 was painted or incised before 1882; no. 7 is a stamped mark used around 1883; no. 8, anchor stamped in ware or raised in relief and used before 1883; no. 9, impressed kiln mark used around 1883. No. 10 is the Rookwood monogram mark with backward "R" and a "P" first used in 1886. No. 11 - In 1887 one flame point was added to the monogram (no. 10) and another was added each year until 1900, making the monogram encircled by fourteen flame points. No. 12 is the copy of the mark filed by Rookwood for copyright on May 14, 1921, "for use on pottery ware made from burnt clay, whether glazed or unglazed," claiming use since January 1900. No. 13 filed for registration on May 14, 1921, for use on pottery ware made from burnt clay, whether glaze or unglazed, claiming use since November 1880. In 1901, the same mark had a Roman numeral added below to indicate the year of the new century (no. 13). No. 14 - in 1965 a registration mark, "R" in a circle, was added. No. 15 was a copy of mark as filed for registration on May 14, 1921, for use on "pottery ware made from burnt clay, whether glazed or unglazed," claiming use since November 1880. Nos. 16, 17 were shown in various directories in the 1940's and 1950's. Nos. 18 to 21. In the circle by Herbert Peck, "Commercial Wares of the Rookwood Pottery," *Antique Trader Annual*, no. 10, pp. 158 to 161, is a discussion about the advertising, promotion and premium ware made by Rookwood Pottery for various customers. No. 18 was found on the bottom of an 1883 Commercial Club presentation jug. This was a club with membership in many cities, such as Boston, Chicago, St. Louis, and Cincinnati. No. 19 on a souvenir mug made for the National Drill and Encampment held in May, 1887. The marking was on the bottom of the highly decorated piece. No. 20 was on the bottom of a small plate or ashtray for a souvenir of the Rookwood Pottery. The decoration on the front was a potter at work. No. 21 on a mug made for the Commercial Club's 25th Anniver-

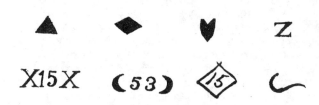

380

sary in 1905. Nos. 22 to 27 are from Edwin J. Kircher, *Rookwood Pottery, An Explanation of Its Marks and Symbols*, a 19 page booklet (no page no.). Kircher said nos. 22 to 24 were used in addition to the regular Rookwood mark after 1920 to help to identify the city with the pottery. Nos. 25 to 27 were used for the various anniversaries at Rookwood Pottery. The 50th year anniversary was in 1930, and the mark used to celebrate it was a kiln with number 50 in it. The 70th year anniversary was in 1950. The work "Rookwood" was sometimes impressed with the kiln mark. In 1962, Rookwood Pottery Company, Starkville, Mississippi, was used to advertise the change of address. In 1965, gold and black paper label containing "R.P." and "Rookwood Pottery." Also, size letters were used from A to F, but Edwin J. Kircher, as cited, p. 7, said that different pattern numbers having the same size number bear no relationship to each other. Size ratio existed only within a given pattern or shape. "A" for one pattern might mean one size and "A" for another pattern would be a different size. The letter "P" was used to designate porcelain, and a letter "L" for standard glaze, according to Kircher, p. 9. Barber, p. 121, shows several process marks such as "X15X" and (53), or ◆15 which would occur on experimental pieces only which seldom left the factory.

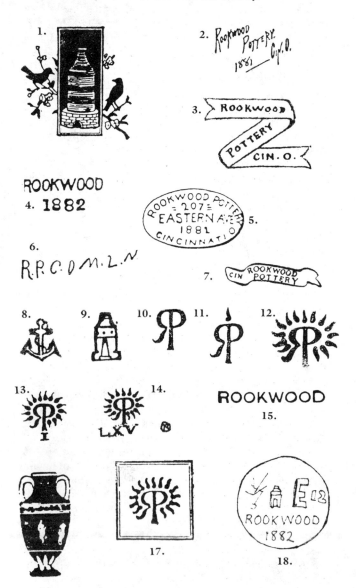

Clay Marks

The clay or body marks consisted of six different letters, G. O. R. S. W. and Y., indicating ginger color, olive, red, sage green, white or yellow, as the case may be:

G   O   R   S   W   Y

Size Marks

The sizes of vases were marked by the letters A to F, inclusive. In connection with these were various numbers, which indicated the shapes and designs. These were entered on the records of the factory.

Process Marks

Esoteric or process marks were occasionally *impressed* on pieces of Rookwood ware, often accompanied by varying record numbers. As these characters only occurred on experimental pieces, they were seldom found on examples which left the factory, and their significance was never divulged. For the benefit of those who may come across such marks, however, they are here shown:

▲   ◆   ♥   Z

X15X   (53)   ◇15   ⌣

Decorator's Marks

It was customary at the Rookwood Pottery for the decorators to incise their initials or monograms on the bottoms of the pieces painted by them. The following is the list compiled by Barber in 1904.

A.R.V.—Albert R. Valentien.
A.H.—Albert Humphreys.
A.B.—Alfred Brennan.
A.M.B.—Miss A.M. Bookprinter (2 marks).
A.M.V.—Mrs. Anna M. Valentien.
A.B.S.—Miss Amelia B. Sprague (4 marks).
A.V.B.—Artus Van Briggle (2 marks).
A.G.—Arthur Goetting.
A.D.S.—Miss Adeliza D. Sehon.
B.—Bruce Horsfall.
C.N.—Miss Clara Chipman Newton (2 marks).
M.M—Miss Marianne Mitchell.
C.S.—Miss Carrie Steinle (3 marks).
C.A.B.—Miss Constance A. Baker.
C.J.D.—Charles John Dibowski.
C.C—Miss Cora Croftop.
C.S.—Charles Schmidt (2 marks).
C.C.L.—Miss Clara C. Lindeman.
D.C.—Daniel Cook.
E.P.C.—Edward P. Cranch (2 marks).
E.D.F.—Miss Emma D. Foertmeyer.
E.A.—Edward Abel.
E.B.I.C.—Miss E. Bertha I. Cranch.
E.D.—E.D. Diers.
E.T.H.—E.T. Hurley.
C.F.B.—Miss Caroline Bonsall.
E.R.F.—Miss Edith R. Felten.
E.W.B.—Miss Elizabeth W. Brain.
E.C.L.—Miss Eliza C. Lawrence.
F.A.—Miss Fannie Auckland.
F.V.—F.W. Vreeland.
H.W.—Miss Harriet Wenderoth.
H.H.—Miss Hattie Horton.
H.E.W.—Miss Harriet E. Willcox.
H.R.S.—Miss Harriet R. Strafer.
H.A.—Howard Altman.
I.B.—Miss Irene Bishop.
J.D.W.—J. Dee Wareham (3 marks).
K.C.M.—Miss Kate Matchette.
k., f.d.k.—Mrs. F.D. Koehler.
G.H.—Miss Grace M. Hall.
K.H.—Miss Katherine Hickman.
L.A.F.—Miss Laura A. Fry (2 marks).
L.N.L.—Miss Lizzie N. Lingenfelter.
L.A.—Miss Leonore Asbury.
L.V.B.—Miss Leona Van Briggle.
L.E.L.—Miss Laura E. Lindeman (2 marks).
M.L.S.—Mrs. Maria Longworth Storer.
M.R.—Martin Rettig.
M.A.D.—Matt A Daly.
M.T., M.A.T.—Miss Mary L. Taylor (2 marks).
M.L.P.—Miss Mary L. Perkins (3 marks).
M.N.—Miss Mary Nourse.
L.E.H.—Miss Lena E. Hanscom.
M.R.—Miss Marie Rauchfuss.
M.F.—Miss Mattie Foglesong.
M.H.S.—Miss Marion H. Smalley.
N.J.H.—N.J. Hirschfeld.
O.G.R.—Miss O. Geneva Reed. (Mrs. Geneva Reed Pinney.
P.P.—Miss Pauline Peters.
F.R.—Fred Rothenbusch.
R.F.—Miss Rose Fechheimer (2 marks).
H.P.S.—Miss H. Pabodie Stuntz.
S.M.—Miss Sadie Markland.
S.E.C.—Miss Sallie Coyne (2 marks).

S.L.—Sturgis Lawrence.
S.S.—Miss Sara Sax (3 marks).
J.S.—Jeannette Swing.
S.T.—Miss Sallie Toohey (3 marks).
T.O.M.—Tom Lunt.
V.B.D.—Miss Virginia B. Demarest (2 marks).
W.H.B.—W.H. Breuer (2 marks).
W.P.McD.—W.P. McDonald (4 marks).
W.K.—William Klemm.
G.Y.—Miss Grace Young.
J.E.Z.—Miss Josephine E. Zettel (2 marks).
Mark of Kataro Shirayamadani, a Japanese artist (see accompanying table).

The decorator's marks as shown by Barber. See previous listing for names.

A.R.V.	Ⓢ	E.R.F.		M.R.	
A.H.	C.F.S.				
A.B.	C.S.	E.C.L		M.H.S	
A.M.B	C.A.B.		L.N.L	N.J.H.	
	C.J.D.	F.V.	L.A.	O.G.R	TOM
a.m.v.		H.W.	I.V.B.		V.B.D—
A.B.S	Ⓢ	H.H	L.E.L.		V.B.D—
	§	H.E.W.	L.E.L	R.F.	WHB
a.s	C.C.L	H.R.S.	M.L.S		
A.B.S	D.C.	I.A.	M.A		W.D
A.V.B	E.P.C	I.B.	M.A.D	S.M.	WPMD
A.M.B.	E.P.C			S.E.C	WPMD
A.G	E.D.F.				WPMD
A.D.S.	E.A	J.D.	M.L.P.	S.L.	W.K.
B—	E.B.I.C.	K.C.M	M.P	5.5.	
C.N		K			
	E.T.H.		m.n.		J.E.
	C.F.B.	G.H.	L.E.H.		

The following decorators are not shown in Barber as cited. They may be found in Edwin J. Kircher, *Rookwood Pottery, An Explanation of its Marks and Symbols* and Herbert Peck, *The Book of Rookwood Pottery*. The last three listed are from Virginia R. Cummins, "Rookwood," *Rookwood Collectors' Newsletter*, June 1976, p. 54.

Abel, Louise Ⓐ

Barrett, Elizabeth 𝓔𝓑

Conant, Arthur P. ⊏C⊐

Conant, Patti M. ⟨PC⟩

Covalenco, Catherine CC

Denzler, Mary Grace

Duell, Cecil A.

Epply, Lorinda

Furukawa, Lois

Harris, Janet

Hentschel, W.E.

Holtkamp, Loretta

Jensen, Jens

Jones, Katherine

King, Flora

Ley, Kay

Lincoln, Elizabeth N.

Lyons, Helen M.

McDermott, Elizabeth F.

McDonald, Margaret Helen

McLaughlin, Charles J.

Menzel, Earl

Noonan, Edith

Pons, Albert F.

Pullman, Wesley

Rehm, Wilhelmine

Sacksteder, Jane

Shirayamadani, Kataro

Stegner, Carolyn

Tischler, Vera

Todd, Charles S.

Van Horne, Katherine

Wildman, Edith L.

Zanetta, Clotilda

Craven, Alice

McDonald, Helen ? **HM** (See Peck list for Herman Moos)

Peachey, Helen W.

The following decorator's marks were sent to this author by letter from Mr. Herbert Peck, author of the *Book of Rookwood Pottery* with the following comment: This lists the artists' marks or monograms collected after the *Book of Rookwood Pottery* was published in 1968. Albert Nunson was never officially a member of the art department; nor was David Seyler; Hicks also signed some pieces with the name Hicks spelled out. Cranch was sometimes stamped into the base with a typestamp. Harriet Wenderoth was also called "Nettie" and some of her early work was signed N.W.

Brennan, Alfred Laurens

Craven, Alice (2nd listing)

Covalenco, Catherine P.

Coyne, Sarah E.

Crabtree, Catherine

Cranch, Edward P.

Epply, Lorinda

Hicks, Orville B.

Klinger, Charles

Moos, Herman

Munson, Albert Cyrus

Pons, Albert F.

Scalf, Virginia

Seyler, David

Wenderoth, Harriet (Nettie)

Willitts, Alice

Rookwood Pottery (No. 2). Cincinnati, Ohio. In late 1982 the Rookwood Pottery building was purchased by Dr. Arthur J. Townley and his three sons from Guy Batchelder and Howard Soltin, who were employees of the Herchede Co. With the purchase, Townley got over 5,000 clay and glaze formulas and more than 1,000 master molds and blocks. The pottery building had been renovated by the Rookwood Realty Co. and converted to an office complex before 1970. He planned a limited production to sell by mail order by advertising in collector's papers and household magazines. Ten percent of the sales were to go to the Cincinnati Art Museum, and the Townley family was never to sell the pottery building again; eventually it was to be given to the Cincinnati Art Museum. One advertisement in the *American Clay Exchange*, October 15, 1986, advertised a limited edition of 500 each of six different miniature paperweights produced by that time.

There were to be 20 in a series with two weights issued each year at $50.00 each. The ad said they were produced from the original Rookwood master molds. The pieces were block ink marked underglaze. Dr. Townley holds the patents on the plain "R.P." mark; the "R.P." and flames mark; and the mark of the single word, "Rookwood." (Information: Duke Coleman, "Rookwood Pottery One More Time Around," *American Art Pottery*, June 1983, p. 3 and Susan Cox, "Rookwood Pottery Back in Production," *American Clay Exchange*, June 1983, p. 4.)

Rosa, Dona. (Indian potter). Oaxaca, Mexico (not New Mexico). Dona Rosa made the now famous black pottery and maintained a small pottery shop in Oaxaca and was still working in 1979 although she was very old at the time. At least one major publication confused this Mexican Indian potter with potters in New Mexico. For more information on this potter see Arthur Guagliumi, "Dona Rosa and the Black Pottery of Oaxaca," *Pottery Collectors' Newsletter*, November, December 1979, pp. 51-53. (Mark: staff written, "Question Box/On Indian Pottery," *Tri State Trader*, November 10, 1979, p. 9.)

DONA ROSA
S B Coyo Tepec
OAX MEX—

Roselane Pottery. Pasadena and Baldwin Park, California. 1938 to 1970's. William Fields and his brother started the pottery in 1938 in Pasadena. Mr. Fields died August 15, 1973, and in November 1973 the pottery was sold to Rod and Audrey Prathos. Sometime later, the state took the property for an expressway, and the pottery was relocated in Baldwin Park. Products were very decorative pieces, many with one color inside and a different color outside. They made animals in solid color, a Chinese Modern line with bowls, vases, ashtrays and candleholders, a "Contemporary" free form line, porcelain bisque birds and animals with jeweled eyes. As many as 5,000 figurines were produced in a day. (Information: Jenny B. Derwich and Dr. Mary Latos, p. 194. Mark 1 on piece sent by Francis Andrews. Mark 2 filed under the name William H. Fields on September 25, 1948, for vases, bowls and trays of pottery, claiming use since July 1, 1946. No. 3 impressed on aqua and black decorative piece with fish design done in slip.

1. *B. Bechtel*
Roselane
PASADENA, CALIF
18-P

2. *Roselane*

3. *Roselane*
PASADENA
CALIF

Rosemary's Ceramics. Mesa, Arizona. 1954. Allen and Rosemary Pringle started the pottery in 1954 making windchimes, vases, mugs, ashtrays, etc. I found listings for them in the *Gift and Tableware Reporter Directory* through 1967. They were not in the other kinds of directories. They used only a paper label-no other mark. (Mark: sent by Francis Andrews.)

MADE IN ARIZONA
by
Rosemary's Ceramics

Rosemeade Pottery. See Wahpeton Pottery Company.

Rosenbloom, Carol. Raleigh, North Carolina. 1971 to present (1983). Studio potter making functional stoneware. She has pieces in the Renwick Gallery and at the Smithsonian Institution. Carol didn't list her shows, etc.

rosenbloom

Rosendahl, Jean. Flag Point. Toms River, New Jersey. Filed for registration of this mark on October 25, 1949, for ceramic corn dish, claiming use since July 19, 1949.

CORN ROLLER

Rosenthal, George. Bronx, New York. Also works in a studio in San Miguel, Mexico. 1953 to present (1983). Makes heavy glazed wheel thrown stoneware into unusual shaped decorative pieces and utilitarian ware.

GEO

Roseville Pottery Company, Inc. Roseville and Zanesville, Ohio. January 4, 1892 to 1954. The pottery was started by George F. Young in the old J.B. Owens plant in Roseville in 1892. Around 1898, the Midland Pottery of Kildow, Williams and McCoy in Roseville, and in 1901 or 1902 a branch of Mosaic Tile Company in Zanesville were purchased. A branch of Roseville Pottery was opened in Putnam. That plant was destroyed in 1917 by fire. After 1917, all Roseville Pottery was made in Zanesville. Roseville Pottery began to operate in Zanesville, as well as Roseville, in 1898 when they purchased the Zanesville branch of Clark Stoneware Company, which had been closed for some time. In 1899, a new three story building was constructed by Roseville Pottery in Zanesville. Roseville made stoneware until around 1900 when they began to make art pottery. In the 1902 *Glass Factory Directory* the Roseville Pottery was listed as operating in Zanesville making dinner sets, jardinieres and novelties. In 1905 and 1906 Roseville Pottery employed 30 to make pottery cookingware in the Roseville plant. But altogether they employed 300 to 350 people in four plants in those years.

A line of "German" cookingware was made in four kilns and operated by 50 workmen, according to Schneider, as cited. They made dinnerware at the start, and again very late in the life of the pottery, a line called "Raymor" was manufactured. The colors included a mixture of earth colors of brown, beige, gray, deep green and medium tan. They are marked "Raymor by Roseville." Also some time between 1912 and 1931, Roseville Pottery made juvenile dinnerware with a plate, a child's bowl (about like an adult soup bowl) and a pitcher, with bands of green and yellow around the shoulder and little chickens at intervals around the plate, which was cream-colored ware. They also made a pitcher with a dog in brown and green colors on cream-colored ware. A rabbit design was used on plates, pitchers, egg cups, etc. All were made for use by children. Roseville Pottery closed on November 1, 1954, and was purchased by the Mosaic Tile Company November 15, 1954. Then on December 12, 1954, the New England Ceramics, Inc. of Torrington, Connecticut, bought the Roseville Pottery with tradename, good will, molds and dies, according to Norris Schneider, "Roseville Pottery," *Zanesville Times Signal*, March 22, 1959 (no page no.). After World War II, imports had reduced sales. In the column by Evan Purviance entitles "American Art Pottery," *Mid-America Reporter*, September 1972, p. 4, is the following list of Roseville Pottery's lines made in Zanesville with approximate dates of the beginning of manufacture and marks where available to the Purviances. From around 1939, on starting with the "Cosmos" line, most pieces were marked "Roseville, U.S.A." in relief.

Roseville (Zanesville) Lines

1930	Sunflower, black sticker
1931	Montacello, black sticker
1931	Windsor
1931	Jonquil, no mark
1931	Blackberry, black sticker
1932	Cherry Blossom
1933	Baneda, black sticker
1933	Falline, black sticker
1933	Ivory, "Roseville, U.S.A." in relief
1933	Tourmaline, gold sticker, Roseville Pottery, "R" with small "v" inside
1933	Wisteria, gold sticker, like on Tourmaline
1934	Artcraft
1934	Laurel, gold sticker, like Tourmaline
1934	Topeo
1934	Luffa
1934	Primrose, "Roseville" impressed
1934	Russco, like Primrose
1935	Pine Cone I, same as Primrose
1935	Velmoss II
1935	Morning Glory, same as Tourmaline
1935	Orian
1936	Clemana, same as Primrose
1936	Moderne, like Primrose
1936	Moss, like Primrose
1937	Thorn Apple, like Primrose
1937	Dawn, "Roseville" impressed
1937	Ixia, "Roseville" impressed
1938	Poppy, "Roseville" impressed
1938	Teasel, "Roseville" impressed
1938	Fuchsia, "Roseville" impressed
1939	Iris, "Roseville" impressed
1939	Crystal Green
1939	Cosmos, "Roseville, U.S.A." in relief - from here on all lines are marked like Cosmos
1940	Bleeding Heart
1940	White Rose
1941	Rozane
1941	Columbine
1941	Bushberry
1942	Peony
1943	Water Lily

1943	Magnolia
1944	Clematis
1945	Freesia
1946	Zephyr Lily
1947	Snowberry
1948	Wincraft
1948	Apple Blossom
1949	Ming Tree
1949	Florane
1949	Mock Orange
1950	Gardenia
1950	Burmese Green
1951	Bittersweet
1951	Artwood
1951	Lotus, marked "Lotus, Roseville U.S.A." in relief
1951	Planters
1952	Silhouette
1953	Pine Cone II, glossy
1953	Raymor dinner ware, marked, "Raymor by Roseville U.S.A." in relief
1954	Gourmet bowls

Roseville Pottery had an impressive list of decorators and designers who worked at the pottery. The very same people had worked at one or more of the other potteries before coming to or after leaving Roseville and are already listed under Weller Pottery, J.B. Owens Pottery, Rookwood Pottery of Cincinnati, and Lonhuda Pottery in Steubenville. E.A. Barber in *Marks of American Potters* was the largest source used by all of the writers in identifying the marks of the various decorators. A few more have been identified over the years and added to the various lists. However, Barber did not list the Roseville decorators because the Roseville Pottery was just becoming a manufacturer of art pottery at the time Barber wrote his book. Many of the decorators who eventually worked at Roseville were identified by Barber under the name of another pottery where they worked before Roseville Pottery. If the decorators were not identified by Barber somewhere, we haven't done too well identifying the Roseville Pottery decorators. There are several marks recorded in various books but the name of the person is marked unknown. Sometimes the name is recorded and the mark is unknown. Chances are, if you find an artist signed piece of Roseville Pottery, you will find the decorator listed under one of the factories previously listed in this discussion. The following decorators, with their marks, are a few not listed under one of the other potteries. I did not include names with unknown marks; or marks where the name was unknown. Schneider listed Hester Pillsbury and Mae and Sarah Timberlake as decorators who worked at Roseville before they came to the Weller plant. See a separate listing for John J. Herold. He worked for Weller a year and another year for Owens and was at the Roseville Pottery as superintendent of the art department from 1900 to 1905 and superintendent of the plant from 1905 to 1908. In 1902, he added the overglaze decorating department. He also devised a copper-red glaze and Herold's ox-blood exhibit won first prize at the St. Louis Exposition in 1904. See the listing Coors Porcelain Company for more on Herold. Christian Nielson, a sculptor, worked at the plant from 1902 to 1906. Harry and Frederick Rhead, two brothers, both designed at Roseville Pottery. Harry worked from around 1902 to 1908, and Fredericka worked from 1908 to 1918. Pieces are found signed by both of these men. See the listings for John J. Herold, designer; Harry Rhead; Frederick Hurten Rhead; Frank Ferrell; and Christian Nielson. (Marks: The patent office registration of the marks prove one thing, there certainly was an overlapping of the use of the various Roseville Pottery marks. The mark used from 1906 to 1910 was just "R.P.CO." In 1912, the rubber-stamped mark was capital "R" and small "v" until after 1931. After 1931, "Roseville U.S.A." was embossed on some pieces and many were marked by a paper label only. About 1904, the mark was changed to include "Rozane Ware," stamped over a rose with a stem. Gold and silver paper labels, oval and triangular in shape marks were used after from 1930. No. 1 was filed October 28, 1904, claiming use since January 1904 for hand decorated underglazed art pottery. No. 2 was filed January 4, 1930, claiming use since December 12, 1921 for use on earthenware, such as vases, pitchers, jugs, jardinieres, pedestals, flower holders, window boxes, cups, saucers, mugs, plates, flower bowls, mixing bowls, hanging baskets, wall pockets, sand jars, umbrella stands, fern dishes, baskets, ice tray. No. 3 was also filed January 4, 1930, claiming use since August 1921 for the same articles. No. 4 was filed March 3, 1930, claiming use since January 2, 1982, for pottery. No. 5 was filed January 19, 1946, claiming use since January 2, 1892 for pottery, namely, jardinieres, jardiniere and pedestal units, cookie jars, baskets, tankards, cornucopias, bowls, pots and saucers, hanging baskets, rose bowls, fruit bowls, urns, tea sets, wall pockets, window boxes, flower holders, vases and bud vases. Nos. 6, 7 were very early marks. No. 8, "Rozane Ware," with various pattern names are pictured in Evans, p. 267, and Kovels, p. 237, including Mongol, Egypto, Mara, Woodland and Royal as shown. No. 9, shown in E.A. Barber, *Marks of American Potters*, was used before 1904. No. 10, Raymor used on dinnereware and some accessory pieces; made in later years before closing. No. 11 was the only mark shown in various directories. No. 12, Lotus, was used around 1951. There was also a block lettered "Lotus," that remains unidentified as to whether it was a Roseville mark. Nos. 13, 14, 15, 16 are from Ralph and Terry Kovel. The Kovel's *Colletors Guide to American Art Pottery*, p. 237. Nos. 13, 14, "Tujiyama," was a black stamped mark used before 1906, according to the Kovels and no. 15 was a red ink stamp used sometime between 1905 and 1939. They said no 16, "Olympic," a black ink stamp was used during the same period. Nos. 17, 18, from Sharon and Bob Huxford, *The Collector's Encyclopedia of Roseville Pottery*, pp. 31, 61. The unusual monogram mark appeared on a piece of decorated artware and was made in very early 1900's.)

6. RVPCO

7. RPCO

8. ROZANE WARE ROYAL

ROSEVILLE 11.

9. ROZANE WARE

10. raymor by Roseville USA OVEN PROOF PAT. PEND.

12. *Lotus*

ROZANE RPC

ROZANE POTTERY

 DONATELLO R.P.C.

raymor modern artware by Roseville USA 416

ROZANE 422

13. *Tujiyama*

14. 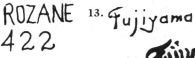 *Tujiyama*

ROSEVILLE POTTERY CO. ZANESVILLE, O.
15.

16. ROZANE "OLYMPIC" POTTERY

THE ROSEVILLE POTTERY Co. — MERCIAN — 545-8
17.

18.

PINE CONE 458 F-5"
19.

20. ROSEVILLE POTTERY R2

ROSEVILLE ROZANE POTTERY 21.

22. R 14S U.S.A.

23. R 14C U.S.A.

24. Roseville U.S.A. 1V2-7

25. Roseville U.S.A. 3-8"

26. 1A Roseville U.S.A. 6LL-0

27. Roseville USA 130-6"

28. Roseville U.S.A. 130-6"

29. Roseville 891-6

Roseville Pottery Decorator Marks
See discussion of other decorator marks in text.

Dutro, E. E O   E D

Duval, Charles C D

Farnsworth, William   F

Gerwick, Gussie	G G G. Gerwick
Hurst, Madge	MH
Martineau, Mignon	A
Miers, W.	W. Miers
Myers, B.	B. MYERS
Myers, H.	H. MYERS
Myers, W.	W. MYERS
Neff, Grace	G N G. NEFF
Shoemaker, R. Lillian	R⌐S
Simpson, Allen	AS
Steinle, Caroline Francis	CFS CS CS

Ross, Laura. Louisville, Kentucky. 1981 to present (1985). Studio potter, Laura Ross, makes stoneware and porcelain which is sawdust fired, producing an unusual beautiful dark color in mottled shades of gray and black. She makes decorative and functional stoneware and porcelain pieces signed with a bronze marker. These pots are fired for 18-24 hours. She adds dyed reeds and caning for handles and various design elements which enhance the coloring and the forms she uses. Laura creates a totally unusual beautiful handmade ware. The round circle shown is a logo not used on pots.

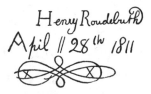

Roudebuth, Henry. Montgomery County, Pennsylvania. Examples of redware, ornamental pie plates, etc. found dated 1811 to 1816. (Information and marks: Barber, *Marks of American Potters*, p. 12.)

ℋ ℛ

Henry Roudebuth
April || 28ᵗʰ 1811

Routson Pottery. Samuel Routson started in Chippewa (near Doylestown), Ohio, in 1841, moved to Wooster in 1856 until 1886. He made brownware, plain and slip decorated stoneware. Other names associated with the pottery were Joseph Routson (mark shown in Thorn, p. 146, is for Joseph Routson, Wooster, Ohio, in a circle) and a Jacob Routson, who had a pottery on Pittsburg Avenue in Wooster, which was said to be the first and only pottery located in Wooster.

A 13″ onion shaped jug impressed, "Rough & Ready/S. Routson/Doylestown, O." was auctioned. (Information: from Mrs. Robert Routson, Wooster. S. Routson mark is on stoneware piece at the Ohio Ceramic Center in Zanesville.)

S ROUTSON
DOYLESTOWN

S ROUTSON

Rowantrees Kiln. Union Street, Blue Hill, Maine. 1934 to 1936. Pottery started by Adelaide Pearson as part of a handicraft program. She was assisted by Laura Paddock. The potters who worked there were village people trained by these two ladies, and they made hand built or wheel thrown tableware and accessories. Glazes were made from manganese available close to the pottery. By 1941, the pottery had become more professional than a handicraft program. The glazes made the pottery outstanding.

Pieces were exhibited many places including New York Society of Ceramic Arts Exhibition, in 1945; the National Exhibition in Washington, in 1941; the Berkshire Museum in Pittsfield, Massachusetts; Museum of Modern Art in New York, etc. Some pieces were marked "R.K., Blue Hill, Maine." Employed eight people in 1974. They were still listed in the telephone directory in 1986. (Information: Marcia Ray, *Collectible Ceramics*, pp. 193, 194; "Rowantrees Pottery Enterprise," *American Ceramic Society Bulletin*, February 15, 1945 (no page no.). Marks shown was sent by Elizabeth Vaughn, Beechwold Antiques.)

Rowantree

Rowe Pottery Works, Inc. Cambridge, Wisconsin. 1973 to present (1985). Jim Rowe has five full potters and four kiln workers on a full time basis who make replicas of salt glazed stoneware used in the 19th century in America. Jim still makes some pots, but mostly manages the business now. The pottery is housed in a 100-year-old blacksmith's shop in Cambridge. Forty designs are made, but each potter makes his own piece from start to finish. The pots are hand decorated or painted with the old fashioned cobalt blue designs of birds, a pig, a cow, hearts, deer, etc. The cobalt is imported from Africa. Each piece is signed by the potter and stamped with the marks shown. The dimensions of each bowl, jar, cup, lamp, etc. must not vary more than half an inch from the original piece used as a model. Each potter turns out at least 100 pieces per day. Each potter is paid on the incentive basis, and they often stay to work after the regular work day. Mark 1 was used from January 1981 to January 1982. Mark 2 was used from January 1982 to present. Individual potters marks are: no. 3, Jim Rowe who started making pottery in 1968. He earned a B.A. degree in ceramics and art history by 1972. In 1972 until 1975, he operated the Rowe Pottery Works. Mark 4 is the mark of Mark Connolly, who started throwing pots in 1977 while earning a degree in history. He came to work for Rowe in 1983. Mark 5 is the mark of Steve Werner, head potter, who went to college in Wisconsin and worked at four different potteries before coming to Rowe Pottery Works in

1981. Mark 6 is that of Ric Lamore who has a degree in art education and taught ceramics in Massachusetts for three years before moving to Wisconsin, where he had his own studio until he came to work for Rowe Pottery Works in 1982. Mark 7 is the mark of Ken Nekola who started making pots in 1974 while in college in Illinois. He came to Rowe Pottery Works in 1980.

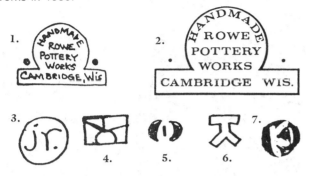

Royal China Company. Sebring, Ohio. 1934 to present (1985). Royal China Company started in the building that was first the Oliver China Company, then the E.H. Sebring Company and in 1934, Royal China Company. The plant was purchased before 1934 but had to be remodeled because it had stood empty for quite some time. In 1964, Royal China Company purchased the capitol stock of the French-Saxon China Company. (See the listing French China Company for previous history.) French-Saxon was operated as a wholly owned subsidiary, and I don't know how long the name French-Saxon was retained or used on ware. After the fire at Royal China in 1970, this building became the nucleus of the operation. On December 31, 1969, the Jeannette Corporation purchased Royal China Company. In the summer of 1969, Jeannette Corp. had also purchased Harker China. Royal China actually was in charge of the operations at Harker Pottery until 1972 when Harker Pottery was closed. (See Harker Pottery listing.) In 1970, Royal China Company suffered a bad fire which destroyed some buildings and all of their records. In 1976 the entire Jeannette Corporation including Royal China Company was purchased by the Coca-Cola Bottling Company of New York. The Jeannette Corporation name continued to be used. In 1981, Royal China Company was sold by the Coca-Cola Company to a group of five private investors called the J. Corporation out of Boston. Then on Dec. 9, 1982, the Jeannette Corporation filed for bankruptcy. In April 1984, Royal China Company underwent another change of ownership when the plant was sold to Nordic Capitol of New York City. The Royal China Company name was retained through all of the changes of ownership and new lines, new products, etc. kept coming from Royal China Company. In August 1986, Royal China Company was no longer producing and only seven employees remained.

Royal China undoubtedly has produced so many different kinds of dinnerware dishes from 1934 until now that the pattern information alone would fill a book. Names for shapes, lines and decorations are sometimes found on the backs of dinnerware. Sometimes it is hard to tell from company to company which one of these is represented by the name found there. Royal China issued what they termed "series." These were composed of the various patterns for a given year. The patterns in a series varied from year to year. The shapes within a series were not identical, so a series could not be considered to be a shape. And the same decoration was sometimes used in two different series, so the whole business gets a little confusing. See *American Kitchen and Dinner Wares*, p. 128, for a long list of series names and the patterns they included. Curt Fahnert, director of dinnerware design development at Royal China until 1986, has been wonderful in helping me to obtain the information on Royal China Company. In a letter in 1981 he stated there were many private stamps made for special customers which would almost be impossible to identify. He also said "no one here knows the old dating code. Records were destroyed in the fire."

In a letter of May 1983, Mr. Fahnert explained to this author how the backstamps made by Kreber Graphics are applied. "They are applied by the same process as the face stamp - direct print. Color is applied automatically to a metal plate and distributed by a roller. The roller then transfers the color to the face of the stamp, and the stamp is placed in position on the ware. This process works at the rate of 20 to 27 pieces per minute. That essentially is the process simplified. The stamps are cut for mounting in the machines. A new stamp is only good for 10,000 pieces maximum."

While Harker China and Royal China Company were both under the ownership of the Jeannette Corporation, work was done under the same management. Just prior to Harker's being closed, they did some work for Royal. Notice the marks with Harker in small print. Kreber made stamps for both companies, and the recent marks could have been for products made at either plant. In December 1982 all backstamps were changed at Royal China to eliminate the Jeannette Corporation name. Royalstone was a trade name used in the 1970's as well as the 1980's. The 1983 lines included some beautiful ceramic lamps called the "New Englander," the "Plymouth Oil Lamp," and "Captain's Oil Lamp," etc. Also that year, other products beside the dinnerware lines were large serving and pasta bowls with quaint Dutch decals, pie bakers with recipes as part of the decoration. These sold so well, the Japanese made them too, and Royal China had to take some legal action against the American distributor. The Japanese pie bakers were unmarked. The old favorite, "Currier and Ives" pattern in all blue design on white background was still continued in 1983 plus many other attractive designs.

Mr. Fahnert said the "Currier and Ives" pattern with a designed border and adapted center by Gordon Parker was started in 1949-1950. The early marks on this ware was date coded. Colonial Homestead was started between 1950 and 1952 and was advertised in Sears all through the 1960's. The Old Curiosity Shop was a pattern of the 1950's also. Both of the latter two were also designed by Gordon Parker. Bluebell was an earlier ware around the 1940's with a blue raised design border and spray of Bluebells in the center. Blue and Pink Willow Ware was started in the 1940's and was advertised as late as 1967. Mr. Curt Fahnert in a letter, February 18, 1983, had this to say about positively identifying the dates the ware was made: "Dating ware can only be done by actual imprinting codes or dates on the stamps. If there are no codes, there would be no way to determine manufacturing dates." Royal Oven Ware was made during the 1940's. (Information: Lehner, *American Kitchen and Dinner Wares*, pp. 127-129 (originally from the company). Marks: from Kreber Graphics, Royal China Company and on dishes. Marks nos. 1-34, are the earlier marks on products started in the 1930's, and 1940's; nos. 35-42 are marks used first in 1950's; nos. 47-50 are marks of the 1960's; nos. 51-52 are on the backs of the 1980's pie bakers, mentioned earlier, reduced in size. No. 12 was filed for registration January 26, 1950 but had been used since July 1, 1934. This shows the form in which this mark was registered for copyright. The other copies are the actual mark. No. 36 "Royal Stetson" had defied explanation even after Mr. Fahnert assured me that Stetson China Company had made some dishes for Royal China Company. Then in the *Crockery and Glass Journal*, March 1944, p. 46 was a news note which told that Stetson China Company of Chicago, Illinois (later in Lincoln, Illinois) had purchased the old French China Company in Sebring. At that time Stetson China Company was a decorating company only. (See Stetson China Company listing.) No. 53 was sent in company material and was probably used in the form of a label. No. 54 was filed for registration November 12, 1965, claiming use just that year for semi-vitreous dinnerware. No. 55 was filed for registration August 1, 1962 claiming use since 1950. So we see the date 1950 in no. 56 was a beginning date, and Colonial Homestead was made for many years. No. 57 was filed December 27, 1968, but had been used since July 1934. No. 58 shows how the registered part of a mark is incorporated in the mark. No. 59 was filed December 23, 1957, claiming use since July, 1957. No. 60 was filed on April 6, 1953 claiming use since January, 1950. No. 61 is the actual copy of the mark. The rest of the marks are later marks of the 1970's and 1980's.)

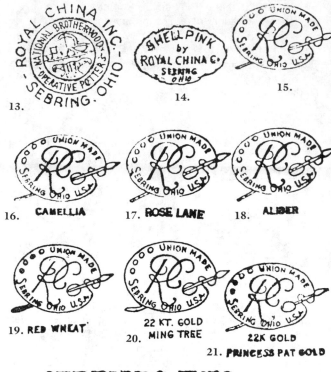

13. 14. 15.

16. CAMELLIA   17. ROSE LANE   18. ALIBER

19. RED WHEAT   20. MING TREE 22 KT. GOLD   22K GOLD

21. PRINCESS PAT GOLD

'CURRIER & IVES
by ROYAL CHINA on
Royal-Ironstone
MADE IN U.S.A.
● DETERGENT·PROOF
● OVEN·PROOF
● DISH WASHER·SAFE
UNDERGLAZE

22.

23. Royal
OVEN WARE
GUARANTEED 100%
OVEN PROOF

24. CURRIER & IVES
"The Old Grist Mill"
UNDERGLAZE PRINT
BY Royal
MADE IN U.S.A.

25. WILLOW WARE BY ROYAL CHINA UNDERGLAZE

26. BLUE WILLOW by Royal SEBRING, OHIO

27. ROYAL CHINA CO SEBRING OHIO ROSE DAWN WARE

ARCADIA 12-36

28.

1. ROYAL BEIGE ROYAL CHINA CO. SEBRING OHIO

2. ROYAL CHINA INC. SEBRING OHIO U S A

3. ROYAL SEBRING CHINA OHIO WARRANTED 22-K GOLD

4. ROYAL CHINA K 55 TWILIGHT UNDERGLAZE

5. ROYAL CHINA A WARRANTED 22-K GOLD DELMAR LACE

6. ROYAL CHINA

7. ROYAL CHINA INC A WARRANTED 22-K-GOLD PRINCESS PAT GOLD

8. ROYAL CHINA

9. TRADEMARK WARRANTED 22-K GOLD GOLD CREST

10. ROYAL CHINA INC DOGWOOD

11. ROYAL CHINA INC B CHIPPENDALE

12. ROYAL CHINA

389

29.

WARRANTED
22-K GOLD
BLUE BELL
C

30.

WHEATLY

31.

SILVER MOON

32.

PLATINUM CREST

33.

SEBRING   OHIO

NOLA

34.

SEBRING OHIO

35.

ROYAL CHINA
INC.
MADE IN U.S.A.
UNDERGLAZE
FALLING LEAVES

36.

ROYAL STETSON
UNDERGLAZE
MADE IN U.S.A.
ROYAL MAYTIME

37.

ROYAL CHINA
INC.
MADE IN U.S.A.
UNDERGLAZE
CAMELOT

38.

ROYAL CHINA
UNDERGLAZE
H   MADE IN U.S.A.   56

39.

ROYAL STETSON
UNDERGLAZE
MADE IN U.S.A.
ROYAL MAYTIME

40.

ROYAL CHINA
INC.
MADE IN U.S.A.
WARRANTED 22 KT.
PLATINUM
EXOTIC

41.

C.O.I. 52
J "Harvest"
UNDERGLAZE PRINT
BY
Royal

42.

BUCKS
COUNTY

UNDERGLAZE
BY ROYAL SEBRING, OHIO
PAT. PEND.

43. ROYAL CHINA

CAVALIER
ironstone

dishwasher safe
ovenproof detergent proof
underglaze decoration

44. ROYAL CHINA
U.S.A.

46.

GOOD
MORNING
BY ROYAL
MADE
IN
USA
SEALED UNDERGLAZE

45.

Memory Lane
ROYAL IRONSTONE
UNDERGLAZE
MADE IN U.S.A.

© 1965   ROYAL CHINA, INC.
SEBRING, OHIO

Royal China
FROLIC

Vendome   47.

ovenproof
dishwasher safe
detergent proof
underglaze decoration

U.S.A.

48.

Royal China Co.
SEBRING OHIO
ROYALSTONE
Naturally

CONVENTIONAL AND
MICROWAVE OVEN APPROVED
DISHWASHER SAFE
USA

49.

ROYAL CHINA
MESA
OMEGASTONE
ovenproof
dishwasher safe
detergent proof
underglaze decoration
U.S.A.

50.

Star Glow
UNDERGLAZE
BY
ROYAL CHINA
SEBRING, O.   MADE IN U.S.A.

51. Country Harvest

FROM ROYAL CHINA CO.

This Royal China ceramic pie baker has been crafted of the highest grade ironstone for durability to give you years of baking pleasure. Made in Sebring, Ohio, the center of the American ceramic industry, its sturdy construction and fluted edging assure perfect, even baking, with that "flavor savor" touch sought by gourmet cooks.
The attractively imprinted recipe is reminiscent of those used by old world master chefs and is one of many equally delicious recipes available in the "Country Harvest" series. Generation-tested, each one has been carefully chosen for its popularity in today's kitchens assuring you of old-fashioned country-style goodness and flavor.
Dishwasher safe, Royal China ceramic bakeware is suitable for a number of entertainment uses and is a colorful, decorative addition to any kitchen decor.
USA

52.

GARDEN CLASSICS

RCGC 8S

GARDEN CLASSICS
This Garden Classic Salad is an American favorite. The recipe has been carefully selected for its taste appeal and kitchen-tested to provide you with a truly fresh, flavor-filled salad. In ancient China and Rome, a salad was any edible herb or plant dressed with salt. Over the years, salads have expanded to include a wide variety of ingredients and dressings. Each recipe in the Garden Classic Series represents the finest of today's gourmet salads.
The ceramic salad bowl is a product of the time-honored American pottery craft centered in Sebring, Ohio. It has been expertly crafted by Royal China for durability and for easy salad mixing. An important feature of the ceramic bowl is its ability to retain cold for a long period of time. Quick chilling of the bowl and salad greens will insure a salad's freshness and flavor throughout any meal.
U.S.A.

53.

ROYAL
STONE
GENUINE STONEWARE
FREEZER-OVEN-SERVE
MADE IN U.S.A.
ROYAL CHINA INC.

54. MEMORY LANE

55. COLONIAL HOMESTEAD

56.

Colonial
Homestead
by
Royal

UNDERGLAZE since 1950
PATENTED
MADE IN U.S.A.

57. ROYAL CHINA

59. FAIR OAKS

58. by ROYAL CHINA on
Royal-Ironstone
MADE IN U.S.A.
● DETERGENT-PROOF
● OVEN-PROOF
● DISH WASHER-SAFE
● UNDERGLAZE

60. The Old Curiosity Shop

61. The Old Curiosity Shop
UNDERGLAZE

Distributed by
Watkins
Winona, MN 55987
Winnipeg, MAN. R3B 001
CONVENTIONAL AND
MICROWAVE OVEN APPROVED
DISHWASHER SAFE
6295 USA 1981

62.

Royal **China** by **Jeannette**
CORPORATION
CONVENTIONAL AND
MICROWAVE OVEN APPROVED
DISHWASHER SAFE
USA

63.

ROYALSTONE
AMERICAN STONEWARE
OVENPROOF DETERGENT PROOF
DISHWASHER PROOF
UNDERGLAZE DECORATION
HARKER
SINCE 1840
SAFARI

64.

ROYALSTONE
AMERICAN STONEWARE
OVENPROOF DETERGENT PROOF
DISHWASHER PROOF
UNDERGLAZE DECORATION
Royal China
TRADE WINDS
U.S.A.

65.

ROYALSTONE
AMERICAN STONEWARE
OVENPROOF DETERGENT PROOF
DISHWASHER PROOF
UNDERGLAZE DECORATION
Royal China
TULIP TIME
U.S.A.

66.

ROYALSTONE
AMERICAN STONEWARE
OVENPROOF DETERGENT PROOF
DISHWASHER PROOF
UNDERGLAZE DECORATION
HARKER
SINCE 1840
MONTEGO

67.

ROYALSTONE
AMERICAN STONEWARE
OVENPROOF DETERGENT PROOF
DISHWASHER PROOF
UNDERGLAZE DECORATION
Royal China
WILLOW BROOK
U.S.A.

68.

Royal **China** by **Jeannette**
CORPORATION
Sunset
CONVENTIONAL AND
MICROWAVE OVEN APPROVED
DISHWASHER SAFE
USA

69.

70. Royal **China** by **Jeannette**
CORPORATION
Frolic
CONVENTIONAL AND
MICROWAVE OVEN APPROVED
DISHWASHER SAFE
USA

71. Royal **China** by **Jeannette**
CORPORATION
Nocturne
CONVENTIONAL AND
MICROWAVE OVEN APPROVED
DISHWASHER SAFE
USA

72. Royal **China** by **Jeannette**
CORPORATION
Windflower
CONVENTIONAL AND
MICROWAVE OVEN APPROVED
DISHWASHER SAFE
USA

73. Royal **China** by **Jeannette**
CORPORATION
Dutch Treat
CONVENTIONAL AND
MICROWAVE OVEN APPROVED
DISHWASHER SAFE
USA

74. Royal **China** by **Jeannette**
CORPORATION
Blue Willow
CONVENTIONAL AND
MICROWAVE OVEN APPROVED
DISHWASHER SAFE
USA

75. Royal **China** by **Jeannette**
CORPORATION
Sussex
CONVENTIONAL AND
MICROWAVE OVEN APPROVED
DISHWASHER SAFE
USA

76. Royal **China** by **Jeannette**
CORPORATION
Stonekraft Java
CONVENTIONAL AND
MICROWAVE OVEN APPROVED
DISHWASHER SAFE
USA

77. Royal **China** by **Jeannette**
CORPORATION
Woodland Magic
CONVENTIONAL AND
MICROWAVE OVEN APPROVED
DISHWASHER SAFE
USA

78. Royal **China** by **Jeannette**
CORPORATION
Vista Java
CONVENTIONAL AND
MICROWAVE OVEN APPROVED
DISHWASHER SAFE
USA

79. Royal **China** by **Jeannette**
CORPORATION
Sweet Morning
CONVENTIONAL AND
MICROWAVE OVEN APPROVED
DISHWASHER SAFE
USA

80. Royal **China** by **Jeannette**
CORPORATION
Sunshine
CONVENTIONAL AND
MICROWAVE OVEN APPROVED
DISHWASHER SAFE
USA

81. Royal **China** by **Jeannette**
CORPORATION
Currier & Ives
CONVENTIONAL AND
MICROWAVE OVEN APPROVED
DISHWASHER SAFE
USA

82. Royal **China** by **Jeannette**
CORPORATION
Fantasy
CONVENTIONAL AND
MICROWAVE OVEN APPROVED
DISHWASHER SAFE
USA

83. Royal **China** by **Jeannette**
CORPORATION
Carousel Java
CONVENTIONAL AND
MICROWAVE OVEN APPROVED
DISHWASHER SAFE
USA

84. Royal **China** by **Jeannette**
CORPORATION
Laurel Valley
CONVENTIONAL AND
MICROWAVE OVEN APPROVED
DISHWASHER SAFE
USA

85. Royal **China** by **Jeannette**
CORPORATION
Sonata
CONVENTIONAL AND
MICROWAVE OVEN APPROVED
DISHWASHER SAFE
USA

86. Royal **China** by **Jeannette**
CORPORATION
Carousel Burnt Orange
CONVENTIONAL AND
MICROWAVE OVEN APPROVED
DISHWASHER SAFE
USA

87. Royal **China** by **Jeannette**
CORPORATION
Santa Fe
CONVENTIONAL AND
MICROWAVE OVEN APPROVED
DISHWASHER SAFE
USA

88. Royal **China** by **Jeannette**
CORPORATION
Prelude
CONVENTIONAL AND
MICROWAVE OVEN APPROVED
DISHWASHER SAFE
USA

89. Royal **China** by **Jeannette**
CORPORATION
Stonekraft Pineapple
CONVENTIONAL AND
MICROWAVE OVEN APPROVED
DISHWASHER SAFE
USA

90. Royal **China** by **Jeannette**
CORPORATION
Vista Pineapple
CONVENTIONAL AND
MICROWAVE OVEN APPROVED
DISHWASHER SAFE
USA

91. Royal **China** by **Jeannette**
CORPORATION
Allegro
CONVENTIONAL AND
MICROWAVE OVEN APPROVED
DISHWASHER SAFE
USA

92. Royal **China** by **Jeannette**
CORPORATION
Countryside
CONVENTIONAL AND
MICROWAVE OVEN APPROVED
DISHWASHER SAFE
USA

93. Royal **China** by **Jeannette**
CORPORATION
Navajo
CONVENTIONAL AND
MICROWAVE OVEN APPROVED
DISHWASHER SAFE
USA

94. Royal **China** by **Jeannette**
CORPORATION
Casablanca
CONVENTIONAL AND
MICROWAVE OVEN APPROVED
DISHWASHER SAFE
USA

95. Royal **China** by **Jeannette**
CORPORATION
Carousel Pineapple
CONVENTIONAL AND
MICROWAVE OVEN APPROVED
DISHWASHER SAFE
USA

96. Royal **China** by **Jeannette**
CORPORATION
Jubilee
CONVENTIONAL AND
MICROWAVE OVEN APPROVED
DISHWASHER SAFE
USA

97. Royal **China** by **Jeannette**
CORPORATION
Nocturne
CONVENTIONAL AND
MICROWAVE OVEN APPROVED
DISHWASHER SAFE
USA

98. Royal **China** by **Jeannette**
CORPORATION
Blue Willow
CONVENTIONAL AND
MICROWAVE OVEN APPROVED
DISHWASHER SAFE
USA

99. Royal **China** by **Jeannette**
CORPORATION
Desert Rose
CONVENTIONAL AND
MICROWAVE OVEN APPROVED
DISHWASHER SAFE
USA

100. Royal China by Jeannette CORPORATION
Hi Spirits
CONVENTIONAL AND MICROWAVE OVEN APPROVED DISHWASHER SAFE
USA

101. Royal China by Jeannette CORPORATION
Queen's Lace
CONVENTIONAL AND MICROWAVE OVEN APPROVED DISHWASHER SAFE
USA

102. Royal China by Jeannette CORPORATION
Nutmeg
CONVENTIONAL AND MICROWAVE OVEN APPROVED DISHWASHER SAFE
USA

103. Royal China by Jeannette CORPORATION
CONVENTIONAL AND MICROWAVE OVEN APPROVED DISHWASHER SAFE
USA

104. Royal China by Jeannette CORPORATION
Margarita
CONVENTIONAL AND MICROWAVE OVEN APPROVED DISHWASHER SAFE
USA

105. Royal China by Jeannette CORPORATION
Intermezzo
CONVENTIONAL AND MICROWAVE OVEN APPROVED DISHWASHER SAFE
USA

106. Royal China by Jeannette CORPORATION
French Garden
CONVENTIONAL AND MICROWAVE OVEN APPROVED DISHWASHER SAFE
USA

107. Royal China by Jeannette CORPORATION
Hampshire
CONVENTIONAL AND MICROWAVE OVEN APPROVED DISHWASHER SAFE
USA

108. Royal China by Jeannette CORPORATION
Dutch Treat
CONVENTIONAL AND MICROWAVE OVEN APPROVED DISHWASHER SAFE
USA

109. Royal China by Jeannette CORPORATION
Blossom Time
CONVENTIONAL AND MICROWAVE OVEN APPROVED DISHWASHER SAFE
USA

110. Royal China by Jeannette CORPORATION
Meadowbrook
CONVENTIONAL AND MICROWAVE OVEN APPROVED DISHWASHER SAFE
USA

111. Royal China by Jeannette CORPORATION
Indian Summer
CONVENTIONAL AND MICROWAVE OVEN APPROVED DISHWASHER SAFE
USA

112. Royal China by Jeannette CORPORATION
Chantilly
CONVENTIONAL AND MICROWAVE OVEN APPROVED DISHWASHER SAFE
USA

113. Royal China by Jeannette CORPORATION
Monterey
CONVENTIONAL AND MICROWAVE OVEN APPROVED DISHWASHER SAFE
USA

114. Royal China by Jeannette CORPORATION
Morning Glory
CONVENTIONAL AND MICROWAVE OVEN APPROVED DISHWASHER SAFE
USA

115. Royal China Co. SEBRING OHIO
AMERICANA
Mount Vernon
CONVENTIONAL AND MICROWAVE OVEN APPROVED DISHWASHER SAFE
USA

116. Royal China Co. SEBRING OHIO
AMERICANA
Sussex
CONVENTIONAL AND MICROWAVE OVEN APPROVED DISHWASHER SAFE
USA
RT-SUS-BS83

117. Royal China Co. SEBRING OHIO
ROYALSTONE
Fashion
CONVENTIONAL AND MICROWAVE OVEN APPROVED DISHWASHER SAFE
USA

118. Royal China Co. SEBRING OHIO
ROYALSTONE
Lancaster
CONVENTIONAL AND MICROWAVE OVEN APPROVED DISHWASHER SAFE
USA

119. Royal China Co. SEBRING OHIO
AMERICANA
Country Charm
CONVENTIONAL AND MICROWAVE OVEN APPROVED DISHWASHER SAFE
USA

120. Royal China Co. SEBRING OHIO
MAJESTIC
Legacy
CONVENTIONAL AND MICROWAVE OVEN APPROVED DISHWASHER SAFE
USA

121. Royal China Co. SEBRING OHIO
MAJESTIC
Woodbury
CONVENTIONAL AND MICROWAVE OVEN APPROVED DISHWASHER SAFE
USA
RT-WOO-BS-83

122. Royal China Co. SEBRING OHIO
ROYALSTONE
Horizon
CONVENTIONAL AND MICROWAVE OVEN APPROVED DISHWASHER SAFE
USA

123. Royal China Co. SEBRING OHIO
AMERICANA
PeachTree
CONVENTIONAL AND MICROWAVE OVEN APPROVED DISHWASHER SAFE
USA

124. Royal China Co. SEBRING OHIO
ROYALSTONE
Rondo J.
CONVENTIONAL AND MICROWAVE OVEN APPROVED DISHWASHER SAFE
USA

125. Royal China Co. SEBRING OHIO
AMERICANA
Autumn Mist
CONVENTIONAL AND MICROWAVE OVEN APPROVED DISHWASHER SAFE
USA

126. Royal China Co. SEBRING OHIO
CONVENTIONAL AND MICROWAVE OVEN APPROVED DISHWASHER SAFE
USA

127. Royal China Co. SEBRING OHIO
MAJESTIC
Newport J.
CONVENTIONAL AND MICROWAVE OVEN APPROVED DISHWASHER SAFE
USA

128. Royal China Co. SEBRING OHIO
MAJESTIC
Newport P.
CONVENTIONAL AND MICROWAVE OVEN APPROVED DISHWASHER SAFE
USA

129. Royal China Co. SEBRING OHIO
MAJESTIC
Keepsake
CONVENTIONAL AND MICROWAVE OVEN APPROVED DISHWASHER SAFE
USA

130. Royal China Co. SEBRING OHIO
AMERICANA
Currier & Ives
CONVENTIONAL AND MICROWAVE OVEN APPROVED DISHWASHER SAFE
USA

131. Royal China Co. SEBRING OHIO
MAJESTIC
Keepsake
CONVENTIONAL AND MICROWAVE OVEN APPROVED DISHWASHER SAFE
USA

132. Royal China Co. SEBRING OHIO
MAJESTIC
Newport S.
CONVENTIONAL AND MICROWAVE OVEN APPROVED DISHWASHER SAFE
USA

133. Royal China
MAJESTIC IRONSTONE
dishwasher safe
ovenproof detergent proof
underglaze decoration
U.S.A.

134. SAXON IRONSTONE
ROYAL CHINA, USA
OVENPROOF UNDERGLAZE DISHWASHERSAFE DETERGENTPROOF

135. ROYAL CHINA CASA DEL SOL
CAVALIER ironstone
ovenproof dishwasher safe detergent proof underglaze decoration
U.S.A.

136. ROYAL CHINA CASABLANCA
CAVALIER ironstone
ovenproof dishwasher safe detergent proof underglaze decoration
U.S.A.

137. ROYAL CHINA JUBILEE
CAVALIER ironstone
ovenproof dishwasher safe detergent proof underglaze decoration
U.S.A.

138. ROYAL CHINA NUTMEG
CAVALIER ironstone
ovenproof dishwasher safe detergent proof underglaze decoration
U.S.A.

139. ROYAL CHINA SANTA FE
CAVALIER ironstone
ovenproof dishwasher safe detergent proof underglaze decoration
U.S.A.

140. ROYAL CHINA CAN CAN
CAVALIER ironstone
ovenproof dishwasher safe detergent proof underglaze decoration
U.S.A.

141. ROYAL CHINA DAMSEL
CAVALIER ironstone
ovenproof dishwasher safe detergent proof underglaze decoration
U.S.A.

142. ROYAL CHINA YUMA
CAVALIER ironstone
ovenproof dishwasher safe detergent proof underglaze decoration
U.S.A.

143. ROYAL CHINA CAROUSEL P
CAVALIER ironstone
ovenproof dishwasher safe detergent proof underglaze decoration
U.S.A.

144. ROYAL CHINA CALYPSO
OMEGASTONE
ovenproof dishwasher safe detergent proof underglaze decoration
U.S.A.

145. ROYAL CHINA CLOVER
OMEGASTONE
ovenproof dishwasher safe detergent proof underglaze decoration
U.S.A.

146. ROYAL CHINA MEXICALI
OMEGASTONE
ovenproof dishwasher safe detergent proof underglaze decoration
U.S.A.

147. ROYAL CHINA AZTEC — OmegaStone — ovenproof, dishwasher safe, detergent proof, underglaze decoration, U.S.A.

148. ROYAL CHINA SNOWFLOWER — OmegaStone — ovenproof, dishwasher safe, detergent proof, underglaze decoration, U.S.A.

149. ROYAL CHINA FINLANDIA — OmegaStone — ovenproof, dishwasher safe, detergent proof, underglaze decoration, U.S.A.

150. Royal China STRAWFLOWER — Vendome — ovenproof, dishwasher safe, detergent proof, underglaze decoration, U.S.A.

151. Royal China SUNWEAVE — Vendome — ovenproof, dishwasher safe, detergent proof, underglaze decoration, U.S.A.

152. Royal China COUNTRYSIDE — Vendome — ovenproof, dishwasher safe, detergent proof, underglaze decoration, U.S.A.

153. Royal China VISTA J — Vendome — ovenproof, dishwasher safe, detergent proof, underglaze decoration, U.S.A.

154. Royal China VISTA P — Vendome — ovenproof, dishwasher safe, detergent proof, underglaze decoration, U.S.A.

155. Royal China SONORA — Vendome — ovenproof, dishwasher safe, detergent proof, underglaze decoration, U.S.A.

156. Royal China ENCHANTED GARDEN — Vendome — ovenproof, dishwasher safe, detergent proof, underglaze decoration, U.S.A.

157. Royal China FANTASY — Vendome — ovenproof, dishwasher safe, detergent proof, underglaze decoration, U.S.A.

158. Royal China NAVAJO — Vendome — ovenproof, dishwasher safe, detergent proof, underglaze decoration, U.S.A.

159. Royal China Regal U.S.A. — underglaze decoration, dishwasher safe, detergent proof, ovenproof

Royal Crown Pottery and Porcelain Company. Merry Oaks, North Carolina. 1939 to 1942. Victor Obler, a Russian immigrant, had a silver business with his brother in New York City. He stocked the contemporary North Carolina pottery in his New York store, the Victor Obler Company. In 1939, he built his own pottery, the Royal Crown Pottery, at Merry Oaks, and employed Jack Kiser as potter. Kiser had worked at A.R. Cole's and J.B. Cole's potteries (see those listings). Charlie Craven started working for Obler in 1940 (see the Craven Family Potteries' listing). In the first year of operation, Obler obtained a profitable contract for supplying florists' ware for the New York Florists' Association. A bright future for the pottery was spoiled by W.W. II. Obler couldn't get materials, such as fuel oil for firing the kilns and ingredients for the glazes, etc. and the pottery was closed in 1942. The original pottery building burned in the middle 1950's, and the ground was later included in a new U.S. Highway 1. The majority of the pieces were not marked. Some were marked with a rubber stamp under lacquer. Some marks were impressed. Charlie Craven made some huge hand thrown vases weighing up to 35 pounds. The pottery also advertised miniatures which may have been made in molds. (Information: Stuart C. Schwartz, "Royal Crown Pottery and Porcelain Company," *Pottery Collectors Newsletter*, February 1974, pp. 57-62. Also, Stuart Schwartz, "Royal Crown Pottery," *American Clay Exchange*, January 1982, pp. 14-16, and Part II, November 1982, pp. 3-5. Marks: no. 1, sent by Stuart Schwartz. The other two marks sent by Edward Blas, pottery collector and researcher. Blas described these marks as ink stamps on clay.)

1. ROYAL CROWN HANDMADE POTTERY
2. ROYAL CROWN HANDMADE POTTERY
3. ROYAL CROWN HAND MADE POTTERY NEW YORK

Roycroft Industries, East Aurora, New York, was founded in 1895 by Elbert Hubbard. The Roycrofters were artists and craftsmen who produced books, furniture and crafts of all sorts. Pottery has been found with various Roycroft marks, but there is some doubt as to who actually made it. The Roycroft Industries was solely owned by Hubbard, directed and managed by him, and his workers were paid wages. This is not to be confused with religious communities such as the Quakers or the Harmony Society, etc. Hubbard wrote and printed over 50 books, which are a bookman's delight for craftsmanship. It is possible since this was strictly a commercial enterprise that the pottery pieces could have been made elsewhere and some decorated and then sold by the Roycrofters. We will never know for sure until the existance of a pottery facility is documented. Hubbard died in 1915 on the Lusitania. (Information and marks: 1, 2, Ann S. Bland, "Roycrofters, Craftsmen of Quality," *Tri State Trader*, December 20, 1975, pp. 1, 13. Marks: 3, 4, Deb and Gini Johnson, *Beginner's Book of American Pottery*, p. 104.)

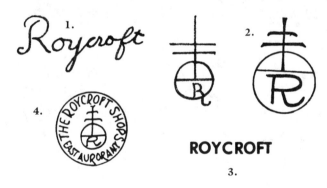

1. Roycroft
2. (Roycroft monogram mark)
3. ROYCROFT
4. THE ROYCROFT SHOPS EAST AURORA N.Y.

Rozart Pottery Studio. Kansas City, Missouri. 1968 to present (1983). Owners George and Rose Rydings became interested in pottery through collecting it. They started to try to make a fine underglaze art work type of ware in a basement studio. They studied endless books and magazines on clay and glaze formulas and pottery making. They kept adding new equipment and improving techniques until they have reached a beautiful product with a clear, creamy soft, semi-matt glaze called "Wax Matt." They paint the decorations in slip glaze directly on the surface of their pieces then glaze them. They produced about 1,000 pieces of scrafitto decorated "Twainware" in 1974 with characters from Mark Twain's novels, then discontinued production. They also made about 100 pieces of slip decorated jasperware pieces. That also was discontinued. In early 1983, George Rydings said by letter they had two lines in production at that time, "Cameoware" and "Rusticware." All else was discontinued. Rose Rydings does most of the painting, but daughters, Susan and Anne help with some decorating. In 1968, 1969 the marks were identified by a rubber stamp; all other marks are incised. The following marks also will be found: 1973-1974, "Twainware" in script (incised); 1973-1977,

"Sylvan" in script (incised); 1975-1980, "Royal" in script (incised, underglaze line); 1980-current mark no. 6 plus "cameo" or "Cameoware" in script; 1981-current mark no. 6 plus "Rustic" or "Rusticware" in script; artists marks are shown under no. 7. (Information and marks: sent by George Rydings.)

1.   2.   3.

4.   5.   6.

7. *Rustic*

8. *Sylvan*

9. *Rusticware*

10. *Cameoware"*

11. *cameo*

12. *Royal*

13. *Twainware*

Artists' Marks

 Rose Rydings

 George Rydings

 Anne Rydings

 Susan Rydings

 Cindy Rydings

Rubel and Company Decorative Accessories, Inc. New York, New York. In business at present (1985). Listed in the 1952 *China, Glass, and Tableware Directory* for art pottery of earthenware and porcelain, figurines, florists ware, salad sets, etc. According to Jenny B. Derwich and Dr. Mary Latos, *A Century of Ceramics in the U.S.*, Tycer Pottery made products for Rubel and Company. The incised mark shown was found on a brown pottery dish, possibly used as a large pottery ashtray, which might have been a Tycer Pottery product. This very large selling agency would have products made in several countries, etc. In the 1945 *Crockery and Glass Journal Directory*, Rubel and Company was listed as representing the following: (several of these companies have industrial listings) Soria and Simon Company; Contintental Art Studios; Blenko Glass Company; Rainbow Art Glass; Glass Display; California Figurine Company; Styson Porcelain; Stafford China; Miracle Patent Lucite Company; Frederick Cooper Studios; Contemporary Arts; Cathay Studios; Marson Ceramics; Carmilroy Novelties; Burchfield Bars; Custom Plastics; Artistic China; Wardle Bars; Barth Art Crystal; Lippe and Company; Glidden Pottery; and Malcolm's. I list all of these to show the complexity of the business. Whenever in one of the books or in this book that a selling agency is mentioned as selling the products of an American Company, it does not mean that was all they sold. And we can't always tell which pieces were made by the American manufacturer if the distributor used his own mark. Nos. 1 and 2, are incised marks found on pieces. Nos. 3, 4, are from directories in the 1960's. No. 5 was filed September 26, 1951, claiming use since March 1950. No. 6 was filed December 28, 1951, claiming use since December 19, 1951. "Trick and Treat" were serving dishes of porcelain and "Laisy Daisy" was used on serving trays of earthenware. This is only a tiny sampling of Rubel marks. See Salem China Company for a Rubel mark.)

Rubel
2009
1.

Rubel
1028
MADE IN USA
2.

RUBEL
...service with a style.
3.

LAIZY DAIZY
4.

RUBEL
5.

Trick 'n Treat 6.

Ruby, Laura. Honolulu, Hawaii. 1973 to present (1982). Studio potter, makes sculptured pieces from all types of clay. She has a B.A. degree from University of Southern California, an M.A. degree from San Francisco State College and M.F.A. degree in art from the Univeristy of Hawaii. She has a sculptured piece installed at the Museums' Association of Hawaii called "Jazzman." She made a large exterior sculpture for the University of Hawaii, Hilo Campus which was commissioned by the Hawaii State Foundation of Culture and Arts. She listed four or five juried exhibitions she has attended every year from 1974 through 1982, along with many invitational exhibitions. She is listed in *Who's Who in American Art*, 15th edition. She also listed several gallery exhibitions.

Ruckel Pottery. See White Hall Pottery Works.

Rudolph, Valentine. Shippensburg, Pennsylvania. Redware potter came from Saxony to the United States and started a pottery employing two men in 1867. The pieces were very plain utilitarian pieces, such as flower pots, mugs, plates, storage jars, cake pans, jugs, some dogs, etc., stamped with "H. Rudolph," or "V. Rudolph." (Information: Jeannette Lasansky, *Redware Pottery, 1780-1904*, pp. 12, 13. Mark: was found on a little redware pot.)

V. RUDOLPH

Rum Rill. Was a sales organization in Little Rock, Arkansas, from 1933 or before to 1942. Ending date furnished by the Little Rock Public Library. From 1933 to 1938 pottery was made for Rum Rill at Red Wing Potteries. From 1938 to 1941, Florence Pottery in Mt. Gilead, Ohio, made some of the Rum Rill pieces. In 1941, Florence Pottery burned. From 1938 until Rum Rill went out of business, the ware was made for the company at Shawnee Pottery in Zanesville, Ohio. Rum Rill owned their own molds and ordered their pieces made to certain specifications. Schwerber and Twiggs did the modeling and made the blocks and casings for the Rum Rill lines. George Rumrill sent representatives to the potteries to make sure the products were what he wanted and various attempts were made until the product suited him. Undoubtedly other potteries will come to light that made products for Rum Rill. A former employee of the pottery gave kitchenware items in the Rum Rill line as mixing bowl sets, cookie jars, salt and pepper sets, coffee pitcher and mugs sets, sugar and creamers, water pitchers, etc. (Information: Lehner, *American Kitchen and Dinner Wares*, p. 129. Marks: no. 1, silver paper label; nos. 2-3, copies as shown in Deb and Gini Johnson, *Beginner's Book of American Pottery*, p. 103. Also see Rum Rill copyrighted marks under Red Wing Pottery listing.)

RUM RILL
MADE IN USA

Rupp Pottery. Harrison, Ohio. Before 1870 until after 1896. Frederick Rupp started this pottery and took his son, William Rupp as a partner. William continued the business of making stoneware and earthenware products after his father's death in 1878. They made flower pots drain pipe, chimney tops, etc. (Information: Lehner, *Ohio Pottery and Glass*, p. 60. "The Question Box," *Tri State Trader*, November 8, 1980, p. 11, staff written. Marks: The marks came from an account ledger book owned and used by Rupp Pottery covering the years 1870 to 1891.)

Rushton Pottery. Henderson, Texas. 1869 to 1900. Joseph Rushton came from Randolph County, Alabama, in 1869 to establish a pottery in Henderson, Texas. The plant closed around 1900 and Rushton died in 1909. The pottery made hand thrown alkaline glazed utilitarian stoneware, crocks, pitchers, etc. The pieces thrown by Joseph Rushton were marked "J.R." Those pieces made by his son-in-law, Jin Haden, were marked "J.H." (Information and impressed mark: L.D. Byrd, *100 Years of Texas Pottery*, p. 114, and by letter.)

J.R.

S

Sabin Industries, Inc. McKeesport, Pennsylvania. 1946 to 1979. In 1946, Sabin Industries, Inc. was founded by Samuel Sabin to decorate china and glass. In 1965 or 1966, Sabin Industries, Inc. was purchased by David T. Chase and Chase Enterprises soon after they purchased Mt. Clemens Pottery. In 1967, this group also purchased McCoy Pottery. By 1974 these three companies were being run as separate companies again with Sabin Industries under the ownership of Mr. David Chase and Sam Sabin. On July 26, 1979, the building of Sabin Industries was burned to the ground, and the operation was moved to Mt. Clemens Pottery in Mt. Clemens, Michigan. See Mt. Clemens Pottery listing for more history. The Sabina Lina of the 1970's, consisted of beautifully decorated ironstone serving pieces which was distributed by Sabin Industries. Sabina II was dinnerware with a lot of stenciled decorations and gold trim. "Microcks" was a heavy ovenware line of all sorts of serving pieces. During the 1950's, Sabin Industries decorated the colonial lady and gentlemen dishes with a great amount of gold trim so widely sought after today. Salem China also made these plates. They are not the Godey Ladies plates, but very similar. One dealer called them the "George and Martha" plates. I doubt the decal ever had a special name. A great many of Sabin's designs were actually stamped on the pieces because we found many of them in the material at the Quality Stamp Company in East Liverpool, Ohio.

Collector Series

made in U S A.

T. Sables & Company. Medford, Masschusetts. 1838-1844. Maker of stoneware. (Information: Lura W. Watkins, "A Check List of New England Stoneware Potters," *Antiques*, 1942, reprinted in Stradling, p. 80. Mark: Stradling, p. 77.)

MEDFORD

Saenger Porcelain/Baker Station Studios. Newark, Delaware. 1974 to present (1984). Peter Saenger, studio potter, is at present making cast table ware in porcelain such as coffee sets, sugars, creamers, etc. in unusual very artistic designs. He has made stoneware tableware, wheel thrown, with a decoration of a mountain, clouds and home. Pieces are marked at present with Saenger inscribed in clay as shown. Peter will be using a stamp in the future that will say Saenger Porcelain.

SAENGER

Safford, Various Potteries. John Safford and John M. Safford. Monmouth, Maine. Around 1824 to 1921. Safford, born 1797, probably trained at the Exeter Pottery of the Dodges'. He moved to Hollis, Maine, and later Bath, Maine, before coming to Monmouth around 1824, where he farmed and also made some pottery. John M. Safford, a cousin of John Safford came to work at the pottery, and by 1830 he had completed an apprenticeship and set up his own pottery. George Llewellyn Safford, a son of John M. became a potter and succeeded his father in his business until 1921. In the 1850 Census, both potteries were still operating, but by 1860 the first John Safford pottery had closed. Both potteries made earthenware and redware with brown or olive green glazed and some impressed designs. Marks impressed. (Information and mark: M. Lelyn Branin, "The Saffords Skilled Earthenware Potters of Monmouth, Maine," *Spinning Wheel*, January, February 1973, p. 14. Marks 2-5, M. Lelyn Branin, *The Early Potters and Potteries of Maine*, p. 222.)

JOHN SAFFORD
MONMOUTH 1.

JOHN SAFFORD
2.

JOHN M SAFFORD
STEW POT NO. 3
3.

JOHN SAFFORD 20
4.

SAFFORD & ALLEN
MONMOUTH ME   5.

Saks and Company. New York, New York. Retail store, filed for registration of this mark on September 26, 1955, for use on china and pottery and vases, claiming use since September 15, 1924.

Saks-Fifth Avenue

Salamander Works. Had factory in Woodbridge, New Jersey, and used the New York City address for selling purposes and possibly an outlet. This was a common practice. Sterling China Company, for example, uses the East Liverpool address of their offices with their factory in Wellsville, Ohio. Woodbridge is not far from New York City. The pottery was established in 1825 and was owned by a William Poillon in 1867. The pottery was incorporated in 1871, and William and his son, Cornelius, continued until a fire destroyed the factory in 1896. Up until the Civil War this pottery had made utilitarian stoneware, flower pots, milk pans, jugs and other household ware. Some of the pieces had relief designs and scroll work. A yellow-gray body was used with a heavy dark brown glaze. Also see the listing Poillon Pottery for later history. (Information: E.A. Barber, *Marks of American Potters*, p. 75-77; and Paul Evans, *Art Pottery of the U.S.*, p. 230. Marks: no. 1, Barber, as cited, p. 76; no. 2, Ramsay, *American Potters and Pottery*, p. 278; no. 3, 4, Thorn, *Handbook of Old Pottery and Porcelain Marks*, p. 146.)

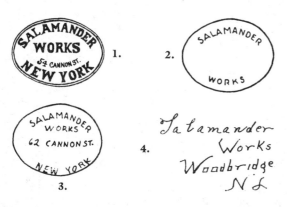

Salem China Company. Salem, Ohio. 1898 to present. The company was founded shortly before 1898 and was in business just long enough to get into financial trouble before August, 1918 when the factory was purchased by F.A. Sebring and Floyd McKee was put in charge. The plant has been operating and prosperous ever since. At first Salem China made just white granite ware. Later fine earthenware and kitchen articles were added. Salem China became an outstanding maker of fine dinnerware, which they stopped manufacturing in 1967. Since 1968, they have been a sales and service organization.

The date code for Salem China Company is as follows: The number signifies the year of manufacture; the letter iden-

tified the decorator. The stars tell the quarter of the year the piece was manufactured, when these are included in the mark. Example: 57*** this signifies that the piece was manufactured in the first quarter of 1957. (3 stars indicates 3 quarters remaining in the year.) 57** indicates it was made in the second quarter of 57; the two stars indicate two remaining quarters. A number with no stars indicates it was made in the last quarter of the year; there are no remaining quarters, thus no stars. Something else that may turn up sometime in the future on a Salem dinner plate would be a broken line cut into the body before glazing (this would be on the back). This was done to identify the year of manufacture; the broken lines were set into the jiggering tool. There is no information at the factory, though, on what marking would signify what year. So much information is lost during the years that might help identify the age of a piece in later years. (Information furnished by Mary Eckstein, long time employee.)

Information: 1-10 may have never been used on dinnerware. They were found in the files at Salem China Company by this author. They were among the papers showing designs by Don or Viktor Schreckengost and were designed by one of them. Several marks are submitted to be used on a new line when it comes out. One is chosen, the rest are not used. Nos. 11, 12 were photos found in the material. They could have been designed for labels etc. Nos. 13 and 15 were on dinner plates in 1981 which were distributed by Salem China.

No. 14 was a Salem China symbol which may not have been used as a mark. No. 16 was the copy patented Dec. 10, 1929 which was supposed to have been in use since 1927. No. 17 was patented Dec. 21, 1929 and was in use since Oct. 1929. The remainder of the marks came from three sources, stamps at the company, on dishes, or from Quality Stamp Company. Nos. 18, 19 were found on the "Victory" shape dinnerware made in the 1940's; 18 from an actual dish and 19 from an ad for "Sun Valley" decorated china in the "Victory" shape. No. 20 is the mark on the Salem China Bicentennial cup that cost $1,500 new, was designed by Don Schreckengost and limited to 750 cups. No. 21 is the type of mark used on "Old Colony Commemorative" plates honoring America's military leaders. Sets of eight included, Generals Marshall, Eisenhower, MacArthur, and Arnold. Admirals King, Nimitz, Leahy and also Pres. Roosevelt. These were made in the 1940's, and the complete set cost only $14.95. That wouldn't buy a single plate of them today. Nos. 25-38 are various distributors marks found on products made by Salem China Company. Remember that Salem China would not be the only manufacturer for these distributors.

Nos. 26, 27 & 37 were on dishes made at Salem China for Sears and Roebuck. Nos. 38-44 may have been decorative stamps used on the top side of dishes. I found them in the Salem China files, but they may or may not have been used as marks on the back of dishes. Nos. 45, 46, were on fine china sold by Salem China Company after 1967. No. 47 was "Ranchstyle" for shape name, made in 1950's. Nos. 48-50 were marks found on beautiful service plates found dated in the 1940's and 1950's. Nos. 52-54 for "Victory" shape name brought out during W.W. II. Nos. 55-57 Quaker china marks were used in a promotion as early as 1952 (letter so dated). Then I found a piece dated as late as 1967 when Salem China quit manufacturing. There were Quaker girl china and specialties used by Clover Farm Stores, Edwards Food Stores, Red and White Stores, Acme Markets, Big Bear Stores Co., Regal Stores, White Villa Grocers Inc., etc. Some of the pattern names sold through this program, which included a china club membership, were Primrose, Rosemont,

Anniversary, Melody Lane, Rosecrest, Zepher, First Lady, Rose Point, Woodhue, Mt. Royal, Seranade, Coin Leaves; this information helps to date the marks seen below for this china. Shape names shown in marks: Tricorne (three sided) in 1930's; Heirloom came after 1963. From a 1958 price sheet, Hostess, Anniversary, Contour, Coronet, Pinehurst, Clover Leaf, Decoration names dated on letters and price sheets: Coronation and Regency (for Sears) in letter 1953. Coronation was a shape, Regency a design or decoration. A great many of the marks shown have the date 1967 below. To my great sorrow a large box of earlier stamps had been thrown away when part of the storage space at Salem China was rented out. There had to be more than 500 marks for Salem China; we have but a few of them.

Nos. 160, 161, were sent by Betty Scott whose family worked at Salem China Company.) No. 162 was the basic mark as it appeared on the patent application filed May 28, 1949, for use on semivitreous china, namely, baby bowls, baby plates, bakers, beer steins, bowls, butter dishes, plates, casseroles, coupes, cups, saucers, coffee pots, teapots, bouillon cups, sugar bowls, cream pitchers, oval dishes, fruit dishes, oatmeal dishes, nappies, sauce boats, salt and pepper shakers, pitchers, chop plates, mugs and service plates, claiming use since 1898 as to "Salem;" since 1934 to "By Salem;" and since April 1944 as shown. No. 163 was verified as a Salem China Company mark by Harrison Keller and he dated the use between 1960 and 1967. No. 161 found on dishes with a picture of an Early American fireside scene with cobalt blue edging around the plate, probably made in the 1930's or before. The "free form" mark was registered for use on dinnerware April 7, 1955 claiming use for one month prior to registration. Mark no. 73 was filed for registration September 8, 1961, claiming use since June 1961 for semivitreous dinnerware. No. 160, Salem Swirl was filed for registration March 6, 1964 claiming use since February. No. 165, Colonial Kitchen, was filed on November 14, 1962. Nos. 164 and 166 for Sturdi-ware a product of the 1960's.)

LADIES NIGHT
ALLIANCE ROTARY CLUB
June 12, 1946

22.

23.

24.

DECORATED
EXPRESSLY FOR
THE C. E. WARD CO.
NEW LONDON, OHIO
ovenproof
67

25.

Jubilee Peach

26.

Whispering Leaves

ovenproof

27.

Marion-Kay
BROWNSTOWN, INDIANA
ovenproof
67

28.

29.

Seneca CHINA
EMPIRE GOLD
23 K.
ovenproof
67

30.

Hostess House, Inc.
Heirloom Platinum
Ovenproof

31.

Distributed By
Whittemore Associates
Boston, Mass.

ovenproof
67

32.

33.

ROYAL
OVINGTON'S
FIFTH AVE.

RUBEL
buffetware

34.

35.

The
Halle Bros.
Co.

Princeton China
Fine dinnerware
known the world over
for quality from our
generation to another.

ovenproof

36.

HARMONY HOUSE
LUCKY CLOVER
by SALEM
MADE IN USA

37.

EDWARD
DON
& COMPANY
ovenproof
67

38.

39.

40.

The
RAIL ROADERS

41.

COFFEE BREAK

42.

43.

HVP
COFFEE BREAK

44.

ENGLISH IRONSTONE
SALEM
ENGLAND
Silver Elegance

45.

INTERNATIONAL
IRONSTONE
Silver Elegance
SALEM 1968
ENGLAND

46.

RANCHSTYLE
by SALEM

47.

Imperial
by Service Plates
SALEM
CHINA CO.
MADE IN USA
23 KARAT GOLD

48.

Imperial
by Service Plates
SALEM
CHINA CO.
MADE IN U.S.A.
23 KARAT GOLD
ovenproof
67

49.

Imperial
by Service Plates
SALEM
CHINA CO.
MADE IN USA
WARRANTED
23 KARAT

50.

SUN VALLEY
by SALEM
CHINA CO.
MADE IN U.S.A.

51.

VICTORY by
SALEM CHINA CO
SALEM OHIO
23 KARAT GOLD
MADE IN U.S.A.

52.

Salem
23 K GOLD
53w

53.

VICTORY
MADE IN U.S.A.

54.

Quaker
Girl

55.

Quaker
Girl
SALEM OHIO
23 KRT GOLD
56U

56.

SALEM
CHINA CO.
SALEM, OHIO
MADE IN U.S.A.

57.

67

58. "Symphony" by SALEM CHINA CO. SALEM, OHIO
MADE IN U.S.A. / 23 KARAT GOLD

59. Sheffield by Salem

60. TRICORNE .By Salem / U.S. PATENT D. 94245

61. TRICORNE by SALEM / PAT. D.94245 MADE IN U.S.A.

62. OVEN PROOF — American Ironstone — MADE IN U.S.A.

63. NEW YORKER by SALEM / MADE USA / WARRANTED 22 CARAT GOLD

64. Salem

65. CENTURY by SALEM / MADE IN U.S.A.

66. CENTURY by SALEM / MADE IN U.S.A. / WARRANTED 22 CARAT GOLD

67. SAPHIRE by SALEM CHINA Co. / MADE IN U.S.A / PLATINUM GOLD

68. Flair by Salem

69. Flair Salem / Peach and Clover / ★★★ 52 X

70. COROT SALEM CHINA COMPANY SALEM

71. VICTORY by SALEM CHINA·CO. SALEM·OHIO

72. NORTH STAR / Salem / ovenproof

73. Salem FLINTSTONE

74. AUTUMN LEAVES / SALEM AMERICAN IRONSTONE / ovenproof ★ 67

75. Salem / AUTUMN LEAVES / © SALEM / ovenproof

76. by SALEM / THE SALEM CHINA CO. SALEM, OHIO

PARSLEY — by SALEM CHINA Co / V / MADE IN U.S.A.

AMERICAN PROVINCIAL — by SALEM / X / MADE IN U.S.A. / ★★ 51

77. STRONG LIKE GIBRALTER / ·STURDI-WARE· / OVEN PROOF / HARMONY HOUSE / Jamaica

78. STRONG LIKE GIBRALTAR / ·STURDI-WARE· / by Salem

79. SALEM AMERICAN IRONSTONE / ·STURDI-WARE· / ovenproof / 67

80. AMERICAN IRONSTONE / Silver Elegance

81. Salem ® / Prints by Pat Prichard / ovenproof / 67

82. GO Salem

83. Flair by Salem

84. PINK BAMBOO / Salem / OVENPROOF / 67

85. Bountiful DINNERWARE / Salem / ovenproof / 67

86. Serenade Dinnerware / SCCo. USA /

87. "christmas eve" / Salem / ORIGINAL BY VIKTOR SCHRECKENGOST / 67

88. SALEM HEIRLOOM

89. FOR 65 years Salem

90. Briar Rose by Salem

91. SALEM HEIRLOOM / WARRANTED 23 KARAT ENCRUSTED GOLD

92. SALEM HEIRLOOM / Made in America

93. LUCERNE CHINA

Made in
America

94.

ANTIQUE
IVORY
FROM
SALEM
PAT. AUG. 9-27

95.

HANDCRAFTED
THE SALEM CHINA CO.
STONEWARE

96.

U. S. PATENT
D. 96722
STREAMLINE
By
SALEM

97.

NORTH STAR
OVENPROOF
★

98.

WOODLAND
DINNERWARE
& CO. USA
★★X54Z

99.

free • form
by
U.S.A.
Patented
ovenproof
hop scotch pink
67

100.

free • form
by
Patented
ovenproof
Southwind
101. 67

free • form
by
USA
Patented
ovenproof
simplicity
67

102.

free • form
by
USA
Patented
ovenproof
Aquaria
67

103.

free • form
by
USA
Patented
ovenproof
hop scotch turquoise
67

104.

free • form
by
USA
Patented
ovenproof
Windblown
67

105.

ovenproof
Heirloom
23 K. GOLD
67

106.

ovenproof
South Seas

107.

ovenproof
Fruitwood
67

108.

ovenproof
Biscayne
67

109.

ovenproof
Burma Lily
67

110.

ovenproof
COMMODORE
23 K. GOLD

111.

112.
ovenproof
Wild Rice

113.
ovenproof
Biscayne
67

ovenproof
Patrician

114.

---

ovenproof
Something Blue
67

115.

ovenproof
April
67

116.

JAMAICA ©
ovenproof
67

117.

OLD SALEM ©

ovenproof
67

118.

MANDARIN
© SALEM
ovenproof
67

119.

ovenproof
Heirloom

120.

CEYLON
by
SALEM
CHINA CO.
MADE IN U.S.A.

121.

NASSAU ©

ovenproof
67

122.

ROYAL WINDSOR ©

ovenproof

123.

CARROUSEL ©

U.S.A.
Pat. Pend.
ovenproof
67

124.

WEATHERVANE ©

ovenproof
67

125.

COTILLION ©
ovenproof
67

126.

CARNIVAL ©

ovenproof
67

127.

ovenproof
Etude
23 K. GOLD
67

128.

MAPLE LEAF ©
ovenproof
67

129.

ovenproof
COIN-FLORA

130.

DAYBREAK
© SALEM
ovenproof
131. 67

MAPLE LEAF ©
ovenproof
132. 67

Ruby Rose ©
ovenproof
67

133.

SIMPLICITY ©
ovenproof
134. 67

ovenproof
Primrose
67

135.

PROVINCIAL ©
Salem
ovenproof
136.

COCK O' THE WALK ©
Salem
ovenproof
67
137.

JAMAICA ©
Salem
ovenproof
67
138.

OLD SALEM ©
Salem
ovenproof
67
139.

TROPICANA ROSE ©
Salem
ovenproof
67
140.

FRUITWOOD ©
Salem
ovenproof
141.

SIMPLICITY ©
Salem
ovenproof
67
142.

Concord ©
Salem
ovenproof
67
143.

Salem
ovenproof
Gold F & V
23 KRT GOLD
67
144.

Salem
ovenproof
Melody Lane
145.

Salem
ovenproof
23 K. GOLD
67
146.

Salem
Aristocrat
23 K. GOLD
52 Z
147.

Salem
ovenproof
Riviera
67
148.

Salem
ovenproof
67
149.

Salem
ovenproof
Castlewood
67
150.

Salem
ovenproof
Whimsey
67
151.

Salem
MANDARIN
ovenproof
67
152.

Salem
ovenproof
Teaberry
67
153.

Salem
ovenproof
Zephyr
PLATINUM
67
154.

Anniversary
Salem
ovenproof
155.

SANDRA
by
SALEM
CHINA CO
W
MADE IN U. S. A.
156.

SHEFFIELD
by
SALEM
V
MADE IN U. S. A.
157.

ROYAL WINDSOR ©
Salem
ovenproof
64
158.

INDIAN TREE
by
SALEM
X
MADE IN U. S. A.
159.

WITH BONE CHINA GLAZE
Salem Swirl
USA
160.

Early American
by SALEM
161.

by
SALEM
162.

Royal Joci
HAND DECORATED
WITH 23 K GOLD
OVENPROOF
67
163.

STURDI-WARE
164.

COLONIAL KITCHEN
165.

STRONG LIKE GIBRALTAR
· STURDI — WARE ·
by Salem
166.

Salt and Mear. East Liverpool, Ohio. 1842 to around 1850. In 1842, James Salt; Joseph Ogden; John Hancock; and Frederick Mear leased the old Mansion House property and started manufacturing pottery. This plant was later managed by Croxall and Cartwright. At the museum in East Liverpool is a piece with the words shown on the side in a large shield as a decoration rather than a mark. (Information: M.K. Zimmerman, "The Pottery Industry of East Liverpool, Ohio," *Crockery and Glass Journal*, December 18, 1924, p. 118.)

SALT & MEAR
EAST
LIVERPOOL
OHIO

Salt O' Thee Earth Pottery. Guernsey (near Cambridge), Ohio. 1975 to present (1985). Jack and Heather Beauchamp are studio potters, making beautiful and functional salt glazed gray stoneware with blue painted decorations. Some pieces are similar to old style ware, pitchers, jugs, etc., all fully marked for identification. The marks shown are "Jax" and the year for Jack. The Salt O Thee Earth Pottery mark is impressed.

Jax 74   Jax 83   Jax 82

Heather + year

SALT O THEE EARTH POTTERY
GUERNSEY, OHIO

Salt of the Earth Pottery. Holyoke, Massachusetts. 1975 to present. Kathy Goos is a studio potter making functional stoneware. Before 1978 she used the interesting mark "Sister Mud" which was the mark of a collective studio which she shared with Kathy Kolman, a potter, who is in Oakland, California, in 1982. From 1978 on the mark has been K. Goos.

Sister Mud   *k. goos*

Salveson-Gerbasi Pottery. Findlay, Ohio. Late 1970's to present (1986). Raye Salveson an Sharon Gerbasi, studio potters, make wheel thrown functional stoneware at present. They attended North Dakota State University in Fargo, North Carolina, and Findlay College in Findlay, Ohio. They listed more than 20 juried shows in which they participated between 1977 and 1984. They also were in group or two person exhibits at the Columbus Cultural Art Center, Ohio Designer Craftsmen Gallery, Ohio State Fair Exhibition, the Appalchian at Bethesda, Maryland, and many more. They won Best of Show at the Lakewood Arts Festival, Lakewood, Ohio, Best of Show at Cain Park, Best of Show at Crosby Gardens and several others. They had a special commission to make dishes for Senator and Mrs. John Glenn. They belong to Ohio Designer Craftsmen and the Craftsmen's Guild of Ann Arbor, and other organizations. Pieces are inscribed as shown.

Salveson

Gerbasi

San Carlos Pottery. San Carlos, California. Around 1948. I have tried every means to find out who Uncle Will was! But at least he gave us a place and approximate date so that he could be included here. There were no directory listings for this pottery. (Marks: staff written, "Super Sleuths," *American Clay Exchange*, May 1983, p. 10. The mark was found on a slip cast vase with a fine glossy gray glaze. The Uncle Will mark was on the front in blue, so this was a dedication piece of some sort.)

SAN-CARLOS-POTTERY
201
CALIFORNIA

UNCLE WILL
CO-FOUNDER OF THE
SAN CARLOS POTTERY
DEC. 3, 1948

Sanders, Herbert Harvey. San Jose, California. Dr. Sanders was born in New Waterford, Ohio, and spent his youth in the area. He worked to pay his way through Ohio State University between 1928 and 1932 when he graduated with a B.S. degree in industrial arts education. He became graduate assistant to William E. Warner, head of the industrial arts department. Sanders was at Ohio State University during the first year that a department which featured ceramics as an art was established. He became a graduate assistant to Arthur E. Baggs until 1937. (See the listings for: O.S.U., Arthur Baggs, Edgar Littlefield and Paul Bogotay.) In 1933, Sanders received an M.A. degree in industrial arts with an area of specialization in ceramic arts. While at O.S.U., Sanders was greatly impressed by a display of the work of Adelaide Robineau (see that listing). He read a treatise by French ceramist, Taxile Doat and started trying to make crystalline glazes. Andrew Pereny (see that listing) and Sanders worked on glaze materials together in 1932. They were making frit, a combination of glaze materials which melted together allow chemical reactions to take place. There is no doubt that working with all the now famous men listed here was a great influence on Sanders as he was on them. From around 1933 to 1938, Sanders taught in high schools in Groveport and Norwood, Ohio, where he established ceramic departments.

From 1934 to 1938 he spent his summers at Ohio State University working on his doctorate degree which he did not receive until 1951. In 1938, he went to teach at San Jose University in California and was made an associate professor in 1943. After fighting for rooms and equipment, etc. he managed to establish a ceramic art department at San Jose University where he taught until 1974. For two years, from 1946 to 1948, he taught and then was director at the School for American Craftsmen in Alfred, New York. He returned to San Jose in 1948. In the 1940's he had many one-man shows and won numerous awards. He became a full professor in 1952 and began writing a series of 29 articles on "Pottery Form and Decoration" for *Ceramic Age*. He wrote *The Sunset Ceramics Book* and *The Practical Pottery Book*.

He conducted workshops on crystalline glazes and other ceramic subjects to the American Ceramic Society, and several other groups. In 1957 he taught a summer session at the University of Hawaii, and in 1958-59 he studied in Japan on a Fulbright Research Scholarship. The result of over 100 interviews with Japanese potters was that Sanders wrote the book, *The World of Japanese Ceramics: Historical and Modern Techniques*, published in 1967. He was made a fellow of the American Ceramic Society in 1966. In the 1960's and 1970's, Sanders worked almost exclusively with porcelain, hand thrown on a wheel, and by this time his crystalline glazes were to perfection, and his shapes were smooth classical forms. He also sculptured animals. Major one-man shows included: the San Jose Art Museum in 1976; the Rochester Art Center in Rochester, Minnesota, in 1977; the Contemporary Artisans Gallery, San Francisco in 1980. His work may be seen at the Oakland Art Museum, National Gallery of Art, Smithsonian Insitution, the San Diego Art Museum, etc. (Information: For a fine long detailed account of Sander's life and work see the following; Tran Turner, "Herbert H. Sanders - Innovator in California Ceramics," *American Clay Exchange*, in four installments, February 15, 1985, pp. 8, 9; February 28, 1985, pp. 8, 9; March 30, 1985, pp. 8, 9; and April 15, 1985, pp. 5-7. Incised marks: nos. 1-3, Tran Turner, as cited. No. 4, Linda Steigleder, from the booklet published by the Everson Museum of Art to accompany the 1978 exhibition, "A Century of Ceramics in the U.S." Turner dated mark 1 as 1930's and 1940's. No. 2 in 1950's and no. 3 as a later mark - early 1950's to early 1970's.)

H. SANDERS
1953

1.   2.

Sanders 3.   4.

Sanders, John. Connecticut. Around 1817. This mark found in Thorn, p. 146, with no definite place. This potter was not in Watkins or any other standard reference.

JOHN SANDERS

Sanders Manufacturing Company. Nashville, Tennessee. Company started in 1918 by three brothers named Sanders. Some time in the 1950's they discontinued decorating plates with various forms of advertising and special orders. Stamped marks taken from plates are shown. Limoges China Company, Canonsburg Pottery, and others furnished blanks for Sanders. The company was still listed as decorators in the 1952 and 1954 *Crockery and Glass Journal Directory*.

 4

Sandstone Creations. Tempe, Arizona. Sandstone Creations makes slip caste and ram pressed ceramic bisque or porcelain pieces, all of which are hand painted. The company started making porcelain bells and chimes around 1975. Since then, tiles, cruits, decorated functional bowls, etc. have been added to their line. The hand painted pictures on the bells, etc. are fabulous, birds, butterflies, horse heads, flowers, little animals, owls, dogs, racoon, etc. In the 1983 brochure, their Designer series has 73 designs available as windbells or wind chimes approximately five inches high. (Mark: is a gold paper label.)

CREATIONS
TEMPE ARIZONA
85282

Sandwich Kiln. Center Sandwich, New Hampshire. 1971 to present. Derek and Linda Marshall, studio potters, make high-fired stoneware, utilitarian pottery for table use, also lamp bases for Norman Perry Company, High Point, North Carolina, which are distributed internationally. They do not use signatures or date the pieces but do have a logo, a leaping fish hallmark located near the foot of each piece. Their list of invitational shows is extensive! Derek, was former vice president for the League of New Hampshire Craftsmen and was their representative at the White House Exhibit in 1977 and the 1977 World Craft Conference in Oaxtepec, Mexico. He has guest lecturer at San Diego State University in 1979 and was a special consultant to National Endowment for the Arts, and this is only a few of his honors. Linda is a member of American Crafts Council, League of New Hampshire Craftsmen, Artists Equity, and New Hampshire Potters' Guild for which she has served as vice president.

Sanford, Peter Peregrine. Barbadoes Neck (now Hackensack), New Jersey. Around 1970's. Moved to White Plains, New York. Made stoneware. (Marks: Thorn, p. 146.)

P.P. SANDFORD
BARBADOESNECK   P.P. SANDFORD

San Gabriel Ceramic Works. Wichita, Kansas. George H. Garcia filed in the name of the pottery on September 6, 1977, for registration of the mark shown for use on ceramic pottery and sculpture, claiming use of mark since June 1976.

San Jose Potteries. San Antonio, Texas. Pottery was listed in the 1945 *Crockery and Glass Journal Directory* for Pan American dinnerware, art pottery, and decorative accessories. James M.A. Cassel was the owner. The company was operated by Michaelian and Kohlberg, Inc. of New York, New York, of which James M.A. Cassel was the manager. This was the only listing in any of the directories that I could find. Pottery must have been shortlived. (Marks: no. 1 shown found on a clown cookie jar; no. 2, was a paper label on a decorative piece; no. 3, "Pottery Puzzlers," *American Clay Exchange*, November 1983, p. 3.)

PAN AMERICAN
ART   1.

SAN JOSE POTTERIES
SAN ANTONIO, TEXAS

2.

SAN JOSE POTTERIES

3.

Santa Anita Pottery. Los Angeles, California. Began around 1939 (Cunningham, *American Dinnerware*, p. 37) to around 1957. Santa Anita Pottery was in business at 3025 Fletcher Drive in Los Angeles, California, in 1948, and by 1951 they were at 3117 San Fernando Road in Los Angeles. All that Floyd McKee, in *A Century of American Dinnerware Manufacture*, 1963, p. 48, had to say about Santa Anita Pottery was that it was controlled by National Silver of New York and managed by Gertrude Gilkey. He noted it had ceased operations several years back (before 1963). Barbara Jean Hayes, author of *Bauer-The California Pottery Rainbow* stated in a letter that in the late 1940's, Santa Anita Pottery shipped their molds to Japan (probably when the address changed), and after that the products were really Japanese. The pottery was still listed in business in 1957 but must have ended very close to that time. Santa Anita Pottery made decorative ware, lazy susans, pepper mills, etc., along with full lines of dinnerware.

(Information: As cited and Lois Lehner, *American Kitchen and Dinner Wares*, p. 131. Marks: Nos. 1-5, on dishes; no. 6 in advertisement shown in *Glaze*, February 1981, p. 11; no. 7 was filed for copyright July 25, 1945, for use on cups, saucers, plates, bowls, dishes, tea and coffee pots, casseroles, and salad sets, made of pottery and dinnerware consisting of cups, saucers, plates, bowls, dishes, tea and coffee pots, casseroles and salad sets, all of which dinnerware is made substantially of earth or clay, claiming use since July 11, 1941. No. 8 was filed May 1, 1948, claiming use since September 7, 1943, for pottery consisting of cups, saucers, plates, bowls, dishes, tea and coffee pots, casseroles and salad sets, all of which dinnerware is made of clay and talcs. No. 9 was filed May 26, 1948, claiming use since January 6, 1948, for same articles as no. 8. No. 10 was filed January 28, 1949, claiming use since January 23, 1948 for use on dinnerware. No. 11 in 1952 *Crockery and Glass Journal Directory*. No. 12 on piece. No. 13 filed September 20, 1952 claiming use since May 1952 for ceramic dinnerware. No. 13 for the same product, was filed at the same time.)

Santa Barbara Ceramic Design. Santa Barbara, California. 1976 to present. The studio was formed in 1976 by its present director, Raymond Markow, to meet a growing demand for the ware which Markow developed during 1973 to 1976 following his graduation from the University of California at Santa Barbara. The decorators who have worked at some time are: Itoko Takeuchi; William Pasini; Michelle Foster; Suzanne Tormey; Anne Collinson; Allison Atwill; Laurie Cosca; Laurie Linn; Margie Gilson; Mary Favero; Gary Ba-Han; Shannon Sargent; Dorie Hutchison. Potters who have worked there are: Raymond Markow; John Cliff; Don Tate and Bob Osig. As explained in a brochure sent by the SBCD, their work consists of the following, ''Each SBCD piece is thrown on the potters wheel and handpainted, using in an innovative variation the traditional majolica technique. The ceramic pigments are blended in a wax emulsion base. These emulsions have a self-masking ''resist'' property that enables the artist to paint intricate details that do not blend into each other as in the majolica technique.

From an historical viewpoint, the pots of SBCD are more closely aligned with the work of the turn of the century art potteries, such as Rookwood, than with the present day studio pottery movement. Like art potteries of the arts and crafts movement, SBCD explores a huge variety of floral motifs, painted on traditional ceramic vessel forms. Though very popular at the turn of the century, this type of work died about 1920 due to a shift in popular tastes. People began to prefer the new ''modern'' look which was based on a machine aesthetic. In a sense, SBCD is a revival of art pottery. It takes up where the art potteries left off. This is due largely to recent technical innovations in the ceramic industry, such as commercial availability of rare earth pigments. These pigments yield a palette of colors undreamed of only a few years ago.'' (Marks: no. 1, Raymond Markow, potter who founded company; nos. 2-5, are the potters who form the pieces; no. 6, SBCD, company initials sometimes used this way; no. 7, company logo; the rest of the marks are for artists who hand paint and decorate the pieces. John Guthrie worked in a sales capacity. Jim Hardman, no. 8 was either a potter or decorator. Laurie Linn became Laurie Linn Ball and her later mark is L.L.B. Anne Collinson became Anne Collinson Fitch and her later mark is A. C. F. Other artists who worked there whose marks I did not have were Phil Krahn, Mark Mackay, Nancy Looker, Christine Adcock, Peggy Brogan. In 1985 three artists were working, Shannon Sargeant, Itoka Takeuchi and Laurie Linn Ball. Itoko Takeuchi painted the beautiful platter shown with the author's picture.

Potters

Ray

1.

2.

J.C.
John Clift

Osif
Bob Osif

3.

4.

ч.
Don Tate

5.

S B
c D

6.

7.

8. J.H.
Jim Hardman

Artists

BH
Dorie Hutchinson

A
Allison Atwill

MG
Margie Gilsom

MF
Mary Pavero

L. L.
Laurie Linn

H
Itoko Takeuchi

MF
Michelle Foster

LC
Laurie Cosca

WP
William Pasini

SS
Shannon Sargent

G or GBH
Gary Ba-Han

AC
Anne Collinson

ST
Suzanne Tormey

KAT
Kat Corcoran

GN
Darcy Neal

B.Rose
Barbara Rose

"Zetta"
Susan Dray

ED
Elena Dhyansky

KC
Kathleen Crea

Santa Clara (Indian) Pottery. Santa Clara Reservation, Santa Clara Pueblo, New Mexico. The art of making pottery is passed down from generation to generation among the Indians of the Southwestern United States (see Acoma and San Ildefonso listings). But each generation has become more and more aware of the aesthetic and saleable value of the pottery pieces. Many of today's Indian potters are well educated, but most still use the old hand coil method to make the pieces. The styles and designs of their ancestors are studied and imitated to honor the old traditions and they appeal to the market as well. Margaret Luther whose mark is shown was on a Santa Clara polychrome pot shown in the Stilwell article cited. She was the daughter of Lela and Van Gutierrez who made pottery between 1900 and 1949. A piece made by these potters sold at Parke Bernet for $850 in 1970. Van died in 1956 and his children, Luther and Margaret, were the family potters. The Tafoya family was also a well known family of Santa Clara potters. Sarafina Tafoya was the mother of Margaret Tafoya whose child was Toni Tafoya Roller. All of these women were potters. Toni's husband is a designer for the Mason Facility at Los Alamos. He helps her to dig clay and accompanies her when she travels for exhibits and demonstrations. Each Pueblo family has its own special clay bed to dig and use. The Santa Clara potters also make the black pieces, fired outdoors. (See the listings mentioned for details.) Camilo Sunflower Tafoya started making pottery in 1964; some of her early pieces are marked "Grace Hoover." Santa Clara potters have used modeling rather than color as decoration, frequently employing a stylized bear paw as a design motif. Varying firing methods result in either black or red coloring. An oxydizing atmosphere produces red or polychrome wares, while an oxygen-reducing atmosphere results in black pottery. No glazes were used. The highly polished surface of many pots comes from burnishing by hand before firing. Many more of these potters are mentioned briefly in the articles cited. (Information: Louise Schaub Witt, "Toni Roller, Santa Clara Potter," *Collectors News*, 1970, pp. 3, 13; Kathleen Stilwell, "Santa Clara Pottery," *American Clay Exchange*, October 30, 1984, pp. 6, 7; also by Stilwell, "Acoma Pottery," *American Clay Exchange*, August 15, 1984, pp. 4, 5.)

Margaret Luther Santa Clara Pottery ?

Santa's Workshop, Inc. North Pole, New York. Filed for registration on this mark on June 5, 1956, for use on dinner plates, utility dishes, mugs, trays, serving sets and dishes of earthenware, claiming use since July 1, 1949.

SANTA'S WORKSHOP

San Vallé Tile Kilns. Los Angeles, California. Sam Greenbaum filed for registration of this mark on March 29, 1952, for use on pottery, such as saucers, bowls, dishes, casseroles, coffee pots, pitchers and mugs, claiming use since February 29, 1952.

San Vallé

Sarosy, Lorri. Painesville, Ohio. 1974 to present on full time basis. Studio potter making handthrown and slab built stoneware pieces both functional and decorative. Graduate of Ohio State University in fine arts. She has shown work at the Cleveland Museum, the Designer Craftsmen Shop of the Columbus Museum of Art and many juried shows, of few of which are: Boston Mills Invitational, Peninsula, Ohio; National Craft Fair, Maryland; Las Olas Festival of the Arts, Ft. Lauderdale, Florida; Valley Arts Center Juried Show, Chagrin Falls, Ohio, 1st in Cramics; 7th Annual Zane Square Festival, Lancaster, Ohio, 1st in Ceramics.

Saturday Evening Girls. See Paul Revere Pottery listing.

Saugatuck Potters. Saugatuck, Michigan. 1950 to 1955. Listed in 1952 *Crockery and Glass Journal Directory*; under decorative china and earthenware such as vases, console sets, etc., also florist ware and decorative wall plates. Had one outlet listed in Evanston, Illinois. Margauerite Ilg Keefe and her husband Herbert Keefe had a studio where they made pottery in Saugatuck. After 1955 they moved to Kenilworth, Illinois, where they made pottery for a few years. (Information: Jenny B. Derwich and Dr. Mary Latos, *Dictionary Guide to U.S. Pottery and Porcelain*, p. 204. Mark: 1952 directory as cited.)

Savidge and Son. Sunbury, Norhumberland County, Pennsylvania. Around 1870. Potter made utilitarian stoneware with an impressed mark. (Information and impressed mark: Jeannette Lasansky, *Made of Mud*, p. 56.)

SAVIDGE & SON
SUNBURY. PA.

Sawyer, H. Mogadore (Akron). Portage County, Ohio. Around 1860 or before. Made stoneware. (Blair, p. 37). This potter is probably the same H. Sawyer listed by Betty Madden in *Art, Crafts and Architecture of Early Illinois*, p. 194, as working in Madison County, Illinois, in the Salamander Pottery around the 1860 era. Many potters moved from Ohio to Illinos to make stoneware because of the clay available there.

1860
Mogadore
H. Sawyer

Saxe, Adrian A. Los Angeles, California. 1962 to present. Adrian Saxe makes one of a kind sculptured pieces from pottery, porcelain or earthenware. He works primarily with Raku. Since 1973, Mr. Saxe has been an associate professor of art at the University of California, Los Angeles. He attended the Chouinard Art School in Los Angeles, from 1965 to 1969. He received his Bachelor of Arts degree from the California Institute of Arts in Valencia, California, in 1974. Before becoming an associate professor of art at U.C.L.A., he had worked as a contract design consultant on mural projects for the Interpace Corporation at the Franciscan Division (formerly Gladding, McBean and Company) in Glendale. He had also taught at the California State University in Long Beach. The work of Mr. Saxe is sold by the Garth Clark Galleries in New York City, and Los Angeles. Also, it is sold by the American Hand, Washington, D.C. Mr. Saxe had a long list of impressive one man shows and selected group exhibitions. There is no way I can relate all that should be told about this artist because of limited space. I can only give a partial listing.

Since 1968 Adrian Saxe listed 14 one man shows in galleries and museums, nine selected Gallery group shows and 32 selected invitational exhibitions. Each of these many shows was an important one. The selected invitational exhibitions were in many different states as well as Japan, Spain, France and England. A few examples are: In 1971, "California Design XI," Pasadena Museum of Modern Art, Pasadena, California / 1971-1972, "Contemporary Ceramic Art: Canada, U.S.A., Mexico, and Japan," The National Museum of Modern Art, Tokyo, Japan. and The National Museum of Modern Art, Kyoto, Japan / 1979-1981, "A Century of Ceramics in the United States: 1878-1978," Everson Museum of Art, Syracuse, New York which traveled to the Renwick Gallery, National Museum of American Art, Smithsonian Institution, Washington, D.C., Cooper-Hewitt Museum, New York, New York, and other museums / 1980-1981, "American Porcelain: New Expressions in an Ancient Art," Renwick Gallery, National Museum of American Art, Smithsonian Institution, Washington, D.C., and a national tour of six museums through S.I.T.E.S.

Also, a selection from this exhibit (pieces including Mr. Saxe's, from the permanent collection of the National Museum of American Art) toured an additional three years in Europe, Asia, and India / 1981, "Animal Imagery: Contemporary Objects and the Beast," Renwick Gallery, National Museum of American Art, Washington, D.C. / 1982, "7th Ceramics National Invitational," Sykes Gallery, Millersville State College, Millersville, Pennsylvania / 1982, "Clay Choices by Clay Artists," Contemporary Crafts Association, Portland, Oregon; 1983, "Echoes: Historical References in Contemporary Ceramics," The Nelson-Atkins Museum of Art, Kansas City, Missouri / 1985, "13th Chuichi International Exhibition of Ceramic Arts," Museum of Art, Nagoya, Japan / 1985, "20th Century American Ceramics," Museu de Ceramica, Barcelona, Spain, and Museum of Art, Madrid, Spain (and other European cities on tour) / 1985, "Pacific Connections," Los Angeles Institute of Contemporary Art, Los Angeles, California, Tacoma Art Museum, Tacoma, Washington, San Diego State University Art Gallery, San Diego, California, University Art Collections, Matthews Centre, Arizona State University, Tempe, Arizona, University of Iowa Museum of Art, Ames, Iowa / 1986, "Contemporary Ceramics," Muscarelle Museum of Art, College of William and Mary, Williamsburg, Virginia; 1986, "American Potters Today," Victoria and Albert Museum, London, England / 1986, "American Artists at Sevres," American Center, Paris, France.

He has pieces in many public collections in the United

States and overseas, including: the National Collection of American Art, Renwick Gallery, Smithsonian Institution, Washington, D.C.; Everson Museum of Art, Syracuse, New York; Los Angeles County Museum of Art, Los Angeles, California; Nelson-Atkins Museum of Art, Kansas City, Missouri; Museum of Art, Carnegie Institute, Pittsburg, Pennsylvania; Musee des Arts Decoratifs, Pavillion de Marsan, Palais du Louvre, Paris, France; Musee National de Ceramique de Sevres, Sevres, France; Cultural Affairs Commission, County of Los Angeles, Los Angeles, California; Times-Mirror Corporation, Los Angeles, California; U.S. News and World Report, Washington, D.C.; Prudential Life Insurance, Newark, New Jersey; American Craft Museum, New York, New York; Victoria and Albert Museum, London, England. Mr. Saxe must be one of the most "written about" workers in clay today which certainly demonstrates his impressive abilities.

Books and catalogues containing material on Saxe, as sent by Mr. Saxes are: California Design, *California Design XI*, Pasadena: Pasadena Art Museum, 1971, pp. 121, 123, 170; National Museum of Modern Art, *Contemporary Ceramic Art: Canada, U.S.A., Mexico and Japan*, Tokyo, Japan, 1971, p. 29; Long Beach Museum of Art, *Ceramic Conjunction*, Long Beach, California, 1977, p. 29; Elaine Levin, *West Coast Clay Spectrum*, Los Angeles: Security Pacific National Bank, 1979, no pagination, cited in text, illustration; Garth Clark, *A Century of Ceramics in the United States; 1878-1978*, New York: E.P. Dutton, 1979, pp. 249, 235; Lloyd E. Herman, *American Porcelain: New Expressions in an Ancient Art*, Forest Grove, Oregon: Timber Press, 1980, pp. 18, 97; Michael W. Monroe, *The Animal Image: Contemporary Objects and the Beast*, Washington, D.C.: Smithsonian Institution Press, 1981, pp. 31, 32, 47; Jan Axel and Karen McCready, *Porcelain: Traditions and New Visions*, New York: Warson-Guptill, 1981, pp. 105, 124, 125; Katherine Pearson, *American Crafts: A Sourcebook for the Home,*, New York: Stewart, Tabori and Chang, 1983, pp. 126-127, 128, 132; Garth Clark, *Ceramics Echoes: Historical References in Contemporary Ceramics*, Kansas City, Missouri: The Contemporary Art Society, 1983, pp. 60, 66-67; Betty Warner Sheinbaum, *Art in Clay: 1950's to 1980's in Southern California; Evolution, Revolution, Continuation*, Los Angeles: Muncipal Art Gallery, 1984, pp. 7, 56-57; Tobi Smith, *Pacific Connections*, Los Angeles: LAICA, 1985, pp. 23, 29-30, 78. Articles in periodicals including material about Saxe, are included in: *Craft Horizons; Coast: Ceramics Monthly; Calendar; Artweek: Craft; Home-Life* (supplement to Washington Star); *Los Angeles Times*; and *Washington Post*.

Saxon China Company. Sebring, Ohio. See French China Company for history. (Marks: nos. 1 and 2, on dishes; a patent was filed on July 9, 1925, for no. 3, for use on china, porcelain and earthenware dishes and sets of dishes, claiming use since January 2, 1925. No. 4, was filed on August 4, 1925, for use on plates, cups, platters, bowls and other tableware pottery, claiming use since June 30, 1925. No. 5, was filed August 4, 1925, for use on same products as no. 4. No claim date was registered but patent was granted in December 29, 1925. No. 6, was also filed August 4, 1925, for same products as no. 4, claiming use since June 30, 1925.)

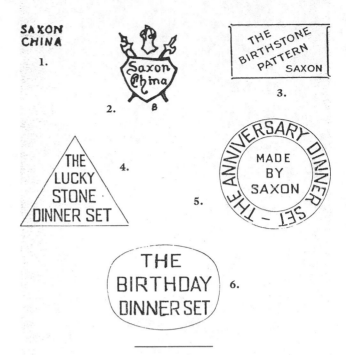

SAXON
CHINA

1.

2.

3.

4.

5.

6.

Sayers, Don and Ruth. Morton, Illinois. Started 1982. Retailers of line of Tea Leaf. Most pieces marked with stamp as shown. The 1982 mark is stamped on with copper lustre. Each year the color of stamp will be changed.

Sayre China Company. East Liverpool, Ohio. 1948 to around middle 1950's. See Pines Pottery for early history. Ira Sayers purchased Pines Pottery from E.S. Carson in 1948 and operated not more than 10 years in the same type of operation as Pines Pottery. (Information: E.S. Carson, Homer Laughlin China Company, Mark: from Quality Stamp Company, East Liverpool, Ohio.)

Scammell China Company. Trenton, New Jersey. 1924 to 1954. In 1923, D. William Scammell purchased the remaining interests in the Maddock Pottery Company and began forming the Scammell China Company, a company engaged in manufacture of hotel and railroad china. In 1939, a line of fine thin translucent china for home use was introduced. The china had a porcelain body with a delicate ivory tone. See Maddock Pottery Company for previous history. (Information: Harold Eberlein and Roger Ramsdell, *The Practical Book of Chinaware*, Philadelphia: J.B. Lippincott, 1948, pp. 303-304; *Trenton City Directory*, 1923-1924: Lehner,

American Kitchen and Dinner Wares, p. 131. Marks: The John Wanamaker mark for railroad china from Sandknop, p. 59. All of the rest of the marks furnished by Larry Paul, who has written a book on Maddock potteries.

SCAMMELL'S
TRENTON CHINA

SCAMMELL'S
Lamberton China

*Lamberton
Ivory
China
made in America*

*Lamberton
Ivory
China
made in America
"Puritan"*

Lenape
SCAMMELL'S
TRENTON CHINA

SCAMMELL'S
TRENTON CHINA

Schaffner, Henry (Heinrich). Salem, North Carolina. 1833 to sometime before death in 1877. Schaffner came from Germany to Salem and was a journeyman potter in 1833 and 1834 and a master potter in Salem after 1834. He operated his own business in Salem, rather than working for the Moravian religious community and therefore the records about him are far less than the other Moravian potters. He took a journeyman potter named Daniel Krause to work for him in 1846 and sometime before Schaffner's death, he turned the pottery over to Krause. (Information and marks: John Bivins, Jr., *The Moravian Potters in North Carolina*, pp. 42, 44, 110 and 133. Mark was incised.)

H.S
SALEM
N.C.

Scheier, Edwin and Mary. Edwin attended the New York School of Industrial Arts and attended classes at Columbia University for no credit when he could. He worked summers as a merchant seaman and winters as an independent craftsman. Still in his early twenties, Edwin was appointed a field supervisor of crafts for the southern states with the Federal Art Project (W.P.A.). He met Mary through this work at Big Stone Gap Federal Art Gallery, where she was director around 1936. They were married shortly after in 1937. Mary had attended the New York School of Fine and Applied Arts in 1928 and 1929 and then studied in Paris one year. Mary had started working with the federal project in 1935. Edwin molded puppets, and for a while they toured the south giving puppet shows. They tried molding in clay and were fascinated. For one and one-half years, they lived in an old house in Glade Spring, Virginia, where they built a kiln and started making beautiful pottery pieces which were shown that very first year at the Contemporary Industrial Arts Exhibit at the Metropolitan Museum of Art in New York City. In 1938, through the League of New Hampshire Arts and Crafts, they went to teach at the University of New Hampshire until 1950 when they retired and moved to Oaxaca, Mexico, where they continued to make pottery. In 1940 at the Ninth Annual National Ceramic Exhibition at the Syracuse Museum of Fine

Arts (now called the Elverson Museum of Art), the Scheiers won second prize. Edwin won for his stoneware bowl, thrown and decorated with fine plaster figures and Mary, for a thrown ribbed vase with fine form and texture. The marks shown are all attributed to Edwin in 1940's and 1951 and are incised. (Information: "Ninth Annual National Ceramic Exhibition," *Bulletin of American Ceramic Society*, Vol. 19, no. 11, 1940, p. 453; and "Edwin and Mary Scheier," *Bulletin of American Ceramic Society*, Vol. 22, no. 7, 1943, pp. 264, 265. Marks: Linda Steigleder, from the booklet published by the Everson Museum of Art to accompany the 1978 exhibition, "A Century of Ceramics in the U.S.")

Scheier   Scheier

Scheier

Schiller Corday Company. See Boleslaw Cybis.

Schneider, Aviva. New Berlin, New York. 1970 to present. Studio potter making one third of a kind porcelain sculptures and plates using colored clay. She also has a line using wheel thrown porcelain of colored clay. One of a kind pieces are signed Aviva Schneider with an underglaze pencil which turns dark on firing. The wheel thrown pieces are stamped "V" with a metal stamp. Aviva has a B.A. degree in ceramics from Kirkland College, Clinton, New York and M.A. degree from Rochester Institute of Technology. She also attended school in Tuscarora, Nevada, at the Tuscarora Pottery School. She listed 14 outstanding invitational and juried shows she has attended. She has pieces in several private collections of colleges and institutes. Awards won include the Orton Foundation Value Purchase Award in 1979, several firsts in Syracuse, New York, etc.

Aviva Schneider   V

Scholl Pottery. Tyler's Port, Montgomery County, Pennsylvania. Around 1811 was earliest known pieces. The pottery started by Michael Scholl followed by his son Jacob Scholl, whose earliest pieces were around 1831. They made redware, sgraffito style. Mark was a Fuchsia flower impressed in the clay with a hardened pottery stamp. (Information: E.A. Barber, "Tulip Ware of the Pennsylvania German Potters,"(first published 1903) New York; Dover Publications, Inc., 1970, pp. 157, 158. Marks: No. 1, Ramsay, p. 278. No. 2, Barber, as cited. I am sure Barber's is the authentic mark. I wanted to show both marks to illustrate what an artist's conception can do to a mark, I really doubt that these were two separate marks.)

 1.   2.

Schonfeld, Max P.H. Los Angeles, California. Distributor who filed for registration on this mark on December 16, 1940, for use on table and cooking china, porcelain vases, urns, hair receivers, cosmetic jars, perfume bottles, powder boxes and soap dishes. This distributor was also listed several times in the 1950's. Gladding, McBean and Company made Kaolena China for Schonfeld from 1939 to 1951, according to company information, and used marks nos. 2 and 3. Most of the pottery that Gladding, McBean and Company shipped for Schonfeld went without identification. "M.S." was the Max Schonfeld trademark, either in script (mark 2) or as seen in marks 4 and 5, used on dinnerware sold by the company. I feel reasonably sure this dinnerware was made by Gladding, McBean and Company for Schonfeld. The "Sierra" pattern was listed in 1952, but I couldn't find a listing for "El Verde" under Gladding, McBean and Company. However, we still do not have all of the company's marks, even though they were furnished to me by the company. The patent reports prove that.

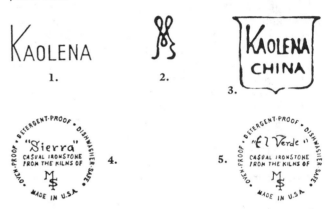

Schoop, Hedi, Art Creations. North Hollywood, California. Started around 1945 to around 1955. Schoop Art Creations was listed in the 1946 *Crockery and Glass Journal Directory*, but not the same directory for 1945. The pottery was still listed in 1954, but I found no listing in 1955. They were no longer listed in the *Manufacturers Directory of California*, in 1955, either. In 1945, Schoop was listed as making figures, figurines and lamps. Pictured in Brown's article cited, was a 10″ Dutch girl with exacting detail done in greens, whites and yellows. (Inscribed mark: Danny Brown, "Those California Figurines," *American Clay Exchange*, October 15, 1985, p. 11.)

Hedi Schoop
S

Schreckengost, Don. East Liverpool, Ohio. Don Schreckengost was born in the pottery town of Sebring, Ohio, son of Adda and Warren Schreckengost. He was the youngest of three sons, Viktor, Paul and Don, all of whom rose to prominence as outstanding designers in the field of ceramics. Majoring in design and sculpture, Don Schreckengost graduated with honors from the Cleveland Institute of Art in 1935 and later did graduate work in Sweden. His first industrial design work was for the Salem China Company. (See the listing for Salem China Company.) He quickly brought unique ideas to the industry, one of the early designers to use bright new colors such as selenium reds.

His revolutionary "Tricorn" shape, designed in 1934, is now a much sought after "collector's item." Schreckengost left the industry, per se, in 1935 to teach at the New York College of Ceramics, Alfred University and to become its first professor of industrial design. During his 10 years at the University, he continued to design for industry and brought to his design students first-hand industrial experience. After leaving the University, he became design director of Homer Laughlin China Company for 15 years, then formed his own company, Design For Industry. His career has been very extensive both in industrial design and fine art, designing not only products, but also packaging, displays and advertising as well as murals, fine art pottery and sculpture.

He is designer for Hall China Company, the Salem China Company and executive design director for the Summitville Tile Company. Other companies with whom he has been associated include: The Dubois Press, Buffalo China Company, Royal China Company, Warwick China, United States Stoneware, Martin-Marietta, Mayer China Company, The O'Hommel Color Company and Universal Rundel. Schreckengost is recognized internationally for his industrial designs and also for his fine creative art. His awards and citations include: the prestigious Charles Fergus Binns award for "High Achievement in the Field of Ceramic Art;" First award for pottery in the Western Hemisphere Exhibition; the Menno Alexander Reeb award for sculpture; Award of Merit at the Graphic Arts Show of New York City; and the Restaurant Association's "Top of The Table Award." He has been recognized by the American Ceramic Society for his outstanding contribution to the art and design of ceramics and was appointed chairman of International Cultural Exchange Exhibition, Geneva, Switzerland by Eisenhower.

The attractive Bicentennial Cup, commissioned by the Salem China Company (one in the Smithsonian Collection) and the 107' mural depicting the early steel industry was designed for Summitville Tile Company have received much publicity. (See the listing for Summitville Tile Company.) His works are exhibited in many museums and private collections -- The Ross Purdy Ceramic Museum; The Smithsonian; The Philadelphia Art Alliance; International Business Machines; The Thomas Watson Collection; and Dartmouth Collection. Well known products were designed by Don Schreckengost for these companies: **Hall China Company** - "Hallcraft" porcelain dinnerware line; "Super-Ceram" high temperature cookware line; "Stak-ups," hotel-restaurant food preparation serve line; collector items such as decorative commemorative whiskey bottles, etc.; "Dura-cast," combination pewter and porcelain line; custom designed lines and specialty items in high temperature porcelain. **Homer Laughlin China Company** - "Rhythm," semi-vitreous dinnerware; "Epicure," colored glazed line of casual and buffet dinnerware; "Charm House," custom designed line of semi-vitreous dinnerware; "Dura-print," line of underglazed mass-produced dinnerware; "Triumph," line of high temperature porcelain dinnerware; "Cavalier," line of formal sophisticated semi-vitreous dinnerware; "American Provincial," decorative "Penn-Dutch" semi-vitreous dinnerware; **The Salem China Company** - "Tri-Corne," early contemporary semi-vitreous; "Esquire," semi-vitreous dinnerware line; "Georgetown," high styled stoneware line; "Noel," special Christmas holiday line of dinnerware, glassware and decorative pieces; "Porcelle," high translucent line of dinnerware; Bicentennial Commemorative cup, a collectors item; line of special decorative dinner stoneware patterns. **Summitville Tiles, Inc.** - custom murals for indoor, outdoor architectural decorative use; new tile pro-

duct lines; Summit forms; sculptured Zodiacs; Bicentennial sculptures; "Heritage," early American line of decorative colored tiles; commemorative sculptures; custom designed interiors, household and commercial. **Royal China Company** - "Royal Stone," colorful stoneware line of buffet and casual dinnerware; numerous semi-vitreous dinnerware patterns; "Royalon," melamine, plastic dinnerware, solid colors and decorated; "Royalon," acrylic line of tumblers, bar ware items; "Royal Cavalier," semi-vitreous dinnerware and special premium items.

D. S

Don Schreckengost

D. Schreckengost

D. Schreckengost + P.

D. Schreckengost. I.D.S.A

STONEWARE COFFEE MUG. 8OZ.
SIGNED EXPRESSLY FOR VICTORIA STATION.
THE SALEM CHINA COMPANY.
DESIGNED BY DON SCHRECKENGOST. IDSA 5/22/73

Schreckengost, Viktor. Viktor Schreckengost was born in Sebring, Ohio, in 1906. His father was a potter, and his brother was Don Schreckengost (see that listing). He studied at the Cleveland Institute of Art from 1924 to 1929. He did post graduate work in Vienna, studying ceramics and sculpture in 1929. He accepted a teaching position at the Cleveland School of Art and also worked as a designer for R. Guy Cowan at the Cowan Pottery, where the production was mainly art pottery. Cowan Pottery closed in 1930. In 1933, Schreckengost reorganized production of Limoges China in Sebring, and also began to design dinnerware for them.

Production increased from 30% to full capacity in one year's time under his direction. Around 1940, 1941, the Sebring Pottery Company, Limoges China Company and Salem China were all under the same management with Schreckengost as designer. He designed dinnerware in the "Manhattan" shape with "Comet" decoration in red flame; also, "Diana" shape with a "Joan of Arc" decoration, and the "Victory" shape with the "Lady Godey" decoration or pattern. For American Limoges China Company, he designed "Jiffy Ware." Schreckengost became so well known because he achieved heights of success in more than one field of ceramics. His sculptures make definite statements and received numerous awards at the Ceramic National Exhibitions at Syracuse. (See those lists in back of this book.) The *Bulletin of American Ceramic Society*, July, (1939), p. 258, tells of Schreckengost's winning the Charles Fergus Binns Medal.

"The award of the Charles Fergus Binns Medal is not the ordinary award of an ordinary Medal. It is a reverent tribute to the memory of a great man. In that tribute all people of Alfred University join both individually and collectively.

The award of the Medal also serves the purpose of recognizing distinguished achievements in ceramic art by the medalist.

The Medal is awarded by a jury consisting of representatives of the National Terra Cotta Society, The United States Potters Association, The American Ceramic Society and the

Ceramic Guild of Alfred University. The members of the jury nominate the candidates and then ballot until one is chosen. The objective is to select the most distinguished ceramic artist in America who has not previously received the Medal.

The Medal this year is awarded to Viktor Schreckengost. Viktor Schreckengost is head of the Department of Design of the Cleveland School of Art and instructor in stage design at Western Reserve University. He won the Cleveland Museum of Art European Travel Scholarship and has studied extensively abroad. For each of the past eight years, he has won first prize for ceramic sculpture at the Cleveland Museum of Art. Last year he won first prize for ceramic sculpture at the National Robineau Exhibition. Specimens of his work which have been included in the traveling exhibition of ceramic artware have won high approval. Mr. Schreckengost is also consulting designer for the Sebring Pottery Corp. Both Fairs commissioned him to do design work. His ceramic art work is of the highest order.''

In Helen Stiles book, *Pottery of the U.S.*, p. 239, is pictured a group of Schreckengost's prize winning sculptures. The works were entitled, ''Keramos,'' a woman's head; ''Smoked Ham,'' a mother sow with six piglets on her back; ''Androcles,'' a lion and man figure; ''Naama,'' a camel and ''Mother Earth.'' These five pieces won first place for a group of five sculptures at the show, Work of Cleveland Artists and Craftsman in 1939. The piece that won first prize at the National Ceramic Exhibition at Syracuse was ''Glory Glory,'' which was a black lady with arms extended to Heaven with her face smiling broadly. In 1983, Schreckengost was one of eight American Clay Sculpturers, who were honored by an exhibit at the Everson Museum of Art in Syracuse, New York. Many of his sculptured pieces are pictured in *The Diversions of Keramos*, 1925 to 1950, published by the Museum in 1983, compiled by Ross Anderson and Barbara Perry.

Recently, Viktor Schreckengost was named a Fellow and Honorary Life Member of the American Ceramic Society. Only 10 other people have received this honor, according to Anderson and Perry in *The Diversions of Keramos*, p. 46. (Information: from books already cited; also, Garth Clark, *A Century of Ceramics in the U.S.*, p. 325. Marks: sent by Viktor Schreckengost. He said the signature was used in conjunction with R. Guy Cowan and the Cowan symbol. These were pieces fired through Limoges China Company and Salem China Company kilns, at which time the company's backstamp was used with Schreckengost's signature. Schreckengost gave the following explanation for his marks: Nos. 1, 2, is signature used on thrown and hand built pottery and sculpture. Each part of letter is into clay with a chisel-like wood tool. Nos. 3, 4, 5, brass die of mark used by Kunstgewerbeschule, Vienna, Austria. Brand like V.S. was his personal mark. Mark of school was usually put on by professor before anything could be fired. Nos. 6, 7, signature used on decorated underglaze and overglaze and sculpture. Applied with stain or underglaze color with brush.)

Schweinfurt, John George. New Market, Virginia. Schweinfurt was an earthenware potter, born 1825, who made miniature toy, small banks, urns with raised or applied flowers, ink wells, clay pipes and small decorative molds that bear his initials. Only the molds were marked, according to Elmer L. Smith, *Pottery, A Utilitarian Folk Craft*, p. 29. Mark: pictured on small mold; Smith, as cited, p. 29.)

Scio Pottery Company. Scio, Ohio. Started in 1932. After the closing of the Albright China Company subsidiary in 1927, there were only 400 people left in the town of Scio. There had been 1,200 in the town while the pottery was operating. In 1932, in the midst of the Depression, the Scio Pottery was started to provide jobs for the town and to compete with the Japanese ware that was flooding our markets. The pottery made underglaze decorated dinnerware by mass production methods with the pottery operating 24 hours a day, seven days a week. Until 1950 the pottery made only plain white dinnerware. The company answered they do not mark or backstamp, and generally they did not. But over the years we have found they did mark two or more special productions for grocery stores, etc., also the mark, ''Mercury,'' was patented to Scio Pottery on December 13, 1938, for pottery vases or jars for use by florists. The ''Golden Wheat'' mark shown was on dinnerware made by Scio Pottery, Homer Laughlin China Company and French Saxon China Company, and they all used this same mark. The factory closed February 28, 1985, but is continuing as a selling agency with overseas products. (Information: company furnished. Marks: no. 1, on dish; no. 2, patent report. No. 3 was filed for registration on April 24, 1969 for non-decorated white dinnerware.)

Golden Wheat MADE IN USA 22 K GOLD 1. **MERCURY** 2.

ENGLISH SWIRL 3.

Scott, George. Cincinnati, Ohio. After 1846 to around 1900. George Scott, a potter, came to this country in 1846 and settled in Cincinnati, Ohio. He did not start making pottery immediately. He sold goods for William Bromley and even imported English wares which he resold. Finally, he was able to purchase an old tavern on Front Street to establish a pottery (Barber, *Pottery and Porcelain of the U.S.*, p. 274). In *American Kitchen and Dinner Wares*, p. 132, I gave the opening date as around 1853 or 1854, according to listings sent to me from the Cincinnati Public Library from directories. He started by making Rockingham and yellowware. In the 1901-1902 *Complete Directory*, the business was listed as the **George Scott Pottery**, making white granite and common china dinner sets, toilet sets and odd dishes, some decorated. In 1889, the pottery was called **George Scott and Sons**. By 1901 the factory was owned by Sarah A. Waite. (Marks: no. 1, Larry Freeman, *China Classics*, New York, New York: Century House, 1959, p. 70; no. 2, Doris A. Lechler, "Playhouse China: American Contributions," *Antique Trader Weekly*, August 29, 1984, pp. 84, 85. Doris gave 1849 as a starting date for Scott's pottery ventures. Apparently they were small enough not to rate directory listing for a few years. Mark 3 is a photostatic copy from plate.)

1.

2.

3.

Scott and Fetzer Company. Cleveland, Ohio. Filed for rights to this mark on November 6, 1941, claiming use since September 26, 1941, for use on ceramic tableware.

Scott, Meg. Canton, Ohio. 1979 to present. Meg Scott, a studio potter makes functional stoneware and sculptures.

Sculptures In Clay. Livonia, Michigan. 1972 to present (1985). Betty Regina, studio potter, attended classes at the Farmington Community Center and the Center for Creative Arts in Detroit. She became interested in making pottery. In the past she has made picture frames, figurines, various pots and decorative pieces, but the sculptured clown figurines and clocks have become so popular, she is making these pieces full time at present. Betty said her clowns are signed, "Regina." (Information and mark from Derwich and Latos, *Dictionary Guide to U.S. Pottery and Porcelain*, p. 189 and from Betty Regina.)

Regina

Seagle, Daniel. Vale, Lincoln County, North Carolina. Started from 1800 to 1805 until 1867. Made earthenware jugs, crocks. (Information: Daisy Wade Bridges, *Potters of the Catawba Valley*, Charlotte, North Carolina: Mint Museum, 1980, pp. 11, 12, 15. Mark: on picture on front cover of same book.)

D S
10

Seagle, James F. Vale, Lincoln County, North Carolina. 1829-1892. Made earthenware. (Information: Daisy Wade Bridges, *Potters of the Catawba Valley*, Charlotte, North Carolina: Mint Museum, 1980, pp. 11, 12, 15. Mark: Bridges as cited, p. 51.)

J.F.S.

Seagrove Pottery/C.C. Cole Pottery. Seagrove, North Carolina. Pottery is operated by Walter and Dorothy Auman. Dorothy Cole Auman, born in 1925, was a daughter of Charles C. Cole, who was a brother to A.C. Cole. She was a member of the fifth generation of the Cole family to produce pottery. Walter Auman, born in 1926, worked for C.C. Cole Pottery from 1952 to 1971. Walter's father and grandfather were potters also, and Walter started making pottery in 1949. When Dorothy was very young, Charles C. Cole took his family to Steeds to make earthenware with his son, Thurston. It was there that an uncle of Dorothy's taught her to throw on the wheel. He taught her to produce miniatures, small baskets and vases. Until the 1930's, all of the various Cole potteries made utilitarian stoneware pieces. In the 1930's, they started making earthenware pieces, some decorative. C.C. Cole worked at the pottery from 1936 until 1971, and the Aumans have continued the business since. In 1953 a retail shop was opened; before that, the pottery sold mostly wholesale. Pieces at present are high fired 2050-2150 degrees earthenware, with various glazes, including tobacco spit, a glossy orange and various other colors. A matt glaze is also used and sometimes pieces are slip decorated. (Information: by letter from Dorothy Auman and Nancy Sweezy, *Raised in Clay, The Southern Pottery Tradition*, pp. 245-250. Mark: sent by pottery. They said mark was written, but didn't say if it was inscribed or written with oxide ink. The Auman Pottery owned by Walter's relatives, 1919 to 1936, stamped pieces "Auman Pottery/Seagrove, N.C." Not to be confused with Seagrove Pottery.)

Seagrove

Sears and Roebuck. Chicago, Illinois. 1886 to present (1987). A distributor. Sears filed for rights on the first four marks shown. No. 1 was the "Sunrise" mark used on semi-porcelain American made dinnerware. Homer Laughlin China Company made dishes for Sears under the Sunrise name. No. 1 filed on May 18, 1928, claiming use since March 3, 1928. No. 2 was filed on March 15, 1933, claiming use since November 18, 1932 for use on earthenware nested bowls, semi-porcelain cups and saucers. No. 3 was filed on Janaury 13, 1941, claiming use since October 8, 1940 for use on table china. This is the Sears mark very familiar to dinnerware collectors. No. 4 was filed on Dember 14, 1929, claiming use since November 4, 1929 for use on semi-porcelain dinnerware. (Marks: nos. 5-14 on dishes and from Quality Stamp Company; marks 15, 16, incised on cookie jars. All but the last two are stamped marks. See Morton Pottery for Vincent Price line sold by Sears. No. 17 was filed for registration February 18, 1970, claiming use of the mark since October, 1969 for snack bowls, flower vases and arrangers made of crockery, earthenware or china.)

MANY MOODS

Seaver, William. Taunton, Massachusetts. 1772 to before 1837. According to Lura W. Watkins in *Early New England Potters and Their Wares*, pp. 81, 82, 86, 87, the mark shown is one *probably* used by William Seaver. She called him the first successful stoneware potter in Massachusetts. He was in partnership with a man named Ebenezer Baker from 1769 to 1772, making redware. In 1772, he built a kiln on what was

called No. 2 Landing Place of Taunton Great River, making stoneware and earthenware pots, jugs, etc. She said there was evidence that the Seaver Pottery in Taunton was continued by another firm in 1837. Other potters in Taunton, whose marks she describes were "A. Standish/Taunton, Mass.," "Standish and Wright," "F.T. Wright and Company/Stoneware/Taunton, Mass." The latter as late as 1866. (Information: Watkins, as cited. Mark: impressed on jug in illustration from Watkins, in section following, p. 291. From the picture I couldn't see the word pot. (abbreviation for pottery). The word Taunton was very clear.

TAUNTON (POT.) ?

Sevey, Amos. Chelsea, Massachusetts. Around 1800. Stoneware potter, listed in "A Check List of New England Potters," by F.H. Norton, in the *Bulletin of American Ceramic Society*, Vol. 18, May 1939, pp. 181-185.

AMOS SEAVEY CHELSEA

Sebring Brothers Pottery. Also called American Pottery Works. East Liverpool, Ohio. See American Pottery Works for marks and information.

Sebring China Company. E.H. Sebring Company dropped the initials soon after founding in 1909, and was known as the Sebring China Company. This name was also used by the Limoges China Company for a very short while in very early 1900's. The five Sebring brothers who owned the potteries in Sebring, Ohio, were famous for changing names and ownership. See that listing.

E.H. Sebring China Company. Operated from around 1909 (Stout said 1911, p. 83) to Depression era. This was formerly the Oliver China Company. In 1934, this company was purchased by the founders of the Royal China Company. The mark no. 1 shown with the word "Art" in it has caused researchers to look for an Art China Company in Sebring, Ohio, that seems not to have existed. This mark was found by this author on a semi-porcelain soup bowl of average quality. (Information: Lehner, *American Kitchen and Dinner Wares*, p. 133. Marks: nos. 1, 3, 4, 5, on dishes; no. 6, Quality Stamp Company; no. 7, from Connie Rogers. No. 2, "Patriot China" was a line of china made by Sebring China Company around 1930. Picture of plate and mark was sent by Al Halpern, had a three little pigs decal on a square plate with rounded corners and a ridged shoulder. Product identified by Harrison Keller of Salem China Company.)

1.

S. C. CO
PATRIOT CHINA
MADE IN AMERICA

2.

MFGD. BY PERMISSION
WALT DISNEY ENTERPRISES

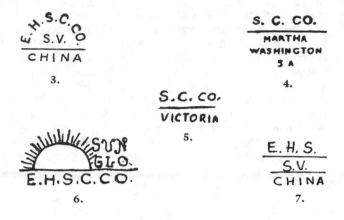

3.

S. C. CO.
MARTHA
WASHINGTON
5 A
4.

S.C. CO.
VICTORIA
5.

E.H.S.C.CO.
6.

E.H.S.
S.V.
CHINA
7.

Sebring Manufacturing Company. Sebring, Ohio. Company was formed out of the consolidation of French China, Saxon China and Strong Manufacturing Company in 1916. They in turn became a part of the American China Corporation which failed in 1931. Sebring Manufacturing Corporation made semi-porcelain dinner sets. See various listings for marks of individual potteries.

Sebring Pottery Company. Operated from 1887 until after the Depression into 1940's. This company was started in East Liverpool and moved to the town of Sebring after the town was founded in 1898 by F.A. Sebring. This company used a great variety of marks on the semi-porcelain that they made. In 1923, after two years of working to perfect it, Sebring Pottery Company introduced "Ivory Porcelain" ware at an exhibit in Pittsburgh. In Helen E. Stiles book, *Pottery of the U.S.*, published in 1941, p. 78, said "the Sebring Pottery Company and the American Limoges China Company of Sebring, Ohio, and Salem China Company of Salem, Ohio, are under the same management. I had previously thought the pottery had ended sooner but it must have lasted into the 1940's. However, it did become absorbed by the Limoges completely and the various lines continued. Because of the joint ownership of the potteries mentioned, we got a duplication of lines and patterns. In other words, they all made some of the same dishes. Just as the Taylor, Smith and Taylor Pottery continued using its own name for a while after being purchased by Anchor Hocking Corporation, then gradually the Taylor, Smith and Taylor marks, etc. were fazed out in preference to the Anchor Hocking name. The buildings were still there operating, the manufacture of lines continued, but the original company was now gone but not quite faded away. All of this makes the writing of pottery history very difficult. (Marks: nos. 1, 2, 3, Barber, *Marks of American Potters*, p. 135; no. 4, Ramsay, p. 279. The Kokus China marks were used around 1900. No. 5, found on dishes which were definitely decoration and shape of the Sebring dishes, but it is hard to tell if they were made at Limoges Pottery Company, Salem China Company, or Sebring Pottery or perhaps all three if they were a distribution for a particular chain of stores. No. 6 is the mark as copyrighted in November, 1923, for use on porcelain and chinaware, namely, dinner sets, teasets, dishes, plates, cups, bowls, teapots, sugar bowls, cream pitchers, platters, tureens, gravy boats, butter dishes and covered dishes, claiming use since June of the same year. No. 7 Jo Cunningham, *American Dinnerware*, p. 48 was used around 1924. The remainder of the marks were from Quality Stamp Company and dishes.

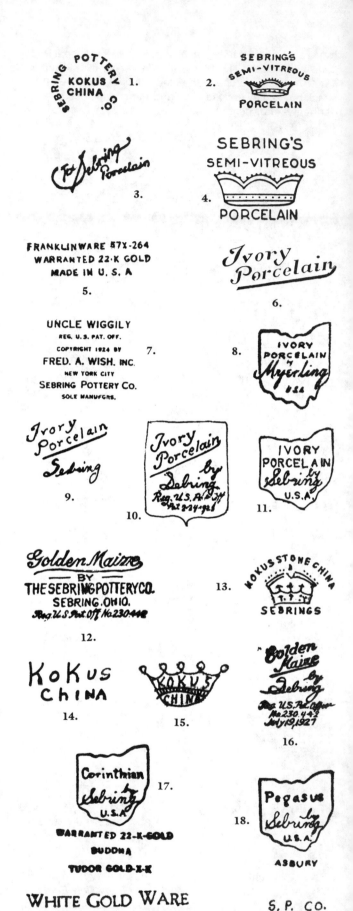

21. GOLDEN WARE *Sebring* U.S.A. WARRANTED 22 CARAT PURE GOLD WILD ROSE

22. THE *Sebring* POTTERY Co. *Sebring Ohio* PATENTED

23. The Jubilee *Sebring* U.S.A.

24. Liberty HOTEL CHINA SEBRING SEBRING, OHIO

25. PROVINCIAL WARE by *Sebring* U.S.A.

26. Rainbo Ware *Sebring* U.S.A.

27. *Ivory Porcelain by Sebring* Reg.U.S. PAT. '24 '25 U.S.A.

28. JADE WARE BY SEBRING U.S.A.

29. 8 Trojan *Sebring* by U.S.A. WARRANTED 22.K.GOLD TOLEDO DELIGHT

30. THE *Sebring* POTTERY CO. U.S.A. WARRANTED 22-K GOLD VERMILLION ROSE-IT208

E. Selby and Company. Hudson, New York. Selby trained under Nathan Clark of Athens, Greene County, New York, and then went to work in Hudson, New York, (Stradling, p. 133). (See Nathan Clark Pottery.) Then in 1834 Edward Selby became a partner in Charles Dillon and Company in Albany. (See explanation under Paul Cushman Pottery and the Charles Dillon listing.) So Selby would have to be in Hudson between his study under Nathan Clark and his partnership with Dillon. There was a **Selby and Sanderson** in Poughkeepsie, New York, from 1839 to 1941. (Information: Robert G. Wheeler, "The Potters of Albany," reprinted from *Antiques* in Stradling book, pp. 126, 131, 133. Marks: Erwin O. Christensen, *Early American Designs*, New York: Pitman Publishing Corporation, 1952, p. 11; no. 2, Stradling, p. 126.)

E. SELBY & CO
HUDSON NY
1.

SELBY & SANDERSON
PO, KEEPSIE N.Y.
2.

Selden Bybee Pottery Company of Lexington, Kentucky. New York City, New York. Late 1920's and early 1930's. Owner, Howard G. Selden had an importing and sales agency which filed a copyright on the word Bybee, preventing the Cornelisons in the Bybee Pottery from using that name for awhile. The mark shown was the one used by Selden Bybee Pottery Company. Around 1930 the Cornelison Bybee Pot-

tery regained legal right to the use of "Bybee Pottery," and the Selden Bybee Pottery Company went out of business during the Depression. The pottery sold by this company was described in Duke Coleman, "Letters and Such," *American Art Pottery*, January 1978, p. 3, as molded, dipped, with unique and interesting colors but not scarce. According to the same article, Cornelison Bybee Pottery manufactured products for Selden Bybee Pottery Company as did the **Tolbert Pottery**, also of Lexington and possibly the California Faience of Berkeley, California. Evans, *American Art Pottery*, p. 42, suggests the latter pottery only as a possible supplier to Selden Bybee. (Information: Chester Davis, "Bybee Pottery," *Spinning Wheel*, July, August 1973, p. 18. Mark: Duke Coleman as cited.)

1927 SELDEN BYBEE 506

Senegal China. Pelham, New York. Started around 1945. Listed as decorators in *1952 Crockery and Glass Journal Directory*, but not listed in 1954. The pottery was listed as making more vitrified decorative pieces such as vases, console sets, candy boxes, ashtrays, etc., also figurines. (Mark 1 found on small, green, heavy glazed cup and saucer in good grade of semi-porcelain. Mark 2 from *1945 Crockery and Glass Journal Directory*.

SENEGAL CHINA
1.

SENEGAL FINE CHINA
2.

Sevres China Company. East Liverpool, Ohio. The pottery existed for a few short years around 1900. Perhaps in this case it would be better to tell the succession that took place in a given building. Around 1862, Agner, Fouts and Company started a pottery in East Liverpool to make Rockingham and yellowware. The firm became Agner and Gaston, then the Sebring brothers arrived on the scene. The plant became the Sebring Pottery in 1887, and in 1900 the building housed Sevres China. Stout said the plant was sold to Sevres China as if it were a company that existed prior to 1900, but Barber said Sevres started in 1900. In 1910, the building belonged to Warner-Keffer China Company until around 1912 when it ceased operations. The Sebring brothers left the building around 1900 to go to the town of Sebring. In the 1908 *East Liverpool Directory*, p. 524, the name was still listed as Sevres China Company. They manufactured semi-porcelain and hotel ware dinner sets, toilet sets and short sets of odd dishes, some decorated.

MELTON

GENEVA

BERLIN

SÈVRES

SEVRES
HOTEL CHINA

Seymour (Israel, George W., Walter J., Henry P). Troy, New York. Between 1823 and 1885. The following information was sent by Warren F. Broderick, researcher and collector. Mark 1 was used by Israel Seymour, William Lundy and Nathan Church, Jr. between 1823 and 1827 known as **I. Seymour and Company**. In 1824, Nathan Church, Jr. opened a pottery of his own in Troy. Israel Seymour operated in Troy from 1818 to 1852, with his address at 44 Ferry Street after 1826. He used several marks: No. 2, "I. Seymour, Troy Factory," was one. He also used, "I. Seymour, Troy." and "I. Seymour, Troy Factory, 44 Ferry St." Walter J. Seymour made pottery from 1852 to 1885. His marks were similar to those of I. Seymour with Troy Factory and 44 Perry St. until 1861 when the marks became "Troy, N Y Pottery," and "Troy Pottery" alone, or "W.J. Seymour and Troy Pottery." Around 1850 to 1852, Israel Seymour's son, Walter, worked with him and the mark was "I. Seymour and Son, Troy." In 1852, Walter took over the pottery until 1858. In 1858, the pottery sold to Isaac Tyler and William Thompson who operated as **Tyler and Thompson**. That same year, Thompson died and Frederick Wetmore joined Tyler to become **Tyler and Company**. In 1860 Tyler died and in 1861 Walter Seymour was the owner again until 1885. When Walter died, Ira Carpenter purchased the pottery. In West Troy, New York, George Seymour made pottery in the **West Troy Pottery** from 1863 to 1867. Several potters who worked there at various times all used the mark, "West Troy Pottery." See the listing West Troy Pottery. There was also N. and A. Seymour in Rome, New York, from 1815 to around 1850 (Stewart and Consentino, p. 126). Also, see Seymour Brothers, Hartford, Connecticut, and Seymour and Stedman, Ravenna, Ohio. (Information: Broderick, as cited; Lura W. Watkins, "A Check List of New England Stoneware Potters," *Antiques*, August 1942, reprinted in Stradling, p. 80; Stewart and Consentino, p. 126. Marks: no. 1, Thorn, p. 147; no. 2, front cover of *Antique Trader Annual*, vol. X; and Guilland, p. 98; no. 3, 4, private collection-name withheld; nos. 5, 6, Broderick as cited. The Everson Museum of Art, Syracuse, New York, has a jug marked "W & A Seymour, Rome."

I. SEYMOUR & CO.
TROY
1.

I. SEYMOUR
TROY FACTORY
2.

W. J. SEYMOUR
TROY   N Y
44 FERRY ST
3.

TROY POTTERY
4.

I. SEYMOUR
5.

I SEYMOUR & SON
TROY
6.

Seymour Potters. Hartford, Connecticut. Israel T. Seymour was a potter in Troy, New York, around 1824 to 1850. His nephew, O.H. Seymour, was associated with Charles T. Webster in New Haven, Connecticut, for around 10 years from approximately 1857 to 1867. The firm then became Seymour and Brothers in 1867. The brother was Henry Phelps Seymour, who died in 1867. O.H. Seymour then took Stanley B. Bosworth as a partner and they operated through the 1880's. (See the listing for M.C. Webster for those marks. Also see the listing Seymour and Stedman, Ravenna, Ohio.)

(Information: Lura W. Watkins, *Early New England Potters and Their Wares*, pp. 194-195. Mark 1 in the column "Antiques and Americana," by George Michael in *Antique Trader Weekly*, November 26, 1980, two double jugs joined at the side are pictured marked "Stedman, Seymour, New Haven." Mark 2, Stewart and Consentino, *Stoneware*, p. 72.)

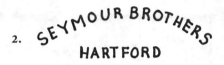

STEDMAN, SEYMOUR
NEW HAVEN   1.

2. **SEYMOUR BROTHERS**
HARTFORD

Seymour and Stedman. Ravenna, Ohio. Around 1850. There was a family of potters named Seymour who made pottery in Hartford and New Haven, Connecticut, in the late 1850's through the 1880's, according to Lura W. Watkins, *Early New England Potters and Their Wares*, p. 195. One of these Seymours was in partnership with a man named Stedman in Ravenna, Ohio, around 1850 making stoneware with the impressed mark shown, according to John Ramsay, p. 228. Ramsay said Seymour came from Connecticut. There was a Absolam Stedman in Hartford, Connecticut, around 1818 who was in partnership with Daniel Goodale, Jr. (Mark: Thorn, p. 147.)

SEYMOUR-STEDMAN
RAVENNA, O.

Shacter, Mayer. 1965 to present (1983). Mayer Shacter, a studio potter, has been making pottery since 1965 in various locations in California. From 1965 to 1968 he operated the **Venice Pottery Gallery** in Venice, California with five assistants. They sold wholesale and also operated a retail business, held classes and fired ware for other potters. From 1968 to 1972 he had the **Point Arena Studio** in Point Arena, California, where he built a home with studio attached. From 1972 to 1975 he operated the **Old Creamery Pottery** in Manchester, California, which was a private studio where he employed five assistants. From 1975 to 1980 he had **Shacter Stoneware and Porcelain** in San Francisco, California, which was a large production studio employing six. From 1980 to present (1983) he has been operating a private studio in Oakland, California. Until 1979, Shacter made functional and decorative stoneware, but since that time he has been working exclusively with porcelain making one of a kind pieces which are both functional and decorative. A copper red porcelain vase made by Shacter was pictured in *Ceramics Monthly*, May 1982, p. 93. Shacter taught at Napa College in Napa, California, in 1982, conducting workshops, teaching classes and training over 30 apprentice potters. He has pieces in 11 collections such as the Oakland Museum and many others. He listed 15 galleries showing his work across the country from Illinois to Texas and Oregon. His education was extensive, including his study under Vivika and Otto Heino at the Chouinard Art Institute. He has produced functional and one of a kind pieces in stoneware from 1970 to 1979. Since then he has been working exclusively in one of a kind, porcelain, functional and non-functional. All major one of a kind pieces are signed since 1970. Some minor work is signed. Since 1965 the stamps shown are on minor pieces.

Shafer, G.C. Pottery Company. Zanesville, Ohio. 1939 to 1980. A decorator working out of a small shop in the rear of his home on Merrick Avenue. He owned his own molds that other companies used to make the ware that Shafer decorated with gold lustre, decals and an overglaze. Mark was stamped on most pieces. (Information: Lehner, *Ohio Pottery and Glass*, p. 99.)

Shafer
23 K Gold
Guaranteed

DECORATED BY
G.C. SHAFER
ZANESVILLE, OHIO

NIAGARA LUSTER
by Shafer

Mc Coy vase
Decorate By
23 K. GOLD
GUARANTEED
SHAFER USA
ZANESVILLE
OHIO

Shafer, Thomas. Columbus, Ohio. 1965 to present. Thomas Shafer, a studio potter, makes functional and decorative stoneware and porcelain. He has won awards for 30 juried and invitational exhibitions in 14 or 15 one-man shows. He has collections in 11 museums. He has had six articles published in the *Ceramics Monthly* and also two books on pottery. "Shafer" an incised signature is the mark he uses and also sometimes the year. This potter gave no further particulars about the exhibitions, awards or articles on the questionnaire he completed.

SHAFER

Shanahan, Mary Jury. Columbus, Ohio. 1980 to present (1987). Mary is a studio potter making wheel thrown stoneware pieces with incised and hand painted decorations. She graduated from Ohio State University in 1970, then taught art for a time and became a full time potter in 1980. She has done Colony Craftsman shows and the Worthington Folk Festival in addition to numerous local arts and crafts shows. Mark is incised.

M J Shan

Shaner, David. David, a professor, studio potter, received his M.F.A. degree in ceramic design from Alfred University, in Alfred, New York, in 1959. From 1959 to 1963 he was assistant professor of art at the University of Illinois in Champaign. From 1963 to 1970, he was the resident potter and director of the Archie Bray Foundation in Helena, Montana. Since 1970 he has operated his own pottery near Big Fork, Montana, making mostly functional ware. Shaner has won many awards, including the Louis Comfort Tiffany scholarship in 1963 and the National Endowment for the Arts Fellowship in 1973 and 1978. The mark shown is a paper sticker. (Information: Garth Clark, *A Century of Ceramics in the U.S.*, pp. 326, 327. Mark: Linda Steigleder, from the booklet published by the Everson Museum of Art to accompany the 1978 exhibition, "A Century of Ceramics in the U.S.")

Shaw, James M., and Company. New York, New York. A selling agency filed for a claim on this mark January 3, 1928, for use on plates, fruit saucers, bowls, platters, butter chips, vegetable dishes, pitchers, sauce boats, sugar bowls, mustard pots, teapots, coffeepots, casseroles, baking dishes, custard cups, cream bottles, bean pots, celery trays, pickle dishes, comports, chop-suey casseroles, cups and saucers made of china, porcelain and earthenware, claiming use of this mark since 1907. See Warwick China Company, D.E. McNicol Pottery and Buffalo China Company, for American companies that made china for this company to sell.

Shawnee Creek Kilns. Germantown, Ohio. A decorating shop of some sort in the 1950's. No listings at all in Montgomery County, Ohio, in the 1960's in the *Dictionary of Ohio Manufacturers*. A letter to Germantown brought no response, only that no listings could be found. (Mark: found on souvenir plate.)

GREENVILLE, OHIO
"The Treaty City"

Greenville is a city steeped in historical background and famed as the site of the signing of the Treaty of Greene Ville in 1795 which cemented peace between the pioneers and the Indians of Ohio. The City Hall, erected in 1875 on the Public Square and torn down in 1951, was one of Greenville's familiar old land marks.

SHAWNEE CREEK KILNS
Germantown, Ohio

Shawnee Pottery Company. Zanesville, Ohio. 1937 to 1961. Made molded decorative ware and kitchenware and cookie jars, etc. Such as casseroles, flower containers, art ware such as fluted bowls in Cameo pattern, tall vases in Fairy Wood, planters in rustic mills and wishing wells and smiling pigs. Several later patterns which were quite successful included Cameo, Fairy Wood, Chantilly and Elegance. Also Touche, which had a rough finish and Petit Point, which resembled a metal finish. The Corn-Queen Ware which has become very much collected was marked just "Oven Proof" most of the time. "Shawnee" in script is the mark most commonly use by Shawnee when they used a mark at all. Much was marked with just a paper label. "Kenwood" so marked was a division of Shawnee. For about a year, around 1941 to 1942, Shawnee made pottery for the Rum Rill Pottery Company which was a distributing company from Little Rock, Arkansas, with a battery of salesmen who sold all over the United States. Mark 1 was filed for a patent on June 27, 1945, for use on kitchenware made of pottery, namely food containers, cooky jars, range sets, teapots, sugars, creamers, milk pitchers, water pitchers, salt cellars, pepper cellars, grease jars, waffle sets, claiming use since May 1, 1945. Mark 2 was filed on January 4, 1944, for use on ceramic table and cooking ware claiming use since September 16, 1943. Mark 3 was filed on November 27, 1937, for pottery table, kitchen and household hollow ware, claiming use since October 11, 1937. Mark 4 was filed on October 21, 1938 for pottery table and kitchen ware, particularly bowls, plates, dishes, pitchers, cups and saucers, claiming use since July 15, 1938. Marks 5 and 6 found on pieces. Marks 7, 8, paper labels. Marks 9, 10, 11 incised. Marks 10, 11, on cookie jars. Mark 12 on Shawnee gold rooster. Mark 13 filed for registration on May 21, 1958 for vases, jardinieres, planters, flower pots, window boxes, etc. made from clay, claiming use of this mark since December 1955.)

1.

2.

3.

MISSION

4.

KENWOOD

5.

6.

7.

8.

9.

10.

PATENTED
Smiley
USA
11.

PATENTED
Chanticlier
USA
12.

SORCERY IN CERAMICS 13.

Shaw, Richard. Shaw received his B.F.A. degree from the San Francsco Art Institute in 1965, and an M.A. from the University of California, in 1968. At an exhibition in the San Francisco Museum of Modern Art in 1973 the ceramic objects shown by Shaw were in the forms of birds, deer hooves, decoy ducks, twigs, branches, etc. Shaw was instrumental in the development of the "Super Object," which was supposed to be some attempt to express the subconscious mental activities and presenting images without order or sequence or congruency. Pictured in Garth Clark, *A Century of Ceramics in the U.S.*, p. 278, is a bottle in the form of an ax in a stump. Also on p. 239 is pictured "Blue Goose" with a blue goose on a striped pole sitting on a book. The pieces seem to come right out of a dream, and I assume that was the idea of the work. See the book cited for a thorough discussion of this artist's work, pp. 328, 329. (Mark: painted; Linda Steigleder, from the booklet published by the Everson Museum of Art to accompany the 1978 exhibition, "A Century of Ceramics in the U.S.," with curators: Garth Clark and Margie Hughto.)

SHAW

Shawsheen Pottery. Pottery was in Billerica, Massachusetts, in 1906 and was moved to Mason City, Iowa, in 1907. Edward and Elizabeth Dahlquist were art students in Minneapolis and later at the Art Institute in Chicago. They turned from painting to hand crafting beautiful art pottery due to the influence of Lucy Perkins of the Brush Guild of New York City. The Guild built clay forms in the earliest Etruscan tradition. They used no machinery in production; not even a potter's wheel was used. The Shawsheen Pottery pieces were hand coiled and had the same Etruscan colors and tones of bronze and copper. Decorations were incised or excised with wooden tools. Later the Dahlquists started throwing some of their pieces on a wheel but they still did all of the aspects of making a piece of pottery by themselves, the throwing, glazing, firing, etc. They also taught classes in ceramics and Edward joined the staff of the University City Pottery as an instructor of hand or slab built pottery for a year or so until 1911. Shortly after, they moved to Chicago and spent most of their time teaching. About 1915 they stopped making any pottery for sale. (Information and imprinted or incised marks: Paul Evans, *Art Pottery of the U.S.*, pp. 270, 271. Many pieces were not marked at all.)

Shearwater Pottery. Ocean Springs, Mississippi. 1928 to present. G.W. Anderson ran the business and his son, Peter, was the potter when the business was founded in 1928. Peter's brothers, Walter I. and James McConnell Anderson (called Mac) worked with Peter after 1930. (No author, "G.W. Anderson," *American Ceramic Society Bulletin*, June 1927, sent with page no.) G.W. died in 1937. In 1941 in Stile's book, p. 190, she describes the unusual shapes covered with glazes the Andersons manufactured. They also made carved decorative designs or added slip for color and texture. They made artistic pottery with fish figures, etc., whatever inspired them in the area in which they lived. The pottery was sold in Boston, Philadelphia, New York and also locally. Then in August 1973, no author, "The Pottery of Shearwater," *Pottery Collectors Newsletter*, p. 138, Peter Anderson and his son, Jim (not to be confused with his Uncle James), were still making pottery digging their own clay and still making their own glazes. But Peter died in December 1984, and Jim became master potter. Mac, a brother of Peter, is still decorating and designing. The younger members of the family are doing most of the potting (from pottery by telephone). Dave Rago, "American Art Pottery," a weekly article in *Antique Trader*, May 14, 1980, p. 74, has this to say about Shearwater marks: "The identification of Shearwater Pottery is easy; however, the definite dating of pieces is not too easy. Ink stamp and impressed marks were used. The marks have the name, "Shearwater," inside a circle. The half inch diameter ink stamp was used before 1960. The three quarter inch ink stamp mark was used after 1960. An impressed circular mark has been used since about 1950. Artist signatures were also used. Peter Anderson marked his pots with the letter "A' connected to the bottom of the letter "P." James McConnell Anderson or Mac first signed pieces with a small "A" attached to an "M." This was changed in the late 1940's to "JMcCA," which he still uses. Walter used no artist signature, but his pieces are distinctive.

(Information: Don Brewer and Burdell Hall by letter. Both are research writers who visited the pottery. Also Rago, as cited. Marks: At one time there was a rectangular stamp, see mark 2, The grandmother of Peter Anderson stated she has only seen it once. This was stamped in the clay. This was followed by a half inch circular stamp with the name "Shearwater" before 1960, followed by a three-fourth inch stamp the same after 1960 in the clay, see mark 3. At times the stamp was misplaced and Shearwater was handwritten on the piece. If it got through the process without a stamp in the clay a half inch circular rubber ink stamp was used. This has been seen on 1929 pieces. Peter Anderson signed his work with a stylized "PA," see mark 4. Very few pieces have been found with this mark. Peter's pieces were also created with molds and repeated as jiggered wares. These have just the Shearwater mark and do not identify the decorator. James McConnell Anderson signed his pieces "J McC A," as shown in mark 5. From the late 1940's figurines designed by Walter and James have only an incised mark as shown in mark 6, or the small block rubber stamp. Currently, pieces are marked with mark 7. Whoever decorates a pot signs it with their initials or name as well as the Shearwater sign. Mark 1 on piece at American Ceramic Society's Ross Purdy Museum in Columbus. Nos. 2-7, Don Brewer, as cited.)

 1.

2.

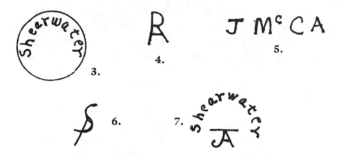

Shelbina Pottery Company, Inc. Shelbina, Missouri. 1947 to 1963. Harold T. Homan had worked as a ceramic consultant in potteries which made sanitary ware for over 25 years before starting his own sanitary ware factory. The company never did make a business of art ware, but did make a few pieces for employees and a very limited amount to sell. Mr. Homan said the last thing they made was a head of Mark Twain, which he molded from clay and built a mold around it, then fired the pieces to a high vitreous china. Another piece he remembered was a Busch Stadium ashtray (home of the St. Louis Cardinals). The pottery also made vases, planters, jardinieres, etc. The art ware was not marked and most of it will not be identified, but they are undoubtedly beautiful pieces. The label shown was used on sanitary ware. In 1963, the pottery was sold to Allied Research and Development Corporation, and closed completely in 1966.

SHELBINA POTTERY Co.

Shenandoah Pottery. See Paden City Pottery.

Shenango China Company. In 1901, two companies were started in New Castle, Pennsylvania. The **New Castle Pottery Company** (1901 to 1905) built a six-kiln plant at the present location of Shenango China on West Grant Street. Also in 1901, Shenango China was incorporated in New Castle on the north side of Emery Street. Shenango China Company and New Castle Pottery Company were both listed in 1902 as making semi-porcelain dinner sets, toilet sets and short sets of odd dishes, some decorated. Shenango employed approximately 150 people. Very quickly Shenango China got into financial difficulty and a receiver was appointed, the company reorganized and a new charter taken under the name **Shenango Pottery Company**. More financial trouble followed until in 1909 when an entire new group took over the property headed by James MacMath Smith as president and treasurer. Under his direction the company began to get established in the industry after nine hard years of struggle. The plant of the New Castle Pottery Company was purchased in 1912, and Shenango moved to Grant Street. In 1913, just as all of the machinery was in place and the plant ready to go, a flood put three feet of water in the entire plant. But under the direction of Smith the plant prospered slowly but surely, because Smith was a man who would not quit trying. If a machine didn't do what he wanted it to, he built his own. He started having raw feldspar shipped directly to the plant and ground there as one of his innovations. Actually, James M. Smith was a novice to the pottery business when he started, but he came to be regarded as the real founder of

Shenango China Company. There were some distinct advantages for the potteries in New Castle, such as soft coal which burned clean, and money from the men of the steel industry for capital. All that was needed was real leadership, and Shenango gained that in James M. Smith. ("James MacMath Smith, President of Shenango Pottery," *Bulletin of the American Ceramic Society*, XX, June 1941, p. 163.) In 1928, the Shenango Pottery Company ran porcelain trials researching a vitrified fine china dinnerware product. The depression and its aftermath kept Shenango manufacturing the same very durable type of hotel ware that they had made since 1909. Then in 1936 a great change came. William Haviland, representing the Theodore Haviland Company of Limoges, France, came to American looking for a company to make Haviland China in America. I found several reasons for this change. McKee suggested that the Havilands may have sensed the coming war with Hitler. The *American Ceramic Society Bulletin*, said the high duties on Haviland china coming to America and mounting costs made it impossible to continue manufacturing in France for American markets. From 1936 to 1958, Shenango Pottery Company made china for the Theodore Haviland Company of France, using their formula, blocks, cases, decals, etc., which the Havilands brought over here. This ware was marketed with the trademark, "Haviland, New York."

In 1939, Mr. Louis E. Hellman, American representative for the famous Rosenthal China of Germany, came to Shenango and arranged to have Rosenthal's shapes and patterns made at Shenango. In 1940, another great collectible was born when the first Castleton China entered the market manufactured by **Castleton China, Inc.** Shenango Pottery had $25,000 invested in this new company, Castleton China, Inc., but not until 1951 did Shenango purchase all of the stock from Louis E. Hellman. At that time, Shenango took over the sales as well as the manufacture of Castleton China, a very fine dinnerware line, which they made until around 1970. The aim in creating Castleton China was to create a fine china by combining the age-old craftsmanship of Europe with the technological superiority of America. Louis E. Hellman, an expert in European porcelains, wanted contemporary design in fine tableware, both in shape and decoration, and he hired the world's outstanding artists to create new designs. (Floyd W. McKee, *A Century of American Dinnerware Manufacture*, privately printed, 1966, p. 38.)

One of the most notable achievements in ceramic art is Castleton "Museum" shape, the first freeform modern shape in fine china. Designed by Eva Zeisel, it was created by Castleton under the auspices of the Museum of Modern Art. It was hailed in Europe and American as marking a new epoch in ceramic history. Castleton studio patterns were entirely hand-crafted and executed to order by skilled craftsmen.

In 1955, Castleton was commissioned by Mamie Eisenhower to create a formal design for gold service plates for the state dining room in the White House. Another design was created to commemorate President Eisenhower's "first birthday" in the White House and was presented to those attending a birthday party given for him by the Pennsylvania Republican Party at Hershey, Pennsylvania, in 1953. The plates are decorated with intertwined doves in a Pennsylvania Dutch symbol signifying love and peace.

In 1968, a set of Castleton China was manufactured by Shenango for the Johnson administration to present to the White House as a state service. This consisted of 216 place settings of 10 pieces each plus large and small centerpiece bowls. Castleton dinnerware also graced the tables of many foreign heads of state.

Castleton China made a series of game plates, all 10¾" in diameter, with the following game: California Quail, Mountain Quail, Woodcock, Prairie Chicken, Dog and Birds, Ring-necked Pheasant. A line of everyday china called "Peter Terris" was made at Shenengo for a short time in the 1950's.

An excerpt taken from company furnished history gives many of the hardships encountered by Shenango. The terrible hard ships caused by today's high energy costs and foreign competition are part of a long struggle endured by all of our American potters and potteries.

"By 1949 Shenango had grown ten times in ten years, but the growth was in sales it did not control; i.e. government ware and dinnerware. Through a number of circumstances, the Company was again in financial straits, one of which was that the very expensive expansion program had been made without any long term financing; second, Haviland and Rosenthal of Europe were back in business; third, huge backlogs were being produced at fixed prices when the final blow was struck. The winter of 1948-49 was an extremely cold one over extended periods of time and the company had been forced to get standby oil to keep operating. Suddenly, the sulphur content in the oil went above normal and every piece of glost ware came out of the kilns with matt glaze and had to be thrown out.

Application was made to Reconstruction Finance Corporation for a long term loan. This was approved with the backing of the Pittsburg First National Bank and short term loans were paid off. A loan of $648,000 was paid off in five years.

In the Fall of 1950, contract negotiations with the C.I.O. -- USWA broke off and the union called a strike which lasted eleven days. This marked the first serious labor problem with the C.I.O. Added to the other financial problems which had been encountered even this comparatively short strike hurt the company.

In 1951 Shenango China purchased all the stock of Castleton China, Inc. from Mr. Louis E. Hellman and took over the sales as well as the manufacture of the Castleton fine china dinnerware line.

In the Fall of 1953, once again contract negotiations with the Union were broken off with a strike that lasted for forty-three days and had a drastic effect on the company fortunes. Let it be noted that the Union finally settled for the offer made by the Company just prior to the strike.

The name of the Company was changed to **Shenango China, Inc.** on August 1, 1954, bringing it back to the same name of September 3, 1901, the date of the bankrupt Shenango China.

In 1956, Shenango's efforts to mechanize were culminated by the development of the first "Fast-Fire" kiln which revolutionized the vitrified china industry. For the first time we had a kiln that would fire glost ware that normally took from thirty-six to forty hours as fast as one hour and ten minutes.

Settlement of the Minority Stockholders suit caused the Trustees of the Smith Estate to sell the controlling interest of Shenango to Sobiloff Brothers, who also offered the same opportunity to other stockholders. Early in 1959, all of the shares were finally purchased by Sobiloff.

In January 1959, Shenango bought Wallace China in California. Operated as a wholly owned subsidiary, adding $1 million in sales, principally on the West Coast.

After Shenango was purchased by Sobiloffs the working capital of the company was pledged for loans to finance other Sobiloff interests.

In 1961, all of the assets of Shenango China, Inc. were transferred to a newly formed, totally held subsidiary, **Shenango Ceramics, Inc.** held by the Sobiloffs.

In September 1964, Mayer China Company, Beaver Falls, PA, was purchased by the Sobiloffs, rounding out $1 million of prestige, quality sales in the Hotelware field.

Following a serious loss in inventory at Wallace China Company during an outside audit, in 1963, which was the result of figuring the inventory incorrectly over a period of years, Wallace China was liquidated late in 1964.

In 1968, the assets of Shenango Ceramics, Inc., including its two wholly owned subsidiaries, Castleton China, Inc. and Mayer China Company, were sold by Sobiloffs to Interpace Corporation, who already manufactured Franciscan earthenware and fine china on the West Coast.''

In June 2,, 1979, Shenango China Company became the property of the Anchor Hocking Corporation and have remained so to the present (January 1985), manufacturing a fine line of hotel, restaurant and institutional ware.

Shenango Date Code

From 1950

Note: First column letter is Jan.-June. Second column is July-Dec. Ex: 20 A was made July-Dec. 1962.

1950	8 M A	1958	16 V I	1967	25 Q F
1951	9 N B	1959	17 W J	1968	26 R 6
1952	10 O C	1960	18 X K	1969	27 T H
1953	11 P D	1961	19 Y L	1970	28 M A
1954	12 Q E	1962	20 Z A	1971	29 N B
1955	13 R F	1963	21 M B	1972	30 O C
Note S not used		1964	22 N C	1973	31 P D
1956	14 T G	1965	23 O D	1974	32 Q E
1957	15 U H	1966	24 P E		

Shenango had a shop in the factory where decals and stamps were made. The marks with the words "Castleton China" would date between 1940 and 1968. Interpace marks would come between 1968 and 1979. The mark "Innkare," was found in Sterling China Company's marks also. "Kenmark China" was found in Homer Laughlin China's marks also. "Arcadian" was also a mark used by Jackson China Company. (Information: company information; and Lehner, *American Kitchen and Dinner Wares*, pp. 136-139. Marks: no. 1, very old mark from Barber, *Marks of American Potters*, p. 34; no. 2 filed by Castle China, Inc., New York, New York, for registration, November 15, 1941, claiming use since September 6, 1940, for use on ceramic tableware; no. 3 filed by Castleton China, Inc., New York, New York, July 5, 1947, claiming use since September 6, 1940, for use on china tableware and china art objects, not ornamented with precious metals, namely vases and centerpieces, consisting of a tray and bowl; no. 4 filed by Castleton China, Inc., New York, New York, on July 5, 1947, claiming use since June 26, 1947, for use on exactly the same objects as mark 3; no. 5 filed for registration on July 26, 1940, claiming use since October 1939 for use on ceramic tableware; no. 6 showing several marks is an advertisement from Hotel Management, July 1946, shown in an effort to help date the marks that follow; nos. 7-8-9 are early marks from Quality Stamp Company, East Liverpool, Ohio; nos. 10-11 are marks for Peter Ferris line made for a short time in the middle 1950's (date furnished by Lou Walls at Shenango); no. 12, probably a paper label as shown in *Crockery and Glass Journal* directories of the 1940's used on a line of cookware; no. 13, sent by Waldorf Stamping Device, New London, Ohio; nos. 14-35 are marks sent by Mr. Lou Walls at Shenango China Company. These marks are small decals. Mr. Walls said only rubber stamps were used on commercial ware after 1948, but some of the fine china still had decaled marks after that time. The decaled marks could have several colors in a single mark. Nos. 36-37 are shown in Father Sandkop's book, *Nothing Could Be Finer*, pp. 59, 64; no. 38, drawn and sent by Jean Fowles; nos. 39-40, marks sent by Larry Paul; nos. 41-45, on dishes. No. 46, for some reason, Homer Laughlin China and Shenango China filed for registration on the word, "Epicure," for ceramic tableware and cookware in the year 1955. Homer Laughlin filed in March and Shenango China in May. The marks are very similar. See Homer Laughlin. Shenango claimed use since March 6, 1950, where as Homer Laughlin claimed use only after March 22, 1955. (Information: company information; and Lehner, *American Kitchen and Dinner Wares*, pp. 136-139. Marks: no. 1, very old mark from Barber, *Marks of American Potters*, p. 34; no. 2 filed by Castle China, Inc.; nos. up to 129 were filed in the Shenango Pottery Company's name before 1950 and Shenango China, Inc. in 1956 and after. Nos. 130 and 131 were filed by Haviland and Company, New York. Nos. 132 to 190 were filed in the name Castleton China Company, Inc. Nos. 191 to 207 were filed by the Interpace Corporation in their name; nos. 208 to 216 were filed by the Anchor Hocking Corporation. No. 47 is an important mark filed in August 1950 because the company claimed use since January 1, 1927. No. 48 was filed August 1, 1950, claiming use since 1912. These two organizations help to date the various Indian marks sent by the company. No. 49, the word Shenango was filed in August 1950, but use was claimed since September 30, 1909. No. 50 was also filed in August 1950, claiming use since January 1942. Most of the balance of the marks filed under the Shenango China, Inc. name for china or restaurant dinnerware were said to be used for only a short time before registration in that case only the registration date is listed including no. 51 filed in September 1954, used only since July of that year. No. 52 through 56 were all filed in 1954 for restaurant china dinnerware. No. 57 was filed in 1954 for clay refractory articles such as saggers, cranks, racks, tilesetters, burner blocks, etc. Nos. 58 through 68 were filed in 1956 for china dinnerware. Nos. 69 to 71 were filed in 1957. No. 72 was used longer before filing. Shepoco was filed in December 1958 and in use on or before 1935. No. 73 also filed in 1958. No. 74 to 77 were filed in 1959, as was no. 78, but no. 78, Rimrol, was used since February 13, 1939. No. 79 to 82 were filed in 1960. Nos. 83 to 88 filed in 1961. No. 89, Independence, was filed in July 1962, but first used in October 1939. Nos. 90 to 93 were also filed in 1962. Nos. 97 to 103 filed in 1963. Nos. 104, 105 filed 1964. Nos. 106 to 113 filed in 1965. Nos. 114 to 122 filed in 1966. Nos. 123 to 129 filed in 1967. No. 130 filed 1958. No. 131 filed 1960. Nos. 132 to 190 were filed in the name of Castleton China, Inc. and were all for fine china tableware. No. 132 was filed July 1950 and used since September 23, 1949. Nos. 133 to 136 were filed in 1956. No. 137 was filed in 1957. Nos. 138 to 144 filed in 1958. Nos. 145 to 147 filed in 1959. Nos. 148 to 150 filed in 1961. Nos. 151 to 160 filed in 1962. Nos. 161 to 165 filed in 1963. Nos. 166, 167 filed in 1964. Nos. 168 to 180 filed in 1965. Nos. 181 to 188 filed in 1966. Nos. 189, 190 filed in 1968. The following nos. 191 to 207 were filed in the name of the Interpace Corporation. Nos. 191 to 197 were all fired in 1968. Desert Rose was filed for dinnerware of earthenware, all of the others were for china dinnerware.

Also, Desert Rose was the only pattern the company claimed long use for prior to registration. First use on Desert Rose was February 1941. The rest were filed within a year or so of first use. Nos. 198 to 206 were filed in 1969. All of the 1970's were not researched for patents. The first half of the 1980's was covered pretty thoroughly though. No. 207 was filed September 1978 for ceramic dinnerware, namely plates, cups, saucers, serving platters, bowls, soup plates, creamers, sugar bowls, etc., claiming use since December 28, 1977. Nos. 208 to 211 were filed in the name Anchor Hocking Corporation in 1980. No. 208, "Cameron," was for ceramic dinnerware. No. 209, "Aunt Jenny's," was for glass and ceramic ovenware, namely bowls, casseroles, platters, tumblers, drinking glasses, also glass and ceramic servingware. No. 212 was filed in 1981. Nos. 213, 214 were filed in 1982. Nos. 212 to 214 were filed for the same glass and ceramic products as listed in no. 209. Nos. 215, 216 were both filed in August 1984 for ceramic dinnerware, claiming first use since June 1984. Nos. 217 to 218 were used on railroad china and are from Richard Luckin, *Dining On Rails*, pp. 131 and 158. The rest are stamped marks sent by Shenango China; a few from Quality Stamp Company of East Liverpool, Ohio; and some are photostatic copies from dishes.)

1.

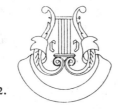

2.

CASTLETON CHINA

3.

MaLin

4.

5.

The Trade Marks
of Supremacy in China

6.

7.

SHENANGO
NEW CASTLE, PA.
CHINA

8.

9.

Peter Terris

10.

Peter Terris,
real china
for everyday
T©14
SHENANGO CHINA INC.

11.

EPICURE
CERAMIC
COOK WARE

12.

SHENANGO CHINA
NEW CASTLE, PA. U.S.A.
ANCHOR HOCKING
A M-41

13.

MADE·USA·REG US PAT OFF
CASTLETON CHINA
BY INTERPACE

14.

SHENANGO CHINA
NEW CASTLE, PA.

15.

Theodore Haviland
New York
MADE IN AMERICA

16.

Inca ware
Shenango China
New Castle, Pa.
U.S.A.

17.

royal sentinel
CHINA MADE IN U.S.A BY SHENANGO

18.

Royal Medallion China
MADE IN USA   BY SHENANGO

19.

Colony House
FINE CHINA
BY CASTLETON, U.S.A

20.

Inca ware
Shenango China
New Castle, Pa.
U.S.A.

21.

Reynolds
FINE CHINA
BY SHENANGO
USA

22.

CASTLETON STUDIOS
BY INTERPACE

23.

CASTLETON STUDIOS
MADE IN U.S.A
EXCLUSIVELY FOR Saladmaster

24.

Castleton China, Inc
Bx 120, New Castle, Pa.

25.

CASTLETON
CHINA
REG. U.S. PAT. OFF

26.

Stonehenge
CHINA FOR Lifetime
SHENANGO U.S.A.

27.

SHENANGO CHINA
NEW CASTLE, PA. U.S.A.
© INTERPACE
C H-35

28.

SHENANGO
FINE CHINA
U.S.A.

29.

SHENANGO
CHINA U.S.A.
BY INTERPACE

30.

31.

32.
GATEWAY CHINA
BY SHENANGO
MADE IN U.S.A.

33.
CRO
BOUTIQUE
FINE CHINA BY SHENANGO
USA

34.
shenango ©

35.
SHENANGO CHINA
NEW CAST. PA.

36.
1827 1927
BALTIMORE AND OHIO
RAILROAD
SHENANGO CHINA
NEW CASTLE, PA.

37.
STATE FLOWER
MOUNTAIN LAUREL
OF PENNSYLVANIA
PRR
MADE FOR THE Pennsylvania Railroad
SHENANGO CHINA
NEW CASTLE PA.

38.
AMERICAN MANOR CHINA
made in USA by shenango
CHANTILLY

39.
IVORY
SHENANGO CHINA

40.
SHENANGO CHINA
NEW CASTLE PA
USA

41.
Staffordshire
A PRODUCT OF
SHENANGO POTTERY CO
NEW CASTLE IN USA

42.
SHENANGO CHINA
NEW CASTLE, PA.

43.
RimRol
PAT NO.

SHENANGO
CHINA USA
INTEPACE
A 28
43.

44.
INDEPENDENCE
IRONSTONE
by Castleton China, Inc.
MADE IN JAPAN

45.
INDEPENDENCE
WHITESTONE
by INTERPACE
MKT JAPAN

46.
Epicure

47.

48.

49.
SHENANGO

50.
Inca

51.

52.
DUO-GRIP

53.
Terraceware

54. UNI-TROL

MICRO-MIX 55.

56. STA-GLAZE

BALTRANITE 57.

58. TROPIC

EL DORADO 59.

60. GOLDMER

NORDIC POINT
61.

62.
VITRIFIED
Lawrence
MADE IN
U.S.A.
CHINA

SWEET GRASS 63.

CHARPINX
64.

CALICO LEAVES
65.

PLATE MATE
66.

WOODMERE
67.

ASTRID 68.

69. VITREX

LINNEA 70.

71. MOONMIST

SHEPOCO
72.

HAWAIIAN HUES
73.

FLEETWOOD 74.

CRESCENT 75.

76. LIDO

MONACO
77.

RIMROL
78.

DEL RAY
79.

MEADOWLARK 80.

81. BUCKINGHAM

PARAKEET 82.   83. TUXEDO GOLD

APOLLO 84. 85. COUNTRY KITCHEN

BEAUTY-LOK 86.   87. TRU-FOOT

CARLTON 88.   89. INDEPENDENCE

LAURENTIAN 90.   91. FRANCINE

FöRM 92.   VICTORIA ROSE 93.

ESQUIRE 94.   SPYR 95.   SVAR 96.

MEDITERRANEAN 97.   98. LYF

NöT 99.   KöNE 100.   TUö 101.

TRIA 102.   SOM 103.   WEXFORD 104.

PAVILION 105.   GILD 106.   CRESTVIEW 107.

AMY 108.   ME TOO 109.   ELSA 110.

STRä 111.   LEMONT 112.   SUTTON 113.

ROUEN 114.   CAROUSEL 115.   CITATION 116.

FRONTENAC 117.   118. C'BON

DUXBURY 119.   120. COVINGTON

GARLAND 121.   PONTCHARTRAIN 122.

AMERICAN MANOR CHINA 123.   LARONDO 124.

CASTILE 125.   GALLANTE 126.   JET SET 127.

DEVEREAUX 128.   PALOS VERDES 129.

RIVIERA 130.   HOME AND HOSTESS 131.

-GREEN THUMB- 132.   LA COSTA 133.

SYMMETRA 134.   135. CONTEMPO

LAVALLIERE 136.   TROUSSEAU 137.

ARIEL 138.   139. CELESTIAL

MAYTIME 140.   CASTELLANA 141.

CERES 142.   143. WOODSPRITE

Everyday China 144.   WHITE LILY 145.

WARDROBE OF CHINA 146.

147. WILD STRAWBERRY

GOLDEN CLASSIC 148.

149. CLASSIC SCROLL

SOPHISTICATE 150.   HICKORY 151.

INDEPENDENCE WHITE 152.

153. OLD ORCHARD

PLYMOUTH ROSE 154.

155. SHENANDOAH

SCANDIA 156.   157. ASH LAWN

NANTUCKET 158.   159. DAUPHINE

160. GOLDEN MEDALLION

POMPEII 161.   ELYSIUM 162.   CORDOVA 163.

CLASSICA 164.   165. RAVENNA

GOLDEN MOMENT 166.

BITTERSWEET 167.   168. CONCERTO

CAPELLA   GOLDEN MELODY
169.   170.

BOLERO CRESCENDO ANDANTE
171.   172.   173.

INTERMEZZO 174.   175. CELESTA

GOLDEN SCROLL 176.

PROVINCIAL FLOWER 177.

FELICITY 178.   179. MUSICALLE

OVERTURE 180.   181. QUADRILLE

LA BOHEME 182.   183. ARIA

FOREVER AFTER   FANTASIA
184.   185.

MADRIGAL 186.   187. WOODSPRITE

FLAMENCO   CROWN WREATH
188.   189.

FILIGREE 190.   191. NOUVELLE

INDIGO   BAROQUE SCROLL
192.   193.

SIBONNET   MIDAS   CHABLIS
194.   195.   196.

DESERT ROSE 197.   198. VERDA

SOUVENIR 199.   200. GRAPHICA

MOON GLOW   NOVA   MAGNA
201.   202.   203.

CARRIAGEHOUSE   MAJESTIC
204.   205.

SIGNA 206.   207. THE NATURALS

CAMERON 208. 209. AUNT JENNY'S

WE SET THE TABLE FOR
AMERICA
210.

WE SET THE TABLE FOR   211.
AMERICA'S FOOD SERVICE

212.   SETTING THE TABLE FOR
AMERICA

KITCHEN CLASSICS   213.

Anchor 214.
Ovenware

ANCHO 215.   216.

217.

Inca ware
Shenango China
New Castle, Pa.
Designed Especially
for
Erie Railroad
218.

CASTLETON
of course
the finest choice
in fine china
219.   220.

CASTLETON
CHINA
the finest choice
in fine china

CASTLETON   CASTLETON   222.
CHINA   CHINA
GLORIA
221.

223.   SHENANGO CHINA
NEW CASTLE PA
Made for
ALBERT PICK & CO.
CHICAGO

CITATION
SHENANGO CHINA
© BY INTERPACE
U.S.A.
B   B-29
224.

OMEGA
by SHENANGO
U.S.A.
© BY INTERPACE ®
A B-29
225.

FÖRM ®
SHENANGO
CHINA U.S.A.
© BY INTERPACE
C   B-29
226.

227.

FÖRM ®
SHENANGO
CHINA U.S.A.
© BY INTERPACE
B   B-29
U.S. PAT. 3,190,486

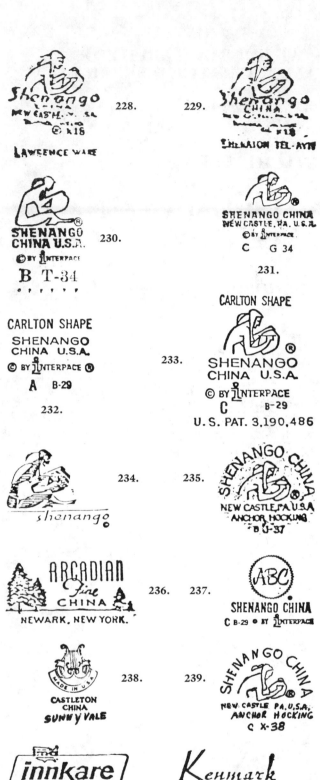

228. Shenango NEW CASTLE N.Y. USA X18
LAWRENCE WARE

229. Shenango CHINA X18
SHERATON TEL-AVIV

230. SHENANGO CHINA U.S.A. © BY INTERPACE
B T-34

231. SHENANGO CHINA NEW CASTLE, PA. U.S.A. © BY INTERPACE
C G 34

232. CARLTON SHAPE SHENANGO CHINA U.S.A. © BY INTERPACE
A B-29

233. CARLTON SHAPE SHENANGO CHINA U.S.A. © BY INTERPACE
C B-29 U.S. PAT. 3,190,486

234. shenango

235. SHENANGO CHINA NEW CASTLE, PA USA ANCHOR HOCKING B J-37

236. ARCADIAN Fine CHINA NEWARK, NEW YORK.

237. ABC SHENANGO CHINA C B-29 BY INTERPACE

238. MADE IN USA CASTLETON CHINA SUNNY VALE

239. SHENANGO CHINA NEW CASTLE PA. U.S.A. ANCHOR HOCKING C X-38

240. innkare Mfg. for DRAKE Memphis Tenn. A Q-32

241. Kenmark China REAL CHINA .. designed for gracious living MADE IN U.S.A. NEW KENSINGTON, PA.

242. Princess China TRU-TONE USA

243. ABC INSTI-WARE BY SHENANGO CHINA C B-29 © BY INTERPACE

244. Nancy Prentiss Fine China MADE IN U.S.A. NEW KENSINGTON, PA.

245. Shenango China NEW CASTLE, PA. U.S.A.

246. SHENANGO CHINA NEW CASTLE, PA.

247. FRANCISCAN GOURMET BY INTERPACE

248. CALA SHENANGO

249. ROYAL PRESTIGE SELECT FINE CHINA made in USA

250. Tradition Silver Ronde MADE IN USA

251. Cathedral FINE CHINA made in U.S.A.

252. SHENANGO CHINA U.S.A. © BY INTERPACE A B-29

253. SHENANGO CHINA NEW CASTLE, PA. U.S.A. INTERPACE C H-35

254. SHENANGO CHINA NEW CASTLE, PA USA ANCHOR HOCKING B J-37

255. SHENANGO CHINA NEW CASTLE, PA. U.S.A. © BY INTERPACE

256. Shenango CHINA NEW CASTLE, PA USA ROYAL WELROC YM F-43

257. Staffordshire A PRODUCT OF SHENANGO POTTERY CO. NEW CASTLE, PA. USA D-19

258. AMERICAN FORESIGHT FINE CHINA made in USA

259. INTERPACE U.S.A.

260. SHENANGO CHINA omega © BY INTERPACE A B-29

261. magna SHENANGO CHINA USA © BY INTERPACE B-29

HOWARD
JOHNSON'S ® 262.

SHENANGO CHINA
© BY ꟼNTERPACE C
B-29

Made Expressly For
International Hotel
Supply Co.
Boston, Mass.
by
SHENANGO
CHINA U.S.A.
© BY ꟼNTERPACE ® 263.
B-29   O IHS-1

SHENANGO AMBERSTONE
ꟼNTERPACE
MADE IN U.S.A.   264.

PAT NO 2,178,274
RIMROL
TRADE MARK

GALA   265.
SHENANGO   266.

SHENANGO CHINA
NEW CASTLE, PA.

Shenfelder, D.P. Reading, Pennsylvania. 1869 to 1900; stock still being sold in 1905, according to Guy F. Reinert, "A History of the Pennsylvania-German Potteries in Berk County," in the *Bulletin of the American Ceramic Society*, January 1940, pp. 26, 27. The potter made slip decorated and plain redware and stoneware. The mark as shown is the correct spelling as seen on a very clear mark on a crock in Smith, p. 8; also the *Regional Aspects of American Folk Pottery*, (no author), p. 52. (Ramsay spelled the name "Schenefelder," in text, p. 178 and "Senefelder" in his marks, p. 279.)

D.P. SHENFELDER
READING, PA.

Sheppard, J. Geddes, New York. 1857 to around 1864 (Stewart and Consentino, p. 126). Made stoneware. (Mark: impressed; front cover of *Antique Trader Annual*, Vol. X, 1979.)

J. SHEPARD
GEDDES, N.Y.

Sherwood Brothers Pottery. New Brighton, Pennsylvania. Founded in 1879 by G.W. and W.D. Sherwood. By 1895 they employed 140 making stoneware. For a while they were associated with the Elversons who were also potters. See Elverson, Sherwood and Barker listing for information. By 1931 they employed only 40 and 32 in 1935. Sherwood Bros. were still listed in 1938 in *Industrial Directory* for Pennsylvania. The next directory I had was 1947 and they were no longer listed. (Mark: on gray stoneware one quart canning jar.)

SHERWOOD BROS.
POTTERY
NEW BRIGHTON, PA.

Shiloh Pottery. Hampstead, Maryland. 1974 to present (1984). O. Kenneth Hankins, studio potter, received an M.S. degree in art education from Alfred University, Alfred, New York, in 1972. Before that he had attended Towson State College in Towson, Maryland, also The Maryland Institute College of Art, where he received his B.F.A. degree, and Frostburg State College in Frostburg, Maryland. He has taught art and pottery making in the Baltimore and Carroll County Schools, Western Maryland College at Westminster, Towson State College in Towson and was chairman of the art department at Garrison Forest School in Garrison, all in Maryland. He is a member of the American Crafts Council, the National Council for Education in Ceramic Arts, the Maryland Crafts Council and Carroll County Arts Council and is very active in community affairs as well. In 1974, he started Shiloh Pottery Farms, an apprenticeship program for young people. He incorporated as Shiloh Pottery, Inc., in 1975 to distribute pottery equipment and supplies, to manufacture clay and pottery wheels, and to produce quality handmade stoneware sold in craftshops and at fairs as well as to continue adult and young peoples' training programs. (Mark is approximately one-half inch square, made of clay, design as shown.)

Shinnick (or Shinnix). Strasburg, Virginia. Before 1870. In Elmer Smith's *Pottery, A Utilitarian Folk Craft*, p. 24, is pictured a stoneware crock with an incised mark scribbled clear across one side. The caption to the picture gives the name, Shinnick, Strasburg, Virginia, but the last couple of letters are barely visible in the picture. In A.H. Rice and John B. Stoudt's book, *The Shenandoah Pottery*, p. 79, they tell that a potter named Shinnix sold his pottery to Samuel H. Sonner in 1870. They said he had made pottery for several years before 1870. I am sure these two authors are talking about the same potter. The conflict is in the spelling of the name. I can't verify the name. None of the authors are living.

Shinnick

Short, Mary, Potteries. Topeka, Kansas. 1938 until in the late 1950's. Mary Short, a sculptress, started in 1938 by sculpting a bust of her young daughter. The piece was entered in an art exhibit of the Topeka Art Guild and won first prize. She opened a shop, bought her own clay beds, mixed her own glazes and created over 300 designs. She was soon hiring 15 helpers and 3 salesmen. She designed and made dinnerware for Carole Stupell, of New York City. But with all the success in the product line, the pottery closed sometime in the 1950's. In the 1952 *Crockery and Glass Journal Directory*, Mary Short Ceramics was listed under earthenware decorative pieces, vases, console sets, bakeware, cups and saucers, center pieces, figures, figurines, salt and peppers, dinnerware and teasets. The pottery was still listed in the 1957 directory as Mary Short Potteries. (Information: Jenny B. Derwich and Dr. Mary Latos, *Dictionary Guide to U.S. Pottery* *and Porcelain*, p. 210, and directories as cited. Mark: from 1957 *Crockery and Glass Journal Directory*.)

Mary Short
POTTERIES
INC.

Shulton, Inc. Clifton, New Jersey. In 1937, Hull Pottery, Crooksville, Ohio, made pottery mugs for Shulton, Inc., manufacturers of the Old Spice products. According to Brenda Roberts, ''Hull Headlines: Old Spice Product Containers,'' *Glaze*, August 1980, p. 6, the mugs were decorated with fired on decals of the 18th century sailing vessels. Hull Pottery also made 11 million pottery containers for Shulton, Inc. during their contract period until W.W. II. In 1983, Regal China Company made a ship decanter and coffee mug for Old Spice. (Information and marks: Roberts as cited.)

EARLY-AMERICAN
Old Spice
SHAVING SOAP
USA

EARLY AMERICAN
Old Spice
MADE IN USA

Sierra Vista Ceramics. Sierra Vista, California, and Phoenix, Arizona. 1942 to 1950's. Reinhold Lenaburg and his son, Leonard, began the business making cookie jars, lazy susans and other utilitarian items. They used domestic clay and made their own glazes. They purchased some molds and made others. The pieces were air brushed and hand sprayed. In 1951, Leonard became sole owner, and he moved to Phoenix, Arizona, and operated under the same name, but I don't know for how long. They were not listed in the 1952 or 1954 *Crockery and Glass Journal Directories*. (Information: Jenny B. Derwich and Dr. Mary Latos, *Dictionary Guide to U.S. Pottery and Porcelain*, p. 210. Mark: sent by Edna Myers, writer for the *Glaze*.)

Sierra Vista
California

Silhouette. Newport News, Virginia. Thomas P. Duncan, Jr., filed for registration of this mark on June 18, 1951, for use on vases, bowls and goblets, made of earthenware and porcelain, claiming use since August 2, 1950. He was doing business under the name Silhouette according to the report.

SILHOUETTE

Sinaco Company, Inc. New York, New York. A distributor, filed for a claim on this mark on April 28, 1944, to be used on china tableware, claiming use since January 28, 1943. Sinaco Company was also listed as a decorating company in the 1952 and 1954 *Crockery and Glass Journal Directories*.

LECOT

Singer, Simon. Haycock, Pennsylvania. Thorn, p. 147, dates this pottery 1809-1852. Made redware, slip decorated and plain. (Ramsay, p. 169. Marks: Thorn, p. 147.)

S. Singer

Charles Laubach
1810 Pattern Durham
Pa. made at Singers
Pottery
Haycock

Singer, Susi. Austria and Pasadena, California. 1925 to 1949. Susi Singer, a studio potter of fame produced ceramics for Wiener Werkstatte as well as independent pieces of her own from 1925 to late 1930's in Austria. She won many outstanding awards in Europe including a first prize in London, a second in Brussels and a first in Paris at the ''Arts and Techniques'' exposition in 1937. In America, she received a Scripps College research grant to experiment on slips and glazes. Thirty figures made under this grant are in the permanent collection of Scripps College Museum, Claremont, California. Susi Singer died in 1949. (Information: all of the foregoing information from Garth Clark, *A Century of Ceramics in the U.S.*, p. 329. Marks: sent by Thomas Turnquist, author and member of American Art Pottery Association. Mark 1 was written in ink on work done in America. Mark 2 was incised on pieces made in Austria.)

SS   *Susi Singer*

Sipe Pottery. Williamsport, Pennsylvania. Around 1867 to 1900. Last listing in directories was 1893. The pottery was started shortly after 1867 by William Sipe. Later he was joined by his two sons Luther and Oscar and operated as **Sipe and Sons Pottery**. Around 1875 Abram Young and Joseph Nichols became Sipe's partners as Sipe, Nichols and Company until 1877, when Nichols became partners with Logan Moore and David P. Hobart. (See that listing.) The Sipe Pottery continued after the departure of Nichols until around 1900 according to Hardcastle. There is a little disagreement between these two authors as to exactly when Nichols was a part of the Sipe Pottery. But I used Lasansky's dates because she discussed further involvements of Nichols. (Information: Jeannette Lasansky, *Made of Mud*, p. 29 and Mildred Veley Hardcastle, ''The Sipe Pottery of Williamsport, Pennsylvania,'' *Antiques Journal*, April 1968, pp. 23, 24. Marks: Hardcastle, as cited, and Lasansky, p. 30.)

SIPE & SON
WMSPORT, PA

SIPE, NICHOLS & CO.
WILLIAMSPORT, PA

SIPE & SONS
WMSPORT, PA.

Slago Pottery. Zanesville, Ohio. In November 1849 *Zanesville Gazette*, Norris Schneider found an advertisement which stated Goetz and Company, proprietors of the Slago Pottery, Marietta Street, Zanesville, were opening a store for wholesale and retail, selling brown and yellowware. In two or three article written in 1957 in the *Zanesville Times Signal*, Norris disputes the interpretations given as to who actually made the beautiful jug which has applied ornament of eagles flanking the shield of the U.S. "Smith and Jones" is on one side of the shield and "Slago Pottery" is on the other. On the back is "Zanesville 1804." A picture of this jug may be seen in Stradling's book, p. 142, and in Schneider's "Early Zanesville Pottery Jug," *Zanesville Times Signal*, November 19, 1957. Schneider contends the first pottery was made in Zanesville around 1808 or 1809 by Samuel Sullivan. In 1804, Zanesville only had 115 people with no potters among them. Schneider said Isaac Jones was in a city directory in 1851 and N.B. and N.K. Smith were listed in Putnam around 1860. This is a very beautiful expensive jug, but according to Schneider, we do not have sufficient explanations so far for the markings.

Smith + Jones / Slago Pottery
Zanesville, 1804

Sleepy Eye Milling Company. Monmouth, Illinois. Sleepy Eye Milling Company started in 1882 and in 1917 was owned by the Kansas Flour Mills but was kept in operation until 1921. The cobalt blue and white pitchers and steins were used as premiums for Sleepy Eye Flour before and after the change of ownership in 1917. Isobel Hellender states in "One Hundred Years of Sleepy Eye," *Western Collector*, May 1972, pp. 4-9, that none of these Indian Head items were produced by Western Stoneware for the milling company after 1937. However, in 1952, the 22-ounce and 40-ounce steins were redesigned (gave the Indian a larger nose) and produced in an overall chestnut brown glaze. Then in 1968 the same 40-ounce design was used to make a few steins to be presented to the company's board of directors and as V.I.P. gifts. These steins were hand-decorated in blue and white with the maple leaf mark of the company and date added to the bottom of the stein (Hellender, pp. 4-9). In 1969, 1970, 1971, 1972, and a very limited quantity in 1973, mugs were made for the same purpose with none available to the public. Another excellent article on "Old Sleepy Eye" (no author) is in *Spinning Wheel*, January-February, 1965, p. 18, for those who are interested mainly in this one aspect of the pottery's production. See Western Pottery Company for more, also for mark on the pitcher. Weir Pottery Company was the first pottery to make the Sleepy Eye products. See Weir Pottery. Weir Pottery, Minnesota Stoneware Company, and Western Stoneware Company all made products for Sleepy Eye Milling Company. The mark shown was impressed on the bottom of the "Standing Indian" pitcher. I don't know what pottery made the pitcher. The mark is pictured on a pitcher in Don and Carol Raycraft, *Decorated Country Stoneware*, p. 49. Jim Martin, co-author of *Monmouth Western Stoneware* had this to say by letter about the standing Indian pitcher,

"The standing Indian pitcher is collected by Old Sleepy Eye collectors but there is no connection with the Sleepy Eye Milling Company or the other pottery pieces. We do not know who made them but assume an Ohio pottery. I have seen five or six different markings on the bottom of them."

FLEMISH WARE

Smith and Day Pottery. Norwalk, Connecticut. Absalom Day operated a pottery from around 1793 to around 1841 and at that time he deeded it to his son, Noah S. Day. In 1812, when Asa E. Smith was 14 years old, he was apprenticed to Absalom Day. By 1825, Asa E. Smith was operating a pottery of his own until around 1843 when Noah S. Day and Asa E. Smith became partners and operated in the Day pottery building until 1849 when it was sold to Norton and Isbell. The pottery burned in the 1850's while under the ownership of The Russell and Irwin Manufacturing Company of New Britain, which made "mineral" knobs. (Information: Lura W. Watkins, *Early New England Potters and Their Wares*, pp. 200, 201. Mark: illustration no. 99 following p. 291 of same book.)

SMITH & DAY MANUFACTURES NORWALK CON

Smith, David. In 1926, studio potter, David Smith, moved to New York City, when he was 20 years old. In 1932, he studied painting at the Art Students League. In 1931, he began to make sculptured metal objects and to add objects to the surface of his paintings. His first showing of welded steel sculptures and drawings was in 1938 at Marian Willard's East River Gallery, in New York City. Through the 1940's and 1950's, he did extensive shows. In 1964, he produced a series of ceramics with David Gil for a project, "Art in America." These were slab and sculptured forms painted with white slip, and then Smith drew on the surface. Smith died in 1965 and these were shown at the Everson Museum's exhibit, "New Works in Clay by Contemporary Painters and Sculptors," sometime after Smith's death. (Information: Garth Clark, *A Century of Ceramcis in the U.S.*, pp. 329, 330. Incised marks: Linda Steigleder, from the booklet published by the Everson Museum of Art to accompany the 1978 exhibition, "A Century of Ceramics in the U.S.")

David Smith 4-11-64

David Smith 4/12 64

Smith, Fife and Company. Philadelphia, Pennsylvania. This company made porcelain around 1830. The porcelain made by them had a yellowish tone but was true hard porcelain although inferior to that of Tucker according to Barber. He mentions pickle dishes and pitchers that were found made by this company and marked with their name. (Information and marks: Barber, *Marks of American Potters*, p. 22.)

Smith, J.C. Mogadore, Portage County, Ohio. Around 1862. Made brownware and stoneware (Thorn, p. 147.)

SMITH

MOGADORE

OHIO

Smith, Joseph. Wrightstown Township, Bucks City, Pennsylvania. Established around 1763 to around 1800. Joseph was succeeded by Thomas Smith Barber, *Tulip Ware of the Pennsylvania-German Potters*, p. 108, said probably a son of Joseph, Barber said there were decorated plates bearing the name, Thomas Smith, maker. Products were slip decorated, sgraffito and plain redware. (Mark 1, Barber as cited, Mark 2, Thorn, p. 147.)

 1.

J. Smith
2.

Smith Phillips China Company. East Liverpool, Ohio. 1901 to 1931. It was started by Josiah T. Smith and W.H. Phillips. In the *1902-1903 Complete Directory* they were listed as making semi-porcelain dinner sets, toilet sets and short sets of odd dishes, some decorated. In the article "Smith Phillips China Company" in the *Pottery, Glass, and Brass Salesman*, December 27, 1917, p. 16, is the announcement of a pattern made by Smith Phillips called the "Cuckoo" design which was described as an overall tropical design in bright colors with a cuckoo as a feature in the design surrounded by wildflowers. Smith Phillips merged with seven other companies in 1929 to form the American China Corporation (see that listing), and at that time they made hotel ware as well as semi-porcelain dinnerware. In "American Pottery Trade Marks" in China, Glass and Lamps, September 3, 1923, p. 19, was the statement that Smith Phillips confined themselves to one distinctive shape which at that time, was known as the "Princess" shape. (Information: Lehner, *American Kitchen and Dinner Wares*, p. 139. Marks: nos. 1-5, Barber. *Marks of American Potters*, p. 106; nos. 6, 7, on dishes.)

1.

FENIX
2.

AMERICAN GIRL
3.

KOSMO
4.

Smith Phillips Semi Porcelain
5.

6.   7.

Smith, Washington. Manhattan, New York. 1833 to 1870. Washington Smith started a pottery to make stoneware in 1833 and was joined by his son, Washington I. Smith, in 1861. The pottery operated until 1870. (Information and impressed mark: on stoneware bottle from Regina Stewart and Geraldine Consentino, *Stoneware*, pp. 94, 95.)

Smith, Willoughby. Womelsdorf, Berks County, Pennsylvania. In 1864, at age 19 he purchased a pottery in Womelsdorf and operated it until he died in 1904. At first, three kick wheels were used and later steam power was introduced making flower pots, pie dishes and crocks of redware, earthenware and stoneware. Potters that worked for Smith were John Snyder who worked there 34 years; Mahlon Pornorman, 32 years; Willoughby's sons, Lewis and Frank Smith. (Information: Guy F. Reinert, "History of the Pennsylvania-German Potteries in Berks County," *Bulletin of American Ceramic Society*, Volume 19, no. 1, 1940, p. 27. Marks: Thorn, p. 148; Barber, *Marks of American Potters*, p. 15.)

Willoughby Smith
Wumelsdorf

SMITH

W. SMITH

WOMELSDORF

W. SMITH
NEW YORK

Snob Hog Pottery. Branson, Missouri. 1975 to present (1984). Dennis E. Thompson is a studio potter who makes sculptured pieces and has worked as a professional artist since 1975. He has a B.A. degree from Northwest Missouri State University in Maryville, Missouri. He listed many shows he has done in Oklahoma, Texas, Nebraska, Ohio, Tennessee, Florida, etc. His work is shown in galleries such as Sidereal Jewels in Eureka Springs, Arkansas; Flat with Clay and The Artful Dodger, Witchita, Kansas; The Clayworks, Nashville, Tennessee; Lake Avenue Gallery, Lake Worth, Florida. He won first place awards in the 1980 Witchita Art

Museum Book and Art Fair, and the 1983 Tennessee Toll Crafts Fair, where he won Exhibitor's Choice as well, also the 1978 Springfield Art Museum, also the 1977 Red Rock Art Rally in Knoxville, Iowa, where he won both Artists Choice and Best Display awards.

Sohn, Ernest, Creations. New York, New York. Selling agency affiliated with Jack Orenstein Associates, Inc., but the 1952 and 1954 *Crockery and Glass Journal Directory* did not explain in what way. Ernest Sohn was listed for bakeware, tableware, glass, metal coasters and a domestic or American made solid colored dinnerware. (Mark: Quality Stamp Company, East Liverpool, Ohio. Mark 2 filed for registration May 1961 and mark 3 was filed the same day for use on pottery buffet and serving accessories, serving trays, coffee warmers, casseroles, lazy susans, salad bowls, etc.

Soini, William. William was a studio potter, born in Finland in 1882, and he died in 1955. Even while he was a youngster in school, he did drawing, carving and clay modeling. He studied at the Trade-Tech Middle School and the Atheneum in Helsinki. His concentration became on pottery, and he was tutored by A.W. Finch, a great Finnish potter. Around 1908 he came to America to be affiliated with the North Dakota School of Mines (see that listing). From there, he studied at the Chicago Art Institute and then moved to Chandler, North Carolina, to work with O.L. Bachelder at the Omar Khayyam Pottery (see that listing). He then went to study at Alfred University for a short time and with all of this as background, he set up his own studios in New York City. He made decorative and utilitarian pieces. He was involved with the Associated American Artists group in the making of Stonelain pottery pieces (see that listing). He was one of the men involved in the production of the pottery by that group. His exhibitions included the New York World's Fair, the San Francisco World's Fair, the Metropolitan Museum of Art, and the various Syracuse Nationals (see lists of these in back of book). His work was described: "The most striking feature of his work is on the one hand its versatility and on the other hand, its starkly noble simplicity." It was called charming and enchantingly beautiful. He signed his studio pieces with a vertical "W" and "S". His Stonelain pieces were marked "Soini." Information and marks: Thomas Turnquist, New York

City Ceramics, Part III, William Soini: A Tribute," *Journal of the American Art Pottery Association*, September, October, 1985, pp. 4, 5.

Soini   W

Somerset Potters' Works. Somerset, Massachusetts. Before 1847-1891. Lura Woodside Watkins in *Early New England Potters and Their Wares*, brings sanity to the confusion that reigns in regard to this pottery! "At Pottersville, the Chace brothers, Leonard, Benjamin G. and Clark added stoneware manufacturing to redware potting in the 1840's. They built a new building in 1847 and incorporated as the Somerset Potters' Works. By 1857 they employed eleven, six of whom made stoneware valued at $9000 per year. In 1882, the Chaces sold the pottery which still operated under the same name. The building was rejuvenated, the kilns modernized, etc. Thirteen men made stoneware by hand except for the sixty gallon crocks which were the specialty. In 1886, an advertisement was for "white, decorated, Rockingham, yellow, stone and earthenware." In 1891 the company merged with a brick factory. All manufacturing ceased in the plant in 1909. (Information: Lura W. Watkins, p. 89. Mark: Stradling, p. 77. There was also a mark "L & B G Chace/Somerset," used by this potter.)

SOMERSET
POTTERS WORKS

Sonner Pottery. Strausburg, Virginia. **Samuel H. Sonner** was not a potter. He acquired the old Samuel Bell Pottery in 1853 with journeymen making ware with Sonner's name. In 1870 Samuel purchased the Shinnick Pottery with the pottery being made by George H. Davidson. According to Smith, Sonner finally did learn to make pottery and produced what Smith termed "the first truly S.H. Sonner pieces." In 1883, **John H. Sonner**, son of Samuel, leased the business and assumed management until 1892. At least two other Sonners made pottery in Strasburg; the sons of William Sonner called George R. and William operated under the name **Sonner Brothers.** These seem to be in different locations from the first pottery listed. Also a **Keister and Sonner Pottery** operated about 1885. (Information: Smith, p. 23 and Doris Devine Fanelli, "John H. Sonner's Stoneware Pottery, Strasburg, Virginia," *Spinning Wheel*, January, February, 1981, pp. 42 and 46. Marks: Smith, p. 23 shows very clear copies of these marks.)

S. H. SONNER
STRASBURG, VA.   J. H. SONNER
                                  STRASBURG, VA.

Soriano Ceramics. Long Island, New York. Started around 1947 until in the 1960's. Listed in the 1952 directory as a maker of florist ware only. In 1958 the company filed registration on mark 2 for use on ceramic tile and book ends, claiming use since 1947 which must have been close to the time

Soriano Ceramics started because they were not listed in 1945 or 1946. In the 1952 *Crockery and Glass Journal Directory*, the company was listed as decorators.

1.

2.

Soto, Ishmael. Lexington, Texas. 1960 to present (1985). Studio potter, makes porcelain and stoneware in dinnerware and functional pieces and sculptured pieces. Ishmael graduated with a B.F.A. degree in applied art from the University of Texas, in Austin and a M.F.A. degree from the Cranbrook Academy of Art, Bloomfield Hills, Michigan, with a major in ceramics and a minor in metal smithing. Between 1960 and 1981, he taught ceramics in private studio classes, also at the following places; San Antonio Art Institute; the University of Texas; Laguna Gloria Art Museum; St. Edwards University; Alabama Coushatta Indian Reservation; Penland School of Crafts; Haystack School of Crafts; Houston Potter's Guild; and Texas Designer Craftsmen. Ishmael listed over 60 shows and exhibits between 1960 and 1980 in places all over Texas, and other states including Tennessee, Maryland, Michigan, also New York City. Ishmael won the ceramic award at the Western Michigan Art Exhibition in 1960, and for four years he won the Sears Roebuck purchase prize at the 22nd, 23rd, 24th and 25th Annual Painting and Sculpture Shows in Dallas. At the 11th Beaumont Art Museum Annual Exhibition, he won the award bronze sculpture. This is only a sampling of the awards this potter has won. He was one of the studio potters featured in the book, *Texas Pottery* by Sherry B. Humphreys and Johnell L. Schmidt, along with other notables, such as Harding Black, Huey Beckham, etc. (Mark is applied with brush.)

Southern California Ceramic Company/California Art Products, Inc. Santa Monaca and Los Angeles, California. In the 1945 *Crockery and Glass Journal*, the listing was California Art Products, Inc. at 2406 E. 58th St. in Los Angeles, with the marks 1 and 2 shown for Hollywood Ware.

Note: In the 1951 *California Manufacturers Directory*, there was a company named Hollywood Ceramic Company at 3061 Riverside Dr. in Los Angeles. Do not confuse the two companies. See Maddux Pottery for more on Hollywood Ceramic Company.

By 1948, the *China and Glass Red Book Directory* listed the Southern California Ceramic Company as being formerly the California Art Products Company. The listing in 1945 said manufacturers of art pottery, figures, figurines and miniatures of earthenware. Also, jardinieres, flower bowl and florists ware. In the 1952 *Crockery and Glass Journal Directory* was a full page ad by the distributors Newland, Schneeloch, and

Pick, Inc. of Broadway, New York, for Orchard dinnerware and Orchard Crystal. The ad said the Orchard dinnerware was made by the Southern California Ceramic Company. In the 1953 *China and Glass Red Book Directory*, William G. Guernsey was listed as president of Southern California Ceramic Company, still making the Orchard dinnerware, semi-porcelain dinnerware and teapots and that was the last listing I could find for the pottery. By 1957 in the *Crockery and Glass Journal Directory*, "Orchard Ware," mark 2, was being made by **California Ceramics** or the **Ceramic Manufacturing Company** in the Craftsmens Center at Calabasas, California, probably for the same distributor. A line of ware owned by a distributor continues after a pottery is gone because the distributor will have another pottery to produce the line. See the listing California Ceramics. (Mark 3 is shown in the directories of the 1950's under the distributor name Newland, Schneeloch, and Pick, Inc.)

Southern California Pottery Company, Inc./B.J. Brock Company. 4513 W. 153 St., Lawndale, California. Before 1945 to around 1955. In the directories I have, the Southern California Pottery Company was first listed in the 1945 *China and Glass Red Book Directory* as manufacturers of bakeware, ovenware and kitchenware. By 1949, the company had expanded their production and were listed for "California Brockware," and "California Rustic," two lines of very nice dinnerware. By August 1950 the company name had become the B.J. Brock Company. Bert J. Brock was president in 1949 and by 1951 the company was listed in the *Crockery and Glass Journal Directory* as the B.J. Brock Company at the same address, and Southern California Pottery Company was no longer listed. B.J. Brock Company was listed in 1954 *Crockery and Glass Journal Directory*. The company was not listed in the 1955 *California Manufacturers Register*. Pattern names included, "Country Charm," "Horizon," "Harvest," "Country Meadow," etc. (Marks: no. 1 is shown in the various directories for Brock. No. 2 is on part of a set of dishes that also has another Brock mark. The rest are from very nice semi-porcelain dishes.)

1.

2.

3.

Brock
OF CALIFORNIA   4.
Oven-Safe

5.   Forever Yours
By Brock
OF CALIFORNIA

Southern Porcelain Manufacturing Company. Kaolin, South Carolina. 1856 to 1876. In Aiken County where the pottery was located, Barber tells that the clay was so white that it was used for whitewashing fences and buildings. William H. Farrar who had been a stockholder of the U.S. Pottery in Bennington started Southern Porcelain after he got the support of some wealthy people in Augusta and some planters in the area to become stockholders. During the first year an English potter was hired and much ware was destroyed in the firing. During the second year, Josiah Jones, a skillful designer and competent potter took over management and made some very fair porcelain, a good white granite, and some cream-colored ware, according to Barber. The business was doomed to failure as Barber tells it because Farrar could not see the need for mixing other imported clay with the South Carolina clay to make a sturdy product. Farrar arranged for other management to come from Vermont in 1857, and the pottery was only reasonably successful until the Civil War. They then started making tableware, toilet ware and a general line of whiteware. During the Civil War, potters were exempt from service according to Ramsay. Southern Porcelain Manufacturing Company made brown insulators and earthenware water pipe for their war effort. In 1863 or 1864 the works were destroyed by fire, but in 1865 a new porcelain company was organized under R.B. Bullock as president. (He later became governor of Georgia.) Under his direction the pottery had varying success as Barber expressed it, and in 1875 the pottery was sold to McNamee and Company of New York. By the time Barber wrote the book in 1893 he said the old kilns and buildings had long since disappeared. (Information and marks: Barber, *Pottery and Porcelain of the U.S.*, p. 187; Ramsay, *American Potters and Pottery*, p. 89.)

S P
COMPANY
KAOLIN
SC

SP Co
KAOLIN
S.C.

Southern Potteries, Inc. Erwin, Tennessee. 1917 to January 1957. In 1910, E.J. Owen, commonly called Ted, went to Erwin to start a pottery. W.P. Jervis, "A Dictionary of Pottery Terms," *Pottery, Glass and Brass Salesman*, June 13, 1918, p. 14, listed Owen as manager of Southern Potteries, Inc. Owen had been one of the organizers of the East End Pottery, in East Liverpool, Ohio; he founded Owen China Company of Minerva, Ohio; he was later manager at the Paden City Pottery for a while, leaving there to go to Erwin, Tennessee. From the book, *A Century of American Dinnerware Manufacture* by Floyd W. McKee, p. 35, we gain a great insight into the inner workings of many of the American potteries. He tells us that the Southern Potteries, Inc. was born out of the idea that the Carolina, Clinchfield and Ohio Railroad should get some industries going that would help to bring traffic through the Johnson City area. The pottery was first called **Clinchfield Pottery** before it became known as the Southern Pottery around 1917 or 1918. The name became

Southern Potteries, Inc. with the incorporation in 1920. McKee tells us that the task of keeping the experienced potters down there while training boys from the hills was a difficult task. He said the pottery had to be reorganized a couple of times. Finally, "Charles Foreman from Minerva, happened along and took a try at it," (in 1922). Foreman was the man who would probably be credited with the success of the pottery. He introduced handpainting on the bisque, using girls from up in the hills in a production line method. The ease in changing patterns, the small wages accepted by the hill people, the growth of the use of dinnerware for theatre premiums, all helped the pottery to succeed. Foreman had a sales agency in Canton, Ohio, which handled a great part of the production. In the 1940's and 1950's Sears and Montgomery Ward sold a great deal of Southern Potteries products. Foreman died in 1953. According to McKee, the decision to liquidate came in January, 1957. The plant was sold to the National Casket Company, and no more pottery was made there. Marks: Many of the marks shown are photostatic copies from dishes. No. 1 reads, "Ruler of the Roost - for centuries has been the symbol of hospitality and good cheer . . . famed gourmets and restaurants have named this emblem to proclaim their ware supreme." No. 2, from Quality Stamp Company, East Liverpool, Ohio. Nos. 3-7, Betty Newbound, author of *Southern Potteries, Inc., Blue Ridge Dinnerware*. This book gives pattern names, history and a great deal of information. No. 8 is the very early mark. Nos. 9, 10 are the only marks we found filed for registration with the patent office. Both were filed December, 20, 1951 claiming they had been used since October 1941.)

1.

2.

3.

4.

Ownen Proof
Underglaze
Hand Painted
Southern Potteries
MADE IN
U. S. A.

5.

6.

Underglaze
Hand Painted
S. P. Inc.
Erwin Tenn
Ownen Proof

Underglaze
Hand Painted
Southern Potteries, Inc.
MADE IN U. S. A.

7.

8.

Blue Ridge 9.

Blue Ridge
10.

11.

HAND PAINTED
UNDER THE GLAZE
Southern
MADE IN U.S.A.
OVEN PROOF
FADE PROOF
14L
12.

13.
HAND PAINTED UNDERGLAZE
S.P.I.
ERWIN, TENN.
MADE IN U.S.A.

Blue Ridge
China
Hand Painted
Underglaze
Southern Potteries, Inc.
MADE IN U.S.A.
14.

15.
Underglaze
Hand Painted
S.P. Inc.
Erwin, Tenn.

Blue Ridge
CHINA
Hand Painted
Underglaze
Southern Potteries, Inc.
MADE IN U.S.A.
16.

Blue Ridge
Hand Painted
Underglaze
Southern Potteries, Inc.
MADE IN U.S.A.
17.

Blue Ridge
UNDERGLAZE
Smoky Mountain Laurel
Southern Potteries Inc.
MADE IN U.S.A.
18.

Blue Ridge
CHINA
19.

Underglaze
Hand Painted
MADE IN
U.S.A.
20.

Mountain
Rose
Hand Painted
Dinnerware
MADE IN U.S.A.
21.

22.

Southern Pottery. Dallas, Texas. **Southern Pottery Tile and Brick Company** was listed in 1890 to 1891 in the *Texas State Gazetteer*, in Athens, Texas, which is about 60 miles from Dallas. In Sherry B. Humphries, *Texas Pottery*, p. 32, is the

following stamped mark dated around 1930 for Southern Pottery, Dallas Texas. I found only the one listing for Southern Pottery Tile and Brick and could make no positive connection between the two potteries at this time.

SOUTHERN POTTERIES
DALLAS
4

South Fork Pottery. Se Ungemach Pottery Company.

Space Needle Corporation. Seattle, Washington. Both marks shown were filed for registration October 16, 1961, claiming use since August 1961, for use on ceramic dinnerware.

SPACE NEEDLE
1.

2.

Sparta Ceramic Tile Company. East Sparta, Ohio. Started in 1922 and became part of U.S. Ceramic Tile Company in December 1954. They had taken over a company which had produced clay and lime and made their first floor tile in 1923. Some specialty items have been produced over the years that are showing up in the hands of collectors. Such as a plate made at Christmas, probably for employees, bearing mark 1. Mark 2 was filed for copyright on October 22, 1945, for hollow pottery ware, namely teapots, sugar bowls and cream pitchers, claiming use since July 1945. The company is beginning this year (1983) to make a line of tile with decals overglaze. "Romany" wall tile has been a major output. See the U.S. Ceramic Tile Company for more history. (Information: Harold C. McCollam, *The Brick and Tile Industry in Stark County, 1809-1976*, Canton, Ohio: Stark County Historical Society, pp. 221-240.)

1.

Spartan
2.

Spaulding China Company, Inc. The plant was in Sebring, Ohio, with offices in the Empire State Building, New York City. The pottery started in 1939 in the old Alliance Vitreous China Company. But according to Leslie C. Wolfe, by letter, all they made until the war started was clock cases and lamps which were sold under the "Miller" trademark for Irving Miller, one of the founders. Morris Feinberg was his partner. By the middle of 1942, Spaulding China Company as we know it was born. In 1941, the plant was moved to the building later occupied by Holiday Designs. In the *1949 Anniversary History of Sebring, Ohio*, p. 16, Clyde Hardy and Margaret Kadisch were in charge of decorating, art and design. Under this direction the Spaulding China produced a variety of figurines and planters and decoration type pieces under the names of Royal Copley and Royal Windsor. Spaulding China Company stopped producing in 1957, but it took close to two years to finish up the business. The actual manufacturing in the last couple of years was done by other factories just to fill outstanding orders. (Marks: no. 1 was filed for registration on July 23, 1945, claiming use since April 1945, for jugs, planters, pots and vases for growing flowers. Mark 2 was filed on July 2, 1947, for use on the same products as no. 1. Nos. 3 and 4 are paper labels. No. 5 is a stamped mark. No. 6 is a raised mark on gray and pink flower holder. Nos. 7-10 are paper labels shown in Leslie Wolfe, *Royal Copley*, privately printed, 1983, p. 21. Mark 11 was filed for registration on November 27, 1948 claiming use since May 1948, for wall pockets and flower holders of ceramics. This mark was filed under the name Windsor China Company, Inc. This fact had me looking for another company that did not really exist but was just a name change or a branch related to Spaulding China Co.)

1. 2. 3. 4. 5. 6. 7. 8. 9.

10.

11.

Spearman, Helen. Hollywood, California. Filed for registration of this mark on October 10, 1932, for handmade pottery, claiming use since February 1, 1931.

Spinner, David. Medford, Pennsylvania. 1800-1811. Was considered a folk artist on pottery, pictured soldiers on horseback, animation hunting scenes, ladies in fashionable dress, etc. He signed some of his pieces with a flowing hand inscription as shown. Made slip decorated and plain redware, some with equestrian designs, etc. (Information: Frances Lichten, *Folk Art of Rural Pennsylvania*, New York: Charles Scribners, 1946, p. 19. Marks: Kaufman, pp. 88, 89.)

David Spinner Potter

David Spinner his Make

Spinski, Victor. Newark, Delaware. Victor, researcher in ceramics and potter, received a B.S. in art and foreign languages from Kansas State Teachers College, Emporia, in 1963, and an M.F.A. from Indiana University, Bloomington, in 1967. He received a Craftsmanship Fellowship from the National Endowment for the Arts for 1974 and 1975. (Information: Garth Clark, *A Century of Ceramics in the U.S.*, p. 331. Incised mark: Linda Steigleder, from the booklet published by the Everson Museum of Art to accompany the 1978 exhibition, "A Century of Ceramics in the U.S.")

Victor Spinski '79

Springfield Pottery Company. Springfield, Missouri. *The Report of Manufacturers of U.S., 10th Census*, Washington: 1880, p. 356, said this pottery started in 1889. (Mark: found on picture on blue stenciled five gallon jug, sent by Henry Heflin, pottery collector and researcher.)

SPRINGFIELD
POTTERY CO.
SPRINGFIELD, MO.

Spring Street Pottery. Cincinnati, Ohio. 1976 to present (1986). Michael Frasca, Richard Aerni and Allan Nairn are working together to make utilitarian, decorative and architectural pieces in stoneware and porcelain, which are wheel thrown, slab built, sculptured or slip cast. In 1985, these three potters worked six months to hand carve and hand decorate the tile to make 120 foot long mural for the Atrium Wintergarden in the middle of downtown Cincinnati. The project took 20,000 pounds of clay! They formulated their own glazes and the tiles were fired over 2,000 degrees F.

Frasca and Aerni were both born in Cincinnati, Ohio. Frasca attended the Art Academy there, and Aerni attended the University of Pennsylvania, in Philadelphia. They were both self taught in clay. In 1976, Frasca and Aerni were working in separate locations in urban Cincinnati, which were about a block apart in an economically depressed area, in damp basements and drafty backrooms. They pooled resources and purchased a huge older three story house for them and their families to live in and still have sufficient room to work. They didn't intend to collaborate on single pieces or specific orders; they only planned to work in the same studio. But eventually they began to combine their efforts to bring a single piece up to their ideal aesthetic form. Allan Nairn was born in England, studied graphic design in London, and later owned and operated Glenmoriston Pottery in Scotland from 1972 to 1982. He became a partner in the Spring Street Studio in 1982. In 1983, they had selected exhibitions in: The Clay Place, Pittsburgh, Pennsylvania; Artifacts, Indianapolis, Indiana; Lombards, Columbus, Ohio. In 1984, they had selected exhibitions in: Smithsonian Institute, Renwick Gallery, Washington, D.C.; Corning Museum of Glass, Corning, New York; K. Lawrence Gallery, Traverse City, Michigan; Toni Birckhead Gallery, Cincinnati, Ohio; Ohio Designer Craftsman Gallery, Columbus, Ohio; Carnegie Art Center, Covington, Kentucky. In 1985, they had selected exhibitions in: Contemporary Art Center, Cincinnati, Ohio; Dayton Art Institute, Dayton, Ohio; Canton Art Institute, Canton, Ohio; The Craftsman Gallery, Scarsdale, New York. They had selected commissions for: 100 large floor planters for Rax Restaurants, Midwest region; 300 large floor planters for Zantigos Restaurants, Midwest region; decorative urns for Jones and Speer, Architects, Cincinnati, Ohio; lobby planters for St. George-St. Francis Hospitals, Cincinnati, Ohio; floor planters and urns for First National Bank, Covington, Kentucky. Any pieces I have seen pictured by Frasca and Aerni are beautiful. In "Collaboration, Two Viewpoints," by Curtis and Susan Benzle, *Dialogue, The Ohio Arts Journal*, March, April 1983, p. 44, is a globular vase of stoneware with red oak ash glaze which stands up like veins creating a beautiful effect. The shape is outstanding.

Spruce Pine Pottery Company/Muscle Shoals Pottery. Spruce Pine, Alabama. Around 1925 to shortly after W.W. II. The pottery was established by C.F. Rauschenberg and his son, Grady, around 1925 to make utilitarian churns, crocks, jugs, pitchers, etc. But for a short time from 1925 to 1927, Frank Long worked at the pottery and made a type of art pottery. Long had worked at the Niloak Pottery in Benton, Arkansas (see that listing). While in Spruce Pine, Long made Niloak swirl type pottery, also some Niloak shapes. Marks used were "Hy Long," "Hy Long Muscle Shoals," "Muscle Shoals," "Marie." Names of potters who followed Long are known, but whether the maufacture of the art pottery continued or not is not certain. Some of the potters were McNeil, Smithwick, Mills, James Boggs, Houston Hamm and Ralph Miller. Two brothers of Boggs also worked at Spruce Pine, Horatio and Virgil. Probably no pieces were marked except the art type pottery, but the names are given just in case one of the potters decided one day to scribble his name into the clay. Horatio Boggs started a pottery of his own in Prattville, Alabama, in 1937 which was still operating in 1986, making unglazed flower pots and concrete mold yard ornaments. (Information: Bob and Linda Doherty and Spencer Glasgow, "Spruce Pine, Alabama Potters and Their Wares," *American Clay Exchange*, May 15, 1986, pp. 8 to 10. Mark: same authors, "To be Niloak or Not to Be Niloak," *American Clay Exchange*, December 1982, p. 2.)

MUSCLE SHOALS

Square-D Company. Peru, Indiana. From 1925 to 1951 this company operated a dry process porcelain plant in Peru, Indiana, making a variety of equipment for the electrical industry including porcelain insulators. (Embossed marks: Tod, *Porcelain Insulators Guide Book for Collectors*, p. 136.)

Squire Ceramics. Los Angeles, California. This pottery was not listed in the 1946 *Crockery and Glass Journal Directory*, but I did find various listings from 1948 through 1952 in the directories I had. They were not listed in 1954. They must have been a very shortlived pottery. In the 1952 *Crockery and Glass Journal Directory Journal*, they were listed as making decorative pottery of earthenware, such as vases, console sets, candy boxes, etc., also earthenware dinnerware. (Marks: from 1952 directory as cited.)

CERAMICS
CALIFORNIA

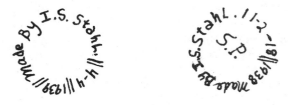

S·Quire
Ceramms
California

Staffel's Pottery (or Staffel's Studio Shop). Charlevois, Michigan. 1949 to present (1983). Bonnie Staffel, studio potter, has been making stoneware and porcelain into sculptured, functional and decorative pieces since 1949 but she opened her shop in 1966. She studied at the Toledo Museum of Art and the Cranbrook Academy. (Marks 1, 2 used before 1956. Marks 3, 4, 5, after 1956 to present.)

Bonnie Staffel

1.   2.   3.

Staffel 4.

Staffel oven ware 5.

Staffel, Rudolf. Staffel, a studio potter, artist, teacher, developed the art of working with porcelain to build and throw what he called "light gatherers." By having different thicknesses in the porcelain pieces, he was able to create various intensities of light and dark in his forms. Clark in the book cited, called Staffel one of the most original vessel makers in American ceramics. In 1931, Staffel studied at the Art Institute in Chicago, under Louis Ripman and Laura Van Papelladam. In 1937, he worked on a part time basis with Paul Cox and taught part time at the Arts and Crafts Club in New Orleans. From 1940 to 1978, he taught at the Tyler School of Art in Philadelphia. See the Clark book for more on this important potter. (Information: Garth Clark, *A Century of Ceramics in the U.S.*, p. 331. Incised mark: Linda Steigleder, from the booklet published by the Everson Museum of Art to accompany the 1978 exhibition, "A Century of Ceramics in the U.S.")

Ruddy Staffel

Stahl Pottery. Powder Mill Valley, about 12 miles south of Allentown, Pennsylvania, was started by Charles Stahl, who made pottery on a wheel for over 40 years. Charles Stahl operated from 1845 to his death in 1896, when Isaac Stahl, son of Charles, operated from 1896 to 1898. In the *Bulletin of the American Ceramic Society*, "Genuine Pennsylvania German Ware," no author, November, 1940, p. 22, the writer contends that the three sons of Charles operated the pottery

after his death. After being closed for years, two of the brothers, opened the pottery again. Isaac and Thomas made the same Pennsylvania German sgrafito ware after 1934 that had been made many years before the pottery had been closed around 1896. They had new kilns, sales rooms, etc. and did a brisk business into the 1940's. In the *Bulletin of the American Ceramic Society*, December 1940, p. 469, was a news note about Thomas Stahl, age 76 and Isaac Stahl, age 67, giving a demonstration with the potter's wheel on the Pennsylvania State College campus, November 10, 1940. (Marks: on pieces at showroom of the American Ceramic Society, Columbus, Ohio.)

Standard Pottery. East Liverpool, Ohio. See Patrick McNicol.

Standard Pottery Company. Brazil, Indiana. Around 1903 to around 1908. In 1902, the buildings were under construction at the pottery site for one of the largest stoneware factories in the state. Ware was hand turned or jollyed by 9 or 10 men, such as jugs, jars, crocks, churns, fruit jars, coolers, etc., ranging in size from two quarts to 30 gallons in size. Albany glaze and white lead glaze were used. No reason was given why the factory ended so soon. The mark stamped in cobalt blue had the outline of an acorn in a circle with the name. (Information and mark: Melvin Davies, *Clay County Indiana Traditional Potters and Their Wares*, pp. 17, 31.)

STANDARD POTTERY CO
30
BRAZIL INDIANA

Stanford Pottery. Sebring, Ohio. Started 1945, was leveled by fire in 1961 and ceased production. Made decorative pieces of semi-porcelain decorated with attractive stencils, namely mugs, vases, planters, etc. They made a line of corn ware very similar to Shawnee's corn line. John F. Bonistall (at one time president or manager of Shawnee Pottery, Stangle Pottery and Terrace Ceramics) said Stanford's corn line was not earlier than Shawnee's. Only a piece in Stanford's Corn line seemed to be marked. The leaves are sculptured and outstanding. Stanford Pottery was listed in the 1965 *China, Glass and Tablewares Directory*; the listing was Stanford Sales, Inc., so the company was continuing to operate in a selling capacity after 1961. According to the 1949 *China and Glass Red Book Directory*, Stanford Pottery made products sold by National Silver marked Nasco. They also made Pantry Parade that year which is a mark owned by China and Glass Distributors, Inc. (See listings for these distributors.)

201A

Stanford Sebring, O.

Stanford Sebring. O.
MADE IN USA

512
STANFORDWARE

STANFORD
SEBRING
OHIO
#246

Stanley Home Products Company. Cannonsburg Pottery Company and Southern Potteries, Erwin, Tennessee, are two of the factories that made dishes for distribution at Stanley Home Products parties, etc., in the 1940's and 1950's. (Mark: Betty Newbound, "Along the Flea Market Trail," *Depression Glass Daze*, Feburary 1980, p. 3.)

Stanwood, James H. Waldoboro, Maine. Around 1860 to until sometime in the 1880's. In the 1860 Census the shop turned out 8,300 pieces of earthenware, valued at $1,141.00. In August 1862, Stanwood went into the army for the Civil War and was wounded in 1865. Around 1866 his name appeared on deeds to land again with Barney C. Mayo and their pottery seems to have flourished because by 1874 they employed eight people to make earthenware. In the early 1880's their names appeared in some directories. In 1890, Stanwood became the postmaster at Waldoboro, and he died in 1898. (Information: M. Lelyn Branin, *The Early Potters and Potteries of Maine*, 1978, pp. 177-179. Mark: Branin, as cited, p. 222.)

Stanwood

Star Encaustic Tile Company. Pittsburgh, Pennsylvania. 1882 to 1905. From 1876 to 1882, the name was **Pittsburgh Encaustic Tile Company**. In 1882, Star Encaustic Tile Company was organized to succeed the former company. Principal products were glazed tile for flooring and pavements. The plant was very small. (Information: Everett Townsend, "Development of the Tile Industry in the U.S.," *American Ceramic Society Bulletin*, Vol. 22, No. 5, May 1943, p. 127, Mark: Barber, *Marks of American Potters*, p. 67.)

S.E.T.
CO.

Stark Ceramics, Incorporated. Canton, Ohio. Had its early beginning as the Osnaburg Brick Company in 1909 which became Stark Brick Company in 1912 which formed a whol-

ly owned subsidiary called Stark Ceramics, Incorporated in 1936. After 1949, Stark Brick Company was liquidated and Stark Ceramics made the brick as well as marketing them. Stark Ceramics, Incorporated was listed in *1960 Directory of Ohio Manufacturers* under ceramic wall and floor tile. Over the years they made some promotional pieces or employee gift pieces. This mark was found on an ashtray.

Stark Pottery. Memphis, Tennessee. 1965 to present (1985). Agnes Gordon Stark is a studio potter, who received a B.F.A. degree from Mellon University of Michigan, in 1963 and Memphis Academy of Arts in 1965-1969, the Louisiana State University in 1969 and 1970, and the Arrowmont School of Crafts in Gatlinburg, Tennessee, under Michael Cardew in 1971. She was listed in *Who's Who of American Women* in 1973-1982. She teaches workshops at schools and universities. Does a lecture circuit around Memphis and has been on Memphis Educational Television, demonstrating how to throw pots on a wheel. The list of exhibitions for this potter is understandingly extensive, including shows in Louisiana, Tennessee, Mississippi, Maryland, Texas, etc., for which she has won many awards throughout her career from the Norman Apell Award for outstanding senior student at Mellon University in 1962, to the Merit Award for a Memphis Artist at the Craftsmen Show in 1980. Agnes makes functional one of a kind pieces of stoneware and porcelain which she signs with "Stark."

Starnes, Walter. Los Angeles, California. Was listed in the 1952 and 1954 Crockery and Glass Journal Directory, under dinnerware made in the U.S., of earthenware. A paper label was found on very pretty hand painted plate. (Mark: paper label, sent by Beechwold Antiques, Columbus, Ohio.)

Star Porcelain Company. Trenton, New Jersey. 1899 to present. Star Porcelain manufactured electrical porcelain, much of which was marked with the name of the company for which it was made. According to Jack H. Tod, *A History of Electrical Porcelain*, p. 94, they also used a marking, "Ideal" in some split electrical knobs. Bay Ridge Specialty Company is a Division of Star Porcelain Company, Trenton, New Jersey.

They are makers of ceramic pottery bathroom accessories, lamp shades and giftware. They employed 80 in 1978. (See separate listing for Bay Ridge Specialty Co.) (Marks: no. 1 filed for registration August 6, 1948, for use on porous absorbent porcelain parts sold as such for parts of dishes for food and like perishable products, claiming use since January 1939. Marks 2, 3, Barber, *Marks of American Potters*, p. 67.)

HUMIDOLAIN STAR

1.   2.   3.

Star, Various Potteries. Various locations. The Star Pottery of Elmendorf, Texas, was dated around 1888-1914 by Stewart and Consentino, *Stoneware*, p. 126. The star within a circle mark was dated 1909 to 1915 by Humphries and Schmidt, as cited. Potter Ernst Richter made stoneware. The wide use of the name "Star" and stars used as part of marks and for decorations has caused a lot of difficulty for the researcher. To name just a few with "Star" as a name: In 1900, there was a Star Pottery in Philadelphia, Pennsylvania, employing 25 to make table and toilet ware. N.K. Smith employed seven in the Star Pottery in Muskingum Ave. in Zanesville, Ohio, in 1868 to make stoneware. Star Porcelain in Trenton, New Jersey, made electrical porcelain and the Bay Ridge Specialties. In 1878, there was a Star Clay Company in Philadelphia, Pennsylvania, who registered a mark in the form of a star but no picture was available in the patent reports back of 1893. Also, there was a Star Pottery Company in East Liverpool, Ohio, which sold in 1870 to Thomas Starkey and P.S. Ourby and the product changed from the older stoneware jugs and crocks to Rockingham and yellowware, according to M.K. Zimmerman, "Pottery Industry in East Liverpool," *Crockery and Glass Journal*, December 18, 1924, p. 223. (Mark 1 is for Star Pottery Elmendorf, Texas, a single star mark, sent by Dave Newkirk, author of *Red Wing Dinnerware*; same mark shown by Humphries and Schmidt, *Texas Pottery*, p. 32; mark 2, shown in Ketchum, *The Pottery and Porcelain Collector's Handbook*, p. 98.)

   1.   2.

Starship Studio. Traverse City, Michigan. 1973 to present (1985). Rosalyn Tyge, studio potter, makes handthrown, hand painted porcelain decorative pieces. She studied three years at the Pewabic Pottery in Detroit, Michigan, from 1975 to 1978. She started selling her pottery commercially in 1973.

Tyge

Star Stoneware. Crooksville, Ohio. 1892 to 1945. The company was operating only part time in 1932 due to the Depression. They made stoneware, utilitarian jugs, churns, crocks, cookingware, etc. Lyndon C. Viel in his second book, *The*

Clay Giants, Book II, p. 77, shows a crock with mark 1. Pieces with this mark can be found in many homes in Crooksville, if one goes looking for stoneware. Mark 2 is claimed by these same people as an older mark used by Star Stoneware of Crooksville. They could show many pieces so marked to prove it. The whole star is recessed or sunken into the bottom and measures about an inch across. There was no lettering or marking on the star. Star Stoneware purchased the controlling interest in the Crooksville Pottery Company, which had been started in 1903. The building was operated as a part of the Star Stoneware until 1938, when it was purchased by the Ferro Enamel Corporation of Cleveland, Ohio, to make pottery saggers and refractory supplies. Star Stoneware also absorbed the Buckeye Stoneware Company (see that listing). Muskingum Pottery burned around 1907 and was rebuilt. Around 1913 they became part of Star Stoneware under Betty Brown. When Star Stoneware closed around 1945 they were operating in more than one building as Star No. 1 and Star No. 2 and had made a great deal more cookingware pieces in the old style than collectors and researchers realize. They had the accumulated knowledge of the old Crooksville-Roseville area cookingware manufacturers. (Marks: no. 1 is on later stoneware jars and churns, etc. of various sizes. They are glazed all white or brown and white, straight sided pieces. The second mark was on a very old little brown stoneware jug glazed across the bottom. Mark 3 was a raised mark on a dark brown 10 gallon jar with a lid and raised flower.)

1.   2.   3.

Stebner Studios. Hartville, Ohio. Bruce Stebner and his wife, Maureen, are studio potters, working in their restored 1830 home to make salt glazed stoneware in the old tradition. Each piece is formed and decorated by hand and salt glazed in firing. The clay is gray or tan and the decorations are cobalt blue. The couple have been featured in national publications such as *Country Living, Early American* and *Creative Ideas for Living*. They have done many shows and have pieces in the Greenfield Village Museum, the Museum of American Folk Art, etc. Bruce has a B.F.A. degree from Kent State University, Bowling Green, Ohio, and worked as a potter at Hale Farm and Village. Their stamped marks and logo are shown.

M. STEBNER
HARTVILLE, OHIO

B. STEBNER
HARTVILLE, OHIO

Stegall's Stoneware Pottery. Tullahoma, Tennessee. 1980 to present (1985). Studio potters, Alan and Nancy Stegall, making functional and nonfunctional artistic pieces. Marks inscribed.

Stegall

Nancy Stegall

Alan Stegall

Stephenson, John H. John, a studio potter, received his B.A. degree in 1951 from the University of Northern Iowa, in Cedar Falls. From 1952 to 1956 he served in the U.S. Air Force and in 1956 he returned to his studies at Cranbrook Academy of Art, Bloominghills, Michigan, where he received his M.A. degree in 1958. Since 1959, he has taught at the University of Michigan in Ann Arbor as a professor of art. His work is mainly sculptured now, and has been widely exhibited. He has received many medals and awards, including the Gold Medal of the City of Faenza at the XXIII Concorso Internazionale Della Ceramica d'Arte Faenza, Faenza, Italy. (Information: Garth Clark, *A Century of Ceramics in the U.S.*, p. 332. Mark: Linda Steigleder, from the booklet published by the Everson Museum of Art to accompany the 1978 exhibition, "A Century of Ceramics in the U.S." Mark is incised.)

STEPHENSON

Stephenson, Suzanne G. Suzanne, a studio potter, studied at Carnegie-Mellon University in Pittsburg, Pennsylvania, and in 1959 she received an M.F.A. degree from Cranbrook Academy of Art in Bloomfield Hills, Michigan. In 1963 she became a professor of art at Michigan University in Ypsilanti, Michigan. In 1962 to 1963, she studied for a time in Japan, and in 1973 she studied lustre glazes in Spain. She has exhibited widely since 1963 and has had several one-woman exhibitions. (Information: Garth Clark, *A Century of Ceramics in the U.S.*, p. 332. Mark: Linda Steigleder, from the booklet published by the Everson Museum of Art to accompany the 1978 exhibition, "A Century of Ceramics in the U.S." Mark is incised.)

SS

Stephen, Walter Benjamin and **Stephen, Nellie Randall** in **Nonconnah Pottery**. Near Memphis, Tennessee. From 1901 to 1910, then moved near Skyland, North Carolina, from 1913 to 1916. Walter and his mother made molded or wheel thrown pieces. Some of them had dark green slip forms, some cameo designs. These pieces were marked with painted letters in paste or slip, "Nonconnah." Nonconnah was an Indian name when translated means Long Stream. Mrs. Nellie Stephens was an artist in her own right who had drawn illustrations for *The Youth's Companion* magazine. In 1913, Nellie Stephen died and Walter moved near Skyland, North Carolina, and began a pottery with C.P. Ryman as a partner for the next three years. From around 1916 to around 1926, Stephen continued to experiment with pottery, but he was in the construction business. In 1926, he started the Pisgah Forest Pottery. See that listing for more information on Stephen. (Information and mark: *The Pottery of Walter Stephen*, published by Ceramic Circle of Charlotte in conjunction with the Mint Museum of History.)

NONCONNAH   **NONCONNAH**

Sterling China Company. Offices in East Liverpool, Ohio, and factory in Wellsville, Ohio. 1917 to present. A large modern maker of hotel and restaurant dinnerware was started by B.E. Allen in 1917 in Wellsville, Ohio. The very early years' products were cups, mugs, bowls, etc. Gradually new items were added to the line; body color and decorations were added and varied. Additional buildings were built and the latest equipment installed. Sterling had the first dipping machine in the hotel china industry, according to the company history. Prior to the machine, all items were dipped by hand in a tub of glass. Sterling started "inlay" patterns in the hotel ware industry. (Colored clay was applied to a piece of clayware and a bond created between the two pieces.) Sterling made a tremendous amount of china for the armed services during World War II. After the war they brought out a new shape designed by Russel Wright.

In the 1950's some of the older hotel china plants went out of business but Sterling continued to grow. In 1954, they took over the Scammell lines of china which had been the leaders in the industry for 80 years (see Scammell). Today Sterling produces the famous Lamberton China along with the large line of Sterling China. In 1947, Iroquois China Company began building a plant in Vega Baja, Puerto Rico to manufacture hotel ware (see Illinois China). In the 1950's this plant was acquired by Sterling China Company and from that time on Caribe China was made at that plant until 1977 when the plant was closed by Sterling China Company. From 1959 to 1969, Sterling China Company owned and operated the Wellsville China Company. See Wellsville China Company for history. (Information: from company. Marks: A large part of these marks were sent by Sterling China Company. Several came from Quality Stamp Company, East Liverpool, Ohio, and some from dishes. The dating code was sent by Sterling China.

(Marks: nos. 1-12, for Caribe China would date between 1951 and 1977. No. 13 came from the company with the backstamps they sent. No. 14, Russel Wright China came shortly after W.W. II. No. 15 was filed for registration by J.L. Pasmantier and Sons in 1933. See that listing. Also see mark no. 28. No. 16, copies of the Jones, McDuffee and Stratton mark was found in 1952 directories. This copy of mark sent by factory. See the listing, Jones, McDuffee and Stratton. Nos. 17, 18, shown in directories in 1950's, but are used until present. Sterling China Company seems to have used some of the same marks over a long period of time for its various customers. None of the marks shown date back of the 1940's. Nos. 9-12, the Lamberton marks would all come after 1954 when Sterling took over Scammell's Lamberton line of china. Nos. 23 to 48 are the stamps made for Sterling China Company by Quality Stamp Company in the 1940's and 1950's.

Nos. 50, 51, backstamps on railroad china. In *Hotel Management*, 1949, was an advertisement sent by Larry Paul (no month or page no. sent). The full page ad said that Sterling China Company had nearly 700 patterns in dinnerware and the leading railroads who used Sterling China Company's dishes were represented in logos shown in numbers 54 to 59. See the listing in back of book to identify railroads. The remainder of the marks were sent by the company and used in 1960's and 1970's. The only patent registration reports we found for Sterling were nos. 60 and 61. The word, "Ultra Dine," and "Ultradine," was filed in two ways on May 3, 1978, both claiming use since April 9, 1973 for china dinnerware.)

	1950	1951	1952	1953	1954	1955	1956
Jan.-March	--	D	K	P	U	Z	A4
April-June	A	E	L	R	V	A1	A5
July-Sept.	B	F	M	S	X	A2	A6
Oct.-Dec.	C	H	O	T	Y	A3	A7

	1957	1958	1959	1960	1961	1962	1963
Jan.-March	A8	B3	B7	C2	C6	D1	D5
April-June	A9	B4	B8	C3	C7	D2	D6
July-Sept.	B1	B5	B9	C4	C8	D3	D7
Oct.-Dec.	B2	B6	C1	C5	C9	D4	D8

	1964	1965	1966	1967	1968	1969
		Jan. E4				
		Feb. E5				
		March E6				
		April E7				
Jan.-March	D9	May E8	F3	F7	G1	G5
April-June	E1	June E9	F4	F8	G2	G6
July-Sept.	E2	July E10	F5	F9	G3	G7
Oct.-Dec.	E3	Aug. F1	F6	F10	G4	G8
		Sept. F1				
		Oct. F2				
		Nov. F2				
		Dec. F2				

	1970	1971	1972	1973	1974	1975	1976
Jan.-March	G9	H4	H8	K4	K8	L3	L7
April-June	H1	H5	K1	K5	K9	L4	L8
July-Sept.	H2	H6	K2	K6	L1	L5	L9
Oct.-Dec.	H3	H7	K3	K7	L2	L6	M1

	1977	1978	1979	1980	1981	1982	1983
Jan.-March	M2	M6	N1	N5	O1	O5	P1
April-June	M3	M7	N2	N6	O2	O6	P2
July-Sept.	M4	M8	N3	N7	O3	O7	P3
Oct.-Dec.	M5	M9	N4	N8	O4	O8	P4

	1984	1985	1986	1987	1988	1989	1990
Jan-March	P5	Q1	Q5	R1	R5	S1	S5
April-June	P6	Q2	Q6	R2	R6	S2	S6
July-Sept.	P7	Q3	Q7	R3	R7	S3	S7
Oct.-Dec.	P8	Q4	Q8	R4	R8	S4	S8

1.

2.

3.

PUERTO RICO U.S.A.
4.

RIVIERA Casuals by Caribe U.S.A.
5.

Caribe China PUERTO RICO U.S.A. D 1
6.

U.S. Caribe MARILITE by Carlos Montes G U.S.A.
7.

Caribe BLUE PUERTO RICO U.S.A.
8.

Caribe China PUERTO RICO USA
9.

Caribe China ANTIQUE PUERTO RICO USA
10.

Caribe China MADE FOR Surfas REFRIGERATION AND RESTAURANT SUPPLY
11.

MADE EXPRESSLY FOR THE UNITED NATIONS BY CARIBE CHINA H FRIEDMAN & SONS NEW YORK SINCE 1889
12.

13.

STERLING CHINA BY Russel Wright MADE U.S.A.
14.

STERLING CHINA B J.L. PASMANTIER AND SONS
15.

16.

STERLING Vitrified China EAST LIVERPOOL, OHIO U.S.A.
17.

STERLING Vitrified China EAST LIVERPOOL OHIO U.S.A.
18.

IVORY LAMBERTON CHINA STERLING MADE IN AMERICA
19.

IVORY LAMBERTON CHINA STERLING MADE IN AMERICA
20.

LAMBERTON CHINA STERLING MADE EXPRESSLY FOR UNITED STATES LINES U.S.A.
21.

LAMBERTON CHINA STERLING MADE IN U.S.A.
22.

Vitrified The Sterling CHINA CO E. LIVERPOOL OHIO
23.

Fultone The Sterling China Co. E. Liverpool Ohio
24.

YORK
BY
STERLING CHINA
U.S.A.
25.

26. *Shell Pink* by STERLING

MADE EXPRESSLY FOR
DELTA AIR LINES
BY
STERLING CHINA CO.
27.

JOHN L. PASMANTIER
AND SONS
NEW YORK CITY;
28.

STERLING
CHINA
EAST LIVERPOOL, O.
MADE EXPRESSLY
FOR
AMERICAN EXPORT
ISBRANDTSEN LINES
U.S.A.
29.

SHILLERWARE
STERLING CHINA CO.
U.S.A.
30.

Furnished by
Atlantic Equipment company
31.

STERLING
Vitrified China
EAST·LIVERPOOL·OHIO
U.S.A.
32.

PAN AM
P/N 873-579140

STERLING
Vitrified China
EDWARD
DON
& COMPANY
33.

LOUBAT,
NEW ORLEANS. LA.
VITRIFIED CHINA
34.

STERLING
CHINA COMPANY
VITRIFIED
EAST LIVERPOOL, O.
35.

BRANIFF INTERNATIONAL
STERLING CHINA CO.
U.S.A.
36.

LOUBAT
NEW ORLEANS
LA.
37.

FRONTIER AIRLINES
905-0S24
DENVER, COLORADO
STERLING CHINA CO.
U.S.A.
38.

STERLING
CHINA COMPANY
EAST LIVERPOOL, O
39.

MADE FOR
INTERNATIONAL
HOTEL SUPPLY CO.
BOSTON, MASS.
STERLING CHINA
IHS - 7.
40.

NORTH CENTRAL FLEET SERVICE
STERLING CHINA CO. U.S.A.
41.

EDGEWOOD
COUNTRY CLUB
42.

"La ROSA de CARIBE"
por
EMPRESS STERLING
EXCLUSIVAMENTE
para
PUERTO RICO
AAA-1 CALIDAD
43.

MEDALLION
STERLING CHINA ©
E.LIVERPOOL, OH. USA
44.

TOWN
STERLING CHINA CO.
MADE IN U.S.A.
45.

STERLING CHINA
MADE FOR
York Kitchen Equipment Co.
NEW YORK
MADE IN U. S. A.
46.

MADE FOR
ALLEGHENY AIRLINES
STERLING CHINA CO.
U.S.A. CR-16
47.

A STERLING CHINA
EXCLUSIVE
EAST LIVERPOOL, O.
U.S.A.
48.

49. Wellsville China Co.
MADE IN U.S.A.

MADE EXPRESSLY FOR
HARRY M. STEVENS INC.
STERLING CHINA
THE BRAMLETT CO.
MIAMI - NEW YORK
50.

51.  Ultra Dine
BY STERLING
USA
N.6

STERLING
VITRIFIED CHINA
FLORIDA EAST COAST
RAILWAY
52.

STERLING
VITRIFIED CHINA
FLORIDA EAST COAST
RAILWAY
53.

54.

55.

56.

57.

58.

59.

ULTRA DINE
60.

ULTRADINE
61.

VITRIFIED CHINA
MADE IN U.S.A.
GANSON
BOSTON, MASS
62.

MORRIS GORDON & SON, INC.
BOSTON MG MASS.
CARIBE CHINA
63.

MADE EXPRESSLY
FOR
TWA
STERLING CHINA CO.
USA
64.

COMPLIMENTS
Wm. ROBERTS, Ltd.
STERLING CHINA
U.S.A.
65.

Rice Islands
Casual CHINA   66.   67.
SEA FLOWER
USA

EXPRESSLY MADE FOR
BRANIFF
INTERNATIONAL
STERLING CHINA
USA

MADE ESPECIALLY FOR
Ben Grass
H. L. HOEGHSTETTER CO.
STERLING CHINA
86.

VITRIFIED CHINA
MADE FOR
TRIPLE CEE
SUPPLY CO.
87.

S.E. RYKOFF & CO.
SER
STERLING CHINA U.S.A.
68.

Berkshire   69.
STERLING CHINA
EAST LIVERPOOL, OHIO

Greenwood's   70.
STAINLESS
VITRIFIED CHINA

STERLING CHINA
MADE
ESPECIALLY FOR
Ackley Equipment Co.
NEW YORK   88.

MARION-KAY
PRODUCTS CO.
BROWNSTOWN, IND.
89.

MADE EXPRESSLY
FOR
H.A.C.   71.
STERLING CHINA
U.S.A.

*Dietary
Products*   72.
D
Div. of Am. Hosp. Sply Corp.
DESIGNED FOR
HOSPITAL USE

THE BARCLAY   90.
FURNISHED BY
JOHN WANAMAKER
PHILADELPHIA

91.   MADE IN AMERICA
EXPRESSLY FOR
WADE PARK MANOR

Mᴇᴅᴀʟʟɪᴏɴ   73.
STERLING
CHINA ©

Erwin   74.
STERLING CHINA
EAST LIVERPOOL,
OHIO

VITRIFIED CHINA BY
Sexton   92.
MADE IN U.S.A.

93.   F.S. LOUIE & CO.
BERKELEY, CALIF.
STERLING CHINA CO. U.S.A.

STERLING CHINA
E. LIVERPOOL, OH.
U.S.A.   75.

innkare   76.

H. LAUBER & CO.   94.
CINCINNATI, OHIO
BY
STERLING CHINA

DESERT TAN   95.
STERLING
Vitrified China
EAST-LIVERPOOL-OHIO
U·S·A·

Ultra Dine   77.
PUERTO RICO
U.S.A.

78.   MADE IN
AMERICA
D. F. McCALLISTER & SONS
PHILA.

STERLING   96.
Vitrified China

97.   T.W.A.
PART #44-1136
STERLING CHINA CO.
MADE IN U.S.A.

Made Expressly For
NEUSTETER'S
By STERLING CHINA
79.

MADE EXPRESSLY FOR
Georgetown Temptations
WASHINGTON, D. C.
80.

MADE ESPECIALLY FOR
PICCADILLY CAFETERIA
FURNISHED BY
HUEY & PHILP   98.
STERLING CHINA

YORK   81.
BY
STERLING CHINA
U. S. A.

82.   MADE EXPRESSLY FOR
LaSalle duBois
E. B. ADAMS CO.
WASHINGTON, D. C.

TRIPLE CHECKED
ABC
APPROVED
Caribe China
PUERTO RICO
U.S.A.
83.

84.   A.L.-361   MADE FOR
ALLEGHENY AIRLINES
STERLING CHINA CO.
U. S. A.

85.
saudia السعودية
الخطوط الجوية العربية السعودية
SAUDI ARABIAN AIRLINES

Sterling China Marks. In a recently published book, mark 1 has been attributed to the Sterling China Company, Sebring, Ohio, an early name used by Limoges China Company (see that listing). I had attributed this mark to Sterling China Company of East Liverpool, Ohio, in one of my earlier books. Then I found a plate with the mark. It is a very poor grade of discolored semi-porcelain with no decoration except an initial in gold. It has no ring to the sound, so it could not have possibly been made by either company. Plus the fact that Sterling China Company in East Liverpool, Ohio, never made anything but hotelware. This mark stays unidentified. No. 2 is a drawn copy. No. 3 is a photostatic copy of the same mark showing the initials "S.C. Co." No. 4 is a mark I believe to be made by the same company as 2 and 3. These marks are on pieces of fine thin highly vitrified china and could not possibly be made by the same company as no. 1, as was suggested. One of these pieces is a very old style sugar bowl. The other is a fine thin plate with delicate decaled flowers and a raised design around the edge. The fine glaze, white clay body and delicate decorations are very similar to the early plates made by Onondago Pottery and marked Syracuse China. I believe these marks belong to Syracuse China Company but at this time I can't prove it. No. 5 mark, "Sterling

Hiawatha Porcelain'' is not really porcelain at all. It is a very good grade of semi-porcelain but does not have the ring to it that the pieces described under 2 and 3 have. This mark is very similar to the early marks used by Homer Laughlin China Company and the quality and appearance of the plate is very good also. So I believe this to be a Homer Laughlin China Company mark. The one thing was may say for sure is that these are American made products. The companies in the old days wanted to fool the public into thinking the ware was English. I'm sure they weren't worried about fooling the writers on American Pottery in the future! As far as I am concerned we still don't know how the early Sterling (later Limoges) China Company pieces were marked or how they looked. See the listing Colonial China Company for another mark involving the word "sterling."

1.   2.   3.

4.   5.

Stern Brothers. New York, New York. Filed for registration of the two marks shown on December 15, 1952, claiming to have used Stern Brothers since 1867, and Stern's since 1932 for ceramic articles, namely, teapots, coffee pots, mustard pots, bean pots, stew pots, cups, saucers, plates, platters, soup dishes, bowls, mugs, dessert dishes, casseroles, tureens, pitchers, creamers, cruets, hors d'oeuvre sets, baking dishes, baking shells, pipkins, petite marmites, salt and pepper holders, jugs and jars.

Stetson China Company. Lincoln, Illinois. Started as a decorator and distributing company in Chicago, Illinois. McKee, p. 30, said that they installed Ladd-Cronin kilns for firing decorated ware. Stetson obtained their blanks in early years from Mount Clemens Pottery. To secure a steady source of supply, Joseph W. Stetson and others took over the Illinois China Company in Lincoln, Illinois, on February 1, 1946. The name was changed shortly to the Stetson China Company. In the 1963 *Polk's Lincoln City Directory*, p. 197, the listing was the **Stetson Corporation** with J.W. Stetson as chairman of the board, Phillip R. Stetson as president, and

Burt Chudacoff as executive vice-president. They advertised themselves as "America's foremost dinnerware manufacturer of small oven-proof semi-porcelain and break resistant Melmac." The Stetson China Company stopped manufacturing in 1966, but a retail outlet was maintained for a period of time in Lincoln, Illinois. In the 1966 *Polk's Lincoln City Directory*, the pottery was called the **Lincoln China Company** with the same executives and same products listed as in the 1963 directory. So unless the compiler of the directory made a mistake, the pottery must have had a new name for a year; perhaps there was an attempt at a reorganization of some sort before closing. The Lincoln China Retail Store was also listed that year. In 1955, Stetson China Company claimed in their advertisement to be the largest manufacturer of individual hand-painted ceramic dinnerware in the U.S. and since Southern Potteries, Inc. was about to reach its time of closing, this may have been a very true claim.

Pieces of Stetson's hand-painted ware are very easily confused with that made by Southern Potteries, Inc. Stetson made a great deal of ware without marks. Southern Potteries seems to have very seldom used a mark on large platters and some accessory pieces and cups. There is room for error in confusing the products of these two companies. (Marks: no. 1 filed for registration December 7, 1942, claiming use since November 1, 1941 on dishes, cups, saucers, plates, platters, serving bowls, made of porcelain; no. 2 filed April 15, 1938, claiming use since March 1, 1933 on china tableware; no. 3 filed April 5, 1938, claiming use since March 1, 1936, for use on tableware; no. 4 filed April 16, 1938, claiming use since November 1936, for use on china tableware; no. 5 filed April 5, 1938, claiming use since March 5, 1933 for use on china tableware; no. 6 filed March 20, claiming use since January 1, 1951; no. 7 filed May 25, 1951, claiming use since August 1949; no. 8 filed May 25, 1951, claiming use since August 1949; nos. 9, 10, 11 were all filed May 2, 1952, claiming use since March 1952; no. 12 filed August 29, 1957, claiming use since March 1, 1933; no. 13 filed June 27, 1957, claiming use since June 20, 1057; no. 14 filed July 15, 1954, claiming use since May 12, 1953; no. 15 filed December 3, 1954, claiming use since September 29, 1954; no. 16 filed January 26, 1955, claiming use since September 24, 1954; no. 17 filed April 14, 1955, claiming use since July 14, 1954; no. 18 filed May 26, 1955, claiming use since April 14, 1955; no.'s 19, 20 filed March 4, 1958, claiming use since September and October 1956; no. 21 filed March 24, 1958, claiming use since March 10, 1958; no. 22 filed April 2, 1958, claiming use since March 26, 1958; nos. 23 and 24 filed April 25, 1958, claiming use since March 1958; no. 25 filed December 19, 1960, claiming use since March 1, 1936; nos. 26, 27 filed December 19, 1960, claiming use since July 1954; no. 28 filed September 26, 1961, claiming use since March 10, 1960; no. 29 filed February 3, 1960, claiming use since May 12, 1953; no. 30 filed July 22, 1960, claiming use since June 9, 1960; no. 31 filed February 24, 1964, claiming use since February 14, 1964; no. 32 filed June 29, 1964, claiming use since March 8, 1963. Most of the marks registered were filed for earthenware. Those claimed for use on china dinnerware were American Heritage, Queen Anne, Linconite, Colonial Lace, Englestown, Royal Stetson, Stetson, La Plume, Heritage by Stetson, California Casual, California Rainbow and Thermaceram. Nos. 33, 34, 35 were from Jo Cunningham's book, pp. 273, 274. No. 36 is the actual version use of the registered mark no. 31. No. 37 is what no. 4 really came to look like. This shows the version filed is not always the complete mark as it appears on the dish. Nos.

445

38, 39, were Melmac marks. Notice "Sun Valley" used on earthenware and melma. The rest of the stamped marks were found on dishes or at Quality Stamp Company, East Liverpool, Ohio.)

Heritage 1.

STETSON 2.

Queen Anne 3.

AIR FLOW 4.

5.

American Bride 6.

S U N VALLEY 7.

AMERICAN HERITAGE 8.

Duchess of Greencastle 9.

Lady Marlowe 10.

Yours truly 11.

STETSON 12.

ROYAL STETSON 13.

TABLE TO TERRACE 14.

COUNTRY CASUAL 15.

LA PLUME 16.

Lady Rose 17.

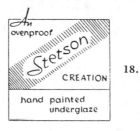
18.

OVENPROOF DINNERWARE Handpainted UNDERGLAZE 19.

Hand Painted underglaze MADE IN U.S.A. 20.

CALIFORNIA RAINBOW 21.

22. CALIFORNIA CASUAL

HERITAGE BY STETSON 23.

ENGLISHTOWN 24.   QUEEN ANNE 25.

LINCONITE 26.   COLONIAL LACE 27.

THERMOCERAM 28.

TABLE TO TERRACE 29.

WONDERWARE 30.

31.

STETSON 32.

Duncan Hines HAND PAINTED Dinnerware BY STETSON TM.DHI MADE IN USA 33.

34.

35.

STETSON DINNERWARE 36.

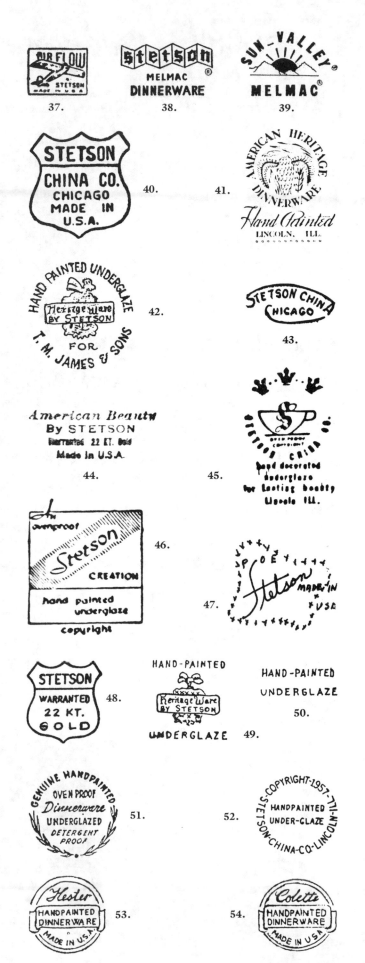

Stetyzenmeyer, F. Rochester, New York. Around 1853 to around 1855 (Stewart and Consentino, p. 126). Became Stetyzenmeyer and Goetzman from 1857 to around 1860 (Stewart and Consentino, p. 126). Mark: found on blue decorated crock at the Ohio Historical Society Museum at Zanesville, Ohio.)

F. STETYZENMEYER

Steubenville Pottery Company. Steubenville, Ohio. 1879-1959. Organized on November 17, 1879. By 1889 they were operating seven kilns and six decorating kilns. By the early 1900's 350 people were employed to make dinner and toilet sets in semi-vitreous and Canton China, cream colored, lightweight, handsomely decorated, which were made in fancy shapes and unique designs. They also made granite ware and other decorated ware. In 1902, they were listed as making semi-porcelain, porcelain and white granite, dinner sets, toilet sets and short sets of odd dishes, some decorated.

American Modern, first made in 1939, was designed by Russel Wright, a New York City designer. The ware came in a variety of colors: Granite Grey, Curry (chartreuse), Bean Brown and Sea Blue. Another pattern, "Woodfield Leaf" with solid colors and very nice leaf shape, by Steubenville is a favorite. According to McKee, p. 46, the Steubenville Pottery had very rough going in the 1950's because sales had always been slanted toward retail distribution under the direction of Harry D. Wintwringer, who died in 1955. The Steubenville Pottery made pieces marked "Final Kiln" on December 15, 1959. By letter from Minnie Merick, Jefferson County Historical Association, Inc. in February 1983 was the information, "When Steubenville Pottery closed the building was purchased by Barium Chemicals, Inc. of Canonsburg, Pa. and all the molds and equipment were moved to Canonsburg." Even the Steubenville Pottery name was used in directories in the 1960's by the Canonsburg plant. See Canonsburg for confusing Steubenville marks of the 1960's, used by Canonsburg Pottery. (Marks: no. 1, stamped mark shown in W.P. Jervis, "World's Pottery Marks," Pottery, Glass and Brass Salesman, May 20, 1915, p. 15. He said present mark-dating mark around 1915. No. 2 is actual photostatic copy of no. 1. No. 3 is a stamped mark used early 1900's. It is a photostatic copy from very old dish. Nos. 4-17, Barber, *Marks of American Potters*, p. 129, 130. All in use before and around 1900. No. 18 was filed for registration October 26, 1931, claiming use since April 9, 1931, for use on earthenware. No.

19 is actual stamped copy of mark, filed in no. 18. Nos. 20-21 are stamped marks of 1920's. No. 22 is a stamped mark on 1930's dishes. Nos. 23, 24 are stamped marks taken from dishes found on wares made from 1930's to closing of the plant. No. 25 is a paper label. Nos. 26 and 27 prove a very important point. The Canonsburg Pottery bought the Steubenville Pottery and continued to use the Steubenville Pottery name for quite some time. In the various directories the mark "by Steubenville." No. 29 was a 1931 mark on a new line of two tone ware called "Inlaid."

1.   2.   3.

4.   5.   6.   7.

8.   9.   10.

11.   12.   13.

14.   15.   16.

17.   18. ROSE DAWN   19.

20.   21.

22.   23.   24.   25.   26.   27.   28.   29.   30.

Stevens, Charles A., and Brothers. Chicago, Illinois. Filed for rights to this mark on July 6, 1927, for use on articles of china, porcelain and earthenware, namely, flowerpots, pitchers, bowls, vases, jugs, jam jars, cup sets, coffee sets, flower containers, cookie jars, salad sets, powder boxes and pottery trays, claiming use since September 17, 1926.

RARITY

Stewart's Northwood's Gift Shop. Lake Geneva, Wisconsin. Filed for rights to this mark January 23, 1948, for use on dishes, vases, flower pots and bowls made of china or pottery, claiming use since 1942.

STEWART'S
NORTHWOOD'S GIFT SHOP

Stine Pottery. White Cottage, Perry County, Ohio (near Crooksville, Roseville area). Before 1868 until after 1910.

C.W. Stine operated a pottery on Kent Run around 1868. Around this time, E. Hall worked for Stine. Hall later made his now famous E. Hall jug at the W.P. Harris Pottery. The mark pictured was found on a beautiful gray stoneware piece with incised lettering and blue decorations. The owner identified the piece as having been made at the Stine Pottery in White Cottage which operated quite a long time for a blue bird type pottery. The W.C. Stine Pottery employed 19 in 1902, as listed in the *Factory Inspection Reports for the State of Ohio.*

FROM
L. S Stine
To
M. W PRINTZ
WHITE COTTAGE, OHIO
DEC. 25, 1899

Stix, Baer and Fuller Company. St. Louis, Missouri. Filed for registration on this mark on January 19, 1962 for use on dishes, cups, saucers, bowls, vases, made of china, porcelain earthenware pots and crocks, claiming use since January 3, 1962.

Stockton Terra Cotta Company/Stockton Art Pottery. Stockton, California. The Stockton Terra Cotta Company was formed in 1890 to make fire brick, sewer and stone pipe. By July 1891 the plant employed 12 men. In 1894, under the direction of Thomas W. Blakely and his son, John W., the pottery started making ornamental pottery and artware of vitrified semi-porcelain with high gloss glazes. Pieces included teapots, creamers, sugars, vases, etc. They made an art line called "Rekston," using yellow California clay with underglaze slip colored decorations with a brown background. See Paul Evans, *Art Pottery of the U.S.*, pp. 273 and 274, for a good description of the products and methods of manufacture. In 1896, **Stockton Art Pottery** was incorporated in California, and the company assumed all debts, etc. held against Stockton Terra Cotta Company. New lines and distributors were added. They started making a monochrome glazed line in several colors. In 1897 the pottery employed 10 women to decorate Rekston, but the output was only about 100 pieces per day. In 1900, economic conditions caused the plant's closing. Another new company was formed called **Stockton Brick and Pottery Company** to make brick, drain tile, crucibles, terra cotta trimmings, furnaces, etc. And the company planned to continue making the art line Rekston. However, an entire plant was destroyed by fire in 1902 and that ended the art pottery manufacture. The pottery did return to making the more structural type of clay pieces as listed previously. Not all Stockton pottery was marked. (Information: Paul Evans, "Stockton Pottery Early California Ware," *Spinning Wheel*, October 1971, pp. 22, 25,

26; also, Thelma Shull, "The Stockton Art Pottery," *Hobbies*, August 1949, pp. 94, 95. Marks: no. 1, Jervis, "Worlds' Pottery Marks," *Pottery Glass and Brass Salesman*, October 22, 1914, p. 13; also, Shull, as cited, p. 94. No. 2, Paul Evans, *Art Pottery of the U.S.*, p. 277.)

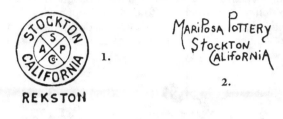

Stockwell, Henry/Humiston and Stockwell. Perth Amboy, New Jersey, and Poughkeepsie, New York. C. Jordan Thorn, *Handbook of Old Pottery and Porcelain Marks*, p. 149, lists Henry Stockwell in the Columbian Factory in Perth Amboy, New Jersey, in 1831. Then John P. Remensnyder, "The Potters of Poughkeepsie," *The Art of the Potter*, edited by Diana and J. Garrison Stradling, p. 125, said that in 1843, Henry Stockwell and Abraham Conover were also in business on Main Street, but I don't think he meant they were working together because he was just listing potters in Poughkeepsie, New York. John Ramsay, p. 180 lists Humiston and Walker making stoneware from 1826 to 1835 in South Amboy, New Jersey. So the partnership of Humiston and Stockwell would be sometime after 1835 until before 1843. (Mark 1, Thorn, p. 149, as cited. Mark 2, from the Ross Purdy Museum at the Ohio Ceramic Society Building in Columbus, Ohio.)

made by Henry Stockwell

HUMISTON & STOCKWELL
AMBOY N.J.

Stoffer, L.D. and Company. Ripley, Illinois. L.D. Stoffer came from Ohio in 1847 and made stoneware jugs, crocks, etc., until around 1860 in Ripley, Illinois. The mark on the picture of the crock sent by Janice T. Wass of the Illinois State Museum was very plain, so evidently this potter's name has been misspelled in other listings. Also, see the listing Tennessee Stoneware and Tile Works. I did not establish whether these were the same family named Stoffer. (Information and mark: Wass, as cited.)

Stofflet, Various Potters. Berks County, Pennsylvania. Around 1814, Heinrick Stofflet was making redware in Berks County. His mark shown below was in Thorn, p. 149. Heinrick's son, Jacob Stofflet, started making pottery with his father from 1830 to 1845. He worked for the Christman Pottery in Bucks County for some time before 1867 and later for Stahl Pottery in Powder Valley, Lehigh County, in 1868. Around 1874 he leased the Lewis Johnson Pottery near Perkiomenville in Montgomery County, where he operated until 1877 when he retired. (Information: Guy F. Reinert, "History of the Pennsylvania-German Potteries in Berks County," *Bulletin of American Ceramic Society*, January 1940, pp. 24-28 Mark: Thorn, p. 149.)

H.S tofflet

Stonegate China Company. Wood Dale, Illinois. Filed for registration on this mark on March 30, 1954, for use on china tableware, claiming use since March 12, 1954.

Stonelain Pottery. See Associated American Artists.

Stoneware By Brown. Anaheim, California. 1972 to present (1983). Studio potters Terry and Larry Brown make functional and decorative wheel thrown pieces, hand painted with beautiful symetrical designs. The largest pieces are dated. The others are signed with a "B" or the word "Brown" by whoever cleans the piece. The Brown's marks are inscribed. When marks are inscribed they vary from one inscription or signature to another, just as we vary every time we sign our names. Several examples are shown here to show the variation that may be found in all inscribed marks.

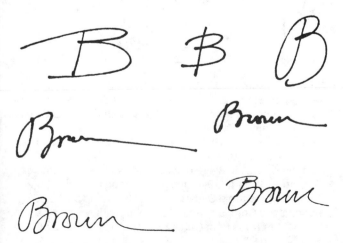

Stork, Edward Leslie. Orange, Cherokee County, Georgia. Around 1870. John Stork and his brother, William, worked for Lemeus Landrum, in the pottery which had been established outside Columbia, South Carolina, by Abner Landrum. John A. Burrison, *Brothers in Clay*, p. 172, called John's son, Edward L. Stork, "a roving potter," so he must have worked in several different potteries in the late 19th and early 20th centuries. A stoneware churn with a lid and Michigan slip is shown in Burrison, p. 70, which was made by this potter. (Information and impress mark: Burrison, as cited.)

E.L. STORK
ORANGE, GA.

J.H. Stouffer Company. Chicago, Illinois. Listed as decorators in 1945 & 1952 *Crockery and Glass Journal Directories*. Not listed in the same directory in 1954.

Stout, Isaac N. Ripley, Illinois. Francis M. Stout started making stoneware in 1848. Isaac was the son of Francis M. Stout, a potter, and Isaac started working with his father in 1878 and the name became F.M. Stout and Son. (Information: W.R. Brink Publishing Co., *History of Schuyler and Brown Counties, Indiana*, 1882. Impressed or stamped mark: on brown glazed stoneware jar, sent by Janice T. Wass, Curator of Decorative Arts, Illinois State Museum.)

I.N. STOUT, MFG.
RIPLEY, ILL.

Straus, Nathan, Inc. New York, New York. In the 1940's or earlier, Warwick China Company and Buffalo China Company made some products for this selling agency. Then on September 7, 1950, the company filed for registration of the mark shown in the name of Nathan Straus-Duparquet, Inc., claiming use since 1921. See McNicol China Company for a mark involving the name, "Duparquet." In 1909, Ben Strauss Company filed for registration of a mark for use on foreign made goods and in 1907 and 1909, Ignaz Strauss filed for "Mikado" ware, also foreign. I established no connection between Nathan Straus (spelled with one "s" in patent report) and these two earlier companies.

DUPARQUET

Studio City Manufacturing Company. Studio City, California. Owner, James E. Kelly, filed for registration on both of these marks in June 1948, claiming use for that month only to be used on ceramic condiment shakers. I found no further listings. In Daniel Rhodes, "California Potters and the Public," *American Ceramic Society Bulletin*, Volume 25, No. 2, 1945, p. 48, Mr. Rhodes said, "There are several hundred plants in the Los Angeles area alone producing glazed pottery objects. A large number of these are small shops making novelties, figurines, ceramic pieces, buttons and other types of ware." This was probably one of them.

SHAKE-RITE

Studio Gallery. Wellington, Kansas. 1974 to present (1985). Studio potters, J. Edward Barker, Jr. and Donna J. Dudley, make various stoneware and sculptured pieces. Donna received a B.F.A. degree from the University of New Mexico in 1961, and Edward acquired an M.A. degree at the same university in 1962. Donna has worked professionally since 1961 and before 1972 Edward worked as a graduate assistant at University of New Mexico, and later as assistant professor at University of Arizona. Altogether, Edward listed 29 invitational or major juried exhibitions and Donna listed 19 besides her various sculptures on public display. Edward's work may be seen on display at First National Bank of Wellington, Kansas, and also, Oklahoma City, Oklahoma, University of New Mexico in Albuquerque, The Hutchinson Art Association in Hutchison, Kansas, Utah State Art Institute in Salt Lake City, and at the Oklahoma City Arts Council. Donna's work is on display at the First National Bank in Oklahoma City, Hutchinson Art Association, Warren Hall Coutts III Memorial Art Gallery, at Park Sculpture in Kansas and Arkansas City. Between the two they have covered many states with their juried exhibitions in Missouri, New Mexico, Washington, Utah, California and Ohio, Kansas, Texas, Louisiana, Arkansas and Oklahoma.

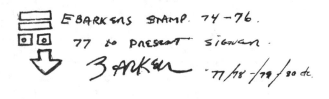

Studio S. Murfreesboro, Tennessee. Lewis D. Snyder is a studio potter, making functional stoneware pieces, such as dinnerware, etc., but he also makes beautiful terra cotta pieces and decorative art pieces on a commission basis. The architectural terra cotta pieces include murals, ceramic veneer or tile for pre-cast walls, columns, etc., all for use on buildings. Studio S is in a renovated barn with the rustic architectural detail in a beautiful setting. Stairways and decks,

an upper and a lower gallery make a beautiful surrounding for the display of this potter's unusual pieces. He makes what he calls, "people pots," which depict humerous expressions in everyday life. Ruffle forms, where he folds collars and ruffles of clay down over the exterior, make some interesting pieces. A very simplified form of Mr. Snyder's training, displays and awards are as follows: B.A. from Glenville State College, Glenville, West Virginia; M.F.A. from Ohio University, Athens, Ohio; Post Graduate Work, International Studies Abroad, Rome, Italy. He was invited to the International Ceramic Symposium, Bechyne, Czechoslovakia. He is a member of the International Academy of Ceramics, Geneva, Switzerland. His works are on display in the International Symposium Museum of Ceramics in Bechyne, Czechoslovakia; Museum of Decorative Arts in Prague, Czechoslovakia; the Everson Museum of Art, Syracuse, New York; Museum of Contemporary Crafts, New York; John Michael Kohler Art Center, Sheboygan, Wisconsin; Renwick Gallery Smithsonian Institute, Washington D.C. Lewis was the winner of numerous purchase awards in competitive and exhibitions including, Craftsmen U.S.A., Museum of Contemporary Crafts, International Exhibition of Ceramic Art, Gdansk, Poland, U.S. Information Service Pottery Exhibition, South America and Africa. He won numerous state and local awards and collections. Most all the signatures on the wheel thrown pieces are enclosed in a circle on the bottom of the piece. Only Snyder's personal pieces are dated. This year he has been experimenting with a new signature for his special pieces. His assistant's pieces are sold under the Studio S mark (no. 1) with their initials at the bottom.

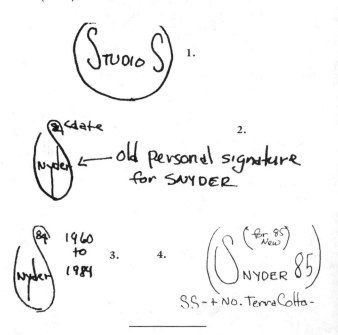

Stupell, Carole, Ltd. New York, New York. Carole Stupell had a specialty shop, bearing her name. Advertised in *House and Gardens* as far back as 1940 to sell American made dinnerware, named "Lorelei." This company was listed at 61 East 57th Street, New York City, in 1983. Other offices listed in 1940 were in Boston and Washington, D.C. (Marks: no. 2, found on earthenware dishes made with an El Patio matt glaze from 1938 to 1940, made by Gladding, McBean and Company for Carole Stupell. No. 3, also made by Gladding, McBean and Company and used on groundlay china pattern in 1941. Mark 1 is from Quality Stamp Company, East Liverpool, Ohio, dated 1976. Marks 2, 3, in company information sent by Gladding, McBean and Company.)

1.

2.

3.

Styson Art Products. New York, New York. This company was found listed in the *Gift and Tableware Reporter Directories* that I had for the years 1949, 1965, 1967. They were not listed in other kinds of directories. They were listed under ice buckets, salad forks and spoons and animal figurines, punch bowls and sets. (Mark sent by B.J. McBride was a paper label.)

Summit China Company. East Akron, and Cleveland, Ohio. 1901 until sometime after 1929. In 1905, they employed 95 people. They made white decorated semi-porcelain, earthenware and granite dinner sets, toilet sets and short sets of odd dishes. They were listed in 1929 *Directory of Manufacturers of Ohio.* (Mark 1 was filed for registration November 28, 1917, claiming use since July 1917 for use on semi-porcelain dinnerware. Information and mark 2, Summit County Historical Society.)

1.

2.

Summitville Tile Company. Summitville, Ohio. 1922 to present. Company manufactures ceramic decorative and plain wall tile and floor tile. The Summit Brick Company was started around 1912 and in 1922, F.H. Johnson and H.K. Lynn organized the Summitville Tile Company. The demand for industrial floor brick determined their production. In 1948, Pete Johnson became the sole owner. Custom murals were added to the line of production. In the 1980's, Don Schreckengost, (see that listing) the executive design director for the company, designed a mural which depicted the history of the area. The mural was built outside the company building in Boardman, Ohio. The mural has 6,000 hand-painted tile made into a series of panels showing a scene with an early iron furnace, one with a horse drawn barge, and an old mill several stories high, made of stone and wood with a background of trees, etc. In decorative tile for the market (other than orders made to custom specifications) the tile com-

pany offers the Heritage Series which features 14 American quilt patterns, a series of 13 or more game birds with a different bird on each tile, herbs and spices on 12 different tiles, and a series of 6 different bird dogs. The company also makes all sorts of tile and brick for building and home decorating. (Information: from company literature and Grace Allison, "Ceramic Tile Custom Murals by Summitville Tile Company," *American Clay Exchange*, April 3, 1985, pp. 4, 5. Marks: sent by company.)

SUMMITVILLE

Suomalainen, Thomas. Walnut Grove, North Carolina. 1963 to present (1985). Tom Suomalainen received a B.A. degree from the University of Minnesota in Deluth, and his M.F.A. degree from Tulane University in New Orleans, Louisiana. Tom began marketing his work as a charter member of the Piedmont Craftsmen, Inc., Winston-Salem, North Carolina, in 1963. His pieces are either functional or sculptural, made of stoneware with a reduction/oxidation process or salt glazed. He makes a limited amount of plates which are decorated with blue on white, also cups, bowls, teapots. His sculptural works are figure oriented, either very abstract or naturalistic with human or animal metamorphic representations. The sculptured pieces are hand built, using thrown sections, slabs, coils and then glazed. His work has been featured in several books and many magazines. The books include: *Penland School of Pottery* (20 pages on Suomalainen), by J. Coyne; *Finding Ones Way with Clay* by Paulus Berensohn; *Salt Glazed Ceramics*, by Jack Troy; and *Red Clay Reader*, by Charlene Whisnat. Magazines include: *The North Carolina Anvil Studio Potter, Ceramics Monthly, American Craft, The Arts Journal*, and *Diversion*. Suomalainen has taught at the Penland School of Crafts, Penland, North Carolina; Arrowmont School of Arts and Crafts, Gatlinburg, Tennessee; and Rochester Institute of Technology, Rochester, New York; Sawtooth Center for Visual Design, Winston-Salem, North Carolina; Salem College, Winston-Salem, North Carolina; High Point College, High Point, North Carolina; North Carolina Governors School, Winston-Salem, North Carolina.

Tom's solo exhibitions include: 1966, Wesley Foundation, Chapel Hill, North Carolina; 1971, Greenwich House, New York City; 1980, High Point Theatre Gallery, High Point, North Carolina; 1967, 1974, 1977, 1981, Southeastern Center for Contemporary Art, Winston-Salem, North Carolina; 1984, Hodges Taylor Gallery, Charlotte, North Carolina; 1968-1984, The Arts, Chapel Hill, North Carolina.

His group exhibitions include: 1968, Everson Museum of Art, Syracuse, New York; also in 1968, Terry Sanford Center, Penland, North Carolina; 1970, New Jersey State Museum, Trenton, New Jersey; also in 1970, Hunterdon Art Center, Clinton, New Jersey; 1972, Fairtree Gallery, New York City; 1976, Scripps College, Claremont, California; 1977, High Museum of Art, Atlanta, Georgia; 1977, The Federal Reserve, Washington, DC; 1979, Kingsborough Community College, Brooklyn, New York; 1979, Southern Arts Federation, Atlanta, Georgia; 1980, Greenville County Museum of Art, Greenville, South Carolina; 1981, Renwick Gallery, National Museum of American Art, Washington, DC; 1982, Western Carolina University, Cullowhee, North Carolina; 1982, Clemson University, Clemson, South Carolina; 1982, Spirit Square Arts Center, Charlotte, North Carolina; 1982, North Carolina Central University, Durham, North Carolina; 1983, North

Carolina Museum of History, Raleigh, North Carolina; 1983, The Federal Reserve, Washington, DC; 1984, Palazzo Venezia, Rome, Italy; Green Hill Center for North Carolina Art, Greensboro, North Carolina; 1984, The Waterworks Gallery, Salisbury, North Carolina.

Tom has collections at: R.J. Reynolds Industries, Winston-Salem, North Carolina; Old Salem Incorporated, Winston-Salem, North Carolina; Wachovia Bank and Trust Company, Winston-Salem, North Carolina; North Carolina National Bank, Charlotte, North Carolina; North Carolina Department of Commerce, Raleigh, North Carolina; Weatherspoon Art Gallery, Greensboro, North Carolina.

His professional affiliations are as follows: Piedmont Craftsmen, Inc., Winston-Salem, North Carolina, charter member, Board of Directors, 1983; Southeastern Center for Contemporary Art, Winston-Salem, North Carolina, Board of Directors, 1979-1981; North Carolina Arts Council, Committee on Crafts, 1965.

Tom's most outstanding award was given to him in 1984, when he was awarded the North Carolina Prize, a $10,000 prize from the New York Times Co. and its North Carolina affiliates, for his contribution to the arts and particularly to the clay arts in North Carolina. This award is juried on an artists entire career contirbutions. He also received an NEA/SECCA Southeast Seven VIII fellowship in 1984. (Information: from the potter, Thomas Suomalainen. Marks: nos. 1, 2, 3 are stamped and nos. 4, 5, 6 are incised.)

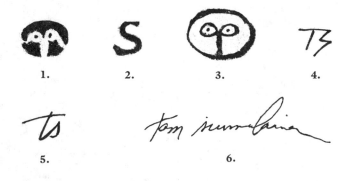

1.   2.   3.   4.

5.   6.

Superware Corporation. Great Neck, New York. Superware Corporation, and **Jacobs Enterprises, Inc.** of Stamford, Connecticut, (a joint venture), filed for registration of this mark on September 4, 1959, for use on ceramic and china dinnerware, claiming use of the mark since July 1959.

ROYAL DUCHESS

Swamp Studio. Columbus, Ohio. Owner, Carol Lynn McDonough is a studio potter, operating since 1978 to present making white earthenware vases, flowerpots and molds. She shows at fairs and craft shows.

Swan Hill Pottery. South Amboy, New Jersey. Before 1849 to after 1876. In using secondary sources for a book of this type I have to make a judgement on the correctness of the author's material used. M. Lelyn Branin was one of the authors who gained my complete and absolute confidence. Because the following goes against the written word of several authors, I have chosen Mr. Branin's account as the one to be authentic. We will quote Mr. Branin exactly from "New Books About Antiques," *Spinning Wheel*, October 1974, p. 36:

"Swan Hill Pottery was constructed by Charles Fish sometime between 1847 and 1849 and it was owned by him until his death in 1876. After his death it was owned by one of his sons-in-law, Harry Clay Perrine, until it was closed during the 1890's. James Carr rented and operated the pottery from mid-1852 until December 1855, and Thomas Locker worked for him. Locker remained at the factory after Carr left South Amboy and he later became superintendent of the manufacturing operations there. John L. Rue, a brother-in-law of Fish was the proprietor of the factory during the 1860's."

See the New York City Pottery, and the International Pottery for James Carr's involvement in those potteries between working at the American Pottery Company in Jersey City and before he established the New York City Pottery in 1853 or 1854 (Barber, p. 77, said 1853). At other potteries, he made Parian, Majolica and cream colored ware. At the Swan Hill Pottery he made yellowware and Rockingham. (Information: Branin, as cited. Marks: C. Jordan Thorn, *Handbook of Old Pottery and Porcelain Marks*, pp. 121, 130.)

SWAN HILL POTTERY

Swan and States Pottery. Stonington, Connecticut. 1824-1935. Joshua Swan and Ichabod States also used the mark W. States not shown here. Makers of stoneware. Also listed in Watkin's list were Adam States 1798; William States, 1811-1824. (Information: Lura W. Watkins, "A Check List of New England Stoneware Potters," *Antiques*, 1942, reprinted in Stradling book, p. 80. Mark: Stewart and Consentino, *Stoneware*, p. 63.)

SWAN & STATES STONINGTON

Swank, Hiram and Sons. Johnstown, Cambria County, Pennsylvania. Started around 1865, according to Ramsay, p. 221, and Thorn, p. 149, to make stoneware marked with the Swank name stenciled in blue. They were listed the same in the 1919 and 1922 Manufacturers Directory. In the 1935 Manufacturers Directory, I found **Hiram Swank's Sons, Inc.**, employing 112 to make terra cotta and fire clay products in Irvona, Clearfield County, Pennsylvania, near Johnstown. They were also listed at Clymer, Indiana County. (Mark: Thorn, p. 149.)

HIRAM SWANK & SONS
JOHNSTOWN, PA.

Swetye Ceramic Artware. Salem, Ohio. Started in 1946, and is not operating at present. Pottery was started by Joseph Swetye in 1946. His son by the same name owns the pottery now. He has not been operating for a few years but plans to open again sometime. The pottery made what Swetye termed semi-vitreous porcelain which is a good quality of semi-porcelain into various decorative pieces such as vases, pitchers, animal figures, decorated with gold finish and silver palladium finish. Between 1946 to 1955 he used Mother of Pearl decoration, blue and yellow lusters, and colored glazes in pink, blue and black. A great deal of the products were sold directly to florists. The family made and decorated the ware in a cement block building located near their home on Depot Road. It was a family business that employed 10 in the heighth of their production in 1940's and 1950's. (Information from owner: mark on piece.)

Sweezy, Nancy. Nancy started making pottery in New Hampshire in 1951. She worked in Cambridge, Massachusetts, from 1959 to 1968 and in Seagrove, North Carolina, from 1968 to 1982, where she made pottery and managed the Jugtown Pottery. In 1982, she moved back to Arlington, Maine, her hometown, where she works at the Radcliffe Pottery Studio at present. She makes utilitarian pieces in plain forms. She stated she did not make pieces for competition or shows, but for trade. She said her pieces were to be used, not shown. Nancy was very modest in the description of her work on the questionnaire she answered. She carried on the tradition of the increasingly well known Jugtown Pottery, started by the Busbees. See the listing, Jugtown Pottery. Nancy is the author of *Raised in Clay, The Southern Pottery Tradition*, published by the Smithsonian Institution Press: Washington, D.C., 1984. Mark is inscribed.

Swift Creek Pottery. McKean, Pennsylvania. 1969 to present (1986). Steven and Susan Kemenyffy are outstanding studio potters, making one-of-a-kind artistic pottery, sculptured pieces of earthenware and Raku. The pieces have colorful paintings of people, plants, etc. on the surface. Two recent pieces were a Raku sculpture of a beautiful woman called, "At the Edge of Spring and Winter," which was shown at the Chautauqua Institute in Chautauqua, New York, in July and August 1985. Another example was, "A Study in Bright," a Raku wall piece with the picture of a colorful woman shown at the Running Ridge Gallery in Ojai, California, in late August

1985. The wall panel is dimensional with parts raised or recessed, then painted. Steven builds the three dimensional forms, and Susan draws the richly decorated female figures on the clay when it is leather hard and glazes them with color. The pieces are Raku fired and then buried in the ground with the smoke and gas to produce brilliant lustrous colors.

Both artists have an M.F.A. degree from the Univeristy of Iowa. Steven is currently a professor of art at Edinboro State College. Susan has also taught in a number of colleges, including the University of Wisconsin; Mercyhurst College, Erie, Pennsylvania; Midwestern University, Wichita Falls, Texas, but she works full time now with the clay. Steven has also taught at Pennsylvania State College where he won a Distinguished Professor Award; University of Wisconsin, Whitewater, Wisconsin; University of Iowa, Iowa City, Iowa; Western New Mexico University, Silver City, New Mexico; Southwestern Crafts Center, San Antonio, Texas; Notre Dame University, South Bend, Indiana; Penn State University, Mt. Alto, Pennsylvania; Naples Mill School of Crafts, Naples Mill, New York; Penland School of Crafts, Penland, North Carolina; Haystack Mountain School of Crafts, Deer Isle, Maine; School of the Art Institute of Chicago, Illinois.

Both are listed in *Who's Who in American Art*, and *Who's Who in the East*, and in *Art in America, Guide to Galleries, Museums and Artists*. Both potters were awarded a National Endowment for the Arts Fellowship Grant, Susan in 1973, and Steven in 1977. I wish I could take the space to list all of the outstanding shows and exhibitions done by these two potters. The list is amazing, not only as to the number of the shows, but also the quality and important places all over the country where they have shown their work. Susan listed 37 one person exhibitions, over 65 invitational and 24 juried exhibitions and 48 workshops which they conducted. Steven has conducted a few more workshops than Susan; he listed 56. No doubt, they did many of them together. While many potters in this book have listed workshops they attended, this couple listed ones they have conducted. Steven had 38 one person exhibitions, 72 invitational and 30 juried exhibitions.

Steven has work in the following collections: Blount Collection, Montgomery, Alabama; Ubukata Industries Company, Inc., Nagoya, Japan; The Museum of Contemporary Crafts, New York, New York; Robert Pfannebacker Collection, Lancaster, Pennsylvania; The Lannan Foundation, Palm Beach, Florida; The Maurer Collection, Los Angeles, California; Marietta College, Marietta, Ohio; Notre Dame University, South Bend, Indiana; The Butler Institute of American Art, Youngstown, Ohio; The Cleveland Clinic, Cleveland, Ohio; The University of North Dakota, Grand Forks, North Dakota; The Charleston Art Center, Charleston, West Virginia; The State University of New York at Cortland; The State University of New York at Geneseo; The Kemper Insurance Company, Long Grove, Illinois, and Osaka, Japan; The Lincoln National Life Insurance Company, Fort Wayne, Indiana; Anshe Hesed Temple, Erie, Pennsylvania.

Susan has work in the following collections: Blount Collection, Montgomery, Alabama; Ubukata Industries Company, Inc., Nagoya, Japan; Robert Pfannebacker Collection, Lancaster, Pennsylvania; The Lannan Foundation, Palm Beach, Florida; The Maurer Collection, Los Angeles, California; Marietta College, Marietta, Ohio; The Butler Institute of American Art, Youngstown, Ohio; The Cleveland Clinic, Cleveland, Ohio; The Kemper Insurance Company, Long Grove, Illinois and Osaka, Japan; The Lincoln National Life Insurance Company, Fort Wayne, Indiana; Anshe Hesed Temple, Erie, Pennsylvania. They have been written about in many publications. Susan has been written about in: *Ceramica Raku; Energy Efficient Ceramics; Low Fire: Other Ways To Work In Clay; History of American Ceramics, The Studio Potter: Pottery Decoration; The Complete Book of Pottery Making; Raku Pottery*. Steven has been written about in: *Personaggi Contemporanei; Ceramica Raku; Energy Efficient Ceramics; Low Fire: Other Ways To Work In Clay; History of American Ceramics, The Studio Potter; Pottery Decoration; The Complete Book of Pottery Making; Raku; Raku Pottery; Objects: U.S.A.* (Information: from Steven and Susan Kemenyffy.)

Swiss Valley Designs. Sugarcreek, Ohio. Lois Lorenz Mason filed for registration of this mark on June 3, 1982, claiming use since March 5, 1977, for use on porcelain and earthenware containers, namely, vases, pitchers, figurines and knick knacks.

Sylvan Ceramics. Pasadena, California. Mr. and Mrs. Sylvan Cohen started the pottery in 1943 (Derwich and Latos, p. 220) to make earthenware figurines, decorative pottery vases, candy boxes, ashtrays, console sets, etc., according to the 1952 *Crockery and Glass Journal Directory*. They were still listed in the 1961 *China, Glass, and Tableware Directory*. (Mark 2 was filed May 23, 1957 for use on ceramic lazy susans, claiming use since April 24, 1957.)

Syracuse China Company. Syracuse, New York. Had its early beginnings in 1841, and is operating at present (1986). In 1841, in Syracuse, New York, W.H. Farrar operated a pottery to make Rockingham in whiskey jugs, butter crocks, mixing bowls, clay animals, etc., from local clay covered with a brown glaze in his little plant on Genesee Street. From 1855 until 1871, the plant was called **Empire Pottery** after being moved to Fayette Street to a building built along the Erie Canal. The Empire Pottery added a line of whiteware to the products. In 1871, the plant was again reorganized when businessmen pooled resources and bought out Empire, and

the name was changed to **Onondaga Pottery Company** until 1966, when the name became Syracuse China Company in order to incorporate the trade name "Syracuse China" into the official name of the company. This is confusing to collectors because the Syracuse China mark was used since 1879 on a particular type of china, and the name of the company didn't change until 1966. Onondaga was organized in 1871 to manufacture white graniteware with the coat of arms of New York as the mark. A high-fired semi-vitreous ware was orginated in 1885, the very first of its kind to carry any kind of a guarantee against crackling and crazing. This was the real beginning of success for the company.

Under James Pass, in 1888, "Imperial Geddo" was created. This was a true vitrified china, thin and translucent, which won an award at the Columbian Exposition in 1893. By 1891 the company had developed a full line of fine china. In 1893, white granite, cream-colored wares in a plain and decorated, dinner and toilet services were introduced.

In 1897, the Syracuse China mark was first used, also according to Barber. Semi-porcelain was made from 1886 to 1898. The *1902-1903 Complete Directory* listed Onondago as making china dinner sets, toilet sets and short sets of odd dishes. In 1921, a new plant was added tò the business called the Court Street plant, which was to be used solely for commercial ware production. In 1979, that plant covered 14 acres under one roof and is the seat of all the company's production. Syracuse China is no longer a privately owned enterprise, and stocks may be purchased by the public. The company has been under the same management since 1971.

After 99 years of manufacturing a fine grade of tableware, Syracuse China discontinued their line of china for home use in 1970. In 1971, they became one of the country's largest producers of beautiful hotel, restaurant, airline and commercial types of tableware. In *A Century of Fine Services*, a booklet from Syracuse China Company, is this explanation: "Stepped-up competition from foreign imports, most notably from Japan, forced closing of fine and casual dinnerware production in 1970. With the closing of the Fayette Street plant, household dinnerware production became a thing of the past. After 99 years of dinnerware production, phasing out procedures began at Fayette, allowing the full energies of Syracuse China to be devoted to continued excellence in commercial ware production."

In 1959, Syracuse China acquired a subsidiary, Vandesca-Syracuse, Ltd., of Joliette, Quebec, Canada, which is also a larger producer of vitrified hotel china. Syracuse China Company purchased the Mayer China Company on December 14, 1984. (See Mayer China Company listing.)

The following dating system is reprinted by permission of Syracuse China for the benefit of China collectors.

Syracuse Dating Coding

For many years Syracuse China has followed the policy of showing the year and month of chinaware manufacture by one "Code" technique or another which appears as a portion of the chinaware back stamp.

This code system enables you to determine how old the ware is and can be related into benefits for your customer. Savings = benefits! Your understanding of the code system may at some future time enable you to change a "negative" customer into a positive one. When the need for replacement of china is apparent, there are some customers who may feel their ware did not hold up long enough. By determining the manufacturing date, you are able in most cases to show the customer the long service life he obtained from his Syracuse China.

Any salesman who can relate benefits in terms of profitability . . . has a lot going for both the customer and himself. (Your Syracuse China Area Manager will be glad to help you in any situations involving date coding.)

The number(s) in the first column represent the year the ware was manufactured. Date coding has been used by Syracuse China for over 75 years.

Today, only one digit is used to denote the year.

6	1977
5	1976
4	1976

In earlier years more digits or initials were used.

103	1974
102	1973
101	1972
100	1971
99	1970
98	1969
97	1968
96	1967
95	1966
94	1965
93	1964
92	1963
91	1962
90	1961
89	1960
00	1959
NN	1958
MM	1957

The Month the ware was produced is indicated by a letter, e.g.: **

A = January
B = February
C = March
D = April
E = May
F = June
G = July
H = August
I = September
J = October
K = November
L = December

**The exception would be:

1930-K	1938-S	1946-AA	1954-II
1931-L	1939-T	1947-BB	1955-JJ
1932-M	1940-U	1948-CC	1956-KK
1933-N	1941-V	1949-DD	1957-LL
1934-O	1942-W	1950-EE	1958-MM
1935-P	1942-X	1951-FF	1959-NN
1936-Q	1944-Y	1952-GG	1960-OO-**
1937-R	1945-Z	1953-HH	

The backstamp changed February, 1960 from OO for 1960 to 89, indicating the 89th year of the company, founded in 1871. For a short period the month was indicated by a series of dots.

Reaching back into history, china that was manufactured from October, 1903 through December, 1911 was marked with a numeral enclosed in a circle. For example: China produced in January through December, 1905 would be marked 16 through 27, the latter denoting it was manufactured December, 1905.

The code marking was changed in January, 1912 with the numeral enclosed in a diamond. China made between and during the dates of January, 1912 through June, 1919 was marked in the following manner.

January to December 1912 - 1 thru 12*
January to December 1913 - 13 thru 24
January to December 1914 - 25 thru 36
January to December 1915 - 37 thru 48
January to December 1916 - 49 thru 60
January to December 1917 - 61 thru 72
January to December 1918 - 73 thru 84
January thru June 1919 - 84 thru 90
January to December 1919 - 1 thru 6
*Manufactured during January of 1912.

EXAMPLE:
Ware manufactured during May, 1977 would carry the code number 6—E. The 6 denotes the year 1977. E refers to the month of May.

Shapes Introduced:

Econorim	1933
Winthrop	1949
Essex	1953
Trend	1955
Signet	1976

1961– 90 (Dots for the months)
1962– 91 (Dots for the months until July then letters, A, B, C, Etc.)
1963– 92 (A, B, C, Etc.)
1964– 93 (A, B, C, Etc.)
1965– 94 (A, B, C, Etc.)
1966– 95 (A, B, C, Etc.)
1967– 96 (A, B, C, Etc.)
1968– 97 (A, B, C, Etc.)
1969– 98 (A, B, C, Etc.)
1970– 99 (A, B, C, Etc.)
1971–100 (A, B, C, Etc.)
1972–101 (A, B, C, Etc.)
1973–102 (A, B, C, Etc.)

Stamp Destination: Effective November 1982.
82-1 82-1 for Syralite holloware and flatware (Mark 1)
82-2 Syralite flatware from #6 plate up (Mark 3)
82-3 on flint holloware and flatware through #5 plate
    Also on all Gibralter ware - item no. to be added. (Mark 2)
82-4 on flint flatware from #6 plate on cup. (Mark 5)
82-5 used on A/D cups and small castware items. (Mark 4)

Date code for 1982 indicated by no. 11. A, B, C, D, tells the quarter of the year. Example: Jan., Feb., and March would be A.

Information: from company as printed in *American Kitchen and Dinner Wares* by Lehner. Marks 1-5 sent by company and explained at end of dating code. Mark 6, 1983 mark taken from a dish. Mark 7 was used from 1873 to 1885 according to a company employee and from 1874 to 1893 according to Barber p. 81. The initials O.P. Co. were filed for registration in December 1914, claiming use since the year 1892. Company information given in 1978 dated the use of O.P. Co. as starting in 1885 and Barber said 1886. No. 10 is the way O.P. Co. was filed. Nos. 7, 8, from Barber, p. 81. The dates for Imperial Geddo do not quite agree either, but give us a good idea of time. Company information said 1888 was the first marketing date for this fragile ware: Barber gave 1890. Mark 11 used on Imperial Geddo. Marks 12, and 13 also in Barber were the first marks used on Syracuse China pieces. No. 13 is a copy taken from a dish, showing the authenticity of the Barber marks. No. 14 is an unusual kind of trademark, but it was registered April 2, 1915 by Onondaga Pottery Company for use on china tableware and ornamental chinaware, claiming use that year. No. 15 was filed in June 1917 for use on chinaware, claiming use since May, 1914. No. 16 was filed on August 15, 1935 for china and porcelain tableware claiming use since July 23, 1935. No. 17, Adobe Ware was filed October, 1932 claiming use since September, 1932 for use on domestic and ornamental china ware. No. 18 was filed September, 1933 for use on domestic and commercial (hotel ware) china and porcelain tableware, claiming use since August 1933. No. 19, 20, marks on Railroad china sent by writer, researcher, Larry Paul. Marks 21 to 30 from Fr. Stephen S. Sandknop, *Nothing Could Be Finer*, 3rd ed. privately printed 1976, pp. 57-64. Marks 31-35, Richard W. Luckin, *Dining On Rails*, p. 248; mark 31, p. 248; mark 32, p. 141; mark 33, p. 126; mark 34, p. 172; mark 35, p. 283. Marks 36-38 were sent by Larry Paul. Marks 39, 40 were from directories before and after the name change to Syracuse. Nos. 41-47 from 1967 *China, Glass and Tablewares Directory*. No. 48 was filed January 23, 1967 and in use since October 24, 1966. No. 49 from Waldorf Stamping Device.

On mark no. 31, one might assume the dish was made in 1931. This could not be so because the Econo-Rim was copyrighted in 1933. (See mark 18.) The design on the plate was copyrighted in 1931 which explains the date. No. 50 from 1945 *Crockery and Glass Journal Directory*; see no. 16 filed in 1935 and still in use in 1945. All of these marks until the year 1979 were filed for dinnerware and tableware made of china: No. 51 filed May 7, 1956, claiming first use February 1956; no. 52 filed January 11, 1957, claiming first use December 1956; no. 53 filed December 27, 1960, claiming first use December 23, 1960; no. 54 filed May 16, 1961, claiming first use February 17, 1961; no. 56 filed October 16, 1961, claiming first use July 15, 1954; no. 55 filed May 1, 1962, claiming first use January 31, 1962; no. 58 filed June 26, 1963, claiming first use March 22, 1963; no. 57 filed May 1, 1964, claiming first use January 22, 1964; nos. 59 and 60 both filed May 1, 1964, claiming first use February 10, 1964; no. 61 filed November 6, 1964, claiming first use September 18, 1964; nos. 62-63 both filed April 6, 1965, claiming first use February 26, 1965; no. 64 filed April 14, 1965, claiming first use February 26, 1965; no. 65 filed April 7, 1966, claiming first use February 16, 1966; no. 66 filed March 31, 1966, claiming first use February 17, 1966; no. 67 filed March 21, 1966, claiming first use February 18, 1966; nos. 68 and 69 both filed April 4, 1966, claiming first use February 17, 1966.

We did not research all of the 1970's for marks. No. 70 filed September 24, 1979, claiming first use May 29, 1979, for oven-proof dinnerware and china tableware, such as casseroles, bakers, Bains Marie, custards, pot pie dishes, ramekins, shirred egg dishes, Welsh Rarebit dishes. Nos. 71 and 72 filed September 24, 1979, claiming first use May 29, 1979 for same products as no. 70. No. 73 filed March 31, 1980, claiming first use December 30, 1979. No. 74 filed June 4, 1980, claiming first use May 1977. Nos. 75-78 all filed in September 1980, claiming use since June 1980. Nos. 79-84 all filed September 30, 1981, claiming use since June and July 1980. No. 85 filed February 9, 1982, claiming first use May 1, 1973. No. 86 filed July 19, 1984, claiming first use May 1, 1971. All of the rest of the marks are from Quality Stamp Company, East Liverpool, Ohio, and from dishes.)

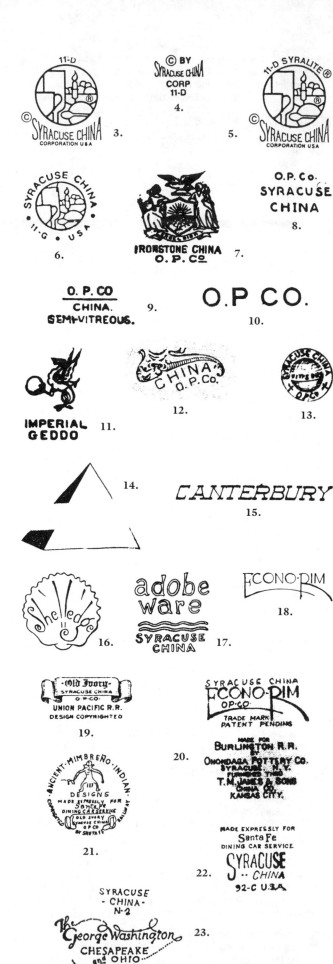

SYRACUSE CHINA
ECONO-RIM
8-Q
TRADE MARK
PAT. PENDING

DESIGNED
ESPECIALLY FOR THE
HIAWATHA

24.

Trend®
SYRACUSE
China
97-D U.S.A.
Made expressly for the
VISTA DOME DENVER ZEPHYR

25.

SYRACUSE
China
DINNER BY STREAMLYNE

MISSOURI
PACIFIC
LINES

26.

Old Ivory
SYRACUSE CHINA
O·P·C·O
Galatea
DESIGN COPYRIGHTED
MADE FOR
C.M.& ST.P.R.R.R.

27.

O.P.CO.
SYRACUSE
-CHINA-
M-9

St ALBANS
COPYRIGHTED
1915

MISSOURI PACIFIC

28.

SYRACUSE CHINA
ECONO-RIM

TRADE MARK

MADE FOR GREAT NORTHERN RAILWAY
Glory of the West
by Syracuse China
ONONDAGA-POTTERY CO.

29.

Old Ivory
SYRACUSE CHINA
O·P·CO
Columbine
THE STATE FLOWER
Colorado.

30.

SYRACUSE CHINA
ECONO-RIM
2-U
TRADE MARK
PATENTED

PRAIRIE MOUNTAIN
WILDFLOWERS
RUBY LILY, CALIFORNIA POPPY,
BABY BLUE EYES, AZALEA
MADE EXPRESSLY FOR
SOUTHERN PACIFIC LINES
DINING CAR SERVICE
BY
ONONDAGA POTTERY CO.
SYRACUSE, N.Y.
DESIGN COPYRIGHTED
1931

31.

SYRACUSE CHINA
ECONO-RIM
TRADE MARK
"The TRAVELER"
DESIGNED
ESPECIALLY FOR
Milwaukee Road
DINING CAR SERVICE

32.

O.P.CO.
SYRACUSE
CHINA
M32

The George Washington
CHESAPEAKE
and OHIO
LINES

33.

34.

Wild Flowers
of
GLACIER NATIONAL PARK

THE RED AND GOLDEN BELLS OF THE GRACEFUL
Columbine MAKES GAY THE BORDERS OF BROOKS
AND STREAMS. SCARCELY BEFORE THE SNOW
HAS MELTED, THE Globeflower DECORATES
THE BANKS OF GRINNELL AND CRACKER
LAKES, WHILE THE Springbeauty ADDS ITS
DELICATE PINK TO THE WONDERLAND OF
WILD FLOWERS OF GLACIER NATIONAL PARK.

SYRACUSE
DESIGNED EXPRESSLY FOR
Great Northern Railway

MOHAWK & HUDSON RAILROAD
SESQUICENTENNIAL
150 YEARS OF
NEW YORK STATE RAILROADING
FIRST TRAIN BETWEEN ALBANY AND SCHENECTADY
PULLED BY LOCOMOTIVE DE WITT CLINTON

1831   1981

MOHAWK & HUDSON CHAPTER
National Railway Historical Society

PRODUCED BY SYRACUSE CHINA CORPORATION

35.

PATRICIA
SYRACUSE
China
MADE IN AMERICA

36.

FEDERAL
SHAPE
SYRACUSE CHINA
MADE IN America

37.

GARDENA
COPYRIGHTED

O.P.CO.
SYRACUSE
-CHINA-
M-1

38.

SYRACUSE
SINCE 1871
China
Onondaga Pottery Co.
1858 W. Fayette St.,
Syracuse, N.Y.

39.

SYRACUSE
SINCE 1871
China
Syracuse China Corp.
1858 W. Fayette St.,
Syracuse, N.Y.

40.

Silhouette®
FINE CHINA
by SYRACUSE
MADE IN U.S.A.

41.

Silhouette®
FINE CHINA
by SYRACUSE
MADE IN U.S.A.

42.

GALLERY
COLLECTION
BY
SYRACUSE
China
MADE IN U.S.A.

43.

GALLERY
COLLECTION
by SYRACUSE
fine china

44.

GRACE
SYRACUSE
China
MADE IN AMERICA

45.

Carefree
TRUE CHINA
by SYRACUSE

46.

Carefree XL
CASUAL CHINA
by SYRACUSE
MADE IN U.S.A.

47.

CAREFREE XL

48.

Trend®
SYRACUSE
CHINA
91-L U.S.A.
PATENTED

49.

Shelledge
SYRACUSE CHINA
PATENTED

50.

TREND

51.

CAREFREE 52.   53. SILHOUETTE

SYRACUSE CHINA

54.

GALLERY COLLECTION

55.

56. HARMONY

57. CONCORD ROSE

GRACE 58.   59. WESTMINSTER

BRAE LOCH 60.   61. SYRALITE

FLIRTATION 62.   63. COURTSHIP

JACKSTRAWS

64.

65.

CANTERBURY   **CHAMPAGNE**

66.   67.

OLD CATHAY 68.   69. **BELCANTO**

CASABLANCA   **INDIAN WELLS**

70.   71.

GOLDEN MAIZE   **BURTON PLACE**

72.   73.

TRUE GOLD 74.   75. **SUN KING**

WOODLANDS 76.   77. **PALOMINO**

SUNDARI   **CRIMSON BLOSSOM**

78.   79.

BEAUVAL 80.   81. **KEY BISCAYNE**

DURANGO 82.   83. **CALVERT COVE**

CHATWIN 84.   85. **SPECTRUM**

CINNAMON

86.

87.

93.

SYRALITE by **SYRACUSE** 100·K   U.S.A.

94.

96.

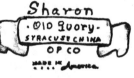

98.

CANTERBURY TRADEMARK PATENTED

O.P.CO SYRACUSE CHINA

100.

NATURE STUDY

95.

Old Jvory SYRACUSE CHINA OP CO

The Hostes ©

97.

O.P.CO. SYRACUSE CHINA 3-F

GLENDALE COPYRIGHTED 1923

99.

ADAM COPYRIGHTED 1926

O.P.CO. SYRACUSE CHINA 3-L

101.

Old Jvory SYRACUSE CHINA OPCO

102.

SYRACUSE CHINA MADE IN AMERICA

89.

WARRANTED 22 CARAT GOLD

88.

SYRACUSE China U.S.A.

10·NN

SYRACUSE CHINA USA 91-C

90.

O.P.CO. SYRACUSE CHINA M-4

91.

103.

Somerset

OPCO SYRACUSE CHINA

104.

105.

Bracelet

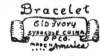

106.

T

Takaezu, Toshiko. Clinton, New Jersey. Around 1950 to present (1985). Studio potter, Toshiko Takaezu, was born in Hawaii, educated at the Honolulu Academy of Arts and the University of Hawaii in Honolulu, and then she studied at the Cranbrook Academy of Art in Bloomfield Hills, Michigan, under Maija Grotell in 1951. At Cranbrook, she began experimenting with glazes and forms and other mediums. Prior to that time she had mostly sculptured with volcanic black sand in Hawaii. At Cranbrook, not only did she expand her work in ceramics, but she started working with weaving and painting as well. Toshiko works in stoneware and porcelain to make hand thrown, coil and slab built and sculptured pieces, both functional and nonfunctional. Many of the pieces are beautifully handpainted. Some of the thrown vessels pictured in the book by John Coyne, *Penland School of Crafts*, were huge, almost as tall as Toshiko.

Among many shows, her work has appeared at the Contemporary Arts Center of Hawaii in Honolulu, 1966; Swarthmore College in Swarthmore, Pennsylvania, 1968; the Boise Art Association in Boise, Idaho, and Lewis and Clark College in Portland, Oregon, 1941; the Benson Gallery in Bridgehampton, New York, 1942; the Honolulu Academy of Arts in Honolulu, 1973.

Her work is in many public collections, among them are: the Smithsonian Institution in Washington, D.C.; the Galleries of the Cranbrook Academy of Art in Bloomfield Hills, Michigan; the Museum of Contemporary Crafts in New York; the Honolulu Academy of Arts in Honolulu; the George Peabody College Museum in Nashville, Tennessee; Detroit Institute of Art in Detroit, Michigan; the Bangkok Museum in Bangkok, Thailand; the Baltimore Museum in Baltimore, Maryland; and the Johnson Wax Collection in Racine.

Toshiko Takaezu has taught at Princeton University in Princeton, New Jersey; Flint Institute of Art in Flint, Michigan; Cranbrook Academy of Art; the University of Wisconsin in Madison; Cleveland Institute of Art in Cleveland, Ohio; Honolulu Academy of Arts; Haystack Mountain School of Crafts in Deer Isle, Maine; the University of Hawaii in Honolulu; and Penland School of Crafts. She lives in Clinton, New Jersey. (Information: John Coyne, "The Penland School of Crafts," *Book of Pottery*, pp. 136-156; Garth Clark, *A Century of Ceramics in the U.S.*, p. 333. Mark: Linda Steigleder, from the booklet accompanying the 1978 exhibit, "A Century of Ceramics in the U.S.," with curators, Garth Clark and Margie Hughto, published by the Everson Museum of Art: Syracuse, New York. This mark was on one piece in the exhibit. This potter may have had more marks not shown.)

Takemoto, Henry. This studio potter-designer worked for the Interpace Corporation (see that listing) as a designer during the 1960's. Interpace Corporation is no longer involved in the pottery business. Henry Takemoto was born in Honolulu, studied at the University of Hawaii where he received a B.F.A. degree in 1957. He received an M.F.A. degree from the Otis Art Institute in Los Angeles in 1959. He taught at San Francisco Art Institute, Montana State University in Missoula, Scripps College in Claremont, California, and at the Claremont College Graduate School. His work of the 1950's was abstract, expressionistic. The piece he had exhibited in the 1978 Century of Ceramics Exhibit at the Everson Museum, was called "First Kumu," made of stoneware with expressionistic designs and very unusual shape, pictured in Garth Clark, book, *A Century of Ceramics in the U.S.*, p. 151. (Information: Garth Clark and Margie Hughto, *A Century of Ceramics in the U.S.*, p. 333. Mark: Linda Steigleder, from the booklet accompanying the 1978 exhibit, "A Century of Ceramics in the U.S.," curators: Garth Clark and Margie Hughto, published by the Everson Museum of Art: Syracuse, New York.)

Talbot, Betty L. Columbus, Ohio. Betty, a studio potter, started throwing in 1968 and opened a studio in 1979. She makes dark functional stoneware with a multilayer glaze fired at cone 10. She has a B.F.A. degree from Ohio State University. She has attended many craft fairs including the Designer Craftsmen Show, Cleveland, etc. She has exhibited at many shows including the Clayworkers Guild Invitational at Northern Illinois University, McHenry County College, Western Illinois University, Blackburn College. She also did the 1981 National Cone Box Show, Purdue University, and many more. Her show pieces and most award pieces are carved porcelain with celadon glaze. Marks one and two are found on stoneware and are painted on with a small brush using fired on iron oxide. Marks three and four are on porcelain using an under glaze pencil which shows up black when fired.

Talisman Pottery. Boulder, Colorado. 1971 to present (1985). Studio potter, Robert C. Baumgartner, makes stoneware and decorated porcelain pieces. He also teaches at the V.M.C. Crafts Center in Boulder.

Tamac Pottery. Perry, Oklahoma. Started around 1946 until 1973. In 1949, the owner was Earl Bechtold until 1963. Robert and Lenita Moore were owners until 1973. Pottery made vases, ashtrays, plates, cups and saucers, glasses, teapots, etc. following something of "free form" shapes in good colors. (Information: Perry, Oklahoma, Chamber of Commerce. Mark: on piece.)

PERRY, OKLA.
U. S. A.

Tanaka Pottery. Minneapolis, Minnesota. 1973 to present. Taeko Tanaka, studio potter, makes utilitarian stoneware and porcelain. She studied at the Tokyo University and also at Duke University under a Fullbright Exchange Scholarship. Mark is Ta - in a Chinese character.

Taney, Jacob and Isaac. Nockamixon, Bucks County, Pennsylvania. (Spelled "Taney," in Thorn, p. 149, and Barber, *Marks of American Potters*, p. 13. Ramsay spelled it "Tawney," p. 173.) Around 1794. Made redware. (Marks: no. 1, Barber, p. 13; nos. 2, 3, Thorn, p. 149.)

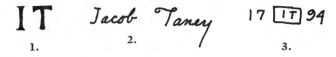

1.   2.   3.

Tariki Stoneware, John O'Leary, Eric O'Leary, and **Robert Pringle**. Meriden, New Hampshire. 1959 to present (1984). John O'Leary, born in 1918, studied for two years in 1946 to 1948 at the School for American Craftsmen in Alfred, New York. In 1949 to 1954 he was a resident potter at Old Sturbridge Village in Sturbridge, Massachusetts. In 1954, he started a pottery in the basement of his home to make functional stoneware for American House, New York City and League of Craftsmen in New Hampshire. At this time he also worked as a research chemist for Goldening-Keene Feldspar Company in Keene, New Hampshire. In 1959, John moved to Meriden, New Hampshire, to have a larger studio which was established by 1961. Demand was increasing from shops in the Eastern U.S. and John's two sons, Eric and Brian, started to work with him in 1969 or 1970. All clays were mixed by hand and glazes prepared in the studio. Workshop programs were offered. By 1973 they were producing ware for over 20 crafts shops. In 1972, they started making restaurant ware of a studio type, and by 1982 they were selling to five restaurants, several shops and galleries.

John did many shows. His biggest two men show was held October 1982, after John had died in September of that same year. One and one-half years were spent in preparation for that show by Eric and John at Quinnipiac College in Hamden, Connecticut. After 1970 the shows listed would be a joint venture for John and his son, Eric. In 1952 to 1954, John had an exhibit in conjunction with a workshop at the Worcester Craft Center in Worcester, Massachusetts.

Other places and dates of exhibits are: Sharon Arts and Crafts Center, Sharon, New Hampshire, 1956; International Craft Exhibit at the National Museum of India in New Delhi, 1958; Centre Arts Visuels, Montreal, 1962; Carneige Hall, University of Maine, 1962; Hopkins Art Center at Dartmouth College in Hanover, New Hampshire in 1965 and 1967; Hanover Art Gallery, 1967; Contemporary Crafts Museum, New York, New York, 1968. John and Eric exhibited at Helen Winnemore's Gallery, Columbus, Ohio, 1969 and 1976; Leverett Craftsman and Artists, Inc., Leverett, Massachusetts, 1970; Lamont Gallery, Exeter, New Hampshire, 1975; American Crafts, The Powerhouse, Cleveland, Ohio, in 1975, which was an exhibit of large architectural work by John and Eric. Two shows were held by England in 1976, in London, private showing for museum curators, gallery owners, and important dignitaries. Then later the Cornwall Exhibition at Cornwall. Other shows included Decordova Museum, Lincoln, Massachusetts, a showing of 30 New England potter's wheel thrown work in April 1976. Between April 1976 and March 1983, 24 more shows were listed for Tariki Stoneware showing the work of Eric and John. At present Robert Pringle is a studio assistant at Tariki Stoneware. The material sent to this author didn't tell when Brian left the family pottery, but the shows listed only John and Eric after early 1970's.

Eric made pottery with his father from the time he was a student in high school. In 1969 or 1970, Eric decided that making pottery was to be his full time profession. He has attended Dartmouth College of Design Studio in Hanover, New Hampshire. Eric has taught at Worcester Craft Center in Worcester, Massachusetts; the Sharon Arts and Crafts Center, Sharon, New Hampshire; a one week workshop at the Visual Arts Center in Montreal, Canada. He was a consultant for one year in 1968 for Fijiwara Yu (Living National Treasures of Japan) at Dartmouth College in Hanover, New Hampshire. The course included methods and techniques of Bizin Ware of Japan. Incoysanete ash glazes and clay bodies were developed by John O'Leary. The pieces were fired at the O'Leary's kiln. Eric listed 20 private collections and 40 galleries and crafts shops that have the O'Leary's work. (Marks: no. 1, John O'Leary; no. 2, Eric O'Leary; no. 3, Robert Pringle; no. 4, handwritten or incised studio mark.)

1.   2.   3.

Tariki Stoneware 4.

Tate, Janette. Kansas City, Missouri. 1983 to present. Studio potter, Janette Tate, received a B.S. Degree from the Kansas City Art Institute in 1983 and started making functional hand thrown ware made of porcelain. I assume the mark shown is a stamped mark.

W.H. Tatler Decorating Company. Trenton, New Jersey. 1874 to 1953. Elijah Tatler, his wife and son started the decorating business in Trenton in 1874. They had been trained to decorate in England. Elijah died in 1876, his wife continued the business with contracts to decorate from Ott and

Brewer, Alpaugh and Magowan, the Columbian Art Pottery and several others. The company went through title changes, all under family ownership and management, and continued until 1953. The firm name was Swan, Whitehead and Tatler in 1882. In 1887, it became the W.H. Tatler Decorating Company. Nelson Lebo, lamp manufacturers in Trenton, purchased the plant in 1953. In *House and Garden*, June 1940 (no page number available), is pictured in an advertisement a set of colorful tulip pattern decorated by Tatler, with hand applied gold borders sold by Davis Collamore and Company, Ltd. of New York. (Information: Jenny B. Derwich and Dr. Mary Latos, *Dictionary Guide to U.S. Pottery and Porcelain*, p. 221. Mark 1 in 1945 *Crockery and Glass Journal Directory*.)

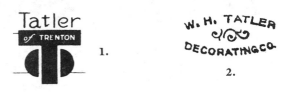

1.

W. H. TATLER DECORATING CO.

2.

Taylor, Lee, Smith. See Taylor, Smith and Taylor for history.

Taylor, Smith, and Taylor. Chester, West Virginia. Started in 1899 or early 1900 to January 1982. Founders were W.L. Smith, John N. Taylor, W.L. Taylor, Homer J. Taylor, and Joseph G. Lee. In 1903, the Taylors bought Lee's interests in the factory, and in 1906, the Taylor interests were purchased by the Smiths. In the *1902-1903 Complete Directory*, the company was listed as Taylor, Smith, and Taylor. In 1907, the company was incorporated in West Virginia with the factory in Chester and offices in East Liverpool. Then in 1973, Anchor Hocking Glass Company purchased Taylor, Smith, and Taylor, and the name Taylor, Smith, and Taylor, was out in preference to the Ceramic Division of Anchor Hocking but marks are as shown. A reference to a dating system in information furnished by Emil Rohrer, who has been with the company since 1937, is reprinted here:

> "There was a dating system used on some of our earlier patterns, but that was discontinued in the fifties. The Taylor, Smith, and Taylor name was encircled in a Laurel wreath then under it, as an example, 11-49-3 indicating November 1949, and I believe the 3 indicated the crew that worked on it. Another backstamp did not spell out the name but used T.S. & T. Co. I am enclosing reproductions of this backstamp showing 5-33-7, obviously May of 1933."

The company made mainly dinnerware and kitchenware. No exact record has been kept over the many years of the long list of patterns, shapes and designs used by Taylor, Smith, and Taylor. In the *1902-1903 Complete Directory*, Taylor, Smith, and Taylor were listed as producing porcelain and white granite dinner sets, toilet sets and short sets of odd dishes, some decorated. Semi-porcelain and ironstone are their later products. There were three big lines by Taylor, Smith, and Taylor that this author thinks will be the most collectible of their ware. "LuRay" was introduced in 1930. "Pebbleford" and "Vistosa" are the other two. Pebbleford is a plain colored ware with specks like sand sprinkled over the color in dark blue green, yellow, light blue green, gray and light tan. Vistosa has a small scalloped edging and lines a little over one-half inch wide. Taylor, Smith & Taylor was closed won permanently by the Anchor Hocking Corporation in January 1982. (Marks: No. 1-4, marks in Barber, *Marks of American Potters*, p. 116, last published in 1909. These are very early marks./ No. 5 is the actual copy of the mark obtained at Quality Stamp Company, East Liverpool, Ohio. Mark is exactly like 3 and 4, only a little larger, found there also./ Pennova was shown in Jervis's *World Pottery Marks* in 1915./ Nos. 7-16 are all earlier marks before 1920. A set of Latona was purchased in 1911./ A wreath was used during the 1930's and 1940's. See marks 17-20./ Lu Ray Pastel, mark 27, came out in 1938, and was manufactured through the 1950's. Vistosa, mark 28 and 29, was made late 1930's until around 1942. Conversation, mark 30, dated in the 1950's as do the Pebbleford marks. See marks 31-38./ Harvey Duke dated the Capitol Ivory mark at the beginning of the 1930's. Also see no. 21 for a 1930's mark. Pastoral in the 1950's was a mark used on a premium for a sales agency. This mark also is seen with just T.S.T. instead of the name written out.

Sometimes, Homer Laughlin China Company and Taylor Smith and Taylor, both made dishes for a single distributor such as grocery chain or food product like Mothers Oats, then we find the mark under both companies. Fortune, Pastoral and Tea Rose are such marks. See marks 23-26./ The exact same mark may be found in more than one size according to the rubber stamp size. Perhaps when new stamps were made the size was varied. These were dishes of the 1950's./ The Bicentennial, 1976 mark shown was on a plate made by T.S.T. and sold by the Cavalier China Company of Chester, West Virginia. See mark 45./ The two marks used on American Greetings Corp. plates "Gigi" and "Holly Hobbie" were sent by Taylor, Smith and Taylor. However, I doubt this pottery was the only one who made these plates for American Greetings Corp. See marks 39, 40./ Marks 41-42 are found recessed in bottom of heavy restaurant type mugs. No. 43 and 44 are found on an individual heavy bakers, like a custard cup. The remainder of the marks from no. 47 on are later marks of the 1960's and 1970's. The same basic mark is used over and over with a different pattern name below or above.

There are undoubtedly many more of each not shown here. Marks are from dishes, Quality Stamp Company, East Liverpool, Ohio, and many later marks were sent by Emil Rohrer of Taylor, Smith and Taylor. No. 46 was filed for registration May 25, 1954 claiming use since March 15, 1954 for semi-porcelain and earthenware tableware, cooky jars and relish dishes. The patent report didn't say if the mark would be a label or how used. No. 47 was registered June 15, 1964 and no. 48 on May 2, 1966. No. 49 filed 1962. Nos. 50 and 51 were the symbols chosen by Taylor, Smith, and Taylor to be shown in the various directories of the 1960's. They didn't say in what form they were to be used, nor did I say in my dinnerware book. I simply showed them as marks for Taylor, Smith and Taylor, just as I am doing here. I did not call them backstamps.

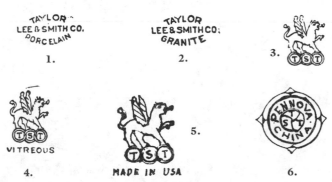

TAYLOR LEE & SMITH CO. PORCELAIN

1.

TAYLOR LEE & SMITH CO. GRANITE

2.

3.

4.

VITREOUS

5.

MADE IN USA

6.

462

7.

8.

9.

10.

P.T.S.T.
PENNOVA
CHINA
11.

12.

CHINA
MADE IN U.S.A. 13.

14.

T.S.T.
LATONA
CHINA
15.

MADE IN U.S.A.
16.

11 49 3
17.

9 37 1
18.

19.

TAYLOR
SMITH
TAYLOR
U.S.A.
10 38 2
20.

T.S.T.
Co.
MADE IN U.S.A.
9 39 2
21.

22.

Fortune
MADE IN USA
T S & T
23.

Fortune
MADE IN U.S.A
T.S.T
24.

Tea Rose
U.S.A
25.

PASTORAL
TAYLOR SMITH & TAYLOR
U.S.A
2-56-1
26.

T.S.&T.
Lu-RAY
PASTELS
U.S.A
27.

28.

29. VISTOSA

30.

TAYLOR·SMITH·TAYLOR
Pebbleford
by GILKES
OVEN PROOF
MADE IN U.S.A.
11-58
PINK 31.

TAYLOR·SMITH·TAYLOR
Pebbleford
by GILKES
OVEN PROOF
8-54-1
SAND 32.

TAYLOR·SMITH·TAYLOR
Pebbleford
by GILKES
OVEN PROOF
33.

3 MARBLE
34.

5-54-1
TEAL
35.

9-54
GRANITE
36.

10-53-1
37.

38.
6-54
SUNBURST

gigi™
Collector's Edition
© AMERICAN GREETINGS CORP.
CLEVELAND USA MCMLXXII
MADE IN U.S.A
39.

HOLLY HOBBIE™
Collector's Edition
MADE IN USA
© AMERICAN GREETINGS CORP.
CLEVELAND, U.S.A. MCMLXXII
40.

GENUINE
Taylor Mug
MADE IN USA
41.

TAYLOR
INTER
NATIONAL
U·S·A
42.

T.S.T.
CHATEAU
BUFFET
USA
43.

T. S. T.
GENUINE
OVEN SERVE WARE
USA
44.

45.

46.

TAYLORSTONE
47.

48.

COLORCRAFT

49.

50.

51.

52.

T.S.T.
Coral-Craft
U.S.A.

53.
T.S.&T
DURABLE EDGE

54.

Classic
Heritage
OVEN PROOF — MADE IN USA
Green

55.

TS&T
Bonnie Green
DESIGNER SERIES
MADE IN USA
OVENPROOF

56.

57.
DUTCH ONION
by Taylor Smith & Taylor
MADE IN USA
Ovenproof

58.

TAYLOR·SMITH·TAYLOR
VERSATILE
OVENPROOF
MADE IN USA

59.

APPALACHIAN·HEIRLOOM
Bonnie
BY
TAYLOR SMITH TAYLOR
22 KARAT GOLD

60.
TAYLOR·SMITH & TAYLOR
U.S.A.
Taylorstone
Ovenproof
"ETRUSCAN"

61.

OVEN PROOF
TS&T
Roaster
MADE IN USA
DETERGENT SAFE

62.
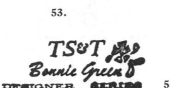
IRONSTONE
OVEN PROOF — MADE IN U.S.A.
Shapes of
Grandeur
Oasis Green

NASSAU
63.
OVEN AND MICROWAVE SAFE
Anchor Hocking
USA
DETERGENT SAFE
IRONSTONE
Glaze Tested Approved

HOLLY WREATH
64.
OVEN AND MICROWAVE SAFE
Anchor Hocking
USA
DETERGENT SAFE
IRONSTONE
Glaze Tested Approved

GREENSPAN
65.
OVEN AND MICROWAVE SAFE
Anchor Hocking
USA
DETERGENT SAFE
IRONSTONE
Glaze Tested Approved

DOGWOOD
66.
OVEN AND MICROWAVE SAFE
Anchor Hocking
USA
DETERGENT SAFE
IRONSTONE
Glaze Tested Approved

RIO
67.
OVEN AND MICROWAVE SAFE
Anchor Hocking
USA
DETERGENT SAFE
IRONSTONE
Glaze Tested Approved

BITTER SWEET
68.
OVEN AND MICROWAVE SAFE
Anchor Hocking
USA
DETERGENT SAFE
IRONSTONE
Glaze Tested Approved

NOSEGAY
69.
OVEN AND MICROWAVE SAFE
Anchor Hocking
USA
DETERGENT SAFE
IRONSTONE
Glaze Tested Approved

HONEY GOLD
70.
OVEN AND MICROWAVE SAFE
Anchor Hocking
USA
DETERGENT SAFE
IRONSTONE
Glaze Tested Approved

RYE TOWN
71.
OVEN AND MICROWAVE SAFE
Anchor Hocking
USA
DETERGENT SAFE
IRONSTONE
Glaze Tested Approved

AUNT JENNY'S
72.
OVEN AND MICROWAVE SAFE
Anchor Hocking
USA
DETERGENT SAFE
IRONSTONE
Glaze Tested Approved

ELEGANCE
73.
OVEN AND MICROWAVE SAFE
Anchor Hocking
USA
DETERGENT SAFE
IRONSTONE
Glaze Tested Approved

MINT
74.
OVEN AND MICROWAVE SAFE
Anchor Hocking
USA
DETERGENT SAFE
IRONSTONE
Glaze Tested Approved

MUMS
75.
OVEN AND MICROWAVE SAFE
Anchor Hocking
USA
DETERGENT SAFE
IRONSTONE
Glaze Tested Approved

BONNIE BLUE
76.
OVEN AND MICROWAVE SAFE
Anchor Hocking
USA
DETERGENT SAFE
IRONSTONE
Glaze Tested Approved

GREEN BOQUET
77.
OVEN AND MICROWAVE SAFE
Anchor Hocking
USA
DETERGENT SAFE
IRONSTONE
Glaze Tested Approved

GARLAND
78.
OVEN AND MICROWAVE SAFE
Anchor Hocking
USA
DETERGENT SAFE
IRONSTONE
Glaze Tested Approved

SUNFLOWER
79.
OVEN AND MICROWAVE SAFE
Anchor Hocking
USA
DETERGENT SAFE
IRONSTONE
Glaze Tested Approved

ZINNIA
80.
OVEN AND MICROWAVE SAFE
Anchor Hocking
USA
DETERGENT SAFE
IRONSTONE
Glaze Tested Approved

BLOSSOM TIME
81.
OVEN AND MICROWAVE SAFE
Anchor Hocking
USA
DETERGENT SAFE
IRONSTONE
Glaze Tested Approved

GREEN BANDSTAND
82.
OVEN AND MICROWAVE SAFE
Anchor Hocking
USA
DETERGENT SAFE
IRONSTONE
Glaze Tested Approved

STRAWFLOWER
83.
OVEN AND MICROWAVE SAFE
Anchor Hocking
USA
DETERGENT SAFE
IRONSTONE
Glaze Tested Approved

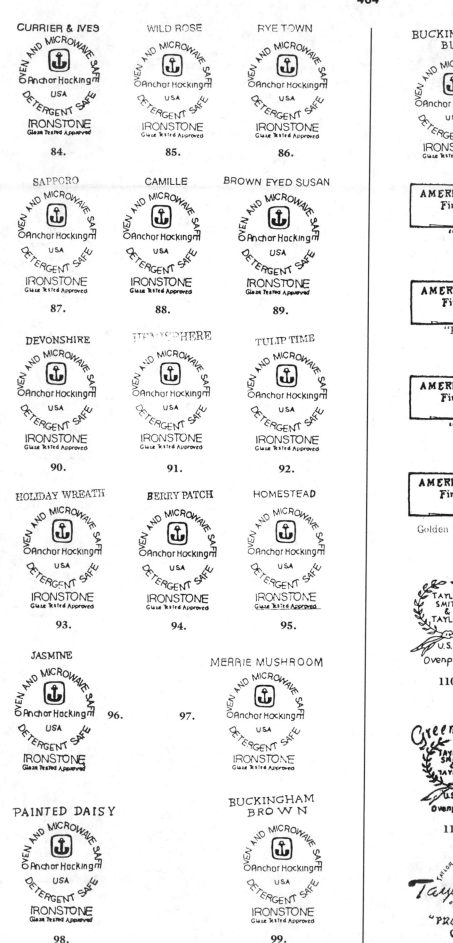

Taylorstone
OVENPROOF

"Summer Morn"

118.

U.S.A.
GLAZE TESTED APPROVED

119. *Ravenscroft, Ltd.*

·OVEN PROOF·
IRONSTONE
Spearmint

Taylorton
American Fine China

A JOHN GRAVE DESIGN

Oven Proof-Craze Proof-Detergent Proof
TAYLOR SMITH & TAYLOR CO. U.S.A.

Masterpiece

134.

U.S.A.

Taylorstone
OVENPROOF

"Daisy Wreath
Green

120.

THE BREMEN GIFT COLLECTION

HOLLY WREATH, MATT GLAZE

MADE IN U.S.A.

121.

135.

Taylorton
American Fine China

A JOHN GRAVE DESIGN

Oven Proof-Craze Proof-Detergent Proof
TAYLOR SMITH & TAYLOR CO. U.S.A.

Ivory Tower

U.S.A.
GLAZE TESTED APPROVED

Ravenscroft, Ltd.

·OVEN PROOF·
IRONSTONE
Spearmint

122.

Chippendale Collection

HALLMARK OF QUALITY

FINE TRANSLUCENT
AMERICAN CHINA

123. "*Heritage*"

Taylorton
American Fine China

A JOHN GRAVE DESIGN

Oven Proof-Craze Proof-Detergent Proof
TAYLOR SMITH & TAYLOR CO. U.S.A.

Rhapsody

136.

Chippendale Collection

HALLMARK OF QUALITY

FINE TRANSLUCENT
AMERICAN CHINA

124.

OVEN
Anchor Hocking
SAFE

USA

DETERGENT SAFE

IRONSTONE
Glaze Tested Approved

125.

Taylorton
American Fine China

A JOHN GRAVE DESIGN

Oven Proof-Craze Proof-Detergent Proof
TAYLOR SMITH & TAYLOR CO. U.S.A.

Silver Wheat

137.

**BLUE BIRD
RENTAL & SALES**

126.

© TAYLOR SMITH & TAYLOR CO.

DESIGN
70

Arboresque

GENUINE CERAMIC IRONWARE

Ovenproof · Detergent Safe
MADE IN U.S.A.

127.

Taylorton
American Fine China

A JOHN GRAVE DESIGN

Oven Proof-Craze Proof-Detergent Proof
TAYLOR SMITH & TAYLOR CO. U.S.A.

Happy Talk

138.

IRONSTONE

HOLIDAY WREATH

OVEN PROOF-DETERGENT SAFE

128.

Holly
& Spruce

TAYLOR SMITH & TAYLOR
· OVEN PROOF ·
U.S.A.

129.

Taylorton
American Fine China

A JOHN GRAVE DESIGN

Oven Proof-Craze Proof-Detergent Proof
TAYLOR SMITH & TAYLOR CO. U.S.A.

Autumn Splendor

139.

ROYAL CRUSADER
FINE CHINA
CRAZE PROOF DETERGENT PROOF
R C
OVEN PROOF GLAZE TESTED

Lady Madeleine

MADE IN U.S.A.

130.

131.

ROYAL CRUSADER
FINE CHINA
GLAZE PROOF DETERGENT PROOF
R C
OVEN PROOF GLAZE TESTED

Lady Dorothy

MADE IN U.S.A.

Taylorton
American Fine China

A JOHN GRAVE DESIGN

Oven Proof-Craze Proof-Detergent Proof
TAYLOR SMITH & TAYLOR CO. U.S.A.

Dianthus

140.

Ever Yours

U.S.A.
BOUTONNEIRE BOUQUET
DETERGENT SAFE
OVEN PROOF
TAYLOR, SMITH & TAYLOR

132.

U.S.A.

133.

Taylorton
American Fine China

A JOHN GRAVE DESIGN

Oven Proof-Craze Proof-Detergent Proof
TAYLOR SMITH & TAYLOR CO. U.S.A.

Pretty Pink

141.

Taylorton
American Fine China
a John Gusing...
Oven Proof-Craze Proof-Detergent Proof
TAYLOR SMITH & TAYLOR CO. U.S.A.
Echo Dell

142.

143.

Taylorton
American Fine China
a John Guove...
Oven Proof-Craze Proof-Detergent Proof
TAYLOR SMITH & TAYLOR CO. U.S.A.
Rose Sachet

Taylorton
American Fine China
a John Guove...
Oven Proof-Craze Proof-Detergent Proof
TAYLOR SMITH & TAYLOR CO. USA
Wild Rice

144.

THE BREMEN GIFT COLLECTION

CURRIER & IVES

Limited Edition

NOT SAFE FOR FOOD USE

Made In U. S. A.

145.

SMUCKERS
Collector Series
The 1972
Christmas Plate
limited edition
of a series portraying
the authentic works
of David Coolidge

146.

Light 'N Lovely
"Mod Green"

147.

148.

Light 'N Lovely
"Love"

OVEN PROOF
IRONSTONE
MADE IN U.S.A.
DISHWASHER SAFE
OCTOGAN AMBER
4567

149.

OVEN PROOF
IRONSTONE
MADE IN U.S.A
DISHWASHER SAFE
BELLE VALLEY
45904

150.

IRONSTONE
MADE IN U.S.A
OCTAGON HOLIDAY

151.

OVEN PROOF
IRONSTONE
MADE IN U.S.A
DISHWASHER SAFE
OCTAGON WHITE
4569

152.

153.

Ever Yours
U.S.A.
BOUTONNIERE
TRUE UNDERGLAZE
OVEN PROOF
TAYLOR, SMITH & TAYLOR

Ever Yours
U.S.A.
AUTUMN HARVEST
TRUE UNDERGLAZE
OVEN PROOF
TAYLOR, SMITH & TAYLOR

154.

Ever Yours
USA
CAPE COD
DETERGENT SAFE
OVEN PROOF
TAYLOR, SMITH & TAYLOR

155.

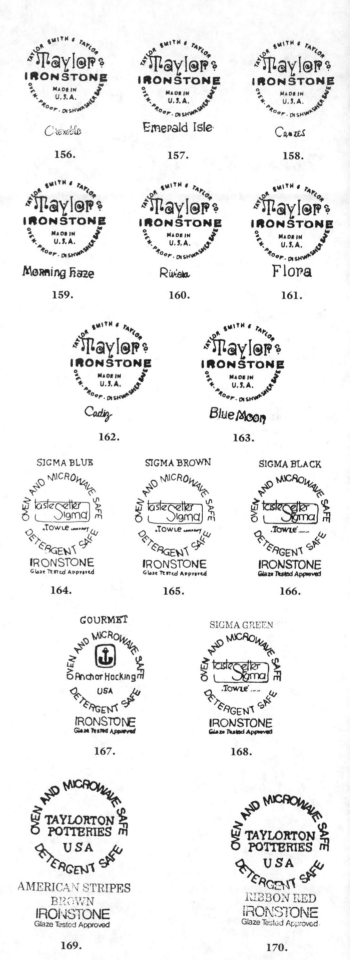

TAYLOR SMITH & TAYLOR
Taylor's IRONSTONE
MADE IN U.S.A.
OVEN-PROOF · DISHWASHER SAFE
Creole

156.

Emerald Isle

157.

Cannes

158.

Morning Haze

159.

Riviera

160.

Flora

161.

Cadiz

162.

Blue Moon

163.

SIGMA BLUE
OVEN AND MICROWAVE SAFE
taste setter Sigma
.TOWLE
DETERGENT SAFE
IRONSTONE
Glaze Tested Approved

164.

SIGMA BROWN
OVEN AND MICROWAVE SAFE
taste setter Sigma
.TOWLE
DETERGENT SAFE
IRONSTONE
Glaze Tested Approved

165.

SIGMA BLACK
OVEN AND MICROWAVE SAFE
taste setter Sigma
.TOWLE
DETERGENT SAFE
IRONSTONE
Glaze Tested Approved

166.

GOURMET
OVEN AND MICROWAVE SAFE
Anchor Hocking
USA
DETERGENT SAFE
IRONSTONE
Glaze Tested Approved

167.

SIGMA GREEN
OVEN AND MICROWAVE SAFE
taste setter Sigma
.TOWLE
DETERGENT SAFE
IRONSTONE
Glaze Tested Approved

168.

OVEN AND MICROWAVE SAFE
TAYLORTON POTTERIES
USA
DETERGENT SAFE
AMERICAN STRIPES
BROWN
IRONSTONE
Glaze Tested Approved

169.

OVEN AND MICROWAVE SAFE
TAYLORTON POTTERIES
USA
DETERGENT SAFE
RIBBON RED
IRONSTONE
Glaze Tested Approved

170.

467

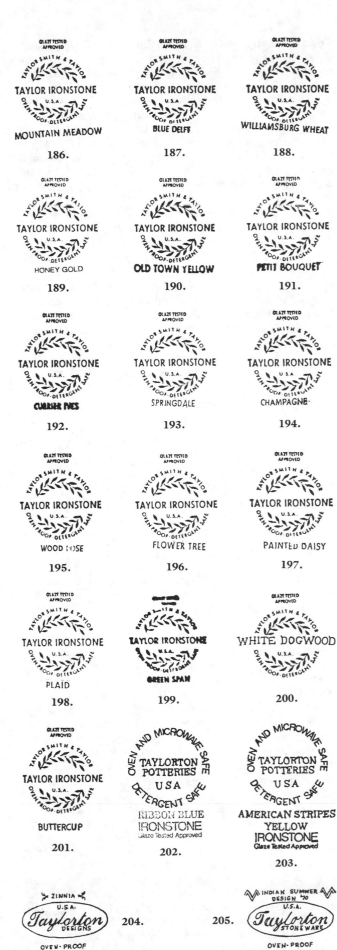

171. BASIC WHITE IRONSTONE — OVEN AND MICROWAVE SAFE, TAYLORTON POTTERIES USA, DETERGENT SAFE, Glaze Tested Approved

172. AMERICAN STRIPES BLUE IRONSTONE — OVEN AND MICROWAVE SAFE, TAYLORTON POTTERIES USA, DETERGENT SAFE, Glaze Tested Approved

173. AZURA DESIGN '70 — Taylorton STONEWARE — OVEN-PROOF DISHWASHER SAFE

174. Lancaster USA Taylorton STONEWARE — OVEN-PROOF DISHWASHER SAFE

175. Taylorton DESIGNS — OVEN-PROOF DISHWASHER SAFE CHECKS & DAISIES

176. Taylorton DESIGNS — OVEN-PROOF DISHWASHER SAFE OLDE PLYMOUTH

177. Taylorton DESIGNS — OVEN-PROOF DISHWASHER SAFE AUTUMN BOUQUET

178. Taylorton DESIGNS — OVEN-PROOF DISHWASHER SAFE RASPBERRY

179. TAYLOR IRONSTONE SPRINGTIME

180. TAYLOR IRONSTONE VICTORIA

181. TAYLOR IRONSTONE GINGHAM GARDEN BR.

182. TAYLOR IRONSTONE NASTURTIUM

183. TAYLOR IRONSTONE MEDALLION

184. TAYLOR IRONSTONE LILY

185. TAYLOR IRONSTONE YELLOW GINGHAM

186. TAYLOR IRONSTONE MOUNTAIN MEADOW

187. TAYLOR IRONSTONE BLUE DELFT

188. TAYLOR IRONSTONE WILLIAMSBURG WHEAT

189. TAYLOR IRONSTONE HONEY GOLD

190. TAYLOR IRONSTONE OLD TOWN YELLOW

191. TAYLOR IRONSTONE PETIT BOUQUET

192. TAYLOR IRONSTONE CURRIER IVES

193. TAYLOR IRONSTONE SPRINGDALE

194. TAYLOR IRONSTONE CHAMPAGNE

195. TAYLOR IRONSTONE WOOD ROSE

196. TAYLOR IRONSTONE FLOWER TREE

197. TAYLOR IRONSTONE PAINTED DAISY

198. TAYLOR IRONSTONE PLAID

199. TAYLOR IRONSTONE GREEN SPAN

200. WHITE DOGWOOD

201. TAYLOR IRONSTONE BUTTERCUP

202. RIBBON BLUE IRONSTONE — OVEN AND MICROWAVE SAFE, TAYLORTON POTTERIES USA, DETERGENT SAFE, Glaze Tested Approved

203. AMERICAN STRIPES YELLOW IRONSTONE — OVEN AND MICROWAVE SAFE, TAYLORTON POTTERIES USA, DETERGENT SAFE, Glaze Tested Approved

204. ZINNIA USA Taylorton DESIGNS — OVEN-PROOF DISHWASHER SAFE

205. INDIAN SUMMER DESIGN '70 USA Taylorton STONEWARE — OVEN-PROOF DISHWASHER SAFE

Teague Pottery. Robbins, North Carolina. 1929 to present. Bryan D. Teague was born in 1898 and learned to be a potter from his father, John Wesley Teague, who worked at J.D. Craven's Shop at a very early age. B.D. Teague married Bessie Craven, grand-daughter of J.D Craven. Their daughter, Zedith Teague Garner (born 1927 and died 1976) was a potter and her son, Daniel, is a potter. In 1929, after various jobs and some service in the marines, B.D. Teague decided to start his own pottery, built a shop and home, and made a ground hog kiln and went into business. For a time during W.W. II, the pottery was closed due to gasoline rationing. But in 1945, B.D. Teague and his daughter, Zedith, reopened to make earthenware for home use. In 1955, Teague became ill, and in 1962 the shop was closed. In 1968, the pottery was reopened by Zedith and her husband, Hobart. Farrell Craven left Ben Owen's shop and came to work with them in 1971. Zedith also taught production-pottery at the local technical school. Zedith died in 1976, but the pottery was still operated by Hobart and Daniel until Hobart died some time before or in 1986. They made hand thrown earthenware pieces from local clay into pitchers, bowls, pie plates, mugs, etc. (Information: Nancy Sweezy, *Raised in Clay, The Southern Pottery Tradition*, pp. 259-264. Roughly incised mark 1, Bob Conway and Ed Gilbreath, *Traditional Pottery in North Carolina*, p. 12. Mark 2, incised mark on a piece made by Hobart Garner.)

Tea, Various Companies. The various tea companies had teapots made for them as advertising promotions. **McCormick and Company, Inc.**, New York, New York, advertised a teapot made for them by Hall China Company in *The Baltimore Sun*, July 1, 1949. **Thomas J. Lipton, Inc.**, known as Lipton Tea Company, Englewood Cliffs, New Jersey, had this mark on teapots circulated by this company. At Quality Stamp Company in East Liverpool, Ohio, we found these marks for the Sexton Company. The same Sexton mark also came from Sterling China. Behind each of these marks is a story of a promotion for that company. Jewell Tea Company, Chicago, Illinois, from 1899 to present had the most widely collected pattern, Autumn Leaf, which came in complete dinner sets and all sorts of accessory pieces, including cake stands, bean pots, butter dishes, canister sets, teapots, coffee pots, etc. Jo Cunningham, long time editor of *The Glaze*, wrote *The Autumn Leaf Story*, a 48 page paperback in 1976, telling the story of the company and the Autumn Leaf pattern. According to Cunningham, the following companies made the Autumn Leaf pattern. See the individual listings: Hall China Company; Crooksville China Company; Crown Potteries; Harker Pottery; Limoges China Company; Paden City Pottery; Universal Potteries. (The McCormick mark and the advertisement cited were sent by Larry Paul, researcher and writer. The various marks shown are backstamps. See Hall China Company for the various Jewell Tea Company's marks.)

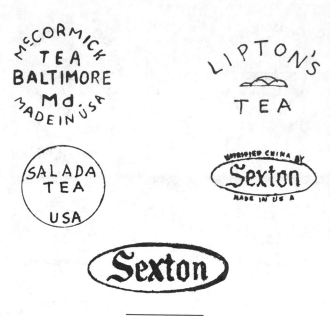

Tebor, Inc. New York, New York. A selling agency. Filed for rights to the first mark on May 26, 1936, for use on ceramic table and cooking ware, jars and vases, claiming use since September 1936. In the 1943 *Crockery and Glass Journal*, p. 33 is an advertisement for Tebor, Inc. in which they advertise themselves as manufacturers of decorative accessories in American Crownford China. The ad also lists Chantilly China. Marks 2, 3, from Quality Stamp Company, East Liverpool, Ohio.

CROWNFORD

1.

2.

3.

Technical Porcelain and Chinaware Company. El Cerrito, California. 1922 until the 1970's. The company started in 1922 and was listed in *California Manufacturers Directory* in 1948 and 1951 as making hotel and institutional dinnerware and technical or sanitary porcelain. (Marks: no. 1, on restaurant ware; no. 2 filed for registration February 7, 1955, claiming use since October 13, 1954, for domestic, household and restaurant chinaware. No. 3 was filed July 8, 1950, claiming use since April of that year, for household, hotel and restaurant chinaware. No. 4 was filed June 30, 1951, claiming use since July 1922 for the same articles. No. 5: Notice the similarity to this mark to one of Southern Potteries. Mark filed January 22, 1963, claiming use since September 20, 1962, for same articles.)

1.

2. U.S.A.

3.

4.

5.

BLUE RIDGE
CHINA
U.S.A.

Teco Pottery. See American Terra Cotta and Ceramic Company.

Temple, Bryon. Lambertville, New Jersey. 1962 to present. Bryon Temple, is a very well known studio potter who makes hand thrown stoneware for table use, cone 10 reduction fired, some salt fired also for table use. He trained at the Bernard Leach Pottery around 1959 and early 1960's in St. Ives, Cronwall, England. Then when Leach lost his eyesight, Temple went back to England in the late 1970's to work with Leach who was 92 years old at the time. In 1962, Temple had started his own pottery in Lambertville, New Jersey. In 1979, a Christie's auction sale gained 1,000 pounds for a large older piece of Leach's pottery. Temple has pieces in major collections across America and in Europe. He very modestly listed only the Cooper-Hewitt/Smithsonian and Museum of Contemporary Crafts of New York City in his questionnaire. His mark is a monogram of a B and T stamped into the ware. In "Ceramactivities," *Ceramics Monthly*, December 1976, p. 87, is a notice of a one man show displaying the "stoneware forms of Byron Temple exhibiting a monumental quality." Temple also worked with Colen Pearson in England.

Tennessee Stoneware and Tile Works. Tennessee, Illinois. Stoffer and Son erected the pottery in 1881 and sold an interest to E.P. Munson in 1883 when the name became Stoffer and Company. In 1884, Munson became the sole owner employing 12 to 14 men with a capacity of 4,500 gallons of clay and two kilns. Munson owned his own clay banks two miles north of Tennessee, Illinois. Also, see L.D. Stoffer and Company. I did not establish whether this was the same family. (Information and mark: Janice T. Wass, curator of Decorative Arts Illinois State Museum. Stenciled mark was on a two gallon stoneware crocks.)

Terrace Ceramics, Inc. Marietta and Zanesville, Ohio. 1960 to January 1, 1975. Until 1965, Terrace Ceramics acted as sole distributor for the products of the American Pottery Company of Marietta, Ohio. In 1964, the offices of Terrace Ceramics were moved from Marietta to Zanesville. The ware was designed by John F. Bonistall, owner of Terrace Ceramics and made by several potteries. The first line marketed by Terrace Ceramics was manufactured in 1961/62 by Haeger Potteries, named "Patricianware," according to Mr. Bonistall. This was a line of horticultural ware. McNicol China Company of Clarksburg, West Virginia, made a line of cookie jars advertised as genuine porcelain for Terrace Ceramics to sell. Terrace Ceramics also marketed a line of "corn ware." Terrace Ceramics is still listed in the *China, Glass and Tableware Directory* (1982). However, according to Mr. Bonistall they are operating a programmed marketing service only and have done no selling since 1975. (Information and mark: from John F. Bonistall. Mark 2 filed for registration July 9, 1962 for Horticultural artware, namely window boxes, jardinieres, urn planters, square planters (and then the patent names all sorts of vases and flower bowls, such as a leaf flower bowl and Rose vase.) All of said articles being in Satin Matte high fired semi-porcelain material. Mark 3 was filed in August 1962 for the same articles. Mark 4 was filed March 19, 1963 claiming use since January 1, 1963 for the same horticulture ware listed. Mark 5 was filed December 26, 1963 for planters, flower bowls, etc. of high fired porcelain material. Mark 6 was filed April 7, 1964 for ceramic ovenware, tableware, bake and serve ware, namely - casseroles, bean pots, teapots, sugar bowls, creamers, salt and pepper shakers, pitchers, etc., claim use since April of that year.

1.

2. **SATIN-WARE**

3. **FERNWARE**

4. **WOODTONES**

5. **COLOR CLAD**

MAIZE-WARE 6.

Terr, Sam and Associates. Austin, Texas. 1955 to present (1983). His most productive years were in Mexico City from 1961 to 1978. Since 1978, Sam Terr, a studio potter has made mostly tiles and small murals in Austin. He also makes beautiful hand thrown dinnerware. The clay body is fired to 1,200 degrees after being glazed in a one fire, high vitrification firing. Sam Terr studied design at the Ceramics School in Alfred, New York, and he won a Bronze Medal, the National IMCE Design Award for 1971. He often combines his ceramic items with wood and silver. He has also designed iron objects and furniture. His mark used on utilitarian stoneware is TERR.

Tessem Stoneware Pottery and Outlet. Westminster, Maryland. 1974 to present (1984). Terry Tessem, studio potter, makes functional stoneware fired to cone 10, also porcelain into sculptured pieces signed with double "T."

Thayer, Pliny. Lansingburgh, New York. 1841 to 1856. Made stoneware and utilitarian pottery. Pliny Thayer came to Lansingburgh and opened a pottery at 103 State Street (now 450 2nd Ave.). From 1848 to 1853 he employed Stephen Pepson and from 1853 to 1855, James and Barney Reiley. On May 14, 1855 he sold his business to James Reiley (see that listing). Reiley took a mortgage from Thayer which was assigned to Samuel Brooks in 1856. (Information and impressed marks: Warren F. Broderick, writer, researcher, which he got from the *Lansingburgh Democrat* and the *Lansingburgh Business Directory*.)

PLINY THAYER   P. THAYER

LANSINGBURGH   LANSINGBURGH

R. Thomas and Sons Company/Thomas China Company. East Liverpool, Ohio. Was founded as **R. Thomas and Sons** in 1873. This plant continued in East Liverpool until 1927. A second plant was owned by R. Thomas and Sons in Lisbon, Ohio, after 1900, and operated there until 1963. The company was founded to make doorknobs and specialties of clay, which after 1885 were primarily insulators. They became one of the largest manufacturers of insulators in the world. But from 1902, for a short span of one and a half years, the company made a complete line of whiteware in the Lisbon factory. At that time the Lisbon factory's name was changed to Thomas China Company. In 1904, when dinnerware was discontinued, both factories were referred to again as R. Thomas and Sons Company. In the *1902 Glass Factory Directory* the Thomas China Company was listed as producing semi-porcelain and hotel ware, dinner sets, toilet sets, short sets of odd dishes and jardinieres, some decorated. These dishes have proved to be very hard to find. (Information: from R.F. Mason, grandson of founder, Richard Thomas, by letter, 1973. There are several pages on the history and technical aspects of the porcelain insulators made by this company in the book by Jack H. Tod, *Porcelain Insulators Guide Book for Collectors*, privately printed, 1976. In Tod's book, there are variations in size of mark 3, "Thomas." The "Q-T" were for the quiet type of insulator. (See the listing for Delta-Star Electric Division for another Thomas mark.) This book is very factual, fine recommended reading. Marks: nos. 1, 2, Barber, *Marks of American Potters*, p. 138; nos. 3-5, from Tod's book as cited, pp. 138-139; no. 3, incuse stamping; no. 4, underglaze in orange ink.)

1. Thomas China Co.

2. U.S.A. THOMAS CHINA Co. LISBON. O.

3. THOMAS

4. Q-T

BOCH PATENT
MARCH 8TH 1898
M'F'D BY
The R. THOMAS & SONS CO.
5.

BOCH PATENT
M'F'D BY
MARCH 8TH 1898
The R. THOMAS & SONS CO.
6.

BOCH PATENT
MARCH 8TH 1898
M'F'D BY
The R. THOMAS & SONS CO.
7.

Thomas, William H. Huntingdon, Pennsylvania. 1871 to 1878. William Thomas and his brothers Ephrim and Edward started a pottery in May 1871 to make utilitarian stoneware in Huntingdon. They operated as Thomas and Brothers but by 1873 both Ephrim and Edward had left Huntingdon. William worked alone until 1878 when he went bankrupt. Over the next 20 years William worked for other pottery owners in the area. (Information and impressed marks: Jeannette Lasansky, *Made of Mud*, pp. 17, 20, 21, 23.)

W.H. THOMAS
HUNTINGDON PA

THOMAS & BRO.
HUNTINGDON, PA.

THOMAS & BRO.

C.C. Thompson Pottery Company. East Liverpool, Ohio. 1868 to 1938. Was started as Thompson and Herbert in 1868 (Stout, p. 69). Their first products were Rockingham and yellowware. By 1878 the plant had five kilns and was very progressive with fine equipment, etc. The name style from 1870 to 1889 was C.C. Thompson and Company. In 1889, it was incorporated as C.C. Thompson Pottery Company and was in business until 1938. Around 1884 the plant began to make cream-colored ware and then semi-porcelain, some decorated. A variety of ware is found for this company. One kind of ware marked "Thompson's Old Liverpool Ware 1868," was really made in 1938. The Sears catalog in a 1938 advertisement describes the flowers as being applied on ivory-toned semi-porcelain in old Liverpool shape, with borders of richly embossed scroll design. The price was $2.98 for 32 pieces! They made a variety of colorful decaled semi-porcelain pieces. (Information: Lehner, *American Kitchen and Dinner Wares*, p. 150. Marks: nos. 1-7, Barber, p. 110; no. 8, Ramsay, p. 281. This author will be very surprised if a mark that looks like this is found, because as I said elsewhere the artist that did the Ramsay marks was not very authentic. Nos. 9-12 on dishes. No. 13 filed on February 27, 1926, for use on pottery, earthenware, chinaware crockery and porcelain, claiming use since February of the same year.)

1. LELAND.

2. SYDNEY.

3. OREGON.

4. MELROSE T

5. MELROSE T.

6. DREXEL

7.

8.

9.

1868
Thompson's
Old Liverpool
Ware

10.

FRANCIS 11.

12.

13. **Nasturtium**

R. Thompson and Company/Thompson Pottery. Gardiner, Maine. 1839 to 1854. Robert Thompson and Charles W. Tarbell made utilitarian stoneware and ovoidal shaped jugs. When Tarbell died in 1844, Thompson purchased his half of pottery. In 1854, Thompson sold the pottery to the Ballard family. (See the listing, Various Ballard Potteries.) (Information: M. Lelyn Branin, *The Early Potters and Potteries of Maine*, p. 127. Mark: Branin, as cited.)

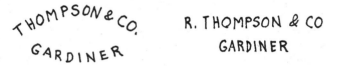

Thompson and Williams. Morgantown, West Virginia. 1875-1878. Robert T. Williams was partners with a man named Thompson in Morgantown for just three years making stoneware pieces with stenciled blue marks and decorations. See the listing Robert T. Williams for more on that potter. (Information and marks: Gordon C. Baker, "Robert T. Williams New Geneva, Pa Potter," *Stoneware Collectors' Journal*, September 1985, p. 29.)

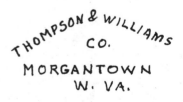

Thorley, Palin. Thorley was born in England in 1892, where he was taught to make pottery by his father and also completed a seven year apprenticeship with Josiah Wedgwood. He served in W.W. I and went back to Wedgwood to work. In 1929, he came to the U.S. to stay to work with Maddock and Miller who were importers. He then moved on to Sebring, Ohio, designed Leigh Ware and worked for various Sebring potteries. He became art director of the American China Corporation. He was also director of art at Hall China Company at one time. He maintained his own studio in East Liverpool, Ohio, and advised many of the potteries in the area on design, such as Hall China, Stetson China, Edwin M. Knowles, etc. In 1946, he started a studio in Williamsburg, Virginia, where he made hand made pieces in the 18th cen-

tury fashion. (Information: Jenny B. Derwich and Dr. Mary Latos, *A Dictionary Guide to U.S. Pottery and Porcelain*, pp. 223, 224. Marks: In 1956, he filed the mark shown for use on pottery, china, porcelain and ceramic dinnerware; tea service sets, flower holders, jugs, jardinieres, pitchers, bowls, vases and ornamental tiles for use as pads for hot dishes and for decorative purposes, claiming use of the mark since October 1955, but claiming pieces made with the plain signature, "Palin Thorley," since 1937.)

Thurston, Carl H. Pasadena, California. Filed for registration of this mark in January 3, 1926 for use on pottery and decorated earthenware, claiming use since the latter part of May 1926.

Tierra Royal Potteries, Inc. Kansas City, Missouri. 1952 to present (1984). Makers of earthenware containers, lamp bases, etc. They manufacture a fine line of ceramics called "Moma" which is an acronym for Missouri Made Artware. It is advertised by Blair Rubel, Ltd., as an American handcrafted product. The vases pictured were in all shapes and sizes in heavily glazed colors of salmon, bone, celadon, blue, burgundy, fizzle and oatmeal. Not to be confused with Tiara Exclusive of Dunkirk, Indiana, distributors of glass, mainly on a hostess plan. (Mark 1, paper label from company. Mark 2, filed August 7, 1952, for glazed pottery planters and vases, claiming use since July 1, 1951.)

 1.

2. *Tierra Royal*

Tiffany and Company. New York, New York. Founded in 1852 by the father of Louis Comfort Tiffany. Louis Comfort Tiffany started his own studio in 1893. Do not confuse Tiffany and Company with Tiffany Studios or the offices and shops belonging to L.C. Tiffany. In the winter of 1882 or 1883 this firm redecorated the White House for President Arthur. They are famous for their jewelry, lamps, etc. Louis Comfort Tiffany was the son of the founder of this store. At age 18 he decided to persue the arts, and he is the one who had the pottery made in his studios (see that listing for Tiffany Studios). Tiffany and Company (the store) filed for registration on May 26, 1928, on the mark shown for use on chinaware, bric-a-brac, earthenware, porcelain, claiming use of the mark since 1900. In *The Antiques Journal*, August 1952, in "Louis Comfort Tiffany," by Valentine Van Tassel, p. 14, we find this statement:

"Any items marked with the word 'Tiffany' alone, even if it is on glassware, should not be taken for the work of the artist and craftsman, Louis C. Tiffany or his company. This trademark (mark 1) belonged to his father's firm. The registration dated August 31, 1920, states that it "has been continously used in the business of said corporation since 1868."

Its use on 'table-glassware' was specifically mentioned. The registration was renewed in August 1940." (Marks: no. 2, filed by Tiffany and Company, February 10, 1920, claiming use since 1868. No. 3, filed by Tiffany and Company, August 12, 1920, claiming use since 1868.)

1.

2. **TIFFANY**

3. TIFFANY & CO.

Tiffany Studios. Corona, New York, and Hobokin, New Jersey. In 1879, Louis Comfort Tiffany produced his first glass. He continued working in glass, and in 1902 he formed Tiffany Studios. In a December 1903 *Country Life In America* magazine, p. 167, the advertisement read "originality of conception and execution endow the productions of the Tiffany Studios with an artistic individuality. The stock now assembled includes lamps, electroliers, Favrile glass in a variety of forms." The selling address in 1903 was 333 to 341 4th Avenue, New York. According to Garth Clark from *Century of Ceramics in U.S.*, p. 334, Louis C. Tiffany began experiments in pottery making in 1898 and first publicly showed them in 1904 at the Louisiana Purchase International Exposition. According to Paul Evans, p. 282, the offering of Tiffany pottery ceased between 1917 and 1920. (Marks: no. 1, from Paul Evans, *Art Pottery of the U.S.*, p. 284; no. 2, from Arthur G. Peterson, *400 Trademarks on Glass*, p. 22. Mark 2 was filed in December 12, 1905, claiming use since 1902 on decorative glass, enamels and pottery. For a discussion of the beautiful art pottery made by Tiffany, see the Evans book, pp. 282-284. Do not confuse with Tiffany and Company.

 1.   2.

Tipp City Novelty. Tipp City, Ohio. 1898 to present. Ceramic and glass decorators who do branding in metal, lustre staining and reshaping by hand of glassware and table accessories, personalized glasses, cups, ashtrays, etc. (Information and mark: Lehner, *Ohio Pottery and Glass*, p. 89.)

 (PAPER LABEL)

Torbert, William R. Brazil Township, Indiana. Around 1855 to around 1899. Torbert was born in Delaware, and moved to Brazil, Indiana, shortly before 1855. By 1860 he had a son, John W., who was listed as a potter. The Torberts made salt glazed stoneware utilitarian pieces. (Information and impressed mark: Melvin Davies, *Clay County Indiana Traditional Potters and Their Wares*, p. 14.)

W. R. TORBERT

Towle Manufacturing Company/Towle-Sigma Giftware Corporation. Boston, Massachusetts. Towle Manufacturing Company filed for registration of mark 1 on November 23, 1981, claiming use since February 1977, for use on stoneware cups, mugs, pitchers, teapots, salt and pepper shakers, butter warmers, salad bowls, soup bowls, cookie jars, napkin rings and coffee and tea sets. By 1982 the name was Towle Sigma Giftware and the products included glass and brass as well as ceramics with mark no. 2. In the Gift and Tableware Reporter, August 21, 1967, Towle Manufacturing Company was listed for American teapots.

BRITTANY   THE DECORATIVE KITCHEN
1.   2.

J.W. Town. Paris, Missouri. Around 1860. Made stoneware. Mark on stoneware piece. (Information and marks: Henry W. Heflin, pottery collector and researcher.)

J.W TOWN
PAT 18 ??   J.W. TOWN

Trapp, Mrs. Howard. Beuhlah, Michigan. Mrs. Trapp filed for registration of the mark, "Muriel Originals," on June 1, 1959, claiming use since February 1955, for use on ceramic ware, cups, plates, bowls, pitchers, jars, lamp bases, vases, ashtrays and figurines.

Treasure Craft or Pottery Craft. Compton, California. 1945 to present. Started by Alfred A. Levin and operated solely by members of the family. Presently selling pottery all over the country. Makers of gourmet cooking accessories, serving items, cookie jars, canister sets, planters, etc., all of excellent quality. One piece of stoneware acquired looked like a perfect piece of studio pottery with swirls of various colors, etc. The microwave cookware is also highly vitrified. Some vases are very artistic. Earthenware products are marked Treasure Craft. The stoneware items are Pottery Craft. This is the 39th year of business with Mr. Alfred A. Levin as head of the firm (1984). (Company furnished information; marks on pieces. No. 1, paper label; other marks impressed or in mold.)

TREASURE CRAFT
© MADE IN USA

TREASURE CRAFT
OF HAWAII © MAUI

Trenle China Company. East Liverpool, Ohio. The predecessor company of Trenle China Company was the **East End China Company** which started in 1894 and became Trenle in Janaury 1909. At that time Trenle filed to change the name of the East End China Company to Trenle China Company. (Secretary of State Report for 1910.) Trenle China Company operated in East Liverpool from 1909 to 1937 when they moved to Ravenswood, West Virginia, to become **Trenle Blake China Company** which was still listed in business in 1967. They made souvenir plates with place names and attractive decals in a very good grade of semi-porcelain. Trenle also made heavy hotel ware and electrical porcelain. (Information: Lehner, *American Kitchen and Dinner Wares*, p. 150 and p. 151. Marks: from Quality Stamp Company and on dishes.)

TRENLE
BLAKE

TRENLE
CHINA

Trenton China Company. Trenton, New Jersey. 1859-1891 (Barber, *Marks of American Potters*, p. 68.) Makers of vitrified and hotel china, white and decorated for table use. From 1888 to 1891 they added electrical porcelain to their regular line.

TRENTON CHINA CO.
TRENTON, N.J.

Trenton Potteries Company. Trenton, New Jersey. There were five potteries that went together in 1892 to form the Trenton Potteries Company. They were Crescent, Delaware, Empire, Enterprise and Equitable. Ideal was built later. The five potteries were all makers of sanitary ware such as bathtubs, etc., but they also made some general pottery. Some of them continued to operate under their original name as a part of the Trenton Potteries Company. I was able to establish ending dates for them from the *Trenton City Directories*. **Crescent Pottery** was organized in 1881 and was listed until 1907, then was not in the directories from 1908 through 1910, then was again listed until 1924. (This is not at all unusual for potteries to be busy, then idle, then back again.) Crescent made white granite and cream-colored ware as well as sanitary ware. **Delaware Pottery** started in 1884 and was a sanitary ware and druggists' ware type of factory, but at one time, according to Barber, they made a limited amount of Belleek porcelain. He doesn't say whether it was made into dinnerware or decorative pieces. I found the Delaware Pottery listed

through 1918. A pottery was established in 1863 by **Coxon and Company** to make white granite and cream-colored ware. Coxon died in 1868 but his widow and sons continued the business with various people. In 1875, the owners were **Coxon and Thompson** until 1884 when they sold to **Alpaugh and McGowan** who had operated another pottery from 1863 to 1883 or 1884 at which time they changed the name to **Empire Pottery**. (Jervis, *Pottery Glass and Brass Salesman*, October 4, 1917, p. 13.) They made thin china dinner sets, tea and toilet wares, and also sanitary ware. Then in 1892, Empire became part of Trenton Potteries Company. Empire was listed in business until 1918 in the *Trenton City Directories*. The **Enterprise**, founded in 1879, and the **Equitable**, founded 1888, were the only two of the five that made sanitary ware before and after the consolidation.

The Enterprise was listed in directories until 1916 and the Equitable until after 1941. **Ideal Pottery** was first listed in 1902 and continued until 1918. Barber said the Ideal was built after the initial consolidation of the first five companies and made only sanitary ware. The *Trenton Directories*, for one year only listed Equitable and Mutual Potteries as part of Trenton Potteries Company in operation. **Mutual Pottery** was listed as Mutual for the first time in 1922. They were sanitary ware manufacturers. Then the Trenton Potteries and the Mutual Pottery were consolidated and operated under the Trenton Potteries's name. The Crane Company was a company that sold sanitary fixtures. They had purchased large interests in the Mutual Pottery and had also acquired the Ideal Pottery. Around 1922 when the Trenton Potteries and Mutual Potteries were consolidated, Dr. M.W. Lerner, in the article cited, said that, Trenton Potteries operated as a Crane subsidiary, with Mutual as plant 1. The company disposed of the already idled Delaware, Crescent and Enterprise Pottery buildings. They were still operating on the Empire Pottery site and at the Equitable Pottery, now plant no. 2. In 1950, the Trenton Potteries was dissolved as such, and operated just as a Division of the Crane Company. They were actually listed as the Trenton Potteries in the *Trenton City Directories* through the 1960's. After two bad fires, one in 1967 and one in 1969, the potteries were closed down permanently.

Products of the Trenton Potteries Company as a unit have been discussed as stated in what each of the consolidated companies made. All except one product, art or decorative pottery, "American Trent Art China," or "Tepeco," made for a short time until right after World War II. There is disagreement at this time as to exactly how long the ware was made, but it spanned less than a 10 year period. According to Dr. M.W. Lerner, the pieces were generally undecorated except for the beautiful colored glazes used. The shapes pictured in his article are fabulous. The products included vases, planters, umbrella stands, candleholders, ashtrays, etc. The pieces are heavy and thick and highly vitrified. Dr. Lerner said marks 10, 11 are found on the Trenton Potteries art ware. (Information: Barber, *Marks of American Potters*, p. 64; Lehner, *American Kitchen and Dinner Wares*, p. 151 and 152; Dr. M.W. Lerner, "The Art Pottery of the Trenton Potteries Company," *Antique Trader*, April 13, 1983, pp. 74-77. Marks 1-9, Barber, *Marks of American Potters*, pp. 64 and 65. At the time Barber wrote his marks book in 1904, the star mark, nos. 3 and 4, were used with the number of the various potteries. He numbered them as: (1) Crescent; (2) Delaware; (3) Empire; (4) Enterprise; (5) Equitable; (6) Ideal. This system was used after 1892. Nos. 6, 7, 8, 9, a circle mark bearing numbers is also shown by Barber. According to Barber, mark 1 was used on the pieces sent to the Paris Exposition in 1904, when the Trenton Potteries Company won two gold medals for sanitary ware. The company entered four beautiful vases, pictured in Dr. Lerner's article. No. 5 was used by both the Trenton Pottery and Trenton Potteries Company. No. 12 was a paper label with black and gold foil found on an attractive green vase. Mark 12 was sent by Francis Andrews. Lerner said these were sometimes on the art pottery line. No. 13 shows the center of the mark (Nos. 6-9) as it was filed for registration on January 7, 1895, claiming use since November 15, 1894, for china, earthenware and pottery for plumbers use and other purposes. Nos. 14, 15 were sent by Elizabeth Vaughn, Beechwold Antiques. No. 16 for American Trent Art China.)

Trenton Pottery Company. Trenton, New Jersey. Two of the owners of the Trenton Pottery from 1852 to 1865 were Taylor and Speeler (Ramsay), and part of that time between 1853 and 1863, John Goodwin was with Taylor and Speeler. A third man, William Bloor was owner from 1856 to 1859. Bloor later went to East Liverpool to form Brunt, Bloor and Martin. The Trenton Pottery Company was incorporated in New Jersey in the old Taylor and Speeler building in 1865 by **Taylor and Company**. In 1870, John Goodwin went to Trenton and purchased interest in the pottery, and it was called **Taylor, Goodwin and Company**. (Barber, *Pottery and Porcelain of the U.S.*, p. 200.) They were manufacturers of ironstone china, cream-colored ware, sanitary and plumbers' earthenware. In

1872, Goodwin sold his interest and went back to East Liverpool. From 1872 to 1879, Ramsay lists **Isaac Davis** as owner. According to Barber, p. 239, **Fell and Thropp Company** were the owners of the Trenton Pottery before 1901, and in 1901 it became **Thropp and Brewer** with the addition of J. Hart Brewer. In the *1902-1903 Complete Directory* is a listing for the **Hart Brewer Pottery Company** making semi-porcelain, hotel ware, white granite dinner and toilet sets, and short sets of odd dishes, decorated. Also see Brewer Pottery Company of Tiffin. Mark shown was used by both the Trenton Pottery and Trenton Potteries Company, according to Barber, *Marks of American Potters*, pp. 56 and 65. (Information: Barber, *Marks of American Potters*, p. 66; Lehner, *American Kitchen and Dinner Wares*, p. 151.)

Trenton Pottery Works. Trenton, New Jersey. This pottery is listed in Barber, *Marks of American Potters*, p. 66, as if it were a separate company from the other Trenton Potteries in 1904 when the book was written. I had a complete run of the *Trenton City Directory* from 1900 to 1975, and there was no listing for such a company. Whether or not it was ever a member of the Trenton Potteries Company, I had no way to determine. The Barber book gave us the marks shown and stated that the company made semi-granite, white granite and opaque porcelain.

Trent Tile Company. Trenton, New Jersey. Company started in 1882. By 1910 Trent Tile Company employed 300 people and was an outstanding company, but by 1912 they were having financial difficulties. Thomas Thropp of the Eureka Flint and Spar Company of Trenton was made receiver, and by 1916 the property was up for sale. Mr. Thropp bought the company and managed it until he died in 1931. The family attempted to keep the company going, but in 1936 it was purchased by Mosaic Tile Company with the Thropps still in management control. In 1939, the plant was closed and taken over by the government. In 1940, **Wenczel Tile Company** purchased the property from the RFC and operated the plant as the Wenczel Tile Company. (Information: Everett Townsend, "Development of the Tile Industry in the U.S.," *American Ceramic Society Bulletin*, May 1943, p. 130. Mark: Thorn, p. 150.)

```
TRENT TILE
TRENTON N.J.
U.S.A
```

Triangle Novelty Company. Carrollton, Ohio. 1933 to 1949. Bert Crawford and Greta Corey started near Carrollton, Ohio, in 1933 and moved to Malvern, Ohio, in 1939. Made Juanita Ware, a multi-colored pottery with a marbleized look. In 1949, Mrs. Corey retired and Crawford went to Dalton, Ohio, and started **Crawford's Pottery** where he made the same type of ware for almost another 20 years. Few pieces were marked. Crawford died in 1972 when he was around 80 years old. Crawford had such a unique formula for making the Juanita Ware that he allowed other potters to watch his complete process, saying they couldn't make it anyway. And they never did. (Information: Grace Allison, "Juanita Ware," *Tri State Trader*, February 26, 1977, p. 1.)

Bert Crawford
1957

Triangle Studios/Vallona Star Ceramics. The company was listed in Los Angeles, California, in 1945 and 1948. By 1949 they were in El Monte, California. Owners were Valeria de Marsa and Everett S. Frost in the 1945 *Crockery and Glass Journal Directory* with Ebeling and Reuss, Inc. as distributors or jobbers. In 1945 Vallona Star was listed as a trade name for the art pottery of the Triangle Studios. By 1951 in the same directory, the company was called Vallona Star Ceramics with the same owners. The products were earthenware art pottery, figurines and miniatures. The company was also listed as decorators. I did not find this company listed in 1954 or after that in the directories I had. (Mark sent by Francis Andrews.)

Vallona
Star
California

Tritt China Company. Niles, Ohio. 1912 to 1922. See Bradshaw China Company for history. (Mark contributed by Grace Allison, writer on American pottery and glass.)

HAND PAINTED
By
TRITT CHINA

Tropico Pottery. See Gladding, McBean and Company for history.

Troxel Potters. Exeter Township, Berks County, Pennsylvania. Before 1866 to 1899. **John Troxel** was not a potter but he started the business. His sons **Daniel and William Troxel** made utilitarian redware from local clay and stoneware. John died in 1886, William continued the pottery until 1899. A Ferdinand Winterhalter did a lot of the potting at the John Troxel Pottery. Barber, p. 12, had a **Samuel Troxel**, 1823-1833, of Montgomery County, Pennsylvania, who made sgraffito earthenware, plain redware and slip decorated ware. Ramsay, p. 184, dates this potter around 1823-1835. Samuel Troxel had marks as shown but according to Hardcastle there is no record of any signed or decorated pieces for John Troxel and his sons. They made strictly utilitarian redware. The one piece Hardcastle had seen was glazed inside only. According to Guy F. Reinert, "History of the Pennsylvania German Potteries of Berks County," *Bulletin of American Ceramic Society*, Volume 19, no. 1 (1940), p. 26, John Link, son of Christian Link, worked at the John Troxel Pottery and two pie dish molds were found signed "John Link, 1867." This may be as close as we can come to a mark for the first Troxel Pottery discussed here. (Information: Mildred Hardcastle, "Potteries of Exeter Township, Berks County, Pennsylvania," *Spinning Wheel*, January, February, 1970, pp. 14, 15, 63. Marks: nos. 1, 2, 3, C. Jordan Thorn, *Handbook of Old Pottery and Porcelain Marks*, p. 150.)

1.

S. T. P.
1 8 2 9   3.

Samuel Troxel
Potter 1825
2.

Tucker, William Ellis in the American China Manufactory. Philadelphia, Pennsylvania. 1825-1832 when Tucker died. Business continued by others. From 1825-1828, William Ellis Tucker and Thomas Tucker; 1828-1829, W.E. Tucker and Thomas Hulme; 1829-1832, William Ellis Tucker (alone); 1832 W.E. Tucker and Joseph Hemphill (Tucker died); 1833-1837, Hemphill with Thomas Tucker as superintendent; 1837-1838, Thomas Tucker, alone. (Berenice M. Ball, "Ceramic Heritage of Chester County, Pa.," *Hobbies*, September 1953, pp. 80-81.) William Ellis Tucker began in a very small way in his American China Manufactory by decorating china and firing it in a kiln built by his father, Benjamin Tucker, on Market Street in Philadelphia. He began experimenting with the manufacture of china and succeeded in making an opaque queensware (white earthenware). By 1825 he was manufacturing a hard-paste, true porcelain. Tucker's wares were described by Elsie Walker Butterworth in an article, "Tucker China," in *Spinning Wheel*, June 1949, p. 3: "The first articles prodcued by Tucker were yellowish in cast and were lacking in finish and artistry. The decorations were done by hand, mostly with landscapes applied by a few strokes of the brush. The models were mostly after the fashion of the English potters of the day." In 1828, William's brother, Thomas Tucker, and Thomas Hulme of Philadelphia became his partners. The product was improved; the decorations became sprays of flowers, roses, birds, some bold decorations, etc. These pieces were sometimes marked "Tucker and Hulme." The partnership lasted a year leaving Tucker alone. For a time in 1832, Joseph Hemphill became a partner. William Ellis Tucker died in 1832 leaving the business to Hemphill. Hemphill had made a trip to Europe to the great porcelain factories, and he brought back workers who were able to produce a more elaborate china which was purchased by the more wealthy American families. In 1837, Hemphill retired and Thomas Tucker leased the building and continued making china for about a year before he closed the business and sold the equipment to Abraham Miller. Charles J. Boulter worked for Abraham Miller in Philadelphia. (Marks: no. 1, Thorn, p. 131; nos. 2-5, Barber, *Marks of American Potters*, p. 16; rest are decorator marks shown in Barber, pp. 17, 18.)

Jos. Hemphill
Philad.

1.

William Ellis Tucker
China Manufacturer
Philadelphia
1828

2.

Tucker & Hulme
China Manufacturers
Philadelphia
1828

3.

Manufactured
by Jos Hemphill
Philad—

4.

Tucker & Hulme.
Philadelphia
1828

5.

Decorator Marks At American China Manufactory

W	Andrew Craig Walker	H	William Hand
W	Andrew Craig Walker		
m	Joseph Moran	V	One Vivian
F	Charles Frederick	CB	Charles J. Boulter

Tunnicliff, Edward. Tunnicliff came from England in 1839 and settled in East Liverpool, Ohio. In 1848, he moved on to Zanesville, Ohio, then to Kewanee, Illinois, in 1853. He made Rockingham, much of which is marked as shown. Pieces were various statues, cookie jars, snuff jars, mugs, teapots, sugar bowls, etc. He made a pair of Russian wolf hounds, a statue of a Greyhound and a bust of Geroge Washington. (Information and mark: Norris Schneider, "Zanesville Potters," *Glaze*, June 30, p. 13.)

E. TUNNICLIFF. ZANESVILLE. OHIO

Tupper, C. Portage County, Ohio. Around 1870. Stoneware. (Information: Ramsay, p. 235. Mark: Thorn, p. 151.)

C. TUPPER
PORTAGE CO.
O

Turner, Robert. Robert Turner, studio potter, received a B.A. degree from Swarthmore College, Swarthmore, Pennsylvania, in 1936. He studied painting from 1937 to 1942 at the Pennsylvania Academy of Fine Arts in Philadelphia and at the Barnes Foundation in Merion, Pennsylvania. He then traveled and painted in Europe, and during this time, he became interested in ceramics. In 1946, he came back to the United States, to study at New York College of Ceramics at Alfred, New York, where he stayed until 1949. From 1949 to 1951, he had a pottery studio at Black Mountain College in North Carolina, where he had come by invitation. In 1951, he set up a pottery studio at Alfred Station, and divided his time between the University and his studio. His pots are made of simple lines in stoneware drawing his themes from nature, such as the desert or seashore, etc. (Information: Garth Clark, *A Century of Ceramics in the U.S.*, pp. 334, 335. Marks: Linda Steigleder, from the booklet published by the Everson Museum of Art to accompany the 1978 exhibition, "A Century of Ceramics in the U.S." Mark is incised.)

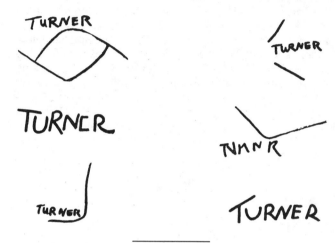

Turn of the Century Pottery. Alexandria, Virginia. 1981 to present (1985). Julie Martin, studio potter, makes white clay stoneware that is glazed to a tannish pink with hand painted decorations in a full range of functional and decorative pieces. She graduated from Marysville College in Marysville, Tennessee, in 1979 with a B.A. degree. She apprenticed with Cabbages and Kings (see that listing).

Julie

Turn of the Wheel Pottery. Springfield, Ohio. Christopher Morrett, owner, is a studio potter operating from 1977 to present to make functional stoneware and porcelain. He listed his shows and awards as "too many to list." He marks his pieces with Morrett as shown and the year the piece was made.

MORReTT 1982

Twin Spout Pottery, Inc. New York, New York. Filed for registration of this mark on August 4, 1939, for use on ceramic teapots, claiming use since July 18, 1939. An advertisement from *Better Homes and Gardens* showing a teapot with two spouts was sent to this author, but unfortunately the ad was not dated. In the 1945 *Crockery and Glass Journal Directory*, this company was listed as manufacturers of earthenware teapots, with many selling agencies representing them.

TEA MASTER

Twin Winton Ceramics. Pasadena and San Juan Capistrano, California. According to the 1977 *California Directory of Manufacturers* the company started in 1946. In 1977, they were employing 65 people and selling one-half million dollars in products per year. They were listed as importers and exporters. In 1953, they were listed in the *Pasadena City Directory*. In the late 1950's they moved to San Juan Capistrano. The pottery was started by Ross and Don Winton who were twin brothers. In 1977, the owner was William F. Bowermaster with John R. Bowermaster and Fred Bowermaster in charge of sales and purchasing. This property has become well known among collectors for their attractive cookie jars in the forms of Smokey the Bear, a sheriff, a rabbit and a cowboy. Twin Winton also made Al Capp type mountain folk figures on a 1½ quart pitcher, a tall mug, a flower container in the form of an outside toilet. These are not as well executed as those made by Imperial Porcelain, Zanesville, but they are attractive. (Information: Rena London and Pasadena City Library. Marks: nos. 1-2, inscribed on a pitcher and mug with mountain folk men for handles; no. 3, inscribed, sent by Rena London on a mug with a cowboy figure for a handle; no. 4, inscribed or scratched into bottom of Smokey the Bear cookie jar. Notice the copyrights 1960 date. No. 5 is a black stamped mark on sailor cookie jar. No. 6 is gold foil and black printing label on rabbit cookie jar.)

Twin, Winton Pasadena Calif

1.

Twin Winton Pasadena, Calif

2.

Open Range W Twin Winton Pasadena

3.

TWIN WINTON
© '60
MADE IN U.S.A.

4.

TWIN WINTON
©
CALIFORNIA U.S.A.

5.

BEAUTIFUL HAND CRAFTED CERAMICS MADE IN U.S.A.
Twin Winton
CALIFORNIA
SAN JUAN CAPISTRANO, CA 92675

6.

Tycer, Warren I. Pottery. Roseville, Ohio, factory; Zanesville, Ohio, offices. Before 1933 to before 1959. Made utilitarian ware such as kitchenware, teapots and mixing bowls. In 1942, Tycer patented a swinging teapot. In a 1943 advertisement a French Drip Earthenware coffee pot with coffee bean and leaf motif was pictured. In 1938, W.I. Tycer Pottery Company of Roseville, Ohio, purchased the Pereny Pottery Company of Columbus, Ohio. (Information from the Andre Pereny by letter, April 1973.) The Tycer plant in Roseville occupied five acres with 22,000 square feet of buildings. In 1959 the Melick Pottery Company purchased the Tycer Pottery Company in Roseville. In the 1952 *Crockery and Glass Journal Directory*, Tycer Pottery has 11 distributors listed in 9 states. (Mark 1 was filed for registration October 14, 1933 for use on ceramic vessels for cooking and similar purposes, claiming use since August 24, 1933. Mark 2 on piece. Mark 3, ''Cook-Rite,'' was used by Tycer in a line of cookware and Bakeware. This mark found on a pie dish and bowl. The pie dish has a dark brown glaze inside, unglazed outside. The bowl is glazed in clear glaze inside over the old yellow clay of the area with a dark brown outside. Marks 1 and 2 cover the whole bottom of the piece.)

1.

W.I. TYCER
POTTERY CO.
ZANESVILLE, OHIO

2.

3.

Tyler, Moses and Dillon, Charles. Albany, New York. Moses Tyler arrived in Albany, in 1822 from Massachusetts. He set up a pottery at 210 Washington Avenue, and operated alone until 1826. Sometime prior to 1834, he became partners with Charles Dillon for a few years at 236 Washington Street which had been the Cushman Pottery. In 1934, Tyler left Dillon and operated alone again using the mark, ''Moses Tyler/Manufacturer/Albany.'' Tyler retired shortly after 1840. When Tyler left Dillon, Dillon became partners with Jacob Henry and Edward Selby as **Dillon, Henry and Company** in 1834 and 1835. Nathan Porter came into the business, and it was called **Dillon, Henry and Porter** from 1835 to 1839. In 1839 to 1841 or 1842 the name was just **Porter and Dillon**. Pieces have been found marked, ''Porter and Dillon, West Troy,'' indicating that Charles Dillon and Porter moved there to work around 1840. In 1845, Nathan Porter was in partnership with Robert Fraser as **Porter and Fraser** in West Troy, New York. That partnership continued until 1863 when the business was sold to George B. Seymour. (Information: Warren F. Broderick, writer, researcher and collector. Marks: no. 1, Guilland, p. 188; nos. 2, 3, Stradling, p. 132.)

M. TYLER & CO.
ALBANY

1.

2. TYLER & DILLON
ALBANY

M. TYLER, ALBANY
MANUFACTURER

3.

U

Unaka Potteries, Inc. High Point, North Carolina and New York, New York. Filed July 7, 1928, for use of the word "Unaka" on pottery vases, urns and lamp bases, claiming use since June 1, 1927.

UNAKA

Underwood, J.A. and C.W. Fort Edward, New York. 1865 to 1867. According to Bill Grande, "Stoneware Pottery," *American Collectors News*, May 1982, p. 9, these two men established the second pottery in Fort Edward, which they sold in 1867 to Haxstun and Ottman. (Mark: Tom Dalton, "Consignment Auction Held Near Grand Rapids, Michigan," *Tri State Trader*, January 2, 1984, p. 20.)

J.A.& C.W. UNDERWOOD
FORT EDWARDS, N.Y.

Ungemach Pottery Company. Roseville, Ohio. Founded by Fred Ungemach in 1937 to May 1, 1984. Fred started by making novelties in what remained of the old National Pottery which had burned down. In 1938, he built a concrete building on the site. From 1937 to 1942 the plant was called *South Fork Pottery*, then became Ungemach Pottery Company. More buildings were added as the business grew. During World War II, planters were made for Walt Disney Productions. Two sons of Fred came into the business in 1946, Robert and Klemm. The pottery survived a disasterous flood in 1950 and a bad fire in 1966. They made mostly garden, floral and decorative pottery. Attractive designs, good glazes and a durable body are characteristic of the products. On May 1, 1984, Ungemach Pottery building and equipment was sold to Terry Zahn and became Friendship Pottery's building number 2. (Information: company furnished. Marks: All of the marks are recessed marks in the molds drawn from various pieces, mostly vases and flower pots.)

USA
Ungemach
UPCo

UNGEMACH
UPCO
241
USA

Ungemach
Roseville
Ohio
USA

UPCO

390
UP CO
USA

THE
UPCO

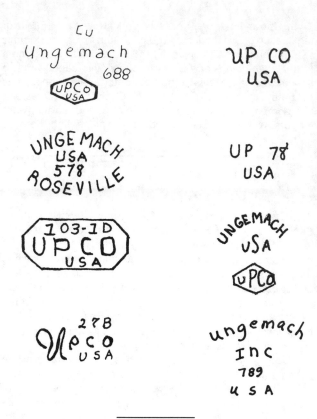

Cu
Ungemach
688
UPCO
USA

UNGEMACH
USA
578
ROSEVILLE

103-1D
UPCO
USA

278
UPCO
USA

UP CO
USA

UP 78
USA

UNGEMACH
USA
UPCo

ungemach
INC
789
USA

Uhl Pottery / Benninghof, Uhl and Company. Around 1850 to 1940's. It has been suggested that there was some connection between Crown Pottery and the Uhl Pottery Company. I find none except that eventually Crown took over the building when Uhl Pottery moved to Huntingburg, Indiana. Uhl Pottery originated in Evansville, Indiana, in 1854 when August Uhl and his brother started a pottery in Vanderburgh County. In 1879, the pottery became **Bennighof, Uhl and Company** according to Barber. Then in 1891 the name was changed to the Uhl Pottery Company and was moved from Evansville to Huntingburg for easier access to clay. In 1891, Crown Pottery was organized in the Uhl Pottery building in Evansville. In searching the *Indiana Directories* for an ending date for Uhl Pottery, I didn't find them listed after 1941, but the building was leased for awhile to the Louisville Pottery in the 1940's, then closed. Uhl Pottery Company made stoneware kitchen items. (Information: Lehner, *American Kitchen and Dinner Wares*, p. 49. Marks: no. 1 sent by Don Brewer. The rest of the marks on various pieces.)

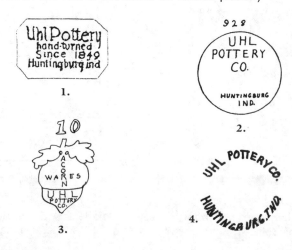

Uhl Pottery
hand-turned
Since 1849
Huntingburg Ind

1.

929
UHL
POTTERY
CO.
HUNTINGBURG
IND.

2.

10
ACORN
WARES
UHL
POTTERY
CO.

3.

UHL POTTERY CO.
HUNTINGBURG, IND.

4.

Union Porcelain Works. Greenpoint, New York. Established by German potters before the Civil War according to Barber. Jervis gives the starting date as 1854. ("A Dictionary of Pottery Terms," *Pottery, Glass and Brass Salesman*, October 24, 1912, p. 33.) Jervis said they were still in business at the time the article was written (1912), and that they made a true hard porcelain. Just before the war broke out the works were purchased by C.H.L. Smith and Thomas C. Smith who introduced the kaolinic body to make translucent bone china. In 1865, they perfected plain whiteware, and in 1866 started to decorate. They made a lot of art pieces, and a table service decorated in overglaze colors and white enameled designs. (Barber, *Pottery and Porcelain of the United States*, pp. 252-259.) Arthur Watts listed the Union Porcelain Works as being at 156 Greene Street, Brooklyn, New York. He said they turned to the manufacture of electrical porcelain insulators around 1900. (Arthur Watts, "Early History of Electrical Porcelain Industry in the United States," *Bulletin of the American Ceramic Society*, XVIII, November 1939, p. 404.) (Marks: nos. 1-5, Barber, pp. 80, 81. No. 6, J.G. Stradling, "American Ceramics at the Philadelphia Centennial," *Antiques*, July 1976, p. 155. The representation of an eagle's head with the letter S in its beak was filed for registration on May 4, 1877, by Thomas Smith and Sons. May 4, 1877, they filed a patent on a milk jug for a term of 14 years.)

Union Potteries Company. 1891-1904. Had plants in East Liverpool and Pittsburgh, according to Barber. In the *1902 Glass Factory Directory* they were listed in both places making semi-porcelain dinner sets, toilet sets and short sets of odd dishes, some decorated. Vodrey, William H., "Record of the Pottery Industry in East Liverpool," *Bulletin of the American Ceramic Society*, XXIV, August 1945, p. 282 has the company listed as being in business from 1891 to 1904 in East Liverpool. Barber stated that they made fine china, and he showed a variety of marks used by them. In "Ohio Ironstone," staff-written, *Spinning Wheel*, June, 1954, p. 25, it is said the Wyllies sold their plant to the Union Potteries Company in 1891. In the *1896 East Liverpool Business Directory*, they were listed as the Union Co-operative Pottery Company making fine decorated ware and white granite at Walnut and Kossuth Streets.

Union Pottery. Newark, New Jersey. 1877 to 1906. Conrad Haidle and John C. Sonn started the Union Pottery in 1871. Jacob Zipf came in 1875. Pieces are found marked "Haidle and Zipf." Zipf operated alone from 1877 to 1906. (Information and mark: Stewart and Consentino, *Stoneware, A Guide for the Beginning Collector*, p. 73.)

JACOB ZIPF
UNION POTT
NEWARK, N.J.

Union Pottery, Various Companies. A Union Pottery was listed in Brooklyn, New York in the *1902-1903 Complete Directory* as making semi-porcelain dinner sets, toilet sets and short sets of odd dishes, some decorated. I did not establish a connection between this pottery and any of several others by the same name. See Union Porcelain, Greenpoint, New York and several others listed for marks involving the name Union.

Union Stoneware Company. Red Wing, Minnesota. 1894 to 1906. This was a selling agency which represented Minnesota Stoneware Company, Red Wing Stoneware Company, and North Star Stoneware Company (see those listings). These three potteries sold their products to Union Stoneware Company, which then put them on the market. (See North Star Pottery listing for further information. Information: David A. Newkirk, *A Guide to Red Wing Markings*, p. 21, and Lyndon C. Viel, *The Clay Giants Book II*, p. 92. Marks: Lyndon C. Viel, as cited, pp. 121, and pp. 92 to 98.)

UNION
STONEWARE CO.
RED WING, MINN.

SUCCESS FILTER,
MANUFACTURED BY
UNION STONEWARE CO.
RED WING, MINN.

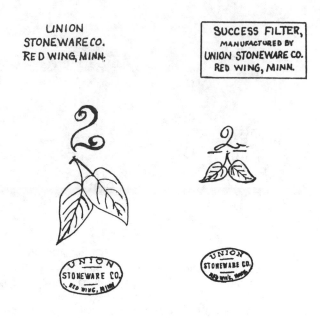

United Flavor Seal Company. Indiana, Pennsylvania. Company filed for registration of this mark on October 1, 1971, claiming use since May 15, 1970, for china tableware.

United States Ceramic Tile Company/Spartek, Inc. Canton, Ohio. U.S. Tile Company and Canton Roofing Tile Company merged to become the U.S. Roofing Tile Company from 1913 to 1926, which became the U.S. Quarry Tile Company from 1926 until December 6, 1954, when it became the U.S. Ceramic Tile Company. In 1954, the U.S. Ceramic Tile Company acquired the Sparta Ceramic Tile Company and operated it as a wholly owned subsidiary. (See that listing.) The U.S. Ceramic Tile Company or Spartek, Inc. had two plants operating in 1983 on Sandyville Road in Sparta. The plants in Huston, Mississippi, and Shreve, Ohio, were no longer operating in 1983. After February 19, 1974, the U.S. Ceramic Tile Company became known as Spartek, Inc., which makes wall, floor and speciality tile, parts of teflon and other plastics, aluminum oxide ceramics with high electrical insulating properties and a line of powdered metal products with a corporate structure. From 1965 to 1968 the U.S. Ceramic Tile Company owned and operated the Western States Ceramic Company in Sacramento to make "Mission Tile." In 1974, the corporate structure of Spartek, Inc. consisted of the U.S. Ceramic Tile Company, Barberton Plastics Products, Inc. in Barberton, Ohio, and the Metal Powder Products Company of Logan, Ohio, which manufacturers the powdered metal parts. Other divisions are Diamonite Products, making aluminum oxide products; Sparta Manufacturing Division; D and H Tool and Die Division. This is such a simplified account of such a complicated company history that I can only recommend reading McCollam, as cited, for a real understanding of the organization of this company. The U.S. Ceramic Tile Company marked products occasionally

other than tile. See the registration for mark 1. (Information: Harold C. McCollam, *The Brick and Tile Industry in Stark County*, pp. 231-242. Marks: no. 1 filed October 6, 1964 by the U.S. Ceramic Tile Company for hollow pottery ware namely teapots, sugar bowls and cream pitchers, claiming use since July 1945. Nos. 2, 3, 4 were found on tile. Mark 3 had one of each of the lines of printing on each side of the back of the tile.)

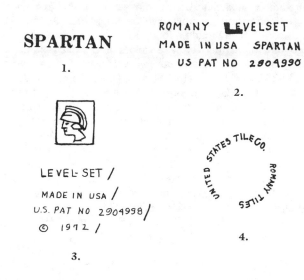

United States Encaustic Tile Company/United States Tile Corporation. Indianapolis, Indiana. 1877 to 1939. Company started in 1877 and was destroyed by fire and rebuilt by 1879. The company was founded by William Harrison, a cousin of President Benjamin Harrison. The firm went into receivership in 1886 when Mr. Harrison's bank, which was affiliated with the tile company, failed. On May 10, 1986 the U.S. Encaustic Tile Works was formed to make unglazed floor tile. Later they began glazing with bright colors, and by 1893 had a matte finish. They also made relief tile. Just before the stock market crash in the depression the company had spent about $125,000 for expansion. Then the owners died, and the tile plant went into hands of a receivership. By December 1932 a reorganizaton had taken place, and the U.S. Tile Corporation was formed. The U.S. Tile Corporation went out of buisiness in 1939. The buildings were being torn down in 1943 and the area was to become a playground. (Information: Everett Townsend, "Development of the Tile Industry in the U.S.," *American Ceramic Society Bulletin*, May 1943, p. 129. Marks: recessed in raised circles; Ralph and Terry Kovel, *The Kovel's Collectors Guide to American Art Pottery*, p. 347.)

U-S-E-T-W
INDIANAPOLIS
IND.

United States Merchandise Corporation. Baltimore, Maryland. A distributor, filed for rights to this mark on May 23, 1939, for use on florists supplies, namely ceramic flower and plant pots, vases, jardinieres and bowls, claiming use since June 6, 1935.

United States Potters Association. Started in 1875 when 41 companies met to organize. Until 1910, Sanitary manufacturers were affiliated but then they formed their own organization, so the United States Potters Association came to represent the dinnerware industry. Since 1912 the offices have been located in East Liverpool, Ohio. (Information: W.A. Betz, "It All Started in East Liverpool," *Crockery and Glass Journal*, April 1955. Their logo is shown. According to the Bulletin of the American Ceramic Society, September 17, 1931, the United States Potters Association recognized the National Brotherhood of Operative Potters, a branch of the American Federation of Labor in 1896, and agreed to deal with them collectively on matters of wages, etc.

United States Pottery Company. Wellsville, Ohio. Started business in 1899 to manufacture a high grade of semi-vitreous porcelain. Their mark was the shield of the United States with "U.S. Pottery Company, Wellsville, O." This company became one of the companies to form the East Liverpool Potteries Company, which also used the mark of the shield of the United States with "East Liverpool Potteries Company." The six potteries were connected from about 1900 to 1903, when the E.L. Potteries Company was dissolved. Some continued on their own; some quit business. No mention of the U.S. Pottery after 1903 was found. (Information: Lehner, Ohio Pottery and Glass, p. 94.)

United States Pottery. Bennington, Vermont. 1848 or 1849 to 1858. Christopher Webber Fenton was in partnership with his brother-in-law, Julius Norton, from around 1844 to 1847,

according to John Spargo, *Early American Pottery and China*, pp. 258-259. Then in 1848 or 1849 (E.A. Barber, *Marks of American Potters*, p. 91) he helped to start another pottery called Lyman, Fenton and Company. In 1849, new buildings were built, and the name became the United States Pottery Company which operated until 1858. The products were Parian ornamental pieces, in a grayish white and pure white, which was decorated in relief. Porcelain biscuit toys were also made. In 1858, when the United States Pottery closed, Fenton went to Peoria, Illinois, to become partners with Decius W. Clark. The products at the United States Pottery in Bennington were made of pottery and porcelain. They made Flint Enamel Ware, Scroddled or Marbled Ware, Rockingham ware and granite ware or stone china and tiles that were inlaid and enameled. They also made white earthenware tableware, pitchers, toilet sets, etc. which was thrown and turned on a wheel. A very small amount of tableware was pressed into moulds. They also made redware pitchers covered with slip, according to John Spargo, *The Potters and Potteries of Bennington*, p. 165. (Marks: Duplicate copies of these marks may be seen in the following references. For instance the three banner marks shown are what three different books showed for the same mark. John Spargo, *Early American Pottery and China*, p. 360; and Thorn, p. 140; Ramsay, p. 267; and E.A. Barber, *Marks of American Potters*, p. 95.)

United States Stoneware Company. Akron, Ohio. The company was incorporated in 1891, but had predecessor companies that dated back to 1856 in Akron. F.J. Knapp operated from around 1860 to late 1880's. Brewster, Knapp and Laudenslager incorporated the company into U.S. Stoneware in 1891. Part of the property that U.S. Stoneware sets on is the site of the old Sperry and Rattle Pottery (1878-1881). In 1902, that property belonged to the Akron Vitrified Clay Manufacturing Company and in 1927 was acquired by the U.S. Stoneware Company. Sometime after 1959, the U.S. Stoneware Company became a part of the Norton Company as it is known today. Mark 1 was used as late as 1953. It was founded on a very old looking dark glazed, highly vitrified, stoneware jar with a clamp on lid that was called a grinding jar used in making industrial pottery. The Norton Company, for many years now, has been manufacturing chemical processing equipment from plastics, metals and ceramics; but in the early years they made utilitarian jugs, crocks, etc. (Mark 2 sent by Elizabeth Boyce on one gallon stoneware crock.)

G4609
M5

US STONEWARE CO.
AKRON, O.

S 1537
1 GAL.
U S
STANDARD
THE U.S. STONEWARE
AKRON, OHIO
L

(PICTURE OF EAGLE BETWEEN U.S.)

1.

Unitile Company. Urichsville, Ohio. This company was a decorative tile company that had a brief existance sometime before 1932. The company was started by William Donahey and his brother James, both of whom came from West Chester, Ohio. The tiles were decorated with various colors in inlaid designs with subjects such as Little Red Riding Hood in a series of tiles which told the whole story. The plant burned and was not rebuilt. James was a pupil of the Cleveland School of Art and a cartoonist for the *Cleveland Plain Dealer*. William Donahey also was an artist with the *Cleveland Plain Dealer* and then became a writer and illustrator for children's features in newspapers, magazines and books. He was author of the *Tennie Weenie Books*. His wife was Mary Dickerson, a writer of children's stories. (Information: Edna Marie Clark, M.A., *Ohio Art and Artists*, pp. 174, 434. Mark on tile.)

UNITILE

Universal Potteries, Inc. Cambridge, Ohio. 1934 to 1976. (For early history, see Bradshaw China.) Producers of a fine grade of semi-porcelain dinnerware, baking dishes and other utilitarian kitchenware with heavy glazes. Marks were intricate and wordy as shown. The company started making tile in 1956, but also made some dinnerware until 1960 when they stopped making dinnerware and manufactured decorative tile only. The name was changed to the **Oxford Tile Company** (1956 to March 5, 1976). Oxford Tile operated successfully for 20 years, officially closing on March 5, 1976, leaving Cam-

bridge without a pottery for the first time since the early 1900's. The "Cat-tail" pattern was advertised in the 1930's and 1940's in *Needlecraft Magazine* and *Sears and Roebuck's* catalogue. "Calico Fruit" was advertised in the 1940's. "Ballerina" marks date from late 1940's through the 1950's (also, see Universal Promotions, Inc.). "Raymor Universal" was advertised in 1950's. "Upico Ivory" was introduced in 1938. "Laurella" was introduced in the middle 1930's and was still advertised in the late 1940's. "Camwood" was in production when the company quit making dinnerware and had been produced for a long period of time. (Information: Lehner, *American Kitchen and Dinner Wares*, p. 155. Marks: photostatic copies from dishes except nos. 1, 2, Jo Cunningham, *American Dinnerware*, pp. 289, 300.)

16.

HARMONY HOUSE
CHERRY RED

17.

WARRANTED
22 CARAT GOLD

18.

BALLERINA
· UNDERGLAZE ·
· OVEN-PROOF ·
· IRONSTONE ·
· DETERGENT ·
AND
DISHWASHER
SAFE
by Universal

Cattail

OXFORD
STONEWARE

19.

20.

21.

BEL AIR
BALLERINA
Ovenproof   by Universal
22   CARAT
PLATINUM

22.

HARVEST
BALLERINA

23.

24.

25.

Moderne

26.

27.

28.

29.

30.

CALICO FRUIT

31.

CALICO FRUIT

32.

33.

THIS PATTERN
WILL NOT FADE
IT IS PERMACAL

34.

35.

36.

37.

38.

39.

40.

41.

42.

43.

Universal Promotions, Inc. Cambridge, Ohio. This company acted as distributors for Universal Potteries products from 1937 until 1956, when Universal Potteries started making floor and wall tile only. No more dinnerware was made at Universal Potteries after that time. Some Universal dinnerware and kitchenware was made by other potteries after 1956 for Universal Promotions, Inc. to sell. In the 1970's, some "Moss Rose" pieces were made with the Ballerina mark to be distributed through groceries, but the promotion was not successful at all and was faded out. Universal Ballerina marks were found for several of the different potteries at Quality Stamp Company, such as Homer Laughlin, Taylor, Smith and Taylor and Hull China Company. These companies were verified as the manufacurers for Universal Promotions, Inc. (Mark: sent from Taylor, Smith and Taylor.)

BALLERINA
· UNDERGLAZE ·
· OVEN-PROOF ·
· IRONSTONE ·
· DETERGENT ·
AND
DISHWASHER
SAFE
by Universal

Universities As Ceramics Training Centers. In 1922, only five major colleges taught ceramics in the United States and these were to train people to make commercial and industrial ceramics not art ware. They were: University of Illinois, Urbana, Ill; Iowa State Colege, Ames, Ia; New York State School of Clay-Working and Ceramics, Alfred, N.Y.; Ohio State University, Columbus, Ohio; Rutgers College, New Brunswick, N.J. But by the end of World War II all major colleges and universities were offering ceramic courses of some type in their curriculum. Ohio State University was one of the very first to offer a ceramic program which included fine arts and art history as well as industrial ceramic courses. The colleges provided training that enabled many people who wanted to work with clay, to work on an individual basis. They didn't have to go into industry to work with clay and the growth of studio potters has been tremendous from the early 1930's to the present time. See the introduction for a discussion on studio potteries.

University City Pottery. People's University, University City, Missouri (St. Louis). The first kiln was fired in April 1910, and all production ceased by 1915, but in the meantime the group of art potters who worked there was astounding, such as Taxile Doat, Emile Diffloth, Eugene Labarriere, Samuel Robineau, Adelaide Robineau, Frederick Rhead, Kathryn Cherry and Julian Zolnay. The founder was Edward Gardner Lewis. See Paul Evans, *Art Pottery of the U.S.*, pp. 286 to 291, for a description of the product and artists. Also by Evans, "American Art Porcelain - The Work of University City Pottery," *Spinning Wheel*, December 1971, pp. 24, 25. Also, Lois H. Kohlenberger, "Ceramics at the People's University," *Ceramics Monthly*, November 1976, pp. 33, 34. (Marks: nos. 1-5, incised marks as shown in staff written article, "University City Pottery," *American Art Pottery*; no. 13, June 1977, pp. 1, 2; no. 1, was shown with date 1913 under it also. Around 1911, pieces were imprinted with the circular Glenmoor Pottery mark. Marks 6-15, as shown in Paul Evans, *Art Pottery of the U.S.*, p. 290; no. 16, was the Taxile Doat mark or monogram as shown in American Art Pottery paper as cited. No. 17 is an incised mark from Linda Steigleder, from the booklet published by the Everson Museum of Art to accompany the 1978 exhibition, "A Century of Ceramics in the U.S.")

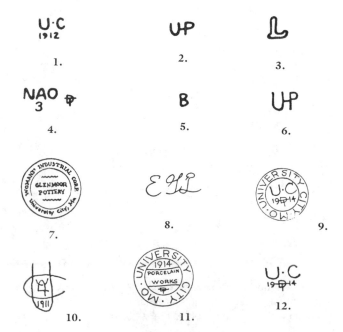

13.   14.   15.   16.

University of North Dakota. See North Dakota School of Mines.

Universities, Various Marks. Quite a few universities and fraternities filed registrations for symbols, decorations or marks to be used on dishes and ceramic pieces, made for them by some factory. The University of Notre Dame in Notre Dame, Indiana, filed for registration of mark 1 on July 16, 1959, claiming use since January 1, 1948, for use on crockery mugs, plates and ashtrays. Sigma Nu Fraternity of Indianapolis, Indiana, filed the next three marks in 1946 and 1947. Marks 2 and 3 were used since 1869 and mark 4 was used after 1915, all on table china.

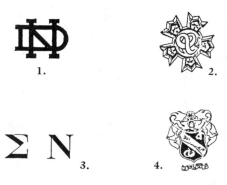

Unser, George. Jeffersonville, Clark County, Indiana. Began operation in 1870 to make stoneware. Employed 3 to 5 full time potters. (Information: Peggy A. Loar, *Indiana Stoneware*, a catalogue of 13 pages for the exhibit held at Indianapolis Museum of Art in 1974, pp. 18, 43. Mark: Melvin L. Davies, research potter.)

G. UNSER
JEFFERSONVILLE
IND.

Usona Art Pottery. Chester, West Virginia. First listed in East Liverpool directories that I had in 1934, but were not listed in 1931. They operated until after 1954. They were still listed in the *Crockery and Glass Journal Directory* in 1954, but were gone shortly after that. Elmer Hoskinson was president. The pottery manufactured earthenware art pottery, figures, figurines, miniatures and special mould pieces. In the 1945

Crockery and Glass Journal Directory, Desert Pottery in Mesa, Arizona, was listed as a branch of Usona Art Pottery. I found no further information on this Desert Pottery. (Mark: sent by June Kass Jackson.)

Utley, Taber. Colorado Springs, Colorado. Studio potter who lived from 1891 to 1978. He taught pottery making and painting at the Pueblo, Colorado Junior College, and at the Broadmoor Art Academy. The pieces were press molded or hand built stamped Tabor Utley in script. (Information and mark: Thomas G. Turnquist, pottery researcher and writer.)

V

Valentien Pottery. San Diego, California. In production about a year in 1911 and 1912. Owners were Albert and Anna Marie Valentien. He was an artist having painted a compendium of California's wildflowers of over 1,000 prints on a commission basis. He painted until he died in 1925. Albert worked for T.J. Wheatley and was a decorator at Rookwood Pottery. Anna also worked at Rookwood. Both studied in Paris. Anna was interested in sculptured forms. She taught art in schools from 1914-1938. The pottery they made is beautiful art pottery with sculptured designs in monochrome matt and vellum - type glazes. They also made plain shapes with the same glazes. Some slip decorated floral and geometric motifs were used. (Information and marks: Staff written, "The Talent of Albert R. Valentien," *American Art Pottery*, pp. 1, 3. Paul Evans, "Valentien Pottery: The Missing Shape Book," *Spinning Wheel*, September 1979, pp. 37-39. Also Dave Rago, "American Art Pottery," *Antique Trader Weekly*, September 9, 1981, p. 91. Marks: no. 1, Rago as cited; no. 2 and 3, signatures or artists shown in Evans as cited.)

1.   2. A.M.V.   3. A R.V.

Van Briggle Pottery. Colorado Springs, Colorado. Artus Van Briggle was a talented decorator at the Rookwood Pottery. So promising was his work that the pottery sent him to Paris to study. He returned to Rookwood Pottery to work until his health forced him to move to a better climate. He moved to Colorado Springs, and he and his wife Anne Gregory founded the Van Briggle Art Pottery around 1900. It was in production by 1901. He died at age 35 in 1904. The dated pieces are greatly sought after by collectors. Van Briggle won awards at the 1904 St. Louis Exposition. He made sculptured figurals and florals in rich colors with thick matte glazes. Anne continued the business until 1913 when it was sold at sheriff's auction. During that period she created 400 or more patterns. The pieces were modeled by the Van Briggles, and a mold was made to make a limited number of pieces. The molded pieces were retouched and remodeled by hand. The pieces were fired, glazed and refired and some color was added.

By 1908 almost all of the ware was cast and emphasis was shifted from art pottery. Pieces were some art pottery, terra cotta pieces, chimney tops, tile, flower pots and garden ware. By 1920 art pottery, as defined by Evans, was replaced with mass produced industrial artware. So much has been written about Van Briggle pottery pieces. In Scott Nelson's "A Comparative Look At the Van Briggle Lorelei," *American Art Pottery*, March 1979, p. 5 is a description of three pieces of the "Lorelei" pattern made in 1902, another between 1912 and 1922, and another after 1940. Also, according to Evans, p. 300, Lorelei could be purchased from the pottery in the 1970's. So we would be remade down through original designs were repeated and are sharper, more detail wears. The older hand made pieces From a fact sheet provided the sizes of the pieces vary. printed by Jo Cunningham in the Van Briggle Pottery and March 1984, p. 15,

are the following which may help collectors to date and identify various pieces.

"The following notes pertain to the older Van Briggle pieces, and these are the only means we have of dating the pieces. We hope this information will be of assistance in any attempts to determine the age of the old Van Briggle pieces.

Every piece bears the Double A trademark. Most pieces also have "Colorado Springs, Colo." sometimes abbreviated.

1901-1907 All pieces were dated and included the design number as well as some Roman numerals. The Roman numeral found on the bottoms of the pottery pieces are also indications of the specific Clay body being used.

1908-1912 Design numbers; no dates.

1912-1914 Dates and design; Numbers sometimes used.

1915-1916 Some dated, some design numbers.

1917-1918 Dates, no design numbers.

1919-1920 Seldom dates; if so apostrophe was used; ('19 or "20).

1901-1920 Bottoms of pieces glazed with same color glaze as body glaze.

1921-1930 Unglazed bottoms, no dates, no design number.

1922-1929 "U.S.A." was used in addition to Colorado Springs on the bottoms of pieces.

1921-and thereafter - white, unglazed bottom or covered with clear glaze.

To give the reader just a little more help in dating Van Briggle, the following is from the article by Abigail E. Foster, "Van Briggle Pottery from 1899," *American Clay Exchange*, December 1982, p. 18:

"From the factory comes this information. The following notes pertain to the older Van Briggle pieces.

The deep Mulberry color was modified in 1946 to a lighter shade called Persian Rose. Persian Rose was made until 1968.

Moonglo glaze was introduced in 1946.

Pieces bearing the high-gloss brown, black or blue-green were introduced at Van Briggle in 1955. Until 1968 the pieces were inscribed "Anna Van Briggle" on the bottom. At that time and forward the items showed the same as the matte glaze items and contained the double A trademark. The high-gloss brown glaze was discontinued in 1978.

Artus and Ann never signed pieces.

The matte Russet glaze was introduced in 1978 and the midnight (matte Black) glaze was introduced in 1979.

A "G" on the base of a piece indicates gold was added to the glaze, a process done for three months. There are many other sub categories such as the "G."

Dating Van Briggle has been so difficult. Larry Lafary in "Van Briggle Part II," *The Glaze*, June 1979, p. 10, had this to say:

"Another age indicator comes to mind. Look at the color of the bottom. Dark clays, including a terra cotta red, were used before 1930. Since then a standard white clay has been used.

A discussion of marks can be very controversial. For example, most sources, and I said most sources, state that pieces made before 1904 marked with a Roman numeral I, II or III indicates the item was crafted by Anne, Harry Bangs or Artus, respectively. This theory was shattered with the discovery of a five page document found in the personal effects of Benjamin Sutton. The document, dated April 21, 1902, covered clay and glaze formulas. The formulas for clay were labeled, I, II and III. Also, in support of this theory is the fact that no one has ever found a piece marked "I."

With the exception of pattern numbers and the dates "1915" and "1916," all marks were hand incised. A metal stamp was used to mark the exceptions. Pattern numbers were discontinued in 1916. As a guide, all pattern numbers below "899" were created prior to 1912. Speaking of pattern numbers reminds me of the number of times I have heard dealers tell customers that the numbers on the bottom indicate the last two digits of the year of manufacture. With the exception of the years 1919 and 1920 which were marked with "19" or "20" below all other markings, all dated marks are a four digit number (i.e. 1902). the numbers on either side of the AA can be the month of manufacture (allows comparison for quality control), the pattern or the finisher.

AA alone or over stock numbers would indicate a pre-1920 piece. "U.S.A." with AA generally means manufacture was between 1922 and 1929."

Some 1984 pieces being made included a figurine soap dish, "The Shell Girl;" "The Hope Maiden" and Indian girl figurine for soap or ashtray, a candleholder in the form of a mushroom, an owl, an Egyptian cat, Bambi, etc. Lamps are an important current product at the factory. (Information: Paul Evans, *Art Pottery of the U.S.*, pp. 297-301 and Eugene Hecht, "Quixote Rides Again," *American Art Pottery*, October 1981, pp. 1, 4, and other articles as cited. Marks: nos. 1-3, E.A. Barber, *Marks of American Potters*, p. 166. These marks are also shown by Jervis in "Worlds Pottery Marks," *Pottery, Glass and Brass Salesman*, April 15, 1915, p. 11 and April 22, 1915, p. 15. Nos. 4-8 are from the booklet by Linda Steigleder, from the booklet published by the Everson Museum of Art to accompany the 1978 exhibition, "The Century of Ceramics in the U.S." Nos. 4-6 incised; No. 7 is a sticker; No. 8 is a stamped mark. Nos. 9-12 shown on Deb and Gini Johnson's *Beginners Book of Pottery*, pp. 54-55. These are incised except no. 11 which is a paper label. No. 13 was dated as a mark used 1908-1911 by Dave Rago, "American Art Pottery," *Antique Trader Weekly*, February 24, 1982, p. 90. No. 14 an incised mark copied from piece at Zanesville. No. 15 identified as 1907-1912 mark in the *American Clay Exchange*, May 1982. The rest are incised marks used on newer pieces of 1960's.)

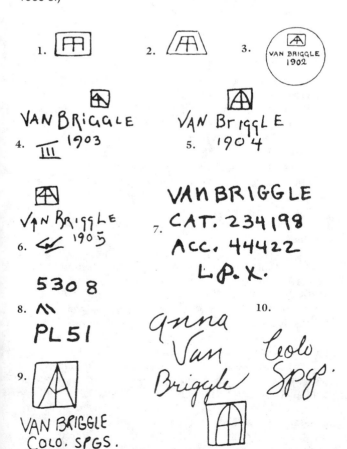

Van Camp Sea Food Company, Inc. Fish Harbor, Terminal Island, California. Filed for a claim on this mark on May 6, 1941, for use on porcelain or chinaware dinnerware and baking dishes, claiming use since March 1, 1939.

Vance Faience Company. See Avon Faience Company.

Vandenberge, Peter. Sacramento, California. Peter was born in Holland. He received a B.S. degree from the Sacramento State College in California, in 1959, and later he received his M.A. degree from the University of California, in Santa Barbara. He was teaching at the San Francisco State College in 1978 at the time Clark wrote the book cited. His early work was low fired vegetable images, and later he made other figurative type work. (Information: Garth Clark, *A Century of Ceramics in the U.S.*, p. 336. Incised marks: Linda Steigleder, from the booklet published by the Everson Museum of Art to accompany the 1978 exhibition, "A Century of Ceramics in the U.S.")

P. V 77   AVB

Vanderkooi, Lenore. Nashville, Tennessee. 1975 to present (1985). Lenore is a studio potter, making functional stoneware. From 1972-1975 she studied ceramics with Robert Freagon at Peabody College in Nashville. She has studied at many one and two week workshops with well known potters, such as Cynthia Bringle, Daniel Rhodes, John Glick and others. Lenore has participated in many juried fairs, and has received numerous awards. In 1981, she was selected for membership in the Southern Highland Handicrafts Guild, and in 1982 she joined the University of Michigan Artist Guild Gallery, the Spring Street Gallery, Montgomery Bell Academy and the Clay Workplace. She has also shown at the Lodestone Gallery, in Boulder, Colorado, and the Ridgeway Gallery, in Oak Ridge, Tennessee. She was invited to show in Functional Ceramics '81 and the 10 year retrospective show Functional Ceramics '83 at the Wooster (Ohio) Museum of Art. She has had a portrait and several pieces pictured in feature articles in *Ceramics Monthly* magazine. At Fall Fair '83, in Nashville, she received the Best of Clay award. The mark shown is stamped on the pots. Some are signed, ''Vanderkooi'' and also stamped.

Van Hunke, Dee and Robert. Pompey, New York. Robert is a teacher in the Fayetteville Manlius School District in Fayetteville, New York. He and his wife Dee have made hand-thrown stoneware utilitarian pieces and hand built sculptures for a number of years. This mark found on a sculptured owl. They are still making pottery in 1983.

$$V\text{-}v^H$$

Van Loon and Boyden. Ashfield, Massachusetts. 1854 to 1856. In 1854 the pottery of Hastings and Belding went into receivership. (See that listing.) The business was taken over by Staats Van Loon and George Washington Boyton with Guilford still holding his 1/3 share. This partnership only lasted for two years. (Information: Lura W. Watkins, Early New England Potters and Their Wares, p. 108. Marks: Thorn, p. 152. In the text, Thorn lists the potter as Van Loon with the correct dates. But whoever drew the marks for him drew ''Van Horn'' which was an error. ''Van Loon'' is correct, according to Watkins, at cited.)

VAN LOON & BOYDEN
ASHFIELD
MASS

Van Nostrand, Morris A. New York, New York. Distributor for Jackson China Company's ''Featherweight'' china. Listed in the 1945 *Crockery and Glass Journal Directory*.

Van Pottery. Trenton, New Jersey. Listed in *Trenton City Directories*, from 1920 to 1932. (Mark: was found on Blue Willow hotel ware plate, sent by Connie Rogers, researcher and writer on Blue Willow ware.)

Vernon Kilns. Vernon, California (southwest of Los Angeles). 1916 to 1960. According to McKee, p. 48, the pottery started in 1916, and until 1928 it was called Poxon China, Ltd. From 1928 to 1948 the name was **Vernon Potteries**. Vernon Kilns was taken over by Metlox Potteries in 1958 and ceased production in 1960. There were two artists who designed ware for Vernon Kilns. Don Blanding, a wandering poet and artist, and Rockwell Kent. Their designs on the shapes created by Gale Turnbull brought into existence some of the most beautiful American dishes made. Two lines designed by Blanding were ''Hawaiian Flowers'' and ''Coral Reef.'' Rockwell Kent adapted his illustrations for the books *Moby Dick* and *Salamina* to decorations for dinnerware for Vernon Kilns.

He also designed the ''Our America'' series which included over 30 scenes; among them was ''Power,'' a picture of a big dam; ''Progress,'' a skyscraper; ''Food,'' a field of harvest; ''History,'' Mesa Indians herding sheep; ''Romance,'' a mansion looking out over cotton fields, etc. Others were ''Florida,'' ''Maple Sugaring in Vermont,'' ''Newport Yacht Races,'' ''The Everglades,'' ''A New England College,'' ''Horse Racing in Kentucky,'' ''New York City,'' ''New Orleans Wharves,'' ''An Indian Herding Sheep,'' etc.

Vernon Kilns issued several plate series including 48 states plates, 44 city plates and 37 ''Bits'' plates such as ''Bits of the Southwest,'' ''Bits of the Old West,'' ''Bits of the Northwest,'' ''Bits of Old England,'' etc. Stiles, p. 143, mentions an artware created by two sisters, Vieve Hamilton and May Hamilton De Causse. Vernon Kilns made flower vases colored and glazed to match the dinnerware, so that it was possible to have a flower container to match dinner dishes.

''Native American'' had 10 designs by Gale Turnbull, including full sets with coffee servers with wooden handles and muffin dishes showing people in dress native to the Southwest, views of missions and three different scenes depicting life in old California. A series of plaid designs stamped ''Vernonware'' included ''Tam O' Shanter,'' in cinnamon, green and yellow-green with a green trim; ''Homespun'' which was green, cinnamon and yellow with a cinnamon trim; ''Gingham,'' a yellow green with yellow bands and green trim; ''Organdie'' with brown and yellow bands and brown trim; ''Calico'' with bands of pink and blue, etc. Another dinnerware pattern was ''Brown Eyed Susan.''

Described in *Good Housekeeping* magazine advertisements are the following lines: ''Early California,'' a bright glazed ware in orange, turquoise, green, brown, blue and yellow, which could be purchased to make a set in solid colors or mixed like a rainbow. ''Modern California'' was in delicate pastel colors in azure blue, sand, straw yellow, orchid, pistachio green and mist gray. ''Casa California'' had a gay, bold design of big, Mexican-type flowers in several designs. ''Ultra California'' was described as having rich halftones in carnation, aster, gardenia and buttercup. ''Vernon Ware'' was made by both Vernon Kilns and Metlox Potteries. (See Metlox Potteries for information and marks on this.) (Information: Maxine Feek Nelson, *Versatile Vernon Kilns*, pp. 1-21; Floyd McKee, *A Century of Dinnerware*; p. 48; Helen Stiles, *Pottery and Porcelain of the U.S.*, p. 143; Virginia Scott, "China Add and Research," *Depression Glass Daze*, August 1977, p. 40; Bess Hunter, "Vernon Kilns," *Glaze*, July-August, 1977, p. 16; Al Fridley, "West Coast Pottery," *The Glaze*, November 1977, p. 7; also information sent by Metlox Potteries. Marks: nos. 1-1 from American Ceramic Society Museum; nos. 2-15, Maxine Nelson, *Versatile Vernon Kilns*, pp. 15, 16, 27, 28, 41, 43, 44, 45, 58 and plate 4; nos. 16-17, Nancy Fowles; nos. 18, also 35 to 42, Elizabeth Vaughn, Beechwold Antiques, Columbus, Ohio; nos. 19-31, Betty Newbound, writer for *Depression Glass Daze*. These are from the special plates made by Vernon Kilns such as the "Famous Men" plates, the "Bits" plates, etc. No. 32 is from the 1954 *Crockery and Glass Journal Directory*. Mark 33 was filed for registration on February 21, 1955, for use on semi-porcelain dinner and tableware, claiming use since January 5, 1955. No. 34 filed September 6, 1955, claiming use since July 1955, for use on dinner and tableware. The remainder were on dishes. The Poxon and the Vernon China marks are the earliest marks. Their use corresponding to dates given. Marks 1 and 4, "Bird Pottery," was a plain colored ware made in early 1930's, Nelson, p. 41. "Early California," "Modern California," "Ultra California," and "Native California," were solid colored wares of late 1930's into the 1940's.)

1.

DESERT POPPY

2.
S A L A M I N A
Designed by
Rockwell Kent
VERNON KILNS
Made in U.S.A.

3.
M O B Y   D I C K
Designed by
Rockwell Kent
VERNON KILNS
Made in USA

4.

VERNON KILNS
CALIFORNIA

5.
HAWAIIAN FLOWERS
Designed by
Aloha
Don Blanding
VERNON KILNS
Made in U.S.A.

6.
V E R N O N
C H I N A

7.

CALIFORNIA

8.
Chatelaine
Sharon Merrill
Design
Vernonware
California, U.S.A.
Jade

9.

HAND PAINTED UNDER GLAZE
VERNON KILNS
CALIF.
MADE IN USA
836
LINDA

10.
DESIGNED BY
WALT DISNEY
COPYRIGHT 1940
VERNON KILNS
MADE IN USA

11.
UNDER GLAZE HAND PAINTED
VINTAGE
VERNONWARE CALIFORNIA U.S.A.

12.

VERNON KILNS
MADE IN CALIFORNIA, U.S.A.

13. Poxon Pottery
Los Angeles
1945

14.
POXON CHINA
VERNON

15.
POXON CHINA
VERNON
CALIFORNIA

16.
VERNON CHINA
VERNON
CALIFORNIA

17.
Daniel Low & Co.
Treasure House of Gifts
Salem, Mass.
By
VERNON KILNS
U.S.A.

THE CAISSONS GO ROLLING ALONG
Copyright 1921 by Egner and Mayer
By Permission of Shapiro, Bernstein & Co. Inc.
Copyright Proprietors

18.

Designed and Engraved
by
VERNON KILNS
U.S.A.

19. HISTORIC SAINT AUGUSTINE
(Founded in 1565)
FLORIDA
The Oldest House featured on this plate is the property of the Saint Augustine Historical Society and Institute of Science. It is famous throughout the nation as a show place rich in historical tradition. Four flags wave over this grand old edifice signifying the reign of four different governments — Spanish, English, Confederate, United States of America. No wonder that the Oldest House abounds in unparalleled grace and charm.
This plate designed exclusively for
J. CARVER HARRIS
by
VERNON KILNS
U.S.A.

20. Made Expressly for
HUDSON'S, DETROIT
by
VERNON KILNS
U.S.A.

21. ALASKA
THE LARGEST COMMONWEALTH UNDER THE STARS AND STRIPES. ITS HISTORY IS RICH IN ROMANCE. ITS WEALTH IS IMMENSE.
1867 — Purchased from Russia for $7,200,000
Designed for
WESTCO KILNS
U.S.A.

22. INDIANA STATE SONG
On the Banks of the Wabash, Far Away
Lyric and Music by Paul Dresser
Oh, the moonlight's fair tonight along the Wabash
From the fields there comes the breath of new mown hay.
Thro' the sycamores the candle lights are gleaming,
On the banks of the Wabash, far away.
Designed Exclusively for
A. C. McCLURG & CO.
by
VERNON KILNS
U.S.A.

23.
AS A MEMENTO OF YOUR VISIT TO VERNON KILNS, LOS ANGELES, CALIFORNIA, WE ARE PLEASED TO PRESENT TO YOU THIS ASH TRAY, WITH ALL OUR GOOD WISHES.
SINCERELY,
Faye G Bennison
PRESIDENT

24.

ST. LOUIS, MISSOURI
COPYRIGHT DESIGN
MARY VANGELDER 1948
by
VERNON KILNS
U.S.A.

25.
CARLSBAD CAVERNS
Distributed by
CAVERN SUPPLY COMPANY
Operators at
CARLSBAD CAVERNS
NATIONAL PARK
CARLSBAD, NEW MEXICO
by
Vernon Kilns
U.S.A.

26.
CORAL REEF
DESIGNED BY
Aloha
Don Blanding
VERNON KILNS
MADE IN U.S.A.

27. ILLINOIS

By thy rivers gently flowing, Illinois, Illinois,
O'er thy prairies verdant growing, Illinois, Illinois,
Comes an echo on the breeze
Rustling thro' the leafy trees,
And its mellow tones are these, Illinois, Illinois,
And its mellow tones are these, Illinois.

. . . . . .

Not without thy wondrous story, Illinois, Illinois,
Can be writ the nation's glory, Illinois, Illinois.

DESIGNED EXCLUSIVELY FOR

A. C. McCLURG & CO.

BY

VERNON KILNS
U.S.A.

WILL ROGERS

28. achieved a unique position
in the hearts of his fellow
Americans. He was born November
4, 1879, near Claremore, Oklahoma, and
worked his way up from the cattle ranges
to become famous as a humorist, a philosopher,
a writer, a world traveler, a star on the lecture plat-
form, on the stage and in motion pictures. His homely
wisdom and philosophy reminded the men in high places
that they were simple folks like the rest of us, and so strong was
his faith in his country and his people, it is not surprising that
America came to rest upon him for his strength and support. On
August 15, 1935, when the news came from a little Alaskan
village that a plane had crashed and that Will Rogers
was gone, for most Americans it was as though a
personal friend had been lost. His statues will
stand as a reminder to our children and to
children's children that good deeds do
not die, nor ever can die. That the
spirit of gratitude endures, and
that gentleness and kind-
ness and compassion
for humanity are
things everlasting.
By
Vernon Kilns
U.S.A.

29.

GEORGIA
"THE EMPIRE STATE OF THE SOUTH"
STATE FLAG
STATE BIRD
STATE FLOWER
Cherokee Rose
BY
VERNON KILNS, U.S.A.

30.
Designed by the Parent Teacher
Association of McAlester for the
city's fiftieth anniversary; spon-
sored by McAlester Anniversary,
Incorporated. The P.T.A., proud
of the city's traditions and prog-
ress, combines the old and the
new in the design. The log cabin
and the pine tree are gone; the old
Busby Hotel is Pittsburg County's
Courthouse; the Dancing Rabbit,
symbol of Indian lands treaty,
remains as title of the High School
Yearbook.
McAlester Indian Territory 1899
Oklahoma, 1949
Vernon Kilns
U.S.A.
This plate is sponsored by
McAlester Anniversary, Inc., in
connection with the Golden Anni-
versary held in McAlester October
1-5, 1949

GENERAL DOUGLAS MacARTHUR

31. The 61-year-old commander, son of Gen. Arthur Mac-
Arthur of Spanish-American war fame, began his military career with his graduation from West Point in 1901.
He was the youngest division commander in the A.E.F.
in 1917, youngest Chief of Staff, U.S.A. (1930-1933).
Sent to the Philippines in 1936, he is now in command
of the United States Far East Forces. For his heroic defense of the Philippines against overwhelming odds, he
will have everlasting fame as one of the great leaders
of military history.

by
VERNON KILNS
U.S.A.
CAMP ROBERTS
CALIFORNIA
1942

32.

HAND PAINTED
UNDER GLAZES
VERNON KILNS
CALIF.
MADE IN U.S.A.
ORGANDIE

HAND PAINTED
UNDER GLAZES
VERNON KILNS
CALIF.
MADE IN U.S.A.
838
BROWN EYED SUSAN

32.
California
Vernonware

33.
TICKLED PINK

34.
"Heavenly Days"

35.
Scenes From
CHATTANOOGA AND CAMP LEWIS
Made Expressly
for
Miller Bros. Co.
By
VERNON KILNS
U.S.A.

36.

Ciudad de
Santa Fe
(City of The Holy Faith)
Founded 1610
✧
Designed for
S. Spitz
Jeweler
by
VERNON KILNS
U.S.A.

37.
Reading, located in the heart of the Pennsylvania Dutch Country, was first planned
in 1748, and became the county seat of
Berks in 1752.

Greater Reading, with its highly diversified
industries, produces all the essentials of life
yet the greatest attribute of Reading and
Berks County is the heart of its people.
By
VERNON KILNS
U.S.A.

FORT DEFIANCE
1794-1944
40.
DEFIANCE, OHIO

Built at confluence of Maumee and
Auglaize rivers by Gen. Anthony
Wayne, during military campaign that
established American rule in the Old
Northwest.
BY
VERNON KILNS
U.S.A.

HISTORIC SAINT AUGUSTINE
38. (Founded in 1565)
FLORIDA

The Oldest House featured on this plate is the property of the
Saint Augustine Historical Society and Institute of Science.
It is famous throughout the nation as a show place rich in his-
torical tradition. Four flags wave over this grand old edifice
signifying the reign of four different governments — Spanish,
English, Confederate, United States of America. No wonder
that the Oldest House abounds in unparalleled grace and charm.
This plate designed exclusively for
J. CARVER HARRIS
by
VERNON KILNS
U.S.A.

39.

NATIONAL
CHINA EQUIPMENT CORP.
MARION, INDIANA
Plate designed
by
Vernon Kilns
U.S.A.

42.

ATLANTA
Gate City of the
South
Designed Exclusively
For
DAVISON-PAXON CO
by
VERNON KILNS
U.S.A.

41.
COLORADO SPRINGS
COLORADO
CITY OF SUNSHINE
DESIGNED EXPRESSLY
FOR
Kaufman's
BY
VERNON KILNS
U.S.A.

ILLINOIS

By thy rivers gently flowing. Illinois. Illinois.
O'er thy prairies verdant growing. Illinois. Illinois.
    Comes an echo on the breeze
    Rustling thro' the leafy trees.
And its mellow tones are these. Illinois. Illinois.
And its mellow tones are these. Illinois.

.   .   .   .   .

Not without thy wondrous story. Illinois. Illinois.
Can be writ the nation's glory. Illinois. Illinois.

DESIGNED EXCLUSIVELY FOR

A. C. McCLURG & CO.

BY

VERNON KILNS
U. S. A.

HONOLULU

Islands Discovered by Captain Cook — 1778
Provisional Government Established — 1893
Republic of Hawaii Established — 1894
Hawaii Annexed to the United States — 1898

Made Exclusively For
the
LIBERTY HOUSE
BY
VERNON KILNS
U. S. A.

Vickers, John and Thomas. Caln and Lionville, Pennsylvania. 1806-1865. Thomas Vickers established pottery in West Whiteland Township, Chester County, Pennsylvania, around 1806. In 1822, the pottery was moved to Lionville, Pennsylvania, and operated as **John Vickers and Son**. The pottery remained in the hands of family members until around 1865 then continued in operation until around 1900. Barber, p. 216 of *Tulip Ware of the Pennsylvania-German Potters* said they operated until a few years ago, and the book was written in 1903. The Vickers made large quantities of commercial slip ware, also sgraffito, plain redware, brown glazed ware and a variegated glazed ware and green enameled ware. Articles were numerous as listed in Barber, *Marks of American Potters*, p. 15, pie plates, milk pots, sugar bowls, cream cups, chimney ornaments, inkstands, tobacco pipes, pitchers and much more. At one time some workman from the Nase Pottery in Montgomery County worked for Vickers and made some ornamental figures in forms of animals and birds

(Barber, *Tulip Ware*, p. 216). (Marks: no. 1, 2, 3, Thorn, p. 152; no. 1 for Thomas Vickers; no. 3 for John Vickers. Ramsay had a much earlier starting date for this pottery, but I chose Barber's dates.)

1. 𝒥𝒱   2. 𝒱   3. 𝒥𝒱

Victor Insulators, Inc. Victor, New York. 1935 to 1953. According to Jack H. Tod, *Porcelain Insulators*, pp. 105, 106, the company incorporated April 1935. In May 1935, General Electric sold the old Locke Insulator plant to a former group of ex-General Electric employees. In 1953, the plant was sold to I-T-E Imperial Corporation and operated as the Victor Insulators Division of this company. The mark used on the insulators was a rectangle-V used from 1935 to 1953, according to Tod. However, on July 26, 1943, this same mark was filed for registration for use on ceramic table and cooking ware, claiming use since September 3, 1942. The word, "Victor" was filed on December 27, 1943. Both registrations were filed under the name Victor Insulators, Inc. Victor Insulators, Inc. never used the "Victor" marks as shown on insulators, but they did use it on porcelain table ware (mostly coffee mugs) which were used in their own plant cafeteria at Victor, and also given as "advertisers." These mugs were widely dispersed. The rectangle-V marking is also found on some of these mugs, and might account for the very belated July 26, 1943 registration of that one. See Tod's book for various types of insulators made and variations in the marking, etc.

VICTOR

Vigland Pottery. Benzonia, Michigan. 1968 to present (1985). Alan G. Vigland and his wife, Susie, are studio potters, who started working with stoneware in 1968, and are now making pieces of porcelain. The pieces are largely functional, but they also make a good line of larger sculptural pieces, which are very colorful with a touch of sophistication. They sell all they can get made and rarely sell through galleries or at shows for that reason. Alan taught part time at Northwestern Michigan College in Traverse City, Michigan for nine years. He has also taught for one year at Michigan State University and a year at Interlochen Arts Academy at Interlochen.

He has held many workshops, which include: Central Michigan University, Creative Arts Gallery, Mt. Pleasant; Michigan Potters Association, held at Oakland Community College, Auburn Heights, Michigan; Ontario Crafts Council, held at the University of Windsor, Ontario, Canada; Midland Art Council, held at the Midland Center for the Arts, Midland, Michigan; Lansing Potters Guild, Lansing, Michigan; Oakland Community College, held at the Royal Oak Campus, Royal Oak, Michigan; Ann Arbor Art Association, held in Ann Arbor, Michigan. He has attended many juried and invitation shows including ones at the Pewabic Society in Detroit; at Eastern Michigan University at Ypsilanti, Michigan; Wooster College, Wooster, Ohio; the Detroit Institute of Arts; Bowling Green University, Bowling Green, Ohio; Delta College at University Center, Michigan. Alan has also had a long list of one man shows. A few of the many awards he has won include: first place, Commemorative Dinnerware Competition, Pewabic Society, Detroit, Michigan; Mary Blakley Ceramic Award, Coconut Grove Art Festival, Miami, Florida; Best of Show, Traverse City Arts Council Exhibit, Traverse City, Michigan; Pottery Award, Birmingham's Art in the Park, Birmingham, Michigan; merit award, Las Olas Art Festival, Ft. Lauderdale, Florida; first place in pottery, Kalamazoo Art Festival, Kalamazoo, Michigan.

Viletta China Company. 1958 to 1978 in Roseberg, Oregon, and 1978 to present in Houston, Texas. Viletta China Company decorates china and glass. At present their blanks are purchased from Germany, England, Japan, Taiwan, China and the United States. (Information and mark: from company vice president, Richard S. Toms.)

Village Potter. Milford, Iowa. 1966 to present (1984). Robert E. Duncan is a studio potter who has won many honors in sculpture and ceramics which may be found in private collections throughout the country and in Europe. He has a B.A. degree from University of Nebraska in Omaha and an M.A. from Wisconsin State University. He has taught ceramics at Drake University, Buena Vista College, also several high schools, including Milford Community School. He makes mostly functional ware and some sculptured pieces, all high fired, some by a reduction process.

Virginia Pottery. New Lexington, Ohio. There is confusion about the Virginia Pottery in New Lexington. It existed sometime before 1910, possibly as early as 1907. A local historian said the Consumer Insulator Company existed there around that time which eventually became a part of the General Porcelain Company. See that listing. The Virginia Pottery is said to have made restaurant and hotel ware marked as shown and electrical porcelain. (Mark was on a very old restaurant sauce dish.)

```
 ¡BERT
 ↓CHINA↑
NEW LEXINGTON
   OHIO
```

Vita Craft Corporation. Shawnee Mission, Kansas. 1939 to present (1986). Started in Williamsport and Ambler, Pennsylvania, in 1939 as a marketing agency for aluminum cookware made by Keewashum Aluminum. In 1940, the company moved to Shawnee Mission. From 1942 to 1946 they didn't operate because of W.W. II. From 1952 to 1958, Picard made "West Port China" cookware for Vita Craft to sell. In 1960, **Belora China**, Glendale, California, started making "Carillon" cookware and continued until early 1980's when Belora went out of business. Vita Craft designed their own products and had them made to their specifications. (Marks: no. 1, Lynnbrooke was filed for registration June 8, 1964, claiming use since March 1964 for china dinnerware. No. 2 was filed Septebmer 4, 1962 for china dinnerware. Information: Secured from Vita Craft by Annise Heaivilin, author of *Grandma's Tea Leaf Ironstone*. Also see General Ceramics for "Carillon" mark.)

1. **LYNNBROOKE**

Vitrefrax Company. Los Angeles, California. The Vitrefrax Company had a subsidiary, Tierra Colorado Company, in 1940 which made high heat firebrick and other products. On March 11, 1926, this mark was filed for registration by Vitrefrax for ceramic products, but no further description was given.

VITROLON

Vodrey and Various Associations. Before going to the Indiana Pottery, Vodrey had a history in several potteries. He came to this country from England in 1827 and built a pottery in East Liberties, Pennsylvania, near Pittsburgh, Pennsylvania. From there, **Vodrey and Frost** moved to Louisville, Kentucky, in 1829 where they made a good grade of creamware. From 1832 to 1836 the firm in Louisville was **Vodrey and Lewis** after Frost retired. In 1836, the Louisville firm was dissolved, and in 1839 Vodrey came to the Indiana Pottery. In 1846, Stout says Vodrey was "forced to abandon" the Indiana Pottery Company and at that time went to East Liverpool and established **Woodland and Vodrey** which began operation in 1848 and then burned out in 1849. After reorganization the firm opened again as **Woodward, Blakely and Company** until 1857 when a financial panic hit. After the panic in 1857, three sons of Jabez; William, James and John, took one of the Woodward, Blakely and Company buildings and operated as Vodrey Brothers until around 1885, when the title was **Vodrey and Brothers**. In 1896, it was Vodrey Pottery Company and remained so until after 1920. There is a great variety of marks shown for this company. The products of the various companies progressed through the usual stages, starting with Rockingham, yellowware and cream-colored ware in the earliest years, then on to white granite and to semi-porcelain. In the *1902-1903 Complete Directory*, Vodrey Pottery Company made semi-porcelain and white granite dinner sets. **Lewis Pottery Company** in Louisville, Kentucky, was a very early pottery which started in 1829 to make queensware and china. The plant was taken over by Vodrey and Lewis and run until 1836. **Phoenix Pottery** was the building's name in East Liverpool, while it operated as Woodward, Blakely and Company. In 1852, Gates, p. 300, tells us the firm had five buildings, three kilns and employed 70 to 80 people. (Information: Lehner,

American Kitchen and Dinner Wares, pp. 98 and 157; Ramsay, pp. 74, 75, 77, 88, 105, 106, 215, 227, 231, 239, 283. Marks: nos. 1, 3, Ramsay. Ramsay's marks lack real accuracy of picture in many cases. No. 2, on dish. Rest of marks are from Barber, *Marks of American Potters*, p. 107.)

1. 2. 3.
4. 5. 6. 7. 8.
9. 10. 11. 12. WARRANTED
13. ADMIRAL V.P.CO.
14. 15. 16.
17. WINONA 18.

Vogue, Various Potteries and Distributors: Vogue Mercantile Company/Vogue Ceramic Industries/Jackson China Company/Vogue Art Ware China Company/Vogue Art Pottery Company. The Vogue Mercantile Company was a selling agency in New York City. They were listed as early as 1945 as importers and wholesalers and factory representatives of china and earthenware dinnerware, blown and pressed table glassware. This company was last listed in 1948 and in 1949 the listing became Vogue Ceramic Industries, which was a subsidiary of Jackson China Company of Falls Creek, Pennsylvania. This was also a selling agency. Philip R. Distillator was president of both companies and owner of Jackson China Company. In the 1943 *China and Glass Red Book Directory*, the ad read: Vogue Ceramic Industries presents Jackson Vitrified China and American Vogue Dinnerware, cake sets, tea sets and the seller was listed as the Vogue Mercantile Company of New York, New York. In 1946, Philip R. Distillator purchased all shares in Jackson China Company and became the sole owner. He doubled the floor space, put in modern equipment and started a decorating plant in New York City, which was destroyed by fire in 1967. This establishes the connection between Jackson China and

the two distributors with the Vogue name. Because they were selling agencies, other companies besides Jackson China made products for Vogue to sell. Homer Laughlin China and others made exclusive patterns which the Vogue Ceramic Industries, Inc, in turn sold to Montgomery Ward and other companies (see mark 4). Marks 1 and 2 were registered under the name, Vogue Mercantile Company, Inc., New York, New York, in 1943 (no. 1), and 1945 (no. 2). No. 1 was used since 1941. Both marks were for dinnerware. No. 3 was found at Quality Stamp Company, East Liverpool, Ohio. No. 5 was the copy of mark 4 as it was registered. It wasn't registered until December 29, 1954, but the company claimed they had used it since July 1941. No. 6 was registered in February 1955, claiming use since 1944. Of course 5 and 6 were registered under the name, Vogue Ceramic Industries, Inc. Feel a little lost? So did I trying to figure this out! But that is not quite all. No. 7 is mark used as the names of a line made by Universal Potteries, Inc., advertised in *Better Homes and Gardens*, May 1952, and sold by Universal Potteries. To make the pottery industry just a little more complicated, there was a Vogue Art Ware and China Company at Fifth and Logan Streets in Dennison, Ohio, in 1960. There was also a Vogue Art Pottery Company of Uhrichsville, Ohio. Two companies named Vogue clear across the state from each other and no connection to the distributors mentioned! Arthur J. Grindley managed the plant in Uhrichsville, for a while after the Grindley Artware Company was destroyed by fire in 1947. The company in Dennison was listed in the 1960 *Ohio Manufacturers Directory*.

In March 1953 *China, Glass and Decorative Accessories Magazine*, p. 28, a new site of interest concerning Vogue Ceramic Industries is as follows:

"An agreement concluded between the French Minister of Fine Arts and Vogue Ceramic Industries, a subsuduary of Jackson Vitrified China Company, Falls Creek, Pennsylvania, has established Vogue as the exclusive United States and Canadian representative for the well-known Sevres fine china line produced in France. This is the first time that Sevres ware is being made available for sale on a retail basis in this country, reports Philip R. Distillator, Vogue president. A permanent exhibit of the line may be seen at the Jackson Galleries, 9 East 55th Street, in New York City."

1. American Vogue
2. Vogue
3. Vogue DINNERWARE WARRANTED 22K GOLD
4. American Vogue Regency Theme / Eggshell Theme Homer Laughlin Made in USA J48N5

6. **VOGUE**

7. *Vogue by UNIVERSAL*

5.

Vohann of California. Capistrano Beach, California. December 1950 to present (1985). They make a fine line of decorative ware, accessories and kitchen pieces, including a frog, sculptured sea otter, sea, birds in flight, monkey, various toothbrush holders in bright vivid colors and well vitrified ware. Plant employs 30 people. They also make ceramic clocks, and several styles of cannister sets for the kitchen. (Mark number 1 is a paper label.)

1.

2. **VOHANN**

Volkmar, Charles, Various Potteries and Associations. Charles Volkmar was born in 1841. He came from a family of artists. Before coming to stay in the United States in 1879, he had worked with a French potter in a suburb of Paris, also he had worked in the Haviland factories. In 1879, he built a kiln on Greenpoint, Long Island, New York, and he designed and built a fireplace of Limoges type tile, for the Salmagundi Club in 1880. In 1881, he was considered the potter of the Club when they secured a Washington Square studio. By 1882 he had his own studio and salesroom in Tremont, New York. In 1888 to 1893 he moved to Menlo Park, New Jersey, to help form the **Menlo Park Ceramic Company** to make art tile and interior ceramic decorations. By 1895 he was back in New York City, and established the **Volkmar Keramic Company.** E.A. Barber, *Pottery and Porcelain of U.S.*, p. 380, said in 1893 Volkmar was organizing the **Volkmar Ceramic Company** to make art tile in Menlo Park, but Evans, p. 312, said there was no indication Volkmar got started.

In 1895, he became partners with Miss Kate Cory, to operate as **Volkmar and Cory** to make art pottery in Corona, New York. They received a Gold Medal at the Atlanta Exposition in their first year of partnership. They made Delft type pieces with white background and American historical scenes in blue. Kate Cory left before the end of 1896, and Volkmar operated alone under the name **Crown Point Pottery.** Volkmar began to produce pottery pieces with subdued colors ungerglaze with a body of New Jersey clay. He made vases, lamp bases, etc. He also introduced a semi-matte glaze. Volkmar acted as a ceramic consultant for other potters in methods of underglazed decorations and continued to make mugs and steins for the Salmagundi Club. For a great deal more on the Volkmar pieces, see Evans as cited. In 1902, Charles and his son, Leon, established the Volkmar Kilns in Metuchen, New Jersey. (See that listing.) (Information: Barber, as cited and Paul Evans, *Art Pottery of the U.S.*, pp. 310-315. Marks: Nos. 1-4, E.A. Barber, *Marks of American Potters*, pp. 82, 83. Mark 1, the "C.V." monogram, was used by Volkmar from 1879 to 1888. Mark 2 was used in 1895, according to Evans, p; 314. No. 3 was used while Charles was in partnership with Cory in 1895 to 1896. No. 4, the styliz-

ed "V" in relief or incised was also used by Leon Volkmar after 1920, sometimes with a date, according to Evans, Nos. 5-7 are three more marks used from 1896 to 1902; as shown in Paul Evan's book. p. 314.)

1. 2. **VOLKMAR** 3. **VOLKMAR & CORY**   4.

5. **CHAS.VOLKMAR**

6. **CROWN POINT WARE** 7. **VOLKMAR**

Volkmar Kilns. Metuchen, New Jersey. Charles and Leon Volkmar started the Volkmar Kilns in 1903 when the Volkmar Pottery in Corona, New York, closed. Leon, the son of Charles, was born in France in 1879 and studied at the National Academy from 1898 to 1901. In 1902, he joined his father at the Volkmar Pottery (see that listing) and served on the staff of the Pratt Institute Art Department until the move to New Jersey. After 1903, both Volkmars taught modeling, glazing, etc., in Metuchen. Also in 1903, Leon became the head of the newly established school of pottery at the Pennsylvania Museum of Industrial Art (see that listing) while he continued his work in Metuchen, also. Charles and Leon worked together until 1911 when Leon joined Mrs. Jean Rice and started to produce art ware under the name **Durant Kilns.** (See that listing.) Charles worked alone in Metuchen, until he died in 1914. Pieces were artware, tiles, panels, plaques, etc., which were made from porcelain body after 1905. Glazes were high gloss and semi-matte. Underglaze decorations were sometimes used. For a better discussion of the work of both Volkmar potteries, see the Evan's book as cited. (Information and marks: Paul Evans, *Art Pottery of the U.S.*, pp. 307-309. Mark 1 was also used by Volkmar Pottery. See that listing.)

1. **V.** 2. **VOLKMAR KILNS, METUCHEN, N.J.** 3. *Volkmar*

Vollrath Company. Sheboygan, Wisconsin. Jacob J. Vollrath was born in Germany in 1824. He came to the United States at age 18 and settled in Sheboygan in 1853. By 1873 he had introduced the process in this country to enamel over cast iron for cooking utensils, etc. In 1886, the Jacob J. Vollrath Company was incorporated. The business remained under family ownership and control and the name became the Vollrath Company. On June 4, 1968 the company filed for registration of the mark shown for dinnerware and serving containers made of china. Several of the Missouri potters had come from Germany in the very early years. George and Nicholas Vollrath purchased the old Marcus Williams pottery in Boonville around 1840 and operated the pottery until 1870. Few Missouri-German potters marked their ware. I found no connection between the Wisconsin Vollraths and those in Missouri, but they probably came from the same family. (Information: staff written, "Jacob J. Vollrath Communication-

Ceramic History,'' *Bulletin of the American Ceramic Society*, May 1937, pp. 226, 227.)

CATHEDRAL

F.J. Von Tury. Metuchen, New Jersey. 1939 to present (1985). Studio in Metuchen and workshop in Edison, New Jersey. Von Tury is a ceramic engineer who does architectural ceramics for interior and exterior use, such as hand decorated tile, panels, murals, etc. These appear in and on buildings throughout the country. His tiles have a texture to the surface that prevents sun glare. He did ''The Ceramic Tree'' mural for the public library in Metuchen which tells the history of ceramics. He helps with very important reconstruction projects such as tiles for the fireplace where Theodore Roosevelt took the oath of office and produced the encaustic type floor needed for replacement of tiles in the U.S. Capitol Building. Von Tury makes porcelain artware for exhibition. These are exhibited in many museums such as the Metropolitan Museum of Art, Purdy Museum of Ceramics in Columbus (Owned by American Ceramic Society), etc. He had ''Art for Use'' Exhibit at the 1980 Olympic Winter Games, Lake Placid, New York. He produces ceramics for the trade also which are sold in stores throughout the country such as bowls, vases, platters, figurines, etc. Von Tury has received many honors, such as American Ceramic Society Design Division Award, twice, in recognition of notable contribution to ceramic art. He is an honorary life member of the American Ceramic Society, a member of the National Institute of Ceramic Engineers, the Architectural League of New York, American Craftsmen's Council, Designer-Craftsmen of New Jersey, and several others. (Information: from the company, sent to this author by Thomas Turnquist. Marks: no. 1, incised mark sent by Turnquist; no. 2, 1967 *China, Glass and Tableware Directory*.)

Voulkos, Peter. Berkeley, California. 1948 to present (1985). Artist, Peter Voulkos, started as a painter, worked next with functional ceramics, then on to more artistic pieces and sculpturing. He sculptures in metal, mostly bronze and clay. Rose Slivka quotes Voulkos on the difference between working wtih clay and metal: ''Clay is an intimate material. It's a very fast moving material, immediately responsive to the touch and it's silent, when I want to work slower and I want more resistance and noise, I turn to metal . . . I started as a painter, and the painting helps the sculpture, the sculpture helps the painting, the pottery helps the sculpture and so on.'' According to Slivka, Peter Voulkos has ''joined craft and art in an inseparable unity while extending the vistas of both.'' In 1978 a sweeping exhibition of his work from 1948 to 1978 including ceramics, bronze sculptures and paintings were shown at the San Francisco Museum of Modern Art, then was taken to the Contemporary Arts Museum in Houston, Texas, and from there to the Museum of Contemporary Crafts in New York, averaging two months showing at each place. He has given workshop demonstrations all across the country. In 1976, he demonstrated at ''Super Mud,'' held at the Pennsylvania State University before some 2,000 potters.

Voulkos received his M.A. degree from California School of Arts and Crafts in 1952 and then went to work at Archie Bray's brickyard in Helena, Montana, where he fired and salt glazed bricks, ran a pottery and conducted workshops for students. In 1953, he went to teach at Black Mountain College, near Asheville, North Carolina, for three weeks, then returned to Archie Bray's brickyard to make production pieces. Slivka said this three weeks at Black Mountain College was a turning point in Voulkos's career. The professional contacts and the work being done excited Voulkos.

Fortunately in 1954, he was asked to head the new ceramic department of Otis Art Institute in Los Angeles. Potters who were not students began to drop in and work with Voulkos and after a while, a whole new art movement came into being in Los Angeles. In 1959, Voulkos sculptured a 5'5'', ''Black Bulerias,'' which won the Rodin Prize at the First Paris Biennale in 1950. Also in 1959, he built a commissioned piece 8' high, ''Gakkas Rock.'' In 1975, Julie Gallas donated it to the University of Los Angeles. Silvka calls it the most intricate, technically stunning and largest ceramic sculpture of that period. In 1959, he became a full professor at the University of California at Berkeley. In a staff written article, ''Ceramactivities,'' *Ceramics Monthly*, April 1977, p. 77, is a description of a series of plates handthrown, stoneware with abstract expressionistic designs, such as holes pressed from underneath and punched and torn openings in monochromatic browns and grays. (Information: Rose Slivka, *Peter Voulkos: A Dialogue With Clay*, New York: Little Brown, 1978; also, Rose Slivka, ''Erasing the Line Separating the Arts from the Crafts,'' *Smithsonian*, March 1978, pp. 87-93. Marks: Linda Steigleder, from the booklet published by the Everson Museum of Art to accompany the 1978 exhibition, ''A Century of Ceramics in the U.S.,'' with Curators: Garth Clark and Margie Hughto. A variety of marks are shown for Voulkos because many of his pieces were in the exhibit. Notice no two marks are inscribed the same. This would be true of most inscribed marks whether we show one or ten examples in this book. The potter wouldn't write it the same each time.)

W

Waco Pottery. Near Bybee, Kentucky. Before 1920 to 1939. About one mile down the road from the Bybee Pottery was another pottery named Waco Pottery, run by a family named Bumstart which operated until 1939, according to James Andrew Cornelison, one of the sons of the owner, Walter Cornelison, II. (See that listing.) This pottery made vases and other decorative pieces that have caused the writers great confusion, this author included. I had attributed the mark to the East Liverpool Potteries Company because of the similarity to their "Waco" mark. Then when I got two of the vases I began to realize this was just not the kind of product made in East Liverpool. The vase is handmade of yellow clay, blue matt glaze, with a dark stamped mark as shown. The vases look old, much older probably than they really are, since the pottery continued until 1939. Chester Davis in "Bybee Pottery," *Spinning Wheel*, July-August 1973, p. 17, shows the vase as being made by Bybee Pottery. It was not. There was no connection between the two potteries. In fact, three potteries existed in the area in the early 1900's to 1920's, but J.A. Cornelison and his mother said the third pottery had no specific name and had been gone for many years.

Wade Ceramics. North Hollywood, California. They were listed in the 1965 and 1967 *Gift and Tableware Reporter Directory* for serving bowls and wall decorations. They were not listed in 1961. (Mark: found on a well vitrified, green glazed flower pot.)

Wade Ceramics

Wagar, Robert. Asheville, North Carolina. Around 1967 to present. Mr. Wagar is a studio potter with M.F.A. and M.A. degrees in ceramics from Northern Illinois University in DeKalb, Illinois. He makes hand made pottery on a wheel, signed with a marking stain as shown. He has done numerous exhibits with various groups. He works in a studio at his home and is open for sales by appointment only. Pieces pictured had hand painted designs. (Information: staff written, "Contemporary Designer Craftsman," *Pottery Collectors Newsletter*, October 1976, p. 83.)

Wagar

Wagner, Art. Zanesville, Ohio. Art Wagner was an artist, who worked as a decorator in many of the plants in the Zanesville area in the 1940's and 1950's. Wagner worked at Weller Pottery, the Pottery Queen, Marco Pottery, Shawnee Pottery and Shaffer Pottery. See the various listings. (Mark: on vase decorated with scene of trees, etc. No factory name was given, only the artists' signature.)

Wagner, Teresa. Columbus, Ohio. 1973 to present. Teresa is a studio potter making functional stoneware with crystalline glazes. She shows at fairs, cultural art exchanges, etc.

Wahpeton Pottery Company/Rosemeade Pottery. Whapeton, North Dakota. 1940 to 1961. The salesroom remained open until 1964. Laura Hughes, the potter, used many wildlife designs in making, shakers, book ends, tea bells, pheasants, hens, miniature animals and birds, mallard ducks, vases, mugs, etc. In 1981, there was a display in the museum at Whapeton. In the 1940's and 1950's, the pottery turned out around 1,000 pieces a day, according to collector of Rosemeade, Fay J. Nygaar. In the column, "Antique Wise," by Dorothy Hammond, *Tri state Trader*, July 12, 1980, p. 5, she said Laura Taylor Hughes was presented an honor roll scroll by the American Artists Professional League for designing more than 200 different designs of Rosemeade Pottery. (Information: Grace M. Weiss, "Rosemeade Pottery," *Antique Trader Annual* for 1973, p. 59. Marks: furnished by letter by Fay J. Nygaar, except no. 1 which was filed for registration March 22, 1951 claiming use since February 1940 for salt and pepper sets, vases, bowls, baskets and dinnereware. Nos. 2, 3 are copies of paper label.)

1.

2.

3.

Rosemeade
4.

Rosemeade
5.

No. Da K.
6.

F. Lantz
7.

Rosemeade
NORTH DAKOTA

8.

Rosemeade
N. D.

10.

Rosemeade
Bad Lands

12.

N. D.

14.

Rosemeade
No. DAK.

9.

NORTH DAKOTA

11.

13.

Wait and Rickets. Akron, Ohio. About 1870. Made stoneware in Springfield Township which became part of Akron. (Information and mark: Thorn, p. 152.)

WAIT & RICKETTS
SPRINGFIELD

Wakefield National Memorial Association. Washington, D.C. Filed for rights to this mark on October 6, 1927, for use on chinaware, claiming use since August 1, 1927. Canonsburg Pottery made a dinnerware line marked Washington Wakefield.

WASHINGTON
WAKEFIELD

Walker China Company. Bedford, Ohio (near Cleveland). The **Bedford China Company** became the **Bailey-Walker China Company** in 1923 when it was reorganized by Harry Bailey and Al Walker (McKee, p. 36). Between 1941 and 1943 the name became Walker China Company. In 1941, Membership Roster for American Ceramic Society, the name was still Bailey Walker China Company. The next listing I had was 1943, and the name had become Walker China Company. Four different bodies for dishes were made there in 1963, fine china, ivory, tan (toltec) and white. Although the company was mainly a producer of hotel type ware, they did make a fine china for homes which McKee, p. 37, says was sold by a house to house selling organization, which McKee does not name. Around 1960 the company employed over 200 people in various automated procedures to make china. On November 15, 1976, the Jeannette Corporation purchased Walker China Company from the Alco Standard Corporation. Jeannette Corporation sold Walker China Company to Mayer China Company of Beaver Falls, Pennsylvania. Walker China Company went out of business on June 13, 1980 and Mayer

China took over all rights to names, patents and equipment, etc. on June 16, 1980. Mayer China made products in the Bedford, Ohio, plant until April 3, 1981, when all equipment was moved back to Beaver Falls. No more china was made with the Walker China Company marks after June 13, 1980. There was a mark used during the transition period which said "Walker China by Mayer." (Information: closing information from Audrey Fulkerson, former employee at Walker China under the direction of John Pezzone, employee of Mayer China; Lehner, *American Kitchen and Dinner Wares*; from various companies involved. Marks: Mark 1 filed for copyright November 22, 1946, claiming use since May 10, 1943, which probably was the time of the name change to Walker China Company; no. 2, furnished by Waldorf Stamping Devices; no. 3, furnished by Larry Paul, researcher and writer; nos. 4, 5, 6, furnished by Mayer China Company from material left in the building after Walker closed. These are the marks used while Jeannette Corp. and Mayer China owned Walker China. The majority of the marks were found on dishes and a few at Quality Stamp Company, East Liverpool, Ohio. Mark 7 was filed for registration on February 20, 1956 claiming prior use for one month for china tableware. The dating code is to add 1922 to the number on the dish. Example: 1-31 would be January 1953. This date code was verified by Audrey Fulkerson, employee at Walker China. Some dealers believe these dishes are older than they actually are. They call 1-31 as being 1931 when it fact it stands for 1953. Nos. 8, 9, Table Rite and Table Light were filed for registration on October 22, 1965.)

1.

WALKER CHINA
VITRIFIED
BEDFORD, OHIO
2-31

2.

3.

Walker China
by Mayer

4.

Table Lite
VITRIFIED ®
Walker
China
"Jeannette"
CORPORATION
USA
8-56

5.

VITRIFIED
Walker
China
Jeannette
CORPORATION
USA
11-56

6.

Table-Rite

8.

WALKER
FINE CHINA

7.

Table-Lite

9.

498

Florma ©
Walker China
VITRIFIED
BEDFORD, OHIO

10.

Walker China
VITRIFIED
BEDFORD, OHIO U.S.A.
JEANNETTE CORPORATION
3-33

11.

Walker China
VITRIFIED
BEDFORD, OHIO
ALCO STANDARD CORP.
1-48

12.

Walker China
BY
MINNERS
NEW YORK
AN ALCO STANDARD COMPANY
4-48

13.

M & G
MACDONALD & GRAHM INC.
NEW YORK
BAILEY-WALKER CHINA

14.

IVORY
Walker China
VITRIFIED
BEDFORD, OHIO
12-33

15.

WALKER
CHINA
BEDFORD, OHIO.
MADE EXPRESSLY FOR
GROSSE POINTE YACHT CLUB
FURNISHED BY
REICHLE SONS. CO.
DETROIT

16.

Table Lite
BY
WALKER
BEDFORD, OHIO.

17.

TOLTEC WARE
BAILEY-WALKER CHINA
Bedford, O.

18.

TOLTEC
WALKER
CHINA
VITRIFIED
BEDFORD, OHIO
11-31

19.

THE BAILEY-WALKER · VITRIFIED CHINA
Bedford, Ohio
1943

20.

IVORY
WALKER
CHINA
VITRIFIED
BEDFORD OHIO
4-42

21.

WALKER
FINE CHINA
MADE IN U.S.A
FURNISHED BY
MINNERS & CO.
NEW YORK, N.Y.

22.

Walker
TRUE CHINA
MADE IN U.S.A.

23.

COMPLIMENTS OF
WALKER
CHINA
VITRIFIED
BEDFORD, OHIO
U.S.A.

24.

Walker China
VITRIFIED
BEDFORD, OHIO
8-40

25.

BAILEY-WALKER
JUS-RITE
PLATE

26.

Walker Potteries. Monrovia, California. In 1945 and 1948 *China and Glass Red Book Directories*, this pottery was listed as manufacturers of earthenware figures, figurines and miniatures and florists' ware. Jessie Robinson Walker was president of Walker Potteries which was listed through 1954. (On October 30, 1946, Jessie R. Walker filed for registration on the marks 1 and 2 shown, for use on chinaware, crockery

or earthenware candleholders, claiming use since September 1946.)

Candlier   *Tarlancy Ware*

Wallace and Chetwynd. East Liverpool, Ohio. 1882-1903. Started in the **Colonial Pottery** in East Liverpool around 1881 or 1882 making a high grade of opaque china, stone china and decorated goods. In 1901, they joined the East Liverpool Potteries Company which was dissolved in 1903. From 1903 to 1929 this building was operated as the **Colonial Company**. Chetwynd had learned the pottery business working for his father in England. (Information: Lehner, *American Kitchen and Dinner Wares*, p. 158. Marks: Barber, *Marks of American Potters*, p. 113; no. 2, stamped on dish.)

1.   2.

Wallace China Company. Vernon, California. Founded around 1931 and completely liquidated in 1964. The company made hotel china, and in 1959 they were purchased by Shenango China Company and operated as a wholly owned subsidiary until the closing. (Information: Lehner, *American Kitchen and Dinner Wares*, p. 158. Marks: No. 1 on dish. No. 2, 3, from Connie Rogers, writer on Willow Ware pattern.) No. 4 was filed for a patent on August 2, 1948 for use on vitrified hotel china, namely plates, cups, saucers, partitioned luncheon plates, serving dishes, creamers, sugar bowls, mugs and teapots, claiming use since April 14, 1931. See Wentz Company for ''Westward Ho.'' No. 5 was filed March 16, 1961 and no. 6 on July 24, 1961, both for vitrified hotel ware, etc. These registrations give the address as Huntington Park, California.

Wallace ®
CHINA
LOS ANGELES, CALIF.
10-U

1.

Wallace ®
CHINA
LOS ANGELES, CALIF.

2.

WALLACE
CHINA

3.

YE OLDE WILLOW
ENGRAVED FROM THE
ORIGINAL PLATES 1832

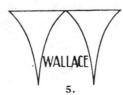

WALLACE
6.

Walley, Joseph William. Walley made pottery pieces in Portland, Maine, in 1873 to before 1885, also in Worcester in 1885 for a short time. Then in 1898 he bought the old Wachusett Pottery in West Sterling, Massachusetts, which had been there since around 1850. He operated the pottery until he died in 1919 making handmade art pottery from local red clay such as candlesticks, vases, planters, lamps, tea tiles, etc. Pieces were cast or handthrown with applied handles and decorations and matt or gloss glazes. (Information and impressed mark: Paul Evans, *Art Pottery of the U.S.*, pp. 316, 317.)

W J W

Walpole, W.L. Roseville, Ohio. Before 1900. The Walpoles were one of the earliest families to settle Roseville, but I found no mention of this man as a potter. The mark stenciled in cobalt blue was shown on a preserve jar pictured in Regina Stewart and Geraldine Consentino, *Stoneware*, p. 85.

W.L. WALPOLE
ROSEVILLE, O

Walrich Pottery. Berkeley, California. 1922 to before 1930. Studio type pottery was started in 1922 by James A. and Gertrude Wall. Porcelain and earthenware pieces were slip caste in molds. The molds had been thrown by James, who also developed all their own glazes. The glazes included matte glazes and a particularly rich color of blue. Two of the sculptors who developed figures and figurines for the pottery were Jacques Schnier and Edgar Tauch. The pottery ended before 1930 at which time, Gertrude was directing Halcyon Pottery (see that listing). (Information and marks: Paul Evans, *Art Pottery of the U.S.*, pp. 318, 319. Nos. 1, 2 are paper labels. No. 3 is impressed. Nos. 4, 5 are incised. No. 6 occasionally appeared as in in-mold mark on a raised disc.)

1.

2.

WALRICH 3.

WALRICH
4. Berkeley, Cal.

5.

6.

Walters, Carl. 1919 to around 1955. Carl Walter's early training was as a painter at the Minneapolis School of Art from 1905 to 1907, and Chase School in New York City, from 1908-1911. He worked as an artist in Portland, Oregon, from 1913-1919. Carl didn't begin experimenting with ceramics until 1919 when he took almost two years developing Egyptian blue. He set up a workshop in Cornish, New Hampshire, in 1921, then moved to Woodstock, New York, in 1922, where he started making ceramic sculptured pieces. By 1924 he showed at the Whitney Museum of American Art in New York. His success was assured and his works are found in collections at the Metropolitan Museum of Art, the Art Institute of Chicago, the Minneapolis Institute of Arts, the Museum of Modern Art in New York. He received a Guggenheim fellowship in 1936 and 1937. Following his death in 1955, a memorial exhibition was held at the Museum of Art in Ogunquit, Maine. Carl Walters used a variety of incised marks. (Information: Garth Clark, *A Century of Ceramics in the U.S.*, pp. 338, 339. Marks: Linda Steigleder, from the booklet published by the Everson Museum of Art to accompany the 1978 exhibition, "A Century of Ceramics in the U.S.")

Wanamaker, John. Philadelphia, Pennsylvania, and New York, New York. Department store. In the November 1954 *Crockery and Glass Journal* article, "Wanamaker Holds Home Fashions Week," staff written, p. 58, the Philadelphia store was selling Red Wing Pottery's "Capistrano," and "Pink Spice"; Sascha Brastoff's, "Wishing Tree"; and Shenango's "Wild Strawberry," in the Peter Terris line by Shenango. From Castleton China (see Shenango China listing), the store had "Royal Medallion," and "Sakarra." (Marks: no. 1 was filed April 15, 1937, claiming use since January 21, 1937. No. 2 was filed July 10, 1929, claiming use since November 15, 1927, for use on chinaware, namely bowls, vases, plates, cups, saucers, sugar bowls, cream pitchers, relish dishes, platters, gravy boats and stands, teapots and jugs. John Wanamaker also sold Morgan Belleek China. (See that listing.) See Buffalo China Company for dishes sold in the 1930's by Wanamaker.)

 **REDLEAF**

VENTURUS

1.   2.

Wands, I.H. Olean, New York. 1852 to 1870 (Stewart and Consentino, p. 126). Made stoneware, utilitarian pottery, such as jars, crocks, butter churns, etc. (Mark: impressed; Guilland, p. 126.)

I. H. WANDS

OLEAN N.Y.

Wannopee Pottery. See the New Milford Pottery Company for history. See Lang and Osgood for further discussion on marks.

Waples-Platier Grocer Company. Fort Worth, Texas. A distributor, filed for rights to this mark on August 5, 1926, for use on china cups and saucers, claiming use since November 23, 1896.

Ward Pottery. See H.A. Graack listing.

Ward, Stephen H. West Brownsville, Pennsylvania. 1860's and 1870's. Made stoneware. (Information and stenciled mark: Schaltenbrand, p. 27.)

Stephen H. Ward

West Brownsville

Warne and Letts. See Cheesequake Potters.

Warner-Keffer China Company. East Liverpool, Ohio. Very short lived company around 1908 to 1910. Makers of semi-porcelain dinnerware. (Information: William H. Vodrey, Jr. ''Record of the Pottery Industry in East Liverpool District,''

American Ceramic Society Bulletin, August 1945, p. 285. Mark: from Edith Michel.)

Warner, William E. (West Troy Pottery). West Troy, New York. 1829 to 1852 (Stewart and Consentino dates, p. 126). Made stoneware, some with impressed mark and blue slip decorations. (Marks: on crocks, Guilland, pp. 117, 121, 125.)

WEST TROY N.Y. POTTERY   **WM. E. WARNER WEST TROY**

WEST TROY, NY POTTERY   **WEST TROY POTTERY**

Warwick China Company. Wheeling, West Virginia. Started in 1884, incorporated in 1887, and closed in 1951. In an article in *The Glaze*, July-August, 1977, p. 9, by Donald C. Hoffman, Sr., entitled, ''Introduction to American Made Warwick China,'' Hoffman states that Warwick produced over 10,000 sets of dinnerware per month at the height of their production. Warwick made beautiful dinner sets of high quality porcelain. They also made semi-porcelain and hotel ware over the years. Warwick's many lines included florals, fraternal order pieces, Indians, monks, nudes, etc. They used decals, hand painting and tintype decorations, at various times. Warwick China Company made three weights of china; hotel or heavier ware; banquet, a medium weight; and a fine thin china. All used a fairly vitrified clay body.

They purchased decals from Palm Brothers Decalcomania Company, but they also made some of their own decals. Warwick China Company did not use pattern names, only numbers to identify most of their china. In Lois Lehner, *American Kitchen and Dinner Wares*, pp. 160-163, is shown four full pages of these decals with the identifying number used. There were actually hundreds of the different decorations used on various dishes. Maybe sometime an author will write a book and assign names to the patterns to help the collectors, because the numbers are not on the dishes either, which makes difficulties in finding a complete set. Shape names for Warwick include Avon, Warwick, Colonial, Sheraton, regency, etc., but I can't say that these were ever included in marks either. According to Don Hoffman, Sr., ''When Warwick Rode the Rails,'' *The Glaze*, December 1977, January 1978, p. 3, Warwick made china for the Erie, Pennsylvania, Baltimore and Ohio railroads. Different sources state the different marks come first at Warwick. According to Barber, the first stamp to be used was a helmet and crossed swords. From 1893 to 1898 the ''Warwick Semi-Porcelain'' mark was in use. Warwick made hotel china after 1912 and some bone china after 1940. The last few years the company was in business, they made mostly hotel ware. Warwick used the mark with "IOGA," on some of their earliest and finest ware, including some tankard pitchers, flow blue (one of the few American companies to attempt flow blue) vases, plates, umbrella holders, etc. (Information: Agnus Schmitt, "Ohio Valley Pottery and China Gain Popularity," *Collectors Weekly*, July 14, 1970, p. 3; and Lehner, as cited. Marks: Quality Stamp Company furnished almost all of the backstamps shown. A few were photostatic copies from dishes. Nos. 1, 8, 9, from Barber, *Marks of American Potters*, p. 152, before 1904. The helmet and crossed swords mark was used over a very long period of time and registered July 12, 1905. As I have stated, Barber said it was the first mark used. See mark 1 for Barber's copy. Then we find similar marks dated in the 1940's. No. 2 is dated 1945. "Santone," nos. 3, 4, and "Permaware," no. 5, were made in the 1940's. Pieces were found with dates, 1946 and 1949. Part of the mark for James M. Shaw and Company, no. 6, was filed for registration in 1928. See the listing for Shaw for the lion part of mark. See McNicol China Company for a similar mark to no. 7, for Barth Equipment Company. See Buffalo China for another mark by Nathan Straus and Sons.)

1.

2.

3.

4.

5.

6.

7.

WARWICK CHINA

8.

WARWICK SEMI PORCELAIN

9.

10.

11.

ADAM PATTERN
WARWICK CHINA
DESIGN PATENTED

12.

13.

THE ROSEWOOD
WARWICK CHINA
WRIGHT TYNDALE
& VAN ROGER CO.
PHILADELPHIA

14.

WARWICK
BURLEY & CO.
CHICAGO
CHINA

15.

16.

WARWICK
Made by
Knglers
N. SHELLENBURG & CO

17.

THE EDGEWOOD
WARWICK CHINA
WRIGHT TYNDALE
& VAN ROGER CO.
PHILADELPHIA

18.

WARWICK
ALBERT PICK COMPANY
CHICAGO

19.

WARWICK CHINA
SPENCER & HURLBUT, N.Y.
SEATTLE, WASH.

20.

WARWICK
L. BARTH & CO. INC.
CHINA
NEW YORK

21.

22.

WARWICK
NEIL HOUSE
BY
HANGERSON & ?
COLUMBUS 4.

23.

SOLD BY
WRIGHT
TYNDALE & VAN ROUEN
PHILA. PA.
WARWICK
CHINA

24.

MADE EXPRESSLY FOR
HOTEL ST. REGIS
WARWICK
CHINA
JAMES M. SHAW
NEW YORK

25.

WARWICK
L. B. KING & Co.
CHINA
DETROIT. MICH.

26.

WARWICK
ALBERT PICK CO. INC.
CHICAGO. ILL.

27.

WARWICK
THE BALLARET
CHINA

28.

McLellan
Stores Co.
WARWICK CHINA

29.

WARWICK CHINA
Nathan Straus & Sons

30.

WARWICK
ALBERT PICK-BARTH COMPANY
CHICAGO INC. NEW YORK

31.

WARWICK CHINA
CHARLES R. LYNDE
BOSTON. MASS.
HOTEL. DEPT

32.

WARWICK CHINA
KOEHLER & HINRICHS Co.
SAINT PAUL

33.

WARWICK
MADE FOR
SPERRY SERVICE
NEW YORK
HORISON PATTERN
VITRIFIED CHINA
DESIGN CONTROLLED

34.

WARWICK CHINA
FORD
ST. LOUIS

35.

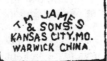
HOTEL PRESIDENT
BEAMISH GLASSWARE CO.
KANSAS CITY, MO.

36.

T. M. JAMES
& SONS
KANSAS CITY, MO.
WARWICK CHINA

37.

THE LEWIS & NEBLETT Co.
WARWICK CHINA

38.

39.

40.

41.
TudorRose

42.
WARWICK NEIL HOUSE by HINTERSCHIED COLUMBUS, O.

43.
WARWICK CHINA

44.
WARWICK

45.
WARWICK WHEELING

46.
WARWICK WHEELING

47.
Loubat NEW ORLEANS WARWICK CHINA

48.
WARWICK L.B KING & Co. CHINA DETROIT MICH

49.
WARWICK L. BARTH & SON CHINA NEW YORK

50.
WARWICK ALBERT PICK COMPANY CHICAGO

51.
WARWICK WHEELING
Southern Hotel 1918 Warwick

52.
WARWICK CHINA AMERICAN CHINA & GLASSWARE Co. CHICAGO, ILL

WARWICK CHINA WHEELING

Washington Company. Washington, Pennsylvania. Decorators of beverage sets, salad sets, ovenware, basketry items, gold rolled bent ware in 1967 *China, Glass and Tableware Directory*, but I believe this company worked mostly with glass or possibly only glass.

Wasserstrom Company. Columbus, Ohio. A sales agency for restaurant supplies, serving fixtures, equipment, dishes, etc. This mark used on china was found at Quality Stamp Company, East Liverpool, Ohio. In 1986, Wasserstrom Company is a family owned company that has sales divisions serving the contract building business, office furniture, restaurant supplies and is currently opening what they call supermarkets for office needs. The mark shown is an older mark.

Watt Pottery. Crooksville, Ohio. In business from 1922 until the pottery burned in 1965. The pottery was located at the site of the old Globe Stoneware Company (1901-1919). The plant then became the Zane W. Burley Pottery (1919-1922), which was followed by Watt Pottery (1922-1965). In "Watt Pottery," *Antique Trader*, September 13, 1978, p. 66, is a fine article by Marv and Bev Tyacke. The Watt pieces were made of local Crooksville clay and were clear glazed and handpainted. In an interview with Mr. and Mrs. W.I. Watt, the Tyackes were able to secure some names and dates for Watt's ware. In 1940, "Kitch-N-Queen," a series of kitchenware banded in turquoise and pink was introduced. In 1950, the "Red Apple," was first offered. In 1955, the "Cherry" design was introduced, and in 1956, the "Star Flower." In 1957, a rooster outlined in black with red and green feathers was brought out. In 1958, the "Dutch" style with tulips was introduced. Other lines are "Kolar Kraft," and "Flav-R-Bake," "Even-Bake," "Gold-N-Bake," "Past L. Kitchenware," and "Wild Rose." / Products could show up with these as marks.

According to the Tyackes, the Japanese copied and made a large spaghetti bowl, they marked theirs with just "U.S.A." An old mark is "Peedeeco," and "U.S.A." See Nelson McCoy Pottery for an "Oven Ware" mark somewhat similar to Watt Pottery's mark. "Cabin Art" was a line of kitchenware made by Watt Pottery and sold by George Borgfeldt, Inc., which was listed in the 1945 *Crockery and Glass Journal Directory*. "Cabin Art" was found incised on a two tone brown pitcher. (Information: Guy E. Crooks, *History of Crooksville*, published by Crooksville Lions Club, around 1945, p. 33, and the Tyackes, as cited. Marks: are incised or in a mold on varous pieces. These are not stamped marks. They are large marks in many cases that cover most of the bottom of the piece with two large indented circles.)

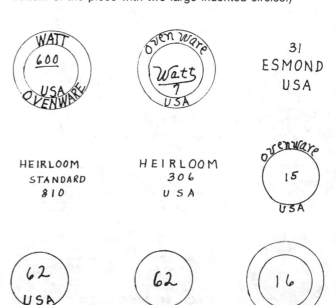

Wayne Manufacturing Company. Staatsburg, New York. Filed for registration of this mark on September 27, 1965, for coated ceramic cookware.

Weaver, Various Potters. Abraham Weaver was listed from around 1824 or 1825 until 1844 in Nockamixon, Bucks Coun-

ty, Pennsylvania. One redware piece described by John Spargo in *Early American Pottery and China*, p. 164, bore the inscription "when this you see, remember me, Abraham Weaver." Pictured is a mark (no. 1) for this potter as shown in C. Jordon Thorn, *Handbook of Old Pottery and Porcelain Marks*, p. 153.

Manchester, Adams County, Ohio, is approximately 40 miles or so from Cincinnati, Hamilton County, Ohio. In Manchester in the 1883 *Ohio State Business Directory*, **Andrew W. Weaver** and **C.C. Parkes** were listed as potters. In 1888, the listing was **Weaver and Bradford**, and by 1890 and 1891 the listing in Manchester was just **J. Weaver**. Two beautiful old stoneware pieces were found with marks nos. 2 and 3, impressed in blue. I made no connection between John Weaver and C. Weaver in Cincinnati with the Weavers listed in Manchester, but a thorough study sometime will probably determine that they were from the same family because they all operated the area in Southern Ohio. I couldn't say for certain that the J. Weaver mark on the beautiful salt glazed five gallon handled jar (mark no. 4) shown in Elmer Smith's *Pottery, A Utilitarian Folk Craft*, p. 7, belonged to John Weaver or was marked for him to sell because I found a **James L. Weaver** in Roseville, Ohio, listed in Ramsay, p. 229.

One more family of potters named Weaver was discussed by A.H. Rice and John B. Stoudt, *The Shenandoah Pottery*, p. 7. This family migrated to the area of Jugtown from Lehigh and Bucks Counties, Pennsylvania, from the area where Abraham Weaver, the first potter listed here, originated. Perhaps a member of the Weaver family will do a through study and write a book one day. (Information and marks: nos. 1 and 2, as cited; nos. 3, 4, from Melvin L. Davies, research potter.)

A. WEAVER
1.

JOHN WEAVER
WHOLESALER
STONEWARE
CINCINNATI, OHIO
2.

C. WEAVER
STONEWARE
DEPOT
CINCINNATI, O.
3.

J. WEAVER

4.

Weber, J.A. Ramsay, p. 164, gives Bedminster, Bucks County, Pennsylvania, as location. Thorn, p. 153, said Barnesville, Pennsylvania. Both gave around 1875 as a date for this potter who made redware, with name impressed as shown in Thorn.

J.A. Weber

Webster, Mack (McCloud) C. Hartford, Connecticut. Around

1810 to 1840 Mack C. Webster purchased a building with Horace Goodwin on Front Street to make pottery. (See the listing Goodwin, Various Potters.) Then around 1840 the name became M.C. Webster and Son when Charles T. Webster joined his father. Mack C. Webster died in 1857 and Orson Hart Seymour became partners with Charles T. Webster for the next 10 years. In 1867 the firm was Seymour and Brother. (Information: Lura W. Watkins, *Early New England Potters and Their Wares*, pp. 194, 195. Marks: Thorn, p. 153.)

WEBSTER & SEYMOUR
HARTFORD

M C WEBSTER & SONS
HARTFORD

Wedgwood Pottery. See Harker Pottery.

Weeks, Cook and Weeks. Akron, Ohio. The pottery started around 1882 or 1883, and in 1910 became the **Maurice A. Knight Company**, still operating. Weeks, Cook, and Weeks, became **Weeks Brothers** and employed 31 to make stoneware. According to Blair, p. 30, Weeks (Arthur and Frederick) Brothers became **F.H. Weeks** from 1891 to 1910. When the brothers separated, **A.J. Weeks** operated on his own until around 1919 (Stout, p. 59). The Weeks Company made stoneware, and the Maurice A. Knight Company is a maker of chemical stoneware. Marks included "F.H. Weeks, Akron" embossed. For Maurice A. Knight, the mark is the name on a shield impressed. Arthur J. Weeks was the first to offer chemical ceramic equipment in the United States. Before that time the materials came from Germany. (Knight Company information.) In the early years the Maurice A. Knight Company made utilitarian type pottery. A cylinder type ink was found marked with name "Maurice A. Knight" in brown glazed pottery. Mark also found on stoneware batter jug, "Mfg. by F.H. Weeks, Akron, Ohio, Patent applied for." A syrup jug with cobalt blue sponging marked "F.H. Weeks" was found. (Information and marks: Lehner, *Ohio Pottery and Glass*, pp. 16, 17.)

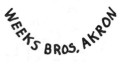   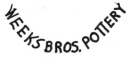

WEEKS, COOK, & WEEKS

Wege Marble and Tile Company. Columbus, Ohio. I found it listed as early as 1927. It was in business before that time and was out of business by 1978. Made decorative ceramic floor and wall tile. Tile found with scene of blue ship, ocean, clouds, etc.

THE WEGE MARBLE & TILE CO.
COLUMBUS, OHIO

Weil, Alfred, J. Chicago, Illinois. In the 1982 *China, Glass and Tableware Directory*, this company was listed, but no specific products were given. I don't know why this distributor didn't have more listings in the directories. The mark shown was in an advertisement in the *Giftware Buyers Guide*, August 31, 1960, and I found the company listed again in 1982. That was all I found. They have permanent showrooms in Chicago and import giftware from around the world. Notice the "W" over "W" similar to the mark for California Figurine, owned by Max Weil, but I made no further connection between any of the four Weil companies. There was also a **Lewis P. Weil** in Philadelphia, Pennsylvania, who was a distributor listed in 1945 *Crockery and Glass Journal Directory* for the Brack Shops in Los Angeles. They were listed as importers, wholesalers of earthenware art pottery, glassware and glass novelties and decorative accessories. I didn't find the mark for this company. In 1953, they were selling French and Italian pottery and Italian glassware. They are listed here because of confusion over the various Weil companies.

Weil Ceramics and Glass, Inc. New York, New York. This was a selling agency with Max Weil as president. (See the listing, Max Weil of California.) They were listed in 1945 as importers of china, earthenware, fancy ware, art pottery, blown and pressed glassware, gifts and specialties. In the 1961 *China, Glass and Tableware*, they were listed as importers of china, glass and pottery from Czechoslovakia, England, France, Italy, Germany, Belgium, Portugal and Sweden. They continued to be listed through all of the directories I had for the 1980's.

Weil, Max, of California/California Figurine Company. 3160 San Fernando Road, Los Angeles, California. Late 1930's until after 1954. Mark 1 was pictured in the 1945 and 1946 *Crockery and Glass Journal Directory*, with the California Figurine Company name. In the 1946 directory, Max Weil of California was also listed at this address. This address was the only connection I could make between California Figurine Company and Max Weil of California, but in "Weil Ware," by Helen Brink, *American Clay Exchange*, October 30, 1984, p. 8, she said California Figurine Company was started by Max Weil in the late 1930's. The last listing I have been able to locate for Max Weil of California was in 1954. The company was not listed in the 1955 *California Manufacturer's Directory*. In the article, "Daring Dishes," *Fortnight Magazine*, August 4, 1950, p. 23, staff written, this company was mentioned as one of the six biggest dinnerware makers in California, at that time. In the *Crockery and Glass Journal Magazine*, December 1947, p. 49, is an advertisement showing "Malay

Bambu'' dinnerware by Max Weil. The dinnerware came in coral, aqua or dawn colors with yellow or black stalks of hand-painted bamboo. In the same magazine for March 1949, p. 67, is an advertisement for ''Malay Blossom'' with the logo of the little donkey and a ''W'' shown in the ad (see mark 2). No. 3 is the actual mark used on this set. They are a beautiful gray with white hand painted blossoms, well vitrified with a good glaze. Max Weil had the very successful and long lived selling agency, Weil Ceramics and Glass. That is probably one of the reasons this California pottery was shortlived. He chose to concentrate his efforts elsewhere. (See the listings, Weil Ceramics and Glass, also Alfred J. Weil Company. Marks: Nos. 3, 4, 5 are backstamps on dishes. Nos. 1 and 6 are paper labels.)

1.

2.

3.

4.

5.

6.

Weil, Walter M. and Sandy Lang Weil. Marietta, Ohio. This very talented husband-wife team are studio potters currently working at the Ohio Ceramic Center at Crooksville, Ohio. They are making some smoke blackened porcelain pieces that are exceptional. Also, Sandy makes beautiful porcelain. Walter graduated from Junior College in Ventura, California, and will graduate from the College of Art and Design in Columbus, Ohio, in 1986, where he received a scholrship. Sandy graduated from the College of Art and Design in 1983. She received a Ford Foundation Scholarship and was on the Dean's list. Both have won awards in several student exhibits.

S Lang

W Weil

Weimer Family Pottery. Snydertown, Pennsylvania. Middle 1860's to 1872. Between or around 1865 to 1868 a pottery was started in Snydertown, Northumberland County, Pennsylvania by two brothers, William R.F. Weimer and George Y. Weimer. William owned the property, and George seems

to have done most of the potting. In Jeannette Lasansky's book, *Made of Mud*, p. 37, is a detailed account of how the brothers came to the area, the property owned by William, etc. William moved to Sunbury, Pennsylvania, in 1868, and George operated the pottery making stoneware utilitarian crocks, jugs, etc. until 1872. (Information and stamped or impressed marks: Lasansky, as cited, pp. 37, 56.)

G.Y. WEIMER   WEIMER & BRO.

W.R.F. WEIMER & BRO.
SNYDERTOWN, PA.

Weir Pottery Company. Monmouth, Illinois. 1899 to 1906. Incorporated September 28, 1899, with W.S. Weir as president. The pottery made canning jars, patented by W.S. Weir in 1892. In 1899 and early 1900, Mr. Weir built a new plant in Monmouth. This plant was destroyed by fire in May 1902 and rebuilt right away on South D. Street, between 6th and 8th Streets, employing 135 people. In 1906, Western Stoneware Company took over the control of Weir Pottery Company, along with six other potteries. See Western Stoneware for information. Weir Pottery became Plant 2, which was operated until 1985 by Western Stoneware Company. According to Jim Martin, ''The Potteries of Monmouth, Illinois,'' *Antique Trader*, December 19, 1979, pp. 62, 63, the Weir Pottery produced mainly pottery canning jars; some had amber glass lids. The pottery also made druggist jugs, vinegar cruets and some Indian Head or Sleepy Eye pitchers with the Weir mark on them. As Plant 2 of Western Stoneware, Monmouth Art and Garden Pottery was made in this building. (Marks: found on old pottery canning jars and sent by Jim Martin.)

Weissman, Beth. 49 West 23rd Street, New York, New York. Was listed as a separate company from the Weissman Company, Inc. (see that listing). In the 1945 *Crockery and Glass Journal Directory*, Beth Weissman was listed as manufacturers of lamps, gifts and hand decorated china. I made no definite connection between the two Weissman companies. (Marks: Company filed for registration of the mark shown on May 3, 1946, claiming use since June 15, 1939.)

BETHWOOD

Weissman Company, Inc. New York, New York, and East Palestine, Ohio. The Weissman Company, Inc. at 189 W. Martin, in East Palestine, and 22 W. 27th Street, New York, New York, went out of business July 1957 when Nat Weissman died. Dwight Morris of Dwight Morris China, East Palestine, Ohio, made products for Weissman China Company to sell. Besides being a selling agency, the Weissman Company in East Palestine was listed as decorators of china and earthenware in the 1952, 1954 *Crockery and Glass Journals*. (Marks: Filed for rights to mark 1 on March 12, 1946, for use on pottery and china, namely bowls, candy boxes, cups, flower pots, jugs, pin trays, pitchers, plates, saucers, salt and pepper shakers and vases, claiming use since March 1941. No. 2 was found at Quality Stamp Company in East Liverpool, and was probably the one that Dwight Morris China Company used on the products they made for Weissman. Mark 3 was the one shown in those directories for Weissman.)

1. 2. 3.

Weller Pottery. Fultonham and Zanesville, Ohio. 1872-1948. Even before 1872, Samuel A. Weller was working with clay. Schneider said he learned to throw crocks, jugs and jars, on a crude kickwheel when he was boy on the farm in Muskingum County. Samuel's brother William also made pottery, and then spent the rest of his life working as a chemist in the Weller Pottery. Vision, business ability and a lot of good luck in finding really talented people to work for him, were the keys to Sam Weller's success story. In 1872, Weller started making pottery as a business in Fultonham, near Zanesville, Ohio. In 1882, he moved to the Putnam part of Zanesville between Pierce Street and Cemetery Drive. By 1891 he was employing 61 people in the pottery, to make hand painted or decorated flowerpots. Later he made jardinieres, umbrella stands, cuspidors, etc. In 1895, Weller bought the Lonhuda Pottery of Steubenville and the former owner, W.A. Long, worked for Weller for about one year.

The pottery manufactured in a part of Weller's organization, which they called the Lonhuda Faience Company organized in January 1895, was an underglaze decoration of flowers, fruits, portraits, etc. During this period, Weller was constantly expanding his facilities. In 1890, he had moved from his Pierce Street plant where he had started in Zanesville to build a three story building. A large addition to make Lonhuda Ware was added in 1895, and in 1901, Weller bought a building from American Encaustic Tiling Company. Between 1895 and 1945, Weller is reported to have brought out 125 different lines. In 1926, plant 3 burned and was rebuilt. In 1948, the plant was sold to the Essex Wire Corporation. Weller was well known for its beautiful art pottery with some of the lines like Louwelsa, consisting of over 500 shapes (Schneider). Weller also made a great deal of kitchen products such as bowls, casseroles, pitchers, etc. In fact, Norris Schneider stated that utility lines comprised half of the Weller production in the 1930's. The company even filled enormous orders for beer mugs when prohibition was over. Weller made a line of baby or juvenile ware in the 1920's. In 1920, the Zanesville Art Pottery Company was purchased

by Weller according to Stout, p. 61. For years, Zanesville Art Pottery had been making culinary articles along with other kinds of ware. Weller continued to make cookware in that plant. Stout p. 61, said Weller had also made such ware in his other plants for a number of years. Weller made an apple design dinnerware which Frederick J. Grant of Gladding, McBean and Company introduced as a type of Franciscan ware with the permission of Weller authorities. (Norris Schneider, "Weller Pottery," *Zanesville Times Signal*, April 6, 1958.) Before showing the Weller marks, there is a paragraph on marks in Paul Evans, *Art Pottery of the U.S.*, p. 327, reprinted here by his permission:

"There is almost no consistency in Weller marks, and the more one attempts to order them the more illogical and confusing they become. In the early period impressed or incised line designations often appear in addition to the impressed Weller name, although in numerous cases pieces bear the mark of one line and the decoration of another; many pieces were not marked at all. Decorator signatures and ciphers do not offer much help in the definite attribution of unmarked pieces as decorators frequently moved from one Zanesville pottery to another, and often the various firm lines were so similar that without a mark they could not be told apart. On the cast ware produced after 1915 usually only the incised, imprinted or in-mold Weller name appears. Paper labels were also used during the 1930's and 1940's, as were the script signature. The Sicardo line is often signed on the face of the piece, as is LaSa. The original Weller Lonhuda line bears the impressed LF -- for Lonhuda Faience - mark within the shield, as well as the impressed Lonhuda designation. The incised Weller Faience mark is found on Jap Birdimal-type ware, often in conjunction with "Rhead," designating F.H. Rhead."

(Information and marks: It was very difficult to credit the following marks because they were included in several books. And each of these books showed almost all of the marks. So I ended up crediting those marks which were shown in one book only. The Barber marks were repeated in all books also, but are shown separately because they are very early marks. Edwin Atlee Barber, *Marks of American Potters*, Philadelphia: Patterson and White, 1904. Ralph and Terry Kovel, *Kovels' Collector's Guide to American Art Pottery*, New York: Crown Publishers; Foster E. Hall and Gladys C. Hall Collector's *Guide to American Pottery Artists, Potters, Designers and Their Marks*. This is a paperback showing all decorators and designers that are included in the other books cited, but in complete alphabetical order. Paul Evans, *Art Pottery of the U.S.*; Sharon and Bob Huxford, *The Collector's Encyclopedia of Weller Pottery*, Paducah, Kentucky: Schroeder Publishing Company. Marks 1-7, Barber, p. 131, all very early marks used in early 1900's; no. 4, by Barber is evidently an error. In *Ohio Pottery and Glass*, p. 101, I said there was a question in the spelling of "Eosian," by Barber. No marks have ever shown up to support Barber's spelling. Many writers have by now supported the "Eocean" spelling. Nos. 8-11 are from marks on pieces from collector, Wilma Hock. No. 8 is a photostatic copy of a round green paper label. No. 9 is a silver foil label. No. 10 is a stamped mark and no. 11, an incised mark. Nos. 12-15 are incised marks on decorative pieces drawn from pieces. The decorator's marks are either incised or written in ink. No. 16 is an incised mark used 1930's and after. No. 17, from a patent office report filed by S.A. Weller Company, Zanesville, on November 5, 1927, claiming use since 1912 for use on pottery. No. 18 was used by the Lonhuda Pottery, according to Barber, p. 131 (see that listing) and also by Weller Pottery when the Lonhuda Faience

Company was formed in Zanesville, and William A. Long, owner of Lonhuda Pottery, went to work with Weller for about one year around 1896. See Huxford, pp. 8, 9, for a comprehensive history on this partnership. Nos. 19, 20 are two very early incised marks dated by the Huxfords, p. 29, around 1903. No. 21 was incised on Greenaway pieces. No. 22, incised on etched mat. Nos. 23-26 are various die stamped marks shown in Huxford, pp. 29, 30. Nos. 27-31 are impressed marks used before 1920 on various art lines. Nos. 32-35 are four ink stamped marks. No. 36, Louwelsea circle seal mark. No. 37, found in ink stamp or paper label. No. 38, embossed on third Dickens. No. 39, on early utility ware. No. 40 impressed. No. 41, ink stamp. No. 42 Jacques Sicard designed the Sicardo line. I have a piece of "Glendale" marked with the single W as mark 47.

The decorator marks that follow are not in complete alphabetical order because they are divided to give credit to the authors that published them. Each time a potter or decorator signed his name, it looked just a little different, just as any signature does, but I found the books mentioned pictured them pretty much alike. Huxfords, Halls and Kovels, give the names of potters whose marks are not yet discovered. They also gave marks of decorators not identified yet. See those books for many more details. Shown separately are the different decorator marks the Kovels had not shown in the other two books. I redrew all decorator marks, but many company marks shown were the copies shown in the Huxford book. Many marks beside those pictured will be found. A vase decorated by artist, A. Wilson, was marked "Weller Decorative Etched Ware," and on the side "A. Wilson After Landseer." The vase pictured a beautiful St. Bernard dog.)

S.A. Weller Pottery decorator's marks as shown on page 132 of E.A. Barber's *Marks of American Potters*.

Decorator	Mark	Decorator	Mark
Virginia Adams.		S. Reid McLaughlin.	
Elizabeth Ayers.		Hattie Mitchell.	
Lizabeth Blake.		Lillie Mitchell.	
Levi J. Burgess.		Minnie Mitchell.	
Anna Dautherty.		Gordon Mull.	
Anthony Dunlavy.		Edwin Pickens.	
Frank Ferrell.		Hester W. Pillsbury.	
Mary Gillie.		Eugene Roberts.	
Albert Haubrich.		Tot Steele.	
Madge Hurst.		C. Minnie Terry.	
Josephine Imlay.		Helen B. Windle.	
Karl Kappes.			

The following marks for decorators are shown in Halls', Kovels' and Huxfords' books as cited already.

Decorator	Mark
Abel	
M. Ansel	
Ruth Azline	
Elizabeth Blake	
John Butterworth	
Charles C. Chilcote	
Laura Cline	
Frank Dedonatis	
Charles John Dibowski	
C.A. Dusenbery	
Dorothy England (Laughead)	
Charles Fouts	
Henry Fuchs	
M. Gibson	
W. Gibson	
Charles Gray	
William F. Hall	
Delores Harvey	
John Herold	
Hugo Herb	
Hood	
Roy Hook	
L. Knaus	
Claude L. Leffler	
John Lessell	

W.A. Long	☆
M. Lybarger	M. LyBARger
Minnie Mitchell	M MM
L. Morris	Morris
M. Myers	M-M
Lizzie Perone	LP
Mary Pierce	AP MP
Albert Radford	AR
Marie Rauchfuss	MR
Frederick Hurten Rhead	FR
Hattie M. Ross	HR
Jacques Sicard	SICARD
Helen Smith	HS
Jessie R. Spaulding	JR
William H. Stemm	WS WHS
E. Sulcer	E. SuLCER
Madaline Thompson	M.T.
Mae Timberlake	M.T. Timberlake
Sarah Timberlake	⚵
Naomi Truitt (Walch)	Walch
R.G. Turner	RG Turner
Charles B. Upjohn	y
Carl Weigelt	CW
Carrie Wilbur	CW
Edna Wilbur	EW
Albert Wilson	A WILSON
Clotilda Marie Zanetta	cZ c.z. M.Z.

Some of these decorators may be in listings already given. These are the marks shown in the Kovel's book that are slightly different.

Virginia Adams	V. ADAMS
A.F. Best	F3 EST
Levi J. Burgess	L J B LJB
Dorothy England	EngLAnd
Frank Ferrell	Ferrell
Mary Gillie	MG M.L.
Charles Gray	G
William F. Hall	W.F Hall
Anna Jewett	J
John Lessell	Lessell LaSa
Claude Leffler	C.L. LEFFlER
L. McLain	L Mc LaIN
Sarah Reid McLaughlin	McLaughLIN
Lillie Mitchell	L MITchell LM
Minnie Mitchel	M. MiTcHEL
Edwin L. Pickens	E L.P.
Frederick H. Rhead	F Rhead
Eugene Roberts	Er
Irvin Smith	Is
Fred Steele	⨎
Mae Timberlake	Mae Timberlake

DICKENS WARE WELLER. 1.

DICKENS WARE WELLER 2.

LOUWELSA WELLER 3.

Eosian WELLER (ERROR?)
4.

TURADA WELLER
5.

SICARDO WELLER.
6.

aurelian WELLER
7.

Weller Ware
8.

WELLER POTTERY
9.

WELLER WARE
10.

Weller Pottery Since 1872
11.

Weller F 68
12.

Weller M K G
13.

P Weller
14.

Weller Pottery
15.

Weller Hand Made
16.

GRAYSTONE
17.

LONHUDA LF
18.

Weller FAIENCE
19.

Weller Rhead Faience
20.

SA Weller
21.

WELLER
22.

WELLER WARE
23.

WELLER
24.

WELLER
25.

ETNA WELLER
26.

ETNA WELLER
27.

ART NOUVEAU WELLER
28.

FLORETTA WELLER
29.

PERFECTO WELLER
30.

LOUWELSA WELLER
31.

WELLER POTTERY
32.

WELLER WARE
33.

Weller
34.

WELLER POTTERY
35.

LOUWELSA WELLER
36.

WELLER WARE
37.

7 WELLER
38.

SA WELLER ZANESVILLE OHIO
39.

LOUWELSA WELLER
40.

WELLER WARE
41.

Sicard
42.

Eocean Weller
43.

LOUWELSA 8 WELLER 530
44.

WELLER ETNA
45.

Eocean Rose Weller
46.

W
47.

AURELIAN WELLER
48.

MATT WELLER
49.

Wellsville China Company. Wellsville, Ohio. The pottery started as **Morley and Company**, 1879 to 1885, making white granite and majolica. In 1885, the company became known as the **Pioneer Pottery Company** until 1896. According to W.B. McCord, *History of Columbiana County, Ohio.* Chicago: Biographical Publishing Company, 1905, p. 173, the pottery must have been in financial difficulty from the time the Pioneer Pottery name was used. He mentions a 10 year litigation in the courts. Around 1900 the Wellsville China Company started in this building and operated until 1969. Wellsville China Company made semi-porcelain dinnerware and accessory pieces.

From 1959 to 1969 the Wellsville China Company was owned by Sterling China Company. Sterling China Company has offices in East Liverpool and the factory in Wellsville, Ohio. The Sterling China Company factory is only three blocks from the Wellsville China Company in Wellsville. The Wellsville plant operated as a wholly subsidiary under its own name, but I am convinced some of the same marks were used in both factories from 1959 to 1969 because marks sent to this author by Sterling China Company as Sterling marks incorporate the name Wellsville China in them. It doesn't help to know the piece is hotel ware because both plants made hotel ware. Wellsville China made semi-vitreous ware, but as far as I can determine, Sterling China Company always made hotel ware. In 1969, the Wellsville plant was closed because of outdated equipment. (Information: Lehner, *American Kitchen and Dinner Wares*, p. 165. Marks: 1-3, Barber, *Marks of American Potters*, p. 128; 4-20, from dishes or Quality Stamp Company, East Liverpool, Ohio; no. 21, 22, from 1952 *Crockery and Glass Journal Directory*; nos. 23-28, sent by Waldorf Stamping Device, New London, Ohio. They sent only more recent marks leading me to believe these marks were used at Wellsville China under Sterling China ownership, and could be considered to be Sterling China products. Notice no. 24 is also shown under Sterling China Company marks having been sent to me by Sterling China Company.)

1.

THE WELLSVILLE CHINA CO
WELLSVILLE
OHIO.

2.

Liberty
S.H.Co.N.K.

3.

WELLSVILLE CHINA
SERWER'S
DETROIT, MICH

4.

WELLSVILLE
CHINA
"BELMONT"

5.

WELLSVILLE
CHINA

6.

Pastel By Wellsville China

7.

WELLSVILLE
CHINA CO.

8.

WELLSVILLE
BAKE RITE
CHINA
OHIO. U.S.A

10.

WELLSVILLE CHINA
Pink Garland
DISTRIBUTED BY
LEWIS BROS.
1212 PENN AVE., PGH., PA.

11.

THE WELLSVILLE CHINA CO.
WELLSVILLE.
OHIO.

12.

WELLSVILLE
DeSOTO
CHINA
OHIO U S A

13.

W. C. CO.

14.

WELLSVILLE
CHINA WELLSVILLE
OHIO
1957

16.

15.

WELLSVILLE
CHINA
"WILLOW"

18.

PRINCESS
W. C. CO.

17.

VITRIFIED
WELLSVILLE CHINA CO OHIO
CHINA

20.

Cosmopolitan
CREATED BY
WELLSVILLE CHINA
WELLSVILLE, OHIO

19.

SAN TAN
WELLSVILLE CHINA
U. S. A.

21.

22.

Wellsville China Co
Wellsville, Ohio

23.

Wellsville
W C Co
MADE IN U S A

24.

WELLSVILLE
CHINA
WELLSVILLE
OHIO

53

25.

510

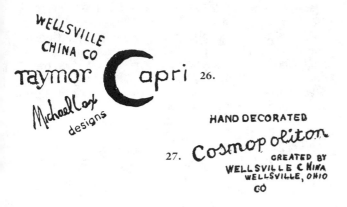

WELLSVILLE CHINA CO
Taymor Capri 26.
Michael Cox designs

HAND DECORATED
27. Cosmopoliton
CREATED BY
WELLSVILLE CHINA
WELLSVILLE, OHIO
CO

Wellsville Pioneer Company. Wellsville, Ohio. See Wellsville China for history and see Pioneer Pottery for marks.

Wendt Pottery. Lewiston, Idaho. 1973 to present (1983). Michael Wendt has been making pottery since 1973. After his business had outgrown two locations, he moved to his present location on Clearwater Street with 2,250 square feet of space and three gas kilns. He makes a high fired porcelain in dinnerware, lamps, vases, etc., from Idaho clay. Since the 1980 eruption of Mt. St. Helens he has been making glaze from the ash of the mountain. On those pieces he mottles with other glazes a picture of the snow capped blue mountain with valleys and trees. He also makes a very nice light colored glazes line of dinnerware in a wheat pattern. Michael makes his own machinery and tools and mines and mixes his own clay. (Marks: 1, 2, incised by hand; no. 3 impressed on wet pot bottom; no. 4, 5, marks stamped on bottom with oxide ink then fired on; no. 6, 7, paper labels. Dates as shown burned right on with mark in oxide ink.)

WENDT 73
1.

WENDT 75
daho Clay & Glaze
2.

WENDT Pottery
1510 Ninth Avenue
Lewiston, Idaho 83501
phone 208 746 3724
NOV 2 9 1980   3.

daho Clay & Glaze
daho Clay & Glaze
WENDT Pottery of
Lewiston, Idaho 83501
LEAD-FREE, DISHWASHER SAFE,
HANDMADE HIGHFIRE STONEWARE
6.

WENDT Pottery made in I...
M. Wendt
daho Clay & Glaze
DEC 19 1982
4.

M. Wendt
daho Clay & Glaze
DEC 19 1982
5.

Mt. Saint Helen's
7. Volcanic Ash Glaze
May 18, 1980 Eruption

Wentz, M.C., Company. Pasadena, California. Before 1939 and operated through 1950's. Wentz Company was a selling agency that registered the "Westward Ho" mark in 1939. I was sadly lacking in directories for the 1930's so I don't know how long before 1939 the company operated. In the directories I had they were listed from 1951 through 1954, but not in 1961. Westward Ho restaurant dinnerware made by Wallace China Company has become well known among collectors, but apparently there are other pieces marked Westward Ho, because mark no. 1 was registered February 28, 1939, to be used on a variety of pieces, namely, ceramic vases, bowls, teapots, sugar and creamer sets, pepper shakers, jam jars, plates and cookie jars. The company claimed use of the mark only one month prior to application. Since Wentz Company was a wholesaler with representatives in San Francisco, California; Dallas, Texas; and New York City, they could have had the products found with a Westward Ho mark made in many places. (Marks: no. 2, in various 1950's directories and no. 3 was sent by a reader. This may not be an exact copy of the mark, but it is very close. In "Westward Ho Dinnerware," *Glaze*, May 1982, p. 7, by Jo Cunningham, is a discussion of the various pieces included in three different decorations designed by Til Goodan, used on Westward Ho, made by Wallace China Company.)

WESTWARD HO   1.

WESTWARD HO
California
2.

WESTWARD HO
RODEO PATTERN
MADE IN CALIF., USA
WALLACE CHINA
3.

Werner Kruger Company. New York, New York. Distributor, filed for registration of this mark on May 6, 1938, for use on ceramic cooking ware, claiming use since October 1, 1937.

"Flamefast"

Wessler and Edwards. Berwick, Pennsylvania. 1882 to around 1890. According to Jeannette Lasansky, *Made in Mud*, p. 13, only one stoneware jug with the mark of these potters has been found at the time her study was done. (Impressed mark: Lasansky, p. 54.)

WESSLER & EDWARDS
BERWICK, PA.

West, Andrea. Mifflinburg, Pennsylvania. Filed for registration of this mark on September 29, 1982, claiming use since October 17, 1978, for ceramic pottery.

Andrea West

West Bend Company and West Bend Thermo Serv., Inc. West Bend, Wisconsin. They had four outlets or representatives in the 1967 *Gift and Tableware Reporter*. (Marks: no. 1 filed for registration August 2, 1963, claiming use since August 1959, for china dinnerware. Mark 2 on heavy brown pot.)

ROYAL SOVEREIGN 1.

West Bend

2.

West Coast Porcelain Manufacturers. Milbrae, California. The pottery made sanitary ware. But for one year in the mid 1920's, the West Coast Porcelain Manufacturers hired Bragdon and Thomas of the California Faience (see that listing) to produce art pottery, a decorative line of porcelain for them at Milbrae for about a year. California Faience continued in operation during this time in Berkeley. (Information: Evans, Paul, *Art Pottery of the U.S.*, p. 41; Turner, Tran, "California Porcelain," *American Art Pottery*, April 1979, p. 4. Mark: Evans, p. 42.)

California
Porcelain

West Coast Pottery, Inc. Burbank, California. Before 1940 until after 1948. They were listed in the 1945 *Crockery and Glass Journal Directory* as manufacturers of earthenware art pottery, figures, figurines, miniature and florists ware. They were listed in the 1948 *California Manufacturer's Register*, but not in 1941 or 1955. (Marks: no. 1, was registered April 28, 1944, for use on ceramic dinnerware, bowls, trays and vases, claiming use since March 15, 1940. Mark 2 is an incised mark on a vase sent by Ed Blas, pottery collector and researcher. Mark 2 is greatly reduced in size as shown, taken from a rubbing of mark. No. 3 is the mark shown in the 1945 directory cited. Ed Blas said it was used as a paper label.)

1.

2.

3.

West End Pottery. East Liverpool, Ohio. 1893 until 1938. Made ironstone and semi-porcelain dinnerwre. In 1929 until 1931 they were a member of the American China Corporation. (Information: Lehner, *Ohio Pottery and Glass*, p. 54. Marks: no. 1, 2, Barber, *Marks of American Potters*, p. 117, no. 3, Jervis, "Worlds Pottery Marks," *Pottery, Glass and Brass Salesman*, May 20, 1915, p. 15; nos. 4, 5, on a plate and bowl of semi-porcelain.)

1.

2.

3.   4.   5.

Western Auto Supply Company. Los Angeles, California. A distributor, filed for rights to this mark on October 2, 1942, for use on china tableware, claiming use since March 15, 1942.

WESTERN ROYAL

Western Pottery Manufacturing Company. Denver, Colorado. Around 1905 to 1936. William Long of the Denver China and Pottery Company sold the assets of his firm to a group that founded the Western Pottery Manufacturing Company at the same address at 16th and Alcott in 1905. Western Pottery Manufacturing Company remained at that address until they went out of business in 1936. Western Pottery Manufacturing Company produced crocks, kitchen items, flower pots and other stoneware items. Their line consisted of 186 items in 1926. The firm was probably Colorado's largest manufacturer of commercial stoneware. (Information: Tom Turnquist, research writer on potters and potteries. Mark: on stoneware jar.)

Western Reserve Pottery, and also the **Brewer Pottery and Clay Manufacturing Company.** The Western Reserve Pottery in Warren, Ohio, was in business from 1898 to around 1906. This pottery made stoneware "Common Sense" washboards as their specialty. They also made jardinieres, teapots, water bottles, hanging baskets, match safes and other novelties from glazed pottery. There was no known trademark except the lettering on the washboard as shown. Marcia Ray, as cited, said the washboard was reddish brown to molasses colored clay, but not Rockingham ware. The

Brewer Pottery and Clay Manufacturing Company of Warren, Ohio, which operated from 1898 until after 1900, also made stoneware washboards, but their specialty was the Brewer Patent Vent Jug. At the point where the handle joined the neck there was an air passage passing into the larger part of the neck through the center of the handle into the jug where the handle joined the jug. When the jug was emptied it made a constant steady stream with no splashing. The jug was patented by William Brewer, who founded the pottery. (Information: Grace C. Allison, researcher and writer on potteries by letter. Mark: printing on washboard pictured in Marcia Ray, *Collectible Ceramics*, p. 241.)

The Common Sense Wash Board
RUB LIGHTLY
It WILL DO the WORK WITH Less Rubbing
then any other Board made
BY
THE WESTERN RESERVE POTTERY CO.

Western Stoneware Company. Monmouth, Illinois. 1906 to 1985. In April 1906, seven small potteries were merged for form Western Stoneware Company. The seven potteries that formed Western Stoneware in 1906 were **Weir Pottery** at 521 West Sixth Avenue, also in Monmouth, Illinois; **Monmouth Pottery Company** at South Third and East Fifth Avenue, Monmouth, Illinois; **Macomb Stoneware Company** at Campbell and Dudley Streets and **Macomb Pottery Company** at the junction of Piper Street and the CB & Q RR tracks, both in Macomb, Illinois; the **D. Culbertson Stoneware Company** in Whitehall, Illinois; **Clinton Stoneware Company** in Clinton, Missouri, and **Fort Dodge Stoneware Company** of Fort Dodge, Iowa. See various listing for history and marks for these potteries. D. Culbertson Stoneware Company in Whitehall, Illinois, seems not to have used a mark involving the name, ''Culbertson.'' Jim Martin, co-author of *Monmouth Western Stoneware*, says no specimens have been found yet with that name. The Culbertson plant was operated until 1916 when it stood idle until it was sold in 1923.

In 1906, Western Stoneware issued no catalog in their first year of production, but they made items in a whiteware clay body with relief trim in Delft blue according to a *Spinning Wheel* article, staff written, ''Old Sleepy Eye,'' January, February 1965, p. 18. The success of the Western Stoneware Company is due in large part to the high quality clay available in Colchester, Illinois.

Stoneware made from this unusual clay is conventional and radar oven heat-resistant, provides superior retention of either heat or cold, and is lead-free, making it completely safe for use with all foods and drink. Western Stoneware Company made a heavy set of dishes made around 1967 bearing the maple leaf mark. The glaze has a beautiful appearance on the pieces because each piece is hand-dipped and the glaze is heavily applied. The company supplied the name ''Mojavi'' for these dishes and added that all dinnerware manufacture was discontinued by Western Stoneware, January 1, 1975. Products were also made for Marshall Burns, Division of Technicolor, a distributor from Chicago, with the Marshall Burns trademark, ''Marcrest.'' Many companies manufactured for Marshall Burns. Marcrest, made at Western Stoneware Company, was an old fashioned oven

proof stoneware, warm brown finish, including a candleflame casserole, 48 ounce size, mugs in two sizes, pitchers in four sizes, dinner plates, lunch plates, saucers, cereal bowls, nested mixing bowls in three sizes, creamer, sugar with a lid, salt and pepper, cookie jar, bean pot, candle holder, ramekins, four inch desserts, a range set, a divided vegetable bowl and a coffee carafe or water jug. In the *American Kitchen and Dinner Wares* book, I had the addresses for the Weir Pottery and Monmouth Pottery turned around because that was the way they were sent to me from the factory.

Barber listed the products of Western Stoneware Company as all kinds of stoneware, and around 1900 they used the mark of two men in a huge stoneware container that looked like a barrel. Western Stoneware suffered major fires which destroyed many records of the company. The company is well known for the premiums made for the Sleepy Eye Milling Company early in the Sleepy Eye Company's history. The ''Flaming Blue'' bowl is one of the first stoneware premiums made by Western Stonewre for Sleepy Eye (company information). See Sleepy Eye Milling Company listing. In 1985, Western Stoneware Company ceased operations. A group of local residents took it over after the shut down and renamed the company **De Novo Ceramics, Ltd.** For a detailed history of each plant and what was made there, see Jim Martin and Bette Cooper, *Monmouth Western Stoneware*, pp. 41-47.

(Marks: no. 1 filed for registration by Western Stoneware Company on January 8, 1948, claiming use since January 30, 1913, for vases, bowls, pitchers, console sets, pots, jardinieres, baskets and ornamental pots. No. 2, stamped on bottom of Sleepy Eye pitcher in Don and Carol Raycraft, *Decorated Country Stoneware*, p. 45; no. 3, Deb and Gini Johnson, *Beginners Books of Pottery*, p. 107; nos. 4-8, these marks were found on the heavy ''Mojavi'' dishes, made around 1967; no. 9, the Eva Zeisel logo or mark shown was in various directories of the 1950's. I don't know exactly how it was used; no. 10, mark sent by Bette Cooper, 32 year employee of Western Stoneware Company and was found on the bottom of a recent bowl; no. 11, mark sent by Dave Newkirk, author of *Red Wing Dinnerware*. I was surprised to find that mark 12 was filed for registration November 1, 1909 because it was used as late as 1967 in very slightly different forms. No. 12 is the copy as it was filed. The rest of the marks were either sent by letters from Jim Martin or Bette Cooper or may be seen in their book, *Monmouth Western Stoneware*, as cited.)

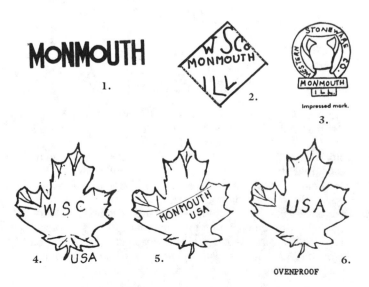

1. MONMOUTH

2. W S Co / MONMOUTH / ILL

3. STONEWARE / WESTERN / CO. / MONMOUTH / ILL.
Impressed mark.

4. W S C / USA

5. MONMOUTH / USA

6. USA
OVENPROOF

OVENPROOF OVENPROOF 8.

9.

OVENPROOF
USA

10.

11.

12.

13.

14.

15.

16.

17.

18.

Westerwald Pottery formerly **Barnyard Pottery.** Brownsville, Pennsylvania. Studio potter, Phil Schaltenbrand started around 1975. He makes primarily cobalt decorated stoneware. Phil is a teacher, and he introduced a course at California State College in folk pottery of Southwestern Pennsylvania. He has written a book entitled *Old Pots*, widely used by this author. The book deals with the old stoneware of potters of the Greensboro, New Geneva region in Pennsylvania. See bibliography for information. The impressed mark shown was used by Phil on pieces made before 1975. From 1975 to 1987 he also signs and dates each piece. He has done numerous one man and group shows.

Westinghouse Electric Corporation. See Pittsburgh High Voltage Insulator Company for early beginning history. In addition to the old Pittsburg HVI Company plant in Derry, Pennsylvania, which operated until 1953, Westinghouse built a plant in Everyville, California, in 1923 which operated until 1944. Westinghouse made a complete line of well designed pin type insulators in these plants. The Westinghouse mark as shown had many slight variations; some had catalog numbers, some were ink stamped and some were incuse. (Information and marks: Tod, *Porcelain Insultors Guide book for Collectors*, pp. 139, 140.)

Westmoore Pottery. Seagrove, North Carolina. 1977 to present (1986). David R. Farrell and Mary Farrell make salt glazed handthrown stoneware and redware or earthenware functional pieces in the style of the 18th and 19th century, American and European potters. David received a B.S. degree in 1973 from the State University of New York at Plattsburgh, where he studied ceramics. He attended the University of Vermont in 1975 to continue studying ceramics. He worked for George Scatchard of Scatchard Stoneware in Underhill, Vermont, for six months in 1975. In 1976, he apprenticed at Jugtown Pottery in Seagrove, North Carolina, and also that year he toured potteries in England for three weeks. In 1976 and 1977 he worked in Beekmantown, New York, with Bill Klock, a potter who studied at the Bernard Leach Pottery.

In the fall of 1977, he established the Westmoore Pottery with Mary Livingstone (now Mrs. Farrell). Mary has a B.A. degree in fine arts from Weslyan University in Middletown, Connecticut. She is an art major who specialized in ceramics and won departmental honors in 1976. She also worked at Jugtown Pottery in the summer of 1975 and was an apprentice there in 1977 before she and David opened their pottery. More then 30 important exhibits, honors and awards were listed for Westmoore Pottery between 1977 and the present, and I'm sure this was only a partial list. Only a few can be included here.

Exhibits include: "Traditional Crafts: Functional Folk Art by Contemporary Craftspeople," Mansfield Art Center, Mansfield, Ohio, June 17-July 22, 1979; Duke University Perkins Library, Durham, North Carolina, March 1980; Carthage Library, Carthage, North Carolina, Spring 1980; Traditional Potters of the Southeast," held by the Smithsonian Insitute in conjunction with the 1981 Folklife Festival, Washington, D.C., July 1981; "Folkcraft Exhibition," at Durham YWCA, sponsored by Durham Technical Institute, Durham, North Carolina, October 1981; Three North Carolina Folk Potters," Folk Craft Gallery, Portland, Oregon, July 1982;

"Wooster Show of Functional Ceramics: A Ten Year Retrospective," traveling exhibit out of Wooster, Ohio, 1983; "Juried Exhibition of North Carolina Crafts," North Carolina Museum of History, Raleigh, North Carolina, March 18 through June 30, 1983; "Southern Traditional Pottery," by Smithsonian Institute, Washington, D.C., in the summer of 1984. It traveled to Mint Museum of History, Charlotte, North Carolina, in the fall of 1984, and Greensboro Historical Museum, Greensboro, North Carolina, in the spring of 1985; North Carolina State University Craft Center, Raleigh, North Carolina, November 12-13, 1983; Davidson County History Museum, Lexington, North Carolina, fall of 1984; Historic Cherry Hill, Inez, North Carolina, October 29 through November 11, 1984; Rocky Mount Art Center, Rocky Mount, North Carolina, December 2-28, 1984; "Clay: Everyday Plus Sunday," John Michael Kohler Art Center, Sheboygans, Wisconsin; "Second Juried Exhibition of North Carolina Crafts," North Carolina Museum of History, Raleigh, North Carolina, April 4 through June 30, 1986.

Writings and publicity about Westmore Pottery include: *Ceramics Monthly*, 1979; featured on "PM Magazine," CBS affiliate, Greensboro, North Carolina, 1979; chapter on Westmoore Pottery included in book *Raised in Clay* by Nancy Sweezy, 1984; and chapter on Westmoore Pottery to be included in book of North Carolina potters by Dr. Leonidas Betts, professor at North Carolina State University, Raleigh, North Carolina. Special honors include: Westmoore Pottery was selected as one example of North Carolina crafts, used to decorate the Governor of North Carolina's office, December 1980-January 1981; served as master craftsmen to National Endowment for the Arts apprenticeship grant recipient Daniel Marley, February 1983 to June 1983. (Marks: no. 1, "Westmoore," was used before 1985; no. 2, "Westmoore Pottery," is in use now. Most items are dated and have the name of the maker inside as shown.)

WESTMOORE
1.

WESTMOORE POTTERY 2.

Weston, D. Ellenville, New York. 1829 to 1848 (Stewart and Consentino, p. 126). Made stoneware. (Mark: impressed; Stewart and Consentino, p. 70; William C, Ketchum, Jr., "Decorative Techniques in American Stoneware," *Antiques Journal*, April 1979, p. 24.)

**D. WESTON
ELLENVILLE, N.Y.**

West Troy Pottery. West Troy, New York. Around 1863 to around 1899. The following stoneware potters worked in the West Troy Pottery at various times: **George Seymour** from 1863 to 1867. See the listing of Various Seymour Potters. In 1867, A.J. and J.L. Russell purchased the West Troy Pottery from George Seymour. They operated until 1879 when the pottery was sold to Daniel Shepley who was first listed in the *West Troy Directory* in 1879 at 14-16 Schenectady Street. From 1880 to 1883 he had a partner, Robert Fleming and the listing was **Shepley and Fleming**. In 1884 to 1896 the name was **Shepley and Smiths**. There were two Smiths, Lewis W. and Frank B. who were in business with Shepley

(and records record the name as Smiths, with an "s" on the end). In 1897, the pottery was owned by Lewis W. Smith and Lysander Luther, and called **Smith and Luther**. In 1897, Shepley had quit to run a saloon at 1285 Broadway. These potters all used the mark, "West Troy Pottery," but some may have also used their own names as did Shepley and Smith. In 1898, John L. Russell took control of the pottery again, then closed it completely in 1899. (Information: Warren F. Broderick, writer, researcher and collector. Mark: Thorn, p. 147. Mr. Broderick thought there probably should be an "s" on the end of the mark shown in Thorn, because of the way the name is encountered in various accounts and records.)

**SHEPLEY & SMITH (s)
WEST TROY
N. Y.**

West Virginia Dealers and General Stores. In West Virginia, more than any other state I have discovered so far, it was fashionable to have pottery crocks, jars, etc. with the name of the dealer or general store. These are all very old gray stoneware with blue stamped or hand lettering and generally are decorated. These jars seem to be very much in the style of the Hamilton and Jones ware, but I do not know who made them all. I loved the Hayman crock, that dealer told it all on one crock! Jackson Court House became part of Ripley. As late as 1922 there was a Proctor Merchandise Company listed in Proctor, West Virginia. At that time, there were seven businesses listed and four of them were general stores for a population of 265 people. In the *Tri State Trader*, April 4, 1981, a crock for Michael Moore General Store of Proctorville, Ohio, was reported as having sold in a sale.

**W W ROGERS
PROCTOR
W. VA.**

**DAN MERCER
WARE
PARKERSBURG
W. VA.**

**W.T. HAYMAN
DEALER IN
DRY GOODS
GROCER
NOTIONS
HATS
BOOTS
SHOES
HARDWARE
LETANT, W. VA.**

**M.+A.J. MOORE
GENERAL
STORE
PROCTOR
WETZEL CO., W. VA.**

**GRAHAM & STONE
GEN' MERCHANDISE
JACKSON C.H
W. VA.**

T.J. Wheatley and Company. Cincinnati, Ohio. See the Dayton Street/Coultry Pottery listing for the early work of T.J. Wheatley in Cincinnati, Ohio. Wheatley was also involved with the Cincinnati Art Pottery Company. (See that listing.) In April 1880 Wheatley opened his own pottery at 23 Hunt Street in Cincinnati where he did all of the work himself at first. He prepared the clay, made the molds, glazed, fired and decorated the pieces. Wheatley made Cincinnati faience decorated in the style of Limoges. He used mostly yellow clay from the area for the body. Then by the end of 1880 he was employing four artists and making good sales to Tiffany and

Company. The Cincinnati Art Pottery was formed in 1879 and incorporated in 1880 to give Wheatley and his students more financing. The name Cincinnati Art Pottery was not generally used until T.J. Wheatley was no longer associated with the pottery in 1882. The name T.J. Wheatley and Company continued to be used until then. In 1882, Wheatley built a pottery at the Covington end of the Suspension Bridge in Cincinnati which was destroyed by flood in 1884. After that time Wheatley seems not to have been associated with any pottery until he worked for Weller around 1897. Also around 1900 he went on to form the Wheatley Pottery Company. (See that listing.) (Information: Paul Evans, *Art Pottery of U.S.*, pp. 331-336 and 66, 67. Incised mark: Evans, as cited, p. 334.)

Wheatley Pottery Company. Cincinnati, Ohio. For the early history of T.J. Wheatley, see the listing for Coultry Pottery, the Cincinnati Art Pottery and the T.J. Wheatley Pottery Company. In 1903, T.J. Wheatley and Isaac Kahn, established the Wheatley Pottery Company which operated until 1927 under that name making art pottery with colored matt glazes over relief design, also garden ware and archectural items. In 1927, Cambridge Tile Manufacturing Company of Covington, Kentucky, purchased the pottery and named it Wheatley Tile and Pottery Company. The Cincinnati Building was idled in 1930 and the operation was transferred to Hartwell, Ohio. Also in 1927, a selling firm was organized Cambridge-Wheatley Company. All of the operations were dissolved by 1936. (Information: Paul Evans, *Art Pottery of the United States*, p. 335-337. Marks: no. 1, Evans, p. 336; no. 2, from copyright report filed June 10, 1921, claiming use since December 1, 1879, for pottery ware made from burned clay, glazed and unglazed.)

WHEATLEY

Wheeler, E.H. "The Potter at Strawbery Banke." Portsmouth, New Hampshire. E.H. Wheeler started in the full time making of high-fired traditional stoneware for use in the home in 1977 as the **Weathervane Stoneware** in Rye, New Hampshire. He moved to his present location in 1979. He also makes artistic pieces for exhibits or on commission basis, such as special orders, etc. On small pieces he puts his initials as shown. On other larger articles he signs Wheeler and the date. Formerly an oceanographer teaching at Stanford, University in New Hampshire, he went on to study in workshops under the various influences of Michael Casson, Michael Cardew, and Karen Karnes. He had pieces selected to represent "Crafts from New Hampshire" in an exhibition at the Renwick Gallery of the Smithsonian National Museum, among his many honors.

EHW   Wheeler 1982

Wheeler, Stu. Dayton, Ohio. 1980 to present (1983). Studio potter who has been making stoneware functional pieces since finishing college in 1973; turned professional in 1980. The numbers found with this potters marks signify the time of production, or how long it took him to make it, and the starting weight off the clay used, as he signified by explanation in parenthesis.

S. Wheeler .2/1.0 (← Time 30 min.) (1.lb. → Starting Wt.)

Wheeling Decorating Company. Market Street in Wheeling, West Virginia. 1905-1960's. They used several marks that might be mistaken for those used by the Wheeling Potteries Company which was out of business before 1910. Wheeling Decorating Company listed in business as late as 1962 in the *West Virginia Manufacturing Directory*, decorating china and glassware. In the 1954 Directory Issue of the *Crockery and Glass Journal*, six different sales outlets were listed for products of the company. (Information: Lehner, *American Kitchen and Dinner Wares*, p. 168. Marks: no. 1, 1954 *Crockery and Glass Journal Directory*; no. 2, sent by Lola Sealy.)

1.

2.

Wheeling Pottery Company and **Associated Companies.** Wheeling, West Virginia. "The Wheeling Pottery Company of Wheeling, West Virginia, made plain and decorated white granite and was organized in November 1879. In 1887, a second company was formed under the same management and called La Belle Pottery Company which made "Adamantine china, plain and decorated, and in 1889 . . . the two companies were consolidated." (Barber, *Marks of American Potters*, p. 149; also *Pottery and Porcelain of the U.S.*, p. 308.) Barber also stated that "on January 1, 1903, the Wheeling Potteries Company was organzied by combining the Wheeling, La Belle, Riverside and Avon Potteries, each of which is now a department of the former." At this time, he stated, the potteries were making utilitarian pottery, semi-porcelain, sanitary wares and artware in the various factories, with each designated to make certain products. Then in 1909, the name of the Wheeling Potteries Company was changed to the

Wheeling Sanitary Manufacturing Company. From the *American Ceramic Society Bulletin*, XX, "Notes for Ceramists," (on Charles Franzheim), May 1941, p. 186, is the following quote:

"When the Wheeling Pottery Company was organized in 1879 in what is known as the "old Wheeling Pottery," it was operated with five kilns and employed about 150 men. At first, only white granite ware or "Queensware," as it is more commonly known, was manufactured. Three or four years later, however, it began to decorate the ware, and in 1904, the plant was making everything from common sanitary ware to the finest china and was employing about 1,200 persons. Although the plant was not the largest in number of kilns, the decorating departments employed a greater number of persons than any similar institution in the country. There were four plants, with 27 biscuit and glost kilns and 20 decorating kilns. Their production covered a wide range of ware, semi-granite (or "C.C"), white granite and semi-porcelain and a line of highly decorated faience ware and sanitary goods. The building, known as the La Belle Pottery, on the South Side, was built in 1889, and the Ohio Valley China Company plant in North Wheeling, now known as the Riverside, was acquired in 1900. A little later, the Tiltonsville, Ohio, plant was added to the Company. C. Merts Franzheim, the eldest son of Charles Franzheim, was assistant general manager in 1904, with direct supervision over the Wheeling and La Belle plants. He spent two years at the ceramic school of the Ohio State University and one year in Germany, at one of the celebrated pottery schools in that country. The Wheeling Pottery Company was the first to make extensive use of the casting process in this country, which was directly due to the continental experience and the assistance given by Rudolph Gaertner."

The *History of West Virginia, Old and New*, published by the American Historical Society, Inc., 1923, p. 465, stated that the Wheeling Potteries Company went into receivership in 1910 with a Mr. Wright, who had been the president of the company, appointed as receiver. He reorganized the company and put them on a profitable basis making sanitary ware under the name of the **Wheeling Sanitary Manufacturing Company**. In 1923, when the history already mentioned was written, The Wheeling Sanitary Manufacturing Company was still operating three of the four plants which had made up the Wheeling Potteries Company. Two were in Wheeling and the other plant was in Tiltonsville. According to an article in the *Antique Trader Annual of Articles*, by Pamela Coates entitled "Wheeling Potteries Company," Vol. IV, 1975, p. 228, she states that the La Belle and Wheeling Pottery plants were operating at capacity right up to the time of reorganization, but that they had been losing money for some years. "Flow Blue" ware was made at Wheeling, as well as tankards, "Virginia Girl" plates, jardinieres, cracker jars, children's items and full lines of dinnerware. Cracker jars are a favorite with collectors.

In the *1902-1903 Complete Directory*, Wheeling Pottery Company was listed as operating the following plants making the goods listed: **Avon Faience Company**, making high grade artware; the **Riverside Pottery**, making sanitary ware; the **Wheeling Pottery Company**, making semi-porcelain, white granite and common china dinner sets, toilet sets, short sets of odd dishes, jardinieres and decorated novelties. (Information: Lehner, *American Kitchen and Dinner Wares*, pp. 168, 169. Marks: All of the marks that follow are for the Wheeling Pottery Company. See the listing Wheeling Potteries Company for that mark. Also, see the listing, Avon Faience Company for a mark used while Avon Faience was part of Wheeling Potteries Company. Mark nos. 1-4 are all copies of the

same mark. Barber, *Marks of American Potters*, p. 150, said this mark was used around 1888 to 1893 on semi-porcelain. No. 1 was a Ramsay, p. 284, mark. I show it here to illustrate the point in the introduction that the artist can lose the look of the original mark by making it too nice! No. 2 is from Hartman, p. 122. No. 3 is from Barber, p. 150. No. 4, copy machine copy of old ironstone bowl. The Ramsay mark is dated 1886 and the Hartman mark 1856. Hartman is obviously wrong, but that still makes Barber's approximate dates of use incorrect, unless Ramsay, is in error, also. No. 4, my mark on dish has to be authentic, and we know it was used before 1903 when Wheeling Pottery Company became the Wheeling Potteries Company. Nos. 5, 6, 7, are the same mark. No. 5, from Hartman, p. 122. No. 6 is from Ramsay, p. 284, and no. 7 is from Barber, p. 149. Here we see Ramsay's artist left out the outline of the United States from the globe. Nos. 8, 9, 10, Barber, p. 150, dated these marks between 1888 to 1893. Nos. 11, 12 are the same mark. We couldn't get a good enlarged copy of this mark from Barber, so we attempt to draw one, and as I said, each artist changes the mark a little. No. 13, on dish. The remainder of the marks are from Barber, pp. 150, 151.)

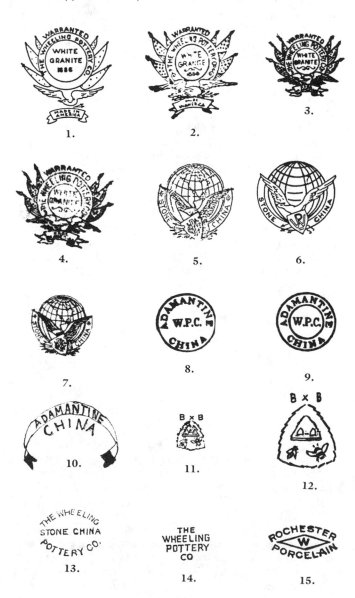

1.   2.   3.

4.   5.   6.

7.   8.   9.

10.   11.   12.

13.   14.   15.

16.

17.

18.

19.

20.

21.

Wheeling Potteries Company. See Wheeling Pottery Company for history. See Avon Faience for mark and information also.

Wheeling Tile Company. Wheeling, West Virginia. Company was organized by Samuel O. Laughlin in 1913. They purchsed two of the old Wheeling Pottery Company's buildings at the corner of Chapline and 32nd Streets and also one block down at LaBelle and 32nd. For a time around 1919 to 1924 the company made some electrical porcelain. After 1924 they made white wall tile with colored glazes. They were still operating in 1944, but I have no real ending date for them. Some beautiful hand painted tiles did come from this company unless some artist just used the tile to paint upon. In the article by Danny Brown, as cited, is a scene signed Hayward with house, trees etc. The one "Wheeling" tile I hve found is white clay glazed tan to yellow with a big decal of flowers over the glaze. (Information: Everett Townsend, "Development of the Tile Industry in the U.S.," *American Ceramic Society Bulletin*, May 1943, p. 144, 145. Mark: no. 1, Danny Brown, Constructing a Collection Tile by Tile," *American Clay Exchange*, April 1983, p. 4. the A.L. Hayward was artists signature on front. Wheeling incised on back. No. 2 on tile.)

WHEELING

A. L. Hayward

WHEELING

CUSHION

Wheelock Pottery. Peoria, Illinois. 1888 to 1971. The business was begun by C.E. Wheelock and Son in 1888, and at first they made all of their own pottery which was a utilitarian type, typical of Illinois's early potteries, in the form of jugs, mugs, crocks, etc. They got into retailing as well as pottery making as the years went along, and they began to import china which was sold under the Wheelock name. In 1971, Fred C. Bodtke, who owned the business at that time, closed it and went into the investment business. A pitcher with a lid and nicely decorated with a basket of flowers was found. The company sold a great deal of commemorative and souvenir ware. (Marks: no. 1 was filed for registration June

12, 1914, claiming use since August 1, 1898, for use on crockery, earthenware, porcelain, namely, plates, cups and saucers, dishes, chamber sets, dinner sets, tea sets, cooking and baking utensils, jars, jugs, pitchers, bowls. Nos. 2, 3, are photostatic copies of marks. No. 4 is a gold paper label found on little decorative vase.)

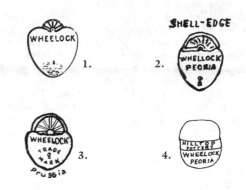

1.

2.

3.

4.

F.J. White and Son Pottery/Denver Art Pottery. Denver, Colorado. Frederick J. White and his son, Francis, established a pottery in Denver in 1893 or 1894 and operated as F.J. White and Son to make jugs, flower pots, Rockingham type teapots and yellow bowls, using Colorado buff clay. By 1909 they were making art pottery, and the name of the firm became the Denver Art Pottery. The plant was moved to several loctions in Denver over the years, and around 1910, F.G. White hoped to establish a pottery in Oklahoma City but was not successful. Frederick died in 1919, and Francis worked on alone until the mid 1950's. Francis died in 1960. The pottery made vases, lamp bases and jardinieres called "Gray Ware," or "Denver Gray Ware." They made a swirled clay line similar to Niloak's Mission ware. A wide range of monochrome glazes were used on pieces. Early work was incised "Denver," with a little "w" in the "D." The impressed "White Denver" mark was used after 1910. Many pieces were dated up to 1920. Much was left unmarked, including all dinner ware. (Information and marks: Paul Evans, *Art Pottery of the U.S.*, pp. 338, 339.)

White
Denver

Denver

White Cloud Farms. Rock Tavern, New York. Before 1928 to after 1932. This pottery was one of the most interesting to write about. I would give a great deal to have the whole story. Information was very scarce. The listing in the 1931 and 1932 Newburgh, New York (close to Rock Tavern) directories was for the White Cloud Farms, fruit growers, poultry raisers and pottery manufacturers on Rough Ride Road, N.W., with post office Rock Tavern Route 1. They were not listed in those directories before or after those two years. With that listing the surprise came with the nude fully sculptured figure attached on the outside of a drinking glass which was patented August 23, 1928. In May and September of the same year, marks 1 and 2 were filed for registration. No doubt, mark 2 was used on the drinking glass, because as the drinker emptied the glass, the nude lady's figure matched the mark! The marks were filed by Will Low Bacher and assigned to White Cloud Farms. Mark 3 was attributed to the White Cloud Farms at the American Ceramic Society's Ross Purdy Museum. It seems fitting since the mark looks like an apple, and an orchard was associated with the pottery.

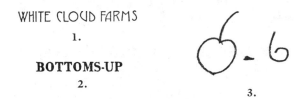

WHITE CLOUD FARMS
1.

BOTTOMS-UP
2.

3.

White Dog Pottery. Northampton, Massachusetts. 1977 to present. Jane E. Hillman, a studio potter, makes one of a kind porcelain pieces and dinnerware of blue and white multi-colored spongeware and handpainted birds in pastel colors. Jane studied ceramics at Alfred University, New York School of Ceramics, Alfred, New York and received a B.F.A. degree in 1972. In 1976, she shared a studio with David Halsey, Salt Potter, Leverett, Massachusetts. In late 1976 and early 1977 Jane had her own studio in Whately, Massachusetts. This very talented potter listed 44 galleries in New York, Massachusetts, Arizona, Ohio, Vermont, New Jersey, Florida, South Carolina, Washington and Maryland where her work has been displayed. Her work is also in private collections in Paris, London, Zurick, Montreal, New York, Kansas City and San Francisco among many places. She has instructed pottery making at Belvoir Terrace Fine Arts Center, Lenox, Massachusetts, also at Leverett Craftsman and Artists, Leverett, Massachusetts, and at her White Dog Pottery.

JANE 81

White, Fr. Jim, S.J. Kansas City, Missouri. 1973 to present (1984). Makes functional and artistic wheel thrown pottery of stoneware and porcelain. Also makes coil, slab and extruded clay pieces fired to cone 10. Father White mixes his own glazes. He has taught pottery at Rockhurst High School, since 1972, and does some commission work on his own. He has front yard sales at the school to sell students' pieces and also has a display case in the high school. He is currently making gray colored utilitarian pieces with a tea leaf design painted in blue. Mark is stamp showing name. Most pieces are dated.

J. WHITE, S.J.

White Hall Pottery Works/Ruckel Pottery. White Hall, Illinois. 1870 to around 1960. The pottery was founded by A.D. Ruckel in 1870. Mr. Ruckel lived in Akron, Ohio, before coming to White Hall. He was a master mechanic in the Railroad shops in Dayton, Ohio, for years. His abilities were used to modernize the pottery making process in his factory. C.A. Ruckel, son of A.D., was in charge of the pottery by 1926 and the name was A.D. Ruckel and Son. By 1926 all ware was made with molds. Janice Tauer Wass, curator of Decorative Arts at Illinois State Museum, said the pottery was believed to be in operation until about 1960. (Information: R.B. Pearce, "One Hundred Years of Clay Products at White Hall, Illinois," written for Illinois Chamber of Commerce, a pamphlet distributed by A.D. Ruckel and Son Pottery in 1926. Marks: no. 1 on beautiful sky blue stoneware bow. No. 2 was sent by Doris and Burdell Hall, authors of *Morton's Potteries: 99 Years.*)

RUCKEL'S POTTERY
1870
WHITE HALL
ILL.

RUCKEL'S
POTTERY
WHITE HALL
ILLINOIS

White Hall Sewer Pipe and Stoneware Company. White Hall, Illinois. 1866 to 1953. The pottery was started in 1866 to make drain tile, sewer pipe, brick, etc. and in 1901 stoneware and specialties were added to their line of ware. In 1903, a new building was built following a bad fire. The pottery closed in 1953, according to Janice T. Wass, curator at the Illinois State Museum. (Information: Bateman and Selby, *Historical Encyclopedia of Illinois and History of McDonough County*, Volume 2, pp. 617-1055. Marks: no. 1 filed January 6, 1936, claiming use since June 7, 1934 for pottery, ant guards, basins, baskets, bean pots, bowls, casseroles, chambers, churns, combinettes, creamers, cups, cuspidors, ewers, flower holders, flower pots, flower pot saucers, hanging baskets, jardinieres, jars, jugs, kegs, pans, pepper shakers, pitchers, plates, salt shakers, saucers, spittoons, steins, sugars, teapots, heat insulated jug liners, tumblers, urns, vases, wall pockets. No. 2 from Don and Carol Raycraft, *Decorated Country Stoneware*, p. 62, on a stoneware poultry fountain and on a handled jar with lid.)

ILLINI
POTTERY
WHITE HALL, ILL.
1.

2.
S P & S
C O
WHITE
HALL
ILL.

Whiteman, T.W. Perth Amboy, New Jersey. Around 1963. Made stoneware utilitarian pieces with impressed mark. (Information and mark: John Ramsay, p. 285; and Thorn, p. 155.)

T. W. WHITEMAN

White Mountain Pottery. Ruidosa, New Mexico. Operating at present (1983). Timothy Wierville, owner, is a studio potter making hand thrown functional stoneware fired to cone 10 or 2,350 degrees. His mark is a combination of his initials. (Information and mark: Dorothy Pryse, "White Mountain Pottery," *American Clay Exchange*, June 1982, p. 4.)

White's Pottery. Utica, New York. 1834-1910. Noah White was first in the family to make pottery in Utica. In 1834, he was listed as one of the stoneware makers at the Samuel H. Addington Pottery. He also worked as an agent for Addington. In 1839, Noah White bought out Addington's Pottery and another factory adjacent to it. Noah's son, Nicholas A. and two more potters made wares marked "N. White." In 1843, William White, another of Noah's sons became part of business. In 1849 he made both sons partners and the name became **N. White and Sons**. After 1856 we got the mark **N. White and Son** because William White sold his share in 1856 and went to Utica, Illinois. In 1863, Noah's grandson, William N. White came into the firm and the name became **Noah White, Son and Company**. Wares made 1850-1870's were marked "White Utica" or "White's Utica." In 1865, Noah died. Nicholas A. White continued under name **N.A. White and Company** in 1866. In 1867, it was **N.A. White and Son** when William N. White became a partner. During the 1870's the plant was expanded, and molds and steam powered kick wheels were introduced in the factory. From 1876 to 1882 the mark was "Whites, Utica, N.Y." In 1882, Nicholas A. White's younger son Charles N. White was made a partner and the mark was "N.A. White and Son, Utica, N.Y." The last owner was Charles N. White. The name was called the **Central New York Pottery** from 1890 to 1899, and then until the closing it was called **Whites Pottery, Inc.** By 1907 the manufacture of stoneware had stopped. The firm was called **C.N. White Clay Products Company**. It was closed in 1910. (Information: Barbara Fanco, "Stoneware made by the White Family in Utica, N.Y.," Stradling book, pp. 134, 135. Marks: Guilland, pp. 102, 103; Stradling, p. 136; Stewart and Consentino, pp. 63, 69.)

WHITE'S UTICA, N.Y.

WHITES. UTICA

N.A. WHITE & SON
UTICA, N.Y.

N.A. WHITE & SON
UTICA, N.Y.

WHITES, UTICA

N.A. WHITE & CO. BINGHAMTON

White and Wood. Binghamton, New York. 1883 to 1887. Charles N. White (also a partner in White Pottery after 1882) and George L. Wood made stoneware. (Information: Barbara Franco, "Stoneware Made by the White Family in Utica, New York," Stradling book, pp. 134, 135. Marks: Lura Woodside Watkins, "The ABC's of American Pottery," *The Antiques Book*, edited by Alice Winchester, p. 48.)

WHITE & WOOD
BINGHAMTON, N.Y.

Whitman, J.M. Havana, New York. Around 1860. Made stoneware utilitarian jugs, etc. with cobalt blue decorations. Mark impressed. (Information: Stewart and Consentino, p. 126.)

J. M. WHITMAN
HAVANA, N.Y.

Whitmore, Robinson & Company. See Johnson, Whitmore & Company.

Whittemore, A.O. Havana, New York. 1869 to around 1893. Made stoneware utilitarian pottery, jugs, etc. with cobalt blue decorations. Mark impressed. (Information: Stewart and Consentino, *Stoneware*, p. 126; crock with mark pictured in same book, p. 80. There is also an artist's drawing of a jug by this potter in Guilland, *Early Americn Folk Pottery*, p. 204. However, the artist spelled Havana as "Gavana.")

A.O. WHITTEMORE
HAVANA, N.Y.

Wick China Company. Located in Wickboro, Pennsylvania. 1899-1913. Wickboro was consolidated into the town of Kittanning on December 29, 1919. Wick China Company was first organized as the **Wick Chinaware Company** in 1889, and it was purchased by W.S. George in 1913 or 1914, then operated as one of his plants under his name. In J.H. Beer and Company's *History of Armstrong County, Pennsylvania,* Philadelphia; 1914, p. 128, is stated that Wick China produced the finest grades of tableware, plain and decorated jardinieres and ornamental vases. They used clay from England and Florida and a little from Pennsylvania. In the 1895 *Factory Inspection Report for Pennsylvania,* Wick China was listed as employing 163 people to make ironstone and decorated ware. By 1900, they employed 263 people. They were a leading producer of Tea Leaf China. This plant was operated by W.S. George until sometime after 1935. (See W.S. George.) (Information: Lehner, *American Kitchen and Dinner Wares,* p. 170. Marks: no. 1, attributed to Wick China by Annise Heaivilin, *Grandma's Tea Leaf,* p. 209; no. 2, Barber, *Marks of American Potters,* p. 35.)

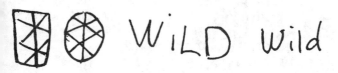

Wickham, Nancy. New York State. Nancy, a studio potter, started making pottery in 1942. She was a student at New York State College of Ceramics at Alfred University during the 1943 to 1945 period. Later she was employed as a designer for Design Technique in New York City. In 1947, she opened her own studio in Greenwich Village, and in 1949 she had a studio in Woodstock, Vermont. She was a winner of several national ceramics prizes. Nancy was well known for incised or rubbed designs. (Information and mark: Tom Turnquist, researcher and writer on American pottery. Pieces are signed incised.)

Wild Pottery. Potter Place, New Hampshire. 1971 to present. Sam Wild, studio potter, makes cone 6 stoneware with a matte white glaze with brown and pastel blue brush work of dragon flies, birds, etc. (Most studio potters fire stoneware between cone 4 and cone 11 for hardness, big commercial potteries can go higher.) Sam has a Master's degree from Ohio University, Athens, Ohio. Most of his work is unmarked but some is marked as shown.

Wild Rose Pottery. Victor, Montana. 1978 to present (1983). Donna Roberts, studio potter, makes stoneware and porcelain functional pieces fired to cone 10. Each piece has etching or hand painted designs. This potter works 10 to 14 hours a day and cannot keep up with sales.

Wild Rose Pottery. Bainbridge, Indiana. 1972 to present (1982). Richard Burkett, a studio potter, makes mostly functional stoneware and porcelain at present. Until 1980 he made mostly salt glazed stoneware fired to cone 9-10. Two-thirds of his work at present is porcelain fired to cone 10. Burkett received a B.A. degree in art from Lawrence University, Appleton, Wisconsin in 1973. (Marks 1 and 2 are used on porcelain pieces. The stamps, mark 3, is used on planters and a few other pieces.)

M. Wille, Inc. New York, New York. Filed for registration on July 22, 1965, claiming use since March 1950. "The name "Georges Briard" is fictitious and does not refer to any particular living individual. Owner of registration no. 632,517." For use on china and porcelain ware, namely, casseroles, tea kettles, sauce pans, percolators, canisters, skillets, canape plates, mugs, cake plates, candy dishes, salad bowls, salt and pepper sets, jam jars, serving trays, cup and saucer sets, coffee sets, dishes, double boilers, colanders, dutch ovens, platters and compotes. Company was listed in the *1961 China, Glass and Tableware Directory,* for George Briard designs on glass, wood, ceramic, brass, tile, etc. Mark 2 from same directory.

Williams and Couch. New Geneva, Pennsylvania. This is a mark found on a tall stoneware crock or churn, pictured in Dr. Carmen A. Guappone's book, *New Geneva and Greensboro Pottery*, p. 41. I have found three men by the name of Williams making pottery in New Geneva (see those listings), also three by the name of Couch, namely, John, Rolby and Edward (Schaltenbrand, p. 87), but I can't say which formed the above combination or when. But by 1890, Schaltenbrand tells us there was only one active firm in New Geneva. So if you find this mark, Guappone classes it rare, and it had to be before 1890.

Willets Manufacturing Company. Trenton, New Jersey. 1879 to around 1909. They made white granite, semi-porcelain and porcelain toilet sets and short sets of odd dishes and novelties, as was recorded in the *1902-1903 Complete Directory*. This company used a great variety of marks as shown in Barber's, *Marks of American Potters*, p. 45. He said they also made majolica door knobs, hardware trimmings and electrical goods.

Williamsburg Pottery Factory, Inc. Lightfoot, Virginia. 1939 to present. The pottery was located in Charlottsville, Virginia, from 1937-1941 and then moved to Lightfoot. The Williamsburg Pottery is a licensed manufacturer for the Colonial Williamsburg Foundation of Williamstown, West Virginia. They reproduce or make items similar to 18th century pottery as souvenirs which are stamped with the C.W. hallmark (see mark 1). The articles are sold in the Colonial Williamsburg Foundation craft house and other Williamsburg shops that are authorized by the foundation. They make salt glazed stoneware fired to 2,000 degrees, slipware, sgraffito, into candle holders, mugs, pitchers, cheese jars, bird bottles, pie plates, etc. (Information: from company. Marks: no. 1 was filed for registration on February 25, 1960, claiming use since December 21, 1946, under the name Williamsburg Restoration, Inc., Williamsburg, Virginia, for use on china and pottery tableware and decorative and miscellaneous pieces of china and pottery, including vases, jardinieres, jugs, trays and candelsticks. Mark 2 was from Quality Stamp Company; no. 3 was sent by the factory and is used at present - stamped in clay; no. 4, on attractive little vase with red clay body and variegated colors of glaze; no. 5, stamped mark sent by factory. The word Williamsburg, as seen in no. 6, was filed February 25, 1960, claiming use since December 21, 1946, for the same articles listed under no. 1.)

 1. 2. 3.

4. 5.

6.

Williams, Charles L. New Geneva, Pennsylvania. Started around 1895 to early 1900's. He succeeded R.T. Williams who disappeared on a boat trip on the Monongahela River in 1895. Following Charles L. Williams and his two partners was a potter named Robbins. Robbins completely quit in 1914. I don't know how much of the time before that the pottery was owned by C.L. Williams. Made stoneware. (Information: Schaltenbrand, *Old Pots*, p. 22; Gordon C. Baker, "Pottery of Greensboro and New Geneva, Pennsylvania," *Spinning Wheel*, November, 1973, p. 15. Marks: Guappone, p. 32 and p. 43.)

Williams, Robert T. This potter made stoneware in several potteries in different locations. In 1869, he learned trade at Lettell (mark on crock, Guappone, p. 27) and Company, Greensboro, Pennsylvania; in 1870, he worked at Hamilton and Jones, Greensboro, Pennsylvania; in 1875, he went to Morgantown, West Virginia to be partners with James Thompson; in 1878, he returned to Hamilton and Jones in Greensboro, Pennsylvania; in 1880, he joined John P. Eberhart in New Geneva, Pennsylvania; in 1882, he purchased Alexander Conrad's New Geneva Pottery. (He is not to be confused with W.T. Williams who became partners with Reppert.) (Information: Gordon C. Baker, "Pottery of Greensboro and New Geneva, Pennsylvania," *Spinning Wheel*, November 1973, p. 15. Marks: Guappone, p. 32, 43; and catalogue for Garth's Auction Barn, Inc. November 28, 1969, no page number.

R.T. WILLIAMS
MANUFACTURERS
NEW GENEVA

R.T. WILLIAMS
GREENSBORO, PA.

Willson, T.H. and Company/John Young and Company/William Moyer. Harrisburg, Pennsylvania. Thomas H. Willson and his brother, Daniel, built a stoneware pottery in Harrisburg in 1852. In 1856, they sold the pottery to John Young and Shem Thomas. But in 1858 the Willsons had the pottery back, and it was under the control of William Moyer for a short time. The year 1861 was the last time the Willsons appeared on the tax records for the pottery. (Information and impressed marks: Jeannette Lasansky, *Made of Mud*, pp. 42, 43, 48, 51. There was a variation of the Willson mark shown without the little house but a number 2 was in its place.)

JOHN YOUNG & CO.

JOHN YOUNG & CO.
HARRISBURG, PA.

W.M. MOYER
HARRISBURG, PA.

MOYER, HARRISBURG

T.H WILLSON & CO.
HARRISBURG. PA.

Wilson, Walter. Pasadena, California. Before 1943 until after 1954. In the directories I had, I found this company listed from 1948 to 1954. My next directory was 1961 and the company no longer listed. They were listed for planters, bowls, wall pockets and household ceramics and Chinese figures on planters. In the May 1951 *China, Glass and Decorative Accessories Magazine*, p. 29, Walter Wilson had an advertisement for a cigarette box, two ashtrays in yellow, white and red, with a sculptured white Hibiscus flower on top of the box. In the 1952 *Crockery and Glass Journal Directory* the listing was domestic earthenware figurines. See listing for McCarty Brothers. (Mark: Francis Andrews; found on planter.)

Walter Wilson
Calif

Winart Pottery. Miami, Oklahoma. 1951-1972. David and Clara Arter started the pottery and made coffee mugs, dinnerware and accessory items. The mugs had decaled cattle, Indians, etc. and came in various sizes. The line was expanded as time went on to make planters, pitchers, etc. They maintained a gift shop called the Serendipity Shop with a large selection of imports. In 1972, they stopped making any of the pottery they sold but continued the gift shop. (Information: Jenny B. Derwich and Dr. Mary Latos, *Dictionary Guide to Pottery and Porcelain of the U.S.*, p. 249. Mark sent by Rena London.)

Winart

Winfred Pottery/American Ceramic Products Company. The Winfield Pottery started in 1929 and operated until 1962 in Pasadena, California. The American Ceramic Products Company started in 1935 as La Mirada Potteries to 1967 in Los Angeles, California. Leslie W. Sample started the Winfield Pottery as a studio and clay working school in 1929. From 1935 until his death in 1939, Sample occupied the El Adobe structure. In 1941, Margaret M. Gabriel, a designer, and her husband took over. Then in 1946 the Winfield line of over

450 shapes was licensed to the American Ceramic Products Company. From that time on until closing, Winfield Pottery used the name "Gabriel-Pasadena" on its products because the Winfield name went to the American Ceramic Products Company. In the 1945 and 1946 *Crockery and Glass Journal Directory* the Winfield Pottery was listed for semi-porcelain dinnerware, ovenware and art pottery at 150 W. Union Street.

In 1939, Tom Hamilton purchased La Mirada and renamed it American Ceramic Products Company. By 1940 they were well established and suffered a bad fire, according to Helen E. Stiles, *Pottery in the U.S.*, p. 149. They moved to a new location in 1946, at 1825 Stanford St., Santa Monica, California. Stiles states that bowls and vases were their principal products; the line also included figurines, smoking equipment and fruit bowls with a beautiful glazes off transparent crackle called "La Mirada" ware. Cecil Jones, an Englishman and founder of La Mirada, was responsible for the fine early glazes and shapes developed by this company. In 1946, when the American Ceramic Products Company purchased the right to use the name "Winfield" on pottery pieces and also the use of some of the Winfield Pottery molds the Winfield Pottery continued to operate under the name Winfield, but they started marking their output "Gabriel." Winfield Pottery was willing to sell some of their rights because they had more orders than they could fill in the 1940's.

Winfield Pottery patterns included "Primitive Pony," "Bamboo," "Grape Ovenware," etc. An advertisement in *House Beautiful*, November, 1942, for Winfield's "Bamboo" pattern, described it as "brilliantly glazed semi-porcelain silhouettes, gray-green bamboo leaves against ivory. After five years, it's still making popularity records." Jack Chipman has added a great deal to our knowledge of these two companies in various articles. In October 1983, he and Gary Booth presented a show and a sale of Winfield Pottery. Also, "Winfield Pottery," *American Clay Exchange*, September 1983, pp. 12 to 14, by Chipman, is a comprehensive article which describes many prodcuts, etc. Most of the artware or giftware came from the Winfield-Gabriel facility. When the Japanese imports began to flood the country again, the facility was closed in 1962 and the American Ceramic Products Company didn't last too much longer either. Most items were marked from the factories. A few early Winfield Pottery pieces are incised "L.S." (for Leslie Sample), along with an inscribed date and the impressed "Winfield Pasadena." After 1946 the words, "Gabriel, Pasadena" were used at the Winfield Pottery building. The American Ceramic Products Company used "Winfield Ware" and "Winfield China," printed in ink. (Marks: nos. 1-5, from Jack Chipman, as cited, p. 14. No. 6 was sent by Esther Boyce, collector. Nos. 7, 8 from dishes and nos. 9 and 10 are from various directories.)

Gabriel
420
Pasadena
1.

Winfield
227
Pasadena
2.

Winfield
211
Pasadena
3.

Winfield
Pasadena
70
4.

WINFIELD
194
PASADENA
5.

TRUE PORCELAIN
Winfield
HAND CRAFTED
FINE CHINA
MADE IN USA
6.

HAND CRAFTED
Winfield
CHINA
CALIFORNIA
7.

HANDCRAFT
Winfield China
CALIFORNIA
8.

Winfield
CHINA
9.

Winfield
HANDCRAFT CHINA
10.

Wingender, Charles and Brother. Haddonfield, New Jersey. E.A. Barber, *Marks of American Potters*, p. 69 showed mark 1 stamped on pieces and said the potters made old fashioned German gray stoneware with cobalt blue decorations, also salt glazed ware around 1900. Regina Stewart and Geraldine Consentino in *Stoneware*, p. 126, lists C. Wingender Sr. and Jr. as operating in Haddonfield from 1890 to 1954. (Mark 2 from Thorn, p. 155.)

‹C.W.& BRO.›
1.

HADDONFIELD , N.J.
C. W. & BRO.
2.

Wingender, J. Marlow, Alabama. Around 1910 made Albany slip glazes stoneware. (Information and mark: E. Henry Willett and Joey Brackner, *The Traditional Pottery of Alabama*, p. 66. The mark looked inscribed in the picture but the printing was so even it could have been stamped in.)

J WINGENDER
[MARLOW AL]
2

Wing's Pottery. Dandridge, Tennessee. 1976 to present (1986). Studio potter, Kathy Wing Strandhagen, makes functional stoneware and dinnerware. Kathy wholesales about 70% of what she makes rather than to do shows full time at present. She didn't list her outlets. This is a decision most studio potters have to make. They can either do shows, etc. to sell their own ware, including maintaining a studio outlet, or they can make twice as many pots and let someone else sell them to the public. Kathy hand signs her pieces with blue slip. The "W" in a circle goes on dinnerware.

Winter, Charlotte D. Paramus, New Jersey. Filed for registration of this mark on June 13, 1952, for use on crockery earthenware of porcelain articles, such as vases, centerpieces for table displays, trays, dishes and flower planters, claiming use since July 26, 1951.

Winterthur, Henry Francis Dupont, Museum. Winterthur, Delaware. Filed for registration of this mark on July 1, 1981, claiming first use November 3, 1980, for use on porcelain dinnerware and figurines.

Winterthur

Wisecarver, Rick. Zanesville, Ohio. Around 1971 to present (1987). Rick started painting on canvas in his early teens. His mother who worked in Zanesville potteries encouraged him to paint on pottery vases. Living in Roseville and Zanesville, Ohio, gave Rick an interest in the art pottery made there. He began to experiment until he was able to duplicate the old glazes and methods. His pieces were first sold in his mother's ceramic shop around 1971-1972 and were signed "Rick Wisecarver, Colony House," with no dates added. In 1972 and 1973 the pieces were marked "WIHO." The "WI" was for Wisecarver and the "HO" for Hoadley which was Rick's mother's maiden name. In 1974 to 1976, letter "A" was added making the mark "WIHOA." The "A" was added for Rick's Aunt Florence Ault. The initials "S.W." appear on some of the vases which are for Steve Wisecarver, Rick's brother, who helped to finish orders and pack. An "S" was added to make it "Wihoa's" for Richard Sims who is now Wisecarver's part-

ner. Since 1976 to present (1983) all pottery is marked "WIHOA'S Art Pottery" with the signature "Rick Wisecarver" and initials "R.S." on the bottom. A few rare pieces may have the Wisecarver name hidden in the feathers of an Indian portrait or in some other place in the portrait. Richard Sims, Rick Wisecarver's partner, pours the molds, cleans the bisque pieces, sprays the background colors and does the glazing. In rush months, all of the family members help finish and pack orders. Wisecarver is now doing reverse paintings on glass lamp shades signed "Rick Wisecarver." The pottery pieces are etched, hand painted, hand sculptured, slip painted, with figures of Indians, buffalos, deer, fox, etc. Shapes resemble old Weller ware or are designed by Wisecarver.

71-72 COLONY HOUSE	(no dates)	RARE	RICK WISECARVER ROSEVILLE, OHIO
72-73 WIHO	(WI) SECARVER	(HO)ADLEY	
74-76 WIHOA	(A)ULT	(S.W.)	ZANESVILLE OHIO
76-83 WIHOAS	(S)IMS	(R.S.)	
82-83 MARKED ONLY	LEE	RARE	ZANESVILLE OHIO
82-83 WIHOA'S SANDS	MADE IN FLORIDA		RICK WISECARVER

ALL OF WIHOA'S ART POTTERY IS SIGNED BY RICK WISECARVER.

(Marks: one and two are examples of a mark found on a special line; no. 3, 4, are examples of the very first mark used. Since these marks are inscribed they will appear a little different each time. "Lee" was a special mark also. No. 6 was a mark found on one of a series of five cookie jars being produced by Wisecarver in 1986, a lady pig in a bonnet, a mammy, an Indian Chief, a covered bridge and a hen on a nest.)

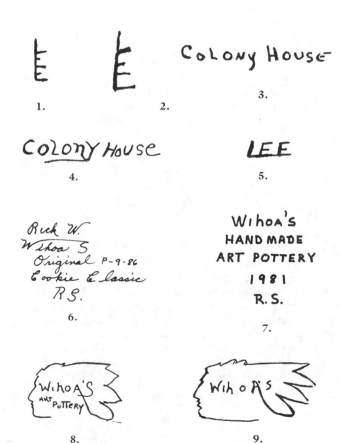

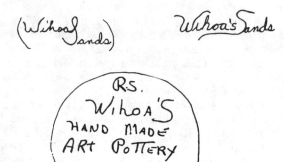

Woideck, George, Stoneware Pottery. Cleveland, Ohio. 1975 to present (1985). George attended Baldwin Wallace College in Berea, Ohio, in 1960-1962. He studied ceramics with the Art Students League in New York City in 1962. In 1963 and 1964 he studied at Kent State University in Athens, Ohio. He makes some very unusual pieces of stoneware with a variety of attractive glazes such as coffee makers, watering cans, a variety of lamps, etc. These are all hand decorated and unique. He makes a full range of functional and decorative pieces. He signs his name to pots. The other mark shown is his logo which is a Chinese symbol for the water well.

Wollard, Lee, China Company. Burbank, California. Listed in 1949 and 1952 *Crockery and Glass Journal*, at 1104 Chestnut Street. Not listed in 1954. They were listed under figurines, figures and miniatures with seven outlets for products in Texas, Nebraska, North Carolina, Ohio, Wisconsin and California. (Mark: sent by Marti Owens.)

Wolper Art Studios. Cockran Avenue, Los Angeles, California. They were listed in the 1948 *China and Glass Red Book Directory*. Norman Wolper made dinnerware ashtrays, boxes, vases, bowls, wall pockets, boudoir accessories, table decorations, barbecue ware are was marked "Speg Amic," or "Spegamic," as shown. The mark shown was a paper label on a little cream colored dish on legs with green raised leaves. (Mark: sent by Jim Gross, collector and researcher.)

Wood. Dayton, Ohio. Around 1870. Made brownware. (Information: Ramsay, p. 213. Mark: Thorn, p. 153.)

WOOD
POTTER
DAYTON
O.

Wood, Beatrice. Ojai, California. Around 1938, Beatrice Wood became interested in making pottery. Before that time she studied art in Paris for a while in her teens. She was part of a French Repertory Theater in New York City. She was accepted as part of a social group of authors and painters and various intellectuals in New York. Around 1924 she established a residence in Ojai. She attended classes at Hollywood High School to learn to make a teapot to match some lustre plates she had purchased. For the next two years she studied with Glen Lukens (see that listing) at the University of Southern California and with the Natzlers (see that listing). Garth Clark said her sense of the theatre is still vividly alive in her work with exotic colors and unconventional forms. Her lusterwares show a personal and uniquely expressive art form. In the 1970's she had exhibitions at the Everson Museum of Art in Syracuse, Hadler Galleries, New York City, and the Philadelphia Museum of Art. (Information: Garth Clark, *A Century of Ceramics in the U.S.*, pp. 341, 342; also, *Beatrice Wood: A Retrospective*, Fullerton, California: California State University, 1983. Mark: sent by Thomas Turnquist, author and member of the American Art Pottery Association.)

BEATO

Wood, Jeanne. Moscow, Idaho. 1971 to present (1983). Studio potter, makes stoneware and porcelain, one of a kind pieces into functional ware.

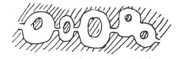

Woodman, Elizabeth. Boulder, Colorado. Woodman, a studio potter and teacher, majored in pottery at the Alfred University, Alfred, New York, from 1948 to 1950. She then set up her own studio on a production basis. She has taught at various times since 1953. From 1957 to 1973, she was a teacher and administrator of the City of Boulder's Recreation Pottery Program, which has evolved to include 350 students, some adults, with eight teachers. Since 1951, Woodman has gone to Italy for two to four months every summer, which has maintained a connection between the two cultures in her work. Her work shows a Mediterranean ceramic tradition. For a better description of the philosophy involved in Woodman's work as regards to the functional and the abstract, see the Clark book cited. (Information: Garth Clark, *A Century of Ceramics in the U.S.*, p. 342. Stamped mark: Linda Steigleder, from the booklet published by the Everson Museum of Art to accompany the 1978 exhibition, "A Century of Ceramics in the U.S.;" also, *The Ceramics of Betty Woodman*, Reading, Pennsylvania: Freedman Gallery, Albright College, 1985.)

WOODMAN

Woodmere China Company, Inc. New Castle, Pennsylvania. Filed for registration of this mark in June 1981, claiming use for one year for decorative china dinner plates.

THE LITTLE PEOPLE

M. Woodruff and Company. Cortland, New York. 1849 to 1870, according to L.G.G. Ramsey, p. 849. Stewart and Consentino, p. 126 gave ending date around 1885. Madison Woodruff was a stoneware potter. He made stoneware jugs, etc. (Marks: no. 1, and dates in business, L.G.G. Ramsey, *The Complete Encyclopedia of Antiques*, p. 849; no. 2, Stewart and Consentino, pp. 61, 69; no. 3, "Crocks, Flasks, Are Among Auction Items," *Bottle News*, November 1976, p. 36. Marks are impressed.)

M. WOODRUFF   M. WOODRUFF & CO
CORTLAND   CORTLAND

1.   2.

CORTLAND 3.

F. Woodworth. Burlington, Vermont. 1872 to before 1895. In 1872, F. Woodworth, stoneware potter, bought the pottery of A.K. Ballard, which had been the pottery of O.L. and A.K. Ballard. See that listing. When the pottery closed in 1895 it was under the ownership of H.E. Sulls. How long he had it was not stated. (Information: Lura W. Watkins, *Early New England Potters and Their Wares*, p. 150. Mark: Smith, *A Utilitarian Folk Craft*, p. 18.)

F. WOODWORTH
BURLINGTON, VT.

F.W. Woolford. 1840's to around 1877. In various locations. This potter made ironstone china in Caledonia, Missouri; redware in Farmington, Missouri and stoneware in Bristol, Missouri. He stayed seven years in Bristol, 1870-1877. Mark

found impressed on stoneware pieces. (Information and mark: Henry W. Heflin, pottery collector and researcher.)

F.W. WOOLFORD
BRISTOL, MO.
STONEWARE
FACTORY

H. Wores. Dover, Ohio. Around 1925-1846. Stoneware. (Information: Thorn, p. 155.)

H. WORES

Works, Laban H. Newport, Ohio. About 1845. Stoneware. (Information: Ramsay, p. 225. Mark: Thorn, p. 155.)

L.H. WORKS

World Wide Art Studios/Division of Atlas Crystal Works. Covington, Kentucky. This company was listed in *Tennessee Directory of Manufacturers* that I had as early as 1949 and through 1975. They were custom decorators of specialty products such as commemorative plates, etc. (Mark: found on 1961 plate with Homer Laughlin Eggshell mark.)

Woronock, David, and William Ansen. New York, New York. Filed for rights to this mark on August 23, 1940, for use on ceramic table and cooking ware, jars and vases, claiming use since 1916. (I don't know if these were distributors or potters.)

HALLMARK

Worth Willow Ware. Oakridge, Oregon. Veryl Marie Worth, owner, started selling Worth Willow Ware in 1976 by mail order only. They produced about 1,000 pieces per month. Some are manufactured by the Worths, some by another Oregon potter and some are imports decorated by the Worths from custom made moulds, made by an Oregon mould maker. They are a small production firm with a special group of collector-consumers. In 1983, Willow Ware production consisted of coffee servers and warmers, two piece creamer sets, cow creamers, elephant creamers, salt boxes, rolling pins, ladles. spoon holders, flower pots, etc., consisting of 500 of each. Veryl Marie Worth is the author of the very helpful book, *Willow Pattern China Collector's Guide*, 1979. (Information and marks: from Veryl Marie Worth.)

W.P.A. Pottery. The Works Progress Administration under the Federal Arts Project was conducted during the Depression. It was a government subsidized program for artists, some of which were potters and potteries. In the *Bulletin of the American Ceramic Society*, No. 5, Volume 21, 1942, p. 113 and 114, is a discussion of an attempt to produce earthenware for W.P.A. nursery schools in the State of Missouri, at the Missouri School of Mines and Metallurgy. The ware proved to be too heavy and the project was abandoned. Centerpieces were made for the tables and they are adorable, including fish, Alice in Wonderland, animals, etc. The idea was to familiarize the children with farm animals and story book charaters. They were covered with a good fritted glaze and made beautiful pieces.

In the article by Karal Ann Marling, "New Deal Ceramics: The Cleveland Workshop," *Ceramics Monthly*, June 1977, pp. 28, 29, we get the story of the program in Cleveland, Ohio. The W.P.A. Workshop in Cleveland, centered around the efforts of Edris Eckhardt, and involved three institutions; the Cleveland School of Fine Arts, the Cleveland Museum of Art, and the Cowan Pottery. Cowan maintained an experimental laboratory encouraging local artists to work there. William Milliken, director of the Cleveland Museum of Art inaugurated a ceramic sculpture category in his annual May show of juried art which ended up bringing in one of a kind specific orders to the artists.

Edris Eckhardt's efforts were centered on two areas. From 1933 to 1939 she attempted to obtain recognition for ceramic sculpture as a legitimate form of fine art and from 1939 to 1941, she promoted large scale architectural murals and decorations for public buildings. Edris initiated the "Alice in Wonderland" series, consisting of five sculptured pieces, 4¾" x 7¼" high. She made molds of several parts of the figures and various members assembled the parts which were made from Ohio clays and 25% flint. As the various students worked in all the different aspects of making the figures, she taught them all phases of ceramic design. (See the listing for Edris Eckhardt.) The W.P.A. artist received $95.00 a month from the government as a subsistence wage. Multiply the effects of this program clear across the country and in many forms of art, and the impact it made on the arts is understandable. In various pottery discussions in this book can be found mentions of the W.P.A. program. The whole story would fill a book. (See index for list.) In the article cited is a description of the various architectural projects under-

taken by the artists in Cleveland. (Information as cited: Karal Ann Marling, is an art historian on the staff at Vassar College. Marks: no. 1, a paper sticker from the booklet published by the Everson Museum of Art to accompany the 1978 exhibition, "A Century of Ceramics in the U.S." Incised mark drawn by Linda Steigleder. Marks 2, 3, from Susan Cox, "W.P.A. Pottery," *American Clay Exchange*, July 1982, p. 14.)

PUBLIC WORKS OF
ART PROJECT

CLEVELAND

WPA
CERAMICS
N. DAK.

F.T. Wright and Son. Tauton, Massachusetts. 1855-1868 (Stewart and Consetino, *Stoneware*, p. 126) The pottery made stoneware utilitarian pieces, jugs, crocks, etc. (Mark: Don and Carol Raycraft, *Decorated Country Stoneware*, Paducah, Kentucky: Collector Books, p. 12.)

F.T. WRIGHT & SON
TAUNTON, MASS.

Wright, Mary S. New York, New York. Filed for rights to this mark on April 2, 1948, for use on pottery serving ware and dinnerware, namely, plates, cups, saucers, soup plates, soup tureens, creamers, sugar bowls, vegetable dishes and pitchers, claiming use since February 25, 1948.

"Country
Cardens"

Mary Wright

Wright, Russel. New York City, New York. A designer. Appears so often in the discussion of American dinnerware, kitchenware and accessory pieces, that he must have a listing of his own. He is a designer from New York City who worked through 1930's to late 1950's.

Steubenville Pottery, Iroquois China, Sterling China Company, Harker Pottery, Paden City Pottery and Bauer Pottery, all employed him at one time or another to design dishes for them. (See the histories of these companies.) Sometimes his name is included in the mark. Helen E. Stiles, in *Pottery in the United States*, p. 179, said "the lamps with a new and modern feeling (1941) are designed by Russel Wright and manufactured by Wright Accessories, Inc. of New York.''

In *Better Homes and Gardens*, September 1946, is an ad for a ''graceful centerpiece in terra cotta, jonquil yellow, or figurex white'' called a ''Flower Boat,'' designed by Russel Wright for Bauer Pottery Company, 1800 Murphy Avenue, S.W., Atlanta, Georgia. The *1954 Crockery and Glass Journal Directory* tells the story of Russel Wright in the listings it contained for him: ''(1) Russel Wright - American Modern dinnerware, Steubenville Pottery Co. and distributed by Richard Morgenthau and Co.; (2) Russel Wright China by Iroquois, Iroquois China Co.; (3) Russel Wright Flame-tumblers, Imperial Glass Corp.; (4) Russel Wright Highlight-pottery dinnerware, Justin Tharaud and Son, Inc. (author's note: Tharaud was a distributor); (6) Russel Wright Pressed Pinch-tumblers, Imperial Glass Corp.'' Russel Wright designed a handled cake tray for Harker Pottery, an oval hotel platter for Sterling China, and for Iroquois China, for ''Casual China''.

According to Betsy Brown in ''Readers Say,'' *Depression Glass Daze*, June 1979, p. 5, Russel Wright was born in Lebanon, Ohio, in April 1905., (He died in 1976.) She goes on to tell us that he attended Columbia and Princeton Universities and studied design under Kenneth Hayes Miller, but was most indebted to Norman Bel Geddes who worked with Wright on his early designs for the theatre. Wright's designs were smooth, clear, sweeping and very utilitarian as opposed to Art Deco. He designed furniture, household appliances, cameras, radios, etc. as well as glassware and ceramic dinnerware. Some of his works are housed at Syracuse University.

Helen Sprackling's article, ''The Glory of Glass,'' *Country Life*, September 1933, p. 33, speaks of Wright as not having abandoned his designing in metal, but having broadened his scope at that time to include glass. She describes the crystal clear stemmed glasses with a fish design by Wright. She praise his ''quick sense of the strategy of line and the play of texture'' as being characteristic of his designing. In a staff-written article, ''Russel Wright's Genius Is Largely Unrecognized,'' *Tri-State Trader*, October 6, 1979, p. 43, the author tells us that Wright designed one of the first stove to tableware lines, the first Wurlitzer piano to be mass-produced and the first three-piece sectional sofa which was for Heywood-Wakefield. From 1939 to 1946, this article tells us, 14 million pieces of his dinnerware were sold. In *Crockery and Glass Journal*, October 1944, p. 38 is a new item, ''Russel Wright Forms Company: Surveys to Determine Design.'' The article goes on to say that Russel Wright, Irving Richards and Eugene Morganthau formed a new corporation in New York state that month. The last two named were both members of the firms, Richards Morganthau and Company and Raymor Manufacturing Division, Inc. The corporation was formed to promote and distribute the dinnerware designed by Wright and manufactured by many of the leading dinnerware manufacturers. (See the listings for the various potteries mentioned.)

Combined with many company names.

H.R. Wyllie China Company. Huntington, West Virginia. From around 1910 until the late 1920's according to Floyd McKee in *A Century of American Dinnerware*. This Wyllie's father had been one of the partners to build a plant in East Liverpool, Ohio which McKee termed unsuccessful. Perhaps this is a reference to John Wyllie and Son. (See John Wyllie and Son for history.) ''Colonel'' H.R. Wyllie had been traveling on the road selling dinnerware when he was induced to come to Huntington by free gas, free taxes and a free site to build the pottery which the townspeople collected money to help construct. The H.R. Wyllie China Company made a nice grade of semi-porcelain dinnerware. (Information: Lehner, *American Kitchen and Dinner Wares*, p. 172. Marks: on dishes and Quality Stamp Company.

Wyllie, John, and Son. East Liverpool, Ohio. Operated 1874 to 1891 (not listed in *1891 East Liverpool Directory*) in the old **Great Western Pottery** in East Liverpool, Ohio, which had been started by the Brunts in 1867. Before 1874, the pottery had made yellowware and Rockingham. Wyllie and Son re-equipped the pottery to make whiteware or ironstone. See ''Ohio Ironstone,'' *Spinning Wheel*, June 1954, p. 26, staff-written, for pictures of Wyllie's ironstone and Lehner, *American Kitchen and Dinner Wares*, p. 172. According to Ramsay in *American Potters and Pottery*, pp. 215-218, the Wyllie Brothers were in East Liverpool from 1848 to 1854, at which time they moved to Pittsburgh. Then in 1874, John Wyllie came back to East Liverpool, Ohio, from Pittsburgh. (Mark: drawn from piece - it wouldn't make a photostatic copy.)

Y

Yates, H.H. Chicago, Cook County, Illinois. Around 1840. Made stoneware with stamped mark. (Information: Betty I. Madden, *Art, Crafts and Architecture of Early Illinois*, p. 190. Mark: p. 186 of the same source.)

H.H. YATES
CHICAGO

Ynez Pottery. Inglewood, California. Before 1948 until around 1953. Started sometime before 1948 and was listed in 1951 and 1952, but was not listed in 1954 or 1955. The 1952 *Crockery and Glass Journal Directory* listed art china, (in this case meaning porcelain or highly vitrified ware), in vases, console sets, ashtrays, candy boxes, etc. Ynez Pottery was also listed under figurines and also florist's ware.

"*Ynez*"
PERSONALITY
PORCELAINS

York Pottery. Lake Butler, Florida (45 miles southwest of Jacksonville). 1870's to before 1890. Henry F. York began making bricks in the 1870's from clay near his home at Lake Butler. Then in the 1880's he started making pottery pieces. He had a $1,500 down draft kiln built and intended that the venture should be a major undertaking. Apparently Henry became ill, but there is some disagreement as to how long the pottery operated, and just when Henry died. Hal Maines, grandson of Henry, said he died in 1890. Pieces described in the article were well decorated with flowers and leaves. One piece had a stipple orange peel appearance with handle that looked like tree bark. Pieces were press-molded and wheel thrown stoneware and earthenware with various colored glazes. At the time of the writing of the article cited for this information, the Museum of Florida History in Tallahassee had a wheel thrown mixing bowl with dark brown glaze inside and unglazed exterior, which they attributed to the York Pottery. This piece had the star mark flanked by three interlocking diamonds which didn't show up well enough in the picture for this author to draw here. A mark inscribed, "Florida," is shown, but must be approached with caution because two more potteries used an impressed mark, "Florida." They are the **Florida Ceramic Company**, Pensacola, Florida, which operated in 1920's and 1930's; and the **Florida Pottery**, St. Petersburg, Florida, which operated around 1930. Both of these companies used a stamped mark, "Florida." York Pottery was the only one which incised the word, "Florida," as identification. (Information and mark: Don Fredgant, "The York Pottery of Lake Butler, Florida," *Antiques Journal*, November 1980, pp. 28-30.)

Florida

Young, William, and Sons. Trenton, New Jersey. 1853-1857. Operated in the old Hattersley Pottery. Then in 1857, they started a new pottery called the **Excelsior Pottery Works** which was operated by the family until 1879. They made crockery, hardware trimmings, pitchers and a few dishes. (Information and marks: Barber, *Marks of American Potters*, p. 44.)

Z

Zane Pottery. See Peters and Reed for history.

Zanesville Art Pottery. Zanesville, Ohio. 1900 to 1920. The Zanesville Roofing Tile Company was organized in 1896, and in 1900 the corporate name was changed to the Zanesville Art Pottery (Evans, p. 340). The pottery made beautiful art pottery similar to some of Weller, old McCoy and others. Various pieces were hand painted, slip decorated, lustre ware and glossy glazed pieces. Pieces were jardinieres, pedestals, umbrella stands, vases, etc. "La Moro" was a hand painted art ware. The pottery suffered two bad fires in 1901 and 1910 and was rebuilt both times. In 1910, they employed 200 people. The plant was sold to Weller in 1920 to become Weller Plant No. 3. (Information: Norris F. Schneider, "Many Small Art Potteries Once Operated in Zanesville," *Zanesville Times Recorder*, February 4, 1962. Impressed Mark: Paul Evans, *Art Pottery of the U.S.*, p. 341.)

LA MORO

Zanesville Stoneware Company. Zanesville, Ohio. Organized in 1887 and incorporated in 1889. Before W.W. I, they made stoneware butter jars, basins, ewers, shoulder jugs, basins and milk pans. As late as 1957 they still made no pressed ware. They used slip casting and jolly wheel, then pieces were dipped or spray glazed. Zanesville Stoneware Company introduced Woodcraft and Zasco lines in early 1920's. In the late 1920's they made tea sets in colors, large jars and vases. Country Fare Hostess Ware sold by Carbone Inc. was made at Zanesville Stoneware, which was an ovenware in yellow-green, glazed with brown trim. At present they make frontier type kitchenware in the hand thrown tradition into casseroles, mixing bowls, pitchers, etc. Several times over the years I have talked to various people at the plant. I have always been assured they never use a mark. Then finally in 1983, I found the mark shown on some heavy stoneware pieces of utilitarian ware. I checked with the factory and was assured it was their mark. I was very happy they finally got a mark so I could include them in this book! (Information: Lehner, Ohio Pottery and Glass, p. 102; Norris F. Schneider, "Zanesville Stoneware Company," *Zanesville Times Signal*, September 8, 1957.)

J.S.Z
3606
ZSC

Zapun Ceramics, Inc. New York, New York. Filed for rights to mark 1 on Janaury 10, 1946 for use on chinaware; urns, vases, fruit and salad bowls, powder jars, coffee and teapots, sugar, cream, salt and pepper containers, dishes, plates, cups and saucers, claiming use since January 1, 1944. In the 1945 *Crockery and Glass Journal Directory* this company was listed as decorators and wholesalers of fine translucent china, gifts and artware. Mark 2 was shown in various directories and some of the dishes decorated by Zapan were made by Taylor, Smith, and Taylor using this mark. See that listing. Mark 3 was in the same directory for 1946.

Zaros Pottery also called **Joetown Pottery.** Malta, Ohio. Rosene and George Zaros started making pottery on a full time basis at the Joetown Hill area in 1971 and are operating there at present. Rosene made her first pot 13 years ago, and George started one year later. At this time, 1982, Rosene is in Spain teaching pottery making. The Zaros are studio potters producing functional stoneware pottery, including dinnerware, and many sculptural hangings such as wind chimes in all sizes. Both sign their pieces with "Zaros" incised into the clay.

Zeisel, Eva. Zeisel was a designer of products for ceramic industry. She designed the "Hallcraft" line for Hall China Company. Western Stoneware Company, Red Wing Pottery, Castleton China Company, and others, benefited from the beautiful designs in dinnerware created for them by Zeisel. A one person show, "Eva, Zeisel: Designer for Industry," opened at the Brooklyn Museum in October 1984, and was to be shown in museums in Chicago, St. Louis, and Providence. In the 1920's, Zeisel studied painting at Budapest, Hungary's Royal Academy of Fine Arts. She opened her own pottery, but very quickly turned to designing for industry. She worked in Germany and Russia and then came to the United States in 1936 where she taught ceramic design for mass production at the Pratt Institute in Brooklyn, New York. In 1946, she was honored by the Museum of Modern Art for the line of tableware she designed. It was named "Museum," and mass produced by Castleton China. (See the listing for Shenango China.) (Marks: The stamped mark shown is used on Hall China's "Hallcraft" line. See Western Stoneware Company for the mark showing Zeisel's name as designer.)

HALLCRAFT
BY
Eva Zeisel
MADE IN U.S.A. BY HALL CHINA CO.

Zent. Huntington, Indiana. Filed for registration of this mark on November 9, 1959, claiming use for one month before for a ceramic pitcher.

"GURGL-JUG"

Zigler, Henry H. Newville, Pennsylvania. 1852-1865. Pictured in Jeannette Lasansky, *Made of Mud*, p. 40 is a pottery jug with Zigler's stamp in both the bottom and side of stoneware jug. (Information and impressed mark: Lasansky as cited, pp. 40, 54.)

H. H. ZIGLER

Zoar Pottery. See Purdy Potters.

Zwojski, Steve. Grant Haven, Michigan. In business in 1985. Studio potter on a full time basis for several years (more than 10). He was formerly from Vermont. Steve makes stoneware pieces with very heavy glaze and fine shapes. (Information: from a relative. Mark: recessed; stamped into stoneware, deep cobalt blue glazed bowl.)

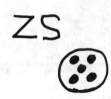

Definitions

These are extremely simplified definitions of some very intricate processes. If the reader is interested, it is easy enough to find lists of definitions in almost any good book on pottery. I was concerned here mainly with the terminology used in this book. In a monthly column entitled "American Art Pottery," which appeared in the *Antique Trader Weekly*, Dave Rago has given definitions dealing with art pottery several times. I suggest the reader see the *Antique Trader Annuals* for these.

"Back stamped," see Introduction and definition for stamping.

Biscuit is made of porcelain or earthenware, fired once and unglazed.

Brownware has a dark brown glaze over a lighter colored buff to brown body. The stony opaque glazing gave the ware its name.

CC ware, cream colored earthenware. See Queensware in this list.

China today has come to mean whatever the plate on the table happens to be, but it was once meant to be identified only with porcelain.

Crazing is the development of hundreds of tiny lines or breaks in the glaze that run in all directions.

Crocks-crockery, various stoneware pieces used for domestic purposes.

Crucible, vessel for melting various materials.

Crystalline glaze is mixed with materials that, when cooled, allows the silicate to crystallize and produce a beautiful crystal gossamer-like quality.

"Custom orders or special mold," earthernware or porcelain made to specific orders given by the distributor to the manufacturer. Sometimes the distributor even owned his own molds and all work was done at a factory to his specifications.

Drawn or painted mark, see Introduction.

Earthenware, all ware made of clay and fired except porcelain, china or stoneware.

Enamel, a metallic color which vitrifies at a low heat. Enameled patterns are sometimes "filled in" over the glaze.

Encaustic means inlaid. On encasutic tile, designs are recessed.

Faience, earthenware covered with tin enamel when piece is unfired or over the glaze after firing.

Functional potters are those whose work is in conventional forms such as dinnerware and objects to be used as opposed to abstractions and works of art.

"Functional or utilitarian pottery" are pieces used in everyday life – mugs, jugs, dinnerware, kitchen ware, etc.

Hand-made pottery is pottery which is thrown or turned on a wheel as opposed to casting or pressing. Some pieces are hand made in molds.

Hardness which keeps being mentioned in connection with porcelain is simply a superior resistance to penetration by liquids and a resistance to pressure.

Hotel china is a hard vitreous ware produced in three different weights and thicknesses.

Impressed mark, see Introduction.

Incised mark, see Introduction.

Ink stamped mark, see Introduction.

Ironstone is a heavy duty, off-white ware. Pieces are fairly well vitrified in comparison with a great deal of semi-porcelain. The ware was generally plain and heavy utilitarian-type pieces.

"Logo" is a sign or symbol used generally on stationary, wrapping products, etc. The logo may sometimes be used as a mark also. (See Conner Prairie Pioneer Settlement for example.)

Marbled ware may be made from different colored slips which are laid on ware and combed together, or the body may be made of different colors of clay and swirled together in the making.

Matt glaze is a dull glaze as opposed to a mirrored glaze with a bright shiny surface.

Mocha ware was cream colored, thinner and more easily broken than yellow ware.

Modeler is a person who sculpts a piece to be reproduced by casting for a wider commercial purpose.

Porcelain is made from hard-paste or soft-paste. It is a ware which is highly vitrified and is sometimes hard to tell from glass. Some porcelain is thin and translucent. Hotel ware was made of porcelain - so are bath fixtures. When it is heavy porcelain, you can't see through it. There are degrees of hardness and quality to porcelain. Our American potteries used the term very loosely calling porcelain what was really semi-porcelain. Hard paste is made with kaolin and other ingredients. Soft paste is made from bone ash plus other materials. "Paste" is just another name for the material used to make the body of the ware.

Queen's ware, ironstone china and white granite ware are terms used indiscriminately by potters to indicate a grade of white earthenware for dining room services one grade higher than cream colored ware. They are made of superior quality materials, the body being slightly stained by a solution of cobalt, which gives it a bluish-white cast.

Red ware is a coarse, porous, lightly fired, pottery similar to common brick. Some pieces are crudely, but colorfully decorated and very few are marked. It is found glazed or unglazed. Bottoms of pieces are generally not glazed. Practically all pieces are utilitarian-type ware except an occasional plate made for a special occassion such as a wedding or birth. Just because a piece of pottery has red clay does not mean it is what we term "red ware." Red clay can be burned to a stoneware consistency. Old type red ware is still being made by a few studio potters today. See Lester Breininger.

"Registered marks" are marks registered with the patent and copyright office which announce the registrant's ownership, his right to use the mark in connection with goods or services specified. Such registration gives the right to sue in U.S. courts to prevent importation of goods bearing an infringing mark. Some marks may be registered as Collective Marks such as the National Brotherhood of Operative Potters which indicate membership in a union or association.

Rockingham ware is made of cheap buff or reddish clay glazed a rich brown to tan for various utilitarian pieces.

Salt glaze is created when common salt is added to the kiln when the temperature is high and a chemical reaction takes place. The result is that free hydrochloric acid is expelled and the soda attacks the alumina, silica and iron of the clay forming the glaze right in the kiln.

Sanitary ware are pottery goods used for sanitary and various domestic purposes. Pieces are generally porcelain, but earthenware was also used. Pieces are bathtubs, sinks, laundry tubs, toilet stools, etc.

Sculptor is an artist who makes original works from marble, stone, metal, wood, terra cotta or ceramics and plaster.

Semi-porcelain is a term that covers lightly fired, easily chipped dishes to ones that are well vitrified but not quite vitrified enough to be called porcelain. Semi-porcelain has a dull body under the glaze when chipped as opposed to porcelain which reveals a shiny body.

Sgraffito was made of red, dark brown or yellow clay with a slip of lighter color. A design was etched in slip so the dark clay body would show through. Sgraffito is the technique of scratching through the slip coating to reveal the clay beneath.

Short sets, often referred to in this book, were sets made by the factory without all of the pieces found in a full set. Perhaps there were no egg cups or dessert dishes or deep dishes made. Any of these missing would make it a short set.

Slab built pottery is made from an approximately one inch thick slab of clay as the starting point, as opposed to starting with a coil which is a piece of clay one foot long and rolled into a half inch or so diameter. Both methods are used in hand making pottery pieces without a wheel.

Slip caste is a process for forming molded pots by filling molds with liquid clay.

Slip glaze is clay mixed with water to a creamy consistancy. Sometimes color is added and then the slip is applied to the surface of the body of the ware by dipping or spraying, etc. Slip clay must be fine grained, with enough mineral additives and alkaline content to make it fuse with the clay of the body and not shrink in the firing.

Stamping is a term inadvertently used in connection with several processes in pottery manufacture. A plate can have a design applied by "stamping" with a rubber stamp. Some of the stamps made at Quality Stamp Company were large and would cover the whole center of a plate. "Stamping" can be used in connection with applying a mark. The old stoneware jug makers sometimes "stamped" their name or initials into a piece with wooden or metal stamps they purchased or made themselves. Dinnerware was "back stamped" underneath a plate or cup with a rubber stamp with the name of the maker or pattern name, etc. Gold and gilt decorations were also stamped around the edges of some pieces.

Stoneware is a more refined clay burned at a high temperature to make a water resistant non-porous vessel. Sometimes various glazes were added or salt could be thrown into the kiln which caused the old jugs and crocks to form their own glazes. Old stoneware was gray to yellowish brown in color. It was refined and lightened in color for cups, plates, etc. and called stone china which was gray or cream-colored. Stoneware has been used and still is to make vases and other decorative objects. Many of the studio potters use either stoneware or porcelain. In this case, the bodies may be made in different colors and the plasticity of stoneware makes it easily modeled. Colored glazes are easily applied to the close grained body.

Studio potter, see Introduction.

"Stylized mark" are letters not written in script or block, but given some personalized treatment.

Terra cotta is an enriched (more vitrified) cast or molded clay brick or block, either glazed or unglazed used for architectural purposes for construction or decoration.

Transfer printing was a method brought over from England by early potters. It involved engraving from a copper plate. The copper plate was warmed and the color worked into the engravings. The excess color was cleaned off. A piece of thin, tissue-type paper was brushed with a soft soap solution. This paper was then laid on the engraved plate and run through a roller press to transfer the color to the paper. The pattern was transferred to the dish and rubbed down into place. Hand work could then be added by filling in the design with color or trimming the piece with gold. There was a decorating kiln, and some of the ware went through that kiln many times. These old transfer designs are delicate and have the look of something engraved. The color, hand painted in, is irregular and runs out of the lines.

Vitrified is a term which applies to the hardness of the ware, how easily it will break, how much pressure and heat it can stand. The more "glass materials" added to clay and the hotter it is heated, the more vitrified a product becomes.

Wedging is a method of working clay to prepare it for throwing or turning on a wheel.

Yellow ware is finer than pottery or redware but coarser than earthenware or stoneware. The pieces are buff colored sometimes running into a deep yellow.

Companies Listed By Location

The following is a list of the potters, factories, distributors, etc. listed by location. This list can be very helpful in identifying marks shown in the book and many not shown. Sometimes the most conclusive information we have about an identifying mark is the location, and sometimes all the information we have in the mark is a location. Locate the potters in the area you are seeking and see the index to locate them in the book. This listing is also instrumental in studying the extent of the pottery made in a certain area, etc.

Alabama

Marlow
Wingender, J.

Mobile
Morrison, Inc.

Montrose
Beasley, James
McAdam, John

Randolf County
Pound, W.P.

Spruce Pine
Muscle Shoals Pottery
Spruce Pine Pottery

Tuscaloosa County
Cribbs, Daniel
Ham Brothers

Arkansas

Benton
Benton Crock & Pottery Co.
Niloak Pottery Co./Hyten-Eagle Pottery Co.
Niloak Pottery and Tile Co.

Camden
Camark Pottery
Camark Pottery II

Conway
Leveritt, Joseph

Hot Springs
Fox Pass Pottery
Hot Springs Pottery
Ouachita Pottery

Little Rock
Rum Rill, George

Arizona

Mesa
Bergstrom and French
La Solana Potteries, Inc.
Rosemary's Ceramics

Phoenix
Copperstate Supply Co.
Loma Mfg. Co.
Sierra Vista Ceramics

Sedona
Oak Creek Kilns (James M. Relph)

Tempe
Sandstone Creations

Tucson
Mallek, Kay Studios

California

Alberhill Pottery

Anaheim
Arita Tabletop
Stoneware by Brown

Barstow
Desert Sands Pottery

Berkley
AW Pottery
California Faience
Hillcrest Pottery (Walden)
Voulkos, Peter
Walrich Pottery

Burbank
Empire China
Haldeman Potteries (also Calabasas)
Leniege China, Inc.
West Coast Pottery, Inc.
Wollard, Lee

Calabasas
California Ceramics
Ceramic Manufacturing Company

Capistrano Beach
Vohann of California

Capitola
Camp Del Mar Pottery

Catalina Island
Catalina Pottery (see listing Catalina Marks)

Chico
Patrick, Vernon

City of Industry
George-Good Corp.

Claremont
Manker, William
McIntosh, Harrison
Pierce, Howard, Ceramics

Corona Del Mar
Finch, Kay, Ceramics

Compton
Pottery Craft
Treasure Craft

Davenport
Big Creek Pottery (McDugal)

El Camino
Capistrano Ceramics

El Cerrito
Pyramid Alloy Mfg. Company
Technical Porcelain and China Company

El Monte
California Cleminsons
Freeman McFarlin Company
Hueckel China and Porcelain (see El Monte various potteries)
Miali Pottery (see El Monte various potteries)
Rio Hondo Potteries
Starr, Vallona, Ceramics

Emeryville
Happy Clay

Fairfax
Arequipa Pottery

Fish Harbor
Van Camp Sea Food Company, Inc.

Fresno
Brown, Cedric and Christy

Glendale
Bergstrom and French
California Dresden
La Salona Potteries
Marsh Industries

Guerneville
Farm Pond Workshop (Wildenhain)

535

Halcyon
Halycon Art Pottery

Hawthorne
Brastoff, Sascha

Hayward
Monefeldt, Jens

Healdsburg
Evans Ceramics, Inc.

Hollywood
Dunn, Vera La Fountain
Hirsch Mfg. Company (also Los Angeles)
Spearman, Helen

Inglewood
Coors, H.F. Co.
Decora Ceramics Inc.
Inez Pottery

Laguna Beach
Ceramic Originals
Knox Leidy Co. (see Ceramic Originals)

Lawndale
B.J. Brock Co. (see Southern Ca. P. Co.)
Southern California Pottery Co.

Los Angeles
Andreson, Laura
Barker Brothers
Batchelder, Ernest (also Pasadena)
Bauer, J. and A., Pottery Co., Inc.
Belmar of California
Brahm, Johannes (also Reseda)
California Belleek
California Figurine Co. (see Max Weil)
Ceramic Art Association
Claycraft Potteries
Commerce-Pacific Inc.
Davidson, Laura
Disney, Walt, Product, Ltd.
Dynasty Ltd.
Eastern Outfitting Co.
Gladding, McBean and Co. (also Glendale)
Grand Feu Art Pottery
Hirsch Mfg. Co. (also Hollywood)
Hollywood Ceramics
Ideas Unlimited
Jaska of California
Keeler, Brad, Artwares
Kinneloa Kiln
Lerner, Claire, Studios
Lotus and Acanthus Studios
Lovett, Robert E.
Lukens, Glen
Maddux of California
Marsh Industries
Oakley, Annie, Enterprises
Pacific Clay Products Co.
Padre Potteries
Peterson, Richard B.
Pillin, Polia
Pixie Potters (also Long Beach)
Price, Kenneth
Registered California, Inc.
Robertson, Fred H.
Robertson P. (see F.H. Robertson)

Santa Anita Pottery
San Valle' Tile Kilns
Sax, Adrian A.
Schonfeld, Max P.H.
Spense and King (see Lotus and Acanthus Studios)
Squire Ceramics
Starnes, Walter
Walker, Jesse Robinson
Weil, Max of California
Western Auto Supply Co.
Wolper Art Studios

Lynwood
Los Angeles Pottery

Manchester
Old Creamery Pottery (Shacter) Also San Francisco and Point Arena

Manhatten Beach
Metlox Potteries

Milbrae
West Coast Porcelain Manufacturers

Monterey
Monterey Art Pottery

Monrovia
Walker Potteries

Montibello
Brudin, Ernest W.

North Hollywood
Frazier Inc.
Wade Ceramics

Oakland
Frey, Viola
Prieto, Antonio

Ojai
Heino, Vivika and Otto
Wood, Beatrice

Pasadena
American Ceramic Products Co. (see Winfield Pottery)
Batchelder Tile Co.
Batchelder-Wilson Co.
Bonzi, William, Co.
Clay Sketches
Flintridge China Co.
Florence Ceramics
Hood, Sylvia, Designs
Roselane Pottery (also Baldwin Park)
Singer, Susi
Sylvan Ceramics
Thurston, Carl H.
Twin Winton Ceramics, also San Juan Capistrano
Wentz, M.C., Co.
Wilson, Walter
Winfield, P.

Point Arena
Point Arena Studio (Shacter) also Venice and Manchester

Sacramento
Jam Ceramic Design (Marquardt)

San Antonio
Brannan, Daniel S.

San Carlos
San Carlos Pottery

San Diego
Celestial China Corp.
G.T. Chemical Products Inc.
Valentian Pottery

San Dimas
Hagen-Renaker Inc.

San Francisco
Bonzi, William, Co.
Burke, Bill
Dohrmann Hotel Supply Co.
Gump, S. and G.
Jalanivich and Olsen
Marks and Rosenfeld
Mova Products
Poor, Henry Varnum (several places)
Roblin Art Pottery (see Robertson)
Robertson, Alexander H.
Robertson, Alexander W.
Shacter, Stoneware and Porcelain

San Gabriel
Claysmith's

San Jose
Gladding Ceramic Insulator Co.
Sanders, Herbert Harvey

San Juan Capistrano
Twin Winton Ceramics (also Pasadena)

Santa Ana
Crest China Co.
Royal Crest China Co.

Santa Barbara
Rhead, Frederick H.
Santa Barbara Ceramic Design

Santa Clara
Knowles, Homer, Pottery Co.

Santa Monica
Block, Richard G., Pottery
California Art Products Co. (see Southern Ca. Cer. Co.)
Southern California Ceramic Co.

Sausalito
Heath Ceramics, Inc.

Sierra Madre
McCarty Brothers

Sierra Vista
Sierra Vista Ceramics (also Phoenix Az.)

South Laguna Beach
Brayton Pottery

Stockton
Laurel Potteries
Stockton Art Pottery
Stockton Terra Cotta Co.

Temple City
Holder, Lily Frona

Torrance
California Original (see Heirlooms of
   Tomorrow)

Van Nuys
Lane and Co.

Vernon
Vernon Kilns
Wallace China Co.

Venice
Venice Pottery Gallery (Shacter) also see
   Point Arena and Manchester

Whittier
Artistic Potteries Co.

Colorado
Boulder
Carol Ann Pottery Ltd.
Talisman Pottery (Baumgartner)
Woodman, Elizabeth

Cotopaxi
A&A Pottery

Colorado Springs
Utley, Tabor
Van Briggle Pottery

Denver
Broadmoor Pottery
Denver China and Pottery Co.
F.J. White and Son Pottery
Geijsbeek Pottery Co. (also Golden)
Western Pottery Mfg. Co.

Golden
Basch, Carol
Coors Porcelain
Geijsbeek Pottery Co. (also Denver)

Loveland
Rocky Mountain Pottery
Loveland Art Pottery

Pueblo
Deer Foot Pottery (Lyle L. Clift)

Connecticut
State Only
Sanders, John

Cheshire
Bovano Ind. Inc.

Darian
Apple Tree Lane Pottery

East Killingly
Farrell Porcelain (Sandra and Richard
   Farrell)

Goshen
Brooks Hervey

Hartford
Barringer, Mary
Bosworth, Stanley
Cross, Peter
Fisher, J.C.
George Street Pottery (New Haven)
Goodale, Daniel
Goodwin Potteries (various)
Goodwin & Webster
Greenleaf Pottery Inc. (East Hartford)
Harrington, T.
Hartford Faience Co.
Kelley, Frank Ruess (Norwalk)
Seymour Potters
Webster, Mack, M.E.

Litchfield
Lord, E.A. (see Lord various Potters)

Meriden
International Silver Co.
Rockwell Silver Co.

New Haven
Pewtress, S.L.

New Milford
Black and Beach Pottery Co.
New Milford Pottery Co.
Wannopee Pottery

Norwalk
Kelly, Frank Reuss
Smith & Day Pottery

Norwich
Armstrong and Wentworth
Norwich Pottery
Risley Stoneware Pottery

Sharon
The Pot Shop (William E. Pitney)

Stonington
Swan and States

Delaware
Newark
Saenger Porcelain/Baker Station Studios
Spinski Victor

Wilmington
Allied Stores Corp.
Gerson Samuel L.
Hare, William

Winterthur
Winterthur, Henry Francis Museum

Florida
Bradenton
Graack, H.A. Art Pottery (also Silver
   Springs)
Ward Pottery (see H.A. Graack)

Hallandale
Mr. Mugs Inc.

Knox Hill
T.B. Odom

Lake Butler
York Pottery

Lake Placid
Brown Jug Pottery

Merritt Island
Merritt Island Pottery

Miami
Dutty, Mary Ellen
Poinciana Chinaware Inc.

Orlando
Colonial Silver Co.

Pensacola
Kohler, J.W.

St. Petersburg
De Lime Studios

Tampa
Hickman, Royal

Georgia
Alvaton
Georgia Art Pottery (see Gordy Family
   Pottery)

Atlanta
Bauer John Andrew (see Bauer Potteries)
Brown Family Potters
Cofield, T.W.
Kline, Charles S.
Lavender, Jane
Lycett, Edward and William
Patch Inc.

Cartersville
Buford, Molly B.
Gordy, D.X.

Clarksburg
The Mark of The Potter (La Rowe)

Crawford County
Avera, John C.
Bustle, (or Bussell) James
Long Family Potters (various)

Jackson County
Addington, William R.

Marietta
Georgianna Ceramics

New Windsor (near North Augusta)
Duche, Andrew (also S. Carolina)

Orange
Stork, Edward L.

Primrose
D.X. Gordy (see Gordy Family Potters)
W.T.B. Gordy (see Gordy Family Potters)

Stone Mountain
Clayhorse Pottery

Thompson
Baggett, Michael

Washington County
Bussell, James M.

White County
Meaders Pottery

Young Cane
Jones, J.A.

Hawaii
Honolulu
Ruby, Laura

Idaho
Lewiston
Beamish, Joan
Wendt Pottery

Moscow
Wood, Jeanne

Sandpoint
First Thought Pottery (K. Stoner)

Illinois
Abingdon
Abingdon Pottery

Addison
A.F.K. Industries

Alexis
Alexis Pottery Co.
Alexis Stoneware Co.
Alexis Stoneware Mfg. Co.

Anna
Anna Pottery

Antioch
Pickard China
Regal China Corp.

Bishop Hill
Hintze Pottery

Campoint
Martin E.G.

Champaign - Urbana
Pilcher, Don

Chicago
American Terra Cotta (N.W. of Chicago)
Atlan Ceramic Art Club
Berggren Trayner Corp.
Bradford Exchange
Carson Pirie Scott & Co.
Chicago Crucible Co.
Chicago Terra Cotta Works
Club Aluminum Products Co.
Consolidated Cosmetics
Deutch, Eugene
Duckworth, Ruth

Fairbanks Ward Industries
Farrell, William
Franklin, Ben Stores
Gates Potteries
Grossman, Edward (the Spitler)
Gustav Hottinger (see N.W. Terra Cotta)
Hartman's Furniture and Carpet Co.
Hill-Shaw Co.
H.M.H. Publishing Co.
Hull House Kilns
Independent Grocers Alliance Distributing
    Co. (I.G.A. Stores)
Kaul, Leo
Kittler, Joseph R.
Leeds China Co.
Lefton China Co.
Marshall Burns Co.
Marshall Field & Co.
McGraw Electric Co.
Midland Terra Cotta Co.
Neff, Grace V.
Northwestern Terra Cotta
Pauline Pottery
Pick, Albert & Co.
Poor & Co.
Red Cliff Co.
Reliable Glassware & Pottery Co.
Sears & Roebuck Co.
Stevens, Chas. A., & Brothers
Stouffer Co.
Weil, Alfred J.
Yates, H.H.

Colchester
Colchester Pottery

Dundee
Haeger Potteries Inc.

Evanston
Albery Novelty Co.

Fowler
Robbins, Carolyn

Galesburg
Galesburg Pottery
Galesburg Stoneware Mfg. Co.

Lincoln
Illinois China Co.
Stetson China Co.

Macomb
Buckeye Pottery
Eagle Pottery
Haeger Potteries Inc.
Illinois Electric Porcelain Co.
Macomb Pottery
Macomb Stoneware

Metropolis
Metropolis Bending Co.

Monmouth
Lowell Stoneware Co.
Monmouth Pottery Co.
Sleepy Eye Milling Co.
Weir Pottery
Western Stoneware Co.

Morton
American Art Potteries
Amish Pottery
Cliftwood Art Potteries
Midwest Pottery
Morton Ceramic Tile Co.
Morton Earthenware Co.
Morton Pottery Co.
Morton Pottery Works
Pilgrin Pottery
Rapp Brothers (various potteries)
Sayers, Don & Ruth

North Lake
Automatic Electric Co.

Peoria
Peoria Pottery
Wheelock Pottery

Ripley
Ripley Illinois (various potters)
Stoffer L.D. & Co.
Stout, Isaac N.

Rockford
Norse Pottery (also Edgerton,   Wisconsin)

Sauk Village
Baldauf, Stephen

Skokie
Play Bear, Inc.

Springfield
Prairie House

Tennessee
Tennessee Stoneware & Tile Works

White Hall
Ruckel Pottery (see White Hall Pottery
    Works)
White Hall Pottery Works
White Hall Sewer Pipe & Stoneware Co.

Wilmette
Jepcor International (see J & H
    International)
J & H International

Wood Dale
Stonegate China Co.

Indiana
Albany
Bethel Pike Pottery

Annapolis
Atcheson and Associates

Bainbridge
Wild Rose Pottery (Burkett)

Bloomington
Martz, Karl

Brazil
Brown, Becky
Husher, Geroge

Standard Pottery Co.
Torbert, William R.

Brownsburg
Marek, J.J.

Cambridge City
Overbeck Pottery

Cannelton
Clark, William & Co.

Chesterton
Clay City Pottery

Clay County
See Clay County Various Potters

Cloverland (Clay County)
Noel, Francis

Evansville
Benninghof, Uhl & Co.
Crown Potteries Co.
Crown Pottery
Koch, George & Sons
Uhl Pottery (also Huntingburg)

Flat Rock
Davies, Melvin L.

Goshen
Doriot, Helen

Greensburg
Mullis, Charles Mfg. Co.

Hartford City
Cline, Wm. W. (see Indiana Redware
   Potters)

Huntington
The Zents

Indianapolis
American Art Clay Co. Inc
Potter's House (T. Thorn)
Ransburg, Harper, J & Co. (also Toledo,
   Ohio)
U.S. Encaustic Tile Co.

Jeffersonville
Unser, George

Lakeville
ʼE-Z Cook Inc.

Madison
Green Hills Pottery
   (McDonough)

Martinsville
Kirchman, Dennis G.

Muncie
Muncie Clay Products Co.
Muncie Potteries Inc.

New Albany
Keller, William

Noblesville
Bastine Pottery
Conner Prairie Pioneer Settlement

Peru
Square D. Co.

Posey Township (Clay County)
Kelsey Family Potters

Porter
Columbia China

Putnamville
Perry, J.S.

Reelsville
Peeler Pottery

Troy
Clews, James
Indiana Pottery Co.

Veedersburg
Marshall Studios Inc. (Martz)

Iowa
Ames
Iowa State College of Agriculture &
   Mechanical Arts

Centerville
Bradley, Mildred

Davenport
Fennell, Helen

Fort Dodge
Fort Dodge Potteries
Fort Dodge Stoneware Co.
Hartwell & Bower Inc.
Plymouth Stoneware Co.
Union Pottery Works
White Pottery Works

Mason City
Shawsheen Pottery

Milford
Village Potter (Duncan)

New Albin
Crystal Springs Studio

Oskaloosa
Farr Pottery

Sioux City
American Dinnerware Service

Ellsworth
Dryden P.

Fort Hayes
Fort Hayes State College Pottery

Miltonvale
Miltonvale Potteries

Olathe
Lauer's Pottery

Pittsburgh
Dickey Clay Co.
Pittsburgh Pottery/Seville Industries

Shawnee Mission
Ferguson, Kenneth
Quality Enterprises Inc.
Vita Craft Corp.

Kentucky
Berea
Berea College
Culbreath, Sarah L.
Deaver Studios

Bybee
Cornelison Bybee Pottery
Seldon-Bybee Pottery Co.
Waco Pottery

Covington
Atlas Crystal Works
Cambridge Tile Mfg. Co.

Erlanger
Kenton Hills Porcelain

Lexington
Seldon Bybee Pottery (and N.Y.C.)

Louisville
Hadley Pottery, Inc.
Lewis Pottery
Louisville Pottery Co.
Louisville Stoneware Co.
Vodrey & Frost
Vodrey & Lewis

Mayfield
Roman Ceramics

New Haven
Big Lick Pottery

Paducah
Paducah Pottery (see Bauer Potteries)

Louisiana
New Orleans
Cox, Paul E. Pottery
New Orleans, Various Potteries including:
   Baronne Street Pottery
   French Porcelain Co.
   Herandez & Co.
   Louisiann Porcelain Mfg. Co,
   New Orleans Art Pottery
Newcomb Pottery

Red Oak
Acorn Pottery

Maine
Arlington
Sweezy, Nancy

Bangor
Bangor Stoneware Co.

Bethal
Bonnema, Garret & Melody

Blue Hill
Rowantrees Kiln

East Boothbay
Andresen, Weston & Barbara

Ellsworth
Daney (see Dana, Dany)

Farmingdale
Horn, Martin

Gardiner
Ballard, Various Potteries (also Burlington Vt.)
Gardiner Stoneware Manufactory
Horn, Martin (also Farmingdale)
Lyman & Clark
Nichols & Alford (see Ballard)
Nichols & Boynton (see Ballard)
Plaisted Pottery
Thompson, R & Co.

Hollis
Alld, John

Kennebunk
Blue Wave

Monmouth
Safford Pottery

Ogunquit
Abbott, Charles

Portland
Clough & Calhoun
Crafts, Martin & Caleb
Dodge Pottery
Lamson & Swasey
Orcutt, Eleazer
Swasey, Lamson & Co. (see Portland Pottery Works)
Portland Pottery Co.
Portland Pottery Works
Portland Stoneware Co.
Winslow & Co. (see Portland Stoneware and Clough & Calhough)

Waldoboro
Stanwood, James H.

Worcester
Walley, Joseph W. (also Portland)

York
Beaumont Heritage Pottery

Maryland

Baltimore
American Wholesale Corp.
Baltimore Bargain House (see American Wholesale Corp.)
Baltimore Clayworks
Bennett, E. Chinaware Factory (see Various Bennett Potteries)
Chesapeake Pottery/D F Haynes & Son Co
Hamill, Brown & Co. (see Maryland Queensware Co.)
Hamill and Bullock (see Maryland Queensware Co.)

Maryland Pottery Co. (see Maryland Queensware Co.)
Maryland Queensware Co.
Miller, Benjamin C.
Morgan, Thomas
Remmey, Henry H.
U.S. Merchandise Corp.

Ellicott City
Delft Blue Ltd.

Frederick
Everedy Co.

Kensington
Diona, Sister Mary

Hagerstown
Bell, Peter Jr.
Leisinger & Bell

Hampstead
Shiloh Pottery (O. Kenneth Hankins)

Massachusetts

Amherst
Cohen, Michael
Fina, Angela

Ashfield
Hastings & Belding

Billerica
Shawsheen Pottery (also Iowa)

Boston
Carbone, Inc.
Dorchester Pottery Works
Fosdick, Marion
Grueby-Faience Co.
Grueby Pottery
Jones McDuffee & Stratton
National Unit Distributors Inc.
New England Pottery Co.
Raymond's Inc.
Schmidt Brothers Inc.
Towle Mfg. Co.
Williams Filene & Son's Co.

Brighton
Revere, Paul, Pottery

Cambridge
Asbury, Carolyn
Hamilton, Nan
Hansen, Gail
Mudville (School)

Charleston
Carpenter, Frederick
Edmunds, Barnabus
Edmunds & Burroughs
Edmunds & Co.
Edmunds & Hooper
Lord, Various Potters
Mystic River Works
Powers & Edmunds

Chelsea
Chelsea Keramic Art Works

Chelsea Pottery
Low Art Tile Co.
Mear, Frederick/Boston Earthenware
Revere, Paul, Pottery
Robertson, James, (see Chelsea Kera Art Works)
Seavey, Amos

Concord
The Potting Shed (C. Star)

Dedham
Dedham Pottery

East Weymouth
Herring Run Pottery (Wyman)

Fitchburg
New Distributor System

Gloucester
Hammond Research Corp.

Holyoke
Salt of the Earth Pottery (K. Goos)

Hyannis
General Housewares Corp.

Marblehead
Marblehead Pottery

Medford
T. Sables & Co.

Merrimac
Merrimac Pottery Co.

Northampton
East Street Clay Studios
Pinch Pottery
White Dog Pottery (Hillman)

Plymouth
Plymouth Pottery

Somerset
Chase, L & B.G.
Somerset Potters' Works

Somerville
McCarthy Brothers

Springfield
Nash, Jonathon

Sturbridge
Old Sturbridge, Inc.

Taunton
Seaver, William
F.T. Wright & Son

Whately
Crafts Potters

Winchester
Clay Craft Studios

Worcester
Norton, F.B. Pottery

Michigan

Ada
Amway Corp.

Ann Arbor
Porcelain Design (S. Hubbard)

Benzonia
Vigland Pottery

Beuhlah
Trapp, Mrs. Howard

Bloomfield Hills
Grotell, Maija

Charlesvois
Staffel's Pottery

Dearborn
Greenfield Village Pottery

Detroit
Borg Warner Corp.
K Mart
Pewabic Pottery
S.S. Kresge Co.

Farmington
Plum Tree Pottery

Grand Ledge
Grand Ledge Clay Products Co.
Grand Ledge Potteries (various)
Grand Ledge Sewer Pipe Co.

Grand Rapids
Irwin, Roberts W.

Grant Haven
Zawojski, Steve

Hanover
Haruta, Yosuke

Holland
Colorcrete Industries Inc.

Kalamazoo
Maloney, Harold J.

Livonia
Sculptures In Clay

Monroe
Ohio China Co.

Mt. Clemens
Jamestown China Co.
Mt. Clemens Pottery

Mt. Morris
Anderson, Ken D.

Petroskey
Kellogg Studios

Pontiac
Carlock, Elaine & Daniel

Royal Oak
Larson, Tyrone & Julie (also N. Carolina)
Luce, Nora

Saugatuck
Saugatuck Potters (Keefe)

Traverse City
Starship Studios (R. Tyge)

Washington
Pine's Earth Studios (Diebboll)

WIlliamston
Good Earth Studios (Terry Emrich)

Minnesota

Anoka
The Pot Shop

Kettle River
Nemadji Earth Pottery Co.

Lindstrom
Christianson Pottery

Milaca
Branum Pottery

Minneapolis
Coiner, John, P.
Daga Design
Earth Works Pottery (Coiner)
General Mills
Handicraft Guild of Minneapolis
Hope Chest Co. Inc.
Tanaka Pottery

New Ulm
Dauffenbach & Gieseke

Red Wing
Minnesota Pottery Co.
Minnesota Stoneware Co.
North Star Stoneware Co.
Red Wing Potteries Inc.
Red Wing Stoneware
Red Wing Union Stoneware
Union Stoneware Co.

St. Paul
Coiner-Deneen Pottery
Deneen Pottery
Mayeron Tile Works

Stillwater
Johnson, Shirley
Mackenzie Pottery

Taylor Falls
Oestreich Pottery

Mississippi

Gautier
Gautier, Josie

Ocean Springs
Shearwater Pottery

Missouri

Avondale
Nichols Pottery

Boonville
Blank Pottery (also California, Missouri)
Jegglin Family Potters

Branson
Snob Hog Pottery

California
Boonville Pottery

Calloway
Caldwell Pottery

Caledonia
F.W. Woolford

Calhoun
Dawson & Sons
Edwards & Minish
Jegglin Family Potters

Carthage
J.S. Brown

Clinton
Clinton Potter Co.

Commerce
Charles Koch Pottery
Commerce Pottery
A.A. Austin & Co.

Dexter
Evans Pottery

Florence
Hummel, John M.

Joplin
Pan's Dell Pottery

Kansas City
Clow, Bonnie L.
Helzberg's Diamond Shops, Inc.
Hill, C.E. & Co.
Rozart Pottery Studio
Tate, Janette
Tierra Royal Potteries Inc.
White, Father Jim, S.J.
Williams, Barbara

Lakenan
D.F. Huggins & Co.

Lee's Summit
Muddy Wheel Pottery

Liberty
China Bull (McNeely)

New York
Abcock
Balsir & Oartar
Hercher, Joseph
Lindsay, W.

New York Pottery
Smith & Fothingham
Smith, S.D.

Ozark
Blair Ceramics Inc.

Paris
Town, J.W.

Parkeville
Doubenmier, Cecil

Pierce City
Purdy, George A.

Rolla
Herold, Paul G.

Savannah
Jansen, Jenny

Shelbina
Shelbina Pottery China Co. Inc.

Springfield
Springfield Pottery Co.

Stoutsville
Conrad, J.W.

St. Joseph
Kemp's Pottery

St. Louis
Ozark Pottery Co.
Paige Pottery Co.
Ralston Purina Co.
Roman Art Co.
Stix, Baer and Fuller Co.

University City
University City Pottery

Washington
Bayer, Joseph

Windsor
Ozark Mountain Store, Inc.

Montana
Cardwell
Clays In Calico

Helena
Archie Bray Foundation

Victor
Bitterroot Pottery (Peggy Steffes)
Pottery by Ward
Rising Sun Pottery (McClain & Loveridge)
Wild Rose Pottery (Roberts)

Nebraska
Brownsville
Potter's Habitat (Jones)

Omaha
Craft, Beverly H.
Phillips, Lz

Nevada
Boulder City
Desert Sands Pottery

New Hampshire
Center Sandwich
Sandwich Kiln (Marshall)

Exeter
Exeter Pottery Works
Lamson Brothers
Lamson & Fields

Fitzwilliam Depot
Pottery Works

Goffstown
Phoenix Pottery (Wild)

Keene
Hampshire Pottery

Lee
Baston, Prescott
Lance Corporation (see Prescott Baston)
Sebastian Miniature (see Prescott Baston)

Madison
Brook Pottery (Flavin)

Mason
Fletcher, Liz

Meriden
Tariki Stoneware (O'Leary's & Pringle)

Nashua
Crafts Potters (also Massachusetts)

Portsmouth
Red Horse Hill Pottery (Niles)
Weathervane Stoneware (Wheeler, E.H.)

Potter Place
Wild Pottery

Walpole
Fenton, Jonathon (also Massachusetts)

Weare
Robinson Studio
Sanford, Peter Peregrine

New Jersey
Absecon
Absecon China & Glass Decorators

Babadoes Neck (near New Hackensack)
Sanford, Peter Peregrin

Camden
Camden Pottery Co.

Carteret
Cardinal China Co.
Carteret China Co.

Chatham
Chatham Potters Inc.
Contemporary Ceramics

Cheesequake
Furman, Noah

Clifton
Shulton, Inc.

Clinton
Takaezu, Toshiko

Dentzville
Amoges China Co.

Elizabeth
Beerbower, L.B. & Co.
Pruden, John

Flag Point
Rosendahl, Jean

Flemington
Hill/Fulpur/Stangl Potteries

Gloucester
American Porcelain Mfg. Co.
Gloucester China Co.

Hackensack
Belcrest Inc.

Haines Port
Creekturn Pottery

Haddonfield
Wingender, Charles & Brothers

Lakewood
Burgues Porcelains Inc.

Lambertville
Temple, Bryon

Little Falls
Abbe, Paul O. Inc.

Metuchen
Gort, Eric China Co.
Volkmar Kilns

Moonsacki
Belcrest Inc. (also Clifton)
Vontury, F.J. Inc.

Morris Plains
Moore, John Hudson, Co.

Mountainside
Mountainside Art Pottery

Newark
Bamberger, L. & Co.
Clifton Art Pottery
Home Decorators Inc.
Krumeich, B.J.
Murchison, Loren & Co.
Union Pottery

New Brunswick
Butler, A.J. & Co.

Paramus
Winter, Charlotte D.

Pennington
Ispanky Porcelains Inc.

Perth Amboy
Humiston & Stockwell (see Henry
  Stockwell)
Paradee, C. Works
Pewtress, John B.
Stockwell, Henry
Whiteman, T.W.

Rahway
Mann, John

Roselle Park
Newcomb, Inc.

Sayreville
Price, Xerpes

Short Hills
Kraus, Anne

South Amboy
Carr, James (see Hill Pottery)
Cheesequake Potters
Congress Pottery
Letts, Joshua
Locker, Thomas (see Swan Hill Pottery)
Swan Hill Pottery (J. Carr)
Warne, Thomas

Trenton
Alpaugh & McGowan
Americana Art China Works
American Crockery Co.
American Porcelain Mfg. Co.
American Pottery Co.
American Pottery Mfg. Co.
Anchor Pottery
Atlantic Mold
Bellmark Pottery Co.
Broome, Isaac
Burroughs & Mountford
Chadwick China Co.
City Pottery
Columbian Art Pottery Co.
Cook Pottery
Cordey China Co. (see Boleslaw Cybis)
Coxon & Co.
Coxon & Thompson
Crescent Pottery
Cybis, Boleslaw
Cybis Porcelains (see Boleslaw Cybis)
Davis, Isaac
Dean, Jesse
Delaware Pottery
East Trenton Pottery
Efcolite Corp.
Empire Pottery
Enterprise Pottery
Eturia Pottery
Equitable Pottery
Fell & Thropp

Glasgow Pottery
Goldcrest Pottery
Goldcrest Ceramics Pottery
Goldscheider Pottery
Greenwood China Co.
Greenwood Pottery (see Greenwood China
  Co.)
Holland Mold
Ideal Pottery
Imperial Porcelain Works
International Pottery Works
Jersey City Pottery Co.
Jersey Porcelain & Earthenware Co.
Keystone Pottery Co.
Lenox Inc.
Lamberton Works
Lincoln Pottery
Maddock Pottery Co.
Maddock, John & Sons
Maddock, Thomas & Sons
Mercer Pottery
Millington & Asbury
Millington, Asbury & Poulson
Nalbone, Charles
Nassau China Co.
New Jersey Pottery Co.
Ott & Brewer
Perlee, Inc.
Providential Tile Co.
Rittenhouse & Evans
Scammell China Co.
Schiller Corday, Inc. (see Boleslaw Cybis)
Star Porcelain Co.
Tatler, W.H.
Taylor & Co.
Taylor, Goodwin & Co.
Thorp & Brewer
Trenton China Co.
Trenton Potteries Co.
Trenton Pottery Co.
Trenton Pottery Works
Van Pottery
Young, William & Sons

Woodbridge
Nancy China
Poillon Pottery
Salamander Works

New Mexico

Acoma
Acoma Pottery (Indian Pottery)

Albuquerque
Muddy Wheel Gallery
Ostrowe, Caryn

La Luz
La Luz Clay Products Co.

Ruidosa
White Mountain Pottery

San Il Defonso Pueblo
Martinez, Marie & Julian

Santa Clara Reservation
Santa Clara Pottery (Indian Pottery)

New York

Alfred
Cushing, Val M.
Glidden Pottery
New York State College

Albany
Boynton, Calvin (also W. Troy)
Dillon, Chas.
Orcutt and Thompson (also Ashfield)
Tyler, (Moses) and Chas. Dillon

Ashfield
Orcutt, Delding and Co.
Orcutt, Guildford and Co.
Orcutt, W. and E.

Athens

Clark, Nathan and Associates (also Lyons)

Bayside, Long Island
Peters, Charles Adolf

Bedford Village
Durant Kilns

Binghamton
Roberts, William
White and Wood

Broadway
Crownford China

Bronx
Confort China Co.
Rosenthal, George

Brooklyn
Abraham and Strauss, Inc.
Graham, Charles

Buffalo
Buffalo Pottery
Larkin Co.
Platecraft of America, Inc.

Chittenango
Chittenango Pottery

Coerlears Hook, Manhatten
Commeraw, Thomas

Cornish
Orchard Kilns Pottery

Corona
American Art Ceramic Co.
Corona Pottery (see Jervis, W.P. listing)
Jervis, W.P. (also Rose Valley, Pa.)
Tiffany Studios (also Hoboken, N.J.)

Cortland
Chollar and Various Associates
Mason and Russell
Woodruff, M. and Co.

East Aurora
Roycroft Industries

East Hampton
Middle Lane Pottery (also Westhampton)

Ellenville
Weston, D.

Fort Edwards
Fort Edward Pottery
Haxstun, Ottman and Co.
New York Stoneware Co.
Ottman Bros.
Underwood, J.A. and G.W.

Fort Ticonderoga
Fort Ticonderoga Pottery

Galesville
Galesville, Various Potters

Geddes
Sheppard, J.

Great Neck
Superware Corp.

Greenpoint
Faience Manufacturing Co.
Union Porcelain Works

Hadon Falls
Halm Art Pottery Co.

Hamburg
Clayworks Production Studios (Linda
   Kitchen)

Hartford
Seymour Brothers

Havanna
Whitman, J.M.
Whittemore, A.O.

Hudson
Selby, E. and Co.

Huntington, Long Island
Brown Brothers (see Huntington Pottery)
Huntington Pottery
Lewis and Gardiner

Hyack
Leeman, Stephen, Products Co.

Lake Success
Mallory Randall Corp.

Le Roy
Lapp Insulator Co.

Lima
Lima Insulator Co.
Porcelain Insulator Corp./Pinco Division

Long Island
Soriano Ceramics

Lyons
Fisher, Jacob
Lyons Pottery

Manhatten
Smith, Washington

Mountaindale
Mountaindale Pottery

Newark
Empire Crafts Corp.

New Berlin
Regan, Peter
Schneider, Aviva

Troy
Lent, George (also Lansingburgh)
Reily, James (also Lansingburgh)
Thayer, Pliny (also Lansignburgh)

New York City
Alexander, S. and Sons
Altman, B. and Co.
American Heritage Publishing Co.
American Home Products Corp.
American House Ltd.
Arcadia Export-Import
Ariston, Inc.
Arlen China Co. (Harlem Crockery Co.)
Associated American Artists
Atlas China Co.
Bacharach, Inc.
Barth Equipment Co., Inc.
Bent and Co., Inc.
Berndae, Inc.
Block China Co.
Block, J. and I. Co.
Blue Arrows Decorating Workshop
Borgfeldt, George, Corp.
Breslauer-Underberg, Inc.
Buckley, Newhall Co.
Carnegie, Hattie, Inc.
Cauter Porcelain Co.
Cavendish Trading Corp.
Chambers Street Pottery, Ltd.
Charleston Decorating Co.
Chelsea Lamo and Shade Co.
Chemical Garden, Inc.
Children's Television Workshop
China and Glass Distributors, Inc.
Continental Ceramics Corp.
Crest Studios
Crolius Pottery
Crownford China Co.
Day, Evangeline
De Lite Mfging. Co., Inc.
De Luxe Decorating Works, Inc.
Design Technic
Eastern China Co., Inc.
East Morrisania China Works
Ebeling and Reuss Co.
Empire State Glass Decorating Co.
Enco, Inc.
Evans, Norris
Everlast
Exclusive China Co.
Farber Brothers
Farber, Samuel P.
Farber, S.W. (see Samuel P. Farber)
Farber, Sydney (see Samuel P. Farber)
Fajans, Caroline R.
Fondeville, Eugene L.
Fortescue, Cecily

Freeman, I. and Co. (also Chicago)
Gallstyn Co., Inc.
General Ceramics
German-American Stoneware Works
Gimbel Bros., Inc.
Goldman Costume Co.
Hall, Charles, Inc.
Harlem Crockery Co.
Harris Strong, Inc. (see Potters of Wall
   Street)
Hellman, Louis E.
Inwood Pottery Studios
Jabeson China Co.
Jensen, George, Inc.
Jervis, Dorothy
Johns-Manville
Kahla China Co.
Keepsake House and Madows
Kupper, Herman C.
Lang and Osgood
Leeman, Stephen, Products Co. (also
   Nyack)
Lefcourte Cosmetics Co.
Lehman, Lewis and Co.
Levy Bros. China Co., Inc.
Lipman, Bernard
Little-Jones Co., Inc.
Lunning, Frederick
MacDougal, Alice Foote, Coffee Shops, Inc.
Macquoid, William and Co.
Macy, R.H. and Co., Inc.
Maddock and Miller
May Dept. Stores
McCrory Stores Corp. (several locations)
McCutcheon, James and Co.
Michaels and Co. Inc.
Midhurst China Co.
Mittledorfer Straus
Morgan, D.
Moss, David L. and Co.
Museum Pieces, Inc.
National Silver Co.
National Specials Co.
Newland, Schneeloch and Piek Inc.
New York Merchandise Co.
New York Pottery
Overseas Mercantile Co.
Ovington Brothers Co.
Packing Products Co.
Pasmantier, John L.
Paul, Edward P. Co.
Penny, J.C. Co. Inc.
Pitman-Dreitzer and Co. Inc.
Plymouth Wholesale Dry Goods Corp.
Potters of Wall Street
Pottery Barn
Princeton China Co.
Reimer, Fred C. and Co.
Remmey Family Various Potters (also
   Philadelphia and Baltimore)
Rogers, John
Rosenthal-Block China Co.
Ross, Howard L. Corp.
Rubel and Co. Decorative Accessories
Saks and Co.
Salamander Works
Shaw, James and Co.
Simon, Alfred and Co.
Sinaco Co. Inc.
Sohn, Earnest
Stern Brothers

Stonelain Pottery
Straub, Paul A. and Co.
Straus, Nathan, Inc.
Stupell, Carole Ltd.
Styson Art Products
Tebor, Inc.
Tiffany and Co.
Twin Spout Pottery Inc.
Van Nostrand, Morris A.
Vogue Mercantile Co.
Wanamaker, John (also Philadelphia)
Weil Ceramics and Glass Inc.
Weissman, Beth
Weissman Co. Inc.
Werner, Kruger Co.
Wille, M. Inc.
Windsor China Co. Inc.
Woronock, David and William Ansen
Wright, Mary S.
Wright, Russel
Zapun Ceramics Inc.

New York State
Levis, Otto V.
Volkmar, Charles (several places)
Wickham, Nancy

Niagara Falls
Carborundum Museum of Ceramics

North Pole
Santa's Workshop Inc.

North Tonowanda
Fleuron, Inc.

Ogdensburg
Hart, various potters (also Sherbourne and
    Fulton)

Olean
Alcas Cutlery Corp.
Wands, I.H.

Oneida
Oneida Community Ltd. (also Sherrill)

Pelham Manor
Jackson Internationale
Senegal China

Pen Yan (Yates County)
Mantell and Thomas
Pen Yan Pottery

Plandome Manor
Fischl, Janet W.

Pittsburgh
Union Potteries Co. (also East Liverpool,
    Ohio)

Pompey
Van Hunke, Dee and Robert

Poughkeepsie
Ball, J.B. and Co.
Boon and Co. T.G.
Caire Pottery

Mabbett and Anthone
Nichols, W.
Reynold, W.

Rochester
Burger, John, Pottery
Glaser, Louis J.
Robeson Rochester Corp. (also Perry)

Rock Tavern
White Cloud Farms

Roundout
Madden, J.M.

Rome
Seymour, N. and A.

Rosendale
April, Nancy

Southampton
Ridgewood Industries Inc.

Straatsburg
Wayne Mfg. Co.

Syracuse
Farrar W.H. and Co.
Iroquois China Co.
Syracuse China Co.

Troy
Boynton, Calvin and Associates
Chapman, Josiah
Coplin, Alexander
Lent, George
Orcutt, Humiston and Co.
Seymour (various potters)
Tyler and Thompson (see Seymour)
West Troy Pottery (see Seymour)

Utica
Brayton and Associates
Central New York Pottery
Field, L.F.
Roberts, David
White Clay Products Co.
White N. and Son
White's Pottery

Victor
General Electric Co. (see Lock Insulator
    Co.)
Locke Insulator Co.
I-T-E Imperial Corp.
Victor Insulators, Inc.

West Troy
Boynton, Calvin
Perry, Sanford S.
Warner, W.M.E.
West Troy Pottery

Woodstock
Byrdcliffe Pottery

North Carolina
Alamance County
Loy, Soloman

Arden
Brown's Pottery (see Brown Family)
Pisgah Forest P.

Asheville
Gray, Verdelle
Wager, Robert

Banner Elk
Potter's Mark Studio (Dicks)

Bethabara
Aust, Gottfried (also Salem)
Christ, Rudolt (also Salem

Blackburn
Ritchie, Luther Seth

Burnsville
Gamza, Steve

Catawaba County
Phillips Pottery
Ritchie, Thomas (also Lincoln County)

Charlotte
Pinewood Pottery (Converse)

Drexel
Drexel Furniture Co.

Hickory
Hilton Potteries
Hyalyn Porcelain

High Point
Unaka Potteries Inc.

Luther
Omar Khayam Pottery (Bachelder)

Penland
Lawton, James
Peiser, Jane
Penland School of Crafts

Merry Oaks
Royal Crown Pottery & Porcelain Co.

Raleigh
Rosenbloom, Carol

Randolf County
Brower, John F.
Fox, Homer Jacob (also Chatham County)

Robbins
Teaque Pottery

Salem
Aust, Gottfried (also Bethabara)
Christ, Rudolf (also Bethabara)
Holland, John Frederic
Schaffner, Henry

Sanford
North State Pottery Co.
Pine State Pottery (see North State Pottery)

Seagrove
A.R. Cole

Jugtown Pottery
Owen & Owens Family Potters
Seagrove Pottery (Auman)
Sweezy, Nancy
Westmoore Pottery

Tyron
Little Mountain Pottery (Graves)

Vale
Craig, B.B.
Hartzog, David
Holly, Daniel
Lefevres, Isaac
Reinhardt Potteries (Various)
Seagle, Daniel
Seagle, James F.

North Dakota

Dickinson
Dickinson Clay Products Co.
Dickota Pottery

Grand Forks
North Dakota School of Mines

Wahpeton
Rosemeade Pottery
Wahpeton Pottery Co.

Ohio

Ada
Minich, Lorna

Akron Area (including Mogadore, Springfield & Middlebury)
Adams, Allison and Co.
Akron China Co.
Akron Pottery Co.
Boss Brothers
Camp and Thompson
Chapman, Upson and Wright
De Haven, Abraham
Harris, Thomas
Johnson, Whitmore and Co.
Knight, Maurice A., Co.
Leitzke Porcelain
Markell, Immon and Co.
Mead, I.M. and Co.
Merrill, E.H. Co.
Moore, W.T.
Myers and Hall
Ohio Brass Co.
Ransbottom Brothers Pottery
Robinson Clay Products Co.
Robinson Merrill Co.
Sawyer, H.
Smith, J.C.
Summitt China Co.
U.S. Stoneware Co.
Wait and Ricketts
Weeks, A.J.
Weeks, Cook and Weeks
Weeks, F.H.
Whitmore, Robinson and Co.

Alliance
Alliance China Co.
Alliance Vitreous China Co.
Century Service Corp.

Crescent China Co.
Cunningham Ind.
Cunningham and Pickett
International China Co.
International D.S. Co.
Kettlesprings Kilns
Laughlin International
Leigh Potters, Inc.
Lifetime China Co.

Antiock
Amos, F.M.

Athens
Mather, Tim, Stoneware and Porcelain
Putnam Pottery (Madonik)

Atwater
Purdy, Various Potters (also Putnam)

Barbarton
Coventry Ware, Inc.
Dior Studios

Bedford
Bailey-Walker China Co.
National Potteries Corp.
Walker China Co.

Beloit
Ilka Ceramics
G. & J. Decorating Co.

Bucyrus
Cookware Associates

Byesville
Cook Porcelain Insulator Co.

Cambridge
Atlas-Globe China Co.
Cambridge Art Pottery
Cook Porcelain Insulator (Byesville)
Globe China Co.
Guernsey Earthenware
Oxford Pottery Co.
Oxford Tile Co., see Universal Potteries, Inc.
Salt of the Earth (Beauchamp)
Universal Potteries Co.
Universal Promotions, Inc.

Canton
Binkley, George
Clewell Pottery
Morgan Belleck China Co.
Scott, Meg
Stark Ceramics
U.S. Ceramics Tile/Spartek Inc.

Carey
Crawford Ceramics
Federal Porcelain Co.
Porcelain Products, Inc.

Carrollton
Albright China Co.
Bahl Potteries, Inc.
Carrollton Pottery
Triangle Novelty Co.

Chesterhill
Open Sky Studio (Pekoc)

Chilicothe
Florentine Pottery

Cincinnati
Avon Pottery
Berninghaus Co.
Brockman Pottery Co.
Cincinnati Art Pottery
Cincinnati Pottery Club
Coultry Pottery
Dallas, Frederick, Pottery
Dayton Street Pottery
Dell, William, Pottery
Franklin Pottery
Frasca and Aerni, see Spring Street Pottery
Hamilton Road Pottery
Healy, Susan G.
Independent Mfrs. Assoc. Inc.
Kendall, Uriah
Korte, Pam, Pottery
McLaughlin, M.L.
Morgan, Matt, Art Pottery
Piper, Lucile Seymour, Co.
Queen City Pottery Co.
Raines, Elsie H.
Rookwood Pottery No. 1
Rookwood Pottery No. 2
Scott, George
Spring Street Pottery
Wheatley Pottery Co.
Wheatley Tile and Pottery Co.
Wheatley, T.J. and Co.

Cleveland
American Chinaware Corp.
American Greeting Card Corp.
Blazys, Alexander, Cleveland
Bogatay, Paul
Bowman, George H./Cleveland China Co.
Brody, E.O., Co.
Cleveland China Co.
Cowan Pottery (also Rocky River)
Eckhardt, Edris
Higgins, A.D.
International Artware Corp.
Kromex Corp.
Schrechengost, Victor
Scott and Fetzer Co.
Woideck, (George), Stoneware Pottery (studio)

Columbus
Aitken, Russell
Albeco Ceramics
Arwood, Barbara
Baggs, Arthur (also Cleveland)
Conaway, Mary S.
Denlinger, Ding
Floch, Jenny
Golden Rule, Inc.
Hand, Russ
Hoffman China
Hunt, William
Hunter Street Pottery (Radca)
Kahiki Restaurant
Leach, Sara Ann

Littlefield, Edgar
McIntosh, Martha L.
Nicodemus, Chester
Pereny Pottery Co.
Potter's Habitat (Jones)
Pots and Stuff (Barnett)
Potter's Wheel (Lynda Schaefer)
Rogers Jewelers
Shafer, Thomas
Shanahan, Mary Jury
Swamp Studio
Talbot, Betty L.
Wagner, Teresa
Wasserstrom's
Wege Marble and Tile Co.

Coshocton
Pope Gosser China Co.

Crooksville
Acme Pottery
Bluebird Pottery
Brown, Tedrow and Crooks
Buckeye Stoneware
Burley Clay Products
Burley Potteries
Burley-Winter Pottery
Crooksville China Co.
Diamond Stoneware Co.
Hicks, E.A.
Hull Pottery Co.
Karen's Kustom Kreations
McGray, H.
Star Stoneware Co.
Watt Pottery

Dalton
Cordelia China Co.
Dalton Pottery
Houghton Pottery

Dayton
Broome, Isaac
Dayton Porcelain Works
Henderson, Alison
Wheeler, Stu
Wood

Delaware
Lehner, Ann Berquist
Long, Doyle

Dennison
Vogue Art Ware and China Co.

Dover
Wores, H.

Doylestown
Routson Pottery

Dublin
Grab, Elaine

East Liverpool
Acacia China Co.
American Pottery Works
Ball and Morris
Bennett, Various Potteries
Bloor, William
Brunt, Bloor, Martin and Co.

Brunt Family Assoc.
Brunt, G.F., Porcelain Co.
Burford Brothers Pottery
Cartwright Brothers
Colonial Pottery Co.
Craft Master of Toledo
Craven Art Pottery
Croxall and Associates, see Ball & Morris
Croxall and Cartwright
Dresden Pottery Works
East End China Co.
East Liverpool Potteries Co.
East Liverpool Pottery Co.
Frederick, Schenkle and Allen, see Globe
  Pottery Co.
Globe Pottery Co.
Goodwin Pottery
Great Western Pottery Co.
Hall China Co.
Harker, George S., Pottery
Harker Pottery Co.
Harker, Taylor and Co.
Harker, Thompson and Co.
International Brotherhood of Pottery and
  Allied Workers
Kass China Co.
Keystone China Co.
Knowles, Taylor, Knowles
Louthan Mfg. Co.
McNicol and Corns
McNicol and Smith
McNicol, Burton and Co.
McNicol, Patrick
McNicol, T.A.
Meric Art Studio
Monarck Dinnerware Co.
Murphy Pottery Co.
National China Co.
Novelty Pottery
Pearl China Co.
Phoenix Pottery
Pioneer Pottery Co.
Potter's Cooperative
Potter's Supply Co.
Riverside Knob Works
Salt and Mear
Sayre China Co.
Schreckengost, Don
Sevres China Co.
Smith Philips China Co.
Standard Pottery
Sterling China Co. (also Wellsville)
Thomas China Co. (also Lisbon)
Thompson, C.C., Pottery Co.
Thorley, Palin
Trenle China Co.
Tunnicliff, Edward
Union Potteries Co.
U.S. Potters Assoc.
Vodrey Brothers
Wallace and Chetwynd
Warner-Keffer China Co.
West End Pottery Co.
Woodward and Vodrey
Woodward, Blakely and Co.
Wyllie, John and Son

East Palestine
Bel Terr China, Inc.
China Artwares Co., see Pa. Dutch
  Potteries

Continental China Co.
East Palestine Pottery Co.
Fitzpatrick Ind., see Pa. Dutch Potteries
Fuestal and Nowling Pottery Co., see East
  Palestine Pottery Co.
George, W.S., Pottery
Harding China
Kingwood Ceramics
Klare China
Morris, Dwight China Co.
Ohio China Co.
Pennsylvania Dutch Potteries

East Sparta
Sparta Ceramic Tile Co.

Findlay
Bell Pottery Co.
Findlay Porcelain Co.
Porcelain Products Co.
Salveson-Gerbasi Pottery

Franklin
Franklin Pottery Co.

Fredericksburg
American Beleek Co.
Fredericksburg Art Pottery

Galena
Lions Head Pottery

Germantown
Shawnee Creek Kilns

Granville
Eerdmans, Jennifer

Hamilton
Hamilton Tile Works
Ohio Tile Works

Harrison
Rupp Pottery

Hartville
Stebner Studios

Hudson
Koenig, Diane

Ironton
Harria, W.P.
Ironton Pottery
Manring, E., and Co.
Silliman, G.W.
Young and Harris

Lakeview
Earl, Jack

Lancaster
Anchor Hocking Corp.
Ravenscroft, Ltd., see Anchor Hocking

Lisbon
Delta Star Electronic Div. (H.K. Porter Co.)
Thomas China Co. (also East Liverpool)

Logan
Bachman, Kathy
Logan Pottery Co.
Magdich, Jean

Malta
Joetown Pottery (Zaros)
Zaros Pottery

Mansfield
McCormick, Annette

Marietta
Weil, Walter and Sandy

Marysville
Entis, Ann

Massillon
Binkley, George, see Massilon, O. potters
Boerner, Andrew, see Massilon, O. potters
Welker, Adam

Medina
Clay and Fiber Studio (Kathleen Totter
  Smith)

Minerva
Cronin China Co.
Owen, Edward J., China Co.

Mount Gilead
Florence Pottery
McGowan Pottery

Muskingum County
Dollings, John & W.C.
Hall, E.
Peterson, James

Newcastle
McCurdy, I.

New Lexington
Liberty China, see Virginia Pottery
Ludowici Celadon Co.
Virginia Pottery

New Philadelphia
Figley, Joseph

Newport
Read, Thomas
Works, Laban H.

Niles
Atlas China Co.
Bradshaw China
Tritt China Co.

Oberlin
Phinney, Tom

Painesville
Harris, Charles W.
Sarosy, Lorri

Portage County
Tupper, C.

Proctorville
Reynolds, J.

Putnam
Bell, Joseph
Rice, Prosper

Ravena
Seymour & Stedman

Ripley
Gamtoft Pottery (Jensen)

Rocky River
Cowan Pottery (also Cleveland)

Roseville
Armstrong, Joe
Brush-McCoy Pottery
Brush Pottery
Bullock, William S.
Chrisshaun Art
D. and D. Pottery
Friendship Pottery
Lowry, Various Potteries
Mayers, W.S.
McCoy, J.W., Pottery
McCoy, Nelson, Pottery
Melick, H.H.
Midland Pottery, see J.W. McCoy
National Pottery
Pace Family Potters
P. and E. Decorators
Ransbottom Brothers Pottery Co.
Robinson-Ransbottom Pottery Co.
Roseville Pottery Co.
South Fork Pottery
Tycer, Warren I.
Ungemach Pottery Co.
Walpole, W.L.

Salem
Salem China Co.
Sweteye Ceramic Artware

Salineville
Dresden China Co., see National China Co.

Scio
Scio Pottery

Sebring
Americana Art China Co.
American Limoges China Co., see Limoges
  China Co.
Art China Co.
China Craft
French China Co.
French Saxon China Co.
Gem Clay Forming Co.
Grindley Artware Mfg. Co.
Holiday Designs, Inc.
Limoges China Co.
Lincoln China Co., see Limoges China Co.
Modern China Co.
Oakwood China Co.
Oliver China Co.
Queens China Co.
Royal China Co.
Saxon China Co.

Sebring Bros. Pottery
Sebring China Co.
Sebring, E.H., China Co.
Sebring Mfg. Co.
Sebring Pottery Co.
Spaulding China Co.
Stanford Pottery

Senaca County
Hopkins, John

Sheffield Lake
Framae Art Pottery (Steel)

Somerset
Heighshoe, S.E.

Sparta
Sparta Ceramic Tile Co.
U.S. Ceramic Tile Co.

Springfield
Turn of the Wheel (Morret)

Steubenville
Lonhuda Art Pottery
Steubenville Pottery Co.

Streetsboro
Clayfield's Pottery

Sugarcreek
Swiss Valley Designs

Summit County
Mead, I.M.

Summitville
Summitville Tile Works

Symmes Creek
Miner, William

Taylorsville
Neff Brothers

Tiffin
Radford Pottery (also Zanesville)

Tiltonsville
Avon Faience Pottery Co.

Tipp City
Jones, Cindy Butler
Tipp City Novelty Co.

Toledo
Daubt Glass and Crockery Co.
Green Thumb Products
Janas, Stephanie
Ransburg, Harper J., and Co.

Toronto
American China Co.

Tuscarawas County
Dick, Jacob
Hamilton, Clem

Uricksville
Unitile Co.
Vogue Art Pottery Co.

Wellsville
Acme Craftware, Inc.
Baum, J.H.
Bunting, W.C., Co.
Chic Pottery
Morley and Co.
Patterson and Sons
Pioneer pottery
Sterling China Co.
U.S. Pottery Co.
Wellsville China Co.
Wellsville Pioneer Pottery

West Lafayette
Moore, Walter B., Inc.

White Cottage
Leica Ceramics
Newton, Dewey
Stine Pottery

Wooster
Coxon Pottery
Routson Pottery (also Doylestown)
Wooster China Co.

Worthington
Butler, Julia B.
Jackson, Sharon
Pincherry Pottery

Youngstown
Cosmopolitan Wares, Inc.
Promotions, Inc.
Vanity Fair Housewares, Inc.

Zanesville
American Encaustic Tiling Co.
Arc-En Ciel
Bohemian Pottery
Brighton Pottery
Brush, George S., Pottery
Chic Pottery, also Wellsville
Clark Stoneware Co.
Dubois & Kinsey
Ferrell, Frank
Fraunfelter China Co.
Gonder Ceramic Arts
Hartstone, Inc.
Herold, John J.
Imperial Porcelain Co.
J & E Decorators
Jones, Cecil
Le Pere Pottery
Lessell, John
Marco Pottery
McCoy, Ltd.
McCoy, William F.
Mosiac Tile Co.
Nielson, Christian
Nouvelle Pottery
Ohio Porcelain
Ohio Pottery
Owens, J.B., Pottery
Peters & Reed/Zane Pottery
Pottery Queen

Radford Pottery (also Tiffin)
Rhead Pottery
Roseville Pottery
Shafer, G.C., Pottery
Shafer, G.C., Pottery
Shawnee Pottery Co.
Slago Pottery
Terrace Ceramics
Wagner, Art
Weller Pottery
Wisecarver, Rick
Zane Pottery, see Peters & Reed
Zanesville Art Pottery
Zanesville Stoneware Co.

Zoar
Zoar Pottery, see Purdy Potters

Oklahoma
Miami
James, Bill Y.
Winart Pottery

Muskogee
Chesnutt, Corinne
Gracetone Pottery

Oklahoma City
Osborne, Beverly

Perry
Tamac Pottery

Porum
Cherokee Nation Pottery (also Tahlequah)

Sapulpa
Frankoma Pottery

Yale
No-Ten-O-Quah Pottery (Thorpe Indian Pottery)

Oregon
Eugene
Myrtle Point
Notkin, Richard T.
Planned Products Inc.

Oakridge
Worth Willow Ware

Roseberg
Viletta China Co. (also Houston, Texas)

Pennsylvania
Beaver Falls
Beaver Falls Art Tile Co.
Mayer China Co.

Bedminster
Drach, Rudolf
Weber, J.A.

Berks County
Troxal potters (various)

Berwick
Stofflet Potters (various)
Wessler & Edwards

Bloomsburg
Rabb and Rehm

Brownsville
Barnyard Pottery (Schaltenbrand)
Ware, Stephen (West Brownsville)
Westerwald Pottery (Schaltenbrand)

Bryn Mawr
Pear Tree

Bucks County
Headman, Andrew
Klinker, Christian
Weaver, Abraham

Cambridge Springs
Campbell, William H., Factory Studios

Canonsburg
Canonsburg Pottery
East Palestine Pottery Co.

Carnegie
Red Bull Inns of America, Inc.

Carversville
Kline, Phillip

Cassville
Hyssong/Hissong, various Potteries (also Huntington)

Chambersburg
Bell, John

Cooksburgh
Cooksburgh Pottery

Derry
Pittsburgh High Voltage Insulators Co.
Westinghouse Electric Corp.

Derry Station
Derry China Co.

Doylestown
Moravian Pottery & Tile Works

Dryville
Dry, John

DuBois
China & Glass Decorators

East Birmingham
Eiler Pottery
Foell & Alt

Edinboro
Nicholas, Donna L.

Falls Creek
Jackson China Co.

Ford City
Ford China Co.

Fredericktown
Bower, J.
Donaghho, A.P.

Gettysburg
Arquette, Cliff

Greensboro
Boughner Pottery
Hamilton, James & Co.
Lettell & Co.
Monon Center Inc.
Reppert Pottery
Reppert & Williams
Vance Pottery
Williams, Robert T. (also New Geneva)

Harrisburgh
Cowden Pottery
Cowden & Wilcox
Moyer, William, Pottery
Willson, T.H. & Co.
Young, John & Co.

Hawthorn
Hawthorn Pottery

Haycock
Singer, Simon

Howard
Leathers Pottery (also Mount Eagle)

Huntingdon
Hyssong/Hissong Potteries
Glazier, Henry
Thomas, William H.

Indiana
United Flavor Seal Co.

Johnstown
Swank, Hiram & Sons

Kittanning
Pennsylvania China Co.

Lancaster County
Eagle Porcelain Works (Gast)
Ganse, Henry
Gast, Henry

Lewistown
Dipple Pottery

Lock Haven
Various Potters (Shroat, Hoffard, Strayer, etc.)

Logansville
Gerstung, John

Masontown
New Geneva Stoneware Co.

McKean
Swift Creek Pottery (The Kemenyffys)

McKeesport
Grant, W.T. Co.
Sabin Industries (also Mt. Clemens, MI)

Maytowne
Klugh, Jesse

Medford
Spinner, David

Mifflinburg
West, Andrea

Milton
Bastian, John

Moorsburg
Ack Potters
Klinker, Christian

Montgomery County
Hubener Pottery
Medinger, Jacob
Roudebush, Henry

Morrisville
Pennsbury Pottery

Mount Pleasant
Howell Porcelain

New Berlin
Maize, William S.
Millheim Pottery
Weiser, H.H.

New Brighton
Elverson, Sherwood & Barker
Enterprise Pottery Co.
Hardesty China Co.
Kirk China Co.
Sherwood Brothers Pottery

New Castle
New Castle Pottery
Shenango China Co.
Woodmere China Co., Inc.

New Geneva
Atchison, HK.
Conrad, A & Co.
Debolt & Atchison
Dilliner, Leander B.
Dilliner, Samuel R.
Eberhart, John R. & Thomas
Eneix & Frankenberry
Eneix, James E.
Williams, Charles L.
Williams & Couch
Williams, Robert T. (also Greensboro)

New Kensington
Aluminum Cooking Utensil Co.

Newport
Miller, George, Family Potters

Newtown
Ramblewood, Anna Mae Burke

Newville
Irvine, Samuel
Zigler, Henry H.

Nockamixon
Taney, Jacob & Isaac

Norristown
Franklin Porcelain Co.

North East
Irish-Hosler Potery

Philadelphia
Allen, George
American China Manufactory (Tucker)
Beech, Ralph B. (also Kensington)
Bonnin & Morris
Bruce, Fisher & Co.
Burnett & Remmey
Capri Creations
Ebeling & Reuss Co.
Fisher, Bruce & Co.
Galloway & Gaff
Haig Pottery
Kelly, Peter
Kurlbaum & Swartz
Marks & Bruhn
McIlvain, William G.
Pennsylvania Museum & School of Industrial Art
Philadelphia City Pottery
Philco Corporation
Plymouth Products
Plymouth Pottery
Port Richmond Pottery Co.
Pardee C. Works (also New Jersey)
Remmey, John Bolgiano
Remmey, Richard Clinton
Remmey, Robert Henry
Tucker, William E. (American China Manufactory)
Wanamaker, John (also N.Y.C.)
Weil, Lewis (see Alfred J. Weil)

Phoenixville
Beerbower & Griffen
Chester Pottery
Griffen Pottery
Griffen China Co.
Griffen, Love & Co.
Griffen, Smith & Hill
Griffen, Smith & Co.
Penn China Co.
Phoenixville Pottery
Schreiber & Betz
Tuxedo Pottery

Pittsburgh
Brinn's China & Glassware Co.
Kaufmann's Department Stores Inc.
Star Encaustic Tile Co.

Pittston
Jones, Evan B.

Plymouth Meeting
Brookcraft Pottery

Powder Mill Valley (near Allentown)
Stahl Pottery

Reading
Shenfelder, D.P.

Rices Landing
Excelsior Works

Robesonia
Breininger, Lester & Barbara

Rochester
Keystone Pottery Co.

Rose Valley
Jervis, William Percival
Rose Valley Pottery (see W.P. Jervis)

Schuylkill County
Boyer, John
Brockville Pottery

Scranton
Millar, George V.

Shartlesville
Henne, T.S.

Shippenburg (Cumberland County)
Rudolf, Valentine

Shippenville
Purinton Pottery Co.

Syndertown
Weimer Family Pottery

South Greenburg
Porcelier Manufacturing Co.

Southampton
Ridgewood China Co.

Stonetown
Link Pottery

Sunbury
Metcalf, Thomas B.
Savidge & Son

Tylersport
Scholl Pottery

Uniontown
Heritage Company

Upper Hanover
Greber Pottery

Villanova
Hoover, Joseph C.
Leman (or Lehman?) Johannes

Warren
Allegheny China Co.

Warrington
American Fine China

Washington
Washington Company

Waynesboro
Bell, John W.
Bell, Upton
Beuter, John

Wicksboro
Wick China Co. (also Kittanning)

Williamsport
Hobart, D.P.
Moore, Nichols & Co.
Sipe, Nichols & Co.
Sipe Pottery

Womelsdorf
Smith, Willoughby

Wrightstown
Smith, Joseph

York
Pfaltzgraff Pottery

Puerto Rico
Caribe China Corp (see Sterling China Co.)

Rhode Island
Pascoag
Holcomb, Jan C.

Providence
Gorham Company

South Carolina
Charleston
Duche, Andrew (also Georgia)
Historic Charleston Foundation

Edgefield District
Chandler, Thomas M.
Miles, Lewis J. Pottery
Potterville (various Potters)
Rhodes, Collin

Kaolin
Southern Porcelain Mfg. Co.

South Dakota
Colome
Cahay Clay Co.

Tennessee
Alexandria
New Hope Studios (Fariello)

Austin
Terr, Sam & Associates

Bell Buckle
Bell Buckle Pottery (White)
Crocket Pottery

Chattanooga
American Lava Corp.

Clarksville
Rice, Tim

Dandridge
Wing's Pottery

Dowelltown
Cosmic Clay Studio (Colombarini)

Erwin
Clouse Pottery
Southern Potteries Inc.

Franklin
Ridge Pottery (Akin)

Friendsville
Monsarrat Pottery

Gatlinburg
Arrowmont School of Crafts

Irwin
Clinchfield Artware Pottery
Southern Potteries Inc.

Jonesboro
Cherokee China Co.

Knoxville
Big Witch Pottery (Gina Anderson)
Knox Porcelain Corp.

Laurel Bloomery
Iron Mountain Stoneware

Lynchburg
Jack Daniel Distillery

Memphis
Stark Pottery (Agnes Stark)

Murfreesboro
Combs, Bill
Studio S (Lewis D. Snyder)

Nashville
Clay Works (Clayton)
Forest Valley Galleries (Lederer)
Nashville Art Pottery
Overcast Clay Sculptureworks & Crocks
Sanders Mfg. Co.
Vanderkooi, Lenore

Nonconnah (near Memphis)
Stephen, Walter

Oak Ridge
Cabbages & Kings Pottery (Knauff)
Paul Menchhofer Pottery

Pigeon Forge
Pigeon Forge Pottery (Ferguson)

Sewanee
Hallelujah P., Goubeaud.

Sevierville
Myhr, David W.

Tullahoma
Stegnall's Stoneware Pottery

Texas
Argyle
Miller, John Brough

Austin
Feats of Clay
Sam Terr Associates

Bastrop
Le Pot Marie (Blazek)

Comanche
Comanche Pottery

Dallas
Fitz & Floyd
Love Field Potteries
Neiman-Marcus Co.
Southern Pottery

Denton
Lambert J.C. (Denton County)
Roark Pottery

Eastland
Horton Ceramics
House of Webster Ceramics

Elmendorf
Star Pottery

Fort Worth
Lincoln, Richard M.
Waples-Platier Grocier Co.

Gilmer
Gilmer Potteries

Henderson
(see the listing Henderson, Texas Various
  Potters for the following)
Cogburn & Protho
Hunt, J.F.
Leopard, John & Son
Rushton Pottery
Russel Pottery

Houston
Viletta China Co. (also Roseberg, Oregon)

Lexington
Soto, Ismael

Limestone County
Oletha Pottery

Marshall
Marshall Pottery

McDade
McDade Pottery

San Antonio
Greer, Georgeanna H.

Vermont
Bennington
Bennington Potters (D. Gill)
Norton Pottery
United States Pottery

Burlington
Ballard, O.L. & A.K.
Nichols & Alford
Nichols & Boynton
Woodworth, F.

Dorset
Fenton, Jonathon
Fenton, R.L. & Co.

Fairfax
Farrar potters, various

St. Johnbury
Fenton & Hancock
Fenton, R.W.

Wallingford
Leonard, S.E.

Virginia
Abingdon
Cumbow Decorating Co.

Albermarle County
Monticello

Alexandria
Milburn, B.C.
Miller E.J.
Miller R.H. & E.J.
Plum, Lewis
Smith, J.W. & H.C.
Swann, John B.
Turn of the Century Pottery (Julie Martin)
Wilkes St. Pottery

Appomattox
Robertson, David T & B. Shearer

Arlington
Baynes, Mary Phelan

Charlottsville
Lingdon, Barbara

Fairfax County
Mt. Vernon Gift Shop

Hopewell
Hopewell China Co.
James Rivers Potteries

Jordan Mines
Fulton, G.N.

Lightfoot
Williamsburg Pottery Factory Inc.

Mechanicsville
Freimarck, John

Mt. Herman
Coffman Potters

New Market
Schweinfurt, John George

Newport News
Silhouette, Thomas P. Duncan

Norfolk
Miller, Marcellus, S.

Richmond
Duval, Benjamin B.

Staunton
Cutting, Heyward Jr.

Strasburg
Bell Potters (various names)
Crisman, W.H.
Eberly Pottery

Funkhouser, L.D. & Co.
Heckerson, James N.
Keister Pottery
Lehew, W.H. & Co.
Miller, George W.
Shinnick
Sonner Pottery

Williamsburg
James Towne Collony Pottery

Washington
Seattle
Space Needle Corp.

Tacoma
Karlinsey Pottery Inc.

Washington D.C.
Capsco, Capital Souvener inc.
Goldenberg's
Patterson, Mignon II
Wakefield National Memorial Assoc.

West Virginia
Cameron
Cameron Clay Products Co.

Chester
Blair, A.C. China Studios
Continential Kilns Inc.
Knowles, Edwin M. (also Newell)
Pine's Pottery
Usona Art Pottery
Taylor, Smith & Taylor

Grafton
Carr China Co.

Huntington
Wyllie, H.R. China Co.

Jackson
Graham & Stone (see West Virginia
  Dealers)

Kenova
Jeffery Dewitt Insulator Co.
Line Material Co/McGraw Electric Co.

Letant
Hayman, W.T. (see West Virginia Dealers)

Morgantown
Morgantown Pottery
Thompson & Williams

New Cumberland
Chelsea China Co.

Newell
Homer Laughlin China Co.

Paden City
F & M Artware Co.
Paden City Artware Co.
Paden City Pottery
Shenandoah Pottery (see Paden City
  Pottery)

Parkersburg
A.B. China Co.
General Porcelain Co.
Lessell Art Ware
Mercer, Dan (see West Virginia Dealers)

Proctor
Rogers, W.W. (see West Virginia Dealers)

Wetzel
Moore, M & A.J. (see West Virginia Dealers)

Wheeling
Conrad Crafters
Davidson, Taylor & Co.
Ohio Valley China Co.
Wheeling Decorating Co.
Wheeling Potteries Co.
Wheeling Potery
Wheelig Tile Co.
Warwick China Co.

Williamstown
American Bisque Co.

Wisconsin

Beldenville
Hillcrest Pottery (Gebbon)

Brookfield
Lamplight Farms

Cambridge
Rockdale Union Stoneware Inc.
Rowe Pottery Works Inc.

Edgerton
American Art Clay Works
Edgerton Potteries
Norse Pottery

Genoa City
Honey Bear Farm

Kenosha
Andrea's Inc.

Kewaskum
Regal Ware Inc.

Lake Geneva
Belvedere inc.
Geneva Porcelain (Belvedere)

Stewart Northwood's Gift Shop

Madison
Ceramic Arts Studio
Hankscraft Co.

Menasha
Bachelder, Carlton

Milwaukee
Baker, Oscar F.
Frankleton, Susan
Hermann Family Potters
Midwoot Pottory Co.

Princeton
Middle Earth/Primus Studio

River Falls
McKeachie-Johnston Pottery

Sheboygan
Gunther & Berns
Vollrath Co.

West Bend
West Bend Co.

Miscellaneous Lists of Various Types of Manufacturers

American Ironstone Manufacturers

American China Co., Toronto, OH
American Crockery Co., Trenton, NJ
Anchor Pottery Co., Trenton, NJ
Beerbower & Griffin, Phoenixville, PA.
Bennett Pottery, Baltimore, MD
Brunt, William, Pottery, East Liverpool, OH
Burroughs & Mountford, Trenton, NJ
City Pottery, Trenton, NJ
Coxon & Co., Trenton, NJ
Crescent Pottery, Trenton, NJ
Crown Pottery, Evansville, IN
East Liverpool Pottery Co., East Liverpool, OH
Eturia Pottery, Trenton, NJ
Fell & Thropp, Trenton, NJ
Glasgow Pottery, Trenton, NJ

Globe Pottery, East Liverpool, OH
Great Western Pottery Co., East Liverpool, OH
Goodwin Pottery, East Liverpool, OH
Greenwood Pottery, Trenton, NJ
Harker Pottery, East Liverpool, OH
International Pottery Co., Trenton, NJ
Jersey City Pottery, Jersey City, NJ
Knowles, Taylor, Knowles, East Liverpool, OH
Laughlin, Homer, China Co., Newell, WV
Maddock, Thomas & Sons, Trenton, NJ
Maryland Pottery Co., Baltimore, MD
Mayer Pottery Co., Beaver Falls, PA
Mercer Pottery Co., Trenton, NJ
Millington & Astbury, Trenton, NJ
Morley & Co., Wellsville

Morrison & Carr, New York, NY
New England Pottery Co.
New York City Pottery, New York, NY
Onondage Pottery Co., Syracuse, NY
Peoria Pottery Co., Peoria, IL
Phoenixville Pottery, Phoenixville, PA
Potter's Cooperative Co., East Liverpool, OH
Steubenville Pottery Co., Steubenville, OH
Trenton Pottery Co., Trenton, NJ
Union Potteries Co., East Liverpool, OH & Pittsburgh, PA
U.S. Pottery Co., Bennington, VT
Vodrey Pottery, East Liverpool, OH
Wheeling Pottery Co., Wheeling, WV
Willets Mfg. Co., Trenton, NJ
Wyllie & Sons, East Liverpool, OH

Decorators and Decorating Factories

It was difficult sometimes to tell the exact involvement of a pottery in the decorating business. This is a suggestive list only. The amount of decorating done by these companies varies from a side-line occupation to a full-time business of decorating. And the type of decorating done may vary widely, also. There were several companies that I wanted to include in this list, but I didn't find marks for them such as the Elbee Art Products Company, Cleveland, Ohio.

Decorating may include many processes from hand painting pictures on the piece, to applying gold lines or trim with the use of decals for decoration. Or it might vary from incised decorating to a simple application of a decal. Some call applying special solid colors and glazes a form of decorating.

Decorators fit into several categories. Very famous people decorated and hand-painted products for the art potteries, such as Newcomb Pottery, Rookwood Pottery, Roseville Pottery, Weller Pottery, Rozart Pottery, Lonhuda Pottery, American China Manufactory, J.B. Owens Pottery, Grueby Pottery, Santa Barbara Ceramic Design, Chelsea Keramic Art Works and Kenton Hills Porcelain. See these individual listings for decorators and their marks.

A second group were factory operations that decaled or decorated custom orders for various groups and businesses, and sometimes they decorated products to sell themselves. These companies did not manufaturer pottery. Also, they generally decorated glass as well as pottery. See G.C. Shafer Pottery, Zanesville, Ohio, or Kass China, East Liverpool, Ohio.

A third group would include decorating departments operated by large potteries almost as a separate business at times, although their main business was to make pottery. They decorated custom orders and had themselves listed under decorators in the directories. For example, see Royal China Company, Sebring, Ohio, and Cronin China Company of Minerva, Ohio.

A group of companies thought of mainly as distributors or selling agencies sometimes did decorating also, such as the Pottery Queen in Zanesville, Ohio, or Eastern China Company, New York, New York.

Absecon China & Glass Decorators, Absecon, NJ
Alexander, S. & Sons, New York, NY
Americana Art China Co., Sebring, OH
Artistic Potteries Co., Whittier, CA
Atlan Ceramic Art Club, Chicago, IL
Atlas China Co., New York, NY
Atlas Crystal Works, Covington, KY
Belcrest, Inc., Clifton, NJ
Belmonte China, East Liverpool, OH

Berggren Trayner Corp., Chicago, IL, & Libertyville, IL
Berndae, Inc., New York, NY
Blair, AC China Studio, Chester, WV
Blue Arrows Decorating Workshop, New York, NY
Bunting, W.C. Co., Wellsville, OH
Cameo China Co., Wellsville, OH
Charleton Decorating Co., New York, NY
Chic Pottery, Zanesville, OH

China & Glass Decorators, Du Bois, PA
Conrad Crafters, Wheeling, WV
Cordey China Co., Philadelphia, PA
Crest Studios, New York, NY
Cronin China Co., Minerva, OH
Crown Potteries, Inc., Evansville, IN
Croyden China Co./Ceramic Decorating Co., Inc., Trenton, NJ
Cumbow China Decorating Co., Abingdon, VA

Dean, Jesse, Trenton, NJ
De Lime Studios, St. Petersburg, FL
De Lite Mfg. Co., New York, NY
De Luxe Decorating Works, New York, NY
De Passe, Inc., New York, NY
Diamond Pottery Co., Crooksville, OH
Eastern China Co., New York, NY
Empire State Glass Decorating Co., New York, NY
Enco, Inc., New York, NY
Gay Fad Studios, Lancaster, OH
G & J Decorating Co., Beloit (near Sebring), OH
Hoffman Ceramics, Columbus, OH
Hyalyn Porcelain, Inc., Hickory, NC
J & E Decorators, Zanesville, OH
Kass China Co., East Liverpool, OH
Kettlesprings Kilns, Alliance, OH
Leica Ceramics, White Cottage, OH
Leneige China Co., Burbank, CA
Le Pere Pottery, Zanesville, OH
Lycett, Edward & William, Atlanta, GA
Mallek, Kay Studios, Tucson, AZ

Marco Pottery, Zanesville, OH
McGray, H., Crooksville, OH
Oakland China & Glass Studio, Oakland, CA
Oakwood China Co., Sebring, OH
Padre Potteries, Los Angeles, CA
Paris Decorators Corp., New York, NY
Paul & Co., New York, NY
P & E Decorators, Roseville, OH
Pitman-Dreitzer & Co., Inc.
Polynesian Arts, Miami, FL
Porcelier Mfg. Co., Greensburg, PA
Pottery Queen, Zanesville, OH
Ransburg, Harper J. Co., Indianapolis, IN
Red Cliff Co., Chicago, IL
Robertson, David T. & Shearer, B. Appomattox, VA
Royal China Co., Sebring, OH
R & N China Co., Inc., Carrollton, OH
Rulon-China Decorator, Trenton, NJ
Sabin Mfg., Co., McKeesport, PA, & Mt. Clemens, MI
Salem China Co., Salem, OH
Sanders Mfg. Co., Nashville, TN

Senegal China Co., Pelham, NY
Shafer, G.C. Pottery Co., Zanesville, OH
Shawnee Creek Kilns, Germantown, OH
Shenango Pottery, New Castle, PA
Short, Mary, Ceramics, Topeka, KS
Sinaco Co., Inc. New York, NY
Soriano Ceramics, New York, NY
Swetye Ceramics Co., East Palestine, OH
Tatler Decorating Co., Trenton, NJ
Tipp City Novelty, Tipp City, Oh
Triangle Studios, Los Angeles, CA
United China & Glass, New Orlean, LA
Viletta China Co., Roseberg, OR
Vogue Ceramic Ind., New York, NY
Washington Co., Washington, PA
Weil of California, Los Angeles, CA
Weissman Co., Inc., New York, NY
Wheeling Decorating Co., Wheeling, WV
World Wide Art Studios, Covington, KY
Zapun Ceramics, New York, NY

Chronology of Whiteware Production Developments

From "William Bloor," *American Ceramic Society Bulletin,* XVI, January 1937, p. 25, the following was found which tells the important dates and the men who contributed to the production of whiteware in the United States. Whiteware, in its broadest sense, includes cream-colored ware, white granite or ironstone, semi-porcelain and porcelain ware.

1671 John Dwight, England. (patented porcelain fluxed with glass)
1695 M. Chicanneau, France. (soft-paste porcelain)
1710 John Frederick Böttger, Germany. (hard porcelain)
1749 Thomas Frye, England. (patented bone china)
1768 William Cookworthy, England. (patented hard-paste porcelain)
1769 Gousse Bonnin, Philadelphia, PA (bone china)
1789 John Curtis, Philadelphia, PA (queensware)
1799 William McFarland, Cincinnati, OH (earthenware)
1800 Josiah Spode, England. (began production of bone china)
1801 James and Robert Caldwell, Cincinnati, OH (earthenware)
1808 Alexander Trotter, Philadelphia, PA (earthernware)
1809 Thomas Vickers & Sons, Downington, PA (queensware)
1810 Daniel Freytag, Philadelphia, PA (earthenware & bone china)
1816 Dr, Mead, New York, NY (hard-paste porcelain)
1816 Abraham Miller, Philadelphia, PA (queensware)

1816 David G. Seixas, Philadelphia, PA (cream-colored earthenware)
1825 Jersey Porcelain & Earthenware, Jersey City, NJ (hard-paste porcelain)
1825 William Ellis Tucker, Philadelphia, PA (hard-paste porcelain)
1829 D. and J. Henderson, Jersey City, NJ (porcelain)
1829 Lewis Pottery Co., Louisville, KY (cream-colored earthenware)
1830 Smith Fife & Co., Philadelphia, PA (porcelain)
1832 Joseph Hemphill, Philadelphia, PA (porcelain
1833 American Pottery Mfg. Co., Jersey City, NJ (porcelain)
1837 Thomas Tucker, Philadelphia, PA (porcelain)
1840 Charles J. Boulter, Philadelphia, PA (soft-paste porcelain)
1845 Norton and Fenton, Bennington, VT (earthenware)
1846 Edwin Bennett, Baltimore, MD (queensware)
1848 Charles Cartlidge & Co., Green Point, LI (porcelain)
1853 Charles Hattersley, Trenton, NJ (earthenware)

1853 Charles Kurbaum and J.T. Schwartz, Philadelphia, PA (porcelain)
1853 Morrison and Carr, New York City (white granite)
1854 American Porcelain Mfg. Co., Gloucester, NJ (soft-paste porcelain)
1857 William Young & Sons, Trenton, NJ (whiteware)
1857 George Allen, Philadelphia, PA (porcelain & Parian ware)
1858 Southern Porcelain Co., Kaolin, SC (porcelain)
1859 Trenton China Co., Trenton, NJ (vitrified ware)
1859 Rhodes and Yates, Trenton, NJ (white granite)
1859 Millington, Astbury & Poulson, Trenton, NJ (whiteware)
1859 Fenton and Clark, Peoria, IL (white granite)
1860 H. Speeler, Trenton, NJ (whiteware)
1860 American Pottery Co., Peoria, IL (white granite)
1861 James Tams and J.P. Stephens, Trenton, NJ (white granite)
1863 Bloor, Ott & Booth, Trenton, NJ (creamware and white granite)

1863 Coxon & Co., Trenton, NJ (creamware and white granite)
1865 Frederick Dallas, Cincinnati, OH (common white)
1865 Trenton Pottery Co., Trenton, NJ (earthenware)
1868 Greenwood Pottery Co., Trenton, NJ (white granite)
1868 James Moses, Trenton, NJ (earthenware)
1869 S.M. Kier, Pittsburgh, PA (earthenware)

1869 Astbury and Maddock, Trenton, NJ (whiteware)
1870 John Wyllie, Pittsburgh, PA (earthenware)
1870 Knowles, Taylor & Knowles, East Liverpool, OH (whiteware)
1870 John Goodwin, Trenton, NJ (earthenware)
1870 Thomas Maddock, Trenton, NJ (sanitary ware)
1871 Yates, Bennett & Allen, Trenton, NJ (white granite)

1874 H. & S. Laughlin, East Liverpool, OH (white granite)
1875 Thomas Gray & L.W. Clark, Boston, MA (white earthenware)
1876 American Crockery Co., Trenton, NJ (white bisque and granite)
1876 Morris and Willmore, Trenton, NJ (Belleek)

Decorative, Wall & Floor, Tile Companies

American Encaustic Tiling Co., Ltd., Zanesville, OH
Batchelder Tile Co./Batchelder Wilson Co., Los Angeles, CA
Beaver Falls Art Tile Co., Beaver Falls, PA
Broome, Isaac, Trenton, NJ
Burke, Ron, Shapleigh, Maine
Cambridge Tile Mfg. Co., Covington, KY
Carlyle Tile Co., Ironton, OH, see Mosiac Tile Co.
Catalina Pottery, Santa Catalina Island
Claycraft Potteries, Winchester, MA
Empire Tile Co. (J.B. Owens), Zanesville, OH
General Tile Co., El Segundo, CA, see Mosaic Tile Co.
Hamilton Tile Works, Hamilton, OH
Heath Ceramics, Inc., Sausalito, CA

Hull Pottery Co., Crooksville, OH
Kinneloa Kiln, see Batchelder
Low Art Tile Co., Chelsea, MA
Lycett, Edmund, Atlanta, GA
Mallek, Kay, Studios, Tucson, AZ
Mayerton Tile Works, St. Paul, MN
Moravian Pottery & Tile Works, Doylestown, PA
Morton Ceramic Tile Co., Morton, IL
Mosaic Tile Co., Zanesville, OH
Moss, David L. & Co., (decorators of tile), New York, NY
Mueller Mosaic Tile Co.
Niloak Pottery & Tile Co., Little Rock, AR
Ohio Tile Co., see Hamilton Tile Co.
Oxford Tile Co., Cambridge, OH
Patch, Inc., Atlanta, GA
Providential Tile Co., Trenton, NJ
Robertson Art Tile Co., Morrisville, PA

Salem China Co., Salem, OH
San Valle Tile Kilns, Los Angeles, CA
Spartek, Inc., Canton, OH
Star Encaustic Tile CO., Pittsburgh, PA
Stark Ceramics, Inc., Canton, OH
Summitville Tile Co., Summitville, OH
Trent Tile Co., Trenton, NJ
Tropico Tile Co., see Gladding, McBean & Co., Glendale, CA
Unitile Co., Urichsville, OH
U.S. Ceramic Tile Co./Spartek, Inc., Canton, OH
U.S. Encaustic Tile Co., Indianapolis, IN
Wege Marble & Tile Co., Columbus, OH
Wenzel Tile Co., see Trent Tile Co., Trenton, NJ
Wheeling Tile Co., Wheeling, WV

New-Old Type Ware Manufacturers

The following potters defy exact classification because some of them are part of families that have made pottery for as many as six generations and are still operating today. They made the very old types of pottery for years and years. A few of them are really studio-type potters. The Robinson Ransbottom Pottery, Pittsburg Pottery and Clay City Pottery are factory operations. But they are listed here as a group because they make stoneware pieces that are in the old style in both decorative or functional pieces, including crocks, jugs, mugs, for a variety of reasons. But the greatest reason is that a wave of nostalgia for the old redware, stoneware and handmade ware that came with the 1970's and the bicentennial created a good market. Lester Breininger, who makes redware, signs all of his pieces and they are widely collected in their own right, as a thing of beauty in a style of pottery manufacture now forgotten. The factories mentioned produce functional, useful pieces for the kitchen which are widely used. The studio potters create beautiful old style pieces with painted birds, cows, etc. None of these potters mean to deceive the buyer in any way. Because their products are quality pieces they cost as much as the older pieces at times. They are not to be thought of as reproductions. They are artful pieces created in the old style, often time by the old methods. the products vary greatly, too. The reader will have to turn to individual listings for a more exact description of the ware.

Breininger, Lester & Barbara (Redware), Robesonia, PA
Brown County Pottery, Nashville, TN
Clay City Pottery, Clay City, IN
Cole, A.R. Pottery, Sanford, NC
Craig, B.B. Pottery, Vale, NC
Craven Family Potters, Steeds, NC
Evans Pottery, Dexter, MO
Gordy Family Potters
Heritage Co., Uniontown, PA
James Towne Collony Pottery, Williamsburg, VA

Jugtown Pottery, Seagrove, NC
Meaders Pottery, White County, GA
New Geneva Stoneware Co., Masontown, PA
Owen & Owens Family Potters, Seagrove, NC
Pine's End Pottery (Diebboll), Washington, MI
Pittsburg Pottery, Pittsburg, KS
Red Cliff Co. (Ironstone)
Robinson Ransbottom Pottery, Roseville, OH

Rockdale Union Stoneware, Inc., Cambridge MA
Rowe Pottery Works, Cambridge, MA
Salt of the Earth Pottery (Beaucamp), Cambridge, OH
Sayers, Don and Ruth, (Tea Leaf)
Seagrove Pottery, Seagrove, NC
Thorley, Palin, at Williamsburg Pottery, Lightfoot, VA

Distributors and Selling Agencies

Abraham & Strauss, Inc., Brooklyn, NY

Abrams, Jess (see Chadwick China)

Alliance China Co., Alliance, OH

Allied Stores Corp., Wilmington, DE

Altman, B., and Company, New York, NY

Aluminum Cooking Utensil Co., Kensington, PA

American Can Co., Greenwich, CT

American Dinnerware Service, Sioux City, IA

American Greeting's Corp., Cleveland, OH

American Heritage Publishing Co., Inc., New York, NY

American Home Products Corp., New York, NY

American House, Ltd., New York, NY

American Wholesale Corp. (Baltimore Bargain House), Baltimore and Cumberland, MD

Amway Corp., Ada OH

Andrea's, Inc., Kenosha, WI

Arcadia Export-Import Corp., New York, NY

Arlen China Co., New York, NY (see Harlem Crockery Co.)

Arquette, Cliff, Gettysburg, PA

Atlas China Co., New York, NY

Atlas Crystal Works, Covington, KY

Atlas Cutlery Corp., Olean, NY

Bacharach, Inc., New York, NY

Baltimore Bargain House (see American Wholesale Corp.)

Bamberger, L., and Co., Newark, NJ

Barker Brothers, Inc., Los Angeles, CA

Barth Equipment Co., Inc., New York, NY

Baynes, Mary Phelan, Arlington, VA

Ben Franklin Stores, Chicago, IL

Bent and Co., Inc., New York, NY

Berndae, Inc. New York, NY

Berninghaus Co., Cincinnati, OH

Black Knight China, New York City and Philadelphia

Block China Co., New York, NY

Block, J & I Co., New York, NY (see Block China Co.)

Blue Wave, Kennebunk, ME

Borgfeldt, George, Corp., New York, NY

Borg-Warner Corp., Inc., Detroit, MI

Bovano Industries, Inc., Cheshire, CT

Boyd, William, Beverly Hills, CA

Breslauer-Underberg, Inc., New York, NY

Bradford Exhange, Chicago, IL

Brinn's China and Glassware Co., Pittsburg, PA

Brody, E.O. Co., Cleveland, OH

Brudin, Ernest W., Montibello, CA

Buckley, Newhall Co., New York, NY

Burroughs, Edgar Rice, Inc., Tarzana, CA

Bybee, Selden, Pottery Co., Lexington, KY; New York City, NY

California Exposition and Fair Corp., Sacramento, CA

California Fruitgrowers Exchange, Los Angeles, CA

Capsco, Capitol Souvenir, Inc., Washington, D.C.

Carbone, Inc., Boston, ME

Cardinal China Co., or Carteret China Co., Carteret, NH

Carmichael, Michael M., Tyler, TX

Carnegie, Hattie, Inc., New York, NY

Carson Pirie Scott and Co., Chicago, IL

Carteret China Co. (see Cardinal China Co.)

Cavendish Trading Corp., NY

Celestial China Corp., San Diego, CA

Century Service Corp., Alliance, OH

Chemical Garden, Inc. New York, NY

Chesnutt, Corinne, Muskogee, OK

Children's Television Workshop, New York, NY

China and Glass Distributors, Inc., New York, NY

Club Aluminum Products Co., Chicago, IL

Colonial Silver Co., Inc., Orlando, FL

Commerce-Pacific, Inc., Los Angeles, CA

Consolidated Cosmetics, Chicago, IL

Continential Ceramics Corp. New York, NY

Copperstate Supply Co., Phoenix, AZ

Craft, Beverly, Omaha, NE

Crownford China Co., Broadway, NY

Cunningham and Pickett and Associated Cos., Alliance, OH

Cunningham Ind. (see Cunningham and Pickett)

Daniel, Jack, Distillery, Lynchburg, TN

Daubt Glass and Crockery Co., Toldeo, OH

Davidson, Taylor and Co., Wheeling, WV

Day, Evangeline, New York, NY

De Lite Mfg. Co., Inc., New York, NY

Disney, Walt, Productions, Ltd., Los Angeles, CA

Dohrmann Hotel Supply Co., San Francisco, CA

Drexel Furniture Co., Drexel, NC

Dunn, Vera La Fountain, Hollywood, CA

Dynasty, Ltd., Los Angeles, CA

Eastern China Co., Inc., New York, NY

Eastern Outfitting Co., Los Angeles, CA

Ebeling and Reuss Co., Philadelphia, PA

Efcolite Corp., Trenton, NJ

Empire Crafts Corp., Newark, NY

Evans, Norris, New York, NY

Everedy Co., Frederick, MD

Everlast Co., New York, NY

Exclusive China Co., Broadway, NY

E-Z Cook, Lakeville, IN

Fairbanks Ward Industries, Inc., Chicago, IL

Fajans, Caroline R., New York, NY

Farber Brothers, New York, NY

Farber, Samuel P., NY

Farber, S.W. (see Samuel P. Farber), NY

Farber, Sydney (see Samuel P. Farber), New York, NY

Feliciano China and Glass, Puerto Rico

Filene's, Wm., Sons Company, Boston, MA

Fischl, Janet W., Plandome Manor, NY

Fisher, Bruce and Co., Philadelphia, PA

Fitz and Floyd, Dallas, TX

Fondeville and Co., New York, NY

Fulkerson, Jude, M.J., Topeka, KS

Gallstyn Co., Inc., New York, NY

General Housewares Corp., Holt-Howard Division, Hyannis, MA

General Mills, Minneapolis, MN

George-Good Corp., City of Industry, CA

Gift Horse Creations, San Mates, CA

Gimbel Bros., Inc. New York, NY

Glaser, Louis J., Rochester, NY

Goldcrest Ceramics Corp., Trenton, NJ

Goldenberg's, Washington, D.C.

Golden Rule, Inc., Columbus, OH

Goldman Costume Co., New York, NY

Grant, W.T. Co., McKeesport, PA

Green Thumb Products, Toledo, OH

Grossman, Edward (The Spitler)), Chicago, IL

G.T. Chemical Products, Inc., San Diego, CA

Gump, S. and G. Co., San Francisco, CA

Hall, Charles, Inc., New York, NY

Hammond Research Corp., Gloucester, MA

Hankscraft Co., Madison, WI

Harlem Crockery Co., New York, NY

Hartman's Furniture and Carpet Co., Chicago, IL

Hellman, Louis E., New York City

Heltzberg's Diamond Shops, Inc., Kansas City, MO

Henry Ford Museum pieces (see Iroquois China Co.)

Historic Charleston Foundation, Charleston, SC

Historic Places, several locations

H.M.H. Publishing Co., Chicago, IL

Holder, Lily Frona, Temple City, CA

Home Decorators, Inc., Newark, NY

Honey Bear Farm, Geona City, WI
Hoover, Joseph C., Villanova, PA
Hope Chest Co., Inc., Minneapolis, MN
Ideas Unlimited, Los Angeles, CA
Independent Grocers' Alliance Distributing Co., Chicago, IL
Independent Mfg. Association, Inc., Cincinnati, OH
International Artware Corp., Cleveland, OH
International D.S. Co., Alliance, OH
International China Co., Alliance, OH
International Silver Co., Meriden, CT
Irwin, Robert W. Co., Grand Rapids, mI
Jabeson China Co., Inc., New York, NY
Jackson Internationale, Pelham Manor, NY
Jensen, George, Inc., New York, NY
Jepcor International (see J. and H. International), Wilmette, IL
J. and H. International, Wilmette, IL
Jones, McDuffee and Stratton, Boston, MA
Kahiki Restaurant, Columbus, OH
Kaufmann's Department Stores, Inc., Pittsburgh, PA
Kaul, Leo, Chicago, IL
Keepsake House and Madow's, New York, NY
Kirk China Company, Brighton, PA
Kittler, Joseph R., Chicago, IL
Koch, George and Sons, Evansville, IN
Kupper, Herman C., New York, NY
La Luz Products Co., La Luz, NM
Lamplight Farms, Brookfield, WI
Lane and Company/Sunkist Creations, Van Nuys, CA
Lang and Osgood, NY
Larkin Co., Buffalo, NY
Laughlin International (see Cunningham and Pickett)
Leeds China Co., Chicago, IL
Leeman, Stephan, Products Co., New York, NY
Lefcourte Cosmetics Co., New York, NY
Lefton China (George Zolton China Co.), Chicago, IL
Levy Brothers China Co., Inc., New York, NY
Lifetime China Co., Alliance, OH
Lipman, Bernard, New York, NY
Little-Jones Co., Inc., New York, NY
Loma Mfg. Co. (see Copperstate Supply)
Lovett, Robert E., Los Angeles, CA
Lunning, Frederick, New York, NY
MacDougal, Alice Foote, Coffee Shops, Inc., New York, NY
Macy, R.H. and Co., New York, NY
Maddock and Miller, Inc., New York, NY
Mallory Randall Corp., Lake Success, NY
Maloney, Harold J., Kalamazoo, MI
Marks and Rosenfield, San Francisco, CA

Marshall Burns Co., Chicago, IL
Marshall Field and Co., Chicago, IL
May Department Stores, New York, NY
McCoy Limited, Zanesville, OH
McCrory Stores, Corp., New York, NY
McCutcheon, James and Co., New York, NY
McIlvain, William Gibbon, Philadelphia, PA
McGraw Electric Co., Chicago, IL
Metropolis Bending Co., Metropolis, IL
Michaels and Co., Inc., Brooklyn, NY
Midhurst China Co., New York, NY
Milk Farm, Dixon, CA
Miller and Rhoads, Inc., Richmond, VA
Mitteldorfer Straus, New York, NY
Monarch Dinnerware Co., East Liverpool, OH
Monefeldt, Jens, Hayward, CA
Monon Center, Inc., Greensboro, PA
Monticello, Albemarle County, VA
Moore, John Hudson, Co., Morris Plains, NJ
Moore, Walter B., Inc., West Lafayette, OH
Morrison, Inc., Mobile, AL
Moses, Grandma, Properties, Inc., New York, NY
Mount Vernon Gift Shop, Fairfax County, VA
Mova Products, San Francisco, CA
Mr. Mugs, Hallandale, FL
Murchison, Loren and Co., Inc., Newark, NJ
Museum Pieces, Inc., New York, NY
Mutual China Co., Indianapolis, IN
Nassau China Co., Trenton, NJ
National Potteries Corp., Bedford, OH
National Silver Co., New York, NY
National Specials Co., New York, NY
National Unit Distributors, Inc., Boston, MA
Neff, Grace V., Chicago, IL
Neiman-Marcus Co., Dallas, TX
New Distributor System, Fitchburg, MA
Newland, Schneeloch and Piek, Inc., New York, NY
Nichols, Elmer L., San Antonio, TX
Oakley, Annie, Enterprises, Inc., Los Angeles, CA
Ohio China Co., Monroe, MI
Old Sleepy Eye Collectors Club of America, Inc., Monmouth, IL
Oneida Community, Ltd., Oneida, NY
Osborne, Beverly, Oklahoma City, OK
Ovington Brothers Co., New York, NY
Ozark Mountain Store, Inc., Windsor, MO
Packing Products Co., New York, NY
Pasmantier, John L., New York, NY
Patterson, Mignon II, Washington, D.C.

Paul, Edward P. and Co., New York, NY
Pear Tree, Inc., Bryn Mawr, PA
Penney, J.C., Co., New York, NY
Peters, Charles Adolph, Long Island, NY
Philco Corp., Philadelphia, PA
Phillips, Lz., Omaha, NE
Pick, Albert and Co., Chicago, IL
Pines Pottery, Chester, WV
Piper, Lucile Seymour, Co., Cincinnati, OH
Pitman-Dreitzer and Co., Inc., New York, NY
Planned Products, Inc., Eugene, OR
Platecraft of America, Inc., Buffalo, NY
Play-Bear, Ltd., Skokie, IL
Plymouth Wholesale Dry Goods Corp., New York, NY
Poor and Co., Chicago, IL
Pottery Barn, New York, NY
Prairie House, Springfield, IL
Princeton China Co., New York, NY (see Lipman, B.)
Promotions, Inc., Youngstown, OH
Pyramid Alloy Mfg. Co., El Cerrito, CA
Quality Enterprises, Inc., Shawnee Mission, KS
Queen City Pottery (outlet for Robinson Ransbottom), Cincinnati, OH
Ralston Purina Co., St. Louis, MO
Ransburg, Harper J. Co., Indianapolis, IN
Ravenscroft, Ltd., Lancaster, OH (Anchor Hocking)
Raymond's, Inc., Boston, MA
Red Bull Inns of America, Carnegie, PA
Regal Ware, Inc., Kewaskum, WI
Reliable Glassware and Pottery Co., Chicago, IL
Rinor Marketing Corp. (see Maddux of California)
Robeson Rochester Corp., Rochester and Perry, NY
Robinson Clay Products Co., Akron, OH
Rockwell Silver Co., Meridan, CT
Rogers Jewelers, Columbus, OH
Rosenthal Block China Co. (see Block China Co.), New York, NY
Rubel and Co., Decorative Accessories, Inc., New York, NY
Rum Rill, Little Rock, AR
Saks and Co., New York, NY
Santa's Workshop, Inc., North Pole, NY
Sayers, Don and Ruth, Morton, IL
Sayre China Co., East Liverpool, OH
Schonfeld, Max P.H., Los Angeles, CA
Scott and Fetzer Co., Cleveland, OH
Sears and Roebuck, Chicago, IL
Shaw, James M. and Co., New York, NY
Shulton, Inc., Clifton, NJ
Sleepy Eye Milling Co., Monmouth, IL

Sohn, Earnest, Creations, New York, NY
Space Needle Corp., Seattle, WA
Stanley Home Products Co., Erwin, TN
Starns, Walter, Los Angeles, CA
Stern Brothers, New York, NY
Stewart's Northwood's Gift Shop, Lake Geneva, WI
Stevens, Charles A. and Brothers, Chicago, IL
Stix, Baer, and Fuller Co., St. Lous, MO
Stouffer, J.II., Co., Chicago, IL
Straub, Paul A. and Co., Inc., New York, NY
Straus, Ben, Inc. (see under Nathan Straus)
Straus, Nathan, Inc., New York, NY
Stupell, Carole, Ltd., New York, NY
Superware Corp., Great Neck, NY
Tebor, Inc., New York, NY
Terrace Ceramics, Inc., Zanesville, OH

Thurston, Carl H., Pasadena, CA
Tiffany and Co., New York, NY
United Flavor Seal Co., Indiana, PA
Universal Promotions, Inc., Cambridge, OH
U.S. Merchandise Corp., Baltimore, MD
Van Camp Sea Food Co., Inc., Terminal Island, CA
Van Nostrand, Morris A., New York, NY
Vita Craft Corp., Shawnee Mission, KS
Vogue, Various Potteries and Distributors, several locations
Wakefield National Memorial Assoc., Washington, D.C.
Walker, Jessie Robinson, Los Angeles, CA
Wanamaker, John, Philadelphia, PA
Waples-Platier Grocer Co., Fort Worth, TX
Wasserstrom's, Columbus, OH

Weil, Alfred J., Chicago, IL
Weil Ceramics and Glass, New York, NY
Weissman, Beth, New York, NY
Weissman Co., Inc., New York, NY
Wentz, M.C., Co., Pasadena, CA
Werner Kruger Co., New York, NY
West Bend Co., West Bend, WI
Western Auto Supply Co., Los Angeles, CA
Wheelock Pottery, Peoria, IL
Wille, M. Inc., New York, NY
Windsor China Co., Inc., New York, NY (see Spaulding China Co.)
Winterthur Museum, Winterthur, DE
Woodmere China Co., Inc., New Castle, PA
Woronock, David and William Ansen, New York, NY
Wright, Mary S., New York, NY
Zapun Ceramics, Inc., New York, NY
Zents, Huntington, IN

Manufacturers of Kitchenware, Dinnerware and Table Accessories

This list includes makers of functional pieces, such as cookie jars and accessory pieces, pitchers, salts and peppers, etc., and all types of dinnerware from Belleek to hotel and restaurant ware, including porcelain, semi-porcelain, creamware, yellowware, whiteware, Rockingham, etc. Every major pottery, even those classified as art potteries such as Rookwood Pottery and Roseville Pottery made some pieces for household use at some time or other, but they are not all listed here. Many studio potters made dinnerware and many distributors used their own marks on dinnerware. See separate listings for these names.

Acme Pottery, Crooksville, OH
Akron China Co., Akron, OH
Akron Pottery Co., see Johnson, Whitmore and Co.
Albright China Co., Carrollton, OH
Allegheny China, Warren, PA
Alliance Vitreous China Co., Alliance, OH
Alpaugh and McGowan, Trenton, NJ, see Trenton Potteries Co.
American Art China Works, Trenton, NJ
American Beleek, Trenton, NJ
American Bisque Co., Williamstown, WV
American Ceramic Products Co., Los Angeles, CA, see Winfield Pottery
American China Co., Toronto, OH
American Chinaware Corp., office in Cleveland, OH
American China Manufactory, see William E. Tucker
American China Products Co., Chesterton, IN
American Chinaware Corp.
American Crockery Co., Trenton, NJ
American Fine China, Warrington, PA
American Haviland, see Shenango
American Porcelain Mfg., Co., Gloucester, NJ
American Pottery Co., Marietta, OH

American Pottery Co., Peoria, IL, see Peoria Pottery Co.
American Pottery Co., Jersey City, NJ, see Jersey City Pottery
American Pottery Mfg. Co., Jersey City, NJ, see Jersey City Pottery
American Pottery Works, East Liverpool, OH
Anchor Hocking Corp., Lancaster, OH
Anchor Pottery, Trenton, NJ
Arita Tabletop, Anaheim, CA
Art China Co., Sebring, OH
Astbury and Maddock, Trenton, NJ, see Thomas Maddock and Sons
Athison Pottery Co., Chittenango, NY, see Chittenango Pottery
Atlas China Co., Niles, OH, see Bradshaw China Co.
Atlas-Globe China Co., Niles, OH, see Bradshaw China Co.
Avalon China, Baltimore, MD, see Chesapeake Pottery
Bahl Potteries, Inc., Carrollton, OH
Bailey-Walker China, Bedford, OH, see Walker China Co.
Ball and Morris, East Liverpool, OH
Bauer, Various Potteries, several places
Baum, J.H., Wellsville, OH
Beck, A.M., Evansville, IN, see Crown Pottery

Bedford China Co., Bedford, OH, see Walker China
Beerbower and Co., Elizabeth, NJ
Beerbower and Griffen, Phoenixville, PA, see Phoenixville Pottery
Bell Pottery, Findlay and Columbus, OH
Bel Terr China, East Palestine, OH
Belvedere, Inc., Lake Geneva, WI
Bennett Potteries, Baltimore, MD
Black and Beach Pottery Co., New Milford, CT, see New Milford Pottery Co.
Blair Ceramics, Ozark, MO
Bloor, Ott and Booth, Trenton, NJ, see William Bloor listing
Bloor, Taylor, Speeler, see William Bloor listing
Bloor, William, East Liverpool, OH
Bockman, N.E., see various Bauer Potteries
Bonnin and Morris, Philadelphia, PA
Boulter, Charles J., Philadelphia, PA, see W.E. Tucker
Bowman, George H., Cleveland, OH, see Cleveland China Co.
Bradshaw China, Niles, OH
Brewer and Tempest, see Brockman Pottery Co.
Brighton Pottery, Zanesville, OH
Brock, B.J. and Co., Lawndale, CA, see Southern Calif. Potteries Co.

Hampshire Pottery, Keene, NH

Hardesty China, New Brighton, PA

Harding China Co., see Kingwood Ceramics

Harker, George S. and Co., East Liverpool, OH

Harker Pottery, East Liverpool, OH

Harker, Taylor, and Co., East Liverpool, OH

Harker, Thompson, and Co., East Liverpool, OH

Harmony House, see Sears and Roebuck

Hartstone, Inc., Zanesville, OII

Hattersley Pottery, Trenton, NH, see City Pottery

Haynes, Bennett, and Co., Baltimore, MD, see Chesapeake Pottery

Haynes, D.F. and Co., Baltimore, MD, see Chesapeake Pottery

Heath Ceramics, Sausalito, CA

Henderson D. and J., Jersey City, NJ, see Jersey City Pottery

Hill/Fulper/Stangl Potteries, Flemington, NJ

Hoffman, China, Columbus, OH

Holiday Designs, Sebring, OH

Hopewell China, Hopewell, VA

Hull House Kilns, Chicago, IL

Hull Pottery, Crooksville, OH

Hyalyn-Cosco, see Hyalyn Porcelain

Hyalyn Porcelain, Hickory, NC

Illinois China Co., Lincoln, IL

Indiana Pottery Co., Troy, IN

International Pottery, Trenton, NJ

Interpace, several locations

Iron Mountain Stoneware, Laurel Bloomery, TN

Iroquois China, Syracuse, NY

Jackson China Co., Falls Creek, PA

James River Potteries, Hopewell, VA, see Hopewell China

Jamestown China Co., see Mt. Clemens Pottery

Jeannette Corp., Incorporated in Pennsylvania

J.E. Jeffords, Philadelphia, PA, see Port Richmond Pottery Co.

Jersey City Pottery, Jersey City, NJ

Jersey City Porcelain & Earthenware Co., Jersey City, NJ, see Jersey City Pottery.

Kass China, East Liverpool, OH

Kenwood Ceramics, see Shawnee Pottery

Keystone China Co., East Liverpool, OH

Kingwood Ceramics, East Palestine, OH

Knowles, Edwin, M. Co., East Liverpool, OH

Knowles, Homer, Santa Clara, CA

Knowles, Taylor, Knowles, East Liverpool, OH

Kurlbaum and Schwartz, Philadelphia, PA

La Belle, Wheeling, WV, see Wheeling Potteries Co.

Lamberton Works, Trenton, NJ

La Solana Potteries, Inc., Mesa, AZ

Laughlin, Homer, Newell, WV

Laurel Potteries of California, San Francisco, CA

Leigh Potters, Inc., Alliance, OH

Lenox, Trenton, NJ

Lewis Pottery, Louisville, KY, see Vodrey and Associations

Liberty China, New Lexington, OH, see Virginia Pottery

Limoges China Co., Sebring, OH

Lincoln China, Sebring, OH, see Limoges China Co.

Lincoln China Co., Lincoln, IL, see Stetson China Co.

Lincoln Pottery, Trenton, NJ

Lion's Valley Stoneware, Lemon Grove, CA, see Lon Valley/Lion's Valley listing

Los Angeles Potteries, Lynwood, CA

Louisiana Porcelain Works, New Orleans, LA, see New Orleans, Various Potteries

Louisville Pottery, Louisville, KY

Louisville Stoneware, Louisville, KY

Ludowici-Celadon Co., New Lexington, OH

Maddock, Various Potteries, Trenton, NJ

Marks on Dishes, Various

Marsh Ind., Los Angeles, CA

Maryland Pottery Co., Baltimore, MD, see Maryland Queensware

Maryland Queensware Factory, Baltimore, MD

Mayer China, Beaver Falls, PA

McCoy, Nelson Pottery, Roseville, OH

McNicol and Corns, see McNicol and Smith

McNicol, Burton and Co., East Liverpool, OH

McNicol, D.E. and Smith, East Liverpool, OH

McNicol Pottery, East Liverpool, Ohio and Clarksburg, WV

McNicol, Patrick, East Liverpool, OH

McNicol, T.A. Pottery Co., East Liverpool, OH

Mellor and Co., Trenton, NJ, see Cook Pottery

Mercer Pottery, Trenton, NJ

Metlox Mfg. Co., Manhattan Beach, CA

Midland Pottery, Roseville, OH, see J.W. McCoy

Millington, Astbury, and Poulson, Trenton, NJ

Modern China Co., Sebring, OH, see American Art China Co.

Morgan Belleek China Co., Canton, OH

Morley and Co., Wellsville, OH

Morris and Willmore, Trenton, NJ, see Columbian Art Pottery

Morrison and Carr, New York City, see New York City Pottery

Moses, John and Sons, Trenton, NJ, see Glasgow Pottery

Mount Clemens Pottery, Mount Clemens, MI

Murphy Pottery, East Liverpool, OH

National China, East Liverpool, OH

New Castle China Co., New Castle, PA

New England Pottery Co., East Boston, MA

New Jersey Pottery Co., Trenton, NJ

New Milford Pottery Co., New Milford, CT

New Orleans Porcelain Co., New Orleans, LA, see New Orleans, Various Potteries

New Orleans, Various Potteries

New York City Pottery, New York City

Novelty Pottery Co., East Liverpool, OH

Oatmeal, Various Co.

Ohio China Co., East Palestine, OH

Ohio Pottery Co., Zanesville, OH, see Fraunfelter China

Ohio Valley China Co., Wheeling, WV

Oliver China Co., Sebring, OH

Onondaga Pottery, Syracuse, NY, see Syracuse China Co.

Ostrow China, see Hopewell China Co.

Ott and Brewer, Trenton, NJ, see Eturia Pottery

Owen, E.J., China Co., Minerva, OH

Oxford Pottery, Cambridge, OH

Pacific Clay Products Co., SC

Paden City Pottery Co., Sisterville, WV

Padre Potteries, Los Angeles, CA

Pearl China Co., East Liverpool, OH

Penn China Co., see Phoenix Pottery

Pennsylvania China Co., Kittanning and Ford City, PA, see Ford China Co.

Peoria Pottery, Peoria, IL

Perlee, Inc., Trenton, NJ

Pfaltzgraff Pottery, York, PA

Philadelphia City Pottery, Philadelphia, PA, see Port Richmond Pottery Co.

Phoenix Pottery, Phoenixville, PA

Pickard China, Antioch, IL

Pioneer Pottery, East Liverpool, OH

Pioneer Pottery, Wellsville, OH

Pope-Gosser, Coshocton, OH

Porcelier Mfg. Co., Greensburg, PA

Port Richmond Pottery, Philadelphia, PA, see Philadelphia City Pottery

Potter's Co-op, East Liverpool, OH, see Brunt, Bloor, Martin and Co.

Prospect Hill Pottery, Trenton, NJ

Purinton Pottery, Shippenville, PA

Queens China Co., Sebring, OH, see Americana Art China Co.

Regal China Corp., Antioch, IL

Rhodes and Yates, Trenton, NJ, see City Pottery

Ridgewood, China Co., Southampton, PA

Rittenhouse, Evans and Co., Trenton, NJ, see Americana Art China Co.

Robinson-Ransbottom, Roseville, OH

Rouse and Turner, Jersey City, NJ, see Jersey City Pottery

Royal China Co., Sebring, OH

Salem China, Salem, OH

Saloy and Hernadez, New Orleans, LA, see Louisiana, Various Potteries

Santa Anita Pottery, Los Angeles, CA

Saxon China, Sebring, OH

Scammell China Co., Trenton, NJ

Schreiber and Betz, Phoenixville, PA, see Phoenix Pottery

Scio Pottery, Scio, OH

Scott, George, Pottery Co., Cincinnati, OH

Sebring Brothers Pottery, East Liverpool, OH, see American Pottery Works

Sebring China Co., Sebring, OH

Sebring, E.H. China Co., Sebring, OH

Sebring Mfg. Co., Sebring, OH

Sebring Pottery, Sebring, OH

Sevres China, East Liverpool, OH

Shawnee Pottery, Zanesville, OH

Shenandoah Pottery, see Paden City Pottery

Shenango China Co., New Castle, PA

Smith, Fife and Co., Philadelphia, PA

Smith, Phillips, East Liverpool, OH

Southern California Ceramics, Santa Monica, CA

Southern California Pottery Co., Lawndale, CA

Southern Porcelain Co., Kaolin, SC

Southern Potteries, Inc., Erwin, TN

Speeler and Taylor, Trenton, NJ, see Trenton Pottery Co.

Standard Pottery, East Liverpool, OH, see Patrick McNicol

Stanford Pottery, Sebring, OH

Stangl Pottery, Trenton, NJ, see Hill/Fulper/Stangl Potteries

Starkey and Howard, Keene, NH, see Hampshire Pottery

Stephens, Tams and Co., Trenton, NJ, see Greenwood Pottery

Sterling China Co., Wellsville and East Liverpool, OH

Sterling China, Sebring, OH, see Limoges China Co.

Sterling China Marks

Stetson China, Lincoln, IL

Steubenville Pottery Co., Steubenville, OH

Strong Mfg. Co., Sebring, OH, see Sebring Mfg. Co.

Summit China, Akron, OH

Syracuse China Co., Syracuse, NY

Taft, J.S. and Co., Keene, NH, see Hampshire Pottery

Tams and Stephens, Trenton, NJ, see Greenwood Pottery

Taylor and Co., Trenton, NJ, see Trenton Pottery Co.

Taylor, Goodwin and Co., Trenton, NJ, see Trenton Pottery Co.

Taylor, Lee and Smith, East Liverpool, OH, see Taylor, Smith and Taylor

Taylor, Smith and Taylor, Newell, WV

Tea Co., Various

Technical Porcelain and Chinaware Co., El Cerito, CA

Tempest, Brockman and Co., see Brockman Pottery Co.

Thomas China Co., Lisbon, OH

Thompson, C.C., and Co., East Liverpool, OH

Thropp and Brewer, see Trenton Pottery Co.

Treasure Craft, Compton, CA

Trenle, Blake, China Co., East Liverpool, OH, see Trenle China Co.

Trenle China Co., East Liverpool, OH

Trenton China Co., Trenton, NJ

Trenton Pottery Co., Trenton, NJ

Trenton Potteries, Trenton, NJ

Trenton Pottery Works, Trenton, NJ

Tritt China, Niles, OH

Tropico Pottery, Los Angeles, CA, see Gladding, McBean and Co.

Trotter, Alexander, Philadelphia, PA, see Columbia Pottery

Tucker and Hulme, Philadelphia, PA, see William Ellis Tucker

Tucker, William Ellis, Philadelphia, PA

Tuxedo Pottery Co., see Phoenix Pottery

Twin Spout Pottery, New York, NY

Twin Winton Ceramics, Pasadena, CA

Tycer Pottery, Roseville, OH

Ungemach Pottery Co., Roseville, OH

Union Porcelain Works, Greenpoint, NY

Union Potteries Co., East Liverpool, OH

Union Pottery, Newark, NJ

Union Pottery Co., Brooklyn, NY, see Union Pottery, several companies

Union Pottery Co., Trenton, NJ, see New Jersey Pottery

U.S. Pottery Co., Bennington, VT

U.S. Pottery Co., Wellsville, OH

Universal Potteries, Inc., Cambridge, OH

Van Pottery, Trenton, NJ

Vernon Kilns, Vernon, CA

Virginia Pottery, New Lexington, OH

Vodrey and Assoc., East Liverpool, OH

Vodrey and Lewis, Louisville, KY, see Vodrey and Associations

Vohann of California, Capistrano Beach, CA

Walker China Co., Bedford, OH

Wallace and Chetwynd, East Liverpool, OH

Wallace China Co., Vernon, CA

Warner-Keffer China Co., East Liverpool, OH

Warwick China Co., Wheeling, WV

Watt Pottery, Crooksville, OH

Wedgwood Pottery, see Harker Pottery

Weil, Max of California/California Figurine Co.

Wellsville China Co., Wellsville, OH

Wellsville Pioneer Pottery, Wellsville, OH, see Wellsville China Co.

West End Pottery Co., East Liverpool, OH

Western Stoneware, Monmouth, IL

West Virginia China Co., Wheeling, WV, see Ohio Valley China Co.

Wheeling Potteries Co., Wheeling, WV, see Wheeling Pottery Co.

Wheeling Pottery Co., Wheeling, WV

Wick China, Kittanning, PA

Willets Mfg. Co., Trenton, NJ

Winfield Pottery, Pasadena, CA

Wooster China Co., see Fredericksburg Art Pottery

Wyllie, H.R. China Co., Huntington, WV

Wyllie, John and Son, East Liverpool, OH

Yates and Titus, Trenton, NJ, see City Pottery

Yates, Bennett, and Allen, Trenton, NJ, see City Pottery

Young, William and Sons. Trenton, NJ

Stoneware and Folk Potters

Abcock, New York, MO

Ack Potters, Mooresburg, PA

Adams, Allison and Company, Middlebury (Akron), OH

Addington, William R., Jug Hill, Jackson County, GA

Akron Pottery Company (see Johnson Whitmore and Company), Akron, OH

Alexandria, Virginia, potters and dealers (Milburn, Miller, Plum and Swann)

Alexis Stoneware Manufacturing Company/Alexis Pottery Company, Alexis, IL

Alld, John, Hollis, ME

Allen, George, Philadelphia, PA

Amos (2 potters)

Armstrong, Joe, Roseville, OH

Armstrong & Wentworth, Norwich, CT

Ashfield Pottery (Orcutt, Guilford and Company), Ashfield, MA

Atcheson and Associates, Annapolis, MD

Atchison, Henry P. (see Debolt and Atchison), New Geneva, PA

Atchison, H.K., New Geneva, PA

Athens Pottery (see Clark Potters), Athens, NY

Aust, Gottfried, Salem, NC

Austin, A.A. & Co., Commerce, MO

Avera, John C., Crawford County, GA

Baker, Oscar P., Milwaukee, WI

Bachelder, Carlton, Menasha, WI

Ballard, Various Potteries, Burlington, VT & Gardener, ME

Ball, J.G., Poughkeepsie, NY

Bangor Stone Ware Co., Bangor, ME

Bastian, Jacob, Milton, PA

Bauer Pottery, Paducah, KY

Bayer, Joseph, Washington, MO

Beasley, James, Montrose, AL

Beech, Ralph B., Philadelphia, PA

L.B. Beerbower and Company, Elizabeth, NJ

Beerbower and Griffin, Elizabeth, NJ

Bell, Joseph, Putnam, OH

Bell (see several Bell Potters), MD & VA

Benjamin, James, Stoneware Depot, Cincinnati, OH

Benninghof, Uhl and Company (see Uhl Pottery), Evansville, IN

Benton Crock & Pottery Co., Benton, AR

Beuter, John, Waynesboro, PA

Binkley, George, see Massillon, OH, various potters

Blair, Sylvester, Cortland, NY

Blank, Pottery, Boonville & California, MO

Boggs Pottery, Prattville, AL

Boerner, A., see Massillon, OH, various potters

Bohemian Pottery, Zanesville, OH

Boon, T.G. & Co., Poughkeepsie, NY

Boonville Pottery, Boonville, MO, see Black Pottery

Boss Brothers, Middlebury (Akron), OH

Boston Earthenware Factory (see Frederick Mear), Boston, MA

Bosworth, Stanley, Hartford, CT

Boughner Pottery/Vance Pottery, Greensboro, PA

Bower, J., Fredericktown, PA

Boyer, John, Schuylkill County, PA

Boynton, Calvin, West Roy & Albany, NY

Brayton, J.F. and Co., Utica, NY

Brockville Pottery, Schuylkill County, PA

Brooks, Hervey, Goshen, CT

Brower, John F., Randolf County, NC

Brown Brothers (see Huntington Pottery), Huntington, Long Island, NY

Brown, J.S., Carthage, MO

Brown Family, Various Potteries, Arden, NC

Buckeye Pottery, Macomb, IL

Buckeye Stoneware, Crooksville, OH

Bullock, William S., Roseville, OH

Burger, J., Jr., (see Burger and Associations), Rochester, NY

Burger and Lang (see Burger and Associations), Rochester, NY

Burley Potteries, Crooksville, OH

Burley & Winter (see Burley Potteries)

Bustle, James & Bussell, James M., Georgia

Butler, A.J. & Co., New Brunswick, NJ

Caire, Adam (see Caire Pottery), Poughkeepsie, NY

Caire, Jacob (see Caire Pottery), Poughkeepsie, NY

Caire Pottery, Poughkeepsie, NY

Caldwell Potters, Callaway County, MO

Camp and Thompson, Akron, OH

Carpenter, Frederick (Mystic River Works), Boston and Charleston, MA

Carr, James (see Swan Hill, P.)

Central New York Pottery (see White's Pottery), Utica, NY

Chandler, Thomas N., Edgefield, SC

Chapman, Josiah, Troy, NY

Chapman, Upson & Wright, Akron, OH

Chase, L. and B.G. (somerset Potters Work), Somerset, MA

Cheesequake, various potters, South Amboy, NJ

Chollar and Associates, Cortland, NY

Christ, Rudolf, Bethabara & Salem, NC

Clark and Fox (see Nathan Clark and Associates), Athens and Lyons, NY

Clark, W.H. (see Ripley, Illinois Potters)

Clark, Nathan, and Associates, Athens and Lyons, NY

Clark Stoneware, Zanesville, OH

Clark, William and Company, Cannelton, IN

Clay City Pottery, Clay City, IN

Clay County, IN (several potters listed)

Cline, William W., Hartford City, IN

Clinton Pottery Company/Clinton Stoneware Company, Clinton, MO

Clough & Calhoun, Portland, ME

Coffman Potters, Rockingham County, VA

Cofield, T.W., Atlanta area, GA

Colchester Pottery, Colchester, IL

Commeraw, Thomas, Coerlears Hook, NY

Commerce Pottery, Commerce, MO

Congress Pottery, South Amboy, NJ

Conrad, A., New Geneva, PA

Conrad, J.W., Stoutsville, MO

Coplin, Alexander, Troy, NY

Cowden and Wilcox (see Cowden Pottery), Harrisburg, PA

Cowden Pottery, Harrisburg, PA

Crafts, Martin & Caleb, Portland, ME

Crafts Potters, Nashua, NH

Craven Family Potters, Steeds, NC

Cribbs, Daniel, Tuscaloosa, AL

Crisman, W.H., Strasburg, VA

Crolius Pottery, Manhatten Wells, NY

Cross, Peter, Hartford, CT

Cushman, Paul, Albany, NY

Dalton Pottery (or Houghton Pottery), Dalton, OH

Dana (sic Daney, Dany), Ellsworth, ME

Dauffenbach and Gieseke, New Ulm, MN

Dave (see Lewis J. Miles Pottery), Edgefield District, SC

Dawson and Sons, Calhoun, MO

Debolt and Atchison, New Geneva, PA

DeHaven, Abraham, Akron, OH

Diamond Novelty Company (see Diamond Stoneware), Crooksville, OH

Diamond Stoneware Company, Crooksville, OH

Dick, Jacob, Tuscarawas County, OH

Dilliner, Samuel R., New Geneva, PA

Dillinger, L.B. and Company, New Geneva, PA

Dillon and Tyler (see Charles Dillon), Albany, NY

Dillon, Charles, Albany, NY

Dillon, Henry and Porter (see Charles Dillon), Albany, NY

Dipple Pottery, Lewisburg, PA

Dodge Pottery, Portland, ME

Dollings, John and W.C., Muskingum County, OH

Donaghho, A.P. (Excelsior Pottery), Parkersburg, WV

Drach, Rudolf, Bedminster, PA

Dry, John, Dryville, PA

Dubois & Kinsey, Zanesville, OH

Duche Family Pottery, Pennsylvania and Georgia

Du Val, B. and Company, Richmond, VA

Eagle Porcelain Works (Henry Gast), Lancaster County, PA

Eagle Pottery, McComb, IL

Eagle Pottery (see James Hamilton), Greensboro, PA

Eberhart, John R., New Geneva, PA

Eberly, J., Strasburg, VA

Edmands and Company, Charlestown, MA

Edwards and Minish, Calhoun, MO

Eiler Pottery, East Birmingham, PA

Elverson Pottery (see Elverson, Sherwood and Barker), New Brighton, PA

Elverson, Sherwood and Barker Pottery, New Brighton, PA

Eneix and Frankenberry (see James E. Eneix), New Geneva, PA

Eneix, J.E., New Geneva, PA

Enterprise Pottery Co., New Brighton, PA

Euler (see Eiler Pottery), East Birmingham, PA

Evans Pottery, Dexter, MO

Excelsior Pottery (see Donaghho), Parkersburg, WV

Excelsior Works, Rices Landing, PA

Exeter Pottery Works, Exeter, NH

Farrar Potters, Various, Fairfax, VT

Farrar, W.H. and Company, Syracuse, NY

Fenton & Hancock, see Fenton, Richard Webber

Fenton, Jonathon, various New England States

Fenton, R.L. & Co., Dorset, VT

Fenton, Richard Webber, St. Johnsbury, VT

Field, L.F. (or T.F.?), Utica, NY

Figley, Joseph, New Philadelphia, OH

Fish, C. (see Swan Hill Pottery)

Fisher, Jacob, Lyons, NY (see Lyons Pottery)

Foell and Alt, East Birmingham, PA

Fort Dodge, IA, various potteries

Fort Edward Pottery Company, Fort Edward, NY

Fox, E.S., see Nathan Clark, Albany, NY

Franklin Factory, Cincinnati, OH

Fulton, G.N., Jordan Mines, VA

Funkhouser, L.D., Strasburg, VA

Furman, Noah, Cheesequake, NJ

Gale, Frederick (see Galesville Potters), Galesville, NY

Galesburg Pottery Co., Galesburg, IL

Galesburg Stoneware Mfg. Co. (see Galesburg Pottery Co.)

Galesville, New York, various potters

Ganse, Henry, Lancaster County, PA

Gardiner Stoneware Manufactory, Gardiner and Farmingdale, ME

Gast, Henry (see Eagle Porcelain Works), Lancaster County, PA

Gerlach, C., PA

German-American Stoneware Works, New York, NY

Gerstung, John, Logansville, Sugar Valley, PA

Glazier, Henry, Huntingdon, PA

Goodale and Stedman (see D. Goodale), Hartford, CT

Goodale, Daniel, Hartford, CT

Goodwin, Various Potteries, Hartford, CT

Gordy Family Potters, GA

Grand Ledge, MI, various potteries

Greber Pottery, Montgomery County, PA

Gunther & Berns, Sheboygan, WI

Haig Pottery, Philadelphia, PA

Hall, E. Muskingum County, OH

Hamilton, Clem, Tuscarawas County, OH

Hamilton, James & Co., Greensboro, PA

Hamilton and Jones, Greensboro, PA

Hamm Brothers, Tuscaloosa County, AL

Hare, William, Wilmington, DE

Harker, George S., East Liverpool, OH

Harker, Taylor & Co., East Liverpool, OH

Harker, Thompson & Co., East Liverpool, OH

Harrington, T., (See Lyons Pottery), Hartford, CT

Harris, Thomas, Cuyahoga Falls (Akron), OH

Hart Family Potters, New York State

Hartsoe, John, Lincolnton, NC

Hartwell and Bower, Inc. (see Fort Dodge Potteries), Fort Dodge, IA

Hartzog, David, Vale, NC

Hastings and Belding, Ashfield, MA

Hawthorn Pottery Co., Hawthorn, PA

Haxstun, Ottman, and Co., Fort Edward, NY

Headman, Andrew, Rock Hill, PA

Heighshoe, S. E., Somerset, OH

Henderson, TX, various potteries

Henne, T. S., Shartlesville, PA

Hercher, Joseph, New York, MO

Hermann Family Potters, Milwaukee, WI

Hewitt, Isaac, see Excelsior Works, Rice's Landing, PA

Hickerson, James N., Strasburg, VA

Hicks, Crooksville, OH

Higgins, A. D., Cleveland, OH

C. E. Hill and Co., Kansas City, MO

Hilton, various potteries, Catawba Valley, N.C.

Hobart, D. P., Williamsport, PA

Holly, Daniel, Vale, NC

Hopkins, John, Senaca County, OH

Horn, Martin, Farmingdale & Gardiner, ME

Houghton Pottery (see Dalton Pottery), Dalton, OH

Howe and Clark (see Nathan Clark), Lyons, NY

Hubener Pottery, Montgomery County, PA

Huggins, D. F. and Son, Lakenan, MO

Humiston & Stockwell (see Henry Stockwell)

Hummel, John M., Florence, MO

Huntington Pottery, Huntington, Long Island, NY

Husher, George, Brazil, IN

Hyssong/Hissong Potteries, Cassville, PA. and Huntingdon, PA

Indiana Redware Potters (various)

Ironton, OH, various potters

Irvine, Samuel, Newville, PA

Jegglin Family Potters, Boonville and Calhoun, MO

Johnson, Whitmore and Co., Akron, OH

Jones, J.A., Young Caine, GA

Jones, Evan B. Pottery, Pittston, PA

Keister & Sonner (see Sonner Pottery), Strausburg, VA

Keller, William, New Albany, IN

Kelly, Peter, Philadelphia, PA

Kelsey Family Potters, Clay County, IN

Kemp's Pottery, St. Joseph, MO

Kendall, Uriah, Cincinnati, OH

Keystone Pottery Co., Rochester, PA

Keystone Pottery (see Burley Potteries), Crooksville, OH

Kline, Charles, Atlanta, GA

Kline, Philip, Carversville, PA

Klinker, Christian, Bucks County, PA

Klugh, Jesse, Maytowne, PA

Knight, Maurice A. Co., Akron, OH

Koch, Charles, Commerce, MO

Kohler, J.W., Pensacola, FL

Krumeich, B.J., Newark, NJ

Lambert, J.C., Denton County, TX

Lamson Brothers (see Exeter Pottery Works), Exeter, NH

Lamson and Field (see Exeter Pottery Works), Exeter, NH

Lamson and Swasey, Portland, ME

Leathers Pottery, Howard and Mt. Eagle, PA

Lefevres, Isaac, Vale, NC

Lewhew, W.H., Strasburg, VA

Lehman and Reidinger (see Caire Pottery)

Lehman, L. and Co., Poughkeepsie and NYC

Leman (or Lehman), Johannes, Tylersport, PA

Lent, George, Troy and Lansingburg, NY

Leonard, S.E., Wallingford, VT

Lettell and Co., Greensboro, PA

Letts, Joshua (see Cheesequake Potters)

Lewis and Gardiner/Lewis and Lewis, Huntington, Long Island, NY

Lewis, O.V., Greenwich, NY

Lindsay, W. (see New York Pottery), New York, MO

Link Pottery, Stonetown, PA

Locker, Thomas (see Swan Hill Pottery)

Lock Haven, PA, various potters

Logan Pottery Co., Logan, OH

Studio Potters and Sculptors

The following studio potters and sculptors are listed by their own name and their studio names also.

A & A Pottery, Cotopaxi, CO
Abbott, Charles, Ogunquit, ME
Aerni, Richard (Spring Street Pottery), Cincinnati, OH
Aitken, Russell Barnett, Cleveland, OH
Akin, Charles (Ridge Pottery), Franklin, TN
Alatoria Pottery (Alan & Toria Friedlander), Topeka, KS
Alden, Katherine (Plymouth Pottery), Philadelphia, PA
Andersen, Weston and Brenda, East Boothbay, ME
Anderson, Gina (Big Witch Pottery), Knoxville, TN
Anderson, Ken D., Mt. Morris, MI
Andreson, Laura, Los Angeles, CA
Apple Tree Lane Pottery (Dorothea O'Hara), Darien, CT
April, Nancy, Rosendale, NY
Ariel of California (see Hillcrest Pottery), Berkeley, CA
Arneson, Robert, CA
Arwood, Barbara, Columbus., OH
Asbury, Carolyn, Cambridge, MA
Associated American Artists (Stonelain), New York, NY
Atwill, Allison (Santa Barbara Ceramics Design), Santa Barbara, CA
Austin, Tom (B. Welsh Studio), Gresham, OR
Autio, Rudy, MT
Aw Pottery, Berkeley, CA
Bacerra, Ralph, Los Angeles, CA
Bachman, Kathy, Logan, OH
Baggett, Michael, Thompson, GA
Baggs, Arthur, Columbus & Cleveland, OH
Ba-Han, Gary (Santa Barbara Ceramic Design), Santa Barbara, CA
Bailey, Clayton, Hayward, CA
Bailey, Ellen (Greenfield Village Pottery), Dearborn, MI
Baker Station Studio (Saenger Porcelain), Newark, DE
Baldauf, Stephen, Sauk Village, IL
Ball, Carlton F., Northern CA
Baltimore Clay Works (Peter Kaiser), Baltimore, MD
Barker, J. Edward (Studio Gallery), Wellington, KS
Barnes, Gayle (Carol Ann Pottery, Ltd.), Boulder, CO
Barnett, Bill (Pots and Stuff), Columbus, OH
Barnyard Pottery (Westerwald Pottery of Schaltenbrand), Brownsville, PA
Barringer, Mary, Hartford, CT
Basch, Carol, Golden, Co. and Anchorage, AK
Bastine Pottery, Noblesville, IN

Bauer, Fred (Bauer and Warashina), several places
Baumgartner, Robert (Talisman Pottery), Boulder, CO
Baynes, Mary Phelan, Arlington, VA
Beamish, Joan (Wendt Pottery), Lewiston, ID
Beaucamp, Jack and Heather (Salt of Thee Earth Pottery), Cambridge, OH
Beaumont Heritage Pottery, York, ME
Beittel, Kenneth R., PA
Bell Buckel Pottery (Anne White), Bell Buckel, TN
Bengston, Billy, Los Angeles, CA
Bennington Potters, Bennington, VT
Berea College, Berea, KY
Bethel Pike Pottery (Alan K. Patrick), Albany, IN
Big Creek Pottery (Bruce McDougal), Davenport, CA
Big Lick Pottery (Mike Imes and Dawn VanKley), New Haven, KY
Big Witch Pottery (Gina Anderson), Knoxville, TN
Binns, Charles Fergus, NJ & CA
Bitterroot Pottery (Peggy Steffes), Victor, MT
Blackburn, Ed, several places
Black, Harding, San Antonio, TX
Blazys, Alexander, Cleveland, OH
Blue Bird Pottery Company (Warren Driggs), Crooksville, OH
Bogatay, Paul, Columbus & Cleveland, OH
Bonnema, Garret and Melody, Bethel, ME
Bradley, Mildred, Centerville, IA
Branum, Wayne (Branum Pottery), Milaca, MN
Breininger, Lester & Barbara, Robesonia, PA
Bringle, Cynthia, Penland, NC
Brookcraft Pottery (Keyser), Plymouth Meeting, PA
Brook Pottery (J. Thomas Flavin), Madison, NH
Brough (see John Brough Miller), Argyle, TX
Brown, Becky, Bloomington, IN
Brown, Terry & Larry (Stoneware by Brown), Anaheim, CA
Brown, Evan Javan, Arden, NC
Brown, Cedric & Christy (Christar Studio), Fresno, CA
Brown Jug Pottery (Margaret Burnham), Lake Placid, FL, & Cookeville, TN
Buford, Molly B., Cartersville, GA
Burke, Bill, San Francisco, CA
Burke, Ron, Shapleigh, ME
Burkett, Richard (Wild Rose Pottery), Bainbridge, IN

Burnham, Margaret S. (Brown Jug Pottery), Lake Placid, FL & Cookeville, TN
Butler, Julia Bolin, Worthington, OH
Cabbages and Kings Pottery (Laurence & Eileen Knauff), Oak Ridge, TN
Cahoy, Emil (Cahoy Pottery), Colome, SD
Campbell, William H., Factory Studios, Cambridge Springs, PA
Carlock, Elaine (Cranberry Hill Studios), Pontiac, MI
Carlson, R. (Middle Earth Studio/Primus Studio), Princeton, WI
Carol Ann Pottery, Ltd. (Carol Ann Wilson), Boulder, CO
Carroll, Carolyn, Palatine, IL
Casper, Melvin (Merritt Island Pottery), Merritt Island, GA
Castle, Nancy Jurs, Scottsville, NY
Cavanaugh, Dorothy (Feats of Clay), Austin, TX
Chambers Street Pottery (Jo Ann Meehan & Jerry Ospa), New York, NY
China Bull (Paul McNeeley), Liberty, MO
Christar Studio (Cedric & Christy Brown), Fresno, CA
Christianson, Linda, Lindstrom, MN
Clay Craft Studios (Hodgdon, Norton, Hollowell, Nickerson), Winchester, MA
Clay and Fiber Studio (Kathleen Totter Smith), Medina, OH
Clayfields Pottery (Larry Schiemann), Streetsboro, OH
Clayhorse Pottery, Stone Mountain, GA
Clays in Calico (Van Gorden), Cardwell, MT
Clayton, Burneta Clore (Clay Works), Nashville, TN
Clay Works (Burneta Clore Clayton), Nashville, TN
Clay Works Production Studios (Linda Kitchen), Hamburg, NY
Cliff, John (Santa Barbara Ceramic Design), Santa Barbara, CA
Clift, Lyle L. (Deer Foot Pottery), Pueblo, CO
Clore, Burneta (Clay Works), Nashville, TN
Clow, Bonnie L., Kansas City, MO
Cohen Pottery (Michael Cohen), Amherst, MA
Coiner, John (Earth Works Pottery), Minneapolis, MN
Cole, Bruce (B. Welsh Studio), Gresham, OR
Collinson, Anne (Santa Barbara Ceramic Design), Santa Barbara, CA

Hillcrest Pottery (Lois Walden), Berkeley, CA

Hillcrest Pottery (William G. Gebben), Beldenville, WI

Hillman, Jane E. (White Dog Pottery), Northampton, MA

Hindes, Charles Austin, Iowa City, IA & several places

Hintze, P. Bishop Hill, IL

Hodgdon, Mary (Clay Craft Studios), Winchester, MA

Holcomb, Jan C., Pascoag, RI

Hollowell, Ruth (Clay Craft Studios), Winchester, MA

Holtz, Martin (Oak Tree Studio), Gresham, OR

Hopwood, David (Greenfield Village Pottery), Dearborn, MI

Horn, Lyle (Carol Ann Pottery, Ltd.), Boulder, Co

Howell, Karen (Howell Porcelain), Mt. Pleasant, PA

Hubbard, Sharon (Porcelain Design), Ann Arbor, MI

Huffman, Dale (Greenfield Village Pottery), Dearborn, MI

Hui, Ka-Kwong, several locations

Hunter Street Pottery (Thomas Radca), Columbus, OH

Hunt, William Company, Columbus, OH

Hutchinson, Dorie (Santa Barbara Ceramic Design), Santa Barbara, CA

Imes, Mike (Big Lick Pottery), New Haven, KY

Ingraham, Gini (Carol Ann Pottery, Ltd.), Boulder, CO

Inwood Pottery Studios (Voorhees), New York, NY

Irish-Hosler Pottery, North East, PA

Ivy Tree (Lehner), Delaware, OH

Jackson, Sharon, Worthington, OH

Jalanivich and Olsen, San Francisco, CA

Jam Ceramic Design (Marquardt), Sacramento, CA

Janas, Stephanie, Toledo, OH

Jansen, Jenny, Savannah, MO

Jervis, Dorothy, New York, NY

Joetown Hill Pottery (George J. Zaros & Rosene Zaros), Malta, OH

Johnston, Randy (McKeachie-Johnston Pottery), River Falls, WI

Johnson, Shirley, Stillwater, MN

Jones, Alan B. (The Potter's Habitat), Columbus, OH

Jones, Cecil, several locations

Jones, Cindy Butler and Bill, Tipp City, OH

Kaiser, Peter (Baltimore Clay Works), Baltimore, MD

Kaneko, Jun, CA & Japan

Karlinsey Pottery, Inc., Tacoma, WA

Kellagher, Kathy (Cooksburg Pottery), Cooksburg, TN

Kelley, Frank Reuss, Norwalk, CT

Kellogg, Stanley, Petoskey, MI

Kemenyffy (Swift Creek Pottery), McKean, PA

King, Sara (Lion's Head Pottery), Galena, OH

Kirby, Orville, CA

Kirchmann, Dennis, G., Martinsville, IN

Kitchen, Linda (Clayworks Production Studios), Hamburg, NY

Knauff, Lawrence & Eileen (Cabbages and Kings Pottery), Oak Ridge, TN

Koenig, Dianne, Hudson, OH

Kolman, Kathy (see Salt of the Earth Pottery)

Korte, Pam, Cincinnati, OH

Kottler, Howard, OH & other states

Kraus, Anne, Short Hills, NJ

Lanham, James S. (Feats of Clay), Austin, TX

Lang, Sandy (see Weil, Walter M. & Sandy), Marietta, OH

Larkin, James & Barbara (Fox Pass Pottery), Hot Springs, AR

La Rowe, John (Mark of the Potter), Clarksburg, GA

Larson, Tyrone & Julie, Bakersville, NC

Lauer, James, Olathe, KS

Lavender, Jane, Atlanta, GA

Lawton, James, Penland, NC

Leach, Bernard (English potter), St. Ives, England

Leach, Janet, H.B., Columbus, OH

Leach, Sara Ann, Columbus, OH

Lederer, Ron & Judy (Forrest Valley Galleries), Nashville, TN

Lehner, Ann Berquist, Delaware, OH

Le Pot Marie (Marie Blazeh), Bastrop, TX

Leveritt, Joseph P., Conway, AR

Lincoln, Richard M., Fort Worth, TX

Lingon, Deborah, Charlottsville, VA

Linn, Laurie (Santa Barbara Ceramic Design), Santa Barbara, CA

Linsoe, Dulcy (Oak Tree Studio), Gresham, OR

Lion's Head Pottery (Sara King), Galena, OH

Littlefield, Edgar, Columbus, OH

Little Mountain Pottery (Graves), Columbus, NC

Long, Doyle, Delware, OH

Loveridge and McClain (Rising Sun Pottery), Victor, MT

Lukens, Glen, Los Angeles, CA

MacKenzie Pottery (Warren MacKenzie)

Macomber, John (Green Leaf Pottery, Inc.), East Hartford, CT

Madonik, Marcia (Putnam Pottery), Athens, OH

Magdich, Jean, Pottery, Logan, OH

Manker, William, Claremont, CA

Marek, J.J., Brownsburg, IN

Mark of the Potter (John La Rowe), Clarksburg, GA

Markow, Raymond (Santa Barbara Ceramic Design), Santa Barbara, CA

Marquardt, Jo Anne (Jam Ceramic Design), Sacramento, CA

Marshall, Derek & Linda (Sandwich Kilns), Center Sandwich, NH

Marshall Studios, Inc. (Gordon Martz), Veedersburg, IN

Martin, Julie (Turn of the Century Pottery), Alexanderia, VA

Martz, Becky Brown, Veedersburg, IN, see Becky Brown

Martz, Gordon (Marshall Studios, Inc.), Veedersburg, IN

Martz, Karl, Bloomington, IN

Mason, John, CA

Mason, Lois (Swiss Valley Designs), Sugarcreek, OH

Mather, Tim, Athens, OH

Maxwell, Jane (Carol Ann Pottery, Ltd.), Boulder, CO

Mayeron, Constance (Mayeron Tile Works), St. Paul, MN

McClain and Loveridge (Rising Sun Pottery), Victor, MT

McCormick, Annette, Mansfield, OH

McDonough, Carol Lynn (Swamp Studio), Columbus, OH

McDonough, Dixie and James (Green Hills Pottery), Madison, IN

McDougal, Bruce (Big Creek Pottery), Davenport, CA

McIntosh, Harrison, Claremont, CA

McIntosh, Martha Lenore, Columbus, OH

McKeachie, Jan (McKeachie-Johnston Pottery Company), River Falls, WI

McKeachie-Johnston Pottery Company, River Falls, WI

McNeeley, Paul (The China Bull), Liberty, MO

Meehan, JoAnn (Chambers Street Pottery), New York, NY

Menchoffer, Paul, Oak Ridge, TN

Merritt-Island Pottery (Melvin Casper), Merritt Island, FL

Middle Earth Studio/Primus Studio (R. Carlson), Princeton, WI

Miller, John Brough, Argyle, TX

Minich, Lorna, Ada, OH

Monsarrat, Allen, Friendsville, TN

Morrett, Christopher (Turn of the Wheel Pottery), Springfield, OH

Muddy Wheel Gallery (Fred R. Wilson), Albuquerque, NM

Muddy Wheel Pottery (William W. Gardner), Lee's Summit, MO

Mudville (School), Cambridge, MA

Musick, Irene, several places

Myhr, David W., Sevierville, TN

Natzler, Gertrud & Otto

New Hope Studios (Maryann Fariello), Alexandria, TN

Nicholas, Donna L., Edinboro, PA

Nichols, Deanna, Avondale, MO

Nickerson, Carol (Clay Craft Studios), Winchester, MA

Nicodemus, Chester, Columbus, OH

Niles, Cheryl Bucklin (Red Horse Hill Pottery), Portsmouth, NH

Niles, George Sanders, Jr. (Red Horse Hill Pottery), Portsmouth, NH

Noguchi, Isamu, several countries

Norton, Ann (Clay Craft Studios), Winchester, MA

No-Ten-O-Quah Pottery (Grace F. Thorpe), Yale, OK

Notkin, Richard T., Myrtle Point, OR

Oak Creek Kilns (James M. Relph), Sedona, AZ

Oaktree Studio (B. Welsh Studio), Gresham, OR

Oestreich Pottery, Taylor Falls, MN

O'Hara, Dorothea Warren (Apple Tree Lane Pottery), Darien, CT

Old Creamery Pottery (Mayer Shacter), CA

O'Leary, John & Eric (Tariki Stoneware), Meriden, NH

Old Sturbridge Inc., Sturbridge, MA

Open Sky Pottery (Bradley and Lynnelle Pekoc), Chesterhill, OH

Orear, Gordon (Greenfield Village Pottery), Dearborn, MI

Osif, Bob (Carol Ann Pottery, Ltd.; also, Santa Barbara Ceramic Design)

Ospa, Jerry (Chambers Street Pottery), New York, NY

Ostrowe, Caryn, Albuquerque, NM

Overcast Clay Sculpture Works and Crocks, Nashville, TN

Pacific Stoneware, Inc. (B. Welsh Studio), Gresham, OR

Paige, Scott, St. Louis, MO

Park Street Potters (see Mary Barringer), Hartford, CT

Parkville Pottery (Cecil Doubenmier), Parkville, MO

Pasini, William (Santa Barbara Ceramic Design), Santa Barbara, CA

Patrick, Alan K. (Bethel Pike Pottery), Albany, IN

Patrick, Vernon, Chico, CA

Peeler Pottery (Richard & Marj Peeler), Reelsville, IN

Peiser, Jane, Penland, NC

Pekoc, Bradley & Lynnelle (Open Sky Pottery), Chesterhill, OH

Pelton's Pottery, San Antonio, TX

Penland School of Crafts (Peiser, Bringle), Larson, Suomalainen

Petterson, Richard B., several locations

Phillips, Jim & Cindy (Feats of Clay), Austin, TX

Phinney, Tom, Oberlin, OH

Phoenix Pottery (Gerry Williams), Goffstown, NH

Pierce, Howard, Claremont & Joshua Tree, CA

Pigeon Forge Pottery (Douglas J. Ferguson & others), Pigeon Forge, TN

Pilcher, Don, Champaign-Urbana, IL

Pillin, Polia, Los Angeles, CA

Pincherry Pottery (Jane & Joseph Cooper), Worthington, OH

Pinch Pottery (East Clay Street Studios; Barbara Walch), Northampton, MA

Pine's End Pottery (Robert H. Dieboll), Washington, MI

Pinewood Pottery (Edith Harwell), Charlotte, NC

Pitney, William E., (The Pot Shop), Sharon, CT

Plum Tree Pottery (John Parker Glick), Farmington, MI

Plymouth Pottery (Katherine Alden), Philadelphia, PA

Point Arena Studio (Mayer Shacter), CA

Poor, Henry Varnum, CA

Porcelain Design (Sharon Hubbard), Ann Arbor, MI

Pots and Stuff (Bill Barnett), Columbus, OH

Pot Shop (Barbara A. Hern), Anoka, MN

Pot Shop (William E. Pitney), Sharon, CT

Potter At Strawbery Banke (Wheeler), Portsmouth, NH

Potter's Habitat (Alan B. Jones), Columbus, OH

Potter's House (Trudy Thorn), Indianapolis, IN

Potter's Mark Studio (Bill Dicks), Banner Elk, NC

Potters of Wall Street (Harris Strong), New York, NY & Ellsworth, ME

Potter's Wheel (Lynda Schaefer Fromm), Columbus, OH

Pottery by Ward (John E. Ward), Victor, MT

Pottery Works (Karen Gregory & Terry Silverman), Fitzwilliam Depot, NH

Potting Shed (Charlotte Star), Concord, MA

Price, Kenneth, CA

Prieto, Antonio, Oakland, CA

Primus Studio (Middle Earth Studio of Carlson), Princeton, WI

Pringle, Robert (Tariki Stoneware), Meriden, NH

Putnam Pottery (Marcia Madonick), Athens, OH

Radca, Thomas (Hunter Street Pottery), Columbus, OH

Radcliffe Pottery (Sweezy), Arlington, ME

Raddatz, Dale A. (Crystal Springs Studio), New Albin, IA

Raines, Elsie H., Cincinnati, OH

Randall, Ruth H., Syracuse, NY

Rauschenberg, Robert, FL

Red Horse Hill Pottery (George S. Niles, Jr.), Portsmouth, NH

Regan, Peter M., New Berlin, NY

Reitz, Donald, several places

Relph, James M. (Oak Creek Kilns), Sedona, AZ

Rice, Tim, Clarksville, TN

Ridge Pottery (Charles Akin), Franklin, TN

Riegger, Harold, San Francisco, CA & several places

Rising Fawn Pottery (Charles Counts), Rising Fawn, GA

Rising Sun Pottery (Randy McClain & Kerry Loveridge), Victor, MT

Robbins, Carolyn, Fowler, IL

Roberts, Donna (Wild Rose Pottery), Victor, MT

Robinson Studios (Robinson and Watanabe), Weare, NH

Rosenbloom, Carol, Raleigh, NC

Rosenthal, George, Bronx, NY

Rowantrees Kiln, Blue Hill, ME

Rowe Pottery Works, Cambridge, MA

Rubenstein, Alice (Carol Ann Pottery, Ltd.), Boulder, CO

Ruby, Laura, Honolulu, Hawaii

Ryan, Michael (Carol Ann Pottery, Ltd.), Boulder, CO

Saenger Porcelain (Baker Station Studios/Peter Saenger), Newark, DE

Salt of the Earth Pottery (Kathy Goos; see Sister Mud & Kathy Kolman), Holyoke, MA

Salt O' Thee Earth (Beaucamp), Cambridge, OH

Salveson-Gerbasi Pottery, Findlay, OH

Sampson, Maia (Carol Ann Pottery, Ltd.), Boulder, CO

Sanders, Herbert, San Jose, CA

Sandwich Kilns (Marshall), Center Sandwich, NH

Santa Barbara Ceramic Design (Raymond Markow & others), Santa Barbara, CA

Sargent, Shannon (Santa Barbara Ceramic Design), Santa Barbara, CA

Sarosy, Lorri, Painesville, OH

Saugatuck Potters, Saugatuck, MI

Saxe, Adrian A., Los Angeles, CA

Schaefer (Lynda Schaefer Fromm, Potter's Wheel), Columbus, OH

Schaltenbrand, Phil (Westerwald Pottery), Brownsville, PA

Scheier, Edwin & Mary, several places

Schieman, Larry (Clayfields Pottery), Streetsboro, OH

Schneider, Aviva, New Berlin, NY

Schreckengost, Don, East Liverpool, OH

Schreckengost, Viktor, Cleveland, OH

Scott, Meg, Canton, OH

Sculpture in Clay (Regina), Livonia, MI

Shacter, Mayer (Shacter Stoneware and Porcelain; Venice Pottery Gallery; Point Arena Studio; Old Creamery Pottery), CA

Shafer, Thomas (Shafer Pottery), Columbus, OH

Shanahan, Mary Jury, Columbus, OH

Shaner, David, Big Fork, MT

Shaw, Richard, CA

Shiloh Pottery (G. Kenneth Hankins), Hampstead, MO

Silverman, Terry & Karen Gregory (The Pottery Works), Fitzwilliam Depot, NH

Singer, Susi, Pasadena, CA
Sister Mud (Kathy Goos; Salt of the Earth Pottery), Holyoke, MA
Smith, David, New York, NY
Snob Hog Pottery (Dennis E. Thompson), Branson, MO
Snyder, Lewis D. (Studio S), Murfreesboro, TN
Sobieniak, Carol (Carol Ann Pottery, Ltd.), Boulder, CO
Soini, William, several locations
Soto, Ishmael, Lexington, TX
Sowinski, Ted (Carol Ann Pottery, Ltd.), Boulder, CO
Spearman, Helen, Hollywood, CA
Spinski, Victor, Newark, DE
Spring Street Pottery (Michael Frasca & Richard Aerni), Cincinnati, OH
Staffel, Bonnie, Charlevois, MI
Staffel, Rudolf, several locations
Strandhagen, Kathy Wing (Wing's Pottery), Dandridge, TN
Star, Charlotte (The Potting Shed), Concord, MA
Stark, Agnus Gordon (Stark Pottery), Memphis, TN
Starship Studio (Rosalyn Tyge), Traverse City, MI
Stebner Studios, Hartville, OH
Steel, Frank & Anna Mae (Framae Art Pottery), Sheffield Lake, OH
Steffes, Peggy (Bitterroot Pottery), Victor, MT
Stegall's Stoneware Pottery (Nancy & Alan Stegall), Tullahoma, TN
Stephenson, John, MI
Stephenson, Suzanne G., MI
Stonelain (Associated American Artists), New York, NY
Stone, Judy (Carol Ann Pottery, Ltd.), Boulder, CO
Stoner, Kaaren (First Thought Pottery), Sandpoint, ID
Stoneware by Brown (Terry & Larry Brown), Anaheim, CA
Strong, Harris (Potters of Wall St.), New York, NY & Ellsworth, ME
Studio Gallery (Barker and Dudley), Wellington, KS
Studio S. (Lewis D. Snyder), Murfreesboro, TN
Sultarski, Peter (Greenfield Village Pottery), Dearborn, MI
Suomalainen, Tom, Walnut Cove, NC
Swamp Studio (Carol Lynn McDonough), Columbus, OH
Sweezy, Nancy, NH, ME, NC
Swift Creek Pottery (Kemenyffy)
Swiss Valley Designs (Lois Mason), Sugarcreek, OH
Takaezu, Toshiko, Clinton, NJ
Takemoto, Henry T., several locations
Takeuchi, Itoko (Santa Barbara Ceramic Design), Santa Barbara, CA
Talbott, Betty L., Columbus, OH
Talisman Pottery (Robert C. Baumgartner), Boulder, CO

Tanaka, Taeko (Tanaka Pottery), Minneapolis, MN
Tariki Stoneware (John & Eric O'Leary & Robert Pringle), Meriden, NH
Tate, Don, (Santa Barbara Ceramic Design), Santa Barbara, CA
Tate, Janette, Kansas City, MO
Temple, Bryon, Lambertville, NJ
Terr, Sam (Sam Terr Associates), Austin, TX
Tessem Stoneware Outlet, Westminster, MD
Thompson, Dennis E. (Snob Hog Pottery), Branson, MO
Thorley, Palin, East Liverpool, OH area (Williamstown, WV
Thorn, Trudy (The Potter's House), Indianapolis, IN
Thorpe, Grace F. (No-Ten-O-Quah Pottery), Yale, OK
Tormey, Suzanne (Santa Barbara Ceramic Design), Santa Barbara, CA
Trapp, Mrs. Howard, Beuhlah, MI
Turner, Jane (Foxhill Pottery), Parkville, MO
Turner, Robert, Afred Station, NY
Turn of the Century Pottery (Julie Martin), Alexandria, VA
Turn of the Wheel Pottery (Christopher Morrett), Springfield, OH
Utley, Taber, Colorado Springs, CO
Valetine, Vey (Greenfield Village Pottery), Dearborn, MI
Van Benschoten, Bryan R. (Greenfield Village Pottery), Dearborn, MI
Vandenberge, Peter, Sacramento, CA
Vanderkooi, Lenore, Nashville, TN
Van Gorden (Clays in Calico), Cardwell, MT
Van Hunke, Dee & Robert, Pompey, NY
Van Kley (Big Lick Pottery), New Haven, KY
Venice Pottery Gallery (Mayer Shacter), CA
Vigland, Alan G. & Susie (Vigland Pottery), Benzonia, MI
Village Potter (Robert E. Duncan)
Voorhees (Inwood Pottery Studio)
Von Tury, F.J., Metuchen, NJ
Voulkos, Peter, Berkeley, CA
Wagar, Robert, Asheville, NC
Wagner, Teresa, Columbus, OH
Walch, Barbara (Pinch Pottery & East Clay Street Studios), Northampton, MA
Walden, Lois (Hillcrest Pottery), Berkeley, CA
Walters, Carl, several places
Warashina, Patti (Fred Bauer & Patti Warashina), several places
Ward, John E. (Pottery by Ward), Victor, MT
Watanabe, Joanne (Robinson Studios), Weare, NH

Weil, Walter M. & Sandy Lang Weil, Marietta, OH
Welsh, Bennett M. (B. Welsh Studio; also, Pacific Stoneware, Inc.), Gresham, OR
Welsh-Fuller (B. Welsh Studio/Oak Tree Studio), Gresham, OR
Wendt, Michael, Pottery, Lewiston, IN
Westmoore Pottery, Seagrove, NC
Westerwald Pottery (Schaltenbrand), Brownsville, PA
Wheeler, E.H. (Wheeler Pottery; also, The Potter at Strawberry Banke), Portsmouth, NH
Wheeler, Stu, Dayton, OH
White, Ann (Bell Buckle Pottery), Bell Buckle, TN
White Dog Pottery (Jane E. Hillman), Northampton, MA
White, Father Jim, S.J., Kansas City, MO
White Mountain Pottery (Timothy Wierwille), Ruidosa, NM
Wickham, Nancy, NY
Wierwille, Timothy (White Mountain Pottery), Ruidosa, NM
Wildenhain, Marguerite (Farm Pond Workshop), Guerneville, CA
Wild Rose Pottery (Donna Roberts), Victor, MT
Wild Rose Pottery (Richard Burkett), Bainbridge, IN
Wild, Sam (Wild Pottery), Potter Place, NH
Williams, Barbara (Pottery by Barbara Williams), Kansas City, MO
Williams, Gerry (Phoenix Pottery), Goffstown, NH
Wilson, Carol Ann (Carol Ann Pottery, Ltd.), Boulder, CO
Wilson, Earnest (Pigeon Forge Pottery), Pigeon Forge, TN
Wilson, Fred R. (Muddy Wheel Gallery), Albuquerque, NM
Wing's Pottery (Kathy Wing Strandhagen), Dandridge, TN
Woideck, George (Stoneware Pottery), Cleveland, OH
Wood, Beatrice, Ojai, CA
Wood, Jeanne, Moscow, IN
Woodman, Betty Elizabeth, Boulder, CO
Wyman, William (Herring Run Pottery), East Weymouth, MA
Yanke, Norman (Greenfield Village Pottery), Dearborn, MI
Yarmark, Alan and Anita (A&A Pottery), Cotopaxi, CO
Zaros, George J. & Rosene (Joetown Pottery), Malta, OH
Zawojski, Steve, Grant Haven, MI

Railroad Letters & Symbols

Initials and names found on **top** of railroad dining car service or business car china. (Information furnished by Larry Paul and Ken Andrews.) The code used in second column is for top marked railroad china. L, marked with railroad logo; N, marked with spelled out name; I, marked with railroad initials; *, indicates more than one known pattern with more than one type of top marking.

Full name used	(L)	Alaska RR.
Full name used	(L)	Algoma Central Railway
A & S		Alton & Southern
A T & SF	(N)	Atchison, Topeka & Santa Fe
A & WP	(L)	Alanta & West Point
ACL	(L)	Atlantic Coast Line
B & O	(L)	Baltimore and Ohio
B & OSW	(I)	Baltimore and Ohio South Western
B & A	(L)	Boston and Albany
B & M	(N, *)	Boston & Maine
BR & P	(L, I, *)	Buffalo Rochester & Pittsburg
CN or CNR	(L, I, *)	Canadian National
CPR	(L, I, *, N)	Canadian Pacific
	(I)	Chicago Milwaukee & Puget Sound
CM & ST P	(L)	Chicago Milwaukee & St. Paul
CM ST P & P	(L)	Chicago Milwaukee St. Paul & Pacific
ELECTROLIN-ER	(N)	Chicago North Shore & Milwaukee
C of G	(L)	Central of Georgia
CRR of NJ	(L)	Central Railroad of New Jersey
CNJ	(L)	Central Railroad of New Jersey
C & O	(I, N, *)	Chesapeake & Ohio
C & A	(L)	Chicago & Alton
CB & Q	(L, N, *)	Chicago Burlington & Quincy
C & EI (THE DIXIE LAND)	(N)	Chicago & Eastern Illinois
C & NW	(L)	Chicago & Northwestern
RI	(I, *)	Chicago, Rock Island & Pacific
SOUTH SHORE LINE	(L)	Chicago South Shore & South Bend RR
CM (MIDLAND ROUTE)	(N)	Colorado Midland
C & S	(I)	Colorado & Southern
D & H	(L, I, *)	Delaware & Hudson
DL & W	(L)	Delaware Lackawanna & Western
D & RG	(L)	Denver & Rio Grande
D & RGW (RIO GRANDE)	(N, L, *)	Denver & Rio Grande Western
D & IR	(L)	Duluth & Iron Range
DM & N - Full name used on china	(L)	Duluth Missabe & Northern
DSS & A - "THE SOUTH SHORE"	(L)	Duluth South Shore & Atlantic RR
Full name used	(L, N, *)	Erie
FEC	(I)	Florida East Coast
FE & MV RR	(L)	Freemansburg Elkhorn & Missouri Valley RR
FRISCO	(L)	St. Louis & San Francisco
GR & I	(L)	Grand Rapids & Indiana
GTR		Grand Trunk
GTP	(L)	Grand Trunk Pacific
GN	(L, I, *)	Great Northern
Full name used	(N)	Gulf Coast Line
GM & O	(L)	Gulf, Mobile & Ohio
IC & ICRR	(I, *)	Illinois Central
ITS or ITRS		Illinois Terminal Railroad
KCS - Full name used	(L)	Kansas City Southern
LV	(L)	Lehigh Valley
L & N		Louisville & Nashville
LA & SL (SALT LAKE ROUTE)	(L)	Los Angeles & Salt Lake
MEC or MC	(N)	Maine Central
Full name used or MC	(N)	Michigan Central
MKT		Missouri Kansas & Texas
MP (THE EAGLE)	(N, L)	Missouri Pacific
MO PAC		Missouri Pacific
IRON MOUNTAIN	(N)	Missouri Pacific, owner, & eventually absorbed by St. Louis, Iron Mountain & Southern
M & O		Mobile & Ohio
MONON	(L)	Monon (Chicago - Indianapolis & Louisville)
MRY (in diamond)	(L)	Munising Railway
N.J.C.		Central Railroad of New Jersey
NYC	(I, *)	New York Central
NC & ST L	(L)	Nashville Chattanooga & St. Louis
NYC & HR RR	(I)	New York Central & Hudson River RR
NYC & ST L (Nickel Plate)	(L)	New York, Chicago & St. Louis
C RR Co. of N.J. - Full name	(L)	New Jersey Central
NYNH & H	(N, I, *)	New York, New Haven & Harford
NYP & N	(I)	New York, Philadelphia & Norfolk Railroad
NKP	(L)	Nickel Plate Road
N & W	(I, *)	Norfolk & Western
NP	(L)	Northern Pacific
ON - Marked with N	(I)	Ontario Northland
O & W RR	(I)	Oregon & Washington
O.R. & N. Co.	(I)	Oregon Railroad & Navigation Co.
O.S.L. R.R.	(L)	Oregon Short Line RR.
PRR	(L, I, *)	Pennsylvania
Full name used	(L)	Pacific Electric Railway

PM - Full name used	(N - SHIP)	Pere Marquette
P & LE	(I)	Pittsburgh & Lake Erie
Full name used	(N)	Pullman
Full name used	(N)	Reading
RF & P	(L)	Richmond, Fredreicksburg & Potomac
RI	(I)	Rock Island
SD & A Ry	(L)	San Diego & Arizona
SAL	(N)	Seaboard
SR or Full name used	(L, N, *)	Southern
SP	(L, *)	Southern Pacific
ST LSW	(I)	St. Louis & South Western

Full name used	(N)	Texas Midland RR.
TP	(L, *)	Texas & Pacific
Full name used	(N)	Uintah Railway (in Rockies, Sandknop, p. 52)
UP (THE CHALLENGER)	(L, N, *)	Union Pacific
Full name used	(L, *)	Wabash
WM	(L)	Western Maryland
WP	(L)	Western Pacific
Y & MV (VICKSBURG ROUTE)	(L)	Yazoo & Mississippi Valley

The following two pages are from *Quiz on Railroads and Railroading*, 11th edition, Washington, D.C., Association of American Railroads, 1956, to help the reader to identify the various logos used by the railroads on tops of dishes. The shapes match from the inside of the page outward. Probably only a few would ever be used in such a way. But if the reader is lucky enough to find such a dish, it is worth a considerable amount of money.

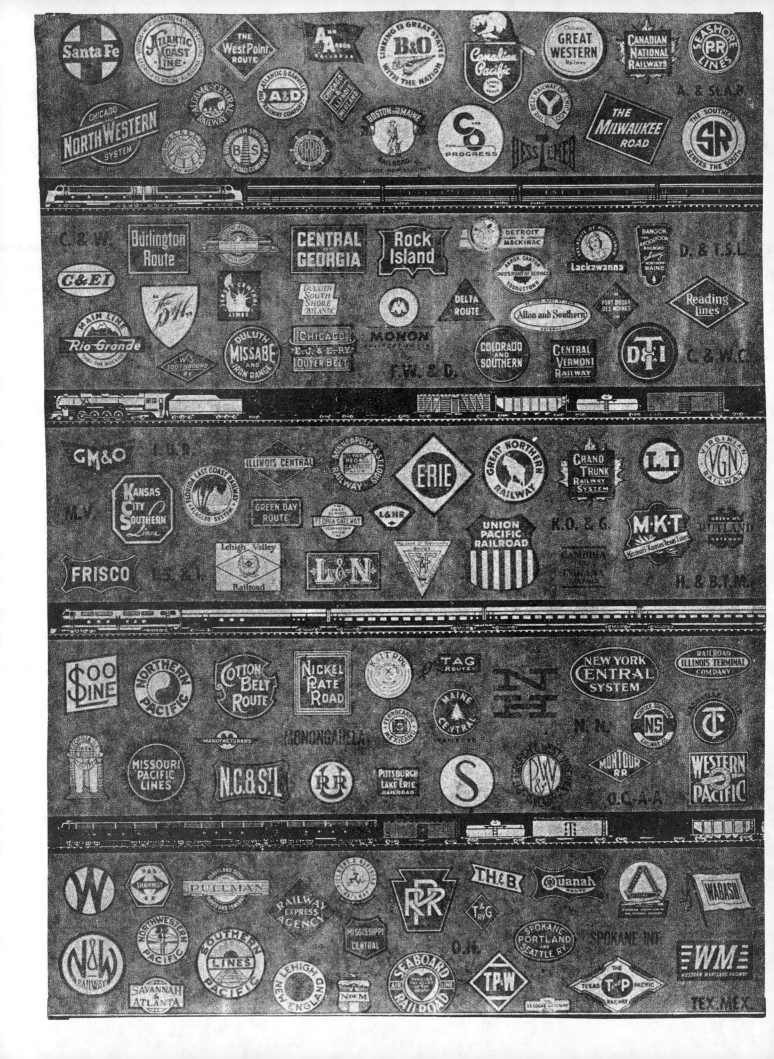

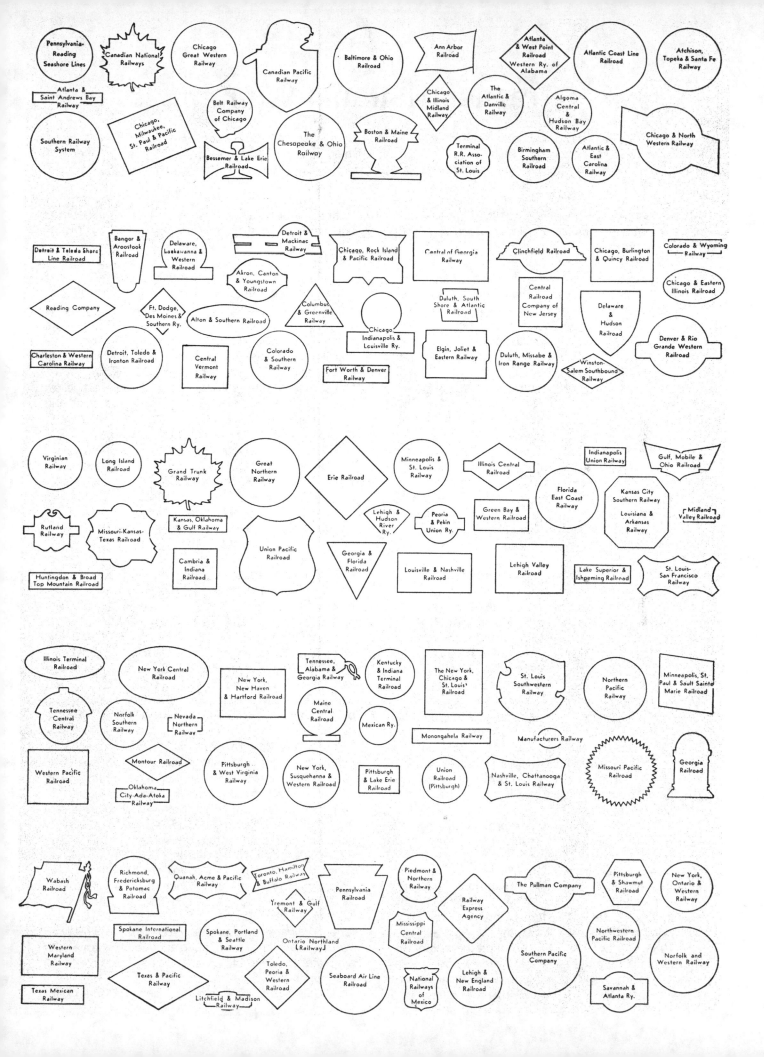

Syracuse National Winners

The following listings are not consistant in the information they contain, but I have included whatever I could obtain on these very important National Ceramic Exhibitions held in Syracuse at the Syracuse Museum, later called the Everson Museum. The majority of the following information was sent with permission for use by Barbara Perry, Curator of Ceramics, Everson Museum of Art, Syracuse, New York.

Before 1932, the work of the artist-potter or studio potter had been shown from time to time in various cities and states. But in 1932, the First National Ceramic Exhibition was held at the Syracuse Museum of Fine Art in Syracuse, New York, through the efforts of Anna Wetherill Olmstead. The exhibition was open to all of the United States, but only potters from 11 states entered. By 1936, when the Fifth National Ceramic Exhibition was held, 26 states made entries and 19 were admitted with 49 potters represented. Following the Fourth National Exhibition, an invitation came to American ceramists to exhibit in Copenhagen, Denmark. The exhibit was taken not only to Denmark, but to Sweden, England and Finland as well. This exhibition marked a milestone in American ceramics. The jury of selection for this fifth exhibition was Richard F. Bach, from the Metropolitan Museum of Art; Arthur E. Baggs, a professor at the Ohio State Univeristy; R. Guy Cowan, a potter from the Onondaga Pottery who represented the American Ceramic Society; William M. Milliken, a curator at the Cleveland Museum of Art; and Anna Wetherill, the director of the Syracuse Museum of Fine Arts.

Starting at the first year of the National Ceramic Exhibition in 1932, the winners were *Charles M. Harder* of Alfred, New York, first prize for pottery a vase, copper red with a thumbed decoration; *Walter P. Suter*, first prize for ceramic sculpture, a fountain figure.

1933: *Arthur E. Baggs,* first prize for pottery, for a group of four, including a copper red, stoneware, globular vase, a copper blue self glazing vase, a copper red stoneware bowl and a handled, selenium red vase with a tale body; *William E. Hentschel*, honorable mention for a decorated porcelain bowl; *Waylande Gregory*, first prize for ceramic sculpture, for "Girl with Olive;" *Russell Barnett Aitken*, first honorable mention, for ceramic sculpture for a group of five pieces, including, "Leopard," "Billy the Kid," "Young Colt," "Young Zebra," and "Ingagi."

1934: *Edgar Littlefield*, first prize for pottery, for a group of five pieces; *William Soini*, Brooklyn, New York, first honorable mention for pottery; *Russell Barnett Aitken*, Cleveland, Ohio, first prize for ceramic sculpture for "Burschenlied Aux Heidelberg" (unique); *Waylande Gregory*, first honorable mention for ceramic sculpture, Metuchen, New Jersey, for "Head of Child," white porcelain-glazed terra cotta.

1935: *Edgar Littlefield*, first prize for pottery, for a crackled plate and blue vase; *Arthur E. Baggs*, second prize for pottery, for a copper blue matt glaze vase; *Charles M. Harder,* third prize for pottery, for a

turquoise earthenware plate, a red lustre earthenware bowl, a slip decoration, hard porcelain jar; *Glen Lukens*, honorable mention, for pottery, a yellow bowl done in raw alkaline; *Paul Bogatay*, first prize for ceramic sculpture, for a native woman figure; *Waylande Gregory*, first honorable mention for ceramic sculpture, for "Kansas Madonna," unique unglazed terra cotta.

1936: For the Fifth National Ceramic Exhibition, I was able to secure the complete list of entries from the Everson Museum of Art. That complete listing follows this list of winners through 1970: *Glen Lukens*, first prize for pottery, for a raw alkaline glazed yellow bowl, raw alkaline glazed blue bowl and gray and platinum bowl; *Maija Grotell*, second prize for pottery, for a bowl with white horses, a gray and lavender bowl with a deer on it, a turquoise and gray bowl with leaves and brown and yellow, also brown and tan geometric vases; *Dorothea Warren O'Hara*, honorable mention for pottery, for a white glazed, carved, tall vase, a flaring, fish design bowl, a black decorated red clay vase, a carved pink glazed bowl, a vase decorated with a deer in a storm on it; *Paul Bogatay*, first prize for ceramic sculpture, for white glazed, "Cow Critter," terra cotta red "Islander," partly glazed, "Javanese Mother and Child;" *Russell Barnett Aitken*, Cleveland, Ohio, honorable mention for ceramic sculpture for a nude on a bull, "Europa," and a baby fawn.

1937: *Roger D. Corsaw*, Norman, Oklahoma, first prize for pottery for a red clay, white engobe, red lustre, sgraffito bowl, a bowl with red clay, yellow and purple lustre, three rings on rim, a bowl with red clay, yellow and purple lustre and brush marks in white center, a bowl with red clay and crackle with white brush mark design on gray background; *Richard C. Smith*, Skaneatales, New York, second prize for pottery for a bowl with yellow and dark blue soda glaze and open center; *Aloys Sacksteder*, Sandusky, Ohio, third prize for pottery for flecked glazed fruit bowl; *Glen Lukens*, first honorable mention for pottery, for an eggshell matte bowl; *Mathilde Parmelee*, Greenwich, Connecticut, first prize for ceramic sculpture for "Pig and Piglets," and "Hen and Henlets;" *Ruth H. Randall*, second prize for ceramic sculpture, for "Armadillo;" *Jean Thalinger*, Cincinnati, Ohio, second prize for ceramic sculpture for "Giraffe;" *Sorcha Boru*, first honorable mention for ceramic sculpture, for "Hansel and Gretel," terra cotta garden piece with glazed flowers; *H. Edward Winter*, Cleveland, Ohio, special prize for enamels for a plaque with decorative head and transparent enamel on copper.

1938: *Arthur E. Baggs*, first prize for pottery, for

a salt glazed stoneware cookie jar; *Herbert H. Sanders*, second prize for pottery, for group of five vases; *Edgar Littlefield* and *Glen Lukens*, third prize for pottery was divided between them, for a group of four bowls; *Laura Andreson*, San Bernardino, California, honorable mention for pottery; *H. Edward Winter*, first prize for enamels, for group of enamel panels; *Russell Barnett Aitken*, first prize for enamels was also divided with him, for enamel panel and two plaques; *Victor Schreckengost*, first prize in ceramic sculpture, for "By the Waterhole," "Glory, Glory," and "The Abduction;" *Carl Schmitz*, New York City, second prize for ceramic sculpture for group for four terra cotta figures; *Thelma Frazier*, Cleveland, Ohio, won the Katherine Q. Payne Memorial Award for group of four figures, "showing unusual humor or whimsy in its conception."

1939: *Gertrud* and *Otto Natzler*, purchase prize for pottery, for a Pompeian turquoise glazed fruit bowl, Pompiean earth glazed vase, stone green glossy glazed vase, blue sea-wave glazed bowl, and turquoise sea-wave glazed bowl; *Henry Varnum Poor*, purchase prize for pottery, for nude platter; *Harold Eaton Riegger*, purchase prize for pottery, for unglazed brown stoneware bottle; *Karl Drerup*, Rockville Center, New York, purchase prize for pottery for enamel, "Idyll," enamel "Horse," and porcelain vase "Shepherd;" *Thelma Frazier*, purchase prize for ceramic sculpture, for tin-copper-cobalt glaze "Night with Young Moon;" *David W. Seyler*, purchase prize for ceramic sculpture, Rookwood Pottery Company, Cincinati, Ohio, for terra cotta "Portrait of Jack Chasnoff;" *Sascha Brastoff*, the Katherine Q. Payne Memorial Award, "for sculpture showing unusual humor or whimsey," for terra cotta figure "Emergence," terra cotta figure "Timid Maiden;" *Waylande Gregory*, special recognition for work in outdoor ceramic sculpture, who had a special exhibit.

1940: *Marion Lawrence Fosdick*, purchase prize for pottery, for a stoneware bowl with slip painting with light brown and gray clay; *Winifred Phillips*, Wanwatosa, Wisconsin, purchase prize for pottery for a stoneware jug with grog body, stoneware bowl with underglaze decoration, stoneware vase with opalescent lining; *Edwin* and *Mary Scheier*, purchase prize for pottery, for a thrown and decorated stoneware bowl, a thrown stoneware vase; *Paul Bogatay*, purchase prize for pottery, for unglazed terra cotta "Colt;" *Gertrude* and *Otto Natzler*, the Katherine Q. Payne Memorial Award for pottery, for turquoise-gray, flowing lava, oval bowl; *Peter Ganine*, Hollywood, California, purchase prize for ceramic scultpure for "Baby Centaur;" *Adolf Odorfer*, Fresno, California, purchase prize for ceramic sculpture for terra cotta "Chorus Girls," terra cotta "Sweet Adeline," and "Family;" *Edward Winter*, purchase prize for enamels for group of six enamel panels.

1941: *Ceramic Sculpture*, Bernard Emerson Frazier; W.W. Swallow; Lyman S. Carpenter; Vally Wieselthier. *Pottery*, Edwin and Mary Scheier; Don Schreckengost; Gertrud and Otto Natzler; Edgar Littlefield; Thomas S. Haile; Crucita T. Cruz.

1946: *Ceramic Sculpture*, William W. Swallow; Carl Walters. *Pottery*, Maiji Grotell; Edwin and Mary Scheier; Laura Andreson; Henry Varnum Poor; Paul Bogatay; Gertrud and Otto Nazler; Sandro Giampietro; Marguerite Wildenhain; William Manker; Herbert H. Sanders; Beatrice Wood; Antonio Prieto.

1947: *Ceramic Sculpture*, Betty Border; Winslow Bryan Eaves; Nancy V. Leitch; Thomas F. McClure; Adolf Odorfer; Miguel Sopo. *Pottery*, Rachel Buegeleisen; Murray Douglas; Marion Fosdick; Irene Kolodziej; Wayne Long; Christine Jane Miller; Minnie Negoro; Glidden Parker; Elleen and Rossi Reynolds; Mary F. Satterly; Edwin and Mary Scheier; Viktor Schreckengost.

1948: *Ceramic Sculpture*, Alexander Archipenko, Betty Davenport Ford; Bernard Frazier; Wayne Long; Henry Fox; Viktor Schreckengost; Egon Weiner. *Honorable Mentions*, Edris Eckhardt; Charles Y. Dusenbury; Peter Lipman-Wulf; Charles Umlauf; William Powers White. *Pottery*, Sascha Brastoff; Margaret H. Jipp; Thomas F. McClure; Harold E. Riegger; Randolph Webb; Nancy Wickham; Donald Wood. *Honorable Mentions*, F. Carlton Ball; Rolf Key-Oberg; Edwin and Mary Scheier; Marguarite Segal; Robert C. Turner.

1949: *Ceramic Sculpture*, Paul Bogatay; Mar Carter; Bruno Mankowski; Carl Schmita; W.W. Swallow Thelma Frazier Winter. *Honorable Mentions*, William M. McVey; Louis B. Raynor; Leah R. Rosen; Elden C. Tefft. *Pottery*, Maija Grotell; John S. Howald; Charles F. Mosgo; Glidden Parker; Edwin Scheier; Mary Scheier; David Weinribl. *Honorable Mentions*, J.T. Abernathy; William E. Ross; Robert C. Turner; Donald G. Wood.

1950: *Ceramic Sculpture*, Betty Davenport Ford; Lois Mahier; Thomas F. McClure; William M. VcVey; Adolf Odorfer; Henry Rox. *Honorable Mentions*, Margaret Stierlin; Ellen V. Walters. *Pottery*, Whitney Atchley; Charles Lakofsky; Polia Pillin; Antonio Prieto; Lee R. Rosen; Viktor Schreckengost; Donald Siegfried; Peter H. Voulkos. *Honorable Mentions*, Edwin Cadogan; Leza S. McVey; Harold E. Riegger; Nancy Wickham.

1951: *Ceramic Sculpture*, William M. McVey; John Cavanaugh; Adolf Odorfer. *Honorable Mentions*, Elah Hale Hays; Donald O. Mavros; Irma Rothstein; A. Gatewood Van Kleeck. *Pottery*, David Gil; Paul D. Holleman; Karen Karnes; Leza S. McVey; Charles F. Mosgo; Stephen J. Polchert; M. Purkiss; Edwin Scheier; Robert C. Turner; Peter H. Voulkos. *Honorable Mentions*, Rupert J. Deese; Kjeld and Erica Deichmann; Elaine E. Healy; Harrison McIntosh; Dorothy Nelson; Elena Montalvo Netherby; Polia Pillin; Betty Anne Travis.

1952: *Special Commendation For Ceramic Sculpture*, Thelma Frazier Winter. *Ceramic Sculpture*, Anne Chapman; Betty Whiteman Feves; Betty Davenport Ford; George K. Stark; W.W. Swallow. *Honorable Mentions*, Paul Bogatay; Ruth Cochran; Clyde Jones;

Mary Kring; Elizabeth C. McFayden; Joan Hang Smith. *Pottery*, Fong Chow; Elizabeth Boyd Greene; Charles Lakofsky; Elizabeth Anne Mesmer; Elena Montalvo Netherby; Stephen Polchert; Theodore Randall; Philip Secrest. *Honorable Mentions*, Elizabeth Ann Baugh; Paul D. Holleman; Albert H. King; E. Ruth Laird; Martha Middleton Lauritzen; Bailey Leslie; James Lovera; Harrison McIntosh;Charles Mosgo; Albert J. Spencer; Peter H. Voulkos.

1954: *Ceramic Sculpture*, Betty Whiteman Feves; Wayne Long; John Risley; Viktor Schreckengost. *Pottery*, Nana Wickham Boyd; Walter and Mary Kring; Hui

Ka Kwong; Harvey K. Littleton; Robert H. Meinhardt; Henry Varnum Poor; Robert Turner; Jayne Van Alstyne; Peter Voulkos. *Architectural Ceramic Sculpture*, Viktor Schreckengost.

1956: *Ceramic Sculpture*, Betty W. Feves; Lillyan Rhodes; Dorothy W. Riester; Alice DeK. Sperry; George K. Stark. *Pottery*, Harris and Ros Barron; Clyde E. Burt; Michael Kan; Charles Kalofsky; Sibyl Laubenthal; Gertrud and Otto Natzler; Elena Montalvo Netherby; James Secrest; Paul C. Volckining; David Weinrib; Marie Woo. *Architectural Ceramic Sculpture*, William M. McVey.

In the years between 1958 and 1964 only the award winners' names were given. The winners were not divided as to pottery pieces or sculpture. For the year 1958 not even the address was given.

1958: *Ceramic National Award Winners*, Carlton Ball; J. Sheldon Carey; Karl Drerup; Florence Gray; Karen Karnes; Ruth Laird; Wayne Long; James McKinnell; Gertrude and Otto Natzler; Lillyan Rhodes; Edwin Scheier; Alice Sperry; Peter Voulkos; Marguerite Wildenhain; Thelma Frazier Winter.

1962-1963: *Ceramic National Award Winners*, Clarence Alling, Topeka, Kansas; Kenneth F. Bares, Euclid; Ohio; Me M. Conner, Cleveland, Ohio; Rupert Deese, Upland, California; Kenneth R. Ferguson, Helena, Montana; John P. Loree, Hornell, New York; James Lovera, Hayward, California; Alex MacKenzie, Stillwater, Minnesota; Warren MacKenzie, Stillwater, Minnesota; Charles McKee, Oakland, California; Gertrud and Otto Natzler, Los Angeles, California; Paul E. Nelson, Seattle, Washington; Win Ng, San Francisco, California; Theodore Randall, Alfred, New York; June Schwarcy, Sausalito, California; William Wyman, Weymouth, Massachusetts.

1963-1964: *Ceramic National Award Winners*, Michael Cohen, Newton Centre, Massachusetts; Daniel Rhodes, Alfred, New York; Bertil Vallien, Los Angeles, California; John H. Stepehenson, Ann Arbor, Michigan; Frans Wildenhain, Rochester, New York; Daye Denning, Plainview, New York; Peter H. Voulkos, Oakland, California; Joseph L. Hysong, San Jose, California; Toshiko Takaezu, Cleveland, Ohio; William Wyman, North Weymouth, Massachusetts; J. Ormond Sanderson, Durham, North Carolina; Antonio Prieto, Oakland, California; Win Ng, San Francisco, California; Herbert H. Sanders, Los Gatos, California; Kenneth John Dierck, El Cerrito, California; Bernard Kypridakis, Sacramento, California; Harris and Ros Barron, Brookline, Massachusetts.

1965-1966: For this year, the list included the piece that won a specific prize but not a place such as first, honorable mention, etc. *Claude Conover*, Cleveland, Ohio, won the B.F. Drakenfield & Company prize for the Everson Museum collection for "Object," a stoneware, handbuilt piece. *Kenneth J. Dierck*, El Cerrito, California, won the Helen S. Everson Museum Memorial purchase prize as well as the Ferro Corporation prize for "Innocent City," a black stoneware relief

with gray, brown and tan accents. *Betty Feves*, Pendleton, Oregon, won the Harris Clay Company prize for "Persona," a stoneware sculpture, which was slab built of stoneware with ash glaze. *Jan Jones*, Galena, Ohio, won the Syracuse China Corporation prize for a wheel thrown stoneware bowl with stamped decoration. *Richard Leach*, Albion, Michigan, won the American Art Clay Company prize for a salt glazed, wheel thrown, stoneware casserole. *Dorothy Midanik*, Toronto, Canada, won the *Ceramic Monthly Magazine* prize for pottery for four stoneware, slab built boxes with iron oxide and white glaze circles for decoration. *Win Ng*, San Francisco, California, won the G. Hammel Company prize for ceramic art. He also won the Syracuse Society of Architects' prize and the William M. Milliken prize for the Everson Museum collection, for "Retreat no. 5," a sculpture with muted polychrome glazes. *George Roby*, Chagrin Fall, Ohio, won the Dansk Designs, Inc. prize for a hand built stoneware bottle with tan and black texture. *Monona Rossol*, Madison, Wisconsin, won the Association of San Francisco Potters prize, for a hand built stoneware vase with black slip and tan glaze. *Jerry Rothman*, Paramount, California, won the A.D. Alpine, Inc. prize, for "Not in Central Park," a stoneware sculpture with yellow ochre slip. *Thomas Shafer*, Iowa City, Iowa, won the Hammond Lead Products, Inc. prize for ceramics, for a hand built stoneware branch pot with iron oxide and iron red glaze, also a hand built stoneware globe with iron oxide slip. *Floyd Shaffer*, Bowling Green, Ohio, won the Mayco Colors Prize for a wheel thrown stoneware bowl with orange and brown glaze. *Paul Soldner*, Claremont, California, won the Canadian Guild of Potters prize, for a wheel thrown and altered raku bottle with unglazed and gray with brown decoration. *John H. Stephenson*, Ann Arbor, Michigan, won the Arcadian Landscaping prize for garden sculpture, for "N is for Neko," a hand built stoneware vase with iron yellow and brown glaze.

1967-1968: *Ceramic National Award Winners*, Frans Wildenhain, Pittsford, New York; Robert C. Turner, Alfred Station, New York; Jun Kaneko, Los Angeles, California; Jean Yates, Santa Rose, California; Kenneth A Hendry, Long Grove, Illinois; William

Creitz, Portland, Oregon; Pat Bauer, Whitmore Lake, Michigan; Mary R. Mintich, Belmont, North Carolina; Gertrude P. Brodsky, Cleveland Heights, Ohio; Philip G. Cornelius, South Pasadena, California; Fred Wollschlager, Paramount, California; Rudy Autio, Missoula, Montana; David Shaner, Helena, Montana; Joe Soldate, Ontario, California; Herbert H. Sanders, San Jose, California; William D. Parry, Alfred, New York; William Lau, New York, New York; Ernie Kim, Richmond, California; Erik Gronborg, Portland, Oregon; Philip G. Cornelius, South Pasadena, California.

1968-1970: *Ceramic National Award Winners,* Joseph Hawley, Mill Valley, California; Donald W. Pilcher, Philo, Illinois; Jun Kaneko, Temple City, Califor-nia; Val M. Cushing, Alfred, New York; Everett O. Snowden, Oakland, California; Ka-Kwong Hui, New York, New York; Ellamarie Wooley, San Diego, Califor-nia; Jim Knecht, Greensboro, North Carolina; William Wilhelmi, Los Angeles, California; Henry K. Gernhardt, LaFayette, New York; Clair Colquitt, Seattle, Washington; Ann Christenson, New York, New York; Jack Earl, Genoa, Ohio; Mick Lamont, San Francisco, California; David Benge, Santa Monica, California; John C. Marshall, Syracus, New York; Beverly Magen-nis, Los Angeles, California; David A. Middlebrook, Ox-ford, Iowa; Ellamarie Wooley, San Diego, California; Jerry Rothman, Los Angeles, California.

The following listing includes all of the entries for the Fifth Ceramic National for the year 1936, with a descrip-tion of the product submitted. The winners for this year were already listed.

1936: *Fifth National Ceramic Exhibition: Sadie Adams,* Flagstaff, Arizona, a pair of Hopi Tiles, black and red on yellow; *Irene Aitken,* Cleveland, Ohio, "Dixie Madonna," "Kentucky Babe," "Primitive Madonna," "Horse with the Braded Mane;" *Russell Barnett Aitken,* Cleveland, Ohio, "Europa, Nude on Bull," "Baby Faun;" *James Anderson,* Shearwater Pottery, Ocean Springs, Mississippi, carved alkaline blue and copper red platters; *Peter Anderson,* Shearwater Pottery, cop-per red, low porous bowl and two copper red vases; *Walter Anderson,* Shearwater Pottery, carved copper red and blue vases, "Negro Group," "Group of Foot-ball Players;" *Alice A. Ayars,* Cleveland, Ohio, Chinese gold vase, and jade and white bowl; *Arthur E. Baggs,* Ohio State University, copper blue, mishima decorated plate, and copper red, grey and copper blue vases; *H. Bailey,* Newcomb Pottery, New Orleans, Louisiana, a formal vase; *Mary Belle Barlow,* Philadelphia, Pen-sylvania, red and white, copper transmutation bottle; *Kenneth Bates,* Cleveland, Ohio, enamel Triptych, enamel Cloisonne, enamel box; *Luke Beckerman,* Scarsdale, New York, porcelain slip under glaze, celadon bowl and a green-blue earthenware, slip under glaze bowl; *A. Lee Bennett,* Gladding, McBean and Company, Los Angeles, California, a white lined ruby and a light green bottle shapevase, a dark ruby and a green round vase, and an old rose, white lined flared beaker vase; *Roberta Board,* Los Angeles, California, "The Gossips;" *Paul Bogatay,* Columbus, Ohio, white glazed "Cow Critter," terra cotta red "Islander," and a partly glazed "Javanese Mother and Child;" *Sorcha Boru,* Menlo Park, California, a 16-piece pottery chess set with silver decoration, a gold "Girl and Fawn" figurine, "Eve," "Ghandi;" *Clivia A. Calder,* Detroit, Michigan, blue and white glazed, "Amelia," red clay figure; *May Hamilton deCausse,* May and Vieve Hamilton Pottery, Vernon Kilns, Los Angeles, Califor-nia, a talc body tropical bowl, and a white talc body carved monkey vase; *Guy Cowan,* Onondaga Pottery Company, Syracuse, New York, a tea set; *Annie Laurie Crawford,* New York, for "Girl with Fruit, African Maid;" "Tom-tom, Ivory coast warrior," "Aunt Chloe and Honey Chile," and a turquoise hair mask; *E. de F. Cur-tis,* Wayne, Pennsylvania, copper red stoneware bowl, and transmutal stoneware bottle; *Maryetta Davidson,* Saratoga Springs, New York, a majolica glaze, terra cotta body flower holder figurine; *Martha Davis,* New York, a slip decorated, Alfred shale bowl; *Emilie Zeckwer Dooner,* Philadelphia, Pennsylvania, a copper red bowl, a copper red cup, red and green transmuta-tion cup, copper red bottle and miniature group; *Mrs. A.R. Dyer,* Cleveland, Ohio, red engobe plate, black engobe bowl, white crackle bowl and flower frog, cop-per red, copper and green celadon jars; *Nancy Bixby Edwards,* Chicago, Illinois, "Child with Rabbit" garden piece; *Winifred Eisert,* New York State College of Ceramics, Alfred, New York, blue green fish plate; *Ruth Eldridge,* New York State College of Ceramics, gray clay with fish plaque; *William Ehrich,* Buffalo, New York, white china glazed "Maternity," and white china glaz-ed "Mother and Child;" *Sadie L. Feldman,* Brooklyn, New York, a modeled vase, "Noah and the Flood," red slip sgraffito bowl, "Let us Enter the Land with Joy," and yellow glaze over sgraffito bread plate; *George Fetzer,* Columbus, Ohio, a brown plate with slip decora-tion, blue decorated jug, and "Katherine," a wheel thrown elephant; *Marion L. Fosdick,* New York State College of Ceramics, Alfred, New York, a carved vase, green and red glaze bowl, and a copper red lamp; *John A. Foster,* Detroit, Michigan, blue crystalline and mir-ror lustre vases, carved lustre and crystalline bowl, white crystalline jar and cover and a red Michigan clay sculptured head; *Norman Foster,* Penwell, New Jersey, "Pig;" *Merle Gage,* San Diego, California, "St. Fran-cis;" *Rose Gonzales,* Laboratory of Anthropology, Sante Fe, New Mexico, a red jar and two red bowls; *Jessie F. Gordon,* Philadelphia, Pennsylvania, gray and blue jar and carved dogwood design blue bowl;

Waylande Gregory, Metuchen, New Jersey, a glazed suntan porcelain "Portrait of a Boy," and black and white procelain pair of zebras; *Maija Grotell*, New York, a white horses bowl, gray and lavendar deer bowl, turquoise and gray leaves bowl, brown and tan geometric vase and a brown and yellow geometric vase; *Katherine B. Grove*, Columbus, Ohio, "Jackass;" *Georgia Grow*, New York State College of Ceramics, Alfred, New York, a deep blue with crayon pattern plaque; *Rowena W. Hallowell*, Clay Craft Studio, Winchester, Masschusetts, wheel thrown ten petal jar; *Vieve Hamilton*, May and Vieve Hamilton Pottery, Vernon Kilns, Los Angeles, California, a carved ovoid vase, white incised pierced plate, sculptured head of Christ, called "The Way-Shower," and a white rythmic bowl; *Charles Harder*, Alfred, New York, a gray vase; *Prue M. Harris*, Philadelphia, Pennsylvania, a copper red, transmutation glaze bottle, copper red, transmutation glaze fluted vase, porcelain translucent pierced bowl, crackle, ashes of roses, porcelain bowl; *Nina Hatfield,* Hoboken, New Jersey, a green and black glaze plate; *Frank G. Holmes*, Lenox, Inc., Trenton, New Jersey, two urns, tea set, classic plate, plates; *Ivan Houser*, Rushmore Pottery, Keystone, South Dakota, a green glazed hand thrown vase; *Richard H. Huebner*, Wheeling, West Virginia, incised white vase, "Noah's Ark," an ivory body, incised cylindrical vase, incised porcelain "May Flowers," red body slip decorated "Satsuma" plate and a red body incised plate; *M.E. Jalanivich* and *Olsen*, San Francisco, California, pair of mountain goats, green fish bowl, purple and blue Chrysanthemum bowl, purple with yellow and red flaring vase; *Virginia Jamison*, New York State College of Ceramics, Alfred, New York, blue and white, crayon pattern plate; *Charles Bartley Jeffery*, Cleveland, Ohio, red bowl with crystals, a hand thrown, blue-green and brown glazed with tooled circles plate; *C. Paul Jennewein*, New York, female head, "Marietta," baby head, "Mimi," male head, "The Victor," a draped figure holding ball of fire, "Fire"; *Ellen Jennings*, Columbus, Ohio, elephant ashtray, elephant match holder, baby elephant; *Edith Keeler*, Marion, Ohio, green glaze on white clay desk piece horse; *Charlotte Kizer*, University of Nebraska, Lincoln, Nebraska, blue-green crackled alkaline glazed bowl and yellow crackled alkaline glazed vase; *Jean Lawyer*, Los Angeles, California, white statuette of "The Tortoise and the Hare;" *Roberta Leber*, Wingarth Studios, West Nyack, New York, sgraffito decorated bowl, and frosted white vase; *Edgar Littlefield*, Ohio State University, Columbus, Ohio, red design on pale blue bowl, gray-white mat glazed vase, brown glazed vase, and an all-over pattern mat glazed vase; *Glen Lukens*, University of Southern California, Los Angeles, California, a raw alkaline glazed yellow bowl and blue bowl, and a gray and platinum bowl; *Marie Martinez*, Laboratory of Anthropology, Santa Fe, New Mexico, two black jars; *Karl Martz*, Nashville, Indiana, an incised border, gray bright glazed vase, a crackled incised zone, white semi-matt with blue lining vase, an incised

zone lavendar semi-matt with brown lining vase, and a polychrome sgraffito bowl; *Vera Odeyne Neff*, Cleveland, Ohio, a blue crystal china moss vase, and an incised orange plate; *Carol M. Nickerson*, Clay Craft Studio, Winchester, Massachusetts, white crackled caste lotus bowl; *Chester Nicodemus*, Columbus, Ohio, rabbit, sealyham, and blue-green jug; *Dorothea Warren O'Hara*, Appletree Lane Pottery, Darien, Ohio, carved white glazed tall vase, carved pink glazed bowl, "Deer in Storm" vase, flaring bowl with fish design, black decorated red clay vase; *Thomas Parker*, Wheeling, West Virginia, "Dawn," an ivory vase, and "Cathedral," a maroon vase; *Katherine Q. Payne*, Harrisburg, Pennsylvania, dormouse, gryphon, mock turtle and white rabbit; *Andrew Pereny*, Columbus, Ohio, incised brown decorated plate, peacock black vase, brown tube decorated vase, turquoise brush decorated plate; *Linn Phelan*, Rochester, New York, "Leaves and Shadow," a pink clay body vase, and "Storm Clouds," a pink clay body vase. *Helen Clark Phillips*, New York, silver lustre on turquoise star plate, and white crackle orange clay giraffe vase; *C. Eleanor Pierce*, Philadelphia, Pennsylvania, scalloped sides green vase; *Henry Varnum Poor*, New York, two plaques; *Vernise Irene Pruitt*, Grand Rapids, Michigan, "Hoosier Milk Maid," decorated in underglaze, and "Adam and Eve," *Georgie V.B. Putney*, New York, green transparent crackle carved jar with open work rim filled in with glaze; *Natalie Pyndus*, Syracuse, New York, white seal and white bear; *Ruth H. Randall*, Syracuse University, Syracuse, New York, "Pair of Cormorants," glazed birds; *Harold Riegger*, New York State College of Ceramics, Alfred, New York, gray and copper red plate; *Yetta Rosenberg*, Cleveland, Ohio, "Oriental Child," with underglaze decoration, alkaline glazed vase; *William E. Ross*, Greenwich, Connecticut, blue pair of fish, and carved brown bowl, *Rose deRossi*, New York State College of Ceramics, Alfred, New York, carved blue vase, and brown crayon pattern vase; *Tonita Roybal*, Laboratory of Anthropology, Santa Fe, New Mexico, two red jars, red bowl and two black jars; *Thomas E. Ryder*, Hershey Industrial School, Hershey, Pennsylvania, incised stoneware bowl; *Aloys Sacksteder*, Sandusky, Ohio, incised design lamp base with oyster white glass; *Herbert H. Sanders*, Norwood, Ohio, blue bowl decorated by black underglaze band of leaves, overall carved decorated blue globular vase, brown globular stoneware vase with flecked brown glaze, copper red stoneware bottle with crushed strawberry glaze, copper red stoneware vase with crushed strawberry glaze; *Viktor Schreckengost*, Cleveland School of Art, Cleveland, Ohio, a dozen unique polo plates, "Harvest" plate, "Abstract still-life," a unique plate, "April," a unique plate, and a circus group consisting of "Madam Kitty," "Little Nell," "Jum and Jumbo," "Henri the Great," "Six Cellinis;" *Frances Serber*, Philadelphia, Pennsylvania, gray bowl; *Lili Shapiro*, Brighton, Massachusetts, mottled blue and green vase, and hand built lamp base; *Agnes J. Shedd*,

Columbus, Ohio, small blue dish, pitcher and bowl; *Shirley Soderstrom*, Hollywood, California, negro caricatures "Adam and Eve," group of three "Fawns," group of five "Shadow Modds;" *William Soini*, Brooklyn, New York, blue bowl and maroon bowl; *Sophie Stemmerman*, New York, a green vase; *Margaret Steenrod*, Ohio State University, Columbus, Ohio, blue fish necklace, and miniature jugs, vases and bottles; *Edgar H. Strong*, Wolcott, New York, red slip banded, red and buff crackle bowl, gray-green stoneware jar, yellow-green slip banded plate, stoneware bowl; *Emily Swift*, Philadelphia, Pennsylvania, for pelican, resting pelican and bowl; *Tewanginema*, Flagstaff, Arizona, black and white on red decorated Hopi bowl; *James C. Thornton*, Newark, Ohio, underglaze stain troubadour; *Robert Trine*, Hollywood, California, vase; *Leon Volkmar*, Bedford Village, New York, black jar, small white bowl, blue bowl, large purple vase; *Carl Walters*, Woodstock, New York, duck; *Randolph Webb*, New York State School of Ceramics, Alfred, New York, white vase, blue gray bowl, blue-green-white slip decorated bowl, red slip decorated globe, and green underglaze sprayed plate; *Walter A. Weldon*, Baltimore, Maryland, blue crystalline vase; *Howard Whalen*, Waylande Gregory Studio, Metuchen, New Jersey, group of three miniature heads; *Kathleen Wheeler*, Washington, D.C., a leopard; *Richard Hendry Williams*, University of Nebraska, Lincoln, Nebraska, transparent glazed bowl; *Helen Williams*, Syracuse, New york, blue-green carved vase, light green carved bowl, and matt white vase; *H. Edward Winter*, Cleveland, Ohio, emerald green bowl and Egyptian lotus plaque.

Electrical Porcelain Insulator Markings

Jack H. Tod, author of books on electrical porcelain has given permission for the following pages to be reprinted from *A History of the Electrical Porcelain Industry of the United States*, pp. 103-115. The reprinting of these pages is in no way a substitute for the fine books written by Mr. Tod.

"*Electrical Porcelain* is the primary collector reference book on all forms of electrical porcelain insulators other than pin types and other high-voltage insulators. It contains the history of evolution of electrical porcelain insulators from their inception to modern times, histories of all companies (over 100) that are known to have made electrical porcelain insulators, every known manufacturer's marking on electrical porcelain, illustrations and descriptions of all wiring insulator types, data and illustrations of every significant insulator patent (nearly 700 in all) from 1880 to date, every pertinent registered trademark, descriptions of the manufacturing processes, etc. The book is well indexed and contains a bibliography of related reference books on insulators." See the bibliography for the books by Mr. Tod and where to purchase them.

Porcelain Insulator Markings

The following tabulation of markings will allow a great many specimens to be attributed to specific companies. The great majority of these markings are taken from actual insulator specimens, but some are trade-names advertised by the company in connection with the indicated class of insulator and which could be expected to turn up on specimens. Some that are listed as "unattributed" appear to match certain company names listed in old directories, but engaging in initial-matching has always led to a frustratingly high degree of errors in the past. Attributions are firmed only with good basis — specimens found in plant dumpage, in the original cartons, shown in company literature, accompanied by patent or cataloging numbers belonging to the company, etc.

The class of insulators shown for each company indicates either the major porcelain items made by the company or the particular types of insulators made by the company on which the marking was used. The following notes will explain the classification terminology used:

Standard porcelain - generally the complete range of standard items such as cleats, knobs, tubes, split knobs, etc. Some large porcelain companies made a very extensive line. Others made only the high-volume items such as split knobs and wiring cleats. Many wiring insulators (especially #334 cleats and split knobs) bear jobber trademarks, and these could have been made by any contracted porcelain company.

Wiring devices - various insulating devices not connected with routing of the wires in a structure. These include ceiling rosettes, pendent switches, wall switches, sockets, plugs, current taps, etc.

Specialty items - all types of special purpose porcelain items made by the company as proprietary items or on contract for others. Relating to electrical porcelain, this could be anything from sparkplug cores to bases for tap-changing switches on a transformer. Most porcelain companies made anything for which they could contract, and non-electrical specialty items are abundant in their plant dumpage.

Radio antenna insulators - as sold separately, or in antenna installation kits with wire, these are guy strains, nail knobs, small screweyes and lightning arrestors. Many have colored glazes, and most markings on them are those of radio companies or wire manufacturers.

Poleline hardware - generally insulators used on pole lines, but also including insulators to services — rack spools, wireholders, etc.

(Abbreviations used by Tod include: porc.-porcelain; wir'g-wiring; elec'c-electric; std-standard; mfg-manufacturer or manufacturing; dev-device.)

 Akron Insulator & Marble Co., Akron, Ohio, standard porc.

 Appleton Electric Co., Chicago, end outlet bushings

ABC - Anderson Mfg., Co., Albert & J M, Boston, plugs & receptacles

A C - unattributed, clamp insulators

A C F Co. - unattributed, telephone cleats & knobs

ACME - Crescent Elec'c Co., Mtn. Grove, MO, rosettes, sockets, etc.

ACME - Reliable Elec'c Co., Chicago, switches, connectors, cutouts

ADAPTI - Adapti Co., The, Cleveland, conduit items unattributed (Boston, MA), guy strains

A.E. Co. - Automatic Elec'c Co, Chicago, tel insulators & specialties

A.I. & M. CO. - Akron Insulator & Marble Co, Akron, OH, standard porcelain

AJAX - Ajax Elec'c Co, Jersey City, NJ, ground'g & wir'g devices

AJAX - Ajax Elec'c Specialty Co, St. Louis, MO, radio & wir'g dev.

ALADDIN - Pass & Seymour, Inc., Syracuse, NY, plug-socket switch

ALLIGATOR -Porcelain Products, Inc., Findlay, Ohio, split knobs

ALPHA - unattributed, radio antenna insulators

AMERICAN - American Porcelain Co, E Liverpool, OH, standard porcelain

AMERICAN ELEC CO INC - (of Chicago), telephone equipment & supplies

AMERICAN SUNDRIES CO - (of Brooklyn), electrical specialties

ANYLITE - Anylite Electric Co, Ft. Wayne, IN, sockets

(AP) - American Porcelain Co, E Liverpool, OH, standard porcelain

A.P.C.L. - unattributed, special knobs

A. P. Co. - Anderson Porcelain Co, E Liverpool, OH, standard porcelain

APPLETON ELECTRIC CO. - (of Chicago), end outlet bushings

ARGUS - Foote, Pierson & Co, Inc, New York Cy, tel & tel arrestors

ARROTYPE - Arrow Electric Co, Hartford, CT, plug fuses

ARROW - Arrow Conductor & Mfg. Co, Chicago, tel & tel arrestors

ARROW - Arrow Electric Co, Hartford, CT, wiring devices

A.S.P.Co - Akron Smoking Pipe Co, Mogador, OH, standard porcelain

B - unattributed, standard porcelain

(B) unattributed, specialties

BABY - Solar Electric Co, Chicago, sign receptacles

B & B - Betts & Betts Corp, New York, NY, bushings, specialties

B D - unattributed, standard porcelain

B & D - Buffinton & Dow patent (licensed), cleats, split knobs

BEAVER - Beaver Machine & Tool Co, Newark, NJ, wiring devices

B.E. Co. - Bryant Elec'c Co, Bridgeport, wiring devices, specialties

BENBOW - Parker & Son, J H, Parkersburg, WV, mine insulators

BENCO - Benjamin Electric Mfg Co, Chicago, sockets

BENDHICK - Fairmount Electric & Mfg Co, Phila, PA, conduit fittings

BENDIX - Bendix Radio Corp, radio antenna insulators

BENJAMIN - Benjamin Elec'c & Mfg Co, Chicago, wiring devices, specialties

BESCO - unattributed, radio antenna insulators

BEST - Best Electric Corp, New York, NY, wiring devices

BINKLEY - Binkley Mfg Co, Warrenton, MD, wireholders

BIRNBACH - Birnbach Radio Co, New York, NY, radio antenna insulators

BOSS - Elec'l Specialty Mfg Co, Prov, RI, cleats, outlet bushings

BRACH - Brach Mfg Co, L S, Newark, NJ, insulators & specialties

BRASCO - unattributed, secondary rack spools

BRUNT - Brunt Porcelain Co, G F, E Liverpool, OH, standard porc.

BRYANT - Bryant Elec'c Co, Bridgeport, wiring devices, specialties

BSCO - Edison Storage Battery Co, Orange, NJ, wet batteries

B & T - Brunt & Thompson, E Liverpool, OH, standard porcelain

BUCKEYE - Findlay Electric Porc Co, E Liverpool, OH, split knobs

BULL DOG - Illinois Electric Porcelain Co, Macomb, IL, split knobs

BULL DOG - Mutual Electric & Machine Co, Detroit, switches, cutouts

BUNNELL - Bunnell & Co, J H, New York, NY, lgtng arrestors, bushings

C - unattributed, split knobs

(C) - unattributed, split knobs

(C) - unattributed, standard porcelain

(C) - Cook Pottery Co, Trenton, standard porcelain, specialties

CAMPBELL - Steel City Electric Co, Pittsburgh, PA, receptacles

CAPLETS - Phelps, James C, Springfield, MA, end outlet bushings

CAREY, O. - Carey Ohio Porcelain Co, Carey, OH, std porc & specialties

CAREY / OHIO - Carey Ohio Porcelain Co, Carey, OH, std porc & specialties

C. C. E. - unattributed, standard porcelain

C E CO. - Central Electric Co, Chicago, standard porc & specialties

Cem Co - Connecticut Elec'c Mfg Co, Bridgeport, CT, wiring devices

CENCO - unattributed, standard porcelain

C.F.W. & M. CO. - Chicago Fuse Mfg Co, Chicago, fuse cutout bases

C.G.R. - Robin, Charles G, New York, NY, end outlet bushings

C - H - Cutler-Hammer Mfg Co, Milwaukee, wiring devices, specialties

CHAPMAN - Bryant Electric Co, Bridgeport, CT, receptables

CHAPMAN - Minnesota Electric Co, Minneapolis, tel & tel arrestors

CHASECO - Chase Electric Co, Chicago, wiring systems

(HH) - Crouse-Hinds Co, Syracuse, NY, end outlet bushings

CHICAGO - Chicago Steel Foundry Co, Chicago, secondary rack spools

(C) - Colonial Insulator Co, Akron, OH, std porc & specialties

C. I. Co. - Colonial Insulator Co, Akron, OH, std porc & specialties

CINCH - Brunt Porcelain Co, G F, E Liverpool, OH, split knobs

COLONIAL - Parker & Son, J H, Parkersburg, WV, split knobs

COLORADO - Flint Electric & Mfg Co, Denver, mine signaling systems

CONDULET - Crouse-Hinds Co, Syracuse, NY, end outlet bushings

CONDULETTO - Crouse-Hinds Co, Syracuse, NY, end outlet bushings, wiring devices

CONLON - Conneaut Metal Works Co, The, Conneaut, OH, wiring devices

CONNECTICUT - Conn Tel & Electric Co, Meriden, CT, lightning arrestors

COOK - Cook Electric Co, Chicago, tel & tel lightning arrestors

FRANK B. COOK CO. / CHICAGO - Cook Electric Co, Chicago, tel & tel lightning arrestors

COOK / TRENTON - Cook Pottery Co, Trenton, NJ, standard porc & specialties

COOKE WILSON, E. S. CO - unattributed (on U-98 mine insulators)

C.O.P. - Carey Ohio Porcelain Co, Carey, OH, stand porc & specialties

CORWICO - Cornish Wire Co, Inc, New York, NY - radio antenna insuls.

COX - Cox arrestor Co, Eaton, OH, tel & tel lightning arrestors

C. P. Co. - Cook Pottery Co, Trenton, NJ, standard porc & specialties

⬦CRL - Centralab, Inc, Milwaukee, radio antenna insulators

CROSS COUNTRY - unattributed, electrical fence insulators

CROUSE-HINDS - Crouse-Hinds Co, Syracuse, NY, end outlet bushings

C.S.I. Co. - Colonial Sign & Insulator Co, Akron, stand porc, speclties

C.S. & I. Co. - Colonial Sign & Insulator Co, Akron, stand porc, speclties

C. S. K. - Knowles Co, C S, Boston, MA, wiring devices

Ⓢ - Knowles Co, C S, Boston, MA, wiring devices, switches, rosettes

C. S. KNOWLES - Knowles Co, C S, Boston, MA, wiring device

CTS - Chicago Tel Supply Co, Chicago, tel insulators & speclties

CUTTER - Cutter, Scott C, Oswego, IL, tree insulators

CUTTER - Westinghouse Elec'c & Mfg Co, E Ptsbg, arc light equipment

C W & A C - Consolidated Wire & Assoc'd Corp, Chicago, radio ant insul

▭D - Square-D Co, Detroit, pin type insulators & specialties

D-2 (etc.) - (standard sizes forestry insulators: D-1, D-2, D-3, etc.)

DAVIDSON - Davidson Porcelain Co, E Liverpool, OH, standard porcelain

DETROIT - Parker & Son, J H, Parkersburg, WV, split knobs

DIAMOND EXPANSION BOLT CO. - (of New York), bridle ring insulators

DOUBLEX - Parker & Son, J H, Parkersburg, WV, strain insulators

D. P. Co. - Davidson Porcelain Co, E Liverpool, OH, standard porcelain

D & S - Davidson & Stevenson Porc Co, E Liverpool, standard porc.

D & S P Co. - Davidson & Stevenson Porc Co, E Liverpool, standard porc.

DUGGAN - Imperial Porcelain Works, Trenton, NJ, cleats

DYKE - Parker & Son, J H, Parkersburg, WV, porcelain knobs

E - East Liverpool Elec'l Porc Co, E Liverpool, stand. porc.

⬦E - Standard Specialty Mfg Co, Cleveland, end outlet bushings

➤E➤ - Arrow Electric Co, Hartford, CT, wiring devices

EAGLE - Eagle Elec'c Mfg Co, L I City, NY, radio antenna insuls.

EDISON - Edison Storage Battery Co, Orange, NJ, wet batteries

E E E - Elec'l Engrs Equipmt Co, Chicago, hi-tension elec'l equip.

E. ENG. CO. - unattributed, standard porcelain

E. E. P. Co. - East End Pottery Co, E Liverpool, OH, standard porcelain

E E & S Co. - Elec'c Engineering & Supply Co, Syracuse, NY, specialties

EFFICIENCY - Efficiency Elec'c Co, The, E Liverpool, porcelain cleats

E.G.B. Co. - Bernard Co, E G, Troy, NY, early cleats (adjustable)

EICO - Electro Importing Co, New York, NY, radio antenna insuls.

ELECTROLET - Killark Electric Mfg Co, St. Louis, MO, end outlet bushings

EL RE CO - Electric Railway Equipment Co, Cincinnati, special knobs

E. M. - Electrical Mfg Co, Battle Creek, MI, wireholders

E. M. Co - Electrical Mfg Co, Battle Creek, MI, wireholders

EMICO - unattributed, end outlet bushings

EMILY - (special class of screweye insulators, all manufacturers)

E.M.W. Co. - unattributed, wireholders

ENDO - Gillette-Vibber Co, New London, CT, end outlet bushings

ENDOULETS - Fralick & Co, S R, Chicago, end outlet bushings

ENSIGN - unattributed, large spools

ENTWISTLE - unattributed, specialties

E. P. Co. - Electrical Porelain Co, E Liverpool, OH, standard porc.

E. R. E. - Electric Railway Equipment Co, Cincinnati, mine insulators

ERIE - Erie Elec'l Equipmt Co, Johnstown, PA, cleats, specialties

E. S. S. Co. - Electric Service Supplies Co, Phila, PA, mine insulators

EUREKA - unattributed, split knobs

EVER READY - Davidson Porcelain Co, E Liverpool, OH, split knobs

F - Findlay Electric Porcelain Co, Findlay, OH, standard porc.

Ⓕ - Freeman Electric Co, E H, Trenton, NJ, wiring devices

◆F◆ - Findlay Elec'c Porcelain Co, Findlay, OH, porcelain insuls

FAIRMONT - Fairmount Electric & Mfg Co, Phila, PA, wiring devices

FARM MASTER - (Wards or Sears), electric fence insulators

F. C. M. - Mesa Co, Fernando C, Irvington, NJ, wiring devices

▷F-E◁ - unattributed, strain insulators

F. E. Co. - Federal Elec'c Co, Chicago, porc bushings, wiring devices

FEDCO - Federal Porcelain Co, Carey, OH, standard porc & speclties

FEDERAL - Federal Electric Co, Chicago, wiring devices

F E P Co - Findlay Elec'c Porc Co, Findlay, OH, stan porc, speclties

FINDLAY - Findlay, Elec'c Porc Co, Findlay, OH, standard porcelain

FIVE HUNDRED - Freeman Electric Co, E H , Trenton, NJ, wiring devices

FLERON - Fleron & Sons, M M, Trenton, NJ, radio antenna insulators

FLETCHER - Fletcher Mfg Co, J R. Dayton, OH, clamp insulators

FLUTO - Pass & Seymour, Inc, Syracuse, NY, sockets

FORT WAYNE ELECTRIC WORKS (of Ft. Wayne, IN) - primary fuse cutouts

⌐⌐∪ - unattributed, dry process secondary rack spools

FRANKLIN - Elec'l Development & Machine Co, Phila, hi-tension spclts

FUSEGUARD - Electric Fuseguard Co, Inc, Newark, NJ, fuse cutouts

G - unattributed, standard porcelain & pin types

[G] - Grabler Mfg Co, The, Cleveland, OH, end outlet bushings

GAMEWELL - Gamewell Co, Newton Upper Falls, MA, signaling systems

GATE INSTALATOR - Accessories Mfg Co, Chicago, electric fence insulators

G. C. F. CO. - unattributed, standard porcelain

G.E. Co. - General Elec'c Co, Schenectady, NY, stand porc & specialty

GEE PEE - General Porcelain Co, Parkersburg, WV, split knobs

GEE - VEE - Gillette-Vibber Co, New London, CT end outlet bushings

GLOBE - Globe Porcelain Co, Trenton, NJ, standard porcelain

GOLIATH - Pass & Seymour, Inc, Syracuse, NY, sockets

GOODRICH/CHICAGO - unattributed, specialties

GORDON - Gordon Electric Mfg Co, Waterville, CT, sws, recepts, etc.

G P Co - General Porcelain Co, Parkersburg, WV, std porc, speclty

GRIP-IT - Parker & Son, J H, Parkersburg, WV, split knobs

GUARDIAN - Muter Co, The, Chicago, radio antenna insulators

G & W - G & W Electric Spclty Co, Chicago, poleline hardware items

⟨H⟩ - Hart Mfg Co, Hartford, CT, switches

⟨H⟩ - Hubbard & Co, Pittsburgh, PA, poleline hardware

HALL - unattributed, special 2-groove knob

HAMILTON - unattributed, specialties

HAMMOND - Hammond Cleat & Insulating Co, Boston, special cleats

HARDWICK HINDLE, INC. - (of Newark, NJ), specialties

HARRIS - (John R. Harris patent #1,302,158), split knobs

HECO - Heineman Electric Co, Phila, PA, wiring devices

HEMCO - Hemco Electric Mfg Co, New York, NY, wiring devices

H.F. - Hartford Faience Co, Hartford, CT, standard porc

H. F. Co. - Hartford Faience Co, Hartford, CT, specialties

H & H - Hart & Hegeman Mfg Co, Hartford, CT, sws, wiring devices

HI-TEN - Hubbard & Co, Pittsburgh, PA, poleline hardware

H & M - Elm City Engineering Co, New Haven, CT, specialties

HOLD FAST - Adamant Porcelain Co, E Liverpool, OH, split knobs

HOLMES - High Tension Elec'l Spclty Co, Newton, MA, tree insuls.

HOPEWELL - Hopewell Insulation & Mfg Co, Hopewell, VA, wiring devices

H. P. CO. - Akron High-Potential Porc Co, Barberton, OH, stand porc

H & S - Hickey & Schneider, Inc, Elizabeth, NJ, lo & hi-volt equip

H.T.P. Co. - Paiste Co, H T, Phila, PA, wiring devices

[HTP] [HTP] - Paiste Co, H T, Phila, PA, wiring devices

HUBBARD - Hubbard & Co, Pittsburgh, PA, poleline hardware

HUBBELL - Hubbell, Inc, Harvey, Bridgeport, CT, wiring devices

HUDSON - unattributed, standard porcelain cleats

(I) or (I) - Imperial Porcelain Works, Trenton, NJ, special insulators

IDEAL - Star Porcelain Co, Trenton, NJ, split knobs

ILLINOIS - Illinois Elec'c Porc Co, Macomb, IL, stand porc, speclty

ISOLANTITE - Isolantite Mfg Co, Stirling, NJ, radio antenna insulators

I T - Electric Appliance Co, Chicago, specialties

J - unattributed, wireholders

J.C.P. - Phelps, James C., Springfield, MA, end outlet bushings

JEFFERSON - Jefferson Electric Mfg Co, Chicago, specialties

J.H.P. & S. - Parker & Son, J H, Parkersburg, WV, specialties

JIFFY - Trenton Porcelain Co, Trenton, NJ, split knobs

J.I.P. INC. - Paulding, Inc. J I, New Bedford, MA, wiring devices

JOHNSON - Johnson Co, E F, Waseca, MN, radio antenna insulators

JOSLYN - Joslyn Mfg & Supply Co, Chicago, poleline hardware

JUNIOR - Bryant Electric Co, Bridgeport, CT, cleat rosettes

JUPITER - Cutter Co, George, South Bend, IN, arc light porc insuls

K - unattributed, wireholders

(K) - unattributed, standard porcelain & specialties

KANT-BREAK - unattributed, specialties

K-C - King-Craymer Electric Mfg Co, S Norwalk, CT, sws, cutouts

K-E - Kirkman Engineering Corp, New York, NY, cutouts, cleat-recepts

KEARNEY - Kearney Corp, James R, St Louis, MO, wireholders

KEYLESS - unattribtued, keyless ceiling switches

KEYSTONE - Electric Service Supplies Co, Phila, PA, poleline hardware

KILLARK - Killark Electric Mfg Co, St Louis, MO, couduit items

KIRKMAN - Kirkman Engineering Corp, New York, NY, wiring devices

K K K - Killock Co, David, New York, NY, porcelain bushings

KLINGEL - Klingel, E L, St. Paul, MN, special knobs

KNAPP - Knapp Foundry Co, Inc, Akron, OH, secondary rack spools

KNOWLES - Knowles Co, C S, Boston, MA, wiring devices

KNOX - Knox Porcelain Corp, Knoxville, TN, stand porc & specialties

KOLUX - Kollarth Bros, Schenectady, NY, sign insulators

KONDU-BOX - unattributed, end outlet bushings

K.P. - Bryant Electric Co, Bridgeport, CT, rosettes

KRETZER BRAND - St Louis Lightning Rod Co, St Louis, MO, lgtng rod access.

 - Kuhlman Electric Co, Bay City, MI, primary fuse cutouts

KWIKON - Fralick & Co, S R, Chicago, wiring devices

L or Ⓛ - unattributed, wireholders

△L - unattributed, wireholders

◇L - unattributed, rack, clamp, wireholder insulators

LEVITON - Leviton Mfg Co, Brooklyn, standard porcelain & specialties

LF or ⒧⒡ - L F Mfg Co (Louis Fort), Jersey City, NJ, clamp insulators

LINGO - unattributed, specialties

LITTLE GEM - Pass & Seymour, Inc, Syracuse, NY, rosettes

L.M. - Line Material Co, Milwaukee, WI, pole line hardware

⊕LM or ▽LM - Line Material Co, Milwaukee, WI, poleline hardware

LOCK SHELL - Hubbell, Inc, Harvey, Bridgeport, CT, switches, sockets

M or △M - Illinois Elec'c Porc Co, Macomb, IL, stand porc & speclty

◇M - unattributed, wireholders

MACOMB - Illinois Elec'c Porc Co, Macomb, IL, standard porcelain

MANDICO - Manufacturer's Distributing Co, New York, sign receptacles

MANHATTAN - Manhattan Elec'l Supply Co, Inc, New York, wiring devices

M. B. Co. - unattributed, standard porcelain & specialties

M. E. Co. - unattributed, specialties

MEMCO - Maxwell Engrg & Mfg Co, New York, NY, tel & tel arrestors

MESCO - Manhattan Elec'l Supply Co, New York, wiring devices

METEOR - unattributed, switches

M I CO - Mogadore Insulators Co, Mogador, OH, stand porc & speclty

MILHAM - American Sign Co, Kalamazoo, MI, sign insulators

MONCUR - unattributed, specialties

MONOWATT - unattributed, standard porcelain & specialties

MULLER - Parker & Son, J H, Parkersburg, WV, strain insulators

MULTI - Multi Electrical Mfg Co, Chicago, conduit items

MULTIPO - Paiste Co, H T, Phila, PA, sockets

MURDOCK - Parker & Son, J H, Parkersburg, WV, misc. insulators

N - Nat'l Electric Porcelain Co, Carey, OH, standard porcelain

NAILIN - unattributed, split knobs

NAILIT - Parker & Son, J H, Parkersburg, WV, split knobs

NAT - Nat'l Electric Porcelain CO, Carey, OH, standard porcelain

NAT'L - National Electric Products Co, Pittsburgh, PA, wireholders

NATIONAL - National Metal Molding Co, Pittsburgh, PA, conduit items

NCO - Nat'l Electric Porcelain Co, Carey, OH, standard porcelain

N.E.E. Co. - New England Electric Co, Littleton, CO, special knobs

N.E.T.&T. CO. - New England Tel & Tel Co, telephone knobs & cleats

N .W. Co. - unattributed, special knobs

O. B. Co. - Ohio Brass Co., Mansfield, OH, mine insulators

OHIO - Frankel Light Co, New York, NY, end outlet bushings

OLIVER - Oliver Elec'l Mfg Co, Battle Creek, MI poleline hardware

O. P. Co. - Ohio Porcelain Co, E Liverpool, pin types & std porcelain

P - Peru Electric Mfg Co, Peru, IN, standard porcelain

P or Ⓟ - Porcelain Products, Inc, Findlay, OH, standard porcelain

Ṕ - Pittsburgh High Voltage Insulator Co, Derry, PA, strains

◇P - unattributed, radio antenna insulators

P A Co. - Pettingell-Andrews Co, Boston, MA, standard porcelain

PAISTE - Paiste Co, H T, Phila, PA, wiring devices

PARAGON - Paragon Electric Co, Chicago, misc. porcelain insulators

PASSMOUR - Pas & Seymour, Inc, Syracuse, NY, sockets

PATTERSON - Stanley & Patterson, New York, NY, specialties

PAULDING - Paulding, Inc, J I, New Bedford, MA, wiring devices

P. B. MFG. Co. - unattributed, end outlet bushings

PEARL - unattributed, wireholders

PEIRCE - Hubbard & Co, Pittsburgh, PA, poleline hardware

PEMCO - Phila Electrical & Mfg Co, Phila, PA, poleline hardware

PERU - Peru Electric Mfg Co, Peru, IN, standard porcelain

PHILCO - Philco Radio Corp, radio antenna insulators

POWERLET - Multi Electrical Mfg Co, Chicago, porcelain bushings

[PP] - Porclain Products Co, Carey, OH, stand porc & specialties

P.P. - Porcelain Products, Inc, Findlay, OH, standard porcelain

P.P. INC. - Porcelain Products, Inc, Findlay, OH, standard porcelain

[PiNcP.] - Porcelain Products, Inc, Findlay, OH, standard porcelain

PRIME - unattributed, electric fence insulators

PRINGLE - Pringle Elec'l Mfg Co, Phila, PA, stand porc & specialties

PRo-TECTO - unattribtued, radio antenna lightning arrestor

P & S - Pass & Seymour, Inc, Syracuse, NY, stand porc & specialty

P S W - unattributed, split knobs

P. T. - C. Co. - unattributed, specialties

QUAD - General Electric Co, Schenectady, NY, receptacles

R - Ravenswood Porcelain Co, Ravenswood, WV, stand, porcelain

RACO - Raco Elec'c Products Div, All Steel Co, Chicago, specialty

RALCO - Central Electric Co, Chicago, wiring devices

READY - National Electric Porcelain Co, Carey, OH, split knobs

R. E. CO. - Reliable Elec'c Co, Chicago, standard porcelain & speclty

(RECO.) - Reliable Elec'c Co, Chicago, standard porcelain, specialties

RED DEVIL - Smith & Hemenway Co, Inc, Irvington, NJ, wiring devices

RELIABLE - Reliable Electric Co, Chicago, standard porcelain

R-H & CO. - Reyburn-Hunter & Co., Pittsburgh, lightning rod equipment

ROCK - unattributed, standard porcelain

RODALE - Rodale Mfg Co, Emmaus, PA, radio antenna insuls, speclties

ROYAL - Royal Electric Mfg Co, Chicago, standard porcelain

R. P. Co. - Ravenswood Porcelain Co, Ravenswood, WV, standard porc.

R R - Radio Receptor Co, New York, NY, radio antenna insulators

R. R. S. Co. - Railroad Supply Co, Chicago, railway signaling systems

R.T. & SONS - R Thomas & Sons, E Liverpool (pre-1892 unicorp), std porc

R T & S CO - R Thomas & Sons, E Liverpool (after 1892 incorporation), standard porcelain

RUBY - Bryant Electric Co, Bridgeport, CT, sign receptacles

RVA - Great Lakes Radio Supplies Co, Inc, Elmhurst, IL, radio

S - unattributed - telephone knobs, wireholders, etc.

SACKETT - "Sackett Patent" mine insulators, various manufacturers

S & C - Schweitzer & Conrad, Inc, Chicago, cutouts, wiring devices

S.C.P. Co. - unattributed, split knobs

SCREWIT - Parker & Son, J.H., Parkersburg, WV, split knobs

SEALET - Butte Electric & Mfg Co, San Francisco, CA, end outlets

Sears/USA - unattributed, electric fence insulators

SEBCO - Star Expansion Bolt Co, New York, NY, misc. insulators

SECURITY - Freeman Electric CO, E H, Trenton, NJ, wiring devices

SENSORY - Heineman Electric Co, Phila, PA, wiring devices, screweyes

SEYLER - Seyler Mfg Co, rack spools, wireholders, etc.

SHAWMUT - Chase-Shawmut Co, Newburyport, MA, cutout bases

S - H Co. - Snyder-Hunt Co, Belle Plaine, IA, special knobs

[SHC] or [SHC] - Stewart-Howland Co, Boston, standard porcelain

SHURLOCK - Pass & Seymour, Inc, Syracuse, NY, sockets & receptacles

SISSELL - Sissell Co, Lloyd D, Los Angeles, CA, rack spools

SKY-ROCKET - Chance Co, A B, Centralia, MO, tel & tel lgtng arrestors

S.M.T. Co. - So Mass Tel Co, telephone knobs

SNAP-CATCH - General Elec'c Co, Schenectady, porc sockets & receptacles

SNAPIT - unattributed, switches

SOLDERALL - Solderall Co, The, Newark, NJ, radio antenna insulators

S.P. - Superior Porcelain Co, Parkersburg, WV, stand porc & spcl

S. P. Co. - Superior Porcelain Co, Parkersburg, WV, stand porc & spcl

SPERO - unattributed (Cleveland, OH), wireholders

S P W - Specialty Porcelain Works, E Liverpool, standard porcelain

<SPW> - Specialty Porcelain Works, E Liverpool, standard porcelain

S. P. W'KS - Specialty Porcelain Works, E Liverpool, standard porcelain, specialties

STANDARD - Standard Electrical Mfg Co, Cleveland, end outlet bushings

STANDARD ELEC. MFG. CO. - (of Chicago, IL), switches

STAR - Star Porcelain Co, Trenton, NJ, standard porcelain & spclty

ST LOUIS - St Louis Malleable Casting Co, MO, secondary rack spools

SUPERIOR - Superior Porcelain Co, Parkersburg, WV, stand porc & spcl

SURGE - Babson Bros Co, Chicago, electric fence insulators

S W P - unattributed, standard porcelain

S.Y. - unattributed, special knobs

(T) - Trumbull Electric Mfg Co, Plainville, CT, switches

T or (T) - Thomas & Sons Co, R E Liverpool, OH, standard porcelain

TAPLET - unattributed, end outlet bushings

TAPON - Jordan Bros, New York, NY, porcelain crossovers

T & B - Thomas & Betts Co, The, New York, NY, wiring devices

TECCO - Trenton Elec'c Conduit Co, NJ, sign & wiring insulators

TEMCO - Trumbull Electric Mfg Co, Plainville, CT, switches

TERMILET - Freeman Electric Co, E H, Trenton, NJ, end outlet bushings

THOMAS - Thomas & Sons Co, R, E Liverpool, OH, standard porcelain

T. P. - Trenton Porcelain Co, Trenton, NJ, stand porc & specialty

T. P. Co. - Trenton Porcelain Co, Trenton, NJ, stand porc & specialty

TRENLE - Trenle Porcelain Co, The, E Liverpool, OH, standard porc

TRIANGLE - Bunnell & Co, J H, New York, NY, lightning arrestors

T.T.P.Co. - Trenle Porcelain Co, The, E Liverpool, std porc & speclty

TULIP - Pass & Seymour, Inc, Syracuse, NY, sign receptacles

TWIN TOWERS - Accessories Mfg Co, K.C., MO, elec'c' fence lgtng arrestors

U or ⓤ - Union Elec'l Porcelain Co, Trenton, NJ, sign specialties

U or ⓤ - Universal Clay Products Co, Sandusky, OH, std porc & spcl

UNILETS - Appleton Electric Co, Chicago, end outlet bushings

UNION - Bunnell & Co, J H, New York, NY, tel & tel arrestors

UNION - Chicago Fuse Mfg Co, Chicago, primary cutouts & cut. bases

UNION - Union Elec'l Porcelain Co, Trenton, NJ, sign & specialties

UNIVERSAL - Universal Clay Products Co, Sandusky, OH, std porc & spcl

U.P.W. - Union Porcelain Works, Brooklyn, NY, early knobs

US U or ⑤ - U S electric Porcelain Co, Findlay, OH, standard porcelain

U S E P Co - U S Electric Porcelain Co, Findlay, OH, standard porcelain

U.S.P.Co. - U S Electric Porcelain Co, Findlay, OH, standard porcelain

U.S. CO. - Utility Services Co, Allentown, PA, rack spools, wirehldrs

VAC-M - Michigan Electric Specialty Co, Muskeegon, tel & tel arrest.

V.V. - V V Fittings Co, Phila, PA, end outlet bushings

W. D. INC. - unattributed, specialties

WEBER - Weber Electric Co, Schenectady, NY, porcelain sockets

WEDGE - Cook Pottery Co, Trenton, NJ, split knobs

W E S Co. - unattributed, standard porcelain

W.E.S. & Co. - unattributed, standard porcelain

WESTERN ELECTRIC - (of New York, NY), standard porcelain cleats

WHITE - White Electrical Supply Co, T C, St Louis, MO, guy strains

WIRT - Wirt Co, Phila, PA, special knobs

WIS-P - Wisconsin Porcelain Co, Sun Prairie, WI, elec fence insuls

WISP - Wisconsin Porcelain Co, Sun Prairie, WI, elec fence insuls

WIS - P - C. - Wisconsin Porcelain Co, Sun Prairie, WI, elec fence insuls

WOODIN - Wood Electric Co, C W, New York, NY, specialties

W P - unattributed, knobs

W. R. CO. - Wheeler Reflector Co, Boston, porcelain sockets

W S - unattributed, wall tubes

⊕ - unattributed, standard porcelain

W S CO. - unattributed, standard porcelain

W. T. Co. - Wheeling Tile Co, Wheeling, WV, standard porcelain

W. VA. P. CO. - West Virginia Porcelain Co, New Haven, WV, standard porc.

YOST - Yost Electric Mfg Co, Toledo, OH, specialties

✪ - unattributed, early 1890's cleats

★ - Star Porcelain Co, Trenton, NJ, standard porcelain

◇ - Diamond Porcelain Co, Trenton, NJ, standard porcelain

△ - unattributed, rack spools

△ - Delta-Star Electric Co, Chicago, poleline hardware

⚓ ⚓ - Anchor Electric Co, Boston, early wiring cleats

⬡ - Electric Service Supplies Co, Phila, PA, line insulators

Bibliography

Magazines

American Antiques

Allison, Grace. "A Rare Bone China in the 1890s, Lotus Ware from Ohio." January 1978, p. 1.

American Art Pottery

Coleman, Duke. "American Art Pottery Gains Wide Range of Attention." July 1980, p. 4.

_____. "Henry Chapman Mercer." January 1979, p. 1.

_____. "Letters and Such." January 1978, pp. 3, 4.

_____. "Matt Morgan, More Than a Potter." November 1977, p. 8.

_____. "Rookwood Pottery One More Time Around." June 1983, p. 3.

Hecht, Eugene. "Quixote Rides Again." October 1981, pp. 1, 4.

Heissenbuttal, Orva. "The Biloxi Art Pottery of George Ohr." October 1976, pp. 1-3.

Hercher, Gail Pike. "Marblehead Pottery." March 1981, pp. 1, 6, 7.

Nelson, Scott. "A Comparative Look at the Van Briggle Lorelei." March 1979, p. 5.

O'Nan, Frederick. "Grace Young." April 1977, p. 4.

Staff-written. "A Rookwood Romance, Elizabeth Barret and Jens Jensen." August 1977, p. 1.

_____. "Maria Martinez." August 1980, p. 4.

_____. "Pewabic Pottery Sold." November 1981, p. 4.

_____. "Pfaltzgraff Not a Dirty Word." July 1976, p. 4.

_____. "Pisgah Forest Cameo." June 1978, p. 3.

_____. "The Talent of Albert R. Valentian." pp. 1, 3.

_____. "University City Pottery." June 1977, pp. 1, 2.

Turner, Tran. "California Porcelain." April 1979, p. 4.

Turnquist, Thomas, G., "Aaron Bohrod and Carlton Ball: Synergism." August 1983, p. 1.

_____. "Broadmoor Pottery." July 1979, p. 5.

_____. "Charles E. Abbott, Vessel Mastery." November 1983, p. 4.

_____. "Clay Craft Studios." July 1983, pp. 1, 3.

_____. "Eugene Deutch, Chicago's Potter." November 1983, pp. 3, 5.

_____. "Frank Reuss Kelley: A Potter Remembered." January 1984, p. 3.

_____. "Harrison McIntosh, A Concerto in Clay." April 1983, pp. 1, 4.

_____. "Mary Yancey Hodgdon." July 1984, p. 5.

_____. "Musick in Clay." March 1984, p. 9.

_____. "The Handicraft Guild of Minneapolis 1904-1919." p. 8.

Wunsch, Allen. "West Coast Florida Art Pottery." December 1980, pp. 1, 3.

American Clay Exchange

Allison, Grace. "Ceramic Tile Custom Murals by Summitville Tile Co." April 3, 1985, pp. 4, 5.

_____. "Cowan-Ohio Pottery of the Roaring Twenties." February 1984, pp. 7, 9.

_____. "The Dwight Morris Porcelain Company, East Palestine, Ohio." May 1985, pp. 4, 5.

Alsbrook, Joseph D. "Camark A Legendary Name in American Pottery." June 15, 1985, pp. 8, 9.

Beetler, Dianne. "Hintze Pottery." March 30, 1986, p. 12.

Brown, Danny. "Constructing a Collection Tile by Tile." April 1983, p. 4.

_____. "Pitcher Potpourri." January 1982, p. 10.

Brewer, Don. "Pinewood Pottery." January 15, 1984, p. 12.

_____. "Pinewood Pottery Update." June 30, 1985, pp. 8, 9.

_____. "What About Muncie." January 1984, pp. 10, 11.

Chipman, Jack. "California Firing Line." January 1986, p. 3.

_____. "Discovering Metlox," March 1983, pp. 12, 13.

_____. "Lotus and Acanthus Studios." August 30, 1986, p. 9.

_____. "The McCarty Brothers." November 15, 1986, pp. 8, 9.

_____. "Winfield Pottery." September 1983, pp. 12, 14.

Cox, Susan. "Bonnema." September 1983, p. 3.

_____. "Louisville Kentucky Potteries." January 1982, p. 10.

_____. "Miltonvale Potteries." January 1982, p. 6.

_____. "Rookwood Pottery Back in Production." June 1983, p. 4.

_____. "Sascha Brastoff, Innovator For All Times." November 1983, p. 10.

_____. "W.P.A. Pottery." June 1982, p. 14.

Derwich, Jenny. "Cleminson Mark." September 15, 1986, p. 9.

Doherty, Linda and Spencer Glasgow. "Spruce Pine, Alabama Potters and Their Wares." May 15, 1986, pp. 8-10.

_____. "To Be Niloak or Not to Be Niloak." December 1982, p. 2.

Doherty, Robert. "Fort Ticonderoga Pottery." February 1984, p. 3.

Foster, Abigail. "Van Briggle Pottery from 1899." December 1982, p. 18.

Hall, Doris and Burdell. "Camark, A New Beginning." September 16, 1986, p. 5.

_____. "New Swirl Pottery from Arkansas." September 30, 1985, pp. 8, 10.

Jennings, Ellen. "Sleuths." September 1984, p. 13.

Polley, Thomas. "Pinewood Pottery." December 1982, p. 22.

Pryse, Dorothy. "White Mountain Pottery." June 1982, p. 4.

Schwartz, Stuart. "Royal Crown Pottery." January 1982, pp. 14-16.

Scott, Douglass. "Claycraft Potteries of California." October 1983, pp. 10, 11.

Staff-written. "Arts and Crafts Auction." May 15, 1986, p. 4.

_____. "Pottery Puzzlers." November 1983, p. 3.

_____. "Super Sleuths." May 1983, p. 10 (on San Carlos Pottery).

Stilwell, Kathleen. "Acoma Pottery." August 15, 1984. pp. 4, 5.

_____. "Santa Clara Pottery." October 30, 1984, pp. 6, 7.

Stone, Alice. "The Sincerity of Purpose, The Work of Ernest Batchelder." November 1982, pp. 10, 11.

Stroughton, Beverly F. "Michael Baggett, The Potter's Art." September 15, 1984, p. 8.

Turner, Tran. "Herbert H. Sanders-Innovator in California Ceramics." Four installments: February 15, 1985, pp. 8, 9; February 28, 1985, pp. 8, 9; March 30, 1985, pp. 8, 9; April 15, 1985, pp. 5, 7.

American Collectors News

Grande, Bill. "Stoneware Pottery." April 1980, p. 12 (On Otto V. Lewis, Also William H. Farrar).

_____. "Stoneware Pottery." May 1982, p. 9 (on J.A. and C.W. Underwood).

Antiques

Many articles on pottery taken from the pages of *Antiques* have been reprinted in two books, *The Art of The Potter* edited by Dianna and J. Garrison Stradling, N.Y., N.Y., Main Street/Universe Books, 1977 and in *The Antiques Book* edited by Alice Winchester, Bonanza Books, N.Y., N.Y., 1950.

Armstrong, Henry R. "The Norwich Pottery Works." *The Art of the Potter*, pp. 99-101.

Clement, Arthur W. "Ceramics in the South." *The Art of the Potter*. pp. 22, 23.

Franco, Barbara. "Stoneware Made by White Family of Utica, New York." *The Art of the Potter*. p. 134.

Macfarlane, Janet R. "Nathan Clark Potter." *The Art of the Potter*. p. 129.

Norton, F.H. "The Crafts Pottery in Nashua, New Hampshire." *The Art of the Potter*. pp. 97, 98.

Remensnyder, John P. "The Potters of Poughkeepsie." *The Art of the Potter*. p. 124.

Sim, Robert J. and Arthur W. Clement. "The Cheesequake Potteries." *The Art of the Potter*. pp. 119-122.

Stradling, J.G. "American Ceramics and the Philadelphia Centennial." July 1970, pp. 146-158.

_____. "East Liverpool, Ohio, An American Pottery Town." June, 1982, p. 1367.

Taylor, Marjorie. "Stoneware of Ripley, Illinois." *The Art of the Potter*. pp. 143-145.

Watkins, Lura W. "A Check List of New England Potters." *The Art of the Potter*. pp. 77-80.

_____. "New Light on Boston Stoneware." *The Art of the Potter*. pp. 81-86.

_____. "The Stoneware of South Ashfield, Massachusetts." *The Art of the Potter*. pp. 102, 103.

Wheeler, Robert G. "The Potters of Albany." *The Art of the Potter*. p. 131-133.

Antiques Journal

Ball, Bernice. "Etruscan Majolica." September 1964, p. 24.

Davidson, Clair. "The Ridge Pottery of Evans Crowley." August 1972, pp. 17, 18.

Fredgant, Don. "T.B. Odom and J.W. Kohler: Two 19th Century West Florida Potters." June 1981, pp. 26-29.

_____. "The York Pottery of Lake Butler, Florida." November 1980, pp. 29-30.

Green, Doris M. "Butter Making." July 1964, p. 27.

Hackley, Mamie. "Tea Leaf Lustre." April 26, 1973, p. 5.

Hamm, Jo. "Desert Sands Pottery." Feburary 1971, pp. 24, 25.

Hardcastle, Mildred Veley. "The Cowden and Wilcox Pottery Story." January, February 1968, pp. 38, 39.

_____. "The Sipe Pottery of Williamsport, Pennsylvania." April 1968, pp. 23, 24.

Harrison, James M. "The Case of the Disappearing Potters." March 1979, pp. 32, 33, 49.

Johnson, Deb and Gini Johnson. "Peters and Reed and the Zane Pottery." April 1975, p. 12.

Johnson, Virginia Coleman. "Niloak Pottery." July 1973, pp. 28-30 and p. 45.

Ketchum, William C. "Decorative Techniques in American Stoneware." April 1979, p. 24.

Poese, Bill. "Flow Blue." March 1972, p. 13.

Rosenow, Jane. "Peoria Pottery and How It Grew." December 1969, p. 30.

Smith, Clarissa. "Etruscan Majolica." June 1957, p. 8.

Thompsen, J.K. "The White House China Room." July 1961, p. 8.

Van Tassel, Valentine. "Louis Comfort Tiffany." August 1952, p. 14.

Wintermute, Ogden H. "Tea Leaf Ironstone." May 1973, p. 14.

Antique Monthly

Green, Janet. "White House China Among World's Best." November 1972, p. 12A.

Antique News (New Carlisle, Ohio)

Crutcher, Jean. "Lotus Ware." October 1964, p. 1.

Antiques Reporter

Hutchinson, Jeanette Ray. "Story of Tea Leaf Ironstone." Nov. 73, p. 16.

Miller, Robert W. "Dedham and Rabbits." June 13, 1973, p. 15.

Antique Trader Weekly

The *Antique Trader Weekly* (formerly called *Antique Trader*) issues *Annuals of Articles* a little more often than once a year. Some of these references are to articles in the Annuals.

Barglof, Elva. "The Four Faces of Fort Dodge." April 2, 1980, pp. 62-64.

_____. "The Prairie-style Art Pottery of Iowa State College." Dec. 1, 1982, pp. 70, 71.

Bartlett, Margaret M. "Onion is Fun to Seek." August 1, 1972, p. 37; or *Annual of Articles*, Vol. V, 1976, p. 292.

_____. "The Early Ironstone and Its Makers." *Annual of Articles*, Vol. V, 1976, p. 292.

Brewer, Don. "Haeger Potteries." Nov. 6, 1985, pp. 74-76.

Carpenter, J.W. "Geo. Ohr's Pot-Ohr-E." September 19, 1972, p. 42.

Caulkins, Donald. "Cowan Pottery." November 30, 1977. *Annual VIII*, p. 4.

Chipman, Jack. "William Manker Ceramics Objects of Timeless Beauty." September 28, 1983, pp. 72-75.

Christian, Donna A. "Jack Daniel Collectibles." Jan. 11, 1984, pp. 47, 49.

Coates, Pamela. "Wheeling Potteries Company." *Annual of Articles*, Vol. IV, 1975, p. 228.

Cook, Peter W. "Bennington's Hound Handled Pitchers." *Annual of Articles*, Vol. V, 1976, p. 332.

Cox, Susan. "Howard Pierce Porcelain." August 3, 1983, pp. 60-63.

Denker, Ellen P. "The Kirkpatrick's Anna P." January 12, 1977, pp. 42, 43.

Dipboye, Marilyn. "Cybis Porcelain Cats." January 1, 1986, p. 50.

Dommel, Darlene. "Dickota Pottery." *Annual of Articles*, 1974, p. 337.

_____. "Teco Pottery." June 8, 1977, p. 76.

Fox, Darlene. "Early 20th Century Premiums and Premium Catalogs." April 8, 1981, pp. 94-100.

Goldblum, Nettie. "American Belleek." *Annual of Articles*, Vol. V, 1976, p. 230.

Havens, Meredith. "The B & O Blue Railroad China." *Annual of Articles*, 1973, p. 84.

Hoffman, Donald C., Sr. "Warwick China." *Annual of Articles*, Vol. V, 1975, p. 194.

Lechler, Doris. "Playhouse China: American Contributions." August 29, 1984, pp. 85, 86.

Lehner, Lois. "A Cookie Jar Update." Feburary 29, 1984, pp. 72-75.

London, Rena. "Cordey." July 16, 1980, pp. 52-55.

Martin, Jim and Bette Cooper. "The Potteries of Monmouth, Illinois." December 19, 1979, pp. 62, 63.

Miller, Robert W. "Willow Ware Plates." *Annual of Articles*, 1972, p. 89.

Mortensen, Rita C. "Dryden Pottery." January 19, 1983, pp. 81-85.

Nelson, Maxine. "Vernon Kilns Americana Plate Collection." *Annual of Articles*, Vol. IV, 1975, p. 161.

Peck, Herbert. "Commercial Wares of the Rookwood Pottery." *Antique Trader Annual No. 10*, pp. 158-161.

Rago, Dave. "American Art Pottery." (column name); May 14, 1980, p. 74 (on Shearwater Pottery); Sept. 9, 1981, p. 91 (on Grand Few Art Pottery, also Valentien Pottery); April 7, 1982, p. 97 (on Susan Frackleton and also M. McLaughlin); April 30, 1980, p. 77 (on Marblehead Pottery); Feb. 6, 1980, p. 69 (on Paul Revere Pottery).

Rogers, Jo Ann. "Evans Family Potters." June 1, 1977, pp. 74-76.

_____. "The Pottery of San Ildelfonso." April 24, 1972, p. 47.

Secrist, Robert and June. "A Rare Pottery Find." March 30, 1977, p. 94.

Smith, Doris W. "Pretty and Practical Bauer Pottery." *Annual of Articles*, 1973, p. 4.

Stipp, Eleanor C. "Cowden Stoneware and Cowden Pottery." June 8, 1976, pp. 52, 53.

Tobias, Morton B. "A Toast to Toby Jugs." Feb. 27, 1985, p. 79.

Thompson, Donna Ashworth. "Collectables for Tomorrow from Frankoma Pottery." July 20, 1976, p. 46.

Turnbull, Margaret E. "Hounds and Pitchers." *Annual of Articles*, 1972, p. 31.

Turnquist, Thomas. "Studio Potter." July 4, 1984, p. 75.

_____. "The Broadmoor and Mountainside Potteries." February 13, 1980, p. 53.

Tyacke, Marv and Bev. "Watt Pottery." September 13, 1978, p. 66.

Weiss, Grace M. "Rosemeade Pottery." *Annual of Articles*, 1973, p. 59.

Appalachia

Harney, Andy Leon. "Appalachian Stoneware for America's Tables. The Iron Mountain Story." October-November 1973 (no page numbers sent to this author).

Avenue

Demarest, Michael. "The Arts." May 1979, pp. 44-47.

Better Homes and Gardens

Huttenlocher, Fae. "A.B.C.'s of Table Furnishings." In three or more issues, March 1947, p. 54; April 1947, p. 54; August 1947, p. 53.

Staff-written. "Pacific Clay Products Co." October, 1935.

Bottle News

Staff-written. "Crocks, Flasks, are Among Auction Items." November 1976, p. 36.

Ceramics Monthly

Bonham, Roger D. "The Mark of the Potter." Nov. 1973, pp. 28-30.

Byrd, Joan Falconer, "Lanier Meaders - Georgia Potter." Oct., 1976, pp. 24, 26, 28.

Caplain, Jerry L. "Don Reitz - New Directions." June 1980, p. 64.

Illian, Clary. "The Three Kilns of Ken Ferguson." March, 1980, pp. 47-50.

Klassen, Jack. "A Conversation with Jack Earl." October 1981, pp. 68-70.

Kohlenberger, Lois H. "Ceramics at the People's University." November 1976, pp. 33, 34.

Levin, Elaine. "Pioneers of Contemporary Ceramics: Arthur Baggs and Glen Lukens." January 1976, pp. 24-30.

_____. "Pioneers of Contemporary Ceramics: Charles Binns and Adelaide Robineau." November 1975, pp. 22-26.

Staff-written. "Pre-Industrial Salt Glazed Ware." April 1977, p. 77.

_____. "Ceramactivities." February 1980, p. 44.

China, Glass, and Decorative Accessories

In a news note with no title. May 1951, p. 35 (on Allied Stores Corp. and Ohio China, Monroe, Michigan), March 1953, p. 28.

China, Glass and Lamps

Staff-written. "Oldest Pottery in America Marks its 125th Anniversary." January 1965 (Reprint sent without page number.).

_____. "American Pottery Trademarks." July 23, 1923, p. 15, August 6, 1923, p. 15, September 10, 1923, p. 15.

China Glass and Tableware

Staff-written. "Newsletter." August 1979, p. 17. (on Haeger Potteries, Inc.).

Collectors News

Bland, Ann S. "Mercer Museum Pennsylvania Wonder." August 1977, pp. 14, 15.

Lynn, Ophelia. "Happiness Was Bluebird in 1900." November 1970, p. 22.

Staff-written. "Pewabic Pottery on Exhibit in Michigan." April 1980, p. 67.

Witt, Louise Schaub. "Toni Roller, Santa Clara Potter." 1970, p. 3, 13.

Collector's Weekly

Bretzger, Judy. "Ott & Brewer Now of Age." November 23, 1971, p. 3.

Roger, JoAnn. "Mutual China Closes." Feburary 1972, p. 4.

_____. "Syracuse China Stops Production of Casual Line." June 29, 1971, p. 11.

Schmitt, Agnes. "Ohio Valley Pottery, China Gain Popularity." July 14, 1970, p. 3.
Staff-written. "The Marks and Signatures of Pickard China." June 1977, p. 13.

Country Home
Brookhauser, Karol K. "Country Potter." (on B.B. Craig) February 1985, pp. 62, 63.

Country Life Magazine
Carrick, Alice Van Lee. "The Orchard Potteries." January 1926, pp. 48-50.
Sprackling, Helen. "The Charm of China." September 1931, p. 65.

Crockery and Glass Journal
Betz, W.A. "It All Started in East Liverpool." April 1955 (reprinted without page numbers).
Staff-written. "Artware Pottery Gossip from Southern California." December 1944, p. 69.
_____. "Atlas China Celebrates 25th Anniversary." January 1943, p. 80.
_____. "Castleton China Exhibit Shown at Barker Brothers." November 1943, p. 21.
_____. "First Showing on Special Castleton China." December 1942, p. 24.
_____. "Industry News." November 1954, p. 36 (on B. Altman & Co.).
_____. "Making American China Artware." January 1943, p. 6.
_____. "New Artware Decoration." January 1943, p. 84.
_____. "News." May 1943, p. 7 (on Paul E. Cox Pottery), August 1950, p. 10 (on Atlas China and Grandma Moses).
_____. "Vincent Broomhill Opens China Firm." December 1944, p. 71.
_____. "Wanamaker Holds Home Fashions Week. November 1954, p. 8.
Zimmerman, M.K. "The Pottery Industry of East Liverpool." December 1924, p. 116 (Fiftieth Anniversary Issue).

Crystal Lake Herald
Staff-written. "Terra Cotta Teco Pottery Brought Early Fame to C.L. (Crystal Lake)." July 1, 1974, p. 8.

Daily Leader, Mount Clemens, Michigan, newspaper
Staff-written. "Old Timer Gazes Back at 1914." 25th anniversary issue, May 22, 1939, pp. 1, 4, 8.

Daily Leader, East Palestine, Ohio, newspaper
Staff-written. "East Palestine's First Pottery." February 1960, p. 1.

Dallas Morning News
Staff-written. "Robert Floyd." October 23, 1983, p. 1.

Depression Glass Daze
Blosser, Jim. "The Mysterious Bauer." November 1977, p. 43.
Brewer, Don. "Camark." June 1982. p. 25.
_____. "More on Van Tellingen." August 1983, p. 8.
_____. "Van Tellingen Uncovered." July 1983, p. 6.
Brink, Helen. "Bluebird China." January 1979, p. 41.
Brown, Betsy. "Russel Wright." June 1979, p.5.
Duke, Harvey. "Chats on China." May 1977, p. 36.
Jinkins, Marlene. "Hopewell China Co." May 1980. p. 42.

Newbound, Betty. "Along the Flea Market Trail." July 1984, p. 5 (on California Cleminsons), August 1984, p. 42 (on Brad Keeler), May 1979 (no. page number available) (on Clinchfield Pottery), August 1980, p. 43 (on Clinchfield Pottery), February 1980, p. 3 (on Stanley Home Products).
Scott, Virginia. "China Ads and Research." May 1977, p. 38, August 1977, p. 40 (on Vernon Kilns).
Sferazza, Julie. "Farber Brothers Facts." July 1980, p. 1.
Staff-written. "Readers Say." June 1979, p. 5, June 1984, p. 44, May 1984, p. 88.
Stanton, Joyce. "Syracuse China." November 1977, p. 43.
_____. "Syracuse China Continued." February 1978, p. 39.

Dialogue, The Ohio Arts Journal
Benzle, Curtis and Susan. "Collaboration, Two Viewpoints." March, April 1983, p. 44 (on Spring Street Pottery).

Early American Life
McCabe, Carol. "Pennsylvania Redware: Continuing a Tradition." October 1984, pp. 34-41.
Staff-written. "Neat Pieces, Plain Style Furniture of 19th Century Georgia." p. 58.

Evening Public Ledger
Ramey, Grace. "Early German Art Revived, Historic Materials Used by Mrs. Keyser." Philadelphia, Pa. November 25, 1939 (no page number sent to author).

Fortnight Magazine
Staff-written. "Daring Dishes." August 4, 1950, p. 23.

Gift and Decorative Accessories
Staff-written. "Pottery Making: A Jensen Attraction." December 1973, p. 170.

Gift and Tableware Reporter
Staff-written. Advertisement for Museum Pieces, Inc. August 16, 1965, p. 152.

The Glaze
Barnett, Jerry. "The Paden City Pottery Company." November 1977, p. 8.
Bartz, Jim. "Treasures of the Dining Car." March 1978, p. 15.
Chipman, Jack and Judy Stangler. "Bauer: A California Success Story." May 1980, pp. 11-14.
Cunningham, Jo. "And the Autumn Leaves Fell." June 1977, p. 5.
Fridley, Al. "West Coast Pottery." November 1977, p. 7.
Hoffman, Sr., Donald. "When Warwick Rode the Rails." December-January 1978, p. 9.
Hunter, Bess. "Vernon Kilns." July-August 1977, p. 16.
Jackson, June. "History of Kass China Co." April 1978, p. 13.
Jeromack, Paul. "Who Was Van Tellingen?" June 1983, p. 6.
Lafray, Larry. "Letters to Editor." February 1979, p. 4.
_____. "Van Briggle part II." June 1979, p. 10.
Latty, Betty. "On the Firing Line." March 1978, p. 10 and April 1981, p. 17.
_____. "Abdingdon, U.S.A." June 1977, p. 6.
Rains, Dona. "Decanter Business Continues to Boom at Roman Ceramics." (reprinted from the Paducah Sun), November 1981, p. 12.
Roberts, Brenda. "Hull Headlines: Old Spice Product Containers." August 1980, p. 6.
Roff, Stephen. "Dorchester Pottery." May 1984, p. 9.
Schneider, Norris. "Zanesville Potters." June 30, p. 13.

Slack, Bonnie. "Traveling China." December-January 1978, p. 8.

Staff-written. "Robeson Rochester Wares." December 1983, p. 7 (reprinted from 1931 article, *Glaze* gave no further bibliography for article).

Viel, Lyndon. "Red Wing Update - Rare." August 1978, p. 8.

Harpers News Monthly Magazine

Staff-written. "Pottery in the United States." December 1880, pp. 357-369. (Reprinted in *Hobbies*, February 1949, pp. 104-120).

Hobbies

Allen, Frederick W. "More About Dedham Pottery." September 1952, p. 80.

Ball, Bernice. "Ceramic Heritage in Chester County, Pa." September 1953, pp. 80, 81.

Farrington, Frank. "American Porcelain." November 1940, p. 53.

Hommel, Rudolf. "Colonial Master Potters." May 1949, p. 80.

La Grange, Marie J. "More About Makers of Majolica." June 1939, p. 54.

Peterson, Arthur G. "Some Pottery in the 1880's. October 1973.

Ramsay, John. "Lotus Ware." October 1942, p. 55.

_____. "American Majolica." May 1945, p. 45.

_____. "Marks of China and Pottery," July 1949, pp. 80, 81.

Ripley, Katherine B. "Canova Pottery." January 1942, p. 58.

Shull, Thelma. "American Scenes for the China Collector." June 1942, p. 66.

_____. "Belleek China." July 1941, p. 64.

"Calendar Plates," January 1947, pp. 60, 61.

_____. "The Pauline Pottery." October 1943, pp. 56-58.

Staff-written. "Presidential Plates." June 1952, p. 82.

Varick, Vernon. "Notes on Early New Jersey Pottery." July 1944, p. 64.

Home Lighting and Accessories

Staff-written. "What Happened to Yesterday's Artistic Craftsmen?" (on Cordey China Company) May 1973. Reprinted with no page numbers.

Home Beautiful

Gough, Marion. "Sixteen Most Popular China Patterns." November 1942, pp. 48-49.

Staff-written. "American Pottery Comes of Age." August 1943, p. 6.

House and Garden

Brown, B.A. "The Story of American China." October 1942, p. 35.

Journal of the American Art Pottery Association

Turnquist, Thomas. "New York City Ceramics, part III, William Soini." September-October 1985, pp. 4, 5.

_____. "Polia Pillin: Clay Eye Treats." September-October 1985, pp. 8, 9.

_____. "New York City Ceramics, Part II, Stonelain Pottery." May 1985, pp. 8, 9.

_____. "New York City Ceramics, Part I, The Inwood Pottery Studios." March 1985, p. 15.

Kansas City Star

Hoffman, Donald. "The Creative Wheel." October 16, 1983, pp. 1E and 7E.

Lincoln-Courier

Staff-written. "Stetson China Was Moved Here from Roodhouse." August 26, 1953, Section 8, p. 11.

Mid America Reporter

Grant, Robert D. "Collecting 19th Century Stoneware." June 1972, p. 8.

Purviance, Evan. "American Art Pottery." September 1972, p. 4, November 1972, p. 7 (on Albert Radford).

Nashville Tribune

Staff-written. "The Mould of a Man's Fortune is in His Own Hands." July 31, 1967 (no page number sent to author).

National Journal (earlier called National Glass, Pottery and Collectables Journal)

Barnett, Gerald. "Leigh Potters Inc." March 1979, p. 22.

_____. "Paden City Pottery Company's Shenandoah Ware." April 6, 1979.

_____. "Spotlight." March 1979, p. 25 (on Gem Clay Forming Co.).

_____. "Collectable American China." April 1979, pp. 25, 27.

Lehner, Lois. "Fredricksburg Art Pottery." June 1981, p. 12.

London, Rena. "Collecting Harker China." September 1980, p. 21.

_____. "Hot Springs Pottery." January 1981, p. 8.

_____. "Out of the Mould." August 1980, p. 4.

_____. "Haeger Pottery - Royal, Doubly Royal and Plain." May 1979, pp. 20, 21.

Rehl, Norma and Connie DeAngelo. "Abingdon." December 1980, pp. 20-21.

Rehl, Norma. "Tabletop Fashions of Bygone Days." August 1981, p. 3.

Staff-written. No title (on *Harker Pottery*). December 1978, p. 12.

_____. "Landmark Exhibit to be Shown at Cooper-Hewitt Museum." April 1980, p. 1.

New Glaze

Roerig, Joyce Herndon. "Collecting Cookie Jars." January-February 1985, p. 14.

New Republic

Cowan, Guy R. "In Defense of American China." July 26, 1922, p. 256.

Hamilton, Alice. "Hazards in American Potteries." July 26, 1922, p. 187.

Paducah Sun

Rains, Dona. "Decanter Business Continues to Boom at Roman Ceramics." Reprinted in *Glaze* (see *Glaze*).

Pottery Collectors Newsletter

Cummins, Virginia R. "Kenton Hills Pottery." October 1972, pp. 1-5.

Derwich, Jenny. "Clinchfield Artware Pottery." October 1974, p. 9.

_____. "Kay Finch Ceramics." July-August 1980, p. 39.

Dryfhout, John H. "Paul St. Gaudens and the Orchard Kiln Pottery." September 1974, pp. 171-173.

Fossett, Mildred Beedle. "The Hilton Craftsmen." March 1978, pp. 19, 21.

Fulgham, Verna M. "Stangl Birds Collect." December 1975, p. 171.

Guagliumi, Arthur. "The Saturday Evening Girls Opening a Door to America." October-November 1975, pp. 149, 151, 152.

_____. "Donna Rosa and Black Pottery of Oaxaca." November-December 1979, p. 7.

Hardcastle, Mildred Veley. "Pottery, Patterson-Brookville-Brockville, near Pottsville, Pa." October 1973, pp. 7, 8.

Henzke, Lucile. "Muncie Pottery." February 1973, p. 51.

Kolakowski, Gail. "Louise Abel." July 1974, p. 139.

Measell, James. "The Hawthorn Pottery Co." March 1976, p. 15. (Same title by Measell in *Glaze*, January 1980, p. 4).

Peck, Herbert. "Rookwood Pottery Paperweights." November 1972, p. 17.

Rauschenberg, Bradford L. "B. Du Val & Co. Richmond: A Newly Discovered Pottery." (Reprinted from the *Journal of Early Southern Decorative Arts*, May 1978 (no page number on insert).

Schwartz, Stuart C. "Royal Crown Pottery and Porcelain Co." February 1974, pp. 57-62.

Smith, Judy. "Niloak Pottery." Benton, Ark., November 1976, p. 97.

Staff-written (Pat Johnson, editor). "American Salt-Glazed Stoneware." March 1978, p. 2.

_____. "Bill Dicks, The Potter's Mark Studio." October 1976, p. 86.

_____. "Contemporary Designer Craftsman." October 1976, p. 83.

_____. "Indiana Earthenware and Stoneware." September-October 1979, pp. 39, 42.

_____. "John Parker Glick, Plum Tree Pottery." November 1972, p. 23.

_____. "Maria, Potter of Ildefonso." March 1973, pp. 65, 66.

_____. "Meader's Pottery, White County, Georgia." March 1974, p. 77.

_____. "Molly B. Buford." October 1976, p. 83.

_____. "Pottery Party Line." August 1977, p. 67.

_____. "Pottery of Shearwater." August 1973, p. 138. (Reprinted from *Southern Living*, May 1973).

_____. "Questions." January-February 1976, p. 10 and April 1978, p. 30.

_____. "Verdelle Gray." October 1976, p. 85.

Pottery, Glass and Brass Salesman

Jervis, W.P. "A Dictionary of Pottery Terms." In many installments, 1917 through 1918.

_____. "Wanopee Pottery." September 26, 1918, p. 11.

_____. "The World's Pottery Marks." In many installments, 1913 through 1916. Published weekly.

Staff-written. "Smith Phillips China Company." December 27, 1917, p. 16.

_____. "The Man Who Saw." May 31, 1917 (A.E. Hull Pottery and Buffalo Pottery Company), p. 16.

Reading Eagle

Lucia, Tony. "Top Potter Craftsman Turns Back Time for Clay Art." August 26, 1984, Section 3, pp. 71, 87.

Sandlapper

Carson, Courtney. "Seven Generations of Pottery Makers." August 1968, pp. 18, 20.

Smith, Thomas G. "Potter's Museum of McClendon." April 1970, pp. 9-11.

Saturday Evening Post

Taylor, Frank J. "Dining off the Rainbow." November 19, 1949, pp. 40, 41, 123, 124, 127.

Sedalia Democrat

Lang, Hazel. "Florence was Pioneer Morgan County Settlement." April 1969, pp. 4, 5.

Smithsonian

Slivka, Rose. "Erasing the Line Separating the Arts from the Crafts." March 1978, pp. 87, 93.

Spinning Wheel

Spinning Wheel (magazine) reprinted a collection of articles edited by Albert Christian Revi in a book entitled *Spinning Wheel's Complete Book of Antiques*, N.Y., N.Y.: Grosset and Dunlap, 1975. There were no page numbers in the book. Some of the following references refer to the book rather than the magazine.

Baker, Gordon C., "Early New Geneva Stoneware Potters." May 1979, pp. 17, 18.

_____. "Dilliner Potters." July, August 1979, p. 29.

_____. "Pottery of Greensboro and New Geneva." November 1973, pp. 14-17.

Ballinger, Phyllis. "Chatter About Spatter." October 1976, p. 10.

Blasberg, Robert. "Twenty Years of Fulper." October 1973, p. 14.

Butterworth, Elsie Walker. "Tucker China." June 1949, p. 3.

Brannin, M. Lelyn. "New Books About Antiques." October 1974, p. 36 (on Swan Hill Pottery).

_____. "The Safford's Skilled Earthenware, Potters of Monmouth, Maine." January, February 1973, p. 14.

Brodbeck, John. "Cowan Pottery." March 1973, pp. 24-27.

Chiolino, Barbara. "Folk Art in Utilitarian Stoneware." April 1968, pp. 16-19.

Davis, Chester. "Bybee Pottery." July, August 1973, p. 17.

_____. "Cordey China." January-February 1973, p. 10.

_____. "The Ceramic Arts Studio of Madison, Wisconsin." January, February 1975, p. 59.

_____. "The Later Years of Rookwood Pottery, 1920-1967." October 1969, pp. 10-12.

_____. "The Orchard Kilns of Paul St. Gaudens." March 1974, pp. 54-56.

Dommel, Darlene. "Red Wing and Rum Rill Pottery." December 1972, pp. 22-24.

_____. "University of North Dakota Pottery." June 1973, pp. 30, 31.

Fanelli, Doris D. "John H. Sonner's Stoneware Pottery, Strasburg, Va." January, February 1981, pp. 42, 46.

Fitzpatrick, Nancy. "The Chesapeake Pottery Company." September 1957, p. 14.

Fitzpatrick, Paul J. "White House China." June 1973, p. 68.

Evans, Paul. "American Art Porcelain - The Work of University City Pottery." December 1971, pp. 24, 25.

_____. "Art Ware of the Ohio Pottery." December 1976, p. 15.

_____. "Hampshire Pottery." September 1970, p. 22.

_____. "Jalan: Transitional Pottery of San Francisco." April 1973, pp. 28, 48, 49.

_____. "The Niloak Pottery." October 1970, pp. 18, 19.

_____. "The Nixon Presidential China." July-August 1976, p. 36.

_____. "Valentian Pottery: The Missing Shape Book." September 1979, pp. 37-39.

Garret, Bruce. "Buffalo Pottery and the Larkin Company." January-February 1963, pp. 18-20.

Gernert, Albert. "Buffalo Pottery's Deldare Ware," *Spinning Wheel's Complete Book of Antiques*, p. 120.

Hardcastle, Mildred Veley. "Phaltzgraff Pottery." 1972.

_____. "Potteries of Exeter Township, Berks County, Pennsylvania." January, February, 197, pp. 14, 15, 63.

_____. "The Hysong Potters," *Spinning Wheel's Complete Book of Antiques*.

Henzke, Lucile. "Stangl Audubon Birds." March 1971, pp. 9-11.

Lawless, Dorothy. "Those Jolly Sportsman Mugs." December 1969, p. 28.

McClinton, Katherine Morrison. "American Hand Painted China." *Spinning Wheel's Complete Book of Antiques*, p. 84.

Meline, Elva. "Art Tile in California, The Work of E.A. Batchelder." November 1971, p. 8-10.

Osborne, Mildred R. "Collecting Calendar Plates," January, February, 1969, pp. 10, 11.

Ray, Marcia. "A.B.C.'s of Ceramics." June 1968, p. 21.

_____. "Memo from Marcia." January, February, 1973, p. 72 (on Glasgow Pottery).

Revi, Albert Christian. "Glass of Class." July, August, 1966, p. 18.

Schaltenbrand, Phil. "Stoneware Potteries of Fredericktown, Pennsylvania." November, December 1982, p. 53.

Staff-written. "Bennett Pottery." November 1958, p. 22.

_____. "Ohio Ironstone." June 1954, p. 26.

_____. "Old Sleepy Eye." January-February 1965, p. 18.

_____. "Rebecca Teapots." July-August 1968, p. 28.

Trapp, Kenneth R. "Rookwood Printed Ware." January, February 1977, pp. 26-28.

Tri-State Trader

Allison, Grace. "Juanita Ware." February 26, 1977, p. 1.

_____. "Lotus Ware." May 6, 1978, p. 1.

_____. "Ohio's Bradshaw Pottery," May 19, 1979, p. 1.

Bland, Ann S. "Roycrafters, Craftsmen of Quality." December 20, 1975, pp. 1, 13.

Dalton, Tom. "Consignment Auction Held Near Grand Rapids, Michigan." January 2, 1984, p. 20.

Hammond, Dorothy, "Antique Wise." July 12, 1980, p. 5 (Wahpeton Pottery information, also Rosemeade Pottery).

Houdeshell, James D. "Houghton Pottery Began in 1942." September 10, 1983.

Hurlburt, Betty. "Collectors of Abingdon Pottery Organize Group." April 15, 1978, p. 10.

Kerfoot, Glenn. "Bybee Pottery: The Old Way." May 19, 1979, p. 23.

Lasker, Faith B. "Presidential China, 38 First Families' Best Shown in Smithsonian Exhibit." August 13, 1977, p. 12.

Postle, Kathleen. Overbeck Motifs Drawn from Nature." July 24, 1971, p. 1.

Shrum, Edison. "Industrial Reformer's Life Traced to S.E. Missouri Tract." October 9, 1982, p. 40.

Staff-written. "Dormant Red Wing Factory Due to become Office Complex." October 16, 1982, p. 9.

_____. "Fire Destroys Pennsbury, Pa. Pottery." August 14, 1971, p. 4.

_____. "First Hampshire Pottery Was Made One Hundred Years Ago." December 21, 1971, p. 2.

_____. "Question Box." November 8, 1980, p. 11 (on Rupp Pottery).

_____. "Russel Wright's Genius is Largely Unrecognized." October 6, 1979, p. 43.

Stefano, Frank, Jr. "Clews Pottery." December 13, 1975, p. 8 (Indiana potteries).

Thompson, Francis. "Lycett Respected Name in China." November 8, 1980, p. 12.

Warner, Betty. "Illinois Pottery Was in Production Nearly 50 Years." March 21, 1981, p. 3.

Western Collector

Ady, Laura S. "Tealeaf Pattern Ironstone Ware." March 1968, p. 11.

Evans, Paul. "The Robertson Saga." May 1967, p. 7.

Hellender, Isobel. "One Hundred Years of Sleepy Eye." May 1972, pp. 4-9.

Kovel, Ralph and Terry. "The Mad Potter of Biloxi." May 1972, p. 1.

York County Coast Star

Le Blanc, Marty. "York Pottery is Well-Known Secret." June 19, 1985, Section B, p. 1.

Youngstown Vindicator Newspaper

Allison, Grace. "Alliance Firm Makes Souvenir Dishes." August 20, 1975, p. 8.

Zanesville Times Recorder

Schneider, Norris. "American Encaustic Tile Company." In several parts: May 14, 1961; May 21, 1961; May 28, 1961; June 4, 1961.

_____. "American Encaustic Tile Company's First Plant Here is Demolished." October 27, 1963.

_____. "D.W. Frank Has 500 Pieces of Weller and Roseville Ware." September 30, 1962.

_____. "H.C. Mueller Contributed to Industrial Life of City." March 7, 1971.

_____. "Many Small Potteries Once Operated in Zanesville." February 4, 1962.

_____. "McCoy Ceramic Collection Features Rare Pieces." July 15, 1973.

Zanesville Times Signal (no page numbers for his articles)

Schneider, Norris F. "Brush Pottery." September 9, 1962.

_____. "Clay Industry." November 3, 1957.

_____. "Early Zanesville Pottery Jug." November 10, 1957.

_____. "J.B. Owens." July 15, 1951.

_____. "John Dollings Credited with Making Stoneware in 1870s." December 8, 1957.

_____. "Lawton Gonder." September 22, 1957.

_____. "Le Pere Plant." November 11, 1956.

_____. "Mosiac Largest U.S. Tile Plant." September 10, 1944.

_____. "Nouvelle Pottery." October 28, 1962.

_____. "Owens Made Pottery Ware." April 7, 1963.

_____. "Peters and Reed Pottery." September 15, 1957.

_____. "Roseville Pottery." March 29, 1959.

_____. "Shawnee Pottery." October 16, 1960.

_____. "Souvenir Tile." October 30, 1966.

_____. "Thirty-One Potteries Operated in City During Late 19th Century." November 24, 1957.

_____. "Weller Pottery." April 6, 1958.

_____. "Zanesville Stoneware Company." September 8, 1957.

Books

Abelson, Cheryl. *Hagen-Renaker, Collector's Catalog*, a 75 page booklet. Privately printed, 1982.

Altman, Seymour and Altman, Violet. *The Book of Buffalo Pottery*. New York: Crown Publishers, Inc. 1969.

Anderson, Ross and Barbara Perry. *The Diversions of Keramos, American Clay Sculpture, 1925-1950*. Syracuse, New York: Everson Museum of Art, 1983.

Andrews, Martha E. *From the Hills of Kansas: The Story of Dryden Pottery*, 46 page booklet, no publisher, no date, distributed by the company.

Barber, Edwin Atlee. *The Pottery and Porcelain of the United States*. New York: G.P. Putnam's Sons, 1893.

_____. *Marks of American Potters*. Philadelphia: Patterson and White, 1904: Reprint. Southampton, N.Y.: Cracker Barrel Press, 1968.

_____. Both of the above books printed in one vol. New York: J. and J. Publishing, 1976.

_____. *Tulipware of the Pennsylvania-German Potters*. New York: Dover Publications, Inc., first published in 1903, reprint 1970.

Barret, Richard Carter. *How to Identify Bennington Pottery*. Brattlesboro, Vt.: Stephen Greene Press, 1964.

Bateman, Newton and Paul Shelby. *Historical Encyclopedia of Illinois and History of McDonough County*. Vol. 21, 1907, pp. 617-1055.

Bausman, Joseph H. *History of Beaver County Pennsylvania*. Vol. 2. New York: n.p., 1904.

Beers, J.H. *The History of Armstrong County Pennsylvania: Her People Past and Present*. Vol. 1. Philadelphia: J.H. Beers and Company, 1914.

Bivins, John, Jr. *The Moravian Potters in North Carolina*. Chapel Hill, North Carolina: University of North Carolina Press, 1972.

Blair, Dean C. *The Potters and Potteries of Summit County, 1825-1915*. Akron: Summit County Historical Society, 1966.

Branin, M. Lelyn. *The Early Potters and Potteries of Maine*. Middletown, Connecticut: Wesleyan University Press, 1978.

Bray, Hazel V. *The Potter's Art in California*. Oakland, Calif.: Women's Board of the Museum Association, 1980.

Bridges, Daisy Wade. *Potter of the Catawba Valley*. Vol. IV of the *Journal of Studies of Ceramics*. Charlotte, N.C.: Mint Museum Historical Dept., 1980.

_____. *The Pottery of Walter Stephen*. Vol. III of the *Journal of Studies of Ceramics*. Charlotte, N.C.: Mint Museum Historical Dept., 1978.

Burrison, John A. *Brothers in Clay*. Athens, Ga.: University of Georgia Press, 1983.

Butler, Joseph G., Jr. *History of Youngstown and Mahoning Valley, Ohio*. Vol. II, 1921.

Butler, Joseph T. *American Antiques, 1800-1900*. New York: Golden Press, 1965.

Byrd, L.D. *100 Years of Texas Pottery*. Winona, Tex.: privately printed, 1976. Copies may be obtained from Thomas Printing, P.O. Box 57, Winona, Tex. 75792.

Caldwell, J.A. *History of Belmont and Jefferson Counties*. Wheeling, W. Va.: Historical Publishing Company, 1880.

Christensen, Edwin O. *Early American Designs*. New York and London: Pitman Publishing Corp., 1952.

Clark, Edna Marie. *Ohio Art and Artists*. Richmond, Va.: Garrett and Massie, 1932.

Clark, Garth and Margie Hughto. *A Century of Ceramics in the United States, 1878-1978*. New York: E.P. Dutton, 1979.

Conway, Bob and Ed Gilbreath. *Traditional Pottery in North Carolina*. Waynesville, N.C.: Mountaineer Publishing Co., 1974.

Cox, Susan. *The Collector's Guide to Frankoma Pottery, Book II*. El Cajon, Calif.: privately printed, 1983.

Cox, Warren E. *The Book of Pottery and Porcelain*, 2 vols. New York: Crown Publishers, 1944; reprint, 1970.

Coyne, John. *The Penland School of Crafts*. Indianapolis and New York City: Bobbs Merrill Company, 1975.

Creswick, Alice M. *Red Book of Fruit Jars*. (No place or copyright notice given in book.).

Crooks, Guy E. *History of Crooksville*. Crooksville, Ohio: Published by Crooksville Lions Club, around 1945. Printed, at least in part, in the Crooksville, Roseville, Ohio Pottery Festival Booklet, 1967.

Cunningham, Jo. *The Collector's Encyclopedia of American Dinnerware*. Paducah, Ky.: Collector Books, 1982.

_____. *Autumn Leaf Story*. Springfield, Mo.: Haf-a-Production, 1976.

Darling, Sharon S. *Chicago Ceramics and Glass*. Chicago, Ill.: Chicago Historical Society, 1979. Marks appearing on pages originally appeared in this book as cited in footnotes on these pages and are reprinted by permission.

Davies, Melvin L. *Clay County Traditional Potters and Their Wares*. A catalogue to accompany 1981 exhibition.

Dearolf, Kenneth. *Wisconsin Folk Pottery*. Kenosha, Wis.: Kenosha Public Museum, 1986.

De Jonge, Eric (editor). *Country Things from the Pages of the Magazine Antiques*. New York: Weathervane Books Div. of Crown Publishers, 1973.

Derwich, Jenny B. and Dr. Mary Latos. *Dictionary Guide to U.S. Pottery and Porcelain*. Detroit, Mich.: privately printed, 1984.

Dockstader, Frederick J. *Indian Art of the Americas*. N.Y., N.Y.: Heye Foundation: New York Museum of Contemporary Crafts, 1973.

Doyle, Joseph B. *Twentieth Century History of Steubenville and Jefferson County, Ohio*. Chicago: Richmond Arnold Publishing Company, 1910.

Dreppard, Carl. *Geography of American Antiques*. Garden City, N.Y.: Doubleday, 1948.

Duke, Harvey. *Superior Quality Hall China*. Otisville, Mich.: privately printed as an Elo book, 1977.

Dworkin, Joan and Martha Horman. *A Guide to Stangl Pottery Birds*. Willow Pond Books, 1977.

Eberlein, Harold and Wearne, Roger. *The Practical Book of Chinaware*. Philadelphia: J.B. Lippincott Co., 1925.

Evans, Paul. *Art Pottery of the United States*. New York: Charles Scribner's Sons, 1974.

Felker, Sharon L. *Lovely Hull Pottery*. Des Moines, Iowa: Wallace Homestead Book Co., 1974.

Ford, Henry and Kate. *History of Hamilton County, Ohio*. Cleveland: L.A. Williams and Company, 1789.

Frank, Donna. *Clay in the Master's Hands*. New York: Vantage House, 1977.

Freeman, Larry. *China Classics*. Watkins Glen, N.Y.: Century House, 1959.

Fridley, A.W. *Catalina Pottery*. Long Beach: privately printed, 1977. Copies may be obtained from author, A.W. Fridley, P.O. Box 7723, Long Beach, Ca.

Guappone, Dr. Carmen A. *New Geneva and Greensboro Pottery*. McClellandtown, Pa.: Guappone Publishers, 1975.

Guild, Lurelle. *The Geography of American Antiques*. New York: Doubleday Page and Co., 1927.

Hall, Foster E. and Gladys C. *Collector's Guide to American Pottery, Artists, Potters and Designers and Their Marks*. Gorda, Fla.: privately printed, no date (1980s).

Guilland, Harold F. *Early American Folk Pottery*. Philadelphia and London: Chilton Book Co., 1971.

Hall, Doris and Burdell. *Morton's Potteries: 99 Years*. Morton, Illinois: privately printed, 1982. Can be obtained from authors, P.O. Box 490, Morton, Illinois 61550.

Hammond, Dorothy. *Price Guide to Country Antiques and American Primitives*. New York: Funk and Wagnalls, 1975.

Hartman, Hazel. *Porcelain and Pottery Marks*. New York City, N.Y.: privately printed, 1943.

Harrington, LaMar. *Ceramics in the Pacific Northwest*. Seattle, Wash.: University of Washington Press, 1979.

Hayes, Barbara. *Bauer--The California Pottery Rainbow*. Venice, Calif.: Salem Witch Antiques, 1977.

Heaivilin, Annise D. *Grandma's Tea Leaf Ironstone*. Des Moines, Iowa: Wallace Homestead Book Co., 1981.

Heald, E.T. "The American Way of Life," *The Stark County Story*, Vol. 4, pt. 3. and Part II, "The Suburban Era, 1917-1958," p. 743. Columbus, Ohio: Stark County Historical Society, 1959.

Hoffman, Donald C. *Why Not Warwick*. Chicago: privately printed, 1975.

Howe, Henry. *Historical Collection of Ohio*. Cincinnati, Ohio: State of Ohio, 1902.

Humphreys, Sherry B. and Johnell L. Schmidt. *Texas Pottery*. Washington, Tex.: Star of Republic Museum, 1976.

Huxford, Sharon and Huxford, Bob. *Brush-McCoy Pottery*. Paducah, Ky.: Collector Books, 1978 (catalog reprints).

_____. *Collector's Encyclopedia of Roseville Pottery*. Paducah, Ky.: Collector Books, 1980.

_____. *The Story of Fiesta*. Paducah, Ky.: Collector Books, 1974.

_____. *Weller Pottery*. Paducah, Ky.: Collector Books, 1979.

Hyde, Hazel. *Maria Making Pottery*. Santa Fe, N. Mex.: Sunstone Press (27 page booklet), 1973.

Johnson, Deb and Johnson, Gini. *Beginners Book of American Pottery*. Newton, Kansas: Minnonite Press, Inc., 1974.

Johnson, Dr. Glen S. *The Sebastian Miniature Collection*. Hudson, Mass.: Lance Corp., 1982.

Kaufman, Henry J. *Pennsylvania Dutch American Folk Art*. New York, N.Y.: Dover Publications, Inc., 1964.

Kester, Walter M. *History of Toronto, Ohio, 1900-1914*. Toronto, Ohio: Toronto Tribune Publishing Co., 1969.

Ketchum, William C., Jr. *The Pottery and Porcelain Collector's Handbook*. New York, N.Y.: Funk and Wagnalls, 1971.

_____. *Early Potters and Potteries of New York State*. New York, N.Y.: Funk and Wagnall, 1970.

Kirscher, Edwin J. *Rookwood Pottery An Explanation of Its Marks and Symbols*. Privately printed by author, 1962.

Kovel, Ralph and Kovel, Terry. *The Kovel's Collector's Guide to American Art Pottery*. New York: Crown Publishers, 1974.

Lamson, Everett, Jr. *The Old Exeter Pottery Works*. Barro, Vt.: Modern Printing Co., 1978.

Lasansky, Jeannette. *Made in Mud, Stoneware Potteries in Central Pennsylvania, 1831-1929*. University Park, Pa.: Pennsylvania University Press, 1979.

_____. *Redware Pottery, 1780-1904*. University Park, Pa.: Pennsylvania State University Press, 1979.

Lehner, Lois. *American Kitchen and Dinner Wares*. Des Moines, Ia: Wallace-Homestead Book Co., 1980.

_____. *Ohio Pottery and Glass, Marks and Manufacturers*. Des Moines, Ia.: Wallace-Homestead Book Co., 1978.

Lichten, Francis. *Folk Art of Rural Pennsylvania*. New York, N.Y.: Charles Scribners Sons, 1946.

Luckin, Richard W. *Dining on Rails*. Denver, Colorado: R.K. Publishing, 1983.

MacDowell, Marsha and C. Kurt Dewhurst. *Cast in Clay: The Folk Pottery of Grand Ledge, Michigan*. East Lansing, Mich.: The Museum of Michigan State University, 1980.

Mack, Horace, *History of Columbian County*. Philadelphia, Pa.: D.W. Ensign and Co., 1879.

Madden, Betty I. *Art, Crafts, and Architecture in Early Illinois*. Urbana, Chicago, Ill.: University of Illinois Press in cooperation with Illinois State Museum, Springfield, Ill., 1974.

Marks, Mariann. *Majolica Pottery*. Paducah, Ky.: Collector Books, 1983.

Martin, James and Bette Cooper. *Monmouth, Western Stoneware*. Des Moines, Iowa: Wallace Homestead Book Company, 1983.

McClinton, Katherine. *American Country Antiques*. New York: Coward-McCann, 1967.

McCollum, Harold C. *The Brick and Tile Industry in Stark County 1809-1976*. Canton, Oh.: Stark County Historical Society, 1976.

McCord, W.B. *History of Columbian County, Ohio*. Chicago: Biographical Publishing Company, 1905.

McKee, Floyd W. *A Century of American Dinnerware Manufacture*. Privately printed, 1966.

McNerney, Kathryn. *Blue and White Stoneware*. Paducah, Ky.: Collector Books, 1981.

Mebane, John. *Ceramics in United States*. Best Sellers in Antiques. Dubuque, Ia.: Babka Publishing Co., 1974.

Middleton, Jefferson. *Clay Products*. 1900 Census of the United States, vol. 3, 1912.

Moody. *Moody's Industrial Manual*, two vols. New York: Moody's Investor's Service, 1977.

Moon, June. *History of Colchester*, Ill.: 1956.

Myers, Suzita. *Alexandria, The Potter's Art*. Alexandria, Virginia: privately printed by the City of Alexandria, Virginia, 1983.

Nelson, Maxine Feek. *Versatile Vernon Kilns*. Costa Mesa, Calif.: Rainbow Publications, 1978.

Newbound, Betty and Newbound, Bill. *Southern Potteries, Inc. - Blue Ridge Dinnerware*. Paducah, Ky.: Schroeder Publishing Co., 1980.

Newkirk, David A. *A Guide to Red Wing Markings*. Monticello, Minn.: Monticello Printing Co., 1979. Copies may be obtained from David A. Newkirk, Route 3, Box 141, Monticello, Minn. 55362.

Newkirk, David A. and Bougie, Stanley J. *Red Wing Dinnerware*. St. Cloud, Minn.: Volkmuth Printers, Inc., 1980.

Pappas, Joan and Kendall, Harold. *Hampshire Pottery Manufactured by J.S. Taft and Company, Keene, New Hampshire*. New York: Crown Publishers, 1971.

Peck, Herbert. *The Book of Rookwood Pottery*. New York: Crown Publishers, 1968.

Perrin, W.H. *History of Alexander, Union and Pulaski Counties, Illinois*. 1883.

Peterson, Arthur G. *400 Trademarks on Glass*. Takoma Park, Md.: Washington College Press, 1968.

Pitkin, Albert Hastings. *Early American Folk Pottery*. Hartford, Conn.: 1918.

Powell, Elizabeth. *Pennsylvania Pottery, Tools and Processes*. Doylestown, Pa.: Bucks County Historical Society, 1972.

Powell, Mary G. *The History of Old Alexandria, Virginia*. Richmond, Va.: William Byrd Press, 1928.

Punchard, Lorraine May. *Playtime Dishes*. Des Moines, Ia.: Wallace-Homestead Book Co., 1978.

Purviance, Evan and Purviance, Louise. *Zanesville Art Pottery in Color*. Des Mointes, Ia.: Wallace-Homestead Book Co., 1968.

_____. *Zanesville Art Tile*. Des Moines, Ia.: Wallace-Homestead Book Co., 1972.

Ramsay, John. *American Potters and Pottery*. New York: Tudor Publishing Co., 1947.

Ramsey, L.G.G. *The Complete Encyclopedia of Antiques*. New York: Hawthorne Books, 1968. Printed in Great Britain.

Ray, Marcia. *Collectible Ceramics*. New York: Crown Publishers, 1974.

Raycraft, Don and Carol. *American Country Pottery*. Des Moines, Iowa: Wallace-Homestead Book Company, 1975.

_____. *Decorated Country Stoneware*. Paducah, Ky.: Collector Books, 1982.

Revi, Albert Christian (editor). *Spinning Wheel's Complete Book of Antiques*. New york: Grosset and Dunlap, 1975.

Rice, A.H. and John B. Stoudt. *The Shenandoah Pottery*. Strasburg, Va.: Shenandoah Publishing House, Inc., 1929. Reprinted in 1974 by the Virginia Book Company, Berryville, Va.

Rickerson, Wildey C. *Majolica*. Chester, Conn.: Pequot Press, 1972.

Robacker, Earl F. *Pennsylvania Dutch Stuff*. N.Y., N.Y.: Bonanza Books, 1946.

Robacker, Earl F. and Ada F. Robacker. *Spatterware and Sponge, Hardy Perennials of Ceramics*. Cranberry, N.J.: A.S. Barnes and Co., Inc. 1978.

Roberts, Brenda. *Collector's Encyclopedia of Hull Pottery*. Paducah, Ky.: Collector Books, 1975.

Roberts, Clarence N. "Developments in the Missouri Pottery Industry, 1800-1950," *Missouri Historical Review*, Vol. 58, July 1951.

Sandknop, Stephen S. *Nothing Could Be Finer: A Compendium of Railroad Dining Car China*. Edina, Mo.: Sandknop Publications, 1977.

Schaltenbrand, Phil. *Old Pots, Salt Glazed Stoneware of Greensboro - New Geneva Region*. Hanover, Pa.: Everybodys Press, 1963.

Schneider, Norris F. *Zanesville Art Pottery*. Zanesville, Ohio: Privately printed, 1963.

Schroeder, William. *800 Insulators Priced and Illustrated*. Paducah, Ky.: Privately printed, 1971.

Schwartz, Stuart C. *North State Pottery Company*. Charlotte, N.C.: Mint Museum, 1977.

Simon, Delores. *Shawnee Pottery*. Paducah, Ky.: Collector Books, 1977.

Slivka, Rose. *Peter Voulkas: A Dialogue With Clay*. New York: Little Brown.

Smith, Elmer L. *Antiques in Pennsylvania*. Lebanon, Pa.: Applied Arts Publishers, 1963.

_____. *Pottery, A Utilitarian Folk Craft*. Lebanon, Pa.: Applied Arts Publishers, 1973.

Spargo, John. *Early American Pottery and China*. New York: Garden City Publishing Co., 1926.

_____. *The Potters and Potteries of Bennington*. New York: Dover Press, (first ed., 1926), (second ed., 1972).

Staff-written. *Regional Aspects of American Folk Pottery*. York, Pa.: The Historical Society of York County. Joseph J. Smith, curator, 1974.

_____. *Time-Life Encyclopedia of Antiques*. Alexandria, Va.: Vol. B, 1977.

Sterling, Regina and Consentino, Geraldine. *Stoneware -- A Guide for Beginning Collectors*. Racine, Wis.: Western Publishing Co., 1977.

Stiles, Helen E. *Pottery in the United States*. New York: E.P. Dutton and Co., Inc., 1941.

Stout, W. *History of Clay Industry in Ohio*. n.p.: Ries and Leighton, around 1921. (Also published in full in the *Geological Survey of Ohio*, Columbus, 1923. Fourth Series, Bulletin 26.).

Stradling, Dianna and Stradling, J. Garrison. *The Art of the Potter*. Clinton, N.J.: Main Street Press, 1977. (Articles from *Antiques Magazine*.) See *Antiques* magazines for individual articles used from this book.

Sweezy, Nancy. *Raised in Clay, The Southern Pottery Tradition*. Washington, D.C.: Smithsonian Institution Press, 1984.

Thorn, C. Jordan. *Handbook of Old Pottery and Porcelain Marks*. New York: Tudor Publishers, 1947.

Tod, Jack H. *Porcelain Insulators, Guide Book for Collectors*. Phoenix, Ariz.: privately printed, 1976.

_____. *A History of the Electrical Porcelain Industry in the U.S.*. Phoenix, Ariz.: privately printed, 1977. Books may be ordered from Jack H. Tod, 3427 N. 47th Place, Phoenix, Ariz., 85018. The *Porcelain Insulators, Guide Book for Collectors* is $22.40 plus $.80 for shipping. *A History of the Electrical Porcelain Industry in the U.S.* is $14.75 plus $1.05 for shipping. Jack H. Tod contributed so much to this book and asked only that this information be included here.

Toulouse, Julian. *Fruit Jars*. Camden, N.J.: Thomas Nelson and Sons, 1969.

Umberger, Art and Jewell Umberger. *The Kitchen Cupboard*. Salem, Oreg.: Old Time Bottle Publishing Co., 1967.

Van Cleaf, Aaron R. *History of Pickaway County and Representative Citizens*. Chicago: Biographical Publishing Co., 1906.

Van Ravenswaay, Charles. *The Arts and Architecture of German Settlements in Missouri: A Survey of a Vanishing Culture*. Hagerstown, Md.: Univeristy of Missouri Press, 1977.

Van Rensselaer, Stephen. *Early American Bottles and Flasks*. Originally printed in 1926. Reprinted at Stratford, Conn.: J. Edmund Edwards Publishing, 1969.

Viel, Lyndon C. *The Stoneware of Red Wing, Goodhue County, Minnesota*. Des Moines, Ia.: Wallace-Homestead Book Co., Book I 1977, Book II 1980.

Watkins, Lura Woodside. *Early New England Potters and Their Wares*. Cambridge, Massachusetts: Harvard University Press, 1950.

Wetherbee, Jean. *A Look at White Ironstone*. Des Moines, Ia.: Wallace-Homestead Book Co., 1980.

Willett, E. Henry and Joey Brackner. *The Traditional Pottery of Alabama*. Montgomery, Ala.: Montgomery Museum of Fine Arts, 1983.

Wiltshire, William E. *Folk Pottery of Shenandoah Valley*. New York: E.P. Dutton and Co., Inc., 1975.

Winchester, Alice. *How to Know American Antiques*. New York: Signet Books, 1951.

_____. *The Antiques Book*. New York: Bonanza Books, 1950. A collection of articles printed in *Antiques* magazine.

Wolfe, William G. *Stories of Guernsey County, Ohio*. Cambridge, Ohio: privately printed, 1934.

Worth, Veryl Marie. *Willow Pattern China Collector's Guide*. Oakridge, Oregon: Fuller Printing, Inc., 1979.

Young, Jennie J. *The Ceramic Art: The History and Manufacture of Pottery and Porcelain*. New York: Harper and Brothers, 1878.

Zug, Charles G., III. *The Traditional Pottery of North Carolina*. Chapel Hill, N.C.: The Ackland Art Museum of the University of North Carolina, 1981.

Further Recommended Reading

Greer, Georgeanna. *American Stonewares, The Art and Craft of Utilitarian Potters*. Exton, Pa.: Schiffer Publishing Co., 1981.

Henzke, Lucile. *Art Pottery of America*. Exton, Pa.: Schiffer Publishing Co., 1982.

Webster, Donald Blake. *Decorated Stoneware Pottery of North America*. Rutland, Vt.: Charles E. Tuttle Company (copyright controlled in Japan).

Bulletin of the American Ceramic Society

Forst, Florence. "Directions in Dinnerware Design." September 1952, p. 320.

Gordy, William J. "A Part of My Experience in the Pottery Business and My Father's Experience." October 1938, p. 374.

Kogan, Belle. "Style Trends and Conditions in Pottery Industry." June 1951, p. 201.

Norton, F.H. "A Check List of Early New England Potteries." May 1939, pp. 181-185.

Reinert, Guy F. "A History of the Pennsylvania-German Potteries in Berks County." January 1940, p. 19.

Robertson, J. Milton. "The Background of Dedham Pottery." November 1941, pp. 411-413.

Townsend, Everett. "Development of the Tile Industry in the U.S." May 1943, p. 127.

Vodrey, William H. "Record of the Pottery Industry in East Liverpool District." August 1945, pp. 282-288.

Watts, Arthur. "Early History of Electrical Porcelain Industry in the U.S." October 1939, pp. 404-408.

Staff-written or no author given. "Centenary Anniversary of Harker Pottery Company." January 1941, p. 25

_____. "Ceramic History, Herman Mueller," January 1942, pp. 1-3.

_____. "Ceramic Plant Purchased by Harbeson-Walker." September 1947, pp. 361, 362.

_____. "Charles W. Franzheim." May 1941, p. 185.

_____. "Company News." (Pfaltzgraff) October 1947, p. 415.

_____. "Cook, Charles Howell." August 1925, p. 48.

_____. "Craft Potters of North Carolina." June 15, 1942, pp. 83, 84.

_____. "Edwin and Mary Scheier." July 1943, pp. 264, 265.

_____. "Edwin M. Knowles." March 1943, p. 78.

_____. "Eugene Hardesty." May 1948, p. 147.

_____. "Francis William Walker." August 1939, pp. 227, 228.

_____. "Frederick Rhead." December 15, 1942, p. 306.

_____. "Genuine Pennsylvania-German Ware." November 1940, p. 22.

_____. "Goldscheiders Produce New Porcelain Base." December 1946, p. 494.

_____. "Gustav Hottinger." December 1936, p. 476.

_____. "G.W. Anderson." June 1037 (sent without page no.).

_____. "Harold Philips Humphry." February 1925, p. 50.

_____. "Herford Hope." February 1925, p. 47.

_____. "History of Haeger Potteries, Inc." October 1945, p. 356.

_____. "History of Hall China." August 1945, p. 280.

_____. "In Memorium - Charles D. Fraunfelter." February 1925, pp. 185, 186.

_____. "James H. Goodwin." February 1925, p. 34.

_____. "James MacMath Smith, President of Shenango." June 1941, p. 163.

_____. "Mildred David Keyser." January 15, 1943, pp. 2-5.

_____. "Necrology - Joseph Mayer." December 1930, pp. 336.

_____. "Ninth Annual National Ceramic Exhibition." November 1940, p. 453.

_____. "Notes for Ceramists." May 1941, p. 186.

_____. "Oregon State College Honors Glen Lukens." July 1939, pp. 258, 259.

_____. "Overbeck Pottery." May 1944, p. 156.

_____. "Radio's Greatest Mural Unveiled." (Gladding, McBean & Co.), February 1942, p. 33.

_____. "Report of the Committee on the Definition of Term Ceramics." July 1920, p. 26.

_____. "Rhodes, Daniel, California Potters and the Public." February 1945, p. 48.

_____. "Rowantrees Pottery Enterprises." February 15, 1945 (no page no.).

_____. "Symposium Held at 48th Annual Meeting of the American Ceramic Society." October 1946, p. 376.

_____. "William Bloor." January 1937, p. 25.

General Directories

China and Glass Red Book Directory. Pittsburgh, Pa.. Published by China, Glass and Decorative Accessories, 1948, 1949, 1951, 1952, 1953, 1961, 1966.

China, Glass and Tableware Directory. Bayonne, N.J.: an Ebel-Doctorow Publication, 1961, 1965, 1966, 1967, 1971-72, 1975-76, 1977-78, 1981-82.

Complete Directory of Glass Factories and Potteries of the United States and Canada. Pittsburgh, Pa.: Commoner Publishing Co., 1902, 1903. (Referred to in text as 1902-1903 Complete Directory.).

Crockery and Glass Journal Directory. East Stroudsburg, Pa.: Haire Publishing Company, 1945, 1946, 1951, 1952, 1954.

Gift and Tableware Reporter Directory. East Stroudsburg, Pa.: Haire Publishing Company, August 16, 1965 and August 21, 1967.

Keller's Annual of the Pottery and Glassware Trader. N.Y., N.Y.: Published by Richard H. Keller, 1913.

The Mercantile Agency, R.G. Dun and Company Reference Book. New York City: R.G. Dun and Company, January 1, 1923, for year 1922.

Directories By State

California

California Manufacturer's Directory. Los Angeles. Times Mirror Press, 1924, 1948, 1951, 1955, 1957, 1960, 1977.

Southern California Business Directory and Buyers Guide. Los Angeles: Civic Data Corp., 1977.

Illinois

Polk's Lincoln City Directory. Lincoln, Illinois: R.L. Polk and Co., 1924, 1929-1930, 1946, 1950, 1955, 1959, 1962, 1963, 1966.

The Fourth Annual Report of the Factory Inspector of Illinois. Chicago: State of Illinois, ending December 15, 1896.

Indiana

Twentieth Annual Report. Indiana Department of Geology and Natural Resources, 1895, p. 173.

Indiana Industrial Directory. Indiana State Chamber of Commerce, 1946, 1948, 1954-55, 1962-63, 1964-65, 1977-78.

Indiana Manufacturers' Directory. Indiana State Chamber of Commerce, 1922, 1941, 1946.

Louisiana

New Orleans City Directory. For all the years from 1880 through 1900.

Michigan

Directory of Michigan Manufactures. For 1959, 1963, 1967, 1971, 1976, 1977.

New Jersey

Industrial Directory of New Jersey. For 1901, 1918, 1931, 1935, 1940-41, 1943-44.

Trenton City Directory. For all years between 1900-1971 except: 1901, 1918.

New York

Newburgh, New York City Directories. Published by Price, Lee and Company, 1931, 1932.

Ohio

Alliance Directory. 1960.

Annual Report of the Factory Inspector of Ohio, 10 vols. Columbus, Ohio: State of Ohio, 1891, 1893, 1896, 1899, 1902, 1903, 1904, 1905, 1906, 1907.

Directory of Manufacturers or *Industrial Directory*. 1944, 1967, 1973.

East Liverpool Directory, R.L. Polk and Co. (Including Chester and Newell, W.Va.), 1908, 1910, 1912, 1914-15, 1916, 1924, 1926, 1929, 1931, 1934, 1937, 1941, 1943, 1945, 1948, 1949, 1951, 1953, 1954, 1956-57, 1958-59, 1960.

Ohio Columbian County Farm and Business Directory. 1948.

Secretary of State Report for Ohio. 1910.

Salem City Directory for 1906. Salem, 1906.

Zanesville City Directory. Akron, Ohio: Burch Directory Company, 1905-06, 1907-08, 1910, 1914, 1916, 1922, 1926, 1928-29, 1930-31,, 1933-34, 1950, 1952, 1954, 1956, 1958, 1961, 1963, 1965, 1967, 1969, 1971, 1973, 1975, 1977, 1979.

Zanesville Ohio Con Survey Directory. Zanesville, Ohio: Danker Printing Company, 1937.

Pennsylvania

Annual Report of the Factory Inspector of Pennsylvania. Philadelphia: State of Pennsylvania, 1893-95, 1900.

Industrial Directory of Pennsylvania. 1916, 1919, 1922, 1931, 1935, 1947, 1950, 1953, 1956, 1959, 1968, 1970, 1973, 1975, 1976.

South Carolina

Handbook of South Carolina. Resources, Institutions and Industries of the State: Columbia, S.C. The State Company, Columbia, S.C.: State Department of Agriculture, 1907.

Industrial Directory of South Carolina. Columbia: S.C. Research, Planning and Development Board, 1947.

South Carolina Industrial Directory. 1972-73, 1976.

Tennessee

Directory of Tennessee Industries. 1943, 1947, 1949, 1952, 1954-55, 1957-58, 1959-60, 1963, 1966, 1969.

Memphis Mid-South Manufacturers Guide. 1970, 1973, 1975.

Texas

Texas State Gazetteer. Chicago: R., L. Polk Company, 1884-85, 1890-91, 1892, 1896-97, 1914-15.

Virginia

Survey of Hopewell, Virginia. Hopewell, Va.: Hopewell Chamber of Commerce, 1938.

West Virginia

West Virginia Manufacturing Directory. 1962, 1967.

West Virginia State Gazetteer and Business Directory. Published by the R.L. Polk Company, 1895-96, 1900, 1910-11, 1918-19, 1923-24.

Company Printed Information

No author. *A Century of Fine Service*. Booklet printed and furnished by Syracuse China Company.

No author. *Heritage of a Century*. Privately printed by Mayer China Company around 1915.

No author. *History of Maddux of California*. Privately printed by Maddux of Calif., 1977.

No author. *History of the Canonsburg Pottery Company*. Printed and furnished by the company, June 20, 1972.

No author. *Stangl, A Portrait in Progress in Pottery*. Privately printed booklet by Stangl Pottery, 1965.

No author. *Sterling China, How It's Made and Suggestions for Proper Use*. East Liverpool, Ohio, no date (around 1950).

No author. *Story of genuine Fiesta Dinnerware, 1936 to 1973*. Printed by the Homer Laughlin China Company.

Special Publications Listed By Author

Andrews, Martha E. *From the Hills of Kansas, The Story of Dryden Pottery*. No publisher, no date, 46 page booklet.

Ayers, E.M. *Art in Southern Illinois, 1865-1914*. Journal of Illinois State Museum, Vol. 36, June 1943, pp. 164-189.

Carson, Edward. *Homer Laughlin, 1873-1893, The First Hundred Years*.

Dooley, Raymond. *The Namesake Town: A Centennial History of Lincoln, Illinois*. Published by the Centennial Booklet Committee, 1953.

Heisey, M. Luther. *The Makers of Pottery in Lancaster County (Pa.)*. Lancaster Historical Society, Vol. 1, nos. 4, 5, 1946, p. 12.

Hyde, Hazel. *Maria Making Pottery*. Santa Fe, N. Mex.: Sunstone Press, 1973, 27 page booklet.

Keen, Kirsten Hoving. *American Art Pottery, 1875-1930*. Wilmington, Delaware: Delaware Art Museum, 1978.

Loar, Peggy A. *Indiana Stoneware*. Published by the Indianapolis Museum of Art with a catalog of an exhibition, April 1974.

Madden, Betty, "Jugs Towns." *The Living Museum*. Illinois State Museum Booklet, January 1968, p. 164.

McClung, D.W. (editor). *The Hamilton Tile Works, Artistic Hearth and Facing Tiles, Centennial Anniversary of Hamilton, Ohio, 1891*. pp. 302, 303.

Milam, Otis H., Jr., *Clay Products*. Prepared by the National Youth Administration, June, 1939.

Pearce, R.B. *One Hundred Years of Clay Products at White Hall, Ill*. A small pamphlet written for the Chamber of Commerce and distributed by the A.D. Ruckel and Son Pottery in 1926.

Pickel, Susan E. *From Kiln to Kitchen, American Ceramic Design in Tableware*. Springfield, Ill.: Illinois State Museum, 1980.

Prentiss, Nancy. *The Perfect Hostess*. New Kensington, Pa. 1954, 78 p. booklet.

Roberts, Clarence N. "Developments in the Missouri Pottery Industry, 1800-1950." *Missouri Historical Review*. Vol. 58, pp. 464-473.

Steigleder, Linda. *Checklist and Marks to Accompany A Century of Ceramics in the U.S.: 1878-1978*. Exhibition with accompanying book by Garth Clark and Margie Hughto. Syracuse, N.Y.: Everson Museum, 1979.

Van Ravenswaay, Charles. "Missouri Potters and Their Wares, 1780-1924." *Missouri Historical Society Bulletin*. July 1951, pp. 453-472.

Wheeler, H.A. "Clay Deposits." *Missouri Geological Survey*. Vol. XI, Jefferson City, 1896, pp. 353-358.

Wheeler, H.A. "Statistics of the Stoneware and Earthenware Potteries of Missouri in 1892." *Missouri Geological Survey*. Vol. II, p. 357.

Special Publications Listed By Publisher Or Those Responsible For Printing With No Author Given

American Historical Society. *History of West Virginia, Old and New*. 1923.

Antique Research Publications. *China and Glassware*. (Reprint of Butler Bros. catalogs for 1925, 1930.) Mentone, Alabama, 1968.

Brink, W.R. Publishing Co. *History of Schuyler and Brown Counties, Indiana*. 1882.

California State University. *Beatrice Wood: A Retrospective*. Fullerton, California, 1893.

Crooksville-Roseville, *Annual Tri-State Pottery Festival Booklet*. Roseville, Ohio, 1967, 1973, 1975, 1979, 1982.

Currier Gallery of Art. *Hampshire Pottery, 1871-1923*. Manchester, New Hampshire, 1986.

Downey Museum of Art. *Southern California Industrial Pottery, 1927-1942*. Downey, California, 1978.

Everson Museum of Art. *Kenneth Beittel*. Syracuse, New York, August 25 to September Exhibition, 1978.

Freedman Gallery, Albright College. *The Ceramics of Billy Wodman*. Reading, Pennsylvania, 1985.

Free Standard Press. *Carrollton Pottery Company*. Carrollton: Centennial Ed., 1915.

Garth's Auction Barn's catalogue. *Early American Antiques*. Stratford, Ohio, August 8, 1970 (no page nos.)

Geological Survey of Ohio. *4th Series Bulletin 26*. Columbus, Ohio, 1923, p. 83.

Heye Foundation, Museum of Contemporary Crafts. *Forms of the Earth, 1000 Years of Pottery in America*. Booklet to accompany exhibit with explanatory material by Frederick J. Dockstader, director of Heye Foundation, Museum of the American Indian; Marvin D. Schwartz, curator at Brooklyn Museum; Dr. Robert Koch, professor at New Haven State Teachers College; Daniel Rhodes, associate professor of art at Alfred University and David R. Campbell, director of the museum, 1979.

Historical Society of York County, Pennsylvania. *Regional Aspects fo American Folk Pottery*. Joseph J. Smith, Curator, 1974.

Industrial Publications, Inc. *Clay Products Cyclopedia*. Chicago, Illinois, 1922.

Inter-Museum Exchange Program and Greenville County Art Association. *Early Decorated Stoneware of the Edgefield District of South Carolina*. A catalogue of thirty pages for exhibition, Greenville, South Carolina, 1976, p. 8.

Moore College of Art. *It's All Part of Clay: Viola Frey*. Philadelphia. Pennsylvania, 1984.

Oberammergau Committee. *Oberammergue*. Grand Central Palace, New York City, December 15 to January 1 Exhibition, 1922.

Pennsylvania State Museum. *Henry Varnum Poor, 1887-1970, A Retrospective Exhibition*. 1983.

Roseville town council. *Roseville*. 20 page booklet, Roseville, Ohio, 1906.

Sebring Historical Society. *Sebring, Ohio, A Brief History*. Sebring, Ohio, a 50th Anniversary Publication, 1949.

Sent by Canonsburg Pottery, with no further information. *Twentieth Century History of Washington and Washington County, Pennsylvania, and Representative Citizens, 1910*.

Index

This index is designed to help the reader find unidentified marks. It does not list a pattern name as long as the mark is identifiable by the pottery's name or mark in the book. Many marks which show pattern names only in this book will have the factory mark with them when found on dishes. Marks registered with the copyright and patent office show only part of a mark as does the material sent to this author by some of the factories such as Metlox Potteries. Those marks are indexed here.

Page numbers are added to the names of the factories which constitute a heading for the alphabetical listing of the companies. A name follows each mark and pattern name shown as a mark. If you are looking for a mark, for instance, "Apollo" and find it listed for Vodrey Pottery Company, then turn to Vodrey Pottery Company for the page number for that pottery.

Sometimes several potteries are discussed under a single heading. So in the index a pottery listed to see for the mark is not necessarily the one that used it. *Turn to the place indicated in the text to determine the owner of the mark.*

Abbreviations used were: P. for Pottery, C. for China.

E

I

J

K

N

O

P

Q

R

U

V

X

Y

Z

Books on Antiques and Collectibles

Most of the following books are available from your local book seller or antique dealer, or on loan from your public library. If you are unable to locate certain titles in your area, you may order by mail from COLLECTOR BOOKS, P.O. Box 3009, Paducah, KY 42001. Add $1.00 for postage for the first book ordered and $.40 for each additional book. Include item number, title and price when ordering. Allow 14 to 21 days for delivery. All books are well illustrated and contain current values.

Books on Glass and Pottery

1810	American Art Glass, Shuman	$29.95
1517	American Belleek, Gaston	$19.95
1312	Blue & White Stoneware, McNerney	$9.95
1432	Blue Willow, Gaston	$9.95
1627	Children's Glass Dishes, China & Furniture II, Lechler	$19.95
1841	Collector's Ency. of Depression Glass, Florence, 8th Ed	$19.95
1373	Collector's Ency. of American Dinnerware, Cunningham	$24.95
1812	Collector's Ency. of Fiesta, Huxford	$19.95
1439	Collector's Ency. of Flow Blue China, Gaston	$19.95
1813	Collector's Encyclopedia of Geisha Girl Porcelain, Litts	$19.95
1664	Collector's Ency. of Heisey Glass, Bredehoft	$24.95
1358	Collector's Ency. of McCoy Pottery, Huxford	$19.95
1039	Collector's Ency. of Nippon Porcelain, Van Patten	$19.95
1350	Collector's Ency. of Nippon Porcelain II, Van Patten	$19.95
1665	Collector's Ency. of Nippon III, Van Patten	$24.95
1447	Collector's Ency. of Noritake, Van Patten	$19.95
1037	Collector's Ency. of Occupied Japan, Florence	$12.95
1038	Collector's Ency. of Occupied Japan, 2nd Ed., Florence	$14.95
1719	Collector's Ency. of Occupied Japan III, Florence	$19.95
1311	Collector's Ency. of R.S. Prussia, Gaston	$24.95
1715	Collector's Ency. of R.S. Prussia II, Gaston	$24.95
1034	Collector's Ency. of Roseville Pottery, Huxford	$19.95
1035	Collector's Ency. of Roseville Pottery, 2nd Ed., Huxford	$19.95
1623	Coll. Guide to Country Stoneware & Pottery, Raycraft	$9.95
1538	Collector's Guide to Hall China, Whitmyer	$9.95
1523	Colors in Cambridge, National Cambridge Society	$19.95
1425	Cookie Jars, Westfall	$9.95
1843	Covered Animal Dishes, Grist	$14.95
1844	Elegant Glassware of the Depression, 3rd. Ed.,Florence	$19.95
1756	Kitchen Glassware of the Depression Years, 3rd, Florence	$19.95
1465	Haviland Collectibles & Art Objects, Gaston	$19.95
1392	Majolica Pottery, Katz-Marks	$9.95
1669	Majolica Pottery, 2nd Series, Katz-Marks	$9.95
1758	Pocket Guide to Depression Glass, 5th Ed., Florence	$9.95
1438	Oil Lamps II, Thuro	$19.95
1670	Red Wing Collectibles, DePasquale	$9.95
1440	Red Wing Stoneware, DePasquale	$9.95
1536	So. Potteries Blue Ridge Dinnerware, 2nd Ed., Newbound	$9.95
1830	Standard Carnival Glass Price Guide, Edwards	$7.95
1814	Wave Crest, Glass of C.F. Monroe, Cohen	$29.95
1848	Very Rare Glassware of the Depression Years, Florence	$24.95

Books on Dolls & Toys

1749	Black Dolls, Gibbs	$14.95
1750	Character Toys & Collectibles, 2nd Series, Longest	$19.95
1529	Collector's Ency. of Barbie Dolls, DeWein	$19.95
1066	Collector's Ency. of Half Dolls, Marion	$29.95
1449	Collector's Ency. of Paper Dolls, 2nd Ed., Young	$9.95
1631	German Dolls, Smith	$9.95
1635	Horsman Dolls, Gibbs	$19.95
1717	Liddle Kiddle Dolls, Storm	$9.95
1067	Madame Alexander Collector's Dolls, Smith	$19.95
1068	Madame Alexander Collector's Dolls II, Smith	$19.95
1840	Madame Alexander Price Guide #13, Smith	$4.95
1080	Modern Collector's Dolls II, Smith	$17.95
1081	Modern Collector's Dolls III, Smith	$17.95
1082	Modern Collector's Dolls IV, Smith	$17.95
1516	Modern Collector's Dolls V, Smith	$19.95
1540	Modern Toys, 1930-1980, Baker	$19.95
1683	Patricia Smith Doll Values IV, Antique to Modern	$9.95
1815	Patricia Smith Doll Values, Antique to Modern, 5th Series	$9.95
1513	Teddy Bears & Steiff Animals, Mandel	$9.95
1817	Teddy Bears & Steiff Animals, Mandel	$19.95
1630	Vogue, Ginny Dolls, Smith	$19.95
1648	World of Alexander-Kins, Smith	$19.95
1808	Wonder of Barbie, Manos	$9.95
1430	World of Barbie Dolls, Manos	$9.95

Other Collectibles

1457	American Oak Furniture, McNerney	$9.95
1846	Antique & Collectible Marbles, Grist, 2nd Ed.	$9.95
1712	Antique & Collectible Thimbles, Mathis	$19.95
1624	Antique Brass, Gaston	$9.95
1628	Antique Copper, Gaston	$9.95
1436	Antique Iron, McNerney	$7.95
1748	Antique Purses, Holiner	$19.95
1154	Antique Tools, Our American Heritage, McNerney	$8.95
1426	Arrowheads & Projectile Points, Hothem	$7.95
1278	Art Nouveau & Art Deco Jewelry, Baker	$9.95
1714	Black Collectibles, Gibbs	$19.95
1666	Book of Country, Raycraft	$19.95
1811	Book of Moxie, Potter	$29.95
1128	Bottle Pricing Guide, 3rd Ed., Cleveland	$7.95
1751	Christmas Collectibles, Whitmyer	$19.95
1752	Christmas Ornaments, Johnston	$19.95
1713	Collecting Barber Bottles, Holiner	$24.95
1634	Coll. Ency. of Salt & Pepper Shakers, Davern	$19.95
1753	Collector's Guide to Baseball Memorabilia, Raycraft	$14.95
1537	Collector's Guide to Country Baskets, Raycraft	$9.95
1437	Collector's Guide to Country Furniture, Raycraft	$9.95
1842	Collector's Guide to Country Furniture II, Raycraft	$14.95
1441	Collector's Guide to Post Cards, Wood	$9.95
1716	Fifty Years of Fashion Jewelry, Baker	$19.95
1638	Flea Market Trader, 5th Ed., Huxford	$8.95
1668	Flint Blades & Proj. Points of the No. Am. Indian, Tully	$24.95
1755	Furniture of the Depression Era, Swedberg	$19.95
1424	Hatpins & Hatpin Holders, Baker	$9.95
1212	Marketplace Guide to Oak Furniture, Blundell	$17.95
1757	Modern Guns, Id. & Values, 6th Ed., Quertermous	$12.95
1181	100 Years of Collectible Jewelry, Baker	$9.95
1124	Primitives, Our American Heritage, McNerney	$8.95
1759	Primitives, Our American Heritage, 2nd Series, McNerney	$14.95
1543	Railroad Collectibles, 3rd Ed., Baker	$17.95
1632	Salt & Pepper Shakers, Guarnaccia	$9.95
1816	Silverplated Flatware, 1987 3rd Ed., Hagan	$14.95
1721	Standard Knife Collector's Guide, Ritchie	$9.95
1279	Victorian Furniture, McNerney	$8.95

Schroeder's Antiques Price Guide

Schroeder's Antiques Price Guide has climbed its way to the top in a field already supplied with several well-established publications! The word is out, *Schroeder's Price Guide* is the best buy at any price. Over 500 categories are covered, with more than 50,000 listings. But it's not volume alone that makes Schroeder's the unique guide it is recognized to be. From ABC Plates to Zsolnay, if it merits the interest of today's collector, you'll find it in Schroeder's. Each subject is represented with histories and background information. In addition, hundreds of sharp original photos are used each year to illustrate not only the rare and the unusual, but the everyday "fun-type" collectibles as well -- not postage stamp pictures, but large close-up shots that show important details clearly.

Each edition is completely re-typeset from all new sources. We have not and will not simply change prices in each new edition. All new copy and all new illustrations make Schroeder's THE price guide on antiques and collectibles.

The writing and researching team behind this giant is proportionately large. It is backed by a staff of more than seventy of Collector Books' finest authors, as well as a board of advisors made up of well-known antique authorities and the country's top dealers, all specialists in their fields. Accuracy is their primary aim. Prices are gathered over the entire year previous to publication from ads and personal contacts. Then each category is thoroughly checked to spot inconsistencies, listings that may not be entirely reflective of actual market dealings, and lines too vague to be of merit. Only the best of the lot remains for publication. You'll find *Schroeder's Antiques Price Guide* the one to buy for factual information and quality.

No dealer, collector or investor can afford not to own this book. It is available from your favorite bookseller or antiques dealer at the low price of $12.95. If you are unable to find this price guide in your area, it's available from Collector Books, P. O. Box 3009, Paducah, KY 42001 at $12.95 plus $2.00 for postage and handling.

8½ x 11, 608 Pages $12.95